10. $MUV = (SP \times AQ) - (SP \times SQ)$

11. Total Labor Variance $= (AR \times AH) - (SR \times SH)$

12. Total Labor Variance = Labor Rate Variance + Labor Efficiency Variance

13. $LRV = (AR \times AH) - (SR \times AH)$

14. $LRV = (AR - SR) \times AH$

15. $LEV = (SR \times AH) - (SR \times SH)$

16. $LEV = (AH - SH) \times SR$

17. Target Cost per Unit = Expected Sales Price per Unit − Desired Profit per Unit

# Chapter 11

**Abbrevations:**

$FOH$ = Fixed Overhead

$VOH$ = Variable Overhead

$AH$ = Actual Direct Labor Hours

$SH$ = Standard Direct Labor Hours that *Should Have Been Worked* for Actual Units Produced

$AVOR$ = Actual Variable Overhead Rate

$SVOR$ = Standard Variable Overhead Rate

1. $AVOR = \dfrac{\text{Actual Variable Overhead}}{\text{Actual Hours}}$

2. Variable Overhead Spending Variance $= (AH \times AVOR) - (AH \times SVOR)$
$= (AVOR - SVOR) \times AH$

3. Variable Overhead Efficiency Variance $= (AH - SH) \times SVOR$

4. Practical Capacity at Standard $= SH_p$

5. $SFOR = \dfrac{\text{Budgeted Fixed Overhead Costs}}{\text{Practical Capacity}}$

6. Applied Fixed Overhead $= SH \times SFOR$

7. Total Fixed Overhead Variance = Actual Fixed Overhead − Applied Fixed Overhead

8. Fixed Overhead Spending Variance $= AFOH - BFOH$

9. Volume Variance = Budgeted Fixed Overhead − Applied Fixed Overhead
$= BFOH - (SH \times SFOR)$

# Chapter 12

1. $ROI = \dfrac{\text{Operating Income}}{\text{Average Operating Assets}}$

2. Average Operating Assets $= \dfrac{(\text{Beginning Assets} + \text{Ending Assets})}{2}$

3.     **Margin**            **Turnover**

$ROI = \dfrac{\text{Operating Income}}{\text{Sales}} \times \dfrac{\text{Sales}}{\text{Average Operating Assets}}$

4. Residual Income = Operating Income − (Minimum Rate of Return × Average Operating Assets)

5. EVA = After-Tax Pperating Income − (Actual Percentage Cost of Capital × Total Capital Employed)

6. $MCE = \dfrac{\text{Processing Time}}{\text{Processing Time} + \text{Move Time} + \text{Inspection Time} + \text{Waiting Time}}$

# Chapter 13

1. Contribution Margin per Unit of Scarce Resource
$= \dfrac{\text{Selling Price per Unit} - \text{Variable Cost per Unit}}{\text{Required Amount of Scarce Resource per Unit}}$

2. Price Using Markup = Cost per Unit + (Cost per Unit × Markup Percentage)

3. Target Cost = Target Price − Desired Profit

# Chapter 14

1. Payback Period $= \dfrac{\text{Original Investment}}{\text{Annual Cash Flow}}$

2. Accounting Rate of Return $= \dfrac{\text{Average Income}}{\text{Initial Investment}}$

3. $NPV = \left[ \sum CF_t / (1 + i)^t \right] - I$
$= \left[ \sum CF_t df_t \right] - I = P - I$

4. $I = \sum [CF_t / (1 + i)^t]$

5. $I = CF(df)$

6. $df = I/CF = \dfrac{\text{Investment}}{\text{Annual Cash Flow}}$

7. $F = P(1 + i)^n$

8. $P = F/(1 + i)^n$

# Chapter 16

**Liquidity ratios:**

1. Current Ratio $= \dfrac{\text{Current Assets}}{\text{Current Liabilities}}$

2. Quick Ratio $= \dfrac{(\text{Cash} + \text{Marketable Securities} + \text{Accounts Receivable})}{\text{Current Liabilities}}$

3. Accounts Receivable Turnover Ratio $= \dfrac{\text{Net Sales}}{\text{Average Accounts Receivable}}$

4. Average Accounts Receivable
$= \dfrac{(\text{Beginning Receivables} + \text{Ending Receivables})}{2}$

5. Turnover in Days $= \dfrac{365}{\text{Receivables Turnover Ratio}}$

6. Inventory Turnover Ratio $= \dfrac{\text{Cost of Goods Sold}}{\text{Average Inventory}}$

7. Average Inventory $= \dfrac{(\text{Beginning Inventory} + \text{Ending Inventory})}{2}$

8. Turnover in Days $= \dfrac{365}{\text{Inventory Turnover Ratio}}$

**Leverage ratios:**

9. Times-Interest-Earned Ratio
$= \dfrac{(\text{Income Before Taxes} + \text{Interest Expense})}{\text{Interest Expense}}$

10. Debt Ratio $= \dfrac{\text{Total Liabilities}}{\text{Total Assets}}$

11. Debt-to-Equity Ratio $= \dfrac{\text{Total Liabilities}}{\text{Total Stockholders' Equity}}$

**Profitability ratios:**

12. Return on Sales $= \dfrac{\text{Net Income}}{\text{Sales}}$

13. Return on Total Assets $= \dfrac{\text{Net Income} + [\text{Interest Expense}(1 - \text{Tax Rate})]}{\text{Average Total Assets}}$

14. Average Total Assets $= \dfrac{(\text{Beginning Total Assets} + \text{Ending Total Assets})}{2}$

15. Return on Stockholders' Equity
$= \dfrac{(\text{Net Income} - \text{Preferred Dividends})}{\text{Average Common Stockholders' Equity}}$

16. Earnings per Share $= \dfrac{(\text{Net Income} - \text{Preferred Dividends})}{\text{Average Common Shares}}$

17. Price-Earnings Ratio $= \dfrac{\text{Market Price per Share}}{\text{Earnings per Share}}$

18. Dividend Yield $= \dfrac{\text{Dividends per Common Share}}{\text{Market Price per Common Share}}$

19. Dividend Payout Ratio $= \dfrac{\text{Common Dividends}}{(\text{Net Income} - \text{Preferred Dividends})}$

FIFTH EDITION

# CORNERSTONES
## OF MANAGERIAL ACCOUNTING

**Maryanne M. Mowen**

Oklahoma State University

**Don R. Hansen**

Oklahoma State University

**Dan L. Heitger**

Miami University

SOUTH-WESTERN
CENGAGE Learning

Australia • Brazil • Japan • Korea • Mexico • Singapore • Spain • United Kingdom • United States

**SOUTH-WESTERN**
CENGAGE Learning·

**Cornerstones of Managerial Accounting, Fifth Edition**
**Maryanne M. Mowen, Don R. Hansen, Dan L. Heitger**

Senior Vice President Learning Acquisitions & Solutions Planning: Jack W. Calhoun

Editorial Director, Business & Economics: Erin Joyner

Editor-in-Chief: Rob Dewey

Executive Editor: Sharon Oblinger

Associate Developmental Editor: Julie Warwick

Editorial Assistant: A.J. Smiley

Brand Management Director: Jason Sakos

Sr. Brand Manager: Kristen Hurd

Market Development Manager: Lisa Lysne

Sr. Market Development Manager: Natalie Livingston

Marketing Coordinator: Eileen Corcoran

Sr. Content Project Manager: Tim Bailey

Media Editor: Bryan England

Manufacturing Planner: Doug Wilke

Production Service: Cenveo Publishing Services

Sr. Art Director: Stacy Jenkins Shirley

Cover and Internal Designer: Mike Stratton

Cover Image: © Pixelfabrik/Alamy

Rights Acquisitions Director: Audrey Pettengill

For product information and technology assistance, contact us at **Cengage Learning Customer & Sales Support, 1-800-354-9706**

For permission to use material from this text or product, submit all requests online at **www.cengage.com/permissions**
Further permissions questions can be emailed to **permissionrequest@cengage.com**

Exam*View*® is a registered trademark of eInstruction Corp. Windows is a registered trademark of the Microsoft Corporation used herein under license. Macintosh and Power Macintosh are registered trademarks of Apple Computer, Inc. used herein under license.

Except where otherwise noted, all content in this title is © Cengage Learning.

Library of Congress Control Number: 2012948984

ISBN 13: 978-1-133-94398-3
ISBN 10: 1-133-94398-5

**South-Western Cengage Learning**

5191 Natorp Boulevard
Mason, OH 45040
USA

Cengage Learning products are represented in Canada by Nelson Education, Ltd.

For your course and learning solutions, visit **www.cengage.com**

Purchase any of our products at your local college store or at our preferred online store **www.cengagebrain.com**

Printed in Canada
1 2 3 4 5 6 7 16 15 14 13 12

This book is dedicated to our students—past, present, and future—who are at the heart of our passion for teaching.

# BRIEF CONTENTS

# NEW TO THIS EDITION

- **Addition of "Why" to Cornerstone Examples:** Each Cornerstone now includes a "Why" portion, reinforcing for students the reasons behind the calculations.

- **Increased Readability and Refined Design:** The new edition features improved design for various features to improve readability including the Q&A inserts, Cornerstones, capitalization of account titles, and better placement of exhibits.

- **Additional Conceptual Material in End-of-Chapter:** Additional Conceptual Connection questions are identified in the end-of-chapter content. These questions ask students to go beyond the calculations to articulate the conceptual context behind the work they've just completed and how that information may impact a company's decision-making.

- **Additional Excel Spreadsheet Templates:** To give students additional practice using Excel to complete their homework, each chapter will have an average of two additional templates.

# NEW TO

- **Author-Revised Feedback:** CengageNOW helps students progress farther outside the classroom and keeps them from getting stuck in their studies by providing them with meaningful, written feedback as they work. In this edition, that feedback has been fully revised by the author team to guide students and to be consistent with material presented in the text.

- **Post-Submission Feedback:** Also available in Cengage-NOW is the ability to show the full solution in addition to newly added source calculations to enhance the learning process. Now students can see where they may have gone wrong so that they can correct it through further practice.

- **Animated Activities:** Animated Activities in Cengage-NOW are the perfect prelecture assignment to expose students to concepts before class! These illustrations visually guide students through selected core topics using a realistic company example to illustrate how the concepts relate to the everyday activities of a business. Animated Activities are assignable or available for self-study and review.

- **Blueprint Connections:** Blueprint Connections in CengageNOW are shorter extensions of the Blueprint Problems that build upon concepts covered and introduced within the Blueprint Problems. These scenario-based exercises help reinforce students' knowledge of the concept, strengthen analytical skills, and are useful as in-class activities or as homework/review after the lecture and before the exam.

- **Conceptual Conversion Questions:** End-of-chapter questions or requirements within larger questions that were previously short answer format have been converted to be assignable and gradable within CengageNOW.

# CHAPTER-BY-CHAPTER ENHANCEMENTS

## Chapter 1: Introduction to Managerial Accounting
- Revised Exhibit 1.2: The Value Chain.
- Revised 10% of the end-of-chapter material.
- Updated chapter opener image.

## Chapter 2: Basic Managerial Accounting Concepts
- Added the 'Why' to each Cornerstone.
- Revised 25% of the end-of-chapter material.
- Revised 'Important Equations.'
- Added new important equation: Conversion Cost = Direct Labor + Manufacturing Overhead.
- Added new important equation: Prime Cost = Direct Materials + Direct Labor.
- Updated chapter opener image.

## Chapter 3: Cost Behavior
- Added the 'Why' to each Cornerstone.
- Revised 25% of the end-of-chapter material.
- New design improves readability of the Q&A feature.
- Revised Exhibit 3.3: Semi-Variable Cost.
- Revised 'Important Equations.'
- Updated chapter opener image.

## Chapter 4: Cost-Volume-Profit Analysis: A Managerial Planning Tool
- Added the 'Why' to each Cornerstone.
- Revised 25% of the end-of-chapter material.
- New design improves readability of the Q&A feature.
- Revised 'Important Equations.'
- Added 3 additional spreadsheet templates.

## Chapter 5: Job-Order Costing
- Added the 'Why' to each Cornerstone.
- Revised 25% of the end-of-chapter material.
- New design improves readability of the Q&A feature.
- Revised 'Important Equations.'

## Chapter 6: Process Costing
- Added the 'Why' to each Cornerstone.
- Revised 25% of the end-of-chapter material.
- New design improves readability of the Q&A feature.
- Added 2 additional spreadsheet templates.
- Updated chapter opener image.

## Chapter 7: Activity-Based Costing and Management
- Added the 'Why' to each Cornerstone.
- Revised 25% of the end-of-chapter material.
- New design improves readability of the Q&A feature.
- Added 4 additional spreadsheet templates.
- Revised 'Important Equations.'

## Chapter 8: Absorption and Variable Costing, and Inventory Management
- Added the 'Why' to each Cornerstone.
- Revised 25% of the end-of-chapter material.
- New design improves readability of the Q&A feature.
- Added 4 additional spreadsheet templates.
- Added new important equation: Variable Costing Product Cost = Direct Materials + Direct Labor + Variable Overhead.
- Added new important equation: Absorption Costing Product Cost = Direct Materials + Direct Labor + Variable Overhead + Fixed Overhead.

## Chapter 9: Profit Planning
- Added the 'Why' to each Cornerstone.
- Revised 25% of the end-of-chapter material.
- New design improves readability of the Q&A feature.
- Added 2 additional spreadsheet templates.
- Added new important equation: Ending Cash Balance = Cash Available − Expected Cash Disbursements.
- Added new important equation: Cash Available = Beginning Cash Balance + Expected Cash Receipts.

## Chapter 10: Standard Costing: A Managerial Control Tool
- Added the 'Why' to each Cornerstone.
- Revised 25% of the end-of-chapter material.
- New design improves readability of the Q&A feature.
- Added 2 additional spreadsheet templates.
- Updated chapter opener image.

## Chapter 11: Flexible Budgets and Overhead Analysis
- Added the 'Why' to each Cornerstone.
- Revised 25% of the end-of-chapter material.
- New design improves readability of the Q&A feature.
- Updated chapter opener image.
- Revised 'Important Equations.'

## Chapter 12: Performance Evaluation and Decentralization
- Added the 'Why' to each Cornerstone.
- Revised 25% of the end-of-chapter material.
- New design improves readability of the Q&A feature.
- Updated chapter opener image.

## Chapter 13: Short-Run Decision Making: Relevant Costing
- Added the 'Why' to each Cornerstone.
- Revised 25% of the end-of-chapter material.
- New design improves readability of the Q&A feature.
- Revised 'Important Equations.'

## Chapter 14: Capital Investment Decisions
- Added the 'Why' to each Cornerstone.
- Revised 25% of the end-of-chapter material.
- New design improves readability of the Q&A feature.
- Revised 'Important Equations.'
- Added 2 additional spreadsheet templates.

## Chapter 15: Statement of Cash Flows
- Added the 'Why' to each Cornerstone.
- Revised 25% of the end-of-chapter material.
- New design improves readability of the Q&A feature.
- Added 2 additional spreadsheet templates.
- Updated chapter opener image.

## Chapter 16: Financial Statement Analysis
- Added the 'Why' to each Cornerstone.
- Revised 25% of the end-of-chapter material.
- New design improves readability of the Q&A feature.
- Added 4 additional spreadsheet templates.
- Updated chapter opener image.
- Updated chapter opener with current data for Apple, Inc.
- Updated dates in Exhibit 16.2: Ratio Analysis.

# SUPERIOR SUPPLEMENTS

## CengageNOW for *Cornerstones of Managerial Accounting, 5e*

CengageNOW offers:

- **Auto-graded Homework** (static and algorithmic), Test Bank, Personalized Study Plan, Gradebook, and eBook are all in one resource.
- **Smart Entry** helps eliminate common data entry errors and prevents students from guessing their way through homework.
- **Learning Outcomes Reporting** provides the ability to analyze student work from the gradebook. Each problem is tagged by topic, learning objective, level of difficulty, time estimates, Bloom's Taxonomy, AICPA, ACBSP, IMA, and other business program standards to allow greater guidance in developing assessments and evaluating student progress.
- **Assignments Options** are the most robust and flexible in the industry.
- **Enhanced Feedback** provides additional pre- and post-submission guidance.
- **Cornerstones Videos** further reinforce concepts and examples for visual learners.
- **Blueprint Problems and Connections** are scenario-based exercises to help reinforce knowledge of the concept, strengthen analytical skills, and are best used as homework or review.
- **Animated Activities** are visual illustrations that guide students through selected core topics using a realistic company example to illustrate how concepts relate to everyday business activities.
- **Conceptual Conversion** to select problems and/or requirements that are short answer in the text are now converted to be assignable and gradeable in CNOW.

## Solutions Manual

Author-written and carefully verified multiple times to ensure accuracy and consistency with the text, the Solutions Manual contains answers to all Discussion Questions, Multiple-Choice Questions, Cornerstone Exercises, Exercises, Problems, and Cases that appear in the text. These solutions help you easily plan, assign, and efficiently grade assignments. All solutions are given in simplified Excel spreadsheets and also are available in PDF format. The Solutions Manual is available electronically for instructors only on the IRCD and on the password protected portion of the text's website at http://login.cengage.com.

## Test Bank

The Test Bank has been revised and verified to ensure accuracy and is available in both Word® and ExamView® formats. It includes questions clearly identified by topic, learning objectives, level of difficulty, **Time Estimate**, **Bloom's Taxonomy**, AICPA, ACBSP, IMA, and other business program standards to allow greater guidance in developing assessments and evaluating student

progress. The Test Bank is available electronically for instructors only on the IRCD and on the password protected portion of the text's website at http://login.cengage.com. ExamView® testing software is available only on the IRCD.

## PowerPoint® Lecture Slides

The PowerPoint® slides have been revised and 'toned down' to allow for greater ease in preparing and presenting lectures to encourage lively classroom discussions. All Cornerstones within each chapter appear in the slides. The slides are available for instructors only on the IRCD and on the password protected portion of the text's website at http://login.cengage.com.

## Spreadsheet Templates and Solutions

All spreadsheet problems and solutions, identified by a spreadsheet icon in the text, are available for instructors only on the IRCD and on the password protected portion of the text's website at http://login.cengage.com. All spreadsheet template files are available for students at www.cengagebrain.com.

## Instructor's Resource CD-ROM (ISBN-10: 1285055098 | ISBN-13: 9781285055091)

Place all of the key teaching resources you need at your fingertips with this all-in-one resource. The IRCD includes everything you need to plan, teach, grade, and assess student understanding and progress. This CD contains:

- Solutions Manual
- Test Bank in Microsoft® Word and ExamView®
- Microsoft® PowerPoint slides
- Instructor's Manual
- Spreadsheet Templates and Solutions

All resources on the IRCD are also available to instructors only on the password protected portion of the text's website at http://login.cengage.com.

## CengageBrain.com Free Study Tools for Students

This robust product website provides immediate access to a rich array of interactive learning resources for students that include flashcards, chapter-by-chapter online quizzes, sample final exam, crossword puzzles, PowerPoint® student slides, and the Cornerstones Videos. Students should go to **www.cengagebrain.com**. At the CengageBrain.com homepage, search by the author, title, or ISBN of the text at the top of the page. CengageBrain.com will lead students to the product page to access the free study resources.

# ACKNOWLEDGMENTS AND THANKS

**We would like to thank the following reviewers whose valuable comments and feedback helped shape and refine this edition:**

Janice Akao, *Butler Community College*

Natalie Allen, *Texas A&M University*

Margaret Andersen, *North Dakota State University*

Dr. Vidya Awasthi, *Seattle University*

Timothy B. Biggart, *Berry College*

Phillip A. Blanchard, *University of Arizona*

John F. Bongorno, *Cuyahoga Community College*

Ann K. Brooks, *University of New Mexico*

Dr. James F. Brown, Jr., *University of Nebraska, Lincoln*

Robert S. Burdette, *Salt Lake Community College*

Charles Caliendo, *University of Minnesota*

Donald P. Campbell, *Brigham Young University*

Dr. Tongyu Cao, *University College Cork, Ireland*

Yu Chen, *Texas A&M International University*

Bea Chiang, *College of New Jersey*

Jay Cohen, *Oakton Community College*

Rafik Elias, *California State University, Los Angeles*

Diane Eure, *Texas State University*

Susan Fennema, *Kalamazoo Valley Community College*

Carlos Ferran, *Governors State University*

Kim W. Gatzke, *Delgado Community College*

Connie S. Hardgrove, *College of Central Florida*

Melvin Houston, *Wayne State University*

Sharon J. Huxley, *Post University*

Dr. Iris Jenkel, *St. Norbert College*

Todd A. Jensen, *Sierra College*

Brian A. Joy, *Henderson Community College*

Mehmet Kocakulah, *University of Southern Indiana*

Gopal Krishnan, *Lehigh University*

Linda Kuechler, *Daemen College*

Meg Costello Lambert, *Oakland Community College*

Thomas F. Largay, *Thomas College*

Dr. Wallace R. Leese, *California State University, Chico*

Roger Lirely, *University of Texas at Tyler*

John Logsdon, *Webber International University*

Dennis M. López, *University of Texas at San Antonio*

Catherine E. Lumbattis, *Southern Illinois University, Carbondale*

Nace Magner, *Western Kentucky University*

Dr. Suneel Maheshwari, *Marshall University*

Steve Markoff, *Montclair State University*

Linda Marquis, *Northern Kentucky University*

Stephen McCarthy, *Kean University*

Dr. L. Kevin McNelis, *New Mexico State University*

Birendra Mishra, *University of California, Riverside*

Mark E. Motluck, *Anderson University*

Gerald M. Myers, *Pacific Lutheran University*

Courtney Greer Naismith, *Collin College*

Mary Beth Nelson, *North Shore Community College*

Richard Newmark, *University of Northern Colorado*

Abbie Gail Parham, *Georgia Southern University*

Nichole Pendleton, *Friends University*

Jeffrey Phillips, *Colby-Sawyer College*

Dr. Jo Ann Pinto, *Montclair State University*

John Plouffe, *California State University*

Sharon Polansky, *Texas A&M University, Corpus Christi*

Barbara Reider, *University of Montana*

Kirsten M. Rosacker, *University of Wisconsin, LaCrosse*

Charles J. Russo, *Towson University*

Dr. Aamir A. Salaria, *Harris-Stowe State University*

Dr. Gerd Schulte, *University of Applied Science*

Ann E. Selk, *University of Wisconsin, Green Bay*

Margaret Shackell, *Cornell University*

Mehdi Sheikholeslami, *Bemidji State University*

Aida Shekib, *Governors State University*

Khim L. Sim, *Western Washington University*

Ercan Sinmaz, *Houston Community College System*

James Smith, *University of San Diego*

Jill Smith, *Missouri Southern State University*

Diane Stark, *Phoenix College*

Leo M. Stenson, *Rosemont College*

Geoff Stephenson, *Olds College*

Dr. Ronald J. Strauss, *Montclair State University*

James C. Sundberg, *Eastern Michigan University*

Karen Grossman Tabak, *Maryville University*

Rita N. Taylor, *University of Cincinnati*

Steven Thoede, *Texas State University*

Donald R. Trippeer, *SUNY, Oneonta*

Vincent Turner, *California Polytechnic University Pomona*

Michael Tyler, *Barry University*

Walt Walczykowski, *Sierra College*

Xinmei Xie, *California State University, Dominguez Hills*

Kenneth Zheng, *University at Buffalo*

**We would also like to thank the following instructors for their careful verification of the textbook and all end-of-chapter materials:**

Eileen Byron, *CPA, PMP*

Kurt Fredricks, *Valencia College*

Patrick Haggerty, *Vance-Granville Community College*

Jeanine M. Metzler, *Northampton Community College*

Tracy Newman, *M.S. Ed*

Richard J. Pettit, Ph.D., *Mountain View College, Dallas, Texas*

Constance Rodriguez, *SUNY Empire State College, Genesee Valley Region*

Domenico Tavella, *Carlow University*

Shunda Ware, *Atlanta Technical College*

# CONTENTS

## CHAPTER 4

# Cost-Volume-Profit Analysis: A Managerial Planning Tool

## CHAPTER 5

# Job-Order Costing

## CHAPTER 8

## Absorption and Variable Costing, and Inventory Management    342

## CHAPTER 9

## Profit Planning    380

# ABOUT THE AUTHORS

**Dr. Maryanne M. Mowen** is Associate Professor Emerita of Accounting at Oklahoma State University. She currently teaches online classes in cost and management accounting for Oklahoma State University. She received her Ph.D. from Arizona State University. Dr. Mowen brings an interdisciplinary perspective to teaching and writing in cost and management accounting, with degrees in history and economics. She has taught classes in ethics and the impact of the Sarbanes-Oxley Act on accountants. Her scholarly research is in the areas of management accounting, behavioral decision theory, and compliance with the Sarbanes-Oxley Act. She has published articles in journals such as *Decision Science, The Journal of Economics and Psychology*, and *The Journal of Management Accounting Research*. Dr. Mowen has served as a consultant to mid-sized and Fortune 100 companies and works with corporate controllers on management accounting issues. She is a member of the Northern New Mexico chapter of SCORE and serves as a mentor, assisting small and start-up businesses. Outside the classroom, she enjoys hiking, traveling, reading mysteries, and working crossword puzzles.

**Dr. Don R. Hansen** is Professor Emeritus of Accounting at Oklahoma State University. He received his Ph.D. from the University of Arizona in 1977. He has an undergraduate degree in mathematics from Brigham Young University. Dr. Hansen's research interests include activity-based costing and mathematical modeling. He has published articles in both accounting and engineering journals including *The Accounting Review, The Journal of Management Accounting Research, Accounting Horizons*, and *Accounting, Organizations, and Society*. He has served on the editorial board of *The Accounting Review*. His outside interests include family, church activities, reading, movies, and watching sports.

**Dr. Dan L. Heitger** is Professor of Accounting and Co-Director of the Center for Business Excellence at Miami University. He received his Ph.D. from Michigan State University and his undergraduate degree in accounting from Indiana University. He actively works with executives and students of all levels in developing and teaching courses in managerial and cost accounting, business sustainability, risk management, and business reporting. He co-founded an organization that provides executive education for large international organizations. Dr. Heitger's interactions with business professionals, through executive education and the Center, allow him to bring a current and real-world perspective to his writing. His published research focuses on managerial accounting and risk management issues and has appeared in *Harvard Business Review, Behavioral Research in Accounting, Accounting Horizons, Issues in Accounting Education, Journal of Accountancy*, and *Management Accounting Quarterly*. His outside interests include hiking with his family in the National Park system.

# 1

# Introduction to Managerial Accounting

© Pixelfabrik/Alamy

After studying Chapter 1, you should be able to:

1. Explain the meaning of managerial accounting.

2. Explain the differences between managerial accounting and financial accounting.

3. Identify and explain the current focus of managerial accounting.

4. Describe the role of managerial accountants in an organization.

5. Explain the importance of ethical behavior for managers and managerial accountants.

6. Identify three forms of certification available to managerial accountants.

Vahkaki/Shutterstock.com

# EXPERIENCE MANAGERIAL DECISIONS
## with BuyCostumes.com

The greatest benefit of managerial accounting is also its biggest challenge—to provide managers with information that improves decisions and creates organizational value. This information helps inform managers about the impact of various strategic and operational decisions on key nonfinancial performance measures and their eventual impact on the organization's financial performance. The information is challenging to prepare and analyze because it requires an understanding of all value chain components that affect the organization, including research and development, production, marketing, distribution, and customer service.

Since its inception in 1999, **BuyCostumes.com** has blended the right managerial accounting information and an innovative business model to provide costumes to customers in over 50 countries. Using

the Internet and marketing creativity, BuyCostumes.com serves a market of 150 million U.S. consumers who spend $3.6 billion on costumes each year.

According to CEO Jalem Getz, BuyCostumes.com measures key performance indicators to guide its decision making. For example, managerial accountants analyze measures of customer satisfaction, average time between order placement and costume arrival for each shipping method, and the profitability of individual customer types. As customer trends change, competitors emerge, and technological advances occur, BuyCostumes.com's managerial accounting information adapts to provide crucial insight into the company's performance and how its strategy should evolve to remain the world's largest Internet costume retailer.

> *"Using the Internet and marketing creativity, BuyCostumes.com serves a market of 150 million U.S. consumers who spend $3.6 billion on costumes each year."*

OBJECTIVE ❶

Explain the meaning of managerial accounting.

# THE MEANING OF MANAGERIAL ACCOUNTING

What do we mean by managerial accounting? Quite simply, **managerial accounting** is the provision of accounting information for a company's internal users. It is the firm's internal accounting system and is designed to support the information needs of managers. Unlike financial accounting, managerial accounting is not bound by any formal criteria such as generally accepted accounting principles (GAAP). Managerial accounting has three broad objectives:

- To provide information for planning the organization's actions.
- To provide information for controlling the organization's actions.
- To provide information for making effective decisions.

Using recent examples from many companies in both the for-profit and not-for-profit sectors, this textbook explains how all manufacturing (e.g., aircraft producer—**Boeing Corporation**), merchandising (e.g., clothing retailer—**Guess**) and service (e.g., healthcare provider—**Cleveland Clinic**) organizations use managerial accounting information and concepts. People in all types of positions—from corporate presidents to graphic designers to hospital administrators—can improve their managerial skills by being well-grounded in the basic concepts and use of managerial accounting information for planning, controlling, and decision making.

Furthermore, thousands of companies increasingly release to the public (i.e., suppliers, regulators, employees, human rights organizations, environmental groups, customers, etc.) very large quantities of managerial accounting information that traditionally either did not exist or was released only internally. This information is released through optional reports known as corporate sustainability reports (e.g., **Starbucks**, **McDonald's**), social responsibility reports (e.g., **Apple**, **Chiquita**), or citizenship reports (e.g., **General Electric**). The release of these reports often occurs because firms want to manage their reputation by preparing and releasing such information themselves, rather than having Internet bloggers, newspapers, and cable news networks publish their own estimates of such information. Some leading companies (e.g., **PepsiCo**, **Novo Nordisk**, **British Telecom**) have even moved so far as to combine their sustainability report with their annual report, thereby resulting in a single, integrated report containing both traditional financial accounting information as well as managerial accounting information.[1] The exciting reality is that the importance and scope of managerial accounting information is growing rapidly around the globe. As a result, the demand for business people who possess the ability to create, understand, use and communicate managerial accounting information continues to grow.

## Information Needs of Managers and Other Users

Managerial accounting information is needed by a number of individuals. In particular, managers and empowered workers need comprehensive, up-to-date information for the following activities:

- planning
- controlling
- decision making

## Planning

The detailed formulation of action to achieve a particular end is the management activity called **planning**. Planning requires setting objectives and identifying methods to achieve those objectives. For example, a firm may set the objective of increasing its

---

[1] For a more in-depth discussion of the future of sustainability accounting, see Robert Eccles and Michael Krzus, *One Report: Integrated Reporting for a Sustainable Strategy* (John Wiley & Sons, Inc., Hoboken, NJ: 2010) or Brian Ballou and Dan Heitger, "Accounting for the Sustainability Continuum," *Journal of Accountancy* (June 2010).

short-term and long-term profitability by improving the overall quality of its products. DaimlerChrysler drastically improved the quality and profitability of its Chrysler automobile division during the beginning of the 21st century to the point where its quality surpassed that of Mercedes-Benz (also owned by DaimlerChrysler).[2] By improving product quality, firms like DaimlerChrysler should be able to reduce scrap and rework, decrease the number of customer complaints and warranty work, reduce the resources currently assigned to inspection, and so on, thus increasing profitability. To realize these benefits, management must develop some specific methods that, when implemented, will lead to the achievement of the desired objective. A plant manager, for example, may start a supplier evaluation program to identify and select suppliers who are willing and able to supply defect-free parts. Empowered workers may be able to identify production causes of defects and to create new methods for producing a product that will reduce scrap and rework and the need for inspection. The new methods should be clearly specified and detailed.

## Controlling

Planning is only half the battle. Once a plan is created, it must be implemented and its implementation monitored by managers and workers to ensure that the plan is being carried out as intended. The managerial activity of monitoring a plan's implementation and taking corrective action as needed is referred to as **controlling**. Control is usually achieved by comparing actual performance with expected performance. This information can be used to evaluate or to correct the steps being taken to implement a plan. Based on the feedback, a manager (or worker) may decide to let the plan continue as is, take corrective action of some type to put the actions back in harmony with the original plan, or do some midstream replanning.

The managerial accounting information used for planning and control purposes can be either financial or nonfinancial in nature. For example, Duffy Tool and Stamping saved $14,300 per year by redesigning a press operation.[3] In one department, completed parts (made by a press) came down a chute and fell into a parts tub. When the tub became full, press operators had to stop operation while the stock operator removed the full tub and replaced it with an empty one. Workers redesigned the operation so that each press had a chute with two branches—each leading to a different tub. Now when one tub is full, completed parts are routed into the other tub. The $14,300 savings are a financial measure of the success of the redesign. The redesign also eliminated machine downtime and increased the number of units produced per hour (operational feedback), both of which are examples of nonfinancial performance. Both types of measures convey important information. Often financial and nonfinancial feedback is given to managers in the form of performance reports that compare the actual data with planned data or other benchmarks.

## Decision Making

The process of choosing among competing alternatives is called **decision making**. This managerial function is intertwined with planning and control in that a manager cannot successfully plan or control the organization's actions without making decisions regarding competing alternatives. For instance, if BMW contemplates the possibility of offering a car that runs on gasoline and hydrogen, its ultimate decision would be improved if information about the alternatives (e.g., pertaining to gasoline versus hydrogen versus hybrid combinations of these two automobile fuel options) is gathered and made available to managers. One of the major roles of the managerial accounting information system is to supply information that facilitates decision making.

---

[2] Sarah A. Webster and Joe Guy Collier, "Fixing a Car Company: Zetsche on Mercedes: 'A Lot of Work Is Ahead,'" *Detroit Free Press.* Taken from http://forums.mbworld.org/forums/showthread.php?t=121650 on April 8, 2008.
[3] George F. Hanks, "Excellence Teams in Action," *Management Accounting* (February 1995): 35.

# YOUDECIDE  What Constitutes Managerial Accounting Information?

You are the **Costco** executive who has been chosen to decide whether or not the company should continue its policy of sourcing its finest coffee from Rwanda.

**What types of information should you consider as you decide how best to structure and analyze this important long-term strategic decision? What challenges do you expect to face in making this decision?**

What constitutes managerial accounting information is growing considerably as organizations must make decisions that include the global consequences of their actions, as well as the impact on an increasingly large number of vocal, well-informed, and powerful stakeholders. Stakeholders include the company's customers, suppliers, employees, regulators, politicians, lawmakers, and local community members. Generally speaking, managerial accounting information can be *financial* in nature, such as sales revenue or cost of sales, or *nonfinancial* in nature, such as the number of quality defects or the percentage of manufacturing plants that are inspected for compliance with human rights policies. One of the most exciting—and yet daunting—aspects of managerial accounting is that one can choose to measure *anything*, assuming the resources, information technology, and creativity exist to capture the desired performance measure.

As a Costco executive, one of the first nonfinancial factors you likely would consider measuring is the quality of the Rwandan coffee to ensure that it fulfills Costco's strategic goal of creating a competitive advantage by providing premium coffee to customers. Quality could be defined by the beans' taste, shelf life longevity, or other factors valued by customers. Other important

nonfinancial performance measures might include the time required to ship the harvested beans from Rwanda to Costco stores around North America and the presence of a local farming workforce in Rwanda critical to successfully sustaining a long-term supply chain between Rwandan fields and Costco customers.

One of the most important financial items to measure would be the importance to Costco's customers of purchasing premium quality coffee, which could be measured by the additional price they are willing to pay for Rwandan coffee over and above more average quality coffee. Other financial measures might include the cost of harvesting, inspecting, and shipping beans, as well as investments in Rwandan farming communities (e.g., physical infrastructure and schools) that ensure the relationship is sustainable for future generations.

Finally, you should consider how the decision to continue sourcing premium coffee from Rwanda will be perceived by Costco's important stakeholders, including its customers who buy the coffee, suppliers who provide the coffee beans, and government officials in the United States and Rwanda who set trading policies between the two countries. Accurately measuring issues like stakeholder perceptions of such decisions can be difficult because the managerial accountant oftentimes must invent new measures, figure out where the data to create such measures might come from, and estimate how accurate these measures will be once collected.

**The managerial accountant's ability to inform executive decision makers by providing innovative, accurate, and timely performance measures can create an important competitive advantage for the organization by improving its key decisions.**

---

OBJECTIVE

Explain the differences between managerial accounting and financial accounting.

# FINANCIAL ACCOUNTING AND MANAGERIAL ACCOUNTING

There are two basic kinds of accounting information systems: financial accounting and managerial accounting.

## Financial Accounting

**Financial accounting** is primarily concerned with producing information (financial statements) for *external* users, including investors, creditors, customers, suppliers, government agencies (Food and Drug Administration, Federal Communications Commission, etc.), and labor unions. This information has a historical orientation and is used for such things as investment decisions, stewardship evaluation, monitoring activity, and regulatory measures. Financial statements must conform to certain rules and conventions that are defined by various agencies, such as the Securities and Exchange Commission (SEC), the Financial Accounting Standards Board (FASB), and the International Accounting Standards Board (IASB). These rules pertain to issues such as the recognition of revenues; timing of expenses; and recording of assets, liabilities, and stockholders' equity.

# Managerial Accounting

The managerial accounting system produces information for *internal* users, such as managers, executives, and workers. Thus, managerial accounting could be properly called *internal accounting*, and financial accounting could be called *external accounting*. Specifically, managerial accounting identifies, collects, measures, classifies, and reports financial and nonfinancial information that is useful to internal users in planning, controlling, and decision making.

# Comparison of Financial and Managerial Accounting

When comparing financial accounting to managerial accounting, several differences can be identified. Some of the more important differences follow and are summarized in Exhibit 1.1.

- *Targeted users.* Managerial accounting focuses on providing information for internal users, while financial accounting focuses on providing information for external users.
- *Restrictions on inputs and processes.* Managerial accounting is not subject to the requirements of generally accepted accounting principles set by the SEC and the FASB that must be followed for financial reporting. The inputs and processes of financial accounting are well defined. Only certain kinds of economic events qualify as inputs, and processes must follow generally accepted methods. Unlike financial accounting, managerial accounting has no official body that prescribes the format, content, and rules for selecting inputs and processes and preparing reports.
- *Type of information.* The restrictions imposed by financial accounting tend to produce objective and verifiable financial information. For managerial accounting, information may be financial or nonfinancial and may be much more subjective in nature.
- *Time orientation.* Financial accounting has a historical orientation (i.e., looking through the rear view mirror). It records and reports events that have already happened. Although managerial accounting also records and reports events that have already occurred, it strongly emphasizes providing information about future events (i.e., looking through the front windshield). Management, for example, may want to know what it will cost to produce a product next year. This future orientation is necessary for planning and decision making.
- *Degree of aggregation.* Managerial accounting provides measures and internal reports used to evaluate the performance of entities, product lines, departments, and managers. Essentially, detailed information is needed and provided. Financial accounting, on the other hand, focuses on overall firm performance, providing a more aggregated viewpoint.
- *Breadth.* Managerial accounting is much broader than financial accounting. It includes aspects of managerial economics, industrial engineering, and management science as well as numerous other areas.

( EXHIBIT 1.1 )

**Comparison of Financial and Managerial Accounting**

| Financial Accounting | Managerial Accounting |
|---|---|
| • Externally focused | • Internally focused |
| • Must follow externally imposed rules | • No mandatory rules |
| • Objective financial information | • Financial and nonfinancial information; subjective information possible |
| • Historical orientation | • Emphasis on the future |
| • Information about the firm as a whole | • Internal evaluation and decisions based on very detailed information |
| • More self contained | • Broad, multidisciplinary |

The accounting system should be designed to provide both financial and managerial accounting information. The key point here is flexibility—the system should be able to supply different information for different purposes.

OBJECTIVE ③

Identify and explain the current focus of managerial accounting.

# CURRENT FOCUS OF MANAGERIAL ACCOUNTING

The business environment in which companies operate has changed dramatically over the past several decades. For instance, advances in technology, the Internet, the opening of markets around the world, increased competitive pressures and increased complexity of strategy (e.g., alliances between **McDonald's** and **The Walt Disney Company** for promotional tie-ins) and operations all have combined to produce a global business environment. Effective managerial accounting systems also have changed in order to provide information that helps improve companies' planning, control, and decision-making activities. Several important uses of managerial accounting resulting from these advances include new methods of estimating product and service cost and profitability, understanding customer orientation, evaluating the business from a cross-functional perspective, and providing information useful in improving total quality.

## New Methods of Costing Products and Services

Today's companies need focused, accurate information on the cost of the products and services they produce. In the past, a company might have produced a few products that were roughly similar to one another. Only the cost of materials and labor might have differed from one product to another and figuring out the cost of each unit was relatively easy. Now, with the increase in technology and automation, it is more difficult to generate the costing information needed by management. As Peter Drucker, internationally respected management guru, points out:

> *Traditional cost accounting in manufacturing does not record the cost of nonproducing such as the cost of faulty quality, or of a machine being out of order, or of needed parts not being on hand. Yet these unrecorded and uncontrolled costs in some plants run as high as the costs that traditional accounting does record. By contrast, a new method of cost accounting developed in the last 10 years—called "activity-based" accounting—records all costs. And it relates them, as traditional accounting cannot, to value-added.[4]*

Activity-based costing (ABC) is a more detailed approach to determining the cost of goods and services. ABC improves costing accuracy by emphasizing the cost of the many activities or tasks that must be done to produce a product or offer a service. **United Parcel Service Inc. (UPS)** used ABC to discover and manage the cost of the activities involved with shipping packages by truck, as opposed to by plane, in order to beat **FedEx** at its overnight delivery business in quick mid-distance (up to 500 miles) overnight deliveries.[5] Process-value analysis focuses on the way in which companies create value for customers. The objective is to find ways to perform necessary activities more efficiently and to eliminate those that do not create customer value.

## Customer Orientation

Customer value is a key focus because firms can establish a competitive advantage by creating better customer value for the same or lower cost than competitors or creating equivalent value for lower cost than that of competitors. Customer value is the difference between what a customer receives and what the customer gives up when buying a product or service. When we talk about customer value, we consider the complete range

---

[4] Peter F. Drucker, "We Need to Measure, Not Count," *The Wall Street Journal* (April 13, 1993): A14.
[5] Charles Haddad and Jack Ewing, "Ground Wars: UPS's Rapid Ascent Leaves FedEx Scrambling," *BusinessWeek* (May 21, 2001): 64–68.

of tangible and intangible benefits that a customer receives from a purchased product. Customers receive basic and special product features, service, quality, instructions for use, reputation, brand name, and other important factors. On the other hand, customers give up the cost of purchasing the product, the time and effort spent acquiring and learning to use the product, and the costs of using, maintaining, and disposing of it.

**Strategic Positioning** Effective cost information can help the company identify strategies that increase customer value and, in so doing, create a sustainable competitive advantage.[6] Generally, firms choose one of two general strategies:

- *Cost leadership*: The objective of the cost leadership strategy is to provide the same or better value to customers at a *lower* cost than competitors.
- *Superior products through differentiation (e.g., highest performance quality, most desired product features, best customer service, etc.)*: A differentiation strategy strives to increase customer value by providing something to customers not provided by competitors. For example, **Best Buy**'s Geek Squad of computer technicians creates a competitive advantage for Best Buy by providing 24-hour in-home technical assistance for its customers. Accurate cost information is important to see whether or not the additional service provided by the Geek Squad adds more to revenue than it does to cost.

**The Value Chain** Successful pursuit of cost leadership and/or differentiation strategies requires an understanding of a firm's value chain. The **value chain** is the set of activities required to design, develop, produce, market, and deliver products and services, as well as provide support services to customers. Exhibit 1.2 illustrates the value chain. A managerial accounting system should track information about a wide variety of activities that span the value chain. For example, **Apple** spent considerable effort researching the cost of developing and manufacturing the iPhone, as well as the amount of money potential customers would be willing to spend to purchase it before releasing the most recent version. Also, customer value can be increased by improving the speed of delivery and response, as many customers believe that delivery delayed is delivery denied. **FedEx** exploited this part of the value chain and successfully developed a service that was not being offered by the **U.S. Postal Service**.

It is important to note that companies have internal customers as well. For example, the procurement process acquires and delivers parts and materials to producing departments. Providing high-quality parts on a timely basis to managers of producing departments is just as vital for procurement as it is for the company as a whole to provide high-quality goods to external customers. The emphasis on managing the internal value chain and servicing internal customers has revealed the importance of a cross-functional perspective.

**( EXHIBIT 1.2 )**

**The Value Chain**

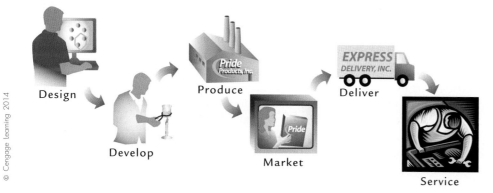

Design

Develop

Produce

Market

Deliver

Service

© Cengage Learning 2014

---

[6] C. Rutledge and R. Williams, "A Seat at the Table," *Outlook Journal* (June 2004). Taken from www.accenture .com/xd/xd.asp?it=enweb&xd=ideas%5Coutlook%5C2_2004%5Cm on October 6, 2005.

The management at **BuyCostumes.com**, for example, focuses on various managerial accounting performance measures to help direct its relationship with customers. Buy-Costumes.com typically records over 20 million unique web viewers each year from its more than 150 million customers. Halloween is its biggest season by far, generating $180 million (half of its total sales for the year), each October. Interestingly, since its creation, BuyCostumes.com management has correctly predicted the outcome of each Presidential election based on the sales data from its Presidential candidate mask collection.

## Cross-Functional Perspective

In managing the value chain, a managerial accountant must understand and measure many functions of the business. Contemporary approaches to costing may include initial design and engineering costs, as well as manufacturing costs, and the costs of distribution, sales, and service. An individual well-schooled in the various definitions of cost, who understands the shifting definitions of cost from the short-run to the long-run, can be invaluable in determining what information is relevant in decision making. For example, strategic decisions may require a cost definition that assigns the costs of all value chain activities. In a long-run decision environment, the banking industry (e.g., **Chase**) spends an estimated $500 million per year across all functional areas to perform customer profitability analyses that identify their most, and least, profitable customers.[7] However, a short-run decision to determine the profitability of a special order (e.g., an offer made to **Bridgestone Firestone North American Tire** at year-end to use idle machinery to produce 1,000 extra tires for a local tire distributor) may require only the incremental costs of the special order in a single functional area.

Why try to relate managerial accounting to marketing, management, engineering, finance, and other business functions? When a value chain approach is taken and customer value is emphasized, we see that these disciplines are interrelated. For example, salespeople may offer deep discounts at the end of the year to meet their sales targets. If customers buy more product, the company's factories may have to work double shifts, incurring overtime pay, to meet this sudden increase in demand. A cross-functional perspective allows us to see the big picture—to see that the increased revenue came at the expense of much higher product costs. This broader vision allows managers to increase quality, reduce the time required to service customers (both internal and external), and improve efficiency.

## Total Quality Management

**Continuous improvement** is the continual search for ways to increase the overall efficiency and productivity of activities by reducing waste, increasing quality, and managing costs. Managerial accounting information about the costs of products, customers, processes, and other objects of management interest can be the basis for identifying problems and alternative solutions.

Continuous improvement is fundamental for establishing excellence. A philosophy of **total quality management**, in which manufacturers strive to create an environment that will enable workers to manufacture perfect (zero-defect) products, has replaced the "acceptable quality" attitudes of the past. This emphasis on quality has also created a demand for a managerial accounting system that provides information about quality, including quality cost measurement and reporting for both manufacturing and service industries. For example, in response to increasing customer complaints regarding its laptop computer repair process, **Toshiba** formed an alliance with **UPS** in which UPS picks up the broken laptop, Toshiba fixes it, and UPS returns the repaired laptop to the customer. In order for this alliance to work effectively, both Toshiba and UPS require relevant managerial accounting information regarding the cost of existing poor quality and efforts to improve future quality.[8]

---

[7] R. Brooks, "Unequal Treatment: Alienating Customers Isn't Always a Bad Idea, Many Firms Discover," *The Wall Street Journal* (January 7, 1999): A1.

[8] T. Friedman, *"The World Is Flat: A Brief History of the Twenty-First Century,"* Farrar, Straus and Giroux: New York, New York, 2005.

Increasingly, companies, such as **DaimlerChrysler**, are using techniques like Six Sigma and Design for Six Sigma (DFSS), together with various types of cost information, to achieve improved quality performance. Chrysler's goal is "to meet customer requirements and improve vehicle and system reliability while reducing development costs and cultivating innovation."[9] On a related note, many companies attempt to increase organizational value by eliminating wasteful activities that exist throughout the value chain. In eliminating such waste, companies usually find that their accounting must also change. This change in accounting, referred to as **lean accounting**, organizes costs according to the value chain and collects both financial and nonfinancial information. The objective is to provide information to managers that supports their waste reduction efforts and to provide financial statements that better reflect overall performance, using both financial and nonfinancial information.

Finally, one of the more recent charges of managerial accountants is to help carry out the company's enterprise risk management (ERM) approach. ERM is a formal way for managerial accountants to identify and respond to the most important threats and business opportunities facing the organization. ERM is becoming increasingly important for long-term success. For example, it is well recognized that **Wal-Mart**'s expert crisis management processes and teams repeatedly responded to the aftermath of Hurricane Katrina throughout Louisiana and Mississippi better and faster than did either local or federal government agencies (e.g., FEMA).[10] The results of many public accounting firm surveys, as well as the *Institute of Management Accountants*, highlight the growing importance that organizations place on conducting effective risk management practices.[11]

## Time as a Competitive Element

Time is a crucial element in all phases of the value chain. World-class firms reduce time to market by compressing design, implementation, and production cycles. These firms deliver products or services quickly by eliminating nonvalue-added time, which is time of no value to the customer (e.g., the time a product spends on the loading dock). Interestingly, decreasing nonvalue-added time appears to go hand in hand with increasing quality.[12]

What about the relationship between time and product life cycles? The rate of technological innovation has increased for many industries, and the life of a particular product can be quite short. Managers must be able to respond quickly and decisively to changing market conditions and will rely on managerial accounting information to accomplish this. For example, **Hewlett-Packard** has found that it is better to be 50% over budget in new product development than to be six months late.

## Efficiency

Improving efficiency is also a vital concern. Both financial and nonfinancial measures of efficiency are needed. Cost is a critical measure of efficiency. Trends in costs over time and measures of productivity changes can provide important measures of the efficacy of continuous improvement decisions. For these efficiency measures to be of value, costs must be properly defined, measured, and assigned; furthermore, production of output must be related to the inputs required, and the overall financial effect of productivity changes should be calculated.

[9] Kevin Kelly, "Chrysler Continues Quality Push," WardsAuto.Com. Taken from http://wardsauto.com/microsites/newsarticle.asp on September 30, 2005.

[10] A. Zimmerman, and V. Bauerlein, "At Wal-Mart, Emergency Plan Has Big Payoff," *The Wall Street Journal* (September 12, 2005): B1.

[11] *Enterprise Risk Management: Tools and Techniques for Effective Implementation.* Institute of Management Accountants, Montvale, New Jersey, 2007: 1–31.

[12] An excellent analysis of time as a competitive element is contained in A. Faye Borthick and Harold P. Roth, "Accounting for Time: Reengineering Business Processes to Improve Responsiveness," *Journal of Cost Management* (Fall 1993): 4–14.

OBJECTIVE ④

Describe the role of managerial accountants in an organization.

# THE ROLE OF THE MANAGERIAL ACCOUNTANT

Managerial accounting is extremely important when making business decisions. For example, Kicker, a real company that makes car stereo systems, relies heavily on managerial accounting information, as we learned in extensive interviews with their top management. Boxes titled "Here's the Real Kicker," like the one below, detail how the company has used managerial accounting information in its operations.

## Here's The Real Kicker

A division of **Stillwater Designs** and **Audio Inc., Kicker** makes car stereo systems. Their signature logo, "Livin' Loud," gives you a hint as to the capabilities of the system. As the company website says, "Livin' Loud has always been the KICKER way—staying one step ahead of the pack—driven to create components that consistently raise the world's expectations for car stereo performance."

Forty years ago, car stereos were underpowered tinny affairs. They could power a radio or an 8-track tape deck. But the in-home listening experience coveted by audio buffs eluded the automobile market. In 1980, Stillwater Designs' founder and president Steve Irby developed the first full-range speaker enclosure designed specifically for automotive use—the Original Kicker®.

Stillwater Designs began in 1973 as a two-person operation, custom designing and building professional sound and musical instrument speaker systems for churches, auditoriums, and entertainers. Building upon the success of the Original Kicker, the company concentrated on the car audio market, applying the same research and design skills that made its first product so successful to the development of a complete line of high-performance components for car audio. What was once a company with two employees in a single-car garage is now a corporation with more than 200 employees in facilities totaling more than 500,000 square feet.

The Kicker brand includes many high-performance car stereo products, including subwoofers, midrange and midbass drivers, tweeters, crossovers, matched component systems, speakers, and power amplifiers. Kicker is proud to have won the prestigious Audio Video International Auto Sound Grand Prix Award, sponsored annually by *Audio-Video International* magazine. Winners are selected by retailers based on fidelity of sound reproduction, design engineering, reliability, craftsmanship and product integrity, and cost/performance ratio. In 2003, seven Kicker products earned Grand Prix awards. Awards emphasizing the performance of the company include the Governor's Award for Excellence in Exporting (2000) and the 1996 Oklahoma City International Trade Association designation as its International Business of the Year.

While Stillwater Designs originally handled research and design (R&D), manufacturing, and sales, it now concentrates primarily on R&D and sales. The bulk of manufacturing has been outsourced (performed by outside firms on a contract basis), although the company still builds some product and plans to build even more as it moves into its new facility for factory-installed audio systems. Engineering and audio research is Kicker president and chief executive officer Steve Irby's first love, and he still heads its design team. The day-to-day involvement of top management, coupled with an energetic workforce of talented individuals in all areas of the company's operations and an innate ability to create truly musical components, has been the reason for the company's remarkable success.

The role of managerial accountants in an organization is one of support. They assist those individuals who are responsible for carrying out an organization's basic objectives. Positions that have direct responsibility for the basic objectives of an organization are referred to as **line positions**. Positions that are supportive in nature and have only indirect responsibility for an organization's basic objectives are called **staff positions**. For Kicker, an organization that designs, produces, and sells audio equipment, the president, general manager, and vice presidents for sales and marketing and operations hold line positions. The purchasing manager and the cost accountant hold staff positions. Kicker's organization chart is shown in Exhibit 1.3.

( EXHIBIT 1.3 )

**Kicker Inc. Organizational Chart**

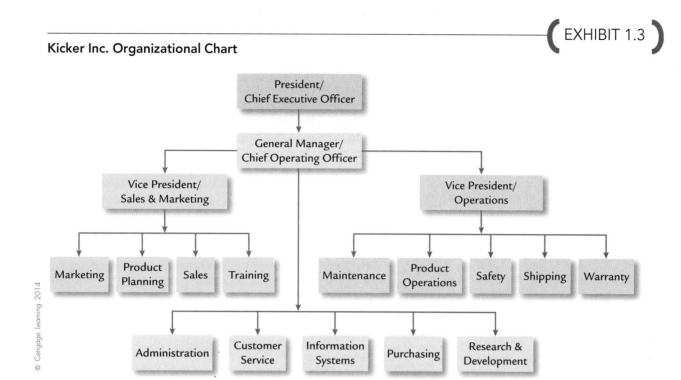

© Cengage Learning 2014

   The **controller**, or chief accounting officer, for **Kicker** is located in the administration department. She supervises all accounting functions and reports directly to the general manager and chief operating officer (COO). Although managerial accountants, such as controllers and cost accounting managers, may wield considerable influence in the organization, they have no authority over the managers in the production area. The managers in line positions are the ones who set policy and make the decisions that impact the company. However, by supplying and interpreting accounting information, managerial accountants can have significant input into policies and decisions.

   Because of the critical role that managerial accounting plays in the operation of an organization, the controller is often viewed as a member of the top management team and is encouraged to participate in planning, controlling, and decision-making activities. As the chief accounting officer, the controller has responsibility for both internal and external accounting requirements. In larger firms, this charge may include direct responsibility for internal auditing, cost accounting, financial accounting (including SEC reports and financial statements), systems accounting (including analysis, design, and internal controls), and taxes. The duties and organization of the controller's office vary from firm to firm. For example, in some firms, the internal audit department may report directly to the financial vice president; similarly, the systems department may report directly to the financial vice president or some other vice president.

   In larger companies, the controller is separate from the treasury department. The **treasurer** is responsible for the finance function. Specifically, the treasurer raises capital and manages cash and investments. The treasurer may also be in charge of credit and collection and insurance.

   No matter which position managerial accountants hold, they must support management in all phases of business decision making. As specialists in accounting, they must be intelligent, well prepared, up-to-date with new developments, and familiar with the customs and practices of all countries in which their firms operate. They are expected to be knowledgeable about the legal environment of business and, in particular, about the Sarbanes-Oxley Act of 2002.

OBJECTIVE 5

Explain the importance of ethical behavior for managers and managerial accountants.

# MANAGERIAL ACCOUNTING AND ETHICAL CONDUCT

Virtually all managerial accounting practices were developed to assist managers in maximizing profits. Traditionally, actions regarding the economic performance of the firm have been the overriding concern. Yet managers and managerial accountants should not become so focused on profits that they develop a belief that the only goal of a business is maximizing its net worth. The objective of profit maximization should be constrained by the requirement that profits be achieved through legal and ethical means.

## Ethical Behavior

**Ethical behavior** involves choosing actions that are right, proper, and just. Behavior can be right or wrong; it can be proper or improper; and the decisions we make can be fair or unfair. Though people often differ in their views of the meaning of the ethical terms cited, there seems to be a common principle underlying all ethical systems. This principle is expressed by the belief that each member of a group bears some responsibility for the well-being of other members. Willingness to sacrifice one's self-interest for the well-being of the group is the heart of ethical action.

This notion of sacrifice produces some core values—values that describe what is meant by right and wrong in more concrete terms. James W. Brackner, writing for the "Ethics Column" in *Management Accounting*, made the following observation:

> *For moral or ethical education to have meaning, there must be agreement on the values that are considered "right." Ten of these values are identified and described by Michael Josephson in "Teaching Ethical Decision Making and Principled Reasoning." The study of history, philosophy, and religion reveals a strong consensus as to certain universal and timeless values essential to the ethical life.*
>
> *These 10 core values yield a series of principles that delineate right and wrong in general terms. Therefore, they provide a guide to behavior.*[13]

The 10 core values referred to in the quotation include the following:

1. Honesty
2. Integrity
3. Promise keeping
4. Fidelity
5. Fairness
6. Caring for others
7. Respect for others
8. Responsible citizenship
9. Pursuit of excellence
10. Accountability

Many of the well-known accounting scandals, such as those involving Adelphia, WorldCom, HealthSouth, Parmalat, and McKesson, provide evidence of the pressures faced by top managers and accountants to produce large net income numbers, especially in the short term. Unfortunately, such individuals often give into these pressures when faced with questionable revenue- and cost-related judgments. For example, the scandal at WorldCom was committed because the CEO, Bernie Ebbers, coerced several of the top accountants at WorldCom to wrongfully record journal entries in the company's books that capitalized millions of dollars in costs as assets (i.e., on the balance sheet) rather than

---

[13] James W. Brackner, "Consensus Values Should Be Taught," *Management Accounting* (August 1992): 19. For a more complete discussion of the 10 core values, see also Michael Josephson, *Teaching Ethical Decision Making and Principled Reasoning, Ethics Easier Said Than Done* (The Josephson Institute, Winter Los Angeles, CA: 1988): 29–30.

as expenses (i.e., on the income statement) that would have dramatically lowered current period net income. Eventually, WorldCom was forced to pay hundreds of millions of dollars to the U.S. government and to shareholders for its illegal and unethical actions. In addition, several of the top executives were sentenced to extensive prison time for their actions. The recent subprime mortgage crisis also highlights the importance of ethical considerations as some banks tried to increase their profits either by lending individuals more money than they could reasonably afford or using terms that were intentionally less clear, or transparent, than many outsiders thought they should be.[14]

In 2002 Congress passed the **Sarbanes-Oxley Act (SOX)**, hoping to limit future securities frauds and accounting misconduct scandals like those associated with Enron, WorldCom, Adelphia, and HealthSouth. SOX led to increased attention on corporate ethics. While successful on many fronts, SOX has not prevented all subsequent frauds. Evidence is in the Allen Stanford securities fraud and the Bernard Maddoff ponzi scheme, which at the time was the world's biggest fraud, allegedly swindling investors out of a total of $50 billion.

Although it may seem contradictory, sacrificing self-interest for the collective good might not only be right and bring a sense of individual worth but might also make good business sense. Companies with a strong code of ethics can create strong customer and employee loyalty. While liars and cheats may win on occasion, their victories often are short-lived. Companies in business for the long term find that it pays to treat all of their constituents with honesty and loyalty.

## Company Codes of Ethical Conduct

One needs only to hear the name "Enron" to be reminded of the importance of ethical conduct. To promote ethical behavior by managers and employees, organizations commonly establish standards of conduct referred to as Company Codes of Conduct. A quick review of various corporate codes of conduct shows some common ground. For example, ChevronTexaco's list of corporate values[15] includes integrity, trust, diversity, high performance, responsibility, and growth. Boeing's Code of Conduct[16] states that it will "conduct its business fairly, impartially, in an ethical and proper manner, and in full compliance with all applicable laws and regulations." All employees must sign the code, and the company "requires that they understand the code, and ask questions, seek guidance, report suspected violations, and express concerns regarding compliance with this policy and the related procedures."

Important parts of corporate codes of conduct are integrity, performance of duties, and compliance with the rule of law. They also uniformly prohibit the acceptance of kickbacks and improper gifts, insider trading, and misappropriation of corporate information and assets. Some such as Motorola,[17] outline employee responsibilities to each other, customers, suppliers, business partners, shareholders, governments, communities, and competitors.

## Standards of Ethical Conduct for Managerial Accountants

In addition to organizations establishing standards of conduct for their managers and employees, professional associations also establish ethical standards. Both the American Institute of Certified Public Accountants (AICPA) and the Institute of Management Accountants (IMA) have established ethical standards for accountants. Professional accountants are bound by these codes of conduct.[18] Both the AICPA and IMA stress the importance of competence, confidentiality, integrity, and credibility or objectivity.

[14] Jane Sasseen, "FBI Widens Net Around Subprime Industry: With 14 Companies Under Investigation, the Bureau's Scope Is the Entire Securitization Process," *BusinessWeek Online* (January 30, 2008). Taken from www.businessweek .com/bwdaily/dnflash/content/jan2008/db20080129_728982.htm?chan=search on February 12, 2008.
[15] Taken from the ChevronTexaco website, www.chevron.com/about/chevtex_way/values.asp (accessed May 12, 2004).
[16] Taken from the Boeing website, www.boeing.com/companyoffices/aboutus/ethics/ (accessed May 12, 2004).
[17] Taken from the Motorola website, www.motorola.com/content/0,75-107,00.html (accessed May 14, 2004).
[18] The AICPA Code of Professional Conduct can be found at www.aicpa.org/about/code. The "Statement of Ethical Professional Practice" is found at www.imanet.org/about_ethics_statement.asp.

In 2005, the IMA revised its Standards of Ethical Conduct for Management Accountants to reflect the impact of the Sarbanes-Oxley Act of 2002. Now called the Statement of Ethical Professional Practice, the revised code considers global issues and incorporates the principles of the code of the International Federation of Accountants, which is the global association of professional accounting groups. In this statement, managerial accountants are told that "they shall not commit acts contrary to these standards nor shall they condone the commission of such acts by others in their organizations." The standards and the recommended resolution of ethical conflicts are presented in Exhibit 1.4.

Suppose a manager's bonus is linked to reported profits, with the bonus increasing as profits increase. Thus, the manager has an incentive to find ways to increase profits, including unethical approaches. A manager could delay promotions of deserving employees or use cheaper parts to produce a product. In either case, if the motive is simply to increase the bonus, the behavior could be labeled as unethical. Neither action is in the best interest of the company or its employees. Yet where should the blame be assigned? After all, the reward system strongly encourages the manager to increase profits. Is the reward system at fault, or is the manager who chooses to increase profits at fault? Or both?

In reality, both the manager and reward system are probably at fault. It is important to design evaluation and reward systems so that incentives to pursue undesirable behavior are minimized. Yet designing a perfect reward system is not a realistic expectation. Managers also have an obligation to avoid abusing the system. Standard III-1 of the code reminds us that members have "a responsibility to (1) mitigate actual conflicts of interest . . . [and to] advise all parties of any potential conflicts." Basically, the prospect of an increased bonus (e.g., a favor) should not influence a manager to engage in unethical actions.

Can ethics be taught? Philosophers and ethicists from Socrates to those studying business ethics today agree that ethics can be taught and, even more importantly, learned. In fact, the IMA now requires continuing education in ethics, as do many of the state boards of accountancy. Perhaps the biggest challenge with ethical dilemmas is that when they arise, employees frequently do not realize (1) that such a dilemma has arisen or (2) the "correct" action that should be taken to rectify the dilemma. Therefore, rather than attempt to study numerous ethical issues in one place, each chapter of this text includes an ethical dilemma or situation designed to increase awareness of the types of conduct considered unethical in business.

OBJECTIVE **6**

Identify three forms of certification available to managerial accountants.

# CERTIFICATION

As with the legal and medical professions, the accounting profession relies on certification to help promote ethical behavior, as well as to provide evidence that the certificate holder has achieved a minimum level of professional competence. The accounting profession offers three major forms of certification to managerial accountants:

- Certificate in Management Accounting
- Certificate in Public Accounting
- Certificate in Internal Auditing

Each certification offers particular advantages to a managerial accountant. In each case, an applicant must meet specific educational and experience requirements and pass a qualifying examination to become certified. Thus, all three certifications offer evidence that the holder has achieved a minimum level of professional competence. Furthermore, all three certifications require the holders to engage in continuing professional education in order to maintain certification. Because certification reveals a commitment to professional competency, most organizations encourage their managerial accountants to become certified.

( EXHIBIT 1.4 )

## Statement of Ethical Professional Practice

Members of IMA shall behave ethically. A commitment to ethical professional practice includes overarching principles that express our values, and standards that guide our conduct.

### PRINCIPLES

IMA's overarching ethical principles include: Honesty, Fairness, Objectivity, and Responsibility. Members shall act in accordance with these principles and shall encourage others within their organizations to adhere to them.

### STANDARDS

A member's failure to comply with the following standards may result in disciplinary action.

### I. COMPETENCE

Each member has a responsibility to:

1. Maintain an appropriate level of professional expertise by continually developing knowledge and skills.
2. Perform professional duties in accordance with relevant laws, regulations, and technical standards.
3. Provide decision support information and recommendations that are accurate, clear, concise, and timely.
4. Recognize and communicate professional limitations or other constraints that would preclude responsible judgment or successful performance of an activity.

### II. CONFIDENTIALITY

Each member has a responsibility to:

1. Keep information confidential except when disclosure is authorized or legally required.
2. Inform all relevant parties regarding appropriate use of confidential information. Monitor subordinates' activities to ensure compliance.
3. Refrain from using confidential information for unethical or illegal advantage.

### III. INTEGRITY

Each member has a responsibility to:

1. Mitigate actual conflicts of interest, regularly communicate with business associates to avoid apparent conflicts of interest. Advise all parties of any potential conflicts.
2. Refrain from engaging in any conduct that would prejudice carrying out duties ethically.
3. Abstain from engaging in or supporting any activity that might discredit the profession.

### IV. CREDIBILITY

Each member has a responsibility to:

1. Communicate information fairly and objectively.
2. Disclose all relevant information that could reasonably be expected to influence an intended user's understanding of the reports, analyses, or recommendations.
3. Disclose delays or deficiencies in information, timeliness, processing, or internal controls in conformance with organization policy and/or applicable law.

### RESOLUTION OF ETHICAL CONFLICT

In applying the Standards of Ethical Professional Practice, you may encounter problems identifying unethical behavior or resolving an ethical conflict. When faced with ethical issues, you should follow your organization's established policies on the resolution of such conflict. If these policies do not resolve the ethical conflict, you should consider the following courses of action:

1. Discuss the issue with your immediate supervisor except when it appears that the supervisor is involved. In that case, present the issue to the next level. If you cannot achieve a satisfactory resolution, submit the issue to the next management level. If your immediate superior is the chief executive officer or equivalent, the acceptable reviewing authority may be a group such as the audit committee, executive committee, board of directors, board of trustees, or owners. Contact with levels above the immediate superior should be initiated only with your superior's knowledge, assuming he or she is not involved. Communication of such problems to authorities or individuals not employed or engaged by the organization is not considered appropriate, unless you believe there is a clear violation of the law.
2. Clarify relevant ethical issues by initiating a confidential discussion with an IMA Ethics Counselor or other impartial advisor to obtain a better understanding of possible courses of action.
3. Consult your own attorney as to legal obligations and rights concerning the ethical conflict.

## The Certified Management Accountant

The Certificate in Management Accounting is designed to meet the specific needs of managerial accountants. A **Certified Management Accountant (CMA)** has passed a rigorous qualifying examination, met an experience requirement, and participates in continuing education.

One of the key requirements for obtaining the CMA is passing a qualifying examination. The following four areas are emphasized:

- economics, finance, and management
- financial accounting and reporting
- management reporting, analysis, and behavioral issues
- decision analysis and information systems

The parts to the examination reflect the needs of managerial accounting and underscore the earlier observation that managerial accounting has more of an interdisciplinary flavor than other areas of accounting.

One of the main purposes of the CMA was to establish managerial accounting as a recognized, professional discipline, separate from the profession of public accounting. Since its inception, the CMA program has been quite successful. Many firms now sponsor and pay for classes that prepare their managerial accountants for the qualifying examination as well as provide other financial incentives to encourage acquisition of the CMA.

## The Certified Public Accountant

The Certificate in Public Accounting is the oldest and most well-known certification in accounting. The purpose of the certificate is to provide minimal professional qualification for external auditors. The responsibility of auditors is to provide assurance concerning the reliability of a firm's financial statements. Only a **Certified Public Accountant (CPA)** is permitted (by law) to serve as an external auditor. CPAs must pass a national examination and be licensed by the state in which they practice. Although the Certificate in Public Accounting does not have a managerial accounting orientation, many managerial accountants also hold this certificate.

## The Certified Internal Auditor

The other certification available to internal accountants is the Certificate in Internal Auditing. Internal auditing differs from external auditing and managerial accounting, and many internal auditors felt a need for a specialized certification. The **Certified Internal Auditor (CIA)** has passed a comprehensive examination designed to ensure technical competence and has 2 years' experience.

# SUMMARY OF LEARNING OBJECTIVES

**LO 1.** Explain the meaning of managerial accounting.

- Managerial accounting information is used to identify problems, solve problems, and evaluate performance.
- Managerial accounting information helps managers in planning, controlling, and decision making.
- Planning is the detailed formulation of action to achieve a particular end.
- Controlling is the monitoring of a plan's implementation.
- Decision making is choosing among competing alternatives.

**LO 2.** Explain the differences between managerial accounting and financial accounting.

- Managerial accounting is
  - intended for internal users.
  - not subject to rules for external financial reporting (e.g., GAAP and SEC regulations).
  - subjective.
  - able to use both financial and nonfinancial measures of performance.
  - able to give a broader, interdisciplinary perspective.
- Financial accounting is
  - directed toward external users.
  - subject to externally imposed rules (e.g., GAAP and SEC regulations).
  - able to provide audited, objective financial information.

**LO 3.** Identify and explain the current focus of managerial accounting.

- It supports management focus on customer value, total quality management, and time-based competition.
- Information about value chain activities and customer sacrifice (such as post-purchase costs) is collected and made available.
- Activity-based management is a major innovative response to the demand for more accurate and relevant managerial accounting information.
- The nature of managerial accounting information system may depend on the strategic position of the firm:
  - Cost leadership strategy
  - Product differentiation strategy
  - Lean accounting

**LO 4.** Describe the role of managerial accountants in an organization.

- They are responsible for identifying, collecting, measuring, analyzing, preparing, interpreting, and communicating information.
- They must be sensitive to the information needs of managers.
- They serve as staff members of the organization and are part of the management team.

**LO 5.** Explain the importance of ethical behavior for managers and managerial accountants.

- A strong ethical sense is needed to resist efforts to change economic information that may present an untrue picture of firm performance.
- Many firms have a written code of ethics or code of conduct.
- The IMA has a code of ethics for managerial accountants.

**LO 6.** Identify three forms of certification available to managerial accountants.

- The Certificate of Management Accounting serves managerial accountants.
- The Certificate of Public Accounting serves and is required for those who practice public accounting.
- The Certificate of Internal Auditing serves internal auditors.

# KEY TERMS

Certified Internal Auditor (CIA), 18
Certified Management Accountant (CMA), 18
Certified Public Accountant (CPA), 18
Continuous improvement, 10
Controller, 13
Controlling, 5
Decision making, 5
Ethical behavior, 14
Financial accounting, 6

Lean accounting, 11
Line positions, 12
Managerial accounting, 4
Planning, 4
Sarbanes-Oxley Act (SOX), 15
Staff positions, 12
Total quality management, 10
Treasurer, 13
Value chain, 9

# DISCUSSION QUESTIONS

1. What is managerial accounting?
2. What are the three broad objectives of managerial accounting?
3. Who are the users of managerial accounting information?
4. Should a managerial accounting system provide both financial and nonfinancial information? Explain.
5. What is meant by controlling?
6. Describe the connection between planning, feedback, and controlling.
7. How do managerial accounting and financial accounting differ?
8. Explain the role of financial reporting in the development of managerial accounting. Why has this changed in recent years?
9. Explain the meaning of customer value. How is focusing on customer value changing managerial accounting?
10. What is the value chain? Why is it important?
11. Explain why today's managerial accountant must have a cross-functional perspective.
12. Briefly explain the practice of enterprise risk management and the role that can be played by managerial accountants in enterprise risk management.
13. What is the difference between a staff position and a line position?
14. The controller should be a member of the top management staff. Do you agree or disagree? Explain.
15. What is ethical behavior? Is it possible to teach ethical behavior in a managerial accounting course?
16. Briefly describe some of the common themes or pressures faced by executives who commit corporate fraud.
17. Identify the three forms of accounting certification. Which form of certification do you believe is best for a managerial accountant? Why?

# MULTIPLE-CHOICE QUESTIONS

**1-1** The provision of accounting information for internal users is known as

a. accounting.
b. financial accounting.
c. managerial accounting.
d. information provision.
e. accounting for planning and control.

**1-2** The users of managerial accounting information include

a. for-profit companies.
b. not-for-profit organizations.
c. city governments.
d. educational institutions.
e. All of these.

**1-3** Setting objectives and identifying methods to achieve those objectives is called

a. planning.
b. decision making.
c. controlling.
d. performance evaluation.
e. None of these.

**1-4** The process of choosing among competing alternatives is called

    a. planning.
    b. decision making.
    c. controlling.
    d. performance evaluation.
    e. None of these.

**1-5** Which of the following is a characteristic of managerial accounting?

    a. There is an internal focus.
    b. Subjective information may be used.
    c. There is an emphasis on the future.
    d. It is broad-based and multidisciplinary.
    e. All of these.

**1-6** An effective managerial accounting system should track information about an organization's activities in which of the following areas?

    a. Development
    b. Marketing
    c. Production
    d. Design
    e. All of these.

**1-7** In terms of strategic positioning, which two general strategies may be chosen by a company?

    a. Revenue production and cost enhancement
    b. Activity-based costing and value chain emphasis
    c. Increasing customer value and decreasing supplier orientation
    d. Cost leadership and product differentiation
    e. Product differentiation and cost enhancement

**1-8** Which of the following is *not* a common form of certification for managerial accountants?

    a. Certificate in Internal Auditing
    b. Certificate in External Auditing
    c. Certificate in Public Accounting
    d. Certificate in Management Accounting

**1-9** The chief accounting officer for a firm is the

    a. chief executive officer.
    b. chief operating officer.
    c. vice president of sales.
    d. production head.
    e. controller.

**1-10** Which of the following is typically found in a corporation's code of ethics?

    a. Compliance with the rule of law
    b. Integrity
    c. Honesty
    d. Competence
    e. All of these.

# EXERCISES

**Exercise 1-11 The Managerial Process**
                                                     OBJECTIVE

Each of the following scenarios requires the use of accounting information to carry out one or more managerial accounting objective.

*(Continued)*

a.  **Laboratory Manager:** An HMO approached me recently and offered us its entire range of blood tests. It provided a price list revealing the amount it is willing to pay for each test. In many cases, the prices are below what we normally charge. I need to know the costs of the individual tests to assess the feasibility of accepting its offer and perhaps suggest some price adjustments on some of the tests.

b.  **Operating Manager:** This report indicates that we have 30% more defects than originally targeted. An investigation into the cause has revealed the problem. We were using a lower-quality material than expected, and the waste has been higher than normal. By switching to the quality level originally specified, we can reduce the defects to the planned level.

c.  **Divisional Manager:** Our market share has increased because of higher-quality products. Current projections indicate that we should sell 25% more units than last year. I want a projection of the effect that this increase in sales will have on profits. I also want to know our expected cash receipts and cash expenditures on a month-by-month basis. I have a feeling that some short-term borrowing may be necessary.

d.  **Plant Manager:** Foreign competitors are producing goods with lower costs and delivering them more rapidly than we can to customers in our markets. We need to decrease the cycle time and increase the efficiency of our manufacturing process. There are two proposals that should help us accomplish these goals, both of which involve investing in computer-aided manufacturing. I need to know the future cash flows associated with each system and the effect each system has on unit costs and cycle time.

e.  **Manager:** At the last board meeting, we established an objective of earning a 25% return on sales. I need to know how many units of our product we need to sell to meet this objective. Once I have the estimated sales in units, we need to outline a promotional campaign that will take us where we want to be. However, in order to compute the targeted sales in units, I need to know the expected unit price and a lot of cost information.

f.  **Manager:** Perhaps the Harrison Medical Clinic should not offer a full range of medical services. Some services seem to be having a difficult time showing any kind of profit. I am particularly concerned about the mental health service. It has not shown a profit since the clinic opened. I want to know what costs can be avoided if I drop the service. I also want some assessment of the impact on the other services we offer. Some of our patients may choose this clinic because we offer a full range of services.

### Required:

Select the managerial accounting objective(s) that are applicable for each scenario: planning, controlling (including performance evaluation), or decision making.

OBJECTIVE  **Exercise 1-12    Differences between Managerial Accounting and Financial Accounting**

Jenna Suarez, the controller for Arben Company, has faced the following situations in the past two weeks:

a.  Ben Heald, head of production, wondered whether it would be more cost effective to buy parts partially assembled or to buy individual parts and assemble them at the Arben factory.

b.  The president of Arben reminded Jenna that the stockholders' meeting was coming up, and he needed her to prepare a PowerPoint® presentation showing the income statement and balance sheet information for last year.

c.  Ellen Johnson, vice president of sales, has decided to expand the sales offices for next year. She sent Jenna the information on next year's rent and depreciation information for budgeting purposes.

d.  Jenna's assistant, Mike, received the information from Ellen on depreciation and added it to depreciation expenses and accumulated depreciation on office equipment.

e.  Jenna compared the budgeted spending on materials used in production with the actual spending on materials used in production. Materials spending was significantly higher than expected. She set up a meeting to discuss this outcome with Ben Heald so that he could explain it.

**Required:**

Determine whether each request is relatively more *managerial accounting oriented* or *financial accounting oriented.*

### Exercise 1-13 Customer Value, Strategic Positioning

OBJECTIVE **3**

Adriana Alvarado has decided to purchase a personal computer. She has narrowed the choices to two: Drantex and Confiar. Both brands have the same processing speed, 6.4 gigabytes of hard-disk capacity, two USB ports, a DVDRW drive, and each comes with the same basic software support package. Both come from mail-order companies with good reputations. The selling price for each is identical. After some review, Adriana discovers that the cost of operating and maintaining Drantex over a 3-year period is estimated to be $300. For Confiar, the operating and maintenance cost is $600. The sales agent for Drantex emphasized the lower operating and maintenance costs. The agent for Confiar, however, emphasized the service reputation of the product and the faster delivery time (Confiar can be purchased and delivered one week sooner than Drantex). Based on all the information, Adriana has decided to buy Confiar.

**Required:**

1. What is the total product purchased by Adriana?
2. **CONCEPTUAL CONNECTION** How does the strategic positioning differ for the two companies?
3. **CONCEPTUAL CONNECTION** When asked why she decided to buy Confiar, Adriana responded, "I think that Confiar offers more value than Drantex." What are the possible sources of this greater value? What implications does this have for the managerial accounting information system?
4. **CONCEPTUAL CONNECTION** Suppose that Adriana's decision was prompted mostly by the desire to receive the computer quickly. Informed that it was losing sales because of the longer time to produce and deliver its products, the management of the company producing Drantex decided to improve delivery performance by improving its internal processes. These improvements decreased the number of defective units and the time required to produce its product. Consequently, delivery time and costs both decreased, and the company was able to lower its prices on Drantex. Explain how these actions translate into strengthening the competitive position of the Drantex PC relative to the Confiar PC. Also discuss the implications for the managerial accounting information system.

### Exercise 1-14 Line versus Staff

OBJECTIVE **4**

The following describes the job responsibilities of two employees of Barney Manufacturing.

*Joan Dennison, Cost Accounting Manager.* Joan is responsible for measuring and collecting costs associated with the manufacture of the garden hose product line. She is also responsible for preparing periodic reports that compare the actual costs with planned costs. These reports are provided to the production line managers and the plant manager. Joan helps to explain and interpret the reports.

*Steven Swasey, Production Manager.* Steven is responsible for the manufacture of the high-quality garden hose. He supervises the line workers, helps to develop the production schedule, and is responsible for seeing that production quotas are met. He is also held accountable for controlling manufacturing costs.

**Required:**

**CONCEPTUAL CONNECTION** Identify Joan and Steven as line or staff and explain your reasons.

### Exercise 1-15 Ethical Behavior

OBJECTIVE **5**

Consider the following scenario between Dave, a printer, and Steve, an assistant in the local university's athletic department.

*(Continued)*

**Steve:** Dave, our department needs to have 10,000 posters printed for the basketball team for next year. Here's the mock-up, and we'll need them in a month. How much will you charge?

**Dave:** Well, given the costs I have for ink and paper, I can come in at around $5,000.

**Steve:** Great, here's what I want you to do. Print me up an invoice for $7,500. That's our budget. Then, when they pay you, you give me a check for $2,500. I'll make sure that you get the job.

**Required:**

CONCEPTUAL CONNECTION Is Steve's proposal ethical? What should Dave do?

OBJECTIVE ⑤    **Exercise 1-16**    **Ethical Behavior**

**Manager:** If I can reduce my costs by $40,000 during this last quarter, my division will show a profit that is 10% above the planned level, and I will receive a $10,000 bonus. However, given the projections for the fourth quarter, it does not look promising. I really need that $10,000. I know of one way that I can qualify. All I have to do is lay off my three most expensive sales-people. After all, most of the orders are in for the fourth quarter, and I can always hire new sales personnel at the beginning of the next year.

**Required:**

CONCEPTUAL CONNECTION What is the right choice for the manager to make? Why did the ethical dilemma arise? Is there any way to redesign the accounting reporting system to discourage the type of behavior that the manager is contemplating?

OBJECTIVE ⑤    **Exercise 1-17**    **Ethical Issues**

The following statements have appeared in newspaper editorials:

1.  Business students come from all segments of society. If they have not been taught ethics by their families and by their elementary and secondary schools, a business school can have little effect.
2.  Sacrificing self-interest for the collective good won't happen unless a majority of Americans also accept this premise.
3.  Competent executives manage people and resources for the good of society. Monetary benefits and titles are simply the by-products of doing a good job.
4.  Unethical firms and individuals, like high rollers in Las Vegas, are eventually wiped out financially.

**Required:**

CONCEPTUAL CONNECTION Assess and comment on each of the statements.

OBJECTIVE ⑤    **Exercise 1-18**    **Ethical Issues**

The Bedron Company is a closely held investment service group that has been quite successful over the past 5 years, consistently providing most members of the top management group with 50% bonuses. In addition, both the chief financial officer and the chief executive officer have received 100% bonuses. Bedron expects this trend to continue.

Recently, Bedron's top management group, which holds 35% of the outstanding shares of common stock, has learned that a major corporation is interested in acquiring Bedron. The other corporation's initial offer is attractive and is several dollars per share higher than Bedron's current share price. One member of management told a group of employees under him about the potential offer. He suggested that they might want to purchase more Bedron stock at the current price in anticipation of the takeover offer.

**Required:**

**CONCEPTUAL CONNECTION** Do you think that the employees should take the action suggested by their boss? Suppose the action is prohibited by Bedron's code of ethics. Now suppose that it is not prohibited by Bedron's code of ethics. Is the action acceptable in that case?

### Exercise 1-19   Company Codes of Conduct                                          OBJECTIVE ⑤

Using the Internet, locate the code of conduct for three different companies.

**Required:**

**CONCEPTUAL CONNECTION** Briefly describe each code of conduct. How are they similar? How are they different?

# 2

# Basic Managerial Accounting Concepts

© Pixelfabrik/Alamy

After studying Chapter 2, you should be able to:

**1** Explain the meaning of cost and how costs are assigned to products and services.

**2** Define the various costs of manufacturing products and providing services as well as the costs of selling and administration.

**3** Prepare income statements for manufacturing and service organizations.

Yuri Arcurs/Shutterstock.com

# EXPERIENCE MANAGERIAL DECISIONS
## with Little Guys Home Electronics

A 60-inch, high-definition, big-screen television creates an aura of intense realism for sports aficionados as they watch with unparalleled clarity the fuzz on the tennis ball as it barely catches the line during a night match at the U.S. Open or the insignia on the football as Tom Brady throws yet another spiral touchdown pass. Using a combination of effective cost-plus pricing and marketplace knowledge, **Little Guys Home Electronics** has, for years, helped to bring such exciting sporting events to life for its thousands of customers. Correct pricing decisions are crucial in the home entertainment market, where the profit margin on video products is only 2 to 3%.

*"Using a combination of effective cost-plus pricing and marketplace knowledge, Little Guys Home Electronics has, for years, helped to bring such exciting sporting events to life for its thousands of customers."*

Little Guys sets prices by marking up full costs and ensuring that the final price falls within a range between the suggested retail price and the minimum advertised price, both of which are affected by the manufacturer and the marketplace. Its managerial accountants must understand cost behavior to be able to predict costs accurately in order for effective markup and pricing decisions to be made. What types of costs does Little Guys consider in its markups? Several examples include product purchases and shipping costs, warehousing costs, labor (including employee health care and retirement benefits as well as other labor support costs), store insurance, advertising, delivery truck investments and maintenance, and customer service trips. Also, future demand must be estimated so that Little Guys can figure out how much to charge for each television, receiver, and the like, such that all costs across the value chain are covered and the desired profit is achieved. Armed with an effective pricing strategy involving judgment about costs, markup percentages, and future market trends, Little Guys hopes to continue delivering exciting home electronics products and services to Chicago-area families for years to come.

OBJECTIVE ❶

Explain the meaning of cost and how costs are assigned to products and services.

# THE MEANING AND USES OF COST

One of the most important tasks of managerial accounting is to determine the cost of products, services, customers, and other items of interest to managers. Therefore, we need to understand the meaning of cost and the ways in which costs can be used to make decisions, both for small entrepreneurial businesses and large international businesses. For example, consider a small gourmet restaurant and its owner Courtney, who also is the head chef. In addition to understanding the complexities of gourmet food preparation, Courtney needs to understand the breakdown of the restaurant's costs into various categories in order to make effective operating decisions. Cost categories of particular interest include:

- direct costs (food and beverages)
- indirect costs (laundry of linens)

On a larger scale, local banks operating in college communities often look at the cost of providing basic checking account services to students. These accounts typically lose money—that is, the accounts cost more to service than they yield in fees and interest revenue. However, the bank finds that students already banking with them are more likely to take out student loans through the bank, and these loans are very profitable. As a result, the bank may actually decide to expand its offerings to students when the related loan business is considered.

## Cost

**Cost** is the amount of cash or cash equivalent sacrificed for goods and/or services that are expected to bring a current or future benefit to the organization. If a furniture manufacturer buys lumber for $10,000, then the cost of that lumber is $10,000 cash. Sometimes, one asset is traded for another asset. Then the cost of the new asset is measured by the value of the asset given up (the cash equivalent). If the same manufacturer trades office equipment valued at $8,000 for a forklift, then the cost of the forklift is the $8,000 value of the office equipment traded for it. Cost is a dollar measure of the resources used to achieve a given benefit. Managers strive to minimize the cost of achieving benefits. Reducing the cost required to achieve a given benefit means that a firm is becoming more efficient.

Costs are incurred to produce future benefits. In a profit-making firm, those benefits usually mean revenues. As costs are used up in the production of revenues, they are said to expire. Expired costs are called **expenses**. On the income statement, expenses are deducted from revenues to determine income (also called *profit*). For a company to remain in business, revenues must be larger than expenses. In addition, the income earned must be large enough to satisfy the owners of the firm.

We can look more closely at the relationship between cost and revenue by focusing on the units sold. The revenue per unit is called **price**. In everyday conversation, we have a tendency to use cost and price as synonyms, because the price of an item (e.g., a CD) is the cost to us. However, accounting courses take the viewpoint of the owner of the company. In that case, cost and price are *not* the same. Instead, for the company, revenue and price are the same. Price must be greater than cost in order for the firm to earn income. Hence, managers need to know cost and trends in cost. For example, the price a consumer pays for a fleece jacket from **The North Face** might be $200, while the total cost that the company incurs to design, manufacture, deliver, and service that jacket is much lower than the $200 price it charges consumers.

## Accumulating and Assigning Costs

**Accumulating costs** is the way that costs are measured and recorded. The accounting system typically does this job quite well. When the company receives a phone bill, for example, the bookkeeper records an addition to the telephone expense account and an addition to the liability account, Accounts Payable. In this way, the cost is *accumulated*. It would be easy to tell, at the end of the year, the total spending on phone calls.

Accumulating costs tells the company what was spent. However, that usually is not enough information. The company also wants to know why the money was spent. In other words, it wants to know how costs were assigned to cost objects.

**Assigning costs** is the way that a cost is linked to some cost object. A cost object is something for which a company wants to know the cost. For example, of the total phone expense, how much was for the sales department, and how much was for manufacturing? *Assigning* costs tells the company why the money was spent. In this case, cost assignment tells whether the money spent on phone calls was to support the manufacturing or the selling of the product. As we will discuss in later chapters, cost assignment typically is more difficult than cost accumulation.

## Here's The Real Kicker

**Kicker** collects and analyzes many types of costs and breaks cost information into a series of accounts that helps Kicker's management in budgeting and decision making. The sales function, for example, is broken down into three areas: selling, customer service, and marketing. Consider the marketing department, which is responsible for advertising, promotions, and tent shows.

Tent shows are small-scale affairs held several times a year in the central and south-central United States. Kicker brings its semi-trailer full of products and sound equipment as well as a couple of show trucks. Then, a large tent is set up to sell Kicker merchandise, explain products, showcase new models, and sell the previous year's models at greatly reduced prices. The cost of each tent show is carefully tracked and compared with that show's revenue. Sites that don't provide sales revenue greater than cost are not booked for the coming year.

Like many of today's companies, Kicker tracks costs carefully for use in decision making. The general cost categories discussed in this chapter help the company to organize cost information and relate it to decision making.

*Jackson Smith/Getty Images*

## Cost Objects

Managerial accounting systems are structured to measure and assign costs to entities called *cost objects*. A **cost object** is any item such as a product, customer, department, project, geographic region, plant, and so on, for which costs are measured and assigned. For example, if **Fifth Third Bank** wants to determine the cost of a platinum credit card, then the cost object is the platinum credit card. All costs related to the platinum card are added in, such as the cost of mailings to potential customers, the cost of telephone lines dedicated to the card, the portion of the computer department that processes platinum card transactions and bills, and so on. In a more personal example, suppose that you are considering taking a course during the summer session. Taking the course is the cost object, and the cost would include tuition, books, fees, transportation, and (possibly) housing. Notice that you could also include the foregone earnings from a summer job (assuming that you cannot work while taking summer classes), which would be an opportunity cost.[1]

# YOUDECIDE   For Which Business Activities Do We Need an Estimate of Cost?

You are the Chief Financial Officer for a major airline company. Managing the company's numerous costs is critically important in this fiercely competitive industry. Therefore, one of your major tasks is deciding which costs to manage in order to achieve the company's profitability targets. In other words, you must identify the airline's most important cost objects to track, measure, and control.

*(Continued)*

---

[1] The concept of opportunity cost will be discussed more fully later in this chapter, as well as in Chapter 13.

**Which cost objects would you select as critical to the company's success?**

Certain airline cost objects are obvious, such as the cost of operating a flight, which includes jet fuel (**Delta** spends over $8 billion annually for jet fuel)[2] and labor costs for pilots, flight crews, and maintenance staffs. However, even the costs of these obvious cost objects can become challenging. For example, when an airline operates multiple types of aircraft, it incurs additional costs to train workers and store spare parts for each aircraft type (i.e., the total cost of training and maintaining 100 aircraft of two different types is greater than the same number of aircraft all of one type). Airlines might be even more specific with certain cost objects, such as when they focus on the cost per available seat mile (or CASM as industry experts refer to it), which typically falls in the 6 to 10 cent range for most airlines.

Other airline cost objects are even more challenging. For example, you likely did not include the cost of managing crises as an important cost object. However, according to the International Air Transit Association, the airline industry took an estimated $1.7 billion hit from disrupted airline travel resulting from the volcanic ash cloud caused by the eruption of the Icelandic volcano Eyjafjallajokull.[3]

Finally, you might consider the cost object of processing customers, such as loading and unloading passengers and their baggage on and off of flights. For example, airlines have charged fees for using curbside check-in services, consuming soft drinks during flight, using pillows and blanks while onboard, selecting seats prior to the day of the flight, and checking bags. **Spirit Airlines** raised many customer (and even regulator) eyebrows by being the first airline to charge passengers ($45) for their carry-on bags.[4]

**Like any company, an airline can identify and manage any cost objects it so desires. Sometimes the most difficult part of effective cost management is the first step—deciding on the exact items for which one needs to understand the cost. Mistakes in selecting the cost objects almost always lead to poor decisions and subpar performance.**

## Assigning Costs to Cost Objects

Costs can be assigned to cost objects in a number of ways. Relatively speaking, some methods are more accurate, and others are simpler. The choice of a method depends on a number of factors, such as the need for accuracy. The notion of accuracy is a relative concept and has to do with the reasonableness and logic of the cost assignment methods used. The objective is to measure and assign costs as well as possible, given management objectives. For example, suppose you and three of your friends go out to dinner at a local pizza parlor. When the bill comes, everything has been added together for a total of $36. How much is your share? One easy way to find your share is to divide the bill evenly among you and your friends. In that case, you each owe $9 ($36/4). But suppose that one of you had a small salad and drink (totaling $5), while another had a specialty pizza, appetizer, and beer (totaling $15). Clearly, it is possible to identify what each person had and assign costs that way. The second method is more accurate, but also more work. Which method you choose will depend on how important it is to you to assign the specific meal costs to each individual. It is the same way in accounting. There are a number of ways to assign costs to cost objects. Some methods are quick and easy but may be inaccurate. Other methods are much more accurate, but involve much more work (in business, more work equals more expense).

**Direct Costs**    **Direct costs** are those costs that can be easily and accurately traced to a cost object. When we say that a cost is easy to trace, we often mean that the relationship between the cost and the object can be physically observed and is easy to track. The more costs that can be traced to the object, the more accurate are the cost assignments. For example, suppose that Chef Courtney, from our earlier discussion, wants to know the cost of emphasizing fresh, in-season fruits and vegetables in her entrees. The purchase cost of the fruits and vegetables would be relatively easy to determine.

**Indirect Costs**    Some costs, however, are hard to trace. **Indirect costs** are costs that cannot be easily and accurately traced to a cost object. For example, Courtney incurs additional costs in scouting the outlying farms and farmers' markets (as opposed to

2 http://images.delta.com.edgesuite.net/delta/pdfs/annual_reports/2009_10K.pdf

3 www.guardian.co.uk/business/2010/apr/21/airline-industry-cost-volcanic-ash (accessed on May 8, 2010).

4 www.msnbc.msn.com/id/37004725/ns/travel-news/

simply ordering fruits and vegetables from a distributor). She must use her own time and automobile to make the trips. Farmers' markets may not deliver, so Courtney must arrange for a coworker with a van to pick up the produce. By definition, fruits and vegetables that are currently in season will be out of season (i.e., unavailable) in a few weeks. This seasonality means that Courtney must spend more time revising menus and developing new recipes that can be adapted to restaurant conditions. In addition, waste and spoilage may increase until Courtney and the kitchen staff learn just how much to order. These costs are difficult to assign to the meals prepared and sold. Therefore, they are indirect costs. Some businesses refer to indirect costs as overhead costs or support costs. Exhibit 2.1 shows direct and indirect costs being assigned to cost objects.

---

**( EXHIBIT 2.1 )**

**Object Costing**

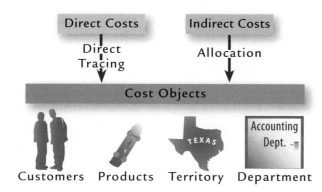

© Cengage Learning 2014

*Assigning Indirect Costs* Even though indirect costs cannot be traced to cost objects, it is still important to assign them. This assignment usually is accomplished by using allocation. **Allocation** means that an indirect cost is assigned to a cost object by using a reasonable and convenient method. Since no clearly observable causal relationship exists, allocating indirect costs is based on convenience or some assumed causal linkage. For example, consider the cost of heating and lighting a plant in which five products are manufactured. Suppose that this utility cost is to be assigned to these five products. It is difficult to see any causal relationship between utility costs and each unit of product manufactured. Therefore, a convenient way to allocate this cost is to assign it in proportion to the direct labor hours used by each product. This method is relatively easy and accomplishes the purpose of ensuring that all costs are assigned to units produced. Allocating indirect costs is important for a variety of reasons. For example, allocating indirect costs to products is needed to determine the value of inventory and of cost of goods sold. Perhaps more importantly, as companies become more complex in the number and types of products and services they offer to customers, the need to understand, allocate, and effectively control indirect costs becomes increasingly important. In addition, indirect costs represent an increasingly large percentage of total costs for many companies.

Returning briefly to the **Little Guys Home Electronics** business from the chapter opening, the prices set by Little Guys management are heavily dependent on understanding the company's costs, both traced direct and allocated indirect, for each product. The more difficult costs to estimate and, therefore, use appropriately in setting prices are the indirect, or overhead, costs. According to David, a partner in Little Guys, the most difficult part of pricing is deciding how accurately the indirect costs—such as inventory warehousing, support role employee labor, store insurance, delivery truck maintenance and rental (when the store owned trucks are in the shop for repair) and healthcare—have been allocated to each home electronics product. For example, if management believes that too few indirect costs have been allocated to a set of Klipsch speakers, then the speaker cost is marked up by a greater percentage than if the correct amount of indirect costs has been assigned. Therefore, accurately tracing direct costs and allocating indirect costs to products and services is important for many management decisions.

Direct and indirect costs occur in service businesses as well. For example, a bank's cost of printing and mailing monthly statements to checking account holders is a direct cost of the product—checking accounts. However, the cost of office furniture in the bank is an indirect cost for the checking accounts.

**ETHICAL DECISIONS**   Tracking costs can also act as an early warning system for unauthorized activity and possible ethical problems. For example, **Metropolitan Life Insurance Company** was dismayed to learn that some of its agents were selling policies as retirement plans. This practice is illegal, and it cost the company more than $20 million in fines as well as $50 million in refunds to policy holders.[5] More accurate and comprehensive data tracking regarding sales, individual agents, types of policies, and policyholders could have alerted Metropolitan Life to a potential problem. Thus, we can see that tracking costs can serve many different and important purposes. •

**Other Categories of Cost**   In addition to being categorized as either direct or indirect, costs often are analyzed with respect to their behavior patterns, or the way in which a cost changes when the level of the output changes.

*Variable Cost*   A **variable cost** is one that increases in total as output increases and decreases in total as output decreases. For example, the denim used in making jeans is a variable cost. As the company makes more jeans, it needs more denim.

*Fixed Cost*   A **fixed cost** is a cost that does not increase in total as output increases and does not decrease in total as output decreases. For example, the cost of property taxes on the factory building stays the same no matter how many pairs of jeans the company makes. How can that be, since property taxes can and do change yearly? While the cost changes, it is not because output changes. Rather, it changes because the city or county government decides to raise taxes.

Variable and fixed costs are covered more extensively in Chapter 3.

*Opportunity Cost*   An **opportunity cost** is the benefit given up or sacrificed when one alternative is chosen over another. For example, an opportunity cost of you participating in a summer study abroad program might include the wages you would have earned during that time if you had stayed home to work rather than participating in the overseas program. On the other hand, an opportunity cost of your staying home to work rather than participating in the study abroad program might include the value that future employers would have placed on the knowledge and experience you would have gathered had you participated in the overseas program. Opportunity cost differs from accounting cost in that the opportunity cost is never included in the accounting records because it is the cost of something that did not occur. Opportunity costs are important to decision making, as we will see more clearly in Chapter 13.

OBJECTIVE ❷

Define the various costs of manufacturing products and providing services as well as the costs of selling and administration.

# PRODUCT AND SERVICE COSTS

Output represents one of the most important cost objects. There are two types of output: products and services.

- **Products** are goods produced by converting raw materials through the use of labor and indirect manufacturing resources, such as the manufacturing plant, land, and machinery. Televisions, hamburgers, automobiles, computers, clothes, and furniture are examples of products.

---

[5] Roush, Chris, "Fields of Green—and Disaster Areas," *BusinessWeek* (January 9, 1995): 94.

- **Services** are tasks or activities performed for a customer or an activity performed by a customer using an organization's products or facilities. Insurance coverage, medical care, dental care, funeral care, and accounting are examples of service activities performed for customers. Car rental, video rental, and skiing are examples of services where the customer uses an organization's products or facilities.

Organizations that produce products are called **manufacturing organizations**. Organizations that provide services are called **service organizations**. Managers of both types of organizations need to know how much individual products or services cost. Accurate cost information is vital for profitability analysis and strategic decisions concerning product design, pricing, and product mix. Incidentally, retail organizations, such as **J. Crew**, buy finished products from other organizations, such as manufacturers, and then sell them to customers. The accounting for inventory and cost of goods sold for retail organizations, often referred to as merchandisers, is much simpler than for manufacturing organizations and is usually covered extensively in introductory financial accounting courses. Therefore, the focus here is on manufacturing and service organizations.

Services differ from products in many ways, including the following:

- *Services are intangible:* The buyers of services cannot see, feel, hear, or taste a service before it is bought.
- *Services are perishable:* Services cannot be stored for future use by a consumer but must be consumed when performed. Inventory valuation, so important for products, is not an issue for services. In other words, because service organizations do not produce and sell products as part of their regular operations, they have no inventory asset on the balance sheet.
- *Services require direct contact between providers and buyers:* An eye examination, for example, requires both the patient and the optometrist to be present. However, producers of products need not have direct contact with the buyers of their goods. Thus, buyers of automobiles never need to have contact with the engineers and assembly line workers that produced their automobiles.

The overall way in which a company costs services in terms of classifying related costs as either direct or indirect is very similar to the way in which it costs products. The main difference in costing is that products have inventories, and services do not.

## Providing Cost Information

Managerial accountants must decide what types of managerial accounting information to provide to managers, how to measure such information, and when and to whom to communicate the information. For example, when making most strategic and operating decisions, managers typically rely on managerial accounting information that is prepared in whatever manner the managerial accountant believes provides the best analysis for the decision at hand. Therefore, the majority of the managerial accounting issues explained in this book do not reference a formal set of external rules, but instead consider the context of the given decision (e.g., relevant versus irrelevant cost information for make-or-buy decisions, full cost versus functional cost information for pricing decisions, etc.).

However, there is one major exception. Managerial accountants must follow specific external reporting rules (i.e., generally accepted accounting principles) when their companies provide outside parties with cost information about the amount of ending inventory on the balance sheet and the cost of goods sold on the income statement. In order to calculate these two amounts, managerial accountants must subdivide costs into functional categories: production and period (i.e., nonproduction). The following section describes the process for categorizing costs as either product or period in nature.

## Determining Product Cost

**Product (manufacturing) costs** are those costs, both direct and indirect, of producing a product in a manufacturing firm or of acquiring a product in a merchandising firm and preparing it for sale. Therefore, only costs in the *production* section of the value chain are included in product costs. A key feature of product costs is that they are inventoried. Product costs initially are added to an inventory account and remain in inventory until they are sold, at which time they are transferred to cost of goods sold (COGS). Product costs can be further classified as direct materials, direct labor, and manufacturing overhead, which are the three cost elements that can be assigned to products for external financial reporting (e.g., inventories or COGS). Exhibit 2.2 shows how direct materials, direct labor, and overhead become product costs.

---

**( EXHIBIT 2.2 )**

**Product Costs Include Direct Materials, Direct Labor, and Overhead**

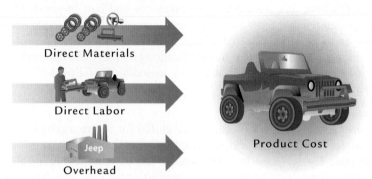

© Cengage Learning 2014

**Direct Materials** **Direct materials** are those materials that are a part of the final product and can be directly traced to the goods being produced. The cost of these materials can be directly charged to products because physical observation can be used to measure the quantity used by each product. Materials that become part of a product usually are classified as direct materials. For example, tires on a new **Porsche** automobile, wood in an **Ethan Allen** dining room table, alcohol in an **Estee Lauder** cologne, and denim in a pair of **American Eagle** jeans are all part of direct materials for manufacturers of these products.

A closely related term is raw materials. Often, the inventory of materials is called the raw materials account. Materials in the raw materials account do not become direct materials until they are withdrawn from inventory for use in production. The raw materials inventory account can include indirect materials as well as direct materials. Indirect materials are used in the production process but the amount used by each unit cannot be easily determined and, as a result, these costs are treated as indirect costs (as discussed later).

**Direct Labor** **Direct labor** is the labor that can be directly traced to the goods being produced. Physical observation can be used to measure the amount of labor used to produce a product. Those employees who convert direct materials into a product are classified as direct labor. For example, workers on an assembly line at **Dell Computers** are classified as direct labor.

Just as there were indirect materials in a company, there may also be indirect labor. This labor is not direct labor since these workers do not actually make the product. However, their contribution is necessary to production. An example of indirect labor in a production setting is the maintenance crew who performs regularly scheduled preventative maintenance every other Wednesday morning in **Georgia Pacific**'s plywood manufacturing plants. Indirect labor is included in overhead and, therefore, is an indirect cost rather than a direct cost.

**Manufacturing Overhead** All product costs other than direct materials and direct labor are put into a category called **manufacturing overhead**. In a manufacturing firm, manufacturing overhead also is known as *factory burden* or *indirect* manufacturing costs. Costs are included as manufacturing overhead if they cannot be traced to the cost object of interest (e.g., unit of product). The manufacturing overhead cost category contains a wide variety of items. Examples of manufacturing overhead costs include depreciation on plant buildings and equipment, janitorial and maintenance labor, plant supervision, materials handling, power for plant utilities, and plant property taxes.

The important thing to remember is that all costs in the factory are classified as direct materials, direct labor, or manufacturing overhead. No product cost can be omitted from classification, no matter how far removed you might think it is from the actual production of a product. Earlier we mentioned that indirect materials and indirect labor are included in overhead. In manufacturing, the glue used in furniture or toys is an example, as is the cost of oil to grease cookie sheets for producing cookies.

*Total Product Cost* The total product cost equals the sum of direct materials, direct labor, and manufacturing overhead:

Total Product Cost = Direct Materials + Direct Labor + Manufacturing Overhead

The unit product cost equals total product cost divided by the number of units produced:

$$\text{Per-Unit Product Cost} = \frac{\text{Total Product Cost}}{\text{Number of Units Produced}}$$

Cornerstone 2.1 shows how to calculate total product cost and per unit product cost.

## Calculating Product Cost in Total and Per Unit

CORNERSTONE

2.1

**Why:**

Product costs are essential to management control and decision making. Managers use product costs to create budgets and analyses. Product costs within manufacturing can then be contrasted with period costs incurred outside of manufacturing.

**Information:**

BlueDenim Company makes blue jeans. Last week, direct materials (denim, thread, zippers, and rivets) costing $48,000 were put into production. Direct labor of $30,000 (50 workers × 40 hours × $15 per hour) was incurred. Overhead equaled $72,000. By the end of the week, BlueDenium had manufactured 30,000 pairs of jeans.

**Required:**

1. Calculate the total product cost for last week.

2. Calculate the cost of one pair of jeans that was produced last week.

**Solution:**

1.

| | |
|---|---|
| Direct materials | $ 48,000 |
| Direct labor | 30,000 |
| Overhead | 72,000 |
| Total product cost | $150,000 |

2. Per-Unit Product Cost = $150,000/30,000 = $5

Product costs include direct materials, direct labor, and manufacturing overhead. Once the product is finished, no more costs attach to it. That is, any costs associated with storing, selling, and delivering the product are not product costs, but instead are period costs.

*Prime and Conversion Costs* Product costs of direct materials, direct labor, and manufacturing overhead are sometimes grouped into prime cost and conversion cost:

- **Prime cost** is the sum of direct materials cost and direct labor cost:

> Prime Cost = Direct Materials + Direct Labor

- **Conversion cost** is the sum of direct labor cost and manufacturing overhead cost:

> Conversion Cost = Direct Labor + Manufacturing Overhead

For a manufacturing firm, conversion cost can be interpreted as the cost of converting raw materials into a final product.

Cornerstone 2.2 shows how to calculate prime cost and conversion cost for a manufactured product.

CORNERSTONE

2.2

## Calculating Prime Cost and Conversion Cost in Total and Per Unit

**Why:**

Managers often categorize product costs into either prime or conversion in nature to compare the relative cost of manufacturing inputs (i.e., direct materials and direct labor) versus processing (i.e., direct labor and manufacturing overhead).

**Information:**

Refer to the information in Cornerstone 2.1 (p. 35) for BlueDenim Company.

**Required:**

1. Calculate the total prime cost for last week.
2. Calculate the per-unit prime cost.
3. Calculate the total conversion cost for last week.
4. Calculate the per-unit conversion cost.

**Solution:**

1.

| | |
|---|---|
| Direct materials | $48,000 |
| Direct labor | 30,000 |
| Total prime cost | $78,000 |

2. Per-Unit Prime Cost = $78,000/30,000 = $2.60

3.

| | |
|---|---|
| Direct labor | $ 30,000 |
| Overhead | 72,000 |
| Total conversion cost | $102,000 |

4. Per-Unit Conversion Cost = $102,000/30,000 units = $3.40

*Note:* Remember that prime cost and conversion cost do NOT equal total product cost. This is because direct labor is part of BOTH prime cost and conversion cost.

**Period Costs** The costs of production are assets that are carried in inventories until the goods are sold. There are other costs of running a company, referred to as *period costs*, that are not carried in inventory. Thus, **period costs** are all costs that are not product costs (i.e., all areas of the value chain except for production). The cost of office supplies, research and development activities, the CEO's salary, and advertising are examples of period costs. For instance, **Victoria's Secret** spent approximately $2.7 million to run a 30-second advertisement during Super Bowl XLII. With the exception of the final episode of M*A*S*H, the Giant's underdog victory over the previously unbeaten Patriots was watched by more viewers (97.5 million) than any television show in history.[6] Despite these record ratings, however, some people considered this $2.7 million period expense to be excessive. Managerial accountants help executives at companies like Victoria's Secret determine whether or not such costly advertising campaigns generate enough additional sales revenue over the long run to make them profitable.

Period costs cannot be assigned to products or appear as part of the reported values of inventories on the balance sheet. Instead, period costs typically are expensed in the period in which they are incurred. However, if a period cost is expected to provide an economic benefit (i.e., revenues) beyond the next year, then it is recorded as an asset (i.e., capitalized) and allocated to expense through depreciation throughout its useful life. The cost associated with the purchase of a delivery truck is an example of a period cost that would be capitalized when incurred and then recognized as an expense over the useful life of the truck. Exhibit 2.3 depicts the distinction between product and period costs and how each type of cost eventually becomes an expense on the income statement. As shown in the exhibit, product costs, which are capitalized as an inventory asset, are expensed on the income statement as cost of goods sold to match against the revenues generated from the sale of the inventory. However, capitalized period costs are depreciated to expense on the income statement over the asset's useful life to match against the revenues generated by the asset over its useful life.

( EXHIBIT 2.3 )

**The Impact of Product versus Period Costs on the Financial Statements**

© Cengage Learning 2014

In a manufacturing organization, the level of period costs can be significant (often greater than 25% of sales revenue), and controlling them may bring greater cost savings than the same effort exercised in controlling production costs. For example, **Nike**'s period expenses are 35% of its revenue ($7,375,000,000/$20,862,000,000).[7] For service organizations, the relative importance of selling and administrative costs depends on the nature of the service produced. Physicians and dentists, for example, do relatively little marketing and thus have very low selling costs. On the other hand, a grocery chain may incur substantial marketing costs. Period costs often are divided into selling costs and administrative costs.

[6] Hiestand, Michael, "Game Attracts Biggest Audience," *USA Today* (February 5, 2008): C1.

[7] From Nike's 2011 Annual Report.

*Selling Costs* Those costs necessary to market, distribute, and service a product or service are **selling costs**. They are often referred to as *order-getting* and *order-filling* costs. Examples of selling costs include salaries and commissions of sales personnel, advertising, warehousing, shipping, and customer service. The first two items are examples of order-getting costs; the last three are order-filling costs.

*Administrative Costs* All costs associated with research, development, and general administration of the organization that cannot reasonably be assigned to either selling or production are **administrative costs**. General administration has the responsibility of ensuring that the various activities of the organization are properly integrated so that the overall mission of the firm is realized. The president of the firm, for example, is concerned with the efficiency of selling, production, and research and development activities. Proper integration of these activities is essential to maximizing the overall profits of a firm. Examples of general administrative costs are executive salaries, legal fees, printing the annual report, and general accounting. Research and development costs are the costs associated with designing and developing new products and must be expensed in the period incurred.

*Direct and Indirect Period Costs* As with product costs, it is often helpful to distinguish between direct period costs and indirect period costs. Service companies also make this important distinction. For example, a surgical center would show that surgical gauze and anesthesia are direct costs used for an operation because it could be determined how much gauze or anesthesia was used for each procedure or patient. Other examples of direct costs in service industries include the chef in a restaurant, a surgical nurse attending an open heart operation, and a pilot for **Southwest Airlines**.

Alternately, although shampoo and hair spray are used in a beauty shop, the exact amount used in each individual's hair cut is not easily determinable. As a result, the costs associated with shampoo and hair spray would be considered indirect, or overhead, costs and allocated, rather than traced, to individual hair cuts. Examples of indirect labor costs in a service setting include the surgical assistants in a hospital who clean up the operating room after surgery, dispose of certain used materials, and sterilize the reusable instruments. Indirect labor is included in overhead. The rental of a Santa suit for the annual company Christmas party would be an example of an indirect cost that would be expensed in the period incurred. Although these costs do not affect the calculation of inventories or COGS (i.e., because they are service companies), their correct classification nonetheless affects numerous decisions and planning and control activities for managers, as we will discuss in detail in future chapters.

OBJECTIVE **3**

Prepare income statements for manufacturing and service organizations.

# PREPARING INCOME STATEMENTS

The earlier definitions of product, selling, and administrative costs provide a good conceptual overview of these important costs. However, the actual calculation of these costs in practice is a bit more complicated. Let's take a closer look at just how costs are calculated for purposes of preparing the external financial statements, focusing first on manufacturing firms.

## Cost of Goods Manufactured

The **cost of goods manufactured** represents the total product cost of goods *completed* during the current period and transferred to finished goods inventory. The only costs assigned to goods completed are the manufacturing costs of direct materials, direct labor, and manufacturing overhead. So, why don't we just add together the current period's costs of direct materials, direct labor, and manufacturing overhead to arrive at cost of goods sold? The reason is inventories of materials and work in process. For instance, some of the materials purchased in the current period likely were used in production (i.e., transferred from materials inventory to work-in-process inventory during the period). However, other materials likely were not used in production, and thus remain in materials inventory at period end. Also, some of the units that were worked on (and thus allocated labor and manufacturing overhead costs) in the current period likely were completed during the period (i.e., transferred from work-in-process inventory to finished goods inventory during the period). However, other units worked on during the period likely were not completed during the period, and thus remain in work-in-process inventory at period end. In calculating cost of goods sold, we need to distinguish between the total manufacturing cost for the current period and the manufacturing costs associated with the units that were completed during the current period (i.e., cost of goods manufactured).

Let's take a look at direct materials. Suppose a company had no materials on hand at the beginning of the month, then bought $15,000 of direct materials during the month, and used all of them in production. The entire $15,000 would be properly called *direct materials*. Usually, though, the company has some materials on hand at the beginning of the month. These materials are the beginning inventory of materials. Let's say that this beginning inventory of materials cost $2,500. Then during the month, the company would have a total of $17,500 of materials that could be used in production ($2,500 from beginning inventory and $15,000 purchased during the month). Typically, the company would not use the entire amount of materials on hand in production. Perhaps they use only $12,000 of materials. Then, the cost of direct materials used in production this month is $12,000, and the remaining $5,500 of materials is the ending inventory of materials. This reasoning can be easily expressed in a formula:

$$\text{Beginning Inventory of Materials} + \text{Purchases} - \text{Direct Materials Used in Production} = \text{Ending Inventory of Materials}$$

While this computation is logical and simple, it does not express the result for which we usually are looking. We are usually trying to figure out the amount of direct materials used in production—not the amount of ending inventory. Cornerstone 2.3 shows how to compute the amount of direct materials used in production.

## Calculating the Direct Materials Used in Production

CORNERSTONE

2.3

**Why:**

The primary use of calculating the direct materials used in production, is to serve as the first number in calculating the cost of goods manufactured. Direct materials used in production also show managers the difference between the amount of materials purchased, and the amount of materials used in manufacturing for the period.

**Information:**

BlueDenim Company makes blue jeans. On May 1, BlueDenim had $68,000 of materials in inventory. During the month of May, BlueDenim purchased $210,000 of materials. On May 31, materials inventory equaled $22,000.

**Required:**

Calculate the cost of direct materials used in production for the month of May.

**Solution:**

| | |
|---|---:|
| Materials inventory, May 1 | $ 68,000 |
| Purchases | 210,000 |
| Materials inventory, May 31 | (22,000) |
| Direct materials used in production | $256,000 |

Once the direct materials are calculated, the direct labor and manufacturing overhead *for the time period* can be added to get the total manufacturing cost for the period. Now we need to consider the second type of inventory—work in process. **Work in process (WIP)** is the cost of the partially completed goods that are still on the factory floor at the end of a time period. These are units that have been started, but are not finished. They have value, but not as much as they will when they are completed. Just as there are beginning and ending inventories of materials, there are beginning and ending inventories of WIP. We must adjust the total manufacturing cost for the time period for the inventories of WIP. When that is done, we will have the total cost of the goods that were completed and transferred from work-in-process inventory to finished goods inventory during the time period. Cornerstone 2.4 shows how to calculate the cost of goods manufactured for a particular time period.

**CORNERSTONE**

**2.4**

## Calculating Cost of Goods Manufactured

**Why:**

The primary use for the statement of cost of goods manufactured is for external financial reporting.

**Information:**

BlueDenim Company makes blue jeans. During the month of May, BlueDenim purchased $210,000 of materials and incurred direct labor cost of $135,000 and manufacturing overhead of $150,000. On May 31, materials inventory equaled $22,000. Inventory information is as follows:

|                  | May 1    | May 31   |
|------------------|----------|----------|
| Materials        | $68,000  | $22,000  |
| Work in process  | 50,000   | 16,000   |

**Required:**

Calculate the cost of goods manufactured for the month of May.

**Solution:**

| | |
|---|---:|
| Direct materials used in production* | $256,000 |
| Direct labor | 135,000 |
| Manufacturing overhead | 150,000 |
| Total manufacturing cost for May | $541,000 |
| WIP, May 1 | 50,000 |
| WIP, May 31 | (16,000) |
| Cost of goods manufactured | $575,000 |

\* Direct Materials = $68,000 + $210,000 − $22,000 = $256,000

## Cost of Goods Sold

To meet external reporting requirements, costs must be classified into three categories:

- production
- selling
- administration

Remember that product costs are initially put into inventory. They become expenses only when the products are sold, which matches the expenses of manufacturing the product to the sales revenue generated by the product at the time it is sold. Therefore, the expense of manufacturing is not the cost of goods manufactured; instead it is the cost of the goods that are sold. **Cost of goods sold** represents the cost of goods that were sold during the period and, therefore, transferred from finished goods inventory on the balance sheet to cost of goods sold on the income statement (i.e., as an inventory expense). Cornerstone 2.5 shows how to calculate the cost of goods sold.

## Calculating Cost of Goods Sold

CORNERSTONE

**2.5**

**Why:**

The primary use for the statement of cost of goods sold is for external financial reporting. It is a critical input to the income statement.

**Information:**

BlueDenim Company makes blue jeans. During the month of May, 115,000 pairs of jeans were completed at a cost of goods manufactured of $575,000. Suppose that on May 1, BlueDenim had 10,000 units in the finished goods inventory costing $50,000 and on May 31, the company had 26,000 units in the finished goods inventory costing $130,000.

**Required:**

1. Prepare a cost of goods sold statement for the month of May.

2. Calculate the number of pairs of jeans that were sold during May.

**Solution:**

1.

**BlueDenim Company**
**Cost of Goods Sold Statement**
**For the Month of May**

| | |
|---|---:|
| Cost of goods manufactured | $ 575,000 |
| Finished goods inventory, May 1 | 50,000 |
| Finished good inventory, May 31 | (130,000) |
| Cost of goods sold | $ 495,000 |

2. Number of units sold:

| | |
|---|---:|
| Finished goods inventory, May 1 | 10,000 |
| Units finished during May | 115,000 |
| Finished goods inventory, May 31 | (26,000) |
| Units sold during May | 99,000 |

The ending inventories of materials, WIP, and finished goods are important because they are assets and appear on the balance sheet (as current assets). The cost of goods sold is an expense that appears on the income statement. Selling and administrative costs are period costs and also appear on the income statement as an expense. Collectively, Cornerstones 2.3, 2.4, and 2.5 (pp. 39–41) depict the flow of costs through the three inventories (materials, work in process, and finished goods) and finally into cost of goods sold.

© Pixelfabrik/Alamy

Exhibit 2.4 uses the information in Cornerstones 2.3, 2.4, and 2.5 to illustrate how the manufacturing costs—direct materials, direct labor, and manufacturing overhead—flow through the inventories—direct materials, work in process, and finished goods—and eventually into cost of goods sold on the income statement. Exhibit 2.4 also shows the difference between when direct materials are purchased (or incurred and put into direct materials inventory—$210,000) versus when they are used in production (i.e., placed into WIP inventory—$256,000). There is no difference between when direct labor and manufacturing overhead costs are incurred versus when they are used in production because they cannot be stored in inventory before use (as can direct materials).

**( EXHIBIT 2.4 )**

**Relationship between the Flow of Costs, Inventories, and Cost of Goods Sold**

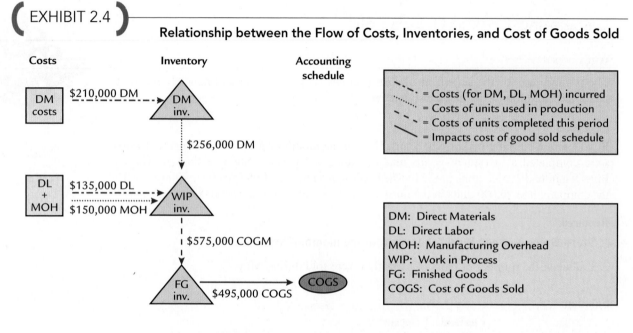

© Cengage Learning 2014

## Income Statement: Manufacturing Firm

The income statement for a manufacturing firm is displayed in Cornerstone 2.6 . This income statement follows the traditional format taught in an introductory financial accounting course. Notice that the income statement covers a certain period of time (i.e., the month of May in Cornerstone 2.6). However, the time period may vary. The key point is that all sales revenue and expenses attached to that period of time appear on the income statement.

**CORNERSTONE**

**2.6**

### Preparing an Income Statement for a Manufacturing Firm

**Why:**

The primary use for the income statement is for external financial reporting. Investors and outside parties use it to determine the financial health of a firm.

**Information:**

Recall that BlueDenim Company sold 99,000 pairs of jeans during the month of May at a total cost of $495,000. Each pair sold at a price of $8. BlueDenim also incurred two types of selling costs: commissions equal to 10% of the sales price, and fixed selling expense of $120,000. Administrative expense totaled $85,000.

*(Continued)*

© Pixelfabrik/Alamy

**Required:**

Prepare an income statement for BlueDenim for the month of May.

**Solution:**

CORNERSTONE

**2.6**

*(Continued)*

**BlueDenim Company**
**Income Statement**
**For the Month of May**

| | | |
|---|---:|---:|
| Sales revenue (99,000 × $8) | | $792,000 |
| Cost of goods sold | | 495,000 |
| Gross margin | | $297,000 |
| Less: | | |
| Selling expense | | |
| Commissions (0.10 × $792,000) | $ 79,200 | |
| Fixed selling expense | 120,000 | 199,200 |
| Administrative expense | | 85,000 |
| Operating income | | $ 12,800 |

Look at the income statement in Cornerstone 2.6. First, the heading tells us what type of statement it is, for what firm, and for what period of time. Then, the income statement itself always begins with "sales revenue" (or "sales" or "revenue"). The sales revenue is calculated as follows:

$$\text{Sales Revenue} = \text{Price} \times \text{Units Sold}$$

After the sales revenue is determined, the firm must calculate expenses for the period. Notice that the expenses are separated into three categories: production (cost of goods sold), selling, and administrative. The first type of expense is the cost of producing the units sold, or the cost of goods sold. This amount was computed and explained in Cornerstone 2.5 (p. 41). Remember that the cost of goods sold is the cost of producing the units that were sold during the time period. It includes direct materials, direct labor, and manufacturing overhead. It does *not* include any selling or administrative expense. In the case of a retail (i.e., a merchandising) firm, the cost of goods sold represents the total cost of the goods sold when they were purchased from an outside supplier. Therefore, the cost of goods sold for a retailer equals the purchase costs adjusted for the beginning and ending balances in its single inventory account. A merchandising firm, such as **Old Navy** or **J. Crew**, has only one inventory account because it does not transform the purchased good into a different form by adding materials, labor, and overhead, as does a manufacturing firm.

**Gross margin** is the difference between sales revenue and cost of goods sold:

$$\text{Gross Margin} = \text{Sales Revenue} - \text{Cost of Goods Sold}$$

It shows how much the firm is making over and above the cost of the units sold. Gross margin does *not* equal operating income or profit. Selling and administrative expenses have not yet been subtracted. However, gross margin does provide useful information. If gross margin is positive, the firm at least charges prices that cover the product cost. In addition, the firm can calculate its gross margin percentage (Gross margin/Sales revenue), as shown in Cornerstone 2.7 , and compare it with the average gross margin percentage for the industry to see if its experience is in the ballpark with other firms in the industry.

## Calculating the Percentage of Sales Revenue for Each Line on the Income Statement

**Why:**

Calculating the percentage of revenue informs managers of the size of each income statement line item relative to sales revenue. This calculation also enables comparisons between fiscal periods and with other firms in the industry.

**Information:**

Refer to the income statement for BlueDenim Company in Cornerstone 2.6.

**Required:**

Calculate the percentage of sales revenue represented by each line of the income statement.

**Solution:**

BlueDenim Company
Income Statement
For the Month of May

|  |  |  | Percent* |
|---|---|---|---|
| Sales revenue (99,000 × $8) |  | $792,000 | 100.0 |
| Cost of goods sold |  | 495,000 | 62.5 |
| Gross margin |  | $297,000 | 37.5 |
| Less: |  |  |  |
| Selling expense |  |  |  |
| Commissions (0.10 × $792,000) | $ 79,200 |  |  |
| Fixed selling expense | 120,000 | 199,200 | 25.2 |
| Administrative expense |  | 85,000 | 10.7 |
| Operating income |  | $ 12,800 | 1.6 |

* Steps in calculating the percentages:
1. Sales Revenue Percent = $792,000/$792,000 = 1.00 or 100% (sales revenue is always 100% of itself)
2. Cost of Goods Sold Percent = $495,000/$792,000 = 0.625 or 62.5%
3. Gross Margin Percent = $297,000/$792,000 = 0.375 or 37.5%
4. Selling Expense Percent = $199,200/$792,000 = 0.252 or 25.2% (rounded)
5. Administrative Expense Percent = $85,000/$792,000 = 0.107 or 10.7% (rounded)
6. Operating Income Percent = $12,800/$792,000 = 0.016 or 1.6% (rounded)

Gross margin percentage varies significantly by industry. For instance, **Kroger**'s gross margin percentage as determined from the income statement in its annual report is 22.2% ($18,262,000,000/$82,189,000,000).[8] However, **Merck**'s gross margin percentage as determined from the income statement in its annual report is 74.3% ($6,905,200,000/$9,290,600,000).[9] One reason for Merck's extremely high gross margin percent is that a large percentage of its costs are related to marketing (e.g., advertising) and research and development ($2.2 billion and $1.4 billion, respectively) and, as such, are expensed as period costs in the period incurred. Thus, Merck's cost of goods sold was relatively small.

[8] Per Kroger's 2010 Annual Report.
[9] Per Merck's 2010 Annual Report.

Finally, selling expense and administrative expense for the period are subtracted from gross margin to arrive at operating income:

> Operating Income = Gross Margin − Selling and Administrative Expense

Operating income is the key figure from the income statement; it is profit, and shows how much the owners are actually earning from the company. Again, calculating the percentage of operating income (i.e., Operating Income/Sales Revenue) and comparing it to the average for the industry gives the owners valuable information about relative profitability.

The income statement can be analyzed further by calculating the percentage of sales revenue represented by each line of the statement, as was done in Cornerstone 2.7. How can management use this information? The first thing that jumps out is that operating income is less than 2% of sales revenue. That's a very small percentage. Unless this is common for the blue jeans manufacturing business, BlueDenim's management should work hard to increase the percentage. Selling expense is a whopping 25.2% of sales. Do commissions really need to be that high? Or is the price too low (compared to competitors' prices)? Can cost of goods sold be reduced? Is 62.5% reasonable? These are questions that are suggested by Cornerstone 2.7, but not answered. Answering the questions is the job of management.

## Income Statement: Service Firm

In a service organization, there is no product to purchase (e.g., a merchandiser like **American Eagle Outfitters**) or to manufacture (e.g., **Toshiba**) and, therefore, there are no beginning or ending inventories. As a result, there is no cost of goods sold or gross margin on the income statement. Instead, the cost of providing services appears along with the other operating expenses of the company. For example, **Southwest Airlines'** income statement begins with Total Operating Revenues of $10,350,000,000 and subtracts Total Operating Expenses of $10,088,000,000 to arrive at an Operating Income of $262,000,000.[10] An income statement for a service firm is shown in Cornerstone 2.8 .

## Preparing an Income Statement for a Service Organization

**CORNERSTONE**

**2.8**

**Why:**

The primary use for the income statement is for external financial reporting. Investors and outside parties use it to determine the financial health of a firm. Cost of goods sold typically does not exist on the income statement because service organizations generate sales by providing services rather than selling products.

**Information:**

Komala Information Systems designs and installs human resources software for small companies. Last month, Komala had software licensing costs of $5,000, service technicians' costs of $35,000, and research and development costs of $55,000. Selling expenses were $5,000, and administrative expenses equaled $7,000. Sales totaled $130,000.

**Required:**

Prepare an income statement for Komala Information Systems for the past month.

*(Continued)*

---

[10] Per Southwest Airlines' 2009 Annual Report: www.southwest.com/investor_relations/if_sec_filings.html.

**CORNERSTONE**

**2.8**

*(Continued)*

**Solution:**

**Komala Information Systems**
**Income Statement**
**For the Past Month**

| | | |
|---|---:|---:|
| Sales revenues: | | $130,000 |
| Less operating expenses: | | |
|    Software licensing | $ 5,000 | |
|    Service technicians | 35,000 | |
|    Research and development | 55,000 | |
|    Selling expenses | 5,000 | |
|    Administrative expenses | 7,000 | 107,000 |
| Operating income | | $ 23,000 |

# SUMMARY OF LEARNING OBJECTIVES

**LO 1.** Explain the meaning of cost and how costs are assigned to products and services.

- Cost is the cash or cash-equivalent value sacrificed for goods and services that are expected to bring a current or future benefit to the organization.
- Managers use cost information to determine the cost of objects such as products, projects, plants, and customers.
- Direct costs are traced to cost objects based on cause-and-effect relationships.
- Indirect (i.e., overhead) costs are allocated to cost objects based on assumed relationships and convenience.

**LO 2.** Define the various costs of manufacturing products and providing services as well as the costs of selling and administration.

- Products are goods that either are purchased or produced by converting raw materials through the use of labor and indirect manufacturing resources, such as plants, land, and machinery. Services are tasks performed for a customer or activities performed by a customer using an organization's products or facilities.
- Product costs are those costs, both direct and indirect, of acquiring a product in a merchandising business and preparing it for sale or of producing a product in a manufacturing business. Product costs are classified as inventory on the balance sheet and then expensed as cost of goods sold on the income statement when the inventory is sold.
- Selling costs are the costs of marketing and distributing goods and services and administrative costs are the costs of organizing and running a company.
- Both selling and administrative costs are period costs.

**LO 3.** Prepare income statements for manufacturing and service organizations.

- The cost of goods manufactured (COGM) represents the total product cost of goods *completed* during the period and transferred to finished goods inventory. The cost of goods sold (COGS) represents the cost of goods that were sold during the period and, therefore, transferred from finished goods inventory to cost of goods sold. For a retailer, there is no COGM, and COGS equals the beginning inventory plus net purchases minus ending inventory.
- For manufacturing and merchandising firms, cost of goods sold is subtracted from sales revenue to arrive at gross margin. In addition, for manufacturing firms, cost of goods manufactured must first be calculated before calculating cost of goods sold.

- Service firms do not calculate gross margin because they do not purchase or produce inventory for sale and, as a result, do not have a cost of goods sold (i.e., inventory expense).
- All firms next subtract selling and administrative expense to arrive at net income.

# SUMMARY OF IMPORTANT EQUATIONS

1. Total Product Cost = Direct Materials + Direct Labor + Manufacturing Overhead

2. Per-Unit Product Cost $= \dfrac{\text{Total Product Cost}}{\text{Number of Units Produced}}$

3. Prime Cost = Direct Materials + Direct Labor

4. Conversion Cost = Direct Labor + Manufacturing Overhead

5. $\dfrac{\text{Beginning Inventory}}{\text{of Materials}}$ + Purchases − $\dfrac{\text{Direct Materials}}{\text{Used in Production}}$ = $\dfrac{\text{Ending Inventory}}{\text{of Materials}}$

6. Gross Margin = Sales Revenue − Cost of Goods Sold

7. Operating Income = Gross Margin − Selling and Administrative Expense

| | |
|---|---|
| CORNERSTONE 2.1 | Calculating product cost in total and per unit, page 35 |
| CORNERSTONE 2.2 | Calculating prime cost and conversion cost in total and per unit, page 36 |
| CORNERSTONE 2.3 | Calculating the direct materials used in production, page 39 |
| CORNERSTONE 2.4 | Calculating cost of goods manufactured, page 40 |
| CORNERSTONE 2.5 | Calculating cost of goods sold, page 41 |
| CORNERSTONE 2.6 | Preparing an income statement for a manufacturing firm, page 42 |
| CORNERSTONE 2.7 | Calculating the percentage of sales revenue for each line on the income statement, page 44 |
| CORNERSTONE 2.8 | Preparing an income statement for a service organization, page 45 |

CORNERSTONES

# KEY TERMS

Accumulating costs, 28
Administrative costs, 38
Allocation, 31
Assigning costs, 29
Conversion cost, 36
Cost, 28
Cost object, 29
Cost of goods manufactured, 38
Cost of goods sold, 41
Direct costs, 30
Direct labor, 34
Direct materials, 34
Expenses, 28
Fixed cost, 32
Gross margin, 43

Indirect costs, 30
Manufacturing organizations, 33
Manufacturing overhead, 34
Opportunity cost, 32
Period costs, 37
Price, 28
Prime cost, 36
Product (manufacturing) costs, 33
Products, 32
Selling costs, 38
Service organizations, 33
Services, 33
Variable cost, 32
Work in process (WIP), 40

# REVIEW PROBLEM

## I. Product Costs, Cost of Goods Manufactured Statement, and the Income Statement

Brody Company makes industrial cleaning solvents. Various chemicals, detergent, and water are mixed together and then bottled in 10-gallon drums. Brody provided the following information for last year:

| | |
|---|---:|
| Raw materials purchases | $250,000 |
| Direct labor | 140,000 |
| Depreciation on factory equipment | 45,000 |
| Depreciation on factory building | 30,000 |
| Depreciation on headquarters building | 50,000 |
| Factory insurance | 15,000 |
| Property taxes: | |
|    Factory | 20,000 |
|    Headquarters | 18,000 |
| Utilities for factory | 34,000 |
| Utilities for sales office | 1,800 |
| Administrative salaries | 150,000 |
| Indirect labor salaries | 156,000 |
| Sales office salaries | 90,000 |
| Beginning balance, Raw materials | 124,000 |
| Beginning balance, WIP | 124,000 |
| Beginning balance, Finished goods | 84,000 |
| Ending balance, Raw materials | 102,000 |
| Ending balance, WIP | 130,000 |
| Ending balance, Finished goods | 82,000 |

Last year, Brody completed 100,000 units. Sales revenue equaled $1,200,000, and Brody paid a sales commission of 5% of sales.

### Required:

1. Calculate the direct materials used in production for last year.
2. Calculate total prime cost.
3. Calculate total conversion cost.
4. Prepare a cost of goods manufactured statement for last year. Calculate the unit product cost.
5. Prepare a cost of goods sold statement for last year.
6. Prepare an income statement for last year. Show the percentage of sales that each line item represents.

### Solution:

1. Direct Materials = $124,000 + $250,000 − $102,000 = $272,000
2. Prime Cost = $272,000 + $140,000 = $412,000
3. First, calculate total overhead cost:

| | |
|---|---:|
| Depreciation on factory equipment | $ 45,000 |
| Depreciation on factory building | 30,000 |
| Factory insurance | 15,000 |
| Factory property taxes | 20,000 |
| Factory utilities | 34,000 |
| Indirect labor salaries | 156,000 |
|    Total overhead | $300,000 |

Conversion Cost = $140,000 + $300,000 = $440,000

4.
| | |
|---|---|
| Direct materials | $272,000 |
| Direct labor | 140,000 |
| Overhead | 300,000 |
| Total manufacturing cost | $712,000 |
| + Beginning WIP | 124,000 |
| − Ending WIP | 130,000 |
| Cost of goods manufactured | $706,000 |

$$\text{Unit Product Cost} = \frac{\$706,000}{100,000 \text{ units}} = \$7.06$$

5.
| | |
|---|---|
| Cost of goods manufactured | $706,000 |
| + Beginning inventory, Finished goods | 84,000 |
| − Ending inventory, Finished goods | 82,000 |
| Cost of goods sold | $708,000 |

6.   First, compute selling expense and administrative expense:

| | |
|---|---|
| Utilities, sales office | $   1,800 |
| Sales office salaries | 90,000 |
| Sales commissions ($1,200,000 × 0.05) | 60,000 |
| Total selling expenses | $151,800 |
| Depreciation on headquarters building | $  50,000 |
| Property taxes, headquarters | 18,000 |
| Administrative salaries | 150,000 |
| Total administrative expenses | $218,000 |

**Brody Company**
**Income Statement**
**For Last Year**

| | | Percent |
|---|---|---|
| Sales | $1,200,000 | 100.00 |
| Cost of goods sold | 708,000 | 59.00 |
| Gross margin | $   492,000 | 41.00 |
| Less: | | |
| Selling expenses | 151,800 | 12.65 |
| Administrative expenses | 218,000 | 18.17* |
| Operating income | $   122,200 | 10.18* |

* Rounded

# DISCUSSION QUESTIONS

1.   Explain the difference between cost and expense.

2.   What is the difference between accumulating cost and assigning cost?

3.   What is a cost object? Give some examples.

4.   What is a direct cost? An indirect cost? Can the same cost be direct for one purpose and indirect for another? Give an example.

5.   What is allocation?

6.   What is the difference between a product and a service? Give an example of each.

7.   Define *manufacturing overhead*.

8.   Explain the difference between direct materials purchased in a month and direct materials used for the month.

9.   Define *prime cost* and *conversion cost*. Why can't prime cost be added to conversion cost to get total product cost?

10. How does a period cost differ from a product cost?

11. Define *selling cost.* Give five examples of selling cost.

12. What is the cost of goods manufactured?

13. What is the difference between cost of goods manufactured and cost of goods sold?

14. What is the difference between the income statement for a manufacturing firm and the income statement for a service firm?

15. Why do firms like to calculate a percentage column on the income statement (in which each line item is expressed as a percentage of sales)?

# MULTIPLE-CHOICE QUESTIONS

**2-1** Accumulating costs means that

   a. costs must be summed and entered on the income statement.
   b. each cost must be linked to some cost object.
   c. costs must be measured and tracked.
   d. costs must be allocated to units of production.
   e. costs have expired and must be transferred from the balance sheet to the income statement.

**2-2** Product (or manufacturing) costs consist of

   a. direct materials, direct labor, and selling costs.
   b. direct materials, direct labor, manufacturing overhead, and operating expense.
   c. administrative costs and conversion costs.
   d. prime costs and manufacturing overhead.
   e. selling and administrative costs.

---

*Use the following information for Multiple-Choice Questions 2-3 and 2-4:*
Wachman Company produces a product with the following per-unit costs:

| | |
|---|---|
| Direct materials | $15 |
| Direct labor | 6 |
| Manufacturing overhead | 19 |

Last year, Wachman produced and sold 2,000 units at a price of $75 each. Total selling and administrative expense was $30,000.

---

**2-3** Refer to the information for Wachman Company above. Conversion cost per unit was

   a. $21.
   b. $25.
   c. $34.
   d. $40.
   e. none of these.

**2-4** Refer to the information for Wachman Company above. Total gross margin for last year was

   a. $40,000.
   b. $70,000.
   c. $80,000.
   d. $88,000.
   e. $100,000.

**2-5** The accountant in a factory that produces biscuits for fast-food restaurants wants to assign costs to boxes of biscuits. Which of the following costs can be traced directly to boxes of biscuits?

   a. The cost of flour and baking soda
   b. The wages of the mixing labor
   c. The cost of the boxes
   d. The cost of packing labor
   e. All of these.

**2-6** Which of the following is an indirect cost?

    a.  The cost of denim in a jeans factory

    b.  The cost of mixing labor in a factory that makes over-the-counter pain relievers

    c.  The cost of bottles in a shampoo factory

    d.  The cost of restriping the parking lot at a perfume factory

    e.  All of the above.

**2-7** Bobby Dee's is an owner-operated company that details (thoroughly cleans—inside and out) automobiles. Bobby Dee's is which of the following?

    a.  Wholesaler              d.  Manufacturing firm

    b.  Retailer                   e.  None of these.

    c.  Service firm

**2-8** **Kellogg's** makes a variety of breakfast cereals. Kellogg's is which of the following?

    a.  Wholesaler              d.  Manufacturing firm

    b.  Retailer                   e.  None of these.

    c.  Service firm

**2-9** **Target** is which of the following?

    a.  Wholesaler              d.  Manufacturing firm

    b.  Retailer                   e.  None of these.

    c.  Service firm

**2-10** Stone Inc. is a company that purchases goods (e.g., chess sets, pottery) from overseas and resells them to gift shops in the United States. Stone Inc. is which of the following?

    a.  Wholesaler              d.  Manufacturing firm

    b.  Retailer                   e.  None of these.

    c.  Service firm

**2-11** JackMan Company produces diecast metal bulldozers for toy shops. JackMan estimated the following average costs per bulldozer:

| | |
|---|---|
| Direct materials | $8.65 |
| Direct labor | 1.10 |
| Manufacturing overhead | 0.95 |

Prime cost per unit is

    a.  $8.65.                  d.  $2.05.

    b.  $1.10.                  e.  $9.75.

    c.  $0.95.

**2-12** Which of the following is a period expense?

    a.  Factory insurance           d.  Factory maintenance

    b.  CEO salary               e.  All of these.

    c.  Direct labor

*Use the following information for Multiple-Choice Questions 2-13 through 2-18:*
Last year, Barnard Company incurred the following costs:

| | |
|---|---|
| Direct materials | $ 50,000 |
| Direct labor | 20,000 |
| Manufacturing overhead | 130,000 |
| Selling expense | 40,000 |
| Administrative expense | 36,000 |

Barnard produced and sold 10,000 units at a price of $31 each.

**2-13** Refer to the information for Barnard Company on the previous page. Prime cost per unit is

   a.  $7.00.                                            d.  $5.00.

   b.  $20.00.                                        e.  $27.60.

   c.  $15.00.

**2-14** Refer to the information for Barnard Company on the previous page. Conversion cost per unit is

   a.  $7.00.                                            d.  $5.00.

   b.  $20.00.                                        e.  $27.60.

   c.  $15.00.

**2-15** Refer to the information for Barnard Company on the previous page. The cost of goods sold per unit is

   a.  $7.00.                                            d.  $5.00.

   b.  $20.00.                                        e.  $27.60.

   c.  $15.00.

**2-16** Refer to the information for Barnard Company on the previous page. The gross margin per unit is

   a.  $24.00.                                       d.  $26.00.

   b.  $11.00.                                      e.  $3.40.

   c.  $16.00.

**2-17** Refer to the information for Barnard Company on the previous page. The total period expense is

   a.  $276,000.                               d.  $40,000.

   b.  $200,000.                              e.  $36,000.

   c.  $76,000.

**2-18** Refer to the information for Barnard Company on the previous page. Operating income is

   a.  $34,000.                                  d.  $270,000.

   b.  $110,000.                              e.  $74,000.

   c.  $234,000.

# CORNERSTONE EXERCISES

> *Use the following information for Cornerstone Exercises 2-19 and 2-20:*
> Slapshot Company makes ice hockey sticks. Last week, direct materials (wood, paint, Kevlar, and resin) costing $32,000 were put into production. Direct labor of $28,000 (10 workers × 200 hours × $14 per hour) was incurred. Manufacturing overhead equaled $60,000. By the end of the week, the company had manufactured 500 hockey sticks.

OBJECTIVE ❷
CORNERSTONE 2.1

**Cornerstone Exercise 2-19   Total Product Cost and Per-Unit Product Cost**

Refer to the information for Slapshot Company above.

**Required:**

1. Calculate the total product cost for last week.
2. Calculate the per-unit cost of one hockey stick that was produced last week.

OBJECTIVE ❷
CORNERSTONE 2.2

**Cornerstone Exercise 2-20   Prime Cost and Conversion Cost**

Refer to the information for Slapshot Company above.

**Required:**

1.  Calculate the total prime cost for last week.
2.  Calculate the per-unit prime cost.
3.  Calculate the total conversion cost for last week.
4.  Calculate the per-unit conversion cost.

### Cornerstone Exercise 2-21    Direct Materials Used in Production

OBJECTIVE 3
CORNERSTONE 2.3

Slapshot Company makes ice hockey sticks. On June 1, Slapshot had $48,000 of materials in inventory. During the month of June, the company purchased $132,000 of materials. On June 30, materials inventory equaled $45,000.

**Required:**

Calculate the direct materials used in production for the month of June.

### Cornerstone Exercise 2-22    Cost of Goods Manufactured

OBJECTIVE 3
CORNERSTONE 2.4

Slapshot Company makes ice hockey sticks. During the month of June, the company purchased $132,000 of materials. Also during the month of June, Slapshot Company incurred direct labor cost of $113,000 and manufacturing overhead of $187,000. Inventory information is as follows:

|  | June 1 | June 30 |
|---|---|---|
| Materials | $48,000 | $45,000 |
| Work in process | 65,000 | 63,000 |

**Required:**

1.  Calculate the cost of goods manufactured for the month of June.
2.  Calculate the cost of one hockey stick assuming that 1,900 sticks were completed during June.

### Cornerstone Exercise 2-23    Cost of Goods Sold

OBJECTIVE 3
CORNERSTONE 2.5

Slapshot Company makes ice hockey sticks. During the month of June, 1,900 sticks were completed at a cost of goods manufactured of $437,000. Suppose that on June 1, Slapshot had 350 units in finished goods inventory costing $80,000 and on June 30, 370 units in finished goods inventory costing $84,000.

**Required:**

1.  Prepare a cost of goods sold statement for the month of June.
2.  Calculate the number of sticks that were sold during June.

---

*Use the following information for Cornerstone Exercises 2-24 and 2-25:*
Slapshot Company makes ice hockey sticks and sold 1,880 sticks during the month of June at a total cost of $433,000. Each stick sold at a price of $400. Slapshot also incurred two types of selling costs: commissions equal to 10% of the sales price, and other selling expense of $65,000. Administrative expense totaled $53,800.

---

### Cornerstone Exercise 2-24    Manufacturing Firm Income Statement

OBJECTIVE 3
CORNERSTONE 2.6

Refer to the information for Slapshot Company above.

**Required:**

Prepare an income statement for Slapshot for the month of June.

### Cornerstone Exercise 2-25    Income Statement Percentages

OBJECTIVE 3
CORNERSTONE 2.7

Refer to the information for Slapshot Company above.

**Required:**

Prepare an income statement for Slapshot for the month of June and calculate the percentage of sales revenue represented by each line of the income statement. (*Note*: Round answers to one decimal place.)

OBJECTIVE ③
CORNERSTONE 2.8

### Cornerstone Exercise 2-26   Service Organization Income Statement

Allstar Exposure designs and sells advertising services to small, relatively unknown companies. Last month, Allstar had sales commissions costs of $50,000, technology costs of $75,000, and research and development costs of $200,000. Selling expenses were $10,000, and administrative expenses equaled $35,000. Sales totaled $410,000.

**Required:**

1. Prepare an income statement for Allstar for the past month.
2. Briefly explain why Allstar's income statement has no line item for Cost of Goods Sold.

# EXERCISES

OBJECTIVE ①

### Exercise 2-27   Cost Assignment

The sales staff of Central Media (a locally owned radio and cable television station) consists of two salespeople, Derek and Lawanna. During March, the following salaries and commissions were paid:

|              | Derek    | Lawanna  |
|--------------|----------|----------|
| Salaries     | $25,000  | $30,000  |
| Commissions  | 6,000    | 1,500    |

Derek spends 100% of his time selling advertising. Lawanna spends two-thirds of her time selling advertising and the remaining one-third on administrative work. Commissions are paid only on sales.

**Required:**

1. Accumulate these costs by account by filling in the following table:

| Cost    | Salaries | Commissions |
|---------|----------|-------------|
| Derek   |          |             |
| Lawanna |          |             |
| Total   |          |             |

2. Assign the costs of salaries and commissions to selling expense and administrative expense by filling in the following table:

| Cost                   | Selling Costs | Administrative Costs |
|------------------------|---------------|----------------------|
| Derek's salary         |               |                      |
| Lawanna's salary       |               |                      |
| Derek's commissions    |               |                      |
| Lawanna's commissions  |               |                      |
| Total                  |               |                      |

OBJECTIVE ①

### Exercise 2-28   Products versus Services, Cost Assignment

Holmes Company produces wooden playhouses. When a customer orders a playhouse, it is delivered in pieces with detailed instructions on how to it together. Some customers prefer that Holmes put the playhouse together. Therefore, these customers purchase the playhouse, as well as pay an additional fee for Holmes to install the playhouse. Holmes then pulls two workers off the production line and sends them to construct the playhouse on site.

**Required:**

1. What two products does Holmes sell? Classify each one as a product or a service.
2. **CONCEPTUAL CONNECTION** Do you think Holmes assigns costs individually to each product or service? Why or why not?
3. **CONCEPTUAL CONNECTION** Describe the opportunity cost of the installation process.

## Exercise 2-29    Assigning Costs to a Cost Object, Direct and Indirect Costs

OBJECTIVE ❶

Hummer Company uses manufacturing cells to produce its products (a *cell* is a manufacturing unit dedicated to the production of subassemblies or products). One manufacturing cell produces small motors for lawn mowers. Suppose that the motor manufacturing cell is the cost object. Assume that all or a portion of the following costs must be assigned to the cell.

a.  Salary of cell supervisor
b.  Power to heat and cool the plant in which the cell is located
c.  Materials used to produce the motors
d.  Maintenance for the cell's equipment (provided by the maintenance department)
e.  Labor used to produce motors
f.  Cafeteria that services the plant's employees
g.  Depreciation on the plant

h.  Depreciation on equipment used to produce the motors
i.  Ordering costs for materials used in production
j.  Engineering support (provided by the engineering department)
k.  Cost of maintaining the plant and grounds
l.  Cost of the plant's personnel office
m.  Property tax on the plant and land

### Required:

Classify each of the costs as a direct cost or an indirect cost to the motor manufacturing cell.

## Exercise 2-30    Total and Unit Product Cost

OBJECTIVE ❷

Martinez Manufacturing Inc. showed the following costs for last month:

| | |
|---|---|
| Direct materials | $7,000 |
| Direct labor | 3,000 |
| Manufacturing overhead | 2,000 |
| Selling expense | 8,000 |

Last month, 4,000 units were produced and sold.

### Required:

1.  Classify each of the costs as product cost or period cost.
2.  What is total product cost for last month?
3.  What is the unit product cost for last month?

## Exercise 2-31    Cost Classification

OBJECTIVE ❷

Loring Company incurred the following costs last year:

| | |
|---|---|
| Direct materials | $216,000 |
| Factory rent | 24,000 |
| Direct labor | 120,000 |
| Factory utilities | 6,300 |
| Supervision in the factory | 50,000 |
| Indirect labor in the factory | 30,000 |
| Depreciation on factory equipment | 9,000 |
| Sales commissions | 27,000 |
| Sales salaries | 65,000 |
| Advertising | 37,000 |
| Depreciation on the headquarters building | 10,000 |
| Salary of the corporate receptionist | 30,000 |
| Other administrative costs | 175,000 |
| Salary of the factory receptionist | 28,000 |

*(Continued)*

**Required:**

1. Classify each of the costs using the following table format. Be sure to total the amounts in each column. *Example:* Direct materials, $216,000.

| Costs | Product Cost | | | Period Cost | |
| --- | --- | --- | --- | --- | --- |
| | Direct Materials | Direct Labor | Manufacturing Overhead | Selling Expense | Administrative Expense |
| Direct materials | $216,000 | | | | |

2. What was the total product cost for last year?
3. What was the total period cost for last year?
4. If 30,000 units were produced last year, what was the unit product cost?

OBJECTIVE **2**    **Exercise 2-32    Classifying Cost of Production**

A factory manufactures jelly. The jars of jelly are packed six to a box, and the boxes are sold to grocery stores. The following types of cost were incurred:

Jars

Sugar

Fruit

Pectin (thickener used in jams and jellies)

Boxes

Depreciation on the factory building

Cooking equipment operators' wages

Filling equipment operators' wages

Packers' wages

Janitors' wages

Receptionist's wages

Telephone

Utilities

Rental of Santa Claus suit (for Christmas party for children of factory workers)

Supervisory labor salaries

Insurance on factory building

Depreciation on factory equipment

Oil to lubricate filling equipment

**Required:**

Classify each of the costs as direct materials, direct labor, or overhead by using the following table. The row for "Jars" is filled in as an example.

| Costs | Direct Materials | Direct Labor | Manufacturing Overhead |
| --- | --- | --- | --- |
| Jars | X | | |

> *Use the following information for Exercises 2-33 and 2-34:*
> Grin Company manufactures digital cameras. In January, Grin produced 4,000 cameras with the following costs:
>
> | | |
> | --- | --- |
> | Direct materials | $400,000 |
> | Direct labor | 80,000 |
> | Manufacturing overhead | 320,000 |
>
> There were no beginning or ending inventories of WIP.

OBJECTIVE **2**    **Exercise 2-33    Product Cost in Total and Per Unit**

Refer to the information for Grin Company above.

**Required:**

1. What was total product cost in January?
2. What was product cost per unit in January?

OBJECTIVE **2**    **Exercise 2-34    Prime Cost and Conversion Cost**

Refer to the information for Grin Company above.

**Required:**

1. What was the total prime cost in January?
2. What was the prime cost per unit in January?
3. What was the total conversion cost in January?
4. What was the conversion cost per unit in January?

### Exercise 2-35    Direct Materials Used

OBJECTIVE **3**

Hannah Banana Bakers makes chocolate chip cookies for cafe restaurants. In June, Hannah Banana purchased $15,500 of materials. On June 1, the materials inventory was $3,700. On June 30, $1,600 of materials remained in materials inventory.

**Required:**

1. What is the cost of the direct materials used in production during June?
2. **CONCEPTUAL CONNECTION** Briefly explain why there is a difference between the cost of direct materials that were *purchased* during the month and the cost of direct materials that were *used* in production during the month.

### Exercise 2-36    Cost of Goods Sold

OBJECTIVE **3**

Allyson Ashley makes jet skis. During the year, Allyson manufactured 94,000 jet skis. Finished goods inventory had the following units:

| | |
|---|---|
| January 1 | 6,800 |
| December 31 | 7,200 |

**Required:**

1. How many jet skis did Allyson sell during the year?
2. If each jet ski had a product cost of $2,200, what was the cost of goods sold last year?

---

*Use the following information for Exercises 2-37 and 2-38:*

In March, Chilton Company purchased materials costing $25,000 and incurred direct labor cost of $10,000. Overhead totaled $42,000 for the month. Information on inventories was as follows:

| | March 1 | March 31 |
|---|---|---|
| Materials | $14,000 | $6,500 |
| Work in process | 8,000 | 4,000 |
| Finished goods | 9,000 | 7,000 |

---

### Exercise 2-37    Direct Materials Used, Cost of Goods Manufactured

OBJECTIVE **3**

Refer to the information for Chilton Company above.

**Required:**

1. What was the cost of direct materials used in March?
2. What was the total manufacturing cost in March?
3. What was the cost of goods manufactured for March?

### Exercise 2-38    Cost of Goods Sold

OBJECTIVE **3**

Refer to the information for Chilton Company above.

**Required:**

What was the cost of goods sold for March?

> *Use the following information for Exercises 2-39 through 2-41.*
> Jasper Company provided the following information for last year:
>
> | | |
> |---|---:|
> | Sales in units | 280,000 |
> | Selling price | $     12 |
> | Direct materials | 180,000 |
> | Direct labor | 505,000 |
> | Manufacturing overhead | 110,000 |
> | Selling expense | 437,000 |
> | Administrative expense | 854,000 |
>
> Last year, beginning and ending inventories of work in process and finished goods equaled zero.

OBJECTIVE ③

### Exercise 2-39    Cost of Goods Sold, Sales Revenue, Income Statement

Refer to the information for Jasper Company above.

**Required:**

Calculate the cost of goods sold for last year.

OBJECTIVE ③

### Exercise 2-40    Income Statement

Refer to the information for Jasper Company above.

**Required:**

1.  Calculate the sales revenue for last year.
2.  Prepare an income statement for Jasper for last year.

OBJECTIVE ③

### Exercise 2-41    Income Statement

Refer to the information for Jasper Company above.

**Required:**

1.  Prepare an income statement for Jasper for last year. Calculate the percentage of sales for each line item on the income statement. (*Note*: Round percentages to the nearest tenth of a percent.)
2.  **CONCEPTUAL CONNECTION** Briefly explain how a manager could use the income statement created for Requirement 1 to better control costs.

OBJECTIVE ③

**ILLUSTRATING RELATIONSHIPS**

### Exercise 2-42    Understanding the Relationship between Cost Flows, Inventories, and Cost of Goods Sold

Ivano Company has collected cost accounting information for the following subset of items for Years 1 and 2.

| | Year 1 | Year 2 |
|---|---:|---:|
| Item: | | |
| Direct materials used in production | a | $50,000 |
| Direct materials: Beginning inventory | $ 10,000 | c |
| Direct materials purchases | 45,000 | d |
| Direct materials: Ending inventory | 15,000 | 17,000 |
| Direct labor used in production | b | 53,000 |
| Manufacturing overhead costs used in production | 80,000 | 76,000 |
| Work in process: Beginning inventory | 17,000 | 14,000 |
| Work in process: Ending inventory | 14,000 | 19,000 |
| Finished goods: Beginning inventory | 8,000 | 7,000 |
| Finished goods: Ending inventory | 7,000 | 11,000 |
| Cost of goods sold | 169,000 | e |

**Required:**

Calculate the values of the missing Items a through e.

# PROBLEMS

**Problem 2-43 Manufacturing, Cost Classification, Income Statement Service Firm Product Costs and Selling and Administrative Costs, Income Statement**

OBJECTIVE ❷ ❸

Pop's Drive-Thru Burger Heaven produces and sells quarter-pound hamburgers. Each burger is wrapped and put in a "burger bag," which also includes a serving of fries and a soft drink. The price for the burger bag is $3.50. During December, 10,000 burger bags were sold. The restaurant employs college students part-time to cook and fill orders. There is one supervisor (the owner, John Peterson). Pop's maintains a pool of part-time employees so that the number of employees scheduled can be adjusted to the changes in demand. Demand varies on a weekly as well as a monthly basis.

A janitor is hired to clean the building early each morning. Cleaning supplies are used by the janitor, as well as the staff, to wipe counters, wash cooking equipment, and so on. The building is leased from a local real estate company; it has no seating capacity. All orders are filled on a drive-thru basis.

The supervisor schedules work, opens the building, counts the cash, advertises, and is responsible for hiring and firing. The following costs were incurred during December:

| | | | |
|---|---|---|---|
| Hamburger meat | $4,500 | Rent | $1,800 |
| Buns, lettuce, pickles, and onions | 800 | Depreciation, cooking equipment | |
| Frozen potato strips | 1,250 | and fixtures | 600 |
| Wrappers, bags, and condiment packages | 600 | Advertising | 500 |
| Other ingredients | 660 | Janitor's wages | 520 |
| Part-time employees' wages | 7,250 | Janitorial supplies | 150 |
| John Peterson's salary | 3,000 | Accounting fees | 1,500 |
| Utilities | 1,500 | Taxes | 4,250 |

Pop's accountant, Elena DeMarco, does the bookkeeping, handles payroll, and files all necessary taxes. She noted that there were no beginning or ending inventories of materials. To simplify accounting for costs, Elena assumed that all part-time employees are production employees and that John Peterson's salary is selling and administrative expense. She further assumed that all rent and depreciation expense on the building and fixtures are part of product cost. Finally, she decided to put all taxes into one category, taxes, and to treat them as administrative expense.

**Required:**

1. Classify each of the costs for Pop's December operations using the table format given below. Be sure to total the amounts in each column.

   *Example:* Hamburger meat, $4,500.

| Cost | Direct Materials | Direct Labor | Manufacturing Overhead | Selling and Administrative |
|---|---|---|---|---|
| Hamburger meat | $4,500 | | | |
| Total | | | | |

2. Prepare an income statement for the month of December.
3. **CONCEPTUAL CONNECTION** Elena made some simplifying assumptions. Were those reasonable? Suppose a good case could be made that the portion of the employees' time spent selling the burger bags was really a part of sales. In that case, would it be better to divide their time between production and selling? Should John Peterson's time be divided between marketing and administrative duties? What difference (if any) would that make on the income statement?

**Problem 2-44 Cost Assignment, Direct Costs**

OBJECTIVE ❶

Harry Whipple, owner of an inkjet printer, has agreed to allow Mary and Natalie, two friends who are pursuing master's degrees, to print several papers for their graduate courses. However, he has imposed two conditions. First, they must supply their own paper. Second, they must pay Harry a fair amount for the usage of the ink cartridge. Harry's printer takes two types of

*(Continued)*

cartridges, a black one and a color one that contains the inks necessary to print in color. Black replacement cartridges cost $25.50 each and print approximately 850 pages. The color cartridge replacement cost $31 and prints approximately 310 color pages. One ream of paper costs $2.50 and contains 500 sheets. Mary's printing requirements are for 500 pages, while Natalie's are for 1,000 pages.

**Required:**

1. Assuming that both women write papers using text only (i.e., black ink), what is the total amount owed to Harry by Mary? By Natalie?
2. What is the total cost of printing (ink and paper) for Mary? For Natalie?
3. Now suppose that Natalie illustrates her writing with many large colorful pie charts and pictures and that about 20% of her total printing is primarily color. Mary uses no color illustrations. What is the total amount owed to Harry by Natalie? What is the total cost of printing (ink and paper) for Natalie?

OBJECTIVE ③  **Problem 2-45   Cost of Direct Materials, Cost of Goods Manufactured, Cost of Goods Sold**

Bisby Company manufactures fishing rods. At the beginning of July, the following information was supplied by its accountant:

| | |
|---|---|
| Raw materials inventory | $40,000 |
| Work-in-process inventory | 21,000 |
| Finished goods inventory | 23,200 |

During July, the direct labor cost was $43,500, raw materials purchases were $64,000, and the total overhead cost was $108,750. The inventories at the end of July were:

| | |
|---|---|
| Raw materials inventory | $19,800 |
| Work-in-process inventory | 32,500 |
| Finished goods inventory | 22,100 |

**Required:**

1. What is the cost of the direct materials used in production during July?
2. What is the cost of goods manufactured for July?
3. What is the cost of goods sold for July?

OBJECTIVE ③  **Problem 2-46   Preparation of Income Statement: Manufacturing Firm**

Laworld Inc. manufactures small camping tents. Last year, 200,000 tents were made and sold for $60 each. Each tent includes the following costs:

| | |
|---|---|
| Direct materials | $18 |
| Direct labor | 12 |
| Manufacturing overhead | 16 |

The only selling expenses were a commission of $2 per unit sold and advertising totaling $100,000. Administrative expenses, all fixed, equaled $300,000. There were no beginning or ending finished goods inventories. There were no beginning or ending work-in-process inventories.

**Required:**

1. Calculate the product cost for one tent. Calculate the total product cost for last year.
2. **CONCEPTUAL CONNECTION** Prepare an income statement for external users. Did you need to prepare a supporting statement of cost of goods manufactured? Explain.
3. **CONCEPTUAL CONNECTION** Suppose 200,000 tents were produced (and 200,000 sold) but that the company had a beginning finished goods inventory of 10,000 tents produced in the prior year at $40 per unit. The company follows a first-in, first-out policy for its inventory (meaning that the units produced first are sold first for purposes of cost flow). What effect does this have on the income statement? Show the new statement.

# EXPERIENCE MANAGERIAL DECISIONS
## with Zingerman's Deli

Have you ever walked by a bakery counter, or even Mom's kitchen, and been stopped in your tracks by the unmistakable aroma of freshly baked bread or homemade cookies? If so, cost behavior was probably the furthest thing from your mind. However, for the owners of **Zingerman's** deli and bakery, founded in 1982 in Ann Arbor, Michigan, cost behavior is critical in making decisions that improve Zingerman's profitability.

In total, Zingerman's tracks and manages over 3,000 distinct costs! For example, Zingerman's pays close attention to variable costs, such as the all-natural, non-alkalized cocoa powder ingredient used in its signature Hot Cocoa Cake, and the size of its hourly workforce, which varies by season. Zingerman's also closely manages its numerous fixed costs, such as recipe "research and development" creation and ovens, across different production and sales levels to be sure that it doesn't make decisions that increase costs to a greater extent than revenues. Still other costs are mixed in nature, and the variable and fixed components must be disentangled before Zingerman's owners can budget for future periods, set prices, and plan for growth in the businesses. So, the next time you bite into a warm chocolate chip cookie, think about—if only for a brief moment—all of the cost behaviors that went into producing, packaging, selling, and distributing that tasty bite of joy!

> *"Zingerman's also closely manages its numerous fixed costs, such as recipe "research and development" creation and ovens, across different production and sales levels to be sure that it doesn't make decisions that increase costs to a greater extent than revenues."*

Chapter 2 discussed various types of costs and took a close look at manufacturing and service costs. The primary concern of the chapter was organizing costs into production, selling, and administrative costs and building related schedules of the cost of goods manufactured, cost of goods sold, and income statements. Now let's focus on cost behavior—the way costs change as the related activity changes.

Cost behavior is the foundation upon which managerial accounting is built. In financial accounting, the theoretical pyramid contains critical assumptions (e.g., economic entity assumption) and principles (e.g., matching principle) necessary for helping financial accountants properly record transactions and prepare financial statements. In much the same way, managers must properly understand cost behavior in order to make wise decisions. For example, The Conference Board's annual survey of over 700 Chief Executive Officers reports the critical importance of understanding various types of costs in order to achieve key business objectives, such as sustainable growth.[1]

Costs can be variable, fixed, or mixed. Knowing how costs change as output changes is essential to planning, controlling, and decision making. For example, suppose that BlueDenim Company expects demand for its jeans product to increase by 10% next year. How will that affect the total costs budgeted for the factory? Clearly, BlueDenim will need 10% more raw materials (denim, thread, zippers, and so on). It will also need more cutting and sewing labor because someone will need to make the additional jeans. These costs are variable. But the factory building will probably not need to be expanded. Neither will the factory need an additional receptionist or plant manager. Those costs are fixed. As long as BlueDenim's accountant understands the behavior of the fixed and variable costs, it will be possible to develop a fairly accurate budget for the next year.

Budgeting, deciding to keep or drop a product line (e.g., **Converse**'s ongoing decision to keep, drop, or alter its Dwyane Wade shoe), and evaluating the performance of a segment (e.g., **Delta Air Lines**' decision to discontinue its low-fare Song Airline business segment) all benefit from knowledge of cost behavior. In fact, failure to know and understand cost behavior can lead to poor—even disastrous—decisions. This chapter discusses cost behavior in depth so that a proper foundation is laid for its use in studying other cost management topics.

 OBJECTIVE **1**

Explain the meaning of cost behavior, and define and describe fixed and variable costs.

# BASICS OF COST BEHAVIOR

**Cost behavior** is the general term for describing whether a cost changes when the level of output changes. A cost that does not change in total as output changes is a *fixed cost*. A *variable cost*, on the other hand, increases in total with an increase in output and decreases in total with a decrease in output. Let's first review the basics of cost and output measures. Then we will look at fixed and variable costs.

## Measures of Output and the Relevant Range

In order to determine the behavior of a cost, we need to have a good grasp of the cost under consideration and a measure of the output associated with the activity. The terms *fixed cost* and *variable cost* do not exist in a vacuum; they only have meaning when related to some output measure. In other words, a cost is fixed or variable with respect to some output measure or driver. In order to understand the behavior of costs, we must first determine the underlying business activity and ask "What causes the cost of this particular activity to go up (or down)?" A **cost driver** is a causal factor that measures the output of the activity that leads (or causes) costs to change. Identifying and managing drivers helps managers better predict and control costs. For instance, weather is a significant driver in the airline industry, especially when storms concentrate in the country's busiest flight corridors such as the Northeast and Midwest. One analyst estimated

[1] The Conference Board CEO Challenge, Research Report TCB-R-1474-11-RR, 2011, www.slideshare.net/kacarter/the-conference-coard-ceo-challenge.

that a particularly snowy January through March period cost **US Airways** $30 million and **Continental Airlines** $25 million in terms of lost revenue and extra costs![2]

Suppose that BlueDenim Company wants to classify its product costs as either variable or fixed with respect to the number of jeans produced. In this case, the number of jeans produced is the driver. Clearly, the use of raw materials (denim, thread, zippers, and buttons) varies with the number of jeans produced. So, materials costs are variable with respect to the number of units produced. How about electricity to run the sewing machines? That, too, is variable with respect to the number of jeans produced because the more jeans that are produced, the more sewing machine time is needed, and the more electricity it takes. Finally, what about the cost of supervision for the sewing department? Whether the company produces many pairs of jeans or fewer pairs of jeans, the cost of supervision is unchanged. So, we would say that supervision is fixed with respect to the number of jeans produced.

How does the relevant range fit into cost relationships? The **relevant range** is the range of output over which the assumed cost relationship is valid for the normal operations of a firm. The relevant range limits the cost relationship to the range of operations that the firm normally expects to occur. Let's consider BlueDenim's cost relationships more carefully. We said that the salary of the supervisor is strictly fixed. But is that true? If the company produced just a few pairs of jeans a year, it would not even need a supervisor. Surely the owner could handle that task (and probably a good number of other tasks as well). On the other hand, suppose that BlueDenim increased its current production by two or three times, perhaps by adding a second and third shift. One supervisor could not possibly handle all three shifts. So, when we talk about supervision cost, we are implicitly talking about it for the range of production that normally occurs. We now take a closer look at fixed, variable, and mixed costs. In each case, the cost is related to only one driver and is defined within the relevant range.

## Here's The Real Kicker

**Kicker** uses information on cost behavior to guide new programs. For example, the variable cost of manufacturing speakers led Kicker to work with its manufacturers to both increase quality and decrease cost. Fixed costs at the Stillwater location also received attention. Several years ago Safety Director Terry Williams faced a problem with worker safety. Cost information based on a number of indicators revealed the problem:

- The cost of workmen's compensation insurance was high.
- The workmen's compensation experience rating was high.
- The number of injuries was up.
- The number of injuries requiring time off was up.
- The number of back injuries (the most serious type) was up.
- The average cost per injury was up.

Terry looked for the root cause of the problem and discovered that improper lifting led to the more serious back injuries. He instituted a comprehensive safety program emphasizing 20 minutes of stretching exercises each day (five minutes before

work, five minutes after each break, and five minutes after lunch).

Was the program a success? At first, the workers resisted the stretching, so Terry got them weight belts. The workers hated them. They went back to stretching. But this time, any worker who refused to stretch had to wear the weight belt for 30 days. This was a highly visible sign of failure to adhere to the program. In addition, Kicker's president was a big proponent of the safety program. He explained the impact of the increased insurance premiums and lost work time on the Kicker profit-sharing program. The profit-sharing program is an important extra for Kicker employees. Each employee makes it his or her job to contribute to the bottom line whenever possible.

Over several months, workers bought into the program. The indicators decreased dramatically. The cost of workmen's compensation insurance decreased by nearly 50% the average cost per injury is less than 5% of the presafety program cost, and there is no lost work time.

**KKICKER** LivinLoud

---

[2] Elizabeth Strott, "Snowy February Slams Airlines." (March 3, 2010): accessed March 12, 2010, from http://articles.moneycentral.msn.com/Investing/Dispatch/market-dispatches.aspx?post=1673400

# Fixed Costs

**Fixed costs** are costs that *in total* are constant within the relevant range as the level of output increases or decreases. For example, **Southwest Airlines** has a fleet of 737s. The cost of these planes represents a fixed cost to the airline because, within the relevant range, the cost does not change as the number of flights or the number of passengers changes. Similarly, the rental cost of warehouse space by a wholesaler is fixed for the term of the lease. If the wholesaler's sales go up or down, the cost of the leased warehouse stays the same.

To illustrate fixed cost behavior, consider a factory operated by Colley Computers Inc., a company that produces unlabeled personal computers for small computer stores across the Midwest. The assembly department of the factory assembles components into a completed personal computer. Assume that Colley Computers wants to look at the cost relationship between supervision cost and the number of computers processed and has the following information:

- The assembly department can process up to 50,000 computers per year.
- The assemblers (direct labor) are supervised by a production-line manager who is paid $32,000 per year.
- The company was established 5 years ago.
- Currently, the factory produces 40,000 to 50,000 computers per year.
- Production has never fallen below 20,000 computers in a year.

The cost of supervision for several levels of production is as follows:

**Colley Computers Inc.**
**Cost of Supervision**

| Number of Computers Produced | Total Cost of Supervision | Unit Cost |
|---|---|---|
| 20,000 | $32,000 | $1.60 |
| 30,000 | 32,000 | 1.07 |
| 40,000 | 32,000 | 0.80 |
| 50,000 | 32,000 | 0.64 |

The cost relationship considered is between supervision cost and the number of computers processed. The number of computers processed is called the *output measure*, or *driver*. Since Colley Computers has been processing between 20,000 and 50,000 computers per year, the relevant range is 20,000 to 50,000. Notice that the *total* cost of supervision remains constant within this range as more computers are processed. Colley Computers pays $32,000 for supervision regardless of whether it processes 20,000, 40,000, or 50,000 computers.

Pay particular attention to the words *in total* in the definition of fixed costs. While the total cost of supervision remains unchanged as more computers are processed, the unit cost does change as the level of output changes. As the example in the table shows, within the relevant range, the unit cost of supervision decreases from $1.60 to $0.64. Because of the behavior of per-unit fixed costs, it is easy to get the impression that the fixed costs themselves are affected by changes in the level of output. But that is not true. Instead, higher output means that the fixed costs can be spread over more units and are thus smaller per unit. Unit fixed costs can often be misleading and may lead to poor decisions. It is often safer to work with total fixed costs.

Let's take a look at the graph of fixed costs given in Exhibit 3.1. For the relevant range, the horizontal line indicates fixed cost behavior. Notice that at 40,000 computers processed, supervision cost is $32,000; at 50,000 computers processed, supervision is also $32,000. This line visually demonstrates that cost remains unchanged as the level of the activity driver varies. For the relevant range, total fixed costs are simply an amount. For Colley Computers, supervision cost amounted to $32,000 for any level of output

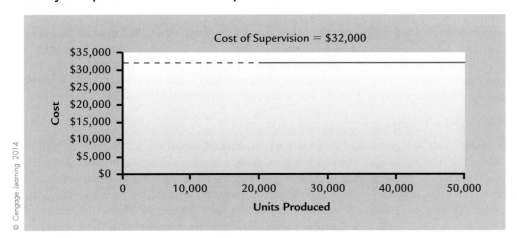

**Colley Computers Fixed Cost of Supervision**

EXHIBIT 3.1

Cost of Supervision = $32,000

between 20,000 and 50,000 computers processed. Thus, supervision is a fixed cost and can be expressed as:

$$\text{Supervision Cost} = \$32,000$$

Strictly speaking, this equation assumes that the fixed costs are $32,000 for all levels (as if the line extends to the vertical axis as indicated by the dashed portion in Exhibit 3.1). Although this assumption is not true, it is harmless if the operating decisions are confined to the relevant range.

Can fixed costs change? Of course, but this possibility does not make them variable. They are fixed at a new higher (or lower) rate. Going back to Colley Computers, suppose that the company gives a raise to the assembly department supervisor. Instead of being paid $32,000 per year, the salary is $34,000 per year. The cost of supervision within the relevant range is $34,000 per year. However, supervision cost is still *fixed* with respect to the number of computers produced.

**Discretionary Fixed Costs and Committed Fixed Costs** By their nature, fixed costs are difficult to change quickly—that is why they are considered fixed. Two types of fixed costs are commonly recognized: discretionary fixed costs and committed fixed costs. **Discretionary fixed costs** are fixed costs that can be changed or avoided relatively easily at management discretion. For example, advertising is a discretionary fixed cost. Advertising cost depends on the decision by management to purchase print, radio, or video advertising. This cost might depend on the size of the ad or the number of times it runs, but it does *not* depend on the number of units produced and sold. Management can easily decide to increase or decrease dollars spent on advertising.

As another example, just before a new season, the **National Football League (NFL)** was forced to make a decision involving discretionary costs when they realized that **Wilson Sporting Goods** had already manufactured 500,000 footballs (of the 900,000 footballs needed for the entire season) with the signature of the outgoing NFL Commissioner—Paul Taglibue—instead of the incoming Commissioner—Roger Goodell. The NFL had to decide whether to play the entire season or only half of the season with the incoming Commissioner's signature on the balls. In the end, the NFL decided give the 500,000 existing balls away to high schools. In this case, the $250,000 additional cost to produce another 500,000 balls with the new signature is a

## concept Q&A

Consider the cost of a wedding reception. What costs are fixed? What costs are variable? What output measure did you use in classifying the costs as fixed or variable?

**Answer:**

Often, the number of guests is the output measure for a wedding reception. The cost of food and drinks varies with the number of guests. The relevant range for a wedding might be the approximate size—perhaps small (less than 100 guests), medium (100–200 guests), and large (200+ guests). Within a relevant range, fixed costs might include rental of the facility, flowers, and the cake.

discretionary cost because it could be changed (i.e., avoided) relatively easily.[3] The $250,000 is a discretionary cost that is entirely fixed because the NFL needed to purchase the additional footballs regardless of the number of games played (the driver for football cost).

**Committed fixed costs**, on the other hand, are fixed costs that cannot be easily changed. Often, committed fixed costs are those that involve a long-term contract (e.g., leasing of machinery or warehouse space) or the purchase of property, plant, and equipment. For example, a construction company may lease heavy-duty earth-moving equipment for a period of 3 years. The lease cost is a committed fixed cost.

## Variable Costs

**Variable costs** are costs that in total vary in direct proportion to changes in output within the relevant range. The costs of producing and assembling the propeller on each boat manufactured by **Boston Whaler** represent variable costs for a manufacturer. In a dentist's office, certain supplies, such as the disposable bib used on each patient, floss, and x-ray film, vary with the number of patients seen. **Binney & Smith**, the maker of Crayola crayons, finds that the cost of wax and pigments varies with the number of crayons produced.

To illustrate, let's expand the Colley Computers example to include the cost of the DVD-ROM drive that is install in each computer. Here the cost is the cost of direct materials—the DVD-ROM drive—and the output measure is the number of computers processed. Each computer requires one DVD-ROM drive costing $40. The cost of DVD-ROM drives for various levels of production is as follows:

**Colley Computers Inc.**
**Cost of DVD-ROM Drives**

| Number of Computers Produced | Total Cost of DVD-ROM Drives | Unit Cost |
|---|---|---|
| 20,000 | $   800,000 | $40 |
| 30,000 | 1,200,000 | 40 |
| 40,000 | 1,600,000 | 40 |
| 50,000 | 2,000,000 | 40 |

As more computers are produced, the total cost of DVD-ROM drives increases in direct proportion. For example, as production doubles from 20,000 to 40,000 units, the *total* cost of DVD-ROM drives doubles from $800,000 to $1,600,000. Notice also that the unit cost of direct materials is constant.

Variable costs can also be represented by a linear equation. Here, total variable costs depend on the level of output. This relationship can be described by the following equation:

$$\text{Total Variable Costs} = \text{Variable Rate} \times \text{Units of Output}$$

The relationship that describes the cost of disk drives is:

$$\text{Total Variable Cost} = \$40 \times \text{Number of Computers}$$

Applying this to Colley, at 50,000 computers processed, the total cost of disk drives is:

$$\$2,000,000 = \$40 \times 50,000 \text{ computers processed}$$

At 30,000 computers processed, the total cost would be $1,200,000.

---

[3] T. Lowry, "Two-Minute Warning," *BusinessWeek* (September 4, 2006): 12.

Exhibit 3.2 shows graphically that variable cost behavior is represented by a straight line extending out from the origin. Notice that at zero units processed, total variable cost is zero. However, as units produced increase, the total variable cost also increases. Total cost increases in direct proportion to increases in the number of computers processed; the rate of increase is measured by the slope of the line.

( EXHIBIT 3.2 )

**Colley Computers Variable Cost of DVD-ROM Drives**

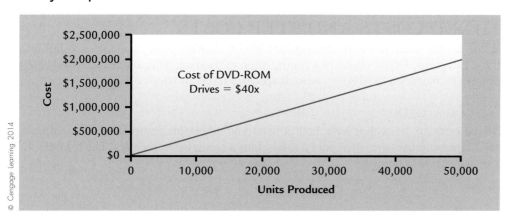

## The Reasonableness of Straight-Line Cost Relationships

The graphs of fixed and variable costs that were just reviewed show cost relationships that are straight lines. Are real-world cost relationships linear?

For Colley Computers, the DVD-ROM drives cost $40 each—no matter how many were purchased. However, if only a few drives were bought, the per-unit cost would be likely higher. So, there are economies of scale in producing larger quantities of output. For example, at extremely low levels of output workers often use more materials per unit or require more time per unit than they do at higher levels of output. Then, as the level of output increases, workers learn how to use materials and time more efficiently so that the variable cost per unit decreases as more and more output is produced. Therefore, when economies of scale are present, the true total cost function is increasing at a decreasing rate, as shown by the nonlinear cost curve in Exhibit 3.3. Some managers refer to costs that behave in this manner as **semi-variable costs**.

( EXHIBIT 3.3 )

**Semi-Variable Cost**

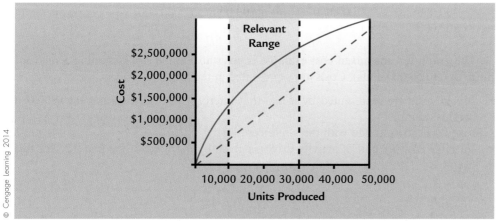

When unit costs change in this way, how do we choose the correct variable rate? Fortunately, the relevant range can help. Recall that *relevant range* is defined as the range of activity for which the assumed cost relationships are valid. Exhibit 3.3 shows how the relevant range can be used to see how well a straight line approximates variable cost. Note that for units of output before 20,000 on the x-axis, the approximation appears to break down. Therefore, managers must be extremely careful in applying cost behavior assumptions to decision making whenever the output level falls outside of the company's relevant range of operations.

OBJECTIVE ②

Define and describe mixed and step costs.

# MIXED COSTS AND STEP COSTS

While strictly fixed and variable costs are easy to handle, many costs do not fall into those categories. Often, costs are a combination of fixed and variable costs (mixed costs) or have an increased fixed component at specified intervals (step costs).

## Mixed Costs

**Mixed costs** are costs that have both a fixed and a variable component. For example, sales representatives are often paid a salary plus a commission on sales. The formula for a mixed cost is as follows:

$$\text{Total Cost} = \text{Total Fixed Cost} + \text{Total Variable Cost}$$

Suppose that Colley Computers has 10 sales representatives, each earning a salary of $30,000 per year plus a commission of $25 per computer sold. The activity is selling, and the output measure is units sold. If 50,000 computers are sold, then the total cost associated with the sales representatives is:

$$= (10 \text{ sales reps} \times \$30{,}000 \text{ salary}) + (\$25 \text{ per unit commission} \times 50{,}000 \text{ computers sold})$$
$$= \$300{,}000 + \$1{,}250{,}000 = \$1{,}550{,}000$$

The cost of Colley's sales representatives is therefore represented by the following equation:

$$\text{Total Cost} = \$300{,}000 + (\$25 \times \text{Number of Computers Sold})$$

The following table shows the selling cost for different levels of sales activity:

**Colley Computers Inc.**

| Fixed Cost of Selling | Variable Cost of Selling | Total Cost | Computers Sold | Selling Cost per Unit |
|---|---|---|---|---|
| $300,000 | $ 500,000 | $ 800,000 | 20,000 | $40.00 |
| 300,000 | 750,000 | 1,050,000 | 30,000 | 35.00 |
| 300,000 | 1,000,000 | 1,300,000 | 40,000 | 32.50 |
| 300,000 | 1,250,000 | 1,550,000 | 50,000 | 31.00 |

The graph for our mixed cost example is given in Exhibit 3.4 (assuming a relevant range of 0 to 50,000 units). Costs are represented in the following ways:

- Mixed costs are represented by a line that intercepts the vertical axis (at $300,000 for this example)
- Fixed costs correspond with the y-intercept
- Variable cost per unit of activity driver is given by the slope of the line ($25 for this example)

EXHIBIT 3.4

**Mixed Cost Behavior**

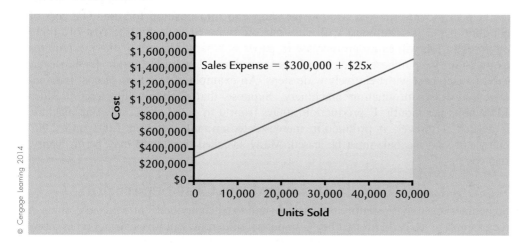

**Step Cost Behavior**

So far, we have assumed that the cost function is continuous. In reality, some cost functions may be discontinuous. These costs are known as *step costs* (or semi-fixed). A **step cost displays** a constant level of cost for a range of output and then jumps to a higher level (or step) of cost at some point, where it remains for a similar range of output. The width of the step defines the range of output for which a particular amount of the resource applies.

Recall the **Zingerman's** deli example at the beginning of the chapter. Zingerman's experiences significant increases in its sales volume during the Christmas holiday season. Because the extra sales demand is temporary, management chooses not to purchase additional freezers, which would permanently increase its fixed costs year-round. Instead, management rents the necessary number of freezer trucks to accommodate its temporary requirements. Renting freezer trucks on an "as needed" basis is an innovative decision for managing Zingerman's fixed costs as they temporarily step up during the holiday season.

Exhibit 3.5 illustrates step costs. Graph A shows a step cost with relatively narrow steps. These narrow steps mean that the cost changes in response to fairly small changes in output. Often, if the steps are very narrow, we can approximate the step

EXHIBIT 3.5

**Step Costs: Narrow Steps and Wide Steps**

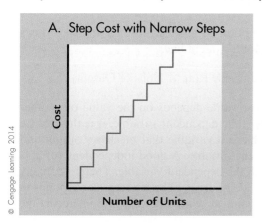

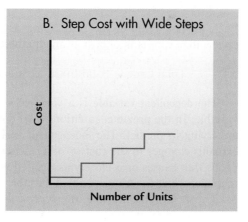

cost as a strictly variable cost. For example, Copy-2-Go, a photocopying shop, buys copy paper in large boxes. The shop typically uses three large boxes per week. Each box is quite heavy and requires the Copy-2-Go owner to incur an additional cost for help in moving the box around the shop and into position for use. The cost of handling paper is a step cost with very narrow steps. Specifically, the cost of taking on an extra job will cause an increase in paper box handling only if the job requires Copy-2-Go to purchase and handle a new box of paper. Graph B, however, shows a step cost with relatively wide steps. An example of this type of cost is a factory that leases production machinery. Suppose that each machine can produce 1,000 units per month. If production ranges from 0 to 1,000 units, only one machine is needed. However, if production increases to amounts between 1,001 and 2,000 units, a second machine must be leased. Many so-called fixed costs may be, in reality, step costs.

## Accounting Records and Need for Cost Separation

Sometimes it is easy to identify the variable and fixed components of a mixed cost, as in the example given earlier for Colley Computers' sales representatives. Many times, however, the only information available is the total cost and a measure of output. For example, the accounting system will usually record both the total cost of maintenance and the number of maintenance hours provided during a given period of time. How much of the total maintenance cost represents a fixed cost and how much represents a variable cost is not revealed by the accounting records. (In fact, the accounting records may not even reveal the breakdown of costs in the sales representative example.)

Therefore, it is necessary to separate the total cost into its fixed and variable components. Only through a formal effort to separate costs can all costs be classified into the appropriate cost behavior categories.

If mixed costs are a very small percentage of total costs, formal cost separation may be more trouble than it's worth. In this case, mixed costs could be assigned to either the fixed or variable cost category without much concern for the classification error or its effect on decision making. Alternatively, the total mixed cost could be arbitrarily divided between the two cost categories. However, this option is seldom available. Mixed costs for many firms are large enough to call for separation.

OBJECTIVE 3

Separate mixed costs into their fixed and variable components using the high-low method, the scattergraph method, and the method of least squares.

# METHODS FOR SEPARATING MIXED COSTS INTO FIXED AND VARIABLE COMPONENTS

Three methods of separating a mixed cost into its fixed and variable components are commonly used:

- the high-low method
- the scattergraph method
- the method of least squares

Each method requires the simplifying assumption of a linear cost relationship. Let's review the expression of cost as an equation for a straight line.

> Total Cost = Total Fixed Cost + (Variable Rate × Units of Output)

The **dependent variable** is a variable whose value depends on the value of another variable. In the previous equation, total cost is the dependent variable; it is the cost we are trying to predict. The **independent variable** is a variable that measures output and explains changes in the cost or other dependent variable. A good independent variable is one that causes or is closely associated with the dependent variable. Therefore, many managers refer to an independent variable as a cost driver. The **intercept** corresponds to fixed cost. Graphically, the intercept is the point at which the cost line intercepts the cost (vertical) axis. The **slope** corresponds to the variable rate (the variable cost per unit of output); it is the slope of the cost line.  Cornerstone 3.1  shows how to create and use a cost formula.

## Creating and Using a Cost Formula

**Why:**

The purpose is to provide managers with a quantitative estimate of both total fixed costs and the variable cost per unit of the cost driver(s). After these cost formula components are determined, managers can predict total costs at various levels of output.

**Information:**

The art and graphics department of State College decided to equip each faculty office with an inkjet color printer (computers were already in place). Sufficient color printers had monthly depreciation of $250. The department purchased paper in boxes of 10,000 sheets (20 reams of 500 sheets each) for $35 per box. Ink cartridges cost $30 and will print, on average, 300 pages.

**Required:**

1. Create a formula for the monthly cost of inkjet printing in the department.

2. If the department expects to print 4,400 pages next month, what is the expected total fixed cost? Total variable cost? Total printing cost?

**Solution:**

1. The cost formula takes the following form:

    Total Cost = Fixed Cost + (Variable Rate × Number of Pages)

    The monthly fixed cost is $250 (the cost of printer depreciation), as it does not vary according to the number of pages printed. The variable costs are paper and ink, as both vary with the number of pages printed.

    Cost of paper per page is $35/10,000 = $0.0035

    Cost of ink per page is $30/300 = $0.10

    Variable rate per page is $0.0035 + $0.10 = $0.1035

    The cost formula is:

    Total Cost of Printing = $250 + ($0.1035 × Number of Pages)

2. Expected fixed cost for next month is $250.

    Expected variable cost for next month is $0.1035 × 4,400 pages = $455.40

    Expected total printing cost for next month is $250 + $455.40 = $705.40

Since the accounting records reveal only total cost and output, those values must be used to estimate the fixed cost and variable rate. To do so, we'll illustrate the high-low method, the scattergraph method, and the method of least squares (i.e., regression) with the following example. The same data will be used with each method so that comparisons among them can be made. The example focuses on materials handling cost for

Anderson Company, a manufacturer of household cleaning products. Materials handling involves moving materials from one area of the factory, say the raw materials storeroom, to another area, such as Workstation 6. Large, complex organizations have found that the cost of moving materials can be quite large. Understanding the behavior of this cost is an important part of deciding how to reduce the cost.

Anderson's controller has accumulated data for the materials handling activity. The plant manager believes that the number of material moves is a good activity driver for the activity. Assume that the accounting records of Anderson Company disclose the following material handling costs and number of material moves for the past 10 months:

| Month | Material Handling Cost | Number of Moves |
|---|---|---|
| January | $2,000 | 100 |
| February | 3,090 | 125 |
| March | 2,780 | 175 |
| April | 1,990 | 200 |
| May | 7,500 | 500 |
| June | 5,300 | 300 |
| July | 3,800 | 250 |
| August | 6,300 | 400 |
| September | 5,600 | 475 |
| October | 6,240 | 425 |

## The High–Low Method

From basic geometry, we know that two points are needed to determine a line. Once we know the two points on a line, then its equation can be determined. Recall that the fixed cost is the *intercept* of the total cost line and that the variable rate is the *slope* of the line. Given two points, the slope and the intercept can be determined. The **high-low method** is a method of separating mixed costs into fixed and variable components by using just the high and low data points. Four steps must be taken in the high-low method.

**Step 1:** Find the high point and the low point for a given data set. The *high point* is defined as the point with the *highest activity* or *output level*. The *low point* is defined as the point with the *lowest activity* or *output level*. It is important to note that the high and low points are identified by looking at the activity levels and not the costs. In some cases the highest (or lowest) activity level might also be associated with the highest (or lowest) cost, whereas in other cases it is not. Therefore, regardless of cost, the managerial accountant must be careful to use the activity level in identifying the high and low data points for the analysis. In the data for maintenance cost, the high output occurred in May, with 500 material moves and total cost of $7,500. The low output was in January with 100 material moves and total cost of $2,000.

**Step 2:** Using the high and low points, calculate the variable rate. To perform this calculation, we recognize that the variable rate, or slope, is the change in the total cost divided by the change in output.

$$\text{Variable Rate} = \frac{\text{High Point Cost} - \text{Low Point Cost}}{\text{High Point Output} - \text{Low Point Output}}$$

Using the high and low points for our example, the variable rate would be as follows:

$$\text{Variable Rate} = \frac{\$7,500 - \$2,000}{500 - 100} = \frac{\$5,500}{400} = \$13.75$$

**Step 3:** Calculate the fixed cost using the variable rate (from Step 2) and either the high point or low point.

> Fixed Cost = Total Cost at High Point − (Variable Rate × Output at High Point)

OR

> Fixed Cost = Total Cost at Low Point − (Variable Rate × Output at Low Point)

Let's use the high point to calculate fixed cost.

$$\text{Fixed Cost} = \$7,500 - (\$13.75 \times 500) = \$625$$

**Step 4:** Form the cost formula for materials handling based on the high-low method.

$$\text{Total Cost} = \$625 + (\$13.75 \times \text{Number of Moves})$$

Cornerstone 3.2 shows how to use the high-low method to construct a cost formula.

## Using the High-Low Method to Calculate Fixed Cost and the Variable Rate and to Construct a Cost Formula

**CORNERSTONE**

**3.2**

**Why:**

The high-low method provides managers with a quick way of estimating cost behavior. Only two data points are needed (high and low activity/driver points) This method is relatively easy and inexpensive for companies to conduct.

**Information:**

BlueDenim Company makes blue jeans. The company controller wants to calculate the fixed and variable costs associated with electricity used in the factory. Data for the past eight months were collected:

| Month | Electricity Cost | Machine Hours |
|---|---|---|
| January | $3,255 | 460 |
| February | 3,485 | 500 |
| March | 4,100 | 600 |
| April | 3,300 | 470 |
| May | 3,312 | 470 |
| June | 2,575 | 350 |
| July | 3,910 | 570 |
| August | 4,200 | 590 |

**Required:**

Using the high-low method, calculate the fixed cost of electricity, calculate the variable rate per machine hour, and construct the cost formula for total electricity cost.

**Solution:**

*Step 1: Find the high and low points:* The high number of machine hours is in March, and the low number of machine hours is in June. (*Hint:* Did you notice that the high cost of $4,200 was for August? Yet August is not the high point because its number of machine hours is not the highest activity level. Remember, the high point is associated with the highest activity level; the low point is associated with the lowest activity level.)

*(Continued)*

**CORNERSTONE**

**3.2**

─────────

*(Continued)*

*Step 2: Calculate the variable rate:*

Variable Rate = (High Cost − Low Cost)/(High Machine Hours − Low Machine Hours)
= ($4,100 − $2,575)/(600 − 350) = $1,525/250
= $6.10 per machine hour

*Step 3: Calculate the fixed cost:*

Fixed Cost = Total Cost − (Variable Rate × Machine Hours)

Let's choose the high point with cost of $4,100 and machine hours of 600.

Fixed Cost = $4,100 − ($6.10 × 600) = $4,100 − $3,660 = $440

(*Hint:* Check your work by computing fixed cost using the low point.)

*Step 4: Construct a cost formula:* If the variable rate is $6.10 per machine hour and fixed cost is $440 per month, then the formula for monthly electricity cost is:

Total Electricity Cost = $440 + ($6.10 × Machine Hours)

Once we have the cost formula, we can use it in budgeting and in performance control. As we determined earlier, the cost formula for materials handling based on the high-low method is:

Total Cost = $625 + ($13.75 × Number of Moves)

Suppose that the number of moves for November is expected to be 350. Budgeted materials handling cost would be:

$5,437.50 = $625 + ($13.75 × 350)

Alternatively, suppose that the controller wondered whether October's materials handling cost of $6,240 was reasonably close to what would have been predicted. Our cost formula would predict October's cost of:

$6,469 (rounded) = $625 + ($13.75 × 425)

The actual cost is just $229 different from the predicted cost and probably would be judged to be reasonably close to the budgeted cost. Cornerstone 3.3 shows how to use the high-low method to calculate predicted total variable cost and total cost for budgeted output.

**CORNERSTONE**

**3.3**

## Using the High-Low Method to Calculate Predicted Total Variable Cost and Total Cost for Budgeted Output

**Why:**
After the cost formula is constructed, its components can be used to predict either total variable costs, total fixed costs, or total costs (both variable and fixed).

*(Continued)*

**Information:**

Recall that BlueDenim Company constructed the following formula for monthly electricity cost. (Refer to Cornerstone 3.2 to see how the fixed cost per month and the variable rate were computed.)

$$\text{Total Electricity Cost} = \$440 + (\$6.10 \times \text{Machine Hours})$$

**Required:**

Assume that 550 machine hours are budgeted for the month of October. Use the previous cost formula to calculate (1) total variable electricity cost for October and (2) total electricity cost for October.

**Solution:**

1. Total Variable Electricity Cost = Variable Rate × Machine Hours
$$= \$6.10 \times 550$$
$$= \$3,355$$

2. Total Electricity Cost = Fixed Cost + (Variable Rate × Machine Hours)
$$= \$440 + (\$6.10 \times 550)$$
$$= \$440 + \$3,355$$
$$= \$3,795$$

CORNERSTONE

**3.3**

*(Continued)*

Let's look at one last point. Notice that monthly data were used to find the high and low points and to calculate the fixed cost and variable rate. This means that the cost formula is the fixed cost *for the month*. Suppose, however, that the company wants to use that formula to predict cost for a different period of time, say a year. In that case, the variable cost rate is just multiplied by the budgeted amount of the independent variable for the year. The intercept, or fixed cost, must be adjusted. To convert monthly fixed cost to yearly fixed cost, simply multiply the monthly fixed cost by 12 (because there are 12 months in a year). If weekly data were used to calculate the fixed and variable costs, one would multiply the weekly fixed cost by 52 to convert it to yearly fixed cost, and so on. Cornerstone 3.4 shows how to use the high-low method to calculate predicted total variable cost and total cost for budgeted output in which the time period differs from the data period.

## Using the High-Low Method to Calculate Predicted Total Variable Cost and Total Cost for a Time Period that Differs from the Data Period

**Why:**

A cost formula can help managers predict total costs for time periods of varying lengths. This flexibility is important because managers often must predict costs for periods of a week, month, quarter, or year in length.

CORNERSTONE

**3.4**

*(Continued)*

CORNERSTONE

**3.4**

*(Continued)*

**Information:**

Recall that BlueDenim Company constructed the following formula for *monthly* electricity cost. (Refer to Cornerstone 3.2 (p. 79) to see how the fixed cost per month and variable rate were computed.)

$$\text{Total Electricity Cost} = \$440 + (\$6.10 \times \text{Machine Hours})$$

**Required:**

Assume that 6,500 machine hours are budgeted for the coming year. Use the previous cost formula to calculate (1) total variable electricity cost for the year, (2) total fixed electricity cost for the year, and (3) total electricity cost for the coming year.

**Solution:**

1. Total Variable Electricity Cost = Variable Rate × Machine Hours
$$= \$6.10 \times 6,500$$
$$= \$39,650$$

2. *Note:* The cost formula is for the month, but we need to budget electricity for the year. Thus, we need to multiply the fixed cost for the month by 12 (the number of months in a year).

$$\text{Total Fixed Electricity Cost} = \text{Fixed Cost} \times 12 \text{ Months in a Year}$$
$$= \$440 \times 12$$
$$= \$5,280$$

3. Total Electricity Cost = 12($440) + ($6.10 × 6,500)
$$= \$5,280 + \$39,650$$
$$= \$44,930$$

The high-low method has several important advantages, including the following:

- **Objectivity:** Any two people using the high-low method on a particular data set will arrive at the same answer.
- **Quick overview:** The high-low method allows a manager to get a quick fix on a cost relationship by using only two data points. For example, a manager may have only two months of data. Sometimes this will be enough to get a crude approximation of the cost relationship.
- **Ease of use:** The high-low method is simple, inexpensive, and easily communicated to other individuals, even those who are not comfortable with numerical analyses.

For these reasons, managerial accountants use the high-low method.

However, the high-low method also has several disadvantages that lead some managers to believe that it is not as good as the other methods at separating mixed costs into fixed and variable components.

- **Occurrence of outliers:** The high and low points often can be what are known as outliers. They may represent atypical cost-activity relationships. For instance, if in the Anderson Company example the high output had been 1,000 moves (rather than 500) due to some extremely unusual business activity during a given month, then this high point likely would have fallen outside of the company's relevant range of operations. It would, therefore, represented an outlier. In the case of outliers, the cost formula computed using these two points will not represent what usually takes place. The scattergraph method can help a manager avoid this trap by selecting two points that appear to be representative of the general cost-activity pattern.

- **Potential for misrepresentative data:** Even if the high and low points are not outliers, other pairs of points may be more representative. To stress the likelihood of this possibility, a high-low analysis of 50 weeks of data would ignore 96% (i.e., 48 out of the 50 weeks) of the data! Again, the scattergraph method allows the choice of more representative points.

## Scattergraph Method

The **scattergraph method** is a way to see the cost relationship by plotting the data points on a graph. The first step in applying the scattergraph method is to plot the data points so that the relationship between materials handling costs and activity output can be seen. This plot is referred to as a scattergraph and is shown in Exhibit 3.6. The vertical axis is total cost (materials handling cost), and the horizontal axis is the driver or output measure (number of moves).

( EXHIBIT 3.6 )

### Anderson Company's Materials Handling Cost

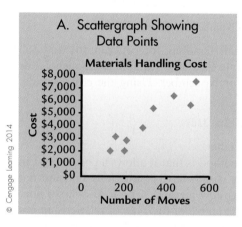

A. Scattergraph Showing Data Points

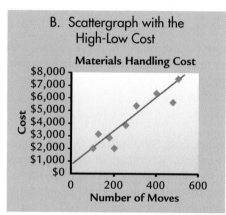

B. Scattergraph with the High-Low Cost

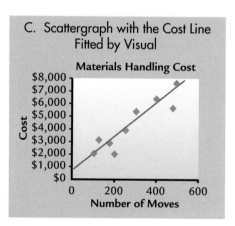

C. Scattergraph with the Cost Line Fitted by Visual

© Cengage Learning 2014

Looking at Graph A, we see that the relationship between materials handling costs and number of moves is reasonably linear. Cost goes up as the number of moves goes up and vice versa.

Now let's examine Graph B to see if the line determined by the high and low points is representative of the overall relationship. Notice that three points lie above the high-low line and five lie below it. This does not give us confidence in the high-low results for fixed and variable costs. In particular, we might wonder if the variable cost (slope) is somewhat higher than it should be and the fixed cost is somewhat lower than it should be.

Thus, one purpose of a scattergraph is to see whether or not a straight line reasonably describes the cost relationship. Additionally, inspecting the scattergraph may reveal one or more points that do not seem to fit the general pattern of behavior. Upon investigation, it may be discovered that these points (the outliers) were due to some irregular occurrences that are not expected to happen again. This knowledge might justify their elimination and perhaps lead to a better estimate of the underlying cost function.

We can use the scattergraph to visually fit a line to the data points on the graph. Of course, the manager or cost analyst will choose the line that appears to fit the points the best, and perhaps that choice will take into account past experience with the behavior of the cost item. Experience may provide a good intuitive sense of how materials handling costs behave. The scattergraph then becomes a useful tool to quantify this intuition. Fitting a line to the points in this way is how the scattergraph method works. Keep in mind that the scattergraph and other statistical aids are tools that can help managers improve their judgment. Using the tools does not restrict the manager from using judgment to alter any of the estimates produced by formal methods.

Examine Graph A carefully. Based only on the information contained in the graph, how would you fit a line to the points in it? Of course, an infinite number of lines might go through the data, but let's choose one that goes through the point for January (100, $2,000) and intersects the y-axis at $800. This gives us the straight line shown in Graph C. The fixed cost, of course, is $800, the intercept. We can use the high-low method to determine the variable rate.

First, remember that our two points are (100, $2,000) and (0, $800). Next, use these two points to compute the variable rate (the slope):

$$\text{Variable Rate} = \frac{\text{High Point Cost} - \text{Low Point Cost}}{\text{High Point Number of Moves} - \text{Low Point Number of Moves}}$$

$$= \frac{\$2,000 - \$800}{100 - 0}$$

$$= \$1,200/100$$

$$= \$12$$

Thus, the variable rate is $12 per material move.

The fixed cost and variable rate for materials handling cost have now been identified. The cost formula for the materials handling activity can be expressed as:

$$\text{Total Cost} = \$800 + \$12 \times \text{Number of Moves}$$

Using this formula, the total cost of materials handling for between 100 and 500 moves can be predicted and then broken down into fixed and variable components. For example, assume that 350 moves are planned for November. Using the cost formula, the predicted cost is:

$$\$5,000 = \$800 + (\$12 \times 350)$$

Of this total cost, $800 is fixed, and $4,200 is variable.

A significant advantage of the scattergraph method is that it allows a cost analyst to inspect the data visually. Exhibit 3.7 illustrates cost behavior situations that are not appropriate for the simple application of the high-low method. Graph A shows a non-linear relationship between cost and output. An example of this type of relationship is a volume discount given on direct materials or evidence of learning by workers (e.g., as more hours are worked, the total cost increases at a decreasing rate due to the increased efficiency of the workers). Graph B shows an upward shift in cost if more than $X_1$ units are made—perhaps because an additional supervisor must be hired or a second shift run. Graph C shows outliers that do not represent the overall cost relationship.

The cost formula for materials handling was obtained by fitting a line to two points [(0, $800) and (100, $2,000)] in Graph C. Judgment was used to select the line. Whereas one person may decide that the best-fitting line is the one passing through those points,

( EXHIBIT 3.7 )

**Scattergraphs with Nonlinear Cost**

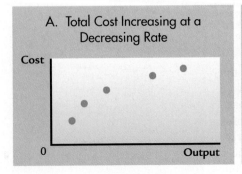

A. Total Cost Increasing at a Decreasing Rate

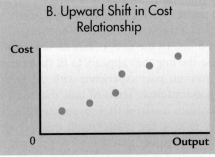

B. Upward Shift in Cost Relationship

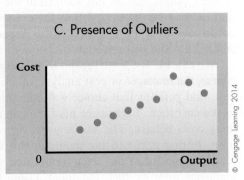

C. Presence of Outliers

others, using their own judgment, may decide that the best line passes through other pairs of points.

The scattergraph method suffers from the lack of any objective criterion for choosing the best-fitting line. The quality of the cost formula depends on the quality of the subjective judgment of the analyst. The high-low method removes the subjectivity in the choice of the line. Regardless of who uses the method, the same line will result.

Looking again at Graphs B and C in Exhibit 3.6 (p. 83), we can compare the results of the scattergraph method with those of the high-low method. There is a difference between the fixed cost components and the variable rates. The predicted materials handling cost for 350 moves is $5,000 according to the scattergraph method and $5,438 according to the high-low method. Which is correct? Since the two methods can produce significantly different cost formulas, the question of which method is the best arises. Ideally, a method that is objective and, at the same time, produces the best-fitting line is needed.

<table>
<tr><td colspan="2">concept Q&A</td></tr>
<tr><td colspan="2">Draw a straight line through the high and low points on each graph in Exhibit 3.7. Can you see that these lines, the high-low lines, could give misleading information on fixed and variable costs?</td></tr>
<tr><td colspan="2">Answer:</td></tr>
<tr><td colspan="2">Yes, it is quite important to consider the relevant range.</td></tr>
</table>

## The Method of Least Squares

The **method of least squares (regression)** is a statistical way to find the *best-fitting* line through a set of data points. One advantage of the method of least squares is that for a given set of data, it will always produce the same cost formula. Basically, the best-fitting line is the one in which the data points are closer to the line than to any other line. What do we mean by closest? Let's take a look at Exhibit 3.8. Notice that there are a series of data points and a line—we'll assume that it is the regression line calculated by the method of least squares. The data points do not all lie directly on the line; this is typical. However, the regression line better describes the pattern of the data than other possible lines. This best description results because the squared deviations between the regression line and each data point are, in total, smaller than the sum of the squared deviations of the data points and any other line. The least squares statistical formulas can find the one line with the smallest sum of squared deviations. In other words, this method identifies the regression line that minimizes the cost prediction errors or differences between predicted costs (i.e., on the regression line) and actual costs (i.e., the actual data points). Given that the method of least squares generates the smallest possible cost prediction errors, many managers refer to it as the most accurate method.

( EXHIBIT 3.8 )

**Line Deviations**

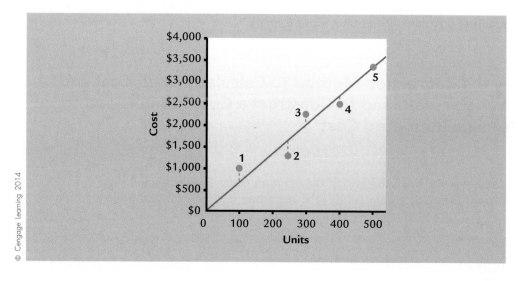

( EXHIBIT 3.9 )

**A Portion of the Summary Output from Excel for Anderson Company**

|   | A | B | C | D |
|---|---|---|---|---|
| 1 | Coefficients: | | | |
| 2 | Intercept | 788.7806 | | |
| 3 | X Variable 1 | 12.38058 | | |
| 4 | | | | |
| 5 | | | | |
| 6 | | | | |
| 7 | | | | |
| 8 | | | | |
| 9 | | | | |

Sheet1   Sheet2   Sheet3

Formerly, the method of least squares had to be calculated by hand. It was a complicated and lengthy process. Today, spreadsheet programs for personal computers have regression packages. It is easy to use them to input data and to let the programs calculate the fixed cost and variable rate.[4] Exhibit 3.9 shows a spreadsheet regression that was run on the data from Anderson Company. Notice that the intercept term is the fixed cost, which is $789 (rounded). The variable rate is shown as "X Variable 1." In other words, it is the first independent variable. So, the variable rate is $12.38 (rounded). We can use the output of regression in budgeting and control the same way that we used the results of the high-low and scattergraph methods.

Suppose that Anderson Company expects the number of moves for November to be 350. Budgeted materials handling cost would be:

$$\text{Total Cost} = \text{Fixed Cost} + (\text{Variable Rate} \times \text{Output})$$
$$= \$789\,(\text{rounded}) + [\$12.38\,(\text{rounded}) \times 350\,\text{moves}]$$
$$= \$789 + 4{,}333$$
$$= \$5{,}122$$

Alternatively, suppose the controller wondered whether October's materials handling cost of $6,240 was reasonably close to what would have been predicted. Our cost formula would predict October cost of $6,051 (rounded):

$$\$6{,}051\,(\text{rounded}) = \$789 + (\$12.38 \times 425)$$

The actual cost is just $189 different from the predicted cost and probably would be judged to be reasonably close to the budgeted cost. Cornerstone 3.5 shows how to use results of regression to construct a cost formula.

CORNERSTONE

## 3.5

## Using the Regression Method to Calculate Fixed Cost and the Variable Rate and to Construct a Cost Formula and to Determine Budgeted Cost

**Why:**

Regression gives the best estimates of the intercept (total fixed cost) and slope (variable cost per unit) for a set of data points. The regression method can yield a more accurate

*(Continued)*

---

[4] See Appendix 3A at the end of this chapter for more information on how to use regression programs in Microsoft Excel®.

cost formula than the high-low method, but it also is more expensive and complicated to perform and explain to other managers.

**CORNERSTONE**

**3.5**

*(Continued)*

**Information:**

BlueDenim Company makes blue jeans. The company controller wanted to calculate the fixed and variable costs associated with electricity used in the factory. Data for the past eight months were collected:

| Month | Electricity Cost | Machine Hours |
|---|---|---|
| January | $3,255 | 460 |
| February | 3,485 | 500 |
| March | 4,100 | 600 |
| April | 3,300 | 470 |
| May | 3,312 | 470 |
| June | 2,575 | 350 |
| July | 3,910 | 570 |
| August | 4,200 | 590 |

Coefficients shown by a regression program are:

| | |
|---|---|
| Intercept | 321 |
| X Variable 1 | 6.38 |

**Required:**

Use the results of regression to perform the following:

1. Calculate the fixed cost of electricity and the variable rate per machine hour.

2. Construct the cost formula for total electricity cost.

3. Calculate the budgeted cost for next month, assuming that 550 machine hours are budgeted.

**Solution:**

1. The fixed cost and the variable rate are given directly by regression.

$$\text{Fixed Cost} = \$321$$
$$\text{Variable Rate} = \$6.38$$

2. The cost formula is:

$$\text{Total Electricity Cost} = \$321 + (\$6.38 \times \text{Machine Hours})$$

3. Budgeted Electricity Cost $= \$321 + (\$6.38 \times 550) = \$3,830$

## Comparison of Methods

Knowing how costs change in relation to changes in output is essential to planning, controlling, and decision making. Each of the methods for separating mixed costs into fixed and variable components help managers understand cost behavior and consequently make good business decisions. Exhibit 3.10 (p. 88) provides an overview of each of these methods, along with the advantages and disadvantages of each.

( EXHIBIT 3.10 )

**Overview of Methods for Separating Mixed Costs into Fixed and Variable Components**

| Method | Overview | Advantages | Disadvantages |
|---|---|---|---|
| High-low method | A method for separating mixed costs into fixed and variable components by using just the low and high data points | • Objective<br>• Quick<br>• Simple<br>• Inexpensive<br>• Easily communicated to others | • Occurrence of outliers<br>• Potential for misrepresentative data |
| Scattergraph method | A method for separating mixed costs into fixed and variable components by fitting a line to a set of data using two points that are selected by judgment | • Simple<br>• Visual representation of the data | • Subjective (choosing the best-fitting line) |
| Method of least squares (regression) | A method for separating mixed costs into fixed and variable components by statistically finding the best-fitting line through a set of data points | • Objective<br>• Regression packages can quickly and easily calculate the fixed cost and variable rate | • Complicated, lengthy process if done by hand |

© Cengage Learning 2014

## Managerial Judgment

Managerial judgment is critically important in determining cost behavior and is by far the most widely used method in practice. Many managers simply use their experience and past observation of cost relationships to determine fixed and variable costs. This method, however, may take a number of forms. Some managers simply assign some costs to the fixed category and others to the variable category. They ignore the possibility of mixed costs. Thus, a chemical firm may regard materials and utilities as strictly variable, with respect to pounds of chemical produced, and all other costs as fixed. Even labor, the textbook example of a strictly variable cost, may be fixed for this firm. The appeal of using a managerial judgment method is simplicity. Before opting for this method, management would do well to make sure that each cost is predominantly fixed or variable and that the decisions being made are not highly sensitive to errors in classifying costs as fixed or variable.

To illustrate the use of judgment in assessing cost behavior, consider companies like **Honda** that use large quantities of manufacturing labor hours in China. Some companies might assume that hourly manufacturing labor cost is strictly variable and, therefore, not worthy of careful cost analysis. However, as workers in China begin to demand significantly higher wages and more lucrative labor deals, some resulting labor costs might (1) increase significantly in amount and (2) change their behavior pattern to become more similar to other countries in which labor unions can guarantee that workers receive certain wages even when manufacturing levels fall dramatically (i.e., labor becomes a mixed, semi-fixed, or even fixed cost).[5] Or more specifically, consider **Elgin Sweeper Company**, a leading manufacturer of motorized street sweepers. Using production volume as the measure of activity output, Elgin revised its chart of accounts to organize costs into fixed and variable components. Elgin's accountants used their knowledge of the company to assign expenses to either a fixed or variable category, using a decision rule that categorized an expense as fixed if it were fixed 75% of the time and as variable if it were variable 75% of the time.[6]

[5] Courtney Rubin. "In China, the Cost of Doing Business Rises: Recent Wage Hikes Combined with Rising Prices Mean China Isn't as Cheap an Option as It Once Was" (June 8, 2010): www.inc.com/news/articles/2010/06/rising-cost-of-business-in-china.html (accessed on July 12, 2010).
[6] John P. Callan, Wesley N. Tredup, and Randy S. Wissinger, "Elgin Sweeper Company's Journey Toward Cost Management," *Management Accounting* (July 1991): 24–27.

Management may instead identify mixed costs and divide these costs into fixed and variable components by deciding what the fixed and variable parts are. That is, they may use experience to say that a certain amount of a cost is fixed and that the rest therefore must be variable. Suppose that a small business had a photocopier with a fixed cost of $3,000 per year. The variable component could be computed by using one or more cost/volume data points. This approach has the advantage of accounting for mixed costs but is subject to a similar type of error as the strict fixed/variable dichotomy. That is, management may be wrong in its assessment.

Finally, management may use experience and judgment to refine statistical estimation results. Perhaps the experienced manager might "eyeball" the data and throw out several points as being highly unusual or revise the results of estimation account for projected changes in cost structure or technology. For example, **Tecnol Medical Products Inc.** radically changed its method of manufacturing medical face masks. Traditionally, face-mask production was labor intensive, requiring hand stitching. Tecnol developed its own highly automated equipment and became the industry's low cost supplier—beating both **Johnson & Johnson** and **3M**. Tecnol's rapid expansion into new product lines and European markets means that historical data on costs and revenues are for the most part irrelevant. Tecnol's management must look forward, not back, to predict the impact of changes on profit.[7] Statistical techniques are highly accurate in depicting the past, but they cannot foresee the future, which, of course, is what management really wants.

The advantage of using managerial judgment to separate fixed and variable costs is its simplicity. In situations in which the manager has a deep understanding of the firm and its cost patterns, this method can give good results. However, if the manager does not have good judgment, errors will occur. Therefore, it is important to consider the experience of the manager, the potential for error, and the effect that error could have on related decisions.

**ETHICAL DECISIONS**   There are ethical implications to the use of managerial judgment. Managers use their knowledge of fixed and variable costs to make important decisions, such as whether to switch suppliers, expand or contract production, or lay off workers. These decisions affect the lives of workers, suppliers, and customers. Ethical managers will make sure that they have the best information possible when making these decisions. In addition, managers will not let personal factors affect the use of cost information. For example, suppose that the purchasing department manager has a good friend who wants to supply some materials for production. The price of the friend's materials is slightly lower than that of the current supplier. However, the friend's company will not ensure 100% quality control—and that will lead to additional costs for rework and warranty repair. The ethical manager will include these additional costs along with the purchase price to calculate the full cost of purchasing from the friend's company. •

---

### concept Q&A

Suppose that you own a small business with a photocopier that a neighboring business owner asks to use occasionally. What is the average cost of copying one page? What cost items would you include? Now consider **Kinko's**: What cost items do you think that it would include?

**Answer:**

If a neighboring business owner only needed a copy rarely, you might consider it a favor and not charge at all. If it happened several times a month, you might charge the variable cost of paper and toner. Finally, if the neighboring business owner used your copier frequently, you might charge 10¢ to 20¢ per page—a price similar to that of an outside photocopying shop. Alternatively, the neighbor might buy you a ream a paper from time to time. **Kinko's** must include all costs in determining the cost of copies, including paper, toner, depreciation on equipment, cost of electricity and utilities, wages of staff, and so on.

---

# YOUDECIDE   Choosing a Cost Estimation Method

Assume that you work as a financial analyst for **Royal Caribbean Cruises Ltd.** The company operates some of the world's biggest cruise ships, such as The Allure of the Seas, which weighs 222,000 tons and carries 5,400 guests, as well as 1,650 crew members. As an internal financial analyst, one of your most important tasks is to estimate the costs that Royal will incur on the many cruises it offers to customers each year. The accuracy with which you predict Royal's most important cruise-related costs will affect many of the strategic and operating decisions made by management. You are familiar with several common cost estimation methods, including

*(Continued)*

---

[7] Stephanie Anderson Forest, "Who's Afraid of J&J and 3M," *BusinessWeek* (December 5, 1994): 66, 68.

scattergraph, high-low, and regression. However, you also are aware that each method has its advantages and disadvantages.

### Which cost estimation method should you employ?

If the scattergraph method were used, the analysis would be quite easy as you could employ Excel to quickly create a plot of the important costs against various potential cost drivers. However, this method does not involve quantitative analysis, which some individuals believe is a significant weakness. If the high-low method were adopted, the analysis would be quantitative in nature and relatively easy to conduct and explain to management. However, this method can be subject to considerable inaccuracy if one or both of the two data points used to construct the cost formula is an outlier. Finally, regression overcomes many of the weaknesses of high-low because it incorporates all of the data into its estimate of the cost formula. Nevertheless, regression can require considerably more time than other methods to collect the necessary

input data, ensure their accuracy, and explain the results to the ultimate users of the results.

To determine which method to employ, you would be wise to consult the managers who will be using your analysis. For example, does management need a general "ball park" estimate or does it need the most accurate estimate possible? The results from your cost analysis, along with the competitive pressures facing **Royal**, will affect important decisions such as how much to pay cruise ship employees to ensure a high quality customer experience, the prices to charge customers to ensure affordability yet exclusivity, and the types and quantities of food, beverages, and shopping to offer onboard the ships.

**There is no obvious, one-size-fits-all answer as to the best cost estimation method to employ. Regardless of the cost estimation method ultimately selected, you likely will supplement the results with a dose of managerial judgment to help management make the best decisions possible.**

---

OBJECTIVE **4**

Use a personal computer spreadsheet program to perform the method of least squares.

# APPENDIX 3A: USING THE REGRESSION PROGRAMS

Computing the regression formula manually is tedious, even with only a few data points. As the number of data points increases, manual computation becomes impractical. Fortunately, spreadsheet packages such as Microsoft Excel® have regression routines that will perform the computations. All you need to do is input the data. The spreadsheet regression program supplies more than the estimates of the coefficients. It also provides information that can be used to see how reliable the cost equation is—a feature that is not available for the scattergraph and high-low methods.

The first step in using the computer to calculate regression coefficients is to enter the data. Exhibit 3.11 shows the computer screen that you would see if you entered the Anderson Company data on material moves into a spreadsheet. It is a good idea to label your variables as is done in the exhibit. The months are labeled, as are column B for moving

( EXHIBIT 3.11 )

**Spreadsheet Data for Anderson Company**

| | A | B | C | D |
|---|---|---|---|---|
| 1 | Month | Cost | # Moves | |
| 2 | January | $2,000 | 100 | |
| 3 | February | 3,090 | 125 | |
| 4 | March | 2,780 | 175 | |
| 5 | April | 1,990 | 200 | |
| 6 | May | 7,500 | 500 | |
| 7 | June | 5,300 | 300 | |
| 8 | July | 3,800 | 250 | |
| 9 | August | 6,300 | 400 | |
| 10 | September | 5,600 | 475 | |
| 11 | | | | |
| 12 | | | | |
| 13 | | | | |
| 14 | | | | |

Sheet1 / Sheet2 / Sheet3

© Cengage Learning 2014

costs and column C for number of moves. The next step is to run the regression. In Excel, if the regression feature needs to be installed, press the Office button, click the Excel Options button at the bottom of the drop down menu, and click Add-Ins from the menu at the left. Click the Go button to the right of the Manage list box at the bottom of the dialog box, click to add a check mark beside Analysis ToolPak, and click OK. Click Yes to install. When the data analysis tools have been added, Data Analysis will appear in the Analysis group on the Data tab. Click on Data Analysis and then choose Regression.

When the regression screen pops up, you can tell the program where the dependent and independent variables are located. Place the cursor at the beginning of the independent rectangle and then (again using the cursor) drag down to select the values under the independent variable column—in this case, cells C2 through C10. Then, move the cursor to the beginning of the dependent rectangle, and select the values in cells B2 through B10. Finally, you need to tell the computer where to place the output. Block a nice-size rectangle, say cells A13 through F20, and click OK. In less than the blink of an eye, the regression output is complete. The regression output is shown in Exhibit 3.12.

Now, let's take a look at the output in Exhibit 3.12. First, let's locate the fixed cost and variable rate coefficients. At the bottom of the exhibit, the intercept and X Variable 1 are shown, and the next column gives their coefficients. Rounding, the fixed cost is 789 and the variable rate is 12.38. Now we can construct the cost formula for materials handling cost. It is:

$$\text{Materials Handling Cost} = \$789 + (\$12.38 \times \text{Number of Moves})$$

We can use this formula to predict the materials handling cost for future months as we did with the formulas for the high-low and scattergraph methods.

Since the regression cost formula is the best-fitting line, it should produce better predictions of materials handling costs. For 350 moves, the total materials handling cost predicted by the least squares line is:

$$\$5,122 = \$789 + (\$12.38 \times 350)$$

Of the total materials handling cost, $789 is fixed and $4,333 is variable. Using this prediction as a standard, the scattergraph line most closely approximates the least squares line.

While the computer output in Exhibit 3.12 can give us the fixed and variable cost coefficients, its major usefulness lies in its ability to provide information about reliability of the estimated cost formula. This is a feature not provided by either the scattergraph or high-low methods.

( EXHIBIT 3.12 )

**Regression Output for Anderson Company**

| | A | B | C | D | |
|---|---|---|---|---|---|
| 1 | SUMMARY OUTPUT | | | | ∧ |
| 2 | | | | | |
| 3 | *Regression Statistics* | | | | |
| 4 | Multiple R | 0.92436 | | | |
| 5 | R Square | 0.854442 | | | |
| 6 | Standard Error | 810.1969 | | | |
| 7 | Observations | 9 | | | |
| 8 | | | | | |
| 9 | | | | | |
| 10 | | *Coefficients* | | | |
| 11 | Intercept | 788.7806 | | | |
| 12 | X Variable 1 | 12.38058 | | | ≡ |
| 13 | | | | | |
| 14 | | | | | |
| 15 | | | | | ∨ |

Sheet1 / Sheet2 / Sheet3 /

## Goodness of Fit

Regression routines provide information on goodness of fit. Goodness of fit tells us how well the independent variable predicts the dependent variable. This information can be used to assess reliability of the estimated cost formula, a feature not provided by either the scattergraph or high-low methods. The summary output in Exhibit 3.12 provides a wealth of statistical information. However, we will look at just one more feature—the coefficient of determination, or $R^2$. (The remaining information is discussed in statistics classes and higher-level accounting classes.)

The Anderson Company example suggests that the number of moves can explain changes in materials handling costs. The scattergraph shown in Graph A in Exhibit 3.6 (p. 83) confirms this belief because it reveals that materials handling costs and activity output (as measured by number of moves) seem to move together. It is quite likely that a significant percentage of the total variability in cost is explained by our output variable. We can determine statistically just how much variability is explained by looking at the coefficient of determination. The percentage of variability in the dependent variable explained by an independent variable (in this case, a measure of activity output) is called the **coefficient of determination ($R^2$)**. The higher the percentage of cost variability explained, the better job the independent variable does of explaining the dependent variable. Since $R^2$ is the percentage of variability explained, it always has a value between 0 and 1.00. In the summary output in Exhibit 3.12, the coefficient of determination is labeled R Square ($R^2$). The value given is 0.85 (rounded), which means that 85% of the variability in the materials handling cost is explained by the number of moves.

How good is this result? There is no cutoff point for a good versus bad coefficient of determination. Clearly, the closer $R^2$ is to 1.00, the better. Is 85% good enough? How about 73%? Or even 46%? The answer is that it depends. If your cost equation yields a coefficient of determination of 75%, you know that your independent variable explains three-fourths of the variability in cost. You also know that some other factor or combination of factors explains the remaining one-fourth. Depending on your tolerance for error, you may want to improve the equation by trying different independent variables (e.g., materials handling hours worked rather than number of moves) or by trying multiple regressions. (Multiple regressions use two or more independent variables. This topic is saved for later courses.)

We note from the summary output in Exhibit 3.12 that the $R^2$ for materials handling cost is 0.85. In other words, material moves explain about 85% of the variability in the materials handling cost. This is not bad. However, something else explains the remaining 15%. Anderson Company's controller may want to keep this in mind when using the regression results.

# SUMMARY OF LEARNING OBJECTIVES

**LO 1.**    Explain the meaning of cost behavior, and define and describe fixed and variable costs.
- Cost behavior is the way a cost changes in relation to changes in activity output.
- Time horizon is important because costs can change from fixed to variable depending on whether the decision takes place over the short run or the long run.
- Variable costs change *in total* as the driver, or output measure, changes. Usually, we assume that variable costs increase in direct proportion to increases in activity output.
- Fixed costs do not change *in total* as activity output changes.

**LO 2.**    Define and describe mixed and step costs.
- Mixed costs have both a variable and a fixed component.
- Step costs remain at a constant level of cost for a range of output and then jump to a higher level of cost at some point, where they remain for a similar range of output.
- Cost objects that display a step cost behavior must be purchased in chunks.
- The width of the step defines the range of output for which a particular amount of the resource applies.

**LO 3.**   Separate mixed costs into their fixed and variable components using the high-low method, the scattergraph method, and the method of least squares.

- In the high-low method, only two data points are used—the high point and the low point with respect to activity level. These two points then are used to compute the intercept and the slope of the line on which they lie.
- The high-low method is objective and easy, but a nonrepresentative high or low point will lead to an incorrectly estimated cost relationship.
- The scattergraph method involves inspecting a graph showing total mixed cost at various output levels and selecting two points that seem to best represent the relationship between cost and output, and drawing a straight line. The intercept gives an estimate of the fixed cost component and the slope an estimate of the variable cost per unit of activity.
- The scattergraph method is a good way to identify nonlinearity, the presence of outliers, and the presence of a shift in the cost relationship. Its disadvantage is that it is subjective.
- The method of least squares uses all of the data points (except outliers) on the scattergraph and produces a line that best fits all of the points.
- The method of least squares offers ways to assess the reliability of cost equations.
- Managers use their experience and knowledge of cost and activity-level relationships to identify outliers, understand structural shifts, and adjust parameters due to anticipated changing conditions.

**LO 4.**   *(Appendix 3A)* Use a personal computer spreadsheet program to perform the method of least squares.

# SUMMARY OF IMPORTANT EQUATIONS

1. Total Variable Costs = Variable Rate × Units of Output
2. Total Cost = Total Fixed Cost + Total Variable Cost
3. Total Cost = Total Fixed Cost + (Variable Rate × Units of Output)
4. $\text{Variable Rate} = \dfrac{\text{High Point Cost} - \text{Low Point Cost}}{\text{High Point Output} - \text{Low Point Output}}$
5. Fixed Cost = Total Cost at High Point − (Variable Rate × Output at High Point)
6. Fixed Cost = Total Cost at Low Point − (Variable Rate × Output at Low Point)

| | |
|---|---|
| CORNERSTONE 3.1 | Creating and using a cost formula, page 77 |
| CORNERSTONE 3.2 | Using the high-low method to calculate fixed cost and the variable rate and to construct a cost formula, page 79 |
| CORNERSTONE 3.3 | Using the high-low method to calculate predicted total variable cost and total cost for budgeted output, page 80 |
| CORNERSTONE 3.4 | Using the high-low method to calculate predicted total variable cost and total cost for a time period that differs from the data period, page 81 |
| CORNERSTONE 3.5 | Using the regression method to calculate fixed cost and the variable rate and to construct a cost formula and to determine budgeted cost, page 86 |

CORNERSTONES

## KEY TERMS

## REVIEW PROBLEM

Kim Wilson, controller for Max Enterprises, has decided to estimate the fixed and variable components associated with the company's shipping activity. She has collected the following data for the past six months:

| Packages Shipped | Total Shipping Costs |
|---|---|
| 10 | $ 800 |
| 20 | 1,100 |
| 15 | 900 |
| 12 | 900 |
| 18 | 1,050 |
| 25 | 1,250 |

**Required:**

1. Estimate the fixed and variable components for the shipping costs using the high-low method. Using the cost formula, predict the total cost of shipping if 14 packages are shipped.
2. Estimate the fixed and variable components using the method of least squares. Using the cost formula, predict the total cost of shipping if 14 packages are shipped.
3. *(Appendix 3A)* For the method of least squares, explain what the coefficient of determination tells us.

**Solution:**

1. The estimate of fixed and variable costs using the high-low method is as follows:

$$\text{Variable Rate} = \frac{\$1,250 - \$800}{25 - 10}$$
$$= \$450/15 \text{ packages}$$
$$= \$30 \text{ per package}$$
$$\text{Fixed Amount} = \$1,250 - \$30(25) = \$500$$
$$\text{Total Cost} = \$500 + \$30X$$
$$= \$500 + \$30(14)$$
$$= \$920$$

2. The output of a spreadsheet regression routine is as follows: Regression output:

| | |
|---|---|
| Constant | 509.911894273125 |
| Std Err of Y Est | 32.1965672507378 |
| R Squared | 0.96928536465981 |
| No. of Observations | 6 |

Degrees of Freedom          4
X Coefficient(s)            29.4052863436125
Std Err of Coef             2.61723229918858
Y = $509.91 + $29.41(14) = $921.65

3. The coefficient of determination ($R^2$) tells us that about 96.9% of total shipping cost is explained by the number of packages shipped.

# DISCUSSION QUESTIONS

1. Why is knowledge of cost behavior important for managerial decision making? Give an example to illustrate your answer.

2. What is a driver? Give an example of a cost and its corresponding output measure or driver.

3. Suppose a company finds that shipping cost is $3,560 each month plus $6.70 per package shipped. What is the cost formula for monthly shipping cost? Identify the independent variable, the dependent variable, the fixed cost per month, and the variable rate.

4. Some firms assign mixed costs to either the fixed or variable cost categories without using any formal methodology to separate them. Explain how this practice can be defended.

5. Explain the difference between committed and discretionary fixed costs. Give examples of each.

6. Explain why the concept of relevant range is important when dealing with step costs.

7. Why do mixed costs pose a problem when it comes to classifying costs into fixed and variable categories?

8. Describe the cost formula for a strictly fixed cost such as depreciation of $15,000 per year.

9. Describe the cost formula for a strictly variable cost such as electrical power cost of $1.15 per machine hour (i.e., every hour the machinery is run, electrical power cost goes up by $1.15).

10. What is the scattergraph method, and why is it used? Why is a scattergraph a good first step in separating mixed costs into their fixed and variable components?

11. Describe how the scattergraph method breaks out the fixed and variable costs from a mixed cost. Now describe how the high-low method works. How do the two methods differ?

12. What are the advantages of the scattergraph method over the high-low method? The high-low method over the scattergraph method?

13. Describe the method of least squares. Why is this method better than either the high-low method or the scattergraph method?

14. What is meant by the best-fitting line?

15. Explain the meaning of the coefficient of determination.

# MULTIPLE-CHOICE QUESTIONS

3-1 A factor that causes or leads to a change in a cost or activity is a(n)
   a. slope.
   b. intercept.
   c. driver.
   d. variable term.
   e. cost object.

3-2 Which of the following would probably be a variable cost in a soda bottling plant?
   a. Direct labor
   b. Bottles
   c. Carbonated water
   d. Power to run the bottling machine
   e. All of these.

3-3 Which of the following would probably be a fixed cost in an automobile insurance company?

   a.　Application forms
   b.　The salary of customer service representatives
   c.　Time spent by adjusters to evaluate accidents
   d.　All of these.
   e.　None of these.

---

*Use the following information for Multiple-Choice Questions 3-4 though 3-7:*
The following cost formula was developed by using monthly data for a hospital.

$$\text{Total Cost} = \$128,000,000 + (\$12,000 \times \text{Number of Patient Days})$$

---

3-4 In the cost formula, the term $128,000,000

   a.　is the total variable cost.
   b.　is the dependent variable.
   c.　is the variable rate.
   d.　is the total fixed cost.
   e.　cannot be determined from the above formula.

3-5 In the cost formula, the term $12,000

   a.　is the variable rate.
   b.　is the dependent variable.
   c.　is the independent variable.
   d.　is the intercept.
   e.　cannot be determined from the above formula.

3-6 In the cost formula, the term "Number of patient days"

   a.　is the variable rate.
   b.　is the intercept.
   c.　is the dependent variable.
   d.　is the independent variable.
   e.　cannot be determined from the formula on the above.

3-7 In the cost formula, the term "Total cost"

   a.　is the variable rate.
   b.　is the intercept.
   c.　is the dependent variable.
   d.　is the independent variable.
   e.　cannot be determined from the formula on the above.

3-8 The following cost formula for total purchasing cost in a factory was developed using monthly data.

$$\text{Total Cost} = \$235,000 + (\$75 \times \text{Number of Purchase Orders})$$

Next month, 8,000 purchase orders are predicted. The total cost predicted for the purchasing department next month

   a.　is $8,000.
   b.　is $235,000.
   c.　is $600,000.
   d.　is $835,000.
   e.　cannot be determined from the above formula.

3-9 An advantage of the high-low method is that it
   a. is subjective.
   b. is objective.
   c. is the most accurate method.
   d. removes outliers.
   e. is descriptive of nonlinear data.

*Use the following information for Multiple-Choice Questions 3-10 and 3-11:*
The following six months of data were collected on maintenance cost and the number of machine hours in a factory:

| Month | Maintenance Cost | Machine Hours |
|---|---|---|
| January | $16,900 | 5,600 |
| February | 13,900 | 4,500 |
| March | 10,900 | 3,800 |
| April | 11,450 | 3,700 |
| May | 13,050 | 4,215 |
| June | 16,990 | 4,980 |

3-10 Select the independent and dependent variables.

| | Independent Variable | Dependent Variable |
|---|---|---|
| a. | Maintenance cost | Machine hours |
| b. | Machine hours | Maintenance cost |
| c. | Maintenance cost | Month |
| d. | Machine hours | Month |
| e. | Month | Maintenance cost |

3-11 Select the correct set of high and low months.

| | High | Low |
|---|---|---|
| a. | January | April |
| b. | January | March |
| c. | June | March |
| d. | June | April |

3-12 An advantage of the scattergraph method is that it
   a. is objective.
   b. is easier to use than the high-low method.
   c. is the most accurate method.
   d. removes outliers.
   e. is descriptive of nonlinear data.

3-13 The total cost for monthly supervisory cost in a factory is $4,500 regardless of how many hours the supervisor works or the quantity of output achieved. This cost
   a. is strictly variable.
   b. is strictly fixed.
   c. is a mixed cost.
   d. is a step cost.
   e. cannot be determined from this information.

3-14 *(Appendix 3A)* In the method of least squares, the coefficient that tells the percentage of variation in the dependent variable that is explained by the independent variable is
   a. the intercept term.
   b. the x-coefficient.
   c. the coefficient of correlation.
   d. the coefficient of determination.
   e. none of these.

# CORNERSTONE EXERCISES

**Cornerstone Exercise 3-15    Creating and Using a Cost Formula**

Big Thumbs Company manufactures portable flash drives for computers. Big Thumbs incurs monthly depreciation costs of $15,000 on its plant equipment. Also, each drive requires materials and manufacturing overhead resources. On average, the company uses 10,000 ounces of materials to manufacture 5,000 flash drives per month. Each ounce of material costs $3.00. In addition, manufacturing overhead resources are driven by machine hours. On average, the company incurs $22,500 of variable manufacturing overhead resources to produce 5,000 flash drives per month.

**Required:**

1.  Create a formula for the monthly cost of flash drives for Big Thumbs.
2.  If the department expects to manufacture 6,000 flash drives next month, what is the expected fixed cost (assume that 6,000 units is within the company's current relevant range)? Total variable cost? Total manufacturing cost (i.e., both fixed and variable)?

---

*Use the following information for Cornerstone Exercises 3-16 through 3-19:*
Pizza Vesuvio makes specialty pizzas. Data for the past eight months were collected:

| Month | Labor Cost | Employee Hours |
|---|---|---|
| January | $ 7,000 | 360 |
| February | 8,140 | 550 |
| March | 9,899 | 630 |
| April | 9,787 | 610 |
| May | 8,490 | 480 |
| June | 7,450 | 350 |
| July | 9,490 | 570 |
| August | 7,531 | 310 |

---

**Cornerstone Exercise 3-16    Using High-Low to Calculate Fixed Cost, Calculate the Variable Rate, and Construct a Cost Function**

Refer to the information for Pizza Vesuvio above. Pizza Vesuvio's controller wants to calculate the fixed and variable costs associated with labor used in the restaurant.

**Required:**

Using the high-low method, calculate the fixed cost of labor, calculate the variable rate per employee hour, and construct the cost formula for total labor cost.

**Cornerstone Exercise 3-17    Using High-Low to Calculate Predicted Total Variable Cost and Total Cost for Budgeted Output**

Refer to the information for Pizza Vesuvio above. Assume that this information was used to construct the following formula for monthly labor cost.

$$\text{Total Labor Cost} = \$5{,}237 + (\$7.40 \times \text{Employee Hours})$$

**Required:**

Assume that 675 employee hours are budgeted for the month of September. Use the total labor cost formula for the following calculations:
1.  Calculate total variable labor cost for September.
2.  Calculate total labor cost for September.

OBJECTIVE ③
CORNERSTONE 3.4

**Cornerstone Exercise 3-18   Using High-Low to Calculate Predicted Total Variable Cost and Total Cost for a Time Period that Differs from the Data Period**

Refer to the information for Pizza Vesuvio on the previous page. Assume that this information was used to construct the following formula for monthly labor cost.

$$\text{Total Labor Cost} = \$5,237 + (\$7.40 \times \text{Employee Hours})$$

**Required:**

Assume that 4,000 employee hours are budgeted for the coming year. Use the total labor cost formula to make the following calculations:
1.   Calculate total variable labor cost for the year.
2.   Calculate total fixed labor cost for the year.
3.   Calculate total labor cost for the coming year.

OBJECTIVE ③
CORNERSTONE 3.5

**Cornerstone Exercise 3-19   Using Regression to Calculate Fixed Cost, Calculate the Variable Rate, Construct a Cost Formula, and Determine Budgeted Cost**

Refer to the information for Pizza Vesuvio on the previous page. Coefficients shown by a regression program for Pizza Vesuvio's data are:

|  |  |
|---|---|
| Intercept | 4,517 |
| X Variable | 8.20 |

**Required:**

Use the results of regression to make the following calculations:
1.   Calculate the fixed cost of labor and the variable rate per employee hour.
2.   Construct the cost formula for total labor cost.
3.   Calculate the budgeted cost for next month, assuming that 675 employee hours are budgeted. (*Note:* Round answers to the nearest dollar.)

# EXERCISES

OBJECTIVE ①

**Exercise 3-20   Variable and Fixed Costs**

What follows are a number of resources that are used by a manufacturer of futons. Assume that the output measure or cost driver is the number of futons produced. All direct labor is paid on an hourly basis, and hours worked can be easily changed by management. All other factory workers are salaried.

a.   Power to operate a drill (to drill holes in the wooden frames of the futons)
b.   Cloth to cover the futon mattress
c.   Salary of the factory receptionist
d.   Cost of food and decorations for the annual Fourth of July party for all factory employees
e.   Fuel for a forklift used to move materials in a factory
f.   Depreciation on the factory
g.   Depreciation on a forklift used to move partially completed goods
h.   Wages paid to workers who assemble the futon frame
i.   Wages paid to workers who maintain the factory equipment
j.   Cloth rags used to wipe the excess stain off the wooden frames

**Required:**

Classify the resource costs as variable or fixed.

OBJECTIVE ①

**Exercise 3-21   Cost Behavior, Classification**

Smith Concrete Company owns enough ready-mix trucks to deliver up to 100,000 cubic yards of concrete per year (considering each truck's capacity, weather, and distance to each job). Total truck depreciation is $200,000 per year. Raw materials (cement, gravel, and so on) cost about $25 per cubic yard of cement.

*(Continued)*

**Required:**

1. Prepare a graph for truck depreciation. Use the vertical axis for cost and the horizontal axis for cubic yards of cement.
2. Prepare a graph for raw materials. Use the vertical axis for cost and the horizontal axis for cubic yards of cement.
3. Assume that the normal operating range for the company is 90,000 to 96,000 cubic yards per year. Classify truck depreciation and raw materials as variable or fixed costs.
4. **CONCEPTUAL CONNECTION** Briefly describe actions that Smith management could take to reduce the truck depreciation cost from year to year.
5. **CONCEPTUAL CONNECTION** Briefly describe actions that Smith management could take to reduce the total raw material cost from year to year.

OBJECTIVE ❶  **Exercise 3-22   Classifying Costs as Fixed and Variable in a Service Organization**

Alva Community Hospital has five laboratory technicians who are responsible for doing a series of standard blood tests. Each technician is paid a salary of $30,000. The lab facility represents a recent addition to the hospital and cost $300,000. It is expected to last 20 years. Equipment used for the testing cost $10,000 and has a life expectancy of 5 years. In addition to the salaries, facility, and equipment, Alva expects to spend $200,000 for chemicals, forms, power, and other supplies. This $200,000 is enough for 200,000 blood tests.

**Required:**

Assuming that the driver (measure of output) for each type of cost is the number of blood tests run, classify the costs by completing the following table. Put an X in the appropriate box for variable cost, discretionary fixed cost, or committed fixed cost.

| Cost Category | Variable Cost | Discretionary Fixed Cost | Committed Fixed Cost |
|---|---|---|---|
| Technician salaries | | | |
| Laboratory facility | | | |
| Laboratory equipment | | | |
| Chemicals and other supplies | | | |

---

*Use the following information for Exercises 3-23 and 3-24:*
Alisha Incorporated manufactures medical stents for use in heart bypass surgery. Based on past experience, Alisha has found that its total maintenance costs can be represented by the following formula: Maintenance Cost = $1,750,000 + $125X, where X = Number of Heart Stents. Last year, Alisha produced 50,000 stents. Actual maintenance costs for the year were as expected. (*Note:* Round all answers to two decimal places.)

---

OBJECTIVE ❶  **Exercise 3-23   Cost Behavior**

Refer to the information for Alisha Incorporated above.

**Required:**

1. What is the total maintenance cost incurred by Alisha last year?
2. What is the total fixed maintenance cost incurred by Alisha last year?
3. What is the total variable maintenance cost incurred by Alisha last year?
4. What is the maintenance cost per unit produced?
5. What is the fixed maintenance cost per unit?
6. What is the variable maintenance cost per unit?
7. **CONCEPTUAL CONNECTION** Briefly explain how Alisha management could improve its cost function to better understand past maintenance costs and predict future maintenance costs.

**Required:**

**CONCEPTUAL CONNECTION** Prepare a scattergraph based on Luisa's data. Use cost for the vertical axis and number of tanning appointments for the horizontal. Based on an examination of the scattergraph, does there appear to be a linear relationship between the cost of tanning services and the number of appointments?

### Exercise 3-32   Method of Least Squares

OBJECTIVE 3

Refer to the information for Luisa Crimini on the previous page.

**Required:**

1. Using a computer spreadsheet program such as Excel, run a regression on these data. Based on the regression output, write the cost formula for tanning. (*Note*: Round the fixed cost to the nearest dollar and the variable rate to the nearest cent.)
2. Using the formula computed in Requirement 1, what is the predicted cost of tanning services for September for 2,500 appointments?

---

*Use the following information for Exercises 3-33 and 3-34:*
During the past year, the high and low use of three different resources for Fly High Airlines occurred in July and April. The resources are airplane depreciation, fuel, and airplane maintenance. The number of airplane flight hours is the driver. The total costs of the three resources and the related number of airplane flight hours are as follows:

| Resource | Airplane Flight Hours | Total Cost |
|---|---|---|
| Airplane depreciation: | | |
| High | 44,000 | $ 18,000,000 |
| Low | 28,000 | 18,000,000 |
| Fuel: | | |
| High | 44,000 | 445,896,000 |
| Low | 28,000 | 283,752,000 |
| Airplane maintenance: | | |
| High | 44,000 | 15,792,000 |
| Low | 28,000 | 11,504,000 |

---

### Exercise 3-33   High-Low Method, Cost Formulas

OBJECTIVE 3

Refer to the information for Fly High Airlines above.

**Required:**

Use the high-low method to answer the following questions.
1. What is the variable rate for airplane depreciation? The fixed cost?
2. What is the cost formula for airplane depreciation?
3. What is the variable rate for fuel? The fixed cost?
4. What is the cost formula for fuel?
5. What is the variable rate for airplane maintenance? The fixed cost?
6. What is the cost formula for airplane maintenance?
7. Using the three cost formulas that you developed, predict the cost of each resource in a month with 36,000 airplane flight hours.

### Exercise 3-34   Changing the Cost Formula for a Month to the Cost Formula for a Year

OBJECTIVE 3

Refer to the information for Fly High Airlines above.

**Required:**

1. Develop annual cost formulas for airplane depreciation, fuel, and airplane maintenance.
2. Using the three annual cost formulas that you developed, predict the cost of each resource in a year with 480,000 airline flight hours.

OBJECTIVE ③   **Exercise 3-35   Method of Least Squares, Developing and Using the Cost Formula**

The method of least squares was used to develop a cost equation to predict the cost of receiving purchased parts at a video game manufacturer. Ninety-six data points from monthly data were used for the regression. The following computer output was received:

| | |
|---|---|
| Intercept | 147,400 |
| Slope | 210 |

The cost driver used was number of parts inspected.

**Required:**

1. What is the cost formula?
2. Using the cost formula from Requirement 1, identify each of the following: independent variable, dependent variable, variable rate, and fixed cost per month.
3. Using the cost formula, predict the cost of receiving for a month in which 6,800 parts are inspected.

OBJECTIVE ③   **Exercise 3-36   Method of Least Squares, Budgeted Time Period Is Different from Time Period Used to Generate Results**

Refer to the company information in **Exercise 3-35**.

**Required:**

1. What is the cost formula for a year?
2. Using the cost formula from Requirement 1, predict the cost of parts inspection for a year in which 13,200 parts are inspected.

OBJECTIVE ③   **Exercise 3-37   Identifying the Parts of the Cost Formula; Calculating Monthly, Quarterly, and Yearly Costs Using a Cost Formula Based on Monthly Data**

Gordon Company's controller, Eric Junior, estimated the following formula, based on monthly data, for overhead cost:

$$\text{Overhead Cost} = \$150{,}000 + (\$52 \times \text{Direct Labor Hours})$$

**Required:**

1. Link each term in column A to the corresponding term in column B.

| Column A | Column B |
|---|---|
| Overhead cost | Fixed cost (intercept) |
| $150,000 | Dependent variable |
| $52 | Independent variable |
| Direct labor hours | Variable rate (slope) |

2. If next month's budgeted direct labor hours equal 8,000, what is the budgeted overhead cost?
3. If next quarter's budgeted direct labor hours equal 23,000, what is the budgeted overhead cost?
4. If next year's budgeted direct labor hours equal 99,000, what is the budgeted overhead cost?

OBJECTIVE ④   **Exercise 3-38   (Appendix 3A) Method of Least Squares Using Computer Spreadsheet Program**

The controller for Beckham Company believes that the number of direct labor hours is associated with overhead cost. He collected the following data on the number of direct labor hours and associated factory overhead cost for the months of January through August.

| Month | Number of Direct Labor Hours | Overhead Cost |
|---|---|---|
| January | 689 | $5,550 |
| February | 700 | 5,590 |

| Month | Number of Direct Labor Hours | Overhead Cost |
|-------|------------------------------|---------------|
| March | 720 | 5,650 |
| April | 690 | 5,570 |
| May | 680 | 5,570 |
| June | 590 | 5,410 |
| July | 750 | 5,720 |
| August | 675 | 5,608 |

**Required:**

1. Using a computer spreadsheet program such as Excel, run a regression on these data. Print out your results.
2. Using your results from Requirement 1, write the cost formula for overhead cost. (*Note*: Round the fixed cost to the nearest dollar and the variable rate to the nearest cent.)
3. **CONCEPTUAL CONNECTION** What is $R^2$ based on your results? Do you think that the number of direct labor hours is a good predictor of factory overhead cost?
4. Assuming that expected September direct labor hours are 700, what is expected factory overhead cost using the cost formula in Requirement 2?

**Exercise 3-39** *(Appendix 3A)* **Method of Least Squares Using Computer Spreadsheet Program**

OBJECTIVE **4**

Susan Lewis, owner of a florist shop, is interested in predicting the cost of delivering floral arrangements. She collected monthly data on the number of deliveries and the total monthly delivery cost (depreciation on the van, wages of the driver, and fuel) for the past year.

| Month | Number of Deliveries | Delivery Cost |
|-------|----------------------|---------------|
| January | 100 | $1,200 |
| February | 550 | 1,800 |
| March | 85 | 1,100 |
| April | 115 | 1,050 |
| May | 160 | 1,190 |
| June | 590 | 1,980 |
| July | 500 | 1,800 |
| August | 520 | 1,700 |
| September | 100 | 1,100 |
| October | 200 | 1,275 |
| November | 260 | 1,400 |
| December | 450 | 2,200 |

**Required:**

1. Using a computer spreadsheet program such as Excel, run a regression on these data. Print out your results.
2. Using your results from Requirement 1, write the cost formula for delivery cost. (*Note*: Round the fixed cost to the nearest dollar and the variable rate to the nearest cent.)
3. **CONCEPTUAL CONNECTION** What is $R^2$ based on your results? Do you think that the number of direct labor hours is a good predictor of delivery cost?
4. Using the cost formula in Requirement 2, what would predicted delivery cost be for a month with 300 deliveries?

# PROBLEMS

**Problem 3-40 Identifying Fixed, Variable, Mixed, and Step Costs**

OBJECTIVE **1** **2**

Consider each of the following independent situations:

a. A computer service agreement in which a company pays $150 per month and $15 per hour of technical time

*(Continued)*

b.  Fuel cost of the company's fleet of motor vehicles
c.  The cost of beer for a bar
d.  The cost of computer printers and copiers in your college
e.  Rent for a dental office
f.  The salary of a receptionist in a law firm
g.  The wages of counter help in a fast-food restaurant
h.  The salaries of dental hygienists in a three-dentist office. One hygienist can take care of 120 cleanings per month
i.  Electricity cost which includes a $15 per month billing charge and an additional amount depending on the number of kilowatt-hours used

**Required:**

1.  For each situation, describe the cost as one of the following: fixed cost, variable cost, mixed cost, or step cost. (*Hint:* First, consider what the driver or output measure is. If additional assumptions are necessary to support your cost type decision, be sure to write them down.)
    *Example:* Raw materials used in production—Variable cost
2.  **CONCEPTUAL CONNECTION** Change your assumption(s) for each situation so that the cost type changes to a different cost type. List the new cost type and the changed assumption(s) that gave rise to it.
    *Example:* Raw materials used in production. Changed assumption—the materials are difficult to obtain, and a year's worth must be contracted for in advance. Now, this is a fixed cost. (This is the case with diamond sales by **DeBeers Inc.** to its sightholders. See the following website for information: www.keyguide.net/sightholders/.)

OBJECTIVE ③    **Problem 3-41    Identifying Use of the High-Low, Scattergraph, and Least Squares Methods**

Consider each of the following independent situations:

a.  Shaniqua Boyer just started her new job as controller for St. Matthias General Hospital. She wants to get a feel for the cost behavior of various departments of the hospital. Shaniqua first looks at the radiology department. She has annual data on total cost and the number of procedures that have been run for the past 15 years. However, she knows that the department upgraded its equipment substantially 2 years ago and is doing a wider variety of tests. So, Shaniqua decides to use data for just the past 2 years.
b.  Francis Hidalgo is a summer intern in the accounting department of a manufacturing firm. His boss assigned him a special project to determine the cost of manufacturing a special order. Francis needs information on variable and fixed overhead, so he gathers monthly data on overhead cost and machine hours for the past 60 months and enters them into his personal computer. A few keystrokes later, he has information on fixed and variable overhead costs.
c.  Ron Wickstead sighed and studied his computer printout again. The results made no sense to him. He seemed to recall that sometimes it helped to visualize the cost relationships. He reached for some graph paper and a pencil.
d.  Lois March had hoped that she could find information on the actual cost of promoting new products. Unfortunately, she had spent the weekend going through the files and was only able to find data on the total cost of the sales department by month for the past 3 years. She was also able to figure out the number of new product launches by month for the same time period. Now, she had just 15 minutes before a staff meeting in which she needed to give the vice president of sales an expected cost of the average new product launch. A light bulb went off in her head, and she reached for paper, pencil, and a calculator.

**Required:**

Determine which of the following cost separation methods is being used: the high-low method, the scattergraph method, or the method of least squares.

**Problem 3-42   Identifying Variable Costs, Committed Fixed Costs, and Discretionary Fixed Costs**

OBJECTIVE **1**

**Required:**

Classify each of the following costs for a jeans manufacturing company as a variable cost, committed fixed cost, or discretionary fixed cost.

a.   The cost of buttons
b.   The cost to lease warehouse space for completed jeans—the lease contract runs for 2 years at $5,000 per year
c.   The salary of a summer intern
d.   The cost of landscaping and mowing the grass—the contract with a local mowing company runs from month to month
e.   Advertising in a national magazine for teenage girls
f.   Electricity to run the sewing machines
g.   Oil and spare needles for the sewing machines
h.   Quality training for employees—typically given for four hours at a time, every six months
i.   Food and beverages for the company Fourth of July picnic
j.   Natural gas to heat the factory during the winter

---

*Use the following information for Problems 3-43 and 3-44:*

Farnsworth Company has gathered data on its overhead activities and associated costs for the past 10 months. Tracy Heppler, a member of the controller's department, has convinced management that overhead costs can be better estimated and controlled if the fixed and variable components of each overhead activity are known. One such activity is receiving raw materials (unloading incoming goods, counting goods, and inspecting goods), which she believes is driven by the number of receiving orders. Ten months of data have been gathered for the receiving activity and are as follows:

| Month | Receiving Orders | Receiving Cost |
|-------|-----------------|----------------|
| 1 | 1,000 | $18,000 |
| 2 | 700 | 15,000 |
| 3 | 1,500 | 28,000 |
| 4 | 1,200 | 17,000 |
| 5 | 1,300 | 25,000 |
| 6 | 1,100 | 21,000 |
| 7 | 1,600 | 29,000 |
| 8 | 1,400 | 24,000 |
| 9 | 1,700 | 27,000 |
| 10 | 900 | 16,000 |

---

**Problem 3-43   Scattergraph, High-Low Method, and Predicting Cost for a Different Time Period from the One Used to Develop a Cost Formula**

OBJECTIVE **3**

Refer the the information for Farnsworth Company above.

**Required:**

1.   Prepare a scattergraph based on the 10 months of data. Does the relationship appear to be linear?
2.   Using the high-low method, prepare a cost formula for the receiving activity. Using this formula, what is the predicted cost of receiving for a month in which 1,450 receiving orders are processed?
3.   Prepare a cost formula for the receiving activity for a quarter. Based on this formula, what is the predicted cost of receiving for a quarter in which 4,650 receiving orders are anticipated? Prepare a cost formula for the receiving activity for a year. Based on this formula, what is the predicted cost of receiving for a year in which 18,000 receiving orders are anticipated?

OBJECTIVE  ❸  **Problem 3-44   Method of Least Squares, Predicting Cost for Different Time Periods from the One Used to Develop a Cost Formula**

Refer to the information for Farnsworth Company on the previous page. However, assume that Tracy has used the method of least squares on the receiving data and has gotten the following results:

|  |  |
|---|---|
| Intercept | 3,212 |
| Slope | 15.15 |

**Required:**

1.  Using the results from the method of least squares, prepare a cost formula for the receiving activity.
2.  Using the formula from Requirement 1, what is the predicted cost of receiving for a month in which 1,450 receiving orders are processed? (*Note:* Round your answer to the nearest dollar.)
3.  Prepare a cost formula for the receiving activity for a quarter. Based on this formula, what is the predicted cost of receiving for a quarter in which 4,650 receiving orders are anticipated? Prepare a cost formula for the receiving activity for a year. Based on this formula, what is the predicted cost of receiving for a year in which 18,000 receiving orders are anticipated?

OBJECTIVE   **Problem 3-45   Cost Behavior, High-Low Method, Pricing Decision**

Fonseca, Ruiz, and Dunn is a large, local accounting firm located in a southwestern city. Carlos Ruiz, one of the firm's founders, appreciates the success his firm has enjoyed and wants to give something back to his community. He believes that an inexpensive accounting services clinic could provide basic accounting services for small businesses located in the barrio. He wants to price the services at cost.

Since the clinic is brand new, it has no experience to go on. Carlos decided to operate the clinic for two months before determining how much to charge per hour on an ongoing basis. As a temporary measure, the clinic adopted an hourly charge of $25, half the amount charged by Fonseca, Ruiz, and Dunn for professional services.

The accounting services clinic opened on January 1. During January, the clinic had 120 hours of professional service. During February, the activity was 150 hours. Costs for these two levels of activity usage are as follows:

|  | 120 Professional Hours | 150 Professional Hours |
|---|---|---|
| Salaries: |  |  |
| Senior accountant | $2,500 | $2,500 |
| Office assistant | 1,200 | 1,200 |
| Internet and software subscriptions | 700 | 850 |
| Consulting by senior partner | 1,200 | 1,500 |
| Depreciation (equipment) | 2,400 | 2,400 |
| Supplies | 905 | 1,100 |
| Administration | 500 | 500 |
| Rent (offices) | 2,000 | 2,000 |
| Utilities | 332 | 365 |

**Required:**

1.  Classify each cost as fixed, variable, or mixed, using hours of professional service as the activity driver.
2.  Use the high-low method to separate the mixed costs into their fixed and variable components. (*Note:* Round variable rates to two decimal places and fixed amounts to the nearest dollar.)
3.  Luz Mondragon, the chief paraprofessional of the clinic, has estimated that the clinic will average 140 professional hours per month. If the clinic is to be operated as a nonprofit organization, how much will it need to charge per professional hour? How much of this charge is variable? How much is fixed? (*Note:* Round answers to two decimal places.)

4. **CONCEPTUAL CONNECTION** Suppose the accounting center averages 170 professional hours per month. How much would need to be charged per hour for the center to cover its costs? Explain why the per-hour charge decreased as the activity output increased. (*Note:* Round answers to two decimal places.)

## Problem 3-46 Flexible and Committed Resources, Capacity Usage for a Service

OBJECTIVE ❶ ❷ ❸

Jana Morgan is about to sign up for cellular telephone service. She is primarily interested in the safety aspect of the phone; she wants to have one available for emergencies. She does not want to use it as her primary phone. Jana has narrowed her options down to two plans:

|  | Plan 1 | Plan 2 |
|---|---|---|
| Monthly fee | $ 20 | $ 30 |
| Free local minutes | 60 | 120 |
| Additional charges per minute: | | |
| Airtime | $ 0.40 | $ 0.30 |
| Long distance | 0.15 | — |
| Regional roaming | 0.60 | — |
| National roaming | 0.60 | 0.60 |

Both plans are subject to a $25 activation fee and a $120 cancellation fee if the service is cancelled before 1 year. Jana's brother will give her a cell phone that he no longer needs. It is not the latest version (and is not Internet capable) but will work well with both plans.

**Required:**

1. Classify the charges associated with the cellular phone service as (a) committed resources or (b) flexible resources.
2. **CONCEPTUAL CONNECTION** Assume that Jana will use, on average, 45 minutes per month in local calling. For each plan, split her minute allotment into used and unused capacity. Which plan will be most cost effective? Why?
3. **CONCEPTUAL CONNECTION** Assume that Jana loves her cell phone and ends up talking frequently with friends while traveling within her region. On average, she uses 60 local minutes a month and 30 regional minutes. For each plan, split her minute allotment into used and unused capacity. Which plan will be most cost effective? Why?
4. **CONCEPTUAL CONNECTION** Analyze your own cellular phone plan by comparing it with other possible options.

## Problem 3-47 Variable and Fixed Costs, Cost Formula, High-Low Method

OBJECTIVE ❶ ❸

Li Ming Yuan and Tiffany Shaden are the department heads for the accounting department and human resources department, respectively, at a large textile firm in the southern United States. They have just returned from an executive meeting at which the necessity of cutting costs and gaining efficiency has been stressed. After talking with Tiffany and some of her staff members, as well as his own staff members, Li Ming discovered that there were a number of costs associated with the claims processing activity. These costs included the salaries of the two paralegals who worked full-time on claims processing; the salary of the accountant who cut the checks; the cost of claims forms, checks, envelopes, and postage; and depreciation on the office equipment dedicated to the processing. Some of the paralegals' time is spent in the routine processing of uncontested claims, but much time is spent on the claims that have incomplete documentation or are contested. The accountant's time appears to vary with the number of claims processed.

Li Ming was able to separate the costs of processing claims from the costs of running the departments of accounting and human resources. He gathered the data on claims processing cost and the number of claims processed per month for the past six months. These data are as follows:

*(Continued)*

| Month | Claims Processing Cost | Number of Claims Processed |
|---|---|---|
| February | $34,907 | 5,700 |
| March | 31,260 | 4,900 |
| April | 37,950 | 6,100 |
| May | 38,250 | 6,500 |
| June | 44,895 | 7,930 |
| July | 44,055 | 7,514 |

**Required:**

1. Classify the claims processing costs that Li Ming identified as variable and fixed.
2. What is the independent variable? The dependent variable?
3. Use the high-low method to find the fixed cost per month and the variable rate. What is the cost formula?
4. **CONCEPTUAL CONNECTION** Suppose that an outside company bids on the claims processing business. The bid price is $4.60 per claim. If Tiffany expects 75,600 claims next year, should she outsource the claims processing or continue to do it in-house?

OBJECTIVE 1 2          Problem 3-48   **Cost Separation**

About 8 years ago, Kicker faced the problem of rapidly increasing costs associated with workplace accidents. The costs included the following:

| State unemployment insurance premiums | $100,000 |
|---|---|
| Average cost per injury | $  1,500 |
| Number of injuries per year | 15 |
| Number of serious injuries | 4 |
| Number of workdays lost | 30 |

   A safety program was implemented with the following features: hiring a safety director, new employee orientation, stretching required four times a day, and systematic monitoring of adherence to the program by directors and supervisors. A year later, the indicators were as follows:

| State unemployment insurance premiums | $50,000 |
|---|---|
| Average cost per injury | $      50 |
| Number of injuries per year | 10 |
| Number of serious injuries | 0 |
| Number of workdays lost | 0 |
| Safety director's starting salary | $60,000 |

**Required:**

1. **CONCEPTUAL CONNECTION** Discuss the safety-related costs listed. Are they variable or fixed with respect to speakers sold? With respect to other independent variables (describe)?
2. **CONCEPTUAL CONNECTION** Did the safety program pay for itself? Discuss your reasoning.

OBJECTIVE 4          Problem 3-49   *(Appendix 3A)* **Method of Least Squares**

Refer to the information for Farnsworth Company (p. 109) for the first 10 months of data on receiving orders and receiving cost. Now suppose that Tracy has gathered two more months of data:

| Month | Receiving Orders | Receiving Cost |
|---|---|---|
| 11 | 1,200 | $28,000 |
| 12 | 950 | 17,500 |

*Note:* For the following requirements, round the intercept terms to the nearest dollar, round the variable rates to the nearest cent, and R-squared to two decimal places.

**Required:**

1. Run two regressions using a computer spreadsheet program such as Excel. First, use the method of least squares on the first 10 months of data. Then, use the method of least squares on all 12 months of data. Write down the results for the intercept, slope, and $R^2$ for each regression. Compare the results.

2. **CONCEPTUAL CONNECTION** Prepare a scattergraph using all 12 months of data. Do any points appear to be outliers? Suppose Tracy has learned that the factory suffered severe storm damage during Month 11 that required extensive repairs to the receiving area— including major repairs on a forklift. These expenses, included in Month 11 receiving costs, are not expected to recur. What step might Tracy, using her judgment, take to amend the results from the method of least squares?

3. **CONCEPTUAL CONNECTION** Rerun the method of least squares, using all the data except for Month 11. (You should now have 11 months of data.) Prepare a cost formula for receiving based on these results, and calculate the predicted receiving cost for a month with 1,450 receiving orders. Discuss the results from this regression versus those from the regression for 12 months of data.

**Problem 3-50  (Appendix 3A) Scattergraph, High-Low Method, Method of Least Squares, Use of Judgment**

OBJECTIVE ③ ④

The management of Wheeler Company has decided to develop cost formulas for its major overhead activities. Wheeler uses a highly automated manufacturing process, and power costs are a significant manufacturing cost. Cost analysts have decided that power costs are mixed. The costs must be broken into their fixed and variable elements so that the cost behavior of the power usage activity can be properly described. Machine hours have been selected as the activity driver for power costs. The following data for the past eight quarters have been collected:

| Quarter | Machine Hours | Power Cost |
|---|---|---|
| 1 | 20,000 | $26,000 |
| 2 | 25,000 | 38,000 |
| 3 | 30,000 | 42,500 |
| 4 | 22,000 | 37,000 |
| 5 | 21,000 | 34,000 |
| 6 | 18,000 | 29,000 |
| 7 | 24,000 | 36,000 |
| 8 | 28,000 | 40,000 |

*Note:* For the following requirements, round the fixed cost to the nearest dollar, round the variable rates to the nearest cent, and the R-squared to two decimal places.

**Required:**

1. Prepare a scattergraph by plotting power costs against machine hours. Does the scattergraph show a linear relationship between machine hours and power cost?

2. Using the high and low points (i.e., the high-low method), compute a power cost formula. (*Note:* Round answers to three decimal places.)

3. Use the method of least squares to compute a power cost formula. Evaluate the coefficient of determination.

4. **CONCEPTUAL CONNECTION** Rerun the regression, and drop the point (20,000, $26,000) as an outlier. Compare the results from this regression to those for the regression in Requirement 3. Which is better?

**Problem 3-51  (Appendix 3A) Separating Fixed and Variable Costs, Service Setting**

OBJECTIVE ③ ④

Louise McDermott, controller for the Galvin plant of Veromar Inc., wanted to determine the cost behavior of moving materials throughout the plant. She accumulated the following data on the number of moves (from 100 to 800 in increments of 100) and the total cost of moving materials at those levels of moves:

*(Continued)*

| Number of Moves | Total Cost |
|---|---|
| 100 | $ 3,000 |
| 200 | 4,650 |
| 300 | 3,400 |
| 400 | 8,500 |
| 500 | 10,000 |
| 600 | 12,600 |
| 700 | 13,600 |
| 800 | 14,560 |

**Required:**

1.  Prepare a scattergraph based on these data. Use cost for the vertical axis and number of moves for the horizontal. Based on an examination of the scattergraph, does there appear to be a linear relationship between the total cost of moving materials and the number of moves?

2.  Compute the cost formula for moving materials by using the high-low method. Calculate the predicted cost for a month with 550 moves by using the high-low formula. (*Note:* Round the answer for the variable rate to three decimal places and the answer for total fixed cost and total cost to the nearest dollar.)

3.  **CONCEPTUAL CONNECTION** Compute the cost formula for moving materials using the method of least squares. (*Note:* For the method of least squares, round the variable rate to two decimal places and total fixed cost and total cost to the nearest dollar.) Using the regression cost formula, what is the predicted cost for a month with 550 moves? What does the coefficient of determination tell you about the cost formula computed by regression?

4.  **CONCEPTUAL CONNECTION** Evaluate the cost formula using the least squares coefficients. Could it be improved? Try dropping the third data point (300, $3,400), and rerun the regression.

# CASES

**Case 3-52    Cost Formulas, Single and Multiple Cost Drivers**

For the past 5 years, Garner Company has had a policy of producing to meet customer demand. As a result, finished goods inventory is minimal, and for the most part, units produced equal units sold.

Recently, Garner's industry entered a recession, and the company is producing well below capacity (and expects to continue doing so for the coming year). The president is willing to accept orders that at least cover their variable costs so that the company can keep its employees and avoid layoffs. Also, any orders above variable costs will increase overall profitability of the company. Toward that end, the president of Garner Company implemented a policy that any special orders will be accepted if they cover the costs that the orders cause.

To help implement the policy, Garner's controller developed the following cost formulas:

$$\text{Direct Material Usage} = \$94X, \quad R^2 = 0.90$$
$$\text{Direct Labor Usage} = \$16X, \quad R^2 = 0.92$$
$$\text{Overhead} = \$350,000 + \$80X, \quad R^2 = 0.56$$
$$\text{Selling Costs} = \$50,000 + \$7X, \quad R^2 = 0.86$$

where X = direct labor hours.

**Required:**

1. Compute the total unit variable cost. Suppose that Garner has an opportunity to accept an order for 20,000 units at $212 per unit. Each unit uses one direct labor hour for production. Should Garner accept the order? (The order would not displace any of Garner's regular orders.)

2. *(Appendix 3A)* Explain the significance of the coefficient of determination measures for the cost formulas. Did these measures have a bearing on your answer in Requirement 1? Should they have a bearing? Why?

3. *(Appendix 3A)* Suppose that a multiple regression equation is developed for overhead costs: $Y = \$100,000 + \$85X1 + \$5,000X2 + \$300X3$, where X1 = Direct Labor Hours, X2 = Number of Setups, and X3 = Engineering Hours. The coefficient of determination for the equation is 0.89. Assume that the order of 20,000 units requires 12 setups and 600 engineering hours. Given this new information, should the company accept the special order referred to in Requirement 1? Is there any other information about cost behavior that you would like to have? Explain.

## Case 3-53   Suspicious Acquisition of Data, Ethical Issues

OBJECTIVE ❶

Bill Lewis, manager of the Thomas Electronics Division, called a meeting with his controller, Brindon Peterson, and his marketing manager, Patty Fritz. The following is a transcript of the conversation that took place during the meeting:

**Bill:** Brindon, the variable costing system that you developed has proved to be a big plus for our division. Our success in winning bids has increased, and as a result our revenues have increased by 25%. However, if we intend to meet this year's profit targets, we are going to need something extra—am I right, Patty?

**Patty:** Absolutely. While we have been able to win more bids, we still are losing too many, particularly to our major competitor, Kilborn Electronics. If we knew more about their bidding strategy, we could be more successful at competing with them.

**Brindon:** Would knowing their variable costs help?

**Patty:** Certainly. It would give me their minimum price. With that knowledge, I'm sure that we could find a way to beat them on several jobs, particularly on those jobs where we are at least as efficient. It would also help us to identify where we are not cost competitive. With this information, we might be able to find ways to increase our efficiency.

**Brindon:** Well, I have good news. I've been talking with Carl Penobscot, Kilborn's assistant controller. Carl doesn't feel appreciated by Kilborn and wants to make a change. He could easily fit into our team here. Plus, Carl has been preparing for a job switch by quietly copying Kilborn's accounting files and records. He's already given me some data that reveal bids that Kilborn made on several jobs. If we can come to a satisfactory agreement with Carl, he'll bring the rest of the information with him. We'll easily be able to figure out Kilborn's prospective bids and find ways to beat them. Besides, I could use another accountant on my staff. Bill, would you authorize my immediate hiring of Carl with a favorable compensation package?

**Bill:** I know that you need more staff, Brindon, but is this the right thing to do? It sounds like Carl is stealing those files, and surely Kilborn considers this information confidential. I have real ethical and legal concerns about this. Why don't we meet with Laurie, our attorney, and determine any legal problems?

**Required:**

1. Is Carl's behavior ethical? What would Kilborn think?
2. Is Bill correct in supposing that there are ethical and/or legal problems involved with the hiring of Carl? (Reread the section on corporate codes of conduct in Chapter 1.) What would you do if you were Bill? Explain.

# 4

# Cost-Volume-Profit Analysis: A Managerial Planning Tool

© Pixelfabrik/Alamy

Paul Burns/Fancy/JupiterImages

After studying Chapter 4, you should be able to:

1. Determine the break-even point in number of units and in total sales dollars.

2. Determine the number of units that must be sold, and the amount of revenue required, to earn a targeted profit.

3. Prepare a profit-volume graph and a cost-volume-profit graph, and explain the meaning of each.

4. Apply cost-volume-profit analysis in a multiple-product setting.

5. Explain the impact of risk, uncertainty, and changing variables on cost-volume-profit analysis.

# EXPERIENCE MANAGERIAL DECISIONS
## with Boyne Resorts

**Boyne USA Resorts** owns and operates ski resorts in British Columbia, Washington, Montana, and Michigan. Boyne earns a significant portion of its revenue from winter skiing. However, winter ski volume depends heavily on natural snowfall, which varies significantly from year to year. As a result, Boyne uses creative thinking along with cost-volume-profit (CVP) analyses to develop activities that generate additional profit. Consider ski lifts at Boyne Highlands, an important source of revenue for the company. What other revenue-generating activities might Boyne develop that revolve around such ski lifts? What additional variable and fixed costs might be involved with these activities, and what are the profit implications?

Boyne develops a variety of lift ticket packages to accommodate as many snow skiers and snow boarders as possible. Lift tickets are interchangeable between multiple Boyne properties and can be used during night skiing in certain areas. Like many ski resorts, Boyne markets spring, summer, and fall activities as well. For instance, many resorts promote mountain biking and hiking where participants purchase lift tickets for enclosed lifts, called gondolas, that carry them and their gear to the top of the mountain to begin their descent. Other ski resorts, such as Aspen, build elaborate children's playgrounds

> *"Other ski resorts, such as Aspen, build elaborate children's playgrounds and bungee trampolines at the top of the lifts to generate additional summer business in ski areas that might otherwise be dormant during the off-season."*

and bungee trampolines at the top of the lifts to generate additional summer business in ski areas that might otherwise be dormant during the off-season. Still other resorts build elaborate mountaintop restaurants and entertainment areas that can be reached only via ski lifts or gondolas, thereby increasing revenues and profits. Using CVP equations and contribution margin formulas, as well as cost-volume-profit and profit-volume graphs, Boyne spends considerable effort analyzing the revenue, cost, volume, and profit implications of these varied activities. With careful CVP analysis and sound judgment, Boyne attempts to make the best decisions possible to continue its profitability and reputation for fun.

# BREAK-EVEN POINT IN UNITS AND IN SALES DOLLARS

**Cost-volume-profit (CVP) analysis** estimates how changes in costs (both variable and fixed), sales volume, and price affect a company's profit. CVP is a powerful tool for planning and decision making. In fact, CVP is one of the most versatile and widely applicable tools used by managerial accountants to help managers make better decisions.

Companies use CVP analysis to reach important benchmarks, such as their break-even point. The **break-even point** is the point where total revenue equals total cost (i.e., the point of zero profit). New companies typically experience losses (negative operating income) initially and view their first break-even period as a significant milestone. For example, online retail pioneer **Amazon.com** was founded in 1994 but did not break even until the fourth quarter of 2001. Also, managers become very interested in CVP analysis during times of economic trouble. For example, to the dismay of many of its shareholders, **SiriusXM Radio** signed shock-jock Howard Stern to a 5-year, $500 million employment contract for joining the young company. As a result of Stern's huge contract cost, some analysts estimated that Sirius would need an additional 2.4 million subscribers (i.e., customers) to reach breakeven. Therefore, CVP analysis helps managers pinpoint problems and find solutions.

CVP analysis can address many other issues as well, including:

- the number of units that must be sold to break even
- the impact of a given reduction in fixed costs on the break-even point
- the impact of an increase in price on profit

Additionally, CVP analysis allows managers to do sensitivity analysis by examining the impact of various price or cost levels on profit.

Since CVP analysis shows how revenues, expenses, and profits behave as volume changes, it is natural to begin by finding the firm's break-even point in units sold.

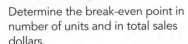
## Here's The Real Kicker

**Kicker** separates cost into fixed and variable components by using judgment. Because the bulk of manufacturing is outsourced, the cost of a set of speakers starts with the purchase price from the manufacturer. This cost is strictly variable in nature. Additional variable costs include duty (ranging from 9 to 30%, electronics are at the high end) and freight (all units are shipped to Stillwater, Oklahoma, for distribution). In-house labor may be needed at Kicker's Stillwater facilities, and that cost has both fixed (salaried workers) and variable (temporary workers) components.

The salaried staff in Stillwater, research and development, depreciation on property, plant and equipment, utilities, and so on, are all fixed.

These fixed and variable costs are used in monthly cost-volume-profit analysis and in management decision making. For example, the monthly cost-volume-profit figures can be used to monitor the effect of changing volume on profit and spotlight increases in fixed and variable costs. If costs are going up, management finds out about the problem early and can make adjustments.

## Using Operating Income in Cost-Volume-Profit Analysis

In CVP analysis, the terms "cost" and "expense" are often used interchangeably. This is because the conceptual foundation of CVP analysis is the economics of breakeven analysis in the short run. For this, it is assumed that all units produced are sold. Therefore, all product and period costs do end up as expenses on the income statement. We will look more closely at the assumptions of CVP later in this chapter. Remember from Chapter 2 that operating income is total revenue minus total expense:

$$\text{Operating Income} = \text{Total Revenue} - \text{Total Expense}$$

For the income statement, expenses are classified according to function; that is, the manufacturing (or service provision) function, the selling function, and the administrative function. For CVP analysis, however, it is much more useful to organize costs into fixed and variable components. The focus is on the firm as a whole. Therefore, the costs refer to all costs of the company—production, selling, and administration. So variable costs are all costs that increase as more units are sold, including:

- direct materials
- direct labor
- variable overhead
- variable selling and administrative costs

Similarly, fixed costs include:

- fixed overhead
- fixed selling and administrative expenses

The income statement format that is based on the separation of costs into fixed and variable components is called the **contribution margin income statement**. Exhibit 4.1 shows the format for the contribution margin income statement.

( EXHIBIT 4.1 )

**The Contribution Margin Income Statement**

| | |
|---|---|
| Sales | $ XXX |
| Total variable cost | (XXX) |
|    Total contribution margin | $ XXX |
| Total fixed cost | (XXX) |
|    Operating income | $ XXX |

© Cengage Learning 2014

**Contribution margin** is the difference between sales and variable expense. It is the amount of sales revenue left over after all the variable expenses are covered that can be used to contribute to fixed expense and operating income. The contribution margin can be calculated in total (as it was in Exhibit 4.1) or per unit.

Let's use Whittier Company, a manufacturer of mulching lawn mowers, as an example. Cornerstone 4.1 illustrates how to calculate the variable and fixed expenses and prepare the contribution margin statement for Whittier.

## Preparing a Contribution Margin Income Statement

CORNERSTONE

**4.1**

**Why:**

A contribution margin income statement helps managers understand the amount contributed to income by higher (lower) sales. Separating out the fixed costs enables managers to easily compute income at various sales quantities.

**Information:**

Whittier Company plans to sell 1,000 mowers at $400 each in the coming year. Product costs include:

| | | |
|---|---|---|
| Direct materials per mower | $ | 180 |
| Direct labor per mower | | 100 |
| Variable factory overhead per mower | | 25 |
| Total fixed factory overhead | | 15,000 |

*(Continued)*

© Pixelfabrik/Alamy

Variable selling expense is a commission of $20 per mower; fixed selling and administrative expense totals $30,000.

**Required:**

1. Calculate the total variable expense per unit.

2. Calculate the total fixed expense for the year.

3. Prepare a contribution margin income statement for Whittier for the coming year.

**Solution:**

1. Total variable expense per unit

$$= \begin{array}{c} \text{Direct} \\ \text{Materials} \end{array} + \begin{array}{c} \text{Direct} \\ \text{Labor} \end{array} + \begin{array}{c} \text{Variable} \\ \text{Factory} \\ \text{Overhead} \end{array} + \begin{array}{c} \text{Variable} \\ \text{Selling} \\ \text{Expense} \end{array}$$

$$= \quad \$180 \quad + \quad \$100 \quad + \quad \$25 \quad + \quad \$20$$

$$= \quad \$325$$

2. Total Fixed Expense = Fixed Factory Overhead
$$+ \text{ Fixed Selling and Administrative Expense}$$
$$= \$15,000 + \$30,000 = \$45,000$$

3.

**Whittier Company**
**Contribution Margin Income Statement**
**For the Coming Year**

|  | Total | Per Unit |
|---|---|---|
| Sales ($400 × 1,000 mowers) | $400,000 | $400 |
| Total variable expense ($325 × 1,000) | 325,000 | 325 |
| Total contribution margin | $ 75,000 | $ 75 |
| Total fixed expense | 45,000 | |
| Operating income | $ 30,000 | |

Notice that the contribution margin income statement in Cornerstone 4.1 shows a total contribution margin of $75,000. The per-unit contribution margin is $75 ($400 − $325). That is, every mower sold contributes $75 toward fixed expense and operating income.

What does Whittier's contribution margin income statement show? First, we see that Whittier will more than break even at sales of 1,000 mowers, since operating income is $30,000. Clearly, Whittier would just break even if total contribution margin equaled the total fixed cost. Let's see how to calculate the break-even point.

## Break-Even Point in Units

If the contribution margin income statement is recast as an equation, it becomes more useful for solving CVP problems. The operating income equation is:

$$\text{Operating Income} = \text{Sales} - \text{Total Variable Expenses} - \text{Total Fixed Expenses}$$

Notice that all we have done is remove the total contribution margin line from Exhibit 4.1 (p. 119), since it is identical to sales minus total variable expense. This equation is the basis of all the coming work on CVP. We can think of it as the basic CVP equation.

We can expand the operating income equation by expressing sales revenues and variable expenses in terms of unit dollar amounts and the number of units sold. Specifically, sales revenue equals the unit selling price times the number of units sold, and total variable costs equal the unit variable cost times the number of units sold. With these expressions, the operating income equation becomes:

> Operating Income = (Price × Number of Units Sold) − (Variable Cost per Unit × Number of Units Sold) − Total Fixed Cost

At the break-even point, operating income equals $0. Cornerstone 4.2 shows how to use the operating income equation to find the break-even point in units for Whittier Company.

## Calculating the Break-Even Point in Units

### Why:

The break-even point in units tells managers exactly how many units must be sold to cover all costs. Any units sold above breakeven will yield a profit.

### Information:

Refer to the Whittier Company information in Cornerstone 4.1. Recall that mowers sell for $400 each, and variable cost per mower is $325. Total fixed cost equals $45,000.

### Required:

1. Calculate the number of mowers that Whittier must sell to break even.

2. Check your answer by preparing a contribution margin income statement based on the break-even point.

### Solution:

1. Break-Even Number of Mowers $= \dfrac{\text{Total Fixed Cost}}{\text{Price} - \text{Variable Cost per Unit}}$

$$= \frac{\$45,000}{\$400 - \$325} = 600$$

2. Contribution margin income statement based on 600 mowers.

| | |
|---|---|
| Sales ($400 × 600 mowers) | $240,000 |
| Total variable expense ($325 × 600) | 195,000 |
| Total contribution margin | $ 45,000 |
| Total fixed expense | 45,000 |
| Operating income | $       0 |

Indeed, selling 600 units does yield a zero profit.

( EXHIBIT 4.2 )

**Contribution Margin and Fixed Cost at Breakeven for Whittier Company**

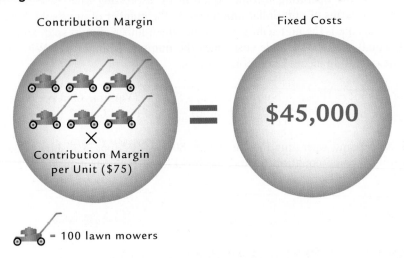

© Cengage Learning 2014

When Whittier breaks even, total contribution margin equals total fixed cost. Exhibit 4.2 illustrates this important observation.

The operating income equation can be rearranged as follows to show the number of units at breakeven:

$$\text{Break-Even Units} = \frac{\text{Total Fixed Cost}}{\text{Price} - \text{Variable Cost per Unit}}$$

In other words, the break-even units are equal to the fixed cost divided by the contribution margin per unit. So, if a company sells enough units for the contribution margin to just cover fixed costs, it will earn zero operating income: it will break even. It is quicker to solve break-even problems using this break-even version of the operating income equation than it is using the original operating income equation.

## Break-Even Point in Sales Dollars

Sometimes, managers using CVP analysis may prefer to use sales revenue as the measure of sales activity instead of units sold. A units sold measure can be converted to a sales revenue measure by multiplying the unit selling price by the units sold:

$$\text{Sales Revenue} = \text{Price} \times \text{Units Sold}$$

For example, the break-even point for Whittier is 600 mulching mowers. Since the selling price for each lawn mower is $400, the break-even volume in sales revenue is $240,000 ($400 × 600).

Any answer expressed in units sold can be easily converted to one expressed in sales revenues, but the answer can be computed more directly by developing a separate formula for the sales revenue case. Here, the important variable is sales dollars, so both the revenue and the variable costs must be expressed in dollars instead of units. Since sales revenue is always expressed in dollars, measuring that variable is no problem. Let's look more closely at variable costs and see how they can be expressed in terms of sales dollars.

**Variable Cost Ratio**  To calculate the break-even point in sales dollars, total variable costs are defined as a percentage of sales rather than as an amount per unit sold. Suppose that a company sells a product for $10 per unit and incurs a variable cost of $6 per unit. The contribution margin would be $4:

$$\text{Price} - \text{Variable Cost per Unit} = \$10 - \$6 = \$4$$

If 10 units are sold, total variable costs are $60:

$$\text{Variable Cost} \times \text{Units Sold} = \$6 \times 10 \text{ units} = \$60$$

Alternatively, since each unit sold earns $10 of revenue and has $6 of variable cost, one could say that 60% of each dollar of revenue earned is attributable to variable cost:

$$\frac{\text{Variable Cost per Unit}}{\text{Price}} = \frac{\$6}{\$10} = 60\%$$

Thus, sales revenues of $100 would result in total variable costs of $60 (0.60 × $100). This 60% is the variable cost ratio.

The **variable cost ratio** is the proportion of each sales dollar that must be used to cover variable costs. The variable cost ratio can be computed using either total data or unit data.

$$\text{Variable Cost Ratio} = \frac{\text{Total Variable Cost}}{\text{Sales}}$$

OR

$$\text{Variable Cost Ratio} = \frac{\text{Unit Variable Cost}}{\text{Price}}$$

**Contribution Margin Ratio**  The percentage of sales dollars remaining after variable costs are covered is the contribution margin ratio. The **contribution margin ratio** is the proportion of each sales dollar available to cover fixed costs and provide for profit. For Whittier, if the variable cost ratio is 60% of sales, then the contribution margin ratio must be the remaining 40% of sales. It makes sense that the complement of the variable cost ratio is the contribution margin ratio. After all, total variable costs and total contribution margin sum to sales revenue.

$$\text{Contribution Margin Ratio} = \frac{\text{Total Contribution Margin}}{\text{Sales}}$$

OR

$$\text{Contribution Margin Ratio} = \frac{\text{Unit Contribution Margin}}{\text{Price}}$$

Just as the variable cost ratio can be computed using total or unit figures, the contribution margin ratio, 40% in our example, can also be computed in these two ways. So, one can divide the total contribution margin by total sales:

$$\frac{\text{Total Contribution Margin}}{\text{Total Sales}} = \frac{\$40}{\$100} = 40\%$$

Alternatively, one can use the unit contribution margin divided by price:

$$\frac{\text{Contribution Margin per Unit}}{\text{Price}} = \frac{\$4}{\$10} = 40\%$$

Naturally, if the variable cost ratio is known, it can be subtracted from 1 to yield the contribution margin ratio:

$$1 - \text{Variable Cost Ratio} = \text{Contribution Margin Ratio}$$
$$1 - 0.60 = 0.40$$

**Cornerstone 4.3** shows how the income statement can be expanded to yield the variable cost ratio and the contribution margin ratio.

---

## concept Q&A

1. If the contribution margin ratio is 30%, what is the variable cost ratio?
2. If the variable cost ratio is 77%, what is the contribution margin ratio?
3. Explain why the contribution margin ratio and the variable cost ratio always total 100%.

**Answer:**

1. Variable Cost Ratio = 1.00 − 0.30 = 0.70, or 70%.
2. Contribution Margin Ratio = 1.00 − 0.77 = 0.23, or 23%.
3. The contribution margin ratio and the variable cost ratio always equal 100% of sales revenue. By definition, total variable cost and total contribution margin sum to sales revenue.

## Calculating the Variable Cost Ratio and the Contribution Margin Ratio

**4.3**

**Why:**

The variable cost ratio tells managers what proportion of each sales dollar goes to covering variable costs. The contribution margin ratio is the proportion of each sales dollar left after variable costs are covered. This proportion goes toward covering fixed costs and profit.

**Information:**

Whittier Company plans to sell 1,000 mowers at $400 each in the coming year. Variable cost per unit is $325. Total fixed cost is $45,000.

**Required:**

1. Calculate the variable cost ratio.

2. Calculate the contribution margin ratio using unit figures.

3. Prepare a contribution margin income statement based on the budgeted figures for next year. In a column next to the income statement, show the percentages based on sales for sales, total variable expense, and total contribution margin.

**Solution:**

1. $\text{Variable Cost Ratio} = \dfrac{\text{Variable Cost per Unit}}{\text{Price}}$

    $= \dfrac{\$325}{\$400} = 0.8125$, or 81.25%

2. Contribution Margin per Unit = Price − Variable Cost per Unit

    $= \$400 - \$325 = \$75$

    $\text{Contribution Margin Ratio} = \dfrac{\text{Contribution Margin per Unit}}{\text{Price}}$

    $= \dfrac{\$75}{\$400} = 0.1875$, or 18.75%

3. Contribution margin income statement based on budgeted figures:

|  |  | Percent of Sales |
|---|---|---|
| Sales ($400 × 1,000 mowers) | $400,000 | 100.00 |
| Total variable expense (0.8125 × $400,000) | 325,000 | 81.25 |
| Total contribution margin | $ 75,000 | 18.75 |
| Total fixed expense | 45,000 |  |
| Operating income | $ 30,000 |  |

Notice in Cornerstone 4.3, Requirement 3, that sales revenue, variable costs, and contribution margin have been expressed as a percent of sales. The variable cost ratio is 0.8125 ($325,000/$400,000); the contribution margin ratio is 0.1875 (computed either as 1 − 0.8125, or $75,000/$400,000).

How do fixed costs relate to the variable cost ratio and contribution margin ratio? Since the total contribution margin is the revenue remaining after total variable costs are covered, it must be the revenue available to cover fixed costs and contribute to profit. How does the relationship of fixed cost to contribution margin affect operating income? There are three possibilities:

- Fixed cost equals contribution margin; operating income is zero; the company breaks even.
- Fixed cost is less than contribution margin; operating income is greater than zero; the company makes a profit.
- Fixed cost is greater than contribution margin; operating income is less than zero; the company makes a loss.

**Calculating Break-Even Point in Sales Dollars**   Now, let's turn to the equation for calculating the break-even point in sales dollars. One way of calculating break-even sales revenue is to multiply the break-even units by the price. However, often the company is a multiple-product firm, and it can be difficult to figure the break-even point for each product sold. The operating income equation can be used to solve for break-even sales for Whittier as follows:

$$\text{Operating Income} = \text{Sales} - \text{Total Variable Expenses} - \text{Total Fixed Expenses}$$
$$\$0 = \text{Break-Even Sales} - (0.8125 \times \text{Break-Even Sales}) - \$45,000$$
$$\$0 = \text{Break-Even Sales} (1.00 - 0.8125) - \$45,000$$
$$\text{Break-Even Sales} = \frac{\$45,000}{(1.00 - 0.8125)}$$
$$= \$240,000$$

So, Whittier Company has sales of $240,000 at the break-even point.

Just as it was quicker to use an equation to calculate the break-even units directly, it is helpful to have an equation to figure the break-even sales dollars. This equation is:

$$\text{Break-Even Sales} = \frac{\text{Total Fixed Expenses}}{\text{Contribution Margin Ratio}}$$

Cornerstone 4.4 shows how to obtain the break-even point in sales dollars for Whittier Company.

## Calculating the Break-Even Point in Sales Dollars

**Why:**

The break-even point in sales dollars makes it easy for managers to see instantly how close they are to breaking even using only sales revenue data. Since sales are typically recorded immediately, the manager does not have to wait to have an income statement prepared in order to see how close the company is to breaking even.

**Information:**

Whittier Company plans to sell 1,000 mowers at $400 each in the coming year. Total variable expense per unit is $325. Total fixed expense is $45,000.

**Required:**

1. Calculate the contribution margin ratio.

CORNERSTONE

**4.4**

*(Continued)*

CORNERSTONE

**4.4**

*(Continued)*

2. Calculate the sales revenue that Whittier must make to break even by using the break-even point in sales equation.

3. Check your answer by preparing a contribution margin income statement based on the break-even point in sales dollars.

**Solution:**

1. Contribution Margin per Unit = Price − Variable Cost per Unit
$$= \$400 - \$325 = \$75$$

$$\text{Contribution Margin Ratio} = \frac{\text{Contribution Margin per Unit}}{\text{Price}}$$

$$= \frac{\$75}{\$400} = 0.1875, \text{ or } 18.75\%$$

[*Hint:* The contribution margin ratio comes out cleanly to four decimal places. Don't round it, and your break-even point in sales dollars will yield an operating income of $0 (rather than being a few dollars off due to rounding).]

Notice that the variable cost ratio equals 0.8125, or the difference between 1.0000 and the contribution margin ratio.

2. Calculate the break-even point in sales dollars:

$$\text{Break-Even Sales Dollars} = \frac{\text{Total Fixed Cost}}{\text{Contribution Margin Ratio}}$$

$$= \frac{\$45,000}{0.8175} = \$240,000$$

3. Contribution margin income statement based on sales of $240,000:

| | |
|---|---:|
| Sales | $240,000 |
| Total variable expense (0.8125 × $240,000) | 195,000 |
| Total contribution margin | $ 45,000 |
| Total fixed expense | 45,000 |
| Operating income | $       0 |

Indeed, sales equal to $240,000 does yield a zero profit.

---

Accountants for the snowsports division of **Boyne USA Resorts** analyze their fixed and variable costs each month as they work to anticipate their break-even point and potential operating income. The contribution margin income statement is a powerful tool to help them with this. They pay close attention to the week between Christmas and New Years, as this is their peak revenue opportunity. Depending on what occurs that week, pricing and cost management for the rest of the season are adjusted.

OBJECTIVE ❷

Determine the number of units that must be sold, and the amount of revenue required, to earn a targeted profit.

## UNITS AND SALES DOLLARS NEEDED TO ACHIEVE A TARGET INCOME

While the break-even point is useful information and an important benchmark for relatively young companies, most companies would like to earn operating income greater than $0. CVP analysis gives us a way to determine how many units must be sold, or how much sales revenue must be generated, to earn a particular target income. Let's look first at the number of units that must be sold to earn a targeted operating income.

## Units to Be Sold to Achieve a Target Income

Remember that at the break-even point, operating income is $0. How can the equations used in our earlier break-even analyses be adjusted to find the number of units that must be sold to earn a target income? The answer is to add the target income amount to the fixed costs. Let's try it two different ways—with the operating income equation and with the basic break-even equation.

Remember that the equation for the operating income is:

$$\text{Operating Income} = (\text{Price} \times \text{Units Sold}) - (\text{Unit Variable Cost} \times \text{Units Sold}) - \text{Fixed Cost}$$

To solve for positive operating income, replace the operating income term with the target income. Recall that Whittier sells mowers at $400 each, incurs variable cost per unit of $325, and has total fixed expense of $45,000. Suppose that Whittier wants to make a target operating income of $37,500. The number of units that must be sold to achieve that target income is calculated as follows:

$$\$37,500 = (\$400 \times \text{Number of Units}) - (\$325 \times \text{Number of Units}) - \$45,000$$

$$\text{Number of Units} = \frac{\$37,500 + \$45,000}{\$400 - \$325} = 1,100$$

Does the sale of 1,100 units really result in operating income of $37,500? The contribution margin income statement provides a good check.

| | |
|---|---:|
| Sales ($400 × 1,100) | $440,000 |
| Total variable expense ($325 × 1,100) | 357,500 |
| Total contribution margin | $ 82,500 |
| Total fixed expense | 45,000 |
| Operating income | $ 37,500 |

Indeed, selling 1,100 units does yield operating income of $37,500.

The operating income equation can be used to find the number of units to sell to earn a targeted income. However, it is quicker to adjust the break-even units equation by adding target income to the fixed cost. This adjustment results in the following equation:

$$\text{Number of Units to Earn Target Income} = \frac{\text{Total Fixed Cost} + \text{Target Income}}{\text{Price} - \text{Variable Cost per Unit}}$$

This equation was used when calculating the 1,100 units needed to earn operating income of $37,500. Cornerstone 4.5 shows how Whittier Company can use this approach.

## Calculating the Number of Units to Be Sold to Earn a Target Operating Income

**Why:**

The number of units needed to earn a target operating income moves managers away from a point of zero profit, toward one of a particular positive profit.

CORNERSTONE

4.5

*(Continued)*

**CORNERSTONE**

**4.5**

*(Continued)*

**Information:**

Whittier Company sells mowers at $400 each. Variable cost per unit is $325, and total fixed cost is $45,000.

**Required:**

1. Calculate the number of units that Whittier must sell to earn operating income of $37,500.

2. Check your answer by preparing a contribution margin income statement based on the number of units calculated.

**Solution:**

1. $$\text{Number of Units} = \frac{\text{Target Income} + \text{Total Fixed Cost}}{\text{Price} - \text{Variable Cost per Unit}}$$

$$= \frac{\$37,500 + \$45,000}{\$400 - \$325} = 1,100$$

2. Contribution margin income statement based on sales of 1,100 units:

| | |
|---|---:|
| Sales ($400 × 1,100) | $440,000 |
| Total variable expense ($325 × 1,100) | 357,500 |
| Total contribution margin | $ 82,500 |
| Total fixed expense | 45,000 |
| Operating income | $ 37,500 |

Indeed, selling 1,100 units does yield operating income of $37,500.

Another way to check the number of units to be sold to yield a target operating income is to use the break-even point. As shown in Cornerstone 4.5, Whittier must sell 1,100 lawn mowers, or 500 more than the break-even volume of 600 units, to earn a profit of $37,500. The contribution margin per lawn mower is $75. Multiplying $75 by the 500 lawn mowers above breakeven produces the operating income of $37,500 ($75 × 500). This outcome demonstrates that contribution margin per unit for each unit above breakeven is equivalent to operating income per unit. Since the break-even point had already been computed, the number of lawn mowers to be sold to yield a $37,500 operating income could have been calculated by dividing the unit contribution margin into the target income and adding the resulting amount to the break-even volume:

$$\text{Units for Income} = \frac{\text{Target Income}}{\text{Unit Contribution Margin}} + \text{Break-Even Volume}$$

In general, assuming that fixed costs remain the same, the impact on a firm's income resulting from a change in the number of units sold can be assessed by multiplying the unit contribution margin by the change in units sold:

$$\text{Change in Operating Income} = \text{Unit Contribution Margin} \times \text{Change in Units Sold}$$

For example, if 1,400 lawn mowers instead of 1,100 are sold, how much more operating income will be earned? The change in units sold is an increase of 300 lawn mowers, and the unit contribution margin is $75. Thus, operating income will increase by $22,500 ($75 × 300) over the $37,500 initially calculated, and total operating income will be $60,000.

# Sales Revenue to Achieve a Target Income

Consider the following question: How much sales revenue must Whittier generate to earn an operating income of $37,500? This question is similar to the one we asked earlier in terms of units but phrases the question directly in terms of sales revenue. To answer the question, add the targeted operating income of $37,500 to the $45,000 of fixed cost and divide by the contribution margin ratio. This equation is:

$$\text{Sales Dollars to Earn Target Income} = \frac{\text{Total Fixed Cost} + \text{Target Income}}{\text{Contribution Margin Ratio}}$$

Cornerstone 4.6 shows how to calculate the sales revenue needed to earn a target operating income of $37,500.

## Calculating Sales Needed to Earn a Target Operating Income

**CORNERSTONE**

**4.6**

**Why:**

The sales needed to earn a target operating income moves managers away from a point of zero profit, toward one of a particular positive profit. Managers find it easy to use actual sales at any point in time to determine how close or far away they are from breakeven.

**Information:**

Whittier Company sells mowers at $400 each. Variable cost per unit is $325, and total fixed cost is $45,000.

**Required:**

1. Calculate the contribution margin ratio.

2. Calculate the sales that Whittier must make to earn an operating income of $37,500.

3. Check your answer by preparing a contribution margin income statement based on the sales dollars calculated.

**Solution:**

1. $\text{Contribution Margin Ratio} = \dfrac{\$400 - \$325}{\$400} = 0.1875$

2. $\text{Sales Dollars} = \dfrac{\text{Target Income} + \text{Total Fixed Cost}}{\text{Contribution Margin Ratio}}$

   $= \dfrac{\$37,500 + \$45,000}{0.1875} = \$440,000$

3. Contribution margin income statement based on sales revenue of $440,000:

| | |
|---|---:|
| Sales | $440,000 |
| Total variable expense (0.8125 × $440,000) | 357,500 |
|    Total contribution margin | $ 82,500 |
| Total fixed expense | 45,000 |
|    Operating income | $ 37,500 |

Indeed, sales revenue of $440,000 does yield operating income of $37,500.

## concept Q&A

Lorna makes and sells decorative candles through gift shops. She knows she must sell 200 candles a month to break even. Every candle has a contribution margin of $1.50. So far this month, Lorna has sold 320 candles. How much has Lorna earned so far this month in operating income? If she sells 10 more candles, by how much will income increase?

**Answer:**

320 candles sold − 200 candles at breakeven = 120 candles above breakeven, 120 × $1.50 = $180. Lorna has earned operating income of $180 so far during the month. An additional 10 candles contribute $15 to operating income ($1.50 × 10).

Whittier must earn revenues equal to $440,000 to achieve a profit target of $37,500. Since break-even sales equals $240,000, additional sales of $200,000 ($440,000 − $240,000) must be earned above breakeven. Notice that multiplying the contribution margin ratio by revenues above breakeven yields the profit of $37,500 (0.1875 × $200,000). Above break even, the contribution margin ratio is a profit ratio; therefore, it represents the proportion of each sales dollar attributable to profit. For Whittier, every sales dollar earned above breakeven increases profits by $0.1875.

In general, assuming that fixed costs remain unchanged, the contribution margin ratio can be used to find the profit impact of a change in sales revenue. To obtain the total change in profits from a change in revenues, multiply the contribution margin ratio times the change in sales:

$$\text{Change in Profits} = \text{Contribution Margin Ratio} \times \text{Change in Sales}$$

For example, if sales revenues are $400,000 instead of $440,000, how will the expected profits be affected? A decrease in sales revenues of $40,000 will cause a decrease in profits of $7,500 (0.1875 × $40,000).

OBJECTIVE **3**

Prepare a profit-volume graph and a cost-volume-profit graph, and explain the meaning of each.

# GRAPHS OF COST-VOLUME-PROFIT RELATIONSHIPS

Graphical representations of CVP relationships can help managers clearly see the difference between variable cost and revenue. It may also help them understand quickly what impact an increase or decrease in sales will have on the break-even point. Two basic graphs are the profit-volume graph and the cost-volume-profit graph.

## The Profit-Volume Graph

A **profit-volume graph** visually portrays the relationship between profits (operating income) and units sold. The profit-volume graph is the graph of the operating income equation:

$$\text{Operating Income} = (\text{Price} \times \text{Units}) - (\text{Unit Variable Cost} \times \text{Units}) - \text{Total Fixed Cost}$$

In this graph, operating income is the dependent variable, and units is the independent variable. Usually, values of the independent variable are measured along the horizontal axis, and values of the dependent variable are measured along the vertical axis.

Assume that Tyson Company produces a single product with the following cost and price data:

| | |
|---|---|
| Total fixed costs | $100 |
| Variable costs per unit | 5 |
| Selling price per unit | 10 |

Using these data, operating income can be expressed as:

$$\text{Operating Income} = (\$10 \times \text{Units}) - (\$5 \times \text{Units}) - \$100$$
$$= (\$5 \times \text{Units}) - \$100$$

This relationship can be graphed by plotting units along the horizontal axis and operating income (or loss) along the vertical axis. Two points are needed to graph a linear equation. While any two points will do, the two points often chosen are those that correspond to zero units sold and zero profits. When units sold are 0, Tyson experiences an operating loss of $100 (or an operating income of −$100). The point corresponding to zero sales volume, therefore, is (0, −$100). When no sales take place, the company suffers a loss equal to its total fixed costs. When operating income is $0, the units sold are equal to 20. The point corresponding to zero profits (breakeven) is (20, $0). These two points, plotted in Exhibit 4.3, define the profit graph.

The graph in Exhibit 4.3 can be used to assess Tyson's profit (or loss) at any level of sales activity. For example, the profit associated with the sale of 40 units can be read from the graph by:

1. drawing a vertical line from the horizontal axis to the profit line and

2. drawing a horizontal line from the profit line to the vertical axis.

As illustrated in Exhibit 4.3, the profit associated with sales of 40 units is $100. The profit-volume graph, while easy to interpret, fails to reveal how costs change as sales volume changes. An alternative approach to graphing can provide this detail.

( EXHIBIT 4.3 )

**Profit-Volume Graph**

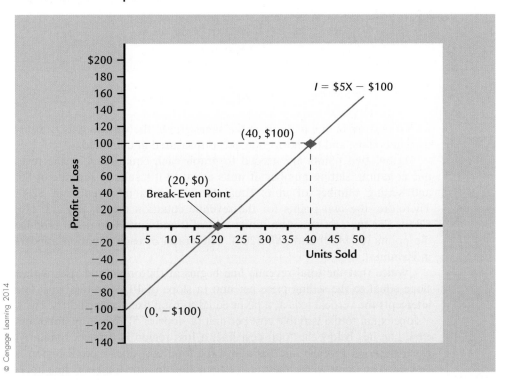

© Cengage Learning 2014

## The Cost-Volume-Profit Graph

The **cost-volume-profit graph** depicts the relationships among cost, volume, and profits (operating income) by plotting the total revenue line and the total cost line on a graph. To obtain the more detailed relationships, it is necessary to graph two separate lines— the total revenue line and the total cost line. These two lines are represented by the following two equations:

$$\text{Revenue} = \text{Price} \times \text{Units}$$
$$\text{Total Cost} = (\text{Unit Variable Cost} \times \text{Units}) + \text{Fixed Cost}$$

Using the Tyson example, the revenue and cost equations are:

$$\text{Revenue} = \$10 \times \text{Units}$$
$$\text{Total Cost} = (\$5 \times \text{Units}) + \$100$$

**( EXHIBIT 4.4 )**

## Cost-Volume-Profit Graph

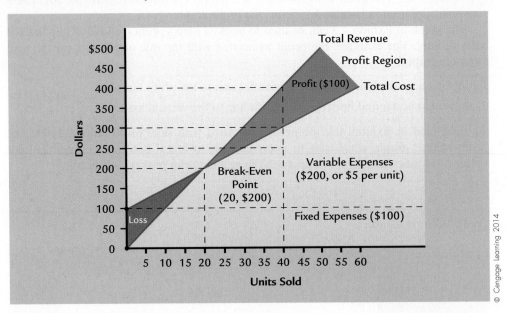

To portray both equations in the same graph, the vertical axis is measured in dollars, and the horizontal axis is measured in units sold.

Again, two points are needed to graph each equation. For the revenue equation, setting number of units equal to 0 results in revenue of $0, and setting number of units equal to 20 results in revenue of $200. Therefore, the two points for the revenue equation are (0, $0) and (20, $200). For the cost equation, units sold of 0 and units sold of 20 produce the points (0, $100) and (20, $200). The graph of each equation appears in Exhibit 4.4.

Notice that the total revenue line begins at the origin and rises with a slope equal to the selling price per unit (a slope of 10). The total cost line intercepts the vertical axis at a point equal to total fixed costs and rises with a slope equal to the variable cost per unit (a slope of 5). When the total revenue line lies below the total cost line, a loss region is defined. Similarly, when the total revenue line lies above the total cost line, a profit region is defined. The point where the total revenue line and the total cost line intersect is the break-even point. To break even, Tyson must sell 20 units and, thus, receive $200 in total revenues.

Now, let's compare the information available from the CVP graph with that available from the profit-volume graph. Consider the sale of 40 units. The profit-volume graph showed that 40 units produced profits of $100. Examine Exhibit 4.4 again. The CVP graph also shows profits of $100, but it reveals more. The CVP graph discloses that total revenues of $400 and total costs of $300 are associated with the sale of 40 units. Furthermore, the total costs can be broken down into fixed costs of $100 and variable costs of $200. The CVP graph provides revenue and cost information not provided by the profit-volume graph. Unlike the profit-volume graph, some computation is needed to determine the profit associated with a given sales volume. However, the greater information content means that managers are likely to find the CVP graph more useful.

## Assumptions of Cost-Volume-Profit Analysis

The profit-volume and cost-volume-profit graphs rely on important assumptions. Some of these assumptions are as follows:

- There are identifiable linear revenue and linear cost functions that remain constant over the relevant range.
- Selling prices and costs are known with certainty.
- Units produced are sold—there are no finished goods inventories.
- Sales mix is known with certainty for multiple-product break-even settings (explained later in this chapter).

**Linear Cost and Revenue Functions** CVP assumes that cost and revenue functions are linear; that is, they are straight lines. But, as was discussed in Chapter 3 on cost behavior, these functions are often not linear. They may be curved or step functions. Fortunately, it is not necessary to consider all possible ranges of production and sales for a firm. Remember that CVP analysis is a short-run decision-making tool. (We know that it is short run in orientation because some costs are fixed.) It is only necessary for us to determine the current operating range, or relevant range, for which the linear cost and revenue relationships are valid. Once a relevant range has been identified, then the cost and price relationships are assumed to be known and constant.

**Prices and Costs Known with Certainty** In reality, firms seldom know prices, variable costs, and fixed costs with certainty. A change in one variable usually affects the value of others. Often, there is a probability distribution to consider. There are formal ways of explicitly building uncertainty into the CVP model. These issues are explored in the section on incorporating risk and uncertainty into CVP analysis.

**Production Equal to Sales** CVP assumes that all units produced are sold. There is no change in inventory over the period. The idea that inventory has no impact on break-even analysis makes sense. Break-even analysis is a short-run decision-making technique, so we are looking to cover all costs of a particular period of time. Inventory embodies costs of a previous period and is not considered in CVP analyses.

**Constant Sales Mix** In single-product analysis, the sales mix is obviously constant—the one product accounts for 100% of sales. Multiple-product break-even analysis requires a constant sales mix. However, it is virtually impossible to predict with certainty the sales mix. Typically, this constraint is handled in practice through sensitivity analysis. By using the capabilities of spreadsheet analysis, the sensitivity of variables to a variety of sales mixes can be readily assessed.

# ILLUSTRATING RELATIONSHIPS AMONG CVP VARIABLES

It is critically important to understand the relationships among the CVP variables of price, unit variable cost, and total fixed costs. Consider Lotts Company, which produces and sells a product with the following costs.

| | |
|---|---|
| Unit sales price | $ 10.00 |
| Unit costs | 5.00 |
| Fixed costs | 10,000 |

Contribution Margin = $10 − $5 = $5

Break-Even Units = $10,000/($10 − $5) = 2,000

This is illustrated in Panel A of Exhibit 4.5 (p. 134). The total revenue line, shown in blue, has a slope of 10 and the total cost line, shown in red, has a slope of 5. The point of intersection is 2,000 units, which is the break-even point. Units sold above breakeven

( EXHIBIT 4.5 )

**Cost-Volume-Profit Relationships**

**Panel A.**

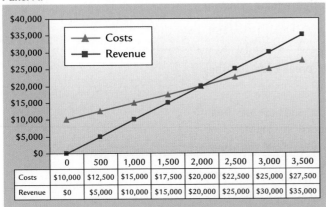

| | 0 | 500 | 1,000 | 1,500 | 2,000 | 2,500 | 3,000 | 3,500 |
|---|---|---|---|---|---|---|---|---|
| Costs | $10,000 | $12,500 | $15,000 | $17,500 | $20,000 | $22,500 | $25,000 | $27,500 |
| Revenue | $0 | $5,000 | $10,000 | $15,000 | $20,000 | $25,000 | $30,000 | $35,000 |

Unit sales price            $10.00
Cost per unit               $5.00
Fixed costs                 $10,000
Break-even point (in units) 2,000 units

**Panel B.**

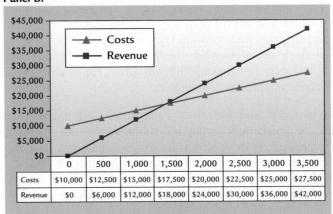

| | 0 | 500 | 1,000 | 1,500 | 2,000 | 2,500 | 3,000 | 3,500 |
|---|---|---|---|---|---|---|---|---|
| Costs | $10,000 | $12,500 | $15,000 | $17,500 | $20,000 | $22,500 | $25,000 | $27,500 |
| Revenue | $0 | $6,000 | $12,000 | $18,000 | $24,000 | $30,000 | $36,000 | $42,000 |

Unit sales price            $12.00
Cost per unit               $5.00
Fixed costs                 $10,000
Break-even point (in units) 1,429 units (rounded)

**Panel C.**

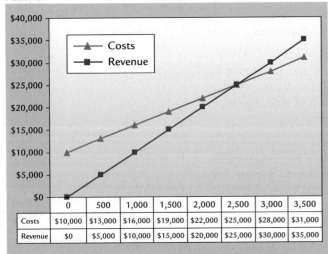

| | 0 | 500 | 1,000 | 1,500 | 2,000 | 2,500 | 3,000 | 3,500 |
|---|---|---|---|---|---|---|---|---|
| Costs | $10,000 | $13,000 | $16,000 | $19,000 | $22,000 | $25,000 | $28,000 | $31,000 |
| Revenue | $0 | $5,000 | $10,000 | $15,000 | $20,000 | $25,000 | $30,000 | $35,000 |

Unit sales price            $10.00
Cost per unit               $6.00
Fixed costs                 $10,000
Break-even point (in units) 2,500 units

**Panel D.**

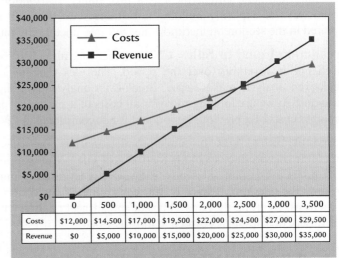

| | 0 | 500 | 1,000 | 1,500 | 2,000 | 2,500 | 3,000 | 3,500 |
|---|---|---|---|---|---|---|---|---|
| Costs | $12,000 | $14,500 | $17,000 | $19,500 | $22,000 | $24,500 | $27,000 | $29,500 |
| Revenue | $0 | $5,000 | $10,000 | $15,000 | $20,000 | $25,000 | $30,000 | $35,000 |

Unit sales price            $10.00
Cost per unit               $5.00
Fixed costs                 $12,000
Break-even point (in units) 2,400 units

© Cengage learning 2014

yield a profit; units sold below breakeven result in a loss. What happens if changes occur in the price, unit variable cost, and fixed costs?

**Impact of Changing Sales Price** In Panel B, price increases to $12, but unit variable cost and total fixed cost are the same. The new unit contribution margin is $7 ($12 − $5). Compare the new, steeper revenue, with a slope of 12, to the original revenue line shown in Panel A. The total cost line remains unchanged. The intersection of the revenue and total cost lines has moved toward the left, resulting in a new, lower break-even point of 1,429 units (rounded).

$$\text{Break-Even Units} = \frac{\$10,000}{\$12 - \$5} = 1,429 \text{ (rounded)}$$

Any increase in price will mean a higher contribution margin and, thus, a lower break-even point.

**Impact of Changing Unit Variable Costs** In Panel C, unit variable cost increases to $6, but price and total fixed costs are the same. The new contribution margin is lower at $4 ($10 – $6). The total revenue line is the same as in Panel A. However, the total cost line has a steeper slope of 6, and it intersects the total revenue line further out to the right, resulting in a higher break-even point. Compare the new total cost line to the original line shown in Panel A.

$$\text{Break-Even Units} = \frac{\$10,000}{\$10 - \$6} = 2,500$$

Thus, any increase in unit variable costs will mean a lower contribution margin and a higher break-even point.

**Impact of Changing Fixed Costs** Finally, in Panel D, total fixed costs increase to $12,000, but price and unit variable cost are the same. The new total cost line intersects the vertical axis at $12,000, not the original $10,000. Since price and unit variable cost remain unchanged, the contribution margin stays at $5 per unit and the total revenue line is unchanged from Panel A. However, the total cost line has shifted upward by $2,000, reflecting the increase in fixed costs. The new break-even point occurs farther out to the right from what it was in Panel A and shows break-even units of 2,400.

$$\text{Break-Even Units} = \frac{\$12,000}{\$10 - \$5} = 2,400$$

Thus, any increase in fixed costs will mean a higher break-even point.

Of course, many changes can be made to this simple data set for Lott Company to see how the contribution margin and break-even point are affected. You can make these changes yourself by going to CengageBrain.com and working with the interactive graph on the *Cornerstones of Managerial Accounting* companion site.

# MULTIPLE-PRODUCT ANALYSIS

OBJECTIVE 4

Apply cost-volume-profit analysis in a multiple-product setting.

Cost-volume-profit analysis is fairly simple in the single-product setting. However, most firms produce and sell a number of products or services. Even though CVP analysis becomes more complex with multiple products, the operation is reasonably straightforward. Let's see how we can adapt the formulas used in a single-product setting to a multiple-product setting by expanding the Whittier example.

Whittier has decided to offer two models of lawn mowers: a mulching mower that sells for $400 and a riding mower that sells for $800. The marketing department is convinced that 1,200 mulching mowers and 800 riding mowers can be sold during the coming year. The controller has prepared the following projected income statement based on the sales forecast:

|  | Mulching Mower | Riding Mower | Total |
|---|---|---|---|
| Sales | $480,000 | $640,000 | $1,120,000 |
| Total variable cost | 390,000 | 480,000 | 870,000 |
| Contribution margin | $ 90,000 | $160,000 | $ 250,000 |
| Direct fixed cost | 30,000 | 40,000 | 70,000 |
| Product margin | $ 60,000 | $120,000 | $ 180,000 |
| Common fixed cost |  |  | 26,250 |
| Operating income |  |  | $ 153,750 |

Note that the controller has separated *direct fixed expenses* from *common fixed expenses*. The **direct fixed expenses** are those fixed costs that can be traced to each segment and would be avoided if the segment did not exist. The **common fixed expenses** are the fixed costs that are not traceable to the segments and would remain even if one of the segments was eliminated.

# Break-Even Point in Units

The owner of Whittier is a bit concerned about adding a new product line and wants to know how many units of each model must be sold to break even. If you were responsible for answering this question, how would you respond? One possibility is to use the equation developed earlier in which fixed costs were divided by the contribution margin. However, this equation was developed for single-product analysis. For two products, there are two prices and two variable costs per unit, calculated as follows:

|  | Equation | Mulching Mower | Riding Mower |
|---|---|---|---|
| Total variable costs | $\dfrac{\text{Variable Cost per Unit}}{\text{Price}}$ | $\dfrac{\$390,000}{1,200} = \$325$ | $\dfrac{\$480,000}{800} = \$600$ |
| Contribution margin | $\dfrac{\text{Total Contribution Margin}}{\text{Sales}}$ | $\$400 - \$325 = \$75$ | $\$800 - \$600 = \$200$ |

One possible solution is to apply the analysis separately to each product line. It is possible to obtain individual break-even points when income is defined as product margin. Breakeven for the mulching mower is as follows:

$$\text{Mulching Mower Break-Even Units} = \frac{\text{Fixed Cost}}{\text{Price} - \text{Unit Variable Cost}}$$

$$= \frac{\$30,000}{\$75}$$

$$= 400 \text{ units}$$

Breakeven for the riding mower can be computed as well:

$$\text{Riding Mower Break-Even Units} = \frac{\text{Fixed Cost}}{\text{Price} - \text{Unit Variable Cost}}$$

$$= \frac{\$40,000}{\$200}$$

$$= 200 \text{ units}$$

Thus, 400 mulching mowers and 200 riding mowers must be sold to achieve a break-even product margin. But a break-even product margin covers only direct fixed costs; the common fixed costs remain to be covered. Selling these numbers of lawn mowers would result in a loss equal to the common fixed costs. This level of sales is not the break-even point for the firm as a whole; somehow the common fixed costs must be factored into the analysis.

We could allocate the common fixed costs to each product line before computing a break-even point. However, the allocation of the common fixed costs is arbitrary. Thus, no meaningful break-even volume is readily apparent.

Another possible solution is to convert the multiple-product problem into a single-product problem. If this can be done, then all of the single-product CVP methodology can be applied directly. The key to this conversion is to identify the expected sales mix, in units, of the products being marketed. **Sales mix** is the relative combination of products being sold by a firm.

**Determining the Sales Mix**    The sales mix is measured in units sold. For example, if Whittier plans on selling 1,200 mulching mowers and 800 riding mowers, then the sales mix in units is 1,200:800. Usually, the sales mix is reduced to the smallest possible whole numbers. Thus, the relative mix, 1,200:800, can be reduced to 12:8, and further reduced to 3:2. That is, Whittier expects that for every three mulching mowers sold, two riding mowers will be sold.

An endless number of different sales mixes can be used to define the break-even volume in a multiple-product setting. For example, a sales mix of 2:1 will define a break-even point of 550 mulching mowers and 275 riding mowers. The total contribution margin produced by this mix is $96,250:

(Mulching Mower Price $\times$ Break-Even Quantity) + (Riding Mower Price $\times$ Break-Even Quantity)

($75 $\times$ 550) + ($200 $\times$ 275)

Similarly, if 350 mulching mowers and 350 riding mowers are sold (corresponding to a 1:1 sales mix), then the total contribution margin is also $96,250:

($75 $\times$ 350) + ($200 $\times$ 350)

Since total fixed costs are $96,250, both sales mixes define break-even points. Fortunately, every sales mix need not be considered. According to Whittier's marketing study, a sales mix of 3:2 can be expected. This is the ratio that should be used; all others can be ignored. The sales mix that is expected to prevail should be used for CVP analysis.

**Sales Mix and Cost-Volume-Profit Analysis** Defining a particular sales mix allows the conversion of a multiple-product problem into a single-product CVP format. Since Whittier expects to sell three mulching mowers for every two riding mowers, it can define the single product it sells as a package containing three mulching mowers and two riding mowers. By defining the product as a package, the multiple-product problem is converted into a single-product one. To use the approach of break-even point in units, the package selling price and the variable cost per package must be known. To compute these package values, the sales mix, individual product prices, and individual variable costs are needed. Cornerstone 4.7 shows how to determine the overall break-even point for each product.

## Calculating the Break-Even Units for a Multiple-Product Firm

CORNERSTONE

4.7

**Why:**

Many firms produce and sell more than one product. In that case, the firm needs to know how many units of each product must be sold to break even.

**Information:**

Recall that Whittier sells two products: mulching mowers priced at $400 and riding mowers priced at $800. The variable cost per unit is $325 per mulching mower and $600 per riding mower. Total fixed cost is $96,250. Whittier's expected sales mix is three mulching mowers to two riding mowers.

**Required:**

1. Form a package of mulching and riding mowers based on the sales mix and calculate the package contribution margin.

2. Calculate the break-even point in units for mulching mowers and for riding mowers.

3. Check your answers by preparing a contribution margin income statement.

*(Continued)*

**Solution:**

1. Each package consists of three mulching mowers and two riding mowers:

| Product | Price | Unit Variable Cost | Unit Contribution Margin | Sales Mix | Package Contribution Margin |
|---|---|---|---|---|---|
| Mulching | $400 | $325 | $ 75 | 3 | $225 |
| Riding | 800 | 600 | 200 | 2 | 400 |
| Package total | | | | | $625 |

The three mulching mowers in the package yield $225 (3 × $75) in contribution margin. The two riding mowers in the package yield $400 (2 × $200) in contribution margin. Thus, a package of five mowers (three mulching and two riding) has a total contribution margin of $625.

2. Break-Even Packages $= \dfrac{\text{Total Fixed Cost}}{\text{Package Contribution Margin}}$

$= \dfrac{\$96,250}{\$625}$

$= 154$ packages

Mulching Mower Break-Even Units $= 154 \times 3 = 462$

Riding Mower Break-Even Units $= 154 \times 2 = 308$

3. Income statement—break-even solution:

| | Mulching Mower | Riding Mower | Total |
|---|---|---|---|
| Sales | $184,800 | $246,400 | $431,200 |
| Total variable cost | 150,150 | 184,800 | 334,950 |
| Contribution margin | $ 34,650 | $ 61,600 | $ 96,250 |
| Total fixed cost | | | 96,250 |
| Operating income | | | $        0 |

The complexity of determining the break-even point in units increases dramatically as the number of products increases. Imagine performing this analysis for a firm with several hundred products. Luckily, computers can easily handle a problem with so much data. Furthermore, many firms simplify the problem by analyzing product groups rather than individual products. Another way to handle the increased complexity is to switch from the units sold to the sales revenue approach. This approach can accomplish a multiple-product CVP analysis using only the summary data found in an organization's income statement.

# Break-Even Point in Sales Dollars

To illustrate the break-even point in sales dollars, the same examples will be used. However, the only information needed is the projected income statement for Whittier Company as a whole.

| | |
|---|---:|
| Sales | $1,120,000 |
| Total variable cost | 870,000 |
| Contribution margin | $ 250,000 |
| Total fixed cost | 96,250 |
| Operating income | $ 153,750 |

Notice that this income statement corresponds to the total column of the more detailed income statement examined previously. The projected income statement rests on the assumption that 1,200 mulching mowers and 800 riding mowers will be sold (a 3:2 sales mix). The break-even point in sales revenue also rests on the expected sales mix. (As with the units sold approach, different sales mixes will produce different results.)

With the income statement, the usual CVP questions can be addressed. For example, how much sales revenue must be earned to break even? Cornerstone 4.8 shows how to calculate the break-even point in sales dollars for a multiple-product firm.

## concept Q&A

Suppose a men's clothing store sells two brands of suits: designer suits with a contribution margin of $600 each and regular suits with a contribution margin of $500 each. At breakeven, the store must sell a total of 100 suits a month. Last month, the store sold 100 suits in total but incurred an operating loss. There was no change in fixed cost, variable cost, or price. What happened?

**Answer:**

Probably, the sales mix shifted toward the relatively lower contribution margin suits. For example, suppose that the break-even point for regular suits was 80, and the break-even point for designer suits was 20. If the mix shifted to 90 regular and 10 designer, it is easy to see that less total contribution margin (and, hence, operating income) would be realized.

## Calculating the Break-Even Sales Dollars for a Multiple-Product Firm

**CORNERSTONE**

**4.8**

**Why:**

The multiple-product firm may not need to know how many units of each product must be sold to break even, but, instead, may be fine with the overall sales revenue that achieves breakeven. Additionally, using this approach does not require individual product information, but uses the overall contribution margin ratio for the firm.

**Information:**

Recall that Whittier Company sells two products that are expected to produce total revenue next year of $1,120,000 and total variable cost of $870,000. Total fixed cost is expected to equal $96,250.

**Required:**

1. Calculate the break-even point in sales dollars for Whittier.

2. Check your answer by preparing a contribution margin income statement.

**Solution:**

1. Contribution Margin Ratio $= \dfrac{\$250,000}{\$1,120,000}$

$= 0.2232$

*(Continued)*

CORNERSTONE
**4.8**

(Continued)

$$\text{Break-Even Sales} = \frac{\text{Fixed Cost}}{\text{Contribution Margin Ratio}}$$

$$= \frac{\$96,250}{0.2232}$$

$$= \$431,228$$

[*Note:* Total break-even sales differ slightly between Cornerstones 4.7 and 4.8 ($431,200 vs. $431,228) due to the rounding of the contribution margin ratio to only four decimal places (0.2232).]

2. Income statement—break-even solution:

| | |
|---|---:|
| Sales | $431,228 |
| Total variable cost (0.7768 × $431,228) | 334,978 |
| Contribution margin | $ 96,250 |
| Total fixed cost | 96,250 |
| Operating income | $ 0 |

The break-even point in sales dollars implicitly uses the assumed sales mix but avoids the requirement of building a package contribution margin. No knowledge of individual product data is needed. The computational effort is similar to that used in the single-product setting. Unlike the break-even point in units, the answer to CVP questions using sales dollars is still expressed in a single summary measure. The sales revenue approach, however, does sacrifice information concerning individual product performance.

# YOU DECIDE   Finding the Break-Even Point for a New Business

You are an accountant in private practice. A friend of yours, Linda, recently started a novelty greeting card business. Linda designs greeting cards that allow the sender to write in his or her own message. She uses heavy card stock, cut to size, and decorates the front of each card with bits of fabric, lace, and ribbon in seasonal motifs (e.g., a heart for Valentine's Day, a pine tree for Christmas). Linda hired several friends to make the cards, according to Linda's instructions, on a piece-work basis. (In piece work, the worker is paid on the basis of number of units produced.) The workers could make the cards at their homes, meaning that no factory facilities were involved. Linda designs the cards and travels around her four-state region to sell the completed cards on consignment. For the few months the company has been in existence, the cards have been selling well, but Linda is operating at a loss.

**What types of information do you need to find the break-even point? How can the business owner use this information to make decisions?**

In order to determine the break-even point, you need to determine the prices and variable costs for the cards. Since creating a multi-product break-even analysis could be complex, it may be easier to determine the average price and the average variable cost for the cards, then find the total fixed cost, and tell Linda how many cards she would need to sell to break even.

Suppose that the break-even number of cards is 250 per month, and that the average contribution margin per card is $0.80. Then, as soon as Linda sells the 250th card, she knows she is in the black. From then on, every card sold adds $0.80 to her profit. This was very important information for Linda—whose business losses are coming right out of her family's checking account. Not only does Linda have a sales goal for each month, she also knows at any point in time how much income she has made.

**Owners of small businesses find break-even analysis and concepts to be very helpful. A knowledge of contribution margin helps owners know how they are doing at any point in time.**

# COST-VOLUME-PROFIT ANALYSIS AND RISK AND UNCERTAINTY

OBJECTIVE ⑤

Explain the impact of risk, uncertainty, and changing variables on cost-volume-profit analysis.

Because firms operate in a dynamic world, they must be aware of changes in prices, variable costs, and fixed costs. They must also account for the effect of risk and uncertainty. The break-even point can be affected by changes in price, unit contribution margin, and fixed cost. Managers can use CVP analysis to handle risk and uncertainty.

For example, France-based **Airbus** reported its first ever loss in 2006. The loss resulted from a decreased sales volume and costly production delays in the redesign of its "extra wide-body" passenger jet to compete with **Boeing**'s 787 Dreamliner. In response to this loss, Airbus used CVP analysis to estimate how a $2.6 billion reduction in its annual variable and fixed costs, as well as various reductions in its $144 million unit jet price, would affect its annual profit.[1] Shipping giant **Maersk** added capacity just before the recession of 2008 hit. As a result, shipping rates were so low that Maersk had a more than $2 billion loss in 2009. Improved economic conditions and an increase in demand above that originally predicted allowed the company to announce that it would break even in 2010.[2]

For a given sales mix, CVP analysis can be used as if the firm were selling a single product. However, when the prices of individual products change, the sales mix can be affected because consumers may buy relatively more or less of the product. Keep in mind that a new sales mix will affect the units of each product that need to be sold in order to achieve a desired profit target. If the sales mix for the coming period is uncertain, it may be necessary to look at several different mixes. In this way, a manager gains insight into the possible outcomes facing the firm.

Suppose that Whittier recently conducted a market study of the mulching lawn mower that revealed three different alternatives:

- *Alternative 1:* If advertising expenditures increase by $8,000, then sales will increase from 1,600 units to 1,725 units.
- *Alternative 2:* A price decrease from $400 to $375 per lawn mower will increase sales from 1,600 units to 1,900 units.
- *Alternative 3:* Decreasing price to $375 *and* increasing advertising expenditures by $8,000 will increase sales from 1,600 units to 2,600 units.

Should Whittier maintain its current price and advertising policies, or should it select one of the three alternatives described by the marketing study?

The first alternative, increasing advertising costs by $8,000 with a resulting sales increase of 125 units, is summarized in Exhibit 4.6 (p. 142). This alternative can be analyzed by using the contribution margin per unit of $75. Since units sold increase by 125, the increase in total contribution margin is $9,375 ($75 × 125 units). However, since fixed costs increase by $8,000, profits only increase by $1,375 ($9,375 − $8,000). Notice that we need to look only at the incremental increase in total contribution margin and fixed expenses to compute the increase in total operating income.

For the second alternative, the price is dropped to $375 (from $400), and the units sold increase to 1,900 (from 1,600). The effects of this alternative are summarized in Exhibit 4.7 (P. 142). Here, fixed expenses do not change, so only the change in total contribution margin is relevant. For the current price of $400, the contribution margin per unit is $75 ($400 − $325), and the total contribution margin is $120,000 ($75 × 1,600). For the new price, the contribution margin drops to $50 per unit ($375 − $325). If 1,900 units are sold at the new price, then the new total contribution margin is $95,000 ($50 × 1,900). Dropping the price results in a profit decline of $25,000 ($120,000 − $95,000).

The third alternative calls for a decrease in the unit selling price and an increase in advertising costs. Like the first alternative, the profit impact can be assessed by looking

---

[1] "Planemaker Airbus to Report Its First Annual Loss," *USA Today* (January 18, 2007): 3B.
[2] Peter T. Leach. "Maersk Line Close to Break Even, CEO Says." *The Journal of Commerce Online* (March 29, 2010). www.joc.com/maritime/maersk-line-close-break-even-says-ceo.

**( EXHIBIT 4.6 )**

### Summary of the Effects of Alternative 1

|  | Before the Increased Advertising | With the Increased Advertising |
|---|---|---|
| Units sold | 1,600 | 1,725 |
| Unit contribution margin | × $75 | × $75 |
| Total contribution margin | $120,000 | $129,375 |
| Less: Fixed expenses | 45,000 | 53,000 |
| Operating income | $ 75,000 | $ 76,375 |

|  | Difference in Profit |
|---|---|
| Change in sales volume | 125 |
| Unit contribution margin | × $75 |
| Change in contribution margin | $ 9,375 |
| Less: Change in fixed expenses | 8,000 |
| Increase in operating income | $ 1,375 |

© Cengage Learning 2014

at the incremental effects on contribution margin and fixed expenses. The incremental profit change can be found by:

1. computing the incremental change in total contribution margin
2. computing the incremental change in fixed expenses
3. adding the two results

As shown in Exhibit 4.8, the current total contribution margin (for 1,600 units sold) is $120,000. Since the new unit contribution margin is $50, the new total contribution margin is $130,000 ($50 × 2,600 units). Thus, the incremental increase in total contribution margin is $10,000 ($130,000 − $120,000). However, to achieve this incremental increase in contribution margin, an incremental increase of $8,000 in fixed costs is needed. The net effect is an incremental increase in operating income of $2,000.

**( EXHIBIT 4.7 )**

### Summary of the Effects of Alternative 2

|  | Before the Proposed Price Decrease | With the Proposed Price Decrease |
|---|---|---|
| Units sold | 1,600 | 1,900 |
| Unit contribution margin | × $75 | × $50 |
| Total contribution margin | $120,000 | $95,000 |
| Less: Fixed expenses | 45,000 | 45,000 |
| Operating income | $ 75,000 | $50,000 |

|  | Difference in Profit |
|---|---|
| Change in contribution margin ($95,000 − $120,000) | $(25,000) |
| Less: Change in fixed expenses | — |
| Decrease in operating income | $(25,000) |

© Cengage Learning 2014

( EXHIBIT 4.8 )

**Summary of the Effects of Alternative 3**

|  | Before the Proposed Price and Advertising Changes | With the Proposed Price Decrease and Advertising Increase |
|---|---|---|
| Units sold | 1,600 | 2,600 |
| Unit contribution margin | × $75 | × $50 |
| Total contribution margin | $120,000 | $130,000 |
| Less: Fixed expenses | 45,000 | 53,000 |
| Profit | $ 75,000 | $ 77,000 |

|  | Difference in Profit |
|---|---|
| Change in contribution margin ($130,000 − $120,000) | $10,000 |
| Less: Change in fixed expenses ($53,000 − $45,000) | 8,000 |
| Increase in profit | $ 2,000 |

Of the three alternatives identified by the marketing study, the third alternative promises the most benefit. It increases total operating income by $2,000. The first alternative increases operating income by only $1,375, and the second *decreases* operating income by $25,000.

These examples are all based on a units sold approach. However, we could just as easily have applied a sales revenue approach. The answers would be the same.

## Introducing Risk and Uncertainty

An important assumption of CVP analysis is that prices and costs are known with certainty. This assumption is seldom accurate. Risk and uncertainty are a part of business decision making and must be dealt with somehow. Formally, risk differs from uncertainty in that under risk, the probability distributions of the variables are known; under uncertainty, they are not known. For purposes of CVP analysis, however, the terms will be used interchangeably.

How do managers deal with risk and uncertainty? There are a variety of methods.

- First, of course, is that management must realize the uncertain nature of future prices, costs, and quantities.
- Next, managers move from consideration of a break-even point to what might be called a "break-even band." In other words, given the uncertain nature of the data, perhaps a firm might break even when 1,800 to 2,000 units are sold instead of at the point estimate of 1,900 units.
- Further, managers may engage in sensitivity or what-if analysis. In this instance, a computer spreadsheet is helpful because managers can set up the break-even (or targeted profit) relationships and then check to see the impact that varying costs and prices have on quantity sold.

Two concepts useful to management are *margin of safety* and *operating leverage*. Both of these concepts may be considered measures of risk. Each requires knowledge of fixed and variable costs.

**Margin of Safety**  The **margin of safety** is the units sold or the revenue earned above the break-even volume. It is calculated as follows.

Margin of Safety = Sales − Breakeven Sales

For example, if the break-even volume for a company is 200 units and the company is currently selling 500 units, then the margin of safety is 300 units:

$$\text{Sales} - \text{Break-Even Units} = 500 - 200$$

The margin of safety can be expressed in sales revenue as well. If the break-even volume is $200,000 and current revenues are $500,000, then the margin of safety is $300,000:

$$\text{Revenues} - \text{Margin of Safety} = \$500,000 - \$200,000$$

In addition, margin of safety sales revenue can be expressed as a percentage of total sales dollars, which some managers refer to as the margin of safety ratio. In this example, the margin of safety ratio would be 60%:

$$\frac{\text{Margin of Safety}}{\text{Revenues}} = \frac{\$300,000}{\$500,000}$$

Exhibit 4.9 illustrates the margin of safety.

## ( EXHIBIT 4.9 )

### The Margin of Safety Illustrated

Cornerstone 4.9 shows the expected margin of safety for Whittier.

## CORNERSTONE

## 4.9

## Computing the Margin of Safety

**Why:**
The margin of safety tells the firm how far above (or below) breakeven it is. The larger the margin of safety, the farther from breakeven and the less risk there is of earning a loss rather than a profit.

**Information:**
Recall that Whittier plans to sell 1,000 mowers at $400 each in the coming year. Whittier has unit variable cost of $325 and total fixed cost of $45,000. Break-even units were previously calculated as 600.

**Required:**

1. Calculate the margin of safety for Whittier in terms of the number of units.

2. Calculate the margin of safety for Whittier in terms of sales revenue.

**Solution:**

1. Margin of Safety in Units = 1,000 − 600 = 400

2. Margin of Safety in Sales Revenue = $400(1,000) − $400(600) = $160,000

The margin of safety can be viewed as a crude measure of risk. There are always events, unknown when plans are made, that can lower sales below the original expected level. In the event that sales take a downward turn, the risk of suffering losses is less if a firm's expected margin of safety is large than if the margin of safety is small. Managers who face a low margin of safety may wish to consider actions to increase sales or decrease costs. These steps will increase the margin of safety and lower the risk of incurring losses.

**Operating Leverage**   In physics, a lever is a simple machine used to multiply force. Basically, the lever multiplies the effort applied to create more work. The larger the load moved by a given amount of effort, the greater is the mechanical advantage. In financial terms, operating leverage is concerned with the relative mix of fixed costs and variable costs in an organization. Sometimes fixed costs can be traded off for variable costs. As variable costs decrease, the unit contribution margin increases, making the contribution of each unit sold that much greater. In such a case, fluctuations in sales have an increased effect on profitability. Thus, firms that have realized lower variable costs by increasing the proportion of fixed costs will benefit with greater increases in profits as sales increase than will firms with a lower proportion of fixed costs. Fixed costs are being used as leverage to increase profits. Unfortunately, it is also true that firms with a higher operating leverage will experience greater reductions in profits as sales decrease. **Operating leverage** is the use of fixed costs to extract higher percentage changes in profits as sales activity changes.

The **degree of operating leverage (DOL)** can be measured for a given level of sales by taking the ratio of contribution margin to operating income, as follows:

$$\text{Degree of Operating Leverage} = \frac{\text{Total Contribution Margin}}{\text{Operating Income}}$$

If fixed costs are used to lower variable costs such that contribution margin increases and operating income decreases, then the degree of operating leverage increases— signaling an increase in risk. Cornerstone 4.10 shows how to compute the degree of operating leverage for Whittier.

## Computing the Degree of Operating Leverage

**Why:**

The greater the degree of operating leverage, the more that a change in sales will affect the firm's operating income.

**Information:**

Recall that Whittier plans to sell 1,000 mowers at $400 each in the coming year. Whittier has unit variable cost per unit of $325 and total fixed cost of $45,000. Operating income at that level of sales was previously computed as $30,000.

**Required:**

Calculate the degree of operating leverage for Whittier.

CORNERSTONE

**4.10**

*(Continued)*

CORNERSTONE

**4.10**

*(Continued)*

**Solution:**

$$\text{Degree of Operating Leverage} = \frac{\text{Total Contribution Margin}}{\text{Operating Income}}$$

$$= \frac{(\$400 - \$325)(1{,}000 \text{ units})}{\$30{,}000}$$

$$= 2.5$$

The greater the degree of operating leverage, the more that changes in sales will affect operating income. Because of this phenomenon, the mix of costs that an organization chooses influences its operating risk and profit level. A company's mix of fixed costs relative to variable costs is referred to as its **cost structure**. Often, a company changes its cost structure by taking on more of one type of cost in exchange for reducing its amount of the other type of cost. For example, as U.S. companies try to compete more effectively with foreign competitors' significantly lower hourly labor costs (a variable cost), many are altering their cost structures by taking on more plant machine automation (a fixed cost) in exchange for using less labor.

To illustrate the impact of these concepts on management decision making, consider a firm that is planning to add a new product line. In adding the line, the firm can choose to rely heavily on automation or on labor. If the firm chooses to emphasize automation rather than labor, fixed costs will be higher, and unit variable costs will be lower. Relevant data for a sales level of 10,000 units follow:

|  | Automated System | Manual System |
|---|---|---|
| Sales | $1,000,000 | $1,000,000 |
| Total variable cost | 500,000 | 800,000 |
| Contribution margin | $ 500,000 | $ 200,000 |
| Total fixed cost | 375,000 | 100,000 |
| Operating income | $ 125,000 | $ 100,000 |
| Unit selling price | $ 100 | $ 100 |
| Unit variable cost | 50 | 80 |
| Unit contribution margin | 50 | 20 |

The degree of operating leverage for the automated system is 4.0 ($500,000/$125,000). The degree of operating leverage for the manual system is 2.0 ($200,000/$100,000). What happens to profit in each system if sales increase by 40%? We can generate the following income statements to see the following:

|  | Automated System | Manual System |
|---|---|---|
| Sales | $1,400,000 | $1,400,000 |
| Total variable cost | 700,000 | 1,120,000 |
| Contribution margin | $ 700,000 | $ 280,000 |
| Total fixed cost | 375,000 | 100,000 |
| Operating income | $ 325,000 | $ 180,000 |

Profits for the automated system would increase by $200,000 ($325,000 − $125,000) for a 160% increase. In the manual system, profits increase by only $80,000

($180,000 − $100,000) for an 80% increase. The automated system has a greater percentage increase because it has a higher degree of operating leverage.

The degree of operating leverage can be used directly to calculate the change in operating income that would result from a given percentage change in sales.

> Percentage Change in Profits = Degree of Operating Leverage ×
> Percent Change in Sales

Since sales are predicted to increase by 40% and the DOL for the automated system is 4.0, operating income increases by 160%. Since operating income based on the original sales level is $125,000, the operating income based on the increased sales level would be $325,000:

$$\text{Operating Income} + (\text{Operating Income} \times \text{Percent Change in Sales})$$
$$= \$125{,}000 + (\$125{,}000 \times 1.6)$$

Similarly, for the manual system, increased sales of 40% and DOL of 2.0 imply increased operating income of 80%. Therefore, operating income based on the increased sales level would be $180,000:

$$\$100{,}000 + (\$100{,}000 \times 0.8)$$

Cornerstone 4.11 illustrates the impact of increased sales on operating income using the degree of operating leverage.

## Calculating the Impact of Increased Sales on Operating Income Using the Degree of Operating Leverage

**CORNERSTONE**

**4.11**

**Why:**

This calculation shows the interplay of degree of operating leverage and the percent change in sales on operating income. Managers can use sensitivity analysis to run various scenarios and see the impact of risk and uncertainty on income.

**Information:**

Recall that Whittier had expected to sell 1,000 mowers and earn operating income equal to $30,000 next year. Whittier's degree of operating leverage is equal to 2.5. The company plans to increase sales by 20% next year.

**Required:**

1. Calculate the percent change in operating income expected by Whittier for next year using the degree of operating leverage.

2. Calculate the operating income expected by Whittier next year using the percent change in operating income calculated in Requirement 1.

**Solution:**

1. Percent Change in Operating Income = DOL × Percent Change in Sales
$$= 2.5 \times 20\% = 50\%$$

2. Expected Operating Income = $30,000 + (0.5 × $30,000) = $45,000

In choosing between the two systems, the effect of operating leverage is a valuable piece of information. Higher operating leverage multiplies the impact of increased sales on income. However, the effect is a two-edged sword. As sales decrease, the automated system will also show much higher percentage decreases. The increased operating leverage is available under the automated system because of the presence of increased fixed costs. The break-even point for the automated system is 7,500 units ($375,000/$50), whereas the break-even point for the manual system is 5,000 units ($100,000/$20). Thus, the automated system has greater operating risk. The increased risk, of course, provides a potentially higher profit level as long as units sold exceed 9,167. Why 9,167? Because that is the quantity for which the operating income for the automated system equals the operating income for the manual system. The quantity at which two systems produce the same operating income is referred to as the **indifference point**. This number of units is computed by setting the operating income equations of the two systems equal and solving for number of units:

$$\$50 \text{ (Units)} - \$375,000 = \$20 \text{ (Units)} - \$100,000$$
$$\text{Units} = 9,167$$

In choosing between the automated and manual systems, the manager must consider the likelihood that sales will exceed 9,167 units. If there is a strong belief that sales will easily exceed this level, then the choice is obviously the automated system. On the other hand, if sales are unlikely to exceed 9,167 units, then the manual system is preferable. Exhibit 4.10 summarizes the relative differences between the manual and automated systems in terms of some of the CVP concepts.

( EXHIBIT 4.10 )

**Differences between a Manual and an Automated System**

|  | Manual System | Automated System |
|---|---|---|
| Price | Same | Same |
| Variable cost | ▲ Relatively higher | ▼ Relatively lower |
| Fixed cost | ▼ Relatively lower | ▲ Relatively higher |
| Contribution margin | ▼ Relatively lower | ▲ Relatively higher |
| Break-even point | ▼ Relatively lower | ▲ Relatively higher |
| Margin of safety | ▲ Relatively higher | ▼ Relatively lower |
| Degree of operating leverage | ▼ Relatively lower | ▲ Relatively higher |
| Down-side risk | ▼ Relatively lower | ▲ Relatively higher |
| Up-side potential | ▼ Relatively lower | ▲ Relatively higher |

© Cengage Learning 2014

## Sensitivity Analysis and Cost-Volume-Profit

The widespread use of personal computers and spreadsheets has placed sensitivity analysis within reach of most managers. An important tool, **sensitivity analysis** is a "what-if" technique that examines the impact of changes in underlying assumptions on an answer. It is relatively simple to input data on prices, variable costs, fixed costs, and sales mix and to set up formulas to calculate break-even points and expected profits. Then, the data can be varied as desired to see how changes impact the expected profit.

In the example on operating leverage, a company analyzed the impact on profit of using an automated versus a manual system. The computations were essentially done by hand, and too much variation is cumbersome. Using the power of a computer, it would be an easy matter to change the sales price in $1 increments between $75 and $125, with related assumptions about quantity sold. At the same time, variable and fixed costs could be adjusted. For example, suppose that the automated system has fixed costs of $375,000 but that those costs could easily double in the first year and come back down in the second and third years as bugs are worked out of the system and workers learn to use it. Again, the spreadsheet can effortlessly handle the many computations.

A spreadsheet, while wonderful for cranking out numerical answers, cannot do the most difficult job in CVP analysis. That job is determining the data to be entered in the first place. The managerial accountant must be aware of the cost and price distributions of the firm as well as of the impact of changing economic conditions on these variables. The fact that variables are seldom known with certainty is no excuse for ignoring the impact of uncertainty on CVP analysis. Fortunately, sensitivity analysis can also give managers a feel for the degree to which a poorly forecast variable will affect an answer. That is also an advantage.

**ETHICAL DECISIONS**   It is important to note that the CVP results are only one input into business decisions. There are many other factors that may bear on decisions to choose one type of process over another, for example, or whether or not to delete certain costs. Businesses and nonprofit entities often face trade-offs involving safety. Ethical concerns also have an important place in CVP analysis. When one company buys another one, it bases its decision in part on the information presented by the to-be-acquired firm. For example, China's **Geely** purchased Volvo from **Ford** in 2010. As the head of Geely stated, "As far as I know, Volvo is in good operating condition and it's possible it could break even in the fourth quarter of this year."[3] Often, however, the costs and probabilities are not known with sufficient certainty. In that case, these factors are included in the ultimate decision-making process. Chapter 13, on short-run decision making, covers this topic in more detail. •

Despite the fact that future conditions cannot be known with certainty, there are various ways of incorporating risk and uncertainty into the analysis. One possibility is that cost of potential problems can be estimated and included in the CVP results. Another is that various scenarios can be considered by running sensitivity analysis—varying costs and prices to see what happens.

# YOUDECIDE    Using Contribution Margin Income Statements to Consider Varying Scenarios

You are the chief accountant for **Boyne Resorts** winter sports. Early in the year, you had budgeted sales prices (lift tickets, restaurant prices), costs, and expected quantity to be sold. However, once the season starts, you will know from week to week more about the actual weather conditions.

**How can you use this information about current weather conditions to better predict budgets for Boyne?**

You can recast the budgeted statements according to how the weather will affect skiing. If the snow is good, some costs will go down. For example, you will lower the predicted cost of running the snow-making machines. However, good weather and more skiers will require additional seasonal hiring as more direct labor will be needed to run the lifts, operate ski equipment rental shops, restaurants, and so on. You can put together contribution margin income statements under various scenarios, increasing volume with good ski weather, decreasing it with poor weather.

**Having the ability to recast budgets will help managers respond quickly to the changing conditions and be able to raise or lower some prices as needed.**

---

[3] Drew Johnson, "Geely: Volvo Could Breakeven by Year's End." *Left Lane News* (March 13, 2010). www.leftlanenews.com/geely-volvo-could-break-even-by-years-end.html.

# SUMMARY OF LEARNING OBJECTIVES

**LO 1.**   Determine the break-even point in number of units and in total sales dollars.
- At breakeven, total costs (variable and fixed) equal total sales revenue.
- Break-even units equal total fixed costs divided by the contribution margin (price minus variable cost per unit).
- Break-even revenue equals total fixed costs divided by the contribution margin ratio.

**LO 2.**   Determine the number of units that must be sold, and the amount of revenue required, to earn a targeted profit.
- To earn a target (desired) profit, total costs (variable and fixed) plus the amount of target profit must equal total sales revenue.
- Units to earn target profit equal total fixed costs plus target profit divided by the contribution margin.
- Sales revenue to earn target profit equals total fixed costs plus target profit divided by the contribution margin ratio.

**LO 3.**   Prepare a profit-volume graph and a cost-volume-profit graph, and explain the meaning of each.
- CVP assumes linear revenue and cost functions, no finished goods ending inventories, constant sales mix, and selling prices and fixed and variable costs that are known with certainty.
- Profit-volume graphs plot the relationship between profit (operating income) and units sold. Break-even units are shown where the profit line crosses the horizontal axis.
- CVP graphs plot a line for total costs and a line for total sales revenue. The intersection of these two lines is the break-even point in units.

**LO 4.**   Apply cost-volume-profit analysis in a multiple-product setting.
- Multiple-product analysis requires the expected sales mix.
- Break-even units for each product will change as the sales mix changes.
- Increased sales of high contribution margin products decrease the break-even point.
- Increased sales of low contribution margin products increase the break-even point.

**LO 5.**   Explain the impact of risk, uncertainty, and changing variables on cost-volume-profit analysis.
- Uncertainty regarding costs, prices, and sales mix affect the break-even point.
- Sensitivity analysis allows managers to vary costs, prices, and sales mix to show various possible break-even points.
- Margin of safety shows how far the company's actual sales and/or units are above or below the break-even point.
- Operating leverage is the use of fixed costs to increase the percentage changes in profits as sales activity changes.

# SUMMARY OF IMPORTANT EQUATIONS

1. Operating Income = (Price × Number of Units Sold) − (Variable Cost per Unit × Number of Units Sold) − Total Fixed Cost

2. $\text{Break-Even Units} = \dfrac{\text{Total Fixed Cost}}{\text{Price} - \text{Variable Cost per Unit}}$

3. Sales Revenue = Price × Units Sold

4. $\text{Variable Cost Ratio} = \dfrac{\text{Total Variable Cost}}{\text{Sales}}$

5. $\text{Variable Cost Ratio} = \dfrac{\text{Unit Variable Cost}}{\text{Price}}$

6. $\text{Contribution Margin Ratio} = \dfrac{\text{Total Contribution Margin}}{\text{Sales}}$

7. $\text{Contribution Margin Ratio} = \dfrac{\text{Unit Contribution Margin}}{\text{Price}}$

8. $\text{Break-Even Sales} = \dfrac{\text{Total Fixed Expenses}}{\text{Contribution Margin Ratio}}$

9. $\text{Margin of Safety} = \text{Sales} - \text{Breakeven Sales}$

10. $\text{Degree of Operating Leverage} = \dfrac{\text{Total Contribution Margin}}{\text{Operating Income}}$

11. $\text{Percentage Change in Profits} = \text{Degree of Operating Leverage} \times \text{Percent Change in Sales}$

**CORNERSTONE 4.1**    Preparing a contribution margin income statement, page 119

**CORNERSTONE 4.2**    Calculating the break-even point in units, page 121

**CORNERSTONE 4.3**    Calculating the variable cost ratio and the contribution margin ratio, page 124

**CORNERSTONE 4.4**    Calculating the break-even point in sales dollars, page 125

**CORNERSTONE 4.5**    Calculating the number of units to be sold to earn a target operating income, page 127

**CORNERSTONE 4.6**    Calculating sales needed to earn a target operating income, page 129

**CORNERSTONE 4.7**    Calculating the break-even units for a multiple-product firm, page 137

**CORNERSTONE 4.8**    Calculating the break-even sales dollars for a multiple-product firm, page 139

**CORNERSTONE 4.9**    Computing the margin of safety, page 144

**CORNERSTONE 4.10**    Computing the degree of operating leverage, page 145

**CORNERSTONE 4.11**    Calculating the impact of increased sales on operating income using the degree of operating leverage, page 147

© Pixelfabrik / Alamy

# KEY TERMS

# REVIEW PROBLEMS

## I. Single-Product Cost-Volume-Profit Analysis

Cutlass Company's projected profit for the coming year is as follows:

|  | Total | Per Unit |
|---|---|---|
| Sales | $200,000 | $20 |
| Total variable cost | 120,000 | 12 |
| Contribution margin | $ 80,000 | $ 8 |
| Total fixed cost | 64,000 | |
| Operating income | $ 16,000 | |

**Required:**

1. Compute the variable cost ratio. Compute the contribution margin ratio.
2. Compute the break-even point in units.
3. Compute the break-even point in sales dollars.
4. How many units must be sold to earn a profit of $30,000?
5. Using the contribution margin ratio computed in Requirement 1, compute the additional profit that Cutlass would earn if sales were $25,000 more than expected.
6. For the projected level of sales, compute the margin of safety in units and in sales dollars.
7. Calculate the degree of operating leverage. Now suppose that Cutlass revises the forecast to show a 30% increase in sales over the original forecast. What is the percent change in operating income expected for the revised forecast? What is the total operating income expected by Cutlass after revising the sales forecast?

**Solution:**

1. $$\text{Variable Cost Ratio} = \frac{\text{Total Variable Cost}}{\text{Sales}}$$
$$= \frac{\$120,000}{\$200,000}$$
$$= 0.60, \text{ or } 60\%$$

$$\text{Contribution Margin Ratio} = \frac{\text{Contribution Margin}}{\text{Sales}}$$
$$= \frac{\$80,000}{\$200,000}$$
$$= 0.40, \text{ or } 40\%$$

2. The break-even point is computed as follows:
$$\text{Units} = \frac{\text{Total Fixed Cost}}{(\text{Price} - \text{Variable Cost per Unit})}$$
$$= \frac{\$64,000}{(\$20 - \$12)}$$
$$= \frac{\$64,000}{\$8} = 8,000$$

3. The break-even point in sales dollars is computed as follows:
$$\text{Break-Even Sales Dollars} = \frac{\text{Total Fixed Cost}}{\text{Contribution Margin Ratio}}$$
$$= \frac{\$64,000}{0.40}$$
$$= \$160,000$$

4. The number of units that must be sold to earn a profit of $30,000 is calculated as follows:
$$\text{Units} = \frac{(\$64,000 + \$30,000)}{\$8}$$
$$= \frac{\$94,000}{\$8}$$
$$= 11,750$$

5. The additional contribution margin on additional sales of $25,000 would be $0.40 \times \$25,000 = \$10,000$.

6. Margin of Safety in Units = Projected Units − Break-Even Units

$$= 10,000 - 8,000 = 2,000$$

   Margin of Safety in Sales Dollars $= \$200,000 - \$160,000 = \$40,000$

7. Degree of Operating Leverage $= \dfrac{\text{Contribution Margin}}{\text{Operating Income}}$

$$= \dfrac{\$80,000}{\$16,000} = 5.0$$

   Percentage Change in Operating Income = Degree of Operating Leverage

$$\times \text{ Percent Change in Sales}$$

$$= 5.0 \times 30\%$$

$$= 150\%$$

   Expected Operating Income $= \$16,000 + (1.5 \times \$16,000)$

$$= \$40,000$$

## II. Multiple-Product Cost-Volume-Profit Analysis

Alpha Company produces and sells two products: Alpha-Basic and Alpha-Deluxe. In the coming year, Alpha expects to sell 3,000 units of Alpha-Basic and 1,500 units of Alpha-Deluxe. Information on the two products is as follows:

|                         | Alpha-Basic | Alpha-Deluxe |
|-------------------------|:-----------:|:------------:|
| Price                   | $120        | $200         |
| Variable cost per unit  | 40          | 80           |

Total fixed cost is $140,000.

### Required:

1. What is the sales mix of Alpha-Basic to Alpha-Deluxe?
2. Compute the break-even quantity of each product.

### Solution:

1. The sales mix of Alpha-Basic to Alpha-Deluxe is 3,000:1,500 or 2:1.
2. Each package consists of two Alpha-Basic and one Alpha-Deluxe:

| Product | Price | Unit Variable Cost | Unit Contribution Margin | Sales Mix | Package Unit Contribution Margin |
|---------|:-----:|:------------------:|:------------------------:|:---------:|:--------------------------------:|
| Alpha-Basic   | $120 | $40 | $ 80 | 2 | $160 |
| Alpha-Deluxe  | 200  | 80  | 120  | 1 | 120  |
| Package total |      |     |      |   | $280 |

$$\text{Break-Even Packages} = \dfrac{\text{Total Fixed Cost}}{\text{Package Contribution Margin}}$$

$$= \dfrac{\$140,000}{\$280}$$

$$= 500$$

Alpha-Basic break-even units $= 500 \times 2 = 1,000$

Alpha-Deluxe break-even units $= 500 \times 1 = 500$

# DISCUSSION QUESTIONS

1. Explain how CVP analysis can be used for managerial planning.
2. Describe the difference between the units sold approach to CVP analysis and the sales revenue approach.
3. Define the term *break-even point.*
4. Explain why contribution margin per unit becomes profit per unit above the break-even point.
5. What is the variable cost ratio? The contribution margin ratio? How are the two ratios related?
6. Suppose a firm with a contribution margin ratio of 0.3 increased its advertising expenses by $10,000 and found that sales increased by $30,000. Was it a good decision to increase advertising expenses? Suppose that the contribution margin ratio is now 0.4. Would it be a good decision to increase advertising expenses?
7. Define the term *sales mix.* Give an example to support your definition.
8. Explain how CVP analysis developed for single products can be used in a multiple-product setting.
9. Since break-even analysis focuses on making zero profit, it is of no value in determining the units a firm must sell to earn a targeted profit. Do you agree or disagree with this statement? Why?
10. How does targeted profit enter into the break-even units equation?
11. Explain how a change in sales mix can change a company's break-even point.
12. Define the term *margin of safety.* Explain how it can be used as a crude measure of operating risk.
13. Explain what is meant by the term *operating leverage.* What impact does increased leverage have on risk?
14. How can sensitivity analysis be used in conjunction with CVP analysis?
15. Why is a declining margin of safety over a period of time an issue of concern to managers?

# MULTIPLE-CHOICE QUESTIONS

**4-1** If the variable cost per unit goes down,

| | **Contribution margin** | **Break-even point** |
|---|---|---|
| a. | increases | increases. |
| b. | increases | decreases. |
| c. | decreases | decreases. |
| d. | decreases | increases. |
| e. | decreases | remains unchanged. |

**4-2** The amount of revenue required to earn a targeted profit is equal to
   a. total fixed cost divided by contribution margin.
   b. total fixed cost divided by the contribution margin ratio.
   c. targeted profit divided by the contribution margin ratio.
   d. total fixed cost plus targeted profit divided by contribution margin ratio.
   e. targeted profit divided by the variable cost ratio.

**4-3** Break-even revenue for the multiple-product firm can
   a. be calculated by dividing total fixed cost by the overall contribution margin ratio.
   b. be calculated by dividing segment fixed cost by the overall contribution margin ratio.
   c. be calculated by dividing total fixed cost by the overall variable cost ratio.
   d. be calculated by multiplying total fixed cost by the contribution margin ratio.
   e. not be calculated; break-even revenue can only be computed for a single-product firm.

**4-4** In the cost-volume-profit graph,

   a.  the break-even point is found where the total revenue curve crosses the x-axis.
   b.  the area of profit is to the left of the break-even point.
   c.  the area of loss cannot be determined.
   d.  both the total revenue curve and the total cost curve appear.
   e.  neither the total revenue curve nor the total cost curve appear.

**4-5** An important assumption of cost-volume-profit analysis is that

   a.  both costs and revenues are linear functions.
   b.  all cost and revenue relationships are analyzed within the relevant range.
   c.  there is no change in inventories.
   d.  the sales mix remains constant.
   e.  all of the above are assumptions of cost-volume-profit analysis.

**4-6** The use of fixed costs to extract higher percentage changes in profits as sales activity changes involves

   a.  margin of safety.                     d.  sensitivity analysis.
   b.  operating leverage.                   e.  variable cost reduction.
   c.  degree of operating leverage.

**4-7** If the margin of safety is 0, then

   a.  the company is precisely breaking even.
   b.  the company is operating at a loss.
   c.  the company is earning a small profit.
   d.  the margin of safety cannot be less than or equal to 0; it must be positive.
   e.  none of the above is true.

**4-8** The contribution margin is the

   a.  amount by which sales exceed total fixed cost.
   b.  difference between sales and total cost.
   c.  difference between sales and operating income.
   d.  difference between sales and total variable cost.
   e.  difference between variable cost and fixed cost.

---

*Use the following information for Multiple-Choice Questions 4-9 and 4-10:*
Dartmouth Company produces a single product with a price of $12, variable cost per unit of $3, and total fixed cost of $7,200.

---

**4-9** Refer to the information for Dartmouth above. Dartmouth's break-even point in units

   a.  is 600.
   b.  is 480.
   c.  is 1,000.
   d.  is 800.
   e.  cannot be determined from the information given.

**4-10** Refer to the information for Dartmouth above. The variable cost ratio and the contribution margin ratio for Dartmouth are

| | Variable cost ratio | Contribution margin ratio |
|---|---|---|
| a. | 80% | 80%. |
| b. | 20% | 80%. |
| c. | 25% | 75%. |
| d. | 75% | 25%. |
| e. | The contribution margin ratio cannot be determined from the information given. | |

**4-11** If a company's total fixed cost decreases by $10,000, which of the following will be true?

    a.  The break-even point will increase.

    b.  The variable cost ratio will increase.

    c.  The break-even point will be unchanged.

    d.  The variable cost ratio will be unchanged.

    e.  The contribution margin ratio will increase.

**4-12** Solemon Company has total fixed cost of $15,000, variable cost per unit of $6, and a price of $8. If Solemon wants to earn a targeted profit of $3,600, how many units must be sold?

    a.  2,500                            d.  18,600

    b.  7,500                             e.  18,750

    c.  9,300

# CORNERSTONE EXERCISES

## Cornerstone Exercise 4-13   Variable Cost, Fixed Cost, Contribution Margin Income Statement

Head-First Company plans to sell 5,000 bicycle helmets at $75 each in the coming year. Product costs include:

| | |
|---|---|
| Direct materials per helmet | $   30 |
| Direct labor per helmet | 8 |
| Variable factory overhead per helmet | 4 |
| Total fixed factory overhead | 20,000 |

Variable selling expense is a commission of $3 per helmet; fixed selling and administrative expense totals $29,500.

**Required:**

1.  Calculate the total variable cost per unit.

2.  Calculate the total fixed expense for the year.

3.  Prepare a contribution margin income statement for Head-First Company for the coming year.

OBJECTIVE ❶
CORNERSTONE 4.2

## Cornerstone Exercise 4-14   Break-Even Point in Units

Head-First Company plans to sell 5,000 bicycle helmets at $75 each in the coming year. Unit variable cost is $45 (includes direct materials, direct labor, variable factory overhead, and variable selling expense). Total fixed cost equals $49,500 (includes fixed factory overhead and fixed selling and administrative expense).

**Required:**

1.  Calculate the break-even number of helmets.

2.  Check your answer by preparing a contribution margin income statement based on the break-even units.

OBJECTIVE ❶
CORNERSTONE 4.3

## Cornerstone Exercise 4-15   Variable Cost Ratio, Contribution Margin Ratio

Head-First Company plans to sell 5,000 bicycle helmets at $75 each in the coming year. Unit variable cost is $45 (includes direct materials, direct labor, variable factory overhead, and variable selling expense). Fixed factory overhead is $20,000 and fixed selling and administrative expense is $29,500.

**Required:**

1.  Calculate the variable cost ratio.

2.  Calculate the contribution margin ratio.

3.  Prepare a contribution margin income statement based on the budgeted figures for next year. In a column next to the income statement, show the percentages based on sales for sales, total variable cost, and total contribution margin.

### Cornerstone Exercise 4-16    Break-Even Point in Sales Dollars

OBJECTIVE ①
CORNERSTONE 4.4

Head-First Company plans to sell 5,000 bicycle helmets at $75 each in the coming year. Variable cost is 60% of the sales price; contribution margin is 40% of the sales price. Total fixed cost equals $49,500 (includes fixed factory overhead and fixed selling and administrative expense).

**Required:**

1. Calculate the sales revenue that Head-First must make to break even by using the break-even point in sales equation.
2. Check your answer by preparing a contribution margin income statement based on the break-even point in sales dollars.

### Cornerstone Exercise 4-17    Units to Earn Target Income

OBJECTIVE ②
CORNERSTONE 4.5

Head-First Company plans to sell 5,000 bicycle helmets at $75 each in the coming year. Unit variable cost is $45 (includes direct materials, direct labor, variable factory overhead, and variable selling expense). Total fixed cost equals $49,500 (includes fixed factory overhead and fixed selling and administrative expense).

**Required:**

1. Calculate the number of helmets Head-First must sell to earn operating income of $81,900.
2. Check your answer by preparing a contribution margin income statement based on the number of units calculated.

### Cornerstone Exercise 4-18    Sales Needed to Earn Target Income

OBJECTIVE ②
CORNERSTONE 4.6

Head-First Company plans to sell 5,000 bicycle helmets at $75 each in the coming year. Variable cost is 60% of the sales price; contribution margin is 40% of the sales price. Total fixed cost equals $49,500 (includes fixed factory overhead and fixed selling and administrative expense).

**Required:**

1. Calculate the sales revenue that Head-First must make to earn operating income of $81,900.
2. Check your answer by preparing a contribution margin income statement based on the sales dollars calculated in Requirement 1.

### Cornerstone Exercise 4-19    Break-Even Point in Units for a Multiple-Product Firm

OBJECTIVE ④
CORNERSTONE 4.7

Suppose that Head-First Company now sells both bicycle helmets and motorcycle helmets. The bicycle helmets are priced at $75 and have variable costs of $45 each. The motorcycle helmets are priced at $220 and have variable costs of $140 each. Total fixed cost for Head-First as a whole equals $58,900 (includes all fixed factory overhead and fixed selling and administrative expense). Next year, Head-First expects to sell 5,000 bicycle helmets and 2,000 motorcycle helmets.

**Required:**

1. Form a package of bicycle and motorcycle helmets based on the sales mix expected for the coming year.
2. Calculate the break-even point in units for bicycle helmets and for motorcycle helmets.
3. Check your answer by preparing a contribution margin income statement.

### Cornerstone Exercise 4-20    Break-Even Sales Dollars for a Multiple-Product Firm

OBJECTIVE ④
CORNERSTONE 4.8

Head-First Company now sells both bicycle helmets and motorcycle helmets. Next year, Head-First expects to produce total revenue of $570,000 and incur total variable cost of $388,000. Total fixed cost is expected to be $58,900.

**Required:**

1. Calculate the break-even point in sales dollars for Head-First. (*Note:* Round the contribution margin ratio to four decimal places and sales to the nearest dollar.)
2. Check your answer by preparing a contribution margin income statement.

OBJECTIVE ⑤
CORNERSTONE 4.9

### Cornerstone Exercise 4-21    Margin of Safety

Head-First Company plans to sell 5,000 bicycle helmets at $75 each in the coming year. Unit variable cost is $45 (includes direct materials, direct labor, variable factory overhead, and variable selling expense). Total fixed cost equals $49,500 (includes fixed factory overhead and fixed selling and administrative expense). Break-even units equal 1,650.

**Required:**

1. Calculate the margin of safety in terms of the number of units.
2. Calculate the margin of safety in terms of sales revenue.

OBJECTIVE ⑤
CORNERSTONE 4.10

### Cornerstone Exercise 4-22    Degree of Operating Leverage

Head-First Company plans to sell 5,000 bicycle helmets at $75 each in the coming year. Unit variable cost is $45 (includes direct materials, direct labor, variable factory overhead, and variable selling expense). Total fixed cost equals $49,500 (includes fixed factory overhead and fixed selling and administrative expense). Operating income at 5,000 units sold is $100,500.

**Required:**

Calculate the degree of operating leverage. (*Note:* Round answer to the nearest tenth.)

OBJECTIVE ⑤
CORNERSTONE 4.11

### Cornerstone Exercise 4-23    Impact of Increased Sales on Operating Income Using the Degree of Operating Leverage

Head-First Company had planned to sell 5,000 bicycle helmets at $75 each in the coming year. Unit variable cost is $45 (includes direct materials, direct labor, variable factory overhead, and variable selling expense). Total fixed cost equals $49,500 (includes fixed factory overhead and fixed selling and administrative expense). Operating income at 5,000 units sold is $100,500. The degree of operating leverage is 1.5. Now Head-First expects to increase sales by 10% next year.

**Required:**

1. Calculate the percent change in operating income expected.
2. Calculate the operating income expected next year using the percent change in operating income calculated in Requirement 1.

# EXERCISES

OBJECTIVE ①

### Exercise 4-24    Basic Break-Even Calculations

Suppose that Adams Company sells a product for $20. Unit costs are as follows:

| | |
|---|---|
| Direct materials | $1.90 |
| Direct labor | 1.40 |
| Variable factory overhead | 2.10 |
| Variable selling and administrative expense | 1.60 |

Total fixed factory overhead is $54,420 per year, and total fixed selling and administrative expense is $38,530.

**Required:**

1. Calculate the variable cost per unit and the contribution margin per unit.
2. Calculate the contribution margin ratio and the variable cost ratio.
3. Calculate the break-even units.
4. Prepare a contribution margin income statement at the break-even number of units.

OBJECTIVE ①

### Exercise 4-25    Price, Variable Cost per Unit, Contribution Margin, Contribution Margin Ratio, Fixed Expense

For each of the following independent situations, calculate the amount(s) required.

**Required:**

1. At the break-even point, Jefferson Company sells 115,000 units and has fixed cost of $349,600. The variable cost per unit is $4.56. What price does Jefferson charge per unit?
2. Sooner Industries charges a price of $120 and has fixed cost of $458,000. Next year, Sooner expects to sell 15,600 units and make operating income of $166,000. What is the variable cost per unit? What is the contribution margin ratio? (*Note:* Round answer to four decimal places)
3. Last year, Jasper Company earned operating income of $22,500 with a contribution margin ratio of 0.25. Actual revenue was $235,000. Calculate the total fixed cost.
4. Laramie Company has variable cost ratio of 0.56. The fixed cost is $103,840 and 23,600 units are sold at breakeven. What is the price? What is the variable cost per unit? The contribution margin per unit?

### Exercise 4-26  Contribution Margin Ratio, Variable Cost Ratio, Break-Even Sales Revenue

OBJECTIVE ❶

The controller of Pelley Company prepared the following projected income statement:

| | |
|---|---|
| Sales | $95,000 |
| Total variable cost | 68,400 |
| Contribution margin | $26,600 |
| Total fixed cost | 14,000 |
| Operating income | $12,600 |

**Required:**

1. Calculate the contribution margin ratio.
2. Calculate the variable cost ratio.
3. Calculate the break-even sales revenue for Pelley.
4. **CONCEPTUAL CONNECTION** How could Pelley increase projected operating income without increasing the total sales revenue?

### Exercise 4-27  Income Statement, Break-Even Units, Units to Earn Target Income

OBJECTIVE ❷

Melford Company sold 26,800 units last year at $16.00 each. Variable cost was $11.50, and total fixed cost was $126,000.

**Required:**

1. Prepare an income statement for Melford for last year.
2. Calculate the break-even point in units.
3. Calculate the units that Melford must sell to earn operating income of $12,150 this year.

### Exercise 4-28  Units Sold to Break Even, Unit Variable Cost, Unit Manufacturing Cost, Units to Earn Target Income

OBJECTIVE ❶

Werner Company produces and sells disposable foil baking pans to retailers for $2.75 per pan. The variable cost per pan is as follows:

| | |
|---|---|
| Direct materials | $0.37 |
| Direct labor | 0.63 |
| Variable factory overhead | 0.53 |
| Variable selling expense | 0.12 |

Fixed manufacturing cost totals $111,425 per year. Administrative cost (all fixed) totals $48,350.

**Required:**

1. Compute the number of pans that must be sold for Werner to break even.
2. **CONCEPTUAL CONNECTION** What is the unit variable cost? What is the unit variable manufacturing cost? Which is used in cost-volume-profit analysis and why?
3. How many pans must be sold for Werner to earn operating income of $13,530?
4. How much sales revenue must Werner have to earn operating income of $13,530?

OBJECTIVE ❺    **Exercise 4-29   Margin of Safety**

Comer Company produces and sells strings of colorful indoor/outdoor lights for holiday display to retailers for $8.12 per string. The variable costs per string are as follows:

| | |
|---|---|
| Direct materials | $1.87 |
| Direct labor | 1.70 |
| Variable factory overhead | 0.57 |
| Variable selling expense | 0.42 |

Fixed manufacturing cost totals $245,650 per year. Administrative cost (all fixed) totals $297,606. Comer expects to sell 225,000 strings of light next year.

**Required:**

1. Calculate the break-even point in units.
2. Calculate the margin of safety in units.
3. Calculate the margin of safety in dollars.
4. **CONCEPTUAL CONNECTION** Suppose Comer actually experiences a price decrease next year while all other costs and the number of units sold remain the same. Would this increase or decrease risk for the company? (*Hint:* Consider what would happen to the number of break-even units and to the margin of safety.)

OBJECTIVE ❶    **Exercise 4-30   Contribution Margin, Unit Amounts, Break-Even Units**

**ILLUSTRATING**
**RELATIONSHIPS**

Information on four independent companies follows. Calculate the correct amount for each question mark. (*Note:* Round unit dollar amounts and ratios to two decimal places; round break-even units to the nearest whole unit.)

| | Laertes | Ophelia | Fortinbras | Claudius |
|---|---|---|---|---|
| Sales | $15,000 | $   ? | $   ? | $10,600 |
| Total variable cost | 5,000 | 11,700 | 9,750 | ? |
| Total contribution margin | $10,000 | $ 3,900 | $   ? | $   ? |
| Total fixed cost | ? | 4,000 | ? | 4,452 |
| Operating income (loss) | $   500 | $   ? | $   364 | $   848 |
| Units sold | ? | 1,300 | 125 | 1,000 |
| Price per unit | $  5.00 | ? | $130.00 | ? |
| Variable cost per unit | $   ? | $  9.00 | $   ? | $   ? |
| Contribution margin per unit | $   ? | $  3.00 | $   ? | $   ? |
| Contribution margin ratio | ? | ? | 40% | ? |
| Break-even units | ? | ? | ? | ? |

OBJECTIVE ❶❷❺    **Exercise 4-31   Sales Revenue Approach, Variable Cost Ratio, Contribution Margin Ratio**

Arberg Company's controller prepared the following budgeted income statement for the coming year:

| | |
|---|---|
| Sales | $415,000 |
| Total variable cost | 302,950 |
| Contribution margin | $112,050 |
| Total fixed cost | 64,800 |
| Operating income | $ 47,250 |

**Required:**

1. What is Arberg's variable cost ratio? What is its contribution margin ratio?
2. Suppose Arberg's actual revenues are $30,000 more than budgeted. By how much will operating income increase? Give the answer without preparing a new income statement.
3. How much sales revenue must Arberg earn to break even? Prepare a contribution margin income statement to verify the accuracy of your answer.
4. What is Arberg's expected margin of safety?
5. What is Arberg's margin of safety if sales revenue is $380,000?

*Use the following information for Exercises 4-32 and 4-33:*
Cherry Blossom Products Inc. produces and sells yoga-training products: how-to DVDs and a basic equipment set (blocks, strap, and small pillows). Last year, Cherry Blossom Products sold 13,500 DVDs and 4,500 equipment sets. Information on the two products is as follows:

|                        | DVDs | Equipment Sets |
| ---------------------- | ---- | -------------- |
| Price                  | $8   | $25            |
| Variable cost per unit | 4    | 15             |

Total fixed cost is $84,920.

## Exercise 4-32    Multiple-Product Breakeven

OBJECTIVE 4

Refer to the information for Cherry Blossom Products above.

**Required:**

1.  What is the sales mix of DVDs and equipment sets?
2.  Compute the break-even quantity of each product.

## Exercise 4-33    Multiple-Product Breakeven, Break-Even Sales Revenue

OBJECTIVE 1 5

Refer to the information for Cherry Blossom Products above. Suppose that in the coming year, the company plans to produce an extra-thick yoga mat for sale to health clubs. The company estimates that 9,000 mats can be sold at a price of $15 and a variable cost per unit of $9. Total fixed cost must be increased by $28,980 (making total fixed cost $113,900). Assume that anticipated sales of the other products, as well as their prices and variable costs, remain the same.

**Required:**

1.  What is the sales mix of DVDs, equipment sets, and yoga mats?
2.  Compute the break-even quantity of each product.
3.  Prepare an income statement for Cherry Blossom Products for the coming year. What is the overall contribution margin ratio? Use the contribution margin ratio to compute overall break-even sales revenue. (*Note*: Round the contribution margin ratio to three decimal places; round the break-even sales revenue to the nearest dollar.)
4.  Compute the margin of safety for the coming year in sales dollars.

## Exercise 4-34    Contribution Margin Ratio, Break-Even Sales Revenue, and Margin of Safety for Multiple-Product Firm

OBJECTIVE 1 4 5

Texas-Q Company produces and sells barbeque grills. Texas-Q sells three models: a small portable gas grill, a larger stationary gas grill, and the specialty smoker. In the coming year, Texas-Q expects to sell 20,000 portable grills, 50,000 stationary grills, and 5,000 smokers. Information on the three models is as follows:

|                        | Portable | Stationary | Smokers |
| ---------------------- | -------- | ---------- | ------- |
| Price                  | $90      | $200       | $250    |
| Variable cost per unit | 45       | 130        | 140     |

Total fixed cost is $2,128,500.

**Required:**

1.  What is the sales mix of portable grills to stationary grills to smokers?
2.  Compute the break-even quantity of each product.
3.  Prepare an income statement for Texas-Q for the coming year. What is the overall contribution margin ratio? Use the contribution margin ratio to compute overall break-even sales revenue. (*Note*: Round the contribution margin ratio to four decimal places; round the break-even sales revenue to the nearest dollar.)
4.  Compute the margin of safety for the coming year.

OBJECTIVE  3    **Exercise 4-35   Cost-Volume-Profit Graphs**

Lotts Company produces and sells one product. The selling price is $10, and the unit variable cost is $6. Total fixed cost is $10,000.

**Required:**

1. Prepare a CVP graph with "Units Sold" as the horizontal axis and "Dollars" as the vertical axis. Label the break-even point on the horizontal axis.
2. Prepare CVP graphs for each of the following independent scenarios: (a) Fixed cost increases by $5,000, (b) Unit variable cost increases to $7, (c) Unit selling price increases to $12, and (d) Fixed cost increases by $5,000 and unit variable cost is $7.

OBJECTIVE 1    **Exercise 4-36   Basic Cost-Volume-Profit Concepts**

Klamath Company produces a single product. The projected income statement for the coming year is as follows:

| | |
|---|---:|
| Sales (54,600 units @ $34) | $1,856,400 |
| Total variable cost | 1,064,700 |
| Contribution margin | $ 791,700 |
| Total fixed cost | 801,850 |
| Operating income | $ (10,150) |

**Required:**

1. Compute the unit contribution margin and the units that must be sold to break even.
2. Suppose 10,000 units are sold above breakeven. What is the operating income?
3. Compute the contribution margin ratio. Use the contribution margin ratio to compute the break-even point in sales revenue. (*Note:* Round the contribution margin ratio to four decimal places, and round the sales revenue to the nearest dollar.) Suppose that revenues are $200,000 more than expected *for the coming year.* What would the total operating income be?

OBJECTIVE 1 5    **Exercise 4-37   Margin of Safety and Operating Leverage**

Medina Company produces a single product. The projected income statement for the coming year is as follows:

| | |
|---|---:|
| Sales (40,000 units @ $45) | $1,800,000 |
| Total variable cost | 1,044,000 |
| Contribution margin | $ 756,000 |
| Total fixed cost | 733,320 |
| Operating income | $ 22,680 |

(*Note*: Round all dollar answers to the nearest dollar. Round fractional answers to two decimal places.)

**Required:**

1. Compute the break-even sales dollars.
2. Compute the margin of safety in sales dollars.
3. Compute the degree of operating leverage (*Note:* Round answer to two decimal places).
4. Compute the new operating income if sales are 20% higher than expected. (*Note:* Round answer to the nearest dollar.)

OBJECTIVE 1 4    **Exercise 4-38   Multiple-Product Breakeven**

Parker Pottery produces a line of vases and a line of ceramic figurines. Each line uses the same equipment and labor; hence, there are no traceable fixed costs. Common fixed cost equals $30,000. Parker's accountant has begun to assess the profitability of the two lines and has gathered the following data for last year:

|  | Vases | Figurines |
|---|---|---|
| Price | $40 | $70 |
| Variable cost | 30 | 42 |
| Contribution margin | $10 | $28 |
| Number of units | 1,000 | 500 |

**Required:**

1. Compute the number of vases and the number of figurines that must be sold for the company to break even.
2. Parker Pottery is considering upgrading its factory to improve the quality of its products. The upgrade will add $5,260 per year to total fixed cost. If the upgrade is successful, the projected sales of vases will be 1,500, and figurine sales will increase to 1,000 units. What is the new break-even point in units for each of the products?

**Exercise 4-39 Break-Even Units, Contribution Margin Ratio, Multiple-Product Breakeven, Margin of Safety, Degree of Operating Leverage**

OBJECTIVE ❶ ❷ ❹ ❺

Jellico Inc.'s projected operating income (based on sales of 450,000 units) for the coming year is as follows:

|  | Total |
|---|---|
| Sales | $11,700,000 |
| Total variable cost | 8,190,000 |
| Contribution margin | $ 3,510,000 |
| Total fixed cost | 2,254,200 |
| Operating income | $ 1,255,800 |

**Required:**

1. Compute: (a) variable cost per unit, (b) contribution margin per unit, (c) contribution margin ratio, (d) break-even point in units, and (e) break-even point in sales dollars.
2. How many units must be sold to earn operating income of $296,400?
3. Compute the additional operating income that Jellico would earn if sales were $50,000 more than expected.
4. For the projected level of sales, compute the margin of safety in units, and then in sales dollars.
5. Compute the degree of operating leverage. (*Note*: Round answer to two decimal places.)
6. Compute the new operating income if sales are 10% higher than expected.

# PROBLEMS

**Problem 4-40 Break-Even Units, Contribution Margin Ratio, Margin of Safety**

OBJECTIVE ❶ ❷ ❺

Khumbu Company's projected profit for the coming year is as follows:

|  | Total | Per Unit |
|---|---|---|
| Sales | $2,040,000 | $24 |
| Total variable cost | 1,530,000 | 18 |
| Contribution margin | $ 510,000 | $ 6 |
| Total fixed cost | 380,400 |  |
| Operating income | $ 129,600 |  |

**Required:**

1. Compute the break-even point in units.
2. How many units must be sold to earn a profit of $240,000?

*(Continued)*

3. Compute the contribution margin ratio. Using that ratio, compute the additional profit that Khumbu would earn if sales were $160,000 more than expected.
4. For the projected level of sales, compute the margin of safety in units.

 OBJECTIVE ❶ ❺     **Problem 4-41   Break-Even Units, Operating Income, Margin of Safety**

Kallard Manufacturing Company produces t-shirts screen-printed with the logos of various sports teams. Each shirt is priced at $13.50 and has a unit variable cost of $9.85. Total fixed cost is $197,600.

**Required:**

1. Compute the break-even point in units. (*Note*: Round answer to the nearest whole unit.)
2. Suppose that Kallard could reduce its fixed costs by $23,500 by reducing the amount of setup and engineering time needed. How many units must be sold to break even in this case? (*Note*: Round answer to the nearest whole unit.)
3. **CONCEPTUAL CONNECTION** How does the reduction in fixed cost affect the break-even point? Operating income? The margin of safety?

 OBJECTIVE ❶ ❷ ❺     **Problem 4-42   Contribution Margin, Break-Even Units, Break-Even Sales, Margin of Safety, Degree of Operating Leverage**

Aldovar Company produces a variety of chemicals. One division makes reagents for laboratories. The division's projected income statement for the coming year is:

| | |
|---|---:|
| Sales (203,000 units @ $70) | $14,210,000 |
| Total variable cost | 8,120,000 |
| Contribution margin | $ 6,090,000 |
| Total fixed cost | 4,945,500 |
| Operating income | $ 1,144,500 |

**Required:**

1. Compute the contribution margin per unit, and calculate the break-even point in units (*Note*: Round answer to the nearest unit.) Calculate the contribution margin ratio and the break-even sales revenue. (*Note*: Round contribution margin ratio to four significant digits, and round the break-even sales revenue to the nearest dollar.)
2. The divisional manager has decided to increase the advertising budget by $250,000. This will increase sales revenues by $1 million. By how much will operating income increase or decrease as a result of this action?
3. Suppose sales revenues exceed the estimated amount on the income statement by $1,500,000. Without preparing a new income statement, by how much are profits underestimated?
4. Compute the margin of safety based on the original income statement.
5. Compute the degree of operating leverage based on the original income statement. If sales revenues are 8% greater than expected, what is the percentage increase in operating income? (*Note*: Round operating leverage to two decimal places.)

  OBJECTIVE ❷ ❹     **Problem 4-43   Multiple-Product Analysis, Changes in Sales Mix, Sales to Earn Target Operating Income**

Basu Company produces two types of sleds for playing in the snow: basic sled and aerosled. The projected income for the coming year, segmented by product line, follows:

| | Basic Sled | Aerosled | Total |
|---|---:|---:|---:|
| Sales | $3,000,000 | $2,400,000 | $5,400,000 |
| Total variable cost | 1,000,000 | 1,000,000 | 2,000,000 |
| Contribution margin | $2,000,000 | $1,400,000 | $3,400,000 |
| Direct fixed cost | 778,000 | 650,000 | 1,428,000 |
| Product margin | $1,222,000 | $ 750,000 | $1,972,000 |
| Common fixed cost | | | 198,900 |
| Operating income | | | $1,773,100 |

The selling prices are $30 for the basic sled and $60 for the aerosled.

**Required:**

1. Compute the number of units of each product that must be sold for Basu to break even.
2. Assume that the marketing manager changes the sales mix of the two products so that the ratio is five basic sleds to three aerosleds. Repeat Requirement 1.
3. **CONCEPTUAL CONNECTION** Refer to the original data. Suppose that Basu can increase the sales of aerosleds with increased advertising. The extra advertising would cost an additional $195,000, and some of the potential purchasers of basic sleds would switch to aerosleds. In total, sales of aerosleds would increase by 12,000 units, and sales of basic sleds would decrease by 5,000 units. Would Basu be better off with this strategy?

**Problem 4-44    Cost-Volume-Profit Equation, Basic Concepts, Solving for Unknowns**          OBJECTIVE ❶❷❸❺

Legrand Company produces hand cream in plastic jars. Each jar sells for $3.40. The variable cost for each jar (materials, labor, and overhead) totals $2.55. The total fixed cost is $58,140. During the most recent year, 81,600 jars were sold.

**Required:**

1. What is the break-even point in units for Legrand? What is the margin of safety in units for the most recent year?
2. Prepare an income statement for Legrand's most recent year.
3. How many units must be sold for Legrand to earn a profit of $25,500?
4. What is the level of sales dollars needed for Legrand to earn operating income of 10% of sales?

**Problem 4-45    Contribution Margin Ratio, Break-Even Sales, Operating Leverage**          OBJECTIVE ❶❺

Elgart Company produces plastic mailboxes. The projected income statement for the coming year follows:

| | |
|---|---|
| Sales | $460,300 |
| Total variable cost | 165,708 |
| Contribution margin | $294,592 |
| Total fixed cost | 150,000 |
| Operating income | $144,592 |

**Required:**

1. Compute the contribution margin ratio for the mailboxes.
2. How much revenue must Elgart earn in order to break even?
3. What is the effect on the contribution margin ratio if the unit selling price and unit variable cost each increase by 15%?
4. **CONCEPTUAL CONNECTION** Suppose that management has decided to give a 4% commission on all sales. The projected income statement does not reflect this commission. Recompute the contribution margin ratio, assuming that the commission will be paid. What effect does this have on the break-even point?
5. **CONCEPTUAL CONNECTION** If the commission is paid as described in Requirement 4, management expects sales revenues to increase by $80,000. How will this affect operating leverage? Is it a sound decision to implement the commission? Support your answer with appropriate computations.

**Problem 4-46    Multiple Products, Break-Even Analysis, Operating Leverage**          OBJECTIVE ❹❺

Carlyle Lighting Products produces two different types of lamps: a floor lamp and a desk lamp. Floor lamps sell for $30, and desk lamps sell for $20. The projected income statement for the coming year follows:

*(Continued)*

| | |
|---|---|
| Sales | $600,000 |
| Total variable cost | 400,000 |
| Contribution margin | $200,000 |
| Total fixed cost | 150,000 |
| Operating income | $ 50,000 |

The owner of Carlyle estimates that 60% of the sales revenues will be produced by floor lamps and the remaining 40% by desk lamps. Floor lamps are also responsible for 60% of the variable cost. Of the fixed cost, one-third is common to both products, and one-half is directly traceable to the floor lamp product line.

**Required:**

1.  Compute the sales revenue that must be earned for Carlyle to break even. (Round the contribution margin ratio to six digits and sales revenue to the nearest dollar.)
2.  Compute the number of floor lamps and desk lamps that must be sold for Carlyle to break even.
3.  Compute the degree of operating leverage for Carlyle. Now assume that the actual revenues will be 40% higher than the projected revenues. By what percentage will profits increase with this change in sales volume?

OBJECTIVE ❶ ❹    Problem 4-47    **Multiple-Product Breakeven**

Polaris Inc. manufactures two types of metal stampings for the automobile industry: door handles and trim kits. Fixed cost equals $146,000. Each door handle sells for $12 and has variable cost of $9; each trim kit sells for $8 and has variable cost of $5.

**Required:**

1.  What are the contribution margin per unit and the contribution margin ratio for door handles and for trim kits?
2.  If Polaris sells 20,000 door handles and 40,000 trim kits, what is the operating income?
3.  How many door handles and how many trim kits must be sold for Polaris to break even?
4.  **CONCEPTUAL CONNECTION** Assume that Polaris has the opportunity to rearrange its plant to produce only trim kits. If this is done, fixed costs will decrease by $35,000, and 70,000 trim kits can be produced and sold. Is this a good idea? Explain.

OBJECTIVE ❶ ❺    Problem 4-48    **Cost-Volume-Profit, Margin of Safety**

Victoria Company produces a single product. Last year's income statement is as follows:

| | |
|---|---|
| Sales (29,000 units) | $1,218,000 |
| Total variable cost | 812,000 |
| Contribution margin | $ 406,000 |
| Total fixed cost | 300,000 |
| Operating income | $ 106,000 |

**Required:**

1.  Compute the break-even point in units and sales dollars calculated using the breakeven units.
2.  What was the margin of safety for Victoria last year in sales dollars?
3.  Suppose that Victoria is considering an investment in new technology that will increase fixed cost by $250,000 per year but will lower variable costs to 45% of sales. Units sold will remain unchanged. Prepare a budgeted income statement assuming that Victoria makes this investment. What is the new break-even point in sales dollars, assuming that the investment is made?

OBJECTIVE ❶ ❺    Problem 4-49    **Cost-Volume-Profit, Margin of Safety**

Abraham Company had revenues of $830,000 last year with total variable costs of $647,400 and fixed costs of $110,000.

**Required:**

1. What is the variable cost ratio for Abraham? What is the contribution margin ratio?
2. What is the break-even point in sales revenue?
3. What was the margin of safety for Abraham last year?
4. **CONCEPTUAL CONNECTION** Abraham is considering starting a multimedia advertising campaign that is supposed to increase sales by $12,000 per year. The campaign will cost $4,500. Is the advertising campaign a good idea? Explain.

**Problem 4-50   Using the Break-Even Equations to Solve for Price and Variable Cost per Unit**

OBJECTIVE

Solve the following independent problems.

**Required:**

1. Andromeda Company's break-even point is 2,400 units. Variable cost per unit is $42; total fixed costs are $67,200 per year. What price does Andromeda charge?
2. Immelt Company charges a price of $6.50; total fixed cost is $314,400 per year, and the break-even point is 131,000 units. What is the variable cost per unit?

**Problem 4-51   Contribution Margin, Cost-Volume-Profit, Margin of Safety**

OBJECTIVE

Candyland Inc. produces a particularly rich praline fudge. Each 10-ounce box sells for $5.60. Variable unit costs are as follows:

| | |
|---|---|
| Pecans | $0.70 |
| Sugar | 0.35 |
| Butter | 1.85 |
| Other ingredients | 0.34 |
| Box, packing material | 0.76 |
| Selling commission | 0.20 |

Fixed overhead cost is $32,300 per year. Fixed selling and administrative costs are $12,500 per year. Candyland sold 35,000 boxes last year.

**Required:**

1. What is the contribution margin per unit for a box of praline fudge? What is the contribution margin ratio?
2. How many boxes must be sold to break even? What is the break-even sales revenue?
3. What was Candyland's operating income last year?
4. What was the margin of safety?
5. **CONCEPTUAL CONNECTION** Suppose that Candyland Inc. raises the price to $6.20 per box but anticipates a sales drop to 31,500 boxes. What will be the new break-even point in units? Should Candyland raise the price? Explain.

**Problem 4-52   Break-Even Sales, Operating Leverage, Change in Income**

OBJECTIVE

Income statements for two different companies in the same industry are as follows:

| | Duncan | Macduff |
|---|---|---|
| Sales | $375,000 | $375,000 |
| Total variable cost | 300,000 | 150,000 |
| Contribution margin | $ 75,000 | $225,000 |
| Total fixed cost | 50,000 | 200,000 |
| Operating income | $ 25,000 | $ 25,000 |

*(Continued)*

**Required:**

1. Compute the degree of operating leverage for each company.
2. **CONCEPTUAL CONNECTION** Compute the break-even point in dollars for each company. Explain why the break-even point for Macduff is higher.
3. **CONCEPTUAL CONNECTION** Suppose that both companies experience a 30% increase in revenues. Compute the percentage change in profits for each company. Explain why the percentage increase in Macduff's profits is so much larger than that of Duncan.

OBJECTIVE ① ⑤

### Problem 4-53   Contribution Margin, Break-Even Sales, Margin of Safety

Suppose that **Kicker** had the following sales and cost experience (in thousands of dollars) for May of the current year and for May of the prior year:

|  | May, Current Year | May, Prior Year |
|---|---|---|
| Total sales | $ 43,560 | $ 41,700 |
| Materials | (17,000) | (16,000) |
| Labor and supplies | (1,400) | (1,200) |
| Commissions | (1,250) | (1,100) |
| Contribution margin | $ 23,910 | $ 23,400 |
| Fixed warehouse cost | (680) | (500) |
| Fixed administrative cost | (4,300) | (4,300) |
| Fixed selling cost | (5,600) | (5,000) |
| Research and development | (9,750) | (4,000) |
| Operating income | $   3,580 | $   9,600 |

In May of the prior year, **Kicker** started an intensive quality program designed to enable it to build original equipment manufacture (OEM) speaker systems for a major automobile company. The program was housed in research and development. In the beginning of the current year, Kicker's accounting department exercised tighter control over sales commissions, ensuring that no dubious (e.g., double) payments were made. The increased sales in the current year required additional warehouse space that Kicker rented in town. (Round ratios to four significant digits. Round sales dollars computations to the nearest dollar.)

**Required:**

1. Calculate the contribution margin ratio for May of both years.
2. Calculate the break-even point in sales dollars for both years.
3. Calculate the margin of safety in sales dollars for both years.
4. **CONCEPTUAL CONNECTION** Analyze the differences shown by your calculations in Requirements 1, 2, and 3.

## CASES

OBJECTIVE ① ④

### Case 4-54   Cost-Volume-Profit with Multiple Products, Sales Mix Changes, Changes in Fixed and Variable Costs

Artistic Woodcrafting Inc. began several years ago as a one-person, cabinet-making operation. Employees were added as the business expanded. Last year, sales volume totaled $850,000. Volume for the first five months of the current year totaled $600,000, and sales were expected to be $1.6 million for the entire year. Unfortunately, the cabinet business in the region where Artistic is located is highly competitive. More than 200 cabinet shops are all competing for the same business.

Artistic currently offers two different quality grades of cabinets: Grade I and Grade II, with Grade I being the higher quality. The average unit selling prices, unit variable costs, and direct fixed costs are as follows:

|            | Unit Price | Unit Variable Cost | Direct Fixed Cost |
|------------|-----------|--------------------|-------------------|
| Grade I    | $3,400    | $2,686             | $95,000           |
| Grade II   | 1,600     | 1,328              | 95,000            |

Common fixed costs (fixed costs not traceable to either cabinet) are $35,000. Currently, for every three Grade I cabinets sold, seven Grade II cabinets are sold.

**Required:**

1. Calculate the number of Grade I and Grade II cabinets that are expected to be sold during the current year.
2. Calculate the number of Grade I and Grade II cabinets that must be sold for Artistic to break even.
3. Artistic can buy computer-controlled machines that will make doors, drawers, and frames. If the machines are purchased, the variable costs for each type of cabinet will decrease by 9%, but common fixed cost will increase by $44,000. Compute the effect on operating income, and also calculate the new break-even point. Assume the machines are purchased at the beginning of the sixth month. Fixed costs for the company are incurred uniformly throughout the year.
4. Refer to the original data. Artistic is considering adding a retail outlet. This will increase common fixed cost by $70,000 per year. As a result of adding the retail outlet, the additional publicity and emphasis on quality will allow the firm to change the sales mix to 1:1. The retail outlet is also expected to increase sales by 30%. Assume that the outlet is opened at the beginning of the sixth month. Calculate the effect on the company's expected profits for the current year, and calculate the new break-even point. Assume that fixed costs are incurred uniformly throughout the year.

## Case 4-55    Ethics and a Cost-Volume-Profit Application

OBJECTIVE ❶

Danna Lumus, the marketing manager for a division that produces a variety of paper products, is considering the divisional manager's request for a sales forecast for a new line of paper napkins. The divisional manager has been gathering data so that he can choose between two different production processes. The first process would have a variable cost of $10 per case produced and total fixed cost of $100,000. The second process would have a variable cost of $6 per case and total fixed cost of $200,000. The selling price would be $30 per case. Danna had just completed a marketing analysis that projects annual sales of 30,000 cases.

Danna is reluctant to report the 30,000 forecast to the divisional manager. She knows that the first process would be labor intensive, whereas the second would be largely automated with little labor and no requirement for an additional production supervisor. If the first process is chosen, Jerry Johnson, a good friend, will be appointed as the line supervisor. If the second process is chosen, Jerry and an entire line of laborers will be laid off. After some consideration, Danna revises the projected sales downward to 22,000 cases.

She believes that the revision downward is justified. Since it will lead the divisional manager to choose the manual system, it shows a sensitivity to the needs of current employees—a sensitivity that she is afraid her divisional manager does not possess. He is too focused on quantitative factors in his decision making and usually ignores the qualitative aspects.

**Required:**

1. Compute the break-even point in units for each process.
2. Compute the sales volume for which the two processes are equally profitable. Identify the range of sales for which the manual process is more profitable than the automated process. Identify the range of sales for which the automated process is more profitable than the manual process. Why does the divisional manager want the sales forecast?
3. Discuss Danna's decision to alter the sales forecast. Do you agree with it? Is she acting ethically? Is her decision justified since it helps a number of employees retain their employment? Should the impact on employees be factored into decisions? In fact, is it unethical not to consider the impact of decisions on employees?

© Pixelfabrik/Alamy

# MAKING THE CONNECTION
## INTEGRATIVE EXERCISE (CHAPTERS 1–4)

## Cost Behavior and Cost-Volume-Profit Analysis for Many Glacier Hotel

| Chapters | Objectives | Cornerstones |
|----------|------------|--------------|
| 2-4 | 2-2 | 3-2 |
| | 3-3 | 4-2 |
| | 4-1 | 4-5 |
| | 4-2 | 4-7 |
| | 4-4 | 4-9 |
| | 4-5 | |

*The purpose of this integrated exercise is to demonstrate the interrelationship between cost estimation techniques and subsequent uses of cost information. In particular, this exercise illustrates how the variable and fixed cost information estimated from a high-low analysis can be used in a single- and multiple-product CVP analysis.*

### Using the High-Low Method to Estimate Variable and Fixed Costs

Located on Swiftcurrent Lake in Glacier National Park, **Many Glacier Hotel** was built in 1915 by the Great Northern Railway. In an effort to supplement its lodging revenue, the hotel decided in 2003 to begin manufacturing and selling small wooden canoes decorated with symbols hand painted by Native Americans living near the park. Due to the great success of the canoes, the hotel began manufacturing and selling paddles as well in 2006. Many hotel guests purchase a canoe and paddles for use in self-guided tours of Swiftcurrent Lake. Because production of the two products began in different years, the canoes and paddles are produced in separate production facilities and employ different laborers. Each canoe sells for $500, and each paddle sells for $50. A 2006 fire destroyed the hotel's accounting records. However, a new system put into place before the 2007 season provides the following aggregated data for the hotel's canoe and paddle manufacturing and marketing activities:

**Manufacturing Data:**

| Year | Number of Canoes Manufactured | Total Canoe Manufacturing Costs | Year | Number of Paddles Manufactured | Total Paddle Manufacturing Costs |
|------|-------------------------------|--------------------------------|------|-------------------------------|---------------------------------|
| 2012 | 250 | $106,000 | 2012 | 900 | $38,500 |
| 2011 | 275 | 115,000 | 2011 | 1,200 | 49,000 |
| 2010 | 240 | 108,000 | 2010 | 1,000 | 42,000 |
| 2009 | 310 | 122,000 | 2009 | 1,100 | 45,500 |
| 2008 | 350 | 130,000 | 2008 | 1,400 | 56,000 |
| 2007 | 400 | 140,000 | 2007 | 1,700 | 66,500 |

**Marketing Data:**

| Year | Number of Canoes Sold | Total Canoe Marketing Costs | Year | Number of Paddles Sold | Total Paddle Marketing Costs |
|------|------|------|------|------|------|
| 2012 | 250 | $45,000 | 2012 | 900 | $ 7,500 |
| 2011 | 275 | 47,500 | 2011 | 1,200 | 9,000 |
| 2010 | 240 | 44,000 | 2010 | 1,000 | 8,000 |
| 2009 | 310 | 51,000 | 2009 | 1,100 | 8,500 |
| 2008 | 350 | 55,000 | 2008 | 1,400 | 10,000 |
| 2007 | 400 | 60,000 | 2007 | 1,700 | 11,500 |

## Required:

1. High-Low Cost Estimation Method

   a. Use the high-low method to estimate the per-unit variable costs and total fixed costs for the *canoe* product line.
   b. Use the high-low method to estimate the per-unit variable costs and total fixed costs for the *paddle* product line.

2. Cost-Volume-Profit Analysis, Single-Product Setting

   Use CVP analysis to calculate the break-even point in units for

   a. The *canoe* product line *only* (i.e., single-product setting)
   b. The *paddle* product line *only* (i.e., single-product setting)

3. Cost-Volume-Profit Analysis, Multiple-Product Setting

   The hotel's accounting system data show an average sales mix of approximately 300 canoes and 1,200 paddles each season. Significantly more paddles are sold relative to canoes because some inexperienced canoe guests accidentally break one or more paddles, while other guests purchase additional paddles as presents for friends and relatives. In addition, for this multiple-product CVP analysis, assume the existence of an additional $30,000 of common fixed costs for a customer service hotline used for both canoe and paddle customers. Use CVP analysis to calculate the break-even point in units for both the canoe and paddle product lines combined (i.e., the multiple-product setting).

4. Cost Classification

   a. Classify the manufacturing costs, marketing costs, and customer service hotline costs either as production expenses or period expenses.
   b. For the period expenses, further classify them into either selling expenses or general and administrative expenses.

5. Sensitivity Cost-Volume-Profit Analysis and Production Versus Period Expenses, Multiple-Product Setting

   If both the variable and fixed *production* expenses (refer to your answer to Requirement 1) associated with the *canoe* product line increased by 5% (beyond the estimate from the high-low analysis), how many canoes and paddles would need to be sold in order to earn a target income of $96,000? Assume the same sales mix and additional fixed costs as in Requirement 3.

6. Margin of Safety

   Calculate the hotel's margin of safety (both in units and in sales dollars) for Many Glacier Hotel, assuming the same facts as in Requirement 3, and it sells 700 canoes and 2,500 paddles next year.

# 5

# Job-Order Costing

© Pixelfabrik/Alamy

After studying Chapter 5, you should be able to:

① Describe the differences between job-order costing and process costing, and identify the types of firms that would use each method.

② Compute the predetermined overhead rate, and use the rate to assign overhead to units or services produced.

③ Identify and set up the source documents used in job-order costing.

④ Describe the cost flows associated with job-order costing.

⑤ (Appendix 5A) Prepare the journal entries associated with job-order costing.

⑥ (Appendix 5B) Allocate support department costs to producing departments.

iStockphoto.com/Kemter

# EXPERIENCE MANAGERIAL DECISIONS

## with Washburn Guitars

Since 1883, **Washburn Guitars** has manufactured high-quality acoustic and electric guitars. Washburn's guitar buyers include musicians ranging from garage bands to some of the world's most famous bands.

Washburn produces many guitar series. Each series has many different models that require the use of varied resources.[1] For example, in 2006 Washburn introduced the Damen Idol, retailing for $2,249. The Damen, named after Damen Avenue in Chicago's Wicker Park—a known hot spot for alternative, pop, and punk musicians, illustrates the complexity and individuality of specialized guitars. It featured a mahogany body, flame maple top, mahogany neck with cream binding, rosewood fingerboard, Seymour Duncan Custom pickups in the bridge and a Seymour Duncan '59 in the neck, a Tone Pros Bridge and Tailpiece, and numerous other options for frets, scaling, finishing, and tuning. Joe Trohman from Fall Out Boy, Aaron Dugan of Matisyahu, Mike Kennerty from The All American Rejects, Shaun Glass from Soil, Marty Casey from the Loveham-

mers and INXS all played the Damen Idol at one time or another.

Many guitar buyers, including most professionals, request various product customizations. For example, Washburn's Custom Shop Pilsen guitar was made especially for Billy Sawilchik to play the National Anthem at Game 2 of the 2005 American League Championship Series between the White Sox and Angels. While customization created great publicity for Washburn, it also created significant design and product differences between guitars, even those within the same model line of a given series. This variability led to differences in the use of materials and labor, which required Washburn to estimate the cost of each guitar job according to the desired degree of customization. Washburn managers relied heavily on their effective job-order costing system to help them understand the costs associated with such product alterations. This ensured that the particular customizations provided a profit after all costs were covered.

> *"While customization created great publicity for Washburn, it also created significant design and product differences between guitars, even those within the same model line of a given series. This variability led to differences in the use of materials and labor, which required Washburn to estimate the cost of each guitar job according to the desired degree of customization."*

---

[1] By 2009, Washburn stopped making the customized guitars favored by top rock musicians. It now concentrates on guitars for a mass audience. While the Damen Idol is no longer in production, it is still an excellent example of job-order production.

**OBJECTIVE ❶**

Describe the differences between job-order costing and process costing, and identify the types of firms that would use each method.

# CHARACTERISTICS OF THE JOB-ORDER ENVIRONMENT

Companies can be divided into two major types, depending on whether their products/ services are unique. Manufacturing and service firms producing unique products or services require a job-order accounting system. When Washburn Guitars was producing its custom guitars, it fell into this category. On the other hand, those firms producing similar products or services can use a process-costing accounting system. **Ben & Jerry's Homemade, Inc.**, a producer of premium ice creams with the whimsical flavor names, falls into this latter category. Each pint of a particular flavor of ice cream, say Cherry Garcia or Triple Caramel Chunk, is indistinguishable from the other pints. The characteristics of a company's actual production process determine whether it needs a job-order or a process-costing accounting system.

## Here's The Real Kicker

In the 1970s, **Kicker** began operations in Steve Irby's garage. Steve was an engineering student at Oklahoma State University and a keyboard player with a local band. The band needed speakers but couldn't afford new ones. Steve and his father built wooden boxes and fitted them with secondhand components. Word spread, and other bands asked for speakers. Steve partnered with a friend to fill the orders. Then, an oil-field worker asked if Steve could rig up speakers for his pickup truck. Long days bouncing over rough fields went more smoothly with music, but the built-in audio systems at the time were awful. Steve designed and built a speaker to fit behind the driver's seat, and Kicker was born.

At first, each job was made to order to fit a particular truck or car. The price Steve charged depended heavily on the cost of the job. Since each job was different, the various costs had to be computed individually. Clearly, the costs of wood, fabric, glue, and components were traceable to each job. Steve could also trace labor time. But the other costs of design time, use of power tools, and space were combined to create an overhead rate. To the extent that the price of a job was greater than its costs, Steve earned a profit.

Jackson Smith/Getty Images

## Job-Order Production and Costing

Firms operating in job-order industries produce a wide variety of services or products that are quite distinct from each other. Customized or built-to-order products fit into this category, as do services that vary from customer to customer, like **Sky Limo Corporation**, which provides air charter services. A **job** is one distinct unit or set of units. For example, a job might be a kitchen remodel for the Ruiz family, or a set of 12 tables for the children's reading room at the local library. Common job-order processes include:

- printing
- construction
- furniture making
- medical and dental services
- automobile repair
- beautician services

Often, a job is associated with a particular customer order. The key feature of job-order costing is that the cost of one job differs from that of another and must be kept track of separately.

For job-order production systems, costs are accumulated by job. This approach to assigning costs is called a **job-order costing system**. In a job-order firm, collecting costs by job provides vital information for management. For example, prices frequently are based on costs in a job-order environment.

## Process Production and Costing

Firms in process industries mass-produce large quantities of similar or homogeneous products. Examples of process manufacturers include:

- food canning and manufacturing
- cement
- petroleum
- pharmaceutical and chemical manufacturing

One gallon of paint is the same as another gallon; one bottle of aspirin is the same as another bottle. The important point is that the cost of one unit of a product is identical to the cost of another. Service firms can also use a process-costing approach. For example, check-clearing departments of banks incur a uniform cost to clear a check, no matter the size of the check or the name of the payee.

Process firms accumulate production costs by process or by department for a given period of time. The output for the process for that period of time is measured. Unit costs are computed by dividing the process costs for the given period by the output of the period:

$$\text{Unit Costs} = \frac{\text{Process Costs}}{\text{Output}}$$

This approach to cost accumulation is known as a **process-costing system** and is examined in detail in Chapter 6. A comparison of job-order costing and process costing is given in Exhibit 5.1.

## Production Costs in Job-Order Costing

While the variety of product-costing definitions discussed in Chapter 2 applies to both job-order and process costing, we will use the traditional definition to illustrate job-order costing procedures. That is, production costs consist of direct materials, direct labor, and overhead. Direct materials and direct labor are typically fairly easy to trace to individual jobs, while overhead, because it consists of all production costs other than direct materials and direct labor, is not always as simple.

# NORMAL COSTING AND OVERHEAD APPLICATION

Unit costs are very important because managers need accurate cost information on materials, labor, and overhead when making decisions. For example, **Bechtel Construction**, whose projects include the Channel Tunnel connecting England and France and Boston's "Big Dig," typically bills its clients at set points throughout construction. As a result, it is important that the unit cost be generated in a timely fashion. Job-order costing using a normal cost system will give the company the unit cost information it needs.

OBJECTIVE

Compute the predetermined overhead rate, and use the rate to assign overhead to units or services produced.

---

( EXHIBIT 5.1 )

**Comparison of Job-Order and Process Costing**

| Job-Order Costing | Process Costing |
| --- | --- |
| • Wide variety of distinct products | • Homogeneous products |
| • Costs accumulated by job | • Costs accumulated by process or department |
| • Unit Cost = Total Job Costs/Output | • Unit Cost = Process Costs/Output |

## Actual Costing versus Normal Costing

Two ways are commonly used to measure the costs associated with production: actual costing and normal costing.

**Actual Costing**  In an **actual cost system**, only *actual* costs of direct materials, direct labor, and overhead are used to determine unit cost. However, there are several issues involved in using actual costing.

*Defining Overhead Costs*  Per-unit computation of the direct materials and direct labor costs is relatively easy to determine. However, defining overhead is much more difficult. Overhead items do not have the direct relationship with units produced that direct materials and direct labor do. For example, how much of a security guard's salary should be assigned to a unit of product or service? Even if the firm averages overhead cost by totaling manufacturing overhead costs for a given period and then divides this total by the number of units produced, distorted costs can occur. The distortion can be traced to uneven incurrence of overhead costs and uneven production from period to period.

*Uneven Overhead Costs*  Many overhead costs are not incurred uniformly throughout the year. For example, actual repair cost occurs whenever a machine breakdown occurs. This timing can make overhead costs in the month of a machine breakdown higher than in other months. The second problem, nonuniform production levels, can mean that low production in one month would give rise to high unit overhead costs, and high production in another month would give rise to low unit overhead costs. Yet the production process and total overhead costs may remain unchanged. One solution would be to wait until the end of the year to total the actual overhead costs and divide by the total actual production, an option that is not realistic for most companies.

*Uneven Production*  Strict actual cost systems are rarely used because they cannot provide accurate unit cost information on a timely basis. A company needs unit cost information throughout the year. This information is needed to prepare interim financial statements and to help managers make decisions such as pricing. Managers must react to day-to-day conditions in the marketplace in order to maintain a sound competitive position. Therefore, they need timely information.

**Normal Costing**  Normal costing solves the problems associated with actual costing. A **normal cost system** determines unit cost by adding actual direct materials, actual direct labor, and estimated overhead. Overhead can be estimated by approximating the year's actual overhead at the *beginning* of the year and then using a predetermined rate throughout the year to obtain the needed unit cost information. Virtually all firms use normal costing.

## Importance of Unit Costs to Manufacturing Firms

Unit cost is a critical piece of information for a manufacturer. Unit costs are essential for valuing inventory, determining income, and making numerous important decisions.

Disclosing the cost of inventories and determining income are financial reporting requirements that a firm faces at the end of each period. In order to report the cost of its inventories, a firm must know the number of units on hand and the unit cost. The cost of goods sold (COGS), used to determine income, requires knowledge of the units sold and their unit cost.

Note that full cost information is useful as an input for a number of important internal decisions as well as for financial reporting. In the long run, for any product to be viable, its price must cover its full cost. Decisions to

---

### concept Q&A

The TV reality series *Trading Spaces* involves two pairs of homeowners who, with the guidance of an interior designer and the help of a professional carpenter, redo one room in each other's house. Each pair has 48 hours and $1,000 to accomplish the renovation. At the end of each show, the host and interior designer total up the "costs" of the redecoration project, which typically comes in at pennies under $1,000. What costs are included in the $1,000? What costs are not? Does each redecoration really cost under $1,000? (*Hint:* Think about direct materials, direct labor, and overhead in your answer.)

**Answer:**

The $1,000 is used to cover the cost of furniture, fabrics, and materials. It does not cover the services of the designer or carpenter. There is clearly a good deal of overhead involved that includes the power tools, carpentry supplies (nails, glue), hand tools, sewing machine(s), and so on. The completed room costs considerably more than $1,000.

introduce a new product, to continue a current product, and to analyze long-run prices are examples of important internal decisions that rely on full unit cost information.

## Importance of Unit Costs to Service Firms

Like manufacturing firms, service and nonprofit firms also require unit cost information. Conceptually, the way companies accumulate and assign costs is the same whether or not the firm is a manufacturer. The service firm must first identify the service "unit" being provided. A hospital would accumulate costs by patient, patient day, and type of procedure (e.g., X-ray, complete blood count test). A governmental agency must also identify the service provided. For example, city government might provide household trash collection and calculate the cost by truck run or number of houses served.

Service firms use cost data in much the same way that manufacturing firms do. They use costs to determine profitability, the feasibility of introducing new services, and so on. However, because service firms do not produce physical products, they do not need to value work-in-process and finished goods inventories. (Inventories of supplies are simply valued at historical cost.)

**ETHICAL DECISIONS** Nonprofit firms must track costs to be sure that they provide their services in a cost-efficient way. Governmental agencies have a fiduciary responsibility to taxpayers to use funds wisely, and that requires accurate accounting for costs. Without such responsibility, questionable results can occur, such as the alleged overcharges by several pharmaceutical firms for common prescription drugs used by Medicaid patients. Under Medicaid rules, the government reimburses companies for the average wholesale price of the drugs used. **Sandoz Pharmaceuticals**, among others, allegedly inflated the prices charged by up to 60,000%. (See Chapter 13 for additional discussion of ethics involving cost-plus pricing).[2] •

A cost accounting system measures and assigns costs so that the unit cost of a product or service can be determined. Unit cost is a critical piece of information for both manufacturing and service firms. Bidding is a common requirement in the markets for specialized products and services (e.g., bids for special tools, audits, legal services, and medical tests and procedures). For example, it would be virtually impossible for **KPMG** to submit a meaningful bid to one of its large audit clients without knowing the unit costs of its services.

## Normal Costing and Estimating Overhead

In normal costing, overhead is estimated and applied to production. The basics of overhead application can be described in three steps:

**Step 1:** Calculate the predetermined overhead rate.
**Step 2:** Apply overhead to production throughout the year.
**Step 3:** Reconcile the difference between the total actual overhead incurred during the year and the total overhead applied to production.

**Step 1: Calculating the Predetermined Overhead Rate** The **predetermined overhead rate** is calculated at the beginning of the year by dividing the total estimated annual overhead by the total estimated level of associated activity or cost driver:

$$\text{Predetermined Overhead Rate} = \frac{\text{Estimated Annual Overhead}}{\text{Estimated Annual Activity Level}}$$

Notice that the predetermined overhead rate includes estimated amounts in *both* the numerator and the denominator. This estimation is necessary because the predetermined overhead rate is calculated in advance, usually at the beginning of the year. It is

---

[2] Jim Edwards, "Sandoz Overcharged Medicaid by 60,000% in $13B Pricing Scam, Says Judge," *BNET*. (January 28, 2010): http://industry.bnet.com/pharma/10006357/sandoz-overcharged-medicaid-by-60000-in-13b-pricing-scam-says-judge/.

impossible to use actual overhead or actual activity level for the year because at that time, the company does not know what the actual levels will be.

Estimated overhead is the firm's best estimate of the amount of overhead (utilities, indirect labor, depreciation, etc.) to be incurred in the coming year. The estimate is often based on last year's figures and is adjusted for anticipated changes in the coming year.

The associated activity level depends on which activity is best associated with overhead. Often, the activity chosen is the number of direct labor hours or the direct labor cost. This makes sense when much of overhead cost is associated with direct labor (e.g., fringe benefits, worker safety training programs, the cost of running the personnel department). The number of machine hours could be a good choice for a company with automated production. Then, much of the overhead cost might consist of equipment maintenance, depreciation on machinery, electricity to run the machinery, and so on. The estimated activity level is the number of direct labor hours, or machine hours, expected for the coming year. **Washburn Guitars** found that much of its overhead was connected to the use of direct labor (e.g., body and neck sanding, fret board assembly, neck joint sanding, taping and painting, wiring and assembly) and of machinery (e.g., CNC body and neck roughing, fret board inlay programming and cutting). Therefore, direct labor and machine hours were good activity choices for overhead application.

**Step 2: Applying Overhead to Production**   Once the overhead rate has been computed, the company can begin to apply overhead to production. **Applied overhead** is found by multiplying the predetermined overhead rate by the actual use of the associated activity for the period:

Applied Overhead = Predetermined Overhead Rate × Actual Activity Level

Suppose that a company has an overhead rate of $5 per machine hour. In the first week of January, the company used 9,000 hours of machine time. The overhead applied to the week's production is computed as:

$$\$5 \times 9{,}000 = \$45{,}000$$

The concept is the same for any time period. So, if the company runs its machines for 50,000 hours in the month of January, applied overhead for January would be $250,000 ($5 × 50,000).

The total cost of product for the period is the actual direct materials and direct labor, plus the applied overhead:

Total Normal Product Costs = Actual Direct Materials + Actual Direct Labor + Applied Overhead

Cornerstone 5.1 shows how to calculate the predetermined overhead rate and how to use that rate to apply overhead to production.

**CORNERSTONE**

**5.1**

## Calculating the Predetermined Overhead Rate and Applying Overhead to Production

**Why:**

Predetermined overhead rates help companies maintain a constant application of overhead throughout the year. These rates do not allow seasonality or variations in production to affect unit cost.

*(Continued)*

**Information:**

At the beginning of the year, Argus Company estimated the following costs:

| | |
|---|---|
| Overhead | $360,000 |
| Direct labor cost | 720,000 |

    Argus uses normal costing and applies overhead on the basis of direct labor cost. (Direct labor cost equals total direct labor hours worked multiplied by the wage rate.) For the month of February, direct labor cost was $56,000.

**Required:**

1. Calculate the predetermined overhead rate for the year.

2. Calculate the overhead applied to production in February.

**Solution:**

1. $\text{Predetermined Overhead Rate} = \dfrac{\$360,000}{\$720,000}$

         $= 0.50,$ or 50% of direct labor cost

2. Overhead Applied to February Production $= 0.50 \times \$56,000 = \$28,000$

## Step 3: Reconciling Actual Overhead with Applied Overhead   Recall that two types of overhead are recorded:

- *Actual overhead:* Costs are tracked throughout the year in the overhead account.
- *Applied overhead:* Costs are computed throughout the year and added to actual direct materials and actual direct labor to get total product cost.

At the end of the year, any difference between actual and applied overhead must be recognized and closed to the cost of goods sold account so that it reflects actual overhead spending.

    Suppose that Proto Company had actual overhead of $400,000 for the year but had applied $390,000 to production. Proto Company has *underapplied* overhead by $10,000. If applied overhead had been $410,000, too much overhead would have been applied to production. The firm would have *overapplied* overhead by $10,000. The difference between actual overhead and applied overhead is called an **overhead variance**:

Overhead Variance = Actual Overhead − Applied Overhead

    If actual overhead is greater than applied overhead, then the variance is called **underapplied overhead**. If actual overhead is less than applied overhead, then the variance is called **overapplied overhead**. If overhead has been underapplied, then product cost has been understated. In this case, the cost appears lower than it really is. Conversely, if overhead has been overapplied, then product cost has been overstated. In this case, the cost appears higher than it really is. Exhibit 5.2 (p. 180) illustrates the concepts of over- and underapplied overhead.

    Because it is impossible to perfectly estimate future overhead costs and production activity, overhead variances are virtually inevitable. However, at year-end, costs reported on the financial statements must be actual amounts. Thus, something must be done with the overhead variance. Usually, the entire overhead variance is assigned to Cost of Goods Sold. This practice is justified on the basis of materiality, the same

( EXHIBIT 5.2 )

**Actual and Applied Overhead**

| Actual Overhead | Underapplied | Underapplied | | Actual Overhead | Overapplied | Overapplied |
|---|---|---|---|---|---|---|
| | Applied Overhead | Cost of Goods Sold | | | Applied Overhead | Cost of Goods Sold |
| If Overhead Is Underapplied | If Overhead Is Underapplied | If Overhead Is Underapplied | | If Overhead Is Overapplied | If Overhead Is Overapplied | If Overhead Is Overapplied |

© Cengage Learning 2014

principle used to justify expensing the entire cost of a stapler in the period acquired rather than depreciating its cost over the life of the stapler. Since the overhead variance is usually relatively small, and all production costs should appear in cost of goods sold eventually, the method of disposition is not a critical matter. Thus,

- Underapplied overhead is added to Cost of Goods Sold.
- Overapplied overhead is subtracted from Cost of Goods Sold.

Adjusted Cost of Goods Sold = Unadjusted Cost of Goods Sold ± Overhead Variance

Suppose Proto Company has an ending balance in its cost of goods sold account equal to $607,000. The underapplied overhead variance of $10,000 would be added to produce a new adjusted balance of $617,000. (Since applied overhead was $390,000, and actual overhead was $400,000, production costs were *understated* by $10,000. Cost of Goods Sold must be increased to correct the problem.) If the variance had been overapplied, it would have been subtracted from Cost of Goods Sold to produce a new balance of $597,000. Cornerstone 5.2 shows how to reconcile actual overhead with applied overhead for Argus Company.

**CORNERSTONE**

**5.2**

## Reconciling Actual Overhead with Applied Overhead

**Why:**
Applied and actual overhead are rarely the same. Since the cost of units sold and of units kept in inventory are carried at historical cost, the difference between actual and applied overhead must be recognized and total cost must be adjusted.

**Information:**
Recall that Argus Company's predetermined overhead rate was 0.50 or 50% of direct labor cost. By the end of the year, actual data are:

| | |
|---|---|
| Overhead | $375,400 |
| Direct labor cost | 750,000 |

Cost of Goods Sold (before adjusting for any overhead variance) is $632,000.

**Required:**

1. Calculate the overhead variance for the year.

2. Dispose of the overhead variance by adjusting Cost of Goods Sold.

*(Continued)*

**Solution:**

1. Overhead Applied for the Year $= 0.50 \times \$750{,}000 = \$375{,}000$

| | |
|---|---:|
| Actual overhead | $375,400 |
| Applied overhead | 375,000 |
| Overhead variance—underapplied | $     400 |

2.

| | |
|---|---:|
| Unadjusted cost of goods sold | $632,000 |
| Add: Overhead variance—underapplied | 400 |
| Adjusted cost of goods sold | $632,400 |

CORNERSTONE

# 5.2

*(Continued)*

If the overhead variance is material, or large, another approach would be taken. That approach, allocating the variance among the ending balances of Work in Process, Finished Goods, and Cost of Goods Sold, is discussed in more detail in later accounting courses.

## Departmental Overhead Rates

The description of overhead application so far has emphasized the plantwide overhead rate. A **plantwide overhead rate** is a single overhead rate calculated by using all estimated overhead for a factory divided by the estimated activity level across the entire factory. However, some companies believe that multiple overhead rates give more accurate costing information. Service firms, or service departments of manufacturing firms, can also use separate overhead rates to charge out their services.

Departmental overhead rates are a widely used type of multiple overhead rate. A **departmental overhead rate** is estimated overhead for a department divided by the estimated activity level for that same department:

$$\text{Departmental Overhead Rate} = \frac{\text{Estimated Department Overhead}}{\text{Estimated Departmental Activity Level}}$$

The steps involved in calculating and applying overhead are the same as those involved for one plantwide overhead rate. The company has as many overhead rates as it has departments. Cornerstone 5.3 shows how to calculate and apply departmental overhead rates.

## Calculating Predetermined Departmental Overhead Rates and Applying Overhead to Production

**Why:**

Departmental overhead rates allow companies to recognize that different producing departments have different overhead costs. These rates allow more precise application of overhead as units pass through one or more departments.

CORNERSTONE

# 5.3

*(Continued)*

## CORNERSTONE
## 5.3

*(Continued)*

**Information:**

At the beginning of the year, Sorrel Company estimated the following:

| | Machining Department | Assembly Department | Total |
|---|---|---|---|
| Overhead | $240,000 | $360,000 | $600,000 |
| Direct labor hours | 135,000 | 240,000 | 375,000 |
| Machine hours | 200,000 | — | 200,000 |

Sorrel uses departmental overhead rates. In the machining department, overhead is applied on the basis of machine hours. In the assembly department, overhead is applied on the basis of direct labor hours. Actual data for the month of June are as follows:

| | Machining Department | Assembly Department | Total |
|---|---|---|---|
| Overhead | $22,500 | $30,750 | $53,250 |
| Direct labor hours | 11,000 | 20,000 | 31,000 |
| Machine hours | 17,000 | — | 17,000 |

**Required:**

1. Calculate the predetermined overhead rates for the machining and assembly departments.

2. Calculate the overhead applied to production in each department for the month of June.

3. By how much has each department's overhead been overapplied? Underapplied?

**Solution:**

1. $\text{Machining Department Overhead Rate} = \dfrac{\$240,000}{200,000 \text{ mhrs}}$

   $= \$1.20 \text{ per machine hour}$

   $\text{Assembly Department Overhead Rate} = \dfrac{\$360,000}{240,000 \text{ DLH}}$

   $= \$1.50 \text{ per direct labor hour}$

2. Overhead Applied to Machining in June $= \$1.20 \times 17,000 = \$20,400$

   Overhead Applied to Assembly in June $= \$1.50 \times 20,000 = \$30,000$

| | Machining Department | Assembly Department |
|---|---|---|
| Actual overhead | $22,500 | $30,750 |
| Applied overhead | 20,400 | 30,000 |
| Underapplied overhead | $ 2,100 | $   750 |

It is important to realize that departmental overhead rates simply carve total overhead into two or more parts. The departments can be added back to get plantwide overhead, as illustrated in Cornerstone 5.4.

2.

| | |
|---|---|
| Direct materials | $730,000 |
| Direct labor ($12 × 5,400 DLH) | 64,800 |
| Overhead ($7.60 × 5,400 DLH) | 41,040 |
|    Total manufacturing costs | $835,840 |
| Unit cost ($835,840/10,000 units) | $   83.58 |

3.  Predetermined Rate for Assembly $= \dfrac{\$330,000}{150,000} = \$2.20$ per DLH

Predetermined Rate for Finishing $= \dfrac{\$1,000,000}{125,000} = \$8$ per machine hour

| | |
|---|---|
| Direct materials | $730,000 |
| Direct labor | 64,800 |
| Overhead: | |
|   Assembly ($2.20 × 5,000 DLH) | 11,000 |
|   Finishing ($8 × 1,200 mhrs) | 9,600 |
|     Total manufacturing costs | $815,400 |
| Unit cost ($815,400/10,000 units) | $   81.54 |

## II. Calculation of Work in Process and Cost of Goods Sold with Multiple Jobs

Kennedy Kitchen and Bath (KKB) Company designs and installs upscale kitchens and bathrooms. On May 1, there were three jobs in process, Jobs 77, 78, and 79. During May, two more jobs were started, Jobs 80 and 81. By May 31, Jobs 77, 78, and 80 were completed. The following data were gathered:

| | Job 77 | Job 78 | Job 79 | Job 80 | Job 81 |
|---|---|---|---|---|---|
| May 1 balance | $875 | $1,140 | $410 | $    0 | $    0 |
| Direct materials | 690 | 320 | 500 | 3,500 | 2,750 |
| Direct labor | 450 | 420 | 80 | 1,800 | 1,300 |

Overhead is applied at the rate of 150% of direct labor cost. Jobs are sold at cost plus 30%. Operating expenses for May totaled $2,700.

### Required:

1.  Prepare job-order cost sheets for each job as of May 31.
2.  Calculate the ending balance in Work in Process (as of May 31) and Cost of Goods Sold for May.
3.  Construct an income statement for KKB for the month of May.

### Solution:

1.

| | Job 77 | Job 78 | Job 79 | Job 80 | Job 81 |
|---|---|---|---|---|---|
| May 1 balance | $  875 | $1,140 | $  410 | $    0 | $    0 |
| Direct materials | 690 | 320 | 500 | 3,500 | 2,750 |
| Direct labor | 450 | 420 | 80 | 1,800 | 1,300 |
| Applied overhead | 675 | 630 | 120 | 2,700 | 1,950 |
|   Totals | $2,690 | $2,510 | $1,110 | $8,000 | $6,000 |

2.  Ending Balance in Work in Process = Job 79 + Job 81

$$= \$1,110 + \$6,000$$
$$= \$7,110$$

Cost of Goods Sold for May = Job 77 + Job 78 + Job 80

$$= \$2,690 + \$2,510 + \$8,000$$
$$= \$13,200$$

3.

**Kennedy Kitchen and Bath Company**
**Income Statement**
**For the Month Ended May 31, 20XX**

| | |
|---|---:|
| Sales* | $17,160 |
| Cost of goods sold | 13,200 |
| Gross margin | $ 3,960 |
| Less: Operating expenses | 2,700 |
| Operating income | $ 1,260 |

\* Sales = $13,200 + 0.30($13,200) = $17,160

## III. Allocation: Direct and Sequential Methods

Barok Manufacturing produces machine parts on a job-order basis. Most business is obtained through bidding. Most firms competing with Barok bid full cost plus a 20% markup. Recently, with the expectation of gaining more sales, Barok reduced its markup from 25% to 20%. The company operates two service departments and two producing departments. The budgeted costs and the normal activity levels for each department are given below.

| | Service Departments | | Producing Departments | |
|---|---|---|---|---|
| | **A** | **B** | **C** | **D** |
| Direct overhead costs | $100,000 | $200,000 | $100,000 | $50,000 |
| Number of employees | 8 | 7 | 30 | 30 |
| Maintenance hours | 2,000 | 200 | 6,400 | 1,600 |
| Machine hours | — | — | 10,000 | 1,000 |
| Labor hours | — | — | 1,000 | 10,000 |

The direct costs of Department A are allocated on the basis of employees. The direct costs of Department B are allocated on the basis of maintenance hours. Departmental overhead rates are used to assign costs to products. Department C uses machine hours, and Department D uses labor hours.

The firm is preparing to bid on a job (Job K) that requires three machine hours per unit produced in Department C and no time in Department D. The expected prime costs per unit are $67.

### Required:

1. Allocate the service costs to the producing departments by using the direct method.
2. What will the bid be for Job K if the direct method of allocation is used?
3. Allocate the service costs to the producing departments by using the sequential method.
4. What will the bid be for Job K if the sequential method is used?

### Solution:

1.

| | Service Departments | | Producing Departments | |
|---|---|---|---|---|
| | **A** | **B** | **C** | **D** |
| Direct overhead costs | $ 100,000 | $ 200,000 | $100,000 | $ 50,000 |
| Department A[a] | (100,000) | — | 50,000 | 50,000 |
| Department B[b] | — | (200,000) | 160,000 | 40,000 |
| Total | $      0 | $      0 | $310,000 | $140,000 |

[a] Department A costs are allocated on the basis of the number of employees in the producing departments, Departments C and D. The percentage of Department A cost allocated to Department C = 30/(30 + 30) = 0.50. Cost of Department A allocated to Department C = 0.50 × $100,000 = $50,000. The percentage of Department A cost allocated to Department D = 30/(30 + 30) = 0.50. Cost of Department A allocated to Department D = 0.50 × $100,000 = $50,000.
[b] Department B costs are allocated on the basis of maintenance hours used in the producing departments, Departments C and D. The percentage of Department B cost allocated to Department C = 6,400/(6,400 + 1,600) = 0.80. Cost of Department B allocated to Department C = 0.80 × $200,000 = $160,000. The percentage of Department B cost allocated to Department D = 1,600/(6,400 + 1,600) = 0.20. Cost of Department B allocated to Department D = 0.20 × $200,000 = $40,000.

2. Department C: Overhead Rate = $310,000/10,000 mhrs = $31 per machine hour. Product cost and bid price:

| | |
|---|---|
| Prime cost | $ 67 |
| Overhead (3 × $31) | 93 |
| Total unit cost | $160 |

Bid Price = $160 × 1.20 = $192

3.

| | Service Departments | | Producing Departments | |
|---|---|---|---|---|
| | **A** | **B** | **C** | **D** |
| Direct overhead costs | $ 100,000 | $ 200,000 | $100,000 | $ 50,000 |
| Department B[a] | 40,000 | (200,000) | 128,000 | 32,000 |
| Department A[b] | (140,000) | — | 70,000 | 70,000 |
| Total | $      0 | $      0 | $298,000 | $152,000 |

[a] Department B ranks first because its direct costs are higher than those of Department A. Department B costs are allocated on the basis of maintenance hours used in Department A, and producing Departments C and D. Percent of Department B cost allocated to Department A is 0.20 [2,000/(2,000 + 6,400 + 1,600)]; cost of Department B allocated to Department A = 0.20 × $200,000 = $40,000. The percentage of Department B cost allocated to Department C = 6,400/(2,000 + 6,400 + 1,600) = 0.64. Cost of Department B allocated to Department C = 0.64 × $200,000 = $128,000. The percentage of Department B cost allocated to Department D = 1,600/(2,000 + 6,400 + 1,600) = 0.16. Cost of Department B allocated to Department D = 0.16 × $200,000 = $32,000.

[b] Department A costs are allocated on the basis of number of employees in the producing departments, Departments C and D. The percentage of Department A cost allocated to Department C = 30/(30 + 30) = 0.50. Cost of Department A allocated to Department C = 0.50 × $140,000 = $70,000. The percentage of Department A cost allocated to Department D = 30/(30 + 30) = 0.50. Cost of Department A allocated to Department D = 0.50 × $140,000 = $70,000. (Note: Department A cost is no longer $100,000. It is $140,000 due to the $40,000 that was allocated from Department B.)

4. Department C: Overhead Rate = $298,000/10,000 mhrs = $29.80 per machine hour. Product cost and bid price:

| | |
|---|---|
| Prime cost | $ 67.00 |
| Overhead (3 × $29.80) | 89.40 |
| Total unit cost | $156.40 |

Bid Price = $156.40 × 1.20 = $187.68

# DISCUSSION QUESTIONS

1. What are job-order costing and process costing? What types of firms use job-order costing? Process costing?

2. Give some examples of service firms that might use job-order costing, and explain why it is used in those firms.

3. What is normal costing? How does it differ from actual costing?

4. Why are actual overhead rates seldom used in practice?

5. Explain how overhead is assigned to production when a predetermined overhead rate is used.

6. What is underapplied overhead? When Cost of Goods Sold is adjusted for underapplied overhead, will the cost increase or decrease? Why?

7. What is overapplied overhead? When Cost of Goods Sold is adjusted for overapplied overhead, will the cost increase or decrease? Why?

8. Suppose that you and a friend decide to set up a lawn mowing service next summer. Describe the source documents that you would need to account for your activities.

9. Why might a company decide to use departmental overhead rates instead of a plantwide overhead rate?

10. What is the role of materials requisition forms in a job-order costing system? Time tickets? Predetermined overhead rates?

11. Carver Company uses a plantwide overhead rate based on direct labor cost. Suppose that during the year, Carver raises its wage rate for direct labor. How would that affect overhead applied? The total cost of jobs?

12. What is an overhead variance? How is it accounted for typically?

13. Is the cost of a job related to the price charged? Explain.

14. If a company decides to increase advertising expense by $25,000, how will that affect the predetermined overhead rate? Eventual cost of goods sold?

15. How can a departmental overhead system be converted to a plantwide overhead system?

16. (Appendix 5B) Describe the difference between producing and support departments.

17. (Appendix 5B) Assume that a company has decided not to allocate any support department costs to producing departments. Describe the likely behavior of the managers of the producing departments. Would this be good or bad? Explain why allocation would correct this type of behavior.

18. (Appendix 5B) Why is it important to identify and use causal factors to allocate support department costs?

19. (Appendix 5B) Identify some possible causal factors for the following support departments:
    a. Cafeteria
    b. Custodial services
    c. Laundry
    d. Receiving, shipping, and storage
    e. Maintenance
    f. Personnel
    g. Accounting

20. (Appendix 5B) Explain the difference between the direct method and the sequential method.

# MULTIPLE-CHOICE QUESTIONS

5-1 Which of the following statements is true?
   a. Job-order costing is used only in manufacturing firms.
   b. Process costing is used only for services.
   c. Job-order costing is simpler to use than process costing because the recordkeeping requirements are less.
   d. The job cost sheet is subsidiary to the work-in-process account.
   e. All of the above are true.

5-2 The ending balance of which of the following accounts is calculated by summing the totals of the open (unfinished) job-order cost sheets?
   a. Raw Materials
   b. Overhead Control
   c. Work in Process
   d. Finished Goods
   e. Cost of Goods Sold

5-3 In a normal costing system, the cost of a job includes
   a. actual direct materials, actual direct labor, and estimated (applied) overhead.
   b. estimated direct materials, estimated direct labor, and estimated overhead.
   c. actual direct materials, actual direct labor, actual overhead, and actual selling cost.
   d. actual direct materials, actual direct labor, and actual overhead.
   e. None of the above. Job-order costing requires the use of actual, not normal, costing.

5-4 The predetermined overhead rate equals
   a. actual overhead divided by actual activity level for a period.
   b. estimated overhead divided by estimated activity level for a period.
   c. actual overhead minus estimated overhead.
   d. actual overhead multiplied by actual activity level for a period.
   e. one-twelfth of estimated overhead.

**5-5** The job-order cost sheet is a subsidiary account to

   a.  Raw Materials.
   b.  Work in Process.
   c.  Finished Goods.
   d.  Cost of Goods Sold.
   e.  Jobs Started.

**5-6** Applied overhead is

   a.  an important part of normal costing.
   b.  never used in normal costing.
   c.  an important part of actual costing.
   d.  the predetermined overhead rate multiplied by estimated activity level.
   e.  the predetermined overhead rate multiplied by estimated activity level for the month.

**5-7** The overhead variance is overapplied if

   a.  actual overhead is less than applied overhead.
   b.  actual overhead is more than applied overhead.
   c.  applied overhead is less than actual overhead.
   d.  estimated overhead is less than applied overhead.
   e.  estimated overhead is more than applied overhead.

**5-8** Which of the following is typically a job-order costing firm?

   a.  Paint manufacturer
   b.  Pharmaceutical manufacturer
   c.  Cleaning products manufacturer
   d.  Cement manufacturer
   e.  Large regional medical center

**5-9** Which of the following is typically a process-costing firm?

   a.  Paint manufacturer
   b.  Custom cabinetmaker
   c.  Large regional medical center
   d.  Law office
   e.  Custom framing shop

**5-10** When materials are requisitioned for use in production in a job-order costing firm, the cost of materials is added to the

   a.  raw materials account.
   b.  work-in-process account.
   c.  finished goods account.
   d.  accounts payable account.
   e.  cost of goods sold account.

**5-11** When a job is completed, the total cost of the job is

   a.  subtracted from the raw materials account.
   b.  added to the work-in-process account.
   c.  added to the finished goods account.
   d.  added to the accounts payable account.
   e.  subtracted from the cost of goods sold account.

**5-12** The costs of a job are accounted for on the

   a.  materials requisition sheet.
   b.  time ticket.
   c.  requisition for overhead application.
   d.  sales invoice.
   e.  job-order cost sheet.

**5-13** Wilson Company has a predetermined overhead rate of $5 per direct labor hour. The job-order cost sheet for Job 145 shows 500 direct labor hours costing $10,000 and materials requisitions totaling $17,500. Job 145 had 1,000 units completed and transferred to Finished Goods. What is the cost per unit for Job 145?

   a.  $20
   b.  $17.50
   c.  $25
   d.  $30
   e.  $22,500

5-14 *(Appendix 5A)* When a job costing $2,000 is finished but not sold, the following journal entry is made:

| | | | |
|---|---|---|---|
| a. | Cost of Goods Sold | 2,000 | |
| | Finished Goods | | 2,000 |
| b. | Finished Goods | 2,000 | |
| | Cost of Goods Sold | | 2,000 |
| c. | Finished Goods | 2,000 | |
| | Work in Process | | 2,000 |
| d. | Work in Process | 2,000 | |
| | Finished Goods | | 2,000 |
| e. | Cost of Goods Sold | 2,000 | |
| | Sales | | 2,000 |

5-15 *(Appendix 5B)* Those departments responsible for creating products or services that are sold to customers are referred to as

   a.   profit making departments.
   b.   producing departments.
   c.   cost centers.
   d.   support departments.
   e.   None of these.

5-16 *(Appendix 5B)* Those departments that provide essential services to producing departments are referred to as

   a.   revenue generating departments.
   b.   support departments.
   c.   profit centers.
   d.   production departments.
   e.   None of these.

5-17 *(Appendix 5B)* An example of a producing department is

   a.   a materials storeroom.         d.   assembly.
   b.   the maintenance department.    e.   All of these.
   c.   engineering design.

5-18 *(Appendix 5B)* An example of a support department is

   a.   data processing.             d.   payroll.
   b.   personnel.                 e.   All of these.
   c.   a materials storeroom.

5-19 *(Appendix 5B)* The method that assigns support department costs only to producing departments in proportion to each department's usage of the service is known as

   a.   the sequential method.      d.   the direct method.
   b.   the proportional method.    e.   None of these.
   c.   the reciprocal method.

5-20 *(Appendix 5B)* The method that assigns support department costs by giving partial recognition to support department interactions is known as

   a.   the sequential method.      d.   the direct method.
   b.   the proportional method.    e.   None of these.
   c.   the reciprocal method.

5-21 *(Appendix 5B)* The method that assigns support department costs by giving full recognition to support department interactions is known as

   a.   the sequential method.      d.   the direct method.
   b.   the proportional method.    e.   None of these.
   c.   the reciprocal method.

# CORNERSTONE EXERCISES

**Cornerstone Exercise 5-22  Predetermined Overhead Rate, Overhead Application**

At the beginning of the year, Ilberg Company estimated the following costs:

| | |
|---|---|
| Overhead | $416,000 |
| Direct labor cost | 520,000 |

Ilberg uses normal costing and applies overhead on the basis of direct labor cost. (Direct labor cost is equal to total direct labor hours worked multiplied by the wage rate.) For the month of December, direct labor cost was $43,700.

**Required:**

1. Calculate the predetermined overhead rate for the year.
2. Calculate the overhead applied to production in December.

OBJECTIVE 2
CORNERSTONE 5.1

**Cornerstone Exercise 5-23  Overhead Variance (Over- or Underapplied), Closing to Cost of Goods Sold**

At the end of the year, Ilberg Company provided the following actual information:

| | |
|---|---|
| Overhead | $423,600 |
| Direct labor cost | 532,000 |

Ilberg uses normal costing and applies overhead at the rate of 80% of direct labor cost. At the end of the year, Cost of Goods Sold (before adjusting for any overhead variance) was $1,890,000.

**Required:**

1. Calculate the overhead variance for the year.
2. Dispose of the overhead variance by adjusting Cost of Goods Sold.

OBJECTIVE 2
CORNERSTONE 5.2

---

*Use the following information for Cornerstone Exercises 5-24 and 5-25:*
At the beginning of the year, Hallett Company estimated the following:

| | Cutting Department | Sewing Department | Total |
|---|---|---|---|
| Overhead | $240,000 | $350,000 | $590,000 |
| Direct labor hours | 31,200 | 100,000 | 131,200 |
| Machine hours | 150,000 | — | 150,000 |

---

**Cornerstone Exercise 5-24  Predetermined Departmental Overhead Rates, Applying Overhead to Production**

Refer to the information for Hallett Company above. Hallett uses departmental overhead rates. In the cutting department, overhead is applied on the basis of machine hours. In the sewing department, overhead is applied on the basis of direct labor hours. Actual data for the month of June are as follows:

| | Cutting Department | Sewing Department | Total |
|---|---|---|---|
| Overhead | $20,610 | $35,750 | $56,360 |
| Direct labor hours | 2,800 | 8,600 | 11,400 |
| Machine hours | 13,640 | — | 13,640 |

**Required:**

1. Calculate the predetermined overhead rates for the cutting and sewing departments.
2. Calculate the overhead applied to production in each department for the month of June.
3. By how much has each department's overhead been overapplied? Underapplied?

OBJECTIVE 2
CORNERSTONE 5.3

CORNERSTONE 5.4

### Cornerstone Exercise 5-25   Convert Departmental Data to Plantwide Data, Plantwide Overhead Rate, Apply Overhead to Production

Refer to the information in **Cornerstone Exercise 5-24** for data. Now, assume that Hallett has decided to use a plantwide overhead rate based on direct labor hours.

**Required:**

1. Calculate the predetermined plantwide overhead rate. (*Note:* Round to the nearest cent.)
2. Calculate the overhead applied to production for the month of June.
3. Calculate the overhead variance for the month of June.

CORNERSTONE 5.5

### Cornerstone Exercise 5-26   Prepare Job-Order Cost Sheets, Predetermined Overhead Rate, Ending Balance of WIP, Finished Goods, and COGS

At the beginning of June, Rhone Company had two jobs in process, Job 44 and Job 45, with the following accumulated cost information:

|                  | Job 44  | Job 45  |
|------------------|---------|---------|
| Direct materials | $5,100  | $1,500  |
| Direct labor     | 1,200   | 3,000   |
| Applied overhead | 780     | 1,950   |
| Balance, June 1  | $7,080  | $6,450  |

During June, two more jobs (46 and 47) were started. The following direct materials and direct labor costs were added to the four jobs during the month of June:

|                  | Job 44  | Job 45  | Job 46  | Job 47  |
|------------------|---------|---------|---------|---------|
| Direct materials | $2,500  | $7,110  | $1,800  | $1,700  |
| Direct labor     | 800     | 6,400   | 900     | 560     |

At the end of June, Jobs 44, 45, and 47 were completed. Only Job 45 was sold. On June 1, the balance in Finished Goods was zero.

**Required:**

1. Calculate the overhead rate based on direct labor cost. (*Note:* Round to three decimal places.)
2. Prepare a brief job-order cost sheet for the four jobs. Show the balance as of June 1 as well as direct materials and direct labor added in June. Apply overhead to the four jobs for the month of June, and show the ending balances.
3. Calculate the ending balances of Work in Process and Finished Goods as of June 30.
4. Calculate the Cost of Goods Sold for June.

---

*Use the following information for Cornerstone Exercises 5-27 and 5-28:*
Quillen Company manufactures a product in a factory that has two producing departments, Cutting and Sewing, and two support departments, S1 and S2. The activity driver for S1 is number of employees, and the activity driver for S2 is number of maintenance hours. The following data pertain to Quillen:

|                     | Support Departments | | Producing Departments | |
|---------------------|----------|----------|----------|----------|
|                     | **S1**   | **S2**   | **Cutting** | **Sewing** |
| Direct costs        | $180,000 | $150,000 | $122,000 | $90,500  |
| Normal activity:    |          |          |          |          |
| Number of employees | —        | 30       | 63       | 147      |
| Maintenance hours   | 1,200    | —        | 16,000   | 4,000    |

### Cornerstone Exercise 5-27    *(Appendix 5B)* Assigning Support Department Costs by Using The Direct Method

OBJECTIVE 6
CORNERSTONE 5.6

Refer to the information for Quillen Company on the previous page.

**Required:**

1. Calculate the cost assignment ratios to be used under the direct method for Departments S1 and S2. (*Note:* Each support department will have two ratios—one for Cutting and the other for Sewing.)
2. Allocate the support department costs to the producing departments by using the direct method.

### Cornerstone Exercise 5-28    *(Appendix 5B)* Sequential Method

OBJECTIVE 6
CORNERSTONE 5.7

Refer to the information for Quillen Company on the previous page. Now assume that Quillen uses the sequential method to allocate support department costs. S1 is allocated first, then S2.

**Required:**

1. Calculate the cost assignment ratios to be used under the sequential method for S2, Cutting, and Sewing. Carry out your answers to four decimal places.
2. Allocate the overhead costs to the producing departments by using the sequential method.

# EXERCISES

### Exercise 5-29    Job-Order Costing versus Process Costing

OBJECTIVE 1

a.  Hospital services
b.  Custom cabinet making
c.  Toy manufacturing
d.  Soft-drink bottling
e.  Airplane manufacturing (e.g., 767s)
f.  Personal computer assembly
g.  Furniture making (e.g., computer desks sold at discount stores)
h.  Custom furniture making
i.  Dental services
j.  Paper manufacturing
k.  Nut and bolt manufacturing
l.  Auto repair
m.  Architectural services
n.  Landscape design services
o.  Flashlight manufacturing

**Required:**

Identify each of these preceding types of businesses as either job-order or process costing.

### Exercise 5-30    Job-Order Costing versus Process Costing

OBJECTIVE 1

a.  Auto manufacturing
b.  Dental services
c.  Auto repair
d.  Costume making

**Required:**

**CONCEPTUAL CONNECTION** For each of the given types of industries, give an example of a firm that would use job-order costing. Then, give an example of a firm that would use process costing.

### Exercise 5-31    Calculating the Predetermined Overhead Rate, Applying Overhead to Production

OBJECTIVE 2

At the beginning of the year, Debion Company estimated the following:

| | |
|---|---|
| Overhead | $522,900 |
| Direct labor hours | 83,000 |

*(Continued)*

Debion uses normal costing and applies overhead on the basis of direct labor hours. For the month of March, direct labor hours were 7,600.

**Required:**

1. Calculate the predetermined overhead rate for Debion.
2. Calculate the overhead applied to production in March.

OBJECTIVE  **Exercise 5-32   Calculating the Predetermined Overhead Rate, Applying Overhead to Production, Reconciling Overhead at the End of the Year, Adjusting Cost of Goods Sold for Under- and Overapplied Overhead**

At the beginning of the year, Horvath Company estimated the following:

| | |
|---|---|
| Overhead | $486,400 |
| Direct labor hours | 95,000 |

Horvath uses normal costing and applies overhead on the basis of direct labor hours. For the month of January, direct labor hours were 7,830. By the end of the year, Horvath showed the following actual amounts:

| | |
|---|---|
| Overhead | $476,100 |
| Direct labor hours | 93,500 |

Assume that unadjusted Cost of Goods Sold for Horvath was $707,000.

**Required:**

1. Calculate the predetermined overhead rate for Horvath.
2. Calculate the overhead applied to production in January. (*Note:* Round to the nearest dollar.)
3. Calculate the total applied overhead for the year. Was overhead over- or underapplied? By how much?
4. Calculate adjusted Cost of Goods Sold after adjusting for the overhead variance.

OBJECTIVE **2** **Exercise 5-33   Calculating Departmental Overhead Rates and Applying Overhead to Production**

At the beginning of the year, Glaser Company estimated the following:

| | Assembly Department | Testing Department | Total |
|---|---|---|---|
| Overhead | $338,000 | $630,000 | $968,000 |
| Direct labor hours | 130,000 | 40,000 | 170,000 |
| Machine hours | 45,000 | 120,000 | 165,000 |

Glaser uses departmental overhead rates. In the assembly department, overhead is applied on the basis of direct labor hours. In the testing department, overhead is applied on the basis of machine hours. Actual data for the month of March are as follows:

| | Assembly Department | Testing Department | Total |
|---|---|---|---|
| Overhead | $29,850 | $58,000 | $87,850 |
| Direct labor hours | 11,700 | 3,450 | 15,150 |
| Machine hours | 4,100 | 10,900 | 15,000 |

**Required:**

1. Calculate the predetermined overhead rates for the assembly and testing departments.
2. Calculate the overhead applied to production in each department for the month of March.
3. By how much has each department's overhead been overapplied? Underapplied?

## Exercise 5-34 Job-Order Costing Variables

On July 1, Job 46 had a beginning balance of $1,235. During July, prime costs added to the job totaled $560. Of that amount, direct materials were three times as much as direct labor. The ending balance of the job was $1,921.

**Required:**

1. What was overhead applied to the job during July?
2. What was direct materials for Job 46 for July? Direct labor?
3. Assuming that overhead is applied on the basis of direct labor cost, what is the overhead rate for the company? (*Note:* Round your answer to two decimal places.)

## Exercise 5-35 Source Documents

For each of the following independent situations, give the source document that would be referred to for the necessary information.

**Required:**

1. Direct materials costing $460 are requisitioned for use on a job.
2. Greiner's Garage uses a job-order costing system. Overhead is applied to jobs based on direct labor hours. Which source document gives the number of direct labor hours worked on Job 2005-276?
3. Pasilla Investigative Services bills clients on a monthly basis for costs to date. Job 3-48 involved an investigator following the client's business partner for a week by automobile. Mileage is billed at number of miles times $0.75.
4. The foreman on the Jackson job wonders what the actual direct materials cost was for that job.

## Exercise 5-36 Applying Overhead to Jobs, Costing Jobs

Jagjit Company designs and builds retaining walls for individual customers. On August 1, there were two jobs in process: Job 93 with a beginning balance of $8,750, and Job 94 with a beginning balance of $7,300. Jagjit applies overhead at the rate of $8 per direct labor hour. Direct labor wages average $18 per hour.

Data on August costs for all jobs are as follows:

|                   | Job 93 | Job 94 | Job 95 | Job 96 |
|-------------------|--------|--------|--------|--------|
| Direct materials  | $ 950  | $4,500 | $3,300 | $1,300 |
| Direct labor cost | 2,160  | 5,400  | 2,610  | 900    |

During August, Jobs 95 and 96 were started. Job 93 was completed on August 17, and the client was billed at cost plus 40%. All other jobs remained in process.

**Required:**

1. Calculate the number of direct labor hours that were worked on each job in August.
2. Calculate the overhead applied to each job during the month of August.
3. Prepare job-order cost sheets for each job as of the end of August.
4. Calculate the balance in Work in Process on August 31.
5. What is the price of Job 93?
6. **CONCEPTUAL CONNECTION** Partway though the year, Jagjit bought a bulldozer to handle larger jobs. The bulldozer cost $38,000 and is needed for larger commercial jobs. Smaller residential jobs can still be done with the smaller bobcat tractor. How could the bulldozer's cost be applied to only those jobs that need the larger equipment?

## Exercise 5-37 Applying Overhead to Jobs, Costing Jobs

Gorman Company builds internal conveyor equipment to client specifications. On October 1, Job 877 was in process with a cost of $18,640 to date.

*(Continued)*

During October, Jobs 878, 879, and 880 were started. Data on costs added during October for all jobs are as follows:

|  | Job 877 | Job 878 | Job 879 | Job 880 |
|---|---|---|---|---|
| Direct materials | $14,460 | $6,000 | $3,500 | $1,800 |
| Direct labor | 14,800 | 8,500 | 1,750 | 2,150 |

Overhead is applied to production at the rate of 80% of direct labor cost. Job 877 was completed on October 28, and the client was billed at cost plus 50%. All other jobs remained in process.

**Required:**

1. Prepare a brief job-order cost sheet showing the October 1 balances of all four jobs, plus the direct materials and direct labor costs during October. (*Note:* There is no need to calculate applied overhead at this point or to total the costs.)
2. Calculate the overhead applied to each job during October.
3. Calculate the balance in Work in Process on October 31.
4. What is the price of Job 877?

OBJECTIVE ④   **Exercise 5-38   Balance of Work in Process and Finished Goods, Cost of Goods Sold**

Derry Company uses job-order costing. At the end of the month, the following information was gathered:

| Job # | Total Cost | Complete? | Sold? |
|---|---|---|---|
| 301 | $1,600 | Yes | No |
| 302 | 1,240 | Yes | Yes |
| 303 | 780 | No | No |
| 304 | 2,300 | Yes | No |
| 305 | 4,150 | Yes | No |
| 306 | 350 | No | No |
| 307 | 710 | Yes | Yes |
| 308 | 620 | No | No |
| 309 | 1,200 | No | No |
| 310 | 515 | No | No |

The beginning balance of Finished Goods was $300, consisting of Job 300 which was not sold by the end of the month.

**Required:**

1. Calculate the balance in Work in Process at the end of the month.
2. Calculate the balance in Finished Goods at the end of the month.
3. Calculate Cost of Goods Sold for the month.

OBJECTIVE ④   **Exercise 5-39   Job-Order Cost Sheets, Balance in Work in Process and Finished Goods**

Golding Company, a job-order costing firm, worked on three jobs in July. Data are as follows:

|  | Job 106 | Job 107 | Job 108 |
|---|---|---|---|
| Balance, July 1 | $21,310 | $ 6,250 | $    0 |
| Direct materials | $10,450 | $12,300 | $16,150 |
| Direct labor | $16,000 | $12,200 | $24,000 |
| Machine hours | 500 | 300 | 1,000 |

Overhead is applied to jobs at the rate of $16 per machine hour. By July 31, Jobs 106 and 108 were completed. Jobs 102 and 106 were sold. Job 107 remained in process. On July 1, the balance in Finished Goods was $49,000 (consisting of Job 102 for $25,600 and Job 104 for $23,400).

Golding prices its jobs at cost plus 30%. During July, variable marketing expenses were 5% of sales, and fixed marketing expenses were $2,000; administrative expenses were $4,800. (Round all amounts to the nearest dollar.)

**Required:**

1. Prepare job-order cost sheets for all jobs in process during July, showing all costs through July 31.
2. Calculate the balance in Work in Process on July 31.
3. Calculate the balance in Finished Goods on July 31.
4. Calculate Cost of Goods Sold for July.
5. Calculate operating income for Golding Company for the month of July.

### Exercise 5-40    Cost Flows

OBJECTIVE **4**

*ILLUSTRATING RELATIONSHIPS*

Consider the following independent jobs. Overhead is applied in Department 1 at the rate of $6 per direct labor hour. Overhead is applied in Department 2 at the rate of $8 per machine hour. Direct labor wages average $10 per hour in each department.

|  | Job 213 | Job 214 | Job 217 | Job 225 |
|---|---|---|---|---|
| Total sales revenue | $? | $4,375 | $5,600 | $1,150 |
| Price per unit | $12 | $? | $14 | $5 |
| Materials used in production | $365 | $? | $488 | $207 |
| Department 1, direct labor cost | $? | $700 | $2,000 | $230 |
| Department 1, machine hours | 15 | 35 | 50 | 12 |
| Department 2, direct labor cost | $50 | $100 | $? | $0 |
| Department 2, machine hours | 25 | 50 | ? | ? |
| Department 1, overhead applied | $90 | $? | $1,200 | $138 |
| Department 2, overhead applied | $? | $400 | $160 | $0 |
| Total manufacturing cost | $855 | $3,073 | $? | $575 |
| Number of units | ? | 350 | 400 | ? |
| Unit cost | $8.55 | $? | $9.87 | $? |

**Required:**

Fill in the missing data for each job.

### Exercise 5-41    Job Cost Flows

OBJECTIVE **4**

Roseler Company uses a normal job-order costing system. The company has two departments through which most jobs pass. Overhead is applied using a plantwide overhead rate of $10 per direct labor hour. During the year, several jobs were completed. Data pertaining to one such job, Job 9-601, follow:

| | |
|---|---|
| Direct materials | $12,000 |
| Direct labor cost: | |
| Department A (450 hours @ $18) | $8,100 |
| Department B (120 hours @ $18) | $2,160 |
| Machine hours used: | |
| Department A | 200 |
| Department B | 800 |
| Units produced | 1,000 |

**Required:**

1. Compute the total cost of Job 9-601.
2. Compute the per-unit manufacturing cost for Job 9-601.

---

*For Requirements 3 and 4, assume that Roseler uses departmental overhead rates. In Department A, overhead is applied at the rate of $3 per direct labor hour. In Department B, overhead is applied at the rate of $7 per machine hour.*

---

*(Continued)*

3. Compute the total cost of Job 9-601.
4. Compute the per-unit manufacturing cost for Job 9-601.

OBJECTIVE 4    **Exercise 5-42   Calculation of Work in Process and Cost of Goods Sold with Multiple Jobs**

Ensign Landscape Design designs landscape plans and plants the material for clients. On April 1, there were three jobs in process, Jobs 39, 40, and 41. During April, two more jobs were started, Jobs 42 and 43. By April 30, Jobs 40, 41, and 43 were completed and sold. The following data were gathered:

|  | Job 39 | Job 40 | Job 41 | Job 42 | Job 43 |
|---|---|---|---|---|---|
| Balance, April 1 | $540 | $3,400 | $2,990 | — | — |
| Direct materials | 700 | 560 | 375 | $3,500 | $6,900 |
| Direct labor | 500 | 600 | 490 | 2,500 | 3,000 |

Overhead is applied at the rate of 110% of direct labor cost. Jobs are sold at cost plus 30%. Selling and administrative expenses for April totaled $4,575. (Round all amounts to the nearest dollar.)

**Required:**

1. Prepare job-order cost sheets for each job as of April 30.
2. Calculate the ending balance in Work in Process (as of April 30) and Cost of Goods Sold for April.
3. Construct an income statement for Ensign Landscape Design for the month of April.

OBJECTIVE 5    **Exercise 5-43   *(Appendix 5A)* Journal Entries**

Yurman Inc. uses a job-order costing system. During the month of May, the following transactions occurred:

a. Purchased materials on account for $29,670.
b. Requisitioned materials totaling $24,500 for use in production. Of the total, $9,200 was for Job 58, $8,900 for Job 59, and the remainder for Job 60.
c. Incurred direct labor for the month of $32,400, with an average wage of $18 per hour. Job 58 used 800 hours; Job 59, 600 hours; and Job 60, 400 hours.
d. Incurred and paid actual overhead of $17,880 (credit Various Payables).
e. Charged overhead to production at the rate of $4.80 per direct labor hour.
f. Completed and transferred Jobs 58 and 59 to Finished Goods.
g. Sold Job 57 (see beginning balance of Finished Goods) and Job 58 to their respective clients on account for a price of cost plus 40%.

Beginning balances as of May 1 were:

| Materials | $ 2,300 |
|---|---|
| Work in Process | 0 |
| Finished Goods (Job 57) | 25,600 |

**Required:**

1. Prepare the journal entries for Transactions a through g.
2. Prepare brief job-order cost sheets for Jobs 58, 59, and 60.
3. Calculate the ending balance of Raw Materials.
4. Calculate the ending balance of Work in Process.
5. Calculate the ending balance of Finished Goods.

OBJECTIVE 6    **Exercise 5-44   *(Appendix 5B)* Direct Method of Support Department Cost Allocation**

Stevenson Company is divided into two operating divisions: Battery and Small Motors. The company allocates power and general factory costs to each operating division using the direct method. Power costs are allocated on the basis of the number of machine hours and general factory costs on the basis of square footage. Support department cost allocations using the direct method are based on the following data:

| | Support Departments | | Operating Divisions | |
| | Power | General Factory | Battery | Small Motors |
|---|---|---|---|---|
| Overhead costs | $160,000 | $430,000 | $163,000 | $84,600 |
| Machine hours | 2,000 | 2,000 | 7,000 | 1,000 |
| Square footage | 1,000 | 1,500 | 5,000 | 15,000 |
| Direct labor hours | | | 18,000 | 60,000 |

**Required:**

1. Calculate the allocation ratios for Power and General Factory. (*Note:* Carry these calculations out to four decimal places.)
2. Allocate the support service costs to the operating divisions. (*Note:* Round all amounts to the nearest dollar.)
3. Assume divisional overhead rates are based on direct labor hours. Calculate the overhead rate for the Battery Division and for the Small Motors Division. (*Note:* Round overhead rates to the nearest cent.)

### Exercise 5-45    *(Appendix 5B)* Sequential Method of Support Department Cost Allocation

OBJECTIVE ➎ 6

Refer to **Exercise 5-44** for data. Now assume that Stevenson uses the sequential method to allocate support department costs to the operating divisions. General Factory is allocated first in the sequential method for the company.

**Required:**

1. Calculate the allocation ratios for Power and General Factory. (*Note:* Carry these calculations out to four decimal places.)
2. Allocate the support service costs to the operating divisions. (*Note:* Round all amounts to the nearest dollar.)
3. Assume divisional overhead rates are based on direct labor hours. Calculate the overhead rate for the Battery Division and for the Small Motors Division. (*Note:* Round overhead rates to the nearest cent.)

# PROBLEMS

### Problem 5-46    Overhead Application and Job-Order Costing

OBJECTIVE ➋ ➍

Heurion Company is a job-order costing firm that uses a plantwide overhead rate based on direct labor hours. Estimated information for the year is as follows:

| | |
|---|---|
| Overhead | $789,000 |
| Direct labor hours | 100,000 |

Heurion worked on five jobs in July. Data are as follows:

| | Job 741 | Job 742 | Job 743 | Job 744 | Job 745 |
|---|---|---|---|---|---|
| Balance, July 1 | $29,870 | $55,215 | $27,880 | $0 | $0 |
| Direct materials | $25,500 | $39,800 | $14,450 | $13,600 | $ 8,420 |
| Direct labor cost | $61,300 | $48,500 | $28,700 | $24,500 | $21,300 |
| Direct labor hours | 4,000 | 3,400 | 1,980 | 1,600 | 1,400 |

By July 31, Jobs 741 and 743 were completed and sold. The remaining jobs were in process.

*(Continued)*

**Required:**

1. Calculate the plantwide overhead rate for Heurion Company. (*Note:* Round to the nearest cent.)
2. Prepare job-order cost sheets for each job showing all costs through July 31. (*Note:* Round all amounts to the nearest dollar.)
3. Calculate the balance in Work in Process on July 31.
4. Calculate Cost of Goods Sold for July.

OBJECTIVE ① ③

### Problem 5-47    Job Cost, Source Documents

Spade Millhone Detective Agency performs investigative work for a variety of clients. Recently, Alban Insurance Company asked Spade Millhone to investigate a series of suspicious claims for whiplash. In each case, the claimant was driving on a freeway and was suddenly rear-ended by an Alban-insured client. The claimants were all driving old, uninsured automobiles. The Alban clients reported that the claimants suddenly changed lanes in front of them, and the accidents were unavoidable. Alban suspected that these "accidents" were the result of insurance fraud. Basically, the claimants cruised the freeways in virtually worthless cars, attempting to cut in front of expensive late-model cars that would surely be insured. Alban believed that the injuries were faked.

Rex Spade spent 37 hours shadowing the claimants and taking pictures as necessary. His surveillance methods located the office of a doctor used by all claimants. He also took pictures of claimants performing tasks that they had sworn were now impossible to perform due to whiplash injuries. Victoria Millhone spent 48 hours using the Internet to research court records in surrounding states to locate the names of the claimants and their doctors. She found a pattern of similar insurance claims for each of the claimants.

Spade Millhone Detective Agency bills clients for detective time at $120 per hour. Mileage is charged at $0.50 per mile. The agency logged in 510 miles on the Alban job. The film and developing amounted to $120.

**Required:**

1. Prepare a job-order cost sheet for the Alban job.
2. **CONCEPTUAL CONNECTION** Why is overhead not specified in the charges? How does Spade Millhone charge clients for the use of overhead (e.g., the ongoing costs of their office—supplies, paper for notes and reports, telephone, utilities)?
3. The mileage is tallied from a source document. Design a source document for this use, and make up data for it that would total the 510 miles driven on the Alban job.

OBJECTIVE ④

### Problem 5-48    Calculating Ending Work in Process, Income Statement

Pavlovich Prosthetics Company produces artificial limbs for individuals. Each prosthetic is unique. On January 1, three jobs, identified by the name of the person being fitted with the prosthetic, were in process with the following costs:

|                    | Carter   | Pelham   | Tillson  |
|--------------------|----------|----------|----------|
| Direct materials   | $ 210    | $ 615    | $1,290   |
| Direct labor       | 440      | 700      | 1,260    |
| Applied overhead   | 374      | 595      | 1,071    |
| Total              | $1,024   | $1,910   | $3,621   |

During the month of January, two more jobs were started, Jasper and Dashell. Materials and labor costs incurred by each job in January are as follows:

|         | Materials | Direct Labor |
|---------|-----------|--------------|
| Carter  | $ 600     | $ 300        |
| Pelham  | 550       | 200          |
| Tillson | 770       | 240          |
| Jasper  | 2,310     | 2,100        |
| Dashell | 190       | 240          |

Tillson and Jasper's prosthetics were completed and sold by January 31.

**Required:**

1.  If overhead is applied on the basis of direct labor dollars, what is the overhead rate? (*Note:* Round your answer to four decimal places.)
2.  Prepare simple job-order cost sheets for each of the five jobs in process during January. (*Note:* Round all amounts to the nearest dollar.)
3.  What is the ending balance of Work in Process on January 31? What is the Cost of Goods Sold in January?
4.  Suppose that Pavlovich Prosthetics Company prices its jobs at cost plus 30%. In addition, during January, marketing and administrative expenses of $2,635 were incurred. Prepare an income statement for the month of January.

## Problem 5-49   Overhead Applied to Jobs, Departmental Overhead Rates

 OBJECTIVE **2**

Xania Inc. uses a normal job-order costing system. Currently, a plantwide overhead rate based on machine hours is used. Xania's plant manager has heard that departmental overhead rates can offer significantly better cost assignments than a plantwide rate can offer. Xania has the following data for its two departments for the coming year:

|                                   | Department A | Department B |
|-----------------------------------|--------------|--------------|
| Overhead costs (expected)         | $75,000      | $33,000      |
| Normal activity (machine hours)   | 10,000       | 8,000        |

**Required:**

1.  Compute a predetermined overhead rate for the plant as a whole based on machine hours.
2.  Compute predetermined overhead rates for each department using machine hours. (*Note:* Carry your calculations out to three decimal places.)
3.  **CONCEPTUAL CONNECTION** Job 73 used 20 machine hours from Department A and 50 machine hours from Department B. Job 74 used 50 machine hours from Department A and 20 machine hours from Department B. Compute the overhead cost assigned to each job using the plantwide rate computed in Requirement 1. Repeat the computation using the departmental rates found in Requirement 2. Which of the two approaches gives the fairer assignment? Why? (*Note:* Round cost to the nearest cent.)
4.  **CONCEPTUAL CONNECTION** Repeat Requirement 3, assuming the expected overhead cost for Department B is $60,000 (not $33,000). For this company, would you recommend departmental rates over a plantwide rate? (*Note:* Round overhead rates to the nearest cent.)

## Problem 5-50   Overhead Rates, Unit Costs

 OBJECTIVE **2**

Folsom Company manufactures specialty tools to customer order. There are three producing departments. Departmental information on budgeted overhead and various activity measures for the coming year is as follows:

|                     | Welding   | Assembly  | Finishing |
|---------------------|-----------|-----------|-----------|
| Estimated overhead  | $220,000  | $62,000   | $150,000  |
| Direct labor hours  | 4,500     | 10,000    | 6,000     |
| Direct labor cost   | $90,000   | $150,000  | $120,000  |
| Machine hours       | 5,000     | 1,000     | 2,000     |

Currently, overhead is applied on the basis of machine hours using a plantwide rate. However, Janine, the controller, has been wondering whether it might be worthwhile to use departmental overhead rates. She has analyzed the overhead costs and drivers for the various departments and decided that Welding and Finishing should base their overhead rates on machine hours and that Assembly should base its overhead rate on direct labor hours.

*(Continued)*

Janine has been asked to prepare bids for two jobs with the following information:

|  | Job 1 | Job 2 |
|---|---|---|
| Direct materials | $6,725 | $9,340 |
| Direct labor cost | $1,800 | $3,100 |
| Direct labor hours: | | |
|   Welding | 20 | 10 |
|   Assembly | 60 | 20 |
|   Finishing | 20 | 70 |
| Number of machine hours: | | |
|   Welding | 50 | 50 |
|   Assembly | 60 | 25 |
|   Finishing | 90 | 125 |

The typical bid price includes a 35% markup over full manufacturing cost. Round all overhead rates to the nearest cent. Round all bid prices to the nearest dollar.

**Required:**

1. Calculate a plantwide rate for Folsom Company based on machine hours. What is the bid price of each job using this rate?
2. Calculate departmental overhead rates for the producing departments. What is the bid price of each job using these rates?

OBJECTIVE ② ④

### Problem 5-51    Calculate Job Cost and Use It to Calculate Price

Suppose that back in the 1970s, Steve was asked to build speakers for two friends. The first friend, Jan, needed a speaker for her band. The second friend, Ed, needed a speaker built into the back of his hatchback automobile. Steve figured the following costs for each:

|  | Jan's Job | Ed's Job |
|---|---|---|
| Materials | $50 | $75 |
| Labor hours | 10 | 20 |

Steve knew that Jan's job would be easier, since he had experience in building the type of speaker she needed. Her job would not require any special equipment or specialized fitting. Ed's job, on the other hand, required specialized design and precise fitting. Steve thought he might need to build a mock-up of the speaker first, to fit it into the space. In addition, he might have to add to his tool collection to complete the job. Normally, Steve figured a wage rate of $6 per hour and charged 20% of labor and materials as an overhead rate.

**Required:**

1. Prepare job-order cost sheets for the two jobs, showing total cost.
2. **CONCEPTUAL CONNECTION** Which cost do you think is more likely to be accurate? How might Steve build in some of the uncertainty of Ed's job into a budgeted cost?

OBJECTIVE ④ ⑤

### Problem 5-52    *(Appendix 5A)* Unit Cost, Ending Work in Process, Journal Entries

During August, Leming Inc. worked on two jobs. Data relating to these two jobs follow:

|  | Job 64 | Job 65 |
|---|---|---|
| Units in each order | 50 | 80 |
| Units sold | 50 | — |
| Materials requisitioned | $3,560 | $785 |
| Direct labor hours | 410 | 583 |
| Direct labor cost | $6,720 | $9,328 |

Overhead is assigned on the basis of direct labor hours at a rate of $11. During August, Job 64 was completed and transferred to Finished Goods. Job 65 was the only unfinished job at the end of the month.

**Required:**

1. Calculate the per-unit cost of Job 64.
2. Compute the ending balance in the work-in-process account.
3. Prepare the journal entries reflecting the completion and sale on account of Job 64. The selling price is 175% of cost. (*Note:* Round all journal entry amounts to the nearest dollar.)

**Problem 5-53   (Appendix 5A) Journal Entries, Job Costs**                    OBJECTIVE ❹ ❺

The following transactions occurred during the month of April for Nelson Company:

a.  Purchased materials costing $4,610 on account.
b.  Requisitioned materials totaling $4,800 for use in production, $3,170 for Job 518 and the remainder for Job 519.
c.  Recorded 65 hours of direct labor on Job 518 and 90 hours on Job 519 for the month. Direct laborers are paid at the rate of $14 per hour.
d.  Applied overhead using a plantwide rate of $6.20 per direct labor hour.
e.  Incurred and paid in cash actual overhead for the month of $973.
f.  Completed and transferred Job 518 to Finished Goods.
g.  Sold on account Job 517, which had been completed and transferred to Finished Goods in March, for cost ($2,770) plus 25%.

**Required:**

1. Prepare journal entries for Transactions a through e.
2. Prepare job-order cost sheets for Jobs 518 and 519. Prepare journal entries for Transactions f and g. (*Note:* Round to the nearest dollar.)
3. Prepare a schedule of cost of goods manufactured for April. Assume that the beginning balance in the raw materials account was $1,025 and that the beginning balance in the work-in-process account was zero.

**Problem 5-54   (Appendix 5A) Predetermined Overhead Rates, Variances, Cost Flows**    OBJECTIVE ❷ ❹ ❺

Barrymore Costume Company, located in New York City, sews costumes for plays and musicals. Barrymore considers itself primarily a service firm, as it never produces costumes without a preexisting order and only purchases materials to the specifications of the particular job. Any finished goods ending inventory is temporary and is zeroed out as soon as the show producer pays for the order. Overhead is applied on the basis of direct labor cost. During the first quarter of the year, the following activity took place in each of the accounts listed:

| Work in Process | | | | Finished Goods | | | |
|---|---|---|---|---|---|---|---|
| Bal. | 17,000 | Complete | 245,000 | Bal. | 40,000 | Sold | 210,000 |
| DL | 80,000 | | | Complete | 245,000 | | |
| OH | 140,000 | | | Bal. | 75,000 | | |
| DM | 40,000 | | | | | | |
| Bal. | 32,000 | | | | | | |

| Overhead | | | Cost of Goods Sold | |
|---|---|---|---|---|
| | 138,500 | 140,000 | 210,000 | |
| | | Bal. 1,500 | | |

Job 32 was the only job in process at the end of the first quarter. A total of 1,000 direct labor hours at $10 per hour were charged to Job 32.

**Required:**

1. Assuming that overhead is applied on the basis of direct labor cost, what was the overhead rate used during the first quarter of the year?

*(Continued)*

2.  What was the applied overhead for the first quarter? The actual overhead? The under- or overapplied overhead?
3.  What was the cost of the goods manufactured for the quarter?
4.  Assume that the overhead variance is closed to the cost of goods sold account. Prepare the journal entry to close out the overhead control account. What is the adjusted balance in Cost of Goods Sold?
5.  For Job 32, identify the costs incurred for direct materials, direct labor, and overhead.

OBJECTIVE ❷❹❺     ### Problem 5-55    *(Appendix 5A)* Overhead Application, Journal Entries, Job Cost

At the beginning of the year, Smith Company budgeted overhead of $129,600 as well as 13,500 direct labor hours. During the year, Job K456 was completed with the following information: direct materials cost, $2,750; direct labor cost, $5,355. The average wage for Smith Company employees is $17 per hour.

By the end of the year, 18,100 direct labor hours had actually been worked, and Smith incurred the following actual overhead costs for the year:

| | |
|---|---|
| Equipment lease | $ 6,800 |
| Depreciation on building | 19,340 |
| Indirect labor | 90,400 |
| Utilities | 14,560 |
| Other overhead | 41,400 |

**Required:**

1.  Calculate the overhead rate for the year.
2.  Calculate the total cost of Job K456.
3.  Prepare the journal entries to record actual overhead and to apply overhead to production for the year.
4.  Is overhead overapplied or underapplied? By how much?
5.  Assuming that the normal cost of goods sold for the year is $635,600, what is the adjusted cost of goods sold?

OBJECTIVE ❶❹❺     ### Problem 5-56    *(Appendix 5A)* Journal Entries, T-Accounts

Lowder Inc. builds custom conveyor systems for warehouses and distribution centers. During the month of July, the following occurred:

a.  Purchased materials on account for $42,630.
b.  Requisitioned materials totaling $27,000 for use in production: $12,500 for Job 703 and the remainder for Job 704.
c.  Recorded direct labor payroll for the month of $26,320 with an average wage of $14 per hour. Job 703 required 780 direct labor hours; Job 704 required 1,100 direct labor hours.
d.  Incurred and paid actual overhead of $19,950.
e.  Charged overhead to production at the rate of $10 per direct labor hour.
f.  Completed Job 703 and transferred it to Finished Goods.
g.  Kept Job 704, which was started during July, in process at the end of the month.
h.  Sold Job 700, which had been completed in May, on account for cost plus 30%.

Beginning balances as of July 1 were:

| | |
|---|---|
| Raw Materials | $ 6,070 |
| Work in Process (for Job 703) | 10,000 |
| Finished Goods (for Job 700) | 6,240 |

**Required:**

1.  Prepare the journal entries for Events a through e.
2.  Prepare simple job-order cost sheets for Jobs 703 and 704.

# EXPERIENCE MANAGERIAL DECISIONS
## with BP

The only consideration that most people give to gasoline is the price charged at the local pump. However, **BP**, one of the largest energy companies in the world, has been thinking about this issue and a lot more for quite a long time. BP was founded in 1901 after William D'Arcy obtained permission from the shah of Persia to dig for oil in what is now the Iranian desert. BP drastically expanded its reach and, as of the early 21st century, had active excavation and production occurring in 22 countries. BP runs its processes nonstop—24 hours a day, 365 days a year—to produce to full capacity, which represents 2.6 million barrels of oil each day or approximately 30 barrels every second. Producing that much of anything is mind-boggling, which hints at the importance of BP's effective process-costing system in determining the costs associated with its numerous products, which include gasoline, heating fuel, greases, and asphalt.

In order to determine costs for a particular process, BP needs to know the total costs of production and the total number of units processed in a specified period of time. The costs include raw crude oil, which varies widely from sweet West Texas crude to heavier Canadian crude, plus labor and management overhead. Other costs include catalysts, which enhance the reactivity to make a molecule turn

*"By calculating process costs and carefully setting production levels and product mixes, BP is able to manage this complex process at its facilities around the globe."*

into something else, and chemicals, which become part of the final product. BP goes to a lot of trouble to combine its process-costing system outputs, current market prices, and a linear programming model in order to calculate the most profitable mix of products to produce from a given mix of raw crude materials. Determining the costs associated with running a refinery with a continuous production process is complex. However, by calculating process costs and carefully setting production levels and product mixes, BP is able to manage this complex process at its facilities around the globe, thereby providing significant profits for use in future energy discovery, distribution efforts, and unexpected and costly events such as the 2010 oil gusher in the Gulf of Mexico.

The recent oil rig explosion and subsequent oil gusher in the Gulf of Mexico have caused tremendous political and financial stress for BP and will continue to do so for some time. The costs associated with stopping the oil from gushing, subsequent cleanup, and ultimate reparations to businesses affected by the gusher are already huge and likely to continue increasing. The image and goodwill of BP have also been negatively impacted. The ultimate effect on BP is not yet known, but BP's ability to deal with these issues is certainly related to the company's significant profitability.

# CHARACTERISTICS OF PROCESS MANUFACTURING

As illustrated by **BP**, production processes help determine the best way of accounting for its costs. For example, BP's refinery in Whiting, Indiana can process up to 400,000 barrels of crude oil per day. A barrel of crude oil is refined into a number of different products such as gasoline, heating oil, greases, and asphalts. In this setting, a large number of similar products pass through an identical set of processes. Since each product within a product line passing through the processes would receive similar "doses" of materials, labor, and overhead, there is no need to accumulate costs by batches (as a job-order costing system does). Instead, costs are accumulated by process. Process costing works well whenever relatively homogeneous products pass through a series of processes and receive similar amounts of manufacturing costs.

Consider the process-costing environment of Healthblend Nutritional Supplements, a company which manufactures minerals, herbs, and vitamins. Healthblend uses the following three processes:

- *Mixing or Picking*: In the mixing or picking department for a given product, the appropriate herbs, vitamins, minerals, and inert materials (typically some binder such as cornstarch) are selected, measured in the prescribed proportions, and then combined in a mixer to blend them thoroughly. When the mix is complete, the resulting mixture is sent to the encapsulation department.
- *Encapsulating*: In encapsulating, the vitamin, mineral, or herb blend is loaded into a machine that fills one-half of a gelatin capsule. The filled half is matched to another half of the capsule, and a safety seal is applied. This process is entirely mechanized. Overhead in this department consists of depreciation on machinery, maintenance of machinery, supervision, fringe benefits, lights, and power. Finally, the filled capsules are transferred to the bottling department.
- *Bottling*: In the bottling department, the capsules are loaded into a hopper, automatically counted into bottles, which are then mechanically capped. Workers then manually pack the correct number of bottles into boxes to ship to retailers.

## Types of Processes

Production at Healthblend is an example of sequential processing. **Sequential processing** requires that units pass through one process before they can be worked on in the next process in the sequence. Exhibit 6.1 shows the sequential pattern of the manufacture of Healthblend's minerals, herbs, and vitamins.

Thus, in a process firm, units typically pass through a series of producing departments where each department or process brings a product one step closer to completion. In each department, materials, labor, and overhead may be needed. Upon completion of a particular process, the partially completed goods are transferred to the next

( EXHIBIT 6.1 )

**Sequential Processing Illustrated**

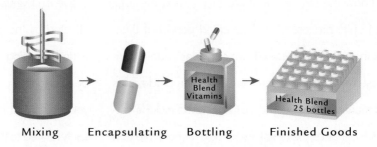

Mixing    Encapsulating    Bottling    Finished Goods

© Cengage Learning 2014

department. After passing through the final department, the goods are completed and transferred to the warehouse.

**Parallel processing** is another processing pattern that requires two or more sequential processes to produce a finished good. Partially completed units (e.g., two subcomponents) can be worked on simultaneously in different processes and then brought together in a final process for completion. Consider, for example, the manufacture of hard disk drives for personal computers. In one series of processes, write heads and cartridge disk drives are produced, assembled, and tested. In a second series of processes, printed circuit boards are produced and tested. These two major subcomponents then come together for assembly in the final process. Exhibit 6.2 portrays this type of process pattern. Notice that the write head and drive processes can occur independently of (or parallel to) the circuit board production and testing processes.

---

( **EXHIBIT 6.2** )

**Parallel Processing Illustrated**

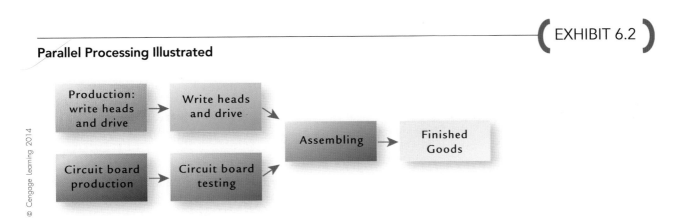

© Cengage Learning 2014

---

Other forms of parallel processes also exist. However, regardless of which processing pattern exists within a firm, all units produced share a common property. Since units are homogeneous and subjected to the same operations for a given process, each unit produced in a period should receive the same unit cost. Understanding how unit costs are computed requires an understanding of the manufacturing cost flows that take place in a process-costing firm.

## How Costs Flow through the Accounts in Process Costing

The manufacturing cost flows for a process-costing system are generally the same as those for a job-order system. As raw materials are purchased, the cost of these materials flows into a raw materials inventory account. Similarly, raw materials, direct labor, and applied overhead costs flow into a work-in-process (WIP) account. When goods are completed, the cost of the completed goods is transferred from WIP to the finished goods account. Finally, as goods are sold, the cost of the finished goods is transferred to the cost of goods sold account. The journal entries generally parallel those described in a job-order costing system.

Although job-order and process cost flows are generally similar, some differences exist. In process costing, each producing department has its own WIP account. As goods are completed in one department, they are transferred to the next department. The costs attached to the goods transferred out are also transferred to the next department. Exhibit 6.3 illustrates this process for Healthblend. By the end of the process, all manufacturing costs end up in the final department (here, bottling) with the final product.

### concept Q&A

Will process costing be the same for sequential and parallel processing systems?

**Answer:**

Yes. Process-costing procedures are the same for both process settings. Costs are collected by process and are assigned to units produced by the process. Each process undergoes this costing action regardless of whether it is a member of a sequential or a parallel process system. Once goods are costed, they are transferred out to the next process.

( EXHIBIT 6.3 )

### Flow of Manufacturing Costs through the Accounts of a Process-Costing Firm

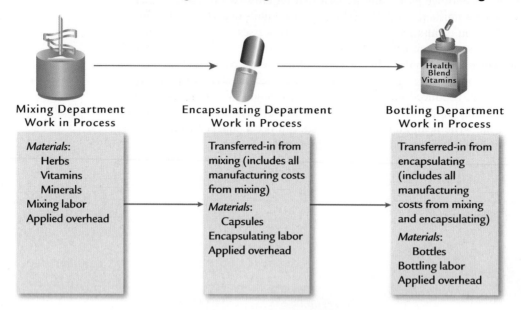

Cornerstone 6.1 attaches costs to the various departments and shows how the costs flow from one department to the next.

## 6.1

## Calculating Cost Flows without Work in Process Inventories

**Why:**

In process costing, each department (process) accumulates its costs in a WIP account. When the work is finsihed in a process, the units and their associated costs are transferred to the next department. Costs are transferred by debiting the WIP account of the department receiving the units and crediting the WIP account of the transferring department.

**Information:**

Suppose that Healthblend decides to produce 2,000 bottles of multivitamins with the following costs (there is no beginning or ending work in process for each department):

|  | Mixing Department | Encapsulating Department | Bottling Department |
|---|---|---|---|
| Direct materials | $1,700 | $1,000 | $800 |
| Direct labor | 50 | 60 | 300 |
| Applied overhead | 450 | 500 | 600 |

**Required:**

1. Calculate the costs transferred out of each department.

2. Prepare journal entries that reflect these cost transfers.

*(Continued)*

**Solution:**

1.

|  | Mixing Department | Encapsulating Department | Bottling Department |
|---|---|---|---|
| Direct materials | $1,700 | $1,000 | $800 |
| Direct labor | 50 | 60 | 300 |
| Applied overhead | 450 | 500 | 600 |
| Costs added | $2,200 | $1,560 | $1,700 |
| Costs transferred in | 0 | 2,200 | 3,760 |
| Costs transferred out | $2,200 | $3,760 | $5,460 |

2.

| | | |
|---|---|---|
| Work in Process (Encapsulating) | 2,200 | |
|     Work in Process (Mixing) | | 2,200 |
| Work in Process (Bottling) | 3,760 | |
|     Work in Process (Encapsulating) | | 3,760 |
| Finished Goods | 5,460 | |
|     Work in Process (Bottling) | | 5,460 |

CORNERSTONE

**6.1**

*(Continued)*

Cornerstone 6.1 shows that when the multivitamin mixture is transferred from the mixing department to the encapsulating department, it takes $2,200 of cost along with it. **Transferred-in costs** are costs transferred from a prior process to a subsequent process. For the subsequent process, transferred-in costs are a type of raw material cost. The same relationship exists between the encapsulating and bottling departments. The completed bottles of multivitamins are transferred to the finished goods warehouse at a total cost of $5,460.

## Accumulating Costs in the Production Report

In process costing, costs are accumulated by department for a period of time. The **production report** is the document that summarizes the manufacturing activity that takes place in a process department for a given period of time. A production report contains information on costs transferred in from prior departments as well as costs added in the department such as direct materials, direct labor, and overhead; similar to the job-order cost sheet, it is subsidiary to the WIP account.

A production report provides information about the physical units processed in a department and their associated manufacturing costs. Thus, a production report is divided into the following sections and subdivisions:

- *Unit information section*: The unit information section has two major subdivisions:
  - units to account for
  - units accounted for
- *Cost information section*: The cost information section has two major subdivisions:
  - costs to account for
  - costs accounted for

A production report traces the flow of units through a department, identifies the costs charged to the department, shows the computation of unit costs, and reveals the disposition of the department's costs for the reporting period.

## Service and Manufacturing Firms

Any product or service that is basically homogeneous and repetitively produced can take advantage of a process-costing approach. Let's look at three possibilities: services, manufacturing firms with a just-in-time (JIT) orientation, and traditional manufacturing firms.

**Service Firms**  Check processing in a bank, teeth cleaning by a hygienist, air travel between Dallas and Los Angeles, and sorting mail by zip code are examples of homogeneous services that are repetitively produced. It is possible for firms engaged in service production to have WIP inventories. For example, a batch of tax returns can be partially completed at the end of a period. However, many services are provided so quickly that there are no WIP inventories. Teeth cleaning, funerals, surgical operations, and carpet cleaning are a few examples where WIP inventories virtually would be nonexistent. Therefore, process costing for services is relatively simple. The total costs for the period are divided by the number of services provided to compute unit cost:

$$\text{Unit Cost} = \frac{\text{Total Costs for the Period}}{\text{Number of Services Provided}}$$

**Manufacturing Firms Using JIT**  Manufacturing firms may also operate without significant WIP inventories. Specifically, firms that have adopted a JIT approach try to reduce WIP inventories to very low levels. Furthermore, JIT firms usually structure their manufacturing so that process costing can be used to determine product costs.

In many JIT firms, work cells are created that produce a product or subassembly from start to finish. Costs are collected by cell for a period of time, and output for the cell is measured for the same period. Unit cost is computed by dividing the costs of the period by output of the period:

$$\text{Unit Cost} = \frac{\text{Total Costs for the Period}}{\text{Total Output of the Period}}$$

There is no ambiguity concerning what costs belong to the period and how output is measured. This simplification illustrates one of the significant benefits of JIT.

**Traditional Manufacturing Firms**  On the other hand, traditional manufacturing firms may have significant beginning and ending WIP inventories. This causes complications in process costing due to several factors such as the presence of beginning and ending WIP inventories and different approaches to the treatment of beginning inventory cost. These complicating factors are discussed in the following sections.

OBJECTIVE ②

Define *equivalent units* and explain their role in process costing. Explain the differences between the weighted average method and the FIFO method of accounting for process costs.

# THE IMPACT OF WORK-IN-PROCESS INVENTORIES ON PROCESS COSTING

The computation of unit cost for the work performed during a period is a key part of the production report. This unit cost is needed both to compute the cost of goods transferred out of a department and to value **ending work-in-process (EWIP)** inventory, the incomplete units on hand at the end of the period. Conceptually, calculating the unit cost is easy—just divide total cost by the number of units produced. However, the presence of WIP inventories causes two problems:

- Defining the units produced can be difficult, given that some units produced during a period are complete, while those in ending inventory are not. This is handled through the concept of equivalent units of production.

- How should the costs and work of **beginning work-in-process (BWIP)**, incomplete units on hand at the beginning of the period, be treated? Should they be counted with the current period work and costs or treated separately? Two methods have been developed to solve this problem: the weighted average method and the FIFO method.

## Equivalent Units of Production

By definition, EWIP is not complete. Thus, a unit completed and transferred out during the period is not identical (or equivalent) to one in EWIP inventory, and the cost attached to the two units should not be the same. In computing the unit cost, the output of the period must be defined, a significant issue for process costing.

To illustrate, assume that Department A had the following data for October:

| | |
|---|---|
| Units in BWIP | — |
| Units completed | 1,000 |
| Units in EWIP (25% complete) | 600 |
| Total manufacturing costs | $11,500 |

What is the output in October for this department? 1,000? 1,600? If the answer is 1,000 units, the effort expended on the units in EWIP is ignored. The manufacturing costs incurred in October belong to both the units completed and to the partially completed units in EWIP. Yet, if the answer is 1,600 units, the fact that the 600 units in EWIP are only partially completed is ignored. Therefore, output must be measured so that it reflects the effort expended on both completed and partially completed units.

The solution is to calculate equivalent units of output. **Equivalent units of output** are the complete units that could have been produced given the total amount of manufacturing effort expended for the period under consideration. Determining equivalent units of output for transferred-out units is easy; a unit would not be transferred out unless it was complete. Thus, every transferred-out unit is an equivalent unit. Units remaining in EWIP inventory, however, are not complete. Thus, someone in production must "eyeball" EWIP to estimate its degree of completion. Cornerstone 6.2 illustrates how to calculate equivalent units of production.

## Calculating Equivalent Units of Production: No Beginning Work in Process

**CORNERSTONE**

**6.2**

**Why:**

Output is the total work of a period and is measured by equivalent units. Equivalent units of output are the complete units that could have been produced given the manufacturing inputs used as illustrated by the following diagram:

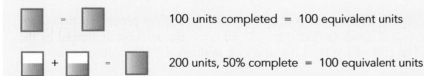

100 units completed = 100 equivalent units

200 units, 50% complete = 100 equivalent units

*Note:* Equivalent Units = Units Completed + Units in EWIP × Fraction Complete

**Information:**

October data: 1,000 units completed; 600 units, 25% complete

*(Continued)*

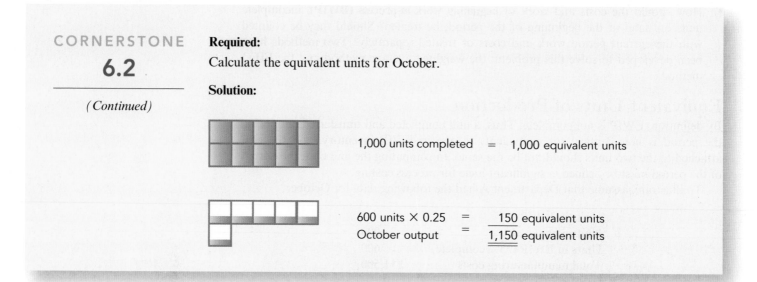

**CORNERSTONE**

**6.2**

*(Continued)*

**Required:**

Calculate the equivalent units for October.

**Solution:**

1,000 units completed  =  1,000 equivalent units

600 units × 0.25  =  150 equivalent units
October output  =  1,150 equivalent units

**ETHICAL DECISIONS**   Estimating the degree of completion is an act that requires judgment and ethical behavior. Overestimating the degree of completion will increase the equivalent units of output and decrease per-unit costs. This outcome, in turn, would cause an increase in both income (cost of goods sold will be less) and in assets (WIP cost will increase). Deliberately overestimating the degree of completion would clearly be in violation of ethical professional practice. ●

Knowing the output for a period and the manufacturing costs for the department for that period, a unit cost can be calculated as:

$$\text{Unit Cost} = \frac{\text{Total Cost}}{\text{Equivalent Units}}$$

The unit cost can then be used to determine the cost of units transferred out and the cost of the units in EWIP. Cornerstone 6.3 shows how the calculations are done when there is no BWIP.

**CORNERSTONE**

**6.3**

## Measuring Output and Assigning Costs: No Beginning Work in Process

**Why:**

Unit cost is calculated by dividing the cost of the period for a given process by the output of the period. The cost of goods (services) transferred out is the unit cost multiplied by the units completed. The cost of EWIP is the unit cost multiplied by the *equivalent units* in EWIP.

**Information:**

Manufacturing costs of the period, $11,500; units transferred out, 1,000; units in EWIP, 600 (25% complete).

*(Continued)*

**Required:**

1. Calculate the unit cost.

2. Calculate the cost of goods transferred out and the cost of EWIP.

**Solution:**

1.

| | |
|---|---|
| Units completed | 1,000 |
| Units in EWIP × 25% (600 × 0.25) | 150 |
| Equivalent units | 1,150 |

$$\text{Cost per Equivalent Unit} = \frac{\text{Total Cost}}{\text{Equivalent Units}}$$

$$\text{Cost per Equivalent Unit} = \frac{\$11,500}{1,150 \text{ units}} = \$10$$

2. Cost of Goods Transferred Out = $10 per unit × 1,000 equivalent units = $10,000

Cost of EWIP = $10 per unit × 150 equivalent units = $1,500

In Cornerstone 6.3, the unit cost of $10 is used to assign a cost of $10,000 ($10 × 1,000) to the 1,000 units transferred out and a cost of $1,500 ($10 × 150) to the 600 units in EWIP. Notice that the cost of the EWIP is obtained by multiplying the unit cost by the *equivalent* units, not the actual number of partially completed units.

## Two Methods of Treating Beginning Work-in-Process Inventory

The calculations illustrated by Cornerstones 6.2 and 6.3 become more complicated when there are BWIP inventories. The work done on these partially completed units represents prior-period work, and the costs assigned to them are prior-period costs. In computing a current-period unit cost for a department, two approaches have evolved for dealing with the prior-period output and prior-period costs found in BWIP:

- The **weighted average costing method** combines beginning inventory costs and work done with current-period costs and work to calculate this period's unit cost. In essence, the costs and work carried over from the prior period are counted as if they belong to the current period. Thus, beginning inventory work and costs are pooled with current work and costs, and an average unit cost is computed and applied to both units transferred out and units remaining in ending inventory.
- The **FIFO costing method** separates work and costs of the equivalent units in beginning inventory from work and costs of the equivalent units produced during the current period. Only current work and costs are used to calculate this period's unit cost. It is assumed that units from beginning inventory are completed first and transferred out. The costs of these units include the costs of the work done in the prior period as well as the current-period costs necessary to complete the units. Units started in the current period are divided into two categories: units started and completed and units started but not finished (EWIP). Units in both of these categories are valued using the current period's cost per equivalent unit.

### concept Q&A

What is the key difference between FIFO and the weighted average costing methods?

**Answer:**

FIFO treats work and costs in BWIP separately from the work and costs of the current period. Weighted average rolls back and picks up the work and costs of BWIP and counts them as if they belong to the current period's work and costs.

If product costs do not change from period to period, or if there is no BWIP inventory, the FIFO and weighted average methods yield the same results. The weighted average method is discussed in more detail in the next section. Further discussion of the FIFO method is found in Appendix 6A.

# YOU DECIDE   Estimating the Degree of Completion

You are the cost accounting manager for a plant that produces riding lawn mowers. The plant manager receives a bonus at the end of each quarter if the plant's income meets or exceeds the quarter's budgeted income. The plant had no work in process at the beginning of the quarter; however, it had 2,500 partially completed units at the end of the quarter. During the quarter, 4,000 units were completed and sold. Manufacturing costs for the quarter totaled $2,750,000. The production line supervisors estimated that the units in process at the end of the quarter were 40% finished. Using this initial estimate, the income for the quarter was $190,000 less than the quarter's budgeted profit. After seeing this tentative result, the plant manager approaches you and argues that the degree of the completion is underestimated and that it should be 60% and not 40%. He explains that he personally examined the partially completed work and that 60% is his best guess. He would prefer that this new estimate be used.

**What effect does the estimated degree of completion have on the quarter's income? Should you use the new estimate?**

The two estimates produce significantly different unit costs, as illustrated below:

| Measure | Equation | 40% degree of completion | 60% degree of completion |
|---|---|---|---|
| Total equivalent units | Equivalent Units<br>= Units Completed + (Units in EWIP<br>× Fraction Complete) | 4,000 + (0.40 × 2,500)<br>= 5,000 equivalent units | 4,000 + (0.60 × 2,500)<br>= 5,500 equivalent units |
| Unit cost | Unit Cost<br>= Total Cost/Equivalent Units | $2,750,000/5,000<br>= $550 | $2,750,000/5,500<br>= $500 |
| Cost of goods sold | Cost of Goods Sold<br>= Units Sold × Unit Cost | 4,000 × $550<br>= $2,200,000 | 4,000 × $500<br>= $2,000,000 |

Compared to the 40% estimate, the 60% estimate increases income by $200,000.

Whether or not, as the cost accounting manager, you would feel comfortable using the new estimate depends on several factors. First, is the 60% estimate better than the 40% estimate? (Suppose the line supervisors insist that their estimate is correct?) Second, does the plant manager regularly participate in estimating degree of completion? If not, what are the motives for doing so this time? Answers to these questions are important. The estimate by the plant manager allows income to increase by a sufficient amount to qualify him for a bonus. If evidence favors the 40% estimate and the plant manager's motive is the bonus, then an ethical dilemma exists. In this case, you would need to follow the organization's established policies on the resolution of such conflicts.

**Estimating the degree of completion is a vital and important part of process costing and needs to be done with care and honesty.**

OBJECTIVE 3

Prepare a departmental production report using the weighted average method.

# WEIGHTED AVERAGE COSTING

The weighted average costing method treats beginning inventory costs and the accompanying equivalent output as if they belong to the current period. This is done for costs by adding the manufacturing costs in BWIP to the manufacturing costs incurred during the current period. The total cost is treated as if it were the current period's total manufacturing cost. Similarly, beginning inventory output and current period output are merged in the calculation of equivalent units. Under the weighted average method, equivalent units of output are computed by adding units completed to equivalent units in EWIP. Notice that the equivalent units in BWIP are included in the computation. Consequently, these units are counted as part of the current period's equivalent units of output.

# Overview of the Weighted Average Method

The essential conceptual and computational features of the weighted average method are illustrated in Cornerstone 6.4 , which uses production data for Healthblend's mixing department for July. The objective is to calculate a unit cost for July and to use this unit cost to value goods transferred out and EWIP.

## Measuring Output and Assigning Costs: Weighted Average Method

CORNERSTONE

6.4

**Why:**

The weighted average method counts prior-period work and costs in BWIP *as if they belong* to the current period. Thus, equivalent units are the units completed of the period plus the equivalent units in EWIP. The unit cost is obtained by dividing the sum of the costs in BWIP and the the current-period costs by the weighted average equivalent units. The resulting unit cost is a blend of the prior-period unit cost and the actual current-period unit cost. Weighted-average valuation of goods transferred out and EWIP follows the same approach described in Cornerstone 6.3 (p. 238).

**Information:**

| | |
|---|---|
| Production: | |
| Units in process, July 1, 75% complete | 20,000 gallons |
| Units completed and transferred out | 50,000 gallons |
| Units in process, July 31, 25% complete | 10,000 gallons |
| Costs: | |
| Work in process, July 1 | $3,525 |
| Costs added during July | $10,125 |

**Required:**

1. Calculate an output measure for July.

2. Assign costs to units transferred out and EWIP using the weighted average method.

**Solution:**

1. *Key:* ▢ = 10,000 units completed    ▢ = 10,000 units, 25% complete

   *Output for July*:

   60,000 total units ⟶ Become 52,500 equivalent units

   Units completed:
   BWIP:

   ▢▢                              = 20,000

   Units Started and Completed:

   ▢▢▢                             = 30,000        50,000

   + EWIP, 25% complete:

   ▢                               =               2,500

   Equivalent Units                               52,500

*(Continued)*

CORNERSTONE
**6.4**
───────
*(Continued)*

2.

Cost/Equivalent Units = $13,650/52,500 units = $0.26 cost per equivalent unit

| | |
|---|---:|
| Transferred out ($0.26 × 50,000) | $13,000 |
| EWIP ($0.26 × 2,500) | 650 |
| Total cost assigned | $13,650 |

Cornerstone 6.4 illustrates that costs from BWIP are pooled with costs added to production during July. These total pooled costs ($13,650) are divided by output to obtain a unit cost which is then used to assign costs to units transferred out and to units in EWIP. On the output side, it is necessary to concentrate on the degree of completion of all units at the *end* of the period. There is no need to be concerned with the percentage of completion of BWIP inventory. The only issue is whether these units are complete or not by the end of July. Thus, equivalent units are computed by pooling manufacturing efforts from June and July.

## Five Steps in Preparing a Production Report

The elements of Cornerstone 6.4 are used to prepare a production report. Recall that the production report summarizes cost and manufacturing activity for a producing department for a given period of time. The production report is subsidiary to the WIP account for a department. The following five steps describe the general pattern of a process-costing production report:

**Step 1.** physical flow analysis
**Step 2.** calculation of equivalent units
**Step 3.** computation of unit cost
**Step 4.** valuation of inventories (goods transferred out and EWIP)
**Step 5.** cost reconciliation

These five steps provide structure to the method of accounting for process costs.

**Step 1: Physical Flow Analysis**   The purpose of Step 1 is to trace the physical units of production. Physical units are not equivalent units. They are units that may be in any stage of completion. The **physical flow schedule**, like the one shown by Cornerstone 6.5 for Healthblend's mixing department, provides an analysis of the physical flow of units. To construct the schedule from the information given, the following two calculations are needed:

> Units Started and Completed = Total Units Completed − Units in BWIP
>
> Units Started = Units Started and Completed + Units in EWIP

## Preparing a Physical Flow Schedule

CORNERSTONE

**6.5**

**Why:**

The physical flow schedule traces the units in process regardless of their stage of completion. It has two parts: (1) units to account for and (2) units accounted for. In the first part, the units started and units in BWIP are listed. In the second part, the units are accounted for by listing the units completed and transferred out and the units started but not completed (EWIP).

**Information:**

| Production: | |
|---|---|
| Units in process, July 1, 75% complete | 20,000 gallons |
| Units completed and transferred out | 50,000 gallons |
| Units in process, July 31, 25% complete | 10,000 gallons |

**Required:**

Prepare a physical flow schedule.

**Solution:**

$$\text{Units Started and Completed} = \text{Units Completed} - \text{Units in BWIP}$$
$$= 50,000 - 20,000$$
$$= 30,000$$
$$\text{Units Started} = \text{Units Started and Completed} + \text{Units in EWIP}$$
$$= 30,000 + 10,000$$
$$= 40,000$$

| Physical flow schedule: | | |
|---|---|---|
| Units to account for: | | |
| Units in BWIP (75% complete) | 20,000 | |
| Units started during the period | 40,000 | |
| Total units to account for | 60,000 | |
| Units accounted for: | | |
| Units completed and transferred out: | | |
| Started and completed | 30,000 | |
| From beginning work in process | 20,000 | 50,000 |
| Units in EWIP (25% complete) | | 10,000 |
| Total units accounted for | | 60,000 |

Notice from Cornerstone 6.5 that the "Total units to account for" must equal the "Total units accounted for." The physical flow schedule is important because it contains the information needed to calculate equivalent units (Step 2).

**Step 2: Calculation of Equivalent Units** Given the information in the physical flow schedule, the weighted average equivalent units for July can be calculated as follows:

Notice that July's output is measured as 52,500 units, 50,000 units completed and transferred out and 2,500 equivalent units from ending inventory (10,000 × 25%). What about beginning inventory? There were 20,000 units in beginning inventory, 75% complete. These units are included in the 50,000 units completed and transferred out during the month. Thus, the weighted average method treats beginning inventory units as if they were started and completed during the current period. Because of this, the equivalent unit schedule shown in Step 2 shows only the total units completed. There is no need to show whether the units completed are from July or from BWIP as was done by Cornerstone 6.4 (p. 241).

**Step 3: Computation of Unit Cost** In addition to July output, July manufacturing costs are needed to compute a unit cost. The weighted average method rolls back and includes the manufacturing costs associated with the units in BWIP and counts these costs as if they belong to July. Thus, as Cornerstone 6.4 illustrated, these costs are pooled to define total manufacturing costs for July:

$$\text{Total Manufacturing Costs for July} = \text{BWIP, July} + \text{Costs Added in July}$$
$$\$13,650 = \$3,525 + \$10,125$$

The manufacturing costs carried over from the prior period ($3,525) are treated as if they were current period costs. The unit cost for July is computed as follows:

$$\text{Unit Cost} = \text{Total Costs/Equivalent Units for July}$$
$$\$0.26 = \$13,650/52,500$$

**Step 4: Valuation of Inventories** Cornerstone 6.4 also showed how to value goods transferred out and EWIP. Using the unit cost of $0.26, we value the two inventories as follows:

- Cost of goods transferred to the encapsulating department is $13,000 (50,000 units × $0.26 per unit)
- Cost of EWIP is $650 (2,500 equivalent units × $0.26 per unit).

Units completed (from Step 1), equivalent units in EWIP (from Step 2), and the unit cost (from Step 3) are all needed to value both goods transferred out and EWIP.

**Step 5: Cost Reconciliation** The total manufacturing costs assigned to inventories are as follows:

| | |
|---|---:|
| Goods transferred out | $13,000 |
| Goods in EWIP | 650 |
| Total costs accounted for | $13,650 |

The manufacturing costs to account for are also $13,650.

| | |
|---|---:|
| BWIP | $ 3,525 |
| Incurred during the period | 10,125 |
| Total costs to account for | $13,650 |

Thus, **cost reconciliation** checks to see if the costs to account for are exactly assigned to inventories. Remember, the total costs assigned to goods transferred out and to EWIP must agree with the total costs in BWIP and the manufacturing costs incurred during the current period.

## Production Report

Steps 1 through 5 provide all of the information needed to prepare a production report for the mixing department for July. The method for preparing this report is shown in Cornerstone 6.6 .

# Preparing a Production Report: Weighted Average Method

**CORNERSTONE**

**6.6**

**Why:**

A production report has two sections: (1) a unit information section and (2) a cost information section. The unit information section presents the physical flow schedule and the equivalent units schedule. The cost information section also has two major subdivisions: (1) costs to account for and (2) costs accounted for. The first cost subdivision includes the calculation of the unit cost, and the second subdivision includes the valuation of goods transferred out and EWIP.

**Information:**

Refer to Steps 1 to 5 of the Healthblend Company example.

**Required:**

Prepare a production report.

**Solution:**

|  |
|---|
| **Healthblend Company**<br>**Mixing Department**<br>**Production Report For July 2013**<br>**(Weighted Average Method)** |
| **UNIT INFORMATION** |

***Physical Flow***

| Units to account for: | | Units accounted for: | |
|---|---|---|---|
| Units in beginning work in process | 20,000 | Units completed | 50,000 |
| Units started | 40,000 | Units in ending work in process | 10,000 |
| Total units to account for | 60,000 | Total units accounted for | 60,000 |

***Equivalent Units***

| | |
|---|---|
| Units completed | 50,000 |
| Units in ending work in process | 2,500 |
| Total equivalent units | 52,500 |

| **COST INFORMATION** |
|---|

| Costs to account for: | |
|---|---|
| Beginning work in process | $ 3,525 |
| Incurred during the period | 10,125 |
| Total costs to account for | $13,650 |
| Cost per equivalent unit | $  0.26 |

| Costs accounted for: | Transferred Out | Ending Work in Process | Total |
|---|---|---|---|
| Goods transferred out ($0.26 × 50,000) | $13,000 | — | $13,000 |
| Goods in ending work in process ($0.26 × 2,500) | — | $650 | 650 |
| Total costs accounted for | $13,000 | $650 | $13,650 |

## Evaluation of the Weighted Average Method

The major benefit of the weighted average method is simplicity. By treating units in BWIP as belonging to the current period, all equivalent units belong to the same category when it comes to calculating unit costs. Thus, unit cost computations are simplified. The main disadvantage of this method is reduced accuracy in computing unit costs for current period output and for units in BWIP. If the unit cost in a process is relatively stable from one period to the next, the weighted average method is reasonably accurate. However, if the price of manufacturing inputs increases significantly from one period to the next, the unit cost of current output is understated, and the unit cost of BWIP units is overstated. If greater accuracy in computing unit costs is desired, a company should use the FIFO method to determine unit costs.

**OBJECTIVE ❹**

Explain how nonuniform inputs and multiple processing departments affect process costing.

# MULTIPLE INPUTS AND MULTIPLE DEPARTMENTS

Accounting for production under process costing is complicated by nonuniform application of manufacturing inputs and the presence of multiple processing departments. How process-costing methods address these complications will now be discussed.

## Nonuniform Application of Manufacturing Inputs

Up to this point, we have assumed that WIP being 60% complete meant that 60% of materials, labor, and overhead needed to complete the process have been used and that another 40% are needed to finish the units. In other words, we have assumed that manufacturing inputs are applied uniformly as the manufacturing process unfolds.

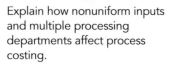

## Here's The Real Kicker

**Stillwater Designs** builds a limited number of items on site. The manufacturing activities include designing and building prototypes and rebuilding of warranty returns (only of certain models such as the square L7s). Rebuilding of warranty returns follows a process manufacturing structure. All units are alike and go through the same steps.

- The woofers are removed from the cabinet, and the cabinet is stripped and cleaned.
- The speaker is torn down to its structures with all chemicals and glues removed.
- The speaker is passed through a demagnetizing process so that all metal pieces and shavings can be removed.
- The speaker is rebuilt using a recone kit to replace damaged and defective parts.

Once the cabinets and speakers are ready, they are assembled, tested, and boxed. Assembly involves placing the speakers in the cabinets and connecting the wire harnesses. There are two tests:

- In-phase test: The in-phase test is to make sure that the power is hooked up correctly.
- Air leak test: The product must be properly sealed because an air leak can damage the woofer.

Notice that the rebuilding and assembly processes are sequential. When finished, the rebuilt speakers and cabinets are transferred from the rebuilding process to the assembly process. Also, note that the cost of the final product is the cost of the materials transferred in from the rebuilding process, plus the cost of the other components and materials added, plus the assembly conversion cost. For example, at the end of the assembly process, the assembled product is packaged for delivery. In this simple process application, it is easy to see that some materials are added at the beginning of the assembly process (the cabinet and components) and some at the end of the process (packaging). The **Kicker** example also shows how process costing handles multiple departments.

**KICKER** *Livin' Loud*

Assuming uniform application of conversion costs (direct labor and overhead) is not unreasonable. Direct labor input is usually needed throughout the process, and overhead is normally assigned on the basis of direct labor hours. Direct materials, on the other hand, are not as likely to be applied uniformly. In many instances, materials are added at either the beginning or the end of the process.

For example, look at the differences in Healthblend's three departments. In the mixing and encapsulating departments, all materials are added at the beginning of the process. However, in the bottling department, materials are added both at the beginning (filled capsules and bottles) and at the end (bottle caps and boxes).

WIP in the mixing department that is 50% complete with respect to conversion inputs would be 100% complete with respect to the material inputs. But WIP in bottling that is 50% complete with respect to conversion would be 100% complete with respect to bottles and transferred-in capsules, but 0% complete with respect to bottle caps and boxes.

Different percentage completion figures for manufacturing inputs pose a problem for the calculation of equivalent units, unit cost, and valuation of EWIP (Steps 2–4). In such cases, equivalent unit calculations are done for each category of manufacturing input. Thus, equivalent units are calculated for each category of materials and for conversion cost. Next, a unit cost for each category is computed. The individual category costs are then used in Step 4 to cost out EWIP. The total unit cost is used to calculate the cost of goods transferred out in the same way as when there was only one input category. Cornerstone 6.7 shows how to calculate Steps 2 through 4 with nonuniform inputs, using the weighted average method.

## Calculating Equivalent Units, Unit Costs, and Valuing Inventories with Nonuniform Inputs

**CORNERSTONE**

**6.7**

**Why:**

If materials are added at the beginning or end of a process, then there will be different completion percentages for materials and conversion costs. Typically, conversion costs are added uniformly and materials are added at discrete points in the production process. Assuming conversion is less than 100% at a given point in time, then materials added at the beginning are 100% complete, and materials added at the end are 0% complete. Accordingly, equivalent units are calculated for each type of input, and a unit cost is calculated for each input. To calculate the unit cost for each category also requires that costs be accounted for by input category. The unit cost is the sum of the input category unit costs. Valuation of goods transferred out uses the unit cost, whereas valuation of EWIP uses input category unit costs.

**Information:**

The mixing department of Healthblend has the following data for September:

| Production: | |
|---|---|
| Units in process, September 1, 50% complete* | 10,000 |
| Units completed and transferred out | 60,000 |
| Units in process, September 30, 40% complete* | 20,000 |

*(Continued)*

**CORNERSTONE**

**6.7**

*(Continued)*

Costs:
|  |  |
|---|---|
| WIP, September 1: |  |
| Materials | $ 1,600 |
| Conversion costs | 200 |
| Total | $ 1,800 |
| Current costs: |  |
| Materials | $12,000 |
| Conversion costs | 3,200 |
| Total | $15,200 |

* With respect to conversion costs, all materials are added at the beginning of the process.

**Required:**

Calculate Steps 2 through 4 using the weighted average method.

**Solution:**

1. *Step 2:* Calculation of equivalent units, nonuniform application:

|  | **Materials** | **Conversion** |
|---|---|---|
| Units completed | 60,000 | 60,000 |
| Add: Units in Ending Work in Process × Fraction Complete: |  |  |
| 20,000 × 100% | 20,000 | — |
| 20,000 × 40% | — | 8,000 |
| Equivalent units of output | 80,000 | 68,000 |

2. *Step 3:* Calculation of unit costs:

Unit Materials Cost = ($1,600 + $12,000)/80,000 = $0.17
Unit Conversion Cost = ($200 + $3,200)/68,000 = $0.05
Total Unit Cost = Unit Materials Cost + Unit Conversion Cost
= $0.17 + $0.05
= $0.22 per completed unit

3. *Step 4:* Valuation of EWIP and goods transferred out:

The cost of EWIP is as follows:

|  |  |
|---|---|
| Materials: $0.17 × 20,000 | $3,400 |
| Conversion: $0.05 × 8,000 | 400 |
| Total cost | $3,800 |

Valuation of Goods Transferred Out:

Cost of Goods Transferred Out = $0.22 × 60,000 = $13,200

For illustrative purposes, a production report, based on Cornerstone 6.7, is shown in Exhibit 6.4. As the example shows, applying manufacturing inputs at different stages of a process poses no serious problems, though it requires more effort.

( EXHIBIT 6.4 )

**Production Report: Weighted Average Method**

### Healthblend Company
### Mixing Department
### Production Report for September 2013
### (Weighted Average Method)

#### UNIT INFORMATION

| Units to account for: | | Units accounted for: | |
|---|---|---|---|
| Units in beginning work in process | 10,000 | Units completed | 60,000 |
| Units started during the period | 70,000 | Units in ending work in process | 20,000 |
| Total units to account for | 80,000 | Total units accounted for | 80,000 |

| | Equivalent Units | |
|---|---|---|
| | **Materials** | **Conversion** |
| Units completed | 60,000 | 60,000 |
| Units in ending work in process | 20,000 | 8,000 |
| Total equivalent units | 80,000 | 68,000 |

#### COST INFORMATION

| | **Materials** | **Conversion** | **Total** |
|---|---|---|---|
| Costs to account for: | | | |
| Beginning work in process | $ 1,600 | $ 200 | $ 1,800 |
| Incurred during the period | 12,000 | 3,200 | 15,200 |
| Total costs to account for | $13,600 | $3,400 | $17,000 |
| Cost per equivalent unit | $ 0.17 | $ 0.05 | $ 0.22 |

| | **Transferred Out** | **Ending Work in Process** | **Total** |
|---|---|---|---|
| Costs accounted for: | | | |
| Goods transferred out ($0.22 × 60,000) | $13,200 | — | $13,200 |
| Goods in ending work in process: | | | |
| Materials ($0.17 × 20,000) | — | $3,400 | 3,400 |
| Conversion ($0.05 × 8,000) | — | 400 | 400 |
| Total costs accounted for | $13,200 | $3,800 | $17,000 |

## Multiple Departments

In process manufacturing, some departments receive partially completed goods from prior departments. The usual approach is to treat transferred-in goods as a separate material category when calculating equivalent units. Thus, the department receiving transferred-in goods would have *three* input categories:

- one for the transferred-in materials
- one for materials added
- one for conversion costs

In dealing with transferred-in goods, two important points should be remembered.

- The cost of this material is the cost of the goods transferred out as computed in the prior department.
- The units started in the subsequent department correspond to the units transferred out from the prior department (assuming that there is a one-to-one relationship between the output measures of both departments).

### concept Q&A

How are transferred-in goods viewed and treated by the department receiving them?

**Answer:**

Transferred-in goods are viewed as materials added at the beginning of the process. They are treated as a separate input category, and equivalent units and a unit cost are calculated for transferred-in materials.

Cornerstone 6.8 shows how to calculate the first three process-costing steps when there are transferred-in goods, where Steps 2 and 3 are restricted to the transferred-in category.

**CORNERSTONE**

**6.8**

## Calculating the Physical Flow Schedule, Equivalent Units, and Unit Costs with Transferred-In Goods

**Why:**

Goods transferred in from a prior department represent a material added at the beginning of the process for the department receiving the goods. The units received become the units started (for the subsequent department), and the cost of the transferred-in materials is the cost of goods transferred out for the transferring department. Finally, transferred-in material is treated as a separate material category for calculating equivalent units.

**Information:**

For September, Healthblend's encapsulating department had 15,000 units in beginning inventory (with transferred-in costs of $3,000) and completed 70,000 units during the month. Further, the mixing department completed and transferred out 60,000 units at a cost of $13,200 in September.

**Required:**

1. Prepare a physical flow schedule with transferred-in goods.

2. Calculate equivalent units for the transferred-in category.

3. Calculate unit cost for the transferred-in category.

**Solution:**

1. In constructing a physical flow schedule for the encapsulating department, its dependence on the mixing department must be considered:

| | |
|---|---|
| Units to account for: | |
|   Units in BWIP | 15,000 |
|   Units transferred in during September | 60,000 |
|     Total units to account for | 75,000 |
| Units accounted for: | |
|   Units completed and transferred out: | |
|     Started and completed | 55,000 |
|     From BWIP | 15,000 |
|   Units in EWIP | 5,000 |
|     Total units accounted for | 75,000 |

2. Equivalent units for the transferred-in category only:

| | |
|---|---|
| Transferred in: | |
|   Units completed | 70,000 |
| Add: Units in EWIP × Fraction Complete (5,000 × 100%)* | 5,000 |
| Equivalent units of output | 75,000 |

\* Remember that the EWIP is 100% complete with respect to transferred-in costs, not to all costs of the encapsulating department.

3. To find the unit cost for the transferred-in category, we add the cost of the units transferred in from mixing in September to the transferred-in costs in BWIP and divide by transferred-in equivalent units:

$$\text{Unit Cost (Transferred-In Category)} = (\$13,200 + \$3,000)/75,000 \text{ units}$$
$$= \$16,200/75,000 \text{ units} = \$0.216$$

The only additional complication introduced in the analysis for a subsequent department is the presence of the transferred-in category. As shown, dealing with this category is similar to handling any other category. However, it must be remembered that the current cost of this special type of raw material is the cost of the units transferred in from the prior process and that the units transferred in are the units started.

# APPENDIX 6A: PRODUCTION REPORT— FIRST-IN, FIRST-OUT COSTING

OBJECTIVE 5

Prepare a departmental production report using the FIFO method.

Under the FIFO costing method, the equivalent units and manufacturing costs in BWIP are excluded from the current period unit cost calculation. This method recognizes that the work and costs carried over from the prior period legitimately belong to that period.

## Differences between the First-In, First-Out and Weighted Average Methods

If changes occur in the prices of the manufacturing inputs from one period to the next, then FIFO produces a more accurate (i.e., more current) unit cost than does the weighted average method. A more accurate unit cost means better cost control, better pricing decisions, and so on. Keep in mind that if the period is as short as a week or a month, however, the unit costs calculated under the two methods will not likely differ much. In that case, the FIFO method has little, if anything, to offer over the weighted average method. Perhaps for this reason, many firms use the weighted average method.

Since FIFO excludes prior-period work and costs, it is necessary to create two categories of completed units:

- BWIP units (FIFO assumes that units in BWIP are completed first, before any new units are started)
- Units started and completed during the current period

For example, assume that a department had 20,000 units in BWIP and completed and transferred out a total of 50,000 units. Of the 50,000 completed units, 20,000 are the units initially found in WIP. The remaining 30,000 were started and completed during the current period.

These two categories of completed units are needed in the FIFO method so that each category can be costed correctly. For the units started and completed, the unit cost is obtained by dividing total current manufacturing costs by the current period equivalent output. However, for the BWIP units, the total associated manufacturing costs are the sum of the prior period costs plus the costs incurred in the current period to finish the units.

## Example of the First-In, First-Out Method

Cornerstone 6.9 shows how FIFO handles output and cost calculations using the same Healthblend data used for the weighted average method (Cornerstone 6.4, p. 241) to highlight the differences between the two methods. Cornerstone 6.9 shows that the equivalent unit calculation measures only the output for the current period.

## Calculating Output and Cost Assignments: First-In, First-Out Method

CORNERSTONE

6.9

**Why:**

Under FIFO, the equivalent units of work in BWIP from the prior period are not counted in calculating this period's equivalent units. Furthermore, the costs in BWIP from the prior period are excluded in calculating the unit cost. The unit cost is the costs of the period divided by the output of the period. *The cost of units transferred out is the sum of three*

*(Continued)*

**CORNERSTONE**

**6.9**

*(Continued)*

*different items:* (1) costs incurred in the prior period found in BWIP, (2) costs of completing the BWIP incurred this period, and (3) costs of the units started and completed this period. The cost of EWIP is the unit cost multiplied by the equivalent units in EWIP.

**Information:**

**Production:**

|   |   |
|---|---|
| Units in process, July 1, 75% complete | 20,000 gallons |
| Units completed and transferred out | 50,000 gallons |
| Units in process, July 31, 25% complete | 10,000 gallons |

**Costs:**

|   |   |
|---|---|
| Work in process, July 1 | $ 3,525 |
| Costs added during July | $10,125 |

**Required:**

1. Calculate the output measure for July.

2. Assign costs to units transferred out and EWIP using the FIFO method.

**Solution:**

1. *Key:* ▨ = 10,000 units completed    ▢ = 10,000 units, 25% complete

*Output for July:*
60,000 total units ⟶ Become 37,500 equivalent units
BWIP: To be completed (20,000 × 25%):

▢▢  =  5,000

+ Units started and completed:

▨▨▨  =  30,000

+ EWIP: Started but not completed (10,000 × 0.25)

▢  =  <u>2,500</u>
     =  <u>37,500</u>

2. Costs for July:

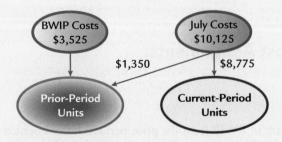

*(Continued)*

CORNERSTONE

6.9

*(Continued)*

Cost/Unit = $10,125/37,500 units = $0.27

| Transferred out: | |
|---|---|
| Cost from BWIP (prior period carryover) | $ 3,525 |
| To complete BWIP ($0.27 × 5,000) | 1,350 |
| Started and completed ($0.27 × 30,000) | 8,100 |
| Total | $12,975 |
| EWIP ($0.27 × 2,500) | 675 |
| Total cost assigned | $13,650 |

Cornerstone 6.9 reveals that costs from the current period and costs carried over from June (beginning inventory costs) are not pooled to calculate July's unit cost. The unit cost calculation uses only July (current period) costs. The five steps to cost out production follow.

**Step 1: Physical Flow Analysis**  The purpose of Step 1 is to trace the physical units of production. As with the weighted average method, in the FIFO method, a physical flow schedule is prepared. This schedule is identical for both methods and is presented again in Exhibit 6.5. (See Cornerstone 6.5, p. 243, for details on how to prepare this schedule.)

( EXHIBIT 6.5 )

**Physical Flow Schedule**

| | | |
|---|---|---|
| Units to account for: | | |
| Units in beginning work in process (75% complete) | | 20,000 |
| Units started during the period | | 40,000 |
| Total units to account for | | 60,000 |
| Units accounted for: | | |
| Units completed: | | |
| Started and completed | 30,000 | |
| From beginning work in process | 20,000 | 50,000 |
| Units in ending work in process (25% complete) | | 10,000 |
| Total units accounted for | | 60,000 |

**Step 2: Calculation of Equivalent Units**  From the equivalent unit computation, one difference between weighted average and FIFO becomes immediately apparent. Under FIFO, the equivalent units in BWIP (work done in the prior period) are not counted as part of the total equivalent work. Only the equivalent work to be completed this period is counted. The equivalent work to be completed for the units from the prior period is computed by multiplying the number of units in BWIP by the percentage of work remaining. Since in this example the percentage of work done in the prior period is 75%, the percentage left to be completed this period is 25%, or an equivalent of 5,000 additional units of work.

The effect of excluding prior period effort is to produce the current period equivalent output. Recall that under the weighted average method, 52,500 equivalent units were computed for this month. Under FIFO, only 37,500 units are calculated for the same month. These 37,500 units represent current period output. The difference, of course, is explained by the fact that the weighted average method rolls back and counts the 15,000 equivalent units of prior period work (20,000 units BWIP $\times$ 75%) as belonging to this period.

**Step 3: Computation of Unit Cost** The additional manufacturing costs incurred in the current period are $10,125. Thus, the current period unit manufacturing cost is $10,125/37,500, or $0.27. Notice that the costs of beginning inventory are excluded from this calculation. Only current period manufacturing costs are used.

**Step 4: Valuation of Inventories** Cornerstone 6.9 shows FIFO values for EWIP and goods transferred out. Since all equivalent units in ending work in process are current period units, the cost of EWIP is simply $0.27 $\times$ 2,500, or $675, the same value that the weighted average method would produce. However, when it comes to valuing goods transferred out, a significant difference emerges between the weighted average method and FIFO.

Under weighted average, the cost of goods transferred out is simply the unit cost times the units completed. Under FIFO, however, there are two categories of completed units:

- Units started and completed (30,000)
- Units from beginning inventory (20,000)

The cost of each category must be calculated separately and then summed to obtain the total cost of goods transferred out. The cost of the first category is calculated as follows:

$$\text{Cost of Units Started and Completed} = \text{Unit Cost} \times \text{Units Started and Completed}$$
$$= \$0.27 \times 30,000$$
$$= \$8,100$$

For these units, the use of the current period unit cost is entirely appropriate. However, the cost of BWIP units that were transferred out is another matter. These units started the period with $3,525 of manufacturing costs already incurred and 15,000 units of equivalent output already completed. To finish these units, the equivalent of 5,000 units were needed. Thus, the cost of these units being transferred out is:

$$\text{Cost of Units in BWIP} = \text{Prior Period Costs} + (\text{Unit Cost} \times \text{Equivalent Units to Complete})$$
$$= \$3,525 + (\$0.27 \times 5,000)$$
$$= \$4,875$$

The unit cost of these 20,000 units, then, is about $0.244 ($4,875/20,000), a blend of prior period and current manufacturing costs.

**Step 5: Cost Reconciliation** The total costs assigned to production are as follows:

| | |
|---|---:|
| Goods transferred out: | |
| Units in BWIP | $ 4,875 |
| Units started and completed | 8,100 |
| Goods in EWIP | 675 |
| Total costs accounted for | $13,650 |

The total manufacturing costs to account for during the period are:

| | |
|---|---:|
| BWIP | $ 3,525 |
| Incurred during the period | 10,125 |
| Total costs to account for | $13,650 |

The costs assigned, thus, equal the costs to account for. With the completion of Step 5, the production report can be prepared. Cornerstone 6.10 shows how to prepare this report for FIFO.

# Preparing a Production Report: First-In, First-Out Method

CORNERSTONE

6.10

**Why:**

A production report has two sections: (1) a unit information section and (2) a cost information section. The unit information section presents the physical flow schedule and the equivalent units schedule. The cost information section also has two major subdivisions: (1) costs to account for and (2) costs accounted for. The first cost subdivision includes the calculation of the unit cost, and the second subdivision includes the valuation of goods transferred out and EWIP.

**Information:**

Refer to the five steps for the Healthblend Company.

**Required:**

Prepare a production report for July 2013 (FIFO method).

**Solution:**

**Healthblend Company**
**Mixing Department**
**Production Report For July 2013**
**(FIFO Method)**

### UNIT INFORMATION

| | | |
|---|---|---|
| Units to account for: | | |
| Units in beginning work in process | | 20,000 |
| Units started during the period | | 40,000 |
| Total units to account for | | 60,000 |

| | Physical Flow | Equivalent Units |
|---|---|---|
| Units accounted for: | | |
| Units started and completed | 30,000 | 30,000 |
| Units completed from beginning work in process | 20,000 | 5,000 |
| Units in ending work in process | 10,000 | 2,500 |
| Total units accounted for | 60,000 | 37,500 |

### COST INFORMATION

| | | |
|---|---|---|
| Costs to account for: | | |
| Beginning work in process | $ 3,525 | |
| Incurred during the period | 10,125 | |
| Total costs to account for | $13,650 | |
| Cost per equivalent unit | $ 0.27 | |

| | Transferred Out | Ending Work in Process | Total |
|---|---|---|---|
| Costs accounted for: | | | |
| Units in beginning work in process: | | | |
| From prior period | $ 3,525 | — | $ 3,525 |
| From current period ($0.27 × 5,000) | 1,350 | — | 1,350 |
| Units started and completed ($0.27 × 30,000) | 8,100 | — | 8,100 |
| Goods in ending work in process ($0.27 × 2,500) | — | $675 | 675 |
| Total costs accounted for | $12,975 | $675 | $13,650 |

# SUMMARY OF LEARNING OBJECTIVES

**LO 1.**  Describe the basic characteristics and cost flows associated with process manufacturing.

- Cost flows under process costing are similar to those under job-order costing.
- Raw materials are purchased and debited to the raw materials account.
- Direct materials used in production, direct labor, and applied overhead are charged to the WIP account.
- In a production process with several processes, there is a WIP account for each department or process. Goods completed in one department are transferred out to the next department.
- When units are completed in the final department or process, their cost is credited to Work in Process and is debited to Finished Goods.

**LO 2.**  Define *equivalent units* and explain their role in process costing. Explain the differences between the weighted average method and the FIFO method of accounting for process costs.

- Equivalent units of production are the complete units that could have been produced given the total amount of manufacturing effort expended during the period.
- The number of physical units is multiplied by the percentage of completion to calculate equivalent units.
- The weighted average costing method combines beginning inventory costs to compute unit costs.
- The FIFO costing method separates units in beginning inventory from those produced during the current period.

**LO 3.**  Prepare a departmental production report using the weighted average method.

- The production report summarizes the manufacturing activity occurring in a department for a given period.
- It discloses information concerning the physical flow of units, equivalent units, unit costs, and the disposition of the manufacturing costs associated with the period.

**LO 4.**  Explain how nonuniform inputs and multiple processing departments affect process costing.

- Nonuniform inputs and multiple departments are easily handled by process-costing methods.
- When inputs are added nonuniformly, equivalent units and unit cost are calculated for each separate input category.
- The adjustment for multiple departments is also relatively simple.
- The goods transferred from a prior department to a subsequent department are treated as a material added at the beginning of the process. Thus, there is a separate transferred-in materials category, where the equivalent units and unit cost are calculated.

**LO 5.**  *(Appendix 6A)* Prepare a departmental production report using the FIFO method.

- A production report prepared according to the FIFO method separates the cost of BWIP from the cost of the current period.
- BWIP is assumed to be completed and transferred out first.
- Costs from BWIP are not pooled with the current period costs in computing unit cost. Additionally, equivalent units of production exclude work done in the prior period.
- When calculating the cost of goods transferred out, the prior period costs are added to the costs of completing the units in BWIP, and then these costs are added to the costs of units started and completed.

# SUMMARY OF IMPORTANT EQUATIONS

1. $\text{Unit Cost} = \dfrac{\text{Total Cost}}{\text{Equivalent Units}}$

2. Units Started and Completed = Total Units Completed − Units in BWIP

   Units Started = Units Started and Completed + Units in EWIP

| | |
|---|---|
| CORNERSTONE 6.1 | Calculating cost flows without work in process inventories, page 234 |
| CORNERSTONE 6.2 | Calculating equivalent units of production: no beginning work in process, page 237 |
| CORNERSTONE 6.3 | Measuring output and assigning costs: no beginning work in process, page 238 |
| CORNERSTONE 6.4 | Measuring output and assigning costs: weighted average method, page 241 |
| CORNERSTONE 6.5 | Preparing a physical flow schedule, page 243 |
| CORNERSTONE 6.6 | Preparing a production report: weighted average method, page 245 |
| CORNERSTONE 6.7 | Calculating equivalent units, unit costs, and valuing inventories with nonuniform inputs, page 247 |
| CORNERSTONE 6.8 | Calculating the physical flow schedule, equivalent units, and unit costs with transferred-in goods, page 250 |
| CORNERSTONE 6.9 | *(Appendix 6A)* Calculating output and cost assignments: first-in, first-out method, page 251 |
| CORNERSTONE 6.10 | *(Appendix 6A)* Preparing a production report: first-in, first-out method, page 255 |

# KEY TERMS

Beginning work-in-process (BWIP), 237
Cost reconciliation, 244
Ending work-in-process (EWIP), 236
Equivalent units of output, 237
FIFO costing method, 239
Parallel processing, 233

Physical flow schedule, 242
Production report, 235
Sequential processing, 232
Transferred-in costs, 235
Weighted average costing method, 239

# REVIEW PROBLEMS

## I. Process Costing

Springville Company, which uses the weighted average method, produces a product that passes through two departments: Blending and Cooking. In the blending department, all materials are added at the beginning of the process. All other manufacturing inputs are added uniformly. The following information pertains to the blending department for February:

a. BWIP, February 1: 100,000 pounds, 40% complete with respect to conversion costs. The costs assigned to this work are as follows:

| | |
|---|---|
| Materials | $20,000 |
| Labor | 10,000 |
| Overhead | 30,000 |

b. EWIP, February 28: 50,000 pounds, 60% complete with respect to conversion costs.
c. Units completed and transferred out: 370,000 pounds. The following costs were added during the month:

| | |
|---|---|
| Materials | $211,000 |
| Labor | 100,000 |
| Overhead | 270,000 |

## Required:

1. Prepare a physical flow schedule.
2. Prepare a schedule of equivalent units.
3. Compute the cost per equivalent unit.
4. Compute the cost of goods transferred out and the cost of EWIP.
5. Prepare a cost reconciliation.

## Solution:

1. Physical flow schedule:

| | | |
|---|---|---|
| Units to account for: | | |
| Units in BWIP | 100,000 | |
| Units started | 320,000 | |
| Total units to account for | 420,000 | |
| Units accounted for: | | |
| Units completed and transferred out: | | |
| Started and completed | 270,000 | |
| From BWIP | 100,000 | 370,000 |
| Units in EWIP | | 50,000 |
| Total units accounted for | | 420,000 |

2. Schedule of equivalent units:

| | Materials | Conversion |
|---|---|---|
| Units completed | 370,000 | 370,000 |
| Units in EWIP × Fraction complete: | | |
| Materials (50,000 × 100%) | 50,000 | — |
| Conversion (50,000 × 60%) | — | 30,000 |
| Equivalent units of output | 420,000 | 400,000 |

3. Cost per equivalent unit:

Materials Unit Cost = ($20,000 + $211,000)/420,000 units

= $0.550

Conversion Unit Cost = ($40,000 + $370,000)/400,000 units

= $1.025

Total Unit Cost = $1.575 per equivalent unit

4. Cost of goods transferred out and cost of EWIP:

Cost of Goods Transferred Out = $1.575 × 370,000

= $582,750

Cost of EWIP = ($0.550 × 50,000) + ($1.025 × 30,000)

= $58,250

5.   Cost reconciliation:

| | |
|---|---:|
| Costs to account for: | |
| BWIP | $ 60,000 |
| Incurred during the period | 581,000 |
| Total costs to account for | $641,000 |
| Costs accounted for: | |
| Goods transferred out | $582,750 |
| WIP | 58,250 |
| Total costs accounted for | $641,000 |

## II. Process Costing

Now suppose that Springville Company uses the FIFO method for inventory valuations. Springville produces a product that passes through two departments: Blending and Cooking. In the blending department, all materials are added at the beginning of the process. All other manufacturing inputs are added uniformly. The following information pertains to the blending department for February:

a.   BWIP, February 1: 100,000 pounds, 40% complete with respect to conversion costs. The costs assigned to this work are as follows:

| | |
|---|---:|
| Materials | $20,000 |
| Labor | 10,000 |
| Overhead | 30,000 |

b.   EWIP, February 28: 50,000 pounds, 60% complete with respect to conversion costs.
c.   Units completed and transferred out: 370,000 pounds. The following costs were added during the month:

| | |
|---|---:|
| Materials | $211,000 |
| Labor | 100,000 |
| Overhead | 270,000 |

### Required:

1.   Prepare a physical flow schedule.
2.   Prepare a schedule of equivalent units.
3.   Compute the cost per equivalent unit.
4.   Compute the cost of goods transferred out and the cost of EWIP.

### Solution:

1.   Physical flow schedule:

| | | |
|---|---:|---:|
| Units to account for: | | |
| Units in BWIP | 100,000 | |
| Units started | 320,000 | |
| Total units to account for | 420,000 | |
| Units accounted for: | | |
| Units completed and transferred out: | | |
| Started and completed | 270,000 | |
| From BWIP | 100,000 | 370,000 |
| Units in EWIP | | 50,000 |
| Total units accounted for | | 420,000 |

(Continued)

2. Schedule of equivalent units:

| | Materials | Conversion |
|---|---|---|
| Units started and completed | 270,000 | 270,000 |
| Units, BWIP × Percentage complete | — | 60,000 |
| Units, EWIP × Percentage to complete: | | |
| Direct materials (50,000 × 100%) | 50,000 | — |
| Conversion costs (50,000 × 60%) | — | 30,000 |
| Equivalent units of output | 320,000 | 360,000 |

3. Cost per equivalent unit:

| | |
|---|---|
| DM unit cost $211,000/320,000 units | $0.659* |
| CC unit cost $370,000/360,000 units | 1.028* |
| Total cost per equivalent unit | $1.687 |

\* Rounded.

4. Cost of goods transferred out and cost of EWIP:

$$\text{Cost of Goods Transferred Out} = (\$1.687 \times 270,000) + (\$1.028 \times 60,000) + \$60,000 = \$577,170$$
$$\text{Cost of EWIP} = (\$0.659 \times 50,000) + (\$1.028 \times 30,000) = \$63,790$$

# DISCUSSION QUESTIONS

1. Describe the differences between process costing and job-order costing.
2. Distinguish between sequential processing and parallel processing.
3. What are the similarities in and differences between the manufacturing cost flows for job-order firms and process firms?
4. What journal entry would be made as goods are transferred out from one department to another department? From the final department to the warehouse?
5. How would process costing for services differ from process costing for manufactured goods?
6. How does the adoption of a JIT approach to manufacturing affect process costing?
7. What are equivalent units? Why are they needed in a process-costing system?
8. Under the weighted average method, how are prior period costs and output treated? How are they treated under the FIFO method?
9. Under what conditions will the weighted average and FIFO methods give the same results?
10. Describe the five steps in accounting for the manufacturing activity of a processing department, and explain how they interrelate.
11. What is a production report? What purpose does this report serve?
12. How is the equivalent unit calculation affected when materials are added at the beginning or end of the process rather than uniformly throughout the process?
13. Explain why transferred-in costs are a special type of raw material for the receiving department.
14. In assigning costs to goods transferred out, how do the weighted average and FIFO methods differ?

# MULTIPLE-CHOICE QUESTIONS

6-1 Process costing works well whenever
   a. heterogeneous products pass through a series of processes and receive different doses of materials, labor, and overhead.
   b. material cost is accumulated by process and conversion cost is accumulated by process.

c. homogeneous products pass through a series of processes and receive similar doses of conversion inputs and different doses of material inputs.

d. homogeneous products pass through a series of processes and receive similar amounts of materials, labor, and overhead.

e. none of the above.

**6-2** Job-order costing works well whenever

a. homogeneous products pass through a series of processes and receive similar doses of conversion inputs and different doses of material inputs.

b. homogeneous products pass through a series of processes and receive similar doses of materials, labor, and overhead.

c. heterogeneous products pass through a series of processes and receive different doses of materials, labor, and overhead.

d. material cost is accumulated by process and conversion cost is accumulated by process.

**6-3** Sequential processing is characterized by

a. a pattern where partially completed units are worked on simultaneously.

b. a pattern where partially completed units must pass through one process before they can be worked on in later processes.

c. a pattern where different partially completed units must pass through parallel processes before being brought together in a final process.

d. a pattern where partially completed units must be purchased from outside suppliers and delivered to the final process in a sequential time mode.

e. none of these.

**6-4** To record the transfer of costs from a prior process to a subsequent process, the following entry would be made:

a. debit Finished Goods and credit Work in Process.

b. debit Work in Process (subsequent department) and credit Transferred-In Materials.

c. debit Work in Process (prior department) and credit Work in Process (subsequent department).

d. debit Work in Process (subsequent department) and credit Work in Process (prior department)

e. none of the above.

**6-5** The costs transferred from a prior process to a subsequent process are

a. treated as another type of materials cost for the receiving department.

b. referred to as transferred-in costs (for the receiving department).

c. referred to as the cost of goods transferred out (for the transferring department).

d. all of the above.

e. none of the above.

**6-6** During the month of May, the grinding department produced and transferred out 2,300 units. EWIP had 500 units, 40% complete. There was no BWIP. The equivalent units of output for May are

a. 2,000.                     d. 2,800.
b. 2,500.                     e. none of these.
c. 2,300.

---

*Use the following information for Multiple-Choice Questions 6-7 through 6-9:*
The mixing department incurred $46,000 of manufacturing costs during the month of September. The department transferred out 2,300 units and had 500 units in EWIP, 40% complete. There was no BWIP.

**6-7** The unit cost for the month of September is

   a. $20.
   b. $18.40.
   c. $16.43.

   d. $200.
   e. $184.

**6-8** The cost of goods transferred out is

   a. $42,320.
   b. $46,000.
   c. $37,789.

   d. $460,000.
   e. none of these.

**6-9** The cost of EWIP is

   a. $9,200.
   b. $10,000.
   c. $3,680.

   d. $3,286.
   e. none of these.

**6-10** During May, Kimbrell Manufacturing completed and transferred out 100,000 units. In EWIP, there were 25,000 units, 40% complete. Using the weighted average method, the equivalent units are

   a. 100,000 units.
   b. 125,000 units.
   c. 105,000 units.

   d. 110,000 units.
   e. 120,000 units.

**6-11** During June, Kimbrell Manufacturing completed and transferred out 100,000 units. In EWIP, there were 25,000 units, 80% complete. Using the weighted average method, the equivalent units are

   a. 100,000 units.
   b. 125,000 units.
   c. 105,000 units.

   d. 110,000 units.
   e. 120,000 units.

**6-12** For August, Kimbrell Manufacturing has costs in BWIP equal to $112,500. During August, the cost incurred was $450,000. Using the weighted average method, Kimbrell had 125,000 equivalent units for August. There were 100,000 units transferred out during the month. The cost of goods transferred out is

   a. $500,000.
   b. $400,000.
   c. $450,000.

   d. $360,000.
   e. $50,000.

**6-13** For September, Murphy Company has manufacturing costs in BWIP equal to $100,000. During September, the manufacturing costs incurred were $550,000. Using the weighted average method, Murphy had 100,000 equivalent units for September. The equivalent unit cost for September is

   a. $1.00.
   b. $7.50.
   c. $6.50.

   d. $6.00.
   e. $6.62.

**6-14** During June, Faust Manufacturing started and completed 80,000 units. In BWIP, there were 25,000 units, 80% complete. In EWIP, there were 25,000 units, 60% complete. Using FIFO, the equivalent units are

   a. 80,000 units.
   b. 95,000 units.
   c. 85,000 units.

   d. 115,000 units.
   e. 100,000 units.

**6-15** During July, Faust Manufacturing started and completed 80,000 units. In BWIP, there were 25,000 units, 20% complete. In EWIP, there were 25,000 units, 80% complete. Using FIFO, the equivalent units are

   a. 80,000 units.
   b. 120,000 units.
   c. 65,000 units.

   d. 85,000 units.
   e. 100,000 units.

6-16 Assume for August that Faust Manufacturing has manufacturing costs in BWIP equal to $80,000. During August, the cost incurred was $720,000. Using the FIFO method, Faust had 120,000 equivalent units for August. The cost per equivalent unit for August is

   a.  $6.12.                              d.  $6.00.
   b.  $6.50.                              e.  $6.67.
   c.  $5.60.

6-17 For August, Lanny Company had 25,000 units in BWIP, 40% complete, with costs equal to $36,000. During August, the cost incurred was $450,000. Using the FIFO method, Lanny had 125,000 equivalent units for August. There were 100,000 units transferred out during the month. The cost of goods transferred out is

   a.  $500,000.                         d.  $400,000.
   b.  $360,000.                         e.  $50,000.
   c.  $450,000.

6-18 When materials are added either at the beginning or the end of the process, a unit cost should be calculated for the

   a.  materials and conversion categories.
   b.  materials category only.
   c.  materials and labor categories.
   d.  conversion category only.
   e.  labor category only.

6-19 With nonuniform inputs, the cost of EWIP is calculated by

   a.  adding the materials cost to the conversion cost.
   b.  subtracting the cost of goods transferred out from the total cost of materials.
   c.  multiplying the unit cost in each input category by the equivalent units of each input found in EWIP.
   d.  multiplying the total unit cost by the units in EWIP.
   e.  none of the above.

6-20 Transferred-in goods are treated by the receiving department as

   a.  units started for the period.
   b.  a material added at the beginning of the process.
   c.  a category of materials separate from conversion costs.
   d.  all of these.
   e.  none of these.

# CORNERSTONE EXERCISES

### Cornerstone Exercise 6-21   Basic Cost Flows

OBJECTIVE ❶
CORNERSTONE 6.1

Pleni Company produces 18-ounce boxes of a wheat cereal in three departments: Mixing, Cooking, and Packaging. During August, Pleni produced 125,000 boxes with the following costs:

|  | Mixing Department | Cooking Department | Packaging Department |
|---|---|---|---|
| Direct materials | $412,500 | $187,500 | $165,000 |
| Direct labor | 60,000 | 37,500 | 90,000 |
| Applied overhead | 75,000 | 41,250 | 116,250 |

**Required:**

1. Calculate the costs transferred out of each department.
2. Prepare journal entries that reflect these cost transfers.

OBJECTIVE ❷
CORNERSTONE 6.2

### Cornerstone Exercise 6-22    Equivalent Units, No Beginning Work in Process

Fried Manufacturing produces cylinders used in internal combustion engines. During June, Fried's welding department had the following data:

| | |
|---|---|
| Units in BWIP | — |
| Units completed | 70,000 |
| Units in EWIP (40% complete) | 10,500 |

**Required:**

Calculate June's output for the welding department in equivalent units of production.

OBJECTIVE ❷
CORNERSTONE 6.3

### Cornerstone Exercise 6-23    Unit Cost, Valuing Goods Transferred Out and EWIP

During April, the grinding department of Moriba Inc. completed and transferred out 105,000 units. At the end of April, there were 37,500 in process, 60% complete. Moriba incurred manufacturing costs totaling $1,530,000.

**Required:**

1. Calculate the unit cost.
2. Calculate the cost of goods transferred out and the cost of EWIP.

OBJECTIVE ❸
CORNERSTONE 6.4

### Cornerstone Exercise 6-24    Weighted Average Method, Unit Cost, Valuing Inventories

Manzer Enterprises produces premier raspberry jam. Output is measured in pints. Manzer uses the weighted average method. During January, Manzer had the following production data:

| | |
|---|---|
| Units in process, January 1, 60% complete | 36,000 pints |
| Units completed and transferred out | 240,000 pints |
| Units in process, January 31, 40% complete | 75,000 pints |
| | |
| Costs: | |
| Work in process, January 1 | $ 54,000 |
| Costs added during January | 351,000 |

**Required:**

1. Using the weighted average method, calculate the equivalent units for January.
2. Calculate the unit cost for January.
3. Assign costs to units transferred out and EWIP.

OBJECTIVE ❸
CORNERSTONE 6.5

### Cornerstone Exercise 6-25    Physical Flow Schedule

Buckner Inc. just finished its second month of operations. Buckner mass produces integrated circuits. The following production information is provided for December:

| | |
|---|---|
| Units in process, December 1, 80% complete | 100,000 |
| Units completed and transferred out | 475,000 |
| Units in process, December 31, 60% complete | 75,000 |

**Required:**

Prepare a physical flow schedule.

OBJECTIVE ❸
CORNERSTONE 6.6

### Cornerstone Exercise 6-26    Production Report, Weighted Average

Murray Inc. manufactures bicycle frames in two departments: Cutting and Welding. Murray uses the weighted average method. Manufacturing costs are added uniformly throughout the process. The following are cost and production data for the cutting department for October:

| | |
|---|---|
| Production: | |
| Units in process, October 1, 40% complete | 10,000 |
| Units completed and transferred out | 68,000 |
| Units in process, October 31, 60% complete | 20,000 |
| Costs: | |
| WIP, October 1 | $ 80,000 |
| Costs added during October | 1,520,000 |

**Required:**

Prepare a production report for the cutting department.

### Cornerstone Exercise 6-27   Nonuniform Inputs, Weighted Average

OBJECTIVE 4
CORNERSTONE 6.7

Integer Inc. had the following production and cost information for its fabrication department during April (materials are added at the beginning of the fabrication process):

Production:

| | |
|---|---|
| Units in process, April 1, 50% complete with respect to conversion | 5,000 |
| Units completed | 32,600 |
| Units in process, April 30, 60% complete | 6,000 |

Costs:

Work in process, April 1:

| | |
|---|---|
| Materials | $ 20,000 |
| Conversion costs | 15,000 |
| Total | $ 35,000 |

Current costs:

| | |
|---|---|
| Materials | $ 62,500 |
| Conversion costs | 105,000 |
| Total | $167,500 |

Integer uses the weighted average method.

**Required:**

1. Prepare an equivalent units schedule.
2. Calculate the unit cost. (*Note:* Round answers to two decimal places).
3. Calculate the cost of units transferred out and the cost of EWIP.

### Cornerstone Exercise 6-28   Transferred-In Cost

OBJECTIVE 4
CORNERSTONE 6.8

Fuerza Inc. produces a protein drink. The product is sold by the gallon. The company has two departments: Mixing and Bottling. For August, the bottling department had 60,000 gallons in beginning inventory (with transferred-in costs of $213,000) and completed 262,500 gallons during the month. Further, the mixing department completed and transferred out 240,000 gallons at a cost of $687,000 in August.

**Required:**

1. Prepare a physical flow schedule for the bottling department.
2. Calculate equivalent units for the transferred-in category.
3. Calculate the unit cost for the transferred-in category.

---

*Use the following information for Cornerstone Exercises 6-29 and 6-30:*

Inca Inc. produces soft drinks. Mixing is the first department and its output is measured in gallons. Inca uses the FIFO method. All manufacturing costs are added uniformly. For July, the mixing department provided the following information:

Production:

| | |
|---|---|
| Units in process, July 1, 80% complete | 24,000 gallons |
| Units completed and transferred out | 138,000 gallons |
| Units in process, July 31, 75% complete | 16,000 gallons |

Costs:

| | |
|---|---|
| Work in process, July 1 | $24,000 |
| Costs added during July | 301,000 |

---

OBJECTIVE ⑤
CORNERSTONE 6.9

**Cornerstone Exercise 6-29    *(Appendix 6A)* First-In, First-Out Method; Equivalent Units**

Refer to the information for Inca Inc. on the previous page.

**Required:**

1.  Calculate the equivalent units for August.
2.  Calculate the unit cost. (*Note:* Round to two decimal places).
3.  Assign costs to units transferred out and EWIP using the FIFO method.

OBJECTIVE ⑤
CORNERSTONE 6.10

**Cornerstone Exercise 6-30    *(Appendix 6A)* FIFO; Production Report**

Refer to the information for Inca Inc. on the previous page.

**Required:**

Prepare a production report.

# EXERCISES

OBJECTIVE ①

**Exercise 6-31    Basic Cost Flows**

Davis Company produces a common machine component for industrial equipment in three departments: molding, grinding, and finishing. The following data are available for November:

|  | Molding Department | Grinding Department | Finishing Department |
|---|---|---|---|
| Direct materials | $143,200 | $ 15,200 | $ 9,800 |
| Direct labor | 13,800 | 33,600 | 22,800 |
| Applied overhead | 17,500 | 136,000 | 19,000 |

During November, 9,000 components were completed. There is no beginning or ending WIP in any department.

**Required:**

1.  Prepare a schedule showing, for each department, the cost of direct materials, direct labor, applied overhead, product transferred in from a prior department, and total manufacturing cost.
2.  Calculate the unit cost. (*Note:* Round the unit cost to two decimal places.)

OBJECTIVE ①

**Exercise 6-32    Journal Entries, Basic Cost Flows**

In December, Davis Company had the following cost flows:

|  | Molding Department | Grinding Department | Finishing Department |
|---|---|---|---|
| Direct materials | $111,600 | $ 30,000 | $ 17,200 |
| Direct labor | 8,000 | 13,600 | 11,600 |
| Applied overhead | 8,400 | 60,400 | 11,200 |
| Transferred-in cost: |  |  |  |
| From Molding |  | 128,000 |  |
| From Grinding |  |  | 232,000 |
| Total cost | $128,000 | $232,000 | $272,000 |

**Required:**

1.  Prepare the journal entries to transfer costs from (a) Molding to Grinding, (b) Grinding to Finishing, and (c) Finishing to Finished Goods.
2.  **CONCEPTUAL CONNECTION** Explain how the journal entries differ from a job-order cost system.

# PROBLEMS

## Problem 6-46    Basic FLows, Equivalent Units

OBJECTIVE ❶ ❷

Thayn Company produces an arthritis medication that passes through two departments: Mixing and Tableting. Thayn uses the weighted average method. Data for February for Mixing is as follows: BWIP was zero; EWIP had 36,000 units, 50% complete; and 420,000 units were started. Tableting's data for February is as follows: BWIP was 24,000 units, 20% complete; and 12,000 units were in EWIP, 40% complete.

**Required:**

1. For Mixing, calculate the (a) number of units transferred to Tableting, and (b) equivalent units of production.
2. For Tableting, calculate the number of units transferred out to Finished Goods.
3. **CONCEPTUAL CONNECTION** Suppose that the units in the mixing department are measured in ounces, while the units in Tableting are measured in bottles of 100 tablets, with a total weight of eight ounces (excluding the bottle). Decide how you would treat units that are measured differently, and then repeat Requirement 2 using this approach.

## Problem 6-47    Steps in Preparing a Production Report

OBJECTIVE ❶ ❷ ❸ ❹

Recently, **Stillwater Designs** expanded its market by becoming an original equipment supplier to **Jeep Wrangler**. Stillwater Designs produces factory upgraded speakers specifically for Jeep Wrangler. The Kicker components and speaker cabinets are outsourced with assembly remaining in-house. Stillwater Designs assemble the product by placing the speakers and other components in cabinets that define an audio package upgrade and that can be placed into the Jeep Wrangler, producing the desired factory-installed appearance. Speaker cabinets and associated Kicker components are added at the beginning of the assembly process.

Assume that **Stillwater Designs** uses the weighted average method to cost out the audio package. The following are cost and production data for the assembly process for April:

| | |
|---|---:|
| Production: | |
| Units in process, April 1, 60% complete | 60,000 |
| Units completed and transferred out | 150,000 |
| Units in process, April 30, 20% complete | 30,000 |
| | |
| Costs: | |
| WIP, April 1: | |
| Cabinets | $ 1,200,000 |
| Kicker components | 12,600,000 |
| Conversion costs | 5,400,000 |
| Costs added during April: | |
| Cabinets | $ 2,400,000 |
| Kicker components | 25,200,000 |
| Conversion costs | 8,640,000 |

**Required:**

1. Prepare a physical flow analysis for the assembly department for the month of April.
2. Calculate equivalent units of production for the assembly department for the month of April.
3. Calculate unit cost for the assembly department for the month of April.
4. Calculate the cost of units transferred out and the cost of EWIP inventory.
5. Prepare a cost reconciliation for the assembly department for the month of April.

## Problem 6-48   Steps for a Production Report

Refer to the data of **Problem 6-47**.

**Required:**

1.  Prepare a production report for the assembly department for the month of April.
2.  **CONCEPTUAL CONNECTION** Write a one-page report that compares the purpose and content of the production report with the job-order cost sheet.

---

*Use the following information for Problems 6-49 and 6-50:*
Alfombra Inc. manufactures throw rugs. The throw-rug department weaves cloth and yarn into throw rugs of various sizes. Alfombra uses the weighted average method. Materials are added uniformly throughout the weaving process. In August, Alfombra switched from FIFO to the weighted average method. The following data are for the throw-rug department for August:

| Production: | |
| --- | --- |
| Units in process, August 1, 60% complete | 40,000 |
| Units completed and transferred out | 120,000 |
| Units in process, August 31, 60% complete | 40,000 |
| Costs: | |
| WIP, August 1 | $144,000 |
| Current costs | 604,800 |
| Total | $748,800 |

---

## Problem 6-49   Equivalent Units, Unit Cost, Weighted Average

Refer to the information for Alfombra Inc. above.

**Required:**

1.  Prepare a physical flow analysis for the throw-rug department for August.
2.  Calculate equivalent units of production for the throw-rug department for August.
3.  Calculate the unit cost for the throw-rug department for August.
4.  Show that the cost per unit calculated in Requirement 3 is a weighted average of the FIFO cost per equivalent unit in BWIP and the FIFO cost per equivalent unit for August. (*Hint:* The weights are in proportion to the number of units from each source.)

## Problem 6-50   Production Report

Refer to the information for Alfombra Inc. above. The owner of Alfombra insisted on a formal report that provided all the details of the weighted average method. In the manufacturing process, all materials are added uniformly throughout the process.

**Required:**

Prepare a production report for the throw-rug department for August using the weighted average method.

## Problem 6-51   Weighted Average Method, Physical Flow, Equivalent Units, Unit Costs, Cost Assignment

Mimasca Inc. manufactures various holiday masks. Each mask is shaped from a piece of rubber in the molding department. The masks are then transferred to the finishing department, where they are painted and have elastic bands attached. Mimasca uses the weighted average method. In May, the molding department reported the following data:

a.  BWIP consisted of 15,000 units, 20% complete. Cost in beginning inventory totaled $1,656.
b.  Costs added to production during the month were $26,094.
c.  At the end of the month, 45,000 units were transferred out to Finishing. Then, 5,000 units remained in EWIP, 25% complete.

**Required:**

1. Prepare a physical flow schedule.
2. Calculate equivalent units of production.
3. Compute unit cost.
4. Calculate the cost of goods transferred to Finishing at the end of the month. Calculate the cost of ending inventory.
5. **CONCEPTUAL CONNECTION** Assume that the masks are inspected at the end of the molding process. Of the 45,000 units inspected, 2,500 are rejected as faulty and are discarded. Thus, only 42,500 units are transferred to the finishing department. The manager of Mimasca considers all such spoilage as abnormal and does not want to assign any of this cost to the 42,500 good units produced and transferred to finishing. Your task is to determine the cost of this spoilage of 2,500 units and then to discuss how you would account for this spoilage cost. Now suppose that the manager feels that this spoilage cost is just part of the cost of producing the good units transferred out. Therefore, he wants to assign this cost to the good production. Explain how this would be handled. (*Hint:* Spoiled units are a type of output, and equivalent units of spoilage can be calculated.)

---

*Use the following information for Problems 6-52 and 6-53:*

Millie Company produces a product that passes through an assembly process and a finishing process. All manufacturing costs are added uniformly for both processes. The following information was obtained for the assembly department for June:

a. WIP, June 1, had 24,000 units (60% completed) and the following costs:

| | |
|---|---|
| Direct materials | $186,256 |
| Direct labor | 64,864 |
| Overhead applied | 34,400 |

b. During June, 70,000 units were completed and transferred to the finishing department, and the following costs were added to production:

| | |
|---|---|
| Direct materials | $267,880 |
| Direct labor | 253,000 |
| Overhead applied | 117,600 |

c. On June 30, there were 10,000 partially completed units in process. These units were 70% complete.

---

## Problem 6-52    Weighted Average Method, Single-Department Analysis

OBJECTIVE

Refer to the information for Millie Company above.

**Required:**

Prepare a production report for the assembly department for June using the weighted average method of costing. The report should disclose the physical flow of units, equivalent units, and unit costs and should track the disposition of manufacturing costs.

## Problem 6-53    First-In, First-Out Method; Single-Department Analysis; One Cost Category

OBJECTIVE

Refer to the information for Millie Company above.

**Required:**

Prepare a production report for the assembly department for June using the FIFO method of costing. The report should disclose the physical flow of units, equivalent units, and unit costs and should track the disposition of manufacturing costs. (*Note:* Carry the unit cost computation to four decimal places.)

OBJECTIVE ❶❷❸ **Problem 6-54 Weighted Average Method, Separate Materials Cost**

Janbo Company produces a variety of stationery products. One product, sealing wax sticks, passes through two processes: blending and molding. The weighted average method is used to account for the costs of production. After blending, the resulting product is sent to the molding department, where it is poured into molds and cooled. The following information relates to the blending process for August:

a. WIP, August 1, had 30,000 pounds, 20% complete. Costs associated with partially completed units were:

| | |
|---|---|
| Materials | $220,000 |
| Direct labor | 30,000 |
| Overhead applied | 20,000 |

b. WIP, August 31, had 50,000 pounds, 40% complete.
c. Units completed and transferred out totaled 480,000 pounds. Costs added during the month were (all inputs are added uniformly):

| | |
|---|---|
| Materials | $5,800,000 |
| Direct labor | 4,250,000 |
| Overhead applied | 1,292,500 |

**Required:**

1. Prepare (a) a physical flow schedule and (b) an equivalent unit schedule.
2. Calculate the unit cost. (*Note:* Round to three decimal places.)
3. Compute the cost of EWIP and the cost of goods transferred out.
4. Prepare a cost reconciliation.
5. Suppose that the materials added uniformly in blending are paraffin and pigment and that the manager of the company wants to know how much each of these materials costs per equivalent unit produced. The costs of the materials in BWIP are as follows:

| | |
|---|---|
| Paraffin | $120,000 |
| Pigment | 100,000 |

The costs of the materials added during the month are also given:

| | |
|---|---|
| Paraffin | $3,250,000 |
| Pigment | 2,550,000 |

Prepare an equivalent unit schedule with cost categories for each material. Calculate the cost per unit for each type of material.

OBJECTIVE ❶❷❸❹ **Problem 6-55 Weighted Average Method, Journal Entries**

Seacrest Company uses a process costing system. The company manufactures a product that is processed in two departments: A and B. As work is completed, it is transferred out. All inputs are added uniformly in Department A. The following summarizes the production activity and costs for November:

| | Department A | Department B |
|---|---|---|
| Beginning inventories: | | |
| Physical units | 5,000 | 8,000 |
| Costs: | | |
| Transferred in | — | $ 45,320 |
| Direct materials | $10,000 | — |
| Conversion costs | $ 6,900 | $ 16,800 |
| Current production: | | |
| Units started | 25,000 | ? |
| Units transferred out | 28,000 | 33,000 |

|  | Department A | Department B |
|---|---|---|
| Costs: |  |  |
| Transferred in | — | ? |
| Direct materials | $57,800 | $ 37,950 |
| Conversion costs | $95,220 | $128,100 |
| Percentage completion: |  |  |
| Beginning inventory | 40% | 50% |
| Ending inventory | 80% | 50% |

**Required:**

1. Using the weighted average method, prepare the following for Department A: (a) a physical flow schedule, (b) an equivalent unit calculation, (c) calculation of unit costs (*Note:* Round to two decimal places), (d) cost of EWIP and cost of goods transferred out, and (e) a cost reconciliation.

2. **CONCEPTUAL CONNECTION** Prepare journal entries that show the flow of manufacturing costs for Department A. Use a conversion cost control account for conversion costs. Many firms are now combining direct labor and overhead costs into one category. They are not tracking direct labor separately. Offer some reasons for this practice.

**Problem 6-56** *(Appendix 6A)* **First-In, First-Out Method; Journal Entries**    OBJECTIVE ❶❷❸❹
Refer to **Problem 6-55.**

**Required:**

1. Using the FIFO method, prepare the following for Department A: (a) a physical flow schedule, (b) an equivalent unit calculation, (c) calculation of unit costs (*Note:* Round to two decimal places), (d) cost of EWIP and cost of goods transferred out, and (e) a cost reconciliation.

2. **CONCEPTUAL CONNECTION** Prepare journal entries that show the flow of manufacturing costs for Department A. Use a conversion cost control account for conversion costs. Many firms are now combining direct labor and overhead costs into one category. They are not tracking direct labor separately. Offer some reasons for this practice.

**Problem 6-57** **Weighted Average Method, Nonuniform Inputs, Multiple Departments**    OBJECTIVE ❶❷❹❺

Benson Pharmaceuticals uses a process-costing system to compute the unit costs of the over-the-counter cold remedies that it produces. It has three departments: Mixing, Encapsulating, and Bottling. In Mixing, the ingredients for the cold capsules are measured, sifted, and blended (materials are thus assumed to be uniformly added throughout the process). The mix is transferred out in gallon containers. The encapsulating department takes the powdered mix and places it in capsules (capsules are necessarily added at the beginning of the process). One gallon of powdered mix converts into 1,500 capsules. After the capsules are filled and polished, they are transferred to Bottling, where they are placed in bottles that are then affixed with a safety seal, lid, and label. Each bottle receives 50 capsules.

During March, the following results are available for the first two departments:

|  | Mixing | Encapsulating |
|---|---|---|
| Beginning inventories: |  |  |
| Physical units | 10 gallons | 4,000 |
| Costs: |  |  |
| Materials | $252 | $32 |
| Labor | $282 | $20 |
| Overhead | ? | ? |
| Transferred in |  | $140 |
| Current production: |  |  |
| Transferred out | 140 gallons | 208,000 |
| Ending inventory | 20 gallons | 6,000 |
| Costs: |  |  |
| Materials | $3,636 | $1,573 |
| Transferred in | — | ? |

*(Continued)*

| | Mixing | Encapsulating |
|---|---|---|
| Labor | $4,618 | $1,944 |
| Overhead | ? | ? |
| Percentage of completion: | | |
| Beginning inventory | 40% | 50% |
| Ending inventory | 50% | 40% |

Overhead in both departments is applied as a percentage of direct labor costs. In the mixing department, overhead is 200% of direct labor. In the encapsulating department, the overhead rate is 150% of direct labor.

**Required:**

1. Prepare a production report for the mixing department using the weighted average method. Follow the five steps outlined in the chapter. (*Note*: Round to two decimal places for the unit cost.)
2. Prepare a production report for the encapsulating department using the weighted average method. Follow the five steps outlined in the chapter. (*Note:* Round to four decimal places for the unit cost.)
3. **CONCEPTUAL CONNECTION** Explain why the weighted average method is easier to use than FIFO. Explain when weighted average will give about the same results as FIFO.

OBJECTIVE **5**        **Problem 6-58    *(Appendix 6A)* First-In, First-Out Method**
Refer to **Problem 6-57.**

**Required:**

Prepare a production report for the mixing and encapsulating departments using the FIFO method. (*Note*: Round the unit cost to four decimal places.) (*Hint:* For the second department, you must convert gallons to capsules.)

## CASES

OBJECTIVE         **Case 6-59    Process Costing versus Alternative Costing Methods, Impact on Resource Allocation Decision**

Golding Manufacturing, a division of Farnsworth Sporting Inc., produces two different models of bows and eight models of knives. The bow-manufacturing process involves the production of two major subassemblies: the limbs and the handles. The limbs pass through four sequential processes before reaching final assembly: layup, molding, fabricating, and finishing. In the layup department, limbs are created by laminating layers of wood. In the molding department, the limbs are heat-treated, under pressure, to form strong resilient limbs. In the fabricating department, any protruding glue or other processing residue is removed. Finally, in the finishing department, the limbs are cleaned with acetone, dried, and sprayed with the final finishes.

The handles pass through two processes before reaching final assembly: pattern and finishing. In the pattern department, blocks of wood are fed into a machine that is set to shape the handles. Different patterns are possible, depending on the machine's setting. After coming out of the machine, the handles are cleaned and smoothed. They then pass to the finishing department, where they are sprayed with the final finishes. In final assembly, the limbs and handles are assembled into different models using purchased parts such as pulley assemblies, weight-adjustment bolts, side plates, and string.

Golding, since its inception, has been using process costing to assign product costs. A predetermined overhead rate is used based on direct labor dollars (80% of direct labor dollars). Recently, Golding has hired a new controller, Karen Jenkins. After reviewing the product-costing procedures, Karen requested a meeting with the divisional manager, Aaron Suhr. The following is a transcript of their conversation:

**Karen:** Aaron, I have some concerns about our cost accounting system. We make two different models of bows and are treating them as if they were the same product. Now I know that the only real difference between the models is the handle. The processing of the handles is the same, but the handles differ significantly in the amount and quality of wood used. Our current costing does not reflect this difference in material input.

**Aaron:** Your predecessor is responsible. He believed that tracking the difference in material cost wasn't worth the effort. He simply didn't believe that it would make much difference in the unit cost of either model.

**Karen:** Well, he may have been right, but I have my doubts. If there is a significant difference, it could affect our views of which model is more important to the company. The additional book-keeping isn't very stringent. All we have to worry about is the pattern department. The other departments fit what I view as a process-costing pattern.

**Aaron:** Why don't you look into it? If there is a significant difference, go ahead and adjust the costing system.

After the meeting, Karen decided to collect cost data on the two models: the Deluxe model and the Econo model. She decided to track the costs for one week. At the end of the week, she had collected the following data from the pattern department:

a. There were a total of 2,500 bows completed: 1,000 Deluxe models and 1,500 Econo models.
b. There was no BWIP; however, there were 300 units in EWIP: 200 Deluxe and 100 Econo models. Both models were 80% complete with respect to conversion costs and 100% complete with respect to materials.
c. The pattern department experienced the following costs:

| | |
|---|---|
| Direct materials | $114,000 |
| Direct labor | 45,667 |

d. On an experimental basis, the requisition forms for materials were modified to identify the dollar value of the materials used by the Econo and Deluxe models:

| | |
|---|---|
| Econo model | $30,000 |
| Deluxe model | 84,000 |

**Required:**

1. Compute the unit cost for the handles produced by the pattern department assuming that process costing is totally appropriate. Round unit cost to two decimal places.
2. Compute the unit cost of each handle using the separate cost information provided on materials. Round unit cost to two decimal places.
3. Compare the unit costs computed in Requirements 1 and 2. Is Karen justified in her belief that a pure process-costing relationship is not appropriate? Describe the costing system that you would recommend.
4. In the past, the marketing manager has requested more money for advertising the Econo line. Aaron has repeatedly refused to grant any increase in this product's advertising budget because its per-unit profit (selling price minus manufacturing cost) is so low. Given the results in Requirements 1 through 3, was Aaron justified in his position?

## Case 6-60   Equivalent Units; Valuation of Work-in-Process Inventories; First-In, First-Out versus Weighted Average

OBJECTIVE ❶❷❸❹

AKL Foundry manufactures metal components for different kinds of equipment used by the aerospace, commercial aircraft, medical equipment, and electronic industries. The company uses investment casting to produce the required components. Investment casting consists of creating, in wax, a replica of the final product and pouring a hard shell around it. After removing the wax, molten metal is poured into the resulting cavity. What remains after the shell is broken is the desired metal object ready to be put to its designated use.

*(Continued)*

Metal components pass through eight processes: gating, shell creating, foundry work, cutoff, grinding, finishing, welding, and strengthening. Gating creates the wax mold and clusters the wax pattern around a sprue (a hole through which the molten metal will be poured through the gates into the mold in the foundry process), which is joined and supported by gates (flow channels) to form a tree of patterns. In the shell-creating process, the wax molds are alternately dipped in a ceramic slurry and a fluidized bed of progressively coarser refractory grain until a sufficiently thick shell (or mold) completely encases the wax pattern. After drying, the mold is sent to the foundry process. Here, the wax is melted out of the mold, and the shell is fired, strengthened, and brought to the proper temperature. Molten metal is then poured into the de-waxed shell. Finally, the ceramic shell is removed, and the finished product is sent to the cutoff process, where the parts are separated from the tree by the use of a band saw. The parts are then sent to the grinding process, where the gates that allowed the molten metal to flow into the ceramic cavities are ground off using large abrasive grinders. In the finishing process, rough edges caused by the grinders are removed by small handheld pneumatic tools. Parts that are flawed at this point are sent to welding for corrective treatment. The last process uses heat to treat the parts to bring them to the desired strength.

In 2013, the two partners who owned AKL Foundry decided to split up and divide the business. In dissolving their business relationship, they were faced with the problem of dividing the business assets equitably. Since the company had two plants—one in Arizona and one in New Mexico—a suggestion was made to split the business on the basis of geographic location. One partner would assume ownership of the plant in New Mexico, and the other would assume ownership of the plant in Arizona. However, this arrangement had one major complication: the amount of WIP inventory located in the Arizona plant.

The Arizona facilities had been in operation for more than a decade and were full of WIP. The New Mexico facility had been operational for only 2 years and had much smaller WIP inventories. The partner located in New Mexico argued that to disregard the unequal value of the WIP inventories would be grossly unfair.

Unfortunately, during the entire business history of AKL Foundry, WIP inventories had never been assigned any value. In computing the cost of goods sold each year, the company had followed the policy of adding depreciation to the out-of-pocket costs of direct labor, direct materials, and overhead. Accruals for the company are nearly nonexistent, and there are hardly ever any ending inventories of materials.

During 2013, the Arizona plant had sales of $2,028,670. The cost of goods sold is itemized as follows:

| | |
|---|---|
| Direct materials | $378,000 |
| Direct labor | 530,300 |
| Overhead | 643,518 |

Upon request, the owners of AKL provided the following supplementary information (percentages are cumulative):

**Costs Used by Each Process as a Percentage of Total Cost**

| | Direct Materials (%) | Direct Total Labor Cost (%) |
|---|---|---|
| Gating | 23 | 35 |
| Shell creating | 70 | 50 |
| Foundry work | 100 | 70 |
| Cutoff | 100 | 72 |
| Grinding | 100 | 80 |
| Finishing | 100 | 90 |
| Welding | 100 | 93 |
| Strengthening | 100 | 100 |

Gating had 10,000 units in BWIP, 60% complete. Assume that all materials are added at the beginning of each process. During the year, 50,000 units were completed and transferred out. The ending inventory had 11,000 unfinished units, 60% complete.

**Required:**

1.  The partners of AKL want a reasonable estimate of the cost of WIP inventories. Using the gating department's inventory as an example, prepare an estimate of the cost of the EWIP. What assumptions did you make? Did you use the FIFO or weighted average method? Why? (*Note*: Round unit cost to two decimal places.)
2.  Assume that the shell-creating process has 8,000 units in BWIP, 20% complete. During the year, 50,000 units were completed and transferred out. (*Note:* All 50,000 units were sold; no other units were sold.) The EWIP inventory had 8,000 units, 30% complete. Compute the value of the shell-creating department's EWIP. What additional assumptions had to be made?

## Case 6-61   Production Report, Ethical Behavior                          OBJECTIVE ❸

Consider the following conversation between Gary Means, manager of a division that produces industrial machinery, and his controller, Donna Simpson, a certified management accountant and certified public accountant:

**Gary:** Donna, we have a real problem. Our operating cash is too low, and we are in desperate need of a loan. As you know, our financial position is marginal, and we need to show as much income as possible—and our assets need bolstering as well.

**Donna:** I understand the problem, but I don't see what can be done at this point. This is the last week of the fiscal year, and it looks like we'll report income just slightly above breakeven.

**Gary:** I know all this. What we need is some creative accounting. I have an idea that might help us, and I wanted to see if you would go along with it. We have 200 partially finished machines in process, about 20% complete. That compares with the 1,000 units that we completed and sold during the year. When you computed the per-unit cost, you used 1,040 equivalent units, giving us a manufacturing cost of $1,500 per unit. That per-unit cost gives us cost of goods sold equal to $1.5 million and ending work in process worth $60,000. The presence of the work in process gives us a chance to improve our financial position. If we report the units in work in process as 80% complete, this will increase our equivalent units to 1,160. This, in turn, will decrease our unit cost to about $1,345 and cost of goods sold to $1.345 million. The value of our work in process will increase to $215,200. With those financial stats, the loan would be a cinch.

**Donna:** Gary, I don't know. What you're suggesting is risky. It wouldn't take much auditing skill to catch this one.

**Gary:** You don't have to worry about that. The auditors won't be here for at least six to eight more weeks. By that time, we can have those partially completed units completed and sold. I can bury the labor cost by having some of our more loyal workers work overtime for some bonuses. The overtime will never be reported. And, as you know, bonuses come out of the corporate budget and are assigned to overhead—next year's overhead. Donna, this will work. If we look good and get the loan to boot, corporate headquarters will treat us well. If we don't do this, we could lose our jobs.

**Required:**

1.  Should Donna agree to Gary's proposal? Why or why not? To assist in deciding, review the corporate code of ethics standards described in Chapter 1. Do any apply?
2.  Assume that Donna refuses to cooperate and that Gary accepts this decision and drops the matter. Does Donna have any obligation to report the divisional manager's behavior to a superior? Explain.
3.  Assume that Donna refuses to cooperate; however, Gary insists that the changes be made. Now what should she do? What would you do?
4.  Suppose that Donna is 63 and that the prospects for employment elsewhere are bleak. Assume again that Gary insists that the changes be made. Donna also knows that his supervisor, the owner of the company, is his father-in-law. Under these circumstances, would your recommendations for Donna differ?

# 7

# Activity-Based Costing and Management

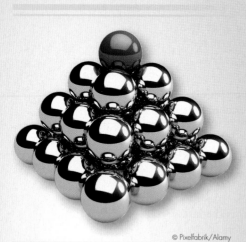

© Pixelfabrik/Alamy

After studying Chapter 7, you should be able to:

**1** Explain why functional (or volume)-based costing approaches may produce distorted costs.

**2** Explain how an activity-based costing system works for product costing.

**3** Describe activity-based customer costing and activity-based supplier costing.

**4** Explain how activity-based management can be used for cost reduction.

Madlen/Shutterstock.com

# EXPERIENCE MANAGERIAL DECISIONS

## with Cold Stone Creamery

Experts believe that ice cream as we know it was invented in the 1600s and was popularized in part by Charles I of England, who made it a staple of the royal table. Ice cream remains as popular as ever today, but trips to the local ice cream parlor have changed dramatically.

**Cold Stone Creamery**, founded in 1988 in Tempe, Arizona, has helped to lead this change with its innovative business model focused on making the ice cream trip an entertainment experience for the entire family. Cold Stone operates nearly 1,500 stores worldwide. Cold Stone executives must understand and control the company's complex cost structure in order to profitably manage its ice cream empire. For example, its most popular product line—ice cream with "mix in" ingredients— boasts 16 basic ice cream flavors with 30 different ingredients and three sizes, which represent thousands of possible ice cream product options! These options are great for customers with varied tastes, but are challenging for Cold Stone to manage given the different types of activities associated with different types of product orders. Therefore, Cold Stone adopted activity-based costing (ABC) to identify the activity drivers associated with each type of ice cream order and to estimate the costs of these activities.

Two important drivers of costs for Cold Stone include ingredients and time, both of which vary significantly across different ice cream product orders. With the insights gained from its ABC analysis, Cold Stone understands the cost of various orders' preparation time, which is measured in seconds. In addition to labor, Cold Stone's ABC system considers the costs associated with training, uniforms, and employee benefits when estimating the cost of each second required in making each product. When combined with other costs, the ABC analysis provides an estimate of profit margin by product type. If a particular product is not making its expected margin, Cold Stone managers know to look at the activities involved in creating the product and to fine-tune that activity. This understanding of Cold Stone's complex cost structure has provided the company with a valuable competitive advantage to become one of the most profitable and fastest-growing franchises in America.

> *"These options are great for customers with varied tastes, but are challenging for Cold Stone to manage given the different types of activities associated with different types of product orders. Therefore, Cold Stone adopted activity-based costing (ABC) to identify the activity drivers associated with each type of ice cream order and to estimate the costs of these activities."*

OBJECTIVE ❶

Explain why functional (or volume)-based costing approaches may produce distorted costs.

# LIMITATIONS OF FUNCTIONAL-BASED COST ACCOUNTING SYSTEMS

Plantwide and departmental rates based on direct labor hours, machine hours, or other volume-based measures have been used for decades to assign overhead costs to products and continue to be used successfully by many organizations. However, for many settings, this approach to costing is equivalent to an averaging approach and may produce distorted, or inaccurate, costs. For example, assume two friends, Lisa and Jessie, go to **Cold Stone Creamery** for dessert. Lisa orders a small chocolate ice cream in a plastic cup with no mix-ins, costing $3.00, and Jessie orders a medium strawberry banana rendezvous in a waffle dish (which has four mix-ins: graham cracker pie crust, white chocolate chips, strawberries, and bananas), costing $10. If the total bill is split evenly between the two, each individual would pay $6.50, which doesn't accurately represent the actual cost of each dessert. Lisa's dessert is overstated by $3.50, and Jessie's is understated by $3.50. If it is important to know the cost of each dessert, the averaging approach is not suitable.

In the same way, plantwide and departmental rates can produce average costs that severely understate or overstate individual product costs. Thus, **Cold Stone Creamery** would be very interested in knowing the cost of its numerous products and likely would not be satisfied with an averaging approach. Without accurate costing, Cold Stone would not be able to properly price its various products. Product cost distortions can be damaging, particularly for those firms whose business environment is characterized by the following:

- intense or increasing competitive pressures (often on a worldwide level)
- small profit margins
- continuous improvement
- total quality management
- total customer satisfaction
- sophisticated technology

Firms operating in theses types of business environments in particular need accurate cost information in order to make effective decisions.

In order for accurate cost information to be produced, it is important that the firm's cost system accurately reflect the firm's underlying business, or economic, reality. Thus, it is important that the managerial accountant continually ask the question, "How well does the cost system's *representation* of my business match the economic *reality* of my business?" If the answer is "not very well," then the cost system needs to be changed. Therefore, in much the same way that financial statements must be transparent for external users, the cost system must be transparent in its assignment of costs for internal users.

The need for more accurate product costs has forced many companies to take a serious look at their costing procedures. Two major factors impair the ability of unit-based plantwide and departmental rates to assign overhead costs accurately:

- The proportion of nonunit-related overhead costs to total overhead costs is large.
- The degree of product diversity is great.

## Nonunit-Related Overhead Costs

The use of either plantwide rates or departmental rates assumes that a product's consumption of overhead resources is related strictly to the units produced. For **unit-level activities**—activities that are performed each time a unit is produced—this assumption makes sense. Traditional, volume-based cost systems label the costs associated with these activities as variable in nature, because they increase or decrease in direct proportion to increases or decreases in the levels of these unit-level activities. All other costs (i.e., ones that are not unit-level) are considered fixed by volume-based cost systems.

But what if there are *nonunit-level activities*—activities that are not performed each time a unit of product is produced? The costs associated with these nonunit-level activities are unlikely to vary (i.e., increase or decrease) with units produced. These costs vary with other factor(s), besides units, and identifying such factor(s) is helpful in predicting and managing these costs. Proponents of activity-based costing (ABC) refer to the ABC cost hierarchy that categorizes costs either as *unit-level* (i.e., vary with output volume), *batch-level* (i.e., vary with the number of groups or batches that are run), *product-sustaining* (i.e., vary with the diversity of the product or service line), or *facility-sustaining* (i.e., do not vary with any factor but are necessary in operating the plant).[1] Exhibit 7.1 shows the activity-based costing hierarchy.

---

( EXHIBIT 7.1 )

**ABC Hierarchy**

| Type of Cost | Description of Cost Driver | Example |
|---|---|---|
| Unit-level | Varies with output volume (e.g., units); traditional variable costs | Cost of indirect materials for labeling each bottle of **Victoria's Secret** perfume |
| Batch-level | Varies with the number of batches produced | Cost of setting up laser engraving equipment for each batch of **Epilog** key chains |
| Product-sustaining | Varies with the number of product lines | Cost of inventory handling and warranty servicing of different brands carried by **Best Buy** electronics store |
| Facility-sustaining | Necessary to operate the plant facility but does not vary with units, batches, or product lines | Cost of **General Motors** plant manager salary |

© Cengage Learning 2014

**Nonunit-Level Activity Drivers** Setting up equipment is one example of a non-unit-level activity because, often, the same equipment is used to produce different products. Setting up equipment means preparing it for the particular type of product being made. For example, a vat may be used to dye t-shirts. After completing a batch of 1,000 red t-shirts, the vat must be carefully cleaned before a batch of 3,000 green t-shirts is produced. Thus, setup costs are incurred each time a batch of products is produced. A batch may consist of 1,000 or 3,000 units, and the cost of setup is the same. Yet as more setups are done, setup costs increase. The number of setups (a batch-level cost), not the number of units produced (a unit-level cost), is a much better measure of the consumption of the setup activity.

Another example of a nonunit-level activity is reengineering products. At times, based on customer feedback, firms face the necessity of redesigning their products. This product reengineering activity is authorized by a document called an *engineering work order*. For example, **Multibras S.A. Electrodomesticos**, a Brazilian appliance manufacturer (and subsidiary of Whirlpool), may issue engineering work orders to correct design flaws of its refrigerators, freezers, and washers. Product reengineering costs may depend on the number of different engineering work orders (a product-sustaining cost) rather than the units produced of any given product.

Similarly, **JetBlue**'s decision to add a second type of jet, the Embraer 190, to its existing fleet of Airbus A320s, caused it to incur significant additional product-sustaining costs that it would not have incurred had it stayed with only one type of

---

[1] R. Cooper, Cost Classification in Unit-Based and Activity-Based Manufacturing Cost Systems, *Journal of Cost Management for the Manufacturing Industry* (Fall 1990): 4–14.

## concept Q&A

At Fitzgerald Inc., Department C inspects each product produced and Department A inspects a small sample of each batch of products produced. Which inspection activity is unit-level, and which is nonunit-level?

**Answer:**

A unit-level activity is performed each time a unit is produced, whereas a nonunit-level activity is performed at times that do not correspond to individual unit production. Thus, inspection is unit-level for Department C and nonunit-level for the Department A.

plane. These additional product-sustaining costs included the costs for doubling the spare parts inventory, maintenance programs, and separate pilot-training tracks.[2]

Therefore, **nonunit-level activity drivers** (i.e., batch, product-sustaining, and facility-sustaining) are factors that measure the consumption of nonunit-level activities by products and other cost objects, whereas **unit-level activity drivers** measure the consumption of unit-level activities. **Activity drivers**, then, are factors that measure the consumption of activities by products and other cost objects and can be classified as either *unit-level* or *nonunit-level*.

Using only unit-based activity drivers to assign nonunit-related overhead costs can create distorted product costs. The severity of this distortion depends on what proportion of total overhead costs these nonunit-based costs represent. For many companies, this percentage can be significant, so care should be exercised in assigning nonunit-based overhead costs. If nonunit-based overhead costs are only a small percentage of total overhead costs, then the distortion of product costs will be quite small. In such a case, using unit-based activity drivers to assign overhead costs is acceptable.

## Product Diversity

The presence of significant nonunit overhead costs is a necessary but not sufficient condition for plantwide and departmental rate failure (i.e., distorted costs). For example, if products consume the nonunit-level overhead activities in the same proportion as the unit-level overhead activities, then no product-costing distortion will occur (with the use of traditional overhead assignment methods). The presence of product diversity is also necessary for product cost distortion to occur. **Product diversity** means that products consume overhead activities in systematically different proportions. This may occur for several reasons, including differences in:

- product size
- product complexity
- setup time
- size of batches

## Illustrating the Failure of Unit-Based Overhead Rates

To illustrate how traditional unit-based overhead rates can distort product costs, refer to the data for Rio Novo's Porto Behlo plant in Exhibit 7.2 (assume that the measures are expected and actual outcomes). The Porto Behlo plant produces two models of washers: a deluxe and a regular model. Because the quantity of regular models produced is 10 times greater than that of the deluxe, the regular model is a high-volume product and the deluxe model is a low-volume product. The models are produced in batches.

Remember that prime costs represent direct materials and direct labor. Given that these costs are direct in nature, they can be traced to each individual unit produced. It is the indirect, or overhead, costs that typically are treated differently by different types of cost systems. Usually, activity-based cost systems generate more accurate cost data than unit-based cost systems because of their more appropriate treatment of overhead costs. For simplicity, only four types of overhead activities, performed by four distinct support departments, are assumed:

- setting up the equipment for each batch (different configurations are needed for the electronic components associated with each model)
- moving a batch
- machining
- assembly (performed after each department's operations)

[2] S. Carey, "Balancing Act: Amid JetBlue's Rapid Ascent, CEO Adopts Big Rivals' Traits," *The Wall Street Journal* (August 25, 2005).

( EXHIBIT 7.2 )

**Product-Costing Data for Rio Novo's Porto Behlo Plant**

| | Activity Usage Measures | | | Activity Cost Data (Overhead Activities) | |
|---|---|---|---|---|---|
| | Deluxe | Regular | Total | Activity | Activity Cost |
| Units produced | 10 | 100 | 110 | Setting up equipment | $1,000 |
| Prime costs | $800 | $8,000 | $8,800 | Moving goods | 1,000 |
| Direct labor hours | 20 | 80 | 100 | Machining | 1,500 |
| Machine hours | 10 | 40 | 50 | Assembly | 500 |
| Setup hours | 3 | 1 | 4 | Total | $4,000 |
| Number of moves | 6 | 4 | 10 | | |

**Problems with Costing Accuracy** The activity usage data in Exhibit 7.2 reveal some serious problems with either plantwide or departmental rates for assigning overhead costs. The main problem with either procedure is the assumption that unit-level drivers such as machine hours or direct labor hours drive or cause all overhead costs.

From Exhibit 7.2, it can be seen that regular models, the high-volume product, use four times as many direct labor hours as deluxe models, the low-volume product (80 hours vs. 20 hours). Thus, if a plantwide rate is used, the regular models will be assigned four times more overhead cost than the deluxe models. But is this reasonable? Do unit-based drivers explain the consumption of all overhead activities? In particular, is it reasonable to assume that each product's consumption of overhead increases in direct proportion to the direct labor hours used? Now consider the four overhead activities to see if the unit-level drivers accurately reflect the demands of regular and deluxe model production.

Examination of the data in Exhibit 7.2 suggests that a significant portion of overhead costs is not driven or caused by direct labor hours. Each product's demands for setup and material-moving activities are more logically related to the setup hours and the number of moves, respectively. These nonunit activities represent 50% ($2,000/$4,000) of the total overhead costs—a significant percentage. Notice that the low-volume product, deluxe models, uses three times more setup hours than the regular models (3/1) and one and a half as many moves (6/4). However, using a plantwide rate based on direct labor hours, a unit-based activity driver assigns four times more setup and material moving costs to the regular models than to the deluxe. Thus, product diversity exists, and we should expect product cost distortion because the quantity of unit-based overhead that each product consumes does not vary in direct proportion to the quantity consumed of nonunit-based overhead.

Regardless of the nature of the product diversity, product cost will be distorted whenever the quantity of unit-based overhead that a product consumes does not vary in direct proportion to the quantity consumed of nonunit-based overhead. The proportion of each activity consumed by a product is defined as the **consumption ratio** and is calculated as:

$$\text{Consumption Ratio} = \frac{\text{Amount of Activity Driver per Product}}{\text{Total Driver Quantity}}$$

Cornerstone 7.1 (p. 286) illustrates how to calculate the consumption ratios for the two products.

# Calculating Consumption Ratios

**Why:**

Logically, the cost of shared resources should be assigned in proportion to the amount of the resources consumed. Since activities represent bundles of resources consumed by products, it is reasonable to assign activity costs in proportion to the amount of activity consumed. Activity drivers measure activity output and thus can be used as measures of activity consumption. Consumption ratios, then, represent the proportion of an activity consumed by individual products, calculated using activity drivers.

**Information:**

Refer to the activity usage information for Rio Novo's Porto Behlo plant in Exhibit 7.2 (p. 285).

**Required:**

Calculate the consumption ratios for each product.

**Solution:**

**Step 1:** Identify the activity driver for each activity.
**Step 2:** Divide the amount of driver used for each product by the total driver quantity.

| | Consumption Ratios | | |
| --- | --- | --- | --- |
| **Overhead Activity** | **Deluxe Model** | **Regular Model** | **Activity Driver** |
| Setting up equipment | 0.75[a] | 0.25[a] | Setup hours |
| Moving goods | 0.60[b] | 0.40[b] | Number of moves |
| Machining | 0.20[c] | 0.80[c] | Machine hours |
| Assembly | 0.20[d] | 0.80[d] | Direct labor hours |

[a] 3/4 (deluxe) and 1/4 (regular).
[b] 6/10 (deluxe) and 4/10 (regular).
[c] 10/50 (deluxe) and 40/50 (regular).
[d] 20/100 (deluxe) and 80/100 (regular).

The consumption ratios in Cornerstone 7.1 suggest that a plantwide rate based on direct labor hours will overcost the regular models and undercost the deluxe models.

**Solving the Problem of Cost Distortion**   This cost distortion can be solved using activity rates. Instead of assigning the overhead costs using a single, plantwide rate, a rate for each overhead activity can be calculated and used to assign overhead costs. Cornerstone 7.2 shows how to calculate these rates.

# Calculating Activity Rates

**Why:**

An activity rate is the means by which activity costs are assigned to products. A rate for each activity is calculated by dividing the activity cost by an activity driver. A cause-and-effect relationship is the basis for choosing the activity driver used in the rate calculation.

*(Continued)*

**Information:**

Rio Novo's Porto Behlo plant activity cost and driver data follow:

| Activity | Activity Cost ($) | Driver | Driver Quantity |
|---|---|---|---|
| Setting up equipment | 1,000 | Setup hours | 4 |
| Moving goods | 1,000 | Number of moves | 10 |
| Machining | 1,500 | Machine hours | 50 |
| Assembly | 500 | Direct labor hours | 100 |

**Required:**

Calculate the activity rates.

**Solution:**

Divide the activity cost by the total driver quantity:

| | |
|---|---|
| Setup rate: | $1,000/4 setup hours = $250 per setup hour |
| Materials handling rate: | $1,000/10 moves = $100 per move |
| Machining rate: | $1,500/50 machine hours = $30 per machine hour |
| Assembly rate: | $500/100 direct labor hours = $5 per direct labor hour |

CORNERSTONE

7.2

*(Continued)*

To assign overhead costs, the amount of activity consumed by each product is needed along with the activity rates. Cornerstone 7.3 shows how to calculate the unit cost for each product by using activity rates.

## Calculating Activity-Based Unit Costs

**Why:**

To increase the accuracy of overhead cost assignments, causal factors, called activity drivers, are chosen that measure the amount of activity consumed by a product. The activity rate multiplied by the amount used of each activity determines the amount of activity cost assigned to a particular product. The sum of all such assigned activity costs is the total amount of overhead consumed by a product. Overhead costs plus prime costs divided by units produced then yields the unit cost.

CORNERSTONE

7.3

**Information:**

Rio Novo's Porto Behlo plant activity rate data for deluxe and regular models follows:

| | Deluxe | Regular | Activity Rate |
|---|---|---|---|
| Units produced per year | 10 | 100 | |
| Prime costs | $800 | $8,000 | |
| Setup hours | 3 | 1 | $250 |
| Number of moves | 6 | 4 | $100 |
| Machine hours | 10 | 40 | $ 30 |
| Direct labor hours | 20 | 80 | $ 5 |

*(Continued)*

CORNERSTONE
**7.3**

*(Continued)*

**Required:**

Calculate the unit cost for deluxe and regular models.

**Solution:**

|  | **Deluxe** | **Regular** |
|---|---|---|
| Prime costs | $ 800 | $ 8,000 |
| Overhead costs: |  |  |
| Setups: |  |  |
| $250 × 3 setup hours | 750 |  |
| $250 × 1 setup hour |  | 250 |
| Moving materials: |  |  |
| $100 × 6 moves | 600 |  |
| $100 × 4 moves |  | 400 |
| Machining: |  |  |
| $30 × 10 machine hours | 300 |  |
| $30 × 40 machine hours |  | 1,200 |
| Assembly: |  |  |
| $5 × 20 direct labor hours | 100 |  |
| $5 × 80 direct labor hours |  | 400 |
| Total manufacturing costs | $2,550 | $10,250 |
| Units produced | ÷ 10 | ÷ 100 |
| Unit cost (Total costs/Units) | $ 255 | $102.50 |

Exhibit 7.3 visually summarizes the calculations in Cornerstones 7.2 and 7.3.

( EXHIBIT 7.3 )

**Activity Rates and Activity-Based Unit Costs for Rio Novo's Porto Behlo Plant**

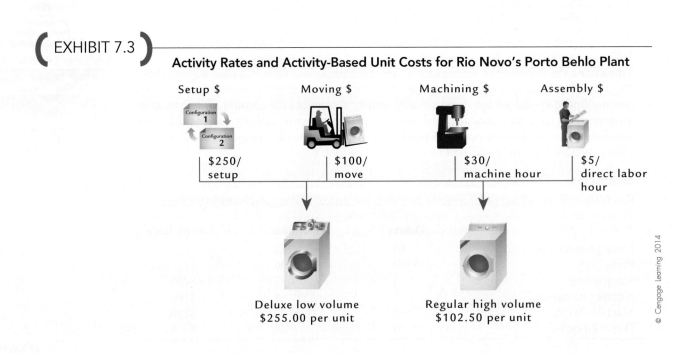

**Comparison of Functional-Based and Activity-Based Product Costs** A plantwide rate based on direct labor hours is calculated as follows:

$$\text{Overhead Rate} = \frac{\text{Total Overhead Costs}}{\text{Total Direct Labor Hours}}$$

$$\frac{\$4,000}{100} = \$40 \text{ per direct labor hour}$$

The product cost for each product using this single unit-level overhead rate is calculated as follows:

|  | Deluxe | Regular |
|---|---|---|
| Prime costs | $ 800 | $ 8,000 |
| Overhead costs: | | |
| $40 × 20 | 800 | |
| $40 × 80 | | 3,200 |
| Total cost | $1,600 | $11,200 |
| Units produced | ÷10 | ÷100 |
| Unit cost | $ 160 | $ 112 |

Now compare these product costs with the activity-based cost of Cornerstone 7.3. This comparison clearly illustrates the effects of using only unit-based activity drivers to assign overhead costs. The activity-based cost assignment reflects the pattern of overhead consumption and is, therefore, the most accurate. Activity-based product costing reveals that functional-based costing undercosts the low volume deluxe models and overcosts the high volume regular models. In fact, the ABC assignment increases the reported cost of the deluxe models by $95 per unit and decreases the reported cost of the regular models by $9.50 per unit—a movement in the right direction given the pattern of overhead consumption.

## Illustrating Relationships: Product Diversity and Product Costing Accuracy

For unit-level overhead rates to fail, products must consume the nonunit-level activities in proportions significantly different than the unit-level activities. The greater the difference in this consumption pattern, the greater the potential product cost distortion. For example, the Regular model of Rio Novo consumes activities in the following proportions:

- 25% of the setup hours
- 40% of the number of moves
- 80% of the machine hours
- 80% of the direct labor hours

Since the plantwide overhead rate uses direct labor hours, a unit-level driver, 80% of the total overhead would be assigned to the Regular model. However, the Regular model consumes only an average of 32.5% of the nonunit-level overhead [(0.25 + 0.40)/2] and so we would expect a significant cost distortion. Intuitively, if the *average* consumption ratio of the nonunit-level activities differs markedly from the unit-level consumption ratio, as 32.5% differs from 80%, then there is greater product diversity and greater product cost distortion. As expected, the distortion is significant because the plantwide rate assigns $3,200 of overhead while the ABC approach assigns only $2,250. Alternatively, if there is little or no product diversity, then products consume unit-level activities and nonunit-level activities in the same (or close to the same) proportion and a plantwide rate works well.

This diversity-accuracy relationship can be seen in the Rio Novo example in Cornerstones 7.2 (p. 286) and 7.3, by allowing the average nonunit-level consumption ratio to vary. We see a special structure characterized by the following features:

- The Deluxe and Regular products have the same consumption ratios (0.20 and 0.80, respectively) for the unit-level activities (machining and assembly).
- The cost of the nonunit-level activities, setting up and moving, is the same ($1,000 for each activity).
- The total cost of the unit-level (nonunit-level) activities is $2,000.

This special structure means that the average consumption ratio for the two unit-level (nonunit-level) activities can be used to assign the activity costs to each product, achieving the same assignment as when done for each individual activity. This can be calculated as follows:

$$\text{Overhead Cost} = \text{Average Consumption Ratio} \times \text{Total Cost of Each Set of Activities}$$

The average consumption ratios for the Regular product are:

$$\text{Unit-Level Activities} = (0.80 + 0.80)/2$$
$$= 0.80$$
$$\text{Nonunit-Level Activities} = (0.25 + 0.40)/2$$
$$= 0.325$$

Thus, for the Regular product:

$$\text{Overhead Cost} = (0.80 \times \$2,000) + (0.325 \times \$2,000)$$
$$= \$1,600 + \$650$$
$$= \$2,250$$

This is the same as the assignments using individual activities and activity rates.

To explore the effect of product diversity on accuracy, hold the unit-level consumption ratios constant and allow the average nonunit-level consumption ratio to vary. This produces the following overhead cost assignment equation for the Regular product:

$$\text{Overhead Cost} = \$1,600 + \text{Average Nonunit Consumption Ratio} \times \$2,000$$

Using this equation, Exhibit 7.4 shows the overhead cost assigned to the Regular model as the average nonunit-level consumption ratio varies. The red line represents the average nonunit consumption ratio function. The blue horizontal line is the overhead cost assignment using the plantwide rate. Notice that when it intersects $3,200 the overhead cost assignment is the same for both ABC and plantwide assignments (the average consumption ratio is 0.80, which is the same as the consumption ratio for the plantwide rate). As the average consumption ratio decreases, the difference between the ABC and plantwide assignments increases. The vertical lines indicate the difference between the ABC and plantwide rate overhead assignments. Clearly, some values can occur that would produce little difference between the plantwide and ABC assignments, and thus it would be cheaper and simpler to use a single-rate costing system. For example, the vertical lines are small between 0.70 and 1.00, indicating that when the average nonunit consumption ratio is in this range, then a plantwide rate would provide good accuracy. The green vertical line represents the accuracy loss when the product diversity corresponds to the original example data.

The key message of the relationship analysis is that in a diverse product environment, activity-based costing promises greater accuracy. Given the importance of making decisions based on accurate facts, a detailed look at activity-based costing is certainly merited.

( EXHIBIT 7.4 )

**Diversity and Product Costing Accuracy**

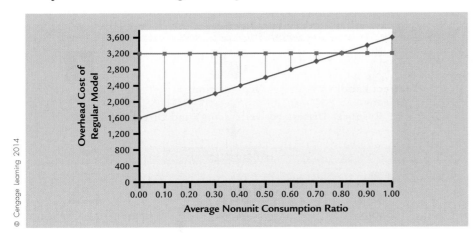

© Cengage Learning 2014

**ETHICAL DECISIONS**   One of the ethical standards of the Institute of Management Accountants (IMA) requires that its members maintain professional expertise by continually developing knowledge and skills. An interesting issue is whether accounting professionals who resist learning different cost management methods are exhibiting ethical behavior. At the very least, cost accounting professionals should learn about different approaches and assess whether the benefit-cost trade-offs justify their use. ●

# ACTIVITY-BASED PRODUCT COSTING

Functional-based overhead costing involves two major stages:

1. Overhead costs are assigned to an organizational unit (plant or department).

2. Overhead costs are then assigned to cost objects.

As Exhibit 7.5 (p. 292) illustrates, an **activity-based costing (ABC) system** is also a two-stage process:

1. Trace costs to activities.

2. Trace activity costs to cost objects.

The underlying assumption is that activities consume resources, and cost objects, in turn, consume activities. An ABC system, however, emphasizes direct tracing and driver tracing (exploiting cause-and-effect relationships), while a volume-based costing system tends to be allocation-intensive (largely ignoring cause-and-effect relationships). Since the focus of ABC is activities, identifying activities must be the first step in designing an ABC system.

## Identifying Activities and Their Attributes

An **activity** is action taken or work performed by equipment or people for other people. Identifying activities usually is accomplished by interviewing managers or representatives of functional work areas (departments). A set of key questions is asked in which answers provide much of the data needed for an ABC system.

**Set of Key Questions**   Interview questions can be used to identify activities and activity attributes needed for costing purposes. The information

OBJECTIVE ❷

Explain how an activity-based costing system works for product costing.

---

concept Q&A

What are some key differences between ABC and volume-based costing?

**Answer:**

ABC uses cause-and-effect relationships to assign overhead costs. Volume-based costing uses unit-based drivers such as direct labor hours, which often have nothing to do with the actual overhead resources consumed by a product.

( **EXHIBIT 7.5** )

### Activity-Based Costing: Assigning Cost of Overhead

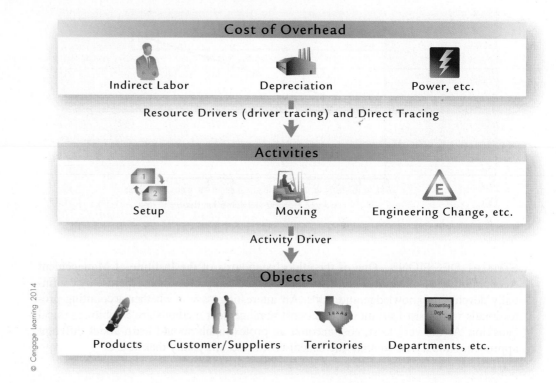

derived from these questions provides data helpful for assigning resource costs to individual activities. To prevent the number of activities from becoming unmanageably large, a common rule of thumb employed by the interviewer is to tell the interviewee to ignore activities that require less than 5% of an individual's time. Examples of questions that interviewers might ask to gather information include the following:

1. How many employees are in your department? (Activities consume labor.)

2. What do they do (please describe)? (Activities are people doing things for other people.)

3. Do customers outside your department use any equipment? (Activities also can be equipment working for other people. In other words, the equipment provides the service for someone by itself).

4. What resources are used by each activity (equipment, materials, energy)? (Activities consume resources in addition to labor.)

5. What are the outputs of each activity? (Helps to identify activity drivers.)

6. Who or what uses the activity output? (Identifies the cost object: products, other activities, customers, etc.)

7. How much time do workers spend on each activity? Time on each activity by equipment? (Information assigns the cost of labor and equipment to activities.)

***Illustrative Example: Hemingway Bank*** Suppose that the manager of Hemingway Bank's credit card department is interviewed and presented with the seven questions just listed. Consider the purpose and response to each question in the order indicated.

- *Question 1 (labor resource):* There are five employees.
- *Question 2 (activity identification):* There are three major activities: processing credit card transactions, issuing customer statements, and answering customer questions.

- *Question 3 (activity identification):* Yes. Automatic bank tellers service customers who require cash advances.
- *Question 4 (resource identification):* Each employee has his or her own computer, printer, and desk. Paper and other supplies are needed to operate the printers. Each employee has a telephone as well.
- *Question 5 (potential activity drivers):* Processing transactions produces a posting for each transaction in our computer system and serves as a source for preparing the monthly statements. The number of monthly customer statements has to be the product for the issuing activity, and I suppose that customers served is the output for the answering activity. The number of cash advances measures the product of the automatic teller activity, although the teller really generates more transactions for other products such as checking accounts. So, perhaps the number of teller transactions is the real output.
- *Question 6 (potential cost objects identified):* We have three products: classic, gold, and platinum credit cards. Transactions are processed for these three types of cards, and statements are sent to clients holding these cards. Similarly, answers to questions are all directed to clients who hold these cards.
- *Question 7 (identifying resource drivers):* I just completed a work survey and have the percentage of time calculated for each worker. All five clerks work on each of the three departmental activities. About 40% of their time is spent processing transactions, with the rest of their time split evenly between preparing statements and answering questions. Phone time is used only for answering client questions, and computer time is 70% transaction processing, 20% statement preparation, and 10% answering questions. Furthermore, my own time and that of my computer are 100% administrative.

> ### concept Q&A
>
> What is the purpose of the interview questions?
>
> **Answer:**
>
> The purpose is to identify activities, drivers, and other important attributes essential for ABC.

**Activity Dictionary**  These interview-derived data are used to prepare an *activity dictionary*. An **activity dictionary** lists the activities in an organization along with some critical activity attributes. Activity attributes are financial and nonfinancial information items that describe individual activities. What attributes are used depends on the purpose. Examples of activity attributes associated with a costing objective include the following:

- types of resources consumed
- amount (percentage) of time spent on an activity by workers
- cost objects that consume the activity output (reason for performing the activity)
- measure of the activity output (activity driver)
- activity name

**Illustrative Example: Hemingway Bank**  Exhibit 7.6 (p. 294) illustrates the activity dictionary for Hemingway's credit card department. The three products, classic, gold, and platinum credit cards, in turn, consume the activities. It is not unusual for a typical organization to produce an activity dictionary containing 200 to 300 activities.

## Assigning Costs to Activities

Once activities are identified and described, the next task is to determine how much it costs to perform each activity. This determination requires identification of the resources being consumed by each activity. Some cost system experts consider this task to be the most difficult one in creating an accurate cost system. Activities consume resources such as labor, materials, energy, and capital. The cost of these resources is found in the general ledger, but the money spent on each activity is not revealed. Thus, it becomes necessary to assign the resource costs to activities by using direct and driver tracing. For labor resources, a *work distribution matrix* often is used. A **work distribution matrix**

**( EXHIBIT 7.6 )**

### Activity Dictionary for Hemingway Bank's Credit Card Department

| Activity Name | Activity Description | Cost Object(s) | Activity Driver |
|---|---|---|---|
| Processing | Sorting, keying, and transactions verifying | Credit cards | Number of transactions |
| Preparing statements | Reviewing, printing, stuffing, and mailing | Credit cards | Number of statements |
| Answering questions | Answering, logging, reviewing database, and making call backs | Credit cards | Number of cards |
| Providing automatic tellers | Accessing accounts, withdrawing funds | Credit cards, checking and savings accounts | Number of teller transactions |

© Cengage Learning 2014

identifies the amount of labor consumed by each activity and is derived from the interview process (or a written survey).

*Illustrative Example: Hemingway Bank*  Exhibit 7.7 provides an example of a work distribution matrix supplied by the manager of Hemingway's credit card department for individual activities (refer to Question 7).

**( EXHIBIT 7.7 )**

### Work Distribution Matrix for Hemingway Bank's Credit Card Department

| Activity | Percentage of Time per Activity |
|---|---|
| Processing transactions | 40% |
| Preparing statements | 30% |
| Answering questions | 30% |

© Cengage Learning 2014

From Exhibit 7.5 (p. 292), we know that both direct tracing and driver tracing are used to assign resource costs to activities. For this example, the time spent on each activity is the basis for assigning the labor costs to the activity. If the time is 100%, then labor is exclusive to the activity, and the assignment method is direct tracing. If the resource is shared by several activities (as is the case of the clerical resource), then the assignment is driver tracing, and the drivers are called *resource drivers*. **Resource drivers** are factors that measure the consumption of resources by activities. Once resource drivers are identified, then the costs of the resource can be assigned to the activity. Cornerstone 7.4 shows how resource drivers and direct tracing are used to assign labor cost to the credit department activities.

**CORNERSTONE**

**7.4**

## Assigning Resource Costs to Activities by Using Direct Tracing and Resource Drivers

**Why:**

Activities consume resources and other cost objects consume activities. Thus, the first step in assigning costs is determining activity cost. The cost of resources is assigned to activities using direct tracing and driver tracing. When resources are exclusively used by an activity, direct tracing is used. For shared resources, resource drivers are used.

*(Continued)*

© Pixelfabrik/Alamy

**Information:**

Refer to the work distribution matrix for Hemingway Bank's credit card department in Exhibit 7.7. Assume that each clerk is paid a salary of $30,000 ($150,000 total clerical cost for five clerks).

**Required:**

Assign the cost of labor to each of the activities in the credit department. Is this assignment driver tracing or direct tracing?

**Solution:**

The amount of labor cost assigned to each activity is given below. (*Note*: The percentages come from the work distribution matrix.)

| | |
|---|---|
| Processing transactions | $60,000 (0.40 × $150,000) |
| Preparing statements | $45,000 (0.30 × $150,000) |
| Answering questions | $45,000 (0.30 × $150,000) |

Labor is a shared resource and is assigned using a resource driver (using labor consumption ratios).

Labor, of course, is not the only resource consumed by activities. Activities also consume materials, capital, and energy. The interview, for example, reveals that the activities within the credit card department use computers (capital), phones (capital), desks (capital), and paper (materials). The automatic teller activity uses the automatic teller (capital) and energy. The cost of these other resources must also be assigned to the various activities. They are assigned in the same way as was described for labor (using direct tracing and resource drivers). The cost of computers could be assigned by using direct tracing (for the supervising activity) and hours of usage for the remaining activities. From the interview, we know the relative usage of computers by each activity. The general ledger reveals that the cost per computer is $1,200 per year. Thus, an additional $6,000 (5 × $1,200) would be assigned to three activities based on relative usage:

- 70% to processing transactions ($4,200)
- 20% to preparing statements ($1,200)
- 10% to answering questions ($600)

Repeating this process for all resources, the total cost of each activity can be calculated. Exhibit 7.8 (p. 296) gives the cost of the activities associated with Hemingway's credit card department under the assumption that all resource costs have been assigned (these numbers are assumed because all resource data are not given for their calculation).

## Assigning Costs to Products

From Cornerstone 7.3 (p. 287), we know that activity costs are assigned to products by multiplying a predetermined activity rate by the usage of the activity, as measured by

**( EXHIBIT 7.8 )**

## Activity Costs for Hemingway Bank's Credit Card Department

| | |
|---|---|
| Processing transactions | $130,000 |
| Preparing statements | 102,000 |
| Answering questions | 92,400 |
| Providing automatic tellers | 250,000 |

© Cengage Learning 2014

activity drivers. Exhibit 7.6 (p. 294) identified the activity drivers for each of the four credit card activities:

- number of transactions for processing transactions
- number of statements for preparing statements
- number of calls for answering questions
- number of teller transactions for the activity of providing automatic tellers

To calculate an activity rate, the practical capacity of each activity must be determined. To assign costs, the amount of each activity consumed by each product must also be known.

*Illustrative Example: Hemingway Bank* Assuming that the practical activity capacity is equal to the total activity usage by all products, the following actual data have been collected for Hemingway's credit card department:

| | Classic Card | Gold Card | Platinum Card | Total |
|---|---|---|---|---|
| Number of cards | 5,000 | 3,000 | 2,000 | 10,000 |
| Transactions processed | 600,000 | 300,000 | 100,000 | 1,000,000 |
| Number of statements | 60,000 | 36,000 | 24,000 | 120,000 |
| Number of calls | 10,000 | 12,000 | 8,000 | 30,000 |
| Number of teller transactions* | 15,000 | 3,000 | 2,000 | 20,000 |

\* The number of teller transactions for the cards is 10% of the total transactions from all sources. Thus, teller transactions total 20,000 (0.10 × 200,000).

Applying Cornerstone 7.2 (p. 287) by using the data and costs from Exhibit 7.8, the activity rates are calculated as follows:

**Rate calculations:**

| | |
|---|---|
| Processing transactions: | $130,000/1,000,000 = $0.13 per transaction |
| Preparing statements: | $102,000/120,000 = $0.85 per statement |
| Answering questions: | $92,400/30,000 = $3.08 per call |
| Providing automatic tellers: | $250,000/200,000 = $1.25 per transaction |

These rates provide the cost of each activity usage. Using these rates, costs are assigned as shown in Exhibit 7.9. However, we now know the whole story behind the development of the activity rates and usage measures. Furthermore, the banking example emphasizes the utility of ABC in service organizations.

EXHIBIT 7.9

**Assigning Costs for Hemingway Bank's Credit Card Department**

| | Gold | Classic | Platinum |
|---|---|---|---|
| **Processing transactions:** | | | |
| $0.13 × 600,000 | $ 78,000 | | |
| $0.13 × 300,000 | | $ 39,000 | |
| $0.13 × 100,000 | | | $13,000 |
| **Preparing statements:** | | | |
| $0.85 × 60,000 | 51,000 | | |
| $0.85 × 36,000 | | 30,600 | |
| $0.85 × 24,000 | | | 20,400 |
| **Answering questions:** | | | |
| $3.08 × 10,000 | 30,800 | | |
| $3.08 × 12,000 | | 36,960 | |
| $3.08 × 8,000 | | | 24,640 |
| **Providing automatic tellers:** | | | |
| $1.25 × 15,000 | 18,750 | | |
| $1.25 × 3,000 | | 3,750 | |
| $1.25 × 2,000 | | | 2,500 |
| Total costs | $178,550 | $110,310 | $60,540 |
| Units | ÷5,000 | ÷3,000 | ÷2,000 |
| Unit cost | $   35.71 | $   36.77 | $   30.27 |

# ACTIVITY-BASED CUSTOMER COSTING AND ACTIVITY-BASED SUPPLIER COSTING

OBJECTIVE ③

Describe activity-based customer costing and activity-based supplier costing.

ABC systems originally became popular for their ability to improve product-costing accuracy by tracing activity costs to the products that consume the activities. However, since the beginning of the 21st century, the use of ABC has expanded into areas upstream (i.e., before the production section of the value chain—research and development, prototyping, etc.) and downstream (i.e., after the production section of the value chain—marketing, distribution, customer service, etc.) from production. Specifically, ABC often is used to more accurately determine the upstream costs of suppliers and the downstream costs of customers. Knowing the costs of suppliers and customers can be vital information for improving a company's profitability.

LSI Logic, a high-tech producer of semiconductors, implemented ABC customer costing and discovered that 10% of its customers were responsible for about 90% of its profits. LSI also discovered that it was actually losing money on about 50% of its customers. It worked to convert its unprofitable customers into profitable ones and invited those who would not provide a fair return to take their business elsewhere. As a consequence, LSI's sales decreased, but its profit tripled.[3] Exhibit 7.10 depicts this interesting yet common relationship between customers and their contribution to company profitability. Some managers refer to this graph as the "whale curve" of customer profitability, likely because of its resemblance to the shape of whale cresting at the water's surface. The important observation from the curve is that the customers to the left of

---

[3] Gary Cokins, "Are All of Your Customers Profitable (To You)?" (June 14, 2001): www.bettermanagment.com/Library (accessed May 2010).

**( EXHIBIT 7.10 )**

### Whale Curve of Cumulative Customer Profitability

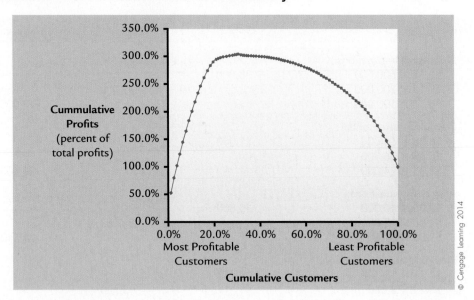

© Cengage Learning 2014

the hump, or peak, increase the company's profitability, while the customers to the right decrease the company's profitability. Therefore, activity-based customer costing is helpful in determining where each customer falls on the curve and, subsequently, how each customer should therefore be treated given its position on the curve. Of particular interest are those customers to the far right because they severely decrease the company's profitability and need to be terminated as unacceptably bad customers or altered in some way so as to become profitable customers for the company.

## Activity-Based Customer Costing

Customers are cost objects of fundamental interest. As the **LSI Logic** experience illustrates, customer management can produce significant gains in profit. It is possible to have customer diversity, just as it is possible to have product diversity. Customers can consume customer-driven activities in different proportions. Sources of customer diversity include order frequency, delivery frequency, geographic distance, sales and promotional support, and engineering support requirements. Knowing how much it costs to service different customers can be vital information for the following purposes:

- setting pricing
- determining customer mix
- improving profitability

Furthermore, because of diversity of customers, multiple drivers are needed to trace costs accurately. This outcome means that ABC can be useful to organizations that have only one product, homogeneous products, or a just-in-time (JIT) structure where direct tracing diminishes the value of ABC for product costing.

**Customer Costing versus Product Costing**  Assigning the costs of customer service to customers is done in the same way that manufacturing costs are assigned to products. Customer-driven activities such as order entry, order picking, shipping, making sales calls, and evaluating a client's credit are identified and listed in an activity dictionary. The cost of the resources consumed is assigned to activities, and the cost of the activities is assigned to individual

### concept Q&A

How are costs assigned to customers by using the ABC approach?

**Answer:**

Costs are traced to activities and then assigned to customers based on their usage of these activities.

customers. The same model and procedures that apply to products apply to customers as well. Cornerstone 7.5 illustrates how ABC assigns costs to customers.

## Calculating Activity-Based Customer Costs

**Why:**

Customer-based activity costs are assigned to customers or customer-types using activity drivers. Knowing the costs of individual customers or customer-types can be helpful in setting prices, determining the best customer mix, and in improving profitability.

**Information:**

Milan Company produces precision parts for 11 major buyers. Of the 11 customers, one accounts for 50% of the sales, with the remaining 10 accounting for the rest of the sales. The 10 smaller customers purchase parts in roughly equal quantities. Orders placed by the smaller customers are about the same size. Data concerning Milan's customer activity follow:

|  | Large Customer | Ten Smaller Customers |
|---|---|---|
| Units purchased | 500,000 | 500,000 |
| Orders placed | 2 | 200 |
| Number of sales calls | 10 | 210 |
| Manufacturing costs | $3,000,000 | $3,000,000 |
| Order filling costs allocated* | $ 202,000 | $ 202,000 |
| Sales force costs allocated* | $ 110,000 | $ 110,000 |

* Allocated based on sales volume.

Currently, customer-driven costs are assigned to customers based on units sold, a unit-level driver.

**Required:**

Assign costs to customers using an ABC approach.

**Solution:**

The appropriate drivers are orders placed and number of sales calls. The activity rates are:

$$\$404,000/202 \text{ orders} = \$2,000 \text{ per order}$$
$$\$220,000/220 \text{ calls} = \$1,000 \text{ per call}$$

Using this information, the customer-driven costs can be assigned to each group of customers as follows:

|  | Large Customer | Ten Smaller Customers |
|---|---|---|
| Order filling costs: |  |  |
| ($2,000 × 2) | $ 4,000 |  |
| ($2,000 × 200) |  | $400,000 |
| Sales force costs: |  |  |
| ($1,000 × 10) | 10,000 |  |
| ($1,000 × 210) |  | 210,000 |
|  | $14,000 | $610,000 |

The activity-based cost assignments reveal a much different picture of the cost of servicing each type of customer. The smaller customers cost more due to their smaller, more frequent orders and the need of the sales force to engage in more negotiations to make a sale.

What does this analysis tell management that it didn't know before? First, the large customer costs much less to service than the smaller customers and perhaps should be charged less. Second, it raises some significant questions relative to the smaller customers. For example, is it possible to encourage larger, less frequent orders? Perhaps offering discounts for larger orders would be appropriate. Why is it more difficult to sell to the smaller customers? Why are more calls needed? Are they less informed than the larger customer about the products? Can we improve profits by influencing our customers to change their buying behavior?

## Activity-Based Supplier Costing

ABC can also help managers identify the true cost of a firm's suppliers. The cost of a supplier is much more than the purchase price of the components or materials acquired. Just like customers, suppliers can affect many internal activities of a firm and significantly increase the cost of purchasing. A more correct view is one where the costs associated with quality, reliability, and late deliveries are added to the purchase costs. Managers are then required to evaluate suppliers based on total cost, not just purchase price. ABC is the key to tracing costs relating to these factors.

**Supplier Costing Methodology**  Assigning the costs of supplier-related activities to suppliers follows the same pattern as ABC product and customer costing. Supplier-driven activities are identified and listed in an activity dictionary. Some examples of supplier-driven activities include the following:

- purchasing
- receiving
- inspection of incoming components
- reworking products (because of defective components)
- expediting products (because of late deliveries of suppliers)
- warranty work (due to defective supplier components)

The cost of the resources consumed is assigned to these activities, and the cost of the activities is assigned to individual suppliers.  Cornerstone 7.6 illustrates how to use ABC for supplier costing.

---

### concept Q&A

How are costs assigned to suppliers by using the ABC approach?

**Answer:**

Costs are traced to activities and are then assigned to suppliers based on a cause-and-effect relationship.

---

## CORNERSTONE 7.6

### Calculating Activity-Based Supplier Costs

**Why:**

Activity drivers are used to trace the costs of activities associated with supplier reliability, quality, and late deliveries to individual suppliers. These costs are then added to direct purchase costs. This outcome enables managers to improve their evaluation and selection of suppliers, with the objective of reducing total supplier costs.

**Information:**

Assume that a purchasing manager uses two suppliers, Murray Inc. and Plata Associates, as the source of two machine parts: Part A1 and Part B2. Consider two activities: repairing products (under warranty) and expediting products. Repairing products occurs because of part failure (bought from suppliers). Expediting products occurs because suppliers are late

*(Continued)*

in delivering needed parts. Activity cost information and other data needed for supplier costing follow:

CORNERSTONE

7.6

*(Continued)*

I. Activity Costs Caused by Suppliers (e.g., failed parts or late delivery)

| Activity | Costs |
|---|---|
| Repairing products | $800,000 |
| Expediting products | $200,000 |

II. Supplier Data

| | Murray Inc. | | Plata Associates | |
|---|---|---|---|---|
| | Part A1 | Part B2 | Part A1 | Part B2 |
| Unit purchase price | $ 20 | $ 52 | $ 24 | $ 56 |
| Units purchased | 80,000 | 40,000 | 10,000 | 10,000 |
| Failed units | 1,600 | 380 | 10 | 10 |
| Late shipments | 60 | 40 | 0 | 0 |

**Required:**

Determine the cost of each supplier by using ABC.

**Solution:**

Using the above data, the activity rates for assigning costs to suppliers are computed as follows:

$$\text{Repair Rate} = \$800,000/2,000^* \text{ unit}$$
$$= \$400 \text{ per failed unit}$$
$$^*(1,600 + 380 + 10 + 10)$$

$$\text{Expediting Rate} = \$200,000/100^{**} \text{ late shipment}$$
$$= \$2,000 \text{ per late shipment}$$
$$^{**}(60 + 40)$$

Using these rates and the activity data, the total purchasing cost per unit of each component is computed:

| | Murray Inc. | | Plata Associates | |
|---|---|---|---|---|
| | Part A1 | Part B2 | Part A1 | Part B2 |
| Purchase cost: | | | | |
| $20 × 80,000 | $1,600,000 | | | |
| $52 × 40,000 | | $2,080,000 | | |
| $24 × 10,000 | | | $240,000 | |
| $56 × 10,000 | | | | $560,000 |
| Repairing products: | | | | |
| $400 × 1,600 | 640,000 | | | |
| $400 × 380 | | 152,000 | | |
| $400 × 10 | | | 4,000 | |
| $400 × 10 | | | | 4,000 |
| Expediting products: | | | | |
| $2,000 × 60 | 120,000 | | | |
| $2,000 × 40 | | 80,000 | | |
| Total costs | $2,360,000 | $2,312,000 | $244,000 | $564,000 |
| Units | ÷80,000 | ÷40,000 | ÷10,000 | ÷10,000 |
| Total unit cost | $ 29.50 | $ 57.80 | $ 24.40 | $ 56.40 |

# YOUDECIDE Managing Customer Profitability

As a consultant, you recently implemented an activity-based customer-profitability system. In your written report to management, you classified the customers of the company into one of four categories based on current profitability and the potential for future profitability[4]:

High Profitability, Substantial Future Potential
Low Profitability, Substantial Future Potential
High Profitability, Limited Future Potential
Low Profitability, Limited Future Potential

After discussing the report with the CEO, he asks you to answer the following question:

**How would you manage the customers in each of the four categories?**

For highly profitable customers, and especially those with long-term potential, special efforts should be made to retain these customers as it is much more expensive to attract new customers. Offering these customers special discounts and new products and service lines coupled with managing their costs-to-serve to a

lower level and improving business processes are ways to increase customer satisfaction while at the same time maintaining or increasing profitability. For customers with low profitability but substantial potential, the goal is to move these customers up to a high profitability state. Pricing policies or initiatives related to both the order and the transactions caused by the order is one way to increase profitability (e.g., activity-based pricing is based on the costs-to-serve, something clearly revealed by the ABC customer model). Another way is to lower the costs to serve by improving activity efficiency and eliminating nonvalue-added activities. The final category of customers (low-profitability and limited potential) is managed up or out—these customers need to be made profitable quickly or simply dropped.

**Knowing customer profitability is important because not every revenue dollar contributes equally to overall profitability. Thus, it is critical for a manager to understand the net profit contribution that each customer makes to the company. Understanding individual customer profitability and the associated drivers allows managers to take actions to sustain and maintain profitable customers and transform unprofitable customers into profitable customers.[5]**

The example in Cornerstone 7.6 (p. 300) shows that Murray, the "low-cost" supplier (as measured by the purchase price of the two parts), actually costs more when the supplier-related activities of repairing and expediting are considered. If all costs are considered, then the choice becomes clear: Plata Associates is the better supplier with a higher-quality product, more on-time deliveries, and, consequently, a lower overall cost per unit.

OBJECTIVE  4

Explain how activity-based management can be used for cost reduction.

# PROCESS-VALUE ANALYSIS

*Process-value analysis* is fundamental to *activity-based management*. **Activity-based management** is a system-wide, integrated approach that focuses management's attention on activities with the objective of improving customer value and profit achieved by providing this value. **Process value analysis** focuses on cost reduction instead of cost assignment and emphasizes the maximization of systemwide performance. As Exhibit 7.11 illustrates, process-value analysis is concerned with:

( EXHIBIT 7.11 )

**Process-Value Analysis Model**

[4] Based on a classification in Cokins, Gary, *Performance Management: Finding the Missing Pieces (to Close the Intelligence Gap)*. Wiley and SAS Business Series, March 29, 2004.
[5] Kaplan, Robert S. and V. G. Narayanan, "Measuring and Managing Customer Profitability," *Journal of Cost Management*, (September/October 2001) 5–15.

- driver analysis
- activity analysis
- performance measurement

## Driver Analysis: The Search for Root Causes

Managing activities requires an understanding of what causes activity costs. Every activity has inputs and outputs. **Activity inputs** are the resources consumed by the activity in producing its output. **Activity output** is the result or product of an activity. For example, if the activity is moving materials, the inputs would be such things as a forklift, a forklift driver, fuel (for the forklift), and crates. The output would be moved goods and materials. An **activity output measure** is the number of times the activity is performed. It is the quantifiable measure of the output. For example, the number of moves or distance moved are possible output measures for the material moving activity.

The output measure effectively is a measure of the demands placed on an activity and is what we have been calling an *activity driver.* As the demands for an activity change, the cost of the activity can change. For example, as the number of programs written increases, the activity of writing programs may need to consume more inputs (labor, CD-ROMs, paper, and so on). However, output measures, such as the number of programs, may not (and usually do not) correspond to the root causes of activity costs. They are the consequences of the activity being performed. The purpose of driver analysis is to reveal root causes. Thus, **driver analysis** is the effort expended to identify those factors that are the root causes of activity costs. For example, an analysis may reveal that the root cause of the cost of moving materials is plant layout. Once the root cause is known, then action can be taken to improve the activity. Specifically, reorganizing plant layout can reduce the cost of moving materials.

> ## concept Q&A
>
> What is the purpose of driver analysis?
>
> **Answer:**
>
> The objective of driver analysis is to find the root causes of activity costs. By knowing root causes, costs can be managed effectively.

Often, the root cause of the cost of an activity is also the root cause of other related activities. For example, the costs of inspecting purchased parts and reordering may both be caused by poor supplier quality. By working with suppliers to reduce the number of defective components supplied (or choosing suppliers that have fewer defects), the demand for both activities may then decrease, allowing the company to save money.

## Activity Analysis: Identifying and Assessing Value Content

The heart of process-value analysis is activity analysis. **Activity analysis** is the process of identifying, describing, and evaluating the activities that an organization performs. Activity analysis produces four outcomes:

1. what activities are done
2. how many people perform the activities
3. the time and resources required to perform the activities
4. an assessment of the value of the activities to the organization, including a recommendation to select and keep only those that add value

Steps 1 through 3 have been described earlier and are common to the information needed for determining and assigning activity costs. Knowing how much an activity costs is clearly an important part of activity-based management. Step 4, determining the value-added content of activities, is concerned with cost reduction rather than cost assignment. Thus, some managerial accountants feel that this is the most important part of activity analysis. Activities can be classified as *value-added* or *nonvalue-added.*

**Value-Added Activities** Those activities necessary to remain in business are called **value-added activities**. Some activities—required activities—are necessary to comply with legal mandates. Activities needed to comply with the reporting requirements of the Securities and Exchange Commission (SEC) and the filing requirements of the Internal Revenue Service (IRS) are examples. These activities are value-added by *mandate*. The remaining activities in the firm are *discretionary*. A discretionary activity is classified as value-added provided it simultaneously satisfies all of the following conditions:

- The activity produces a change of state.
- The change of state was not achievable by preceding activities.
- The activity enables other activities to be performed.

For example, consider the production of rods used in hydraulic cylinders. The first activity, cutting rods, cuts long rods into the correct lengths for the cylinders. Next, the cut rods are welded to cut plates. The cutting rods activity is value-added because:

- It causes a change of state—uncut rods become cut rods.
- No prior activity was supposed to create this change of state.
- It enables the welding activity to be performed.

Though the value-added properties are easy to see for an operational activity like cutting rods, what about a more general activity like supervising production workers? A managerial activity is specifically designed to manage other value-added activities—to ensure that they are performed in an efficient and timely manner. Supervision certainly satisfies the enabling condition. Is there a change in state? There are two ways of answering affirmatively:

- First, supervising can be viewed as an enabling resource that is consumed by the operational activities that do produce a change of state. Thus, supervising is a secondary activity that serves as an input that is needed to help bring about the change of state expected for value-added primary activities.
- Second, it could be argued that the supervision brings order by changing the state from uncoordinated activities to coordinated activities.

Once value-added activities are identified, we can define value-added costs. **Value-added costs** are the costs to perform value-added activities with perfect efficiency.

**Nonvalue-Added Activities**   All activities other than those that are absolutely essential to remain in business, and therefore considered unnecessary, are referred to as **nonvalue-added activities**. A nonvalue-added activity can be identified by its failure to satisfy any one of the three previous defining conditions for adding value. Violation of the first two conditions is the usual case for nonvalue-added activities. Inspecting cut rods (for correct length), for example, is a nonvalue-added activity. Inspection is a state-detection activity, not a state-changing activity. (It tells us the state of the cut rod—whether it is the right length.) Thus, it fails the first condition (activity produced a change of state). Consider the activity of reworking goods or subassemblies. Rework is designed to bring a good from a nonconforming state to a conforming state. Thus, a change of state occurs. Yet the activity is nonvalue-added because it repeats work; it is doing something that should have been done by preceding activities Condition 2 (change of state was not achievable by preceding activities) is violated.

**Nonvalue-added costs** are costs that are caused either by nonvalue-added activities or the inefficient performance of valued-added activities. For nonvalue-added activities, the nonvalue-added cost is the cost of the activity itself. For inefficient value-added activities, the activity cost must be broken into its value-added and nonvalue-added components. For example, if Receiving should use 10,000 receiving orders but uses 20,000, then half of the cost of Receiving is value-added and half is nonvalue-added. The value-added component is the waste-free component of the value-added activity and is, therefore, the *value-added standard*. Due to increased competition, many firms are attempting to eliminate nonvalue-added activities because they add unnecessary cost and impede performance. Firms are also striving to optimize value-added activities. Thus activity analysis identifies and eventually eliminates all unnecessary activities and, simultaneously, increases the efficiency of necessary activities.

The theme of activity analysis is waste elimination. As waste is eliminated, costs are reduced. The cost reduction *follows* the elimination of waste. Note the value of managing the causes of the costs rather than the costs themselves. Though managing costs may increase the efficiency of an activity, if the activity is unnecessary, what does it matter if it's performed efficiently? An unnecessary activity is wasteful and should be eliminated. For example, moving raw materials and partially finished goods is often cited as a nonvalue-added activity. Installing an automated materials handling system may increase the efficiency of this activity, but changing to cellular manufacturing with on-site, just-in-time delivery of raw materials could virtually eliminate the activity. It's easy to see which is preferable.

*Examples of Nonvalue-Added Activities*   Reordering parts, expediting production, and rework because of defective parts are all examples of nonvalue-added activities. Other examples include warranty work, handling customer complaints, and reporting defects. Nonvalue-added activities can exist anywhere in the organization. In the manufacturing operation, the following major activities are often cited as wasteful and unnecessary:

- *Scheduling:* An activity that uses time and resources to determine when different products have access to processes (or when and how many setups must be done) and how much will be produced.
- *Moving:* An activity that uses time and resources to move raw materials, work in process, and finished goods from one department to another.
- *Waiting:* An activity in which raw materials or work in process use time and resources by waiting on the next process.
- *Inspecting:* An activity in which time and resources are spent ensuring that the product meets specifications.
- *Storing:* An activity that uses time and resources while a good or raw material is held in inventory.

None of these activities adds any value for the customer. (Note that inspection would not be necessary if the product were produced correctly the first time and, therefore, adds no value for the customer.) The challenge of activity analysis is to find ways to produce the good without using any of these activities.

## Here's The Real Kicker

For **Stillwater Designs**, warranty work is a significant cost. Warranty work associated with defective products is typically labeled a nonvalue-added cost. Stillwater Designs recognizes the nonvalue-added nature of this activity and takes measures to eliminate the causes of the defective units. The company tracks return failures (over time) and provides this information to its research and development (R&D) department. R&D then uses this information to make design improvements on existing models (running changes) as well as to change the design on future models. The objective of the design changes is to reduce the demand for the warranty activity, thus reducing warranty cost.

However, not all **Kicker** warranty costs can be classified as nonvalue-added. When products are returned, customer service decides whether or not the problem is covered under warranty. Sometimes, problems are covered even though they are not attributable to a defective product. When the company decides to replace a nondefective product, it is making a conscious decision to increase customer satisfaction and brand loyalty. This part of the warranty cost is a "marketing warranty cost" and could be classified as a value-added cost. For example, customers sometimes buy amplifiers that are more powerful than the subwoofers can handle, resulting in burnt voice coils. By replacing the product (even though technically it's the customer's fault), the customer will be more likely to buy again and to provide good word-of-mouth advertising for Kicker products.

**Cost Reduction**   Activity management carries with it the objective of cost reduction. Competitive conditions dictate that companies must deliver customer desired products on time and at the lowest possible cost. These conditions mean that an organization must continually strive for cost improvement. Activity management can reduce costs in four ways:[6]

- activity elimination
- activity selection
- activity reduction
- activity sharing

*Activity Elimination*   **Activity elimination** focuses on nonvalue-added activities. Once activities that fail to add value are identified, measures must be taken to rid the organization of these activities. For example, the activity of inspecting incoming parts seems necessary to ensure that the product using the parts functions according to specifications. Use of a bad part can produce a bad final product. Yet this activity is necessary only because of the poor quality performance of the supplying firms. Selecting suppliers who are able to supply high-quality parts or who are willing to improve their quality performance to achieve this objective will eventually allow the elimination of incoming inspection. Cost reduction then follows.

*Activity Selection*   **Activity selection** involves choosing among different sets of activities that are caused by competing strategies. Different strategies cause different activities. Different product design strategies, for example, can require significantly different activities. Activities, in turn, cause costs. Each product design strategy has its own set of activities and associated costs. All other things being equal, the lowest-cost design strategy should be chosen. In a continual-improvement environment, redesign of existing products and processes can lead to a different, cheaper set of activities. Thus activity selection can have a significant effect on cost reduction.

*Activity Reduction*   **Activity reduction** decreases the time and resources required by an activity. This approach to cost reduction should be primarily aimed at improving the efficiency of necessary activities or a short-term strategy for improving nonvalue-added activities until they can be eliminated. Setup activity is a necessary activity that is often cited as an example for which less time and fewer resources need to be used. Finding ways to reduce setup time—and thus lower the cost of setups—is another example of the concept of gradual reductions in activity costs.

*Activity Sharing*   **Activity sharing** increases the efficiency of necessary activities by using economies of scale. Specifically, the quantity of the cost driver is increased without increasing the total cost of the activity itself. This lowers the per-unit cost of the cost driver and the amount of cost traceable to the products that consume the activity. For example, a new product can be designed to use components already being used by other products. By using existing components, the activities associated with these components already exist, and the company avoids the creation of a whole new set of activities.

**Assessing Nonvalue-Added Costs**   Cornerstone 7.7 shows how to determine the nonvalue-added cost of activities. Determining the cost is followed by a root-cause analysis and then by the selection of an approach to reduce the waste found in the activity. For example, defective products cause warranty work. Defective products, in turn, are caused by such factors as defective internal processes, poor product design, and defective supplier components. Correcting the causes will lead to the elimination of the warranty activity. Inefficient purchasing could be attributable to such root causes as poor product design (too many components), orders that are incorrectly filled out, and defective supplier components (producing additional orders). Correcting the causes will reduce the demand for the purchasing activity, and as the activity is reduced, cost reduction will follow.

---

[6] Peter B. B. Turney, "How Activity-Based Costing Helps Reduce Cost," *Journal of Cost Management* (Winter 1991): 29–35.

## Assessing Nonvalue-Added Costs

**CORNERSTONE**

**7.7**

**Why:**

Nonvalue-added costs are caused either by nonvalue-added activities or value-added activities performed inefficiently. Determining the nonvalue-added costs allows managers to see the amount of waste, assess its importance, and identify opportunities for improvement.

**Information:**

Consider the following two activities: (1) Performing warranty work, cost: $120,000. The warranty cost of the most efficient competitor is $20,000. (2) Purchasing components, cost: $200,000 (10,000 purchase orders). A benchmarking study reveals that the most efficient level will use 5,000 purchase orders and entail a cost of $100,000.

**Required:**

Determine the nonvalue-added cost of each activity.

**Solution:**

Determine the value content of each activity: Is the activity nonvalue-added or value-added?

1. Performing warranty work is nonvalue-added; it is done to correct something that wasn't done right the first time. Thus, the nonvalue-added cost of performing warranty work is $120,000. The cost of the competitor has no bearing on the analysis. Root causes for warranty work are defective products.

2. Purchasing components is necessary so that materials are available to produce products and, thus, is value-added. However, the activity is not performed efficiently, as revealed by the benchmarking study. The cost per purchase order is $20 ($100,000/5,000). The nonvalue-added cost is calculated as:

$$\text{(Actual Quantity} - \text{Value-Added Quantity)} \times \text{Cost per Purchase Order}$$
$$(10,000 - 5,000) \times \$20 = \$100,000$$
$$(\text{or simply, } \$200,000 - \$100,000)$$

## Activity Performance Measurement

Assessing how well activities (and processes) are performed is fundamental to management's efforts to improve profitability. Activity performance measures exist in both financial and nonfinancial forms. These measures are designed to assess how well an activity was performed and the results achieved. They are also designed to reveal if constant improvement is being realized. Measures of activity performance center on three major dimensions:

- efficiency
- time
- quality

**Efficiency**   *Efficiency* focuses on the relationship of activity inputs to activity outputs. For example, one way to improve activity efficiency is to produce the same activity output with lower cost for the inputs used. Thus cost and trends in cost become important measures of efficiency.

**Time**  The *time* required to perform an activity is also critical. Longer times usually mean more resource consumption and less ability to respond to customer demands. Time measures of performance tend to be nonfinancial, whereas efficiency and quality measures are both financial and nonfinancial.

*Cycle time* and *velocity* are two operational measures of time-based performance. Cycle time can be applied to any activity or process that produces an output, and it measures how long it takes to produce an output from start to finish. In a manufacturing process, **cycle time** is the length of time that it takes to produce a unit of output from the time raw materials are received (starting point of the cycle) until the good is delivered to finished goods inventory (finishing point of the cycle). Thus, cycle time is the time required to produce one unit of a product (Time/Units produced). **Velocity** is the number of units of output that can be produced in a given period of time (Units produced/Time). Notice that velocity is the reciprocal of cycle time. For the cycle time example, the velocity is two units per hour. Cornerstone 7.8 demonstrates how to compute cycle time and velocity.

**CORNERSTONE**

**7.8**

## Calculating Cycle Time and Velocity

**Why:**

Cycle time (Time/Units Produced) and velocity (Units Produced/Time) measure the time it takes for a firm to respond to such things as customer orders, customer complaints, and the development of new products. The objective is to reduce cycle time (increase velocity) and thus improve response time, making the firm more competitive.

**Information:**

Assume that Frost Company takes 10,000 hours to produce 20,000 units of a product.

**Required:**

What is the velocity in hours? Cycle time in hours? Cycle time in minutes?

**Solution:**

$$\text{Velocity} = 20{,}000/10{,}000 = 2 \text{ units per hour}$$
$$\text{Cycle Time} = 10{,}000/20{,}000 = 1/2 \text{ hour}$$
$$= 10{,}000(60 \text{ minutes})/20{,}000 = 30 \text{ minutes}$$

**Quality**  *Quality* is concerned with doing the activity right the first time it is performed. If the activity output is defective, then the activity may need to be repeated, causing unnecessary cost and reduction in efficiency. Quality cost management is a major topic and is discussed in more detail next.

## Quality Cost Management

Activity-based management also is useful for understanding how quality costs can be managed. Quality costs can be substantial *in size* and a source of significant savings *if managed effectively.* Improving quality can produce significant improvements in profitability and overall efficiency. Quality improvement can increase profitability in two ways:

- by increasing customer demand *and thus sales revenues*
- by decreasing costs

---

**concept Q&A**

What are the three dimensions of performance for activities? Explain why they are important.

**Answer:**

Efficiency, time, and quality are the three performance dimensions. All three relate to the ability of a manager to reduce activity cost.

For example, when **Toyota** sold more cars and trucks than **General Motors** for the first time ever in 2007, some automotive industry experts attributed this crowning achievement to Toyota's long-time commitment to quality-related issues, such as quality cost management.[7]

**Quality-Related Activities** Quality-linked activities are those activities performed because poor quality may or does exist. The costs of performing these activities are referred to as **costs of quality**. The definitions of *quality-related activities* imply four categories of quality costs:

- prevention costs
- appraisal costs
- internal failure costs
- external failure costs

Thus, the costs of quality are associated with two subcategories of quality-related activities: *control activities and failure activities.*

**Control Activities** **Control activities** are performed by an organization to prevent or detect poor quality (because poor quality may exist). **Control costs** are the costs of performing control activities. Control activities are made up of prevention and appraisal activities.

**Prevention costs** are incurred to prevent poor quality in the products or services being produced. As prevention costs increase, we would expect the costs of failure to decrease. Examples of prevention costs are quality engineering, quality training programs, quality planning, quality reporting, supplier evaluation and selection, quality audits, quality circles, field trials, and design reviews.

**Appraisal costs** are incurred to determine whether products and services are conforming to their requirements or customer needs. Examples include inspecting and testing raw materials, packaging inspection, supervising appraisal activities, product acceptance, process acceptance, measurement (inspection and test) equipment, and outside endorsements. The main objective of the appraisal function is to prevent nonconforming goods from being shipped to customers.

**Failure Activities** **Failure activities** are performed by an organization or its customers in response to poor quality (poor quality does exist). **Failure costs** are the costs incurred by an organization because failure activities are performed. Notice that the definitions of *failure activities* and *failure costs* imply that customer response to poor quality can impose costs on an organization.

**Internal failure costs** are incurred when products and services do not conform to specifications or customer needs. This nonconformance is detected *before* the bad products or services (nonconforming, unreliable, not durable, and so on) are shipped or delivered to outside parties. These are the failures detected by appraisal activities. Examples of internal failure costs are scrap, rework, downtime (due to defects), reinspection, retesting, and design changes. These costs disappear if no defects exist.

**External failure costs** are incurred when products and services fail to conform to requirements or satisfy customer needs *after* being delivered to customers. Of all the costs of quality, this category can be the most devastating. For example, costs of recalls can run into the hundreds of millions of dollars. Other examples include lost sales because of poor product performance, returns and allowances because of poor quality, warranties, repairs, product liability, customer dissatisfaction, lost market share, and complaint adjustment. **Northwest Airlines** is notorious for placing near the bottom of customer satisfaction rankings, which some analysts believe consistently hurts its ticket sales. External failure costs, like internal failure costs, disappear if no defects exist.

---

[7] D. Jones, "Toyota's Success Pleases Proponents of 'Lean'," *USA Today* (May 3, 2007): 2B.

# Environmental Cost Management

For many organizations, management of environmental costs is becoming a matter of high priority and a significant competitive issue. Many executives now believe that improving environmental quality may actually reduce environmental costs rather than increase them. For example, between 2002 and 2008, **Baxter International Inc.**, a producer of medical products, reduced toxic wastes emitted to air, water, and soil; increased recycling activity; and, as a consequence, reported environmental income, savings, and cost avoidance for the 7-year period of $91.9 million.[8]

Before environmental cost information can be provided to management, environmental costs must be defined. Various possibilities exist; however, an appealing approach is to adopt a definition consistent with a total environmental quality model. Accordingly, environmental costs can be referred to as *environmental quality costs.* Similar to product quality, environmentally linked activities are those activities performed because poor environmental quality may or does exist. The costs of performing these activities are referred to as *environmental costs.* **Environmental costs** are associated with the creation, detection, remediation, and prevention of environmental degradation. With this definition, environmental costs, like quality costs, are classified into four analogous categories:

- prevention costs
- detection costs
- internal failure costs
- external failure costs

External failure costs, in turn, can be subdivided into realized and unrealized categories. As with quality costs, environmental costs are associated with two subcategories of environmentally related activities: *control activities* and *failure activities.*

**Control Activities** **Environmental prevention costs** are the costs of activities carried out to prevent the production of contaminants and/or waste that could cause damage to the environment. Examples of prevention activities include evaluating and selecting suppliers, evaluating and selecting equipment to control pollution, designing processes and products to reduce or eliminate contaminants, training employees, studying environmental impacts, auditing environmental risks, undertaking environmental research, developing environmental management systems, and recycling products.

**Environmental detection costs** are the costs of activities executed to determine if products, processes, and other activities within the firm are in compliance with appropriate environmental standards. The environmental standards and procedures that a firm seeks to follow are defined in three ways:

- regulatory laws of governments
- voluntary standards developed by private organizations
- environmental policies developed by management

Examples of detection activities are auditing environmental activities, inspecting products and processes (for environmental compliance), developing environmental performance measures, carrying out contamination tests, verifying supplier environmental performance, and measuring levels of contamination.

**Failure Activities** **Environmental internal failure costs** are costs of activities performed because contaminants and waste have been produced but not discharged into the environment. Thus, internal failure costs are incurred to eliminate and manage contaminants or waste once produced. Internal failure activities have one of two goals:

- to ensure that the contaminants and waste produced are not released to the environment
- to reduce the level of contaminants released to an amount that complies with environmental standards

[8] Baxter Environmental Financial Statement, 2008, at www.baxter.com/sustainability (accessed May 2010).

Examples of internal failure activities include operating equipment to minimize or eliminate pollution, treating and disposing of toxic materials, maintaining pollution equipment, licensing facilities for producing contaminants, and recycling scrap.

**Environmental external failure costs** are the costs of activities performed after discharging contaminants and waste into the environment. **Realized external failure costs**, or private costs, are those incurred and paid for by the firm. Examples of realized external failure activities are cleaning up a polluted lake, cleaning up oil spills, cleaning up contaminated soil, using materials and energy inefficiently, settling personal injury claims from environmentally unsound practices, settling property damage claims, restoring land to its natural state, and losing sales from a bad environmental reputation. **Unrealized external failure costs**, or **societal costs**, are caused by the firm but are incurred and paid for by parties outside the firm. Examples of societal costs include receiving medical care because of polluted air (individual welfare), losing a lake for recreational use because of contamination (degradation), losing employment because of contamination (individual welfare), and damaging ecosystems from solid waste disposal (degradation).

> ## concept Q&A
>
> Why are there two categories of external failure costs?
>
> **Answer:**
>
> One category represents those external environmental costs that the firm causes and pays for, and the other category is those external environmental costs caused by the firm but paid for by parties outside the firm.

# SUMMARY OF LEARNING OBJECTIVES

**LO 1.** Explain why functional (or volume)-based costing approaches may produce distorted costs.

- Overhead costs have increased in significance over time and in many firms represent a much higher percentage of product costs than direct labor.
- Many overhead activities are unrelated to the units produced.
- Functional-based costing systems are not able to assign the costs of these nonunit-based overhead activities properly.
- Nonunit-based overhead activities often are consumed by products in different proportions than are unit-based overhead activities. Because of this nonproportionality, assigning overhead by using only unit-based drivers can distort product costs.
- If the nonunit-based overhead costs are a significant proportion of total overhead costs, the inaccuracy in cost assignments can be a serious matter.

**LO 2.** Explain how an activity-based costing system works for product costing.

- Activities are identified and defined through the use of interviews and surveys. This information allows an activity dictionary to be constructed.
- The activity dictionary lists activities and potential activity drivers, classifies activities as primary or secondary, and provides any other attributes deemed to be important.
- Resource costs are assigned to activities by using direct tracing and resource drivers.
- The costs of secondary activities are ultimately assigned to primary activities by using activity drivers.
- Finally, the costs of primary activities are assigned to products, customers, and other cost objects.
- The cost assignment process is described by the following general steps: (1) identifying the major activities and building an activity dictionary, (2) determining the cost of those activities, (3) identifying a measure of consumption for activity costs (activity drivers), (4) calculating an activity rate, (5) measuring the demands placed on activities by each product, and (6) calculating product costs.

**LO 3.** Describe activity-based customer costing and activity-based supplier costing.

- Tracing customer-driven costs to customers can provide significant information to managers.
- Accurate customer costs allow managers to make better pricing decisions, customer-mix decisions, and other customer-related decisions that improve profitability.
- Tracing supplier-driven costs to suppliers can enable managers to choose the true low-cost suppliers, producing a stronger competitive position and increased profitability.

**LO 4.** Explain how activity-based management can be used for cost reduction.

- Assigning costs accurately is vital for good decision making.
- Assigning the costs of an activity accurately does not address the issue of whether or not the activity should be performed or whether it is being performed efficiently.
- Activity-based management focuses on process-value analysis.
- Process-value analysis has three components: driver analysis, activity analysis, and performance evaluation. These three steps determine what activities are being done, why they are being done, and how well they are done.
- Understanding the root causes of activities provides the opportunities to manage activities so that costs can be reduced.
- Quality and environmental activities are particularly susceptible to activity-based management.
- Quality costs are costs that are incurred because poor product quality exists or may exist.
- Environmental costs are costs that are incurred because environmental degradation exists or may exist.

## SUMMARY OF IMPORTANT EQUATIONS

1. $\text{Consumption Ratio} = \dfrac{\text{Amount of Activity Driver per Product}}{\text{Total Driver Quantity}}$

2. $\text{Overhead Rate} = \dfrac{\text{Total Overhead Costs}}{\text{Total Direct Labor Hours}}$

**CORNERSTONES**

| | |
|---|---|
| CORNERSTONE 7.1 | Calculating consumption ratios, page 286 |
| CORNERSTONE 7.2 | Calculating activity rates, page 286 |
| CORNERSTONE 7.3 | Calculating activity-based unit costs, page 287 |
| CORNERSTONE 7.4 | Assigning resource costs to activities by using direct tracing and resource drivers, page 294 |
| CORNERSTONE 7.5 | Calculating activity-based customer costs, page 299 |
| CORNERSTONE 7.6 | Calculating activity-based supplier costs, page 300 |
| CORNERSTONE 7.7 | Assessing nonvalue-added costs, page 307 |
| CORNERSTONE 7.8 | Calculating cycle time and velocity, page 308 |

## Cornerstone Exercise 7-29 Consumption Ratios

OBJECTIVE **1**
CORNERSTONE 7.1

Refer to the information for Botas Company on the previous page.

**Required:**

1. Calculate the consumption ratios for the four drivers.
2. Is there evidence of product diversity? Explain.

## Cornerstone Exercise 7-30 Activity Rates

OBJECTIVE **1**
CORNERSTONE 7.2

Refer to the information for Botas Company on the previous page. The following activity data have been collected:

| | |
|---|---|
| Cutting | $150,000 |
| Assembling | 187,500 |
| Inspecting | 45,000 |
| Reworking | 22,500 |

**Required:**

Calculate the activity rates that would be used to assign costs to each product.

## Cornerstone Exercise 7-31 Calculating ABC Unit Costs

OBJECTIVE **1**
CORNERSTONE 7.3

Perry National Bank has collected the following information for four activities and two types of credit cards:

| Activity | Driver | Classic | Gold | Activity Rate |
|---|---|---|---|---|
| Processing transactions | Transactions processed | 8,000 | 4,800 | $0.15 |
| Preparing statements | Number of statements | 8,000 | 4,800 | 0.90 |
| Answering questions | Number of calls | 16,000 | 24,000 | 3.00 |
| Providing ATMs | ATM transactions | 32,000 | 9,600 | 1.20 |

There are 5,000 holders of Classic cards and 20,000 holders of the Gold cards.

**Required:**

Calculate the unit cost (rounded to the nearest cent) for Classic and Gold credit cards.

## Cornerstone Exercise 7-32 Assigning Costs to Activities

OBJECTIVE **2**
CORNERSTONE 7.4

Baker Company produces small engines for lawnmower producers. The accounts payable department at Baker has six clerks who process and pay supplier invoices. The total cost of their salaries is $320,000. The work distribution for the activities that they perform is as follows:

| Activity | Percentage of Time on Each Activity |
|---|---|
| Comparing source documents | 15% |
| Resolving discrepancies | 65 |
| Processing payment | 20 |

**Required:**

Assign the cost of labor to each of the three activities in the accounts payable department.

## Cornerstone Exercise 7-33 Activity-Based Customer Costing

OBJECTIVE **3**
CORNERSTONE 7.5

Dormirbien Company produces mattresses for 20 retail outlets. Of the 20 retail outlets, 19 are small, separately owned furniture stores and one is a retail chain. The retail chain buys 60% of the mattresses produced. The 19 smaller customers purchase mattresses in approximately equal quantities, where the orders are about the same size. Data concerning Dormirbien's customer activity are as follows:

*(Continued)*

| | Large Retailer | Smaller Retailers |
|---|---|---|
| Units purchased | 36,000 | 24,000 |
| Orders placed | 12 | 1,200 |
| Number of sales calls | 6 | 294 |
| Manufacturing costs | $14,400,000 | $9,600,000 |
| Order filling costs allocated* | $484,800 | $323,200 |
| Sales force costs allocated* | $240,000 | $160,000 |

\* Currently allocated on sales volume (units sold).

Currently, customer-driven costs are assigned to customers based on units sold, a unit-level driver.

**Required:**

Assign costs to customers by using an ABC approach. Round activity rates and activity costs to the nearest dollar.

OBJECTIVE ③
CORNERSTONE 7.6

### Cornerstone Exercise 7-34    Activity-Based Supplier Costing

LissenPhones uses Alpha Electronics and La Paz Company to buy two electronic components used in the manufacture of its cell phones: Component 125X and Component 30Y. Consider two activities: testing and reordering components. After the two components are inserted, testing is done to ensure that the two components in the phones are working properly. Reordering occurs because one or both of the components have failed the test and it is necessary to replenish component inventories. Activity cost information and other data needed for supplier costing are as follows:

I. Activity Costs Caused by Suppliers (testing failures and reordering as a result)

| Activity | Costs |
|---|---|
| Testing components | $1,500,000 |
| Reordering components | 375,000 |

II. Supplier Data

| | Alpha Electronics | | La Paz Company | |
|---|---|---|---|---|
| | 125X | 30Y | 125X | 30Y |
| Unit purchase price | $10 | $26 | $12 | $28 |
| Units purchased | 150,000 | 75,000 | 18,750 | 18,750 |
| Failed tests | 1,500 | 975 | 13 | 12 |
| Number of reorders | 75 | 50 | 0 | 0 |

**Required:**

Determine the cost of each supplier by using ABC. Round unit costs to two decimal places.

OBJECTIVE ④
CORNERSTONE 7.7

### Cornerstone Exercise 7-35    Nonvalue-Added Costs

Boothe Inc. has the following two activities: (1) Retesting reworked products, cost: $480,000. The retesting cost of the most efficient competitor is $150,000. (2) Welding subassemblies, cost: $900,000 (45,000 welding hours). A benchmarking study reveals that the most efficient level for Boothe would use 36,000 welding hours and entail a cost of $720,000.

**Required:**

Determine the nonvalue-added cost of each activity.

OBJECTIVE ④
CORNERSTONE 7.8

### Cornerstone Exercise 7-36    Velocity and Cycle Time

Karsen Company takes 7,200 hours to produce 28,800 units of a product.

**Required:**

What is the velocity? Cycle time?

# EXERCISES

### Exercise 7-37  Consumption Ratios; Activity Rates

Bienestar Company produces two types of get-well cards: scented and regular. Drivers for the four activities are as follows:

|  | Scented Cards | Regular Cards |
|---|---|---|
| Inspection hours | 180 | 120 |
| Setup hours | 70 | 30 |
| Machine hours | 160 | 480 |
| Number of moves | 480 | 120 |

The following activity data have been collected:

| | |
|---|---|
| Inspecting products | $7,500 |
| Setting up equipment | 4,750 |
| Machining | 5,120 |
| Moving materials | 2,700 |

**Required:**

1. Calculate the consumption ratios for the four drivers.
2. **CONCEPTUAL CONNECTION** Is there evidence of product diversity? Explain the significance of product diversity for decision making if the company chooses to use machine hours to assign all overhead.
3. Calculate the activity rates that would be used to assign costs to each product.
4. Suppose that the activity rate for inspecting products is $20 per inspection hour. How many hours of inspection are expected for the coming year?

### Exercise 7-38  Activity Rates

Patten Company uses activity-based costing (ABC). Patten manufactures toy cars using two activities: plastic injection molding and decal application. Patten's 2013 total budgeted overhead costs for these two activities are $675,000 (80% for injection molding and 20% for decal application). Molding overhead costs are driven by the number of pounds of plastic that are molded together. Decal application overhead costs are driven by the number of decals applied to toys. The budgeted activity data for 2013 are as follows:

| | |
|---|---|
| Pounds of plastic molded | 3,000,000 |
| Number of decals applied | 375,000 |

**Required:**

1. Calculate the activity rate for the plastic injection molding activity.
2. Calculate the activity rate for the decal application activity.

### Exercise 7-39  Comparing ABC and Plantwide Overhead Cost Assignments

The Sabroso Chocolate Company uses activity-based costing (ABC). The controller identified two activities and their budgeted costs:

| | |
|---|---|
| Setting up equipment | $270,000 |
| Other overhead | $900,000 |

Setting up equipment is based on setup hours, and other overhead is based on oven hours.

Oscuro produces two products, Fudge and Cookies. Information on each product is as follows:

|  | Fudge | Cookies |
|---|---|---|
| Units produced | 5,000 | 25,000 |
| Setup hours | 4,000 | 1,000 |
| Oven hours | 1,000 | 5,000 |

*(Continued)*

**Required:**

(*Note:* Round answers to two decimal places.)

1. Calculate the activity rate for (a) setting up equipment and (b) other overhead.
2. How much total overhead is assigned to Fudge using ABC?
3. What is the unit overhead assigned to Fudge using ABC?
4. Now, ignoring the ABC results, calculate the plantwide overhead rate, based on oven hours.
5. How much total overhead is assigned to Fudge using the plantwide overhead rate?
6. **CONCEPTUAL CONNECTION** Explain why the total overhead assigned to Fudge is different under the ABC system (i.e., using the activity rates) than under the nonABC system (i.e., using the plantwide rate).

OBJECTIVE ① ②

### Exercise 7-40    Activity-Based Product Costing

Suppose that a surgical ward has gathered the following information for four nursing activities and two types of patients:

| | | Patient Category | | |
| | Driver | Normal | Intensive | Activity Rate |
| --- | --- | --- | --- | --- |
| Treating patients | Treatments | 6,400 | 8,000 | $4.00 |
| Providing hygienic care | Hygienic hours | 4,800 | 17,600 | 5.00 |
| Responding to requests | Requests | 32,000 | 80,000 | 2.00 |
| Monitoring patients | Monitoring hours | 6,000 | 72,000 | 3.00 |

**Required:**

1. Determine the total nursing costs assigned to each patient category.
2. Output is measured in patient days. Assuming that the normal patient category uses 8,000 patient days and the intensive patient category uses 6,400 patient days, calculate the nursing cost per patient day for each type of patient.
3. **CONCEPTUAL CONNECTION** The supervisor of the surgical ward has suggested that patient days is the only driver needed to assign nursing costs to each type of patient. Calculate the charge per patient day (rounded to the nearest cent) using this approach and then explain to the supervisor why this would be a bad decision.

OBJECTIVE ②

### Exercise 7-41    Assigning Costs to Activities, Resource Drivers

The Receiving Department has three activities: unloading, counting goods, and inspecting. Unloading uses a forklift that is leased for $15,000 per year. The forklift is used only for unloading. The fuel for the forklift is $3,600 per year. Other operating costs (maintenance) for the forklift total $1,500 per year. Inspection uses some special testing equipment that has a depreciation of $1,200 per year and an operating cost of $750. Receiving has three employees who have an average salary of $50,000 per year. The work distribution matrix for the receiving personnel is as follows:

| Activity | Percentage of Time on Each Activity |
| --- | --- |
| Unloading | 40% |
| Counting | 25 |
| Inspecting | 35 |

No other resources are used for these activities.

**Required:**

1. Calculate the cost of each activity.
2. **CONCEPTUAL CONNECTION** Explain the two methods used to assign costs to activities.

## Exercise 7-42 Activity-Based Customer-Driven Costs

OBJECTIVE 2

Suppose that **Stillwater Designs** has two classes of distributors: JIT distributors and nonJIT distributors. The JIT distributor places small, frequent orders, and the nonJIT distributor tends to place larger, less frequent orders. Both types of distributors are buying the same product. Stillwater Designs provides the following information about customer-related activities and costs for the most recent quarter:

|  | JIT Distributors | NonJIT Distributors |
|---|---|---|
| Sales orders | 700 | 70 |
| Sales calls | 70 | 70 |
| Service calls | 350 | 175 |
| Average order size | 750 | 7,500 |
| Manufacturing cost/unit | $125 | $125 |
| Customer costs: |  |  |
| Processing sales orders | $3,080,000 |  |
| Selling goods | 1,120,000 |  |
| Servicing goods | 1,050,000 |  |
| Total | $5,250,000 |  |

### Required:

1. Calculate the total revenues per distributor category, and assign the customer costs to each distributor type by using revenues as the allocation base. Selling price for one unit is $150.
2. **CONCEPTUAL CONNECTION** Calculate the customer cost per distributor type using activity-based cost assignments. Discuss the merits of offering the nonJIT distributors a $2 price decrease (assume that they are agitating for a price concession).
3. **CONCEPTUAL CONNECTION** Assume that the JIT distributors are simply imposing the frequent orders on **Stillwater Designs**. No formal discussion has taken place between JIT customers and Stillwater Designs regarding the supply of goods on a JIT basis. The sales pattern has evolved over time. As an independent consultant, what would you suggest to Stillwater Designs' management?

## Exercise 7-43 Activity-Based Supplier Costing

OBJECTIVE 3

Bowman Company manufactures cooling systems. Bowman produces all the parts necessary for its product except for one electronic component, which is purchased from two local suppliers: Manzer Inc. and Buckner Company. Both suppliers are reliable and seldom deliver late; however, Manzer sells the component for $89 per unit, while Buckner sells the same component for $86. Bowman purchases 80% of its components from Buckner because of its lower price. The total annual demand is 4,000,000 components.

To help assess the cost effect of the two components, the following data were collected for supplier-related activities and suppliers:

I. Activity Data

|  | Activity Cost |
|---|---|
| Inspecting components (sampling only) | $ 480,000 |
| Reworking products (due to failed component) | 6,084,000 |
| Warranty work (due to failed component) | 9,600,000 |

II. Supplier Data

|  | Manzer Inc. | Buckner Company |
|---|---|---|
| Unit purchase price | $89 | $86 |
| Units purchased | 800,000 | 3,200,000 |
| Sampling hours* | 80 | 3,920 |
| Rework hours | 360 | 5,640 |
| Warranty hours | 800 | 15,200 |

* Sampling inspection for Manzer's product has been reduced because the reject rate is so low.

*(Continued)*

**Required:**

1.  Calculate the cost per component for each supplier, taking into consideration the costs of the supplier-related activities and using the current prices and sales volume. (*Note*: Round the unit cost to two decimal places.)
2.  Suppose that Bowman loses $4,000,000 in sales per year because it develops a poor reputation due to defective units attributable to failed components. Using warranty hours, assign the cost of lost sales to each supplier. By how much would this change the cost of each supplier's component? (Round to two decimal places.)
3.  **CONCEPTUAL CONNECTION** Based on the analysis in Requirements 1 and 2, discuss the importance of activity-based supplier costing for internal decision making.

---

*Use the following information for Exercises 7-44 through 7-46:*
The following six situations at Diviney Manufacturing Inc. are independent.

a.  A manual insertion process takes 30 minutes and 8 pounds of material to produce a product. Automating the insertion process requires 15 minutes of machine time and 7.5 pounds of material. The cost per labor hour is $12, the cost per machine hour is $8, and the cost per pound of materials is $10.
b.  With its original design, a gear requires 8 hours of setup time. By redesigning the gear so that the number of different grooves needed is reduced by 50% the setup time is reduced by 75%. The cost per setup hour is $50.
c.  A product currently requires 6 moves. By redesigning the manufacturing layout, the number of moves can be reduced from 6 to 0. The cost per move is $20.
d.  Inspection time for a plant is 16,000 hours per year. The cost of inspection consists of salaries of 8 inspectors, totaling $320,000. Inspection also uses supplies costing $5 per inspection hour. The company eliminated most defective components by eliminating low-quality suppliers. The number of production errors was reduced dramatically by installing a system of statistical process control. Further quality improvements were realized by redesigning the products, making them easier to manufacture. The net effect was to achieve a close to zero-defect state and eliminate the need for any inspection activity.
e.  Each unit of a product requires 6 components. The average number of components is 6.5 due to component failure, requiring rework and extra components. Developing relations with the right suppliers and increasing the quality of the purchased component can reduce the average number of components to 6 components per unit. The cost per component is $500.
f.  A plant produces 100 different electronic products. Each product requires an average of 8 components that are purchased externally. The components are different for each part. By redesigning the products, it is possible to produce the 100 products so that they all have 4 components in common. This will reduce the demand for purchasing, receiving, and paying bills. Estimated savings from the reduced demand are $900,000 per year.

---

OBJECTIVE ❹     Exercise 7-44    **Nonvalue-Added Costs**

Refer to the information for Diviney Manufacturing above.

**Required:**

Estimate the nonvalue-added cost for each situation.

OBJECTIVE ❹     Exercise 7-45    **Driver Analysis**

Refer to the information for Diviney Manufacturing above.

**Required:**

**CONCEPTUAL CONNECTION** For each situation, identify the possible root cause(s) of the activity cost (such as plant layout, process design, and product design).

### Exercise 7-46 Type of Activity Management

OBJECTIVE 4

Refer to the information for Diviney Manufacturing on the previous page.

**Required:**

For each situation, identify the cost reduction measure: activity elimination, activity reduction, activity sharing, or activity selection.

### Exercise 7-47 Cycle Time and Velocity

OBJECTIVE 1 2 4

In the first quarter of operations, a manufacturing cell produced 80,000 stereo speakers, using 20,000 production hours. In the second quarter, the cycle time was 10 minutes per unit with the same number of production hours as were used in the first quarter.

ILLUSTRATING RELATIONSHIPS

**Required:**

1.  Compute the velocity (per hour) for the first quarter.
2.  Compute the cycle time for the first quarter (minutes per unit produced).
3.  How many units were produced in the second quarter?

### Exercise 7-48 Product-Costing Accuracy, Consumption Ratios

OBJECTIVE 4

Plata Company produces two products: a mostly handcrafted soft leather briefcase sold under the label Maletin Elegant and a leather briefcase produced largely through automation and sold under the label Maletin Fina. The two products use two overhead activities, with the following costs:

| | |
|---|---|
| Setting up equipment | $ 3,000 |
| Machining | 18,000 |

The controller has collected the expected annual prime costs for each briefcase, the machine hours, the setup hours, and the expected production.

| | Elegant | Fina |
|---|---|---|
| Direct labor | $9,000 | $3,000 |
| Direct materials | $3,000 | $3,000 |
| Units | 3,000 | 3,000 |
| Machine hours | 500 | 4,500 |
| Setup hours | 100 | 100 |

**Required:**

1.  **CONCEPTUAL CONNECTION** Do you think that the direct labor costs and direct materials costs are accurately traced to each briefcase? Explain.
2.  Calculate the consumption ratios for each activity.
3.  Calculate the overhead cost per unit for each briefcase by using a plantwide rate based on direct labor costs. Comment on this approach to assigning overhead.
4.  **CONCEPTUAL CONNECTION** Calculate the overhead cost per unit for each briefcase by using overhead rates based on machine hours and setup hours. Explain why these assignments are more accurate than using the direct labor costs.

### Exercise 7-49 Product-Costing Accuracy, Consumption Ratios, Activity Rates, Activity Costing

OBJECTIVE 1 2

Tristar Manufacturing produces two types of battery-operated toy soldiers: infantry and special forces. The soldiers are produced by using one continuous process. Four activities have been

*(Continued)*

identified: machining, setups, receiving, and packing. Resource drivers have been used to assign costs to each activity. The overhead activities, their costs, and the other related data are as follows:

| Product | Machine Hours | Setups | Receiving Orders | Packing Orders |
|---|---|---|---|---|
| Infantry | 20,000 | 300 | 900 | 1,600 |
| Special forces | 20,000 | 100 | 100 | 800 |
| Costs | $80,000 | $24,000 | $18,000 | $30,000 |

### Required:

1. Calculate the total overhead assigned to each product by using only machine hours to calculate a plantwide rate.
2. Calculate consumption ratios for each activity. (Round to two significant digits.)
3. Calculate a rate for each activity by using the associated driver.
4. Assign the overhead costs to each product by using the activity rates computed in Requirement 3.
5. **CONCEPTUAL CONNECTION** Comment on the difference between the assignment in Requirement 1 and the activity-based assignment.

OBJECTIVE  **Exercise 7-50   Formation of an Activity Dictionary**

A hospital is in the process of implementing an ABC system. A pilot study is being done to assess the effects of the costing changes on specific products. Of particular interest is the cost of caring for patients who receive in-patient recovery treatment for illness, surgery (noncardiac), and injury. These patients are housed on the third and fourth floors of the hospital (the floors are dedicated to patient care and have only nursing stations and patient rooms). A partial transcript of an interview with the hospital's nursing supervisor is as follows:

1. How many nurses are in the hospital?

   *There are 101 nurses, including me.*

2. Of these 100 nurses, how many are assigned to the third and fourth floors?

   *Fifty nurses are assigned to these two floors.*

3. What do these nurses do (please describe)?

   *Provide nursing care for patients, which, as you know, means answering questions, changing bandages, administering medicine, changing clothes, etc.*

4. And what do you do?

   *I supervise and coordinate all the nursing activity in the hospital. This includes surgery, maternity, the emergency room, and the two floors you mentioned.*

5. What other lodging and care activities are done for the third and fourth floors by persons other than the nurses?

   *The patients must be fed. The hospital cafeteria delivers meals. The laundry department picks up dirty clothing and bedding once each shift. The floors also have a physical therapist assigned to provide care on a physician-directed basis.*

6. Do patients use any equipment?

   *Yes. Mostly monitoring equipment.*

7. Who or what uses the activity output?

   *Patients. But there are different kinds of patients. On these two floors, we classify patients into three categories according to severity: intensive care, intermediate care, and normal care. The more severe the illness, the more activity is used. Nurses spend much more time with intermediate care patients than with normal care. The more severe patients tend to use more of the laundry service as well. Their clothing and bedding need to be changed more frequently. On the other hand, severe patients use less food. They eat fewer meals. Typically, we measure each patient type by the number of days of hospital stay. And you have to realize that the same patient contributes to each type of product.*

**Required:**

Prepare an activity dictionary with three categories: activity name, activity description, and activity driver.

### Exercise 7-51    Activity Rates and Activity-Based Product Costing

OBJECTIVE ▶ 2

Hammer Company produces a variety of electronic equipment. One of its plants produces two laser printers: the deluxe and the regular. At the beginning of the year, the following data were prepared for this plant:

|  | Deluxe | Regular |
| --- | --- | --- |
| Quantity | 100,000 | 800,000 |
| Selling price | $900 | $750 |
| Unit prime cost | $529 | $483 |

In addition, the following information was provided so that overhead costs could be assigned to each product:

| Activity Name | Activity Driver | Activity Cost | Deluxe | Regular |
| --- | --- | --- | --- | --- |
| Setups | Number of setups | $ 2,000,000 | 300 | 200 |
| Machining | Machine hours | 80,000,000 | 100,000 | 300,000 |
| Engineering | Engineering hours | 6,000,000 | 50,000 | 100,000 |
| Packing | Packing orders | 100,000 | 100,000 | 400,000 |

**Required:**

1. Calculate the overhead rates for each activity.
2. Calculate the per-unit product cost for each product. (Round to the nearest dollar.)

### Exercise 7-52    Value- and Nonvalue-Added Costs

OBJECTIVE ▶ 4

Waterfun Technology produces engines for recreational boats. Because of competitive pressures, the company was making an effort to reduce costs. As part of this effort, management implemented an activity-based management system and began focusing its attention on processes and activities. Receiving was among the processes (activities) that were carefully studied. The study revealed that the number of receiving orders was a good driver for receiving costs. During the last year, the company incurred fixed receiving costs of $630,000 (salaries of 15 employees). These fixed costs provide a capacity of processing 72,000 receiving orders (7,200 per employee at practical capacity). Management decided that the efficient level for receiving should use 36,000 receiving orders.

**Required:**

1. **CONCEPTUAL CONNECTION** Explain why receiving would be viewed as a value-added activity. List all possible reasons. Also, list some possible reasons that explain why the demand for receiving is more than the efficient level of 36,000 orders.
2. Break the cost of receiving into its value-added and nonvalue-added components.

## PROBLEMS

### Problem 7-53    Functional-Based versus Activity-Based Costing

OBJECTIVE ▶ 1 2

For years, Tamarindo Company produced only one product: backpacks. Recently, Tamarindo added a line of duffel bags. With this addition, the company began assigning overhead costs by using departmental rates. (Prior to this, the company used a predetermined plantwide rate based on units produced.) Surprisingly, after the addition of the duffel-bag line and the switch to departmental rates, the costs to produce the backpacks increased, and their profitability dropped.

*(Continued)*

Josie, the marketing manager, and Steve, the production manager, both complained about the increase in the production cost of backpacks. Josie was concerned because the increase in unit costs led to pressure to increase the unit price of backpacks. She was resisting this pressure because she was certain that the increase would harm the company's market share. Steve was receiving pressure to cut costs also, yet he was convinced that nothing different was being done in the way the backpacks were produced. After some discussion, the two managers decided that the problem had to be connected to the addition of the duffel-bag line.

Upon investigation, they were informed that the only real change in product costing procedures was in the way overhead costs are assigned. A two-stage procedure was now in use. First, overhead costs are assigned to the two producing departments, Patterns and Finishing. Second, the costs accumulated in the producing departments are assigned to the two products by using direct labor hours as a driver (the rate in each department is based on direct labor hours). The managers were assured that great care was taken to associate overhead costs with individual products. So that they could construct their own example of overhead cost assignment, the controller provided them with the information necessary to show how accounting costs are assigned to products:

|  | Department | | Total |
|  | Patterns | Finishing | |
| --- | --- | --- | --- |
| Accounting cost | $30,000 | $90,000 | $120,000 |
| Transactions processed | 20,000 | 60,000 | 80,000 |
| Total direct labor hours | 15,000 | 30,000 | 45,000 |
| Direct labor hours per backpack* | 0.10 | 0.20 | 0.30 |
| Direct labor hours per duffel bag* | 0.20 | 0.40 | 0.60 |

\* Hours required to produce one unit of each product.

The controller remarked that the cost of operating the accounting department had doubled with the addition of the new product line. The increase came because of the need to process additional transactions, which had also doubled in number.

During the first year of producing duffel bags, the company produced and sold 100,000 backpacks and 25,000 duffel bags. The 100,000 backpacks matched the prior year's output for that product.

**Required:**

1. **CONCEPTUAL CONNECTION** Compute the amount of accounting cost assigned to a backpack before the duffel-bag line was added by using a plantwide rate approach based on units produced. Is this assignment accurate? Explain.
2. Suppose that the company decided to assign the accounting costs directly to the product lines by using the number of transactions as the activity driver. What is the accounting cost per unit of backpacks? Per unit of duffel bags?
3. Compute the amount of accounting cost assigned to each backpack and duffel bag by using departmental rates based on direct labor hours.
4. **CONCEPTUAL CONNECTION** Which way of assigning overhead does the best job—the functional-based approach by using departmental rates or the activity-based approach by using transactions processed for each product? Explain. Discuss the value of ABC before the duffel-bag line was added.

OBJECTIVE ❶ ❷       **Problem 7-54    Plantwide versus Departmental Rates, Product-Costing Accuracy: Activity-Based Costing**

Ramsey Company produces speakers (Model A and Model B). Both products pass through two producing departments. Model A's production is much more labor-intensive than that of Model B. Model B is also the more popular of the two speakers. The following data have been gathered for the two products:

|  | Product Data | |
|---|---|---|
|  | **Model A** | **Model B** |
| Units produced per year | 10,000 | 100,000 |
| Prime costs | $150,000 | $1,500,000 |
| Direct labor hours | 140,000 | 300,000 |
| Machine hours | 20,000 | 200,000 |
| Production runs | 40 | 60 |
| Inspection hours | 800 | 1,200 |
| Maintenance hours | 10,000 | 90,000 |
| Overhead costs: | | |
| Setup costs | $270,000 | |
| Inspection costs | 210,000 | |
| Machining | 240,000 | |
| Maintenance | 270,000 | |
| Total | $990,000 | |

**Required:**

1. Compute the overhead cost per unit for each product by using a plantwide rate based on direct labor hours. (*Note*: Round to two decimal places.)
2. Compute the overhead cost per unit for each product by using ABC. (*Note:* Round rates and unit overhead cost to two decimal places.)
3. Suppose that Ramsey decides to use departmental overhead rates. There are two departments: Department 1 (machine intensive) with a rate of $3.50 per machine hour and Department 2 (labor intensive) with a rate of $0.90 per direct labor hour. The consumption of these two drivers is as follows:

|  | **Department 1**<br>**Machine Hours** | **Department 2 Direct**<br>**Labor Hours** |
|---|---|---|
| Model A | 10,000 | 130,000 |
| Model B | 170,000 | 270,000 |

Compute the overhead cost per unit for each product by using departmental rates. (*Note:* Round to two decimal places.)

4. **CONCEPTUAL CONNECTION** Using the activity-based product costs as the standard, comment on the ability of departmental rates to improve the accuracy of product costing. Did the departmental rates do better than the plantwide rate?

**Problem 7-55    Production-Based Costing versus Activity-Based Costing, Assigning Costs to Activities, Resource Drivers**

OBJECTIVE ❶ ❷

Willow Company produces lawn mowers. One of its plants produces two versions of mowers: a basic model and a deluxe model. The deluxe model has a sturdier frame, a higher horsepower engine, a wider blade, and mulching capability. At the beginning of the year, the following data were prepared for this plant:

|  | **Basic Model** | **Deluxe Model** |
|---|---|---|
| Expected quantity | 40,000 | 20,000 |
| Selling price | $180 | $360 |
| Prime costs | $80 | $160 |
| Machine hours | 5,000 | 5,000 |
| Direct labor hours | 10,000 | 10,000 |
| Engineering support (hours) | 1,500 | 4,500 |
| Receiving (orders processed) | 250 | 500 |
| Materials handling (number of moves) | 1,200 | 4,800 |
| Purchasing (number of requisitions) | 100 | 200 |
| Maintenance (hours used) | 1,000 | 3,000 |
| Paying suppliers (invoices processed) | 250 | 500 |
| Setting up equipment (number of setups) | 16 | 64 |

*(Continued)*

Additionally, the following overhead activity costs are reported:

| | |
|---|---|
| Maintaining equipment | $114,000 |
| Engineering support | 120,000 |
| Materials handling | ? |
| Setting up equipment | 96,000 |
| Purchasing materials | 60,000 |
| Receiving goods | 40,000* |
| Paying suppliers | 30,000 |
| Providing space | 20,000 |
| Total | $       ? |

\* Receiving activity cost includes allocated share of forklift operators' salaries.

Facility-level costs are allocated in proportion to machine hours (provides a measure of time the facility is used by each product). Receiving and materials handling use three inputs: two forklifts, gasoline to operate the forklift, and three operators. The three operators are paid a salary of $40,000 each. The operators spend 25% of their time on the receiving activity and 75% on moving goods (materials handling). Gasoline costs $3 per move. Depreciation amounts to $8,000 per forklift per year.

### Required:

(*Note:* Round answers to two decimal places.)
1. Calculate the cost of the materials handling activity. Label the cost assignments as driver tracing or direct tracing. Identify the resource drivers.
2. Calculate the cost per unit for each product by using direct labor hours to assign all overhead costs.
3. Calculate activity rates, and assign costs to each product. Calculate a unit cost for each product, and compare these costs with those calculated in Requirement 2.
4. Calculate consumption ratios for each activity.
5. **CONCEPTUAL CONNECTION** Explain how the consumption ratios calculated in Requirement 4 can be used to reduce the number of rates. Calculate the rates that would apply under this approach.

OBJECTIVE    **Problem 7-56   Activity Costing, Assigning Resource Costs, Primary and Secondary Activities**

Elmo Clinic has identified three activities for daily maternity care: occupancy and feeding, nursing, and nursing supervision. The nursing supervisor oversees 150 nurses, 25 of whom are maternity nurses (the other nurses are located in other care areas such as the emergency room and intensive care). The nursing supervisor has three assistants, a secretary, several offices, computers, phones, and furniture. The three assistants spend 75% of their time on the supervising activity and 25% of their time as surgical nurses. They each receive a salary of $60,000. The nursing supervisor has a salary of $80,000. She spends 100% of her time supervising. The secretary receives a salary of $35,000 per year. Other costs directly traceable to the supervisory activity (depreciation, utilities, phone, etc.) average $170,000 per year.

Daily care output is measured as "patient days." The clinic has traditionally assigned the cost of daily care by using a daily rate (a rate per patient day). Daily rates can differ between units, but within units the daily rates are the same for all patients. Under the traditional approach, the daily rate is computed by dividing the annual costs of occupancy and feeding, nursing, and a share of supervision by the unit's capacity expressed in patient days. The cost of supervision is assigned to each care area based on the number of nurses. A single driver (patient days) is used to assign the costs of daily care to each patient.

A pilot study has revealed that the demands for nursing care vary within the maternity unit, depending on the severity of a patient's case. Assume that the maternity unit has three levels of increasing severity: normal patients, cesarean patients, and patients with complications. The pilot study provided the following activity and cost information:

| Activity | Annual Cost | Activity Driver | Annual Quantity |
|---|---|---|---|
| Occupancy and feeding | $1,500,000 | Patient days | 10,000 |
| Nursing care (maternity) | 1,200,000 | Hours of nursing care | 50,000 |
| Nursing supervision | ? | Number of nurses | 150 |

The pilot study also revealed the following information concerning the three types of patients and their annual demands:

| Patient Type | Patient Days Demanded | Nursing Hours Demanded |
|---|---|---|
| Normal | 7,000 | 17,500 |
| Cesarean | 2,000 | 12,500 |
| Complications | 1,000 | 20,000 |
| Total | 10,000 | 50,000 |

**Required:**

1. Calculate the cost per patient day by using a functional-based approach.
2. Calculate the cost per patient day by using an activity-based approach.
3. **CONCEPTUAL CONNECTION** The hospital processes 1,250,000 pounds of laundry per year. The cost for the laundering activity is $600,000 per year. In a functional-based cost system, the cost of the laundry department is assigned to each user department in proportion to the pounds of laundry produced. Typically, maternity produces 240,000 pounds per year. How much would this change the cost per patient day calculated in Requirement 1? Now, describe what information you would need to modify the calculation made in Requirement 2. Under what conditions would this activity calculation provide a more accurate cost assignment?

## Problem 7-57    Customers as a Cost Object                              OBJECTIVE ❶ ❷ ❸

Morrisom National Bank has requested an analysis of checking account profitability by customer type. Customers are categorized according to the size of their account: low balances, medium balances, and high balances. The activities associated with the three different customer categories and their associated annual costs are as follows:

| | |
|---|---|
| Opening and closing accounts | $  300,000 |
| Issuing monthly statements | 450,000 |
| Processing transactions | 3,075,000 |
| Customer inquiries | 600,000 |
| Providing automatic teller machine (ATM) services | 1,680,000 |
| Total cost | $6,105,000 |

Additional data concerning the usage of the activities by the various customers are also provided:

| | Account Balance | | |
|---|---|---|---|
| | Low | Medium | High |
| Number of accounts opened/closed | 22,500 | 4,500 | 3,000 |
| Number of statements issued | 675,000 | 150,000 | 75,000 |
| Processing transactions | 27,000,000 | 3,000,000 | 750,000 |
| Number of telephone minutes | 1,500,000 | 900,000 | 600,000 |
| Number of ATM transactions | 2,025,000 | 300,000 | 75,000 |
| Number of checking accounts | 57,000 | 12,000 | 6,000 |

**Required:**

(*Note:* Round answers to two decimal places.)

1. Calculate a cost per account per year by dividing the total cost of processing and maintaining checking accounts by the total number of accounts. What is the average fee per month that the bank should charge to cover the costs incurred because of checking accounts?

*(Continued)*

2. Calculate a cost per account by customer category by using activity rates.
3. Currently, the bank offers free checking to all of its customers. The interest revenues average $90 per account; however, the interest revenues earned per account by category are $80, $100, and $165 for the low-, medium-, and high-balance accounts, respectively. Calculate the average profit per account (average revenue minus average cost from Requirement 1). Then calculate the profit per account by using the revenue per customer type and the unit cost per customer type calculated in Requirement 2.
4. **CONCEPTUAL CONNECTION** After the analysis in Requirement 3, a vice president recommended eliminating the free checking feature for low-balance customers. The bank president expressed reluctance to do so, arguing that the low-balance customers more than made up for the loss through cross-sales. He presented a survey that showed that 50% of the customers would switch banks if a checking fee were imposed. Explain how you could verify the president's argument by using ABC.

OBJECTIVE     Problem 7-58   **Activity-Based Costing and Customer-Driven Costs**

Grundvig Manufacturing produces several types of bolts used in aircrafts. The bolts are produced in batches and grouped into three product families. Because the product families are used in different kinds of aircraft, customers also can be grouped into three categories, corresponding to the product family that they purchase. The number of units sold to each customer class is the same. The selling prices for the three product families range from $0.50 to $0.80 per unit. Historically, the costs of order entry, processing, and handling were expensed and not traced to individual customer groups. These costs are not trivial and totaled $9,000,000 for the most recent year. Recently, the company started emphasizing a cost reduction strategy with an emphasis on creating a competitive advantage.

Upon investigation, management discovered that order-filling costs were driven by the number of customer orders processed with the following cost behavior:

Step-fixed cost component: $50,000 per step (2,000 orders define a step)*
Variable cost component: $20 per order

* Grundvig currently has sufficient steps to process 200,000 orders.

The expected customer orders for the year total 200,000. The expected usage of the order-filling activity and the average size of an order by customer category follow:

|  | Category I | Category II | Category III |
|---|---|---|---|
| Number of orders | 100,000 | 60,000 | 40,000 |
| Average order size | 600 | 1,000 | 1,500 |

As a result of cost behavior analysis, the marketing manager recommended the imposition of a charge per customer order. The charge was implemented by adding the cost per order to the price of each order (computed by using the projected ordering costs and expected orders). This ordering cost was then reduced as the size of the order increased and was eliminated as the order size reached 2,000 units. Within a short period of communicating this new price information to customers, the average order size for all three product families increased to 2,000 units.

**Required:**

1. **CONCEPTUAL CONNECTION** Grundvig traditionally has expensed order-filling costs. What is the most likely reason for this practice?
2. Calculate the cost per order for each customer category. (*Note:* Round to two decimal places.)
3. **CONCEPTUAL CONNECTION** Calculate the reduction in order-filling costs produced by the change in pricing strategy (assume that resource spending is reduced as much as possible and that the total units sold remain unchanged). Explain how exploiting customer activity information produced this cost reduction. Would any other internal activities benefit from this pricing strategy?

## Problem 7-59   Activity-Based Supplier Costing

OBJECTIVE ❷ ❸

Levy Inc. manufactures tractors for agricultural usage. Levy purchases the engines needed for its tractors from two sources: Johnson Engines and Watson Company. The Johnson engine has a price of $1,000. The Watson engine is $900 per unit. Levy produces and sells 22,000 tractors. Of the 22,000 engines needed for the tractors, 4,000 are purchased from Johnson Engines, and 18,000 are purchased from Watson Company. The production manager, Jamie Murray, prefers the Johnson engine. However, Jan Booth, purchasing manager, maintains that the price difference is too great to buy more than the 4,000 units currently purchased. Booth also wants to maintain a significant connection with the Johnson source just in case the less expensive source cannot supply the needed quantities. Jamie, however, is convinced that the quality of the Johnson engine is worth the price difference.

Frank Wallace, the controller, has decided to use activity costing to resolve the issue. The following activity cost and supplier data have been collected:

| Activity | Cost |
|---|---|
| Replacing engines[a] | $    800,000 |
| Expediting orders[b] | 1,000,000 |
| Repairing engines[c] | 1,800,000 |

[a] All units are tested after assembly, and some are rejected because of engine failure. The failed engines are removed and replaced, with the supplier replacing any failed engine. The replaced engine is retested before being sold. Engine failure often causes collateral damage, and other parts often need to be replaced.
[b] Due to late or failed delivery of engines.
[c] Repair work is for units under warranty and almost invariably is due to engine failure. Repair usually means replacing the engine. This cost plus labor, transportation, and other costs make warranty work very expensive.

| | Watson | Johnson |
|---|---|---|
| Engines replaced by source | 1,980 | 20 |
| Late or failed shipments | 198 | 2 |
| Warranty repairs (by source) | 2,440 | 60 |

### Required:

1. **CONCEPTUAL CONNECTION** Calculate the activity-based supplier cost per engine (acquisition cost plus supplier-related activity costs). (Round to the nearest cent.) Which of the two suppliers is the low-cost supplier? Explain why this is a better measure of engine cost than the usual purchase costs assigned to the engines.
2. **CONCEPTUAL CONNECTION** Consider the supplier cost information obtained in Requirement 1. Suppose further that Johnson can only supply a total of 20,000 units. What actions would you advise Levy to undertake with its suppliers?

## Problem 7-60   Activity-Based Management, Nonvalue-Added Costs

OBJECTIVE ❹

Danna Martin, president of Mays Electronics, was concerned about the end-of-the year marketing report that she had just received. According to Larry Savage, marketing manager, a price decrease for the coming year was again needed to maintain the company's annual sales volume of integrated circuit boards (CBs). This would make a bad situation worse. The current selling price of $18 per unit was producing a $2-per-unit profit—half the customary $4-per-unit profit. Foreign competitors kept reducing their prices. To match the latest reduction would reduce the price from $18 to $14. This would put the price below the cost to produce and sell it. How could these firms sell for such a low price? Determined to find out if there were problems with the company's operations, Danna decided to hire a consultant to evaluate the way in which the CBs were produced and sold. After two weeks, the consultant had identified the following activities and costs:

| | |
|---|---|
| Setting up equipment | $   125,000 |
| Materials handling | 180,000 |
| Inspecting products | 122,000 |
| Engineering support | 120,000 |
| Handling customer complaints | 100,000 |

*(Continued)*

| | |
|---|---:|
| Filling warranties | 170,000 |
| Storing goods | 80,000 |
| Expediting goods | 75,000 |
| Using materials | 500,000 |
| Using power | 48,000 |
| Manual insertion labor[a] | 250,000 |
| Other direct labor | 150,000 |
| Total costs | $1,920,000[b] |

[a] Diodes, resistors, and integrated circuits are inserted manually into the circuit board.
[b] This total cost produces a unit cost of $16 for last year's sales volume.

The consultant indicated that some preliminary activity analysis shows that per-unit costs can be reduced by at least $7. Since the marketing manager had indicated that the market share (sales volume) for the boards could be increased by 50% if the price could be reduced to $12, Danna became quite excited.

**Required:**

1.  **CONCEPTUAL CONNECTION** What is activity-based management? What phases of activity analysis did the consultant provide? What else remains to be done?
2.  **CONCEPTUAL CONNECTION** Identify as many nonvalue-added costs as possible. Compute the cost savings per unit that would be realized if these costs were eliminated. Was the consultant correct in the preliminary cost reduction assessment? Discuss actions that the company can take to reduce or eliminate the nonvalue-added activities.
3.  Compute the unit cost required to maintain current market share, while earning a profit of $4 per unit. Now compute the unit cost required to expand sales by 50%, assuming a per unit profit of $4. How much cost reduction would be required to achieve each unit cost?
4.  Assume that further activity analysis revealed the following: switching to automated insertion would save $60,000 of engineering support and $90,000 of direct labor. Now, what is the total potential cost reduction per unit available from activity analysis? With these additional reductions, can Mays achieve the unit cost to maintain current sales? To increase it by 50%? What form of activity analysis is this: reduction, sharing, elimination, or selection?
5.  **CONCEPTUAL CONNECTION** Calculate income based on current sales, prices, and costs. Then calculate the income by using a $14 price and a $12 price, assuming that the maximum cost reduction possible is achieved (including Requirement 4's reduction). What price should be selected?

OBJECTIVE     **Problem 7-61    Nonvalue-Added Costs, Activity Costs, Activity Cost Reduction**

John Thomas, vice president of Mallett Company (a producer of a variety of plastic products), has been supervising the implementation of an ABC management system. John wants to improve process efficiency by improving the activities that define the processes. To illustrate the potential of the new system to the president, John has decided to focus on two processes: production and customer service.

Within each process, one activity will be selected for improvement: materials usage for production and sustaining engineering for customer service (sustaining engineers are responsible for redesigning products based on customer needs and feedback). Value-added standards are identified for each activity. For materials usage, the value-added standard calls for six pounds per unit of output (the products differ in shape and function, but their weight is uniform). The value-added standard is based on the elimination of all waste due to defective molds. The standard price of materials is $5 per pound. For sustaining engineering, the standard is 58% of current practical activity capacity. This standard is based on the fact that about 42% of the complaints have to do with design features that could have been avoided or anticipated by the company.

Current practical capacity (at the end of 2013) is defined by the following requirements: 6,000 engineering hours for each product group that has been on the market or in development for 5 years or less and 2,400 hours per product group of more than 5 years. Four product groups have less than 5 years' experience, and 10 product groups have more. Each of the 24 engineers is paid a salary of $60,000. Each engineer can provide 2,000 hours of service per year. No other significant costs are incurred for the engineering activity.

Actual materials usage for 2013 was 25% above the level called for by the value-added standard; engineering usage was 46,000 hours. A total of 80,000 units of output were produced. John and the operational managers have selected some improvement measures that promise to reduce nonvalue-added activity usage by 40% in 2014. Selected actual results achieved for 2014 are as follows:

| | |
|---|---|
| Units produced | 80,000 |
| Materials used | 584,800 |
| Engineering hours | 35,400 |

The actual prices paid for materials and engineering hours are identical to the standard or budgeted prices.

**Required:**

1. For 2013, calculate the nonvalue-added usage and costs for materials usage and sustaining engineering.
2. **CONCEPTUAL CONNECTION** Using the budgeted improvements, calculate the expected activity usage levels for 2014. Now, compute the 2014 usage variances (the difference between the expected and actual values), expressed in both physical and financial measures, for materials and engineering. Comment on the company's ability to achieve its targeted reductions. In particular, discuss what measures the company must take to capture any realized reductions in resource usage.

## Problem 7-62    Cycle Time, Velocity, Product Costing

OBJECTIVE ▶ 4

Goldman Company has a JIT system in place. Each manufacturing cell is dedicated to the production of a single product or major subassembly. One cell, dedicated to the production of telescopes, has four operations: machining, finishing, assembly, and qualifying (testing).

For the coming year, the telescope cell has the following budgeted costs and cell time (both at theoretical capacity):

| | |
|---|---|
| Budgeted conversion costs | $7,500,000 |
| Budgeted raw materials | $9,000,000 |
| Cell time | 12,000 hours |
| Theoretical output | 90,000 telescopes |

During the year, the following actual results were obtained:

| | |
|---|---|
| Actual conversion costs | $7,500,000 |
| Actual materials | $7,800,000 |
| Actual cell time | 12,000 hours |
| Actual output | 75,000 telescopes |

**Required:**

(*Note:* Round answers to two decimal places.)

1. Compute the velocity (number of telescopes per hour) that the cell can theoretically achieve. Now, compute the theoretical cycle time (number of hours or minutes per telescope) that it takes to produce one telescope.
2. Compute the actual velocity and the actual cycle time.
3. **CONCEPTUAL CONNECTION** Compute the budgeted conversion costs per minute. Using this rate, compute the conversion costs per telescope if theoretical output is achieved. Using this measure, compute the conversion costs per telescope for actual output. Does this product costing approach provide an incentive for the cell manager to reduce cycle time? Explain.

OBJECTIVE ④     **Problem 7-63    Classification of Environmental Costs**

Consider the following independent environmental activities:

a.   A company takes actions to reduce the amount of material in its packages.

b.   After its useful life, a soft-drink producer returns the activated carbon used for purifying water for its beverages to the supplier. The supplier reactivates the carbon for a second use in nonfood applications. As a consequence, many tons of material are prevented from entering landfills.

c.   An evaporator system is installed to treat wastewater and to collect usable solids for other uses.

d.   The inks used to print snack packages (for chips) contain heavy metals.

e.   Processes are inspected to ensure compliance with environmental standards.

f.   Delivery boxes are used five times and then recycled. This prevents 112 million pounds of cardboard from entering landfills and saves two million trees per year.

g.   Scrubber equipment is installed to ensure that air emissions are less than the level permitted by law.

h.   Local residents are incurring medical costs from illnesses caused by air pollution from automobile exhaust pollution.

i.   As part of implementing an environmental perspective for a balanced performance measurement system, environmental performance measures are developed.

j.   Because of liquid and solid residues being discharged into a local lake, it is no longer fit for swimming, fishing, and other recreational activities.

k.   To reduce energy consumption, magnetic ballasts are replaced with electronic ballasts, and more efficient light bulbs and lighting sensors are installed. As a result, 2.3 million kilowatt-hours of electricity are saved per year.

l.   Because of a legal settlement, a chemical company must spend $20,000,000 to clean up contaminated soil.

m.   A soft-drink company uses the following practice: In all bottling plants, packages damaged during filling are collected and recycled (glass, plastic, and aluminum).

n.   Products are inspected to ensure that the gaseous emissions produced during operation follow legal and company guidelines.

o.   Costs are incurred to operate pollution-control equipment.

p.   An internal audit is conducted to verify that environmental policies are being followed.

**Required:**

Classify these environmental activities as prevention, detection, internal failure, or external failure costs. For external failure costs, classify the costs as societal or realized. Also, label those activities that are compatible with sustainable development with "SD."

# CASES

OBJECTIVE ②③④     **Case 7-64    Activity-Based Costing, Distorted Product Costs**

Sharp Paper Inc. has three paper mills, one of which is located in Memphis, Tennessee. The Memphis mill produces 300 different types of coated and uncoated specialty printing papers. Management was convinced that the value of the large variety of products more than offset the extra costs of the increased complexity.

During 2013, the Memphis mill produced 120,000 tons of coated paper and 80,000 tons of uncoated paper. Of the 200,000 tons produced, 180,000 were sold. Sixty products account for 80% of the tons sold. Thus, 240 products are classified as low-volume products.

Lightweight lime hopsack in cartons (LLHC) is one of the low-volume products. LLHC is produced in rolls, converted into sheets of paper, and then sold in cartons. In 2013 the cost to produce and sell one ton of LLHC was as follows:

| Direct materials: | | |
|---|---|---|
| Furnish (3 different pulps) | 2,225 pounds | $ 450 |
| Additives (11 different items) | 200 pounds | 500 |
| Tub size | 75 pounds | 10 |
| Recycled scrap paper | (296 pounds) | (20) |
| Total direct materials | | $ 940 |
| Direct labor | | $ 450 |
| Overhead: | | |
| Paper machine ($100 per ton × 2,500 pounds) | | $ 125 |
| Finishing machine ($120 per ton × 2,500 pounds) | | 150 |
| Total overhead | | $ 275 |
| Shipping and warehousing | | $ 30 |
| Total manufacturing and selling cost | | $1,695 |

Overhead is applied by using a two-stage process. First, overhead is allocated to the paper and finishing machines by using the direct method of allocation with carefully selected cost drivers. Second, the overhead assigned to each machine is divided by the budgeted tons of output. These rates are then multiplied by the number of pounds required to produce one good ton.

In 2013, LLHC sold for $2,400 per ton, making it one of the most profitable products. A similar examination of some of the other low-volume products revealed that they also had very respectable profit margins. Unfortunately, the performance of the high volume products was less impressive, with many showing losses or very low profit margins. This situation led Ryan Chesser to call a meeting with his marketing vice president, Jennifer Woodruff, and his controller, Kaylin Penn.

**Ryan:** The above-average profitability of our low-volume specialty products and the poor profit performance of our high-volume products make me believe that we should switch our marketing emphasis to the low-volume line. Perhaps we should drop some of our high-volume products, particularly those showing a loss.

**Jennifer:** I'm not convinced that solution is the right one. I know our high-volume products are of high quality, and I'm convinced that we are as efficient in our production as other firms. I think that somehow our costs are not being assigned correctly. For example, the shipping and warehousing costs are assigned by dividing these costs by the total tons of paper sold. Yet . . .

**Kaylin:** Jennifer, I hate to disagree, but the $30-per-ton charge for shipping and warehousing seems reasonable. I know that our method to assign these costs is identical to a number of other paper companies.

**Jennifer:** Well, that may be true, but do these other companies have the variety of products that we have? Our low-volume products require special handling and processing, but when we assign shipping and warehousing costs, we average these special costs across our entire product line. Every ton produced in our mill passes through our mill shipping department and is either sent directly to the customer or to our distribution center and then eventually to customers. My records indicate quite clearly that virtually all of the high-volume products are sent directly to customers, whereas most of the low-volume products are sent to the distribution center. Now, all of the products passing through the mill shipping department should receive a share of the $2,000,000 annual shipping costs. I'm not convinced, however, that all products should receive a share of the receiving and shipping costs of the distribution center as currently practiced.

**Ryan:** Kaylin, is this true? Does our system allocate our shipping and warehousing costs in this way?

**Kaylin:** Yes, I'm afraid it does. Jennifer may have a point. Perhaps we need to reevaluate our method to assign these costs to the product lines.

**Ryan:** Jennifer, do you have any suggestions concerning how the shipping and warehousing costs should be assigned?

*(Continued)*

**Jennifer:** It seems reasonable to make a distinction between products that spend time in the distribution center and those that do not. We should also distinguish between the receiving and shipping activities at the distribution center. All incoming shipments are packed on pallets and weigh one ton each (there are 14 cartons of paper per pallet). In 2013, the receiving department processed 56,000 tons of paper. Receiving employs 15 people at an annual cost of $600,000. Other receiving costs total about $500,000. I would recommend that these costs be assigned by using tons processed.

Shipping, however, is different. There are two activities associated with shipping: picking the order from inventory and loading the paper. We employ 30 people for picking and 10 for loading, at an annual cost of $1,200,000. Other shipping costs total $1,100,000. Picking and loading are more concerned with the number of shipping items than with tonnage. That is, a shipping item may consist of two or three cartons instead of pallets. Accordingly, the shipping costs of the distribution center should be assigned by using the number of items shipped. In 2013, for example, we handled 190,000 shipping items.

**Ryan:** These suggestions have merit. Kaylin, I would like to see what effect Jennifer's suggestions have on the per-unit assignment of shipping and warehousing for LLHC. If the effect is significant, then we will expand the analysis to include all products.

**Kaylin:** I'm willing to compute the effect, but I'd like to suggest one additional feature. Currently, we have a policy to carry about 25 tons of LLHC in inventory. Our current costing system totally ignores the cost of carrying this inventory. Since it costs us $1,665 to produce each ton of this product, we are tying up a lot of money in inventory—money that could be invested in other productive opportunities. In fact, the return lost is about 16% per year. This cost should also be assigned to the units sold.

**Ryan:** Kaylin, this also sounds good to me. Go ahead and include the carrying cost in your computation.

To help in the analysis, Kaylin gathered the following data for LLHC for 2013:

| | |
|---|---|
| Tons sold | 10 |
| Average cartons per shipment | 2 |
| Average shipments per ton | 7 |

**Required:**

1. Identify the flaws associated with the current method of assigning shipping and warehousing costs to Sharp's products.
2. Compute the shipping and warehousing cost per ton of LLHC sold by using the new method suggested by Jennifer and Kaylin.
3. Using the new costs computed in Requirement 2, compute the profit per ton of LLHC. Compare this with the profit per ton computed by using the old method. Do you think that this same effect would be realized for other low-volume products? Explain.
4. Comment on Ryan's proposal to drop some high-volume products and place more emphasis on low-volume products. Discuss the role of the accounting system in supporting this type of decision making.
5. After receiving the analysis of LLHC, Ryan decided to expand the analysis to all products. He also had Kaylin reevaluate the way in which mill overhead was assigned to products. After the restructuring was completed, Ryan took the following actions: (a) the prices of most low-volume products were increased, (b) the prices of several high-volume products were decreased, and (c) some low-volume products were dropped. Explain why his strategy changed so dramatically.

OBJECTIVE ② ③ ④        **Case 7-65    Activity-Based Product Costing and Ethical Behavior**

Consider the following conversation between Leonard Bryner, president and manager of a firm engaged in job manufacturing, and Chuck Davis, certified management accountant, the firm's controller.

**Leonard:** Chuck, as you know, our firm has been losing market share over the past 3 years. We have been losing more and more bids, and I don't understand why. At first, I thought that other firms were undercutting simply to gain business, but after examining some of the public financial reports, I believe that they are making a reasonable rate of return. I am beginning to believe that our costs and costing methods are at fault.

**Chuck:** I can't agree with that. We have good control over our costs. Like most firms in our industry, we use a normal job-costing system. I really don't see any significant waste in the plant.

**Leonard:** After talking with some other managers at a recent industrial convention, I'm not so sure that waste by itself is the issue. They talked about activity-based management, activity-based costing, and continuous improvement. They mentioned the use of something called "activity drivers" to assign overhead. They claimed that these new procedures can help to produce more efficiency in manufacturing, better control of overhead, and more accurate product costing. A big deal was made of eliminating activities that added no value. Maybe our bids are too high because these other firms have found ways to decrease their overhead costs and to increase the accuracy of their product costing.

**Chuck:** I doubt it. For one thing, I don't see how we can increase product costing accuracy. So many of our costs are indirect costs. Furthermore, everyone uses some measure of production activity to assign overhead costs. I imagine that what they are calling "activity drivers" is just some new buzzword for measures of production volume. Fads in costing come and go. I wouldn't worry about it. I'll bet that our problems with decreasing sales are temporary. You might recall that we experienced a similar problem about 12 years ago—it was 2 years before it straightened out.

**Required:**

1. Do you agree or disagree with Chuck Davis and the advice that he gave Leonard Bryner? Explain.
2. Was there anything wrong or unethical in the behavior that Chuck Davis displayed? Explain your reasoning.
3. Do you think that Chuck was well informed—that he was aware of the accounting implications of ABC and that he knew what was meant by cost drivers? Should he have been well informed? Review (in Chapter 1) the first category of the Statement of Ethical Professional Practice for management accountants. Do any of these standards apply in Chuck's case?

# 8

# Absorption and Variable Costing, and Inventory Management

© Pixelfabrik/Alamy

Chris Borrelli/MCT/Newscom

After studying Chapter 8, you should be able to:

1. Explain the difference between absorption and variable costing.

2. Prepare segmented income statements.

3. Discuss inventory management under the economic order quantity and just-in-time (JIT) models.

# EXPERIENCE MANAGERIAL DECISIONS

## with Zingerman's

Income statements used in financial accounting typically show all of the sales and expenses for the company as a whole. This may be enough for external parties, such as investors and banks. However, managers of companies with more than one business segment need to know how each segment is performing as well.

**Zingerman's** deli, the company introduced in Chapter 3, has eight separate businesses. Seven of these segments—the Delicatessen, Mail Order, Bakehouse, ZingTrain, Roadhouse Restaurant, Creamery, and Coffee Company—sell products and services to external customers. Each segment has both variable and fixed costs. For example, variable costs of the Roadhouse Restaurant include food, beverages, paper products, and some labor. Direct fixed costs for Roadhouse include rent/depreciation for the building, furniture, and equipment.

The eighth segment, ZingNet, is internal and provides support services, such as human resources, payroll, organizational marketing, graphics brand design, information technology, administration, accounting, and office rental to the other seven segments. ZingNet costs are common to the overall company and they are allocated on the basis of revenues for each business.

> *"The eighth segment, ZingNet, is internal and provides support services, such as human resources, payroll, organizational marketing, graphics brand design, information technology, administration, accounting, and office rental to the other seven segments."*

This method of allocation occasionally causes problems among the external businesses—especially those that do not use much of the ZingNet services, but have high sales (thereby getting a larger share of ZingNet cost allocation). The use of variable costing and segmented income statements can help to overcome this kind of problem, since a properly developed segmented income statement separates direct fixed costs from common fixed costs. Treating the ZingNet costs as common fixed costs would also be consistent with Zingerman's belief that ZingNet costs are an investment in future profitability.

OBJECTIVE **1**

Explain the difference between absorption and variable costing.

# MEASURING THE PERFORMANCE OF PROFIT CENTERS BY USING VARIABLE AND ABSORPTION INCOME STATEMENTS

Many companies consist of separate business units called profit centers. It is important for these companies to determine both the overall performance of the business and the performance of the individual profit centers. The overall income statement is useful for looking at overall company performance. However, this income statement is of little use for determining the viability of the individual business units or segments. Instead, it is important to develop a segmented income statement for each profit center. Two methods of computing income have been developed: one based on variable costing and the other based on full or absorption costing. These are costing methods because they refer to the way in which product costs are determined. Recall that *product costs* are inventoried; they include direct materials, direct labor, and overhead. *Period costs*, such as selling and administrative expense, are expensed in the period incurred. The difference between variable and absorption costing hinges on the treatment of one particular cost: fixed factory overhead.

## Absorption Costing

**Absorption costing** assigns *all* manufacturing costs to the product. Direct materials, direct labor, variable overhead, and fixed overhead define the cost of a product. Thus, under absorption costing, fixed overhead is viewed as a product cost, not a period cost. Under this method, fixed overhead is assigned to the product through the use of a predetermined fixed overhead rate and is not expensed until the product is sold. In other words, fixed overhead is an inventoriable cost.

## Variable Costing

Variable costing stresses the difference between fixed and variable manufacturing costs. **Variable costing** assigns only variable manufacturing costs to the product; these costs include direct materials, direct labor, and variable overhead. Fixed overhead is treated as a period expense and is *excluded* from the product cost. The rationale for this is that fixed overhead is a cost of capacity, or staying in business. Once the period is over, any benefits provided by capacity have expired and should not be inventoried. Under variable costing, fixed overhead of a period is seen as expiring that period and is charged in total against the revenues of the period.

## Comparison of Variable and Absorption Costing Methods

Exhibit 8.1 illustrates the classification of costs as product or period costs under absorption and variable costing.

Generally accepted accounting principles (GAAP) require absorption costing for external reporting. The Financial Accounting Standards Board (FASB), the Internal Revenue Service (IRS), and other regulatory bodies do not accept variable costing as a

**( EXHIBIT 8.1 )**

**Classification of Costs under Absorption and Variable Costing as Product or Period Costs**

|  | Absorption Costing | Variable Costing |
|---|---|---|
| Product costs | Direct materials<br>Direct labor<br>Variable overhead<br>Fixed overhead | Direct materials<br>Direct labor<br>Variable overhead |
| Period costs | Selling expenses<br>Administrative expenses | Fixed overhead<br>Selling expenses<br>Administrative expenses |

product-costing method for external reporting. Yet variable costing can supply vital cost information for decision making and control, information not supplied by absorption costing. For *internal* application, variable costing is an important managerial tool.

## Inventory Valuation

Inventory is valued at product or manufacturing cost. (Recall that inventory cost *never* includes the period costs of selling or administration.) Under absorption costing, that product cost includes direct materials, direct labor, variable overhead, and fixed overhead.

> Absorption Costing Product Cost = Direct Materials + Direct Labor
> + Variable Overhead + Fixed Overhead

Under variable costing, the product cost includes only direct materials, direct labor, and variable overhead.

> Variable Costing Product Cost = Direct Materials + Direct Labor + Variable Overhead

Cornerstone 8.1 shows how to compute inventory cost under absorption costing.

## Computing Inventory Cost under Absorption Costing

CORNERSTONE

8.1

**Why:**

Unit cost under absorption costing includes all product costs, both fixed and variable. It is a long run measure of product costing.

**Information:**

During the most recent year, Fairchild Company had the following data associated with the product it makes:

| | |
|---|---:|
| Units in beginning inventory | — |
| Units produced | 10,000 |
| Units sold ($300 per unit) | 8,000 |
| Variable costs per unit: | |
|    Direct materials | $50 |
|    Direct labor | $100 |
|    Variable overhead | $50 |
| Fixed costs: | |
|    Fixed overhead per unit produced | $25 |
|    Fixed selling and administrative | $100,000 |

**Required:**

1. How many units are in ending inventory?

2. Using absorption costing, calculate the per-unit product cost.

3. What is the value of ending inventory?

**Solution:**

1. Units Ending Inventory = Units Beginning Inventory + Units Produced − Units Sold

$$= 0 + 10{,}000 - 8{,}000$$

$$= 2{,}000 \text{ units}$$

*(Continued)*

CORNERSTONE

**8.1**

*(Continued)*

2. Absorption costing unit cost:

| | |
|---|---:|
| Direct materials | $ 50 |
| Direct labor | 100 |
| Variable overhead | 50 |
| Fixed overhead | 25 |
| Unit product cost | $225 |

3. Value of Ending Inventory = Units Ending Inventory × Absorption Unit Product Cost

$$= 2{,}000 \text{ units} \times \$225$$

$$= \$450{,}000$$

Notice that the inventory cost computed under absorption costing is the traditional product cost used for external financial statements and for GAAP. Each unit includes all variable manufacturing costs as well as a portion of fixed factory overhead. Cornerstone 8.2 shows how to calculate inventory cost under variable costing.

CORNERSTONE

**8.2**

## Computing Inventory Cost under Variable Costing

**Why:**

Unit cost under variable costing includes only variable product cost. Fixed product cost is a period cost that is not attached to inventory.

**Information:**

Refer to the data in Cornerstone 8.1 for Fairchild Company (p. 345).

**Required:**

1. How many units are in ending inventory?

2. Using variable costing, calculate the per-unit product cost.

3. What is the value of ending inventory?

**Solution:**

1. Units Ending Inventory = Units Beginning Inventory + Units Produced − Units Sold

$$= 0 + 10{,}000 - 8{,}000$$

$$= 2{,}000 \text{ units}$$

2. Variable costing unit cost:

| | |
|---|---:|
| Direct materials | $ 50 |
| Direct labor | 100 |
| Variable overhead | 50 |
| Unit product cost | $200 |

3. Value of Ending Inventory = Units Ending Inventory × Variable Unit Product Cost

$$= 2{,}000 \text{ units} \times \$200$$

$$= \$400{,}000$$

Looking carefully at Cornerstone 8.1 and 8.2, we can see that the only difference between the two approaches is the treatment of fixed factory overhead. Thus, the unit product cost under absorption costing is always greater than the unit product cost under variable costing. Exhibit 8.2 shows this difference pictorially for a simplified example.

( EXHIBIT 8.2 )

**Product Cost under Absorption and Variable Costing**

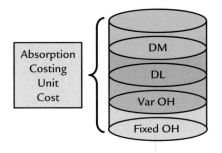
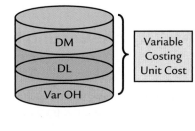

## Income Statements Using Variable and Absorption Costing

Because unit product costs are the basis for cost of goods sold, the variable- and absorption-costing methods can lead to different operating income figures. The difference arises because of the amount of fixed overhead recognized as an expense under the two methods. Cornerstone 8.3 shows how to develop cost of goods sold and income statements for absorption costing.

## Preparing an Absorption-Costing Income Statement

**Why:**

Absorption-costing income statements are used for external reporting. All product costs are included in Cost of Goods Sold.

CORNERSTONE

8.3

**Information:**

Refer to the data in Cornerstone 8.1 for Fairchild Company (p. 345).

**Required:**

1. Calculate the cost of goods sold under absorption costing.

2. Prepare an income statement using absorption costing.

**Solution:**

1. Cost of Goods Sold = Absorption Unit Product Cost × Units Sold

$$= \$225 \times 8,000$$

$$= \$1,800,000$$

2.

**Fairchild Company**
**Absorption-Costing Income Statement**

| | |
|---|---:|
| Sales ($300 × 8,000) | $2,400,000 |
| Less: Cost of goods sold | 1,800,000 |
| Gross margin | $  600,000 |
| Less: Selling and administrative expenses | 100,000 |
| Operating income | $  500,000 |

As we see in Cornerstone 8.3, the cost of goods sold includes some but not all fixed factory overhead. Total fixed factory overhead is $250,000 ($25 × 10,000 units produced). However, only $200,000 ($25 × 8,000 units sold) of fixed overhead was expensed in cost of goods sold. Where did the other $50,000 of fixed overhead go? It is included in the cost of ending inventory.

Cornerstone 8.4 shows how to prepare a variable-costing income statement.

**CORNERSTONE**

**8.4**

## Preparing a Variable-Costing Income Statement

**Why:**
Variable-costing income statements are useful for internal decision making. All fixed costs are considered period costs. When the time period is over, fixed costs' usefulness has expired.

**Information:**
Refer to the data in Cornerstone 8.1 for Fairchild Company (p. 345).

**Required:**
1. Calculate the cost of goods sold under variable costing.

2. Prepare an income statement using variable costing.

**Solution:**
1. Cost of Goods Sold = Variable Unit Product Cost × Units Sold

$$= \$200 \times 8,000$$

$$= \$1,600,000$$

2.

**Fairchild Company**
**Variable-Costing Income Statement**

| | | |
|---|---:|---:|
| Sales ($300 × 8,000) | | $2,400,000 |
| Less variable expenses: | | |
|   Variable cost of goods sold | | 1,600,000 |
| Contribution margin | | $  800,000 |
| Less fixed expenses: | | |
|   Fixed overhead | $250,000 | |
|   Fixed selling and administrative | 100,000 | 350,000 |
| Operating income | | $  450,000 |

Compare Cornerstone 8.3 (p. 347) and 8.4. Operating income under absorption costing is $500,000 whereas operating income under variable costing is only $450,000. Remember that $50,000 of current period product cost in fixed factory overhead went into inventory under absorption costing. However, all of the fixed factory overhead is included in the costs for variable costing. Notice that selling and administrative expenses are never included in product cost. They are always expensed on the income statement and never appear on the balance sheet.

## Production, Sales, and Income Relationships

The relationship between variable-costing income and absorption-costing income changes as the relationship between production and sales changes. If more is sold than was produced, variable-costing income is greater than absorption-costing income. This situation is just the opposite of the Fairchild example. Selling more than was produced means that beginning inventory and units produced are being sold. Under absorption costing, units coming out of inventory have attached to them fixed overhead from a prior period. In addition, units produced and sold have all of the current period's fixed overhead attached. Thus, the amount of fixed overhead expensed by absorption costing is greater than the current period's fixed overhead by the amount of fixed overhead flowing out of inventory. Accordingly, variable-costing income is greater than absorption-costing income by the amount of fixed overhead flowing out of beginning inventory.

If production and sales are equal, of course, no difference exists between the two reported incomes. Since the units produced are all sold, absorption costing, like variable costing, will recognize the total fixed overhead of the period as an expense. No fixed overhead flows into or out of inventory.

The relationships between production, sales, and the two reported incomes are summarized in Exhibit 8.3. Note that if production is greater than sales, then inventory has increased. If production is less than sales, then inventory must have decreased. If production is equal to sales, then the number of units in beginning inventory is equal to the number of units in ending inventory.

( EXHIBIT 8.3 )

**Production, Sales, and Income Relationships**

| If | Then |
|---|---|
| 1. Production > Sales | Absorption income > Variable income |
| 2. Production < Sales | Absorption income < Variable income |
| 3. Production = Sales | Absorption income = Variable income |

© Cengage Learning 2014

The difference between absorption and variable costing centers on the recognition of expense associated with fixed factory overhead. Under absorption costing, fixed factory overhead must be assigned to units produced. This presents two problems that we have not explicitly considered.

- First, how do we convert factory overhead applied on the basis of direct labor hours or machine hours into factory overhead applied to units produced?
- Second, what is done when actual factory overhead does not equal applied factory overhead?

The solution to these problems is reserved for a more advanced accounting course.

## Evaluating Profit-Center Managers

The evaluation of managers is often tied to the profitability of the units that they control. How income changes from one period to the next and how actual income compares with planned income are frequently used as signals of managerial ability. To be meaningful signals, however, income should reflect managerial effort. For example, if a manager has worked hard and increased sales while holding costs in check, income should increase over the prior period, signaling success. In general terms, if income performance is expected to reflect managerial performance, then managers have the right to expect the following:

- As sales revenue increases from one period to the next, all other things being equal, income should increase.
- As sales revenue decreases from one period to the next, all other things being equal, income should decrease.
- As sales revenue remains unchanged from one period to the next, all other things being equal, income should remain unchanged.

Variable costing ensures that the above relationships hold; however, absorption costing may not.

OBJECTIVE **2**

Prepare segmented income statements.

# SEGMENTED INCOME STATEMENTS USING VARIABLE COSTING

Variable costing is useful in preparing segmented income statements because it gives useful information on variable and fixed expenses. A **segment** is a subunit of a company of sufficient importance to warrant the production of performance reports. Segments can be divisions, departments, product lines, customer classes, and so on. In segmented income statements, fixed expenses are broken down into two categories: *direct fixed expenses* and *common fixed expenses*. This additional subdivision highlights controllable versus noncontrollable costs and enhances the manager's ability to evaluate each segment's contribution to overall firm performance.

## Direct Fixed Expenses

**Direct fixed expenses** are fixed expenses that are directly traceable to a segment. These are sometimes referred to as *avoidable fixed expenses* or *traceable fixed expenses* because they vanish if the segment is eliminated. For example, if the segments were sales regions, a direct fixed expense for each region would be the rent for the sales office, salary of the sales manager of each region, and so on. If one region were to be eliminated, then those fixed expenses would disappear. **Zingerman's Bakehouse**, from the opening scenario, bakes and sells cakes and pastries. The ovens and cooking equipment are fixed costs for the Bakehouse. If the Bakehouse were eliminated, those costs would disappear.

## Common Fixed Expenses

**Common fixed expenses** are jointly caused by two or more segments. These expenses persist even if one of the segments to which they are common is eliminated. For example, depreciation on the corporate headquarters building, the salary of the CEO, and the cost of printing and distributing the annual report to shareholders are common fixed expenses for **Walt Disney Company**. If Walt Disney Company were to sell a theme park or open a new one, those common expenses would not be affected. In addition, ZingNet, from the opening scenario, is a support service used by all of **Zingerman's** business segments. If one segment, say the Bakehouse, were eliminated, the costs of ZingNet would be unaffected. These are common fixed costs of the company.

## Preparing Segmented Income Statements

Cornerstone 8.5 shows how to prepare a segmented income statement where the segments are product lines. In the example, Audiomatronics produces both MP3 players and DVD players.

---

### concept Q&A

Suppose that a department store decides to drop a department, such as the furniture department. What are the direct fixed costs involved? What are the common fixed costs that would not be reduced if the department is dropped?

**Answer:**

The direct fixed costs of the furniture department include the wages of the clerks working in that department, the special fixtures that might be required to display some items (e.g., bedding), and the cost of display samples. Common fixed costs include utilities for the store as a whole, the cost of advertising the Memorial Day sales event, and the cost of the overall store manager.

---

CORNERSTONE

**8.5**

## Preparing a Segmented Income Statement

**Why:**

Segmented income statements allow managers to see the profitability of individual segments of the company. Segments can be products, regions, customer type, and so on.

**Information:**

Audiomatronics Inc. produces MP3 players and DVD players in a single factory. The following information was provided for the coming year.

*(Continued)*

| | MP3 Players | DVD Players |
|---|---|---|
| Sales | $400,000 | $290,000 |
| Variable cost of goods sold | 200,000 | 150,000 |
| Direct fixed overhead | 30,000 | 20,000 |

A 5% sales commission is paid for each of the product lines. Direct fixed selling and administrative expense was estimated to be $10,000 for the MP3 line and $15,000 for the DVD line. Common fixed overhead for the factory was estimated to be $100,000; common selling and administrative expense was estimated to be $20,000.

**Required:**

Prepare a segmented income statement for Audiomatronics Inc. for the coming year, using variable costing.

**Solution:**

**Audiomatronics Inc.**
**Segmented Income Statement**
**For the Coming Year**

| | MP3 Players | DVD Players | Total |
|---|---|---|---|
| Sales | $ 400,000 | $ 290,000 | $ 690,000 |
| Variable cost of goods sold | (200,000) | (150,000) | (350,000) |
| Variable selling expense* | (20,000) | (14,500) | (34,500) |
| Contribution margin | $ 180,000 | $ 125,500 | $ 305,500 |
| Less direct fixed expenses: | | | |
| Direct fixed overhead | (30,000) | (20,000) | (50,000) |
| Direct selling and administrative | (10,000) | (15,000) | (25,000) |
| Segment margin | $ 140,000 | $  90,500 | $ 230,500 |
| Less common fixed expenses: | | | |
| Common fixed overhead | | | (100,000) |
| Common selling and administrative | | | (20,000) |
| Operating income | | | $ 110,500 |

\* Variable Selling Expense for MP3 Players = 0.05 × Sales = 0.05 × $400,000 = $20,000
Variable Selling Expense for DVD Players = 0.05 × Sales = 0.05 × $290,000 = $14,500

Notice that Cornerstone 8.5 shows that both products have large positive contribution margins ($180,000 for MP3 players and $125,500 for DVD players). Both products are providing revenue above variable costs that can be used to help cover the firm's fixed costs. However, some of the firm's fixed costs are caused by the segments themselves. Thus, the real measure of the profit contribution of each segment is what is left over after these direct fixed costs are covered.

The profit contribution each segment makes toward covering a firm's common fixed costs is called the **segment margin**. A segment should at least be able to cover both its own variable costs and direct fixed costs. A negative segment margin drags down the firm's total profit, making it time to consider dropping the product. Ignoring any effect a segment may have on the sales of other segments, the segment margin measures the change in a firm's profits that would occur if the segment were eliminated.

# YOUDECIDE Using Segmented Income Statements to Make Decisions

You are the Financial Vice President for Folsom Company, which sells three products, Alpha, Beta, and Gamma. You have just received the income statement shown in Panel A of Exhibit 8.4. Clearly, Gamma is unprofitable. In fact, the company is losing $13,740 a year on Gamma.

**Should you drop Gamma? Will income go up if you do?**

Take a closer look at the income statement. Notice that both the direct fixed costs and the allocated common fixed costs are subtracted from each segment's contribution margin. This is misleading; it seems that dropping any segment would result in losing the operating income associated with the segment. However, if one segment is dropped, the allocated common fixed costs will remain.

A more useful income statement is presented in Panel B of Exhibit 8.4. Here, the segment margin for all three products is positive, as is overall income. While Gamma is not as profitable as Alpha and Beta, it is profitable. Dropping Gamma will result in a decrease in operating income of $12,000, the amount of the segment margin.

**Separating the direct fixed costs from the common fixed costs, and focusing on the segment margin, will give a truer picture of a segment's profitability.**

( **EXHIBIT 8.4** )

### Comparison of Segmented Income Statement With and Without Allocated Common Fixed Expense

**Folsom Company information for last year:**

|  | Alpha | Beta | Gamma |
|---|---|---|---|
| Units produced and sold | 10,000 | 30,000 | 26,000 |
| Price | $30 | $25 | $14 |
| Variable cost per unit | $20 | $18 | $12 |
| Direct fixed expense | $35,000 | $38,000 | $40,000 |

|  | A. Segmented Income Statement with Allocation of Common Fixed Expense: | | | | B. Segmented Income Statement without Allocation of Common Fixed Expense: | | | |
|---|---|---|---|---|---|---|---|---|
|  | Alpha | Beta | Gamma | Total | Alpha | Beta | Gamma | Total |
| Sales | $300,000 | $750,000 | $364,000 | $1,414,000 | $300,000 | $750,000 | $364,000 | $1,414,000 |
| Less: Variable cost | 200,000 | 540,000 | 312,000 | 1,052,000 | 200,00 | 540,000 | 312,000 | 1,052,000 |
| Contribution margin | $100,000 | $210,000 | 52,000 | $ 362,000 | $100,000 | $210,000 | 52,000 | $ 362,000 |
| Less: Direct fixed cost | 35,000 | 38,000 | 40,000 | 113,000 | 35,000 | 38,000 | 40,000 | 113,000 |
| Segment margin | $ 65,000 | $172,000 | $ 12,000 | 249,000 | $ 65,000 | $172,000 | $ 12,000 | 249,000 |
| Less: Allocated common cost | 21,220 | 53,040 | 25,740 | 100,000 |  |  |  | 100,000 |
| Operating income | $ 43,780 | $118,960 | $ (13,740) | $ 149,000 |  |  |  | $ 149,000 |

**OBJECTIVE**

Discuss inventory management under the economic order quantity and just-in-time (JIT) models.

# DECISION MAKING FOR INVENTORY MANAGEMENT

The prior discussion of absorption and variable costing makes it clear that inventory can affect operating income. In addition to the product cost of inventory, there are other types of costs that relate to inventories of raw materials, work in process, and finished goods. For example, inventory must be bought, received, stored, and moved.

## Inventory-Related Costs

When the demand for a product or material is known with near certainty for a given period of time (usually a year), two major costs are associated with inventory. If the inventory is a material or good purchased from an outside source, then these inventory-related costs are known as *ordering costs* and *carrying costs*. (If the material or good is produced internally, then the costs are called *setup costs* and *carrying costs*.)

- **Ordering costs** are the costs of placing and receiving an order. Examples include order processing costs (clerical costs and documents), the cost of insurance for shipment, and unloading and receiving costs.
- **Carrying costs** are the costs of keeping and storing inventory. Examples include insurance, inventory taxes, obsolescence, the opportunity cost of funds tied up in inventory, handling costs, and storage space.

If demand is not known with certainty, then a third category of inventory costs—called *stockout costs*—exists.

- **Stockout costs** are the costs of not having a product available when demanded by a customer or the cost of not having a raw material available when needed for production. Examples are lost sales (both current and future), the costs of expediting (increased transportation charges, overtime, and so on), and the costs of interrupted production (e.g., idled workers).

It is important to realize that the purchase price of raw materials is not a part of the total cost associated with carrying inventory. That price must be paid anyway. Similarly, the product cost of units produced is not an inventory-related cost.

Exhibit 8.5 summarizes the reasons typically offered for carrying inventory. It's important to realize that these reasons are given to *justify* carrying inventories. A host of other reasons can be offered that *encourage* the carrying of inventories. For example, performance measures such as measures of machine and labor efficiency may promote the buildup of inventories.

> ### concept Q&A
>
> Has a store ever been out of an item that you wanted to buy? What did you do? What is the impact of the stockout on the store?
>
> **Answer:**
>
> You might have gone to another store or tried to buy the item online. The stockout cost for the first store is not only the profit to be made from selling to you, but also, potentially, your future business.

( EXHIBIT 8.5 )

**Traditional Reasons for Carrying Inventory**

- To balance ordering or setup costs and carrying costs.
- To satisfy customer demand (for example, meet delivery dates).
- To avoid shutting down manufacturing facilities because of:
  - machine failure.
  - defective parts.
  - unavailable parts.
  - late delivery of parts.
- To buffer against unreliable production processes.
- To take advantage of discounts.
- To hedge against future price increases.

© Cengage Learning 2014

## Economic Order Quantity: The Traditional Inventory Model

Once a company decides to carry inventory, two basic questions must be addressed:

1. How much should be ordered?
2. When should the order be placed?

The first question must be answered before the second. Assume that demand is known. In choosing an order quantity, managers need to be concerned only with ordering and carrying costs. The formulas for calculating these are as follows:

Total Inventory-Related Cost = Ordering Cost + Carrying Cost

Ordering Cost = Number of Orders per Year × Cost of Placing an Order

$$\text{Average Number of Units in Inventory} = \frac{\text{Units in Order}}{2}$$

Carrying Cost = Average Number of Units in Inventory
× Cost of Carrying One Unit in Inventory

The cost of carrying inventory can be computed for any organization that carries inventories, including retail, service, and manufacturing organizations. Cornerstone 8.6 illustrates the application for a service organization and shows how to calculate total ordering cost, carrying cost, and inventory cost.

CORNERSTONE
8.6

## Calculating Ordering Cost, Carrying Cost, and Total Inventory-Related Cost

**Why:**

Ordering and carrying costs are part of the overall cost of obtaining inventory. Larger orders mean lower annual ordering costs but higher annual carrying costs.

**Information:**

Mall-o-Cars Inc. sells a number of automotive brands and provides service after the sale for those brands. Part X7B is used to repair water pumps. Each year, 10,000 units of Part X7B are used; they are currently purchased from external suppliers in lots of 1,000 units. It costs Mall-o-Cars $25 to place the order, and carrying cost is $2 per part per year.

**Required:**

1. How many orders for Part X7B does Mall-o-Cars place per year?

2. What is the total ordering cost of Part X7B per year?

3. What is the total carrying cost of Part X7B per year?

4. What is the total cost of Mall-o-Cars' inventory policy for Part X7B per year?

**Solution:**

1. Number of Orders = Annual Number of Units Used/Number of Units in an Order
   = 10,000/1,000
   = 10 orders per year

2. Total Ordering Cost = Number of Orders × Cost per Order
   = 10 orders × $25
   = $250

3. Total Carrying Cost = Average Number of Units in Inventory ×
   Cost of Carrying One Unit in Inventory
   = (1,000/2) × $2
   = $1,000

4. Total Inventory-Related Cost = Total Ordering Cost + Total Carrying Cost
   = $250 + $1,000
   = $1,250

The total carrying cost for the year is figured by multiplying the average number of units on hand by the cost of carrying one unit in inventory for a year. But what is the average number of units on hand? Given the policy of ordering 1,000 units at a time, the maximum number on hand would be 1,000 units—the amount on hand just after an order is delivered. Ideally, the minimum amount on hand would be zero, the amount the company has just moments before the new order arrives. Therefore, the average amount in inventory is the maximum plus the minimum divided by two:

$$\text{Average Inventory} = \frac{(\text{Maximum Amount} - \text{Minimum Amount})}{2}$$

See Exhibit 8.6 for an illustration of this concept.

( EXHIBIT 8.6 )

**Illustration of Average Inventory**

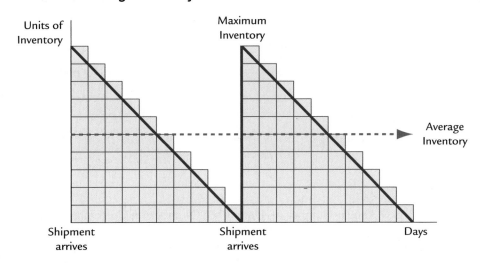

© Cengage Learning 2014

## The Economic Order Quantity

The total cost of Mall-o-Cars' current policy is $1,250 ($250 + $1,000). An order quantity of 1,000 with a total cost of $1,250, however, may not be the best choice. Some other order quantity may produce a lower total cost. The objective is to find the order quantity that minimizes the total cost. The number of units in the optimal size order quantity is called the **economic order quantity (EOQ)**. Since EOQ is the quantity that minimizes total inventory-related costs, a formula[1] for computing it is as follows.

$$EOQ = \sqrt{2 \times CO \times D/CC}$$

where

$\quad EOQ$ = The optimal number of units to be ordered at one time
$\quad\quad CO$ = The cost of placing one order
$\quad\quad\quad D$ = The annual demand for the item in units
$\quad\quad CC$ = The cost of carrying one unit in inventory for a year

Cornerstone 8.7 shows how to use the EOQ formula.

---

[1] This formula is derived by using calculus. Its derivation is reserved for a later course.

CORNERSTONE

8.7

## Calculating the Economic Order Quantity (EOQ)

**Why:**

The economic order quantity is the number of units that should be ordered at one time to minimize total inventory-related costs of ordering and carrying inventory.

**Information:**

Refer to the data in Cornerstone 8.6 for Mall-o-Cars Inc. (p. 354).

**Required:**

1. What is the EOQ for Part X7B?

2. How many orders per year for Part X7B will Mall-o-Cars place under the EOQ policy?

3. What is the total annual ordering cost of Part X7B for a year under the EOQ policy?

4. What is the total annual carrying cost of Part X7B per year under the EOQ policy?

5. What is the total annual inventory-related cost for Part X7B under the EOQ policy?

**Solution:**

1. $EOQ = \sqrt{2 \times CO \times D/CC}$

$\quad EOQ = \sqrt{2 \times \$25 \times 10{,}000/\$2}$

$\qquad = \sqrt{500{,}000/2}$

$\qquad = 500 \text{ units}$

2. Number of Orders = Annual Number of Units Used/Number of Units in an Order

$\qquad = 10{,}000/500$

$\qquad = 20 \text{ orders per year}$

3. Total Ordering Cost = Number of Orders × Cost per Order

$\qquad = 20 \text{ orders} \times \$25$

$\qquad = \$500$

4. Total Carrying Cost = Average Number of Units in Inventory ×

$\qquad$ Cost of Carrying One Unit in Inventory

$\qquad = (500/2) \times \$2$

$\qquad = \$500$

5. Total Inventory-Related Cost = Total Ordering Cost + Total Carrying Cost

$\qquad = \$500 + \$500$

$\qquad = \$1{,}000$

© Pixelfabrik/Alamy

Look carefully at Cornerstone 8.7. Notice that at the EOQ, the carrying cost equals the ordering cost. This is always true for the simple EOQ model described here. Now compare Cornerstone 8.7 with Cornerstone 8.6. The EOQ order quantity of 500 is less costly than an order quantity of 1,000 ($1,000 vs. $1,250).

# Reorder Point

The EOQ answers the question of how much to order (or produce). Knowing when to place an order (or setup for production) is also an essential part of any inventory policy. The **reorder point** is the point in time when a new order should be placed (or setup started). It is a function of the EOQ, the lead time, and the rate at which inventory is used. **Lead time** is the time required to receive the economic order quantity once an order is placed or a setup is started.

To avoid stockout costs and to minimize carrying costs, an order should be placed so that it arrives just as the last item in inventory is used. Knowing the rate of usage and lead time allows us to compute the reorder point that accomplishes these objectives:

$$\text{Reorder Point} = \text{Rate of Usage} \times \text{Lead Time}$$

Cornerstone 8.8 shows how to calculate the reorder point when usage is known with certainty.

## Calculating the Reorder Point When Usage Is Known with Certainty

**CORNERSTONE**

**8.8**

**Why:**

The time to reorder is linked to the amount of inventory left in stock. When inventory is drawn down to a particular point, more must be ordered or the company will run out.

**Information:**

Mall-o-Cars Inc. sells a number of automotive brands and provides service after the sale for those brands. Part X7B is used to repair water pumps. Each year, 10,000 units of Part X7B are used; they are used at the rate of 40 parts per day. It takes Mall-o-Cars five days from the time of order to the time of the arrival of the order.

**Required:**

Calculate the reorder point.

**Solution:**

Reorder Point = Daily Usage $\times$ Lead Time
Reorder Point = 40 $\times$ 5 days = 200 units

Thus, when Mall-o-Cars' supply of Part X7B drops to 200 units, it is time to reorder.

If the demand for the part or product is not known with certainty, a stockout may occur. For example, if 45 units of the part were used per day instead of 40, the firm would use 200 parts after nearly four and a half days. Since the new order would not arrive until the end of the fifth day, production would be idled for half a day. To avoid this problem, organizations often choose to carry safety stock. **Safety stock** is extra inventory carried to serve as insurance against changes in demand. Safety stock is computed by multiplying the lead time by the difference between the maximum rate of usage and the average rate of usage:

$$\text{Safety Stock} = (\text{Maximum Daily Usage} - \text{Average Daily Usage}) \times \text{Lead Time}$$

Cornerstone 8.9 shows how to calculate safety stock and the reorder point with safety stock.

**CORNERSTONE**

**8.9**

## Calculating Safety Stock and the Reorder Point with Safety Stock

### Why:

Safety stock helps firms cope with uncertainty in the amount used or in the amount of time it takes for an inventory order to arrive.

### Information:

Mall-o-Cars Inc. sells a number of automotive brands and provides service after the sale for those brands. Part X7B is used to repair water pumps. Each year, 10,000 units of Part X7B are used; they are used at the rate of 40 parts per day. However, some days, as many as 50 parts are used. It takes Mall-o-Cars five days from the time of order to the time of the arrival of the order.

### Required:

1. Calculate the amount of safety stock.

2. Calculate the reorder point with safety stock.

### Solution:

1. Safety Stock = (Maximum Daily Usage − Average Daily Usage) × Lead Time

$$= (50 − 40) × 5 \text{ days}$$

$$= 50 \text{ units}$$

2. Reorder Point = Maximum Daily Usage × Lead Time

Reorder Point = 50 × 5 days = 250 units

or

Reorder Point = (Average Daily Usage × Lead Time) + Safety Stock

Reorder Point = (40 × 5 days) + 50 = 250 units

**ETHICAL DECISIONS**    There is a dark side to purchasing and inventory management. Sometimes unscrupulous agents choose suppliers based on side payments or kickbacks. That is, a purchasing manager who chooses to buy from a particular supplier is paid separately by the supplier for making a favorable decision. These kickbacks are typically illegal as well as unethical, and can result in lawsuits and prosecution. For example, the Department of Justice charged **Johnson & Johnson** with making illegal kickbacks to **Omnicare**, a large pharmacy supplier to nursing homes, to encourage Omnicare pharmacists to recommend particular drugs to nursing home physicians. These drugs, including risperdol, were expensive and not necessarily better than competing drugs.[2] •

[2] Michael Muskal, "Drug maker Johnson & Johnson Paid Kickbacks to Mega-pharmacy, U.S. Charges in Civil Complaint." *The Los Angeles Times*, January 15, 2010. http://latimesblogs.latimes.com/dcnow/2010/01/government-alleges-jj-paid-kickbacks.html

# Economic Order Quantity and Inventory Management

The EOQ model is very useful in identifying the optimal trade-off between inventory ordering costs and carrying costs. It also is useful in helping to deal with uncertainty by using safety stock. The historical importance of the EOQ model in many American industries can be better appreciated by understanding the nature of the traditional manufacturing environment. This environment has been characterized by the mass production of a few standardized products that typically have a very high setup cost. The high setup cost encouraged a large batch size. Thus, production runs for these firms tended to be quite long, and the excess production was placed in inventory.

# Just-in-Time Approach to Inventory Management

The economic environment for many traditional, large-batch, high setup cost firms has changed dramatically in the past few decades. Advances in transportation and communication have contributed significantly to the creation of global competition. Advances in technology have contributed to shorter life cycles for products, and product diversity has increased. These competitive pressures have led many firms to abandon the EOQ model in favor of a just-in-time (JIT) approach.

The **just-in-time (JIT)** approach maintains that goods should be pulled through the system by present demand rather than being pushed through on a fixed schedule based on anticipated demand. Many fast-food restaurants, like **McDonald's**, use a pull system to control their finished goods inventory. When a customer orders a hamburger, it is taken from the warming rack. When the number of hamburgers gets too low, the cooks cook more hamburgers. Customer demand pulls the materials through the system. This same principle is used in manufacturing settings. Each operation produces only what is necessary to satisfy the demand of the succeeding operation. The material or subassembly arrives just in time for production to occur so that demand can be met.

**Comparing Just-in-Time and Traditional Inventory Approaches** The hallmark of JIT is to reduce all inventories to very low levels. This idea of maintaining smaller inventories, however, challenges the traditional reasons for holding inventories illustrated in Exhibit 8.5 (p. 353). JIT inventory management offers alternative solutions that do not require high inventories.

*Ordering Costs* For example, in a traditional system, inventory resolves the conflict between ordering or setup costs and carrying costs by selecting an inventory level that minimizes the sum of these costs. If demand is greater than expected or if production is reduced by breakdowns and production inefficiencies, then inventories serve as buffers, providing products to customers that may otherwise not have been available. In a JIT environment, however, ordering costs are reduced by developing close relationships with suppliers. Negotiating long-term contracts for the supply of outside materials will obviously reduce the number of orders and the associated ordering costs. Some retailers have reduced ordering costs by allowing the manufacturer to handle inventory management for the retailer. The manufacturer tells the retailer when and how much stock to reorder. The retailer reviews the recommendation and approves the order if it makes sense. **Wal-Mart** and **Procter & Gamble**, for example, use this arrangement to reduce inventories as well as stockout problems.

*Uncertainty in Demand* According to the traditional view, inventories prevent shutdowns caused by machine failure, defective material or subassembly, and unavailability of a raw material or subassembly. Those espousing the JIT approach claim that inventories do not solve these problems but rather cover up or hide them. JIT solves the three problems by emphasizing total preventive maintenance and total quality control and by building the right kind of relationship with suppliers. In JIT, reduced setup times allow manufacturers to literally produce to order.

*Lower Cost of Inventory* Traditionally, inventories are carried so that a firm can take advantage of quantity discounts and hedge against future price increases of the items purchased. The objective is to lower the cost of inventory. JIT achieves the same objective without carrying inventories. The JIT solution is to negotiate long-term contracts with a few chosen suppliers located as close to the production facility as possible and to establish more extensive supplier involvement. Suppliers are not selected on the basis of price alone. Performance—the quality of the component and the ability to deliver as needed—and commitment to JIT purchasing are vital considerations. Other benefits of long-term contracts exist. They stipulate prices and acceptable quality levels. Long-term contracts also reduce dramatically the number of orders placed, which helps to drive down the ordering cost.

**Limitations of the Just-in-Time Approach** JIT does have limitations. It is often referred to as a program of simplification—yet this does not imply that JIT is simple or easy to implement. Time is required, for example, to build sound relationships with suppliers. Insisting on immediate changes in delivery times and quality may not be realistic and may cause difficult confrontations between a company and its suppliers. Workers also may be affected by JIT. Studies have shown that sharp reductions in inventory buffers may cause a regimented workflow and high levels of stress among production workers. If the workers perceive JIT as a way of simply squeezing more out of them, then JIT efforts may be doomed. Perhaps a better strategy for JIT implementation is one where inventory reductions follow the process improvements that JIT offers. It requires careful and thorough planning and preparation. Companies should expect some struggle and frustration.

## HERE'S THE REAL KICKER

Inventory management is an important activity at **Kicker**. Because many of the speakers are made overseas, Kicker must schedule production and shipments to match demand. Demand for speakers is seasonal. Imagine a typical Kicker customer. He's a young man, aged 16–24, who wants great, loud sound in his car or truck. He drives around with the volume up and the windows down. From this description, we can see why sales decrease by 15% during the winter months. But in mid-March, sales ramp up. California, Florida, and New York are major markets. Spring and summer will start earlier in the first two states and continue into May and June in the latter. It's vital that Kicker have the units available for customers when they want speakers.

Now let's focus on the production side. Many speakers are made in China. The Chinese New Year typically begins in late January or early February. There are major festivals and the speaker factory closes down for a month. Since Kicker sales increase during the spring months, they need a fair amount of inventory on hand early in the year to meet demand and coordinate with production shutdown. Inventory is a fact of life for Kicker in the spring and can range as high as 50 to 100% of anticipated sales. In essence, Kicker has a sizeable safety stock. The executive team hates lost sales. In fact, that was emphasized in their discussion of inventory policy. They did have previous stockouts, and vividly remember the lost sales.

In summary, stockouts are a problem to be avoided. The cost of lost sales is high. Production and sales are seasonal. Overall, Kicker believes that the traditional reasons for holding inventory are best solved by substantial inventory.

**KICKER** *Livin'Loud*

Jackson Smith/Getty Images

The most glaring deficiency of JIT is the absence of inventory to buffer production interruptions. Current sales are constantly being threatened by an unexpected interruption in production. In fact, if a problem occurs, JIT's approach consists of trying to find and solve the problem before any further production activity occurs. Retailers who use JIT tactics also face the possibility of shortages. (JIT retailers order what they need now, not what they expect to sell; the idea is to flow goods through the channel as late as possible, keeping inventories low and decreasing the need for markdowns.) If demand increases well beyond the retailer's supply of inventory, then the retailer may be unable to make order adjustments quickly enough to avoid lost sales and irritated customers. The JIT manufacturing company is also willing to place current sales at risk to achieve assurance of future sales. This assurance comes from higher quality, quicker response time, and less operating costs. Even so, we must recognize that a sale lost today is a sale lost forever. Installing a JIT system so that it operates with little interruption is not a short-run project. Thus, losing sales is a real cost of installing a JIT system.

# SUMMARY OF LEARNING OBJECTIVES

**LO 1.** Explain the difference between absorption and variable costing.

- Absorption costing treats fixed factory overhead as a product cost. Unit product cost consists of direct materials, direct labor, variable factory over head, and fixed factory overhead.
- The absorption-costing income statement groups expenses according to function:
  - Production cost—cost of goods sold, including variable and fixed product cost.
  - Selling expense—variable and fixed cost of selling and distributing product.
  - Administrative expense—variable and fixed cost of administration.
- Variable costing treats fixed factory overhead as a period expense. Unit product cost consists of direct materials, direct labor, and variable factory over head.
- The variable-costing income statement groups expenses according to cost behavior:
  - Variable expenses of manufacturing, selling, and administration.
  - Fixed expenses of manufacturing (fixed factory overhead), selling, and administration.
- Impact of units produced and units sold on absorption-costing income and variable-costing income:
  - If units produced > units sold, then absorption-costing income > variable-costing income.
  - If units produced < units sold, then absorption-costing income < variable-costing income.
  - If units produced = units sold, then absorption-costing income = variable-costing income.

**LO 2.** Prepare segmented income statements.

- Segments are subunits of a firm large enough to affect income.
  - Products
  - Divisions
  - Geographical areas
  - Any other type of important subunit
- Using a variable-costing income statement gives managers important information.
- Fixed expenses are divided into two parts.
  - Direct fixed expenses (these would be eliminated if the segment is eliminated).
  - Common fixed expenses (apply to two or more subunits).
- Segment margin (contribution margin minus direct fixed expense) is important for evaluating subunits.

**LO 3.** Discuss inventory management under the economic order quantity and just-in-time (JIT) models.

- EOQ balances the cost of ordering inventory with the cost of carrying inventory.
- Ordering cost is the cost of placing an order.
- Carrying cost is the cost of holding one unit in inventory for a year.
- At the EOQ, ordering cost equals carrying cost.
- Safety stock protects against running out of inventory due to uncertainty in demand.
- The EOQ approach uses inventory to solve problems:
  - Uneven demand for the product
  - Avoiding shutdown of factories
  - Hedging against future price increases
  - Taking advantage of discounts

- JIT models solve problems of uneven demand, production failures, and so on, without using inventory.
  - Long-term contracts
  - Supplier relationships
  - Reduce setup times to produce on demand
  - Creation of manufacturing cells
  - Maximizing quality and productivity

## SUMMARY OF IMPORTANT EQUATIONS

1. Absorption Costing Product Cost = Direct Materials + Direct Labor + Variable Overhead + Fixed Overhead

2. Variable Costing Product Cost = Direct Materials + Direct Labor + Variable Overhead

3. Total Inventory-Related Cost = Ordering Cost + Carrying Cost

Ordering Cost = Number of Orders per Year × Cost of Placing an Order

$$\text{Average Number of Units in Inventory} = \frac{\text{Units in Order}}{2}$$

Carrying Cost = Average Number of Units in Inventory × Cost of Carrying One Unit in Inventory

4. $EOQ = \sqrt{2 \times CO \times D/CC}$

5. Reorder Point = Rate of Usage × Lead Time

6. Safety Stock = (Maximum Daily Usage − Average Daily Usage) × Lead Time

**CORNERSTONES**

| | |
|---|---|
| CORNERSTONE 8.1 | Computing inventory cost under absorption costing, page 345 |
| CORNERSTONE 8.2 | Computing inventory cost under variable costing, page 346 |
| CORNERSTONE 8.3 | Preparing an absorption-costing income statement, page 347 |
| CORNERSTONE 8.4 | Preparing a variable-costing income statement, page 348 |
| CORNERSTONE 8.5 | Preparing a segmented income statement, page 350 |
| CORNERSTONE 8.6 | Calculating ordering cost, carrying cost, and total inventory-related cost, page 354 |
| CORNERSTONE 8.7 | Calculating the economic order quantity (EOQ), page 356 |
| CORNERSTONE 8.8 | Calculating the reorder point when usage is known with certainty, page 357 |
| CORNERSTONE 8.9 | Calculating safety stock and the reorder point with safety stock, page 358 |

© Pixelfabrik/Alamy

## KEY TERMS

Absorption costing, 344
Carrying costs, 353
Common fixed expenses, 350
Direct fixed expenses, 350
Economic order quantity (EOQ), 355
Just-in-time (JIT), 359
Lead time, 357

Ordering costs, 353
Reorder point, 357
Safety stock, 357
Segment, 350
Segment margin, 351
Stockout costs, 353
Variable costing, 344

# REVIEW PROBLEMS

## I. Absorption and Variable Costing; Segmented Income Statements

Fine Leathers Company produces a ladies' wallet and a men's wallet. Selected data for the past year follow:

|  | Ladies' Wallet | Men's Wallet |
|---|---|---|
| Production (units) | 100,000 | 200,000 |
| Sales (units) | 90,000 | 210,000 |
| Selling price | $5.50 | $4.50 |
| Direct labor hours | 50,000 | 80,000 |
| Manufacturing costs: | | |
| Direct materials | $75,000 | $100,000 |
| Direct labor | 250,000 | 400,000 |
| Variable overhead | 20,000 | 24,000 |
| Fixed overhead: | | |
| Direct | 50,000 | 40,000 |
| Common[a] | 20,000 | 20,000 |
| Nonmanufacturing costs: | | |
| Variable selling | 30,000 | 60,000 |
| Direct fixed selling | 35,000 | 40,000 |
| Common fixed selling[b] | 25,000 | 25,000 |

[a] Common overhead totals $40,000 and is divided equally between the two products.
[b] Common fixed selling costs total $50,000 and are divided equally between the two products.

Budgeted fixed overhead for the year, $130,000, equaled the actual fixed overhead. Fixed overhead is assigned to products using a plantwide rate based on expected direct labor hours, which were 130,000. The company had 10,000 men's wallets in inventory at the beginning of the year. These wallets had the same unit cost as the men's wallets produced during the year.

### Required:

1. Compute the unit cost for the ladies' and men's wallets using the variable-costing method. Compute the unit cost using absorption costing.
2. Prepare an income statement using absorption costing.
3. Prepare an income statement using variable costing.
4. Prepare a segmented income statement using products as segments.

### Solution:

1.  The unit cost for the ladies' wallet is as follows:

$$\text{Direct Materials} = (\$75,000/100,000) = \$0.75$$
$$\text{Direct Labor} = (\$250,000/100,000) = \$2.50$$
$$\text{Variable Overhead} = (\$20,000/100,000) = \$0.20$$
$$\text{Variable Cost per Unit} = (\$0.75 + \$2.50 + \$0.20) = \$3.45$$
$$\text{Fixed Overhead} = [(50,000 \times \$1.00)/100,000] = \$0.50$$
$$\text{Absorption Cost per Unit} = (\$3.45 + \$0.50) = \$3.95$$

The unit cost for the men's wallet is as follows:

$$\text{Direct Materials} = (\$100,000/200,000) = \$0.50$$
$$\text{Direct Labor} = (\$400,000/200,000) = \$2.00$$
$$\text{Variable Overhead} = (\$24,000/200,000) = \$0.12$$
$$\text{Variable Cost per Unit} = (\$0.50 + \$2.00 + \$0.12) = \$2.62$$
$$\text{Fixed Overhead} = [(80,000 \times \$1.00)/200,000] = \$0.40$$
$$\text{Absorption Cost per Unit} = (\$2.62 + \$0.40) = \$3.02$$

Notice that the only difference between the two unit costs is the assignment of the fixed overhead cost. Notice also that the fixed overhead unit cost is assigned using the predetermined fixed overhead rate ($130,000/130,000 hours = $1 per hour).

For example, the ladies' wallets used 50,000 direct labor hours and so receive $1 × 50,000, or $50,000, of fixed overhead. This total, when divided by the units produced, gives the $0.50 per-unit fixed overhead cost. Finally, observe that variable nonmanufacturing costs are not part of the unit cost under variable costing. For both approaches, only manufacturing costs are used to compute the unit costs.

2. The income statement under absorption costing is as follows:

| | |
|---|---:|
| Sales [($5.50 × 90,000) + ($4.50 × 210,000)] | $1,440,000 |
| Less: Cost of goods sold [($3.95 × 90,000) + ($3.02 × 210,000)] | 989,700 |
| Gross margin | $ 450,300 |
| Less: Selling expenses* | 215,000 |
| Operating income | $ 235,300 |

\* The sum of selling expenses for both products.

3. The income statement under variable costing is as follows:

| | |
|---|---:|
| Sales [($5.50 × 90,000) + ($4.50 × 210,000)] | $1,440,000 |
| Less variable expenses: | |
| Variable cost of goods sold [($3.45 × 90,000) + ($2.62 × 210,000)] | 860,700 |
| Variable selling expenses | 90,000 |
| Contribution margin | $ 489,300 |
| Less fixed expenses: | |
| Fixed overhead | 130,000 |
| Fixed selling | 125,000 |
| Operating income | $ 234,300 |

4. Segmented income statement:

| | Ladies' Wallet | Men's Wallet | Total |
|---|---:|---:|---:|
| Sales | $495,000 | $945,000 | $1,440,000 |
| Less variable expenses: | | | |
| Variable cost of goods sold | 310,500 | 550,200 | 860,700 |
| Variable selling expenses | 30,000 | 60,000 | 90,000 |
| Contribution margin | $154,500 | $334,800 | $ 489,300 |
| Less direct fixed expenses: | | | |
| Direct fixed overhead | 50,000 | 40,000 | 90,000 |
| Direct selling expenses | 35,000 | 40,000 | 75,000 |
| Segment margin | $ 69,500 | $254,800 | $ 324,300 |
| Less common fixed expenses: | | | |
| Common fixed overhead | | | 40,000 |
| Common selling expenses | | | 50,000 |
| Operating income | | | $ 234,300 |

## II. Inventory Costs, EOQ, Reorder Point

A local TV repair shop uses 36,000 units of a part each year (an average of 100 units per working day). It costs $20 to place and receive an order. The shop orders in lots of 400 units. It costs $4 to carry one unit per year in inventory.

### Required:

1. Calculate the total annual ordering cost.
2. Calculate the total annual carrying cost.
3. Calculate the total annual inventory cost.

4.  Calculate the EOQ.
5.  Calculate the total annual inventory cost using the EOQ inventory policy.
6.  How much is saved per year using the EOQ versus an order size of 400 units?
7.  Compute the reorder point, assuming the lead time is three days.
8.  Suppose that the usage of the part can be as much as 110 units per day. Calculate the safety stock and the new reorder point.

**Solution:**

1.  Ordering Cost = Cost of Placing an Order × (Demand in Units/Number of Units in One Order)
    $$= \$20 \times 36,000/400$$
    $$= \$1,800$$

2.  Carrying Cost = (Carrying Cost per Unit × Average Units in Inventory)/2
    $$= \$4 \times 400/2$$
    $$= \$800$$

3.  Total Cost = Ordering Cost + Carrying Cost = $1,800 + $800 = $2,600

4.  $EOQ = \sqrt{2 \times CO \times D/CC}$
    $$= \sqrt{2 \times \$20 \times 36,000/\$4}$$
    $$= \sqrt{360,000}$$
    $$= 600 \text{ units}$$

5.  Total Annual Inventory Cost = (Cost per Order × Total Units/Units per Order)
    $$+ \text{(Carrying Cost} \times \text{Units per Order/2)}$$
    $$= [(\$20 \times 36,000)/600] + [(\$4 \times 600)/2]$$
    $$= \$1,200 + \$1,200$$
    $$= \$2,400$$

6.  Savings = $2,600 − $2,400 = $200

7.  Reorder Point = 100 × 3 = 300 units

8.  Safety Stock = (110 − 100)3 = 30 units
    Reorder Point = 110 × 3 = 330 units or 300 + 30 = 330 units

# DISCUSSION QUESTIONS

1.  What is the difference between the unit cost of a product under absorption costing and variable costing?

2.  If a company produces 10,000 units and sells 8,000 units during a period, which method of computing operating income (absorption costing or variable costing) will result in the higher operating income? Why?

3.  What is a segment?

4.  What is the difference between contribution margin and segment margin?

5.  What are ordering costs? Carrying costs? Give examples of each.

6.  What are stockout costs?

7.  Does the purchase price of the part being ordered enter into the EOQ equation? Why or why not?

8.  What are the reasons for carrying inventory?

9.  Explain why, in the traditional view of inventory, carrying costs increase as ordering costs decrease.

*(Continued)*

10. What is the economic order quantity?

11. Explain how safety stock is used to deal with demand uncertainty.

12. What approach does JIT take to minimize total inventory costs?

# MULTIPLE-CHOICE QUESTIONS

**8-1** Yates Company shows the following unit costs for its product:

| | |
|---|---|
| Direct materials | $40 |
| Direct labor | 30 |
| Variable overhead | 2 |
| Fixed overhead | 5 |

Yates started the year with 8,000 units in inventory, produced 50,000 units during the year, and sold 55,000 units. The value of ending inventory is

a. greater under variable costing than absorption costing.

b. greater under absorption costing than variable costing.

c. the same under both variable and absorption costing.

d. There is no ending inventory.

e. This situation cannot happen.

**8-2** In a segmented income statement, which of the following statements is true?

a. Segment margin is greater than contribution margin.

b. Common fixed expenses must be allocated to each segment.

c. Contribution margin is equal to sales less all variable and direct fixed expenses of a segment.

d. Segment margin is equal to contribution margin less direct and common fixed expenses.

e. Segment margin is equal to contribution margin less direct fixed expenses.

**8-3** The EOQ for Part B-22 is 2,500 units, and four orders are placed each year. The total annual ordering cost is $1,200. Which of the following is true?

a. The cost of placing one order is $4,800.

b. The annual demand for the part is 2,500 units.

c. The cost of placing one order is $1,200.

d. The total carrying cost is $1,200.

e. It is impossible to calculate the annual carrying cost given the above information.

**8-4** Which of the following is a reason for carrying inventory?

a. To balance setup and carrying costs

b. To satisfy customer demand

c. To avoid shutting down manufacturing facilities

d. To take advantage of discounts

e. All of these.

**8-5** Suppose that a material has a lead time of four days and that the average usage of the material is 12 units per day. What is the reorder point?

a. 3

b. 12

c. 15

d. 36

e. 48

**8-6** Suppose that a material has a lead time of four days and that the average usage of the material is 12 units per day. The maximum usage is 15 units per day. What is the safety stock?

a. 3

b. 12

c. 9

d. 15

e. 5

**8-7** A segment could be which of the following?

a. Product

b. Customer type

c. Geographic region

d. All of these.

e. None of these.

**8-8** Garrett Company provided the following information:

|  | Product 1 | Product 2 |
|---|---|---|
| Units sold | 10,000 | 20,000 |
| Price | $20 | $15 |
| Variable cost per unit | $10 | $10 |
| Direct fixed cost | $35,000 | $75,000 |

Common fixed cost totaled $46,000. Garrett allocates common fixed cost to Product 1 and Product 2 on the basis of sales. If Product 2 is dropped, which of the following is true?

a. Sales will increase by $300,000.

b. Overall operating income will increase by $2,600.

c. Overall operating income will decrease by $25,000.

d. Overall operating income will not change.

e. Common fixed cost will decrease by $27,600.

**8-9** Companies may choose to use variable costing because it

a. accords with GAAP.

b. is most useful for management decision making.

c. provides the gross margin.

d. is useful for external reporting.

e. None of these.

---

*Use the following information for Multiple-Choice Questions 8-10 through 8-12:*
McCartney Company produces a number of products and provides the following information:

| | |
|---|---|
| Annual demand for Product C | 20,000 |
| Cost of setting up to make Product C | $ 45 |
| Cost of carrying one unit of Product C in inventory | $ 5 |

Currently, McCartney produces 1,000 units of Product C per production run.

---

**8-10** Refer to the information for McCartney Company above. Inventory-related cost for Product C under the current inventory policy is

a. $900.

b. $2,500.

c. $3,400.

d. $45,000.

e. $100,000.

**8-11** Refer to the information for McCartney Company above. The economic order quantity (EOQ) for Product C is

a. 500.

b. 600.

c. 700.

d. 800.

e. 1,000.

**8-12** Refer to the information for McCartney Company above. What is the total inventory-related cost at the EOQ? (*Note*: Round the number of setups to the nearest whole number.)

a. $1,500

b. $3,330

c. $2,985

d. $3,400

e. $5,000

# CORNERSTONE EXERCISES

> *Use the following information for Cornerstone Exercises 8-13 and 8-14:*
> During the most recent year, Judson Company had the following data associated with the product it makes:
>
> | | |
> |---|---:|
> | Units in beginning inventory | 300 |
> | Units produced | 15,000 |
> | Units sold ($300 per unit) | 12,700 |
> | Variable costs per unit: | |
> |    Direct materials | $20 |
> |    Direct labor | $60 |
> |    Variable overhead | $12 |
> | Fixed costs: | |
> |    Fixed overhead per unit produced | $30 |
> |    Fixed selling and administrative | $140,000 |

OBJECTIVE ❶
CORNERSTONE 8.1

**Cornerstone Exercise 8-13    Inventory Valuation under Absorption Costing**

Refer to the data for Judson Company above.

**Required:**

1. How many units are in ending inventory?
2. Using absorption costing, calculate the per-unit product cost.
3. What is the value of ending inventory under absorption costing?

OBJECTIVE ❶
CORNERSTONE 8.2

**Cornerstone Exercise 8-14    Inventory Valuation under Variable Costing**

Refer to the data for Judson Company above.

**Required:**

1. How many units are in ending inventory?
2. Using variable costing, calculate the per-unit product cost.
3. What is the value of ending inventory under variable costing?

> *Use the following information for Cornerstone Exercises 8-15 and 8-16:*
> During the most recent year, Osterman Company had the following data:
>
> | | |
> |---|---:|
> | Units in beginning inventory | — |
> | Units produced | 10,000 |
> | Units sold ($47 per unit) | 9,300 |
> | Variable costs per unit: | |
> |    Direct materials | $9 |
> |    Direct labor | $6 |
> |    Variable overhead | $4 |
> | Fixed costs: | |
> |    Fixed overhead per unit produced | $5 |
> |    Fixed selling and administrative | $138,000 |

OBJECTIVE ❶
CORNERSTONE 8.3

**Cornerstone Exercise 8-15    Absorption-Costing Income Statement**

Refer to the data for Osterman Company above.

**Required:**

1. Calculate the cost of goods sold under absorption costing.
2. Prepare an income statement using absorption costing.

## Cornerstone Exercise 8-16    Variable-Costing Income Statement

OBJECTIVE ❶

CORNERSTONE 8.4

Refer to the data for Osterman Company on the previous page.

**Required:**

1.  Calculate the cost of goods sold under variable costing.
2.  Prepare an income statement using variable costing.

## Cornerstone Exercise 8-17    Segmented Income Statement

OBJECTIVE ❷

CORNERSTONE 8.5

Gorman Nurseries Inc. grows poinsettias and fruit trees in a green house/nursery operation. The following information was provided for the coming year.

|                              | Poinsettias | Fruit Trees |
| ---------------------------- | ----------- | ----------- |
| Sales                        | $970,000    | $3,100,000  |
| Variable cost of goods sold  | 460,000     | 1,630,000   |
| Direct fixed overhead        | 160,000     | 200,000     |

A sales commission of 4% of sales is paid for each of the two product lines. Direct fixed selling and administrative expense was estimated to be $146,000 for the poinsettia line and $87,000 for the fruit tree line.

Common fixed overhead for the nursery operation was estimated to be $800,000; common selling and administrative expense was estimated to be $450,000.

**Required:**

Prepare a segmented income statement for Gorman Nurseries for the coming year, using variable costing.

---

*Use the following information for Cornerstone Exercises 8-18 and 8-19:*
La Cucina Company sells kitchen supplies and housewares. Lava stone is used in production of molcajetes (mortars and pestles used in the making of guacamole) and is purchased from external suppliers. Each year, 8,000 pounds of lava stone is used; it is currently purchased in lots of 500 pounds. It costs La Cucina $5 to place the order, and carrying cost is $2 per pound per year.

---

## Cornerstone Exercise 8-18    Ordering Cost, Carrying Cost, and Total Inventory-Related Cost

OBJECTIVE ❸

CORNERSTONE 8.6

Refer to the data for La Cucina Company above.

**Required:**

1.  How many orders for lava stone does La Cucina place per year?
2.  What is the total ordering cost of lava stone per year?
3.  What is the total carrying cost of lava stone per year?
4.  What is the total cost of La Cucina's inventory policy for lava stone per year?

## Cornerstone Exercise 8-19    Economic Order Quantity

OBJECTIVE ❸

CORNERSTONE 8.7

Refer to the data for La Cucina Company above.

**Required:**

1.  What is the EOQ for lava stone?
2.  How many orders per year for lava stone will La Cucina place under the EOQ policy?
3.  What is the total annual ordering cost of lava stone for a year under the EOQ policy?
4.  What is the total annual carrying cost of lava stone per year under the EOQ policy?
5.  What is the total annual inventory-related cost for lava stone under the EOQ?

OBJECTIVE ③
CORNERSTONE 8.8

### Cornerstone Exercise 8-20   Reorder Point

La Cucina Company sells kitchen supplies and housewares. Lava stone is used in production of molcajetes (mortars and pestles used in the making of guacamole) and is purchased from external suppliers. Each year, 8,000 pounds of lava stone is used; it is used evenly at the rate of 30 pounds per day. It takes La Cucina 5 days from the time of order to the time of arrival of the order.

**Required:**

Calculate the reorder point.

OBJECTIVE ③
CORNERSTONE 8.9

### Cornerstone Exercise 8-21   Safety Stock and the Reorder Point with Safety Stock

La Cucina Company sells kitchen supplies and housewares. Lava stone is used in production of molcajetes (mortars and pestles used in the making of guacamole) and is purchased from external suppliers. Each year, 8,000 pounds of lava stone is used; it is used evenly at the rate of 30 pounds per day. However, some days as many as 35 pounds are used. It takes La Cucina 5 days from the time of order to the time of arrival of the order.

**Required:**

1.  Calculate the amount of safety stock.
2.  Calculate the reorder point with safety stock.

## EXERCISES

OBJECTIVE ❶

### Exercise 8-22   Inventory Valuation under Absorption Costing

Amiens Company produced 20,000 units during its first year of operations and sold 18,900 at $17 per unit. The company chose practical activity—at 20,000 units—to compute its predetermined overhead rate. Manufacturing costs are as follows:

| | |
|---|---:|
| Direct materials | $ 80,000 |
| Direct labor | 101,400 |
| Variable overhead | 15,600 |
| Fixed overhead | 54,600 |

**Required:**

1.  Calculate the unit cost for each of these four costs.
2.  Calculate the cost of one unit of product under absorption costing.
3.  How many units are in ending inventory?
4.  Calculate the cost of ending inventory under absorption costing.

OBJECTIVE ❶

### Exercise 8-23   Inventory Valuation under Variable Costing

Lane Company produced 50,000 units during its first year of operations and sold 47,300 at $12 per unit. The company chose practical activity—at 50,000 units—to compute its predetermined overhead rate. Manufacturing costs are as follows:

| | |
|---|---:|
| Direct materials | $123,000 |
| Direct labor | 93,000 |
| Variable overhead | 65,000 |
| Fixed overhead | 51,000 |

**Required:**

1.  Calculate the cost of one unit of product under variable costing.
2.  Calculate the cost of ending inventory under variable costing.

### Exercise 8-24  Inventory Valuation under Absorption and Variable Costing

OBJECTIVE ❶

Overton Company produced 80,000 units last year. The company sold 79,000 units and there was no beginning inventory. The company chose practical activity—at 80,000 units—to compute its predetermined overhead rate. Manufacturing costs are as follows:

| | |
|---|---|
| Direct materials | $596,000 |
| Direct labor | 104,000 |
| Variable overhead | 88,000 |
| Fixed overhead | 228,800 |

**Required:**

1. Calculate the cost of one unit of product under absorption costing.
2. Calculate the cost of one unit of product under variable costing.
3. Calculate the cost of ending inventory under absorption costing.
4. Calculate the cost of ending inventory under variable costing.

### Exercise 8-25  Income Statements under Absorption and Variable Costing

OBJECTIVE ❶

In the coming year, Kalling Company expects to sell 28,700 units at $32 each. Kalling's controller provided the following information for the coming year.

| | |
|---|---|
| Units production | 30,000 |
| Unit direct materials | $9.95 |
| Unit direct labor | $2.75 |
| Unit variable overhead | $1.65 |
| Unit fixed overhead* | $2.50 |
| Unit selling expense (variable) | $2.00 |
| Total fixed selling expense | $ 65,500 |
| Total fixed administrative expense | $231,000 |

\* The unit fixed overhead is based on 30,000 units produced.

**Required:**

1. Calculate the cost of one unit of product under absorption costing.
2. Calculate the cost of one unit of product under variable costing.
3. Calculate operating income under absorption costing for next year.
4. Calculate operating income under variable costing for next year.

### Exercise 8-26  Inventory Valuation under Absorption and Variable Costing with Decrease in Ending Inventory

OBJECTIVE ❶

The following information pertains to Chacon Inc. for last year:

| | |
|---|---|
| Beginning inventory in units | 5,000 |
| Units produced | 20,000 |
| Units sold | 23,700 |
| Costs per unit: | |
|   Direct materials | $8.00 |
|   Direct labor | $4.00 |
|   Variable overhead | $1.50 |
|   Fixed overhead* | $4.15 |
|   Variable selling expenses | $3.00 |
| Fixed selling and administrative expenses | $24,300 |

\* Fixed overhead totals $83,000 per year.

**Required:**

1. Calculate the cost of one unit of product under absorption costing.
2. Calculate the cost of one unit of product under variable costing.
3. How many units are in ending inventory?
4. Calculate the cost of ending inventory under absorption costing.
5. Calculate the cost of ending inventory under variable costing.

*(Continued)*

OBJECTIVE ❷

### Exercise 8-27    Income Statements under Absorption and Variable Costing with Decrease in Ending Inventory

The following information pertains to Chacon Inc. for last year:

| | |
|---|---|
| Beginning inventory in units | 5,000 |
| Units produced | 20,000 |
| Units sold | 23,700 |
| Costs per unit: | |
|    Direct materials | $8.00 |
|    Direct labor | $4.00 |
|    Variable overhead | $1.50 |
|    Fixed overhead* | $4.15 |
|    Variable selling expenses | $3.00 |
| Fixed selling and administrative expenses | $24,300 |

\* Fixed overhead totals $83,000 per year.

Assume that the selling price is $27 per unit.

**Required:**

1. Calculate operating income using absorption costing.
2. Calculate operating income using variable costing.

OBJECTIVE ❶

ILLUSTRATING RELATIONSHIPS

### Exercise 8-28    Solving for Missing Values Using Absorption and Variable Costing Relationships

Each of the following situations is independent.

**Required:**

1. Kester Company had ending inventory cost of $5,000 under absorption costing. Ending inventory cost $3,400 under variable costing. Kester produced 16,000 units and sold 15,200. What was fixed overhead per unit? If unit fixed overhead is based on normal production of 16,000 units, what was total fixed overhead?
2. Gonsalves Company has prime cost of $6 per unit. Total fixed overhead is $23,000 and is allocated based on normal production of 20,000 units. Ending inventory consists of 6,000 units which cost $8.00 per unit under absorption costing. What is variable overhead cost per unit?
3. Last year, Shermer Company's operating income was $45,000 under absorption costing and $42,500 under variable costing. Fixed overhead was applied at the rate of $2.50 per unit. Beginning inventory was zero. How many units were in ending inventory?

OBJECTIVE ❷

### Exercise 8-29    Segmented Income Statement

Knitline Inc. produces high-end sweaters and jackets in a single factory. The following information was provided for the coming year.

| | Sweaters | Jackets |
|---|---|---|
| Sales | $210,000 | $450,000 |
| Variable cost of goods sold | 145,000 | 196,000 |
| Direct fixed overhead | 25,000 | 47,000 |

A sales commission of 5% of sales is paid for each of the two product lines. Direct fixed selling and administrative expense was estimated to be $20,000 for the sweater line and $50,000 for the jacket line.

Common fixed overhead for the factory was estimated to be $45,000. Common selling and administrative expense was estimated to be $15,000.

**Required:**

1. Prepare a segmented income statement for Knitline for the coming year, using variable costing.

## Problem 8-40   Ordering and Carrying Costs, EOQ

OBJECTIVE 3

A-Tech Company uses 36,000 circuit boards each year in its production of stereo units. The cost of placing an order is $15. The cost of holding one unit of inventory for one year is $3. Currently, A-Tech orders 3,000 circuit boards in each order.

**Required:**

1. Compute the annual ordering cost.
2. Compute the annual carrying cost.
3. Compute the cost of A-Tech's current inventory policy.
4. Compute the economic order quantity.
5. Compute the ordering cost and the carrying cost for the EOQ.
6. How much money does using the EOQ policy save the company over the policy of purchasing 3,000 circuit boards per order?
7. **CONCEPTUAL CONNECTION** Suppose that the supplier charges an extra $0.05 per unit to purchase circuit boards in orders of 1,500 or less. Should A-Tech switch to the EOQ policy or not?

## Problem 8-41   Economic Order Quantity

OBJECTIVE 3

Italia Pizzeria is a popular pizza restaurant near a college campus. Brandon Thayn, an accounting student, works for Italia Pizzeria. After several months at the restaurant, Brandon began to analyze the efficiency of the business, particularly inventory practices. He noticed that the owner had more than 50 items regularly carried in inventory. Of these items, the most expensive to buy and carry was cheese. Cheese was ordered in blocks at $17.50 per block. Annual usage totals 14,000 blocks.

Upon questioning the owner, Brandon discovered that the owner did not use any formal model for ordering cheese. It took five days to receive a new order when placed, which was done whenever the inventory of cheese dropped to 200 blocks. The size of the order was usually 400 blocks. The cost of carrying one block of cheese is 10% of its purchase price. It costs $40 to place and receive an order.

Italia Pizzeria stays open seven days a week and operates 50 weeks a year. The restaurant closes for the last two weeks of December.

**Required:**

1. Compute the total cost of ordering and carrying the cheese inventory under the current policy.
2. Compute the total cost of ordering and carrying cheese if the restaurant were to change to the EOQ. How much would the restaurant save per year by switching policies?
3. If the restaurant uses the EOQ, when should it place an order? (*Note:* Assume that the amount of cheese used per day is the same throughout the year.) How does this compare with the current reorder policy?
4. **CONCEPTUAL CONNECTION** Suppose that storage space allows a maximum of 600 blocks of cheese. Discuss the inventory policy that should be followed with this restriction.
5. **CONCEPTUAL CONNECTION** Suppose that the maximum storage is 600 blocks of cheese and that cheese can be held for a maximum of 10 days. The owner will not hold cheese any longer than 10 days in order to ensure the right flavor and quality. Under these conditions, evaluate the owner's current inventory policy.

# CASES

## Case 8-42   Ethical Issues, Absorption Costing, Performance Measurement

OBJECTIVE

Ruth Swazey, divisional controller and certified management accountant, was upset by a recent memo she received from the divisional manager, Paul Chesser. Ruth was scheduled to present

*(Continued)*

the division's financial performance at headquarters in one week. In the memo, Paul had given Ruth some instructions for this upcoming report. In particular, she had been told to emphasize the significant improvement in the division's profits over last year. Ruth, however, didn't believe that there was any real underlying improvement in the division's performance and was reluctant to say otherwise. She knew that the increase in profits was because of Paul's conscious decision to produce for inventory.

In an earlier meeting, Paul had convinced his plant managers to produce more than they knew they could sell. By doing so, more of the fixed factory overhead could be moved into inventory with the extra units produced. He argued that by deferring some of this period's fixed costs, reported profits would jump. He pointed out two significant benefits. First, by increasing profits, the division could exceed the minimum level needed so that all the managers would qualify for the annual bonus. Second, by meeting the budgeted profit level, the division would be better able to compete for much needed capital. Ruth had objected but had been overruled. The most persuasive counterargument was that the increase in inventory could be liquidated in the coming year as the economy improved. However, Ruth considered this event unlikely. Based on past experience, she believed that it would take at least two years of improved market demand before the productive capacity of the division was exceeded.

**Required:**

1. Discuss the behavior of Paul, the divisional manager. Was the decision to produce for inventory an ethical one?
2. What should Ruth do? Should she comply with the directive to emphasize the increase in profits? If not, what options does she have?
3. In Chapter 1, the Statement of Ethical Professional Practice was given. Identify any standards that apply in this situation.

OBJECTIVE ❸    **Case 8-43    Ethical Issues, Absorption Costing, Performance Measurement**

Mac Ericson and Tammy Ferguson met at an IMA conference two months ago and began dating. Mac is the controller for Longley Enterprises, and Tammy is a marketing manager for Sharp Products. Longley is a major supplier for Piura Products, a competitor of Sharp's. Longley has entered into a long-term agreement to supply certain materials to Piura. Piura has been developing a JIT purchasing and manufacturing system. As part of its development, Piura and Longley have established EDI capabilities. The following conversation took place during a lunch date:

**Tammy:** "Mac, I understand that you have EDI connections with Piura. Is that right?"

**Mac:** "Sure. It's part of the partners-in-profits arrangement that we have worked so hard to get. It's working real well. Knowing Piura's production schedule helps us stabilize our own schedule. It has actually cut some of our overhead costs. It has also decreased Piura's costs. I estimate that we both have decreased production costs by about 7 to 10%."

**Tammy:** "That's interesting. You know, I have a real chance of getting promoted to VP of marketing . . . .."

**Mac:** "Hey, that's great. When will you know?"

**Tammy:** "It all depends on this deal that I am trying to cut with Balboa—if I win the contract, then I think I have it. My main problem is with Piura. If I knew what its production schedule was, I could get a pretty good idea as to how long it would take it to deliver. I could then make sure that we beat its delivery offer—even if we had to work overtime and do all kinds of expediting. I know that our delivery speed is very, very important to Balboa. Our quality is as good as Piura's, but it tends to beat us on delivery time. My boss would love to kick Piura. It has beat us too many times recently. I am wondering if you would be willing to help me out."

**Mac:** "Tammy, you know that I would help if I could, but Piura's production schedule is confidential information. If word got out that I had leaked that kind of stuff to you, I would be history."

**Tammy:** "Well, no one would ever know. Besides, I have already had a chat with Tom Anderson, our CEO. Our VP of finance is retiring. He knows about you and your capabilities. I think he would be willing to hire you—especially if he knew that you helped swing this Balboa deal. You could increase your salary by 40%."

**Mac:** "I don't know. I have my doubts about the propriety of all this. It might look kind of funny if I take over as VP of finance not long after Piura loses the Balboa deal. But a VP position and a big salary increase are tempting. It's unlikely that I'll ever have a shot at the VP position in my company."

**Tammy:** "Think it over. If you are interested, I'll arrange a dinner with Tom Anderson. He said he'd like to meet you. He knows a little about this. I'm sure that he has the ability to keep it quiet. I don't think there is much risk."

**Required:**

1. Based on this information, has Mac violated any part of the IMA's Statement of Ethical Professional Practice? Explain.
2. Suppose that Mac decides to provide information in exchange for the VP position. What IMA standards would he violate?

# 9 Profit Planning

After studying Chapter 9, you should be able to:

1. Define budgeting and discuss its role in planning, control, and decision making.

2. Define and prepare the operating budget, identify its major components, and explain the interrelationships of its various components.

3. Define and prepare the financial budget, identify its major components, and explain the interrelationships of its various components.

4. Describe the behavioral dimension of budgeting.

# EXPERIENCE MANAGERIAL DECISIONS
## with High Sierra

Have you ever wondered where that huge backpack you use to lug 50 pounds of books all over campus originated? If so, you might be surprised by the history behind the company. After World War II, Army and Navy Surplus stores supplied consumers with tents, canteens, and canvas bags. One of these stores was Seaway Importing, a company founded in 1978 by Harry Bernbaum. Harry and his son Hank recognized the need to develop more durable products and founded the **High Sierra Sport Company**.

Budgeting plays an important role in High Sierra's decision making process. Throughout the 1980s, High Sierra developed its brand reputation as a manufacturer and supplier of numerous types of quality outdoor and foul weather gear, including backpacks, duffel bags, book bags, and hydration gear. During the mid-1990s, budgeting played a key role in helping High Sierra realize it needed to streamline its brand identity in order to keep its competitive edge in quality and

> *"High Sierra's management used its budgeting process to eliminate poor performing products and to analyze new products, such as a winter sports product line that focused more directly on the company's brand and target market."*

price. High Sierra's management used its budgeting process to eliminate poor performing products and to analyze new products, such as a winter sports product line that focused more directly on the company's brand and target market (e.g., alliances with the U.S. Ski and Snowboard Association). During the early 2000s, High Sierra's budgeting process showed management that it needed to expand operations by outsourcing some of its production overseas in order to remain cost competitive. To ensure that its budgeting process continues to provide useful insights, High Sierra frequently adopts new and evolving techniques, such as participative budgeting and continuous budgeting. In summary, High Sierra uses budgeting as an effective planning and control tool to promote successful new product development that creates value for the company and keeps students buying those huge backpacks every year.

OBJECTIVE ①

Define budgeting and discuss its role in planning, control, and decision making.

# DESCRIPTION OF BUDGETING

All businesses should prepare budgets. Budgets help business owners and managers to plan ahead, and later, exercise control by comparing what actually happened to what was expected in the budget. Budgets formalize managers' expectations regarding sales, prices, and costs. Even small businesses and nonprofit entities can benefit from the planning and control provided by budgets.

## Budgeting and Planning and Control

Planning and control are linked. *Planning* is looking ahead to see what actions should be taken to realize particular goals. *Control* is looking backward, determining what actually happened and comparing it with the previously planned outcomes. This comparison can then be used to adjust the budget, looking forward once more. Exhibit 9.1 illustrates the cycle of planning and control using budgets.

**Budgets** are financial plans for the future and are a key component of planning. They identify objectives and the actions needed to achieve them. Before preparing a budget, an organization should develop a strategic plan. The **strategic plan** plots a direction for an organization's future activities and operations; it generally covers at least 5 years. The overall strategy is then translated into the long- and short-term objectives that form the basis of the budget. The budget and the strategic plan should be tightly linked. Since budgets, especially 1-year plans, are short run in nature, this linkage is important because it helps management to ensure that not all attention is focused on the short run. For example, in early 2009 **Home Depot Inc.** planned to open 12 new stores in that year. By November, however, the economic situation had deteriorated badly. The number of transactions was down as was the size of the average sale. Home Depot slashed its capital expenditure by 52% and its administrative expenses by 8.4%. When the economy improves and sales increase, the company will be better positioned to return to the earlier budgeted amounts.[1]

( EXHIBIT 9.1 )

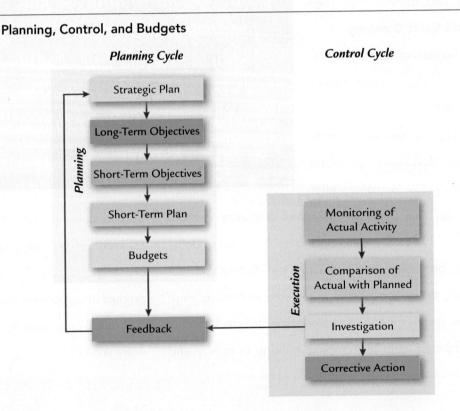

**Planning, Control, and Budgets**

*Planning Cycle*  *Control Cycle*

© Cengage Learning 2014

[1] Chris Burritt, "Home Depot Says Profit Fell as Shoppers Spent Less." November 17, 2009. Bloomberg.Com. www.bloomberg.com/apps/news?pid=20601103&sid=au1udfheLWj0

## Advantages of Budgeting

A budgetary system gives an organization several advantages.

**Planning**  Budgeting forces management to plan for the future. It encourages managers to develop an overall direction for the organization, foresee problems, and develop future policies.

**Information for Decision Making**  Budgets improve decision making. For example, a restaurant owner who knows the expected revenues and the costs of meat, vegetables, cheeses, and so on might make menu changes that play up the less expensive items and reduce the use of more expensive ingredients. These better decisions, in turn, may keep customers happy while still providing a profitable living for the chefs, waiters, and others who work at the restaurant.

**Standards for Performance Evaluation**  Budgets set standards that can control the use of a company's resources and motivate employees. A vital part of the budgetary system, **control** is achieved by comparing actual results with budgeted results on a periodic basis (e.g., monthly). A large difference between actual and planned results is feedback that prompts managers to take corrective action. For example, **High Sierra, Inc.** saw that sales of certain items were not meeting the budgeted amounts. Further market research showed that few customers needed the features of those particular products. As a result, the company could reduce its budgeted production in units and phase out the products.

**Improved Communication and Coordination**  Budgets also serve to communicate and coordinate the plans of the organization to each employee. Accordingly, employees can be aware of their particular role in achieving those objectives. Since budgets for the various areas and activities of the organization must all work together to achieve organizational objectives, coordination is promoted. Managers can see the needs of other areas and are encouraged to subordinate their individual interests to those of the organization. The role of communication and coordination becomes more even more important as an organization grows.

| concept Q&A |
|---|
| How can a budget help in planning and control? |
| **Answer:** |
| A budget requires a plan. It also sets benchmarks that can be used to evaluate performance. |

## The Master Budget

The **master budget** is the comprehensive financial plan for the organization as a whole. Typically, the master budget is for a 1-year period, corresponding to the fiscal year of the company. Yearly budgets are broken down into quarterly and monthly budgets. The use of smaller time periods allows managers to compare actual data with budgeted data more frequently, so problems may be noticed and resolved sooner.

Some organizations have developed a continuous budgeting philosophy. A **continuous budget** is a moving 12-month budget. As a month expires in the budget, an additional month in the future is added so that the company always has a 12-month plan on hand. Proponents of continuous budgeting maintain that it forces managers to plan ahead constantly.

**Directing and Coordinating**  Most organizations prepare the master budget for the coming year during the last four or five months of the current year. The **budget committee** reviews the budget, provides policy guidelines and budgetary goals, resolves differences that arise as the budget is prepared, approves the final budget, and monitors the actual performance of the organization as the year unfolds. The president of the organization appoints the members of the committee, who are usually the president, vice president of marketing, vice president of manufacturing, other vice presidents, and the controller. The controller usually serves as the **budget director**, the person responsible for directing and coordinating the organization's overall budgeting process.

| concept Q&A |
|---|
| What is the main objective of continuous budgeting? |
| **Answer:** |
| It forces managers to plan ahead constantly—something especially needed when firms operate in rapidly changing environments. |

**Major Components of the Master Budget** A master budget can be divided into operating and financial budgets:

- **Operating budgets** describe the income-generating activities of a firm: sales, production, and finished goods inventories. The ultimate outcome of the operating budgets is a pro forma or budgeted income statement.
- **Financial budgets** detail the inflows and outflows of cash and the overall financial position. Planned cash inflows and outflows appear in the cash budget. The expected financial position at the end of the budget period is shown in a budgeted, or pro forma, balance sheet.

Since many of the financing activities are not known until the operating budgets are known, the operating budget is prepared first. Describing and illustrating the individual budgets that make up the master budget will reveal the interdependencies of the component budgets. A diagram displaying these interrelationships is shown in Exhibit 9.2. Details of the capital budget are covered in a separate chapter.

( EXHIBIT 9.2 )

**The Master Budget and Its Interrelationships**

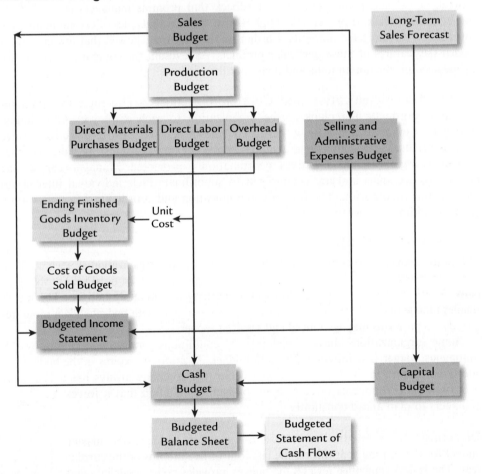

© Cengage Learning 2014

OBJECTIVE ❷

Define and prepare the operating budget, identify its major components, and explain the interrelationships of its various components.

# PREPARING THE OPERATING BUDGET

The operating budget consists of a budgeted income statement accompanied by the following supporting schedules:

- sales budget
- production budget
- direct materials purchases budget

- direct labor budget
- overhead budget
- selling and administrative expenses budget
- ending finished goods inventory budget
- cost of goods sold budget

We illustrate the master budgeting process with an example based on the activities of Texas Rex Inc., a trendy restaurant in the Southwest that sells t-shirts with the Texas Rex logo (a dinosaur that engages in a variety of adventures while eating the Mexican food for which the restaurant is known). The example focuses on the Texas Rex clothing manufacturing plant.

## Sales Budget

The **sales budget** is approved by the budget committee and describes expected sales in units and dollars. Because the sales budget is the basis for all of the other operating budgets and most of the financial budgets, it is important that it be as accurate as possible.

The first step in creating a sales budget is to develop the sales forecast. This is usually the responsibility of the marketing department. One approach to forecasting sales is the *bottom-up approach*, which requires individual salespeople to submit sales predictions. These are aggregated to form a total sales forecast. The accuracy of this sales forecast may be improved by considering other factors such as the general economic climate, competition, advertising, pricing policies, and so on. Some companies use more formal approaches, such as time-series analysis, correlation analysis, and econometric modeling. For example, the regression technique studied in the Appendix of Chapter 3 can be applied to forecasting sales, in addition to costs.

The sales forecast is just the initial estimate, and it is often adjusted by the budget committee. The budget committee may decide that the forecast is too pessimistic or too optimistic and revise it appropriately. For example, **Nintendo** set very conservative sales estimates for 2008 and later had to increase its sales forecast. Wii hardware sales alone were so robust that sales were expected to increase by one million units more than the company's original forecast.[2]

### concept Q&A

Why is the sales budget not necessarily the same as the sales forecast?

**Answer:**

The sales forecast is a starting point and an important input to the budgetary process. However, it is usually adjusted up or down, depending on the strategic objectives and plans of management.

## HERE'S THE REAL KICKER

**Stillwater Designs** has 14 departments. Each department is given a budget for the coming fiscal year. The budgeting process begins with a sales forecast prepared by the president and vice presidents. The fiscal year for the company is October 1 through September 30, which is driven by the seasonal nature of the business. In January of each year, there is a consumer electronics show in Las Vegas, Nevada. New products are introduced, and initial orders from distributors are taken. The sales season starts earnestly in March, reaches its peak in June or July, and drops to its lowest level in the fall. The sales season is driven by the anticipation of warm weather. The young men buying the Kicker speakers and amplifiers want to drive with windows down—with the apparent hope of impressing young women. The budget is therefore prepared during August and September, the last two months of the fiscal year.

Each department is given a percentage of sales as its budget. The amount ultimately decided upon is not simply a top-down decision. Department managers submit a request for their desired budget. Negotiation takes place between the department managers and their associated vice presidents (each departmental manager is answerable to a specific vice president). Whether or not the desired levels are provided depends on how well the departmental manager can justify the expenditures. An important criterion is the notion that resources are expended to make profits.

The budget is reviewed monthly. Any large deviations from the budget (usually more than a 10% deviation) are investigated. However, no formal incentive system is tied to budgetary performance. The budget is viewed as a guideline. If more resources are needed, then they can be obtained provided the request is backed up with a good idea and a promising payout.

Jackson Smith/Getty Images

---

[2] "Pachter finds Nintendo's Sales Forecast Too Humble." Posted January 31, 2008 at 02:57 pm by Pulkit Chandna: www.gamertell.com/gaming/comment/analyst-nintendos-forecasts-remain-too-low/, accessed March 16, 2008.

Cornerstone 9.1 shows how to prepare the sales budget for Texas Rex's standard t-shirt line. For simplicity, assume that Texas Rex has only one product: a standard short-sleeved t-shirt with the Texas Rex logo screen printed on the back. (For a multiple-product firm, the sales budget reflects sales for each product in units and sales dollars.)

**CORNERSTONE**

**9.1**

## Preparing a Sales Budget

**Why:**

Managers use a sales budget to determine estimated units to be sold and forecast prices for the coming year.

**Information:**

Budgeted units to be sold for each quarter of the year 2014: 1,000, 1,200, 1,500, and 2,000. Selling price is $10 per t-shirt.

**Required:**

Prepare a sales budget for each quarter and for the year.

**Solution:**

**Texas Rex Inc.**
**Sales Budget**
**For the Year Ended December 31, 2014**

|  | Quarter | | | | |
|---|---|---|---|---|---|
|  | **1** | **2** | **3** | **4** | **Year** |
| Units | 1,000 | 1,200 | 1,500 | 2,000 | 5,700 |
| Unit selling price | ×$10 | ×$10 | ×$10 | ×$10 | ×$10 |
| Budgeted sales | $10,000 | $12,000 | $15,000 | $20,000 | $57,000 |

Notice that the sales budget in Cornerstone 9.1 reveals that Texas Rex's sales fluctuate seasonally. Most sales take place in the summer and fall quarters. This is due to the popularity of the t-shirts in the summer and the sales promotions that Texas Rex puts on for "back to school" and Christmas.

# YOU DECIDE    Budgeting in a Service Industry

You are the controller for a large, regional medical center. The chief of cardiology has been pushing to have a free-standing heart hospital built on the medical center campus. However, you are concerned that taking the heart cases away from the main hospital will hurt its bottom line. While the medical center is non-profit, it does need to cover all of its costs to stay in business. You also wonder whether the heart hospital will break even.

**What information do you need to forecast revenues and costs of the heart hospital?**

This is a two part problem. The first question, what impact will the heart hospital have on the main hospital's revenues, requires knowledge of the number and types of heart cases seen at the main hospital each year. This information could come from the sales revenue

(Continued)

budget from the previous year, assuming that the total number of patient days and procedures are broken out by type of case and procedure. Since so many of the costs of a hospital are fixed, there will probably be little decrease in costs as those heart patients leave for the free-standing heart hospital. The second question requires a forecast of the number of patients and probably reimbursement rates expected for procedures to be performed by the heart hospi-

tal. This information can be compared with budgeted operating costs to see if the heart hospital's revenues can cover its costs.

**Forecasts of sales revenues and costs are dependent on detailed information provided by sources like the marketing or sales department and past accounting information and need to be revised and updates as new information or circumstances dictate.**

## Production Budget

The **production budget** tells how many units must be produced to meet sales needs and to satisfy ending inventory requirements. The Texas Rex production budget would show how many t-shirts are needed to satisfy sales demand for each quarter and for the year. If there were no beginning or ending inventories, the t-shirts to be produced would exactly equal the units to be sold. This would be the case in a just-in-time (JIT) firm. However, many firms use inventories as a buffer against uncertainties in demand or production. Thus, they need to plan for inventory levels as well as sales.

To compute the units to be produced, both unit sales and units of beginning and ending finished goods inventory are needed:

> Units to Be Produced = Expected Unit Sales + Units in Desired Ending
> Inventory (EI) − Units in Beginning Inventory (BI)

Cornerstone 9.2 shows how to prepare a production budget using this formula. Consider the first column (Quarter 1) of the budget in Cornerstone 9.2. Texas Rex anticipates sales of 1,000 t-shirts. In addition, the company wants 240 t-shirts in ending inventory at the end of the first quarter (0.20 × 1,200). Thus, 1,240 t-shirts are needed during the first quarter. Where will these 1,240 t-shirts come from? Beginning inventory can provide 180 of them, leaving 1,060 to be produced during the quarter. Notice that the production budget is expressed in terms of units.

Two important points regarding Cornerstone 9.2 should be emphasized:

- The beginning inventory for one quarter is always equal to the ending inventory of the previous quarter. For Quarter 2, the beginning inventory is 240 t-shirts, which is identical to the desired ending inventory for Quarter 1.
- The column for the year is not simply the addition of the amounts for the four quarters. Notice that the desired ending inventory for the year is 200 t-shirts, which is, of course, equal to the desired ending inventory for the fourth quarter.

## Direct Materials Purchases Budget

After the production budget is completed, the budgets for direct materials, direct labor, and overhead can be prepared. The **direct materials purchases budget** tells the amount and cost of raw materials to be purchased in each time period. It depends on the expected use of materials in production and the raw materials inventory needs of the firm. The company needs to prepare a separate direct materials purchases budget for every type of raw material used. The formula used for calculating purchases is as follows:

> Purchases = Direct Materials Needed for Production
> + Direct Materials in Desired Ending Inventory
> − Direct Materials in Beginning Inventory

# Preparing a Production Budget

**9.2**

### Why:
Once a sales budget has been prepared, a production budget tells managers how many units must be produced to satisfy anticipated sales and ending inventory needs.

### Information:
Budgeted units to be sold for each quarter: 1,000, 1,200, 1,500, and 2,000. Assume that company policy requires 20% of the next quarter's sales in ending inventory and that beginning inventory of t-shirts for the first quarter of the year was 180. Assume also that sales for the first quarter of 2015 are estimated at 1,000 units.

### Required:
1. Calculate the desired ending inventory in units for the each quarter of the year. What is the ending inventory in units for the year?

2. Prepare a production budget for each quarter and for the year.

### Solution:
1. Ending inventory, Quarter 1 = 0.20 × 1,200 units = 240

   Ending inventory, Quarter 2 = 0.20 × 1,500 units = 300

   Ending inventory, Quarter 3 = 0.20 × 2,000 units = 400

   Ending inventory, Quarter 4 = 0.20 × 1,000 units = 200

   Ending inventory for the year = Ending inventory for Quarter 4 = 200 units

2.

**Texas Rex Inc.**
**Production Budget**
**For the Year Ended December 31, 2014**

|  | Quarter | | | | |
|---|---|---|---|---|---|
|  | **1** | **2** | **3** | **4** | **Year** |
| Sales in units | 1,000 | 1,200 | 1,500 | 2,000 | 5,700 |
| Desired ending inventory | 240 | 300 | 400 | 200 | 200 |
| Total needs | 1,240 | 1,500 | 1,900 | 2,200 | 5,900 |
| Less: Beginning inventory* | (180) | (240) | (300) | (400) | (180) |
| Units to be produced | 1,060 | 1,260 | 1,600 | 1,800 | 5,720 |

\* Beginning inventory for Quarter 1 is given in information. Beginning inventory for the remaining quarters is equal to ending inventory for the previous quarter.

The quantity of direct materials in inventory is determined by the firm's inventory policy.

Texas Rex uses two types of raw materials: plain t-shirts and ink. The direct materials purchases budgets for these two materials are presented in Cornerstone 9.3 .

# Preparing a Direct Materials Purchases Budget

**CORNERSTONE**

**9.3**

**Why:**

The direct materials budget shows managers how much must be bought to support production and ending inventory needs for materials.

**Information:**

Budgeted units to be produced for each quarter: 1,060, 1,260, 1,600, and 1,800. Plain t-shirts cost $3 each, and ink (for the screen printing) costs $0.20 per ounce. On a per-unit basis, the factory needs one plain t-shirt and five ounces of ink for each logoed t-shirt that it produces. Texas Rex's policy is to have 10% of the following quarter's production needs in ending inventory. The factory has 58 plain t-shirts and 390 ounces of ink on hand on January 1. At the end of the year, the desired ending inventory is 106 plain t-shirts and 530 ounces of ink.

**Required:**

1. Calculate the ending inventory of plain t-shirts and of ink for Quarters 2 and 3.

2. Prepare a direct materials purchases budget for plain t-shirts and one for ink.

**Solution:**

1. Ending inventory plain t-shirts, Quarter 2 = 0.10 × (1,600 units × 1 t-shirt) = 160
   Ending inventory plain t-shirts, Quarter 3 = 0.10 × (1,800 units × 1 t-shirt) = 180
   Ending inventory ink, Quarter 2 = 0.10 × (1,600 units × 5 ounces) = 800
   Ending inventory ink, Quarter 3 = 0.10 × (1,800 units × 5 ounces) = 900

2.

**Texas Rex Inc.**
**Direct Materials Purchases Budget**
**For the Year Ended December 31, 2014**

| Plain t-shirts | Quarter | | | | |
| --- | --- | --- | --- | --- | --- |
| | **1** | **2** | **3** | **4** | **Year** |
| Units to be produced | 1,060 | 1,260 | 1,600 | 1,800 | 5,720 |
| Direct materials per unit | ×1 | ×1 | ×1 | ×1 | ×1 |
| Production needs | 1,060 | 1,260 | 1,600 | 1,800 | 5,720 |
| Desired ending inventory | 126 | 160 | 180 | 106 | 106 |
| Total needs | 1,186 | 1,420 | 1,780 | 1,906 | 5,826 |
| Less: Beginning inventory | (58) | (126) | (160) | (180) | (58) |
| Direct materials to be purchased | 1,128 | 1,294 | 1,620 | 1,726 | 5,768 |
| Cost per t-shirt | ×$3 | ×$3 | ×$3 | ×$3 | ×$3 |
| Total purchase cost plain t-shirts | $3,384 | $3,882 | $4,860 | $5,178 | $17,304 |

| Ink | Quarter | | | | |
| --- | --- | --- | --- | --- | --- |
| | **1** | **2** | **3** | **4** | **Year** |
| Units to be produced | 1,060 | 1,260 | 1,600 | 1,800 | 5,720 |
| Direct materials per unit | ×5 | ×5 | ×5 | ×5 | ×5 |
| Production needs | 5,300 | 6,300 | 8,000 | 9,000 | 28,600 |
| Desired ending inventory | 630 | 800 | 900 | 530 | 530 |
| Total needs | 5,930 | 7,100 | 8,900 | 9,530 | 29,130 |

*(Continued)*

**CORNERSTONE**

**9.3**

*(Continued)*

| Ink | Quarter | | | | Year |
|---|---|---|---|---|---|
| | **1** | **2** | **3** | **4** | **Year** |
| Less: Beginning inventory | (390) | (630) | (800) | (900) | (390) |
| Direct materials to be purchased | 5,540 | 6,470 | 8,100 | 8,630 | 28,740 |
| Cost per ounce | ×$0.20 | ×$0.20 | ×$0.20 | ×$0.20 | ×$0.20 |
| Total purchase cost of ink | $1,108 | $1,294 | $1,620 | $1,726 | $5,748 |
| Total direct materials purchase cost | $4,492 | $5,176 | $6,480 | $6,904 | $23,052 |

Notice how similar the direct materials purchases budget is to the production budget. Consider the first quarter, starting with the plain t-shirts. It takes one plain t-shirt for every logo t-shirt, so the 1,060 logo t-shirts to be produced are multiplied by one to obtain the number of plain t-shirts needed for production. Next, the desired ending inventory of 126 (10% of the next quarter's production needs) is added. Thus, 1,186 plain t-shirts are needed during the first quarter. Of this total, 58 are already in beginning inventory, meaning that the remaining 1,128 must be purchased. Multiplying the 1,128 plain t-shirts by the cost of $3 each gives Texas Rex the $3,384 expected cost of plain t-shirt purchases for the first quarter of the year. The direct materials purchases budget for ink is done in the same way as t-shirts except that each unit produced requires 5 ounces of ink. So the total units to be produced must be multiplied by 5 to get the production needs of ink.

## Direct Labor Budget

The **direct labor budget** shows the total direct labor hours and the direct labor cost needed for the number of units in the production budget. As with direct materials, the budgeted hours of direct labor are determined by the relationship between labor and output. The direct labor budget for Texas Rex is shown in Cornerstone 9.4 .

## Overhead Budget

The **overhead budget** shows the expected cost of all production costs other than direct materials and direct labor. Many companies use direct labor hours as the driver for overhead. Then costs that vary with direct labor hours are pooled and called variable overhead. The

**CORNERSTONE**

**9.4**

### Preparing a Direct Labor Budget

**Why:**
The direct labor budget shows how many hours are required for production in the coming year. The average wage is multiplied by direct labor hours to determine total anticipated direct labor cost.

**Information:**
Recall from Cornerstone 9.2 (p. 387) that budgeted units to be produced for each quarter are: 1,060, 1,260, 1,600, and 1,800. It takes 0.12 hour to produce one t-shirt. The average wage cost per hour is $10.

*(Continued)*

**Required:**

Prepare a direct labor budget.

**Solution:**

**Texas Rex Inc.**
**Direct Labor Budget**
**For the Year Ended December 31, 2014**

|  | Quarter | | | | |
|---|---|---|---|---|---|
|  | 1 | 2 | 3 | 4 | Year |
| Units to be produced | 1,060 | 1,260 | 1,600 | 1,800 | 5,720 |
| Direct labor time per unit in hours | ×0.12 | ×0.12 | ×0.12 | ×0.12 | ×0.12 |
| Total hours needed | 127.2 | 151.2 | 192.0 | 216.0 | 686.4 |
| Average wage per hour | ×$10 | ×$10 | ×$10 | ×$10 | ×$10 |
| Total direct labor cost | $1,272 | $1,512 | $1,920 | $2,160 | $6,864 |

remaining overhead items are pooled into fixed overhead. The method for preparing an overhead budget using this approach to cost behavior is shown in Cornerstone 9.5 .

## Preparing an Overhead Budget

**Why:**

The overhead budget shows forecast variable and fixed overhead costs for the coming year. Taken together with the materials and labor budgets, total production cost can be determined.

**Information:**

Refer to Cornerstone 9.4 for the direct labor budget. The variable overhead rate is $5 per direct labor hour. Fixed overhead is budgeted at $1,645 per quarter (this amount includes $540 per quarter for depreciation).

CORNERSTONE

9.5

**Required:**

Prepare an overhead budget.

**Solution:**

**Texas Rex Inc.**
**Overhead Budget**
**For the Year Ended December 31, 2014**

|  | Quarter | | | | |
|---|---|---|---|---|---|
|  | 1 | 2 | 3 | 4 | Year |
| Budgeted direct labor hours | 127.2 | 151.2 | 192.0 | 216.0 | 686.4 |
| Variable overhead rate | ×$ 5 | ×$ 5 | ×$ 5 | ×$ 5 | ×$ 5 |
| Budgeted variable overhead | $ 636 | $ 756 | $ 960 | $1,080 | $ 3,432 |
| Budgeted fixed overhead* | 1,645 | 1,645 | 1,645 | 1,645 | 6,580 |
| Total overhead | $2,281 | $2,401 | $2,605 | $2,725 | $10,012 |

* Includes $540 of depreciation in each quarter.

## concept Q&A

What operating budgets are needed to calculate a budgeted unit cost?

**Answer:**

Materials, labor, and overhead budgets. It could be argued that sales and production budgets are needed also because the three budgets listed cannot be developed until the sales and production budgets are known.

## Ending Finished Goods Inventory Budget

The **ending finished goods inventory budget** supplies information needed for the balance sheet and also serves as an important input for the preparation of the cost of goods sold budget. To prepare this budget, the unit cost of producing each t-shirt must be calculated by using information from the direct materials, direct labor, and overhead budgets. The way to calculate the unit cost of a t-shirt and the cost of the planned ending inventory is shown in Cornerstone 9.6 .

Notice that the Ending Finished Goods Inventory Budget brings together information from the production, direct labor, and overhead budgets to compute the unit product cost for the year.

**CORNERSTONE**

**9.6**

### Preparing an Ending Finished Goods Inventory Budget

**Why:**

The Ending Finished Goods Budget helps managers determine the predicted unit cost of production. This amount is used in valuing ending inventory on the budgeted balance sheet.

**Information:**

Refer to Cornerstones 9.3 (p. 389), 9.4 (p. 390), and 9.5 (p. 391) for the direct materials, direct labor, and overhead budgets.

**Required:**

1. Calculate the unit product cost.

2. Prepare an ending finished goods inventory budget.

**Solution:**

1.

| | | |
|---|---|---|
| Direct materials: | | |
| Plain t-shirt | $3 | |
| Ink (5 oz. @ $0.20) | 1 | $4.00 |
| Direct labor (0.12 hr. @ $10) | | 1.20 |
| Overhead: | | |
| Variable (0.12 hr. @ $5) | | 0.60 |
| Fixed (0.12 hr. @ $9.59*) | | 1.15** |
| Total unit cost | | $6.95 |

\* Budgeted Fixed Overhead/Budgeted Direct Labor Hours = $6,580/686.4 = $9.

\*\* Rounded

2.

**Texas Rex Inc.**
**Ending Finished Goods Inventory Budget**
**For the Year Ended December 31, 2014**

| | |
|---|---|
| Logo t-shirts | 200 |
| Unit cost | ×$6.95 |
| Total ending inventory | $1,390 |

## Cost of Goods Sold Budget

Assuming that the beginning finished goods inventory is valued at $1,251, the budgeted cost of goods sold schedule can be prepared using information from Cornerstones 9.3 to 9.6. The **cost of goods sold budget** reveals the expected cost of the goods to be sold and is shown in Cornerstone 9.7 .

### Preparing a Cost of Goods Sold Budget

**CORNERSTONE**

**9.7**

**Why:**

The Cost of Goods Sold Budget is used to determine the predicted cost of units to be sold in the coming year. It is an input to the budgeted income statement.

**Information:**

Refer to Cornerstones 9.3 through 9.6 (beginning p. 389) for the direct materials, direct labor, overhead, and ending finished goods budgets. The cost of beginning finished goods inventory is $1,251.

**Required:**

Prepare a cost of goods sold budget.

**Solution:**

**Texas Rex Inc.**
**Cost of Goods Sold Budget**
**For the Year Ended December 31, 2014**

| | |
|---|---|
| Direct materials used (Cornerstone 9.3)* | $22,880 |
| Direct labor used (Cornerstone 9.4) | 6,864 |
| Overhead (Cornerstone 9.5) | 10,012 |
|    Budgeted manufacturing costs | $39,756 |
| Beginning finished goods | 1,251 |
|    Cost of goods available for sale | $41,007 |
| Less: Ending finished goods (Cornerstone 9.6) | (1,390) |
|    Budgeted cost of goods sold | $39,617 |

* Production Needs = (5,720 plain t-shirts × $3) + (28,600 oz. ink × $0.20)

The output of the Cost of Goods Sold Budget, the budgeted cost of goods sold, will appear in the budgeted income statement.

## Selling and Administrative Expenses Budget

The next budget to be prepared, the **selling and administrative expenses budget**, outlines planned expenditures for nonmanufacturing activities. As with overhead, selling and administrative expenses can be broken down into fixed and variable components. Such items as sales commissions, freight, and supplies vary with sales activity. The selling and administrative expenses budget is illustrated in Cornerstone 9.8 .

## CORNERSTONE

## 9.8

# Preparing a Selling and Administrative Expenses Budget

**Why:**

The Selling and Administrative Expense Budget is becoming a larger portion of modern business. This budget helps managers determine the amounts to be spent on these nonproduction categories.

**Information:**

Refer to Cornerstone 9.1 (p. 386) for the sales budget. Variable expenses are $0.10 per unit sold. Salaries average $1,420 per quarter; utilities, $50 per quarter; and depreciation, $150 per quarter. Advertising for Quarters 1 through 4 is $100, $200, $800, and $500, respectively.

**Required:**

Prepare a selling and administrative expenses budget.

**Solution:**

**Texas Rex Inc.**
**Selling and Administrative Expenses Budget**
**For the Year Ended December 31, 2014**

|  | Quarter | | | | |
| --- | --- | --- | --- | --- | --- |
|  | **1** | **2** | **3** | **4** | **Year** |
| Planned sales in units (Cornerstone 9.1) | 1,000 | 1,200 | 1,500 | 2,000 | 5,700 |
| Variable selling and administrative |  |  |  |  |  |
| expenses per unit | ×$ 0.10 | ×$ 0.10 | ×$ 0.10 | ×$ 0.10 | ×$ 0.10 |
| Total variable expenses | $ 100 | $ 120 | $ 150 | $ 200 | $ 570 |
| Fixed selling and administrative |  |  |  |  |  |
| expenses: |  |  |  |  |  |
| Salaries | $1,420 | $1,420 | $1,420 | $1,420 | $5,680 |
| Utilities | 50 | 50 | 50 | 50 | 200 |
| Advertising | 100 | 200 | 800 | 500 | 1,600 |
| Depreciation | 150 | 150 | 150 | 150 | 600 |
| Total fixed expenses | $1,720 | $1,820 | $2,420 | $2,120 | $8,080 |
| Total selling and administrative |  |  |  |  |  |
| expenses | $1,820 | $1,940 | $2,570 | $2,320 | $8,650 |

## concept Q&A

Why is it not possible to prepare a budgeted income statement by using only operating budgets?

**Answer:**

Interest expense comes from the financial budgets. Only operating income can be computed by using operating budgets.

Notice how the selling and administrative expenses budget follows a very similar format as that of the overhead budget. In both cases, variable and fixed expenses are calculated. Notice also that depreciation, a non-cash expense, is shown separately. This will be important later on when the company prepares the cash budget.

## Budgeted Income Statement

With the completion of the budgeted cost of goods sold schedule and the budgeted selling and administrative expenses budget, Texas Rex has all the operating budgets needed to prepare an estimate of *operating* income. The way to prepare this budgeted income statement is shown in Cornerstone 9.9 . The eight budgets already prepared, along with the budgeted operating income statement, define the operating budget for Texas Rex.

Cornerstone 9.12 reveals that much of the information needed to prepare the cash budget comes from the operating budgets and from the schedules for cash receipts on accounts receivable and cash payments on accounts payable. It is important to recall that only cash expenditures are included in the cash budget. The operating budgets for overhead and selling and administrative expenses included depreciation expense, which is a noncash expense. Therefore, depreciation expense was subtracted from the totals to yield the cash expenditures for overhead and for selling and administrative expense.

The cash budget underscores the importance of breaking down the annual budget into smaller time periods. The cash budget for the year gives the impression that sufficient operating cash will be available to finance the acquisition of the new equipment. Quarterly information, however, shows the need for short-term borrowing ($1,000) because of both the acquisition of the new equipment and the timing of the firm's cash flows. Most firms prepare monthly cash budgets, and some even prepare weekly and daily budgets.

Texas Rex's cash budget provides another piece of useful information. By the end of the third quarter, the firm has more cash ($3,762) than needed to meet operating needs. Management should consider investing the excess cash in an interest-bearing account. Once plans are finalized for use of the excess cash, the cash budget should be revised to reflect those plans. Budgeting is a dynamic process. As the budget is developed, new information becomes available, and better plans can be formulated.

## Budgeted Balance Sheet

The budgeted balance sheet depends on information contained in the current balance sheet and in the other budgets in the master budget. Exhibit 9.4 shows the budgeted balance sheets as of December 31, 2013 and December 31, 2014. Explanations for the budgeted figures are provided in the footnotes.

# YOUDECIDE   Cash Budgeting for a Small Painting Company

You are the accountant for a number of small businesses in your town, one of which is Ramon's Paint and Plaster. Ramon has been through a tough year as construction in the town has been down. However, new home construction is picking up and Ramon has been asked to bid on twice as many jobs in the past month as he was last year at this time. Ramon needs to know what his cash flow will be for the coming year. You are starting to amass information to help you forecast monthly cash inflows and outflows for the next six months.

**What information do you need to forecast cash inflows and outflows for the paint and plaster business for the next six months?**

This is a two part problem. The first question, what inflows of cash are expected, depends on the number and size of the jobs Ramon can successfully bid on. Ramon's business has been primarily residential, so you'll need to know the number of housing starts (or the number of building permits applied for) and the number of remodeling jobs expected. You will also need to consider the price Ramon charges as well as the probability of prompt payment. Some builders have a good reputation for paying promptly in the first ten days of the month following work by Ramon's crew. Others lag behind. While you can encourage Ramon to work primarily with the better builders, he may be forced to accept some jobs with contractors who frequently pay later.

The second question requires a forecast of the potential cash outflows. Ramon has a crew of six workers and the hourly rate is known. He also can figure out the cost of the paint and plaster materials fairly accurately, once the size of the job is known. It will be difficult to forecast the cash inflows and outflows too far in advance. As a result, you will probably want to set up the cash budget for one to three months in advance and then update the forecasted numbers as the year progresses.

**Forecasts of cash inflows and outflows depend on the economic conditions, the reputation of the payment patterns of the customers, and the prices charged both for the jobs obtained as well as for the supplies used. Information from the past year can be used as a baseline, however, changing economic conditions will affect future amounts.**

( EXHIBIT 9.4 )

## Budgeted Balance Sheet

### Texas Rex Inc.
### Balance Sheet
### December 31, 2013

#### Assets

| | | |
|---|---:|---:|
| Current assets: | | |
| Cash | $ 5,200 | |
| Accounts receivable | 1,350 | |
| Raw materials inventory | 252 | |
| Finished goods inventory | 1,251 | |
| Total current assets | | $ 8,053 |
| Property, plant, and equipment (PP&E): | | |
| Land | $ 1,100 | |
| Building and equipment | 30,000 | |
| Accumulated depreciation | (5,000) | |
| Total PP&E | | 26,100 |
| Total assets | | $34,153 |

#### Liabilities and Owner's Equity

| | | |
|---|---:|---:|
| Current liabilities: | | |
| Accounts payable | | $ 1,000 |
| Owner's equity: | | |
| Retained earnings | | 33,153 |
| Total liabilities and owner's equity | | $34,153 |

### Texas Rex Inc.
### Budgeted Balance Sheet
### December 31, 2014

#### Assets

| | | |
|---|---:|---:|
| Current assets: | | |
| Cash | $ 6,584[a] | |
| Accounts receivable | 1,500[b] | |
| Raw materials inventory | 424[c] | |
| Finished goods inventory | 1,390[d] | |
| Total current assets | | $ 9,898 |
| Property, plant, and equipment (PP&E): | | |
| Land | $ 1,100[e] | |
| Building and equipment | 36,500[f] | |
| Accumulated depreciation | (7,760)[g] | |
| Total PP&E | | 29,840 |
| Total assets | | $39,738 |

#### Liabilities and Owner's Equity

| | | |
|---|---:|---:|
| Current liabilities: | | |
| Accounts payable | | $ 1,381[h] |
| Owner's equity: | | |
| Retained earnings | | 38,357[i] |
| Total liabilities and owner's equity | | $39,738 |

[a]Ending balance from Cornerstone 9.12.
[b]Ten percent of fourth-quarter credit sales (0.75 × $20,000)—see Cornerstones 9.1 and 9.12.
[c]From Cornerstone 9.3 [(106 × $3) + (530 × $0.20)].
[d]From Cornerstone 9.6.
[e]From the December 31, 2013, balance sheet.
[f]December 31, 2013, balance ($30,000) plus new equipment acquisition of $6,500 (see the 2013 ending balance sheet and Cornerstone 9.12).
[g]From the December 31, 2013, balance sheet, Cornerstone 9.5, and Cornerstone 9.8 ($5,000 + $2,160 + $600).
[h]Twenty percent of fourth-quarter purchases (0.20 × $6,904)—see Cornerstones 9.3 and 9.12.
[i]$33,153 + $5,204 (December 31, 2013, balance plus net income from Cornerstone 9.9).

# USING BUDGETS FOR PERFORMANCE EVALUATION

OBJECTIVE ❹
Describe the behavioral dimension of budgeting.

Budgets are often used to judge the performance of managers. Bonuses, salary increases, and promotions are all affected by a manager's ability to achieve or beat budgeted goals. Since a manager's financial status and career can be affected, budgets can have a significant behavioral effect. Whether that effect is positive or negative depends in large part on how budgets are used.

Positive behavior occurs when the goals of each manager are aligned with the goals of the organization and each manager has the drive to achieve them. The alignment of managerial and organizational goals is often referred to as **goal congruence**. If the budget is improperly administered, subordinate managers may subvert the organization's goals. **Dysfunctional behavior** is individual behavior that is in basic conflict with the goals of the organization.

An ideal budgetary system is one that achieves complete goal congruence and, simultaneously, creates a drive in managers to achieve the organization's goals in an ethical manner. While an ideal budgetary system probably does not exist, research and practice have identified some key features that promote a reasonable degree of positive behavior. These features include:

- frequent feedback on performance
- monetary and nonmonetary incentives
- participative budgeting
- realistic standards
- controllability of costs
- multiple measures of performance

## concept Q&A

In the last quarter of the fiscal year, a divisional manager chose to delay budgeted preventive maintenance expenditures so that the budgeted income goals could be achieved. Is this an example of goal congruent behavior or dysfunctional behavior?

**Answer:**

Assuming that the budgeted maintenance expenditures were well specified, the manager is sacrificing the long-run well-being of the division to achieve a short-run benefit (dysfunctional behavior).

## Frequent Feedback on Performance

Managers need to know how they are doing as the year progresses. Frequent, timely performance reports allow managers to know how successful their efforts have been, to take corrective actions, and to change plans as necessary.

## Monetary and Nonmonetary Incentives

A sound budgetary system encourages goal-congruent behavior. **Incentives** are the means an organization uses to influence a manager to exert effort to achieve an organization's goal Traditional organizational theory assumes that employees are primarily motivated by monetary rewards, they resist work, and they are inefficient and wasteful. Thus, **monetary incentives** are used to control a manager's tendency to shirk and waste resources by relating budgetary performance to salary increases, bonuses, and promotions. The threat of dismissal is the ultimate economic sanction for poor performance. In reality, employees are motivated by more than economic factors. Employees are also motivated by intrinsic psychological and social factors, such as the satisfaction of a job well done, recognition, responsibility, self-esteem, and the nature of the work itself. Thus **nonmonetary incentives**, including job enrichment, increased responsibility and autonomy, recognition programs, and so on, can be used to enhance a budgetary control system.

## concept Q&A

Assume that a company evaluates and rewards its managers based on their ability to achieve budgeted goals. Why would the same company ask its managers to participate in setting their budgeted standards?

**Answer:**

Participation encourages managers to internalize the goals and make them their own, leading to improved performance.

## Participative Budgeting

Rather than imposing budgets on subordinate managers, **participative budgeting** allows subordinate managers considerable say in how the budgets are established. Typically, overall objectives are communicated to the manager, who helps develop a budget that will accomplish these objectives.

Participative budgeting communicates a sense of responsibility to subordinate managers and fosters creativity. Since the subordinate manager creates the budget, the budget's goals will more likely become the manager's personal goals, resulting in greater goal congruence. The increased responsibility and challenge inherent in the process provide nonmonetary incentives that lead to a higher level of performance.

Participative budgeting has three potential problems:

- setting standards that are either too high or too low
- building slack into the budget (often referred to as padding the budget)
- pseudoparticipation

**Standard Setting**    Some managers may tend to set the budget either too loose or too tight. Since budgeted goals tend to become the manager's goals when participation is allowed, making this mistake in setting the budget can result in decreased performance levels. If goals are too easily achieved, a manager may lose interest, and performance may actually drop. Feeling challenged is important to aggressive and creative individuals. Similarly, setting the budget too tight ensures failure to achieve the standards and frustrates the manager. This frustration, too, can lead to poorer performance (see Exhibit 9.5). The trick is to get managers in a participative setting to set high but achievable goals.

( EXHIBIT 9.5 )

**The Art of Standard Setting**

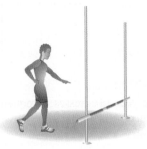

Standard Set Too Loose
Goals Too Easily Achieved

Standard Set Too Tight
Frustration

© Cengage Learning 2014

**Budgetary Slack**    The second problem with participative budgeting is the opportunity for managers to build slack into the budget. **Budgetary slack** (or *padding the budget*) exists when a manager deliberately underestimates revenues or overestimates costs in an effort to make the future period appear less attractive in the budget than they think it will be in reality. Either approach increases the likelihood that the manager will achieve the budget and consequently reduces the risk that the manager faces. Top management should carefully review budgets proposed by subordinate managers and provide input, where needed, in order to decrease the effects of building slack into the budget.

**ETHICAL DECISIONS**    The act of padding the budget is questionable when considering what is viewed as ethical professional practice. Padding the budget is a deliberate misrepresentation of costs and/or revenues. It is certainly not communicating information fairly and objectively and constitutes a violation of the credibility standard. The motive for such behavior is also not consistent with the professional responsibility to exhibit integrity. While it might be useful to estimate some costs at a little higher amount than expected to factor in uncertainty, excessive padding is misrepresentation and can lead to failure to spend resources in other areas that may need them. ●

**Pseudoparticipation**    The third problem with participation occurs when top management assumes total control of the budgeting process, seeking only superficial participation from lower-level managers. This practice is termed **pseudoparticipation**. Top management is simply obtaining formal acceptance of the budget from subordinate managers, not seeking real input. Accordingly, none of the behavioral benefits of participation will be realized.

## Realistic Standards

Budgeted objectives are used to gauge performance. Accordingly, they should be based on realistic conditions and expectations. Budgets should reflect operating realities, including the following:

- *Actual Levels of Activity:* Flexible budgets are used to ensure that budgeted costs can be realistically compared with costs for actual levels of activity.
- *Seasonal Variations:* Interim budgets should reflect seasonal effects. **Toys "R" Us**, for example, would expect much higher sales in the quarter that includes Christmas than in other quarters.
- *Efficiencies:* Budgetary cuts should be based on *planned* increases in efficiency and not simply arbitrary across-the-board reductions. Across-the-board cuts without any formal evaluation may impair the ability of some units to carry out their missions.
- *General Economic Trends:* General economic conditions also need to be considered. Budgeting for a significant increase in sales when a recession is projected is not only foolish but also potentially dangerous.

## Controllability of Costs

Ideally, managers are held accountable only for costs that they can control. **Controllable costs** are costs whose level a manager can influence. For example, divisional managers have no power to authorize such corporate-level costs as research and development and salaries of top managers. Therefore, they should not be held accountable for the incurrence of those costs. If noncontrollable costs are put in the budgets of subordinate managers to help them understand that these costs also need to be covered, then they should be separated from controllable costs and labeled as *noncontrollable*.

## Multiple Measures of Performance

Often, organizations make the mistake of using budgets as their only measure of managerial performance. While financial measures of performance are important, overemphasis can lead to a form of dysfunctional behavior called *milking the firm* or *myopia*. **Myopic behavior** occurs when a manager takes actions that improve budgetary performance in the short run but bring long-run harm to the firm. For example, to meet budgeted cost objectives or profits, managers can delay promoting deserving employees or reducing expenditures for preventive maintenance, advertising, and new product development. Using measures that are both financial and nonfinancial and that are long term and short term can alleviate this problem. For example, **Starwood Hotels** incurs considerable costs every year to research consumer trends and to train its hotel staff members to help ensure sustainable growth in room revenue for its luxury St. Regis brand. Budgetary measures alone cannot prevent myopic behavior.

# SUMMARY OF LEARNING OBJECTIVES

**LO 1.**    Define budgeting and discuss its role in planning, control, and decision making.
- Budgeting is the creation of a plan of action expressed in financial terms.
- Budgeting plays a key role in planning, control, and decision making.
- Budgets serve to improve communication and coordination, a role that becomes increasingly important as organizations grow in size.
- The master budget, which is the comprehensive financial plan of an organization, is made up of the operating and financial budgets.

**LO 2.** Define and prepare the operating budget, identify its major components, and explain the interrelationships of its various components.

- The operating budget is the budgeted income statement and all supporting budgets.
- The sales budget consists of the anticipated quantity and price of all products to be sold. It is done first, and the results feed directly into the production budget.
- The production budget gives the expected production in units to meet forecasted sales and desired ending inventory goals. Expected production is supplemented by beginning inventory. The results of the production budget are needed for the direct materials purchases budget and the direct labor budget.
- The direct materials purchases budget gives the necessary purchases during the year for every type of raw material to meet production and desired ending inventory goals.
- The direct labor budget shows the number of direct labor hours, and the direct labor cost needed to support production. The resulting direct labor hours are needed to prepare the overhead budget.
- The overhead budget may be broken down into fixed and variable components to facilitate preparation of the budget.
- The selling and administrative expenses budget gives the forecasted costs for these functions.
- The finished goods inventory budget and the cost of goods sold budget detail production costs for the expected ending inventory and the units sold, respectively.
- The budgeted income statement outlines the net income to be realized if budgeted plans come to fruition.

**LO 3.** Define and prepare the financial budget, identify its major components, and explain the interrelationships of its various components.

- The financial budget includes the cash budget, the capital expenditures budget, and the budgeted balance sheet.
- The cash budget is the beginning balance in the cash account, plus anticipated receipts, minus anticipated disbursements, plus or minus any necessary borrowing.
- The budgeted (or pro forma) balance sheet gives the anticipated ending balances of the asset, liability, and equity accounts if budgeted plans hold.

**LO 4.** Describe the behavioral dimension of budgeting.

- The success of a budgetary system depends on how seriously human factors are considered.
- To discourage dysfunctional behavior, organizations should avoid overemphasizing budgets as a control mechanism.
- Budgets can be improved as performance measures by using participative budgeting and other nonmonetary incentives, providing frequent feedback on performance, using flexible budgeting, ensuring that the budgetary objectives reflect reality, and holding managers accountable for only controllable costs.

# SUMMARY OF IMPORTANT EQUATIONS

1. Units to Be Produced = Expected Unit Sales + Units in Desired Ending Inventory (EI)
$$- \text{Units in Beginning Inventory (BI)}$$

2. Purchases = Direct Materials Needed for Production
$$+ \text{Direct Materials in Desired Ending Inventory}$$
$$- \text{Direct Materials in Beginning Inventory}$$

3. Cash Available = Beginning Cash Balance + Expected Cash Receipts

4. Ending Cash Balance = Cash Available − Expected Cash Disbursements

CORNERSTONES

# KEY TERMS

# REVIEW PROBLEMS

## I. Select Operational Budgets

Joven Products produces coat racks. The projected sales for the first quarter of the coming year and the beginning and ending inventory data are as follows:

| | |
|---|---|
| Unit sales | 100,000 |
| Unit price | $15 |
| Units in beginning inventory | 8,000 |
| Units in targeted ending inventory | 12,000 |

The coat racks are molded and then painted. Each rack requires four pounds of metal, which costs $2.50 per pound. The beginning inventory of materials is 4,000 pounds. Joven Products wants to have 6,000 pounds of metal in inventory at the end of the quarter. Each rack produced requires 30 minutes of direct labor time, which is billed at $9 per hour.

### Required:

1. Prepare a sales budget for the first quarter.
2. Prepare a production budget for the first quarter.
3. Prepare a direct materials purchases budget for the first quarter.
4. Prepare a direct labor budget for the first quarter.

### Solution:

1.

**Joven Products**
**Sales Budget**
**For the First Quarter**

| | |
|---|---|
| Units | 100,000 |
| Unit price | ×$15 |
| Sales | $1,500,000 |

2.

**Joven Products**
**Production Budget**
**For the First Quarter**

| | |
|---|---|
| Sales (in units) | 100,000 |
| Desired ending inventory | 12,000 |
| Total needs | 112,000 |
| Less: Beginning inventory | 8,000 |
| Units to be produced | 104,000 |

3.

**Joven Products**
**Direct Materials Purchases Budget**
**For the First Quarter**

| | |
|---|---|
| Units to be produced | 104,000 |
| Direct materials per unit (lb.) | ×4 |
| Production needs (lb.) | 416,000 |
| Desired ending inventory (lb.) | 6,000 |
| Total needs (lb.) | 422,000 |
| Less: Beginning inventory (lb.) | 4,000 |
| Materials to be purchased (lb.) | 418,000 |
| Cost per pound | ×$2.50 |
| Total purchase cost | $1,045,000 |

4.

**Joven Products**
**Direct Labor Budget**
**For the First Quarter**

| | |
|---|---|
| Units to be produced | 104,000 |
| Labor hours per unit | ×0.5 |
| Total hours needed | 52,000 |
| Cost per hour | ×$9 |
| Total direct labor cost | $468,000 |

## II. Cash Budgeting

Kylles Inc. expects to receive cash from sales of $45,000 in March. In addition, Kylles expects to sell property worth $3,500. Payments for materials and supplies are expected to total $10,000, direct labor payroll will be $12,500, and other expenditures are budgeted at $14,900. On March 1, the cash account balance is $1,230.

### Required:

1. Prepare a cash budget for Kylles Inc. for the month of March.
2. Assume that Kylles Inc. wanted a minimum cash balance of $15,000 and that it could borrow from the bank in multiples of $1,000 at an interest rate of 12% per year. What would the adjusted ending balance for March be for Kylles? How much interest would Kylles owe in April, assuming that the entire amount borrowed in March would be paid back?

### Solution:

1.

**Kylles Inc.**
**Cash Budget for the Month of March**

| | |
|---|---|
| Beginning cash balance | $ 1,230 |
| Cash sales | 45,000 |
| Sale of property | 3,500 |
| Total cash available | $49,730 |
| Less disbursements: | |
| Materials and supplies | $10,000 |
| Direct labor payroll | 12,500 |
| Other expenditures | 14,900 |
| Total disbursements | $37,400 |
| Ending cash balance | $12,330 |

2.

| | |
|---|---|
| Unadjusted ending balance | $12,330 |
| Plus borrowing | 3,000 |
| Adjusted ending balance | $15,330 |

In April, interest owed would be $(1/12 \times 0.12 \times \$3,000) = \$30$.

# DISCUSSION QUESTIONS

1. Define the term *budget*. How are budgets used in planning?
2. Define *control*. How are budgets used to control?
3. Explain how both small and large organizations can benefit from budgeting.
4. Discuss some reasons for budgeting.
5. What is a master budget? An operating budget? A financial budget?
6. Explain the role of a sales forecast in budgeting. What is the difference between a sales forecast and a sales budget?
7. All budgets depend on the sales budget. Is this true? Explain.
8. Why is goal congruence important?
9. Why is it important for a manager to receive frequent feedback on his or her performance?
10. Discuss the roles of monetary and nonmonetary incentives. Do you believe that nonmonetary incentives are needed? Why?
11. What is participative budgeting? Discuss some of its advantages.

12.  A budget too easily achieved will lead to diminished performance. Do you agree? Explain.

13.  What is the role of top management in participative budgeting?

14.  Explain why a manager has an incentive to build slack into the budget.

15.  Explain how a manager can milk the firm to improve budgetary performance.

# MULTIPLE-CHOICE QUESTIONS

**9-1** A budget

a. is a long-term plan.
b. covers at least 2 years.
c. is only a control tool.
d. is a short-term financial plan.
e. is necessary only for large firms.

**9-2** Which of the following is part of the control process?

a. Monitoring of actual activity
b. Comparison of actual with planned activity
c. Investigating
d. Taking corrective action
e. All of these.

**9-3** Which of the following is *not* an advantage of budgeting?

a. It forces managers to plan.
b. It provides information for decision making.
c. It guarantees an improvement in organizational efficiency.
d. It provides a standard for performance evaluation.
e. It improves communication and coordination.

**9-4** The budget committee

a. reviews the budget.
b. resolves differences that arise as the budget is prepared.
c. approves the final budget.
d. is directed (typically) by the controller.
e. does all of these.

**9-5** A moving, 12-month budget that is updated monthly is

a. not used by manufacturing firms.
b. waste of time and effort.
c. a master budget.
d. a continuous budget.
e. always used by firms that prepare a master budget.

**9-6** Which of the following is *not* part of the operating budget?

a. The direct labor budget
b. The cost of goods sold budget
c. The production budget
d. The capital budget
e. The selling and administrative expenses budget

**9-7** Before a direct materials purchases budget can be prepared, you should first

a. prepare a sales budget.
b. prepare a production budget.
c. decide on the desired ending inventory of materials.
d. obtain the expected price of each type of material.
e. do all of these.

**9-8** The first step in preparing the sales budget is to

a. prepare a sales forecast.
b. review the production budget carefully.
c. assess the desired ending inventory of finished goods.
d. talk with past customers.
e. increase sales beyond the forecast level.

**9-9** Which of the following is needed to prepare the production budget?

a.  Direct materials needed for production

b.  Direct labor needed for production

c.  Expected unit sales

d.  Units of materials in ending inventory

e.  None of these.

**9-10** A company requires 100 pounds of plastic to meet the production needs of a small toy. It currently has 10 pounds of plastic inventory. The desired ending inventory of plastic is 30 pounds. How many pounds of plastic should be budgeted for purchasing during the coming period?

a.  80 pounds

b.  110 pounds

c.  120 pounds

d.  130 pounds

e.  None of these.

**9-11** A company plans to sell 220 units. The selling price per unit is $24. There are 50 units in beginning inventory, and the company would like to have 20 units in ending inventory. How many units should be produced for the coming period?

a.  250

b.  200

c.  230

d.  220

e.  None of these.

**9-12** Which of the following is needed to prepare a budgeted income statement?

a.  The production budget

b.  Budgeted selling and administrative expenses

c.  The budgeted balance sheet

d.  The capital expenditures budget

e.  Last year's income statement

**9-13** Select the one budget below that is *not* an operating budget.

a.  Cost of goods sold budget

b.  Cash budget

c.  Production budget

d.  Overhead budget

e.  All of these are operating budgets.

**9-14** The cash budget serves which of the following purposes?

a.  Documents the need for liberal inventory policies.

b.  Reveals the amount of depreciation expense.

c.  Reveals the amount lost due to uncollectible accounts.

d.  Provides information about the ability to repay loans.

e.  None of the above.

**9-15** Assume that a company has the following accounts receivable collection pattern:

| | |
|---|---|
| Month of sale | 40% |
| Month following sale | 60% |

All sales are on credit. If credit sales for January and February are $100,000 and $200,000, respectively, the cash collections for February are

a.  $140,000.

b.  $300,000.

c.  $120,000.

d.  $160,000.

e.  $80,000.

**9-16** The percentage of accounts receivable that are uncollectible can be ignored for cash budgeting because

a.  no cash is received from an account that defaults.

b.  it is included in cash sales.

c.  it appears on the budgeted income statement.

d.  for most companies, it is not a material amount.

e.  none of the above is correct.

**9-17** An ideal budgetary system is one that

    a. encourages dysfunctional behavior.

    b. encourages goal-congruent behavior.

    c. encourages myopic behavior.

    d. encourages subversion of an organization's goals.

    e. does none of these.

**9-18** Some key budgetary features that tend to promote positive managerial behavior are

    a. frequent feedback on performance.

    b. participative budgeting.

    c. realistic standards.

    d. well-designed monetary and non-monetary incentives.

    e. all of these.

**9-19** Which of the following is *not* an advantage of participative budgeting?

    a. It encourages budgetary slack.

    b. It tends to lead to a higher level of performance.

    c. It fosters a sense of responsibility.

    d. It encourages greater goal congruence.

    e. It fosters a sense of creativity in managers.

**9-20** Which of the following items is a possible example of myopic behavior?

    a. Failure to promote deserving employees

    b. Reducing expenditures on preventive maintenance

    c. Cutting back on new product development

    d. Buying cheaper, lower-quality materials so that the company does not exceed the materials purchases budget

    e. All of these.

# CORNERSTONE EXERCISES

**Cornerstone Exercise 9-21   Preparing a Sales Budget**

Patrick Inc. sells industrial solvents in five-gallon drums. Patrick expects the following units to be sold in the first three months of the coming year:

|  |  |
|---|---|
| January | 41,000 |
| February | 38,000 |
| March | 50,000 |

The average price for a drum is $35.

**Required:**

Prepare a sales budget for the first three months of the coming year, showing units and sales revenue by month and in total for the quarter.

**Cornerstone Exercise 9-22   Preparing a Production Budget**

Patrick Inc. makes industrial solvents. In the first four months of the coming year, Patrick expects the following unit sales:

|  |  |
|---|---|
| January | 41,000 |
| February | 38,000 |
| March | 50,000 |
| April | 51,000 |

Patrick's policy is to have 25% of next month's sales in ending inventory. On January 1, it is expected that there will be 6,700 drums of solvent on hand.

**Required:**

Prepare a production budget for the first quarter of the year. Show the number of drums that should be produced each month as well as for the quarter in total.

## Cornerstone Exercise 9-23   Preparing a Direct Materials Purchases Budget

OBJECTIVE ❷
CORNERSTONE 9.3

Patrick Inc. makes industrial solvents sold in five-gallon drums. Planned production in units for the first three months of the coming year is:

| | |
|---|---|
| January | 43,800 |
| February | 41,000 |
| March | 50,250 |

Each drum requires 5.5 gallons of chemicals and one plastic drum. Company policy requires that ending inventories of raw materials for each month be 15% of the next month's production needs. That policy was met for the ending inventory of December in the prior year. The cost of one gallon of chemicals is $2.00. The cost of one drum is $1.60. (*Note:* Round all unit amounts to the nearest unit. Round all dollar amounts to the nearest dollar.)

**Required:**

1. Calculate the ending inventory of chemicals in gallons for December of the prior year, and for January and February. What is the beginning inventory of chemicals for January?
2. Prepare a direct materials purchases budgets for chemicals for the months of January and February.
3. Calculate the ending inventory of drums for December of the prior year, and for January and February.
4. Prepare a direct materials purchases budgets for drums for the months of January and February.

## Cornerstone Exercise 9-24   Preparing a Direct Labor Budget

OBJECTIVE ❷
CORNERSTONE 9.4

Patrick Inc. makes industrial solvents. Planned production in units for the first three months of the coming year is:

| | |
|---|---|
| January | 43,800 |
| February | 41,000 |
| March | 50,250 |

Each drum of industrial solvent takes 0.3 direct labor hours. The average wage is $18 per hour.

**Required:**

Prepare a direct labor budget for the months of January, February, and March, as well as the total for the first quarter.

## Cornerstone Exercise 9-25   Preparing an Overhead Budget

OBJECTIVE ❷
CORNERSTONE 9.5

Patrick Inc. makes industrial solvents. Budgeted direct labor hours for the first three months of the coming year are:

| | |
|---|---|
| January | 13,140 |
| February | 12,300 |
| March | 15,075 |

The variable overhead rate is $0.70 per direct labor hour. Fixed overhead is budgeted at $2,750 per month.

**Required:**

Prepare an overhead budget for the months of January, February, and March, as well as the total for the first quarter. (*Note*: Round all dollar amounts to the nearest dollar.)

## Cornerstone Exercise 9-26   Preparing an Ending Finished Goods Inventory Budget

OBJECTIVE ❷
CORNERSTONE 9.6

Andrews Company manufactures a line of office chairs. Each chair takes $14 of direct materials and uses 1.9 direct labor hours at $16 per direct labor hour. The variable overhead rate is $1.20

*(Continued)*

per direct labor hour and the fixed overhead rate is $1.60 per direct labor hour. Andrews expects to have 675 chairs in ending inventory. There is no beginning inventory of office chairs.

**Required:**

1.  Calculate the unit product cost. (*Note:* Round to the nearest cent.)
2.  Calculate the cost of budgeted ending inventory. (*Note:* Round to the nearest dollar.)

OBJECTIVE ❷
CORNERSTONE 9.7

### Cornerstone Exercise 9-27    Preparing a Cost of Goods Sold Budget

Andrews Company manufactures a line of office chairs. Each chair takes $14 of direct materials and uses 1.9 direct labor hours at $16 per direct labor hour. The variable overhead rate is $1.20 per direct labor hour and the fixed overhead rate is $1.60 per direct labor hour. Andrews expects to produce 20,000 chairs next year and expects to have 675 chairs in ending inventory. There is no beginning inventory of office chairs.

**Required:**

Prepare a cost of goods sold budget for Andrews Company.

OBJECTIVE ❷
CORNERSTONE 9.8

### Cornerstone Exercise 9-28    Preparing a Selling and Administrative Expenses Budget

Fazel Company makes and sells paper products. In the coming year, Fazel expects total sales of $19,730,000. There is a 3% commission on sales. In addition, fixed expenses of the sales and administrative offices include the following:

| | |
|---|---:|
| Salaries | $ 960,000 |
| Utilities | 365,000 |
| Office space | 230,000 |
| Advertising | 1,200,000 |

**Required:**

Prepare a selling and administrative expenses budget for Fazel Company for the coming year.

OBJECTIVE ❷
CORNERSTONE 9.9

### Cornerstone Exercise 9-29    Preparing a Budgeted Income Statement

Oliver Company provided the following information for the coming year:

| | |
|---|---:|
| Units produced and sold | 160,000 |
| Cost of goods sold per unit | $   6.30 |
| Selling price | $  10.80 |
| Variable selling and administrative expenses per unit | $   1.10 |
| Fixed selling and administrative expenses | $423,000 |
| Tax rate | 35% |

**Required:**

Prepare a budgeted income statement for Oliver Company for the coming year. (*Note:* Round all income statement amounts to the nearest dollar.)

OBJECTIVE ❸
CORNERSTONE 9.10

### Cornerstone Exercise 9-30    Preparing a Schedule of Cash Collections on Accounts Receivable

Kailua and Company is a legal services firm. All sales of legal services are billed to the client (there are no cash sales). Kailua expects that, on average, 20% will be paid in the month of billing, 50% will be paid in the month following billing, and 25% will be paid in the second month following billing. For the next five months, the following sales billings are expected:

| | |
|---|---:|
| May | $ 84,000 |
| June | 100,800 |
| July | 77,000 |
| August | 86,800 |
| September | 91,000 |

**Required:**

Prepare a schedule showing the cash expected in payments on accounts receivable in August and in September.

### Cornerstone Exercise 9-31    Preparing an Accounts Payable Schedule

OBJECTIVE ③
CORNERSTONE 9.11

Wight Inc. purchases raw materials on account for use in production. The direct materials purchases budget shows the following expected purchases on account:

|        |           |
|--------|-----------|
| April  | $374,400  |
| May    | 411,200   |
| June   | 416,000   |

Wight typically pays 20% on account in the month of billing and 80% the next month.

**Required:**

1. How much cash is required for payments on account in May?
2. How much cash is expected for payments on account in June?

### Cornerstone Exercise 9-32    Preparing a Cash Budget

OBJECTIVE ③
CORNERSTONE 9.12

La Famiglia Pizzeria provided the following information for the month of October:

a. Sales are budgeted to be $157,000. About 85% of sales are cash; the remainder are on account.
b. La Famiglia expects that, on average, 70% of credit sales will be paid in the month of sale, and 28% will be paid in the following month.
c. Food and supplies purchases, all on account, are expected to be $116,000. La Famiglia pays 25% in the month of purchase and 75% in the month following purchase.
d. Most of the work is done by the owners, who typically withdraw $6,000 a month from the business as their salary. (*Note:* The $6,000 is a payment in total to the two owners, not per person.) Various part-time workers cost $7,300 per month. They are paid for their work weekly, so on average 90% of their wages are paid in the month incurred and the remaining 10% in the next month.
e. Utilities average $5,950 per month. Rent on the building is $4,100 per month.
f. Insurance is paid quarterly; the next payment of $1,200 is due in October.
g. September sales were $181,500 and purchases of food and supplies in September equaled $130,000.
h. The cash balance on October 1 is $2,147.

**Required:**

1. Calculate the cash receipts expected in October. (*Hint*: Remember to include both cash sales and payments from credit sales.)
2. Calculate the cash needed in October to pay for food purchases.
3. Prepare a cash budget for the month of October.

# EXERCISES

### Exercise 9-33    Planning and Control

OBJECTIVE ①

a. Dr. Jones, a dentist, wants to increase the size and profitability of his business by building a reputation for quality and timely service.
b. To achieve this, he plans on adding a dental laboratory to his building so that crowns, bridges, and dentures can be made in-house.
c. To add the laboratory, he needs additional money, which he decides must be obtained by increasing revenues. After some careful calculation, Dr. Jones concludes that annual revenues must be increased by 10%.

*(Continued)*

d.  Dr. Jones finds that his fees for fillings and crowns are below the average in his community and decides that the 10% increase can be achieved by increasing these fees.

e.  He then identifies the quantity of fillings and crowns expected for the coming year, the new per-unit fee, and the total fees expected.

f.  As the year unfolds (on a month-by-month basis), Dr. Jones compares the actual revenues received with the budgeted revenues. For the first three months, actual revenues were less than planned.

g.  Upon investigating, he discovered that he had some reduction in the number of patients because he had also changed his available hours of operation.

h.  He returned to his old schedule and found out that the number of patients was restored to the original expected levels.

i.  However, to make up the shortfall, he also increased the price of some of his other services.

### Required:

Match each statement with the following planning and control elements (*Note:* A letter may be matched to more than one item):

1.  Corrective action
2.  Budgets
3.  Feedback
4.  Investigation
5.  Short-term plan
6.  Comparison of actual with planned
7.  Monitoring of actual activity
8.  Strategic plan
9.  Short-term objectives
10.  Long-term objectives

---

*Use the following information for Exercises 9-34 and 9-35:*

Assume that **Stillwater Designs** produces two automotive subwoofers: S12L7 and S12L5. The S12L7 sells for $475, and the S12L5 sells for $300. Projected sales (number of speakers) for the coming five quarters are as follows:

|                        | S12L7 | S12L5 |
|------------------------|-------|-------|
| First quarter, 2014    | 800   | 1,300 |
| Second quarter, 2014   | 2,200 | 1,400 |
| Third quarter, 2014    | 5,600 | 5,300 |
| Fourth quarter, 2014   | 4,600 | 3,900 |
| First quarter, 2015    | 900   | 1,200 |

The vice president of sales believes that the projected sales are realistic and can be achieved by the company.

OBJECTIVE ❶ ❷

### Exercise 9-34    Sales Budget

Refer to the information regarding **Stillwater Designs** above.

### Required:

1.  Prepare a sales budget for each quarter of 2014 and for the year in total. Show sales by product and in total for each time period.
2.  **CONCEPTUAL CONNECTION** How will Stillwater Designs use this sales budget?

## Exercise 9-35    Production Budget

OBJECTIVE 2

Refer to the information regarding **Stillwater Designs** on the previous page. Stillwater Designs needs a production budget for each product (representing the amount that must be outsourced to manufacturers located in Asia). Beginning inventory of S12L7 for the first quarter of 2014 was 340 boxes. The company's policy is to have 20% of the next quarter's sales of S12L7 in ending inventory. Beginning inventory of S12L5 was 170 boxes. The company's policy is to have 30% of the next quarter's sales of S12L5 in ending inventory.

**Required:**

Prepare a production budget for each quarter for 2014 and for the year in total.

## Exercise 9-36    Production Budget and Direct Materials Purchases Budgets

OBJECTIVE 2

Peanut-Fresh Inc. produces all-natural organic peanut butter. The peanut butter is sold in 12-ounce jars. The sales budget for the first four months of the year is as follows:

|          | Unit Sales | Dollar Sales ($) |
|----------|-----------|------------------|
| January  | 48,000    | 100,800          |
| February | 46,000    | 96,600           |
| March    | 55,000    | 121,000          |
| April    | 58,000    | 125,200          |

Company policy requires that ending inventories for each month be 20% of next month's sales. At the beginning of January, the inventory of peanut butter is 14,500 jars.

Each jar of peanut butter needs two raw materials: 24 ounces of peanuts and one jar. Company policy requires that ending inventories of raw materials for each month be 10% of the next month's production needs. That policy was met on January 1.

**Required:**

1. Prepare a production budget for the first quarter of the year. Show the number of jars that should be produced each month as well as for the quarter in total.
2. Prepare separate direct materials purchases budgets for jars and for peanuts for the months of January and February.

## Exercise 9-37    Production Budget

OBJECTIVE 2

Aqua-pro Inc. produces submersible water pumps for ponds and cisterns. The unit sales for selected months of the year are as follows:

|       | Unit Sales |
|-------|-----------|
| April | 180,000   |
| May   | 220,000   |
| June  | 200,000   |
| July  | 240,000   |

Company policy requires that ending inventories for each month be 25% of next month's sales. However, at the beginning of April, due to greater sales in March than anticipated, the beginning inventory of water pumps is only 21,000.

**Required:**

Prepare a production budget for the second quarter of the year. Show the number of units that should be produced each month as well as for the quarter in total.

## Exercise 9-38    Direct Materials Purchases Budget

OBJECTIVE 2

Langer Company produces plastic items, including plastic housings for humidifiers. Each housing requires about 15 ounces of plastic costing $0.08 per ounce. Langer molds the plastic into the proper shape. Langer has budgeted production of the housings for the next four months as follows:

*(Continued)*

|  | Units |
|---|---|
| July | 3,500 |
| August | 4,400 |
| September | 4,900 |
| October | 6,300 |

Inventory policy requires that sufficient plastic be in ending monthly inventory to satisfy 20% of the following month's production needs. The inventory of plastic at the beginning of July equals exactly the amount needed to satisfy the inventory policy.

**Required:**

Prepare a direct materials purchases budget for July, August, and September, showing purchases in units and in dollars for each month and in total.

**OBJECTIVE ❷**   **Exercise 9-39   Direct Labor Budget**

Evans Company produces asphalt roofing materials. The production budget in bundles for Evans' most popular weight of asphalt shingle is shown for the following months:

|  | Units |
|---|---|
| March | 4,000 |
| April | 13,000 |
| May | 14,400 |
| June | 17,000 |

Each bundle produced requires (on average) 0.40 direct labor hours. The average cost of direct labor is $20 per hour.

**Required:**

Prepare a direct labor budget for March, April, and May, showing the hours needed and the direct labor cost for each month and in total.

**OBJECTIVE ❷**   **Exercise 9-40   Sales Budget**

Alger Inc. manufactures six models of leaf blowers and weed eaters. Alger's budgeting team is finalizing the sales budget for the coming year. Sales in units and dollars for last year follow:

| Product | Number Sold | Price ($) | Revenue |
|---|---|---|---|
| LB-1 | 14,700 | 32 | $  470,400 |
| LB-2 | 18,000 | 20 | 360,000 |
| WE-6 | 25,200 | 15 | 378,000 |
| WE-7 | 16,200 | 10 | 162,000 |
| WE-8 | 6,900 | 18 | 124,200 |
| WE-9 | 4,000 | 22 | 88,000 |
| Total |  |  | $1,582,600 |

In looking over the previous year's sales figures, Alger's sales budgeting team recalled the following:

a.   Model LB-1 is a newer version of the leaf blower with a gasoline engine. The LB-1 is mounted on wheels instead of being carried. This model is designed for the commercial market and did better than expected in its first year. As a result, the number of units of Model LB-1 to be sold was forecast at 250% of the previous year's units.

b.   Models WE-8 and WE-9 were introduced on July 1 of last year. They are lighter versions of the traditional weed eater and are designed for smaller households or condo units. Alger estimates that demand for both models will continue at the previous year's rate.

c.   A competitor has announced plans to introduce an improved version of model WE-6, Alger's traditional weed eater. Alger believes that the model WE-6 price must be cut 30% to maintain unit sales at the previous year's level.

d.  It was assumed that unit sales of all other models would increase by 5%, prices remaining constant.

**Required:**

Prepare a sales budget by product and in total for Alger Inc. for the coming year.

### Exercise 9-41    Production Budget and Direct Materials Purchases Budget

OBJECTIVE 2

Jani Subramanian, owner of Jani's Flowers and Gifts, produces gift baskets for various special occasions. Each gift basket includes fruit or assorted small gifts (e.g., a coffee mug, deck of cards, novelty cocoa mixes, scented soap) in a basket that is wrapped in colorful cellophane. Jani has estimated the following unit sales of the standard gift basket for the rest of the year and for January of next year.

| | |
|---|---|
| September | 250 |
| October | 200 |
| November | 230 |
| December | 380 |
| January | 100 |

Jani likes to have 5% of the next month's sales needs on hand at the end of each month. This requirement was met on August 31.

Two materials are needed for each fruit basket:

| | |
|---|---|
| Fruit | 1 pound |
| Small gifts | 6 items |

The materials inventory policy is to have 5% of the next month's fruit needs on hand and 30% of the next month's production needs of small gifts. (The relatively low inventory amount for fruit is designed to prevent spoilage.) Materials inventory on August 31 met this company policy.

**Required:**

1.  Prepare a production budget for September, October, November, and December for gift baskets. (*Note*: Round all answers to the nearest whole unit.)
2.  Prepare a direct materials purchases budget for the two types of materials used in the production of gift baskets for the months of September, October, and November. (*Note:* Round answers to the nearest whole unit.)
3.  **CONCEPTUAL CONNECTION** Why do you think there is such a big difference in budgeted units from November to December? Why did Jani budget fewer units in January than in December?

### Exercise 9-42    Schedule of Cash Collections on Accounts Receivable and Cash Budget

OBJECTIVE 3

Bennett Inc. found that about 15% of its sales during the month were for cash. Bennett has the following accounts receivable payment experience:

| | |
|---|---|
| Percent paid in the month of sale | 25 |
| Percent paid in the month after the sale | 68 |
| Percent paid in the second month after the sale | 5 |

Bennett's anticipated sales for the next few months are as follows:

| | |
|---|---|
| April | $250,000 |
| May | 290,000 |
| June | 280,000 |
| July | 295,000 |
| August | 300,000 |

**Required:**

1.  Calculate credit sales for May, June, July, and August.
2.  Prepare a schedule of cash receipts for July and August.

OBJECTIVE ③   **Exercise 9-43   Schedule of Cash Collections on Accounts Receivable and Cash Budget**

Roybal Inc. sells all of its product on account. Roybal has the following accounts receivable payment experience:

| | |
|---|---|
| Percent paid in the month of sale | 20 |
| Percent paid in the month after the sale | 55 |
| Percent paid in the second month after the sale | 23 |

To encourage payment in the month of sale, Roybal gives a 2% cash discount. Roybal's anticipated sales for the next few months are as follows:

| | |
|---|---|
| April | $190,000 |
| May | 248,000 |
| June | 260,000 |
| July | 240,000 |
| August | 300,000 |

**Required:**

1. Prepare a schedule of cash receipts for July.
2. Prepare a schedule of cash receipts for August.

OBJECTIVE ③   **Exercise 9-44   Cash Payments Schedule**

Fein Company provided the following information relating to cash payments:

a. Fein purchased direct materials on account in the following amounts:

| | |
|---|---|
| June | $68,000 |
| July | 77,000 |
| August | 73,000 |

b. Fein pays 20% of accounts payable in the month of purchase and the remaining 80% in the following month.
c. In July, direct labor cost was $32,300. August direct labor cost was $35,400. The company finds that typically 90% of direct labor cost is paid in cash during the month, with the remainder paid in the following month.
d. August overhead amounted to $71,200, including $6,350 of depreciation.
e. Fein had taken out a four-month loan of $15,000 on May 1. Interest, due with payment of principal, accrued at the rate of 9% per year. The loan and all interest were repaid on August 31. (*Note:* Use whole months to compute interest payment.)

**Required:**

Prepare a schedule of cash payments for Fein Company for the month of August.

OBJECTIVE ③   **Exercise 9-45   Cash Budget**

The owner of a building supply company has requested a cash budget for June. After examining the records of the company, you find the following:

a. Cash balance on June 1 is $736.
b. Actual sales for April and May are as follows:

| | April | May |
|---|---|---|
| Cash sales | $10,000 | $18,000 |
| Credit sales | 28,900 | 35,000 |
| Total sales | $38,900 | $53,000 |

c. Credit sales are collected over a three-month period: 40% in the month of sale, 30% in the second month, and 20% in the third month. The sales collected in the third month are subject to a 2% late fee, which is paid by those customers in addition to what they owe. The remaining sales are uncollectible.

d.  Inventory purchases average 64% of a month's total sales. Of those purchases, 20% are paid for in the month of purchase. The remaining 80% are paid for in the following month.

e.  Salaries and wages total $11,750 per month, including a $4,500 salary paid to the owner.

f.  Rent is $4,100 per month.

g.  Taxes to be paid in June are $6,780.

The owner also tells you that he expects cash sales of $18,600 and credit sales of $54,000 for June. No minimum cash balance is required. The owner of the company doesn't have access to short-term loans.

**Required:**

1.  Prepare a cash budget for June. Include supporting schedules for cash collections and cash payments.

2.  **CONCEPTUAL CONNECTION** Did the business show a negative cash balance for June? Suppose that the owner has no hope of establishing a line of credit for the business, what recommendations would you give the owner for dealing with a negative cash balance?

# PROBLEMS

### Problem 9-46    Cash Budget

OBJECTIVE 3

Aragon and Associates has found from past experience that 25% of its services are for cash. The remaining 75% are on credit. An aging schedule for accounts receivable reveals the following pattern:

a.  Ten percent of fees on credit are paid in the month that service is rendered.

b.  Sixty percent of fees on credit are paid in the month following service.

c.  Twenty-six percent of fees on credit are paid in the second month following service.

d.  Four percent of fees on credit are never collected.

Fees (on credit) that have not been paid until the second month following performance of the legal service are considered overdue and are subject to a 3% late charge.

Aragon has developed the following forecast of fees:

| | |
|---|---|
| May | $180,000 |
| June | 200,000 |
| July | 190,000 |
| August | 194,000 |
| September | 240,000 |

**Required:**

Prepare a schedule of cash receipts for August and September.

### Problem 9-47    Operating Budget, Comprehensive Analysis

OBJECTIVE 1 2 3 4

Allison Manufacturing produces a subassembly used in the production of jet aircraft engines. The assembly is sold to engine manufacturers and aircraft maintenance facilities. Projected sales in units for the coming five months follow:

| | |
|---|---|
| January | 40,000 |
| February | 50,000 |
| March | 60,000 |
| April | 60,000 |
| May | 62,000 |

The following data pertain to production policies and manufacturing specifications followed by Allison Manufacturing:

a.  Finished goods inventory on January 1 is 32,000 units, each costing $166.06. The desired ending inventory for each month is 80% of the next month's sales.

*(Continued)*

b.  The data on materials used are as follows:

| Direct Material | Per-Unit Usage | Unit Cost ($) |
|---|---|---|
| Metal | 10 lbs. | 8 |
| Components | 6 | 5 |

Inventory policy dictates that sufficient materials be on hand at the end of the month to produce 50% of the next month's production needs. This is exactly the amount of material on hand on December 31 of the prior year.

c.  The direct labor used per unit of output is three hours. The average direct labor cost per hour is $14.25.

d.  Overhead each month is estimated using a flexible budget formula. (*Note:* Activity is measured in direct labor hours.)

| | Fixed-Cost Component ($) | Variable-Cost Component ($) |
|---|---|---|
| Supplies | — | 1.00 |
| Power | — | 0.50 |
| Maintenance | 30,000 | 0.40 |
| Supervision | 16,000 | — |
| Depreciation | 200,000 | — |
| Taxes | 12,000 | — |
| Other | 80,000 | 0.50 |

e.  Monthly selling and administrative expenses are also estimated using a flexible budgeting formula. (*Note:* Activity is measured in units sold.)

| | Fixed Costs ($) | Variable Costs ($) |
|---|---|---|
| Salaries | 50,000 | — |
| Commissions | — | 2.00 |
| Depreciation | 40,000 | — |
| Shipping | — | 1.00 |
| Other | 20,000 | 0.60 |

f.  The unit selling price of the subassembly is $205.

g.  All sales and purchases are for cash. The cash balance on January 1 equals $400,000. The firm requires a minimum ending balance of $50,000. If the firm develops a cash shortage by the end of the month, sufficient cash is borrowed to cover the shortage. Any cash borrowed is repaid at the end of the quarter, as is the interest due (cash borrowed at the end of the quarter is repaid at the end of the following quarter). The interest rate is 12% per annum. No money is owed at the beginning of January.

**Required:**

1.  Prepare a monthly operating budget for the first quarter with the following schedules. (*Note:* Assume that there is no change in work-in-process inventories.)

a.  Sales budget
b.  Production budget
c.  Direct materials purchases budget
d.  Direct labor budget
e.  Overhead budget

f.  Selling and administrative expenses budget
g.  Ending finished goods inventory budget
h.  Cost of goods sold budget
i.  Budgeted income statement
j.  Cash budget

2.  **CONCEPTUAL CONNECTION** Form a group with two or three other students. Locate a manufacturing plant in your community that has headquarters elsewhere. Interview the controller for the plant regarding the master budgeting process. Ask when the process starts each year, what schedules and budgets are prepared at the plant level, how the controller forecasts the amounts, and how those schedules and budgets fit in with the overall corporate

budget. Is the budgetary process participative? Also, find out how budgets are used for performance analysis. Write a summary of the interview.

**Problem 9-48   Understanding Relationships, Cash Budget, Pro Forma Balance Sheet**

OBJECTIVE ❸

ILLUSTRATING
RELATIONSHIPS

Ryan Richards, controller for Grange Retailers, has assembled the following data to assist in the preparation of a cash budget for the third quarter of 2014:

a.   Sales:

| | |
|---|---|
| May (actual) | $100,000 |
| June (actual) | 120,000 |
| July (estimated) | 90,000 |
| August (estimated) | 100,000 |
| September (estimated) | 135,000 |
| October (estimated) | 110,000 |

b.   Each month, 30% of sales are for cash and 70% are on credit. The collection pattern for credit sales is 20% in the month of sale, 50% in the following month, and 30% in the second month following the sale.

c.   Each month, the ending inventory exactly equals 50% of the cost of next month's sales. The markup on goods is 25% of cost.

d.   Inventory purchases are paid for in the month following the purchase.

e.   Recurring monthly expenses are as follows:

| | |
|---|---|
| Salaries and wages | $10,000 |
| Depreciation on plant and equipment | 4,000 |
| Utilities | 1,000 |
| Other | 1,700 |

f.   Property taxes of $15,000 are due and payable on July 15, 2014.

g.   Advertising fees of $6,000 must be paid on August 20, 2014.

h.   A lease on a new storage facility is scheduled to begin on September 2, 2014. Monthly payments are $5,000.

i.   The company has a policy to maintain a minimum cash balance of $10,000. If necessary, it will borrow to meet its short-term needs. All borrowing is done at the beginning of the month. All payments on principal and interest are made at the end of a month. The annual interest rate is 9%. The company must borrow in multiples of $1,000.

j.   A partially completed balance sheet as of June 30, 2014, follows. (*Note:* Accounts payable is for inventory purchases only.)

| | | | |
|---|---|---|---|
| Cash | $    ? | | |
| Accounts receivable | ? | | |
| Inventory | ? | | |
| Plant and equipment, net | 425,000 | | |
| Accounts payable | | $    ? | |
| Common stock | | 210,000 | |
| Retained earnings | | 268,750 | |
| Total | $    ? | $    ? | |

**Required:**

1.   Complete the balance sheet given in Item j.

2.   Prepare a cash budget for each month in the third quarter and for the quarter in total (the third quarter begins on July 1). Prepare a supporting schedule of cash collections.

3.   Prepare a pro forma balance sheet as of September 30, 2014.

4.   **CONCEPTUAL CONNECTION** Form a group with two or three other students. Discuss why a bank might require a cash budget for businesses that are seeking short-term loans. Determine what other financial reports might be useful for a loan decision. Also, discuss how the reliability of cash budgets and other financial information can be determined.

OBJECTIVE ① ④   **Problem 9-49   Participative Budgeting, Not-for-Profit Setting**

Dwight D. Eisenhower was the 34th president of the United States and the Supreme Commander of the Allied Forces during World War II. Much of his army career was spent in planning. He once said that "planning is everything; the plan is nothing."

**Required:**

CONCEPTUAL CONNECTION What do you think he meant by this? Consider his comment with respect to the master budget. Do you agree or disagree? Be sure to include the impact of the master budget on planning and control.

OBJECTIVE ③   **Problem 9-50   Cash Budget**

The controller of Feinberg Company is gathering data to prepare the cash budget for July. He plans to develop the budget from the following information:

a.  Of all sales, 40% are cash sales.
b.  Of credit sales, 45% are collected within the month of sale. Half of the credit sales collected within the month receive a 2% cash discount (for accounts paid within 10 days). Thirty percent of credit sales are collected in the following month; remaining credit sales are collected the month thereafter. There are virtually no bad debts.
c.  Sales for the second two quarters of the year follow. (*Note:* The first three months are actual sales, and the last three months are estimated sales.)

| | Sales |
|---|---|
| April | $ 450,000 |
| May | 580,000 |
| June | 900,000 |
| July | 1,140,000 |
| August | 1,200,000 |
| September | 1,134,000 |

d.  The company sells all that it produces each month. The cost of raw materials equals 26% of each sales dollar. The company requires a monthly ending inventory of raw materials equal to the coming month's production requirements. Of raw materials purchases, 50% are paid for in the month of purchase. The remaining 50% is paid for in the following month.
e.  Wages total $105,000 each month and are paid in the month incurred.
f.  Budgeted monthly operating expenses total $376,000, of which $45,000 is depreciation and $6,000 is expiration of prepaid insurance (the annual premium of $72,000 is paid on January 1).
g.  Dividends of $130,000, declared on June 30, will be paid on July 15.
h.  Old equipment will be sold for $25,200 on July 4.
i.  On July 13, new equipment will be purchased for $173,000.
j.  The company maintains a minimum cash balance of $20,000.
k.  The cash balance on July 1 is $27,000.

**Required:**

Prepare a cash budget for July. Give a supporting schedule that details the cash collections from sales.

OBJECTIVE ① ② ③   **Problem 9-51   Understanding Relationships, Master Budget, Comprehensive Review**

Optima Company is a high-technology organization that produces a mass-storage system. The design of Optima's system is unique and represents a breakthrough in the industry. The units Optima produces combine positive features of both compact and hard disks. The company is completing its fifth year of operations and is preparing to build its master budget for the coming year (2014). The budget will detail each quarter's activity and the activity for the year in total. The master budget will be based on the following information:

a.  Fourth-quarter sales for 2013 are 55,000 units.
b.  Unit sales by quarter (for 2014) are projected as follows:

| First quarter | 65,000 |
|---|---|
| Second quarter | 70,000 |
| Third quarter | 75,000 |
| Fourth quarter | 90,000 |

The selling price is $400 per unit. All sales are credit sales. Optima collects 85% of all sales within the quarter in which they are realized; the other 15% is collected in the following quarter. There are no bad debts.

c.  There is no beginning inventory of finished goods. Optima is planning the following ending finished goods inventories for each quarter:

| First quarter | 13,000 units |
|---|---|
| Second quarter | 15,000 units |
| Third quarter | 20,000 units |
| Fourth quarter | 10,000 units |

d.  Each mass-storage unit uses five hours of direct labor and three units of direct materials. Laborers are paid $10 per hour, and one unit of direct materials costs $80.

e.  There are 65,700 units of direct materials in beginning inventory as of January 1, 2014. At the end of each quarter, Optima plans to have 30% of the direct materials needed for next quarter's unit sales. Optima will end the year with the same amount of direct materials found in this year's beginning inventory.

f.  Optima buys direct materials on account. Half of the purchases are paid for in the quarter of acquisition, and the remaining half are paid for in the following quarter. Wages and salaries are paid on the 15th and 30th of each month.

g.  Fixed overhead totals $1 million each quarter. Of this total, $350,000 represents depreciation. All other fixed expenses are paid for in cash in the quarter incurred. The fixed overhead rate is computed by dividing the year's total fixed overhead by the year's budgeted production in units.

h.  Variable overhead is budgeted at $6 per direct labor hour. All variable overhead expenses are paid for in the quarter incurred.

i.  Fixed selling and administrative expenses total $250,000 per quarter, including $50,000 depreciation.

j.  Variable selling and administrative expenses are budgeted at $10 per unit sold. All selling and administrative expenses are paid for in the quarter incurred.

k.  The balance sheet as of December 31, 2013, is as follows:

| Assets | |
|---|---|
| Cash | $    250,000 |
| Direct materials inventory | 5,256,000 |
| Accounts receivable | 3,300,000 |
| Plant and equipment, net | 33,500,000 |
| Total assets | $42,306,000 |

| Liabilities and Stockholders' Equity | |
|---|---|
| Accounts payable | $  7,248,000* |
| Capital stock | 27,000,000 |
| Retained earnings | 8,058,000 |
| Total liabilities and stockholders' equity | $42,306,000 |

\* For purchase of direct materials only.

l.  Optima will pay quarterly dividends of $300,000. At the end of the fourth quarter, $2 million of equipment will be purchased.

*(Continued)*

**Required:**

Prepare a master budget for Optima Company for each quarter of 2014 and for the year in total. The following component budgets must be included:

1. Sales budget
2. Production budget
3. Direct materials purchases budget
4. Direct labor budget
5. Overhead budget
6. Selling and administrative expenses budget
7. Ending finished goods inventory budget
8. Cost of goods sold budget (*Note:* Assume that there is no change in work-in-process inventories.)
9. Cash budget
10. Pro forma income statement (using absorption costing) (*Note:* Ignore income taxes.)
11. Pro forma balance sheet (*Note:* Ignore income taxes.)

OBJECTIVE **2**      **Problem 9-52    Direct Materials and Direct Labor Budgets**

Willison Company produces stuffed toy animals; one of these is Betty Rabbit. Each rabbit takes 0.2 yards of fabric and six ounces of polyfiberfill. Fabric costs $3.50 per yard, and polyfiberfill is $0.05 per ounce. Willison has budgeted production of stuffed rabbits for the next four months as follows:

|  | Units |
|---|---|
| October | 20,000 |
| November | 40,000 |
| December | 25,000 |
| January | 30,000 |

Inventory policy requires that sufficient fabric be in ending monthly inventory to satisfy 15% of the following month's production needs and sufficient polyfiberfill be in inventory to satisfy 30% of the following month's production needs. Inventory of fabric and polyfiberfill at the beginning of October equals exactly the amount needed to satisfy the inventory policy.

Each rabbit produced requires (on average) 0.10 direct labor per hour. The average cost of direct labor is $15.50 per hour.

**Required:**

1. Prepare a direct materials purchases budget of fabric for the last quarter of the year, showing purchases in units and in dollars for each month and for the quarter in total.
2. Prepare a direct materials purchases budget of polyfiberfill for the last quarter of the year, showing purchases in units and in dollars for each month and for the quarter in total.
3. Prepare a direct labor budget for the last quarter of the year, showing the hours needed and the direct labor cost for each month and for the quarter in total.

OBJECTIVE **3**      **Problem 9-53    Cash Budgeting**

Jordana Krull owns The Eatery in Miami, Florida. The Eatery is an affordable restaurant located near tourist attractions. Jordana accepts cash and checks. Checks are deposited immediately. The bank charges $0.50 per check; the amount per check averages $65. Bad checks that Jordana cannot collect make up 2% of check revenue.

During a typical month, The Eatery has sales of $75,000. About 75% are cash sales. Estimated sales for the next three months are as follows:

| July | $60,000 |
|---|---|
| August | 75,000 |
| September | 80,000 |

Jordana thinks that it may be time to refuse to accept checks and to start accepting credit cards. She is negotiating with a credit card processing service that will allow her to accept all major credit cards. She would start the new policy on July 1. Jordana estimates that with the drop in sales from the no-checks policy and the increase in sales from the acceptance of credit cards, the net increase in sales will be 20%. The credit card processing service will charge no setup fee, however the following fees and conditions apply:

- Monthly gateway and statement fee totaling $19, paid on the first day of the month.
- Discount fee of 2% of the total sale. This is not paid separately, instead, the amount that Jordana receives from each credit sale is reduced by 2%. For example, on a credit card sale of $150, the processing company would take $3 and remit a net amount of $147 to Jordana's account.
- Transaction fee of $0.25 per transaction paid at the time of the transaction.

There will be a two-day delay between the date of the transaction and the date on which the net amount will be deposited into Jordana's account. On average, 94% of a month's net credit card sales will be deposited into her account that month. The remaining 6% will be deposited the next month.

If Jordana adds credit cards, she believes that cash sales will average just 5% of total sales, and that the average credit card transaction will be $50.

**Required:**

1. Prepare a schedule of cash receipts for August and September under the current policy of accepting checks.
2. Assuming that Jordana decides to accept credit cards,
   a. Calculate revised total sales, cash sales, and credit card sales by month for August and September.
   b. Calculate the total estimated credit card transactions for August and September.
3. Prepare a schedule of cash receipts for August and September that incorporates the changes in policy.

# CASES

### Case 9-54   Budgeting in the Government Sector, Internet Research

OBJECTIVE

Similar to companies, the U.S. government must prepare a budget each year. However, unlike private, for-profit companies, the budget and its details are available to the public. The entire budgetary process is established by law. The government makes available a considerable amount of information concerning the federal budget. Most of this information can be found on the Internet. Using Internet resources (e.g., consider accessing the Office of Management and Budget at www.whitehouse.gov/omb), answer the following questions:

**Required:**

1. When is the federal budget prepared?
2. Who is responsible for preparing the federal budget?
3. How is the final federal budget determined? Explain in detail how the government creates its budget.
4. What percentage of the gross domestic product (GDP) is represented by the federal budget?
5. What are the revenue sources for the federal budget? Indicate the percentage contribution of each of the major sources.
6. How does U.S. spending as a percentage of GDP compare with spending of other countries?
7. How are deficits financed?

OBJECTIVE

### Case 9-55   **Cash Budget**

Dr. Roger Jones is a successful dentist but is experiencing recurring financial difficulties. For example, Jones owns his office building, which he leased to the professional corporation that housed his dental practice (he owns all shares in the corporation). After the corporation's failure to pay payroll taxes for the past six months, however, the Internal Revenue Service is threatening to impound the business and sell its assets. Also, the corporation has had difficulty paying its suppliers, owing one of them over $200,000 plus interest. In the past, Jones had borrowed money on the equity in either his personal residence or his office building, but he has grown weary of these recurring problems and has hired a local consultant for advice.

According to the consultant, the financial difficulties facing Jones have been caused by the absence of proper planning and control. Budgetary control is sorely needed. The following financial information is available for a typical month:

| **Revenues** | | |
| --- | --- | --- |
| | **Average Fee ($)** | **Quantity** |
| Fillings | 50 | 90 |
| Crowns | 300 | 19 |
| Root canals | 170 | 8 |
| Bridges | 500 | 7 |
| Extractions | 45 | 30 |
| Cleaning | 25 | 108 |
| X-rays | 15 | 150 |

| **Costs** | | |
| --- | --- | --- |
| Salaries: | | |
| Two dental assistants | $1,900 | |
| Receptionist/bookkeeper | 1,500 | |
| Hygienist | 1,800 | |
| Public relations (Mrs. Jones) | 1,000 | |
| Personal salary | 6,500 | |
| Total salaries | | $12,700 |
| Benefits | | 1,344 |
| Building lease | | 1,500 |
| Dental supplies | | 1,200 |
| Janitorial | | 300 |
| Utilities | | 400 |
| Phone | | 150 |
| Office supplies | | 100 |
| Lab fees | | 5,000 |
| Loan payments | | 570 |
| Interest payments | | 500 |
| Miscellaneous | | 200 |
| Depreciation | | 700 |
| Total costs | | $24,964 |

Benefits include Jones's share of social security and a health insurance premium for all employees. Although all revenues billed in a month are not collected, the cash flowing into the business is approximately equal to the month's billings because of collections from prior months. The office is open Monday through Thursday from 9:00 A.M. to 4:00 P.M. and on Friday from 9:00 A.M. to 12:30 P.M. A total of 32 hours are worked each week. Additional hours could be worked, but Jones is reluctant to do so because of other personal endeavors that he enjoys.

Jones has noted that the two dental assistants and receptionist are not fully utilized. He estimates that they are busy about 65 to 70% of the time. Jones's wife spends about 5 hours each week on a monthly newsletter that is sent to all patients. She also maintains a birthday list and sends cards to patients on their birthdays.

Jones recently attended an informational seminar designed to teach dentists how to increase their revenues. An idea from that seminar persuaded Jones to invest in promotion and public relations (the newsletter and the birthday list).

**Required:**

1. Prepare a monthly cash budget for Dr. Jones.
2. Using the cash budget prepared in Requirement 1 and the information given in the case, recommend actions to solve Dr. Jones's financial problems. Prepare a cash budget that reflects these recommendations and demonstrates to Jones that the problems can be corrected. Do you think that Jones will accept your recommendations? Do any of the behavioral principles discussed in the chapter have a role in this type of setting? Explain.

### Case 9-56 Budgetary Performance, Rewards, Ethical Behavior

OBJECTIVE  1 4

Linda Ellis, division manager, is evaluated and rewarded on the basis of budgetary performance. Linda, her assistants, and the plant managers are all eligible to receive a bonus if actual divisional profits are between budgeted profits and 120% of budgeted profits. The bonuses are based on a fixed percentage of actual profits. Profits above 120% of budgeted profits earn a bonus at the 120% level (in other words, there is an upper limit on possible bonus payments). If the actual profits are less than budgeted profits, no bonuses are awarded. Consider the following actions taken by Linda:

a. Linda tends to overestimate expenses and underestimate revenues. This approach facilitates the ability of the division to attain budgeted profits. Linda believes that the action is justified because it increases the likelihood of receiving bonuses and helps to keep the morale of the managers high.
b. Suppose that toward the end of the fiscal year, Linda saw that the division would not achieve budgeted profits. Accordingly, she instructed the sales department to defer the closing of a number of sales agreements to the following fiscal year. She also decided to write off some inventory that was nearly worthless. Deferring revenues to next year and writing off the inventory in a no-bonus year increased the chances of a bonus for next year.
c. Assume that toward the end of the year, Linda saw that actual profits would likely exceed the 120% limit and that she took actions similar to those described in Item b.

**Required:**

1. Comment on the ethics of Linda's behavior. Are her actions right or wrong? What role does the company play in encouraging her actions?
2. Suppose that you are the marketing manager for the division, and you receive instructions to defer the closing of sales until the next fiscal year. What would you do?
3. Suppose that you are a plant manager, and you know that your budget has been padded by the division manager. Further, suppose that the padding is common knowledge among the plant managers, who support it because it increases the ability to achieve the budget and receive a bonus. What would you do?
4. Suppose that you are the division controller, and you receive instructions from the division manager to accelerate the recognition of some expenses that legitimately belong to a future period. What would you do?

# 10

# Standard Costing: A Managerial Control Tool

© Pixelfabrik/Alamy

After studying Chapter 10, you should be able to:

1. Explain how unit standards are set and why standard cost systems are adopted.

2. Explain the purpose of a standard cost sheet.

3. Describe the basic concepts underlying variance analysis, and explain when variances should be investigated.

4. Compute the materials variances, and explain how they are used for control.

5. Compute the labor variances, and explain how they are used for control.

6. (Appendix 10A) Prepare journal entries for materials and labor variances.

Radius Images/Jupiterimages

**Required:**

1. **CONCEPTUAL CONNECTION** Why did Tom Rich purchase the large quantity of raw materials? Do you think that this behavior was the objective of the price standard? If not, what is the objective(s)?

2. **CONCEPTUAL CONNECTION** Suppose that Tom is right and that the only way to meet the price standards is through the use of quantity discounts. Also, assume that using quantity discounts is not a desirable practice for this company. What would you do to solve this dilemma?

3. **CONCEPTUAL CONNECTION** Should Tom be fired? Explain.

---

*Use the following information for Exercises 10-35 and 10-36:*

Deporte Company produces single-colored t-shirts. Materials for the shirts are dyed in large vats. After dying the materials for a given color, the vats must be cleaned and prepared for the next batch of materials to be colored. The following standards for changeover for a given batch have been established:

| | |
|---|---|
| Direct materials (2.4 lbs. @ $0.95) | $2.28 |
| Direct labor (0.75 hr. @ $7.40) | 5.55 |
| Standard prime cost | $7.83 |

During the year, 79,500 pounds of material were purchased and used for the changeover activity. There were 30,000 batches produced, with the following actual prime costs:

| | |
|---|---|
| Direct materials | $ 63,000 |
| Direct labor | $163,385 (for 22,450 hrs.) |

---

## Exercise 10-35  Materials and Labor Variances

OBJECTIVE **4** **5**

Refer to the information for Deporte Company above.

**Required:**

Compute the materials and labor variances associated with the changeover activity, labeling each variance as favorable or unfavorable.

## Exercise 10-36  *(Appendix 10A)* Journal Entries

OBJECTIVE **6**

Refer to the information for Deporte Company above.

**Required:**

1. Prepare a journal entry for the purchase of raw materials.
2. Prepare a journal entry for the issuance of raw materials.
3. Prepare a journal entry for the addition of labor to Work in Process.
4. Prepare a journal entry for the closing of variances to Cost of Goods Sold.

## Exercise 10-37  *(Appendix 10A)* Materials Variances, Journal Entries

OBJECTIVE **4** **6**

Esteban Products produces instructional aids, including white boards, which use colored markers instead of chalk. These are particularly popular for conference rooms in educational institutions and executive offices of large corporations. The standard cost of materials for this product is 12 pounds at $8.25 per pound.

During the first month of the year, 3,200 boards were produced. Information concerning actual costs and usage of materials follows:

| | |
|---|---|
| Materials purchased | 38,000 lbs. @ $8.35 |
| Materials used | 37,500 lbs. |

*(Continued)*

**Required:**

1. Compute the materials price and usage variances.
2. Prepare journal entries for all activity relating to materials.

OBJECTIVE ❺ ❻

### Exercise 10-38   *(Appendix 10A)* Labor Variances, Journal Entries

Escuchar Products, a producer of DVD players, has established a labor standard for its product—direct labor: 2 hrs at $9.65 per hour. During January, Escuchar produced 12,800 DVD players. The actual direct labor used was 25,040 hours at a total cost of $245,392.

**Required:**

1. Compute the labor rate and efficiency variances.
2. Prepare journal entries for all activities relating to labor.

# PROBLEMS

OBJECTIVE ❶

### Problem 10-39   Setting Standards and Assigning Responsibility

Cabanarama Inc. designs and manufactures easy-to-set-up beach cabanas that families can set up for picnicking, protection from the sun, and so on. The cabanas come in a kit that includes canvas, lacing, and aluminum support poles. Cabanarama has expanded rapidly from a two-person operation to one involving over a hundred employees. Cabanarama's founder and owner, Frank Love, understands that a more formal approach to standard setting and control is needed to ensure that the consistent quality for which the company is known continues.

Frank and Annette Wilson, his financial vice president, divided the company into departments and designated each department as a cost center. Sales, Quality Control, and Design report directly to Frank. Production, Shipping, Finance, and Accounting report to Annette. In the production department, one of the supervisors was assigned the materials purchasing function. The job included purchasing all raw materials, overseeing inventory handling (receiving, storage, etc.), and tracking materials purchases and use.

Frank felt that control would be better achieved if there were a way for his employees to continue to perform in such a way that quality was maintained and cost reduction was achieved. Annette suggested that Cabanarama institute a standard costing system. Variances for materials and labor could then be calculated and reported directly to her, and she could alert Frank to any problems or opportunities for improvement.

**Required:**

1.  a. **CONCEPTUAL CONNECTION** When Annette designs the standard costing system for Cabanarama, who should be involved in setting the standards for each cost component?

    b. **CONCEPTUAL CONNECTION** What factors should be considered in establishing the standards for each cost component?

2. **CONCEPTUAL CONNECTION** Assume that Cabanarama develops the standards for materials use, materials price, labor use, and labor wages. Who will be assigned responsibility for each and for any resulting variances? Why?

OBJECTIVE ❸❹❺

### Problem 10-40   Basics of Variance Analysis, Variable Inputs

Basuras Waste Disposal Company has a long-term contract with several large cities to collect garbage and trash from residential customers. To facilitate the collection, Basuras places a large plastic container with each household. Because of wear and tear, growth, and other factors, Basuras places about 200,000 new containers each year (about 20% of the total households). Several years ago, Basuras decided to manufacture its own containers as a cost-saving measure. A strategically located plant involved in this type of manufacturing was acquired. To help ensure cost efficiency, a standard cost system was installed in the plant. The following standards have been established for the product's variable inputs:

| | Standard Quantity | Standard Price (rate in $) | Standard Cost |
|---|---|---|---|
| Direct materials | 12 lbs. | $ 3.50 | $42.00 |
| Direct labor | 1.70 hrs. | 11.00 | 18.70 |
| Variable overhead | 1.70 hrs. | 3.00 | 5.10 |
| Total | | | $65.80 |

During the first week in January, Basuras had the following actual results:

| | |
|---|---|
| Units produced | 6,000 |
| Actual labor costs | $118,800 |
| Actual labor hours | 10,800 |
| Materials purchased and used | 69,000 lbs. @ $3.55 |
| Actual variable overhead costs | $ 39,750 |

The purchasing agent located a new source of slightly higher-quality plastic, and this material was used during the first week in January. Also, a new manufacturing process was implemented on a trial basis. The new process required a slightly higher level of skilled labor. The higher-quality material has no effect on labor utilization. However, the new manufacturing process was expected to reduce materials usage by 0.25 pound per container.

**Required:**

1. **CONCEPTUAL CONNECTION** Compute the materials price and usage variances. Assume that the 0.25 pound per container reduction of materials occurred as expected and that the remaining effects are all attributable to the higher-quality material. Would you recommend that the purchasing agent continue to buy this quality, or should the usual quality be purchased? Assume that the quality of the end product is not affected significantly.

2. **CONCEPTUAL CONNECTION** Compute the labor rate and efficiency variances. Assuming that the labor variances are attributable to the new manufacturing process, should it be continued or discontinued? In answering, consider the new process's materials reduction effect as well. Explain.

3. **CONCEPTUAL CONNECTION** Refer to Requirement 2. Suppose that the industrial engineer argued that the new process should not be evaluated after only one week. His reasoning was that it would take at least a week for the workers to become efficient with the new approach. Suppose that the production is the same the second week and that the actual labor hours were 9,000 and the labor cost was $99,000. Should the new process be adopted? Assume the variances are attributable to the new process. Assuming production of 6,000 units per week, what would be the projected annual savings? (Include the materials reduction effect.)

**Problem 10-41  Setting Standards, Materials and Labor Variances**          OBJECTIVE ❶ ❹ ❺

Tom Belford and Tony Sorrentino own a small business devoted to kitchen and bath granite installations. Recently, building contractors have insisted on up-front bid prices for a house rather than the cost-plus system that Tom and Tony were used to. They worry because natural flaws in the granite make it impossible to tell in advance exactly how much granite will be used on a particular job. In addition, granite can be easily broken, meaning that Tom or Tony could ruin a slab and would need to start over with a new one. Sometimes the improperly cut pieces could be used for smaller installations, sometimes not. All their accounting is done by a local certified public accounting firm headed by Charlene Davenport. Charlene listened to their concerns and suggested that it might be time to implement tighter controls by setting up a standard costing system.

*(Continued)*

Charlene reviewed the invoices pertaining to a number of Tom and Tony's previous jobs to determine the average amount of granite and glue needed per square foot. She then updated prices on both materials to reflect current conditions. The standards she developed for one square foot of counter installed were as follows:

| | |
|---|---:|
| Granite, per square foot | $50.00 |
| Glue (10 oz. @ $0.15) | 1.50 |
| Direct labor hours: | |
|    Cutting labor (0.10 hr. @ $15) | 1.50 |
|    Installation labor (0.25 hr. @ $25) | 6.25 |

These standards assumed that one seamless counter requires one sink cut (the space into which the sink will fit) as well as cutting the counter to fit the space available.

Charlene tracked the actual costs incurred by Tom and Tony for granite installation for the next six months. She found that they completed 50 jobs with an average of 32 square feet of granite installed in each one. The following information on actual amounts used and cost was gathered:

| | |
|---|---:|
| Granite purchased and used (1,640 sq. ft.) | $79,048 |
| Glue purchased and used (16,000 oz.) | $ 2,560 |
| Actual hours cutting labor | 180 |
| Actual hours installation labor | 390 |

The actual wage rate for cutting and installation labor remained unchanged from the standard rate.

**Required:**

1. Calculate the materials price variances and materials usage variances for granite and for glue for the past six months.
2. Calculate the labor rate variances and labor efficiency variances for cutting labor and for installation labor for the past six months.
3. **CONCEPTUAL CONNECTION** Would it be worthwhile for Charlene to establish standards for atypical jobs (such as those with more than one sink cut or wider than normal)?

OBJECTIVE  **Problem 10-42    Setting a Direct Labor Standard, Learning Curve Effects, Service Company**

Mantenga Company provides routine maintenance services for heavy moving and transportation vehicles. Although the vehicles vary, the maintenance services provided follow a fairly standard pattern. Recently, a potential customer has approached the company, requesting a new maintenance service for a radically different type of vehicle. New servicing equipment and some new labor skills will be needed to provide the maintenance service. The customer is placing an initial order to service 150 vehicles and has indicated that if the service is satisfactory, several additional orders of the same size will be placed every three months over the next 3 to 5 years.

Mantenga uses a standard costing system and wants to develop a set of standards for the new vehicle. The usage standards for direct materials such as oil, lubricants, and transmission fluids were easily established. The usage standard is 25 quarts per servicing, with a standard cost of $4 per quart. Management has also decided on standard rates for labor and overhead: The standard labor rate is $15 per direct labor hour, the standard variable overhead rate is $8 per direct labor hour, and the standard fixed overhead rate is $12 per direct labor hour. The only remaining decision is the standard for labor usage. To assist in developing this standard, the engineering department has estimated the following relationship between units serviced and average direct labor hours used:

| Units Serviced | Cumulative Average Time per Unit (hours) |
|:---:|:---:|
| 40 | 2.500 |
| 80 | 2.000 |
| 160 | 1.600 |
| 320 | 1.280 |
| 640 | 1.024 |

As the workers learn more about servicing the new vehicles, they become more efficient, and the average time needed to service one unit declines. Engineering estimates that all of the learning effects will be achieved by the time that 320 units are produced. No further improvement will be realized past this level.

**Required:**

1. Assume that the average labor time is 0.768 hour per unit after the learning effects are achieved. Using this information, prepare a standard cost sheet that details the standard service cost per unit. (*Note:* Round costs to two decimal places.)
2. **CONCEPTUAL CONNECTION** Given the per-unit labor standard set, would you expect a favorable or an unfavorable labor efficiency? Explain. Calculate the labor efficiency variance for servicing the first 320 units.
3. **CONCEPTUAL CONNECTION** Assuming no further improvement in labor time per unit is possible past 320 units, explain why the cumulative average time per unit at 640 is lower than the time at 320 units. Show that the standard labor time should be 0.768 hour per unit. Explain why this value is a good choice for the per-unit labor standard.

**Problem 10-43  Unit Costs, Multiple Products, Variance Analysis, Service Setting**   OBJECTIVE ❷ ❹ ❺

The maternity wing of the city hospital has two types of patients: normal and cesarean. The standard quantities of labor and materials per delivery for 2013 are:

|  | Normal | Cesarean |
|---|:---:|:---:|
| Direct materials (lbs.) | 9.0 | 21 |
| Nursing labor (hrs.) | 2.5 | 5 |

The standard price paid per pound of direct materials is $10. The standard rate for labor is $16. Overhead is applied on the basis of direct labor hours. The variable overhead rate for maternity is $30 per hour, and the fixed overhead rate is $40 per hour.

Actual operating data for 2013 are as follows:

a. Deliveries produced: normal, 4,000; cesarean, 8,000.
b. Direct materials purchased and used: 200,000 pounds at $9.50—35,000 for normal maternity patients and 165,000 for the cesarean patients; no beginning or ending raw materials inventories.
c. Nursing labor: 50,700 hours—10,200 hours for normal patients and 40,500 hours for the cesarean; total cost of labor, $580,350.

**Required:**

1. Prepare a standard cost sheet showing the unit cost per delivery for each type of patient.
2. Compute the materials price and usage variances for each type of patient.
3. Compute the labor rate and efficiency variances for each type of patient.
4. **CONCEPTUAL CONNECTION** Assume that you know only the total direct materials used for both products and the total direct labor hours used for both products. Can you compute the total materials usage and labor efficiency variances? Explain.
5. **CONCEPTUAL CONNECTION** Standard costing concepts have been applied in the health-care industry. For example, diagnostic-related groups (DRGs) are used for prospective payments for Medicare patients. Select a search engine (such as Yahoo! or Google), and

(Continued)

conduct a search to see what information you can obtain about DRGs. You might try "Medicare DRGs" as a possible search topic. Write a memo that answers the following questions:

a. What is a DRG?
b. How are DRGs established?
c. How many DRGs are used?
d. How does the DRG concept relate to standard costing concepts discussed in the chapter? Can hospitals use DRGs to control their costs? Explain.

OBJECTIVE ③④⑤    **Problem 10-44   Control Limits, Variance Investigation**

Buenolorl Company produces a well-known cologne. The standard manufacturing cost of the cologne is described by the following standard cost sheet:

| Direct materials: | |
|---|---|
| Liquids (4.5 oz. @ $0.40) | $1.80 |
| Bottles (1 @ $0.05) | 0.05 |
| Direct labor (0.2 hr. @ $15.00) | 3.00 |
| Variable overhead (0.2 hr. @ $5.00) | 1.00 |
| Fixed overhead (0.2 hr. @ $1.50) | 0.30 |
| Standard cost per unit | $6.15 |

Management has decided to investigate only those variances that exceed the lesser of 10% of the standard cost for each category or $20,000.

During the past quarter, 250,000 four-ounce bottles of cologne were produced. Descriptions of actual activity for the quarter follow:

a. A total of 1.35 million ounces of liquids was purchased, mixed, and processed. Evaporation was higher than expected (no inventories of liquids are maintained). The price paid per ounce averaged $0.42.
b. Exactly 250,000 bottles were used. The price paid for each bottle was $0.048.
c. Direct labor hours totaled 48,250, with a total cost of $733,000.

Normal production volume for Buenolorl is 250,000 bottles per quarter. The standard overhead rates are computed by using normal volume. All overhead costs are incurred uniformly throughout the year. (*Note:* Round unit costs to the nearest cent and total amounts to the nearest dollar.)

**Required:**

1. Calculate the upper and lower control limits for materials and labor.
2. Compute the total materials variance, and break it into price and usage variances. Would these variances be investigated?
3. Compute the total labor variance, and break it into rate and efficiency variances. Would these variances be investigated?

OBJECTIVE ③④⑤    **Problem 10-45   Control Limits, Variance Investigation**

The management of Golding Company has determined that the cost to investigate a variance produced by its standard cost system ranges from $2,000 to $3,000. If a problem is discovered, the average benefit from taking corrective action usually outweighs the cost of investigation. Past experience from the investigation of variances has revealed that corrective action is rarely needed for deviations within 8% of the standard cost. Golding produces a single product, which has the following standards for materials and labor:

| Direct materials (8 lbs. @ $0.25) | $2 |
|---|---|
| Direct labor (0.4 hr. @ $7.50) | 3 |

Actual production for the past three months with the associated actual usage and costs for materials and labor follow. There were no beginning or ending raw materials inventories.

|                      | April     | May       | June      |
|----------------------|-----------|-----------|-----------|
| Production (units)   | 90,000    | 100,000   | 110,000   |
| Direct materials:    |           |           |           |
| Cost                 | $189,000  | $218,000  | $230,000  |
| Usage (lbs.)         | 723,000   | 870,000   | 885,000   |
| Direct labor:        |           |           |           |
| Cost                 | $270,000  | $323,000  | $360,000  |
| Usage (hrs.)         | 36,000    | 44,000    | 46,000    |

**Required:**

1. What upper and lower control limits would you use for materials variances? For labor variances?
2. Compute the materials and labor variances for April, May, and June. Identify those that would require investigation by comparing each variance to the amount of the limit computed in part 1. Compute the actual percentage deviation from standard. Round all unit costs to four decimal places. Round variances to the nearest dollar. Round variance rates to three decimal places so that percentages will show to one decimal place.
3. **CONCEPTUAL CONNECTION** Let the horizontal axis be time and the vertical axis be variances measured as a percentage deviation from standard. Draw horizontal lines that identify upper and lower control limits. Plot the labor and material variances for April, May, and June. Prepare a separate graph for each type of variance. Explain how you would use these graphs (called *control charts*) to assist your analysis of variances.

## Problem 10-46   Standard Costing, Planned Variances

OBJECTIVE ② ④ ⑤

Phono Company manufactures a plastic toy cell phone. The following standards have been established for the toy's materials and labor inputs:

|                  | Standard Quantity | Standard Price (rate in $) | Standard Cost |
|------------------|-------------------|----------------------------|---------------|
| Direct materials | 0.5 lb.           | $ 1.50                     | $0.75         |
| Direct labor     | 0.15 hr.          | 10.00                      | 1.50          |

During the first week of July, the company had the following results:

| Units produced            | 90,000                    |
|---------------------------|---------------------------|
| Actual labor costs        | $138,000                  |
| Actual labor hours        | 13,400                    |
| Materials purchased and used | 44,250 lbs. @ $1.55 per lb |

*Other information:* The purchasing agent located a new source of slightly higher-quality plastic, and this material was used during the first week in July. Also, a new manufacturing layout was implemented on a trial basis. The new layout required a slightly higher level of skilled labor. The higher-quality material has no effect on labor utilization. Similarly, the new manufacturing approach has no effect on material usage. (*Note:* Round all variances to the nearest dollar.)

**Required:**

1. **CONCEPTUAL CONNECTION** Compute the materials price and usage variances. Assuming that the materials variances are essentially attributable to the higher quality of materials, would you recommend that the purchasing agent continue to buy this quality, or should the usual quality be purchased? Assume that the quality of the end product is not affected significantly.
2. **CONCEPTUAL CONNECTION** Compute the labor rate and efficiency variances. Assuming that the labor variances are attributable to the new manufacturing layout, should it be continued or discontinued? Explain.
3. **CONCEPTUAL CONNECTION** Refer to Requirement 2. Suppose that the industrial engineer argued that the new layout should not be evaluated after only one week. His reasoning was that it would take at least a week for the workers to become efficient with the new approach. Suppose that the production is the same the second week and that the actual

*(Continued)*

labor hours were 13,200 and the labor cost was $132,000. Should the new layout be adopted? Assume the variances are attributable to the new layout. If so, what would be the projected annual savings?

OBJECTIVE ❶❹❺

### Problem 10-47    Standard Costing

Botella Company produces plastic bottles. The unit for costing purposes is a case of 18 bottles. The following standards for producing one case of bottles have been established:

| | |
|---|---|
| Direct materials (4 lbs. @ $0.95) | $ 3.80 |
| Direct labor (1.25 hours @ $15.00) | 18.75 |
| Standard prime cost | 22.55 |

During December, 78,000 pounds of material were purchased and used in production. There were 15,000 cases produced, with the following actual prime costs:

| | |
|---|---|
| Direct materials | $ 74,000 |
| Direct labor | $315,000 (for 22,500 hrs.) |

### Required:

1. Compute the materials variances.
2. Compute the labor variances.
3. **CONCEPTUAL CONNECTION** What are the advantages and disadvantages that can result from the use of a standard costing system?

OBJECTIVE ❹❺❻

### Problem 10-48    *(Appendix 10A)* Variance Analysis, Revision of Standards, Journal Entries

The Lubbock plant of Morril's Small Motor Division produces a major subassembly for a 6.0 horsepower motor for lawn mowers. The plant uses a standard costing system for production costing and control. The standard cost sheet for the subassembly follows:

| | |
|---|---|
| Direct materials (6.0 lbs. @ $5) | $30.00 |
| Direct labor (1.6 hrs. @ $12) | 19.20 |

During the year, the Lubbock plant had the following actual production activity:

a. Production of subassemblies totaled 50,000 units.
b. A total of 260,000 pounds of raw materials was purchased at $4.70 per pound.
c. There were 60,000 pounds of raw materials in beginning inventory (carried at $5 per lb.). There was no ending inventory.
d. The company used 82,000 direct labor hours at a total cost of $1,066,000.

The Lubbock plant's practical activity is 60,000 units per year. Standard overhead rates are computed based on practical activity measured in standard direct labor hours.

### Required:

1. **CONCEPTUAL CONNECTION** Compute the materials price and usage variances. Of the two materials variances, which is viewed as the most controllable? To whom would you assign responsibility for the usage variance in this case? Explain.
2. **CONCEPTUAL CONNECTION** Compute the labor rate and efficiency variances. Who is usually responsible for the labor efficiency variance? What are some possible causes for this variance?
3. **CONCEPTUAL CONNECTION** Assume that the purchasing agent for the small motors plant purchased a lower-quality raw material from a new supplier. Would you recommend that the plant continue to use this cheaper raw material? If so, what standards would likely need revision to reflect this decision? Assume that the end product's quality is not significantly affected.
4. Prepare all possible journal entries.

# CASES

### Case 10-49   Establishment of Standards, Variance Analysis

Paul Golding and his wife, Nancy, established Crunchy Chips in 1938. Over the past 60 years, the company has established distribution channels in 11 western states, with production facilities in Utah, New Mexico, and Colorado. In 1980, Paul's son, Edward, took control of the business. By 2013, it was clear that the company's plants needed to gain better control over production costs to stay competitive. Edward hired a consultant to install a standard costing system. To help the consultant establish the necessary standards, Edward sent her the following memo:

**To:**       Diana Craig, Certified Management Accountant
**From:**    Edward Golding, President, Crunchy Chips
**Subject:** Description and Data Relating to the Production of Our Plain Potato Chips
**Date:**     September 28, 2013

The manufacturing process for potato chips begins when the potatoes are placed into a large vat in which they are automatically washed. After washing, the potatoes flow directly to an automatic peeler. The peeled potatoes then pass by inspectors, who manually cut out deep eyes or other blemishes. After inspection, the potatoes are automatically sliced and are dropped into the cooking oil. The frying process is closely monitored by an employee. After the chips are cooked, they pass under a salting device and then pass by more inspectors, who sort out the unacceptable finished chips (those that are discolored or too small). The chips then continue on the conveyor belt to a bagging machine that bags them in one-pound bags. After bagging, the bags are placed in a box and shipped. The box holds 15 bags.

The raw potato pieces (eyes and blemishes), peelings, and rejected finished chips are sold to animal feed producers for $0.16 per pound. The company uses this revenue to reduce the cost of potatoes; we would like this reflected in the price standard relating to potatoes.

Crunchy Chips purchases high-quality potatoes at a cost of $0.245 per pound. Each potato averages 4.25 ounces. Under efficient operating conditions, it takes four potatoes to produce one 16-ounce bag of plain chips. Although we label bags as containing 16 ounces, we actually place 16.3 ounces in each bag. We plan to continue this policy to ensure customer satisfaction. In addition to potatoes, other raw materials are the cooking oil, salt, bags, and boxes. Cooking oil costs $0.04 per ounce, and we use 3.3 ounces of oil per bag of chips. The cost of salt is so small that we add it to overhead. Bags cost $0.11 each and boxes $0.52 each.

Our plant produces 8.8 million bags of chips per year. A recent engineering study revealed that we would need the following direct labor hours to produce this quantity if our plant operates at peak efficiency:

| | |
|---|---|
| Raw potato inspection | 3,200 |
| Finished chip inspection | 12,000 |
| Frying monitor | 6,300 |
| Boxing | 16,600 |
| Machine operators | 6,300 |

I'm not sure that we can achieve the level of efficiency advocated by the study. In my opinion, the plant is operating efficiently for the level of output indicated if the hours allowed are about 10% higher.

The hourly labor rates agreed upon with the union are:

| | |
|---|---|
| Raw potato inspectors | $15.20 |
| Finished chip inspectors | 10.30 |
| Frying monitor | 14.00 |
| Boxing | 11.00 |
| Machine operators | 13.00 |

Overhead is applied on the basis of direct labor dollars. We have found that variable overhead averages about 116% of our direct labor cost. Our fixed overhead is budgeted at $1,135,216 for the coming year.

*(Continued)*

**Required:**

1. Discuss the benefits of a standard costing system for Crunchy Chips.
2. Discuss the president's concern about using the result of the engineering study to set the labor standards. What standard would you recommend?
3. Form a group with two or three other students. Develop a standard cost sheet for Crunchy Chips' plain potato chips.
4. Suppose that the level of production was 8.8 million bags of potato chips for the year as planned. If 9.5 million pounds of potatoes were used, compute the materials usage variance for potatoes.

OBJECTIVE

### Case 10-50    Standard Costing, Ethical Behavior, Usefulness of Costing

Pat James, the purchasing agent for a local plant of the Oakden Electronics Division, was considering the possible purchase of a component from a new supplier. The component's purchase price, $0.90, compared favorably with the standard price of $1.10. Given the quantity that would be purchased, Pat knew that the favorable price variance would help to offset an unfavorable variance for another component. By offsetting the unfavorable variance, his overall performance report would be impressive and good enough to help him qualify for the annual bonus. More importantly, a good performance rating this year would help him to secure a position at division headquarters at a significant salary increase.

Purchase of the part, however, presented Pat with a dilemma. Consistent with his past behavior, Pat made inquiries regarding the reliability of the new supplier and the part's quality. Reports were basically negative. The supplier had a reputation for making the first two or three deliveries on schedule but being unreliable from then on. Worse, the part itself was of questionable quality. The number of defective units was only slightly higher than that for other suppliers, but the life of the component was 25% less than what normal sources provided.

If the part were purchased, no problems with deliveries would surface for several months. The problem of shorter life would cause eventual customer dissatisfaction and perhaps some loss of sales, but the part would last at least 18 months after the final product began to be used. If all went well, Pat expected to be at headquarters within six months. He saw little personal risk associated with a decision to purchase the part from the new supplier. By the time any problems surfaced, they would belong to his successor. With this rationalization, Pat decided to purchase the component from the new supplier.

**Required:**

1. Do you agree with Pat's decision? Why or why not? How important was Pat's assessment of his personal risk in the decision? Should it be a factor?
2. Do you think that the use of standards and the practice of holding individuals accountable for their achievement played major roles in Pat's decision?
3. Review the discussion on corporate ethical standards in Chapter 1. Identify the standards that might apply to Pat's situation. Should every company adopt a set of ethical standards that apply to its employees, regardless of their specialty?
4. The usefulness of standard costing has been challenged in recent years. Some claim that its use is an impediment to the objective of continuous improvement (an objective that many feel is vital in today's competitive environment). Write a short paper (individually or in a small group with two or three other students) that analyzes the role and value of standard costing in today's manufacturing environment. Address the following questions:
   a. What are the major criticisms of standard costing?
   b. Will standard costing disappear, or is there still a role for it in the new manufacturing environment? If so, what is the role?
   c. Given the criticisms, can you explain why its use continues to be so prevalent? Will this use eventually change?

In preparing your paper, the following references may be useful; however, do not restrict your literature search to these references. They are simply to help you get started.

- Robin Cooper and Robert S. Kaplan, "Activity-Based Systems: Measuring the Costs of Resource Usage," *Accounting Horizons* (September 1992): 1–13.
- Forrest B. Green and Felix E. Amenkhienan, "Accounting Innovations: A Cross-Sectional Survey of Manufacturing Firms," *Journal of Cost Management* (Spring 1992): 59–64.
- Bruce R. Gaumnitz and Felix P. Kollaritsch, "Manufacturing Variances: Current Practice and Trends," *Journal of Cost Management* (Spring 1991): 59–64.
- Chris Guilding, Dane Lamminmaki, and Colin Drury, "Budgeting and Standard Costing Practices in New Zealand and the United Kingdom," *Journal of International Accounting, Vol.* 33, No. 5 (1998): 569–588.

## Cost System Choices, Budgeting, and Variance Analyses for Sacred Heart Hospital

| Chapters | Objectives | Cornerstones |
|----------|-----------|--------------|
| 7 | 7-1 | 7-2 |
| 9 | 7-2 | 7-3 |
| 10 | 7-4 | 10-1 |
| | 9-1 | 10-3 |
| | 10-1 | 10-4 |
| | 10-3 | 10-5 |
| | 10-4 | 10-6 |
| | 10-5 | |

*The purpose of this integrated exercise is to demonstrate how a change in the cost system's allocation base can result in significantly different reported costs for control purposes (e.g., the cost of various service lines), as well as significantly different budgeted costs for planning purposes (e.g., flexible budgets and variance analyses).*

## The Two Cost Systems

**Sacred Heart Hospital (SHH)** faces skyrocketing nursing costs, all of which relate to its two biggest nursing service lines—the Emergency Room (ER) and the Operating Room (OR). SHH's current cost system assigns total nursing costs to the ER and OR based on the number of patients serviced by each line. Total hospital annual nursing costs for these two lines are expected to equal $300,000. The table below shows expected patient volume for both lines.

| Measure | ER | OR | Total |
|---------|-----|-----|-------|
| Number of patients (ER visits or OR surgeries) | 1,000 | 1,000 | 2,000 |
| Number of vital signs checks | 2,000 | 4,000 | 6,000 |
| Number of nursing hours | 10,000 | 5,000 | 15,000 |

### Required:

1. Using the current cost system, calculate the hospital-wide rate based on number of patients.

2. Calculate the amount of nursing costs that the current cost system assigns to the ER and to the OR.

3. Using the results from Requirement 2, calculate the cost per OR nursing hour under the current cost system.

After discussion with several experienced nurses, Jack Bauer (SHH's accountant) decided that assigning nursing costs to the two service lines based on the number of times that nurses must check patients' vital signs might more closely match the underlying use of costly hospital resources. Therefore, for comparative purposes, Jack decided to develop a second cost system on his computer that assigns total nursing costs to the ER and OR based on the number of times nurses check patients' vital signs. This system is referred to as the "vital-signs costing system." The earlier table also shows data for vital signs checks for lines.

4. Using the vital-signs costing system, calculate the hospital-wide rate based on the number of vital signs checks.

5. Calculate the amount of nursing costs that the vital-signs costing system assigns to the ER and to the OR.

6. Using the results from Requirement 5, calculate the cost per OR nursing hour under the vital-signs costing system.

## Budgeting and Variance Analysis

In an effort to better plan for and control OR costs, SHH management asked Jack to calculate the flexible budget variance (i.e., flexible budget costs-actual costs) for OR nursing costs, including the price variance and efficiency variance that make up the flexible budget variance for OR nursing costs. Given that Jack is interested in comparing the reported costs of both systems, he decided to prepare the requested OR variance analysis for both the current cost system and the vital signs costing system. In addition, Jack chose to use each cost system's estimate of the cost per OR nursing hour as the standard cost per OR nursing hour. Jack collected the following additional information for use in preparing the flexible budget variance for both systems:

Actual number of surgeries performed = 950
Standard number of nursing hours allowed for each OR surgery = 5
Actual number of OR nursing hours used = 5,000
Actual OR nursing costs = $190,000

7. For the OR service line, use the information above and the cost per OR nursing hour under the current cost system to calculate the

   a. flexible budget variance. (*Hint:* Use your answer to Requirement 3 as the standard cost per OR nursing hour for the current cost system.)
   b. price variance.
   c. efficiency variance.

8. For the OR service line, use the information above and the cost per OR nursing hour under the vital signs cost system to calculate the

   a. flexible budget variance. (*Hint:* Use your answer to Requirement 6 as the standard cost per OR nursing hour for the vital signs cost system.)
   b. price variance.
   c. efficiency variance.

## Discussion of Reported Costs and Variances from the Two Systems

9. Consider SHH's need to control its skyrocketing costs, Jack's discussion with experienced nurses regarding their use of hospital resources, and the reported costs that you calculated from each cost system. Based on these considerations, which cost system (current or vital signs) should Jack choose? Briefly explain the reasoning behind your choice.

10. What does each of the calculated variances suggest to Jack regarding actions that he should or should not take with respect to investigating and improving each variance? Also, briefly explain why the variances differ between the two cost systems.

# 11

# Flexible Budgets and Overhead Analysis

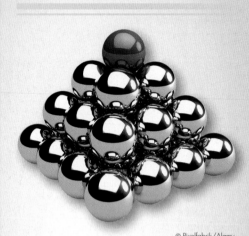

© Pixelfabrik/Alamy

After studying Chapter 11, you should be able to:

1. Prepare a flexible budget, and use it for performance reporting.

2. Calculate the variable overhead variances, and explain their meaning.

3. Calculate the fixed overhead variances, and explain their meaning.

4. Prepare an activity-based flexible budget.

# EXPERIENCE MANAGERIAL DECISIONS
## with The Second City

**The Second City** has been North America's premiere live improvisational and sketch comedy theater company for the past 50 years. Many famous stars began their careers at The Second City, including John Candy, Tina Fey, Mike Myers, Eugene Levy, and Bill Murray. More than just The Second City Television (SCTV), The Second City includes training centers, national touring companies, media and entertainment offshoots, and a corporate communication division. The Second City is an entrepreneurial organization, as evidenced most recently by its decision to provide comedy theater aboard Norwegian Cruise Line ships.

Given the nature of its businesses, The Second City is extremely dependent on overhead costs. These overhead costs must be allocated to each business to create accurate budgets, which is followed by variance analyses when actual overhead costs differ significantly from budgeted overhead costs. Its fixed overhead costs are associated with capacity and relate primarily to its home and resident stages in Chicago, Toronto, Las Vegas, Denver, and Detroit, rather than to its traveling shows. Examples of The Second City's fixed overhead costs include salaries, stage and other facilities rent, facilities maintenance,

*"Given the nature of its business, The Second City is extremely dependent on overhead costs. These overhead costs must be allocated to each business to create accurate budgets, which is followed by variance analyses when actual overhead costs differ significantly from budgeted overhead costs."*

depreciation, taxes, and insurance. These overhead costs then are assigned to individual business budgets by using allocation bases such as square footage, number of employees, and percentage of earnings. The Second City then uses overhead cost variances to "red flag" potential problems that might need managerial attention.

For example, The Second City Theatricals might have a slow year because the producers are too busy with other ventures to mount a new production, while at the same time, The Second City Training Center might have a surge in enrollment. Such a scenario likely would lead The Second City financial executives to shift some assigned overhead costs from the theatrical business to the training center business. The Second City uses flexible budgets for planning and control of its businesses that experience fluctuating volumes, such as the seasonality present in some of its traveling and cruise activities. While the managerial accountants likely do not provide too many jokes, they do provide the critical function of budgeting and examining variances for overhead costs. That allows the comic talent of The Second City to continue to do what it does best—make us laugh.

OBJECTIVE ❶

Prepare a flexible budget, and use
it for performance reporting.

# USING BUDGETS FOR PERFORMANCE EVALUATION

Budgets are useful for both planning and control, where they are used as benchmarks for performance evaluation. Determining how budgeted amounts should be compared with actual results is a major consideration that must be addressed.

## Static Budgets versus Flexible Budgets

In Chapter 9, we learned how companies prepare a master budget based on their best estimate of the level of sales and production activity for the coming year. We also discussed some behavioral issues associated with performance reporting. However, no detailed discussion was provided on how to prepare budgetary *performance reports*. A **performance report** compares actual costs with budgeted costs. There are two ways to make this comparison:

- Compare actual costs with the budgeted costs for the budgeted level of activity.
- Compare actual costs with the actual level of activity.

The first choice is a report based on *static budgets,* whereas the second choice is for a report based on *flexible budgets*. The two approaches for variance calculation are illustrated in Exhibit 11.1. Notice the relationship between the actual number of units produced (10,000) and the two types of budgets. The static budget compares actual costs for production of 10,000 units with the budgeted costs for 8,000 units. Unsurprisingly, the variance is unfavorable. The flexible budget, on the other hand, compares actual costs for production of 10,000 units with the budgeted costs for 10,000 units. This is a much more meaningful comparison.

( **EXHIBIT 11.1** )

**The Relationship between Static and Flexible Budget Variances for the Actual Quantity Produced**

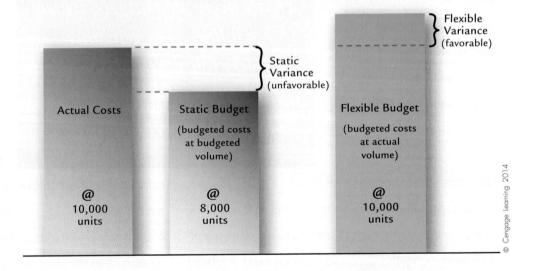

© Cengage Learning 2014

**Static Budgets and Performance Reports**  A **static budget** is a budget created in advance that is based on a particular level of activity. Master budgets are generally created for a particular level of activity. Thus, one way to prepare a performance report is to compare the actual costs with the budgeted costs from the master budget. As an example, the production of Cool-U screen-printed t-shirts will be considered. In setting up the master budget for the first quarter of the year, Cool-U expected to produce 1,060 t-shirts. When the quarter had ended, Cool-U found that it had actually produced 1,200 t-shirts. Cornerstone 11.1 shows how to prepare a performance report based on a static budget for the first quarter of operations for Cool-U's clothing manufacturing plant. For simplicity, the report only considers production costs.

## Preparing a Performance Report Based on a Static Budget (Using Budgeted Production)

CORNERSTONE

11.1

**Why:**

Managers often use this budget to compare actual with budgeted amounts.

**Information:**

| Relationships from the Master Budget | Actual Data for Quarter 1 |
|---|---|
| Budgeted production for Quarter 1: 1,060 | Production: 1,200 units |
| Materials: | |
|   1 plain t-shirt @ $3.00 | Materials cost: $4,830 |
|   5 ounces of ink @ $0.20 | |
| Labor: | |
|   0.12 hr. @ $10.00 | Labor cost: $1,500 |
| Variable overhead (*VOH*): | |
|   Maintenance: | |
|     0.12 hr. @ $3.75 | Maintenance cost: $535 |
|   Power: | |
|     0.12 hr. @ $1.25 | Power cost: $170 |
| Fixed overhead (*FOH*): | |
|   Grounds keeping: $1,200 per quarter | Grounds keeping: $1,050 |
|   Depreciation: $600 per quarter | Depreciation: $600 |

**Required:**

Prepare a performance report using a budget based on expected production.

**Solution:**

| | Actual | Budgeted | Variance |
|---|---|---|---|
| Units produced | 1,200 | 1,060 | 140 *F*[a] |
| Direct materials cost | $4,830 | $4,240[b] | $ 590 *U*[c] |
| Direct labor cost | 1,500 | 1,272[d] | 228 *U* |
| *VOH*: | | | |
|   Maintenance | 535 | 477[e] | 58 *U* |
|   Power | 170 | 159[f] | 11 *U* |
| *FOH*: | | | |
|   Grounds keeping | 1,050 | 1,200 | (150) *F* |
|   Depreciation | 600 | 600 | 0 |
| Total | $8,685 | $7,948 | $ 737 *U* |

[a] *F* means the variance is favorable.
[b] Budgeted Units (T-shirt Cost + Ink Cost) = 1,060[($3 + (5 oz. × $0.20)].
[c] *U* means the variance is unfavorable.
[d] Budgeted Units (Number of Direct Labor Hours × Cost per Hour) + 1,060(0.12 × $10.00).
[e] Budgeted Units (Number of Direct Labor Hours × Variable Maintenance Rate) = 1,060(0.12 × $3.75).
[f] Budgeted Units (Number of Direct Labor Hours × Variable Power Rate) = 1,060(0.12 × $1.25).

Why are static budgets usually not a good choice for benchmarks in preparing a performance report?

**Answer:**

The actual output may differ from the budgeted output, thus causing significant differences in cost. Comparing planned costs for one level of activity with the actual costs of a different level of activity does not provide good control information.

According to Cornerstone 11.1, there were unfavorable variances for direct materials, direct labor, maintenance, and power. However, actual costs for production of 1,200 t-shirts are being compared with planned costs for production of 1,060. Because direct materials, direct labor, and *VOH* are variable costs, they should be higher at higher production levels. Thus, even if cost control were perfect for the production of 1,200 units, unfavorable variances would be produced for at least some of the variable costs. To create a meaningful performance report, actual costs and expected costs must be compared at the *same* level of activity. Since actual output often differs from planned output, a method is needed to compute what the costs should have been for the actual output level.

**ETHICAL DECISIONS**    Companies that use static budgets as the benchmark for performance evaluation invite potential abuse by managers. Although unethical, a manager could deliberately produce less than the planned output—producing, for example, 1,000 t-shirts instead of the planned 1,060. By producing less, the actual costs will be less than the budgeted amounts, creating a favorable performance outcome. Using flexible budgeting allows the benchmark to be adjusted to reflect the expected costs for the actual level of output. ●

**Flexible Budgets**    A **flexible budget** enables a firm to compute expected costs for a range of activity levels. The key to flexible budgeting is knowledge of fixed and variable costs. The two types of flexible budgets are:

- before-the-fact, in which the budget gives expected outcomes for a range of activity levels
- after-the-fact, in which a budget is based on the actual level of activity

A before-the-fact flexible budget allows managers to generate financial results for a number of potential scenarios. The after-the-fact flexible budget is used to compute what costs should have been for the actual level of activity. Those expected costs are then compared with the actual costs in order to assess performance. Flexible budgeting is the key to providing the frequent feedback that managers need to exercise control and effectively carry out the plans of an organization.

To illustrate a before-the-fact flexible budget, suppose that the management of Cool-U wants to know the cost of producing 1,000 t-shirts, 1,200 t-shirts, and 1,400 t-shirts. To compute the expected cost for these different levels of output, managers need to know the cost behavior pattern of each item in the budget. Knowing the variable cost per unit and the total fixed costs allows the calculation of the expected costs for any level of activity within the relevant range. Cornerstone 11.2 shows how budgets can be prepared for different levels of activity, using cost formulas for each item.

## CORNERSTONE 11.2

## Preparing a Before-the-Fact Flexible Production Budget

**Why:**
This type of flexible budget allows managers to determine the effect of varying output levels on costs.

**Information:**
Levels of output: 1,000, 1,200, and 1,400.

*(Continued)*

Materials:
   1 plain t-shirt @ $3.00
   5 ounces of ink @ $0.20 per oz.:

Labor:
   0.12 hr. @ $10.00

*VOH*:
   Maintenance: 0.12 hr. @ $3.75
   Power: 0.12 hr. @ $1.25

*FOH*:
   Grounds keeping: $1,200 per quarter
   Depreciation: $600 per quarter

CORNERSTONE

**11.2**

*(Continued)*

**Required:**

Prepare a budget for three levels of output: 1,000, 1,200, and 1,400 units.

**Solution:**

| Production Costs | Variable Cost per Unit | Range of Production (units) | | |
|---|---|---|---|---|
| | | **1,000** | **1,200** | **1,400** |
| Variable: | | | | |
|   Direct materials | $4.00[a] | $4,000[b] | $4,800 | $5,600 |
|   Direct labor | 1.20[c] | 1,200[d] | 1,440 | 1,680 |
| *VOH*: | | | | |
|   Maintenance | 0.45[e] | 450[f] | 540 | 630 |
|   Power | 0.15[g] | 150[h] | 180 | 210 |
|     Total variable costs | $5.80 | $5,800 | $6,960 | $8,120 |
| *FOH*: | | | | |
|   Grounds keeping | | $1,200 | $1,200 | $1,200 |
|   Depreciation | | 600 | 600 | 600 |
|     Total fixed costs | | $1,800 | $1,800 | $1,800 |
| Total production costs | | $7,600 | $8,760 | $9,920 |

[a] T-shirt Cost + Ink Cost = [($3.00 × 1 t-shirt) × ($0.20 × 5 oz.)]
[b] ($4 × 1,000 units)
[c] ($10.00 per direct labor hour × 0.12 direct labor hours per unit)
[d] ($1.20 × 1,000 units)
[e] ($3.75 per direct labor hour × 0.12 direct labor hours per unit)
[f] ($0.45 × 1,000 units)
[g] ($1.25 per direct labor hour × 0.12 direct labor hours per unit)
[h] ($0.15 × 1,000 units)

    Cornerstone 11.2 shows that total budgeted production costs increase as the production level increases. Budgeted costs change because total variable costs go up as output increases. Because of this, flexible budgets are sometimes referred to as **variable budgets**. Since Cool-U has a mix of variable and fixed costs, the overall average cost of producing one t-shirt goes *down* as production goes *up*. This makes sense. As production increases, there are more units over which to spread the fixed production costs.

    Often, the flexible budget formulas are based on direct labor hours instead of units. This is easy to do because direct labor hours are correlated with units produced. For example, the variable cost formulas for *VOH* are $3.75 and $1.25 per direct labor hour ($5.00 per direct labor hour in total) for maintenance and power, respectively. When standard hours are used, we need to convert units into direct labor hours. For Cool-U, the production of 1,000 budgeted units means that 120 direct labor hours will be needed (0.12 direct labor hours per unit × 1,000 budgeted units).

## Here's the Real Kicker

**Stillwater Designs** has a Product Steering Committee that decides on the timing for upgrades and redesigns for its various **Kicker** speaker models. About every 4 years, a complete redesign is done for a Kicker speaker. A complete redesign takes about 16 to 18 months. A specification workshop is held that identifies features, benefits, customers, and competitors. Additionally, the costs of the new model, including the design costs (research and development), acquisition costs, freight, and duties, are estimated for various sales volumes. During this phase, the company will work closely with the manufacturers to control the design so that manufacturing costs are carefully set. A financial analysis is run over the expected life cycle of the new product (2 to 3 years) to see what the profit potential is. Thus, both expected revenues and costs for various levels of activity are assessed. This before-the-fact flexible budgeting analysis is especially important for those products with which the company has less experience. At times, a new product may be produced even if at the most likely volume the product is not expected to be profitable. The reason? The new product may complete a line or may enhance the overall image of the Kicker speakers.

Flexible budgets are powerful control tools because they allow management to compute what the costs should be for the level of *output that actually occurred*. Recall that Cool-U thought that 1,060 units would be produced, and budgeted for that amount. However, actual production was 1,200 units. It does not make sense to compare the actual costs for 1,200 t-shirts to the budgeted costs for 1,060 t-shirts. Management needs a performance report that compares actual and budgeted costs for the actual level of activity. This is the second type of flexible budget and preparation of this report is shown in Cornerstone 11.3 .

**CORNERSTONE**

**11.3**

## Preparing a Performance Report Using a Flexible Budget

**Why:**

This type of flexible budget is better than a static budget for performance evaluation. It compares actual results with the amount that would have been budgeted for the actual level of production.

**Information:**

From Cornerstones 11.1 (p. 479) and 11.2 (p. 480), the actual costs for 1,200 units and the budgeted costs for the actual level of activity are as follows:

|  | Actual Costs | Budgeted Costs |
| --- | --- | --- |
| Units produced | 1,200 | 1,200 |
| Direct materials cost | $4,830 | $4,800 |
| Direct labor cost | 1,500 | 1,440 |
| *VOH*: |  |  |
| Maintenance | 535 | 540 |
| Power | 170 | 180 |
| *FOH*: |  |  |
| Grounds keeping | 1,050 | 1,200 |
| Depreciation | 600 | 600 |

*(Continued)*

**Required:**

Prepare a performance report using budgeted costs for the actual level of activity.

**Solution:**

| | Actual | Budget | Variance |
|---|---|---|---|
| Units produced | 1,200 | 1,200 | — |
| Production costs: | | | |
|   Direct materials | $4,830 | $4,800 | $  30 U |
|   Direct labor | 1,500 | 1,440 | 60 U |
| *VOH*: | | | |
|   Maintenance | 535 | 540 | (5) F |
|   Power | 170 | 180 | (10) F |
|     Total variable costs | $7,035 | $6,960 | $  75 U |
| *FOH*: | | | |
|   Grounds keeping | $1,050 | $1,200 | $(150) F |
|   Depreciation | 600 | 600 | (0) |
|     Total fixed costs | $1,650 | $1,800 | $(150) F |
| Total production costs | $8,685 | $8,760 | $ (75) F |

The revised performance report in Cornerstone 11.3 paints a much different picture than the one in Cornerstone 11.1 (p. 479). All of the variances are fairly small. Had they been larger, management should search for the cause and try to correct the problems.

A difference between the actual amount and the flexible budget amount is the **flexible budget variance**. The flexible budget provides a measure of the efficiency of a manager. That is, how well did the manager control costs for the actual level of production? To measure whether or not a manager accomplishes his or her goals, the static budget is used. The static budget represents certain goals that the firm wants to achieve. A manager is effective if the goals described by the static budget are achieved or exceeded. In the Cool-U example, production volume was 140 units greater than the original budgeted amount; the manager exceeded the original budgeted goal. Therefore, the effectiveness of the manager is not in question.

# YOU DECIDE   Flexible Budgeting for Entertainment

You are the chief accountant for **The Second City**, the company described in the chapter opener. Your job includes budgeting for the live performances, including the national touring companies and the customized comedy shows put on by the company. (See www.secondcity.com/ for examples of the live performances.) At the beginning of each year, you must put together budgets for these performances based on projected demand for the shows and projected costs. As the year unfolds, you want to update the budgets in accordance with new information and create performance reports that compare the actual costs with projected costs.

**What information will you need to create flexible budgets for the live performances?**

You will need to consider the fixed and variable costs associated with putting on live performances away from The Second City's Chicago base. The variable costs will include travel and salary

*(Continued)*

costs for the performers, stage and facilities rent for each venue, and other variable costs associated with the shows (e.g., costs of hiring ticket sellers and ushers, supplies such as programs and tickets). Clearly, the variable costs will increase with an increase in the number of shows and venues. Some fixed costs must also be determined. These include the salaries of the writers, insurance, costs of props and costumes, costs of marketing the shows to prospective customers including corporations and regional theatres.

**Knowing the difference between the fixed and variable costs will enable you to create budgets that are useful to management in planning for the year ahead, as well as controlling costs as the year unfolds.**

OBJECTIVE

Calculate the variable overhead variances, and explain their meaning.

# VARIABLE OVERHEAD ANALYSIS

In Chapter 10, total variances for direct materials and direct labor were broken down into price and efficiency variances. In a standard cost system, the total overhead variance, or the difference between applied and actual overhead, is also broken down into component variances. There are several methods of overhead variance analysis; the four-variance method is described in this chapter. First, overhead is divided into fixed and variable categories. Next, two variances are calculated for each category.

- Variable overhead variances
  - Variable overhead spending variance
  - Variable overhead efficiency variance
- Fixed overhead variances
  - Fixed overhead spending variance
  - Fixed overhead volume variance

## Total Variable Overhead Variance

The total variable overhead variance is simply the difference between the *actual variable overhead* and *applied variable overhead*. *VOH* is applied by using hours allowed in a standard cost system. The total variable overhead variance can be divided into spending and efficiency variances. Variable overhead spending and efficiency variances can be calculated by using either the three-pronged (columnar) approach or formulas. The best approach is a matter of preference. However, the formulas first need to be expressed specifically for *VOH*.

Because the equations for variable overhead variances can be long if expressed in words, abbreviations are often used. Here are some common abbreviations that you will find in the rest of this section:

$FOH$ = Fixed Overhead

$VOH$ = Variable Overhead

$AH$ = Actual Direct Labor Hours

$SH$ = Standard Direct Labor Hours that *Should Have Been Worked* for Actual Units Produced

$AVOR$ = Actual Variable Overhead Rate

$SVOR$ = Standard Variable Overhead Rate

Cornerstone 11.4 illustrates how to calculate the total variable overhead variance using the first quarter data for Cool-U. The unit prices and quantities used for the flexible budget are assumed to be the standards associated with Cool-U's standard cost system.

## Calculating the Total Variable Overhead Variance

**Why:**

The total variable overhead variance shows managers the difference between what was actually spent on variable overhead items and what was expected to have been spent. It combines the effect of differences in the prices of overhead items and in the use of direct labor hours which are typically used to apply overhead.

**CORNERSTONE**

**11.4**

**Information:**

| | |
|---|---|
| Standard variable overhead rate ($SVOR$) | $5.00 per direct labor hour |
| Actual variable overhead costs ($AH$) | $705 |
| Standard hours allowed per unit | 0.12 hour |
| Actual direct labor hours worked ($AH$) | 150 hours |
| Actual production | 1,200 units |

**Required:**

Calculate (1) the actual variable overhead rate and (2) the total variable overhead variance.

**Solution:**

1.  Actual Variable Overhead Rate = Actual Variable Overhead Cost/Actual Direct Labor Hours

$$AVOR = \$705/150 \text{ hours}$$
$$AVOR = \$4.70$$

2.

| | |
|---|---|
| Actual variable overhead ($AH \times AVOR$) | $705 |
| Applied variable overhead ($SH \times SVOR$)* | 720 |
| Total variable overhead variance [($AH \times AVOR$) − ($SH \times SVOR$)] | $(15) F |

\* $SH \times SVOR$ = (0.12 hours per unit × 1,200 units) × $5.

**Variable Overhead Spending Variance**  The **variable overhead spending variance** measures the aggregate effect of differences between the actual variable overhead rate ($AVOR$) and the standard variable overhead rate ($SVOR$). The actual variable overhead rate is computed as follows:

$$AVOR = \frac{\text{Actual Variable Overhead}}{\text{Actual Hours}}$$

As shown by Cornerstone 11.4, this rate is $4.70 per hour ($705/150 $AH$). The formula for computing the variable overhead spending variance is:

$$\text{Variable Overhead Spending Variance} = (AH \times AVOR) - (AH \times SVOR)$$
$$= (AVOR - SVOR) \times AH$$

**Variable Overhead Efficiency Variance**  $VOH$ is assumed to vary in proportion to changes in the direct labor hours used. The **variable overhead efficiency variance** measures the change in the actual variable overhead cost ($VOH$) that occurs because of efficient (or inefficient) use of direct labor. The variable overhead efficiency variance is computed by using the following formula:

$$\text{Variable Overhead Efficiency Variance} = (AH - SH) \times SVOR$$

Cornerstone 11.5 shows how to calculate the variable overhead variances for Cool-U using both a columnar and a formula approach.

## Calculating Variable Overhead Spending and Efficiency Variances: Columnar and Formula Approaches

**Why:**

The total variable overhead variance can be broken down into the variable overhead spending and efficiency variances. These give managers a better idea of the reasons for the overall variance.

**Information:**

| | |
|---|---|
| Standard variable overhead rate (*SVOR*) | $5.00 per direct labor hour |
| Actual variable overhead rate (*AVOR*) | $4.70 |
| Actual hours worked (*AH*) | 150 hours |
| Number of t-shirts produced | 1,200 units |
| Hours allowed for production (*SH*) | 144 hours[a] |

[a] $0.12 \times 1,200$.

**Required:**

Calculate the variable overhead spending and efficiency variances.

**Solution:**

*Columnar:*

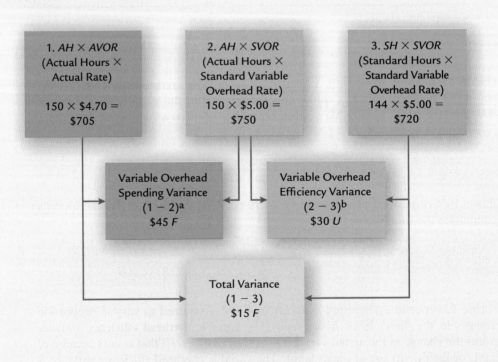

© Pixelfabrik/Alamy

**Formulas:**

[a]$VOH$ Spending Variance $= (AVOR - SVOR) \times AH$

$\qquad = (\$4.70 - \$5.00) \times 150$

$\qquad = \$45 \; F$

[b]$VOH$ Efficiency Variance $= (AH - SH) \times SVOR$

$\qquad = (150 - 144) \times \$5.00$

$\qquad = \$30 \; U$

CORNERSTONE

# 11.5

*(Continued)*

## Comparison of the Variable Overhead Spending Variance with the Price Variances of Materials and Labor

While the variable overhead spending variance is similar to the price variances of materials and labor, there are some conceptual differences. $VOH$ is not a single input—it is made up of a large number of individual items, such as indirect materials, indirect labor, electricity, maintenance, and so on. The standard variable overhead rate represents the weighted cost per direct labor hour that should be incurred for all variable overhead items. The difference between what should have been spent per hour and what actually was spent per hour is a type of price variance.

One reason that a variable overhead spending variance can arise is that prices for individual variable overhead items have increased or decreased. Assume that the price changes of individual overhead items are the only cause of the spending variance. If the spending variance is unfavorable, price increases for individual variable overhead items are the cause. If the spending variance is favorable, price decreases are dominating.

The second reason for a variable overhead spending variance is the use of the items that comprise variable overhead. Waste or inefficiency in the use of $VOH$ increases the actual variable overhead cost. This increased cost, in turn, is reflected in an increased actual variable overhead rate. Thus, even if the actual prices of the individual overhead items were equal to the budgeted or standard prices, an unfavorable variable overhead spending variance could still take place. For example, more kilowatt-hours of power may be used than should be, yet this is not captured by any change in direct labor hours. However, the effect is reflected by an increase in the total cost of power and, thus, the total cost of $VOH$. Similarly, efficiency can decrease the actual variable overhead cost and decrease the actual variable overhead rate. Efficient use of variable overhead items contributes to a favorable spending variance. If the waste effect dominates, then the net contribution will be unfavorable. If efficiency dominates, then the net contribution is favorable. Therefore, the variable overhead spending variance is the result of both price and efficiency.

### concept Q&A

How does the variable overhead spending variance differ from the materials and labor price variances?

**Answer:**

The variable overhead spending variance is affected by price changes of individual items as well as efficiency issues.

## Responsibility for the Variable Overhead Spending Variance

Variable overhead items may be affected by several responsibility centers. For example, utilities are a joint cost. To the extent that consumption of $VOH$ can be traced to a responsibility center, responsibility can be assigned. Consumption of indirect materials is an example of a traceable variable overhead cost.

Controllability is a prerequisite for assigning responsibility. Price changes of variable overhead items are essentially beyond the control of supervisors. If price changes are small (as they often are), then the spending variance is primarily a matter of the efficient use of overhead in production. This is controllable by production supervisors. Accordingly, responsibility for the variable overhead spending variance is generally assigned to production departments.

## Responsibility for the Variable Overhead Efficiency Variance

The variable overhead efficiency variance is directly related to the direct labor efficiency or usage variance. If $VOH$ is truly proportional to direct labor consumption, then like the labor usage variance, the variable overhead efficiency variance is caused by efficient or inefficient use of direct labor. If more (or fewer) direct labor hours are used than the standard calls for, then the total variable overhead cost will increase (or decrease). The validity of the measure depends on the validity of the relationship between variable overhead costs and direct labor hours. In other words, do variable overhead costs really change in proportion to changes in direct labor hours? If so, responsibility for the variable overhead efficiency variance should be assigned to the individual who has responsibility for the use of direct labor: the production manager.

## A Performance Report for the Variable Overhead Spending and Efficiency Variances

Cornerstone 11.5 (p. 486) showed a favorable $45 variable overhead spending variance and an unfavorable $30 variable overhead efficiency variance. The $45 $F$ spending variance means that overall Cool-U spent less than expected on variable overhead. The reasons for the $30 unfavorable variable overhead efficiency variance are the same as those offered for an unfavorable labor usage variance. An unfavorable variance means that more hours were used than called for by the standard. Even if the total variable overhead spending and efficiency variances are insignificant, they reveal nothing about how well costs of *individual* variable overhead items were controlled. It is possible for two large variances of opposite sign to cancel each other out. Control of $VOH$ requires line-by-line analysis for each item. Cornerstone 11.6 shows how to prepare a performance report that supplies the line-by-line information essential for detailed analysis of the variable overhead variances.

**CORNERSTONE**

**11.6**

## Preparing a Performance Report for the Variable Overhead Variances

**Why:**

This kind of report allows managers to examine the differences between budgeted and actual overhead on an item by item basis. It gives managers greater control.

**Information:**

| | |
|---|---|
| Standard variable overhead rate (*SVOR*) | $5.00 per direct labor hour |
| Actual costs: | |
|     Maintenance | $535 |
|     Power | $170 |
| Actual hours worked (*AH*) | 150 hours |
| Number of t-shirts produced | 1,200 units |

*(Continued)*

| Hours allowed for production (*SH*) | 144 hours[a] | CORNERSTONE |
| Variable overhead (*VOH*): | | **11.6** |
| Maintenance | 0.12 hr. @ $3.75 | |
| Power | 0.12 hr. @ $1.25 | |

[a] 0.12 × 1,200

*(Continued)*

**Required:**

Prepare a performance report that shows the variances on an item-by-item basis.

**Solution:**

**Performance Report for the Quarter Ended March 31, 20XX**

| Cost | Cost Formula[a] | Actual Costs | Budget for Actual Hours[b] | Spending Variance[c] | Budget for Standard Hours[d] | Efficiency Variance[e] |
|---|---|---|---|---|---|---|
| Maintenance | $3.75 | $535 | $562.50 | $27.50 F | $540 | $22.50 U |
| Power | 1.25 | 170 | 187.50 | 17.50 F | 180 | 7.50 U |
| Total | $5.00 | $705 | $750.00 | $45.00 F | $720 | $30.00 U |

[a] Per direct labor hour.
[b] Computed using the cost formula and 150 actual hours.
[c] Spending Variance = Actual Costs − Budget for Actual Hours.
[d] Computed using the cost formula and an activity level of 144 standard hours.
[e] Efficiency Variance = Budget for Actual Hours − Budget for Standard Hours.

The analysis on a line-by-line basis reveals no unusual problems such as two large individual item variances with opposite signs. No individual item variance is more than 10% of its budgeted amount. Thus, no single variance appears large enough to be of concern.

# FIXED OVERHEAD ANALYSIS

OBJECTIVE ③
Calculate the fixed overhead variances, and explain their meaning.

Fixed overhead costs are capacity costs acquired in advance of usage. For example, **The Second City**, described in the chapter opener, has fixed overhead costs that include salaries, stage and facilities rent, depreciation, and taxes. Recall from Chapter 5 that the predetermined overhead rate is calculated at the beginning of the year by dividing budgeted overhead by the budgeted amount of the base (e.g., direct labor hours). Now, however, we need to divide that predetermined overhead rate into variable and fixed overhead rates. It was easy to find the variable overhead rate since that rate is unchanged even though the number of units produced, and thus direct labor hours, changes. However, the fixed overhead rate changes as the underlying production level changes. To keep a stable fixed overhead rate throughout the year, companies typically use practical capacity to determine the number of direct labor hours in the denominator of the fixed overhead rate.

Suppose that Cool-U can produce 1,500 t-shirts per quarter under efficient operating conditions. Practical capacity measured in standard hours ($SH_p$) is calculated by the following formula:

Practical Capacity at Standard = $SH_p$

$$= 0.12 \times 1,500$$
$$= 180 \text{ hours}$$

Recall from Cornerstone 11.2 (p. 480) that Cool-U's total fixed costs per quarter equal $1,800. The standard fixed overhead rate (*SFOR*) is calculated as follows:

$$SFOR = \frac{\text{Budgeted Fixed Overhead Costs}}{\text{Practical Capacity}}$$

$$SFOR = \frac{\$1,800}{180}$$

$$= \$10 \text{ per direct labor hour}$$

Some firms use average or expected capacity instead of practical capacity to calculate fixed overhead rates. In this case, the standard hours used to calculate the fixed overhead rate typically will be less than the standard direct labor hours at practical capacity.

## Total Fixed Overhead Variances

The total fixed overhead variance is the difference between actual fixed overhead and applied fixed overhead, when applied fixed overhead is obtained by multiplying the standard fixed overhead rate (*SFOR*) times the standard hours allowed for the actual output (*SH*). Thus, the applied fixed overhead is:

$$\text{Applied Fixed Overhead} = SH \times SFOR$$

The total fixed overhead variance is the difference between the actual fixed overhead and the applied fixed overhead:

$$\text{Total Fixed Overhead Variance} = \text{Actual Fixed Overhead} - \text{Applied Fixed Overhead}$$

The total fixed overhead variance can be divided into spending and volume variances. Spending and volume variances can be calculated by using either the three-pronged (columnar) approach or formulas. The best approach to use is a matter of preference. However, the formulas first need to be expressed specifically for *FOH*. Cornerstone 11.7 illustrates how to calculate the total fixed overhead variance for Cool-U.

**CORNERSTONE**

**11.7**

## Calculating the Total Fixed Overhead Variance

**Why:**
The total fixed overhead variance shows the difference between actual spending on fixed overhead and the amount of fixed overhead applied. It gives managers an initial overview of potential problems.

**Information:**

| | |
|---|---|
| Standard fixed overhead rate (*SFOR*) | $10.00 per direct labor hour |
| Actual fixed overhead costs | $1,650 |
| Standard hours allowed per unit | 0.12 hour |
| Actual production | 1,200 units |

**Required:**

Calculate the (1) standard hours for actual units produced, (2) total applied fixed overhead, and (3) total fixed overhead variance.

*(Continued)*

**Solution:**

1. $SH$ = Actual Units × Standard Hours Allowed per Unit
    = 1,200 units  × 0.12 hour
    = 144 hours

2. Applied Fixed Overhead = $SH \times SFOR$
    = 144 × \$10
    = \$1,440

3.

| | |
|---|---:|
| Actual fixed overhead cost | \$1,650 |
| Applied fixed overhead | 1,440 |
| Total variance | \$  210 $U$ |

CORNERSTONE

**11.7**

*(Continued)*

**Fixed Overhead Spending Variance**  The fixed overhead spending variance is defined as the difference between the actual fixed overhead ($AFOH$) and the budgeted fixed overhead ($BFOH$):

$$\text{Fixed Overhead Spending Variance} = AFOH - BFOH$$

**Fixed Overhead Volume Variance**  The fixed overhead volume variance is the difference between budgeted fixed overhead ($BFOH$) and applied fixed overhead:

$$\text{Volume Variance} = \text{Budgeted Fixed Overhead} - \text{Applied Fixed Overhead}$$
$$= BFOH - (SH \times SFOR)$$

The volume variance measures the effect of the actual output differing from the output used at the beginning of the year to compute the predetermined standard fixed overhead rate. If you think of the output used to calculate the fixed overhead rate as the capacity acquired (practical capacity) and the actual output as the capacity used, then the volume variance is the cost of unused capacity. Cornerstone 11.8 illustrates how to calculate the fixed overhead variances using either a columnar or a formula approach.

## Calculating Fixed Overhead Variances: Columnar and Formula Approaches

**Why:**

The total fixed overhead variance can be broken down into the fixed overhead spending and volume variances. Knowing these components helps managers determine what, if anything, can be done to correct large variances.

**Information:**

| | |
|---|---|
| Actual fixed overhead ($AH$) | \$1,650 |
| Standard fixed overhead rate ($SFOR$) | \$10.00 per direct labor hour |
| Budgeted fixed overhead ($BFOH$) | \$1,800 |
| Number of t-shirts produced | 1,200 units |
| Hours allowed for production ($SH$) | 144 hours[a] |

[a] 0.12 × 1,200.

CORNERSTONE

**11.8**

*(Continued)*

**CORNERSTONE**

**11.8**

_(Continued)_

**Required:**

Calculate the fixed overhead spending and volume variances.

**Solution:**

_Columnar:_

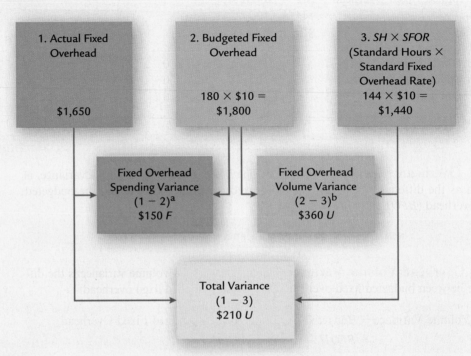

**Formulas:**

[a]FOH Spending Variance = Actual Fixed Overhead − Budgeted
    Fixed Overhead
    = \$1,650 − \$1,800
    = \$150 _F_

[b]FOH Volume Variance = Budgeted Fixed Overhead − Applied Fixed Overhead
    = _BFOH_ − (_SH_ × _SFOR_)
    = \$1,800 − (144 × \$10)
    = \$1,800 − \$1,440
    = \$360 _U_

## Responsibility for the Fixed Overhead Spending Variance

_FOH_ is made up of items such as salaries, depreciation, taxes, and insurance. Many fixed overhead items—long-run investments, for instance—cannot be changed in the short run. Consequently, fixed overhead costs are often beyond the immediate control of management. Since many fixed overhead costs are affected primarily by long-run decisions, and not by changes in production levels, the budget variance is usually small. For example, actual depreciation, salaries, taxes, and insurance costs are not likely to be much different from planned costs.

## Analysis of the Fixed Overhead Spending Variance

Because *FOH* is made up of many individual items, a line-by-line comparison of budgeted costs with actual costs provides more information concerning the causes of the spending variance. The *FOH* section of Cornerstone 11.3 (p. 482) provides such a report. The report reveals that the fixed overhead spending variance is out of line with expectations. Less was spent on grounds keeping than expected. In fact, the entire spending variance is attributable to this one item. Since the amount is more than 10% of budget, it merits investigation. An investigation, for example, might reveal that the weather was especially wet and thus reduced the cost of watering for the period involved. In this case, no action is needed, as a natural correction would be forthcoming.

## Responsibility for the Fixed Overhead Volume Variance

Assuming that volume variance measures capacity utilization implies that the general responsibility for this variance should be assigned to the production department. At times, however, a significant volume variance may be due to factors beyond the control of production. For example, if the purchasing department buys lower-quality raw materials than usual, significant rework time may result. This will cause lower production and an unfavorable volume variance. In this case, responsibility for the variance rests with purchasing, not production.

## Analysis of the Volume Variance

The $360 *U* variance (Cornerstone 11.8) occurs because the production capacity is 180 hours and only 144 hours should have been used. Why the company failed to use all of its capacity is not known. Given that unused capacity is about 20% of the total, investigation seems merited. Exhibit 11.2 graphically illustrates the volume variance. Notice that the volume variance occurs because fixed overhead is treated as if it were a variable cost. In reality, fixed costs do not change as activity changes, as a predetermined fixed overhead rate allows.

---

$\left(\text{EXHIBIT 11.2}\right)$

**Graphical Analysis of the Volume Variance**

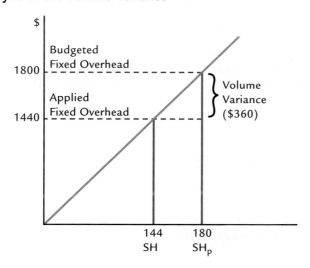

## ACTIVITY-BASED BUDGETING

The traditional approach to budgeting (explained in Chapter 9) emphasizes:

- estimation of revenues and costs by organizational units (e.g., departments, plants)
- use of a single unit-based driver such as direct labor hours

OBJECTIVE

Prepare an activity-based flexible budget.

Companies that have implemented an activity-based costing (ABC) system may also wish to install an *activity-based budgeting system*. An **activity-based budgeting (ABB) system** focuses on:

- estimation of the costs of activities rather than the costs of departments and plants
- use of multiple drivers, both unit-based and nonunit-based

The ABB approach supports continuous improvement and process management. Because activities consume resources (which cause cost), ABB can be used to reduce cost through the elimination of wasteful activities and improving the efficiency of necessary activities.

## Static Activity Budgets

Assuming that activity-based costing (ABC) has been implemented, the major emphasis for ABB is estimating the workload (demand) for each activity and then determining the resources required for this workload. The workload for each activity must be set to support the sales and production activities expected for the coming period.

As with traditional budgeting, ABB begins with sales and production budgets. Direct materials and direct labor budgets are also compatible with an activity-based costing framework because these inputs can be directly traced to the individual products. The major differences between traditional and ABB are found in the overhead and selling and administration categories. In a traditional-based approach, budgets within these categories are typically detailed by cost categories. These cost categories are classified as variable or fixed, using production or sales output measures as the basis for determining cost behavior. Furthermore, traditional budgets are usually constructed by budgeting for a cost item within a department and then rolling these items up into the master overhead budget. For example, the cost of supervision in an overhead budget is the sum of all the supervision costs of the various departments. ABB, on the other hand, identifies the overhead, selling, and administrative *activities* and then builds a budget for each activity, based on the resources needed to provide the required output levels. Costs are classified as variable or fixed with respect to the *activity* output measure or driver.

Consider, for example, purchasing materials. The demand for this activity is based on the materials requirements for the various products and services produced. An activity driver, such as number of purchase orders, measures the output demanded. Cornerstone 11.9 illustrates how to prepare a budget at the activity level for the purchasing activity.

---

### concept Q&A

What are the main differences between ABB and traditional budgeting?

**Answer:**

ABB differs primarily with overhead and selling and administrative budgets. ABB builds a budget for each activity based on the demands of the activity for resources. Traditional budgeting focuses on cost items required by organizational units such as departments.

---

**CORNERSTONE**

**11.9**

## Preparing a Static Budget for an Activity

**Why:**

The static budget for activities is often used by managers to get a rough picture of whether or not results are occurring according to plan.

**Information:**

1. Demand for purchase orders based on materials requirements: 15,000 purchase orders.

2. Resources needed:

   a. Five purchasing agents, each capable of processing 3,000 orders per year; salary, $40,000 each

*(Continued)*

b.  Supplies (forms, paper, stamps, envelopes, etc.); projected to cost $1.00 per purchase order

c.  Desks and computers; depreciation $5,000 per year

d.  Office space, rent, and utilities, $6,000

**Required:**

Prepare a budget for the purchasing activity.

**Solution:**

Purchasing budget:

| | |
|---|---:|
| Salaries | $200,000 |
| Supplies | 15,000 |
| Depreciation | 5,000 |
| Occupancy | 6,000 |
| Total | $226,000 |

CORNERSTONE

## 11.9

*(Continued)*

For the purchasing activity in Cornerstone 11.9, Supplies is a variable cost, and the other resources are fixed costs (a step-fixed cost behavior in the case of salaries and depreciation). However, one important difference should be mentioned: Fixed and variable purchasing costs are defined with respect to the *number of purchase orders* and not direct labor hours or units produced or other measures of production output. In budgeting at the activity level, the cost behavior of each activity is defined with respect to *its own* output measure. Knowing the output measure helps control activity costs by controlling the underlying activities. For example, by redesigning products so that they use more common components, the number of purchase orders can be decreased. Decreasing the number of purchase orders reduces the use of resources used by the Purchasing Department. Furthermore, decreasing the number of purchase orders demanded reduces the activity capacity needed. Thus, activity costs will decrease.

## Activity Flexible Budgeting

Understanding the relationship between changes in activity costs and changes in activity drivers allows managers to more carefully plan and monitor activity improvements. **Activity flexible budgeting** is the prediction of what activity costs will be as related output changes. Variance analysis within an activity framework makes it possible to improve traditional budgetary performance reporting, and enhances the ability to manage activities.

In a traditional-based approach, budgeted costs for the actual level of activity are obtained by assuming that a single unit-based driver (e.g., units of product or direct labor hours) drives all costs. A cost formula is developed for each cost item as a function of units produced or direct labor hours. Cornerstone 11.2 (p. 480) illustrated a traditional flexible budget for production based on direct labor hours. If, however, costs vary with respect to more than one driver, and the drivers are not highly correlated with direct labor hours, then the predicted costs can be misleading.

The solution is to build flexible budget formulas for more than one driver. Cost estimation procedures (high-low method, the method of least squares, and so on) can be used to estimate cost formulas for each activity. This multiple-formula approach allows

---

### concept Q&A

Why does activity-based flexible budgeting provide a more accurate prediction of costs?

**Answer:**

Activity-based flexible budgeting is more accurate if costs vary with more than one driver and the drivers are not highly correlated with direct labor hours (which is often the case).

managers to predict more accurately what costs should be for different levels of activity, as measured by the drivers. These costs can then be compared with the actual costs to help assess budgetary performance. Cornerstone 11.10 illustrates how to prepare an activity flexible budget. Notice that flexible budgets are computed for *each driver*.

# CORNERSTONE 11.10

## Preparing an Activity Flexible Budget

**Why:**
The activity flexible budget compares the actual results for an activity with the amount that would have been budgeted for actual production. It is superior to the static activity budget since it compares budgeted to actual results for the same level of activity.

**Information:**
Information on four overhead activities for Kellman Company is given below.

| Activity | Driver | Fixed Cost | Variable Rate |
|---|---|---|---|
| Maintenance | Machine hours | $ 20,000 | $ 5.50 |
| Machining | Machine hours | 15,000 | 2.00 |
| Setting up | Setups | — | 1,800 |
| Inspection | Setups | 80,000 | 2,100 |
| Purchasing | Purchase Orders | 211,000 | 1.00 |

**Required:**
Prepare an activity-based flexible budget for the following production levels:

| Driver | 32,000 units | 64,000 units |
|---|---|---|
| Machine hours | 8,000 | 16,000 |
| Setups | 25 | 30 |
| Purchase orders | 15,000 | 25,000 |

**Solution:**
Steps in forming the activity-based flexible budget include:

1. Set up a table showing the activities under their related driver.

2. Calculate total activity cost by multiplying the variable rate times the driver level and adding the fixed amount. For example, at 8,000 machine hours,

$$\text{Maintenance} = \$20,000 + (\$5.50 \times 8,000 \text{ machine hours}) = \$64,000$$

And at 16,000 machine hours,

$$\text{Maintenance} = \$20,000 + (\$5.50 \times 16,000 \text{ machine hours}) = \$108,000$$

| | | | Required for | |
|---|---|---|---|---|
| | | | **32,000 units** | **64,000 units** |
| *Driver: Machine Hours* | | | | |
| | **Fixed** | **Variable** | **8,000** | **16,000** |
| Maintenance | $20,000 | $5.50 | $64,000 | $108,000 |
| Machining | 15,000 | 2.00 | 31,000 | 47,000 |
| Subtotal | $35,000 | $7.50 | $95,000 | $155,000 |

*(Continued)*

*Driver: Number of Setups*

| | Fixed | Variable | 25 | 30 |
|---|---|---|---|---|
| Setups | $  — | $1,800 | $ 45,000 | $ 54,000 |
| Inspections | 80,000 | 2,100 | 132,500 | 143,000 |
| Subtotal | $80,000 | $3,900 | $177,500 | $197,000 |

*Driver: Number of Purchase Orders*

| | Fixed | Variable | 15,000 | 25,000 |
|---|---|---|---|---|
| Purchasing | $211,000 | $1.00 | $226,000 | $236,000 |
| Total | | | $498,500 | $588,000 |

CORNERSTONE

**11.10**

*(Continued)*

The flexible budget shown in Cornerstone 11.10 will be more accurate than one based on just a single unit-based driver. This will also give managers information that can be used in cost control because they can see what effect an increase or decrease in each driver has on total cost.

An activity-based performance report is shown in Cornerstone 11.11 . It compares the budgeted costs for the actual activity usage levels with the actual costs.

## Preparing an Activity-Based Performance Report

CORNERSTONE

**11.11**

**Why:**

The activity-based performance report allows managers to compare actual with budgeted amounts activity by activity. This gives better control than overall spending amounts.

**Information:**

Actual activity level is the first one for each activity listed in Cornerstone 11.10. For example, budgeted costs for maintenance would be based on 8,000 machine hours and would equal $64,000.

Actual costs:

| | | | |
|---|---|---|---|
| Maintenance | $ 55,000 | Setups | $ 46,500 |
| Machining | 29,000 | Purchasing | 220,000 |
| Inspections | 125,500 | | |

**Required:**

Prepare an activity-based performance report.

**Solution:**

*Note:* For this performance report, just input the actual costs as given above. Then input the budgeted costs for the activity levels required. The budget variance is the difference between the actual costs and the budgeted costs. If actual costs are greater than budgeted costs, the budget variance is unfavorable (*U*). If actual costs are less than budgeted costs, the budget variance is favorable (*F*).

*(Continued)*

|  | Actual Costs | Budgeted Costs | Budget Variance |
|---|---|---|---|
| Maintenance | $ 55,000 | $ 64,000 | $ 9,000 *F* |
| Machining | 29,000 | 31,000 | 2,000 *F* |
| Inspections | 125,500 | 132,500 | 7,000 *F* |
| Setups | 46,500 | 45,000 | 1,500 *U* |
| Purchases | 220,000 | 226,000 | 6,000 *F* |
| Total | $476,000 | $498,500 | $22,500 *F* |

Looking at Cornerstone 11.11, we see that the variances for the five items are mixed. The net outcome is a favorable variance of $22,500. The preparation of the activity-based performance report follows the pattern and approach of the traditional report shown in Cornerstone 11.3 (p. 482). The difference is that the comparison is for *each* activity.

One can also compare the actual fixed activity costs with the budgeted fixed activity costs and the actual variable activity costs with the budgeted variable costs. For example, assume that the actual fixed inspection costs are $82,000 (due to a midyear salary adjustment, reflecting a more favorable union agreement than anticipated) and that the actual variable inspection costs are $43,500. The variable and fixed budget variances for the inspection activity are computed as follows:

| Activity | Actual Cost | Budgeted Cost | Variance |
|---|---|---|---|
| Inspection |  |  |  |
| Fixed | $ 82,000 | $ 80,000 | $2,000 *U* |
| Variable | 43,500 | 52,500 | 9,000 *F* |
| Total | $125,500 | $132,500 | $7,000 *F* |

Breaking each variance into fixed and variable components provides more insight into the source of the variation in planned and actual expenditures.

# YOUDECIDE Activity Flexible Budgeting for Museums

Museums do much more than simply present art to the public. Today's art museums put on shows, provide access to the public to view the collections, sell art-related merchandise in the museum store and online, and may put on special events and performances. The annual budget for a museum can easily run into millions of dollars, so cost understanding and control are crucial.[1] As an accountant for a large metropolitan museum, you would be responsible for budgeting and controlling costs. Splitting costs into fixed and variable components would be a first step in budgeting. However, what driver would you use? Number of patrons going through the museum? That would be a good driver for a few costs, especially those related to printing tickets and explanatory materials (such as maps of the museum to help people navigate through the collections). However, the vast majority of costs would be fixed with respect to the number of people going through the museum. ABC and budgeting would give a much richer view of the costs of running the various activities of the museum.

**What type of information would you need to create activity-based budgets?**

Your first step would be to determine the various activities of the museum. These might include: providing access to the public, selling merchandise through the museum store, putting on special events (e.g., concerts, lectures, benefits), acquiring and cataloging pieces of art, and so on. For example, the activity of cataloguing new art pieces would include the salaries of staff who catalog the pieces, or clean and restore them, insurance on the art, and so on. Many of these costs vary with the number of newly donated or purchased pieces. The activity of selling merchandise would have

[1] The newly opened National Museum of 21st Century Arts in Rome (dubbed the "Maxxi") has an annual operating budget of 9 million euros (about $11 million). Kelly Crow, "Rome turns to the art of today," *The Wall Street Journal*, May 21, 2010. http://online.wsj.com/article/SB10001424052748703691804575254362971810080.html

costs of staff to run the store, cost of the items purchased for sale, advertising, and so on. Those costs might vary with the number of items sold or with the revenue earned. Putting on special events would have a different set of costs attached and those might vary with the number of events and the number of attendees.

**Recognizing the different activities associated with the museum and relating the costs to specific activity drivers will give you a much better idea of what costs to expect. This understanding can help the museum director exercise good stewardship of the funds donated and provide important services to the public.**

# SUMMARY OF LEARNING OBJECTIVES

**LO 1.** Prepare a flexible budget, and use it for performance reporting.

- Static budgets provide expected cost for a given level of activity. If the actual level of activity differs from the static budget level, then comparing actual costs with budgeted costs does not make sense. The solution is flexible budgeting.
- Flexible budgets divide costs into those that vary with units of production (or direct labor hours) and those that are fixed with respect to unit-level drivers. These relationships allow the identification of a cost formula for each item in the budget.
- Cost formulas calculate expected costs for various levels of activity. There are two applications of flexible budgets: before-the-fact and after-the-fact.

  - Before-the-fact applications allow managers to see what costs will be for different levels of activity, thus helping in planning.
  - After-the-fact applications allow managers to see what the cost should have been for the actual level of activity. Knowing these after-the-fact expected or budgeted costs provides the opportunity to evaluate efficiency by comparing actual costs with budgeted costs.

**LO 2.** Calculate the variable overhead variances, and explain their meaning.

- Overhead costs are often a significant proportion of budget costs.
- Comparing actual variable and fixed overhead costs with applied overhead costs yields a total overhead variance.
- In a standard cost system, it is possible to break down overhead variances into component variances.
- For variable overhead, the two component variances are the spending variance and the efficiency variance.
- The spending variance is the result of comparing the actual costs with budgeted costs.
- The variable overhead efficiency variance is the result of efficient or inefficient use of labor because variable overhead is assumed to vary with direct labor hours.

**LO 3.** Calculate the fixed overhead variances, and explain their meaning.

- For fixed overhead, the two component variances are the spending variance and the volume variance.
- The spending variance is the result of comparing the actual costs with budgeted costs.
- The fixed overhead volume variance is the result of producing a level different than that used to calculate the predetermined fixed overhead rate. It can be interpreted as a measure of capacity utilization.

**LO 4.** Prepare an activity-based flexible budget.

- Activity-based budgeting is done at the activity level.

  - First, demand for products is assessed.
  - Next, the level of activity output needed to support the expected production level is estimated.
  - Finally, the resources needed to support the required activity output are estimated. This then becomes the activity budget.
  - Activity flexible budgets differ from traditional flexible budgets because the cost formulas are based on the activity drivers for the respective activities rather than being based only on a single unit-based driver, such as direct labor hours.

# SUMMARY OF IMPORTANT EQUATIONS

**Abbrevations:**

$$FOH = \text{Fixed Overhead}$$
$$VOH = \text{Variable Overhead}$$
$$AH = \text{Actual Direct Labor Hours}$$
$$SH = \text{Standard Direct Labor Hours that } \textit{Should Have Been Worked} \text{ for Actual}$$
$$\text{Units Produced}$$
$$AVOR = \text{Actual Variable Overhead Rate}$$
$$SVOR = \text{Standard Variable Overhead Rate}$$

1. $AVOR = \dfrac{\text{Actual Variable Overhead}}{\text{Actual Hours}}$

2. Variable Overhead Spending Variance $= (AH \times AVOR) - (AH \times SVOR)$
$$= (AVOR - SVOR) \times AH$$

3. Variable Overhead Efficiency Variance $= (AH - SH) \times SVOR$

4. Practical Capacity at Standard $= SH_p$

5. $SFOR = \dfrac{\text{Budgeted Fixed Overhead Costs}}{\text{Practical Capacity}}$

6. Applied Fixed Overhead $= SH \times SFOR$

7. Total Fixed Overhead Variance $=$ Actual Fixed Overhead $-$ Applied Fixed Overhead

8. Fixed Overhead Spending Variance $= AFOH - BFOH$

9. Volume Variance $=$ Budgeted Fixed Overhead $-$ Applied Fixed Overhead
$$= BFOH - (SH \times SFOR)$$

CORNERSTONES

| | |
|---|---|
| **CORNERSTONE 11.1** | Preparing a performance report based on a static budget (using budgeted production), page 479 |
| **CORNERSTONE 11.2** | Preparing a before-the-fact flexible production budget, page 480 |
| **CORNERSTONE 11.3** | Preparing a performance report using a flexible budget, page 482 |
| **CORNERSTONE 11.4** | Calculating the total variable overhead variance, page 485 |
| **CORNERSTONE 11.5** | Calculating variable overhead spending and efficiency variances: columnar and formula approaches, page 486 |
| **CORNERSTONE 11.6** | Preparing a performance report for the variable overhead variances, page 488 |
| **CORNERSTONE 11.7** | Calculating the total fixed overhead variance, page 490 |
| **CORNERSTONE 11.8** | Calculating fixed overhead variances: columnar and formula approaches, page 491 |
| **CORNERSTONE 11.9** | Preparing a static budget for an activity, page 494 |
| **CORNERSTONE 11.10** | Preparing an activity flexible budget, page 496 |
| **CORNERSTONE 11.11** | Preparing an activity-based performance report, page 497 |

© Pixelfabrik / Alamy

# KEY TERMS

Activity flexible budgeting, 495
Activity-based budgeting (ABB) system, 494
Flexible budget, 480
Flexible budget variance, 483
Performance report, 478

Static budget, 478
Variable budgets, 481
Variable overhead efficiency variance, 485
Variable overhead spending variance, 485

## Exercise 11-32    Flexible Budget for Various Levels of Activity

OBJECTIVE ①

Refer to the information for Palladium Inc. on the previous page.

**Required:**

1. Prepare an overhead budget for the expected level of direct labor hours for the coming year.
2. Prepare an overhead budget that reflects production that is 15% higher than expected, and for production that is 15% lower than expected.

## Exercise 11-33    Performance Report Based on Actual Production

OBJECTIVE ①

Refer to the information for Palladium Inc. on the previous page. Assume that actual production required 93,000 direct labor hours at standard. The actual overhead costs incurred were as follows:

| | | | |
|---|---|---|---|
| Maintenance | $107,000 | Indirect labor | $336,000 |
| Power | 41,200 | Rent | 35,000 |

**Required:**

Prepare a performance report for the period based on actual production.

---

*Use the following information for Exercises 11-34 and 11-35:*

Rostand Inc. operates a delivery service for over 70 restaurants. The corporation has a fleet of vehicles and has invested in a sophisticated, computerized communications system to coordinate its deliveries. Rostand has gathered the following actual data on last year's delivery operations:

| | |
|---|---|
| Deliveries made | 38,600 |
| Direct labor | 31,000 direct labor hours @ $9.00 |
| Actual variable overhead | $157,700 |

Rostand employs a standard costing system. During the year, a variable overhead rate of $5.10 per hour was used. The labor standard requires 0.80 hour per delivery.

---

## Exercise 11-34    Variable Overhead Variances, Service Company

OBJECTIVE ②

Refer to the information for Rostand Inc. above.

**Required:**

1. Compute the standard hours allowed for actual deliveries made last year.
2. Compute the variable overhead spending and efficiency variances.

## Exercise 11-35    Fixed Overhead Variances

OBJECTIVE ③

Refer to the information for Rostand Inc. above. Assume that the actual fixed overhead was $403,400. Budgeted fixed overhead was $400,000, based on practical capacity of 32,000 direct labor hours.

**Required:**

1. Calculate the standard fixed overhead rate based on budgeted fixed overhead and practical capacity.
2. Compute the fixed overhead spending and volume variances.

## Exercise 11-36    Overhead Variances

OBJECTIVE ② ③

At the beginning of the year, Lopez Company had the following standard cost sheet for one of its chemical products:

| | |
|---|---|
| Direct materials (4 lbs. @ $2.80) | $11.20 |
| Direct labor (2 hrs. @ $18.00) | 36.00 |
| FOH (2 hrs. @ $5.20) | 10.40 |
| VOH (2 hrs. @ $0.70) | 1.40 |
| Standard cost per unit | $59.00 |

**ILLUSTRATING RELATIONSHIPS**

*(Continued)*

Lopez computes its overhead rates using practical volume, which is 80,000 units. The actual results for the year are as follows: (a) Units produced: 79,600; (b) Direct labor: 158,900 hours at $18.10; (c) *FOH*: $831,000; and (d) *VOH*: $112,400.

**Required:**

1. Compute the variable overhead spending and efficiency variances.
2. Compute the fixed overhead spending and volume variances.

OBJECTIVE ❷ ❸

ILLUSTRATING
RELATIONSHIPS

### Exercise 11-37   Overhead Application, Fixed and Variable Overhead Variances

Zepol Company is planning to produce 600,000 power drills for the coming year. The company uses direct labor hours to assign overhead to products. Each drill requires 0.75 standard hour of labor for completion. The total budgeted overhead was $1,777,500. The total fixed overhead budgeted for the coming year is $832,500. Predetermined overhead rates are calculated using expected production, measured in direct labor hours. Actual results for the year are:

| | | | |
|---|---|---|---|
| Actual production (units) | 594,000 | Actual variable overhead | $928,000 |
| Actual direct labor hours (*AH*) | 446,000 | Actual fixed overhead | $835,600 |

**Required:**

1. Compute the applied fixed overhead.
2. Compute the fixed overhead spending and volume variances.
3. Compute the applied variable overhead.
4. Compute the variable overhead spending and efficiency variances.

OBJECTIVE ❷ ❸

ILLUSTRATING
RELATIONSHIPS

### Exercise 11-38   Understanding Relationships between Overhead Variances, Budgeted Amounts, and Actual Units Produced and Direct Labor Hours Worked

Last year, Gladner Company had planned to produce 140,000 units. However, 143,000 units were actually produced. The company uses direct labor hours to assign overhead to products. Each unit requires 0.9 standard hour of labor for completion. The fixed overhead rate was $11 per direct labor hour and the variable overhead rate was $6.36 per direct labor hour.

The following variances were computed:

| | | | |
|---|---|---|---|
| Fixed overhead spending variance | $24,000 *U* | Variable overhead spending variance | $9,196 *U* |
| Fixed overhead volume variance | 29,700 *F* | Variable overhead efficiency variance | 1,272 *U* |

**Required:**

1. Calculate the total applied fixed overhead.
2. Calculate the budgeted fixed overhead.
3. Calculate the actual fixed overhead.
4. Calculate the total applied variable overhead.
5. Calculate the number of actual direct labor hours.
6. Calculate the actual variable overhead.

OBJECTIVE ❶

### Exercise 11-39   Performance Report for Variable Overhead Variances

Anker Company had the data below for its most recent year, ended December 31:

| **Actual costs:** | | **Variable overhead standards:** | |
|---|---|---|---|
| Indirect labor | $36,000 | Indirect labor | 0.15 hr. @ $24.00 |
| Supplies | $3,800 | Supplies | 0.15 hr. @ $2.40 |
| Actual hours worked | 1,490 hours | Standard variable overhead rate | $26.40 per direct labor hour |
| Units produced | 10,000 units | | |
| Hours allowed for production | 1,500 hours | | |

**Required:**

Prepare a performance report that shows the variances on an item-by-item basis.

## Exercise 11-40    Activity-Based Budgeting

OBJECTIVE 4

Fermi Company decided to look more closely at the materials receiving activity in its factory. The driver for receiving is the number of receiving orders. The following information for a year was collected:

Demand for receiving orders: 130,000
Resources needed:

a.   6 workers capable of completing 25,000 receiving orders per year. (The completion of a receiving order requires unloading the materials onto the receiving dock, checking the receiving order against the purchase order and invoice, and carrying the materials to the materials storeroom.) Salary is $27,000 for each worker
b.   Supplies (paper, grease markers, small tools, rags) expected to cost $0.80 per receiving order
c.   Workbenches, dollies, computers, etc.; depreciation $14,400 per year
d.   Space for the receiving dock, utilities; $9,800 per year

**Required:**

1.   Prepare a static budget for the receiving activity for the year.
2.   Calculate the cost per receiving order based on annual demand for receiving orders. (*Note:* Round to the nearest cent.)

## Exercise 11-41    Activity Flexible Budget

OBJECTIVE 4

Healder Company provided information on the following three overhead activities.

| Activity | Driver | Fixed Cost | Variable Rate |
|---|---|---|---|
| Engineering | Engineering hours | $67,000 | $5.50 |
| Machining | Machine hours | 36,000 | 1.40 |
| Receiving | Receiving orders | 51,000 | 3.75 |

Healder has found that the following driver levels are associated with two different levels of production.

| Driver | 40,000 units | 50,000 units |
|---|---|---|
| Engineering hours | 500 | 750 |
| Machine hours | 30,000 | 37,500 |
| Receiving orders | 9,000 | 12,000 |

**Required:**

Prepare an activity-based flexible budget for the two levels of activity.

## Exercise 11-42    Activity-Based Performance Report

OBJECTIVE 4

Inchon produced 312,000 units last year. The information on the actual costs and budgeted costs at actual production of four activities follows.

| Activity | Actual Cost | Budgeted Cost for Actual Production |
|---|---|---|
| Maintenance | $179,600 | $176,700 |
| Machining | 90,500 | 89,800 |
| Setting up | 119,500 | 121,000 |
| Purchasing | 75,750 | 74,600 |

**Required:**

Prepare an activity-based performance report for the four activities for the past year.

# PROBLEMS

> *Use the following information for Problems 11-43 through 11-45:*
> Ladan Suriman, controller for Healthy Pet Company, has been instructed to develop a flexible budget for overhead costs. The company produces two types of dog food. BasicDiet is a standard mixture for healthy dogs. SpecialDiet is a reduced protein formulation for older dogs with health problems. The two dog foods use common raw materials in different proportions. The company expects to produce 80,000 bags of each product during the coming year. BasicDiet requires 0.20 direct labor hours per bag, and SpecialDiet requires 0.30 direct labor hours per bag. Ladan has developed the following fixed and variable costs for each of the four overhead items:
>
> | Overhead Item | Fixed Cost | Variable Rate per Direct Labor Hour |
> |---|---|---|
> | Maintenance | $57,250 | $0.50 |
> | Power | | 0.40 |
> | Indirect labor | 43,500 | 2.10 |
> | Rent | 39,000 | |

OBJECTIVE ❶  **Problem 11-43   Overhead Budget for a Particular Level of Activity**

Refer to the information for Healthy Pet Company above.

**Required:**

1.  Calculate the total direct labor hours required for the production of 80,000 bags of Basic-Diet and 80,000 bags of SpecialDiet.
2.  Prepare an overhead budget for the expected activity level (calculated in Requirement 1) for the coming year.

OBJECTIVE ❶  **Problem 11-44   Flexible Budget for Various Production Levels**

Refer to the information for Healthy Pet Company above.

**Required:**

1.  Calculate the direct labor hours required for production that is 10% higher than expected. Calculate the direct labor hours required for production that is 20% lower than expected.
2.  Prepare an overhead budget that reflects production that is 10% higher than expected, and for production that is 20% lower than expected. (*Hint*: Use total direct labor hours calculated in Requirement 1.)

OBJECTIVE ❶  **Problem 11-45   Performance Report Based on Actual Production**

Refer to the information for Healthy Pet Company above. Assume that Healthy Pet actually produced 100,000 bags of BasicDiet and 90,000 bags of SpecialDiet. The actual overhead costs incurred were as follows:

| | | | |
|---|---|---|---|
| Maintenance | $81,300 | Indirect labor | $143,600 |
| Power | 18,700 | Rent | 39,000 |

**Required:**

1.  Calculate the number of direct labor hours budgeted for actual production of the two products.
2.  Prepare a performance report for the period based on actual production.
3.  **CONCEPTUAL CONNECTION** Based on the report, would you judge any of the variances to be significant? Can you think of some possible reasons for the variances?

OBJECTIVE 1

## Problem 11-46   Overhead Budget, Flexible Budget

Spelzig Company manufactures radio-controlled toy cars. Spelzig has developed the following flexible budget for overhead for the coming year. Activity level is measured in direct labor hours.

| | Variable Cost Formula | Activity Level (hours) | | |
| --- | --- | --- | --- | --- |
| | | 15,000 | 20,000 | 25,000 |
| Variable costs: | | | | |
| Maintenance | $3.80 | $ 57,000 | $ 76,000 | $ 95,000 |
| Supplies | 4.25 | 63,750 | 85,000 | 106,250 |
| Power | 0.08 | 1,200 | 1,600 | 2,000 |
| Total variable costs | $8.13 | $121,950 | $162,600 | $203,250 |
| Fixed costs: | | | | |
| Depreciation | | $144,700 | $144,700 | $144,700 |
| Salaries | | 188,900 | 188,900 | 188,900 |
| Total fixed costs | | $333,600 | $333,600 | $333,600 |
| Total overhead costs | | $455,550 | $496,200 | $536,850 |

The factory produces two different toy cars. The production budget for November is 30,000 units for Car W23 and 60,000 units for Car Z280. Car W23 requires 12 minutes of direct labor time, and Car Z280 requires 24 minutes. Fixed overhead costs are incurred uniformly throughout the year.

**Required:**

1. Calculate the number of direct labor hours needed in November to produce Car W23 and the number of direct labor hours needed in November to produce Car Z280. What are the total direct labor hours budgeted for November?
2. Prepare an overhead budget for November. Round all amounts to the nearest dollar. (*Hint*: The budgeted fixed costs given are for the year.)

OBJECTIVE 1

## Problem 11-47   Kicker Speakers, Before-the-Fact Flexible Budgeting, Flexible Budgeting for the New Solo X18 Model

**Stillwater Designs** is considering a new **Kicker** speaker model: Solo X18, which is a large and expensive subwoofer (projected price is $760 to distributors). The company controls the design specifications of the model and contracts with manufacturers in mainland China to produce the model. Stillwater Designs pays the freight and custom duties. The product is shipped to Stillwater and then sold to distributors throughout the United States.

The market for this type of subwoofer is small and competitive. It is expected to have a 3-year life cycle. Market test reviews were encouraging. One potential customer noted that the speaker could make a deaf person hear again. Another remarked that the bass could be heard two miles away. Another customer was simply impressed by the size and watts of the subwoofer (a maximum of 10,000 watts capability). Encouraged by the results of market tests, the Product Steering Committee also wanted to review the financial analysis. The projected revenues and costs at three levels of sales volume are as follows (for the 3-year life cycle):

| | Pessimistic | Most Likely | Optimistic |
| --- | --- | --- | --- |
| Sales volume (units) | 72,000 | 150,000 | 250,000 |
| Variable costs (total): | | | |
| Acquisition cost | $43,200,000 | $ 90,000,000 | $150,000,000 |
| Freight | 4,320,000 | 9,000,000 | 15,000,000 |
| Duties | 1,800,000 | 3,750,000 | 6,250,000 |
| Total | $49,320,000 | $102,750,000 | $171,250,000 |
| Fixed costs (total): | | | |
| Engineering (R&D) | $10,000,000 | $ 10,000,000 | $ 10,000,000 |
| Overhead | 3,000,000 | 3,000,000 | 3,000,000 |
| Total | $13,000,000 | $ 13,000,000 | $ 13,000,000 |

*(Continued)*

**Required:**

1. Prepare flexible budget formulas for the cost items listed for the Solo X18 model. Also, provide a flexible budget formula for total costs.
2. **CONCEPTUAL CONNECTION** Prepare an income statement for each of the three levels of sales volume. Discuss the value of before-the-fact flexible budgeting and relate this to the current example.
3. **CONCEPTUAL CONNECTION** Form a group with two to four other students. Assume that the group is acting as a Product Steering Committee. Evaluate the feasibility of producing the Solo X18 model (using the given financial data and the results of Requirements 1 and 2.) If the financial performance of the model is questionable, discuss possible courses of action that the company might take to improve the financial performance of the product. Also, discuss some reasons why the company might wish to produce the model even if it does not promise a good financial return.

OBJECTIVE ① **Problem 11-48  Flexible Budgeting**

ILLUSTRATING
RELATIONSHIPS

Quarterly budgeted overhead costs for two different levels of activity follow. The 2,000 level was the expected level from the master budget.

| | Cost Formula ($) | | Direct Labor Hours | |
| --- | --- | --- | --- | --- |
| | **Fixed** | **Variable** | **1,000 Hours** | **2,000 Hours** |
| Maintenance | 7,500 | 5.00 | $12,500 | $17,500 |
| Depreciation | 5,600 | — | 5,600 | 5,600 |
| Supervision | 22,000 | — | 22,000 | 22,000 |
| Supplies | — | 2.30 | 2,300 | 4,600 |
| Power | — | 0.60 | 600 | 1,200 |
| Other | 18,000 | 1.25 | 19,250 | 20,500 |

The actual activity level was 1,700 hours.

**Required:**

1. Prepare a flexible budget for an activity level of 1,700 direct labor hours.
2. Suppose that all of the formulas for each item are missing. You only have the budgeted costs for each level of activity. Show how you can obtain the formulas for each item by using the information given for the budgeted costs for the two levels.

OBJECTIVE ① **Problem 11-49  Flexible Budgeting**

Orchard Fresh Inc. purchases fruit from numerous growers and packs fruit boxes and fruit baskets for sale. Orchard Fresh has developed the following flexible budget for overhead for the coming year. Activity level is measured in direct labor hours.

| | | Activity Level (hours) | | |
| --- | --- | --- | --- | --- |
| | | **2,000** | **2,500** | **3,000** |
| Variable costs: | | | | |
| Maintenance | $0.76 | $ 1,520 | $ 1,900 | $ 2,280 |
| Supplies | 0.45 | 900 | 1,125 | 1,350 |
| Power | 0.20 | 400 | 500 | 600 |
| Total variable costs | $1.41 | $ 2,820 | $ 3,525 | $ 4,230 |
| Fixed costs: | | | | |
| Depreciation | | $ 4,800 | $ 4,800 | $ 4,800 |
| Salaries | | 24,500 | 24,500 | 24,500 |
| Total fixed costs | | $29,300 | $29,300 | $29,300 |
| Total overhead costs | | $32,120 | $32,825 | $33,530 |

**Required:**

1. Prepare a flexible budget for May, using 200, 240, and 280 direct labor hours. (Round answers to the nearest cent.)

2. **CONCEPTUAL CONNECTION** The Cushing High School Parent-Teacher Organization ordered 200 gift baskets from Orchard Fresh to be given to high school teachers and support staff as a thank you for a successful school year. These gift baskets must be ready by May 31 and were not included in the original production budget for May. Describe how Orchard Fresh could adjust the total budgeted overhead for May to include the new order.

### Problem 11-50  Performance Reporting

OBJECTIVE ①

Fernando's is a tiny sandwich shop just off the State University campus. Customers enter and place their orders at a small counter area. All orders are take-out because there is no space for dining in.

The owner of Fernando's, Luis Azaria, is attempting to construct a series of budgets. He has accumulated the following information:

a. The average sandwich (which sells for $4.50) requires 1 roll, 4 ounces of meat, 2 ounces of cheese, 0.05 head of lettuce, 0.25 of a tomato, and a healthy squirt (1 ounce) of secret sauce.
b. Each customer typically orders one soft drink (average price $1.50) consisting of a cup and 12 ounces of soda. Refills are free, but this offer is seldom taken advantage of because the typical customer carries out his/her sandwich and soda.
c. Use of paper supplies (napkins, bag, sandwich wrap, cups) averages $1,650 per month.
d. Fernando's is open for two 4-hour shifts. The noon shift on Monday through Friday requires two workers earning $10 per hour. The evening shift is only worked on Friday, Saturday, and Sunday nights. The two evening shift employees also earn $10 per hour. There are 4.3 weeks in a month.
e. Rent is $575 per month. Other monthly cash expenses average $1,800.
f. Food costs are:

| | | | |
|---|---|---|---|
| Meat | $7.00/lb | Tomatoes (a box contains about | |
| Cheese | $6.00/lb | 20 tomatoes) | $4/box |
| Rolls | $28.80/gross | Secret sauce | $6.40/gallon |
| Lettuce (a box contains 24 heads) | $12.00/box | Soda (syrup and carbonated water) | $2.56/gallon |

In a normal month when school is in session, Fernando's sells 5,000 sandwiches and 5,000 sodas. In October, State U holds its homecoming celebration. Luis figures that if he adds a noon shift on Saturday and Sunday of homecoming weekend, October sales will be 30% higher than normal. To advertise his noon shifts during homecoming weekend, Luis will buy cups emblazoned with the State U Homecoming schedule. This will add $200 to paper costs for the month. Last year, he added two additional shifts, and his sales goal was realized.

**Required:**

1. Prepare a flexible budget for a normal school month.
2. Prepare a flexible budget for October.
3. **CONCEPTUAL CONNECTION** Do you think it was worthwhile for Luis to add the additional shifts for homecoming weekend last October?

### Problem 11-51  Traditional versus Activity Flexible Budgeting

OBJECTIVE ① ④

Carly Davis, production manager, was upset and puzzled by the latest performance report, which indicated that she was $100,000 over budget. She and her staff had worked hard to beat the budget. Now she saw that three items—direct labor, power, and setups—were over budget. The actual costs for these three items were as follows:

| | |
|---|---|
| Direct labor | $210,000 |
| Power | 135,000 |
| Setups | 140,000 |
| Total | $485,000 |

Carly felt that the additional labor and power cost were due to the fact that her team produced more units than originally budgeted. Uncertainty in scheduling had led to more setups

*(Continued)*

than planned. She asked Sean Carpenter, the controller, why the performance report did not take the additional production into account. Sean assured Carly that he did adjust the report for increased production and showed her the budget formulas he used to predict the costs for different levels of activity. The formulas were based on direct labor hours as follows:

$$\text{Direct Labor Cost} = \$10X$$
$$\text{Power Cost} = \$5,000 + \$4X$$
$$\text{Setup Cost} = \$100,000$$

Carly pointed out that power costs were unrelated to direct labor hours, but that they seemed to vary with machine hours instead. She also pointed out that setup costs were not fixed. They varied with the number of setups—which had increased due to scheduling changes. The increase in setups required her team to work overtime, adding to the costs. Each setup also took supplies that added significantly to overhead costs.

Sean agreed that the formulas did not adequately take care of Carly's concerns. He agreed to develop a new set of cost formulas based on better explanatory variables. After a few days, Sean shared the following cost formulas with Carly:

$$\text{Direct Labor Cost} = \$10X, \text{ where } X = \text{Direct Labor Hours}$$
$$\text{Power Cost} = \$68,000 + 0.9Y, \text{ where } Y = \text{Machine Hours}$$
$$\text{Setup Cost} = \$98,000 + \$400Z, \text{ where } Z \text{ Number of Setups}$$

The actual measure of each activity driver is as follows:

| | |
|---|---|
| Direct labor hours | 20,000 |
| Machine hours | 90,000 |
| Number of setups | 110 |

**Required:**

1. Prepare a performance report for direct labor, power, and setups using the direct labor-based formulas.
2. Prepare a performance report for direct labor, power, and setups using the multiple cost driver formulas that Sean developed.
3. **CONCEPTUAL CONNECTION** Of the two approaches, which provides the more accurate picture of Carly's performance? Why?

OBJECTIVE ❹    **Problem 11-52    Activity Flexible Budgeting**

Billy Adams, controller for Westcott Inc., prepared the following budget for manufacturing costs at two different levels of activity for 2014:

**DIRECT LABOR HOURS**

| | Level of Activity | |
|---|---|---|
| | **50,000** | **100,000** |
| Direct materials | $300,000 | $ 600,000 |
| Direct labor | 200,000 | 400,000 |
| Depreciation (plant) | 100,000 | 100,000 |
| Subtotal | $600,000 | $1,100,000 |

**MACHINE HOURS**

| | Level of Activity | |
|---|---|---|
| | **200,000** | **300,000** |
| Maintenance equipment | $360,000 | $510,000 |
| Machining | 112,000 | 162,000 |
| Subtotal | $472,000 | $672,000 |

**MATERIAL MOVES**

| | Level of Activity | |
|---|---|---|
| | **20,000** | **40,000** |
| Materials handling | $165,000 | $290,000 |

**NUMBER OF BATCHES INSPECTED**

| | Level of Activity | |
|---|---|---|
| | **100** | **200** |
| Inspecting products | $ 125,000 | $ 225,000 |
| Total | $1,362,000 | $2,287,000 |

During 2014, Westcott employees worked a total of 80,000 direct labor hours, used 250,000 machine hours, made 32,000 moves, and performed 120 batch inspections. The following actual costs were incurred:

| | | | |
|---|---|---|---|
| Direct materials | $440,000 | Machining | $142,000 |
| Direct labor | 355,000 | Materials handling | 232,500 |
| Depreciation | 100,000 | Inspecting products | 160,000 |
| Maintenance | 425,000 | | |

Westcott applies overhead using rates based on direct labor hours, machine hours, number of moves, and number of batches. The second level of activity (the far right column in the preceding table) is the practical level of activity (the available activity for resources acquired in advance of usage) and is used to compute predetermined overhead pool rates.

**Required:**

1.  Prepare a performance report for Westcott's manufacturing costs in 2014.
2.  Assume that one of the products produced by Westcott is budgeted to use 10,000 direct labor hours, 15,000 machine hours, and 500 moves and will be produced in 5 batches. A total of 10,000 units will be produced during the year. Calculate the budgeted unit manufacturing cost (rounded to the nearest cent).
3.  **CONCEPTUAL CONNECTION** One of Westcott's managers said: "Budgeting at the activity level makes a lot of sense, but this budget needs to provide more detailed information. For example, the materials handling activity requires forklifts and operators, and this information is lost with simply reporting the total cost of the activity for various levels of output. We have four forklifts; each is rented for $10,000 per year and can provide 10,000 moves per year. Furthermore, for our two shifts, we need up to eight operators if we run all four forklifts. Each operator is paid a salary of $30,000 per year. Fuel costs us about $0.25 per move."

    Based on these comments, explain how this additional information may help Westcott to better manage its costs. Also, assuming that these are the only three items, expand the detail of the flexible budget for materials handling to reveal the cost of these three resource items for 20,000 moves and 40,000 moves, respectively. (*Note:* You may wish to review the concepts of flexible, committed, and discretionary resources found in Chapter 3.)

## Problem 11-53  Flexible Budgeting

OBJECTIVE ❶

At the beginning of last year, Jean Bingham, controller for Thorpe Inc., prepared the following budget for conversion costs at two levels of activity for the coming year:

| | Direct Labor Hours | |
|---|---|---|
| | **100,000** | **120,000** |
| Direct labor | $1,000,000 | $1,200,000 |
| Supervision | 180,000 | 180,000 |
| Utilities | 18,000 | 21,000 |
| Depreciation | 225,000 | 225,000 |
| Supplies | 25,000 | 30,000 |
| Maintenance | 240,000 | 284,000 |
| Rent | 120,000 | 120,000 |
| Other | 60,000 | 70,000 |
| Total manufacturing cost | $1,868,000 | $2,130,000 |

During the year, the company worked a total of 112,000 direct labor hours and incurred the following actual costs:

| | | | |
|---|---|---|---|
| Direct labor | $963,200 | Supplies | $ 24,640 |
| Supervision | 190,000 | Maintenance | 237,000 |
| Utilities | 20,500 | Rent | 120,000 |
| Depreciation | 225,000 | Other | 60,500 |

Thorpe applied overhead on the basis of direct labor hours. Normal volume of 120,000 direct labor hours is the activity level to be used to compute the predetermined overhead rate.

*(Continued)*

**Required:**

1. Determine the cost formula for each of Thorpe's conversion costs. (*Hint*: Use the high-low method.)
2. **CONCEPTUAL CONNECTION** Prepare a performance report for Thorpe's conversion costs for last year. Should any cost item be given special attention? Explain.

OBJECTIVE ❷ ❸  **Problem 11-54    Overhead Application, Overhead Variances**

Moleno Company produces a single product and uses a standard cost system. The normal production volume is 120,000 units; each unit requires five direct labor hours at standard. Overhead is applied on the basis of direct labor hours. The budgeted overhead for the coming year is as follows:

|  |  |
|---|---|
| FOH | $2,160,000* |
| VOH | 1,440,000 |

\* At normal volume.

During the year, Moleno produced 118,600 units, worked 592,300 direct labor hours, and incurred actual fixed overhead costs of $2,150,400 and actual variable overhead costs of $1,422,800.

**Required:**

1. Calculate the standard fixed overhead rate and the standard variable overhead rate.
2. Compute the applied fixed overhead and the applied variable overhead. What is the total fixed overhead variance? Total variable overhead variance?
3. **CONCEPTUAL CONNECTION** Break down the total fixed overhead variance into a spending variance and a volume variance. Discuss the significance of each.
4. **CONCEPTUAL CONNECTION** Compute the variable overhead spending and efficiency variances. Discuss the significance of each.
5. Journal entries for overhead variances were not discussed in this chapter. Typically, the overhead variance entries happen at the end of the year. Assume that applied fixed (variable) overhead is accumulated on the credit side of the fixed (variable) overhead control account. Actual fixed (variable) overhead costs are accumulated on the debit side of the respective control accounts. At the end of the year, the balance in each control account is the total fixed (variable) variance. Create accounts for each of the four overhead variances and close out the total variances to each of these four variance accounts. These four variance accounts are then usually closed to Cost of Goods Sold.

    Form a group with two to four other students, and prepare the journal entries that isolate the four variances. Finally, prepare the journal entries that close these variances to Cost of Goods Sold.

OBJECTIVE ❷ ❸  **Problem 11-55    Overhead Variance Analysis**

 The Lubbock plant of Morril's Small Motor Division produces a major subassembly for a 6.0 horsepower motor for lawn mowers. The plant uses a standard costing system for production costing and control. The standard cost sheet for the subassembly follows:

|  |  |
|---|---|
| Direct materials (6.0 lbs. @ $5.00) | $30.00 |
| Direct labor (1.6 hrs. @ $12.00) | 19.20 |
| VOH (1.6 hrs. @ $10.00) | 16.00 |
| FOH (1.6 hrs. @ $6.00) | 9.60 |
| Standard unit cost | $74.80 |

During the year, the Lubbock plant had the following actual production activity: (a) Production of motors totaled 50,000 units; (b) The company used 82,000 direct labor hours at a total cost of $1,066,000; (c) Actual fixed overhead totaled $556,000; and (d) Actual variable overhead totaled $860,000.

The Lubbock plant's practical activity is 60,000 units per year. Standard overhead rates are computed based on practical activity measured in standard direct labor hours.

**Required:**

1. Compute the variable overhead spending and efficiency variances.
2. **CONCEPTUAL CONNECTION** Compute the fixed overhead spending and volume variances. Interpret the volume variance. What can be done to reduce this variance?

### Problem 11-56   Overhead Variances

 OBJECTIVE ❷ ❸

Extrim Company produces monitors. Extrim's plant in San Antonio uses a standard costing system. The standard costing system relies on direct labor hours to assign overhead costs to production. The direct labor standard indicates that four direct labor hours should be used for every monitor produced. (The San Antonio plant produces only one model.) The normal production volume is 120,000 units. The budgeted overhead for the coming year is as follows:

|  |  |
|---|---|
| *FOH* | $1,286,400 |
| *VOH* | 888,000* |

\* At normal volume.

Extrim applies overhead on the basis of direct labor hours.

During the year, Extrim produced 119,000 units, worked 487,900 direct labor hours, and incurred actual fixed overhead costs of $1.3 million and actual variable overhead costs of $927,010.

**Required:**

1. Calculate the standard fixed overhead rate and the standard variable overhead rate.
2. Compute the applied fixed overhead and the applied variable overhead. What is the total fixed overhead variance? Total variable overhead variance?
3. **CONCEPTUAL CONNECTION** Break down the total fixed overhead variance into a spending variance and a volume variance. Discuss the significance of each.
4. **CONCEPTUAL CONNECTION** Compute the variable overhead spending and efficiency variances. Discuss the significance of each.

### Problem 11-57   Understanding Relationships, Incomplete Data, Overhead Analysis

 OBJECTIVE ❷ ❸

Lynwood Company produces surge protectors. To help control costs, Lynwood employs a standard costing system and uses a flexible budget to predict overhead costs at various levels of activity. For the most recent year, Lynwood used a standard overhead rate of $18 per direct labor hour. The rate was computed using practical activity. Budgeted overhead costs are $396,000 for 18,000 direct labor hours and $540,000 for 30,000 direct labor hours. During the past year, Lynwood generated the following data: (a) Actual production: 100,000 units; (b) Fixed overhead volume variance: $20,000 *U*; (c) Variable overhead efficiency variance: $18,000 *F*; (d) Actual fixed overhead costs: $200,000; and (e) Actual variable overhead costs: $310,000.

**Required:**

1. Calculate the fixed overhead rate.
2. Determine the fixed overhead spending variance.
3. Determine the variable overhead spending variance.
4. Determine the standard hours allowed per unit of product.

### Problem 11-58   Flexible Budget, Overhead Variances

OBJECTIVE ❶ ❷ ❸

Shumaker Company manufactures a line of high-top basketball shoes. At the beginning of the year, the following plans for production and costs were revealed:

|  |  |
|---|---|
| Pairs of shoes to be produced and sold | 55,000 |
| Standard cost per unit: |  |
| Direct materials | $15 |
| Direct labor | 12 |
| *VOH* | 6 |
| *FOH* | 3 |
| Total unit cost | $36 |

*(Continued)*

During the year, a total of 50,000 units were produced and sold. The following actual costs were incurred:

| | | | |
|---|---|---|---|
| Direct materials | $775,000 | *VOH* | $310,000 |
| Direct labor | 590,000 | *FOH* | 180,000 |

There were no beginning or ending inventories of raw materials. In producing the 50,000 units, 63,000 hours were worked, 5% more hours than the standard allowed for the actual output. Overhead costs are applied to production using direct labor hours.

**Required:**

1. Using a flexible budget, prepare a performance report comparing expected costs for the actual production with actual costs.
2. Determine the following: (a) Fixed overhead spending and volume variances and (b) Variable overhead spending and efficiency variances.

# CASES

OBJECTIVE ③ **Case 11-59   Fixed Overhead Spending and Volume Variances, Capacity Management**

Lorale Company, a producer of recreational vehicles, recently decided to begin producing a major subassembly for jet skis. The subassembly would be used by Lorale's jet ski plants and also would be sold to other producers. The decision was made to lease two large buildings in two different locations: Little Rock, Arkansas, and Athens, Georgia. The company agreed to a 11-year, renewable lease contract. The plants were of the same size, and each had 10 production lines. New equipment was purchased for each line and workers were hired to operate the equipment. The company also hired production line supervisors for each plant. A supervisor is capable of directing up to two production lines per shift. Two shifts are run for each plant. The practical production capacity of each plant is 300,000 subassemblies per year. Two standard direct labor hours are allowed for each subassembly. The costs for leasing, equipment depreciation, and supervision for a single plant are as follows (the costs are assumed to be the same for each plant):

| | |
|---|---|
| Supervision (10 supervisors @ $50,000) | $ 500,000 |
| Building lease (annual payment) | 800,000 |
| Equipment depreciation (annual) | 1,100,000 |
| Total fixed overhead costs* | $2,400,000 |

\* For simplicity, assume these are the only fixed overhead costs.

After beginning operations, Lorale discovered that demand for the product in the region covered by the Little Rock plant was less than anticipated. At the end of the first year, only 240,000 units were sold. The Athens plant sold 300,000 units as expected. The actual fixed overhead costs at the end of the first year were $2,500,000 (for each plant).

**Required:**

1. Calculate a fixed overhead rate based on standard direct labor hours.
2. Calculate the fixed overhead spending and volume variances for the Little Rock and Athens plants. What is the most likely cause of the spending variance? Why are the volume variances different for the two plants?
3. Suppose that from now on the sales for the Little Rock plant are expected to be no more than 240,000 units. What actions would you take to manage the capacity costs (fixed overhead costs)?
4. Calculate the fixed overhead cost per subassembly for each plant. Do they differ? Should they differ? Explain. Do ABC concepts help in analyzing this issue?

## Case 11-60 Ethical Considerations; Flexible Budgeting and the Environment

Harry Johnson, the chief financial officer of Ur Thrift Inc, a large retailer, had just finished a meeting with the Roger Swasey, the chief financial officer of the large retailer, and Connie Baker, its environmental officer. Over the years, Harry had overseen the development of a number of cost formulas that allowed Ur Thrift to budget the variable costs of a variety of items. For example, packaging for one of its private line of dolls had a cost formula of $Y = \$2.20X$, where $X$ represented the number of dolls sold. The formula was used to calculate the expected packaging costs which were then compared with the actual packaging costs. Over the last several years, the actual costs and budgeted costs were virtually on target, prompting Harry to claim that packaging costs were well controlled.

Connie Baker, however, argued that the packaging costs were not well controlled. In fact, she was adamant in her view that the packaging was excessive and that by reducing the packaging, costs could be reduced and the environmental impacts reduced as well. She argued that the company had an ethical obligation to reduce environmental impacts and that cost savings would also be captured, improving the profitability of the company. As another example, Connie discussed the fleet of semitrailer trucks used by Ur Thrift to move goods from its warehouses to retail outlets. The fuel cost formula was $\$3X$, where $X$ represented gallons of fuel consumed. She pointed out that the performance data also revealed that fuel costs were in control. Yet her office had recently recommended the installation of an auxiliary power unit to heat and cool the cabs of the trucks during the mandatory 10-hour breaks required of its drivers. This avoided the need to have the engine idle during this rest period. She claimed that this would significantly reduce fuel costs and easily pay for the new auxiliary units in a short period of time.

Connie had also made some comments that caused Harry to pause and do some soul searching. She noted that the financial officers of the company should be more concerned about reducing costs than simply predicting what they should be. Thus (according to her view), cost formulas are useful only to tell us where we currently are so that they can be used to assess how to reduce costs. The so-called flexible budgets are simply a means of enforcing static standards. She also said that the company's managers had an ethical obligation to not overconsume the resources of the planet. She urged both Harry and Roger to help position the company so that it could reduce its environmental impacts.

### Required:

1. Do financial officers have an ethical obligation to help in reducing negative environmental impacts? Identify and discuss which parts of the IMA's Statement of Ethical Professional Practice might apply. Also, describe the role that flexible budgeting may play in reducing environmental impacts.
2. Suppose that Harry and Connie embark on a cooperative effort to eliminate any excessive packaging. The projected results are impressive. The expected reductions will save $3 million in shipping costs ($0.50 per package), $1.5 million in packaging materials ($0.40 per package), 5,000 trees, and 1.25 million barrels of oil. Are there any ethical issues associated with these actions? What standards might apply?
3. Identify two potential ethical dilemmas that might surface in the use of flexible budgeting for performance evaluation (the dilemmas do not need to be connected with environmental activities).

# 12

# Performance Evaluation and Decentralization

© Pixelfabrik/Alamy

After studying Chapter 12, you should be able to:

**1** Explain how and why firms choose to decentralize.

**2** Compute and explain return on investment.

**3** Compute and explain residual income and economic value added.

**4** Explain the role of transfer pricing in a decentralized firm.

**5** (*Appendix 12A*) Explain the uses of the Balanced Scorecard, and compute cycle time, velocity, and manufacturing cycle efficiency.

Courtesy Herman Miller, Inc.

# EXPERIENCE MANAGERIAL DECISIONS
## with Herman Miller

The goal of performance evaluation is to provide information useful for assessing the effectiveness of past decisions so that future decisions can be improved. As you might guess, this goal is difficult to achieve because of the sheer quantity of information present in organizations and the complexity of the business environment in which most decisions are made. However, **Herman Miller, Inc.**, a large furniture manufacturer headquartered in western Michigan with business activities in over 100 countries, uses an increasingly popular performance evaluation technique—economic value added (EVA)—to help it make better decisions. For example, the entire office furniture market experienced a devastating slump in the early 2000s as a result of the dot-com bust and the 9/11 disaster. EVA measures provided Herman Miller with information beyond traditional accounting performance metrics that was critical to its dramatic and quick recovery from the negative operating margins it experienced during the slump to the near double-digit positive margins it enjoyed only a few years later. EVA identifies the return generated by the company's assets and then subtracts the cost of all capital, both debt (e.g., money raised from loans, leases, and bonds) and equity (e.g., money raised from investors), used by the company to finance those assets in order to determine whether value is being created or destroyed. More specifically, EVA helps Herman Miller to quantify the long-term financial benefits of carrying less inventory and employing fewer fixed assets in its business. As a result of such EVA analyses, Herman Miller makes fundamentally different strategic and operating decisions involving its furniture production processes than it would if it relied solely on traditional accounting metrics. The ability to impact decisions in such a positive fashion has catapulted EVA into a position of prominence in Herman Miller's successful performance evaluation system.

> *"Herman Miller, Inc., a large furniture manufacturer headquartered in western Michigan with business activities in over 100 countries, uses an increasingly popular performance evaluation technique—economic value added (EVA)—to help it make better decisions."*

# DECENTRALIZATION AND RESPONSIBILITY CENTERS

In general, a company is organized along lines of responsibility. Traditional organizational charts illustrate the flow of responsibilities from the chief executive officer down through the vice presidents to middle- and lower-level managers. Today, most companies use a flattened hierarchy—emphasizing teams. This structure is consistent with decentralization. **GE Capital**, for example, is essentially a group of smaller businesses. Ideally, the responsibility accounting system mirrors and supports the structure of an organization.

Firms with multiple responsibility centers usually choose one of two decision-making approaches to manage their diverse and complex activities: *centralized* or *decentralized*.

- In centralized decision making, decisions are made at the very top level, and lower-level managers are charged with implementing these decisions.
- Decentralized decision making allows managers at lower levels to make and implement key decisions pertaining to their areas of responsibility. This practice of delegating decision-making authority to the lower levels of management in a company is called **decentralization**.

Exhibit 12.1 illustrates the difference between centralized and decentralized companies.

( EXHIBIT 12.1 )

**Centralization and Decentralization**

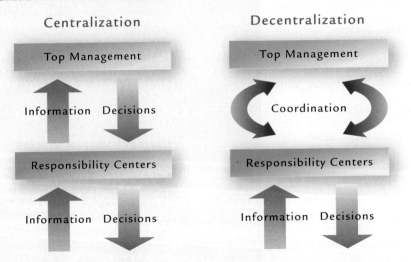

© Cengage Learning 2014

Organizations range from highly centralized to strongly decentralized. Most firms fall somewhere in between, with the majority tending toward decentralization. The reasons for the popularity of decentralization and the ways in which a company may choose to decentralize are discussed next.

## Reasons for Decentralization

Firms decide to decentralize for several reasons, including the following:

- ease of gathering and using local information
- focusing of central management
- training and motivating of segment managers
- enhanced competition, exposing segments to market forces

**Gathering and Using Local Information**  The quality of decisions is affected by the quality of information available. As a firm grows in size and operates in different markets and regions, central management may not understand local conditions. Lower-level managers, however, are in contact with immediate operating conditions (such as the strength and nature of local competition, the nature of the local labor force, and so on). As a result, they often are better positioned to make local decisions. For example, **McDonald's** has restaurants around the world. The tastes of people in China or France differ from those of people in the United States. So, McDonald's tailors its menu to different countries. The result is that the McDonald's in each country can differentiate to meet the needs of its local market.

**Focusing of Central Management**   By decentralizing the operating decisions, central management is free to engage in strategic planning and decision making. The long-run survival of the organization should be of more importance to central management than day-to-day operations.

**Training and Motivating of Managers**   Organizations always need well-trained managers to replace higher-level managers who leave to take advantage of other opportunities. What better way to prepare a future generation of higher-level managers than by providing them the opportunity to make significant decisions? These opportunities also enable top managers to evaluate local managers' capabilities and promote those who make the best decisions.

**Enhanced Competition**   In a highly centralized company, overall profit margins can mask inefficiencies within the various subdivisions. Large companies now find that they cannot afford to keep a noncompetitive division. One of the best ways to improve performance of a division or factory is to expose it more fully to market forces. At **Koch Industries Inc.**, each unit is expected to act as an autonomous business unit and to set prices both externally and internally. Units whose services are not required by other Koch units may face possible elimination.

## Divisions in the Decentralized Firm

Decentralization involves a cost-benefit trade-off. As a firm becomes more decentralized, it passes more decision authority down the managerial hierarchy. As a result, managers in a decentralized firm make and implement more decisions than do managers in a centralized firm. The benefit of decentralization is that decisions are more likely to be made by managers who possess the specific local knowledge—not possessed by high level managers—to use the firm's resources in the best way possible to maximize firm value. However, the cost of decentralization is that lower-level managers who have the knowledge to make the best decisions with the firm's resources are less likely to possess the same incentive as high-level managers to maximize firm value. Stated differently, as compared to high-level managers, lower-level managers are more likely to use the firm's resources for personal gain than for increasing the firm's stock value.

Decentralization usually is achieved by creating units called *divisions*. Divisions can be differentiated a number of different ways, including the following:

- types of goods or services
- geographic lines
- responsibility centers

## Types of Goods or Services

One way in which divisions are differentiated is by the types of goods or services produced. For example, divisions of **PepsiCo** include the Snack Ventures Europe Division (a joint venture with **General Mills**), **Frito-Lay Inc.**, and **Tropicana**, as well as its flagship soft-drink division. Exhibit 12.2 (p. 526) shows decentralized divisions of PepsiCo. These divisions are organized on the basis of product lines. Notice that some divisions depend on other divisions. For example, PepsiCo spun off its restaurant divisions to **YUM! Brands**. As a result, the cola you drink at **Pizza Hut**, **Taco Bell**, and **KFC** will be Pepsi—not Coke. In a decentralized setting, some interdependencies usually exist; otherwise, a company would merely be a collection of totally separate entities.

## EXHIBIT 12.2

**Decentralized Divisions**

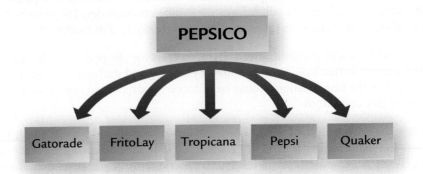

© Cengage Learning 2014

## Geographic Lines

Divisions may also be created along geographic lines. For example, **UAL Inc.** (parent of **United Airlines**) has a number of regional divisions: Asian/Pacific, Caribbean, European, Latin American, and North American. The presence of divisions spanning one or more regions creates the need for performance evaluation that can take into account differences in divisional environments.

## Responsibility Centers

A third way divisions differ is by the type of responsibility given to the divisional manager. As a firm grows, top management typically creates areas of responsibility, known as responsibility centers, and assigns subordinate managers to those areas. A **responsibility center** is a segment of the business whose manager is accountable for specified sets of activities. The results of each responsibility center can be measured according to the information that managers need to operate their centers. The four major types of responsibility centers are as follows:

- **Cost center**: Manager is responsible only for costs.
- **Revenue center**: Manager is responsible only for sales, or revenue.
- **Profit center**: Manager is responsible for both revenues and costs.
- **Investment center**: Manager is responsible for revenues, costs, and investments.

The choice of responsibility center typically mirrors the actual situation and the type of information available to the manager. Information is the key to appropriately holding managers responsible for outcomes. For example, a production department manager is held responsible for departmental *costs* but not for sales. This responsibility choice occurs because the production department manager understands and directly controls some production costs but does not set prices. Any difference between actual and expected costs can best be explained at this level.

The marketing department manager sets the price and projected sales *revenue*. Therefore, the marketing department may be evaluated as a revenue center. Direct costs of the marketing department and overall sales are the responsibility of the sales manager.

In some companies, plant managers are given the responsibility for manufacturing and marketing their products. These plant managers control both *costs and revenues*, putting them in control of a profit center. Operating income is an important performance measure for profit center managers.

Finally, divisions sometimes are cited as examples of investment centers. In addition to having control over cost and pricing decisions, divisional managers have the power to make *investment* decisions such as plant closings and openings and decisions to keep or drop a product line. As a result, both operating income and some type of return on investment are important performance measures for investment center managers. Exhibit 12.3 displays these centers along with the type of information that managers need to manage their operations. As the exhibit shows, investment centers represent the greatest degree of decentralization (followed by profit centers and finally by cost and revenue centers) because their managers have the freedom to make the greatest variety of decisions.

( EXHIBIT 12.3 )

**Types of Responsibility Centers and Accounting Information Used to Measure Performance**

| | Cost | Sales | Capital Investment | Other |
|---|---|---|---|---|
| Cost center | X | | | |
| Revenue center | | X | | |
| Profit center | X | X | | |
| Investment center | X | X | X | X |

© Cengage Learning 2014

It is important to realize that while the responsibility center manager has responsibility only for the activities of that center, decisions made by that manager can affect other responsibility centers. For example, the sales force at a floor care products firm routinely offers customers price discounts at the end of the month. Sales increase dramatically, which is good for revenue and the sales force. However, the factory is forced to institute overtime shifts to keep up with demand. These overtime shifts increase the costs of the factory as well as the cost per unit of product.

Organizing divisions as responsibility centers creates the opportunity to control the divisions through the use of responsibility accounting. Revenue center control is achieved by evaluating the efficiency and the effectiveness of divisional managers on the basis of sales revenue. Cost center control is based on control of costs and frequently employs variance analysis, as described in Chapters 9 and 10. This chapter focuses on the evaluation of profit centers and investment centers.

# YOUDECIDE  Organizational Structure

You have been chosen as the CEO of a new hospital. One important decision you face early is determining the optimal level of decentralization for your various levels of supporting management.

**What factors should you consider as you decide how best to structure the hospital management?**

There is no easy, one-size-fits all answer. However, some of the top ranked hospitals in the world, such as the **Cleveland Clinic**, recognize that much of the specific knowledge critically important for making the best patient care decisions resides with the hospital's physicians, surgeons, and nurses rather than with the Chief Executive Officer or other "C-Suite" executives (e.g., Chief Financial Officer, Chief Operations Officer, Chief Integrity Officer, etc.). Such hospitals choose a highly decentralized organizational structure so that many important decisions that affect patient treatment are made by individuals far removed from top management. The biggest challenge to effectively managing a highly decentralized decision making structure like this one is to create quantitative performance measures for the decision makers—in this case the physicians, surgeons, and nurses—to assess the quality of their decisions. Furthermore, these performance measures need to be used as part of the decision makers' compensation packages to reward (or punish) their wise (or unwise) decisions that hopefully are taken in the best interest of the patients and, ultimately, the hospital. A growing number of publicly-traded companies, such as **Starbucks**, offer lower level employees—even part-time employees—incentives such as healthcare benefits and stock options to motivate them to take actions that are in the companies' best long-term interests.

**In decentralized organizations, managerial accounting is important in designing effective performance measures and incentive systems to help ensure that lower-level managers use their decision-making authority to improve the organization's performance.**

OBJECTIVE ② 

Compute and explain return on investment.

# MEASURING THE PERFORMANCE OF INVESTMENT CENTERS BY USING RETURN ON INVESTMENT

Typically, investment centers are evaluated on the basis of return on investment (ROI). Other common measures include residual income and economic value added (EVA).

## Return on Investment

Divisions that are investment centers will have an income statement and a balance sheet. So, could those divisions be ranked on the basis of income? Suppose, for example, that a company has two divisions—Alpha and Beta. Alpha's income is $100,000, and Beta's income is $200,000. Did Beta perform better than Alpha? What if Alpha used an investment of $500,000 to produce the contribution of $100,000, while Beta used an investment of $2 million to produce the $200,000 contribution? Does your response change? Clearly, it does. Relating the reported operating profits to the assets used to produce them is a more meaningful measure of performance.

One way to relate operating profits to assets employed is to compute the **return on investment (ROI)**, which is the profit earned per dollar of investment. ROI is the most common measure of performance for an investment center. It can be defined as follows:

$$\text{ROI} = \frac{\text{Operating Income}}{\text{Average Operating Assets}}$$

**Operating income** refers to earnings before interest and taxes. **Operating assets** are all assets acquired to generate operating income, including cash, receivables, inventories, land, buildings, and equipment. Average operating assets is computed as follows:

$$\text{Average Operating Assets} = \frac{(\text{Beginning Assets} + \text{Ending Assets})}{2}$$

Opinions vary regarding how long-term assets (plant and equipment) should be valued (e.g., gross book value vs. net book value or historical cost vs. current cost). Most firms use historical cost and net book value.[1]

Going back to our example, Alpha's ROI is 0.20, calculated as:

$$\frac{\text{Operating Income}}{\text{Average Operating Assets}} = \frac{\$100,000}{\$500,000}$$

Beta's ROI is only 0.10 ($200,000/$2,000,000). The formula for ROI is quick and easy to use.

## Margin and Turnover

A second way to calculate ROI is to separate the formula (Operating Income/Average Operating Assets) into margin and turnover. **Margin** is the ratio of operating income to sales. It tells how many cents of operating income result from each dollar of sales; it expresses the portion of sales that is available for interest, taxes, and profit. Some managers also refer to margin as return on sales. **Turnover** is a different measure; it is found by dividing sales by average operating assets. Turnover tells how many dollars of sales result from every dollar invested in operating assets. It shows how productively assets are being used to generate sales.

| | Margin | Turnover |
|---|---|---|
| $\text{ROI} =$ | $\dfrac{\text{Operating Income}}{\text{Sales}}$ | $\times \quad \dfrac{\text{Sales}}{\text{Average Operating Assets}}$ |

Notice that "Sales" in the above formula can be cancelled out to yield the original ROI formula of Operating Income/Average Operating Assets.

---

[1] There is no one correct way to calculate ROI. The important thing is to be sure that one method is applied consistently, which allows the company to compare the ROIs among divisions and over time.

Suppose, for example, that Alpha had sales of $400,000. Then, margin would be 0.25, calculated as

$$\frac{\text{Operating Income}}{\text{Sales}} = \frac{\$100,000}{\$400,000}$$

Turnover would be 0.80, calculated as

$$\frac{\text{Sales}}{\text{Average Operating Assets}} = \frac{\$400,000}{\$500,000}$$

Alpha's ROI would still be 0.20 (0.25 × 0.80). Cornerstone 12.1 shows how to calculate these ratios.

## Calculating Average Operating Assets, Margin, Turnover, and Return on Investment

**CORNERSTONE**

**12.1**

**Why:**

Return on investment is a key measure of performance. It relates the income earned to the investment needed to produce that income. It is appropriate for companies and for investment centers.

**Information:**

Celimar Company's Western Division earned operating income last year as shown in the following income statement:

| | |
|---|---:|
| Sales | $ 480,000 |
| Cost of goods sold | (222,000) |
| Gross margin | $ 258,000 |
| Selling and administrative expense | (210,000) |
| Operating income | $  48,000 |

At the beginning of the year, the value of operating assets was $277,000. At the end of the year, the value of operating assets was $323,000.

**Required:**

For the Western Division, calculate the following: (1) average operating assets, (2) margin, (3) turnover, and (4) return on investment.

**Solution:**

1. Average Operating Assets = (Beginning Assets + Ending Assets)/2
   = ($277,000 + $323,000)/2
   = $300,000

2. Margin = Operating Income/Sales = $48,000/$480,000
   = 0.10, or 10%

3. Turnover = Sales/Average Operating Assets = $480,000/$300,000 = 1.6

4. ROI = Margin × Turnover = 0.10 × 1.6 = 0.16, or 16%

   *Note:* ROI can also be calculated as

   ROI = Operating Income/Average Operating Assets
   = $48,000/$300,000
   = 0.16, or 16%

While both approaches yield the same ROI, the calculation of margin and turnover gives a manager valuable information. To illustrate this additional information, consider the data presented in Exhibit 12.4. The Electronics Division improved its ROI from 18% in Year 1 to 20% in Year 2. The Medical Supplies Division's ROI, however, dropped from 18 to 15%. Computing the margin and turnover ratios for each division gives a better picture of what caused the change in rates. As with variance analysis, understanding the causes of managerial accounting measures (i.e., variances, margins, turnover, etc.) helps managers take actions to improve the division. These ratios also are presented in Exhibit 12.4.

Notice that the margins for both divisions dropped from Year 1 to Year 2. In fact, the divisions experienced the *same* percentage of decline (16.67%). A declining margin could be explained by increasing expenses, competitive pressures (forcing a decrease in selling prices), or both.

Despite the declining margin, the Electronics Division was able to increase its rate of return. The reason is that the increase in turnover more than compensated for the decline in margin. One explanation for the increased turnover could be a deliberate policy to reduce inventories.

(Notice that the average assets employed remained the same for the Electronics Division even though sales increased by $10 million.)

The experience of the Medical Supplies Division was less favorable. Because its turnover rate remained unchanged, its ROI dropped. This division, unlike the Electronics Division, could not overcome the decline in margin.

( EXHIBIT 12.4 )

## Comparison of Divisional Performance

| | Comparison of ROI | |
| --- | --- | --- |
| | **Electronics Division** | **Medical Supplies Division** |
| Year 1: | | |
| Sales | $30,000,000 | $117,000,000 |
| Operating income | 1,800,000 | 3,510,000 |
| Average operating assets | 10,000,000 | 19,510,000 |
| ROI[a] | 18% | 18% |
| Year 2: | | |
| Sales | $40,000,000 | $117,000,000 |
| Operating income | 2,000,000 | 2,925,000 |
| Average operating assets | 10,000,000 | 19,500,000 |
| ROI[a] | 20% | 15% |

| | Margin and Turnover Comparisons | | | |
| --- | --- | --- | --- | --- |
| | **Electronics Division** | | **Medical Supplies Division** | |
| | **Year 1** | **Year 2** | **Year 1** | **Year 2** |
| Margin[b] | 6.0% | 5.0% | 3.0% | 2.5% |
| Turnover[c] | ×3.0 | ×4.0 | ×6.0 | ×6.0 |
| ROI | 18.0% | 20.0% | 18.0% | 15.0% |

[a]Operating Income/Average Operating Assets
[b]Operating Income/Sales
[c]Sales/Average Operating Assets

# Advantages of Return on Investment

At least three positive results stem from the use of ROI:

- It encourages managers to focus on the relationship among sales, expenses, and investment, as should be the case for a manager of an investment center.
- It encourages managers to focus on cost efficiency.
- It encourages managers to focus on operating asset efficiency.

These advantages are illustrated by the following three scenarios.

## Illustrating Relationships: Focus on Return on Investment Relationships

Della Barnes, manager of the Plastics Division, is mulling over a suggestion from her marketing vice president to increase the advertising budget by $100,000. The marketing vice president is confident that this increase will boost sales by $200,000. Della realizes that the increased sales will also raise expenses. She finds that the increased variable cost will be $80,000.

The division also will need to purchase additional machinery to handle the increased production. The equipment will cost $50,000 and will add $10,000 of depreciation expense. As a result, the proposal will add $10,000 ($200,000 − $80,000 − $10,000 − $100,000) to operating income. Currently, the division has sales of $2 million, total expenses of $1,850,000, and operating income of $150,000. Operating assets equal $1 million.

|  | **Without Increased Advertising** | **With Increased Advertising** |
|---|---|---|
| Sales | $2,000,000 | $2,200,000 |
| Less: Expenses | 1,850,000 | 2,040,000 |
| Operating income | $ 150,000 | $ 160,000 |
| Average operating assets | $1,000,000 | $1,050,000 |

ROI:

$$\$150,000/\$1,000,000 = 0.15, \text{ or } 15\%$$

$$\$160,000/\$1,050,000 = 0.1524, \text{ or } 15.24\%$$

The ROI without the additional advertising is 15%. The ROI with the additional advertising and $50,000 investment in assets is 15.24%. Since ROI is increased by the proposal, Della decides to authorize the increased advertising. In effect, the current ROI, without the proposal, is the hurdle rate. **Hurdle rate** indicates the minimum ROI necessary to accept an investment.

**Focus on Cost Efficiency** Kyle Chugg, manager of Turner's Battery Division, groaned as he reviewed the projections for the last half of the current fiscal year. The recession was hurting his division's performance. Adding the projected operating income of $200,000 to the actual operating income of the first half produced expected annual earnings of $425,000. Kyle then divided the expected operating income by the division's average operating assets to obtain an expected ROI of 12.15%. "This is awful," muttered Kyle. "Last year our ROI was 16%. And I'm looking at a couple more bad years before business returns to normal. Something has to be done to improve our performance."

Kyle directed all operating managers to identify and eliminate nonvalue-added activities. As a result, lower-level managers found ways to reduce costs by $150,000 for the remaining half of the year. This reduction increased the annual operating income from $425,000 to $575,000, increasing ROI from 12.15% to 16.43% as a result. Interestingly, Kyle found that some of the reductions could be maintained after business returned to normal.

**Focus on Operating Asset Efficiency** The Electronic Storage Division prospered during its early years. In the beginning, the division developed portable external disk drives for storing data; sales and ROI were extraordinarily high. However, during the past several years, competitors had developed similar technology, and the division's ROI had plunged from 30 to 15%. Cost cutting had helped initially, but all of the fat had been removed, making further improvements from cost reductions impossible. Moreover, any increase in sales was unlikely—competition was too stiff. The divisional manager searched for some way to increase the ROI by at least 3 to 5%. Only by raising the ROI so that it compared favorably with that of the other divisions, could the division expect to receive additional capital for research and development (R&D).

The divisional manager initiated an intensive program to reduce operating assets. Most of the gains were made in the area of inventory reductions. However, one plant was closed because of a long-term reduction in market share. By installing a just-in-time purchasing and manufacturing system, the division was able to reduce its asset base without threatening its remaining market share. Finally, the reduction in operating assets meant that operating costs could be decreased still further. The end result was a 50% increase in the division's ROI, from 15% to more than 22%.

## Disadvantages of the Return on Investment Measure

Overemphasis on ROI can produce myopic behavior. Two negative aspects associated with ROI frequently are:

- It can produce a narrow focus on divisional profitability at the expense of profitability for the overall firm.
- It encourages managers to focus on the short run at the expense of the long run.

These disadvantages are illustrated by the following two scenarios.

**Narrow Focus on Divisional Profitability**  A Cleaning Products Division has the opportunity to invest in two projects for the coming year. The outlay required for each investment, the dollar returns, and the ROI are as follows:

|  | Project I | Project II |
|---|---|---|
| Investment | $10,000,000 | $4,000,000 |
| Operating income | 1,300,000 | 640,000 |
| ROI | 13% | 16% |

The division currently earns ROI of 15%, with operating assets of $50 million and operating income on current investments of $7.5 million. The division has approval to request up to $15 million in new investment capital. Corporate headquarters requires that all investments earn at least 10% (this rate represents the corporation's cost of acquiring the capital). Any capital not used by a division is invested by headquarters, and it earns exactly 10%.

The division manager has four alternatives: (1) invest in Project I, (2) invest in Project II, (3) invest in both Projects I and II, or (4) invest in neither project. The divisional ROI was computed for each alternative.

| | Alternatives | | | |
|---|---|---|---|---|
|  | **Select Project I** | **Select Project II** | **Select Both Projects** | **Select Neither Project** |
| Operating income | $8,800,000 | $8,140,000 | $9,440,000 | $7,500,000 |
| Operating assets | $60,000,000 | $54,000,000 | $64,000,000 | $50,000,000 |
| ROI | 14.67% | 15.7% | 14.75% | 15.00% |

The divisional manager chose to invest only in Project II, since it would boost ROI from 15.00% to 15.07%.

While the manager's choice maximized divisional ROI, it did not maximize the profit the company could have earned. If Project I had been selected, the company would have earned $1.3 million in profits. By not selecting Project I, the $10 million in capital is invested at 10%, earning only $1 million (0.10 × $10,000,000). The single-minded focus on divisional ROI, then, cost the company $300,000 in profits ($1,300,000 − $1,000,000).

**Encourages Short-Run Optimization**   Ruth Lunsford, manager of a Small Tools Division, was displeased with her division's performance during the first three quarters. Given the expected income for the fourth quarter, the ROI for the year would be 13%, at least two percentage points below where she had hoped to be. Such an ROI might not be strong enough to justify the early promotion she wanted. With only three months left, drastic action was needed. Increasing sales for the last quarter was unlikely. Most sales were booked at least two to three months in advance. Emphasizing extra sales activity would benefit next year's performance. What was needed were some ways to improve this year's performance.

After careful thought, Ruth decided to take the following actions:

- Lay off five of the highest paid salespeople.
- Cut the advertising budget for the fourth quarter by 50%.
- Delay all promotions within the division for three months.
- Reduce the preventive maintenance budget by 75%.
- Use cheaper raw materials for fourth-quarter production.

In the aggregate, these steps would reduce expenses, increase income, and raise the ROI to about 15.2% for the current year.

While Ruth's actions increase the profits and ROI in the short run, they have some long-run negative consequences. Laying off the highest paid (and possibly the best) salespeople may harm the division's future sales-generating capabilities. Future sales could also be hurt by cutting back on advertising and using cheaper raw materials. Delaying promotions could hurt employee morale, which could, in turn, lower productivity and future sales. Finally, reducing preventive maintenance will likely increase downtime and decrease the life of the productive equipment.

**ETHICAL DECISIONS**   Ethical considerations also come into play when managers attempt to "game" ROI. Ruth's five top-earning salespeople probably were her best salespeople. Letting them go meant that sales probably would decrease, an outcome not in the best interest of the firm. Thus, her action is directly contrary to her obligation to take actions in the best interests of the company. The layoffs also might violate the implicit contract a company has with workers that outstanding work will lead to continued employment. ●

# MEASURING THE PERFORMANCE OF INVESTMENT CENTERS BY USING RESIDUAL INCOME AND ECONOMIC VALUE ADDED

OBJECTIVE ❸

Compute and explain residual income and economic value added.

To compensate for the tendency of ROI to discourage investments that are profitable for the company but that lower a division's ROI, some companies have adopted alternative performance measures such as residual income. EVA is an alternate way to calculate residual income that is being used in a number of companies, such as **Herman Miller**.

## Residual Income

**Residual income** is the difference between operating income and the minimum dollar return required on a company's operating assets:

> Residual Income = Operating Income – (Minimum Rate of Return ×
> Average Operating Assets)

Cornerstone 12.2  shows how to calculate residual income.

## Calculating Residual Income

**12.2**

**Why:**

Residual income is measured in dollar amounts rather than percentages. It relates the income earned to the minimum required return on investment and overcomes the tendency for managers to turn down profitable projects that might lower divisional ROI.

**Information:**

Celimar Company's Western Division earned operating income last year as shown in the following income statement:

| | |
|---|---:|
| Sales | $480,000 |
| Cost of goods sold | 222,000 |
| Gross margin | $258,000 |
| Selling and administrative expense | 210,000 |
| Operating income | $ 48,000 |

At the beginning of the year, the value of operating assets was $277,000. At the end of the year, the value of operating assets was $323,000. Celimar Company requires a minimum rate of return of 12%.

**Required:**

For the Western Division, calculate (1) average operating assets and (2) residual income.

**Solution:**

1. Average Operating Assets = (Beginning Assets + Ending Assets)/2
   $$= (\$277,000 + \$323,000)/2$$
   $$= \$300,000$$

2. Residual Income = Operating Income − (Minimum Rate of Return × Average Operating Assets
   $$= \$48,000 - (0.12 \times \$300,000)$$
   $$= \$48,000 - \$36,000$$
   $$= \$12,000$$

The minimum rate of return is set by the company and is the same as the hurdle rate (see the section on ROI). If residual income is greater than zero, then the division is earning more than the minimum required rate of return (or hurdle rate). If residual income is less than zero, then the division is earning less than the minimum required rate of return. Finally, if residual income equals zero, then the division is earning precisely the minimum required rate of return.

**Advantage of Residual Income**   Recall that the manager of the Cleaning Products Division rejected Project I because it would have reduced divisional ROI. However, that decision cost the company $300,000 in profits. The use of residual income as the performance measure would have prevented this loss. The residual income for each project is computed as follows:

*Project I*
Residual Income = Operating Income − (Minimum Rate of Return × Average Operating Assets)
$$= \$1,300,000 - (0.10 \times \$10,000,000)$$
$$= \$1,300,000 - \$1,000,000$$
$$= \$300,000$$

*Project II*

Residual Income = $640,000 − (0.10 × $4,000,000)

$= \$640,000 - \$400,000$

$= \$240,000$

Notice that both projects have positive residual income. For comparative purposes, the divisional residual income for each of the four alternatives identified is as follows:

| | Alternatives | | | |
| | Select Only Project I | Select Only Project II | Select Both Projects | Select Neither Project |
|---|---|---|---|---|
| Operating assets | $60,000,000 | $54,000,000 | $64,000,000 | $50,000,000 |
| Operating income | $ 8,800,000 | $ 8,140,000 | $ 9,440,000 | $ 7,500,000 |
| Minimum return* | 6,000,000 | 5,400,000 | 6,400,000 | 5,000,000 |
| Residual income | $ 2,800,000 | $ 2,740,000 | $ 3,040,000 | $ 2,500,000 |

\* 0.10 × Operating Assets

As shown on page 532, selecting both projects produces the greatest increase in residual income. The use of residual income encourages managers to accept any project that earns a return that is above the minimum rate.

**Disadvantages of Residual Income**   Residual income, like ROI, can encourage a short-run orientation. If Ruth Lunsford were being evaluated on the basis of residual income, she could have taken the same actions.

Another problem with residual income is that, unlike ROI, it is an absolute measure of profitability. Thus, direct comparison of the performance of two different investment centers becomes difficult, as the level of investment may differ. For example, consider the residual income computations for Division A and Division B where the minimum required rate of return is 8%.

| | Division A | Division B |
|---|---|---|
| Average operating assets | $15,000,000 | $2,500,000 |
| Operating income | $ 1,500,000 | $  300,000 |
| Minimum return[a] | (1,200,000) | (200,000) |
| Residual income | $   300,000 | $  100,000 |
| Residual return[b] | 2% | 4% |

[a] 0.08 × Operating Assets
[b] Residual Income/Operating Assets

It is tempting to claim that Division A is outperforming Division B since its residual income is three times higher. Notice, however, that Division A is considerably larger than Division B and has six times as many assets. One possible way to correct this disadvantage is to compute both ROI and residual income and to use both measures for performance evaluation. ROI could then be used for interdivisional comparisons.

## Economic Value Added (EVA)

Another financial performance measure that is similar to residual income is *economic value added.* **Economic value added (EVA)**[2] is after tax operating income minus the dollar cost of capital employed. The dollar cost of capital employed is the actual percentage cost of capital[3] multiplied by the total capital employed, expressed as follows:

> EVA = After-Tax Operating Income − (Actual Percentage Cost of Capital × Total Capital Employed)

[2] EVA was developed by Stern Stewart & Co. in the 1990s. More information can be found on the firm's website, www.sternstewart.com/evaabout/whatis.php.
[3] The computation of a company's actual cost of capital is reserved for advanced accounting courses.

Cornerstone 12.3 shows how to calculate EVA.

## CORNERSTONE 12.3

## Calculating Economic Value Added

**Why:**

Economic value added adjusts earnings by the true cost of capital employed. As a result, it is a measure of wealth created or destroyed by a company during a given time period.

**Information:**

Celimar Company's Western Division earned net income last year as shown in the following income statement:

| | |
|---|---|
| Sales | $480,000 |
| Cost of goods sold | 222,000 |
| Gross margin | $258,000 |
| Selling and administrative expense | 210,000 |
| Operating income | $ 48,000 |
| Less: Income taxes (@ 30%) | 14,400 |
| Net income | $ 33,600 |

Total capital employed equaled $300,000. Celimar Company's actual cost of capital is 10%.

**Required:**

Calculate EVA for the Western Division.

**Solution:**

$$\text{EVA} = \text{After-Tax Operating Income} - (\text{Actual Percentage Cost of Capital} \times \text{Total Capital Employed})$$
$$= \$33,600 - (0.10 \times \$300,000)$$
$$= \$33,600 - \$30,000$$
$$= \$3,600$$

## concept Q&A

What are the differences and similarities between the basic residual income calculation and EVA?

**Answer:**

Residual income can use either before-tax income (operating income) or after-tax income. In addition, residual income uses a minimum required rate of return set by upper management. EVA, on the other hand, uses after-tax income and requires the company to compute its actual cost of capital.

Basically, EVA is residual income with the minimum rate of return equal to the actual cost of capital for the firm (as opposed to some minimum rate of return desired by the company for other reasons). If EVA is positive, then the company has increased its wealth during the period. If EVA is negative, then the company has decreased its wealth during the period. Consider the old saying, "It takes money to make money." EVA helps the company to determine whether the money it makes is more than the money it takes to make it. Over the long term, only those companies creating capital, or wealth, can survive.

As a form of residual income, EVA is a dollar figure, not a percentage rate of return. However, it does bear a resemblance to rates of return such as ROI because it links net income (return) to capital employed. The key feature of EVA is its emphasis on *after-tax* operating profit and the *actual* cost of capital. Residual income, on the other hand, uses a minimum expected rate of return.

Investors like EVA because it relates profit to the amount of resources needed to achieve it. A number of companies are evaluated on the basis of EVA. For example, companies such as **General Electric, Wal-Mart, Merck & Co., IBM, Verizon Communications, Disney Company, JetBlue Airways Corp.,** and **Pixar** use EVA metrics in some capacity. One important caveat for EVA metrics is that their calculation is not based on Generally Accepted Accounting Principles (GAAP), which means that ten different organizations likely will calculate EVA in ten different ways, unlike GAAP metrics that must be calculated in the same manner by all organizations.

**Behavioral Aspects of Economic Value Added**   A number of companies have discovered that EVA helps to encourage the right kind of behavior from their divisions in a way that emphasis on operating income alone cannot. The underlying reason is EVA's reliance on the true cost of capital. In some companies, the responsibility for investment decisions rests with corporate management. As a result, the cost of capital is considered a corporate expense rather than an expense attributable to particular divisions. If a division builds inventories and investment, the cost of financing that investment is passed along to the overall income statement and does not show up as a reduction from that division's operating income as it would under an EVA analysis. Without an EVA analysis, the result is to make investment seem free to the divisions, and of course, they want more.

Let's return briefly to **Herman Miller**'s use of EVA that was introduced at the beginning of the chapter. Before developing its EVA metrics (as part of its lean manufacturing initiative), Herman Miller would purchase or build in large batches to capture savings resulting from bulk transactions. For example, managers often would order a batch of 1,000 parts when only 200 actually were needed for custom orders. However, with the introduction of EVA, a capital charge was assessed on the fixed warehousing- and equipment-related assets required to process, transport, store, replace (in the event of obsolescence), and repair (if damaged) these large quantities of excess inventory. In so doing, EVA helped managers quickly realize that the costs of processing excess inventory often outweigh any benefits of purchasing or building in unnecessarily large quantities. Manager behavior at Herman Miller has changed dramatically as a result of EVA, as each part in the production process now is produced or purchased to match the customer order and that part moves through the entire process without significant delay, usually going out the door within a single day.

Not surprisingly, research indicates that more firms continue to adopt EVA measures as part of their overall performance evaluation package.[4] It should be cautioned, however, that research also shows that some firms that collect EVA measures struggle to integrate these relatively complex measures into managerial decision making without considerable training for the managers.[5]

# TRANSFER PRICING

In many decentralized organizations, the output of one division is used as the input of another. For example, assume that one division of **Sony** manufactures batteries for its VAIO computers, which in turn sells the batteries to another Sony division that uses them to complete the computer manufacturing process. This internal transfer between two divisions within Sony raises an accounting issue. How is the transferred good valued? When divisions are treated as responsibility centers, they are evaluated on the basis

**OBJECTIVE ❹**

Explain the role of transfer pricing in a decentralized firm.

---

[4] Stern Stewart Research, "Stern Stewart's EVA Clients Outperform the Market and Their Peers," *EVAluation: Special Report* (October 2002).
[5] Alexander Mersereau, "Pushing the Art of Management Accounting," *CMA Management,* Volume 79, Issue 9 (February 1, 2006).

of their contribution to costs, revenues, operating income, ROI, and residual income or EVA, depending on the particular center type. As a result, the value of the transferred good is revenue to the selling division and cost to the buying division. This value, or internal price, is called the *transfer price*. In other words, a **transfer price** is the price charged for a component by the selling division to the buying division of the same company. Transfer pricing is a complex issue and has an impact on divisions and the company as a whole.

## Impact of Transfer Pricing on Divisions and the Firm as a Whole

When one division of a company sells to another division, both divisions as well as the company as a whole are affected. The price charged for the transferred good affects both

- the costs of the buying division
- the revenues of the selling division

Thus, the profits of both divisions, as well as the evaluation and compensation of their managers, are affected by the transfer price. Since profit-based performance measures of the two divisions are affected (for example, ROI and residual income), transfer pricing often can be an emotionally charged issue. Exhibit 12.5 illustrates the effect of the transfer price on two divisions of ABC Inc. Division A produces a component and sells it to another division of the same company, Division C. The $30 transfer price is revenue to Division A; clearly, Division A wants the price to be as high as possible. Conversely, the $30 transfer price is cost to Division C, just like the cost of any raw material. Division C prefers as low a transfer price as possible.

( EXHIBIT 12.5 )

**Impact of Transfer Price on Transferring Divisions and the Company, ABC Inc., as a Whole**

| Division A | Division C |
| --- | --- |
| Produces component and transfers it to C for transfer price of $30 per unit. | Purchases component from A at transfer price of $30 per unit and uses it in production of final product. |
| Transfer price = $30 per unit | Transfer price = $30 per unit |
| Revenue to A | Cost to C |
| Increases income | Decreases income |
| Increases ROI | Decreases ROI |

© Cengage Learning 2014

Note: Transfer Price Revenue = Transfer Price Cost; zero dollar impact on ABC Inc.

The actual transfer price nets out for the company *as a whole* in that total *pretax* income for the company is the same regardless of the transfer price. However, transfer pricing can affect the level of *after-tax* profits earned by the multinational company that operates in multiple countries with different corporate tax rates and other legal requirements set by the countries in which the various divisions generate income. For example, if the selling division operates in a low-tax country and the buying division operates in a high-tax country, the transfer price may be set quite high. Then, the high transfer price (a revenue for A) would increase profit in the division in the low-tax country, and the high transfer price (a cost for B) would decrease profit in the division in the high-tax country. This transfer pricing strategy reduces overall corporate income taxes. The international transfer pricing situation is examined in detail in more advanced courses.

# Transfer Pricing Policies

Recall that a decentralized company allows much more authority for decision making at lower management levels. It would be counterproductive for the decentralized company to then decide on the actual transfer prices between two divisions. As a result, top management usually sets the transfer pricing policy, but the divisions still decide whether or not to transfer. For example, top management at Verybig Inc. may set the corporate transfer pricing policy at full manufacturing cost. Then, if Mediumbig Division wants to transfer a product to Somewhatbig Division, the transfer price would be the product cost. However, neither division is forced to transfer the product internally. The transfer pricing policy only says that *if* the product is transferred, it must be at cost.

Several transfer pricing policies are used in practice, including the following:

- market price
- cost-based transfer prices
- negotiated transfer prices

**Market Price** If there is a competitive outside market for the transferred product, then the best transfer price is the market price. In such a case, divisional managers' actions will simultaneously optimize divisional profits and firmwide profits. Furthermore, no division can benefit at the expense of another. In this setting, top management will not be tempted to intervene.

Suppose that the Furniture Division of a corporation produces futons. The Mattress Division of that same corporation produces mattresses, including a mattress model that fits into the futon. If mattresses are transferred from the Mattress Division to the Furniture Division, a transfer pricing opportunity exists. In this case, the Mattress Division is the selling division, and the Furniture Division is the buying division. Suppose that the mattresses can be sold to outside buyers at $50 each; this $50 is the market price. Clearly, the Mattress Division would not sell the mattresses to the Furniture Division for less than $50 each. Just as clearly, the Furniture Division would not pay more than $50 for the mattresses. The transfer price is easily set at the market price.

The market price, if available, is the best approach to transfer pricing. Since the selling division can sell all that it produces at the market price, transferring internally at a lower price would make the division worse off. Similarly, the buying division can always acquire the good at the market price, so it would be unwilling to pay more for an internally transferred good.

Will the two divisions transfer at the market price? It really does not matter, since the divisions and the company as a whole will be as well off whether or not the transfer takes place internally. However, if the transfer is to occur, it will be at the market price.

**Cost-Based Transfer Prices** Frequently, there is no good outside market price. The lack of a market price might occur because the transferred product uses patented designs owned by the parent company. Then, a company might use a cost-based transfer pricing approach. For example, suppose that the Mattress Division uses a high-density foam padding in the futon mattress and that outside companies do not produce this type of mattress in the appropriate size. If the company has set a cost-based transfer pricing policy, then the Mattress Division will charge the full cost of producing the mattress. (Full cost includes the cost of direct materials, direct labor, variable overhead, and a portion of fixed overhead.) Suppose that the full cost of the mattress is as follows:

| | |
|---|---|
| Direct materials | $15 |
| Direct labor | 5 |
| Variable overhead | 3 |
| Fixed overhead | 5 |
| Full cost | $28 |

Now, the transfer price is $28 per mattress. This amount will be paid to the Mattress Division by the Furniture Division. Notice that this transfer price does not allow for any profit for the selling division (here, the Mattress Division). The Mattress Division may well try to scale back production of the futon mattress and increase production of mattresses available for sale to outside parties. To reduce this desire, top management may define cost as "cost plus." In this case, suppose that the company allows transfer pricing at cost plus 10%. Then, the transfer price is $30.80, calculated as:

$$\text{Transfer Price} + (\text{Transfer Price} + 10\%) = \$28 + (\$28 \times 0.10)$$

If the policy is cost-based transfer pricing, will the transfer take place? It depends. Suppose the Furniture Division wants to purchase lower-quality mattresses in the external market for $25 each. Then, no transfer will occur. Also, suppose the Mattress Division is producing at capacity and can sell the special mattresses for $40 each. The Mattress Division will refuse to transfer any mattresses to the Furniture Division and instead will sell all it can produce to outside parties.

**Negotiated Transfer Prices**   Finally, top management may allow the selling and buying division managers to negotiate a transfer price. This approach is particularly useful in cases with market imperfections, such as the ability of an in-house division to avoid selling and distribution costs that external market participants would have to incur. Using a negotiated transfer price then allows the two divisions to share any cost savings resulting from avoided costs.

Using the example of the Mattress and Furniture divisions, suppose that the futon mattress typically sells for $50 and has full product cost of $28. Normally, a sales commission of $5 is paid to the salesperson, but that cost will not be incurred for any internal transfers. Now, a bargaining range exists. That range goes from the minimum transfer price to the maximum. The two divisions will negotiate the transfer price, deciding how much of the cost savings will go to each division.

- Minimum Transfer Price (Floor): The transfer price that would leave the selling division no worse off if the good were sold to an internal division than if the good were sold to an external party. This is sometimes referred to as the "floor" of the bargaining range.
- Maximum Transfer Price (Ceiling): The transfer price that would leave the buying division no worse off if an input were purchased from an internal division than if the same good were purchased externally. This is sometimes referred to as the "ceiling" of the bargaining range.

In the example, the minimum transfer price is $45:

$50 market price − $5 selling commission that can be avoided on internal sales

The maximum transfer price is $50, which is the outside market price that the Furniture Division would have to pay if the mattresses were bought externally. What is the actual transfer price? That depends on the negotiating skills of the Mattress and Furniture division managers. Any transfer price between $45 and $50 is possible. Cornerstone 12.4 shows how to calculate several types of transfer prices.

CORNERSTONE
12.4

## Calculating Transfer Price

**Why:**
Transfer price represents the price of goods that are sold, or transferred, between different divisions within the same company. Transfer price allows for each division to calculate its own profitability.

*(Continued)*

CORNERSTONE

12.4

(Continued)

**Information:**

Omni Inc. has a number of divisions, including Alpha Division, a producer of circuit boards, and Delta Division, a heating and air-conditioning manufacturer. Alpha Division produces the cb-117 model that can be used by Delta Division in the production of thermostats that regulate the heating and air-conditioning systems. The market price of the cb-117 is $14, and the full cost of the circuit board is $9.

**Required:**

1. If Omni has a transfer pricing policy that requires transfer at full cost, what will the transfer price be? Would the Alpha and Delta divisions choose to transfer at that price?

2. If Omni has a transfer pricing policy that requires transfer at market price, what would the transfer price be? Would the Alpha and Delta divisions choose to transfer at that price?

3. Assume Omni allows negotiated transfer pricing and Alpha Division can avoid $3 of selling expense by selling to Delta Division. Which division sets the minimum transfer price, and what is it? Which division sets the maximum transfer price, and what is it? Would the Alpha and Delta divisions choose to transfer somewhere in the bargaining range?

**Solution:**

1. The full cost transfer price is $9. Delta Division would be delighted with that price, but Alpha Division would refuse to transfer since $14 could be earned in the outside market.

2. The market price is $14. Both Delta and Alpha divisions would transfer at that price (since neither would be worse off than if it bought/sold in the outside market).

3. Minimum transfer price = $14 − $3 = $11. This price is set by Alpha, the selling division.

   Maximum transfer price = $14. This price is the market price and is set by Delta, the buying division.

   Both divisions would accept a transfer price within the bargaining range. Precisely what the transfer price would be depends on the negotiating skills of the division managers.

# Here's The Real Kicker

**Kicker**'s top management is closely involved in all aspects of the company, from design and development through production, sales, delivery, and aftermarket activities. Profit performance, as measured by periodic income statements, is an important measure, but Kicker also keeps track of a number of other measures of performance.

For example, financial information is very important. Financial statements are presented to the president and vice presidents every month. These are reviewed carefully for trends and are compared with the budgeted amounts. Worrisome increases in

expenses or decreases in revenue are analyzed to see what the underlying factors might be.

Customer satisfaction is also continually measured. Kicker has two major types of customers—dealers who sell Kicker products and end users who have Kicker car speakers installed. Each customer type has specific needs. For example, dealers have the exclusive right to sell Kicker products and Kicker offers a 1-year warranty on speakers sold through a dealer. However, end users want as low a price as possible and will occasionally find speakers available on the Internet (called "gray market" speakers because the seller is not authorized to sell them). In the past, no warranty

(Continued)

was available on nondealer-sold speakers, but problems arose when customers purchased obviously new products through the Internet, and they were not covered under warranty when something went wrong. Kicker therefore decided to offer a shorter warranty for new products sold by unauthorized sellers in order to keep the customer base happy and increase satisfaction.

Kicker focuses on strategic objectives for the long term. For example, engineers in R&D take continuing education to stay current in their fields. When Kicker approached producing and selling original equipment manufacture (OEM) speakers to a major automobile maker, a number of employees had to learn International Organization for Standardization (ISO) quality concepts quickly. They took classes, met with consultants, and traveled to the site of other ISO-qualified firms to learn how to meet quality standards.

Jackson Smith/Getty Images

Explain the uses of the Balanced Scorecard, and compute cycle time, velocity, and manufacturing cycle efficiency.

# APPENDIX 12A: THE BALANCED SCORECARD—BASIC CONCEPTS

Segment income, ROI, residual income, and EVA are important measures of managerial performance, but they lead managers to focus only on dollar figures, which may not tell the whole story for the company. In addition, lower-level managers and employees may feel helpless to affect income or investment. As a result, nonfinancial operating measures that look at such factors as market share, customer complaints, personnel turnover ratios, and personnel development have been developed. Letting lower-level managers know that attention to long-run factors is also vital reduces the tendency to overemphasize financial measures.

Managers in an advanced manufacturing environment are especially likely to use multiple measures of performance and to include nonfinancial as well as financial measures. For example, **General Motors** evaluated Robert Lutz, then head of product development, on the basis of 12 criteria. These criteria include how well he used existing parts in new vehicles and how many engineering hours he cut from the development process.[6]

The **Balanced Scorecard** is a strategic management system that defines a strategic-based responsibility accounting system. The Balanced Scorecard *translates* an organization's mission and strategy into operational objectives and performance measures for the following four perspectives:

- The **financial perspective** describes the economic consequences of actions taken in the other three perspectives.
- The **customer perspective** defines the customer and market segments in which the business unit will compete.
- The **internal business process perspective** describes the internal processes needed to provide value for customers and owners.
- The **learning and growth (infrastructure) perspective** defines the capabilities that an organization needs to create long-term growth and improvement. This perspective is concerned with three major *enabling factors:* employee capabilities, information systems capabilities, and employee attitudes (motivation, empowerment, and alignment).

Exhibit 12.6 shows a Balanced Scorecard for a typical hotel based on questionnaire data provided by a research survey of three- and four-star hotels.[7] The scorecard includes the four basic scorecard categories and objectives with key measures for each category.

---

[6] David Welch and Kathleen Kerwin, "Rick Wagoner's Game Plan," *BusinessWeek* (February 10, 2003): 52–60.
[7] N. Evans, "Assessing the Balanced Scorecard as a Management Tool for Hotels," *International Journal of Contemporary Hospitality Management*, Vol. 17 (Issue 4/5, 2005): 376–390.

**EXHIBIT 12.6**

### Balanced Scorecard for Ashley Hotel*

| Objective | Measure |
|---|---|
| **Financial Perspective** | |
| Operating Revenues | • Total daily operating revenue<br>• Revenue per available room |
| Operating Costs | • Operating expenses relative to budget<br>• Cost per occupant |
| **Customer Perspective** | |
| Customer Satisfaction | • Customer satisfaction ratings<br>• Number of monthly complaints |
| Customer Loyalty | • Number of new reward club members<br>• Percent of returning guests |
| **Internal Perspective** | |
| Employee Turnover | • Employee turnover rate<br>• Number of employee complaints |
| Response to Customer Complaint | • Percentage of complaints receiving response<br>• Average response time |
| **Learning and Growth** | |
| New Market Identification | • Growth in reward club membership for new demographic segments |
| Employee Training and Advancement | • Percentage of employees participating in training courses<br>• Survey scores pre- and post-training sessions |

* Measures are based on survey data reported from actual hotels—N. Evans, Assessing the Balanced Scorecard as a Management Tool for Hotels, *International Journal of Contemporary Hospitality Management*. 2005. Vol. 17 (Issue 4/5): 376–390.

## Strategy Translation

**Strategy**, according to the creators of the Balanced Scorecard framework, is defined as:[8]

> . . . *choosing the market and customer segments the business unit intends to serve, identifying the critical internal and business processes that the unit must excel at to deliver the value propositions to customers in the targeted market segments, and selecting the individual and organizational capabilities required for the internal, customer, and financial objectives.*

Strategy specifies management's desired relationships among the four perspectives. *Strategy translation,* on the other hand, means specifying objectives, measures, targets, and initiatives for each perspective. Consider, for example, the financial perspective.

- Objective: For the financial perspective, a company's *objective* may be to grow revenues by introducing new products.
- Measure: The *performance measure* may be the percentage of revenues from the sale of new products.

[8] Robert S. Kaplan and David P. Norton, *The Balanced Scorecard* (Boston: Harvard Business School Press, 1996), p. 37.

- Target: The *target* or *standard* for the coming year for the measure may be 20% (i.e., 20% of the total revenues for the coming year must be from the sale of new products).
- Initiative: The *initiative* describes *how* this is to be accomplished. The "how," of course, involves the other three perspectives.

The company must now identify the customer segments, internal processes, and individual and organizational capabilities that will permit the realization of the revenue growth objective. This illustrates the fact that the financial objectives serve as the focus for the objectives, measures, and initiatives of the other three perspectives.

**The Role of Performance Measures**    The Balanced Scorecard is not simply a collection of critical performance measures. The performance measures are derived from a company's vision, strategy, and objectives. These measures must be *balanced* between the following measures:

- performance driver measures (i.e., lead indicators of future financial performance) and outcome measures (i.e., lagged indicators of financial performance)
- objective and subjective measures
- external and internal measures
- financial and nonfinancial measures

The performance measures must also be carefully *linked* to the organization's strategy. Doing so creates significant advantages for an organization. For example, each quarter, **Analog Devices'** senior managers discuss Balanced Scorecard results for the various divisions. On one occasion, managers noted problems with their new-product ratios—used to measure the effectiveness of R&D spending. They quickly discovered that one division lagged in developing new products. The division's manager focused heavily on R&D by investing more money and exploring new market segments, new product sales, and marketing strategies. Analog Devices' corporate vice president for marketing, quality, and planning noted that they wouldn't have been able to catch the problem so early if they just looked at financials.[9] Other companies, such as **Bank of Montreal, Hilton Hotels Corporation**, and **Duke University Children's Hospital** have had similar success.

The rapid and widespread adoption of this strategic management system is a strong testimonial of its worth. For example, companies like **General Electric, Verizon,** and **Microsoft** have adapted their initial Balanced Score-cards into risk dashboards that contain key financial and nonfinancial measures pertaining to the important risks that threaten organizational success.[10] In addition, other organizations, like **Wal-Mart**, adapt their Balanced Scorecards to include measures that help their suppliers focus on increasingly important sustainability issues like using less packaging materials and more effective packaging techniques.[11]

**Linking Performance Measures to Strategy**    Balancing outcome measures with performance drivers is essential to linking with the organization's strategy. Performance drivers make things happen and are indicators of how the outcomes are going to be realized. Thus, they tend to be unique to a particular strategy. Outcome measures are also important because they reveal whether the strategy is being implemented successfully with the desired economic consequences. For example, if the number of defective products is decreased, does this produce a greater market share? Does this, in turn, produce more revenues and profits? These questions suggest that the most important principle of linkage is the usage of cause-and-effect relationships. In fact, a **testable strategy** can be defined as a set of linked objectives aimed at an overall goal. The testability of the

[9] Joel Kurtzman, "Is Your Company Off Course: Now You Can Find Out Why," *Fortune* (February 17, 1997), http://money.cnn.com/magazines/fortune/fortune_archive/1997/02/17/222180/index.htm (accessed December 13, 2006).
[10] Ante Spencer, "Giving the Boss the Big Picture," *BusinessWeek* (February 13, 2006).
[11] "Getting Leaner—Ahead of the Pack: Suppliers Adjust to New Packaging Priorities," *Retailing Today* (2006): 16–18.

strategy is achieved by restating the strategy into a set of cause-and-effect hypotheses that are expressed by a sequence of if-then statements.[12] Consider, for example, the following sequence of if-then statements that link quality training with increased profitability:

> *If design engineers receive quality training, then they can redesign products to reduce the number of defective units; if the number of defective units is reduced, then customer satisfaction will increase; if customer satisfaction increases, then market share will increase; if market share increases, then sales will increase; if sales increase, then profits will increase.*

Exhibit 12.7 illustrates the quality improvement strategy described by a sequence of if-then statements. First, notice how each of the four perspectives is linked through the cause-and-effect relationships hypothesized:

- The learning and growth perspective is present through the training dimension.
- The internal perspective is represented by the redesign and manufacturing processes.
- The customer perspective is represented by customer satisfaction and market share.
- The financial perspective is present because of revenues and profits.

---

**( EXHIBIT 12.7 )**

**Testable Strategy Illustrated**

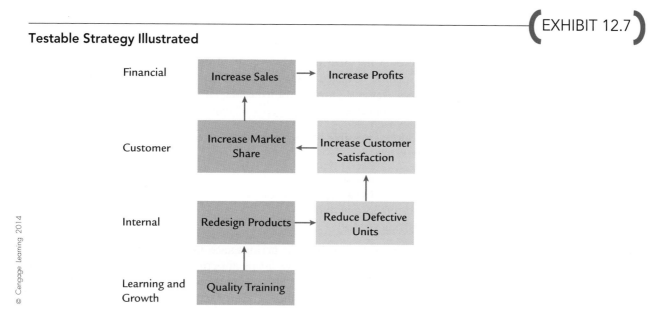

© Cengage Learning 2014

Second, viability of the strategy is testable. Strategic feedback is available that allows managers to test the reasonableness of the strategy. Hours of quality training, the number of products redesigned, the number of defective units, customer satisfaction, market share, revenues, and profits all are observable measures. Thus, the claimed relationships can be checked to see if the strategy produces the expected results. If not, it could be due to one of two causes—implementation problems or an invalid strategy.

**Implementation Problems** It is possible that key *performance drivers* such as training and redesign of products did not achieve their targeted levels (i.e., fewer hours of training and fewer products redesigned than planned). In this case, the failure to produce the targeted *outcomes* for defects, customer satisfaction, market share, revenues, and profits could be merely an implementation problem.

**Invalid Strategy** If the targeted levels of performance drivers were achieved and the expected outcomes did not materialize, then the problem could very well lie with the

---

[12] Robert S. Kaplan and David P. Norton, *The Balanced Scorecard* (Boston: Harvard Business School Press, 1996), p. 149. Kaplan and Norton describe the sequence of if-then statements only as a strategy. Calling it a testable strategy distinguishes it from the earlier, more general definition offered, and, in our opinion, properly so.

strategy itself. This example depicts a *double-loop feedback*. **Double-loop feedback** occurs whenever managers receive information about both the *effectiveness* of strategy implementation as well as the *validity* of the assumptions underlying the strategy. In a functional-based responsibility accounting system, typically only *single-loop feedback* is provided. **Single-loop feedback** emphasizes only effectiveness of implementation. In single-loop feedback, actual results deviating from planned results are a signal to take corrective action so that the plan (strategy) can be executed as intended. The validity of the assumptions underlying the plan is usually not questioned.

## The Four Perspectives and Performance Measures

The four perspectives define the strategy of an organization and provide the structure or framework for developing an integrated, cohesive set of performance measures. These measures, once developed, become the means for articulating and communicating the strategy of the organization to its employees and managers. The measures also serve the purpose of aligning individual objectives and actions with organizational objectives and initiatives.

### The Financial Perspective
The financial perspective establishes the long- and short-term financial performance objectives. The financial perspective is concerned with the global financial consequences of the other three perspectives. Thus, the objectives and measures of the other perspectives must be linked to the financial objectives. The financial perspective has three strategic themes—revenue growth, cost reduction, and asset utilization—which serve as the building blocks for the development of specific operational objectives and measures.

*Revenue Growth* Several possible objectives are associated with revenue growth, including the following:

- increase the number of new products
- create new applications for existing products
- develop new customers and markets
- adopt a new pricing strategy

Once operational objectives are known, performance measures can be designed. For example, possible measures for the above list of objectives (in the order given) are percentage of revenue from new products, percentage of revenue from new applications, percentage of revenue from new customers and market segments, and profitability by product or customer.

*Cost Reduction* Examples of cost reduction objectives include:

- reducing the cost per unit of product
- reducing the cost per customer
- reducing the cost per distribution channel

The appropriate measure is the cost per unit of the particular cost object. Trends in this measure will tell whether or not the costs are being reduced. For these objectives, the accuracy of cost assignments is especially important. Activity-based costing can play an essential measurement role, especially for selling and administrative costs—costs not usually assigned to cost objects like customers and distribution channels.

*Asset Utilization* Improving asset utilization is the principal objective. Financial measures such as ROI and EVA are used. The objectives and measures for the financial perspective are summarized in Exhibit 12.8.

### Customer Perspective
The customer perspective is the source of the revenue component for the financial objectives. This perspective defines and selects the customer and market segments in which the company chooses to compete.

© Cengage Learning 2014

EXHIBIT 12.8

**Summary of Objectives and Measures: Financial Perspective**

| Objectives | Measures |
|---|---|
| *Revenue Growth:* | |
| Increase the number of new products | Percentage of revenue from new products |
| Create new applications | Percentage of revenue from new applications |
| Develop new customers and markets | Percentage of revenue from new sources |
| Adopt a new pricing strategy | Product and customer profitability |
| | |
| *Cost Reduction:* | |
| Reduce unit product cost | Unit product cost |
| Reduce unit customer cost | Unit customer cost |
| Reduce distribution channel cost | Cost per distribution channel |
| | |
| *Asset Utilization:* | |
| Improve asset utilization | Return on investment |
| | Economic value added |

***Core Objectives and Measures***  Once the customers and segments are defined, then *core objectives and measures* are developed. Core objectives and measures are those that are common across all organizations. The five key core objectives are as follows:

- increase market share
- increase customer retention
- increase customer acquisition
- increase customer satisfaction
- increase customer profitability

Possible core measures for these objectives, respectively, are market share (percentage of the market), percentage growth of business from existing customers and percentage of repeating customers, number of new customers, ratings from customer satisfaction surveys, and individual and segment profitability. Activity-based costing is a key tool in assessing customer profitability (Chapter 7). Notice that customer profitability is the only financial measure among the core measures. This measure, however, is critical because it emphasizes the importance of the *right* kind of customers. What good is it to have customers if they are not profitable? The obvious answer spells out the difference between being customer focused and customer obsessed.

***Customer Value***  In addition to the core measures and objectives, measures are needed that drive the creation of *customer value* and, thus, drive the core outcomes. For example, increasing customer value builds customer loyalty (increases retention) and increases customer satisfaction. **Customer value** is the difference between realization and sacrifice, where realization is what the customer receives and sacrifice is what is given up in return. Realization includes such things as product functionality (features), product quality, reliability of delivery, delivery response time, image, and reputation. Sacrifice includes product price, time to learn to use the product, operating cost, maintenance cost, and disposal cost. The costs incurred by the customer *after* purchase are called **postpurchase costs**.

The attributes associated with the realization and sacrifice value propositions provide the basis for the objectives and measures that will lead to improving the core outcomes. The objectives for the sacrifice value proposition are the simplest:

- decrease price
- decrease postpurchase costs

Selling price and postpurchase costs are important measures of value creation. Decreasing these costs decreases customer sacrifice and, thus, increases customer value. Increasing customer value should impact favorably on most of the core objectives.

Similar favorable effects can be obtained by increasing realization. Realization objectives, for example, would include the following:

- improve product functionality
- improve product quality
- increase delivery reliability
- improve product image and reputation

Possible measures for these objectives include, respectively, feature satisfaction ratings, percentage of returns, on-time delivery percentage, and product recognition ratings. Of these objectives and measures, delivery reliability will be used to illustrate how measures can affect managerial behavior, indicating the need to be careful in the choice and use of performance measures.

Delivery reliability means that output is delivered on time. On-time delivery is a commonly used operational measure of reliability. To measure on-time delivery, a firm sets delivery dates and then calculates on-time delivery performance by dividing the orders delivered on time by the total number of orders delivered. The goal, of course, is to achieve a ratio of 100%. Some, however, have found that use of this measure may produce undesirable behavioral consequences.[13] Specifically, plant managers were giving priority to filling orders not yet late over orders that were already late. The performance measure was encouraging managers to have one very late shipment rather than several moderately late shipments. A chart measuring the age of late deliveries could help mitigate this problem. Exhibit 12.9 summarizes the objectives and measures for the customer perspective.

( EXHIBIT 12.9 )

**Summary of Objectives and Measures: Customer Perspective**

| Objectives | Measures |
|---|---|
| *Core:* | |
| Increase market share | Market share (percentage of market) |
| Increase customer retention | Percentage growth of business from existing customers |
| | Percentage of repeating customers |
| Increase customer acquisition | Number of new customers |
| Increase customer satisfaction | Ratings from customer surveys |
| Increase customer profitability | Customer profitability |
| | |
| *Customer Value:* | |
| Decrease price | Price |
| Decrease postpurchase costs | Postpurchase costs |
| Improve product functionality | Ratings from customer surveys |
| Improve product quality | Percentage of returns |
| Increase delivery reliability | On-time delivery percentage |
| | Aging schedule |
| Improve product image and reputation | Ratings from customer surveys |

© Cengage Learning 2014

**Internal (Process) Perspective**  The internal perspective typically focuses on identifying the organization's core internal business processes needed for creating customer and shareholder value to achieve the customer and financial objectives. To provide the framework needed for this perspective, a *process value chain* is defined. The **process value chain** is made up of three processes:

- The **innovation process** anticipates the emerging and potential needs of customers and creates new products and services to satisfy those needs. It represents what is called the *long-wave* of value creation.

---

[13] Joseph Fisher, "Nonfinancial Performance Measures," *Journal of Cost Management* (Spring 1992): 31–38.

- The **operations process** produces and delivers *existing* products and services to customers. It begins with a customer order and ends with the delivery of the product or service. It is the *short-wave* of value creation.
- The **postsales service process** provides critical and responsive services to customers after the product or service has been delivered.

*Innovation Process: Objectives and Measures* Objectives for the innovation process include the following:

- increase the number of new products
- increase percentage of revenue from proprietary products
- decrease the time to develop new products

Associated measures are actual new products developed versus planned products, percentage of total revenues from new products, percentage of revenues from proprietary products, and development cycle time (time to market).

*Operations Process: Objectives and Measures* The three operations process objectives that typically are mentioned and emphasized include the following:

- increase process quality
- increase process efficiency
- decrease process time

Examples of process quality measures are quality costs, output yields (good output divided by good input), and percentage of defective units (good output divided by total output). Measures of process efficiency are concerned mainly with process cost and process productivity. Activity-based costing and process-value analysis facilitate measuring and tracking process costs. Common process time measures are cycle time, velocity, and manufacturing cycle effectiveness (MCE).

**Cycle Time and Velocity** The time to respond to a customer order is referred to as *responsiveness. Cycle time* and *velocity* are two operational measures of responsiveness. **Cycle time** is the length of time it takes to produce a unit of output from the time raw materials are received (starting point of the cycle) until the good is delivered to finished goods inventory (finishing point of the cycle). Thus, cycle time is the time required to produce a product (Time divided by Units produced). **Velocity** is the number of units of output that can be produced in a given period of time (Units produced divided by Time). Cornerstone 12.5 shows how to compute cycle time and velocity.

## Computing Cycle Time and Velocity

**Why:**
Cycle time (Time/Units Produced) and velocity (Units Produced/Time) measure the time it takes for a firm to respond to such things as customer orders, customer complaints, and the development of new products.

**Information:**

A company has the following data for one of its manufacturing cells:

Maximum units produced in a quarter (3-month period): 200,000 units

Actual units produced in a quarter: 160,000 units

Productive hours in one quarter: 40,000 hours

CORNERSTONE

12.5

*(Continued)*

CORNERSTONE

**12.5**

*(Continued)*

**Required:**

1. Compute the theoretical cycle time (in minutes).

2. Compute the actual cycle time (in minutes).

3. Compute the theoretical velocity in units per hour.

4. Compute the actual velocity in units per hour.

**Solution:**

1.  Theoretical Cycle Time = (40,000 hours)(60 minutes per hour)/200,000 units
    = 12 minutes per unit

2.  Actual Cycle Time = (40,000 hours)(60 per hour)/160,000 units
    = 15 minutes per unit

3.  Theoretical Velocity = 60 minutes per hour/12 minutes per unit
    = 5 units per hour

    (Or, 200,000 units per quarter/40,000 hours per quarter = 5 units per hour)

4.  Actual Velocity = 60 minutes per hour/15 minutes per unit
    = 4 units per hour

    (Or 160,000 units per quarter/40,000 hours per quarter = 4 units per hour)

Incentives can be used to encourage operational managers to reduce manufacturing cycle time or to increase velocity, thus improving delivery performance. A natural way to accomplish this objective is to tie product costs to cycle time and reward operational managers for reducing product costs. For example, in a just-in-time (JIT) firm, conversion costs of the cell can be assigned to products on the basis of the time that it takes a product to move through the cell. Using the theoretical productive time available for a period (in minutes), a value-added standard cost per minute can be computed.

$$\text{Standard Cost per Minute} = \frac{\text{Cell Conversion Costs}}{\text{Minutes Available}}$$

To obtain the conversion cost per unit, this standard cost per minute is multiplied by the actual cycle time used to produce the units during the period. By comparing the unit cost computed using the actual cycle time with the unit cost possible using the theoretical or optimal cycle time, a manager can assess the potential for improvement. Note that the more time it takes a product to move through the cell, the greater the unit product cost. With incentives to reduce product cost, this approach to product costing encourages operational managers and cell workers to find ways to decrease cycle time or increase velocity.

**Manufacturing Cycle Efficiency** Another time based operational measure calculates **MCE (manufacturing cycle efficiency)**. MCE is measured as value-added time divided by total time. Total time includes both value-added time (the time spent efficiently producing the product) and nonvalue-added time (such as move time, inspection time, and waiting time). The formula for computing MCE is:

$$MCE = \frac{\text{Processing Time}}{\text{Processing Time} + \text{Move Time} + \text{Inspection Time} + \text{Waiting Time}}$$

In this equation, processing time is the time that it takes to convert raw materials into a finished good. The other activities and their times are viewed as wasteful, and the goal is to reduce those times to zero. If this is accomplished, the value of MCE will be 1.0, or 100%. As MCE improves (moves toward 1.0), cycle time decreases. Furthermore, since the only way MCE can improve is by decreasing waste, cost reduction must also follow. Cornerstone 12.6 shows how to calculate MCE.

## Calculating Manufacturing Cycle Efficiency

CORNERSTONE

12.6

**Why:**

MCE measures the proportion of manufacturing cycle time attributable to value-added processing. Without waste, the ratio should be equal to 1.0.

**Information:**

A company provided the following information:

Maximum units produced in a quarter (3-month period): 200,000 units

Actual units produced in a quarter: 160,000 units

Productive hours in one quarter: 40,000 hours

Actual cycle time = 15 minutes

Theoretical cycle time = 12 minutes

**Required:**

1. Calculate the amount of processing time and the amount of nonprocessing time.

2. Calculate MCE.

**Solution:**

1. Processing time is equal to theoretical cycle time. That is, if everything goes smoothly and there is no wasted time, it takes 12 minutes to produce one unit. Nonprocessing time, therefore, must be the difference between actual cycle time (which includes some waste) and theoretical cycle time.

$$\text{Processing Time} = \text{Theoretical Cycle Time} = 12 \text{ minutes}$$
$$\text{Nonprocessing Time} = \text{Actual Cycle Time} - \text{Theoretical Cycle Time}$$
$$= 15 - 12 = 3 \text{ minutes}$$

2. MCE = Processing Time/(Processing Time + Nonprocessing Time)
   = 12/(12 + 3) = 0.8, or 80%

Cornerstone 12.6 illustrates a fairly efficient process, as measured by MCE. Many manufacturing companies have MCEs less than 0.05.[14]

***Postsales Service Process: Objectives and Measures*** Increasing quality, increasing efficiency, and decreasing process time are also objectives that apply to the post-sales service process. Service quality, for example, can be measured by first-pass yields, where first-pass yields are defined as the percentage of customer requests resolved with a single service call. Efficiency can be measured by cost trends and productivity measures. Process time can be measured by cycle time, where the starting point of the cycle is defined as the receipt of a customer request, and the finishing point is when the customer's problem is solved. The objectives and measures for the process perspective are summarized in Exhibit 12.10.

## (EXHIBIT 12.10)

### Summary of Objectives and Measures: Internal Perspective

| Objectives | Measures |
|---|---|
| *Innovation:* | |
| Increase the number of new products | Number of new products vs. planned |
| Increase proprietary products | Percentage revenue from proprietary products |
| Decrease new product development time | Time to market (from start to finish) |
| *Operations:* | |
| Increase process quality | Quality costs |
| | Output yields |
| | Percentage of defective units |
| Increase process efficiency | Unit cost trends |
| | Output/input(s) |
| Decrease process time | Cycle time and velocity |
| | MCE |
| *Postsales Service:* | |
| Increase service quality | First-pass yields |
| Increase service efficiency | Costs trends |
| | Output/input |
| Decrease service time | Cycle time |

© Cengage Learning 2014

**Learning and Growth Perspective** The fourth and final category in a typical balanced scorecard is the learning and growth perspective, which represents the source of the capabilities that enable the accomplishment of the other three perspectives' objectives. This perspective has three major objectives:

- increase employee capabilities
- increase motivation, empowerment, and alignment
- increase information systems capabilities

***Employee Capabilities*** Three core *outcome* measurements for employee capabilities are employee satisfaction ratings, employee turnover percentages, and employee productivity (e.g., revenue per employee). Examples of lead measures or performance drivers for employee capabilities are hours of training and strategic job coverage ratios (percentage of critical job requirements filled). As new processes are created, new skills are often required. Training and hiring are sources of these new skills. Furthermore, the percentage of the employees needed in certain key areas with the requisite skills signals the capability of the organization to meet the objectives of the other three perspectives.

[14] Robert S. Kaplan and David P. Norton, *The Balanced Scorecard* (Boston: Harvard Business School Press, 1996), p. 117.

*Motivation, Empowerment, and Alignment*  Employees must not only have the necessary skills, but they must also have the freedom, motivation, and initiative to use those skills effectively. The number of suggestions per employee and the number of suggestions implemented per employee are possible measures of motivation and empowerment. Suggestions per employee provide a measure of the degree of employee involvement, whereas suggestions implemented per employee signal the quality of the employee participation. The second measure also signals to employees whether or not their suggestions are being taken seriously.

*Information Systems Capabilities*  Increasing information system capabilities means providing more accurate and timely information to employees so that they can improve processes and effectively execute new processes. Measures should be concerned with the *strategic information availability*. For example, possible measures include percentage of processes with real-time feedback capabilities and percentage of customer-facing employees with online access to customer and product information. Exhibit 12.11 summarizes the objectives and measures for the learning and growth perspective.

**( EXHIBIT 12.11 )**

**Summary of Objectives and Measures: Learning and Growth Perspective**

| Objectives | Measures |
|---|---|
| *Employee Capabilities:*<br>Increase employee capabilities | Employee satisfaction ratings<br>Employee productivity (Revenue/Employee)<br>Hours of training<br>Strategic job coverage ratio (percentage of critical job requirements filled) |
| *Motivation:*<br>Increase motivation and alignment | Suggestions per employee<br>Suggestions implemented per employee |
| *Information Systems Capabilities:*<br>Increase information systems capabilities | Percentage of processes with real-time feedback capabilities<br>Percentage of customer-facing employees with online access to customer and product information |

# SUMMARY OF LEARNING OBJECTIVES

**LO 1.**  Explain how and why firms choose to decentralize.
- In a decentralized organization, lower-level managers make and implement decisions. In a centralized organization, lower-level managers are responsible only for implementing decisions.
- Reasons why companies decentralize:
  - Local managers can make better decisions using local information.
  - Local managers can provide a more timely response.
  - It is impossible for one central manager to be fully knowledgeable about all products and markets.
- Decentralization can train and motivate local managers and free top management from day-to-day operating conditions so that they can spend time on long-range activities, such as strategic planning. Managerial accounting is important in designing

effective performance measures and incentive systems to help ensure that managers in a decentralized organization use their decision-making authority to improve the organization's performance.

- Four types of responsibility centers are:
  - Cost centers—manager is responsible for costs.
  - Revenue centers—manager is responsible for price and quantity sold.
  - Profit centers—manager is responsible for costs and revenues.
  - Investment centers—manager is responsible for costs, revenues, and investment.

**LO 2.**   Compute and explain return on investment.

- ROI is the ratio of operating income to average operating assets.
- Margin is operating income divided by sales *or* margin times turnover.
- Turnover is sales divided by average operating assets.
- Advantage: ROI encourages managers to focus on improving sales, controlling costs, and using assets efficiently.
- Disadvantage: ROI can encourage managers to sacrifice long-run benefits for short-run benefits.

**LO 3.**   Compute and explain residual income and economic value added.

- Residual income is operating income minus a minimum percentage cost of capital times capital employed.
  - If residual income > 0, then the division is earning more than the minimum cost of capital.
  - If residual income < 0, then the division is earning less than the minimum cost of capital.
  - If residual income = 0, then the division is earning just the minimum cost of capital.
- Economic value added is *after-tax* operating profit minus the *actual* total annual cost of capital.
  - If EVA > 0, then the company is creating wealth (or value).
  - If EVA < 0, then the company is destroying wealth.

**LO 4.**   Explain the role of transfer pricing in a decentralized firm.

- Transfer price is charged by the selling division of a company to a buying division of the same company.
  - Increases revenue to the selling division
  - Increases cost to the buying division
- Common transfer pricing policies are:
  - Cost based (e.g., total product cost)
  - Market based (price charged in the outside market)
  - Negotiated (between the buying and selling divisions' managers)

**LO 5.**   *(Appendix 12A)* Explain the uses of the Balanced Scorecard, and compute cycle time, velocity, and manufacturing cycle efficiency.

- Balanced Scorecard is a strategic management system.
- Objectives and measures are developed for four perspectives:
  - financial perspective
  - customer perspective
  - internal perspective
  - learning and growth perspective
- Velocity is the number of units produced in a period of time.
- Cycle time is the time needed to produce one unit.
- MCE is measured as value-added time divided by total time. The higher the MCE, the greater the firm's efficiency.

# SUMMARY OF IMPORTANT EQUATIONS

1. $\text{ROI} = \dfrac{\text{Operating Income}}{\text{Average Operating Assets}}$

2. $\text{Average Operating Assets} = \dfrac{(\text{Beginning Assets} + \text{Ending Assets})}{2}$

3. $\text{ROI} = \underset{\text{Margin}}{\underbrace{\dfrac{\text{Operating Income}}{\text{Sales}}}} \times \underset{\text{Turnover}}{\underbrace{\dfrac{\text{Sales}}{\text{Average Operating Assets}}}}$

4. Residual Income = Operating Income − (Minimum Rate of Return × Average Operating Assets)

5. EVA = After-Tax Operating Income − (Actual Percentage Cost of Capital × Total Capital Employed)

6. $\text{MCE} = \dfrac{\text{Processing Time}}{\text{Processing Time} + \text{Move Time} + \text{Inspection Time} + \text{Waiting Time}}$

**CORNERSTONE 12.1**  Calculating average operating assets, margin, turnover, and return on investment, page 529

**CORNERSTONE 12.2**  Calculating residual income, page 534

**CORNERSTONE 12.3**  Calculating economic value added, page 536

**CORNERSTONE 12.4**  Calculating transfer price, page 540

**CORNERSTONE 12.5**  *(Appendix 12A)* Computing cycle time and velocity, page 549

**CORNERSTONE 12.6**  *(Appendix 12A)* Calculating manufacturing cycle efficiency, page 551

# KEY TERMS

© Pixelfabrik / Alamy

# REVIEW PROBLEMS

## I. ROI

Flip Flop Politics Inc. had gross margin of $550,000 and selling and administrative expense of $300,000 last year. Also, Flip Flop began last year with $1,400,000 of operating assets and ended the year with $1,100,000 of operating assets.

### Required:

Calculate return on investment for Flip Flop Politics.

### Solution:

$$\text{Return on Investment} = \frac{\text{Operating Income}}{\text{Average Operating Assets}}$$

| | |
|---|---:|
| Gross margin | $550,000 |
| Selling and administrative expense | 300,000 |
| Operating income | $250,000 |

$$\text{Average Operating Assets} = \frac{(\text{Beginning Operating Assets} + \text{Ending Operating Assets})}{2}$$

$$= \frac{(\$1,400,000 + \$1,100,000)}{2}$$

$$= \frac{\$2,500,000}{2}$$

$$= \$1,250,000$$

$$\text{Therefore, Return on Investment} = \frac{\text{Operating Income}}{\text{Average Operating Assets}}$$

$$= \frac{\$250,000}{\$1,250,000}$$

$$= 0.20, \text{ or } 20\%$$

## II. Economic Value Added

El Suezo Inc. had sales of $5,000,000, cost of goods sold of $3,500,000, and selling and administrative expense of $500,000 for its most recent year of operations. El Suezo faces a tax rate of 40%. Also, El Suezo employed $2,000,000 of debt capital and $4,000,000 of equity capital in generating its return. Finally, the company's actual cost of capital is 8%.

### Required:

1. Calculate after-tax operating income for El Suezo.
2. Calculate EVA for El Suezo.

### Solution:

| | | |
|---|---|---:|
| 1. | Sales | $5,000,000 |
| | Cost of goods sold | 3,500,000 |
| | Gross margin | $1,500,000 |
| | Selling and administrative expense | 500,000 |
| | Operating income | $1,000,000 |
| | Income taxes (@ 40%) | 400,000 |
| | Net income | $  600,000 |

2.   EVA = After-Tax Operating Income − (Actual Percentage Cost of Capital × Total Capital Employed)

   = $600,000 − [0.08 × ($2,000,000 + $4,000,000)]

   = $600,000 − (0.08 × $6,000,000)

   = $600,000 − $480,000

   = $120,000

## III. Transfer Pricing

The Components Division produces a part that is used by the Goods Division. The cost of manufacturing the part follows:

| | |
|---|---|
| Direct materials | $10 |
| Direct labor | 2 |
| Variable overhead | 3 |
| Fixed overhead* | 5 |
| Total cost | $20 |

\* Based on a practical volume of 200,000 parts.

Other costs incurred by the Components Division are as follows:

| | |
|---|---|
| Fixed selling and administrative | $500,000 |
| Variable selling (per unit) | 1 |

The part usually sells for between $28 and $30 in the external market. Currently, the Components Division is selling it to external customers for $29. The division is capable of producing 200,000 units of the part per year. However, because of a weak economy, only 150,000 parts are expected to be sold during the coming year. The variable selling expenses are avoidable if the part is sold internally.

The Goods Division has been buying the same part from an external supplier for $28. It expects to use 50,000 units of the part during the coming year. The manager of the Goods Division has offered to buy 50,000 units from the Components Division for $18 per unit.

### Required:

1.   Determine the minimum transfer price that the Components Division would accept.
2.   Determine the maximum transfer price that the manager of the Goods Division would pay.
3.   Should an internal transfer take place? Why or why not? If you were the manager of the Components Division, would you sell the 50,000 components for $18 each? Explain.
4.   Suppose that the average operating assets of the Components Division total $10 million. Compute the ROI for the coming year, assuming that the 50,000 units are transferred to the Goods Division for $21 each.

### Solution:

1.   The minimum transfer price is $15. The Components Division has idle capacity and so must cover only its incremental costs, which are the variable manufacturing costs. (Fixed costs are the same whether or not the internal transfer occurs; the variable selling expenses are avoidable.)
2.   The maximum transfer price is $28. The Goods Division would not pay more for the part than it has to pay an external supplier.
3.   Yes, an internal transfer should occur; the opportunity cost of the selling division is less than the opportunity cost of the buying division. The Components Division would earn an additional $150,000 profit ($3 × 50,000). The total joint benefit, however, is $650,000 ($13 × 50,000). The manager of the Components Division should attempt to negotiate a more favorable outcome for that division.

4. Income statement:

| | |
|---|---:|
| Sales [($29 × 150,000) + ($21 × 50,000)] | $ 5,400,000 |
| Less: Variable cost of goods sold ($15 × 200,000) | (3,000,000) |
| Less: Variable selling expenses ($1 × 150,000) | (150,000) |
| Contribution margin | $ 2,250,000 |
| Less: Fixed overhead ($5 × 200,000) | (1,000,000) |
| Less: Fixed selling and administrative | (500,000) |
| Operating income | $ 750,000 |

$$\text{ROI} = \text{Operating Income/Average Operating Assets}$$
$$= \$750,000/\$10,000,000$$
$$= 0.075$$

# DISCUSSION QUESTIONS

1. Discuss the differences between centralized and decentralized decision making.
2. What is decentralization?
3. Explain why firms choose to decentralize.
4. What are margin and turnover? Explain how these concepts can improve the evaluation of an investment center.
5. What are the three benefits of ROI? Explain how each benefit can lead to improved profitability.
6. What is residual income? What is EVA? How does EVA differ from the general definition of residual income?
7. Can residual income or EVA ever be negative? What is the meaning of negative residual income or EVA?
8. What is a transfer price?
9. Briefly explain three common transfer pricing policies used by organizations.
10. *(Appendix 12A)* What is the Balanced Scorecard?
11. *(Appendix 12A)* Describe the four perspectives of the Balanced Scorecard.

# MULTIPLE-CHOICE QUESTIONS

**12-1** The practice of delegating authority to division-level managers by top management is

a. decentralization.
b. good business practice.
c. centralization.
d. autonomy.
e. never done in business today.

**12-2** Which of the following is *not* a reason for decentralizing?

a. Training and motivating managers
b. Unmasking inefficiencies in subdivisions of an overall profitable company
c. Allowing top management to focus on strategic decision making
d. Allowing top management to make all key operating decisions throughout the company
e. All of the above are reasons for decentralizing.

**12-3** A responsibility center in which a manager is responsible only for costs is a(n)

a. investment center.
b. revenue center.
c. profit center.
d. cost center.

**12-4** A responsibility center in which a manager is responsible for revenues, costs, and investments is a(n)

a.  investment center.
b.  revenue center.
c.  profit center.
d.  cost center.

**12-5** If sales and average operating assets for Year 2 are identical to their values in Year 1, yet operating income is higher, Year 2 return on investment (compared with Year 1 ROI) will

a.  decrease.
b.  increase.
c.  stay the same.
d.  The direction of change in ROI cannot be determined by this information.

**12-6** If sales and average operating assets for Year 2 are identical to their values in Year 1, yet operating income is higher, Year 2 turnover (compared with Year 1 turnover) will

a.  decrease.
b.  increase.
c.  stay the same.
d.  The direction of change in turnover cannot be determined by this information.

**12-7** The key difference between residual income and EVA is that EVA

a.  uses the actual cost of capital for the company rather than a minimum required cost of capital.
b.  uses the minimum required cost of capital for a company rather than the actual percentage cost of capital.
c.  is a ratio rather than an absolute dollar amount.
d.  cannot be negative.
e.  There is no difference between residual income and EVA.

**12-8** If ROI for a division is 15% and the company's minimum required cost of capital is 18%, then

a.  residual income for the division is negative.
b.  residual income for the division takes on a value between zero and positive one.
c.  residual income cannot be computed.
d.  EVA must be negative.
e.  residual income is positive.

---

*Use the following information for Multiple-Choice Questions 12-9 and 12-10:*
Division A manufactures an aircraft engine component with unit variable product cost of $38 and market price of $50. Division A incurs shipping costs of $3 per unit for sales to outside parties only. Division B uses this component in the manufacture of its own engine production activities. Top management allows negotiated transfer pricing.

---

**12-9** Refer to the information above. If Division A is operating at full capacity, the maximum transfer price (the ceiling of the bargaining range) is

a.  $38.
b.  $50.
c.  $44.
d.  $47.
e.  There is no bargaining range.

**12-10** Refer to the information above. If Division A is operating at less than full capacity, the minimum transfer price (the floor of the bargaining range) is

a.  $38.
b.  $50.
c.  $44.
d.  $47.
e.  There is no bargaining range.

**12-11** *(Appendix 12A)* Which of the following is a perspective of the Balanced Scorecard?

a. Learning and growth (infrastructure)

b. Internal business process

c. Customer

d. Financial

e. All of these are perspectives of the Balanced Scorecard.

**12-12** *(Appendix 12A)* The length of time it takes to produce a unit of output from the time raw materials are received until the good is delivered to finished goods inventory is called

a. velocity.

b. cycle time.

c. manufacturing cycle efficiency.

d. theoretical cycle time.

e. theoretical MCE.

# CORNERSTONE EXERCISES

*Use the following information for Cornerstone Exercises 12-13 through 12-15:*
East Mullett Manufacturing earned operating income last year as shown in the following income statement:

| | |
|---|---:|
| Sales | $3,750,000 |
| Cost of goods sold | 2,250,000 |
| Gross margin | $1,500,000 |
| Selling and administrative expense | 1,200,000 |
| Operating income | $ 300,000 |
| Less: Income taxes (@ 40%) | 120,000 |
| Net income | $ 180,000 |

At the beginning of the year, the value of operating assets was $1,600,000. At the end of the year, the value of operating assets was $1,400,000.

OBJECTIVE ❷
CORNERSTONE 12.1

**Cornerstone Exercise 12-13   Calculating Average Operating Assets, Margin, Turnover, and Return on Investment**

Refer to the information for East Mullett Manufacturing above. Round answers to two decimal places.

**Required:**

Calculate (1) average operating assets, (2) margin, (3) turnover and (4) return on investment.

OBJECTIVE ❸
CORNERSTONE 12.2

**Cornerstone Exercise 12-14   Calculating Residual Income**

Refer to the information for East Mullett Manufacturing above. East Mullett requires a minimum rate of return of 5%.

**Required:**

Calculate (1) average operating assets and (2) residual income.

OBJECTIVE ❸
CORNERSTONE 12.3

**Cornerstone Exercise 12-15   Calculating Economic Value Added**

Refer to the information for East Mullett Manufacturing above. Total capital employed equaled $1,200,000. East Mullett's actual cost of capital is 4%.

**Required:**

Calculate the EVA for East Mullett Manufacturing.

## Cornerstone Exercise 12-16    Calculating Transfer Price

OBJECTIVE ④
CORNERSTONE 12.4

Burt Inc. has a number of divisions, including the Indian Division, a producer of liquid pumps, and Maple Division, a manufacturer of boat engines.

Indian Division produces the h20-model pump that can be used by Maple Division in the production of motors that regulate the raising and lowering of the boat engine's stern drive unit. The market price of the h20-model is $720, and the full cost of the h20-model is $540.

### Required:

1.  If Burt has a transfer pricing policy that requires transfer at full cost, what will the transfer price be? Do you suppose that Indian and Maple divisions will choose to transfer at that price?
2.  If Burt has a transfer pricing policy that requires transfer at market price, what would the transfer price be? Do you suppose that Indian and Maple divisions would choose to transfer at that price?
3.  Now suppose that Burt allows negotiated transfer pricing and that Indian Division can avoid $120 of selling expense by selling to Maple Division. Which division sets the minimum transfer price, and what is it? Which division sets the maximum transfer price, and what is it? Do you suppose that Indian and Maple divisions would choose to transfer somewhere in the bargaining range?

> *Use the following information for Cornerstone Exercises 12-17 and 12-18:*
> Indy Company has the following data for one of its manufacturing plants:
>
> Maximum units produced in a quarter (3-month period): 250,000 units
> Actual units produced in a quarter (3-month period): 200,000 units
> Productive hours in one quarter: 25,000 hours

## Cornerstone Exercise 12-17    *(Appendix 12A)* Calculating Cycle Time and Velocity

OBJECTIVE ⑤
CORNERSTONE 12.5

Refer to the information for Indy Company above.

### Required:

Compute the (1) theoretical cycle time (in minutes), (2) actual cycle time (in minutes), (3) theoretical velocity in units per hour, and (4) actual velocity in units per hour.

## Cornerstone Exercise 12-18    *(Appendix 12A)* Calculating Manufacturing Cycle Efficiency

OBJECTIVE ⑤
CORNERSTONE 12.6

Refer to the information for Indy Company above. The actual cycle time for Indy Company is 7.5 minutes and the theoretical cycle time is 6 minutes.

### Required:

1.  Calculate the amount of processing time and the amount of nonprocessing time.
2.  Calculate the MCE.

# EXERCISES

## Exercise 12-19    Types of Responsibility Centers

OBJECTIVE ①

Consider each of the following independent scenarios:

a.  Terrin Belson, plant manager for the laser printer factory of Compugear Inc., brushed his hair back and sighed. December had been a bad month. Two machines had broken down, and some factory production workers (all on salary) were idled for part of the month.

*(Continued)*

Materials prices increased, and insurance premiums on the factory increased. No way out of it; costs were going up. He hoped that the marketing vice president would be able to push through some price increases, but that really wasn't his department.

b. Joanna Pauly was delighted to see that her ROI figures had increased for the third straight year. She was sure that her campaign to lower costs and use machinery more efficiently (enabling her factories to sell several older machines) was the reason why. Joanna planned to take full credit for the improvements at her semiannual performance review.

c. Gil Rodriguez, sales manager for ComputerWorks, was not pleased with a memo from headquarters detailing the recent cost increases for the laser printer line. Headquarters suggested raising prices. "Great," thought Gil, "an increase in price will kill sales and revenue will go down. Why can't the plant shape up and cut costs like every other company in America is doing? Why turn this into my problem?"

d. Susan Whitehorse looked at the quarterly profit and loss statement with disgust. Revenue was down, and cost was up—what a combination! Then she had an idea. If she cut back on maintenance of equipment and let a product engineer go, expenses would decrease—perhaps enough to reverse the trend in income.

e. Shonna Lowry had just been hired to improve the fortunes of the Southern Division of ABC Inc. She met with top staff and hammered out a 3-year plan to improve the situation. A centerpiece of the plan is the retiring of obsolete equipment and the purchasing of state-of-the-art, computer-assisted machinery. The new machinery would take time for the workers to learn to use, but once that was done, waste would be virtually eliminated.

**Required:**

For each of the above independent scenarios, indicate the type of responsibility center involved (cost, revenue, profit, or investment).

 OBJECTIVE 2    **Exercise 12-20    Margin, Turnover, Return on Investment**

Pelak Company had sales of $25,000,000, expenses of $17,500,000, and average operating assets of $10,000,000.

**Required:**

Compute the (1) operating income, (2) margin and turnover ratios, and (3) ROI.

 OBJECTIVE 2    **Exercise 12-21    Margin, Turnover, Return on Investment, Average Operating Assets**

Elway Company provided the following income statement for the last year:

| | |
|---|---|
| Sales | $1,040,000,000 |
| Less: Variable expenses | 700,250,000 |
| Contribution margin | $ 339,750,000 |
| Less: Fixed expenses | 183,750,000 |
| Operating income | $ 156,000,000 |

At the beginning of last year, Elway had $28,300,000 in operating assets. At the end of the year, Elway had $23,700,000 in operating assets.

**Required:**

1. Compute average operating assets.
2. Compute the margin and turnover ratios for last year. (*Note:* Round the answer for margin ratio to two decimal places.)
3. Compute ROI. (*Note:* Round answer to two decimal places.)
4. **CONCEPTUAL CONNECTION** Briefly explain the meaning of ROI.
5. **CONCEPTUAL CONNECTION** Comment on why the ROI for Elway Company is relatively high (as compared to the lower ROI of a typical manufacturing company).

## Exercise 12-22   Return on Investment, Margin, Turnover

OBJECTIVE ❷

Data follow for the Construction Division of D. Jack Inc.:

|  | Year 1 | Year 2 |
|---|---|---|
| Sales | $148,500,000 | $162,250,000 |
| Operating income | 8,910,000 | 8,112,500 |
| Average operating assets | 337,500,000 | 405,625,000 |

(*Note:* Round all answers to two decimal places.)

**Required:**

1.   Compute the margin and turnover ratios for each year.
2.   Compute the ROI for the Construction Division for each year.

## Exercise 12-23   Residual Income

OBJECTIVE ❸

The Tuxedo Division of Shamus O'Toole Company had operating income last year of $152,250,000 and average operating assets of $2,175,000,000. O'Toole's minimum acceptable rate of return is 8%. (*Note:* Round all answers to two decimal places.)

**Required:**

1.   Calculate the residual income for the Tuxedo Division.
2.   Was the ROI for the Tuxedo Division greater than, less than, or equal to 8%?

## Exercise 12-24   Economic Value Added

OBJECTIVE ❸

Falconer Company had net (after-tax) income last year of $12,375,400 and total capital employed of $111,754,000. Falconer's actual cost of capital was 9%.

**Required:**

1.   Calculate the EVA for Falconer Company.
2.   **CONCEPTUAL CONNECTION** Is Falconer creating or destroying wealth?

---

*Use the following information for Exercises 12-25 and 12-26:*
Washington Company has two divisions: the Adams Division and the Jefferson Division. The following information pertains to last year's results:

|  | Adams Division | Jefferson Division |
|---|---|---|
| Net (after-tax) income | $ 605,000 | $ 315,000 |
| Total capital employed | 4,000,000 | 3,250,000 |

Washington's actual cost of capital was 12%.

---

## Exercise 12-25   Economic Value Added

OBJECTIVE ❸

Refer to the information for Washington Company above.

**Required:**

1.   Calculate the EVA for the Adams Division.
2.   Calculate the EVA for the Jefferson Division.
3.   **CONCEPTUAL CONNECTION** Is each division creating or destroying wealth?
4.   **CONCEPTUAL CONNECTION** Describe generally the types of actions that Washington's management team could take to increase Jefferson Division's EVA?

## Exercise 12-26   Residual Income

OBJECTIVE ❸

Refer to the information for Washington Company above. In addition, Washington Company's top management has set a minimum acceptable rate of return equal to 8%.

*(Continued)*

**Required:**

1.  Calculate the residual income for the Adams Division.
2.  Calculate the residual income for the Jefferson Division.

---

*Use the following information for Exercises 12-27 through 12-29:*
Aulman Inc. has a number of divisions, including a Furniture Division and a Motel Division. The Motel Division owns and operates a line of budget motels located along major highways. Each year, the Motel Division purchases furniture for the motel rooms. Currently, it purchases a basic dresser from an outside supplier for $40. The manager of the Furniture Division has approached the manager of the Motel Division about selling dressers to the Motel Division. The full product cost of a dresser is $29. The Furniture Division can sell all of the dressers it makes to outside companies for $40. The Motel Division needs 10,000 dressers per year; the Furniture Division can make up to 50,000 dressers per year.

---

OBJECTIVE **4**     **Exercise 12-27   Transfer Pricing**
Refer to the information for Aulman Inc. above.

**Required:**

1.  Which division sets the maximum transfer price? Which division sets the minimum transfer price?
2.  Suppose the company policy is that all transfers take place at full cost. What is the transfer price?
3.  **CONCEPTUAL CONNECTION** Do you think that the transfer will occur at the company-mandated transfer price? Why or why not?

OBJECTIVE **4**     **Exercise 12-28   Transfer Pricing**
Refer to the information for Aulman Inc. above. Also, assume that the company policy is that all transfer prices are negotiated by the divisions involved.

**Required:**

1.  What is the maximum transfer price? Which division sets it?
2.  What is the minimum transfer price? Which division sets it?
3.  **CONCEPTUAL CONNECTION** If the transfer takes place, what will be the transfer price? Does it matter whether or not the transfer takes place?

OBJECTIVE **4**     **Exercise 12-29   Transfer Pricing**
Refer to the information for Aulman Inc. above. Also, although the Furniture Division has been operating at capacity (50,000 dressers per year), it expects to produce and sell only 40,000 dressers for $40 each next year. The Furniture Division incurs variable costs of $14 per dresser. The company policy is that all transfer prices are negotiated by the divisions involved.

**Required:**

1.  What is the maximum transfer price? Which division sets it?
2.  What is the minimum transfer price? Which division sets it?
3.  Suppose that the two divisions agree on a transfer price of $35. What is the benefit for the Furniture Division? For the Motel Division? For Aulman Inc. as a whole?

OBJECTIVE **5**     **Exercise 12-30   (Appendix 12A) Cycle Time and Velocity**
Prakesh Company has the following data for one of its manufacturing cells:

> Maximum units produced in a month: 50,000 units
> Actual units produced in a month: 40,000 units
> Hours of production labor in one month: 10,000 hours

# EXPERIENCE MANAGERIAL DECISIONS

## with Navistar, Inc.

Relevant decision analysis represents one of the most exciting and widely applicable managerial accounting tools in existence. One big proponent of relevant analysis is **Navistar, Inc.**, a multi-billion Fortune 300 Company founded in 1902. More than 100 years later, the company has grown to manufacture components and electronics for a wide variety of vehicles, including buses, tractor trailers, military vehicles, and trucks, to its diverse customers all around the world.

Faced with important, long-term, growth issues, Navistar, Inc. used relevant analysis to decide whether to expand axle production at its truck assembly plant in Ontario or to outsource its extra axle production requirements to an outside supplier company. Before the analysis could be conducted, Navistar, Inc.'s managerial accountants first had to identify all relevant factors, both quantitative and qualitative, as well as the short-term and long-term impacts of these factors. Some factors were relatively easy to identify and measure, such as the labor cost that would be required if the additional axles were made in-house or the cost of acquiring the extra factory space needed to produce the additional axles in-house. However, other factors, such as the need to eliminate bottlenecks that would be created from producing the additional axles in-house, complicated the in-house analysis.

> *"Faced with important, long-term growth issues, Navistar, Inc. used relevant analysis to decide whether to expand axle production at its truck assembly plant in Ontario."*

In addition, if Navistar, Inc. decided to make the additional axles in-house, it would require significant capacity-related capital expenditures. That carried a risk associated with the possibility that the current demand for additional axles might not persist in the long term. In this case, Navistar, Inc. would be stuck with the cost of the additional capacity without the business to generate additional revenues to cover those costs. On the other hand, if the additional axle production were outsourced, Navistar, Inc. would have to ensure that its new axle supplier partnered with the Canadian Auto Workers union to minimize the outsourcing effect on Navistar, Inc.'s existing workforce labor agreements. Furthermore, suppliers would have to be trained to deliver parts and subassemblies in sequence with Navistar, Inc.'s demanding schedule. This training represented a considerable outsourcing cost to Navistar, Inc.

In the end, the relevant costing analysis helped Navistar, Inc.'s executives decide to outsource its additional axle production. As a result, Navistar, Inc.'s Ontario plant has enjoyed annual cost savings of over $3 million! A careful analysis of all relevant factors helped the company make the right decision and avoid being burdened in the long run by the costs of excess capacity that occur in the always cyclical truck assembly business.

OBJECTIVE ❶

Describe the short-run decision-making model, and explain how cost behavior affects the information used to make decisions.

# SHORT-RUN DECISION MAKING

Short-run decision making consists of choosing among alternatives with an immediate or limited end in view. Short-term decisions sometimes are referred to as tactical decisions because they involve choosing between alternatives with an immediate or limited time frame in mind. Strategic decisions, on the other hand, usually are long-term in nature because they involve choosing between different strategies that attempt to provide a competitive advantage over a long time frame. Accepting a special order for less than the normal selling price to utilize idle capacity and to increase this year's profits is an example of a tactical decision. While such decisions tend to be *short run* in nature, it should be emphasized that they often have long-run consequences. Consider a second example. Suppose that a company is thinking about producing a component instead of buying it from suppliers. The immediate objective may be to lower the cost of making the main product. Yet this decision may be a small part of the overall strategy of establishing a cost leadership position for the firm. Therefore, short-run decisions are often *small-scale actions* that serve a larger purpose.

## The Decision–Making Model

How does a company go about making good short-run decisions? A **decision model**, a specific set of procedures that produces a decision, can be used to structure the decision maker's thinking and to organize the information to make a good decision. The following is an outline of one decision-making model.

**Step 1.**   Recognize and define the problem.
**Step 2.**   Identify alternatives as possible solutions to the problem. Eliminate alternatives that clearly are not feasible.
**Step 3.**   Identify the costs and benefits associated with each feasible alternative. Classify costs and benefits as relevant or irrelevant, and eliminate irrelevant ones from consideration.
**Step 4.**   Estimate the relevant costs and benefits for each feasible alternative.
**Step 5.**   Assess qualitative factors.
**Step 6.**   Make the decision by selecting the alternative with the greatest overall net benefit.

The decision-making model just described has six steps. Nothing is special about this particular listing. You may find it more useful to break the steps into 8 or 10 segments. Alternatively, you may find it useful to aggregate them into a shorter list. For example, you could use a three-step model:

**Step 1.**   Identify the decision.
**Step 2.**   Identify alternatives and their associated relevant costs
**Step 3.**   Make the decision.

The key point is to find a comfortable way for you to remember the important steps in the decision-making model.

## Here's The Real Kicker

Two years ago, the loan officer at **Kicker**'s bank left for another job out of state. This was an excellent time for Kicker to reevaluate its banking relationship. The company took a number of bids from the four major banks in town. In the process, Kicker executives learned a great deal about various banking services and the way that banks charged for them. Some examples include Internet service, loan rates, credit card transac-tions, returned check fees, and wire fees. Qualitative factors played a role in the ultimate decision. For example, how quickly does the bank respond? Does Kicker feel comfortable with its banking officer (is she or he knowledgeable about the speaker and electronics industry and attuned to Kicker's special needs)? After weighing both the monetary and nonmonetary factors, Kicker switched banks.

**K KICKER**
*LIVIN LOUD*

To illustrate the decision-making model, consider Audio-Blast Inc., a company that manufactures speaker systems for new automobiles. Recently, Audio-Blast was approached by a major automobile manufacturer about the possibility of installing Audio-Blast's main product—the mega-blast speaker system—into its new sports car. Audio-Blast speakers would be installed at the factory. Suppose that Audio-Blast decides to pursue the speaker order from the automobile manufacturer. Currently, the company does not have sufficient productive and storage capacity to fulfill the order. How might the decision-making model help Audio-Blast find the best way of obtaining that capacity?

## Step 1: Recognize and Define the Problem

The first step is to recognize and define a specific problem. For example, the members of Audio-Blast's management team recognized the need for additional productive capacity as well as increased space for raw materials and finished goods inventories. The number of workers and the amount of space needed, the reasons for the need, and how the additional space would be used are all important dimensions of the problem. However, the central question is *how* to acquire the additional capacity.

## Step 2: Identify the Alternatives as Possible Solutions

The second step is to list and consider possible solutions. Suppose that the production head and the consulting engineer identified the following possible solutions:

1. Build a new factory with sufficient capacity to handle current and foreseeable needs.

2. Lease a larger facility, and sublease its current facility.

3. Lease an additional, similar facility.

4. Institute a second shift in the main factory, and lease an additional building that would be used for storage of raw materials and finished goods inventories only, thereby freeing up space for expanded production.

5. Outsource production to another company, and resell the speakers to the auto manufacturer.

As part of this step, Audio-Blast's upper management team met to discuss and eliminate alternatives that clearly were not feasible. The first alternative was eliminated because it carried too much risk for the company. The order had not even been secured, and the popularity of the new sports car model was not proven. Audio-Blast's president refused to "bet the company" on such a risky proposition. The second alternative was rejected because the economy in Audio-Blast's small town was such that subleasing a facility of its size was not possible. The third alternative was eliminated because it went too far in solving the space problem and, presumably, was too expensive. The fourth and fifth alternatives were feasible; they were within the cost and risk constraints and solved the needs of the company. Notice that the president linked the short-run decision (increase productive capacity) to the company's overall growth strategy by rejecting alternatives that involved too much risk at this stage of the company's development.

## Step 3: Identify the Costs and Benefits Associated with Each Feasible Alternative

In the third step, the costs and benefits associated with each feasible alternative are identified. At this point, clearly irrelevant costs can be eliminated from consideration. (It is fine to include irrelevant costs and benefits in the analysis as long as they are included for *all* alternatives. We usually do not include them because focusing only on the relevant costs and benefits reduces the amount of data to be collected.) Typically, the controller is responsible for gathering necessary data.

Assume that Audio-Blast determines that the costs of making 20,000 speakers include the following:

| | |
|---|---|
| Direct materials | $ 60,000 |
| Direct labor | 110,000 |
| Variable overhead | 10,000 |
| Total variable production cost | $180,000 |

In addition, a second shift must be put in place and a warehouse must be leased to store raw materials and finished goods inventories if Audio-Blast continues to manufacture the speakers internally. Additional costs of the second shift, including a production supervisor and part-time maintenance and engineering, amount to $90,000 per year. A building that could serve as a warehouse is sitting empty across the street and can be rented for $20,000 per year. Costs of operating the building for inventory storage, including telephone and Internet access as well as salaries of materials handlers, would amount to $80,000 per year. The second alternative is to purchase the speakers externally and use the freed-up production space for inventory. An outside supplier has offered to supply sufficient volume for $360,000 per year.

Note that when the cash flow patterns become complicated for competing alternatives, it is difficult to produce a stream of equal cash flows for each alternative. In such a case, more sophisticated procedures can and should be used for the analysis. These procedures are discussed in Chapter 14, which deals with the long-run investment decisions referred to as *capital expenditure decisions.*

## Step 4: Estimate the Relevant Costs and Benefits for Each Feasible Alternative

We now see that the fourth alternative—continuing to produce internally and leasing more space—costs $370,000. The fifth alternative—purchasing outside and using internal space—costs $360,000. The comparison follows:

| Alternative 4 | | Alternative 5 | |
|---|---|---|---|
| Variable cost of production | $180,000 | Purchase price | $360,000 |
| Added second shift costs | 90,000 | | |
| Building lease and operating costs | 100,000 | | |
| Total | $370,000 | | |

The **differential cost** is the difference between the summed costs of two alternatives in a decision. Notice that the differential cost is $10,000 in favor of the fifth alternative. Typically, a differential cost compares the sum of each alternative's *relevant* costs only, as in the differential cost comparison of Alternatives 4 and 5. Emphasis on differential cost allows decision makers to occasionally include irrelevant costs in the alternatives if they choose to do so. However, the inclusion of irrelevant costs is acceptable *only if all irrelevant costs are included for each alternative.* For example, suppose that the controller had included fixed manufacturing cost that must be paid whether or not the speakers are made internally or externally. Then, the total cost of each alternative would increase, but the differential cost would still be $10,000. Again, as noted earlier in the chapter, it is recommended to compare only relevant costs because the inclusion of irrelevant costs often adds unnecessary data collection expenses and confusion in communicating additional information that is not relevant to the given analysis.

## Step 5: Assess Qualitative Factors

While the costs and revenues associated with the alternatives are important, they do not tell the whole story. Qualitative factors can significantly affect the manager's decision.

Qualitative factors are simply those factors that are hard to put a number on, including things like political pressure and product safety.

- *Political Pressure*: Companies like **Levi's** that relocate some or all of their U.S. manufacturing facilities to countries outside of the U.S. with cheaper labor often face stiff political pressure in the United States as a result of such offshoring decisions. Some managers worry that such political pressure from customers can have long-term negative effects on sales that more than offset the labor cost savings that spurred the decision to offshore.
- *Product Safety*: Product safety represents another key qualitative factor for outsourcing organizations, as illustrated by the trouble **Toyota** faced when it appeared to let its product quality slip by postponing safety recalls to save money in the short-term. **Mattel** also discovered the importance of safety as a key qualitative factor when it discovered that its Chinese suppliers used illegal lead paint on thousands of its toys, which lead to an onslaught of toy recalls and a decrease in parents' trust of Mattel's products.

Returning to Audio-Blast, its president likely would be concerned with qualitative considerations such as the quality of the speakers purchased externally, the reliability of supply sources, the expected stability of prices over the next several years, labor relations, community image, and so on. To illustrate the possible impact of qualitative factors on Audio-Blast's decision, consider the first two factors, quality and reliability of supply:

- *Quality:* If the quality of speakers is significantly less when purchased externally from what is available internally, then the quantitative advantage from purchasing may be more fictitious than real. Reselling lower-quality speakers to such a high-profile buyer could permanently damage Audio-Blast's reputation. Because of this possibility, Audio-Blast may choose to continue to produce the speakers internally.
- *Reliability of Supply:* If supply sources are not reliable, production schedules could be interrupted, and customer orders could arrive late. For example, the tsunami off the coast of Japan significantly disrupted supply chains across the globe for numerous companies from **Sony** to **Honda** to **Apple**. The eruption of the Icelandic volcano also posed tremendous business interruption challenges.[1] These factors can increase labor costs and overhead and hurt sales. Again, depending on the perceived trade-offs, Audio-Blast may decide that producing the speakers internally is better than purchasing them, even if relevant cost analysis gives the initial advantage to purchasing.

How should qualitative factors be handled in the decision-making process? First, they must be identified. Secondly, the decision maker should try to quantify them. Often, qualitative factors are simply more difficult to quantify, not impossible. For example, possible unreliability of the outside supplier might be quantified as the probable number of late delivery days multiplied by the penalty Audio-Blast would be charged by the auto manufacturer for later delivery. More difficult measurement challenges exist. For example, **Mobil Corporation** decided to implement a strategic change of focusing on a new target audience, including "road warriors" (employees who drive a lot), "true blues" (affluent, loyal customers), and generation F3 (yuppies on the go who want fuel, want food, and want them fast).[2] However, successful implementation required that the company find a way to measure the experience of new target customers at newly designed Mobil gas pumps and convenience stores. After considerable thought, an innovative manager developed one of the first recognized "secret shopper" programs in which Mobil employees secretly dressed as customers in order to live the Mobil gas station "experience." These secret shoppers then recorded numerous aspects

[1] Dave Lenckus, "Coverage Trends in Manufacturing's 'Big 3' Risks: Workers' Comp, Product Recall, and Supply Chains." (February 9, 2012): Life Health Pro. Accessed online at: www.lifehealthpro.com/2012/02/09/coverage-trends-in-manufacturings-big-3-risks-work.
[2] Marc Epstein and Bill Birchard, *Counting What Counts: Turning Corporate Accountability to Competitive Advantage.* Perseus Books, New York, NY. 2000.

of their experience on quantitative scales for feedback to station managers. Without such evaluative data, it would have been extremely difficult for Mobil managers to assess the causes of success or failure of the new strategy implementation. Finally, truly qualitative factors, such as the impact of late orders on customer relations, must be taken into consideration in the final step of the decision-making model—the selection of the alternative with the greatest overall benefit.

## Step 6: Make the Decision

Once all relevant costs and benefits for each alternative have been assessed and the qualitative factors weighed, a decision can be made.

**ETHICAL DECISIONS**    Ethical concerns revolve around the way in which decisions are implemented and the possible sacrifice of long-run objectives for short-run gain. Relevant costs are used in making short-run decisions. However, decision makers should always maintain an ethical framework. Reaching objectives is important, but how you get there is perhaps more important. Unfortunately, many managers have the opposite view. Part of the reason for the problem is the extreme pressure to perform that many managers face. Often, the individual who is not a top performer may be laid off or demoted. Under such conditions, there is great temptation to engage in questionable behavior today and to let the future take care of itself. Unfortunately, as the historic banking regulatory upheaval of the late 2000s demonstrates, many financial services institutions in the mid-2000s yielded to unethical temptations to lend excessive amounts of money to prospective homeowners who in the end could not afford such loans. Whenever relevant costing is used, it is important to include all costs that are relevant—including those involving ethical ramifications. ●

---

---

## Relevant Costs Defined

The decision-making approach just described emphasized the importance of identifying and using relevant costs. **Relevant costs** possess two characteristics: (1) they are *future* costs AND (2) they *differ* across alternatives. All pending decisions relate to the future. Accordingly, only future costs can be relevant to decisions. However, to be relevant, a cost must not only be a future cost but must also differ from one alternative to another. If a future cost is the same for more than one alternative, then it has no effect on the decision. Such a cost is *irrelevant*. The same relevance characteristics also apply to benefits. One alternative may produce an amount of future benefits different from another alternative (e.g., differences in future revenues). If future benefits differ across alternatives, then they are relevant and should be included in the analysis. The ability to identify relevant and irrelevant costs (and revenues) is a very important decision-making skill.

**Relevant Costs Illustrated**    Consider Audio-Blast's make-or-buy alternatives. The cost of direct labor to produce the additional 20,000 speakers is $110,000. In order to determine if this $110,000 is a relevant cost, we need to ask the following:

1. *Is the direct labor cost a future cost?*
   It is certainly a future cost. Producing the speakers for the auto manufacturer requires the services of direct laborers who must be paid.

2. *Does it differ across the two alternatives?*
   If the speakers are purchased from an external supplier, then a second shift, with its direct labor, will not be needed. Thus, the cost of direct labor *differs* across alternatives ($110,000 for the make alternative, and $0 for the buy alternative).

Therefore, it is a relevant cost.

Implicit in this analysis is the use of a past cost to estimate a future cost. The most recent cost of direct labor has averaged $5.50 per speaker; for 20,000 speakers, the direct labor will cost $110,000. This past cost was used as the estimate of next year's cost. Although past costs are not relevant, they often are used to predict what future costs will be.

*Opportunity Costs*  Another type of relevant cost is opportunity cost. **Opportunity cost** is the benefit sacrificed or foregone when one alternative is chosen over another. Therefore, an opportunity cost is relevant because it is both a future cost and one that differs across alternatives. While an opportunity cost is not an accounting cost, because accountants do not record the cost of what might happen in the future (i.e., they do not appear in financial statements), it is an important consideration in relevant decision making.

For example, if you are deciding whether to work full time or to go to school full time, the opportunity cost of going to school would be the wages you give up by not working. Companies also include opportunity costs in many of their decision analyses. When **Ernst & Young** estimates the net benefit of sending thousands of its accountants to week-long training courses, it includes the opportunity cost of the tens of millions of dollars in lost revenue that it foregoes by not being able to bill clients for the time accountants spend in training. Oftentimes, opportunity costs are quite challenging to estimate. However, their inclusion can change the final result of the analysis, such as whether to accept or reject a special sales opportunity or to outsource a product rather than make it in-house. Therefore, managerial accountants have the ability to add significant value to relevant decision making by finding ways to measure particularly challenging opportunity costs.

**Irrelevant Past Cost Illustrated**  Audio-Blast uses large power saws to cut the lumber that forms the housings for speakers. These saws were purchased 3 years ago and are being depreciated at an annual rate of $25,000. In order to determine if this $25,000 is a relevant cost, we need to ask the following:

1. *Is the direct labor cost a future cost?*
   Depreciation represents an allocation of a cost already incurred. It is a **sunk cost**, a cost that cannot be affected by any future action. Although we allocate this sunk cost to future periods and call that allocation depreciation, none of the original cost is avoidable.

2. *Does it differ across the two alternatives?*
   Sunk costs are always the same across alternatives and, therefore, always irrelevant.

Thus, depreciation costs, like all sunk costs, fail to possess the two characteristics required of relevant costs and, therefore, always are irrelevant.

In choosing between the two alternatives, the original cost of the power saws and their associated depreciation are not relevant factors. However, it should be noted that salvage value of the machinery is a relevant cost for certain decisions. For example, if Audio-Blast decides to transform itself into a distributor, not a producer, of speakers, the amount that can be realized from the sale of the power equipment will be relevant and will be included as a benefit of the switch to distributor status.

*Sunk Costs*  It is important to note the psychology behind managers' treatment of sunk costs. Although managers *should ignore* sunk costs for relevant decisions, such as whether or not to continue funding a particular product in the future, it unfortunately is human nature to allow sunk costs to affect these decisions. For example, **Toshiba** and its HD DVD product team engaged in a fierce, multi-year battle with **Sony** and its Blu-ray product team for recognition as the universally accepted format in the growing next-generation high-definition DVD market. Throughout the battle, both sides spent millions of dollars developing, manufacturing, and advertising its own format. However, Sony's Blu-ray sales trounced Toshiba's HD DVD sales one Christmas shopping season, which prompted Hollywood giant **Warner Bros.** to decide to release its films only on Sony's Blu-ray format, rather than on both formats as it had done previously (the other major production companies had already sided with Sony as well). Around the same time, **Blockbuster Video** announced that it would only carry DVDs with the Blu-ray format. To objective entertainment business experts outside of Toshiba, these decisions by Warner Bros. and Blockbuster were the final blow to Toshiba's format and it was obvious that the HD DVD product line should be discontinued immediately to cut its losses and stop the financial bleeding. However, rather than ignore its significant sunk costs by cutting its future losses, Toshiba announced that it was "unwilling to concede defeat in the next-generation-DVD battle" and decided to launch an "aggressive advertising campaign to promote its [Toshiba's] HD DVD players and slash prices about 50%."[3] Therefore, not only did Toshiba continue to spend money developing, manufacturing, and marketing its failed product, it expected to earn only about half of the regular sales revenue per unit sold. Eventually, even Toshiba recognized the handwriting on the wall and dropped its HD DVD format, but only after throwing away a considerable amount of money on a product that most experts believed should have been dropped much earlier.

Another classic example of inappropriately honoring sunk costs is **Coca-Cola**'s New Coke debacle in the mid-1980s. The development and launching of New Coke was very costly and also an undeniably huge failure. However, Coca-Cola unwisely elected to continue to spend money to advertise and maintain its failed new product simply because it had already spent so much money on the product in the past. As business experts repeatedly noted, no amount of advertising cost was going to change the company's past expenditures to develop and launch New Coke and the company would have been far better off to scrap New Coke as soon as its failure was apparent.

The **XFL** football league and the **Concorde** supersonic jet over a period of 20 years are additional examples of companies that failed to cut their losses and drop their product or service and instead continued to pour money into past failed ideas because of their large associated sunk costs.

**Irrelevant Future Cost Illustrated**    Suppose that Audio-Blast currently pays an Internet provider $5,000 per year to store its website on the server. Since Audio-Blast intends to keep the web page no matter what is decided regarding the potential speaker order, that cost is not relevant to the decision.

The same concepts apply to benefits. One alternative may produce an amount of future benefits different from another alternative (e.g., differences in future revenues). If future benefits differ across alternatives, then they are relevant and should be included in the analysis.

## Cost Behavior and Relevant Costs

Most short-run decisions require extensive consideration of cost behavior. It is easy to fall into the trap of believing that variable costs are relevant and fixed costs are not. But this assumption is not true. For example, the variable costs of production were relevant to Audio-Blast's decision. The fixed costs associated with the existing factory were not relevant. However, the additional fixed cost of the supervisor for a second shift was relevant to the decision.

The key point is that changes in supply and demand for resources must be considered when assessing relevance. If changes in demand and supply for resources across alternatives bring about changes in spending, then the changes in resource spending are the relevant costs that should be used in assessing the relative desirability of the two alternatives.

---

[3] Michelle Kessler, "Toshiba Turns Up Heat in DVD War," *USA Today* (January 15, 2008): 4B.

Flexible resources can be easily purchased in the amount needed and at the time of use. For example, electricity used to run stoves that boil fruit in the production of jelly is a resource that can be acquired and used as needed. Thus, if the jelly manufacturer wants to increase production of jelly, electricity will increase just enough to satisfy that demand. This type of resource is typically referred to as a strictly variable cost.

Some resources are purchased before they are used. Clearly, investment in a factory of a particular size falls into this category; so does a year-to-year lease of office space or equipment. These costs usually are treated as fixed costs. If the decision covers a situation shorter than the time period for which the resource is fixed, then this cost usually is irrelevant.

Still other resources are acquired in advance of usage through implicit contracting; they are usually acquired in lumpy amounts. In Chapter 3, these costs were shown as step costs. This category may include an organization's salaried and hourly employees. The implicit understanding is that the organization will maintain employment levels even though there may be temporary downturns in the quantity of an activity used. This understanding means that an activity may have unused capacity available. Recall that the relevant range is important in considering step costs. As long as a company remains within the relevant range, it will not go up or down a step, so the cost is fixed for all intents and purposes.

For example, assume that a company has three purchasing agents each of whom can process 15,000 purchase orders a year. This assumption means that the existing staff can handle 45,000 purchase orders a year. If the company is processing only 40,000 purchase orders, then there is some unused capacity in purchasing. If the company is considering a special order that will require an additional 2,000 purchase orders, then there is no increased cost to purchasing. However, if the company considers an expansion that will require an additional 8,000 purchase orders per year, then an additional staffing cost will need to be incurred in purchasing.

# SOME COMMON RELEVANT COST APPLICATIONS

OBJECTIVE 2

Apply relevant costing and decision-making concepts in a variety of business situations.

Relevant costing is of value in solving many different types of problems. Traditionally, these applications include decisions:

- to make or buy a component.
- to accept a special order at less than the usual price.
- to keep or drop a segment or product line.
- to further process joint products or sell them at the split-off point.

Though by no means an exhaustive list, many of the same decision-making principles apply to a variety of problems.

## Make-or-Buy Decisions

Managers often face the decision of whether to make a particular product (or provide a service) or to purchase it from an outside supplier. A manufacturer may need to consider whether to make or buy components used in manufacturing. A manager of a service firm may need to decide whether to provide a service in-house or to outsource it. For example, many large accounting firms increasingly are sending certain accounting service tasks overseas in an effort to reduce their U.S. staff accountant labor costs, as well as to free up U.S. staff accountants' time for more challenging, value-adding service tasks. **Make-or-buy decisions** are those decisions involving a choice between internal and external production. Exhibit 13.1 illustrates the make-or-buy decision.

Let's return briefly to **Navistar, Inc.**'s use of relevant analysis in making the make-or-buy decision for its additional axle needs. In question was whether it should

## ( EXHIBIT 13.1 )

**Make-or-Buy Decisions**

 OR

manufacture (i.e., "make") the additional axles it needed or purchase (i.e., "buy") them from an external vendor. After a careful discussion with a cross functional team representing personnel from Human Resources, Accounting, Purchasing, and Finance, managers decided that the key costs of on the "make" side included one-time capital and start-up expenditures on machines and ongoing expenditures for labor, repairs and maintenance, utilities, depreciation, and insurance. Key costs on the "buy" side included one-time vendor tooling expenditures and ongoing expenditures for freight, logistics, inventory storage and movement, and training. In addition, managers considered important qualitative characteristics such as ensuring high quality, which was particularly relevant for the training costs because Navistar, Inc. wanted to be sure that any purchased axles were of a high quality and delivered to the right place at the appropriate time. After these relevant costs were identified, quantified, and analyzed, Navistar, Inc. confidently elected to outsource its additional axle production.

**Make-or-Buy Decision Illustrated** Assume that Swasey Manufacturing currently produces an electronic component used in one of its printers. In one year, Swasey will switch production to another type of printer, and the electronic component will not be used. However, for the coming year, Swasey must produce 10,000 of these parts to support the production requirements for the old printer.

A potential supplier has approached Swasey about the component. The supplier will build the electronic component to Swasey's specifications for $4.75 per unit. The offer sounds very attractive since the full manufacturing cost per unit is $8.20. Should Swasey Manufacturing make or buy the component?

Recall the steps involved in short-run decision making (p. 574). The problem (Step 1) and the feasible alternatives (Step 2) are both readily identifiable. Since the horizon for the decision is only one period, there is no need to be concerned about periodically recurring costs (Step 3). Relevant costing is particularly useful for short-run analysis. We simply need to identify the relevant costs (Step 4), total them, and make a choice (Step 6) [assuming no overriding qualitative concerns (Step 5)].

The full absorption cost of the component is computed as follows:

|  | Total Cost | Unit Cost |
|---|---|---|
| Direct materials | $10,000 | $1.00 |
| Direct labor | 20,000 | 2.00 |
| Variable overhead | 8,000 | 0.80 |
| Fixed overhead | 44,000 | 4.40 |
| Total | $82,000 | $8.20 |

Fixed overhead consists of common factory costs that are allocated to each product line. No matter what happens to the component line, overall fixed overhead will not be affected. As a result, the fixed overhead is irrelevant; it can be ignored in structuring the problem.

All other costs in this example are relevant. The costs of direct materials and direct labor are relevant because they will not be needed if the part is purchased externally. Similarly, variable overhead is relevant, because its cost would not be incurred if the component were purchased externally.

Now, what about the purchase of the component? Of course, the purchase price is relevant. If the component were made, this cost would not be incurred. Are there any other costs associated with an outside purchase? A check with the purchasing department and receiving dock confirmed that there was sufficient slack in the system to easily handle the additional purchase, suggesting that there are no additional relevant costs of purchasing the component. Cornerstone 13.1 shows how to structure this make-or-buy problem.

## Structuring a Make-or-Buy Problem

**CORNERSTONE**

**13.1**

**Why:**

The make-or-buy decision situation requires the company to focus on the relevant items (usually costs) associated with either making or purchasing a given product. Typically, the alternative (make or buy) with the lower relevant costs represents the best decision for the company.

**Information:**

Swasey Manufacturing needed to determine if it would be cheaper to make 10,000 units of a component in-house or to purchase them from an outside supplier for $4.75 each. Cost information on internal production includes the following:

|  | Total Cost | Unit Cost |
|---|---|---|
| Direct materials | $10,000 | $1.00 |
| Direct labor | 20,000 | 2.00 |
| Variable overhead | 8,000 | 0.80 |
| Fixed overhead | 44,000 | 4.40 |
| Total | $82,000 | $8.20 |

Fixed overhead will continue whether the component is produced internally or externally. No additional costs of purchasing will be incurred beyond the purchase price.

**Required:**

1. What are the alternatives for Swasey Manufacturing?

2. List the relevant cost(s) of internal production and of external purchase.

3. Which alternative is more cost effective and by how much?

4. Now assume that the fixed overhead includes $10,000 of cost that can be avoided if the component is purchased externally. Which alternative is more cost effective and by how much?

**Solution:**

1. There are two alternatives: make the component in-house or purchase it externally.

*(Continued)*

CORNERSTONE
**13.1**

*(Continued)*

2. Relevant costs of making the component in-house include direct materials, direct labor, and variable overhead. Relevant costs of purchasing the component externally include the purchase price.

|  | Alternatives | | Differential |
|  | Make | Buy | Cost to Make |
| --- | --- | --- | --- |
| Direct materials | $10 000 | — | $ 10,000 |
| Direct labor | 20,000 | — | 20,000 |
| Variable overhead | 8,000 | — | 8,000 |
| Purchase cost | — | $47,500 | (47,500) |
| Total relevant cost | $38,000 | $47,500 | $ (9,500) |

3. It is cheaper (by $9,500) to make the component in-house.

4.

|  | Alternatives | | Differential |
|  | Make | Buy | Cost to Make |
| --- | --- | --- | --- |
| Direct materials | $10,000 | — | $ 10,000 |
| Direct labor | 20,000 | — | 20,000 |
| Variable overhead | 8,000 | — | 8,000 |
| Avoidable fixed overhead | 10,000 | — | 10,000 |
| Purchase cost | — | $47,500 | (47,500) |
| Total relevant cost | $48,000 | $47,500 | $   500 |

Now it is cheaper (by $500) to purchase the component.

Be sure to read the analysis in Cornerstone 13.1 carefully. At first, the fixed overhead remains whether or not the component is made internally. In this case, fixed overhead is not relevant, and making the product is $9,500 cheaper than buying it. Later, in Requirement 4, part of the fixed overhead is avoidable. This condition means that purchasing the component externally will save $10,000 in fixed cost (i.e., Swasey can avoid $10,000 of fixed overhead if it buys the component). Now, the $10,000 of fixed cost is relevant—it is a future cost and it differs between the two alternatives—and the offer of the supplier should be accepted; it is $500 cheaper to buy the component.

The same analysis can be performed on a unit-cost basis. Once the relevant costs are identified, relevant unit costs can be compared. For this example, these costs are $3.80 ($38,000/10,000) for the "make" alternative and $4.75 ($47,500/10,000) for the "buy" alternative.

One type of relevant cost that is becoming increasingly large due to globalization and the green environmental movement concerns the disposal costs associated with electronic waste (or e-waste). Increasingly government agencies are assessing manufacturers of computers, televisions, digital music devices, etc., a costly fee at production to cover product disposal costs that public landfills eventually incur once the products reach the end of their life cycle, become obsolete, and are thrown out to pollute the environment. **Hewlett-Packard Co.** has taken a strategic leadership position by recycling approximately 10% of its sales as a more cost effective means than incurring the aforementioned governmental fees at production.[4] The failure to include relevant life cycle costs

[4] Lorraine Woellert, "HP Wants Your Old PCs Back," *BusinessWeek Online* (April 10, 2006).

can cause the make side of the make-or-buy analysis to appear more attractive (i.e., less costly) than it is in reality.

## Special-Order Decisions

From time to time, a company may consider offering a product or service at a price different from the usual price. Prices can vary to customers in the same market, and firms often have the opportunity to consider special orders from potential customers in markets not ordinarily served. For example, **General Motors** contracted with the Pentagon to use excess production capacity to manufacture its popular 4-wheel drive pickup truck for use by U.S. troops in desert combat situations, except that these trucks were altered to include bulletproof windows, mounts for machine guns, and night vision capability. A potentially important qualitative factor in this example is that certain customer segments might hold strong opinions about General Motors' association with combat activities. Such opinions might help or hurt regular sales, but their effect should be estimated and included in the relevant analysis if they are deemed to be significant. **Special-order decisions** focus on whether a specially priced order should be accepted or rejected. These orders often can be attractive, especially when the firm is operating below its maximum productive capacity. Exhibit 13.2 illustrates the special-order decision.

**Special-Order Decision Illustrated** Suppose that an ice cream company produces only premium ice cream. Its factory has a capacity of 20 million half-gallon units but only plans to produce 16 million units. The total costs associated with producing and selling 16 million units are as follows (in thousands of dollars):

|  | Total | Unit Cost |
|---|---|---|
| Variable costs: |  |  |
| Ingredients | $15,200 | $0.95 |
| Packaging | 3,200 | 0.20 |
| Direct labor | 4,000 | 0.25 |
| Variable overhead | 1,280 | 0.08 |
| Selling commission | 320 | 0.02 |
| Total variable costs | $24,000 | $1.50 |
| Total fixed costs | 1,552 | 0.097 |
| Total costs | $25,552 | $1.597 |
| Selling price |  | $2.00 |

### concept Q&A

You also have make-or-buy decisions to make. For example, do you change the oil in your car yourself, or do you take it to the shop? Choose one such decision, and explain why you have chosen to "make it" or "buy it." What factors could influence you to change your mind?

**Answer:**

Suppose that you choose the oil-change decision. You might decide to change it yourself because (1) you know how to, (2) you have the appropriate tools to do the job, (3) you have the time, and (4) you don't mind messing around under the hood. Alternatively, you might decide to have it done because (1) you don't have confidence in your ability to do it, (2) you don't own the equipment (nozzle, pan to hold oil), (3) you are unsure which oil to choose, or (4) you don't want to do the job. A factor that could influence your decision from changing your own oil to taking it to a shop might be that, after graduation, you will be working full time and will want to use your free time for other things.

$\left(\text{EXHIBIT 13.2}\right)$

**Accept or Reject a Special Order**

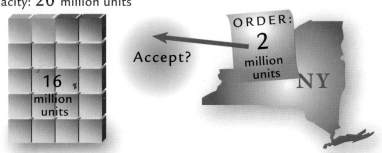

Capacity: **20** million units

An ice cream distributor from a geographic region not normally served by the company has offered to buy 2 million units at $1.55 per unit, provided its own label can be attached to the product. Since the distributor approached the company directly, there is no sales commission. As the manager of the ice cream company, would you accept or reject this order?

The offer of $1.55 is well below the normal selling price of $2.00; in fact, it is even below the total unit cost. Even so, accepting the order may be profitable. The company has idle capacity, and the order will not replace, or cannibalize, other units being produced to sell at the normal price. Additionally, many of the costs are not relevant; fixed costs will continue regardless of whether the order is accepted or rejected.

If the order is accepted, a benefit of $1.55 per unit will be realized that otherwise wouldn't be. However, all of the variable costs except for commissions ($0.02) also will be incurred, producing a cost of $1.48 per unit. The net benefit is $0.07 ($1.55 − $1.48) per unit. The relevant cost analysis can be summarized as follows:

| | Accept | Reject | Differential Benefit to Accept |
|---|---|---|---|
| Revenues | $ 3,100,000 | $— | $ 3,100,000 |
| Ingredients | (1,900,000) | — | (1,900,000) |
| Packaging | (400,000) | — | (400,000) |
| Direct labor | (500,000) | — | (500,000) |
| Variable overhead | (160,000) | — | (160,000) |
| Profit | $ 140,000 | $ 0 | $ 140,000 |

We see that for this company, accepting the special order will increase profits by $140,000 ($0.07 × 2,000,000).

Cornerstone 13.2 shows how to apply relevant costing to a special-order problem.

---

**CORNERSTONE**

**13.2**

## Structuring a Special-Order Problem

**Why:**

A special order occurs when a company uses its excess capacity to produce a "one-time" order for another company. The challenge in a special order analysis is to estimate the relevant costs and benefits associated with the order because many of the company's costs will be unaffected (and therefore irrelevant) by whether the order is accepted or rejected.

**Information:**

Leibnitz Company has been approached by a new customer with an offer to purchase 20,000 units of model TR8 at a price of $9 each. The new customer is geographically separated from the company's other customers, and existing sales would not be affected. Leibnitz normally produces 100,000 units of TR8 per year but only plans to produce and sell 75,000 in the coming year. The normal sales price is $14 per unit. Unit cost information for the normal level of activity is as follows:

| | |
|---|---|
| Direct materials | $3.00 |
| Direct labor | 2.80 |
| Variable overhead | 1.50 |
| Fixed overhead | 2.00 |
| Total | $9.30 |

*(Continued)*

Fixed overhead will not be affected by whether or not the special order is accepted.

**Required:**

1. What are the relevant costs and benefits of the two alternatives (accept or reject the special order)?

2. By how much will operating income increase or decrease if the order is accepted?

**Solution:**

1. Relevant costs and benefits of accepting the special order include the sales price of $9, direct materials, direct labor, and variable overhead. No relevant costs or benefits are attached to rejecting the order.

2. If the problem is analyzed on a unit basis:

|  | Accept | Reject | Differential Benefit to Accept |
|---|---|---|---|
| Price | $9.00 | $— | $9.00 |
| Direct materials | (3.00) | — | (3.00) |
| Direct labor | (2.80) | — | (2.80) |
| Variable overhead | (1.50) | — | (1.50) |
| Increase in operating income | $1.70 | $ 0 | $1.70 |

Operating income will increase by $34,000 ($1.70 × 20,000 units) if the special order is accepted.

CORNERSTONE

**13.2**

*(Continued)*

## Keep-or-Drop Decisions

Often, a manager needs to determine whether a segment, such as a product line, should be kept or dropped. Keep-or-drop decisions can be relatively small scale in nature, such as when **Nike** decides what to do with particular existing celebrity- and athlete-sponsored clothing or equipment lines. On the other hand, these decisions can be very large scale in nature, such as when **Ford Motor Company** contemplated the sale of its luxury Jaguar and Land Rover automobile lines. Such decisions also can involve large physical assets, such as when **MGM Resorts International** in Las Vegas contemplated whether or not to raze its luxury hotel (the Harmon) before it even opened as a result of alleged construction and engineering problems.[5] Segmented reports prepared on a variable-costing basis provide valuable information for these **keep-or-drop decisions**. Both the segment's contribution margin and its segment margin are useful in evaluating the performance of segments. However, while segmented reports provide useful information for keep-or-drop decisions, relevant costing describes how the information should be used to arrive at a decision.

**Keep-or-Drop Decision Illustrated**  Consider Norton Materials Inc., which produces concrete blocks, bricks, and roofing tile. The controller has prepared the following estimated segment income statement for next year (in thousands of dollars):

[5] Alexandra Berzon, "MGM Folds Vegas Tower," (August 16, 2011), B1, *The Wall Street Journal.*

|                          | Blocks | Bricks | Tile   | Total   |
| ------------------------ | ------ | ------ | ------ | ------- |
| Sales revenue            | $500   | $800   | $150   | $1,450  |
| Less: Variable expenses  | 250    | 480    | 140    | 870     |
| Contribution margin      | $250   | $320   | $ 10   | $ 580   |
| Less direct fixed expenses: |     |        |        |         |
|   Advertising   | (10)   | (10)   | (10)   | (30)    |
|   Salaries      | (37)   | (40)   | (35)   | (112)   |
|   Depreciation  | (53)   | (40)   | (10)   | (103)   |
| Segment margin           | $150   | $230   | $ (45) | $ 335   |

The projected performance of the roofing tile line shows a negative segment margin. This occurrence would be the third consecutive year of poor performance for that line. The president of Norton Materials, Tom Blackburn—concerned about this poor performance—is trying to decide whether to keep or drop the roofing tile line.

His first reaction is to try to increase the sales revenue of roofing tiles, possibly through an aggressive sales promotion coupled with an increase in the selling price. The marketing manager thinks that this approach would be fruitless, however. The market is saturated, and the level of competition is too keen to hold out any hope for increasing the firm's market share.

Increasing the product line's profits through cost cutting is not feasible either. Costs were cut the past 2 years to reduce the loss to its present anticipated level. Any further reductions would lower the quality of the product and adversely affect sales.

With no hope for improving the profit performance of the line beyond its projected level, Tom has decided to drop it. He reasons that the firm will lose a total of $10,000 in contribution margin but will save $45,000 by dismissing the line's supervisor and eliminating its advertising budget. (The depreciation cost of $10,000 is not relevant because it represents an allocation of a sunk cost.) Thus, dropping the product line has a $35,000 advantage over keeping it. Cornerstone 13.3 shows how to structure this information as a keep-or-drop product line problem.

CORNERSTONE

13.3

## Structuring a Keep-or-Drop Product Line Problem

**Why:**

Companies often must consider whether a segment or product line should remain. The most important aspect of this analysis is determining which costs will be eliminated (i.e., be relevant) and which costs will remain (i.e., be irrelevant) if the segment or product is dropped.

**Information:**

Shown below is a segmented income statement for Norton Materials Inc.'s three product lines:

|                          | Blocks    | Bricks    | Tile      | Total       |
| ------------------------ | --------- | --------- | --------- | ----------- |
| Sales revenue            | $500,000  | $800,000  | $150,000  | $1,450,000  |
| Less: Variable expenses  | 250,000   | 480,000   | 140,000   | 870,000     |
| Contribution margin      | $250,000  | $320,000  | $ 10,000  | $ 580,000   |
| Less direct fixed expenses: |        |           |           |             |
|   Advertising   | (10,000)  | (10,000)  | (10,000)  | (30,000)    |
|   Salaries      | (37,000)  | (40,000)  | (35,000)  | (112,000)   |
|   Depreciation  | (53,000)  | (40,000)  | (10,000)  | (103,000)   |
| Segment margin           | $150,000  | $230,000  | $ (45,000)| $ 335,000   |

*(Continued)*

The roofing tile line has a contribution margin of $10,000 (sales of $150,000 minus total variable costs of $140,000). All variable costs are relevant. Relevant fixed costs associated with this line include $10,000 in advertising and $35,000 in supervision salaries.

**Required:**

1. List the alternatives being considered with respect to the roofing tile line.

2. List the relevant benefits and costs for each alternative.

3. Which alternative is more cost effective and by how much?

**Solution:**

1. The two alternatives are to keep the roofing tile line or to drop it.

2. The relevant benefits and costs of keeping the roofing tile line include sales of $150,000, variable costs of $140,000, advertising cost of $10,000, and supervision cost of $35,000. None of the relevant benefits and costs of keeping the roofing tile line would occur under the drop alternative.

3.

| | Keep | Drop | Differential Amount to Keep |
|---|---|---|---|
| Sales | $150,000 | $— | $150,000 |
| Less: Variable expenses | 140,000 | — | 140,000 |
| Contribution margin | $ 10,000 | $— | $ 10,000 |
| Less: Advertising | (10,000) | — | (10,000) |
| Cost of supervision | (35,000) | — | (35,000) |
| Total relevant benefit (loss) | $ (35,000) | $ 0 | $ (35,000) |

The difference is $35,000 in favor of dropping the roofing tile line.

**CORNERSTONE**

**13.3**

*(Continued)*

A merger between companies is another type of keep-or-drop decision that requires managerial accountants to estimate relevant costs, such as which costs would go away when two companies merge and which costs would remain. For example, when **XM Satellite Radio** and **Sirius Satellite Radio** first considered merging into one giant satellite radio company, proponents argued that the merger would create significant cost savings to the new company that could be passed along to consumers in the form of lower prices.[6] They reasoned that many of the costs that XM and Sirius incurred as separate companies would either decrease or be eliminated because the new combined company would need only one research and development group, one marketing department, etc. Any costs that would decrease or go away after the merger would be relevant costs for the merger analysis, while any costs that would remain unchanged after the merger would be irrelevant.

**Keep or Drop with Complementary Effects** Suppose that dropping Norton's roofing tile line would lower sales of blocks by 10% and bricks by 8%, as many customers buy roofing tile at the same time that they purchase blocks or bricks. Some customers will go elsewhere if they cannot buy both products at the same location. How does this information affect the keep-or-drop decision? Cornerstone 13.4 shows the impact on all product lines.

---

[6] Kim Peterson, "XM Plus Sirius Doesn't Equal Monopoly?" (March 24, 2008): accessed April 5, 2008, from http://blogs.moneycentral.msn.com/topstocks/archive/2008/03/24/xm-plus-sirius-doesn-t-equal-monopoly-feds-say.aspx.

CORNERSTONE

## 13.4

# Structuring a Keep-or-Drop Product Line Problem with Complementary Effects

**Why:**

A potential complication of a keep-or-drop analysis is the implication such a decision might have on other aspects of the business. Such implications must be included in the analysis before making a final decision.

**Information:**

Refer to Norton Materials' segmented income statement in Cornerstone 13.3 (p. 588). Assume that dropping the product line reduces sales of blocks by 10% and sales of bricks by 8%. All other information remains the same.

**Required:**

1. If the roofing tile line is dropped, what is the contribution margin for the block line? For the brick line?

2. Which alternative (keep or drop the roofing tile line) is now more cost effective and by how much?

**Solution:**

1. Previous contribution margin of blocks was $250,000. A 10% decrease in sales implies a 10% decrease in total variable costs, so the contribution margin decreases by 10%.

    New Contribution Margin for Blocks = $250,000 − 0.10($250,000) = $225,000

    The reasoning is the same for the brick line, but the decrease is 8%.

    New Contribution Margin for Bricks = $320,000 − 0.08($320,000) = $294,400

    Therefore, if the roofing tile product line were dropped, the resulting total contribution margin for Norton Materials would equal $519,400 ($225,000 + $294,400).

2.

|  | Keep | Drop | Differential Amount to Keep |
|---|---|---|---|
| Contribution margin | $ 580,000 | $519,400 | $ 60,600 |
| Less: Advertising | (30,000) | (20,000) | (10,000) |
| Cost of supervision | (112,000) | (77,000) | (35,000) |
| Total | $ 438,000 | $422,400 | $ 15,600 |

Notice that the contribution margin for the drop alternative equals the new contribution margins of the block and brick lines ($225,000 + $294,400). Also, advertising and supervision remain relevant across these alternatives.

Now the analysis favors keeping the roofing tile line. In fact, company income will be $15,600 higher if all three lines are kept as opposed to dropping the roofing tile line.

The example provides some insights beyond the simple application of the decision model. The initial analysis, which focused on two feasible alternatives, led to a tentative decision to drop the product line. Additional information provided by the marketing manager led to a reversal of the first decision. Perhaps other feasible alternatives exist as well. These additional alternatives would require still more analyses.

# YOUDECIDE   Relevant Decision Making

You are an elected official in a major city that is considering whether or not to move forward with a proposed plan to demolish the city's existing professional sports stadium and build an elaborate new stadium. One of the most difficult aspects of this decision is estimating the new stadium's incremental revenues and costs that would result if it were built.

**What specific types of relevant revenues and costs would you consider in making this important decision?**

There are many stadium events for which the associated relevant revenues and costs must be estimated accurately if the correct decision is to be made. These stadium events (and their relevant revenues and costs) include:

- Main attraction sporting events (e.g., ticket revenues from baseball, basketball, and/or football games for which the stadium would be built; additional staffing, cleanup, and insurance costs)
- Concessions and other sales (e.g., contribution margins or fees earned from product and service sales—most new stadiums boast as many high-end shopping opportunities as an upscale mall!)
- Television contract terms (e.g., the amount and percentage of revenue brought in by *additional* games being televised in the new stadium, perhaps in primetime slots)
- Offseason events (e.g., the ticket revenue from boxing matches, music concerts, etc.).

For this relevant stadium decision, estimating the relevant revenues might be even more difficult than estimating the relevant costs. For instance, projecting how many *more* people will want to attend games in a new stadium can be unclear, as well as how much money they would be willing to spend for various seats located around the stadium.

Several New York City area stadiums experienced tremendous difficulty in accurately estimating these same items. For example, the **New York Yankees** and **New York Mets** organizations built new stadiums with price tags of over $1.2 billion and $800 million, respectively! However, in the new Yankee stadium, many of the more expensive seats—the ones behind the batter and, thus, most visible on television—remained empty because of their hefty $2,500 per seat price tag. In fact, the Yankee organization decreased some of its highest ticket prices by 50% during the stadium's first season in an attempt to fill these high profile empty seats. In other words, decision makers struggled to estimate the amount of incremental revenue that would result from some of the more important seats in a new Yankee stadium. Undaunted by such challenging relevant analyses, however, the New York area also built a $1.6 billion new Meadowlands Stadium to be shared by the **New York Jets** and **New York Giants**.

In addition to the previously mentioned relevant items, some citizens raise objections to such large amounts of money being spent on replacing existing fully functional sporting facilities with gargantuan sports palaces. They argue that $1 billion could be better spent on different causes. Such sentiments, whether you agree or disagree with them, represent potentially important qualitative factors that effective managerial accountants should take into account when performing relevant analyses for proposed new stadiums, especially when these citizens represent tax payers or potential fans the stadium builders count on for purchasing expensive tickets in the future.

**When making such an important decision, relevant costs for things like sporting events, concessions, television contracts, and off-season events must be considered in addition to qualitative factors like citizen sentiment.**

## Further Processing of Joint Products

**Joint products** have common processes and costs of production up to a split-off point. At that point, they become distinguishable as separately identifiable products. For example, certain minerals such as copper and gold may both be found in a given ore. The ore must be mined, crushed, and treated before the copper and gold are separated. The point of separation is called the **split-off point**. The costs of mining, crushing, and treatment are common to both products and, therefore, are incurred regardless of whether the ore is sold at the split-off point or further processed into copper, gold and any other substances that exist in the ore. As a result, joint costs are irrelevant to the decision of whether to sell at the split-off point or to process further.

Many joint products are sold at the split-off point. However, sometimes it is more profitable to process a joint product further, beyond the split-off point, prior to selling it. A **sell-or-process-further decision** is an important relevant decision that a manager must make.

**Sell-or-Process-Further Decision Illustrated** Consider Appletime Corporation, a large corporate farm that specializes in growing apples. Each plot produces approximately one ton of apples. The trees in each plot must be sprayed, fertilized, watered, and pruned. When the apples are ripened, workers are hired to pick them. The apples are then transported to a warehouse, where they are washed and sorted. The approximate cost of all these activities (including processing) is $300 per ton per year.

Apples are sorted into three grades (A, B, and C), determined by size and blemishes. Large apples without blemishes (bruises, cuts, wormholes, and so on) are sorted into one bin and classified as Grade A. Small apples without blemishes are sorted into a second bin and classified as Grade B. All remaining apples are placed in a third bin and classified as Grade C. Every ton of apples produces 800 pounds of Grade A, 600 pounds of Grade B, and 600 pounds of Grade C apples.

Grade A apples are sold to large supermarkets for $0.40 per pound. Grade B apples are packaged in five-pound bags and sold to supermarkets for $1.30 per bag. (The cost of each bag is $0.05.) Grade C apples are processed further and made into applesauce. The sauce is sold in 16-ounce cans for $0.75 each. The cost of processing is $0.10 per pound of apples. The final output is 500 sixteen-ounce cans.

A large supermarket chain recently requested that Appletime supply 16-ounce cans of apple pie filling for which the chain is willing to pay $0.90 per can. Appletime determined that the Grade B apples would be suitable for this purpose and estimated that it would cost $0.24 per pound to process the apples into pie filling. The output would be 500 cans. Exhibit 13.3 illustrates the decision to sell Grade B apples at the split-off point or to process them further into pie filling.

In deciding whether to sell Grade B apples at split-off or to process them further and sell them as pie filling, the common costs of spraying, pruning, and so on are not relevant. The company must pay the $300 per ton for these activities regardless of whether it sells at split-off or processes further. However, the revenues earned at

( EXHIBIT 13.3 )

**Further Processing of Joint Products**

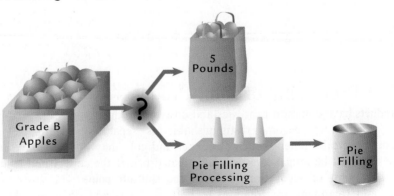

© Cengage Learning 2014

split-off are likely to differ from the revenues that would be received if the Grade B apples were further processed and sold as pie filling. Therefore, revenues are a relevant consideration. Similarly, the processing costs occur only if further processing takes place. Hence, processing costs are relevant. Cornerstone 13.5 shows how to structure the sell-or-process-further decision for the Grade B apples.

## Structuring the Sell-or-Process-Further Decision

**Why:**

Because joint costs are incurred prior to the split-off point, they are sunk costs in determining whether to sell a product at split-off or process it further. Only the sales value at split-off, the further processing costs, and the eventual sales value are relevant to this decision.

**Information:**

Appletime grows apples and then sorts them into one of three grades, A, B, or C, based on their condition. Appletime must decide whether to sell the Grade B apples at split-off or to process them into apple pie filling. The company normally sells the Grade B apples in 120 five-pound bags at a per-unit price of $1.25. If the apples are processed into pie filling, the result will be 500 cans of filling with additional costs of $0.24 per can. The buyer will pay $0.90 per can.

**Required:**

1. What is the contribution to income from selling the Grade B apples in five-pound bags?

2. What is the contribution to income from processing the Grade B apples into pie filling?

3. Should Appletime continue to sell the Grade B apples in bags or process them further into pie filling?

**Solution:**

1. Revenue from Apples in Bags = $1.25 × 120 = $150

2. Revenue from Further Processing = $0.90 × 500 = $450
   Further Processing Cost = $0.24 × 500 = $120
   Income from Further Processing = $450 − $120 = $330

3. Appletime should process the Grade B apples into pie filling because the company will make $330 versus the $150 it would make by selling the apples in bags.

# PRODUCT MIX DECISIONS

 OBJECTIVE ③

Choose the optimal product mix when faced with one constrained resource.

Most of the time, organizations have wide flexibility in choosing their product mix. Product mix refers to the relative amount of each product manufactured (or service provided) by a company. Decisions about product mix can have a significant impact on an organization's profitability.

Each mix represents an alternative that carries with it an associated profit level. A manager should choose the alternative that maximizes total profits. Since fixed costs do not vary with activity level, the total fixed costs of a firm will be the same for all

## concept Q&A

Consider your, or a friend's, cell phone plan. Often, there are different types of minutes—priced at different levels. For example, a plan might include 300 "anytime" minutes and 1,000 "night and weekend minutes." Discuss these different types of minutes as constraints. What do they constrain? Do these constraints affect the decision to call a friend?

**Answer:**

They constrain the amount of time that you can talk per month. Early in the month, you might phone friends regularly. Later in the month, you might try to figure out how many minutes you have left and try harder to time your calls. For example, calls that must be made at a particular time may use "anytime minutes" (e.g., to set up a job interview appointment between 9 A.M. and 5 P.M.). Calls to friends and family might be postponed to the evening or the weekend.

possible mixes and, therefore, are not relevant to the decision. Thus, a manager needs to choose the alternative that maximizes total contribution margin.

**Product Mix Decision Illustrated** Assume that Jorgenson Company produces two types of gears: X and Y, with unit contribution margins of $25 and $10, respectively. If the firm possesses unlimited resources and the demand for each product is unlimited, then the product mix decision is simple—produce an infinite number of each product. Unfortunately, every firm faces limited resources and limited demand for each product. These limitations are called **constraints**. A manager must choose the optimal mix given the constraints found within the firm.

Assuming that Jorgenson can sell all that is produced, some individuals might argue that only Gear X should be produced and sold—it has the larger contribution margin. However, this solution is not necessarily the best choice. The selection of the optimal mix can be significantly affected by the relationships of the constrained, or scarce, resources to the individual products. These relationships affect the quantity of each product that can be produced and, consequently, the total contribution margin that can be earned. This point is most vividly illustrated when faced with one resource constraint. Cornerstone 13.6 shows how to determine the optimal product mix with one constrained resource.

## CORNERSTONE

## 13.6

## Determining the Optimal Product Mix with One Constrained Resource

**Why:**

A company often faces a situation where one of its processes (or resources) cannot handle all of the demands placed on it. Therefore, a company must decide how best to allocate this scarce resource to production operations in order to maximize company profit.

**Information:**

Jorgenson Company produces two types of gears, X and Y, with unit contribution margins of $25 and $10, respectively. Each gear must be notched by a special machine. The firm owns eight machines that together provide 40,000 hours of machine time per year. Gear X requires two hours of machine time, and Gear Y requires 0.5 hour of machine time. There are no other constraints.

**Required:**

1. What is the contribution margin per hour of machine time for each gear?

2. What is the optimal mix of gears?

3. What is the total contribution margin earned for the optimal mix?

**Solution:**

1.

|  | Gear X | Gear Y |
| --- | --- | --- |
| Contribution margin per unit | $25.00 | $10.00 |
| Required machine time per unit | ÷ 2 | ÷ 0.5 |
| Contribution margin per hour of machine time | $12.50 | $20.00 |

*(Continued)*

2. Since Gear Y yields $20 of contribution margin per hour of machine time, all machine time should be devoted to the production of Gear Y.

Units Gear Y = 40,000 total hours/0.5 hour per Gear Y = 80,000 units

The optimal mix is Gear Y = 80,000 units and Gear X = 0 units.

3. Total Contribution Margin of Optimal Mix = (80,000 units Gear Y)$10
$$= \$800,000$$

**CORNERSTONE**

# 13.6

*(Continued)*

Cornerstone 13.6 clearly illustrates a fundamentally important point involving relevant decision making with a constrained resource. This point is that the contribution margin *per unit* of each product is not the critical concern when deciding how much of each product type to produce and sell. Instead, the contribution margin *per unit of the scarce resource* is the deciding factor, which means that the product yielding the highest contribution margin per unit of the scarce resource should be selected. Returning to Cornerstone 13.6, Gear X earns contribution margin per unit of $25, which is 2.5 times greater than the $10 contribution margin per unit earned by Gear Y. However, each Gear X unit requires *more* than 2.5 times as much machine time (the constrained factor) to produce than does each Gear Y unit, thereby making Gear Y more attractive financially than Gear X. Specifically, Gear X earns $12.50 of contribution margin per machine hour ($25/2), but Gear Y earns $20 of contribution margin per machine hour ($10/0.5). Thus, Gear Y is the more attractive product and the optimal mix is 80,000 units of Gear Y and no units of Gear X.

$$\text{Contribution Margin per Unit of Scarce Resource} = \frac{\text{Selling Price per Unit} - \text{Variable Cost per Unit}}{\text{Required Amount of Scarce Resource per Unit}}$$

Suppose, however, that there is also a demand constraint. Only 60,000 units of Gear Y can be sold.  Cornerstone 13.7  shows how to incorporate this additional constraint.

# Determining the Optimal Product Mix with One Constrained Resource and a Sales Constraint

**CORNERSTONE**

# 13.7

**Why:**

A complication of the scarce resource question arises when there also is a sales constraint that indicates the maximum sales that can be achieved. Keeping both the constrained resource and the sales constraint in mind is essential if the best decision is to be made.

**Information:**

Jorgenson Company produces two types of gears, X and Y, with unit contribution margins of $25 and $10, respectively. Each gear must be notched by a special machine. The firm owns eight machines that together provide 40,000 hours of machine time per year. Gear X requires two hours of machine time, and Gear Y requires 0.5 hour of machine time. A maximum of 60,000 units of each gear can be sold.

**Required:**

1. What is the contribution margin per hour of machine time for each gear?

2. What is the optimal mix of gears?

3. What is the total contribution margin earned for the optimal mix?

*(Continued)*

CORNERSTONE

## 13.7

*(Continued)*

**Solution:**

1.

|  | Gear X | Gear Y |
|---|---|---|
| Contribution margin per unit | $25.00 | $10.00 |
| Required machine time per unit | $\div 2$ | $\div 0.5$ |
| Contribution margin per hour of machine time | $12.50 | $20.00 |

2. Since Gear Y yields $20 of contribution margin per hour of machine time, the first priority is to produce all of Gear Y that the market will take (i.e., demands).

$$\text{Machine Time Required for Maximum Amount of Gear Y} = 60,000 \text{ units} \times 0.5 \text{ machine hours required for each Gear Y unit}$$
$$= 30,000 \text{ hours needed to manufacture } 60,000 \text{ Gear Y units}$$

$$\text{Remaining Machine Time for Gear X} = 40,000 \text{ hours} - 30,000 \text{ hours}$$
$$= 10,000 \text{ hours}$$

$$\text{Units of Gear X to Be Produced in Remaining } 10,000 \text{ Hours} = 10,000 \text{ hours}/2 \text{ hours per unit}$$
$$= 5,000 \text{ units}$$

Now the optimal mix is 60,000 units of Gear Y and 5,000 units of Gear X. This mix will precisely exhaust the machine time available.

3. Total Contribution Margin of Optimal Mix = (60,000 units Gear Y × $10)
$$+ (5,000 \text{ units Gear X} \times \$25)$$
$$= \$725,000$$

Coffee chain **Caribou Coffee**, as well as other retail businesses, pays careful attention to profitability and sales per square foot of cafe floor space, which often is the most important constrained resource. The importance of this metric explains why fast-food restaurants like **McDonald's** push their drive-through service—customers using the drive-through option do not require any internal store floor space. In fact, some restaurants generate more than 80% of sales from this service.

## Multiple Constrained Resources

The presence of only one constrained resource might not be realistic. Organizations often face multiple constraints: limitations of raw materials, limitations of skilled labor, limited demand for each product, and so on. The solution of the product mix problem in the presence of multiple constraints is considerably more complicated and requires the use of a specialized mathematical technique known as *linear programming,* which is reserved for advanced cost management courses.

OBJECTIVE ④

Explain the impact of cost on pricing decisions.

# THE USE OF COSTS IN PRICING DECISIONS

One of the more difficult decisions faced by a company is pricing. This section examines the impact of cost on price and the role of the accountant in gathering the needed information.

## Cost-Based Pricing

Demand is one side of the pricing equation; supply is the other side. Since revenue must cover all costs for the firm to make a profit, many companies start with cost to determine price. That is, they calculate product cost and add the desired profit. The mechanics of this approach are straightforward. Usually, there is a cost base and a markup. The **markup** is a percentage applied to the base cost and is calculated as follows:

> Price Using Markup = Cost per Unit + (Cost per Unit × Markup Percentage)

It includes desired profit and any costs not included in the base cost. Companies that bid for jobs routinely base bid price on cost. Law firms and public accounting firms are service organizations that use cost-plus pricing to bid for clients. Cornerstone 13.8 shows how to apply a markup percentage to cost to obtain price.

## Calculating Price by Applying a Markup Percentage to Cost

**Why:**

Many organizations set prices on their products and services by marking up the estimated cost of producing or providing such products and services. The challenges of cost-based pricing include accurately estimating these costs and selecting an appropriate markup percentage.

**Information:**

Elvin Company assembles and installs computers to customer specifications. Elvin has decided to price its jobs at the cost of direct materials and direct labor plus 20%. The job for a local vocational-technical school included the following costs:

| | |
|---|---|
| Direct materials | $65,000 |
| Direct labor (assembly and installation) | 4,000 |

**Required:**

Calculate the price charged by Elvin Company to the vocational-technical school.

**Solution:**

Price = Cost + (Markup Percentage × Cost)
    = $69,000 + 0.20($69,000)
    = $69,000 + $13,800
    = $82,800

Notice in Cornerstone 13.8 that the markup of 20% is not pure profit. Instead, it includes other costs not specified, such as overhead (including Elvin's offices and management salaries) as well as any marketing and administrative expenses. The markup percentage can be calculated using a variety of bases.

Retail stores often use markup pricing, and typical markup is 100% of cost. Thus, if Graham Department Store purchases a sweater for $24, the retail price marked is $48 [$24 + (1.00 × $24)]. Again, the 100% markup is not pure profit—it goes toward the salaries of the clerks, payment for space and equipment (cash registers, furniture, and fixtures), utilities, advertising, and so on. A major advantage of markup pricing is that standard markups are easy to apply. Consider the difficulty of setting a price for every piece of merchandise in a hardware or department store. It is much simpler to apply a uniform markup to cost and then to adjust prices upward (downward) if demand is more (less) than anticipated.

Several important observations are in order at this point concerning the relationship between the base cost, the markup percentage, and the firm's cost system. First, when the firm includes relatively few costs in the base cost (rather than a large number of costs), it usually becomes very important that the firm selects a large enough markup percentage to ensure that the markup covers all of the remaining costs not included in the base cost. Determining a price that is large enough to cover significant other costs with the markup requires considerable judgment and cost estimation. Second, on a related note, the effectiveness of cost-plus pricing relies heavily on the accuracy of the cost system and pricing managers' understanding of the firm's cost structure. For example, assume that a firm marks up only its direct manufacturing costs and does not understand well the behavior of its indirect manufacturing costs or its nonmanufacturing costs (e.g., research and development costs, distribution costs, customer service costs, etc.). In this case, it is likely that the firm will encounter problems in setting prices either too high—and will be undercut by competitors with more appropriate lower prices—or too low—and will not cover all costs, thereby resulting in a net loss.

## Target Costing and Pricing

Many American and European firms set the price of a new product as the sum of the costs and the desired profit. The rationale is that the company must earn sufficient revenues to cover all costs and yield a profit. Peter Drucker writes, "This is true but irrelevant: Customers do not see it as their job to ensure manufacturers a profit. The only sound way to price is to start out with what the market is willing to pay."[7]

**Target costing** is a method of determining the cost of a product or service based on the price (target price) that customers are willing to pay. The marketing department determines what characteristics and price for a product are most acceptable to consumers. Then, it is the job of the company's engineers to design and develop the product such that cost and profit can be covered by that price. Japanese firms have practiced this approach for years; American companies increasingly use target costing. For example, **Olympus, Toyota, Boeing, Nissan,** and **Caterpillar** have used a value chain perspective to implement target costing. Target costing recognizes that between 75 and 90% of a product's cost becomes "committed" or "locked into" by the time it finishes the design stage.[8] Therefore, it is most effective to make such large changes in the design and development stage of the product life cycle because at this point the features of the product, as well as its costs, still are fairly easy to adjust. Typical target costing efforts to reduce costs focus on redesigning the product to require fewer or less costly materials, labor, and processes during production, delivery and customer service. **Mercedes,** for instance, used target costing extensively in the design of its popular M-class sports utility vehicle series, which made its public debut in the blockbuster movie *Jurassic Park*.

**Target Costing Illustrated**  Consider the target costing experience used by Digitime Company in developing a wristwatch that incorporates a PDA (personal digital assistant). The "cool factor" on this item is high, but actually inputting data on the watch is difficult. So, the company expects to be able to charge a premium price to a relatively small number of early adopters. The marketing vice president's price estimate is $200.

---

[7] Peter Drucker, "The Five Deadly Business Sins," *The Wall Street Journal* (October 21, 1993): A22.
[8] Antonio Davila and Marc Wouters, "Designing Cost-Competitive Technology Products through Cost Management," *Accounting Horizons*, Vol. 18, No. 1 (2004): 13–26.

Digitime's management requires a 15% profit on new products. Therefore, target cost is calculated using the following equation:

$$\text{Target Cost} = \text{Target Price} - \text{Desired Profit}$$

Cornerstone 13.9 shows how to calculate a target cost.

## Calculating a Target Cost

CORNERSTONE

13.9

**Why:**

When prices are set by the market, a company might use target costing to determine the cost at which it must be able to produce and sell its product in order to achieve its desired profit margin given the market determined price.

**Information:**

Digitime manufactures wristwatches and is designing a new watch model that incorporates a PDA (personal digital assistant), which Digitime hopes consumers will view as a cool and valuable design feature. As such, the new PDA watch has a target price of $200. Management requires a 15% profit on new product revenues.

**Required:**

1. Calculate the amount of desired profit.

2. Calculate the target cost.

**Solution:**

1. Desired Profit = 0.15 × Target Price
   = 0.15 × $200
   = $30

2. Target Cost = Target Price − Desired Profit
   = $200 − $30
   = $170

Target costing involves much more up front work than cost-based pricing. If Digitime can't make the watch for $170, then the engineers and designers will have to go back to the drawing board and find a way to get it done on budget. However, let's not forget the additional work that must be done if the cost-based price turns out to be higher than what customers will accept. Then, the arduous task of bringing costs into line to support a lower price, or the opportunity cost of missing the market altogether, begins. For example, in the 1980s, the U.S. consumer electronics market became virtually nonexistent because cost-based pricing led to increasingly higher prices. Japanese (and later Korean) firms practicing target costing offered lower prices and just the features wanted by consumers to win the market.

Target costing can be used most effectively in the design and development stage of the product life cycle. At that point, the features of the product, as well as its costs, still are relatively easy to adjust.

# SUMMARY OF LEARNING OBJECTIVES

**LO 1.**   Describe the short-run decision-making model, and explain how cost behavior affects the information used to make decisions.
- Six steps of the decision making model are:
  - Recognize and define the problem.
  - Identify feasible alternatives.
  - Identify costs and benefits with each feasible alternative.
  - Estimate the relevant costs and benefits for each feasible alternative.
  - Assess qualitative factors.
  - Make the decision by selecting the alternative with the greatest overall net benefit.
- Relevant costs:
  - These are future costs that differ across alternatives
  - They frequently are variable costs—called flexible resources.

**LO 2.**   Apply relevant costing and decision-making concepts in a variety of business situations.
- Make-or-buy decision
- Special-order decision
- Keep-or-drop decision
- Further processing of joint products

**LO 3.**   Choose the optimal product mix when faced with one constrained resource.
- Single constraint leads to production of product with the greatest contribution margin per unit of scarce resource.
- Multiple constraints require linear programming.

**LO 4.**   Explain the impact of cost on pricing decisions.
- Markup costing applies markup to cost to determine price.
- Target costing works backward from desired price to find allowable cost.

# SUMMARY OF IMPORTANT EQUATIONS

1. $\text{Contribution Margin per Unit of Scarce Resource} = \dfrac{\text{Selling Price per Unit} - \text{Variable Cost per Unit}}{\text{Required Amount of Scarce Resource per Unit}}$
2. Price Using Markup = Cost per Unit + (Cost per Unit × Markup Percentage)
3. Target Cost = Target Price − Desired Profit

**CORNERSTONES**

| | |
|---|---|
| CORNERSTONE 13.1 | Structuring a make-or-buy problem, page 583 |
| CORNERSTONE 13.2 | Structuring a special-order problem, page 586 |
| CORNERSTONE 13.3 | Structuring a keep-or-drop product line problem, page 588 |
| CORNERSTONE 13.4 | Structuring a keep-or-drop product line problem with complementary effects, page 590 |
| CORNERSTONE 13.5 | Structuring the sell-or-process-further decision, page 593 |
| CORNERSTONE 13.6 | Determining the optimal product mix with one constrained resource, page 594 |
| CORNERSTONE 13.7 | Determining the optimal product mix with one constrained resource and a sales constraint, page 595 |
| CORNERSTONE 13.8 | Calculating price by applying a markup percentage to cost, page 597 |
| CORNERSTONE 13.9 | Calculating a target cost, page 599 |

# KEY TERMS

Constraints, 594

Decision model, 574

Differential cost, 576

Joint products, 591

Keep-or-drop decisions, 587

Make-or-buy decisions, 581

Markup, 597

Opportunity cost, 579

Relevant costs, 578

Sell-or-process-further decision, 592

Special-order decisions, 585

Split-off point, 591

Sunk cost, 579

Target costing, 598

# REVIEW PROBLEMS

## I. Special-Order Decision

Pastin Company produces a light-weight travel raincoat with the following unit cost:

| | |
|---|---|
| Direct materials | $4.00 |
| Direct labor | 1.00 |
| Variable overhead | 1.75 |
| Fixed overhead | 2.00 |
| Unit cost | $8.75 |

While production capacity is 200,000 units per year, Pastin expects to produce only 170,000 raincoats for the coming year. The fixed selling costs total $85,000 per year, and variable selling costs are $0.50 per unit sold. The raincoats normally sell for $12 each.

At the beginning of the year, a customer from a geographic region outside the area normally served by the company offered to buy 20,000 raincoats for $8 each. The customer would pay all transportation costs, and there would be no variable selling costs.

### Required:

1. Should the company accept the order? Provide both qualitative and quantitative justification for your decision. Assume that no other orders are expected beyond the regular business and the special order.

### Solution:

1. The company expects idle capacity. Accepting the special order would bring production up to near capacity. The two options are to accept or reject the order. If the order is accepted, then the company could avoid laying off employees and would enhance and maintain its community image. However, the order is considerably below the normal selling price of $12. Because the price is so low, the company needs to assess the potential impact of the sale on its regular customers and on the profitability of the firm. Considering the fact that the customer is located in a region not usually served by the company, the likelihood of an adverse impact on regular business is not high. Thus, the qualitative factors seem to favor acceptance.

   To assess profitability, the firm should identify the relevant costs and benefits of each alternative. This analysis is as follows:

| | Accept | Reject |
|---|---|---|
| Revenues | $160,000 | $— |
| Direct materials | (80,000) | — |
| Direct labor | (20,000) | — |
| Variable overhead | (35,000) | — |
| Total benefits | $ 25,000 | $ 0 |

Accepting the order would increase profits by $25,000. (The fixed overhead and selling costs are all irrelevant because they are the same across both alternatives.) *Conclusion:* The order should be accepted because both qualitative and quantitative factors favor it.

### II. Optimal Mix

Two types of gears are produced: A and B. Gear A has a unit contribution margin of $200, and Gear B has a unit contribution margin of $400. Gear A uses two hours of grinding time, and Gear B uses five hours of grinding time. There are 200 hours of grinding time available per week. This is the only constraint.

**Required:**

1. Is the grinding constraint an internal constraint or an external constraint?
2. Determine the optimal mix. What is the total contribution margin?
3. Suppose that there is an additional demand constraint: Market conditions will allow the sale of only 80 units of each gear. Now, what is the optimal mix? The total contribution margin per week?

**Solution:**

1. It's an internal constraint.
2. Gear A: $200/2 hours = $100 per grinding hour
   Gear B: $400/5 hours = $80 per grinding hour
   Since Gear A earns more contribution margin per unit of scarce resource than Gear B, only Gear A should be produced and sold (this is based on the fact that we can sell all we want of each product).
   Optical mix: Gear A = 100 units* and Gear B = 0

   Total Contribution Margin = $200 × 100 units = $20,000 per week

   *200 hours/2 hours per unit = 100 units of A can be produced per week
3. Now, we should sell 80 units of Gear A using 160 hours (2 × 80) and 8 units of Gear B (40 hours/5 hours per unit).

   Total Contribution Margin = (80 × $200) + (8 × $400) = $19,200 per week

## DISCUSSION QUESTIONS

1. What is the difference between tactical and strategic decisions?
2. What are some ways that a manager can identify a feasible set of decision alternatives?
3. What role do past costs play in relevant costing decisions?
4. Explain why depreciation on an existing asset is always irrelevant.
5. Give an example of a future cost that is not relevant.
6. Can direct materials ever be irrelevant in a make-or-buy decision? Explain.
7. Why would a firm ever offer a price on a product that is below its full cost?
8. Discuss the importance of complementary effects in a keep-or-drop decision.
9. Should joint costs be considered in a sell-or-process-further decision? Explain.
10. Suppose that a product can be sold at split-off for $5,000 or processed further at a cost of $1,000 and then sold for $6,400. Should the product be processed further?
11. Suppose that a firm produces two products. Should the firm always place the most emphasis on the product with the largest contribution margin per unit? Explain.

## MULTIPLE-CHOICE QUESTIONS

**13-1** Which of the following is *not* a step in the short-run decision-making model?

a. Defining the problem.
b. Identifying alternatives.
c. Identifying the costs and benefits of feasible alternatives.
d. Assessing qualitative factors.
e. All of these are steps in the short-run decision-making model.

**13-2** Costs that *cannot* be affected by any future action are called

a.  differential costs.
b.  sunk costs.
c.  inventory costs.
d.  relevant costs.
e.  joint costs.

---

*Use the following information for Multiple-Choice Questions 13-3 through 13-5:*
Sandy is considering moving from her apartment into a small house with a fenced yard. The apartment is noisy, and she has difficulty studying. In addition, the fenced yard would be great for her dog. The distance from school is about the same from the house and from the apartment. The apartment costs $750 per month, and she has two months remaining on her lease. The lease cannot be broken, so Sandy must pay the last two months of rent whether she lives there or not. The rent for the house is $450 per month, plus utilities, which should average $100 per month. The apartment is furnished; the house is not. If Sandy moves into the house, she will need to buy a bed, dresser, desk, and chair immediately. She thinks that she can pick up some used furniture for a good price.

---

**13-3** Refer to the information for Sandy above. Which of the following costs is *irrelevant* to Sandy's decision to stay in the apartment or move to the house?

a.  House rent of $450 per month
b.  Utilities for the house of $100 per month
c.  The noise in the apartment house
d.  The cost of the used furniture
e.  The last two months of rent in the apartment

**13-4** Refer to the information for Sandy above. Which of the following is a qualitative factor?

a.  House rent of $450 per month
b.  Utilities for the house of $100 per month
c.  The noise in the apartment house
d.  The cost of the used furniture
e.  The last two months of rent in the apartment

**13-5** Refer to the information for Sandy above. Suppose that the apartment building was within walking distance to campus and the house was five miles away. Sandy does not own a car. How would that affect her decision?

a.  It would make the house more desirable.
b.  It would make the apartment more desirable.
c.  It would make both choices less desirable.
d.  It would make both choices more desirable.
e.  It would have no effect on the decision; buying or not buying a car is a separate decision.

**13-6** Which of the following statements is false?

a.  Fixed costs are never relevant.
b.  Variable costs are never relevant.
c.  Usually, variable costs are irrelevant.
d.  Step costs are irrelevant when a decision alternative requires moving outside of the existing relevant range.
e.  All of the above.

**13-7** In a make-or-buy decision,

a.  the company must choose between expanding or dropping a product line.
b.  the company must choose between accepting or rejecting a special order.
c.  the company would consider the purchase price of the externally provided good to be relevant.
d.  the company would consider all fixed overhead to be irrelevant.
e.  None of the above.

**13-8** Carroll Company, a manufacturer of vitamins and minerals, has been asked by a large drugstore chain to provide bottles of vitamin E. The bottles would be labeled with the name of the drugstore chain, and the chain would pay Carroll $2.30 per bottle rather than the $3.00 regular price. Which type of a decision is this?

    a.  Make-or-buy
    b.  Special-order
    c.  Keep-or-drop
    d.  Economic order quantity
    e.  Markup pricing

**13-9** Jennings Hardware Store marks up its merchandise by 30%. If a part costs $25.00, which of the following is true?

    a.  The price is $7.50.
    b.  The markup is $32.50.
    c.  The price is $32.50.
    d.  The markup is pure profit.
    e.  All of the above.

**13-10** When a company faces a production constraint or scarce resource (e.g., only a certain number of machine hours are available), it is important to

    a.  produce the product with the highest contribution margin in total.
    b.  produce the product with the lowest full manufacturing cost.
    c.  produce the product with the highest contribution margin per unit of scarce resource.
    d.  produce the product with the highest contribution margin per unit.
    e.  The constraint is not relevant to the production problem.

**13-11** In the keep-or-drop decision, the company will find which of the following income statement formats most useful?

    a.  A segmented income statement in the contribution margin format
    b.  A segmented income statement in the full costing format that is used for financial reporting
    c.  An overall income statement in the contribution margin format
    d.  An overall income statement in the full costing format that is used for financial reporting
    e.  Income statements are of no use in making this type of decision.

**13-12** In the sell-or-process-further decision,

    a.  joint costs are always relevant.
    b.  total costs of joint processing and further processing are relevant.
    c.  all costs incurred prior to the split-off point are relevant.
    d.  the most profitable outcome may be to further process some separately identifiable products beyond the split-off point, but sell others at the split-off point.
    e.  None of the above.

# CORNERSTONE EXERCISES

OBJECTIVE ❷
CORNERSTONE 13.1

**Cornerstone Exercise 13-13   Structuring a Make-or-Buy Problem**

Fresh Foods, a large restaurant chain, needed to determine if it would be cheaper to produce 5,000 units of its main food ingredient for use in its restaurants or to purchase them from an outside supplier for $12 each. Cost information on internal production includes the following:

|  | Total Cost | Unit Cost |
| --- | --- | --- |
| Direct materials | $25,000 | $ 5.00 |
| Direct labor | 15,000 | 3.00 |
| Variable manufacturing overhead | 7,500 | 1.50 |
| Variable marketing overhead | 10,000 | 2.00 |
| Fixed plant overhead | 30,000 | 6.00 |
| Total | $87,500 | $17.50 |

Fixed overhead will continue whether the ingredient is produced internally or externally. No additional costs of purchasing will be incurred beyond the purchase price.

**Required:**

1. What are the alternatives for Fresh Foods?
2. List the relevant cost(s) of internal production and of external purchase.
3. Which alternative is more cost effective and by how much?
4. Now assume that 20% of the fixed overhead can be avoided if the ingredient is purchased externally. Which alternative is more cost effective and by how much?

## Cornerstone Exercise 13-14    Structuring a Special-Order Problem

OBJECTIVE **2**

CORNERSTONE 13.2

Harrison Ford Company has been approached by a new customer with an offer to purchase 10,000 units of its model IJ4 at a price of $5 each. The new customer is geographically separated from the company's other customers, and existing sales would not be affected. Harrison normally produces 75,000 units of IJ4 per year but only plans to produce and sell 60,000 in the coming year. The normal sales price is $12 per unit. Unit cost information for the normal level of activity is as follows:

| | |
|---|---|
| Direct materials | $1.75 |
| Direct labor | 2.50 |
| Variable overhead | 1.50 |
| Fixed overhead | 3.25 |
| Total | $9.00 |

Fixed overhead will not be affected by whether or not the special order is accepted.

**Required:**

1. What are the relevant costs and benefits of the two alternatives (accept or reject the special order)?
2. By how much will operating income increase or decrease if the order is accepted?

---

*Use the following information for Cornerstone Exercises 13-15 and 13-16:*
Shown below is a segmented income statement for Hickory Company's three wooden flooring product lines:

| | Strip | Plank | Parquet | Total |
|---|---|---|---|---|
| Sales revenue | $400,000 | $200,000 | $300,000 | $900,000 |
| Less: Variable expenses | 225,000 | 120,000 | 250,000 | 595,000 |
| Contribution margin | $175,000 | $ 80,000 | $ 50,000 | $305,000 |
| Less direct fixed expenses: | | | | |
| Machine rent | (5,000) | (20,000) | (50,000) | (75,000) |
| Supervision | (15,000) | (10,000) | (20,000) | (45,000) |
| Depreciation | (35,000) | (10,000) | (25,000) | (70,000) |
| Segment margin | $120,000 | $ 40,000 | $ (45,000) | $115,000 |

---

## Cornerstone Exercise 13-15    Structuring a Keep-or-Drop Product Line Problem

OBJECTIVE **2**

CORNERSTONE 13.3

Refer to the information for Hickory Company above. Hickory's management is deciding whether to keep or drop the parquet product line. Hickory's parquet flooring product line has a contribution margin of $50,000 (sales of $300,000 less total variable costs of $250,000). All variable costs are relevant. Relevant fixed costs associated with this line include 80% of parquet's machine rent and all of parquet's supervision salaries.

**Required:**

1. List the alternatives being considered with respect to the parquet flooring line.
2. List the relevant benefits and costs for each alternative.
3. Which alternative is more cost effective and by how much?

**Cornerstone Exercise 13-16    Structuring a Keep-or-Drop Product Line Problem with Complementary Effects**

Refer to the information for Hickory Company on the previous page. Relevant fixed costs associated with this line include 80% of parquet's machine rent and all of parquet's supervision salaries. In addition, assume that dropping the parquet product line would reduce sales of the strip line by 10% and sales of the plank line by 5%. All other information remains the same.

**Required:**

1. If the parquet product line is dropped, what is the contribution margin for the strip line? For the plank line?
2. Which alternative (keep or drop the parquet product line) is now more cost effective and by how much?

**Cornerstone Exercise 13-17    Structuring the Sell-or-Process-Further Decision**

Jack's Lumber Yard receives 8,000 large trees each period that it subsequently processes into rough logs by stripping off the tree bark and leaves (i.e., one tree equals one log). Jack's then must decide whether to sell its rough logs (for use in log cabin construction) at split-off or to process them further into refined lumber (for use in regular construction framing). Jack's normally sells logs for a per-unit price of $495. Alternately, each log can be processed further into 800 feet of lumber at an additional cost of $0.15 per board foot. Also, lumber can be sold for $0.75 per board foot.

**Required:**

1. What is the contribution to income from selling the logs for log cabin construction?
2. What is the contribution to income from processing the logs into lumber?
3. Should Jack's continue to sell the logs or process them further into lumber?

> *Use the following information for Cornerstone Exercises 13-18 and 13-19:*
> Comfy Fit Company manufactures two types of university sweatshirts, the Swoop and the Rufus, with unit contribution margins of $5 and $15, respectively. Regardless of type, each sweatshirt must be fed through a stitching machine to affix the appropriate university logo. The firm leases seven machines that each provides 1,000 hours of machine time per year. Each Swoop sweatshirt requires 6 minutes of machine time, and each Rufus sweatshirt requires 20 minutes of machine time. (*Note:* For all answers that are less than 1.0, round the answer to 2 decimal places. For all unit answers (e.g., the answer is greater than 1.0), round the answer to the nearest whole number.)

**Cornerstone Exercise 13-18    Determining the Optimal Product Mix with One Constrained Resource**

Refer to the information for Comfy Fit Company above. Assume that there are no other constraints.

**Required:**

1. What is the contribution margin per hour of machine time for each type of sweatshirt?
2. What is the optimal mix of sweatshirts?
3. What is the total contribution margin earned for the optimal mix?

**OBJECTIVE ❸**
**CORNERSTONE 13.7**

**Cornerstone Exercise 13-19    Determining the Optimal Product Mix with One Constrained Resource and a Sales Constraint**

Refer to the information for Comfy Fit Company above. Assume that a maximum of 40,000 units of each sweatshirt can be sold.

**Required:**

1. What is the contribution margin per hour of machine time for each type of sweatshirt?
2. What is the optimal mix of sweatshirts?
3. What is the total contribution margin earned for the optimal mix?

**Cornerstone Exercise 13-20   Calculating Price by Applying a Markup Percentage to Cost**

OBJECTIVE ④
CORNERSTONE 13.8

Integrity Accounting Firm provides various financial services to organizations. Integrity has decided to price its jobs at the total variable costs of the job plus 15%. The job for a medium-sized dance club client included the following costs:

| | |
|---|---|
| Direct materials | $ 20,000 |
| Direct labor (partners and staff accountants) | 150,000 |
| Depreciation (using straight-line method) on Integrity's office building | 50,000 |

**Required:**

Calculate the price charged by Integrity Accounting to the dance club.

**Cornerstone Exercise 13-21   Calculating a Target Cost**

OBJECTIVE ④
CORNERSTONE 13.9

Yuhu manufactures cell phones and is developing a new model with a feature (aptly named Don't Drink and Dial) that prevents the phone from dialing an owner-defined list of phone numbers between the hours of midnight and 6:00 A.M. The new phone model has a target price of $380. Management requires a 25% profit on new product revenues.

**Required:**

1. Calculate the amount of desired profit.
2. Calculate the target cost.

# EXERCISES

**Exercise 13-22   Model for Making Tactical Decisions**

OBJECTIVE ①

The model for making tactical decisions described in the text has six steps. These steps are listed, out of order, below.

**Required:**

Put the steps in the correct order, starting with the step that should be taken first.
1. Select the alternative with the greatest overall benefit.
2. Identify the costs and benefits associated with each feasible alternative.
3. Assess qualitative factors.
4. Recognize and define the problem.
5. Identify alternatives as possible solutions to the problem.
6. Total the relevant costs and benefits for each alternative.

**Exercise 13-23   Model for Making Tactical Decisions**

OBJECTIVE ①

Austin Porter is a sophomore at a small Midwestern university (SMWU). He is considering whether to continue at this university or to transfer to one with a nationally recognized engineering program. Austin's decision-making process included the following:

a. He surfed the web to check out the sites of a number of colleges and universities with engineering programs.
b. Austin wrote to five of the universities to obtain information on their engineering colleges, tuition and room and board costs, the likelihood of being accepted, and so on.
c. Austin compared costs of the five other schools with the cost of his present school. He totaled the balance in his checking and savings accounts, estimated the earnings from his work-study job, and asked his parents whether or not they would be able to help him out.
d. Austin's high-school sweetheart had a long heart-to-heart talk with him about their future—specifically, that there might be no future if he left town.
e. Austin thought that while he enjoyed his present college, its engineering program did not have the national reputation that would enable him to get a good job on either the East or West Coast. Working for a large company on the coast was an important dream of his.

*(Continued)*

f.   Austin's major advisor agreed that a school with a national reputation would make job hunting easier. However, he reminded Austin that small college graduates had occasionally gotten the kind of jobs that Austin wanted.

g.   Austin had a number of good friends at SMWU, and they were encouraging him to stay.

h.   A friend of Austin's from high school returned home for a long weekend. She attends a prestigious university and told Austin of the fun and opportunities available at her school. She encouraged Austin to check out the possibilities elsewhere.

i.   A friendly professor outside of Austin's major area ran into him at the student union. She listened to his thinking and reminded him that a degree from SMWU would easily get him into a good graduate program. Perhaps he should consider postponing the job hunt until he had his master's degree in hand.

j.   Two of the three prestigious universities accepted Austin and offered financial aid. The third one rejected his application.

k.   Austin made his decision.

**Required:**

Classify the events a through k under one of the six steps of the model for making tactical decisions described in your text.

> *Use the following information for Exercises 13-24 and 13-25:*
> Zion Manufacturing had always made its components in-house. However, Bryce Component Works had recently offered to supply one component, K2, at a price of $25 each. Zion uses 10,000 units of Component K2 each year. The cost per unit of this component is as follows:
>
> | | |
> |---|---:|
> | Direct materials | $12.00 |
> | Direct labor | 8.25 |
> | Variable overhead | 4.50 |
> | Fixed overhead | 2.00 |
> | Total | $26.75 |

OBJECTIVE     **Exercise 13-24    Make-or-Buy Decision**

Refer to the information for Zion Manufacturing above. The fixed overhead is an allocated expense; none of it would be eliminated if production of Component K2 stopped.

**Required:**

1.   What are the alternatives facing Zion Manufacturing with respect to production of Component K2?

2.   List the relevant costs for each alternative. If Zion decides to purchase the component from Bryce, by how much will operating income increase or decrease?

3.   **CONCEPTUAL CONNECTION** Which alternative is better?

OBJECTIVE     **Exercise 13-25    Make-or-Buy Decision**

Refer to the information for Zion Manufacturing above. Assume that 75% of Zion Manufacturing's fixed overhead for Component K2 would be eliminated if that component were no longer produced.

**Required:**

1.   **CONCEPTUAL CONNECTION** If Zion decides to purchase the component from Bryce, by how much will operating income increase or decrease? Which alternative is better?

2.   **CONCEPTUAL CONNECTION** Briefly explain how increasing or decreasing the 75% figure affects Zion's final decision to make or purchase the component.

3.   **CONCEPTUAL CONNECTION** By how much would the per unit relevant fixed cost have to decrease before Zion would be indifferent (i.e., incur the same cost) between "making" versus "purchasing" the component? Show and briefly explain your calculations.

*Use the following information for Exercises 13-26 and 13-27:*

Smooth Move Company manufactures professional paperweights and has been approached by a new customer with an offer to purchase 15,000 units at a per-unit price of $7.00. The new customer is geographically separated from Smooth Move's other customers, and existing sales will not be affected. Smooth Move normally produces 82,000 units but plans to produce and sell only 65,000 in the coming year. The normal sales price is $12 per unit. Unit cost information is as follows:

| | |
|---|---|
| Direct materials | $3.10 |
| Direct labor | 2.25 |
| Variable overhead | 1.15 |
| Fixed overhead | 1.80 |
| Total | $8.30 |

## Exercise 13-26   Special-Order Decision

OBJECTIVE 2

Refer to the information for Smooth Move Company above. If Smooth Move accepts the order, no fixed manufacturing activities will be affected because there is sufficient excess capacity.

**Required:**

1. What are the alternatives for Smooth Move?
2. **CONCEPTUAL CONNECTION** Should Smooth Move accept the special order? By how much will profit increase or decrease if the order is accepted?
3. **CONCEPTUAL CONNECTION** Briefly explain the significance of the statement in the exercise that "existing sales will not be affected" (by the special sale).

## Exercise 13-27   Special Order

OBJECTIVE 2

Refer to the information for Smooth Move Company above. Suppose a customer wants to have its company logo affixed to each paperweight using a label. Smooth Move would have to purchase a special logo labeling machine that will cost $12,000. The machine will be able to label the 15,000 units and then it will be scrapped (with no further value). No other fixed overhead activities will be incurred. In addition, each special logo requires additional direct materials of $0.20.

**Required:**

**CONCEPTUAL CONNECTION** Should Smooth Move accept the special order? By how much will profit increase or decrease if the order is accepted?

*Use the following information for Exercises 13-28 through 13-30:*

Petoskey Company produces three products: Alanson, Boyne, and Conway. A segmented income statement, with amounts given in thousands, follows:

| | Alanson | Boyne | Conway | Total |
|---|---|---|---|---|
| Sales revenue | $1,280 | $185 | $300 | $1,765 |
| Less: Variable expenses | 1,115 | 45 | 225 | 1,385 |
| Contribution margin | $ 165 | $140 | $ 75 | $ 380 |
| Less direct fixed expenses: | | | | |
| Depreciation | 50 | 15 | 10 | 75 |
| Salaries | 95 | 85 | 80 | 260 |
| Segment margin | $ 20 | $ 40 | $(15) | $ 45 |

Direct fixed expenses consist of depreciation and plant supervisory salaries. All depreciation on the equipment is dedicated to the product lines. None of the equipment can be sold.

*(Continued)*

OBJECTIVE ② **Exercise 13-28    Keep-or-Drop Decision**

Refer to the information for Petoskey Company on the previous page. Assume that each of the three products has a different supervisor whose position would *remain* if the associated product were dropped.

**Required:**

**CONCEPTUAL CONNECTION** Estimate the impact on profit that would result from dropping Conway. Explain why Petoskey should keep or drop Conway.

OBJECTIVE ② **Exercise 13-29    Keep-or-Drop Decision**

Refer to the information for Petoskey Company on the previous page. Assume that, each of the three products has a different supervisor whose position would *be eliminated* if the associated product were dropped.

**Required:**

**CONCEPTUAL CONNECTION** Estimate the impact on profit that would result from dropping Conway. Explain why Petoskey should keep or drop Conway.

OBJECTIVE ② **Exercise 13-30    Keep-or-Drop Decision**

Refer to the information for Petoskey Company from **Exercise 13-29**. Assume that 20% of the Alanson customers choose to buy from Petoskey because it offers a full range of products, including Conway. If Conway were no longer available from Petoskey, these customers would go elsewhere to purchase Alanson.

**Required:**

**CONCEPTUAL CONNECTION** Estimate the impact on profit that would result from dropping Conway. Explain why Petoskey should keep or drop Conway.

OBJECTIVE ② **Exercise 13-31    Sell at Split-Off or Process Further**

Bozo Inc. manufactures two products from a joint production process. The joint process costs $110,000 and yields 6,000 pounds of LTE compound and 14,000 pounds of HS compound. LTE can be sold at split-off for $55 per pound. HS can be sold at split-off for $9 per pound. A buyer of HS asked Bozo to process HS further into CS compound. If HS were processed further, it would cost $34,000 to turn 14,000 pounds of HS into 4,000 pounds of CS. The CS would sell for $45 per pound.

**Required:**

1. What is the contribution to income from selling the 14,000 pounds of HS at split-off?
2. **CONCEPTUAL CONNECTION** What is the contribution to income from processing the 14,000 pounds of HS into 4,000 pounds of CS? Should Bozo continue to sell the HS at split-off or process it further into CS?

> *Use the following information for Exercises 13-32 and 13-33:*
> Billings Company produces two products, Product Reno and Product Tahoe. Each product goes through its own assembly and finishing departments. However, both of them must go through the painting department. The painting department has capacity of 2,460 hours per year. Product Reno has a unit contribution margin of $120 and requires five hours of painting department time. Product Tahoe has a unit contribution margin of $75 and requires three hours of painting department time. There are no other constraints.

OBJECTIVE ③ **Exercise 13-32    Choosing the Optimal Product Mix with One Constrained Resource**

Refer to the information for Billings Company above.

**Required:**

1. What is the contribution margin per hour of painting department time for each product?
2. What is the optimal mix of products?
3. What is the total contribution margin earned for the optimal mix?

**Exercise 13-33   Choosing the Optimal Product Mix with a Constrained Resource and a Demand Constraint**

OBJECTIVE 3

Refer to the information for Billings Company on the previous page. Assume that only 500 units of each product can be sold.

**Required:**

1.   What is the optimal mix of products?
2.   What is the total contribution margin earned for the optimal mix?

**Exercise 13-34   Calculating Price Using a Markup Percentage of Cost**

OBJECTIVE 4

Grinnell Lake Gift Shop has decided to price the candles that it sells at cost plus 80%. One type of carved bear-shaped candle costs $12, and huckleberry-scented votive candles cost $1.10 each.

**Required:**

1.   What price will Grinnell Lake Gift Shop charge for the carved bear candle?
2.   What price will Grinnell Lake Gift Shop charge for each scented votive candle?
3.   **CONCEPTUAL CONNECTION** Briefly explain two specific challenges that the financial manager of Grinnell Lake Gift Shop might encounter in employing this cost-plus pricing approach.

**Exercise 13-35   Target Costing**

OBJECTIVE 4

H. Banks Company would like to design, produce, and sell versatile toasters for the home kitchen market. The toaster will have four slots that adjust in thickness to accommodate both slim slices of bread and oversized bagels. The target price is $60. Banks requires that new products be priced such that 20% of the price is profit.

**Required:**

1.   Calculate the amount of desired profit per unit of the new toaster.
2.   Calculate the target cost per unit of the new toaster.

**Exercise 13-36   Keep or Buy, Sunk Costs**

OBJECTIVE 1 2

Heather Alburty purchased a previously owned, 2004 Grand Am for $8,900. Since purchasing the car, she has spent the following amounts on parts and labor:

| | |
|---|---|
| New stereo system | $1,200 |
| Trick paint | 400 |
| New wide racing tires | 800 |
| Total | $2,400 |

Unfortunately, the new stereo doesn't completely drown out the sounds of a grinding transmission. Apparently, the Grand Am needs a considerable amount of work to make it reliable transportation. Heather estimates that the needed repairs include the following:

| | |
|---|---|
| Transmission overhaul | $2,000 |
| Water pump | 400 |
| Master cylinder work | 1,100 |
| Total | $3,500 |

In a visit to a used car dealer, Heather has found a 2005 Neon in mint condition for $9,400. Heather has advertised and found that she can sell the Grand Am for only $6,400. If she buys the Neon, she will pay cash, but she would need to sell the Grand Am.

**Required:**

1.   **CONCEPTUAL CONNECTION** In trying to decide whether to restore the Grand Am or to buy the Neon, Heather is distressed because she already has spent $11,300 on the Grand Am. The investment seems too much to give up. How would you react to her concern?

*(Continued)*

2. **CONCEPTUAL CONNECTION** Assuming that Heather would be equally happy with the Grand Am or the Neon, should she buy the Neon, or should she restore the Grand Am?

---

*Use the following information for Exercises 13-37 and 13-38:*
Blasingham Company is currently manufacturing Part Q108, producing 35,000 units annually. The part is used in the production of several products made by Blasingham. The cost per unit for Q108 is as follows:

| | |
|---|---|
| Direct materials | $ 6.00 |
| Direct labor | 2.00 |
| Variable overhead | 1.50 |
| Fixed overhead | 3.50 |
| Total | $13.00 |

---

OBJECTIVE ❷

### Exercise 13-37   Make or Buy

Refer to the information for Blasingham Company above. Of the total fixed overhead assigned to Q108, $77,000 is direct fixed overhead (the lease of production machinery and salary of a production line supervisor—neither of which will be needed if the line is dropped). The remaining fixed overhead is common fixed overhead. An outside supplier has offered to sell the part to Blasingham for $11. There is no alternative use for the facilities currently used to produce the part.

**Required:**

1. **CONCEPTUAL CONNECTION** Should Blasingham Company make or buy Part Q108?
2. What is the most that Blasingham would be willing to pay an outside supplier?
3. If Blasingham buys the part, by how much will income increase or decrease?

OBJECTIVE ❶ ❷

### Exercise 13-38   Make or Buy

Refer to the information for Blasingham Company above. All of the fixed overhead is common fixed overhead. An outside supplier has offered to sell the part to Blasingham for $11. There is no alternative use for the facilities currently used to produce the part.

**Required:**

1. **CONCEPTUAL CONNECTION** Should Blasingham Company make or buy Part Q108?
2. What is the most Blasingham would be willing to pay an outside supplier?
3. If Blasingham buys the part, by how much will income increase or decrease?

# PROBLEMS

OBJECTIVE ❶ ❷

### Problem 13-39   Special-Order Decision

Rianne Company produces a light fixture with the following unit cost:

| | |
|---|---|
| Direct materials | $2 |
| Direct labor | 1 |
| Variable overhead | 3 |
| Fixed overhead | 2 |
| Unit cost | $8 |

The production capacity is 300,000 units per year. Because of a depressed housing market, the company expects to produce only 180,000 fixtures for the coming year. The company also has fixed selling costs totaling $500,000 per year and variable selling costs of $1 per unit sold. The fixtures normally sell for $12 each.

At the beginning of the year, a customer from a geographic region outside the area normally served by the company offered to buy 100,000 fixtures for $7 each. The customer also offered to pay all transportation costs. Since there would be no sales commissions involved, this order would not have any variable selling costs.

**Required:**

1. **CONCEPTUAL CONNECTION** Based on a quantitative (numerical) analysis, should the company accept the order?
2. **CONCEPTUAL CONNECTION** What qualitative factors might impact the decision? Assume that no other orders are expected beyond the regular business and the special order.

**Problem 13-40    Make or Buy, Qualitative Considerations**

Hetrick Dentistry Services operates in a large metropolitan area. Currently, Hetrick has its own dental laboratory to produce porcelain and gold crowns. The unit costs to produce the crowns are as follows:

|                   | Porcelain | Gold  |
| ----------------- | --------- | ----- |
| Raw materials     | $ 70      | $130  |
| Direct labor      | 27        | 27    |
| Variable overhead | 8         | 8     |
| Fixed overhead    | 22        | 22    |
| Total             | $127      | $187  |

Fixed overhead is detailed as follows:

| Salary (supervisor) | $26,000 |
| Depreciation        | 5,000   |
| Rent (lab facility) | 32,000  |

Overhead is applied on the basis of direct labor hours. These rates were computed by using 5,500 direct labor hours.

A local dental laboratory has offered to supply Hetrick all the crowns it needs. Its price is $125 for porcelain crowns and $150 for gold crowns; however, the offer is conditional on supplying both types of crowns—it will not supply just one type for the price indicated. If the offer is accepted, the equipment used by Hetrick's laboratory would be scrapped (it is old and has no market value), and the lab facility would be closed. Hetrick uses 2,000 porcelain crowns and 600 gold crowns per year.

**Required:**

1. **CONCEPTUAL CONNECTION** Should Hetrick continue to make its own crowns, or should they be purchased from the external supplier? What is the dollar effect of purchasing?
2. **CONCEPTUAL CONNECTION** What qualitative factors should Hetrick consider in making this decision?
3. **CONCEPTUAL CONNECTION** Suppose that the lab facility is owned rather than rented and that the $32,000 is depreciation rather than rent. What effect does this have on the analysis in Requirement 1?
4. **CONCEPTUAL CONNECTION** Refer to the original data. Assume that the volume of crowns used is 4,200 porcelain and 600 gold. Should Hetrick make or buy the crowns? Explain the outcome.

**Problem 13-41    Sell or Process Further**

Zanda Drug Corporation buys three chemicals that are processed to produce two types of analgesics used as ingredients for popular over-the-counter drugs. The purchased chemicals are blended for two to three hours and then heated for 15 minutes. The results of the process are two separate analgesics, depryl and pencol, which are sent to a drying room until their moisture content is reduced to 6 to 8%. For every 1,300 pounds of chemicals used, 600 pounds of depryl and 600 pounds of pencol are produced. After drying, depryl and pencol are sold to companies

*(Continued)*

that process them into their final form. The selling prices are $12 per pound for depryl and $30 per pound for pencol. The costs to produce 600 pounds of each analgesic are as follows:

| | |
|---|---|
| Chemicals | $8,500 |
| Direct labor | 6,735 |
| Overhead | 9,900 |

The analgesics are packaged in 20-pound bags and shipped. The cost of each bag is $1.30. Shipping costs $0.10 per pound.

Zanda could process depryl further by grinding it into a fine powder and then molding the powder into tablets. The tablets can be sold directly to retail drug stores as a generic brand. If this route were taken, the revenue received per bottle of tablets would be $4.00, with 10 bottles produced by every pound of depryl. The costs of grinding and tableting total $2.50 per pound of depryl. Bottles cost $0.40 each. Bottles are shipped in boxes that hold 25 bottles at a shipping cost of $1.60 per box.

**Required:**

1. **CONCEPTUAL CONNECTION** Should Zanda sell depryl at split-off, or should depryl be processed and sold as tablets?
2. If Zanda normally sells 265,000 pounds of depryl per year, what will be the difference in profits if depryl is processed further?

OBJECTIVE ❶ ❷   Problem 13-42   **Keep or Drop**

AudioMart is a retailer of radios, stereos, and televisions. The store carries two portable sound systems that have radios, tape players, and speakers. System A, of slightly higher quality than System B, costs $20 more. With rare exceptions, the store also sells a headset when a system is sold. The headset can be used with either system. Variable-costing income statements for the three products follow:

| | System A | System B | Headset |
|---|---|---|---|
| Sales | $45,000 | $ 32,500 | $8,000 |
| Less: Variable expenses | 20,000 | 25,500 | 3,200 |
| Contribution margin | $25,000 | $ 7,000 | $4,800 |
| Less: Fixed costs* | 10,000 | 18,000 | 2,700 |
| Operating income | $15,000 | $(11,000) | $2,100 |

\* This includes common fixed costs totaling $18,000, allocated to each product in proportion to its revenues.

The owner of the store is concerned about the profit performance of System B and is considering dropping it. If the product is dropped, sales of System A will increase by 30%, and sales of headsets will drop by 25%. (*Note:* Round all answers to the nearest whole number.)

**Required:**

1. Prepare segmented income statements for the three products using a better format.
2. **CONCEPTUAL CONNECTION** Prepare segmented income statements for System A and the headsets assuming that System B is dropped. Should B be dropped?
3. **CONCEPTUAL CONNECTION** Suppose that a third system, System C, with a similar quality to System B, could be acquired. Assume that with C the sales of A would remain unchanged; however, C would produce only 80% of the revenues of B, and sales of the headsets would drop by 10%. The contribution margin ratio of C is 50%, and its direct fixed costs would be identical to those of B. Should System B be dropped and replaced with System C?

OBJECTIVE ❶ ❷   Problem 13-43   **Accept or Reject a Special Order**

Steve Murningham, manager of an electronics division, was considering an offer by Pat Sellers, manager of a sister division. Pat's division was operating below capacity and had just been given an opportunity to produce 8,000 units of one of its products for a customer in a market not normally served. The opportunity involves a product that uses an electrical component produced by Steve's division. Each unit that Pat's division produces requires two of the components. However, the price that the customer is willing to pay is well below the price that is usually charged. To make a reasonable profit on the order, Pat needs a price concession from Steve's division. Pat had offered to pay full manufacturing cost for the parts. So Steve would know that everything was above board, Pat supplied the following unit cost and price information concerning the special order, excluding the cost of the electrical component:

| | |
|---|---:|
| Selling price | $32 |
| Less costs: | |
| Direct materials | 17 |
| Direct labor | 7 |
| Variable overhead | 2 |
| Fixed overhead | 3 |
| Operating profit | $ 3 |

The normal selling price of the electrical component is $2.30 per unit. Its full manufacturing cost is $1.85 ($1.05 variable and $0.80 fixed). Pat argued that paying $2.30 per component would wipe out the operating profit and result in her division showing a loss. Steve was interested in the offer because his division was also operating below capacity (the order would not use all the excess capacity).

**Required:**

1. **CONCEPTUAL CONNECTION** Should Steve accept the order at a selling price of $1.85 per unit? By how much will his division's profits be changed if the order is accepted? By how much will the profits of Pat's division change if Steve agrees to supply the part at full cost?

2. **CONCEPTUAL CONNECTION** Suppose that Steve offers to supply the component at $2. In offering this price, Steve says that it is a firm offer, not subject to negotiation. Should Pat accept this price and produce the special order? If Pat accepts the price, what is the change in profits for Steve's division?

3. **CONCEPTUAL CONNECTION** Assume that Steve's division is operating at full capacity and that Steve refuses to supply the part for less than the full price. Should Pat still accept the special order? Explain.

## Problem 13-44   Cost-Based Pricing Decision

OBJECTIVE ❹

Jeremy Costa, owner of Costa Cabinets Inc., is preparing a bid on a job that requires $1,800 of direct materials, $1,600 of direct labor, and $800 of overhead. Jeremy normally applies a standard markup based on cost of goods sold to arrive at an initial bid price. He then adjusts the price as necessary in light of other factors (e.g., competitive pressure). Last year's income statement is as follows:

| | |
|---|---:|
| Sales | $130,000 |
| Cost of goods sold | 48,100 |
| Gross margin | $ 81,900 |
| Selling and administrative expenses | 46,300 |
| Operating income | $ 35,600 |

**Required:**

1. Calculate the markup that Jeremy will use.
2. What is Jeremy's initial bid price?

## Problem 13-45   Product Mix Decision, Single Constraint

OBJECTIVE ❸

Sealing Company manufactures three types of DVD storage units. Each of the three types requires the use of a special machine that has a total operating capacity of 15,000 hours per year. Information on the three types of storage units is as follows:

*(Continued)*

|                        | Basic  | Standard | Deluxe  |
|------------------------|--------|----------|---------|
| Selling price          | $9.00  | $30.00   | $35.00  |
| Variable cost          | $6.00  | $20.00   | $10.00  |
| Machine hours required | 0.10   | 0.50     | 0.75    |

Sealing's marketing director has assessed demand for the three types of storage units and believes that the firm can sell as many units as it can produce.

**Required:**

1.  How many of each type of unit should be produced and sold to maximize the company's contribution margin? What is the total contribution margin for your selection?
2.  Now suppose that Sealing Company believes that it can sell no more than 12,000 of the deluxe model but up to 50,000 each of the basic and standard models at the selling prices estimated. What product mix would you recommend, and what would be the total contribution margin?

OBJECTIVE **Problem 13-46    Special-Order Decision, Qualitative Aspects**

Randy Stone, manager of Specialty Paper Products Company, was agonizing over an offer for an order requesting 5,000 boxes of calendars. Specialty Paper Products was operating at 70% of its capacity and could use the extra business. Unfortunately, the order's offering price of $4.20 per box was below the cost to produce the calendars. The controller, Louis Barns, was opposed to taking a loss on the deal. However, the personnel manager, Yatika Blaine, argued in favor of accepting the order even though a loss would be incurred. It would avoid the problem of layoffs and would help to maintain the company's community image. The full cost to produce a box of calendars follows:

| | |
|------------------|--------|
| Direct materials | $1.15  |
| Direct labor     | 2.00   |
| Variable overhead| 1.10   |
| Fixed overhead   | 1.00   |
| Total            | $5.25  |

Later that day, Louis and Yatika met over coffee. Louis sympathized with Yatika's concerns and suggested that the two of them rethink the special-order decision. He offered to determine relevant costs if Yatika would list the activities that would be affected by a layoff. Yatika eagerly agreed and came up with the following activities: an increase in the state unemployment insurance rate from 1% to 2% of total payroll, notification costs to lay off approximately 20 employees, and increased costs of rehiring and retraining workers when the downturn was over. Louis determined that these activities would cost the following amounts:

*   Total payroll is $1,460,000 per year.
*   Layoff paperwork is $25 per laid-off employee.
*   Rehiring and retraining is $150 per new employee.

**Required:**

1.  **CONCEPTUAL CONNECTION** Assume that the company will accept the order only if it increases total profits (without taking the potential layoffs into consideration). Should the company accept or reject the order? Provide supporting computations.
2.  **CONCEPTUAL CONNECTION** Consider the new information on activity costs associated with the layoff. Should the company accept or reject the order? Provide supporting computations.

OBJECTIVE **Problem 13-47    Sell or Process Further, Basic Analysis**

Shenista Inc. produces four products (Alpha, Beta, Gamma, and Delta) from a common input. The joint costs for a typical quarter follow:

| | |
|------------------|---------|
| Direct materials | $95,000 |
| Direct labor     | 43,000  |
| Overhead         | 85,000  |

The revenues from each product are as follows: Alpha, $100,000; Beta, $93,000; Gamma, $30,000; and Delta, $40,000.

Management is considering processing Delta beyond the split-off point, which would increase the sales value of Delta to $75,000. However, to process Delta further means that the company must rent some special equipment that costs $15,400 per quarter. Additional materials and labor also needed will cost $8,500 per quarter.

**Required:**

1.  What is the operating profit earned by the four products for one quarter?
2.  **CONCEPTUAL CONNECTION** Should the division process Delta further or sell it at split-off? What is the effect of the decision on quarterly operating profit?

## Problem 13-48    Product Mix Decision, Single Constraint
OBJECTIVE 3

Norton Company produces two products (Juno and Hera) that use the same material input. Juno uses two pounds of the material for every unit produced, and Hera uses five pounds. Currently, Norton has 16,000 pounds of the material in inventory. All of the material is imported. For the coming year, Norton plans to import an additional 8,000 pounds to produce 2,000 units of Juno and 4,000 units of Hera. The unit contribution margin is $30 for Juno and $60 for Hera. Also, assume that Norton's marketing department estimates that the company can sell a maximum of 2,000 units of Juno and 4,000 units of Hera.

Norton has received word that the source of the material has been shut down by embargo. Consequently, the company will not be able to import the 8,000 pounds it planned to use in the coming year's production. There is no other source of the material.

**Required:**

1.  Compute the total contribution margin that the company would earn if it could manufacture 2,000 units of Juno and 4,000 units of Hera.
2.  Determine the optimal usage of the company's inventory of 16,000 pounds of the material. Compute the total contribution margin for the product mix that you recommend.

## Problem 13-49    Sell at Split-Off or Process Further
OBJECTIVE 2

Eunice Company produces two products from a joint process. Joint costs are $70,000 for one batch, which yields 1,000 liters of germain and 4,000 liters of hastain. Germain can be sold at the split-off point for $24 or be processed further, into geraiten, at a manufacturing cost of $4,100 (for the 1,000 liters) and sold for $33 per liter.

If geraiten is sold, additional distribution costs of $0.80 per liter and sales commissions of 10% of sales will be incurred. In addition, Eunice's legal department is concerned about potential liability issues with geraiten—issues that do not arise with germain.

**Required:**

1.  **CONCEPTUAL CONNECTION** Considering only gross profit, should germain be sold at the split-off point or processed further?
2.  **CONCEPTUAL CONNECTION** Taking a value-chain approach (by considering distribution, marketing, and after-the-sale costs), determine whether or not germain should be processed into geraiten.

## Problem 13-50    Differential Costing
OBJECTIVE 1 2

As pointed out earlier in "Here's the Real Kicker," **Kicker** changed banks a couple of years ago because the loan officer at its bank moved out of state. Kicker saw that as an opportunity to take bids for its banking business and to fine-tune the banking services it was using. This problem uses that situation as the underlying scenario but uses three banks: FirstBank, Community Bank, and RegionalOne Bank. A set of representative data was presented to each bank for the purpose of preparing a bid. The data are as follows:

*(Continued)*

Checking accounts needed: 6
Checks per month:* 2,000
Foreign debits/credits on checking accounts per month: 200
Deposits per month:* 300
Returned checks:* 25 per month
Credit card charges per month: 4,000
Wire transfers per month: 100, of which 60 are to foreign bank accounts
Monthly credit needs (line of credit availability and cost): $100,000 average monthly usage

*These are overall totals for the six accounts during a month.

Internet banking services?
Knowledgeable loan officer?
Responsiveness of bank?

**FirstBank Bid:**
Checking accounts:  $5 monthly maintenance fee per account
$0.10 foreign debit/credit
$0.50 earned for each deposit
$3 per returned check

Credit card fees: $0.50 per item

Wire transfers: $15 to domestic bank accounts, $50 to foreign bank accounts

Line of credit:  Yes, this amount is available,
interest charged at prime plus 2%,
subject to a 6% minimum interest rate

Internet banking services?  Yes, full online banking available:
$15 one-time setup fee for each account
$20 monthly fee for software module

The loan officer assigned to the potential **Kicker** account had 10 years of experience with medium to large business banking and showed an understanding of the audio industry.

**Community Bank Bid:**
Checking accounts:  No fees for the accounts, and no credits earned on deposits
$2.00 per returned check

Credit card fees:  $0.50 per item,
$7 per batch processed. Only manual processing was available, and
Kicker estimated 20 batches per month

Wire transfers: $30 per wire transfer

Line of credit:  Yes, this amount is available:
interest charged at prime plus 2%
subject to a 7% minimum interest rate

Internet banking services? Not currently, but within the next six months

The loan officer assigned to the potential **Kicker** account had 4 years of experience with medium to large business banking, none of which pertained to the audio industry.

**RegionalOne Bank Bid:**
Checking accounts:  $5 monthly maintenance fee per account to be waived for Kicker
$0.20 foreign debit/credit
$0.30 earned for each deposit
$3.80 per returned check

Credit card fees: $0.50 per item

Wire transfers: $10 to domestic bank accounts, $55 to foreign bank accounts

Line of credit:  Yes, this amount is available:
                     interest charged at prime plus 2%
                     subject to a 6.5% minimum interest rate

Internet banking services?  Yes, full online banking available:
                                 one-time setup fee for each account waived for Kicker
                                 $20 monthly fee for software module

The loan officer assigned to the potential **Kicker** account had 2 years of experience with large business banking. Another branch of the bank had expertise in the audio industry and would be willing to help as needed. This bank was the first one to submit a bid.

**Required:**

1.  Calculate the predicted monthly cost of banking with each bank. Round answers to the nearest dollar.
2.  **CONCEPTUAL CONNECTION** Suppose **Kicker** felt that full online Internet banking was critical. How would that affect your analysis from Requirement 1? How would you incorporate the subjective factors (e.g., experience, access to expertise)?

# CASES

### Case 13-51    Make or Buy: Ethical Considerations

OBJECTIVE  ❶ ❷

Pamela McDonald, chief management accountant and controller for Murray Manufacturing Inc., was having lunch with Roger Branch, manager of the company's power department. Over the past six months, Pamela and Roger had developed a romantic relationship and were making plans for marriage. To keep company gossip at a minimum, Pamela and Roger had kept the relationship very quiet, and no one in the company was aware of it. The topic of the luncheon conversation centered on a decision concerning the company's power department that Larry Johnson, president of the company, was about to make.

**Pamela:** Roger, in our last executive meeting, we were told that a local utility company offered to supply power and quoted a price per kilowatt-hour that they said would hold for the next 3 years. They even offered to enter into a contractual agreement with us.

**Roger:** This is news to me. Is the bid price a threat to my area? Can they sell us power cheaper than we make it? And why wasn't I informed about this matter? I should have some input. This burns me. I think I should give Larry a call this afternoon and lodge a strong complaint.

**Pamela:** Calm down, Roger. The last thing I want you to do is call Larry. Larry made us all promise to keep this whole deal quiet until a decision had been made. He did not want you involved because he wanted to make an unbiased decision. You know that the company is struggling somewhat, and they are looking for ways to save money.

**Roger:** Yeah, but at my expense? And at the expense of my department's workers? At my age, I doubt that I could find a job that pays as well and has the same benefits. How much of a threat is this offer?

**Pamela:** Jack Lacy, my assistant controller, prepared an analysis while I was on vacation. It showed that internal production is cheaper than buying, but not by much. Larry asked me to review the findings and submit a final recommendation for next Wednesday's meeting. I've reviewed Jack's analysis, and it's faulty. He overlooked the interactions of your department with other service departments. When these are considered, the analysis is overwhelmingly in favor of purchasing the power. The savings are about $300,000 per year.

**Roger:** If Larry hears that, my department's gone. Pam, you can't let this happen. I'm 3 years away from having a vested retirement. And my workers—they have home mortgages, kids in college, families to support. No, it's not right. Pam, just tell him that your assistant's analysis is on target. He'll never know the difference.

**Pamela:** Roger, what you're suggesting doesn't sound right either. Would it be ethical for me to fail to disclose this information?

**Roger:** Ethical? Do you think it's right to lay off employees that have been loyal, faithful workers simply to fatten the pockets of the owners of this company? The Murrays already are so rich that they don't know what to do with their money. I think that it's even more unethical to penalize me and my workers. Why should we have to bear the consequences of some bad marketing decisions? Anyway, the effects of those decisions are about gone, and the company should be back to normal within a year or so.

**Pamela:** You may be right. Perhaps the well-being of you and your workers is more important than saving $300,000 for the Murrays.

### Required:

1.  Should Pamela have told Roger about the impending decision concerning the power department? What do you think most corporate codes of ethics would say about this?
2.  Should Pamela provide Larry with the correct data concerning the power department? Or should she protect its workers? What would you do if you were Pamela?

OBJECTIVE ❶ ❷

### Case 13-52   Keep or Drop a Division

Jan Shumard, president and general manager of Danbury Company, was concerned about the future of one of the company's largest divisions. The division's most recent quarterly income statement follows:

| | |
|---|---:|
| Sales | $3,751,500 |
| Less: Cost of goods sold | 2,722,400 |
| Gross profit | $1,029,100 |
| Less: Selling and administrative expenses | 1,100,000 |
| Operating (loss) | $  (70,900) |

Jan is giving serious consideration to shutting down the division because this is the ninth consecutive quarter that it has shown a loss. To help him in his decision, the following additional information has been gathered:

-   The division produces one product at a selling price of $100 to outside parties. The division sells 50% of its output to another division within the company for $83 per unit (full manufacturing cost plus 25%). The internal price is set by company policy. If the division is shut down, the user division will buy the part externally for $100 per unit.
-   The fixed overhead assigned per unit is $20.
-   There is no alternative use for the facilities if shut down. The facilities and equipment will be sold and the proceeds invested to produce an annuity of $100,000 per year. Of the fixed selling and administrative expenses, 30% represent allocated expenses from corporate headquarters. Variable selling expenses are $5 per unit sold for units sold externally. These expenses are avoided for internal sales. No variable administrative expenses are incurred.

### Required:

1.  Prepare an income statement that more accurately reflects the division's profit performance.
2.  Should the president shut down the division? What will be the effect on the company's profits if the division is closed?

## Case 13-53   Internet Research, Group Case

Often, websites for major airlines contain news of current special fares and flights. A decision to run a brief "fare special" is an example of a tactical decision. Form a group with one to three other students. Have each member of the group choose one or two airlines and check their websites for recent examples of fare specials. Have the group collaborate in preparing a presentation to the class discussing the types of cost and revenue information that would go into making this type of tactical decision.

# 14

# Capital Investment Decisions

© Pixelfabrik/Alamy

After studying Chapter 14, you should be able to:

1. Explain the meaning of *capital investment decisions,* and distinguish between independent and mutually exclusive capital investment decisions.

2. Compute the payback period and accounting rate of return for a proposed investment, and explain their roles in capital investment decisions.

3. Use net present value analysis for capital investment decisions involving independent projects.

4. Use the internal rate of return to assess the acceptability of independent projects.

5. Explain the role and value of postaudits.

6. Explain why net present value is better than internal rate of return for capital investment decisions involving mutually exclusive projects.

7. (*Appendix 14A*) Explain the relationship between current and future dollars.

mary981/Shutterstock.com

# EXPERIENCE MANAGERIAL DECISIONS

## with Hard Rock International

Launched in 1971 in London, England, nearly everyone has visited, or at least seen t-shirts for, one of **Hard Rock International**'s world-famous cafe restaurants located around the globe, from the U.S. to Europe to Asia and Australia. What visitors likely appreciate most is Hard Rock's impressive collection of rock 'n' roll memorabilia and its tasty fare. However, for Hard Rock's managerial accountants and the readers of this textbook, what is most likely to be appreciated is Hard Rock's masterful use of effective capital budgeting techniques to make decisions on a very big scale that are critical to the company's continued success. One of those decisions concerns the opening of new cafes all over the world from Mumbai, India, to Louisville, Kentucky.

New cafes require advanced planning concerning anticipated cash flows, both for future costs and revenues. Future cost-related cash flow projections include items such as labor and materials from different countries, licensing laws, utilities, kitchen and bar equipment, computers, construction, and audio-visual equipment. Future cash flows for food and beverage sales are even more difficult to project than costs because of uncer-

> *"New cafes require advanced planning concerning anticipated cash flows, both for future costs and revenues. Future cash flows for food and beverage sales are even more difficult to project than costs because of uncertainties involving demographics, economic conditions, and competition."*

tainties involving demographics, economic conditions, and competition. Another complicating factor is the challenge of estimating local awareness of the Hard Rock brand. Brand awareness is important because it drives Hard Rock's merchandise sales. Estimates of future cash flows for revenues and expenses are combined to calculate a proposed cafe's payback period and net present value (NPV). These metrics then are compared with Hard Rock's decision model requirements to help determine whether or not the proposed cafe is a wise decision.

Another capital investment decision for Hard Rock surrounds the acquisition of its rock 'n' roll memorabilia. Hard Rock uses its memorabilia to generate food and merchandise revenues by attracting more customers into the cafe. The collection has grown from a single Eric Clapton guitar to more than 72,000 instruments, stage outfits, platinum and gold LPs, music and lyric sheets, and photographs.

All of these decisions require effective capital budgeting practices.

OBJECTIVE

Explain the meaning of *capital investment decisions*, and distinguish between independent and mutually exclusive capital investment decisions.

# TYPES OF CAPITAL INVESTMENT DECISIONS

Organizations, like **Hard Rock**, often are faced with the opportunity (or need) to invest in assets or projects that represent long-term commitments. New production systems, new plants, new equipment, new product development, and, in the case of Hard Rock, new cafes are examples of assets and projects that fit this category. Usually, many alternatives are available. Hard Rock, for example, may be faced with the decision of whether or not to develop a new cafe in a certain location. Manufacturing firms, on the other hand, may need to decide whether to invest in a flexible manufacturing system or to continue with an existing traditional manufacturing system. These long-range decisions are examples of *capital investment decisions*.

**Capital investment decisions** are concerned with the process of planning, setting goals and priorities, arranging financing, and using certain criteria to select long-term assets. Because capital investment decisions place large amounts of resources at risk for long periods of time and simultaneously affect the future development of the firm, they are among the most important decisions made by managers. Poor capital investment decisions can be disastrous. For example, a failure to invest in automated manufacturing when other competitors do so may result in significant losses in market share because of the inability to compete on the basis of quality, cost, and delivery time. Making the right capital investment decisions is absolutely essential for long-term survival.

## Independent and Mutually Exclusive Projects

The process of making capital investment decisions often is referred to as **capital budgeting**. Two types of capital budgeting projects will be considered: *independent projects* and *mutually exclusive projects*.

- **Independent projects** are projects that, if accepted or rejected, do not affect the cash flows of other projects. For example, a decision by **Hard Rock** to develop a cafe in Argentina is not affected by its decision to build a new cafe in Singapore. These are independent capital investment decisions.
- **Mutually exclusive projects** are those projects that, if accepted, preclude the acceptance of all other competing projects. For example, each time **Hard Rock** develops a new cafe, it installs kitchen and bar equipment. Some equipment uses standard technology while other options offer advanced technology for energy efficiency. Once one type of equipment is chosen the other type is excluded; they are mutually exclusive.

## Making Capital Investment Decisions

In general terms, a sound capital investment will earn back its original capital outlay over its life and, at the same time, provide a reasonable return on the original investment. After making this assessment, managers must decide on the acceptability of independent projects and compare competing projects on the basis of their economic merits.

But what is meant by reasonable return? Generally, any new project must cover the opportunity cost of the funds invested. For example, if a company takes money from a money market fund that is earning 4% and invests it in a new project, then the project must provide at least a 4% return (the return that could have been earned had the money been left in the money market fund). In reality, funds for investment often come from different sources—each representing a different opportunity cost. The return that must be earned is a blend of the opportunity costs of the different sources. Thus, if a company uses two sources of funds, one with an opportunity cost of 4% and the other with an opportunity cost of 6%, then the return that must be earned is somewhere between 4 and 6%, depending on the relative amounts used from each source. Furthermore, it is usually assumed that managers should select projects that maximize the wealth of the firm's owners.

To make a capital investment decision, a manager must

- estimate the quantity and timing of cash flows
- assess the risk of the investment
- consider the impact of the project on the firm's profits

**Hard Rock** has little difficulty estimating what a new cafe will cost (the investment required). However, estimating future cash flows is much more challenging. For example, Hard Rock projects sales for a new cafe by first looking at sales from existing cafes with a similar size and location. Next, local factors such as demographics, economic conditions, competition, and awareness of the Hard Rock brand are considered. After taking all these factors into account, two sets of sales estimates are made for a 10-year horizon: (1) a likely scenario, and (2) a worst case scenario. Sales are also broken out into four sources: Restaurant, Catering, Bar, and Retail. This breakout is important because each revenue area has a different labor and materials cost structure. This facilitates the estimating of operating costs. Given the estimated revenues and costs, the future cash flows can then calculated. Obviously, as the accuracy of cash flow forecasts increases, the reliability of the decision improves.

Managers must set goals and priorities for capital investments. They also must identify some basic criteria for the acceptance or rejection of proposed investments. In this chapter, we will study four basic methods to guide managers in accepting or rejecting potential investments. The methods include both nondiscounting and discounting decision approaches (two methods are discussed for each approach). The discounting methods are applied to investment decisions involving both independent and mutually exclusive projects.

Note that, for simplicity, although forecasting future cash flows is a critical part of the capital investment process, we will reserve discussions of forecasting methodologies for more advanced courses. Furthermore, the cash flows projected must be *after-tax cash flows*. Taxes have an important role in developing cash flow assessments. Here, however, tax effects either are assumed away or the cash flows can be thought of as after-tax cash flows. Consequently, after-tax cash flows are assumed to be known and the focus in this chapter will be on making capital investment decisions *given* these cash flows.

# NONDISCOUNTING MODELS: PAYBACK PERIOD AND ACCOUNTING RATE OF RETURN

The basic capital investment decision models can be classified into two major categories: *nondiscounting models* and *discounting models*:

- **Nondiscounting models** ignore the time value of money.
- **Discounting models** explicitly consider the time value of money.

Although many accounting theorists disparage the nondiscounting models because they ignore the time value of money, many firms continue to use these models in making capital investment decisions. However, the use of discounting models has increased over the years, and few firms use only one model. Indeed, most firms seem to use both types.[1] This pattern suggests that both categories—nondiscounted and discounted—supply useful information to managers as they struggle to make a capital investment decision.

OBJECTIVE ❷

Compute the payback period and accounting rate of return for a proposed investment, and explain their roles in capital investment decisions.

[1] From the mid-1950s to 1988, surveys reveal that the use of discounting models as the primary evaluation method for capital projects went from about 9 to 80%. See A. Robichek and J. G. McDonald, "Financial Planning in Transition, Long Range Planning Service," Report No. 268 (Stanford Research Institute, Menlo Park, CA: January 1966); and T. Klammer, B. Koch, and N. Wilner, "Capital Budgeting Practices—A Survey of Corporate Use," published in the Proceedings of Decision Sciences National Meeting, November 21–24, 1988, North Texas State University.

## Payback Period

One type of nondiscounting model is the *payback period.* The **payback period** is the time required for a firm to recover its original investment. If the cash flows of a project are an equal amount each period, then the following formula can be used to compute its payback period:

$$\text{Payback Period} = \frac{\text{Original Investment}}{\text{Annual Cash Flow}}$$

If, however, the cash flows are unequal, the payback period is computed by adding the annual cash flows until such time as the original investment is recovered. If a fraction of a year is needed, it is assumed that cash flows occur evenly within each year. Cornerstone 14.1 shows how payback analysis is done for both even and uneven cash flows.

CORNERSTONE

14.1

## Calculating Payback

**Why:**

The payback period is the time required to recover a project's initial investment. It is often used to assess things such as (1) financial risk, (2) impact of an investment on liquidity, (3) obsolescence risk, and (4) impact of investment on performance measures.

**Information:**

Suppose that a new car wash facility requires an investment of $100,000 and either has: (a) even cash flows of $50,000 per year or (b) the following expected annual cash flows: $30,000, $40,000, $50,000, $60,000, and $70,000.

**Required:**

Calculate the payback period for each case.

**Solution:**

a.   Payback Period = Original Investment/Annual Cash Flow
            = $100,000/$50,000 = 2 years

b.

| Year | Unrecovered Investment (beginning of year) | Annual Cash Flow | Time Needed for Payback (years) |
|------|-------------------------------------------|------------------|--------------------------------|
| 1 | $ 100,000 | $ 30,000 | 1.0 |
| 2 | 70,000 | 40,000 | 1.0 |
| 3 | 30,000 | 50,000 | 0.6* |
| 4 | 0 | 60,000 | 0.0 |
| 5 | 0 | 70,000 | 0.0 |
| | | | 2.6 |

* At the beginning of Year 3, $30,000 is needed to recover the investment. Since a net cash flow of $50,000 is expected, only 0.6 year ($30,000/$50,000) is needed to recover the remaining $30,000, assuming a uniform cash inflow throughout the year.

**Using the Payback Period to Assess Risk** One way to use the payback period is to set a maximum payback period for all projects and to reject any project that exceeds this level. Why would a firm use the payback period in this way? Some analysts suggest that the payback period can be used as a rough measure of risk, with the notion that the longer it takes for a project to pay for itself, the riskier it is. Also, firms with riskier cash flows in general could require a shorter payback period than normal. Additionally, firms with liquidity problems would be more interested in projects with quick paybacks. Another critical concern is obsolescence. In some industries, the risk of obsolescence is high. Firms within these industries, such as computer and MP3 player manufacturers, would be interested in recovering funds rapidly.

**ETHICAL DECISIONS** Another reason, less beneficial to the firm, may also be involved. Many managers in a position to make capital investment decisions may choose investments with quick payback periods out of self-interest. If a manager's performance is measured using such short-run criteria as annual net income, projects with quick paybacks may be chosen to show improved net income and cash flow as quickly as possible. Consider that divisional managers often are responsible for making capital investment decisions and are evaluated on divisional profit. The tenure of divisional managers, however, is typically short—3 to 5 years on average. Consequently, an incentive exists for self-interested managers to shy away from investments that promise healthy long-run returns but relatively meager returns in the short run. New products and services that require time to develop a consumer following fit this description. However, ethical managers would avoid responding to these types of incentives. Corporate budgeting policies and a budget review committee can mitigate these problems by clearly communicating expected behaviors. ●

**Using the Payback Period to Choose Among Alternatives** The payback period can be used to choose among competing alternatives. Under this approach, the investment with the shortest payback period is preferred over investments with longer payback periods. However, this use of the payback period is less defensible because this measure suffers from two major deficiencies:

- It ignores the cash flow performance of the investments beyond the payback period.
- It ignores the time value of money.

These two significant deficiencies are easily illustrated. Assume that an engineering firm is considering two different types of computer-aided design (CAD) systems: CAD-A and CAD-B. Each system requires an initial outlay of $150,000, has a 5-year life, and displays the following annual cash flows:

| Investment | Year 1 | Year 2 | Year 3 | Year 4 | Year 5 |
|---|---|---|---|---|---|
| CAD-A | $90,000 | $ 60,000 | $50,000 | $50,000 | $50,000 |
| CAD-B | 40,000 | 110,000 | 25,000 | 25,000 | 25,000 |

Both investments have payback periods of 2 years. In other words, if a manager uses the payback period to choose among competing investments, the two investments would be equally desirable. In reality, however, the CAD-A system should be preferred over the CAD-B system for two reasons:

- The CAD-A system provides a much larger dollar return for the Years 3, 4, and 5 beyond the payback period ($150,000 vs. $75,000).
- The CAD-A system returns $90,000 in the first year, while B returns only $40,000. The extra $50,000 that the CAD-A system provides in the first year could be put to productive use, such as investing in another project. It is better to have a dollar now than to have it 1 year from now, because the dollar on hand can be invested to provide a return 1 year from now.

In summary, the payback period provides information to managers that can be used as follows:

- To help control the risks associated with the uncertainty of future cash flows.
- To help minimize the impact of an investment on a firm's liquidity problems.
- To help control the risk of obsolescence.
- To help control the effect of the investment on performance measures.

However, the method suffers significant deficiencies: It ignores a project's total profitability and the time value of money. While the computation of the payback period may be useful to a manager, relying on it solely for a capital investment decision would be foolish.

## Accounting Rate of Return

The *accounting rate of return* is the second commonly used nondiscounting model. The **accounting rate of return (ARR)** measures the return on a project in terms of income, as opposed to using a project's cash flow. The accounting rate of return is computed by the following formula:

$$\text{Accounting Rate of Return} = \frac{\text{Average Income}}{\text{Initial Investment}}$$

Income is not equivalent to cash flows because of accruals and deferrals used in its computation. The average income of a project is obtained by adding the net income for each year of the project and then dividing this total by the number of years. Cornerstone 14.2 shows how to calculate the accounting rate of return.

**CORNERSTONE**

**14.2**

## Calculating the Accounting Rate of Return

**Why:**

The accounting rate of return for a project is average income for a project divided by the initial investment. Unlike the payback period, the accounting rate of return considers the profitability of an investment; however, like the payback period, it ignores the time value of money. It may be useful as a screening measure to ensure that a new investment does not adversely debt covenants (covenants may use accounting ratios that can be affected by the income reported and the level of long-term assets).

**Information:**

An investment requires an initial outlay of $100,000 and has a 5-year life with no salvage value. The yearly cash flows are $50,000, $50,000, $60,000, $50,000 and $70,000.

**Required:**

1. Calculate the annual net income for each of the 5 years.

2. Calculate the accounting rate of return.

*(Continued)*

**Solution:**

1. Yearly Depreciation Expense = ($100,000 – $0)/5 years = $20,000

   Annual Net Income = Net Cash Flow – Depreciation Expense

   Year 1 Net Income = $50,000 – $20,000 = $30,000

   Year 2 Net Income = $50,000 – $20,000 = $30,000

   Year 3 Net Income = $60,000 – $20,000 = $40,000

   Year 4 Net Income = $50,000 – $20,000 = $30,000

   Year 5 Net Income = $70,000 – $20,000 = $50,000

2. Total Net Income (5 years) = $180,000

   Average Net Income = $180,000/5 = $36,000

   $$\text{Accounting Rate of Return} = \frac{\$36,000}{\$100,000} = 0.36$$

**Limitations of Accounting Rate of Return**   Unlike the payback period, the ARR does consider a project's profitability. However, the ARR has other potential drawbacks, including the following.

- *Ignoring Time Value of Money:* Like the payback period, it ignores the time value of money. Ignoring the time value of money is a critical deficiency in this method as well. It can lead a manager to choose investments that do not maximize profits. The ARR and payback model are referred to as *nondiscounting models* because they ignore the time value of money.

- *Dependency on Net Income:* ARR is dependent upon net income, which is the financial measure most likely to be manipulated by managers. Some of the reasons for manipulating net income include debt contracts (i.e., debt covenants) and bonuses. Often, debt contracts require that a firm maintain certain financial accounting ratios, which can be affected by the income reported and by the level of long-term assets. Accordingly, the ARR may be used as a screening measure to ensure that any new investment will not adversely affect these ratios.

- *Managers' Incentive:* Additionally, because bonuses to managers often are based on accounting income or return on assets, managers may have a personal interest in seeing that any new investment contributes significantly to net income. A manager seeking to maximize personal income is likely to select investments that return the highest net income per dollar invested, even if the selected investments are not the ones that produce the greatest cash flows and return to the firm in the long-run.

---

**concept Q&A**

Why would a manager choose only investments that return the highest income per dollar invested?

**Answer:**

It might be an action that helps the company to comply with debt covenants or have something to do with the manager's incentive compensation.

---

# DISCOUNTING MODELS: THE NET PRESENT VALUE METHOD

Discounting models use **discounted cash flows** which are future cash flows expressed in terms of their present value. The use of discounting models requires an understanding of the present value concepts. Present value concepts are reviewed in Appendix 14-A (p. 644). Review these concepts and make sure that you understand them before

**OBJECTIVE ③**

Use net present value analysis for capital investment decisions involving independent projects.

studying capital investment discount models. Present value tables [Exhibits 14B.1 (p. 647) and 14B.2 (p. 648)] are presented in Appendix 14-B (p. 646). These tables are referred to and used throughout the rest of this chapter. Two discounting models will be considered: *net present value* and *internal rate of return*.

## Net Present Value Defined

**Net present value (NPV)** is the difference between the present value of the cash inflows and outflows associated with a project:

$$NPV = \left[\sum CF_t/(1+i)^t\right] - I$$
$$= \left[\sum CF_t df_t\right] - I$$
$$= P - I$$

where

$I$ = The present value of the project's cost (usually the initial cash outlay)
$CF_t$ = The cash inflow to be received in period $t$, with $t = 1 \ldots n$
$i$ = The required rate of return
$t$ = The time period
$P$ = The present value of the project's future cash inflows
$df_t = 1/(1+i)^t$, the discount factor

NPV measures the profitability of an investment. A positive NPV indicates that the investment increases the firm's wealth. To use the NPV method, a *required rate of return* must be defined. The **required rate of return** is the minimum acceptable rate of return. It also is referred to as the *discount rate, hurdle rate*, and *cost of capital.* In theory, if future cash flows are known with certainty, then the correct required rate of return is the firm's **cost of capital**. In practice, future cash flows are uncertain, and managers often choose a discount rate higher than the cost of capital to deal with the uncertainty. However, if the rate chosen is excessively high, it will bias the selection process toward short-term investments. Because of the risk of being overly conservative, it may be better to use the cost of capital as the discount rate and find other approaches to deal with uncertainty.

Once the NPV for a project is computed, it can be used to determine whether or not to accept and investment:

- If the NPV is greater than zero the investment is profitable and, therefore, acceptable. A positive NPV signals that (1) the initial investment has been recovered, (2) the required rate of return has been recovered, and (3) a return in excess of (1) and (2) has been received.
- If the NPV equals zero, the decision maker will find acceptance or rejection of the investment equal.
- If the NPV is less than zero, the investment should be rejected. In this case, it is earning less than the required rate of return.

---

### concept Q&A

Suppose that the NPV of an investment is $2,000. Why does this mean that the investment should be accepted?

**Answer:**

NPV greater than zero means that the investment recovers its capital while simultaneously earning a return in excess of the required rate.

---

## Net Present Value Illustrated

Brannon Company has developed new earphones for portable MP3 players that it believes are superior to anything on the market. The earphones have a projected product life cycle of 5 years. Although the marketing manager is excited about the new product's prospects, a decision to manufacture the new product depends on whether it can earn a positive NPV given the company's required rate of return of 12%. In order to make a decision regarding the earphones, two steps must be taken:

**Step 1:** The cash flows for each year must be identified.
**Step 2:** The NPV must be computed using the cash flows from Step 1.

Cornerstone 14.3 shows how to calculate the NPV.

## Assessing Cash Flows and Calculating Net Present Value

CORNERSTONE

14.3

**Why:**

NPV is the present value of future cash flows minus the initial outlay. The required rate of return, usually the cost of capital, is used to calculate the present value. Projects with a positive (negative) NPV should be accepted (rejected). A positive NPV signals that the investment will increase the value of the firm.

**Information:**

A detailed market study revealed expected annual revenues of $300,000 for new earphones. Equipment to produce the earphones will cost $320,000. After 5 years, the equipment can be sold for $40,000. In addition to equipment, working capital is expected to increase by $40,000 because of increases in inventories and receivables. The firm expects to recover the investment in working capital at the end of the project's life. Annual cash operating expenses are estimated at $180,000. The required rate of return is 12%.

**Required:**

Estimate the annual cash flows, and calculate the NPV.

**Solution:**

### STEP 1. CASH FLOW IDENTIFICATION

| Year | Item | Cash Flow |
|---|---|---|
| 0 | Equipment | $(320,000) |
| | Working capital | (40,000) |
| | Total | $(360,000) |
| 1–4 | Revenues | $ 300,000 |
| | Operating expenses | (180,000) |
| | Total | $ 120,000 |
| 5 | Revenues | $ 300,000 |
| | Operating expenses | (180,000) |
| | Salvage | 40,000 |
| | Recovery of working capital | 40,000 |
| | Total | $ 200,000 |

### STEP 2A. NPV ANALYSIS

| Year | Cash Flow[a] | Discount Factor[b] | Present Value |
|---|---|---|---|
| 0 | $(360,000) | 1.00000 | $(360,000) |
| 1 | 120,000 | 0.89286 | 107,143 |
| 2 | 120,000 | 0.79719 | 95,663 |
| 3 | 120,000 | 0.71178 | 85,414 |
| 4 | 120,000 | 0.63552 | 76,262 |
| 5 | 200,000 | 0.56743 | 113,486 |
| Net present value | | | $ 117,968 |

*(Continued)*

| | **STEP 2B. NPV ANALYSIS** | | |
|---|---|---|---|
| Year | Cash Flow | Discount Factor[c] | Present Value |
| 0 | $(360,000) | 1.00000 | $(360,000) |
| 1–4 | 120,000 | 3.03735 | 364,482 |
| 5 | 200,000 | 0.56743 | 113,486 |
| Net present value | | | $ 117,968 |

CORNERSTONE
**14.3**

*(Continued)*

[a] From Step 1.
[b] From Exhibit 14B.1.
[c] Years 1–4 from Exhibit 14B.2; Year 5 from Exhibit 14B.1.

In Cornerstone 14.3, notice that Step 2 offers two approaches for computing NPV. Step 2A computes NPV by using discount factors from Exhibit 14B.1. Step 2B simplifies the computation by using a single discount factor from Exhibit 14B.2 for the even cash flows occurring in Years 1 through 4.

ILLUSTRATING
RELATIONSHIPS

## Illustrating Relationships: NPV, Discount Rates, and Cash Flows

Estimating cash flows is often difficult and certainly a major source of risk for capital budgeting decisions. The discount rate is the minimum acceptable required rate of return and, under certainty, would correspond to the firm's cost of capital. Because of uncertain future cash flows, firms may use a higher discount rate than its cost of capital. It is also common to provide pessimistic and most likely cash flow scenarios to help assess a project's risk (as **Hard Rock** does). As the discount rate increases, the present value of future cash flows decreases, making it harder for a project to achieve a positive NPV. Alternatively, providing pessimistic and likely assessments of cash flows also allows managers to see the effect of differences in cash flow estimates on project viability as measured by NPV. Illustrating the relationship between the discount rate and cash flows affords rich insight about the economic feasibility of a project.

For purposes of illustration, suppose that an amusement park is considering an investment in a new ride that has the following data:

| | |
|---|---|
| Investment: | $3,500,000 |
| Likely annual cash flow: | $1,200,000 |
| Pessimistic annual cash flow: | $800,000 |
| Discount rate range: | 0.08 to 0.18, increments of 0.02 |
| Expected cost of capital: | 0.10 |
| Project life: | 6 years |

Using this information, the NPV is calculated and plotted as the discount rate varies (increasing by increments of 0.02 for the range indicated) for each series of cash flows. Exhibit 14.1 illustrates the relationships. For the likely cash flow scenario, the project has a positive NPV for all discount rates. For the worst case scenario, the NPV is negative for the four highest discount rates, about zero (actually slightly negative) for the 10% rate and positive only for the 8% rate.

Knowing these relationships, what decision should be made? For the expected cost of capital of 10%, the worst prediction is a NPV of about zero (−$16,000). Thus, it appears to be a fairly safe investment since there seems to be very little likelihood of

( EXHIBIT 14.1 )

**NPV, Discount Rates and Cash Flow**

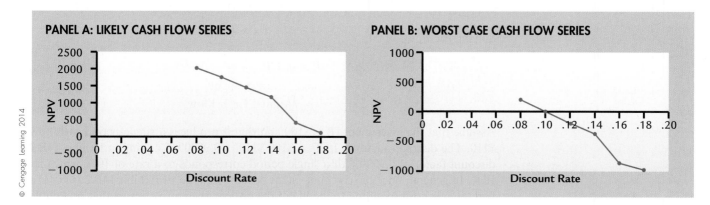

PANEL A: LIKELY CASH FLOW SERIES

PANEL B: WORST CASE CASH FLOW SERIES

losing on the project. Using both Panels A and B provides good insight into the risk and economic viability of the proposed project.

# INTERNAL RATE OF RETURN

Another discounting model is the *internal rate of return* method.

OBJECTIVE

Use the internal rate of return to assess the acceptability of independent projects.

## Internal Rate of Return Defined

The **internal rate of return (IRR)** is defined as the interest rate that sets the present value of a project's cash inflows equal to the present value of the project's cost. In other words, it is the interest rate that sets the project's NPV at zero. The following equation can be used to determine a project's IRR:

$$I = \sum [CF_t/(1+i)^t]$$

where $t = 1, \ldots, n$

The right side of this equation is the present value of future cash flows, and the left side is the investment. $I$, $CF_t$, and $t$ are known. Thus, the IRR (the interest rate, $i$, in the equation) can be found using trial and error. Once the IRR for a project is computed, it is compared with the firm's required rate of return:

- If the IRR is greater than the required rate, the project is deemed acceptable.
- If the IRR is less than the required rate of return, the project is rejected.
- If the IRR is equal to the required rate of return, the firm is indifferent between accepting or rejecting the investment proposal.

The IRR is the most widely used of the capital investment techniques. One reason for its popularity may be that it is a rate of return, a concept that managers are comfortable with using. Another possibility is that managers may believe (in most cases, incorrectly) that the IRR is the true or actual compounded rate of return being earned by the initial investment. Whatever the reasons for its popularity, a basic understanding of the IRR is necessary.

## Internal Rate of Return Illustrated: Multiple-Period Setting with Uniform Cash Flows

Assume initially that the investment produces a series of uniform cash flows. Since the series of cash flows is uniform, a single discount factor from the present value table in Exhibit 14B.2 (p. 648) can be used to compute the present value of the annuity.

Letting *df* be this discount factor and *CF* be the annual cash flow, the IRR equation assumes the following form:

$$I = CF(df)$$

Solving for *df*, we obtain:

$$df = I/CF$$
$$= \frac{\text{Investment}}{\text{Annual Cash Flow}}$$

Assume that the investment (*I*) is $100 and that it produces a single-period cash flow of $110. The discount factor is I/CF = $100/$110 = 0.90909. Looking in Exhibit 14B.2, a discount factor of 0.90909 for a single period corresponds to a rate of 10%, which is the IRR. In general, once the discount factor is computed, go to Exhibit 14B.2 (p. 648) and find the row corresponding to the life of the project, then move across that row until the computed discount factor is found. The interest rate corresponding to this discount factor is the IRR. Cornerstone 14.4 illustrates how to calculate the IRR for multiple-period uniform cash flows.

## CORNERSTONE 14.4

## Calculating Internal Rate of Return with Uniform Cash Flows

**Why:**
The IRR is the interest rate (discount rate) where NPV = 0. Acceptable investments should have an IRR greater than the required rate of return (cost of capital).

**Information:**
Assume that a hospital has the opportunity to invest $205,570.50 in a new ultrasound system that will produce net cash inflows of $50,000 at the end of each of the next 6 years.

**Required:**
Calculate the IRR for the ultrasound system.

**Solution:**

$$df = I/CF$$
$$= \$205,570.50/\$50,000$$
$$= 4.11141$$

Since the life of the investment is 6 years, find the sixth row in Exhibit 14B.2 and then move across this row until *df* = 4.11141 is found. The interest rate corresponding to 4.11141 is 12%, which is the IRR.

Exhibit 14B.2 does not provide discount factors for every possible interest rate. To illustrate, assume that the annual cash inflows expected by the hospital (in Cornerstone 14.4) are $51,000 instead of $50,000. The new discount factor is 4.03079 ($205,570.50/$51,000). Going once again to the sixth row in Exhibit 14B.2, it is clear that the discount factor—and thus the IRR—lies between 12 and 14%. Although it is possible to approximate the IRR by interpolation, for simplicity, we can identify the range for the

IRR as indicated by the table values. In practice, business calculators or spreadsheet programs like Excel can provide the values of IRR without the use of tables such as Exhibit 14B.2.

## Internal Rate of Return Illustrated: Multiple-Period Setting with Uneven Cash Flows

If the cash flows are not uniform, then the IRR equation must be used. For a multiple-period setting, this equation can be solved by trial and error or by using a business calculator or a spreadsheet program. To illustrate the solution by trial and error, assume that a $10,000 investment in a PC system produces clerical savings of $6,000 and $7,200, respectively, for the 2 years. The IRR is the interest rate that sets the present value of these two cash inflows equal to $10,000:

$$P = \left[\frac{\$6,000}{(1 + i)}\right] + \left[\frac{\$7,200}{(1 + i)^2}\right]$$

$$= \$10,000$$

To solve this equation by trial and error, start by selecting a possible value for $i$. Given this first guess, the present value of the future cash flows is computed and then compared with the initial investment. If the present value is greater than the initial investment, then the interest rate is too low. If the present value is less than the initial investment, then the interest rate is too high. The next guess is adjusted accordingly.

Assume that the first guess is 18%. Using $i$ equal to 0.18, the present value table in Exhibit 14B.1 (p. 647) yields the following discount factors: 0.84746 and 0.71818. These discount factors produce the following present value for the two cash inflows:

$$P = (0.84746 \times \$6,000) + (0.71818 \times \$7,200)$$

$$= \$10,256$$

Since $P$ is greater than $10,000, the interest rate selected is too low. A higher guess is needed. If the next guess is 20%, we obtain the following:

$$P = (0.83333 \times \$6,000) + (0.69444 \times \$7,200)$$

$$= \$9,999.95$$

Since this value is very close to $10,000, we can say that the IRR is 20%. (The IRR is, in fact, exactly 20%. The present value is slightly less than the investment because the discount factors found in Exhibit 14B.1 have been rounded to 5 decimal places.)

## YOUDECIDE IRR and Uncertainty in Estimates of Cash Savings and Project Life

As a manager of a plant producing cooking oils and margarines, you are concerned about the emission of contaminated water effluents. On a regular basis, your plant violates its discharge permit and dumps many times the allowable waste (organic solids) into a local river. This practice is beginning to draw increased attention and criticism from the state environmental agency. You are considering the acquisition and installation of a zero-discharge system, closed-loop system with an expected life of 10 years and a required investment of $250,000. The closed-loop system is expected to produce the following expected annual savings:

| | |
|---|---:|
| Water (from the ability to recycle the water): | $20,000 |
| Materials (from the ability to use extracted materials): | 5,000 |
| Avoidance of fines and penalties: | 15,000 |
| Reduction in demand for laboratory analysis: | 10,000 |
| Total Savings | $50,000 |

To accept any project, the IRR must be greater than the cost of capital, which is 10%.

Upon calculating the IRR, you find that it is about 15%, significantly greater than the 10% benchmark rate. However, upon

(Continued)

seeking approval for the project from the divisional manager, he asks you how certain you are about the projected cash savings. He also questions the estimated life, arguing that based on his experience the expected life of the particular closed-loop system is usually closer to 8 years than 10.

**How would you address the divisional manager's concerns about projected cash savings and estimated life?**

The concerns of the divisional manager relate to the uncertainty surrounding both the cash flow and project life estimates. The savings from recycling water and the fines and penalties probably have very little uncertainty attached to them. The same may also be true of the lab costs, especially if the analysis is outsourced. The major source of uncertainty probably is attached to the quantity of organic solids that once extracted can be used to produce additional margarines and cooking oils. Assuming that the extraction process does not produce any usable organic solids, the annual savings would be $45,000 ($50,000 − $45,000), yielding the worst case scenario for cash flows. This uncertainty in the cash flows can be dealt with by first calculating the minimum annual cash savings that must be realized to earn a rate equal to the firm's cost of capital and then comparing this minimum cash savings with the cash flows of the worst case scenario ($45,000). Calculating this minimum cash flow for an 8 year life simultaneously addresses the project life issue.

The minimum cash flow is calculated as follows (where *df* is the discount factor for 8 years and 10%, from Exhibit 14B.2, p. 648):

$$I = CF(df)$$
$$CF = I/df$$
$$= \$250,000/5.33493$$
$$= \$48,861 \text{ (rounded)}$$

In the worst case scenario, the project will not meet the minimum cash savings requirement. The cash savings from the extraction of organic solids can only be off by about 20% to retain project viability. As a plant manager, you might argue that there is a likely *underestimation* of future fines and penalties resulting from the increased political attention to polluting of the local river. Also, there may be a positive benefit, not included in the savings, of a more favorable public image (e.g., increased sales because of the favorable environmental action). Taken together, you should have a strong position for winning approval of the project.

**Sensitivity analysis thus provides a powerful tool for assessing the impact of uncertainty in capital investment analysis.**

---

OBJECTIVE

Explain the role and value of postaudits.

# POSTAUDIT OF CAPITAL PROJECTS

A key element in the capital investment process is a follow-up analysis of a capital project once it is implemented. This analysis is called a *postaudit*. A **postaudit** compares the actual benefits with the estimated benefits and actual operating costs with estimated operating costs. It evaluates the overall outcome of the investment and proposes corrective action if needed. The following real-world case illustrates the usefulness of a postaudit activity.

## Postaudit Illustrated

Allen Manesfield and Jenny Winters were discussing a persistent and irritating problem present in the process of producing intravenous (IV) needles. Allen and Jenny are employed by Honley Medical, which specializes in the production of medical products and has three divisions: the IV Products Division, the Critical Care Monitoring Division, and the Specialty Products Division. Allen and Jenny are associated with the IV Products Division—Allen as the senior production engineer and Jenny as the marketing manager.

The IV Products Division produces needles of five different sizes. During one stage of the manufacturing process, the needle itself is inserted into a plastic hub and is bonded by using epoxy glue. According to Jenny, the use of epoxy to bond the needles was causing the division all kinds of problems. In many cases, the epoxy wasn't bonding correctly. The rejects were high and the division was receiving a large number of complaints from its customers. Corrective action was needed to avoid losing sales. After some discussion and analysis, a recommendation was made to use induction welding in lieu of epoxy bonding. In induction welding, the needles are inserted into the plastic hub, and an RF generator is used to heat the needles. The RF generator works on the same principle as a microwave oven. As the needles get hot, the plastic melts and the needles are bonded.

Switching to induction welding required an investment in RF generators and the associated tooling. The investment was justified by the IV Products Division based on the savings associated with the new system. Induction welding promised to reduce the cost of direct materials by eliminating the need to buy and use epoxy. Savings of direct labor costs also were predicted because the welding process is more automated. Adding to these savings were the avoidance of daily cleanup costs and the reduction in rejects. Allen presented a formal NPV analysis showing that the welding system was superior to the epoxy system. Headquarters approved its purchase.

One year later, Allen and Jenny had the following conversation regarding the induction welding decision.

**Jenny:** Allen, I'm quite pleased with induction welding for bonding needles. In the year since the new process was implemented, we've had virtually no complaints from our customers. The needles are firmly bonded.

**Allen:** I wish that positive experience were true for all other areas as well. Unfortunately, implementing the process has uncovered some rather sticky and expensive problems that I didn't anticipate. The Internal Audit Department recently completed a postaudit of the project, and now my feet are being held to the fire.

**Jenny:** That's too bad. What's the problem?

**Allen:** You mean problems. Let me list a few for you. One is that the RF generators interfered with the operation of other equipment. To eliminate this interference, we had to install filtering equipment. But that's not all. We also discovered that the average maintenance person doesn't know how to maintain the new equipment. Now we're faced with the need to initiate a training program to upgrade the skills of our maintenance people. Upgrading skills implies higher wages. Although the RF bonding process is less messy, it is more complex. The manufacturing people complained to the internal auditors about that. They maintain that a simple process, even if messy, is preferred—especially now that demand for the product is increasing by leaps and bounds.

**Jenny:** What did the internal auditors conclude?

**Allen:** They concluded that many of the predicted savings did take place but that significant costs were not foreseen. Because of these unforeseen problems, they recommended that I look carefully at the possibility of moving back to using epoxy. They indicated that NPV analysis using actual data appears to favor that process. With production expanding, the acquisition of additional RF generators and filtering equipment plus the necessary training is simply not as attractive as returning to epoxy bonding. This conclusion is reinforced by the fact that the epoxy process is simpler and by the auditors' conclusion that the mixing of the epoxy can be automated, avoiding the quality problem we had in the first place.

**Jenny:** Well, Allen, you can't really blame yourself. You had a real problem and took action to solve it. It's difficult to foresee all the problems and hidden costs of a new process.

**Allen:** Unfortunately, the internal auditors don't agree. In fact, neither do I. I probably jumped too quickly. In the future, I intend to think through new projects more carefully.

In the case of the RF bonding decision for Honley Medical, some of the estimated capital investment benefits did materialize: complaints from customers decreased, rejects were fewer, and direct labor and materials costs decreased. However, the investment was greater than expected because filtering equipment was needed, and actual operating costs were much higher because of the increased maintenance cost and the increased complexity of the process. Overall, the internal auditors concluded that the investment was a poor decision. The corrective action that they recommended was to abandon the new process and return to epoxy bonding. Based on this recommendation, the firm abandoned inductive welding and returned to epoxy bonding, which was improved by automating the mix.

## Postaudit Benefits

Firms that perform postaudits of capital projects experience a number of benefits, including the following.

- *Resource Allocation:* By evaluating profitability, postaudits ensure that resources are used wisely. If the project is doing well, it may call for additional funds and additional attention. If the project is not doing well, corrective action may be needed to improve performance or abandon the project.
- *Positive Impact on Managers' Behavior:* If managers are held accountable for the results of a capital investment decision, they are more likely to make such decisions in the best interests of the firm. Additionally, postaudits supply feedback to managers that should help to improve future decision making. Consider Allen's reaction to the postaudit of the RF bonding process. Certainly, we would expect him to be more careful and more thorough in making future investment recommendations. In the future, Allen will probably consider more than one alternative, such as automating the mixing of the epoxy. Also, for those alternatives being considered, he will probably be especially alert to the possibility of hidden costs, such as increased training requirements for a new process.
- *Independent Perspective:* For Honley Medical, the postaudit was performed by the internal audit staff. Generally, more objective results are obtainable if the postaudit is done by an independent party. Since considerable effort is expended to ensure as much independence as possible for the internal audit staff, that group is usually the best choice for this task.

## Postaudit Limitations

Postaudits, however, are costly. Moreover, even though they may provide significant benefits, they have other limitations. Most obvious is the fact that the assumptions driving the original analysis may often be invalidated by changes in the actual operating environment. Accountability must be qualified to some extent by the impossibility of foreseeing every possible eventuality.

---

### concept Q&A

**Why do a postaudit?**

**Answer:**

Postaudits allow a company to assess the quality of capital investment decisions and also produce corrective actions where some of the initial assumptions prove to be wrong. They also encourage managerial accountability and provide useful information for improving future capital budgeting decisions.

---

OBJECTIVE

Explain why net present value is better than internal rate of return for capital investment decisions involving mutually exclusive projects.

# MUTUALLY EXCLUSIVE PROJECTS

Up to this point, we have focused on independent projects. Many capital investment decisions deal with mutually exclusive projects. How NPV analysis and IRR are used to choose among competing projects is an interesting question. An even more interesting question to consider is whether NPV and IRR differ in their ability to help managers make wealth-maximizing decisions in the presence of competing alternatives. For example, we already know that the nondiscounting models can produce erroneous choices because they ignore the time value of money. Because of this deficiency, the discounting models are judged superior. Similarly, it can be shown that the NPV model is generally preferred to the IRR model when choosing among mutually exclusive alternatives.

## Net Present Value Compared with Internal Rate of Return

NPV and IRR both yield the same decision for independent projects. For example, if the NPV is greater than zero, then the IRR is also greater than the required rate of return. Both models signal the correct decision. However, for competing projects, the two methods can produce different results. Intuitively, we believe that for mutually exclusive projects, the project with the highest NPV or the highest IRR should be chosen. Since it is possible for the two methods to produce different rankings of mutually exclusive projects, the method that consistently reveals the wealth-maximizing project is preferred.

NPV differs from IRR in two major ways:

- The NPV method assumes that each cash inflow received is reinvested at the required rate of return, whereas the IRR method assumes that each cash inflow is reinvested at the computed IRR. Reinvesting at the required rate of return is more realistic and produces more reliable results when comparing mutually exclusive projects.
- The NPV method measures profitability in absolute terms, whereas the IRR method measures it in relative terms. NPV measures the amount by which the value of the firm changes.

These differences are summarized in Exhibit 14.2.

---

**( EXHIBIT 14.2 )**

**Net Present Value Compared with Internal Rate of Return**

|  | NPV | IRR |
|---|---|---|
| Type of measure | *Absolute* dollars | *Relative* percentage |
| Cash flow reinvestment assumption | At required rate of return | At internal rate of return |

© Cengage Learning 2014

Since NPV measures the impact that competing projects have on the value of the firm, choosing the project with the largest NPV is consistent with maximizing the wealth of shareholders. On the other hand, IRR does not consistently result in choices that maximize wealth. IRR, as a relative measure of profitability, has the virtue of measuring accurately the rate of return of funds that remain internally invested. However, maximizing IRR will not necessarily maximize the wealth of firm owners because it cannot, by nature, consider the absolute dollar contributions of projects. In the final analysis, what counts are the total dollars earned—the absolute profits—not the relative profits. Accordingly, NPV, not IRR, should be used for choosing among competing, mutually exclusive projects or competing projects when capital funds are limited.

An independent project is acceptable if its NPV is positive. For mutually exclusive projects, the project with the largest NPV is chosen. There are three steps in selecting the best project from several competing projects:

**Step 1:** Assess the cash flow pattern for each project.
**Step 2:** Compute the NPV for each project.
**Step 3:** Identify the project with the greatest NPV.

concept Q&A

Why is NPV better than IRR for choosing among competing projects?

**Answer:**

NPV uses a more realistic reinvestment assumption, and its signal is consistent with maximizing the wealth of firm owners (IRR does not measure absolute profits).

## NPV Analysis for Mutually Exclusive Projects Illustrated

Bintley Corporation has committed to improving its environmental performance. One environmental project identified a manufacturing process as being the source of both liquid and gaseous residues. After six months of research activity, the engineering department announced that it is possible to redesign the process to prevent the production of contaminating residues. Two different process designs (A and B) that prevent the production of contaminants are being considered. Both process designs are more expensive to operate than the current process. However, because the designs prevent production of contaminants, significant annual benefits are created. These benefits stem from eliminating the need to operate and maintain expensive pollution control equipment, treat and dispose of toxic liquid wastes, and pay the annual fines for exceeding allowable contaminant releases. Increased sales to environmentally conscious customers also are factored into the benefit estimates. Cornerstone 14.5 shows how NPV and IRR analyses are carried out for this setting.

**CORNERSTONE**

**14.5**

## Calculating Net Present Value and Internal Rate of Return for Mutually Exclusive Projects

**Why:**

For competing projects, the discounting method that consistently chooses the wealth-maximizing project should be used. NPV measures profitability in absolute terms, while IRR measures relative profitability. NPV measures the amount by which the value of the firm changes and thus is consistent with maximizing wealth.

**Information:**

Consider two pollution prevention designs: Design A and Design B. Both designs have a project life of 5 years. Design A requires an initial outlay of $180,000 and has a net annual after-tax cash inflow of $60,000 (revenues of $180,000 minus cash expenses of $120,000). Design B, with an initial outlay of $210,000, has a net annual cash inflow of $70,000 ($240,000 − $170,000). The after-tax cash flows are summarized as follows:

| CASH FLOW PATTERN | | |
|---|---|---|
| Year | Design A | Design B |
| 0 | $(180,000) | $(210,000) |
| 1 | 60,000 | 70,000 |
| 2 | 60,000 | 70,000 |
| 3 | 60,000 | 70,000 |
| 4 | 60,000 | 70,000 |
| 5 | 60,000 | 70,000 |

The cost of capital for the company is 12%.

**Required:**

Calculate the NPV and the IRR for each project.

*(Continued)*

**Solution:**

### DESIGN A: NPV ANALYSIS

| Year | Cash Flow | Discount Factor* | Present Value |
|------|-----------|------------------|---------------|
| 0 | $(180,000) | 1.00000 | $(180,000) |
| 1–5 | 60,000 | 3.60478 | 216,287 |
| Net present value | | | $ 36,287 |

### DESIGN A: IRR ANALYSIS

Discount Factor = Initial Investment/Annual Cash Flow

$$= \$180,000/\$60,000$$

$$= 3.00000$$

From Exhibit 14B.2 (p. 648), $df = 3.00000$ for 5 years implies that IRR $\approx$ 20%.

### DESIGN B: NPV ANALYSIS

| Year | Cash Flow | Discount Factor* | Present Value |
|------|-----------|------------------|---------------|
| 0 | $(210,000) | 1.00000 | $(210,000) |
| 1–5 | 70,000 | 3.60478 | 252,335 |
| Net present value | | | $ 42,335 |

### DESIGN B: IRR ANALYSIS

Discount Factor = Initial Investment/Annual Cash Flow

$$= \$210,000/\$70,000$$

$$= 3.00000$$

From Exhibit 14B.2, $df = 3.00000$ for 5 years implies that IRR $\approx$ 20%.

*From Exhibit 14B.2.

Based on the NPV analysis in Cornerstone 14.5, Design B is more profitable; it has the larger NPV. Accordingly, the company should select Design B over Design A. Interestingly, Designs A and B have identical internal rates of return. As shown by Cornerstone 14.5, both designs have a discount factor of 3.00000. From Exhibit 14B.2, it is seen that a discount factor of 3.00000 and a life of 5 years yields an IRR of about 20%. Even though both projects have an IRR of 20%, the firm should not consider the two designs to be equally desirable. The analysis demonstrates that Design B produces a larger NPV and, therefore, will increase the value of the firm more than Design A. Design B should be chosen. This illustrates the conceptual superiority of NPV over IRR for analysis of competing projects.

## Special Considerations for Advanced Manufacturing Environment

For advanced manufacturing environments, like those using automated systems, capital investment decisions can be more complex because they must take special considerations into account.

## Here's The Real Kicker

During the period of 2001–2003, **Stillwater Designs** experienced high sales of their Kicker products. As a result, the levels of inventory filled all storage areas to capacity. Consequently, Stillwater Designs began plans to add another building on existing property with 50,000 square feet of capacity. This new facility had an estimated construction cost between $1 and $1.5 million. During this preliminary planning phase, a shipping strike placed extra storage demands on existing facilities, and Stillwater Designs began looking for a warehousing facility that could be leased on a short-term basis.

They identified a 250,000-square-foot facility on 22 acres that was owned by Moore Business Forms. This facility was an attractive leasing option, and it quickly became a competing alternative to adding the 50,000-square-foot facility to Stillwater's current complex. In fact, the company began looking at the possibility of buying and renovating the Moore facility and moving all of its operations into the one facility. Renovation required such actions as installing a new HVAC system, bringing the building up to current fire codes, painting and resealing the floor, and adding a large number of offices. After careful financial analysis, Stillwater Designs decided that the buy-and-renovate option was more profitable than adding the 50,000-square-foot building to its current complex. Two economic factors affecting the decision were (1) selling the current complex of five buildings would help pay for the needed renovations, and (2) the purchase cost of the non-renovated Moore facility was less than the cost of building the 50,000-square-foot facility.

**How Investment Differs** Investment in automated manufacturing processes is much more complex than investment in the standard manufacturing equipment of the past. For standard equipment, the direct costs of acquisition represent virtually the entire investment. For automated manufacturing, the direct costs can represent as little as 50 or 60% of the total investment. Software, engineering, training, and implementation are a significant percentage of the total costs. Thus, great care must be exercised to assess the actual cost of an automated system. It is easy to overlook the peripheral costs, which can be substantial.

**How Estimates of Operating Cash Flows Differ** Estimates of operating cash flows from investments in standard equipment typically have relied on directly identifiable tangible benefits, such as direct savings from labor, power, and scrap. However, when investing in automated systems, the intangible and indirect benefits can be material and critical to the viability of the project. Greater quality, more reliability, reduced lead time, improved customer satisfaction, and an enhanced ability to maintain market share all are important intangible benefits of an advanced manufacturing system. Reduction of labor in support areas such as production scheduling and stores are indirect benefits. More effort is needed to measure these intangible and indirect benefits in order to assess more accurately the potential value of investments.

Consider, for example, Zielesch Manufacturing, which is evaluating a potential investment in a flexible manufacturing system (FMS). The choice facing the company is to continue producing with its traditional equipment, expected to last 10 years, or to switch to the new system, which also is expected to have a useful life of 10 years. Zielesch's discount rate is 12%. The data pertaining to the investment are presented in Exhibit 14.3. Notice that for Zielesch, the *incremental cash flows* are used to compare the new project with the old. Instead of calculating the NPV for each alternative and comparing, an equivalent approach is to calculate the NPV of the incremental cash flows of the new system (cash flows of new system minus cash flows of old system). If the NPV for the incremental cash flows is positive, then the new equipment is preferred to the old.

( EXHIBIT 14.3 )

**Investment Data; Direct, Intangible, and Indirect Benefits**

| | FMS | Status Quo |
|---|---|---|
| Investment (current outlay): | | |
|    Direct costs | $10,000,000 | — |
|    Software, engineering | 8,000,000 | — |
|      Total current outlay | $18,000,000 | — |
| Net after-tax cash flow | $ 5,000,000 | $1,000,000 |
| Less: After-tax cash flows for status quo | 1,000,000 | n/a |
|    Incremental benefit | $ 4,000,000 ← | n/a |
| **Incremental Benefit Explained** | | |
| Direct benefits: | | |
|    Direct labor | $ 1,500,000 | |
|    Scrap reduction | 500,000 | |
|    Setups | 200,000 | |
| | $ 2,200,000 | |
| Intangible benefits (quality savings): | | |
|    Rework | $    200,000 | |
|    Warranties | 400,000 | |
|    Maintenance of competitive position | 1,000,000 | |
| | 1,600,000 | |
| Indirect benefits: | | |
|    Production scheduling | $    110,000 | |
|    Payroll | 90,000 | |
| | 200,000 | |
| Total | $ 4,000,000 ← | |

Using the incremental data in Exhibit 14.3, the NPV of the proposed system can be computed as follows:

| | |
|---|---|
| Present value ($4,000,000 × 5.65022*) | $22,600,880 |
| Investment | 18,000,000 |
|   NPV | $ 4,600,880 |

  * This number is the discount factor for an interest rate of 12% and a life of
    10 years (see Exhibit 14B.2, p. 648).

The NPV is positive and large in magnitude, and it clearly signals the acceptability of the FMS. This outcome, however, is strongly dependent on explicit recognition of both intangible and indirect benefits. If those benefits are eliminated, then the direct savings total $2.2 million, and the NPV is negative:

| | |
|---|---|
| Present value ($2,200,000 × 5.65022) | $12,430,484 |
| Investment | 18,000,000 |
|   NPV | $ (5,569,516) |

The rise of activity-based costing has made identifying indirect benefits easier with the use of cost drivers. Once they are identified, they can be included in the analysis if they are material.

Examination of Exhibit 14.3 reveals the importance of intangible benefits. One of the most important intangible benefits is maintaining or improving a firm's competitive position. A key question is what will happen to the cash flows of the firm if the investment is not made. That is, if Zielesch chooses to forego an investment in technologically advanced equipment, will it be able to continue to compete with other firms on the basis of quality, delivery, and cost? (The question becomes especially relevant if competitors choose to invest in advanced equipment.) If the competitive position deteriorates, Zielesch's current cash flows will decrease.

If cash flows will decrease if the investment is not made, this decrease should show up as an incremental benefit for the advanced technology. In Exhibit 14.3, Zielesch estimates this competitive benefit as $1,000,000. Estimating this benefit requires some serious strategic planning and analysis, but its effect can be critical. If this benefit had been ignored or overlooked, then the NPV would have been negative and the investment alternative rejected:

| | |
|---|---|
| Present value ($3,000,000 × 5.65022) | $16,950,660 |
| Investment | 18,000,000 |
| NPV | $(1,049,340) |

OBJECTIVE 7

Explain the relationship between current and future dollars.

# APPENDIX 14A: PRESENT VALUE CONCEPTS

An important feature of money is that it can be invested and can earn interest. A dollar today is not the same as a dollar tomorrow. This fundamental principle is the backbone of discounting methods. Discounting methods rely on the relationships between current and future dollars. Thus, to use discounting methods, we must understand these relationships.

## Future Value

Suppose that a bank advertises a 4% annual interest rate. If a customer invests $100, he or she would receive, after 1 year, the original $100 plus $4 interest [$100 + (0.04)($100)] = (1 + 0.04)$100 = (1.04)($100) = $104. This result can be expressed by the following equation, where $F$ is the future amount, $P$ is the initial or current outlay, and $i$ is the interest rate:

$$F = P(1 + i)$$

For the example, $F = \$100(1 + 0.04) = \$100(1.04) = \$104$.

Now suppose that the same bank offers a 5% rate if the customer leaves the original deposit, plus any interest, on deposit for a total of 2 years. How much will the customer receive at the end of 2 years? Again assume that a customer invests $100. Using the future value equation, the customer will earn $105 at the end of Year 1:

$$F = \$100(1 + 0.05) = \$100(1.05) = \$105$$

If this amount is left in the account for a second year, this equation is used again with $P$ now assumed to be $105. At the end of the second year, then, the total is $110.25:

$$F = \$105(1 + 0.05) = \$105(1.05) = \$110.25$$

In the second year, interest is earned on both the original deposit and the interest earned in the first year. The earning of interest on interest is referred to as **compounding of interest**. The value that will accumulate by the end of an investment's life, assuming a specified compound return, is the **future value**. The future value of the $100 deposit in the second example is $110.25.

A more direct way to compute the future value is possible. Since the first application of the future value equation can be expressed as F = $105 = $100(1.05), the second application can be expressed as $F = \$105(1.05) = \$100(1.05)(1.05) = \$100(1.05)^2 = P(1 + i)^2$. This suggests the following compounding interest formula for computing amounts for $n$ periods into the future:

$$F = P(1 + i)^n$$

# Present Value

Often, a manager needs to compute not the future value but the amount that must be invested now in order to yield some given future value. The amount that must be invested now to produce the future value is known as the **present value** of the future amount. For example, how much must be invested now in order to yield $363 2 years from now, assuming that the interest rate is 10%? Or, put another way, what is the present value of $363 to be received 2 years from now?

In this example, the future value, the years, and the interest rate are all known. We want to know the current outlay that will produce that future amount. In the compounding interest equation, the variable representing the current outlay (the present value of $F$) is $P$. Thus, to compute the present value of a future outlay, all we need to do is solve the compounding interest equation for $P$:

$$P = F/(1 + i)^n$$

Using this present value equation, we can compute the present value of $363:

$$P = \frac{\$363}{(1 + 0.1)^2}$$
$$= \$363/1.21$$
$$= \$300$$

The present value, $300, is what the future amount of $363 is worth today. All other things being equal, having $300 today is the same as having $363 2 years from now. Put another way, if a firm requires a 10% rate of return, the most the firm would be willing to pay today is $300 for any investment that yields $363 2 years from now.

The process of computing the present value of future cash flows is often referred to as **discounting**. Thus, we say that we have discounted the future value of $363 to its present value of $300. The interest rate used to discount the future cash flow is the **discount rate**. The expression $1/(1 + i)^n$ in the present value equation is the **discount factor**. By letting the discount factor, called $df$, equal $1/(1 + i)^n$, the present value equation can be expressed as $P = F(df)$. To simplify the computation of present value, a table of discount factors is given for various combinations of $i$ and $n$ [refer to Exhibit 14B.1 (p. 647) in Appendix 14B]. For example, the discount factor for $i = 10\%$ and $n = 2$ is 0.82645 (go to the 10% column of the table and move down to the second row). With the discount factor, the present value of $363 is computed as follows:

$$P = F(df)$$
$$= \$363 \times 0.82645$$
$$= \$300 \text{ (rounded)}$$

# Present Value of an Uneven Series of Cash Flows

Exhibit 14B.1 can be used to compute the present value of any future cash flow or series of future cash flows. A series of future cash flows is called an **annuity**. The present value of an annuity is found by computing the present value of each future cash flow and then summing these values. For example, suppose that an investment is expected to produce the following annual cash flows: $110, $121, and $133.10. Assuming a discount rate of 10%, the present value of this series of cash flows is computed in Exhibit 14A.1.

**Present Value of an Uneven Series of Cash Flows**

| Year | Cash Receipt | Discount Factor | Present Value* |
|------|-------------|----------------|---------------|
| 1 | $110.00 | 0.90909 | $100.00 |
| 2 | 121.00 | 0.82645 | 100.00 |
| 3 | 133.10 | 0.75131 | 100.00 |
| | | 2.48685 | $300.00 |

© Cengage Learning 2014

*Rounded.

## Present Value of a Uniform Series of Cash Flows

If the series of cash flows is even, the computation of the annuity's present value is simplified. For example, assume that an investment is expected to return $100 per year for 3 years. Using Exhibit 14B.1 and assuming a discount rate of 10%, the present value of the annuity is computed in Exhibit 14A.2.

**Present Value of an Annuity**

| Year | Cash Receipt* | Discount Factor | Present Value* |
|------|--------------|----------------|---------------|
| 1 | $100 | 0.90909 | $ 90.91 |
| 2 | 100 | 0.82645 | 82.65 |
| 3 | 100 | 0.75131 | 75.13 |
| | | 2.48685 | $248.69 |

© Cengage Learning 2014

*The annual cash flow of $100 can be multiplied by the sum of the discount factors (2.48685) to obtain the present value of the uniform series ($248.69).

As with the uneven series of cash flows, the present value in Exhibit 14A.2 was computed by calculating the present value of each cash flow separately and then summing them. However, in the case of an annuity displaying uniform cash flows, the computations can be reduced from three to one as described in the footnote to the exhibit. The sum of the individual discount factors can be thought of as a discount factor for an annuity of uniform cash flows. A table of discount factors that can be used for an annuity of uniform cash flows is available in Exhibit 14B.2.

## APPENDIX 14B: PRESENT VALUE TABLES

The present value tables are found on pages 647 and 648.

## EXHIBIT 14B.1

### Present Value of a Single Amount*

| n/i | 1% | 2% | 3% | 4% | 5% | 6% | 7% | 8% | 9% | 10% | 12% | 14% | 16% | 18% | 20% | 25% | 30% |
|---|---|---|---|---|---|---|---|---|---|---|---|---|---|---|---|---|---|
| 1 | 0.99010 | 0.98039 | 0.97087 | 0.96154 | 0.95238 | 0.94340 | 0.93458 | 0.92593 | 0.91743 | 0.90909 | 0.89286 | 0.87719 | 0.86207 | 0.84746 | 0.83333 | 0.80000 | 0.76923 |
| 2 | 0.98030 | 0.96117 | 0.94260 | 0.92456 | 0.90703 | 0.89000 | 0.87344 | 0.85734 | 0.84168 | 0.82645 | 0.79719 | 0.76947 | 0.74316 | 0.71818 | 0.69444 | 0.64000 | 0.59172 |
| 3 | 0.97059 | 0.94232 | 0.91514 | 0.88900 | 0.86384 | 0.83962 | 0.81630 | 0.79383 | 0.77218 | 0.75131 | 0.71178 | 0.67497 | 0.64066 | 0.60863 | 0.57870 | 0.51200 | 0.45517 |
| 4 | 0.96098 | 0.92385 | 0.88849 | 0.85480 | 0.82270 | 0.79209 | 0.76290 | 0.73503 | 0.70843 | 0.68301 | 0.63552 | 0.59208 | 0.55229 | 0.51579 | 0.48225 | 0.40960 | 0.35013 |
| 5 | 0.95147 | 0.90573 | 0.86261 | 0.82193 | 0.78353 | 0.74726 | 0.71299 | 0.68058 | 0.64993 | 0.62092 | 0.56743 | 0.51937 | 0.47611 | 0.43711 | 0.40188 | 0.32768 | 0.26933 |
| 6 | 0.94205 | 0.88797 | 0.83748 | 0.79031 | 0.74622 | 0.70496 | 0.66634 | 0.63017 | 0.59627 | 0.56447 | 0.50663 | 0.45559 | 0.41044 | 0.37043 | 0.33490 | 0.26214 | 0.20718 |
| 7 | 0.93272 | 0.87056 | 0.81309 | 0.75992 | 0.71068 | 0.66506 | 0.62275 | 0.58349 | 0.54703 | 0.51316 | 0.45235 | 0.39964 | 0.35383 | 0.31393 | 0.27908 | 0.20972 | 0.15937 |
| 8 | 0.92348 | 0.85349 | 0.78941 | 0.73069 | 0.67684 | 0.62741 | 0.58201 | 0.54027 | 0.50187 | 0.46651 | 0.40388 | 0.35056 | 0.30503 | 0.26604 | 0.23257 | 0.16777 | 0.12259 |
| 9 | 0.91434 | 0.83676 | 0.76642 | 0.70259 | 0.64461 | 0.59190 | 0.54393 | 0.50025 | 0.46043 | 0.42410 | 0.36061 | 0.30751 | 0.26295 | 0.22546 | 0.19381 | 0.13422 | 0.09430 |
| 10 | 0.90529 | 0.82035 | 0.74409 | 0.67556 | 0.61391 | 0.55839 | 0.50835 | 0.46319 | 0.42241 | 0.38554 | 0.32197 | 0.26974 | 0.22668 | 0.19106 | 0.16151 | 0.10737 | 0.07254 |
| 11 | 0.89632 | 0.80426 | 0.72242 | 0.64958 | 0.58468 | 0.52679 | 0.47509 | 0.42888 | 0.38753 | 0.35049 | 0.28748 | 0.23662 | 0.19542 | 0.16192 | 0.13459 | 0.08590 | 0.05580 |
| 12 | 0.88745 | 0.78849 | 0.70138 | 0.62460 | 0.55684 | 0.49697 | 0.44401 | 0.39711 | 0.35553 | 0.31863 | 0.25668 | 0.20756 | 0.16846 | 0.13722 | 0.11216 | 0.06872 | 0.04292 |
| 13 | 0.87866 | 0.77303 | 0.68095 | 0.60057 | 0.53032 | 0.46884 | 0.41496 | 0.36770 | 0.32618 | 0.28966 | 0.22917 | 0.18207 | 0.14523 | 0.11629 | 0.09346 | 0.05498 | 0.03302 |
| 14 | 0.86996 | 0.75788 | 0.66112 | 0.57748 | 0.50507 | 0.44230 | 0.38782 | 0.34046 | 0.29925 | 0.26333 | 0.20462 | 0.15971 | 0.12520 | 0.09855 | 0.07789 | 0.04398 | 0.02540 |
| 15 | 0.86135 | 0.74301 | 0.64186 | 0.55526 | 0.48102 | 0.41727 | 0.36245 | 0.31524 | 0.27454 | 0.23939 | 0.18270 | 0.14010 | 0.10793 | 0.08352 | 0.06491 | 0.03518 | 0.01954 |
| 16 | 0.85282 | 0.72845 | 0.62317 | 0.53391 | 0.45811 | 0.39365 | 0.33873 | 0.29189 | 0.25187 | 0.21763 | 0.16312 | 0.12289 | 0.09304 | 0.07078 | 0.05409 | 0.02815 | 0.01503 |
| 17 | 0.84438 | 0.71416 | 0.60502 | 0.51337 | 0.43630 | 0.37136 | 0.31657 | 0.27027 | 0.23107 | 0.19784 | 0.14564 | 0.10780 | 0.08021 | 0.05998 | 0.04507 | 0.02252 | 0.01156 |
| 18 | 0.83602 | 0.70016 | 0.58739 | 0.49363 | 0.41552 | 0.35034 | 0.29586 | 0.25025 | 0.21199 | 0.17986 | 0.13004 | 0.09456 | 0.06914 | 0.05083 | 0.03756 | 0.01801 | 0.00889 |
| 19 | 0.82774 | 0.68643 | 0.57029 | 0.47464 | 0.39573 | 0.33051 | 0.27651 | 0.23171 | 0.19449 | 0.16351 | 0.11611 | 0.08295 | 0.05961 | 0.04308 | 0.03130 | 0.01441 | 0.00684 |
| 20 | 0.81954 | 0.67297 | 0.55368 | 0.45639 | 0.37689 | 0.31180 | 0.25842 | 0.21455 | 0.17843 | 0.14864 | 0.10367 | 0.07276 | 0.05139 | 0.03651 | 0.02608 | 0.01153 | 0.00526 |
| 21 | 0.81143 | 0.65978 | 0.53755 | 0.43883 | 0.35894 | 0.29416 | 0.24151 | 0.19866 | 0.16370 | 0.13513 | 0.09256 | 0.06383 | 0.04430 | 0.03094 | 0.02174 | 0.00922 | 0.00405 |
| 22 | 0.80340 | 0.64684 | 0.52189 | 0.42196 | 0.34185 | 0.27751 | 0.22571 | 0.18394 | 0.15018 | 0.12285 | 0.08264 | 0.05599 | 0.03819 | 0.02622 | 0.01811 | 0.00738 | 0.00311 |
| 23 | 0.79544 | 0.63416 | 0.50669 | 0.40573 | 0.32557 | 0.26180 | 0.21095 | 0.17032 | 0.13778 | 0.11168 | 0.07379 | 0.04911 | 0.03292 | 0.02222 | 0.01509 | 0.00590 | 0.00239 |
| 24 | 0.78757 | 0.62172 | 0.49193 | 0.39012 | 0.31007 | 0.24698 | 0.19715 | 0.15770 | 0.12640 | 0.10153 | 0.06588 | 0.04308 | 0.02838 | 0.01883 | 0.01258 | 0.00472 | 0.00184 |
| 25 | 0.77977 | 0.60953 | 0.47761 | 0.37512 | 0.29530 | 0.23300 | 0.18425 | 0.14602 | 0.11597 | 0.09230 | 0.05882 | 0.03779 | 0.02447 | 0.01596 | 0.01048 | 0.00378 | 0.00142 |
| 26 | 0.77205 | 0.59758 | 0.46369 | 0.36069 | 0.28124 | 0.21981 | 0.17220 | 0.13520 | 0.10639 | 0.08391 | 0.05252 | 0.03315 | 0.02109 | 0.01352 | 0.00874 | 0.00302 | 0.00109 |
| 27 | 0.76440 | 0.58586 | 0.45019 | 0.34682 | 0.26785 | 0.20737 | 0.16093 | 0.12519 | 0.09761 | 0.07628 | 0.04689 | 0.02908 | 0.01818 | 0.01146 | 0.00728 | 0.00242 | 0.00084 |
| 28 | 0.75684 | 0.57437 | 0.43708 | 0.33348 | 0.25509 | 0.19563 | 0.15040 | 0.11591 | 0.08955 | 0.06934 | 0.04187 | 0.02551 | 0.01567 | 0.00971 | 0.00607 | 0.00193 | 0.00065 |
| 29 | 0.74934 | 0.56311 | 0.42435 | 0.32065 | 0.24295 | 0.18456 | 0.14056 | 0.10733 | 0.08215 | 0.06304 | 0.03738 | 0.02237 | 0.01351 | 0.00823 | 0.00506 | 0.00155 | 0.00050 |
| 30 | 0.74192 | 0.55207 | 0.41199 | 0.30832 | 0.23138 | 0.17411 | 0.13137 | 0.09938 | 0.07537 | 0.05731 | 0.03338 | 0.01963 | 0.01165 | 0.00697 | 0.00421 | 0.00124 | 0.00038 |

* $P_n = A/(1 + i)^n$

© Cengage Learning 2014

## EXHIBIT 14B.2

### Present Value of an Annuity*

| n/i | 1% | 2% | 3% | 4% | 5% | 6% | 7% | 8% | 9% | 10% | 12% | 14% | 16% | 18% | 20% | 25% | 30% |
|---|---|---|---|---|---|---|---|---|---|---|---|---|---|---|---|---|---|
| 1 | 0.99010 | 0.98039 | 0.97087 | 0.96154 | 0.95238 | 0.94340 | 0.93458 | 0.92593 | 0.91743 | 0.90909 | 0.89286 | 0.87719 | 0.86207 | 0.84746 | 0.83333 | 0.80000 | 0.76923 |
| 2 | 1.97040 | 1.94156 | 1.91347 | 1.88609 | 1.85941 | 1.83339 | 1.80802 | 1.78326 | 1.75911 | 1.73554 | 1.69005 | 1.64666 | 1.60523 | 1.56564 | 1.52778 | 1.44000 | 1.36095 |
| 3 | 2.94099 | 2.88388 | 2.82861 | 2.77509 | 2.72325 | 2.67301 | 2.62432 | 2.57710 | 2.53129 | 2.48685 | 2.40183 | 2.32163 | 2.24589 | 2.17427 | 2.10648 | 1.95200 | 1.81611 |
| 4 | 3.90197 | 3.80773 | 3.71710 | 3.62990 | 3.54595 | 3.46511 | 3.38721 | 3.31213 | 3.23972 | 3.16987 | 3.03735 | 2.91371 | 2.79818 | 2.69006 | 2.58873 | 2.36160 | 2.16624 |
| 5 | 4.85343 | 4.71346 | 4.57971 | 4.45182 | 4.32948 | 4.21236 | 4.10020 | 3.99271 | 3.88965 | 3.79079 | 3.60478 | 3.43308 | 3.27429 | 3.12717 | 2.99061 | 2.68928 | 2.43557 |
| 6 | 5.79548 | 5.60143 | 5.41719 | 5.24214 | 5.07569 | 4.91732 | 4.76654 | 4.62288 | 4.48592 | 4.35526 | 4.11141 | 3.88867 | 3.68474 | 3.49760 | 3.32551 | 2.95142 | 2.64275 |
| 7 | 6.72819 | 6.47199 | 6.23028 | 6.00205 | 5.78637 | 5.58238 | 5.38929 | 5.20637 | 5.03295 | 4.86842 | 4.56376 | 4.28830 | 4.03857 | 3.81153 | 3.60459 | 3.16114 | 2.80211 |
| 8 | 7.65168 | 7.32548 | 7.01969 | 6.73274 | 6.46321 | 6.20979 | 5.97130 | 5.74664 | 5.53482 | 5.33493 | 4.96764 | 4.63886 | 4.34359 | 4.07757 | 3.83716 | 3.32891 | 2.92470 |
| 9 | 8.56602 | 8.16224 | 7.78611 | 7.43533 | 7.10782 | 6.80169 | 6.51523 | 6.24689 | 5.99525 | 5.75902 | 5.32825 | 4.94637 | 4.60654 | 4.30302 | 4.03097 | 3.46313 | 3.01900 |
| 10 | 9.47130 | 8.98259 | 8.53020 | 8.11090 | 7.72173 | 7.36009 | 7.02358 | 6.71008 | 6.41766 | 6.14457 | 5.65022 | 5.21612 | 4.83323 | 4.49409 | 4.19247 | 3.57050 | 3.09154 |
| 11 | 10.36763 | 9.78685 | 9.25262 | 8.76048 | 8.30641 | 7.88687 | 7.49867 | 7.13896 | 6.80519 | 6.49506 | 5.93770 | 5.45273 | 5.02864 | 4.65601 | 4.32706 | 3.65640 | 3.14734 |
| 12 | 11.25508 | 10.57534 | 9.95400 | 9.38507 | 8.86325 | 8.38384 | 7.94269 | 7.53608 | 7.16073 | 6.81369 | 6.19437 | 5.66029 | 5.19711 | 4.79322 | 4.43922 | 3.72512 | 3.19026 |
| 13 | 12.13374 | 11.34837 | 10.63496 | 9.98565 | 9.39357 | 8.85268 | 8.35765 | 7.90378 | 7.48690 | 7.10336 | 6.42355 | 5.84236 | 5.34233 | 4.90951 | 4.53268 | 3.78010 | 3.22328 |
| 14 | 13.00370 | 12.10625 | 11.29607 | 10.56312 | 9.89864 | 9.29498 | 8.74547 | 8.24424 | 7.78615 | 7.36669 | 6.62817 | 6.00207 | 5.46753 | 5.00806 | 4.61057 | 3.82408 | 3.24867 |
| 15 | 13.86505 | 12.84926 | 11.93794 | 11.11839 | 10.37966 | 9.71225 | 9.10791 | 8.55948 | 8.06069 | 7.60608 | 6.81086 | 6.14217 | 5.57546 | 5.09158 | 4.67547 | 3.85926 | 3.26821 |
| 16 | 14.71787 | 13.57771 | 12.56110 | 11.65230 | 10.83777 | 10.10590 | 9.44665 | 8.85137 | 8.31256 | 7.82371 | 6.97399 | 6.26506 | 5.66850 | 5.16235 | 4.72956 | 3.88741 | 3.28324 |
| 17 | 15.56225 | 14.29187 | 13.16612 | 12.16567 | 11.27407 | 10.47726 | 9.76322 | 9.12164 | 8.54363 | 8.02155 | 7.11963 | 6.37286 | 5.74870 | 5.22233 | 4.77463 | 3.90993 | 3.29480 |
| 18 | 16.39827 | 14.99203 | 13.75351 | 12.65930 | 11.68959 | 10.82760 | 10.05909 | 9.37189 | 8.75563 | 8.20141 | 7.24967 | 6.46742 | 5.81785 | 5.27316 | 4.81219 | 3.92794 | 3.30369 |
| 19 | 17.22601 | 15.67846 | 14.32380 | 13.13394 | 12.08532 | 11.15812 | 10.33560 | 9.60360 | 8.95011 | 8.36492 | 7.36578 | 6.55037 | 5.87746 | 5.31624 | 4.84350 | 3.94235 | 3.31053 |
| 20 | 18.04555 | 16.35143 | 14.87747 | 13.59033 | 12.46221 | 11.46992 | 10.59401 | 9.81815 | 9.12855 | 8.51356 | 7.46944 | 6.62313 | 5.92884 | 5.35275 | 4.86958 | 3.95388 | 3.31579 |
| 21 | 18.85698 | 17.01121 | 15.41502 | 14.02916 | 12.82115 | 11.76408 | 10.83553 | 10.01680 | 9.29224 | 8.64869 | 7.56200 | 6.68696 | 5.97314 | 5.38368 | 4.89132 | 3.96311 | 3.31984 |
| 22 | 19.66038 | 17.65805 | 15.93692 | 14.45112 | 13.16300 | 12.04158 | 11.06124 | 10.20074 | 9.44243 | 8.77154 | 7.64465 | 6.74294 | 6.01133 | 5.40990 | 4.90943 | 3.97049 | 3.32296 |
| 23 | 20.45582 | 18.29220 | 16.44361 | 14.85684 | 13.48857 | 12.30338 | 11.27219 | 10.37106 | 9.58021 | 8.88322 | 7.71843 | 6.79206 | 6.04425 | 5.43212 | 4.92453 | 3.97639 | 3.32535 |
| 24 | 21.24339 | 18.91393 | 16.93554 | 15.24696 | 13.79864 | 12.55036 | 11.46933 | 10.52876 | 9.70661 | 8.98474 | 7.78432 | 6.83514 | 6.07263 | 5.45095 | 4.93710 | 3.98111 | 3.32719 |
| 25 | 22.02316 | 19.52346 | 17.41315 | 15.62208 | 14.09394 | 12.78336 | 11.65358 | 10.67478 | 9.82258 | 9.07704 | 7.84314 | 6.87293 | 6.09709 | 5.46691 | 4.94759 | 3.98489 | 3.32861 |
| 26 | 22.79520 | 20.12104 | 17.87684 | 15.98277 | 14.37519 | 13.00317 | 11.82578 | 10.80998 | 9.92897 | 9.16095 | 7.89566 | 6.90608 | 6.11818 | 5.48043 | 4.95632 | 3.98791 | 3.32970 |
| 27 | 23.55961 | 20.70690 | 18.32703 | 16.32959 | 14.64303 | 13.21053 | 11.98671 | 10.93516 | 10.02658 | 9.23722 | 7.94255 | 6.93515 | 6.13636 | 5.49189 | 4.96360 | 3.99033 | 3.33054 |
| 28 | 24.31644 | 21.28127 | 18.76411 | 16.66306 | 14.89813 | 13.40616 | 12.13711 | 11.05108 | 10.11613 | 9.30657 | 7.98442 | 6.96066 | 6.15204 | 5.50160 | 4.96967 | 3.99226 | 3.33118 |
| 29 | 25.06579 | 21.84438 | 19.18845 | 16.98371 | 15.14107 | 13.59072 | 12.27767 | 11.15841 | 10.19828 | 9.36961 | 8.02181 | 6.98304 | 6.16555 | 5.50983 | 4.97472 | 3.99381 | 3.33168 |
| 30 | 25.80771 | 22.39646 | 19.60044 | 17.29203 | 15.37245 | 13.76483 | 12.40904 | 11.25778 | 10.27365 | 9.42691 | 8.05518 | 7.00266 | 6.17720 | 5.51681 | 4.97894 | 3.99505 | 3.33206 |

* $P_n = (1/i)[1 - 1/(1 + i)^n]$

# SUMMARY OF LEARNING OBJECTIVES

**LO 1.** Explain the meaning of *capital investment decisions,* and distinguish between independent and mutually exclusive capital investment decisions.

- Capital investment decisions are concerned with the acquisition of long-term assets and usually involve a significant outlay of funds.
- The two types of capital investment projects are independent and mutually exclusive.
- Independent projects are projects that, whether accepted or rejected, do not affect the cash flows of other projects.
- Mutually exclusive projects are projects that, if accepted, preclude the acceptance of all other competing projects.

**LO 2.** Compute the payback period and accounting rate of return for a proposed investment, and explain their roles in capital investment decisions.

- Managers make capital investment decisions by using formal models to decide whether to accept or reject proposed projects.
- These decision models are classified as nondiscounting and discounting, depending on whether they address the question of the time value of money.
- The two nondiscounting models are the payback period and the ARR.
- The payback period is the time required for a firm to recover its initial investment. For even cash flows, it is calculated by dividing the investment by the annual cash flow. For uneven cash flows, the cash flows are summed until the investment is recovered. If only a fraction of a year is needed, then it is assumed that the cash flows occur evenly within each year.
- The payback period ignores the time value of money and the profitability of projects because it does not consider the cash inflows available beyond the payback period. The payback period is useful for assessing and controlling risk, minimizing the impact of an investment on a firm's liquidity, and controlling the risk of obsolescence.
- The ARR is computed by dividing the average income expected from an investment by either the original or average investment.
- Unlike the payback period, the ARR does consider the profitability of a project; however, it ignores the time value of money.
- The ARR may be useful to managers for screening new investments to ensure that certain accounting ratios are not adversely affected (specifically, accounting ratios that may be monitored to ensure compliance with debt covenants).

**LO 3.** Use net present value analysis for capital investment decisions involving independent projects.

- NPV is the difference between the present value of future cash flows and the initial investment outlay.
- To use the NPV model, a required rate of return must be identified (usually the cost of capital). The NPV method uses the required rate of return to compute the present value of a project's cash inflows and outflows.
- If the present value of the inflows is greater than the present value of the outflows, then the NPV is greater than zero, and the project is profitable. If the NPV is less than zero, then the project is not profitable and should be rejected.

**LO 4.** Use the internal rate of return to assess the acceptability of independent projects.

- The IRR is computed by finding the interest rate that equates the present value of a project's cash inflows with the present value of its cash outflows.
- If the IRR is greater than the required rate of return (cost of capital), then the project is acceptable; if the IRR is less than the required rate of return, then the project should be rejected.

**LO 5.** Explain the role and value of postaudits.

- Postauditing of capital projects is an important step in capital investment.
- Postaudits evaluate the actual performance of a project in relation to its expected performance.

- A postaudit may lead to corrective action to improve the performance of the project or to abandon it.
- Postaudits also serve as an incentive for managers to make capital investment decisions prudently.

**LO 6.** Explain why net present value is better than internal rate of return for capital investment decisions involving mutually exclusive projects.

- In evaluating mutually exclusive or competing projects, managers have a choice of using NPV or IRR.
- When choosing among competing projects, the NPV model correctly identifies the best investment alternative.
- IRR may choose an inferior project. Thus, since NPV always provides the correct signal, it should be used.

**LO 7.** *(Appendix 14A)* Explain the relationship between current and future dollars.

- The value of an investment at the end of its life is called its future value.
- Present value is the amount that must be invested now to yield some future value.
- Present value is computed by discounting the future value using a discount rate. The discount rate is the interest rate used to discount the future amount.
- An annuity is a series of future cash flows. If the annuity is uneven, then each future cash flow must be discounted using individual discount rates (the present value for each cash flow is calculated separately and then summed). For even cash flows, a single discount rate, which is the sum of each discount rate for each cash flow, can be used.

# SUMMARY OF IMPORTANT EQUATIONS

1. $\text{Payback Period} = \dfrac{\text{Original Investment}}{\text{Annual Cash Flow}}$

2. $\text{Accounting Rate of Return} = \dfrac{\text{Average Income}}{\text{Initial Investment}}$

3. $NPV = \left[\sum CF_t/(1+i)^t\right] - I$

   $\quad\ = \left[\sum CF_t df_t\right] - I$

   $\quad\ = P - I$

4. $I = \sum[CF_t/(1+i)^t]$

5. $I = CF(df)$

6. $df = I/CF$

   $\quad = \dfrac{\text{Investment}}{\text{Annual Cash Flow}}$

7. $F = P(1+i)^n$

8. $P = F/(1+i)^n$

**CORNERSTONES**

CORNERSTONE 14.1   Calculating payback, page 626

CORNERSTONE 14.2   Calculating the accounting rate of return, page 628

CORNERSTONE 14.3   Assessing cash flows and calculating net present value, page 631

CORNERSTONE 14.4   Calculating internal rate of return with uniform cash flows, page 634

CORNERSTONE 14.5   Calculating net present value and internal rate of return for mutually exclusive projects, page 640

# KEY TERMS

Accounting rate of return (ARR), 628
Annuity, 645
Capital budgeting, 624
Capital investment decisions, 624
Compounding of interest, 644
Cost of capital, 630
Discount factor, 645
Discount rate, 645
Discounted cash flows, 629
Discounting, 645
Discounting models, 625

Future value, 644
Independent projects, 624
Internal rate of return (IRR), 633
Mutually exclusive projects, 624
Net present value (NPV), 630
Nondiscounting models, 625
Payback period, 626
Postaudit, 636
Present value, 645
Required rate of return, 630

# REVIEW PROBLEMS

## I. Basics of Capital Investment

Kenn Day, manager of Day Laboratory, is investigating the possibility of acquiring some new test equipment. The equipment requires an initial outlay of $300,000. To raise the capital, Kenn will sell stock valued at $200,000 (the stock pays dividends of $24,000 per year) and borrow $100,000. The loan for $100,000 would carry an interest rate of 6%. Kenn figures that his weighted average cost of capital is 10% [(2/3 × 0.12) + (1/3 × 0.06)]. This weighted cost of capital is the discount rate that will be used for capital investment decisions.

Kenn estimates that the new test equipment will produce a cash inflow of $50,000 per year. Kenn expects the equipment to last for 20 years.

### Required:

1. Compute the payback period.
2. Assuming that depreciation is $14,000 per year, compute the ARR (on total investment).
3. Compute the NPV of the test equipment.
4. Compute the IRR of the test equipment.
5. Should Kenn buy the equipment?

### Solution:

1. The payback period is $300,000/$50,000, or 6 years.
2. The ARR is ($50,000 − $14,000)/$300,000, or 12%.
3. From Exhibit 14B.2 (p. 648), the discount factor for an annuity with $i$ at 10% and $n$ at 20 years is 8.51356. Thus, the NPV is (8.51356 × $50,000) − $300,000, or $125,678.
4. The discount factor associated with the IRR is 6.00000 ($300,000/$50,000). From Exhibit 14B.2, the IRR is between 14 and 16% (using the row corresponding to Period 20).
5. Since the NPV is positive and the IRR is greater than Kenn's cost of capital, the test equipment is a sound investment. This, of course, assumes that the cash flow projections are accurate.

## II. Capital Investments with Competing Projects

A hospital is considering the possibility of two new purchases: new x-ray equipment and new biopsy equipment. Each project would require an investment of $750,000. The expected life for each is 5 years with no expected salvage value. The net cash inflows associated with the two independent projects are as follows:

*(Continued)*

| Year | X-Ray Equipment | Biopsy Equipment |
|------|-----------------|------------------|
| 1 | $375,000 | $ 75,000 |
| 2 | 150,000 | 75,000 |
| 3 | 300,000 | 525,000 |
| 4 | 150,000 | 600,000 |
| 5 | 75,000 | 675,000 |

## Required:

1. Compute the net present value of each project, assuming a required rate of 12%.
2. Compute the payback period for each project. Assume that the manager of the hospital accepts only projects with a payback period of 3 years or less. Offer some reasons why this may be a rational strategy even though the NPV computed in Requirement 1 may indicate otherwise.

## Solution:

1. X-ray equipment:

| Year | Cash Flow | Discount Factor | Present Value |
|------|-----------|-----------------|---------------|
| 0 | $(750,000) | 1.00000 | $(750,000) |
| 1 | 375,000 | 0.89286 | 334,823 |
| 2 | 150,000 | 0.79719 | 119,579 |
| 3 | 300,000 | 0.71178 | 213,534 |
| 4 | 150,000 | 0.63552 | 95,328 |
| 5 | 75,000 | 0.56743 | 42,557 |
| NPV | | | $  55,821 |

Biopsy equipment:

| Year | Cash Flow | Discount Factor | Present Value |
|------|-----------|-----------------|---------------|
| 0 | $(750,000) | 1.00000 | $(750,000) |
| 1 | 75,000 | 0.89286 | 66,965 |
| 2 | 75,000 | 0.79719 | 59,789 |
| 3 | 525,000 | 0.71178 | 373,685 |
| 4 | 600,000 | 0.63552 | 381,312 |
| 5 | 675,000 | 0.56743 | 383,015 |
| NPV | | | $ 514,766 |

2. X-ray equipment:

| Payback Period = | $375,000 | 1.00 year |
|------------------|----------|-----------|
| | 150,000 | 1.00 |
| | 225,000 | 0.75 ($225,000/$300,000) |
| | $750,000 | 2.75 years |

Biopsy equipment:

| Payback Period = | $ 75,000 | 1.00 year |
|------------------|----------|-----------|
| | 75,000 | 1.00 |
| | 525,000 | 1.00 |
| | 75,000 | 0.13 ($75,000/$600,000) |
| | $750,000 | 3.13 years |

This might be a reasonable strategy because payback is a rough measure of risk. The assumption is that the longer it takes a project to pay for itself, the riskier the project is. Other reasons might be that the firm might have liquidity problems, the cash flows might be risky, or there might be a high risk of obsolescence.

# DISCUSSION QUESTIONS

1. Explain the difference between independent projects and mutually exclusive projects.

2. Explain why the timing and quantity of cash flows are important in capital investment decisions.

3. The time value of money is ignored by the payback period and the ARR. Explain why this is a major deficiency in these two models.

4. What is the payback period? Compute the payback period for an investment requiring an initial outlay of $80,000 with expected annual cash inflows of $30,000.

5. Name and discuss three possible reasons that the payback period is used to help make capital investment decisions.

6. What is the accounting rate of return? Compute the ARR for an investment that requires an initial outlay of $300,000 and promises an average net income of $100,000.

7. The NPV is the same as the profit of a project expressed in present dollars. Do you agree? Explain.

8. Explain the relationship between NPV and a firm's value.

9. What is the cost of capital? What role does it play in capital investment decisions?

10. What is the role that the required rate of return plays in the NPV model? In the IRR model?

11. Explain how the NPV is used to determine whether a project should be accepted or rejected.

12. The IRR is the true or actual rate of return being earned by the project. Do you agree or disagree? Discuss.

13. Explain what a postaudit is and how it can provide useful input for future capital investment decisions, especially those involving advanced technology.

14. Explain why NPV is generally preferred over IRR when choosing among competing or mutually exclusive projects. Why would managers continue to use IRR to choose among mutually exclusive projects?

15. Suppose that a firm must choose between two mutually exclusive projects, both of which have negative NPVs. Explain how a firm can legitimately choose between two such projects.

# MULTIPLE-CHOICE QUESTIONS

**14-1** Capital investments should

a. always produce an increase in market share.

b. only be analyzed using the ARR.

c. earn back their original capital outlay plus a reasonable return.

d. always be done using a payback criterion.

e. do none of these.

**14-2** To make a capital investment decision, a manager must

a. estimate the quantity and timing of cash flows.

b. assess the risk of the investment.

c. consider the impact of the investment on the firm's profits.

d. choose a decision criterion to assess viability of the investment (such as payback period or NPV).

e. do all of these.

**14-3** Mutually exclusive capital budgeting projects are those that

a. if accepted or rejected do not affect the cash flows of other projects.

b. if accepted will produce a negative NPV.

c. if rejected preclude the acceptance of all other competing projects.

d. if accepted preclude the acceptance of all other competing projects.

e. if rejected imply that all other competing projects have a positive NPV.

**14-4** An investment of $6,000 produces a net annual cash inflow of $2,000 for each of 5 years. What is the payback period?

    a.  2 years

    b.  1.5 year

    c.  Unacceptable

    d.  3 years

    e.  Cannot be determined.

**14-5** An investment of $1,000 produces a net cash inflow of $500 in the first year and $750 in the second year. What is the payback period?

    a.  1.67 years

    b.  0.50 year

    c.  2.00 years

    d.  1.20 years

    e.  Cannot be determined.

**14-6** The payback period suffers from which of the following deficiencies?

    a.  It is a rough measure of the uncertainty of future cash flows.

    b.  It helps control the risk of obsolescence.

    c.  It ignores the uncertainty of future cash flows.

    d.  It ignores the financial performance of a project beyond the payback period.

    e.  Both c and d.

**14-7** The ARR has one specific advantage *not* possessed by the payback period in that it

    a.  considers the time value of money.

    b.  measures the value added by a project.

    c.  is always an accurate measure of profitability.

    d.  is more widely accepted by financial managers.

    e.  considers the profitability of a project beyond the payback period.

**14-8** An investment of $2,000 provides an average net income of $400. Depreciation is $40 per year with zero salvage value. The ARR using the original investment is

    a.  44%.

    b.  22%.

    c.  20%.

    d.  40%.

    e.  none of these.

**14-9** If the NPV is positive, it signals

    a.  that the initial investment has been recovered.

    b.  that the required rate of return has been earned.

    c.  that the value of the firm has increased.

    d.  all of these.

    e.  both a and b.

**14-10** NPV measures

    a.  the profitability of an investment.

    b.  the change in wealth.

    c.  the change in firm value.

    d.  the difference in present value of cash inflows and outflows.

    e.  all of these.

**14-11** NPV is calculated by using

    a.  the required rate of return.

    b.  accounting income.

    c.  the IRR.

    d.  the future value of cash flows.

    e.  none of these.

**14-12** Using NPV, a project is rejected if it is

    a.  equal to zero.

    b.  negative.

    c.  positive.

    d.  equal to the required rate of return.

    e.  greater than the cost of capital.

**14-13** If the present value of future cash flows is $4,200 for an investment that requires an outlay of $3,000, the NPV

a.   is $200.
b.   is $1,000.
c.   is $1,200.
d.   is $2,200.
e.   cannot be determined.

**14-14** Assume that an investment of $1,000 produces a future cash flow of $1,000. The discount factor for this future cash flow is 0.80. The NPV is

a.   $0.
b.   $110.
c.   ($200).
d.   $911.
e.   none of these.

**14-15** Which of the following is *not* true regarding the IRR?

a.   The IRR is the interest rate that sets the present value of a project's cash inflows equal to the present value of the project's cost.
b.   The IRR is the interest rate that sets the NPV equal to zero.
c.   The popularity of IRR may be attributable to the fact that it is a rate of return, a concept that is comfortably used by managers.
d.   If the IRR is greater than the required rate of return, then the project is acceptable.
e.   The IRR is the most reliable of the capital budgeting methods.

**14-16** Using IRR, a project is rejected if the IRR

a.   is equal to the required rate of return.
b.   is less than the required rate of return.
c.   is greater than the cost of capital.
d.   is greater than the required rate of return.
e.   produces an NPV equal to zero.

**14-17** A postaudit

a.   is a follow-up analysis of a capital project, once implemented.
b.   compares the actual benefits with the estimated benefits.
c.   evaluates the overall outcome of the investment.
d.   proposes corrective action, if needed.
e.   does all of these.

**14-18** Postaudits of capital projects are useful because

a.   they are not very costly.
b.   they have no significant limitations.
c.   the assumptions underlying the original analyses are often invalidated by changes in the actual working environment.
d.   they help to ensure that resources are used wisely.
e.   of all of these.

**14-19** For competing projects, NPV is preferred to IRR because

a.   maximizing IRR maximizes the wealth of the owners.
b.   in the final analysis, relative profitability is what counts.
c.   choosing the project with the largest NPV maximizes the wealth of the shareholders.
d.   assuming that cash flows are reinvested at the computed IRR is more realistic than assuming that cash flows are reinvested at the required rate of return.
e.   of all of the above.

**14-20** Assume that there are two competing projects, A and B. Project A has a NPV of $1,000 and an IRR of 15%. Project B has an NPV of $800 and an IRR of 20%. Which of the following is true?

a.   Project A should be chosen because it has a higher NPV.
b.   Project B should be chosen because it has a higher IRR.
c.   It is not possible to use NPV or IRR to choose between the two projects.
d.   Neither project should be chosen.
e.   None of these.

# CORNERSTONE EXERCISES

### Cornerstone Exercise 14-21    Payback Period

Ventura Manufacturing is considering an investment in a new automated manufacturing system. The new system requires an investment of $3,000,000 and either has (a) even cash flows of $750,000 per year or (b) the following expected annual cash flows: $375,000, $375,000, $1,000,000, $1,000,000, and $250,000.

**Required:**

Calculate the payback period for each case.

### Cornerstone Exercise 14-22    Accounting Rate of Return

Eyring Company invested $7,500,000 in a new product line. The life cycle of the product is projected to be 7 years with the following net income stream: $300,000, $300,000, $500,000, $900,000, $1,000,000, $2,100,000, and $1,200,000.

**Required:**

Calculate the ARR.

### Cornerstone Exercise 14-23    Net Present Value

Holland Inc. has just completed development of a new cell phone. The new product is expected to produce annual revenues of $1,350,000. Producing the cell phone requires an investment in new equipment, costing $1,440,000. The cell phone has a projected life cycle of 5 years. After 5 years, the equipment can be sold for $180,000. Working capital is also expected to increase by $180,000, which Holland will recover by the end of the new product's life cycle. Annual cash operating expenses are estimated at $810,000. The required rate of return is 8%.

**Required:**

1. Prepare a schedule of the projected annual cash flows.
2. Calculate the NPV using only discount factors from Exhibit 14B.1 (p. 647).
3. Calculate the NPV using discount factors from both Exhibit 14B.1 and 14B.2 (p. 648).

### Cornerstone Exercise 14-24    Internal Rate of Return

Randel Company produces a variety of gardening tools and aids. The company is examining the possibility of investing in a new production system that will reduce the costs of the current system. The new system will require a cash investment of $3,455,400 and will produce net cash savings of $600,000 per year. The system has a projected life of 9 years.

**Required:**

Calculate the IRR for the new production system.

### Cornerstone Exercise 14-25    NPV and IRR, Mutually Exclusive Projects

Weeden Inc. intends to invest in one of two competing types of computer-aided manufacturing equipment: CAM X and CAM Y. Both CAM X and CAM Y models have a project life of 10 years. The purchase price of the CAM X model is $2,400,000, and it has a net annual after-tax cash inflow of $600,000. The CAM Y model is more expensive, selling for $2,800,000, but it will produce a net annual after-tax cash inflow of $700,000. The cost of capital for the company is 10%.

**Required:**

1. Calculate the NPV for each project. Which model would you recommend?
2. Calculate the IRR for each project. Which model would you recommend?

# EXERCISES

Round all present value calculations to the nearest dollar.

## Exercise 14-26   Payback Period

OBJECTIVE ❶ ❷

ILLUSTRATING
RELATIONSHIPS

Each of the following scenarios is independent. Assume that all cash flows are after-tax cash flows.

a.  Colby Hepworth has just invested $400,000 in a book and video store. She expects to receive a cash income of $120,000 per year from the investment.
b.  Kylie Sorensen has just invested $1,400,000 in a new biomedical technology. She expects to receive the following cash flows over the next 5 years: $350,000, $490,000, $700,000, $420,000, and $280,000.
c.  Carsen Nabors invested in a project that has a payback period of 4 years. The project brings in $960,000 per year.
d.  Rahn Booth invested $1,300,000 in a project that pays him an even amount per year for 5 years. The payback period is 2.5 years.

### Required:

1.  What is the payback period for Colby?
2.  What is the payback period for Kylie?
3.  How much did Carsen invest in the project?
4.  How much cash does Rahn receive each year?

## Exercise 14-27   Accounting Rate of Return

OBJECTIVE ❶ ❷

ILLUSTRATING
RELATIONSHIPS

Each of the following scenarios is independent. Assume that all cash flows are after-tax cash flows.

a.  Cobre Company is considering the purchase of new equipment that will speed up the process for extracting copper. The equipment will cost $3,600,000 and have a life of 5 years with no expected salvage value. The expected cash flows associated with the project are as follows:

| Year | Cash Revenues | Cash Expenses |
|---|---|---|
| 1 | $6,000,000 | $4,800,000 |
| 2 | 6,000,000 | 4,800,000 |
| 3 | 6,000,000 | 4,800,000 |
| 4 | 6,000,000 | 4,800,000 |
| 5 | 6,000,000 | 4,800,000 |

b.  Emily Hansen is considering investing in one of the following two projects. Either project will require an investment of $75,000. The expected cash revenues minus cash expenses for the two projects follow. Assume each project is depreciable.

| Year | Project A | Project B |
|---|---|---|
| 1 | $22,500 | $22,500 |
| 2 | 30,000 | 30,000 |
| 3 | 45,000 | 45,000 |
| 4 | 75,000 | 22,500 |
| 5 | 75,000 | 22,500 |

c.  Suppose that a project has an ARR of 30% (based on initial investment) and that the average net income of the project is $120,000.
d.  Suppose that a project has an ARR of 50% and that the investment is $150,000.

### Required:

1.  Compute the ARR on the new equipment that Cobre Company is considering.
2.  **CONCEPTUAL CONNECTION** Which project should Emily Hansen choose based on the ARR? Notice that the payback period is the same for both investments (thus equally

*(Continued)*

preferred). Unlike the payback period, explain why ARR correctly signals that one project should be preferred over the other.

3. How much did the company in Scenario c invest in the project?
4. What is the average net income earned by the project in Scenario d?

OBJECTIVE ❶ ❸

### Exercise 14-28    Net Present Value

Each of the following scenarios is independent. Assume that all cash flows are after-tax cash flows.

a. Southward Manufacturing is considering the purchase of a new welding system. The cash benefits will be $400,000 per year. The system costs $2,250,000 and will last 10 years.

b. Kaylin Day is interested in investing in a women's specialty shop. The cost of the investment is $180,000. She estimates that the return from owning her own shop will be $35,000 per year. She estimates that the shop will have a useful life of 6 years.

c. Goates Company calculated the NPV of a project and found it to be $21,300. The project's life was estimated to be 8 years. The required rate of return used for the NPV calculation was 10%. The project was expected to produce annual after-tax cash flows of $45,000.

### Required:

1. Compute the NPV for Southward Manufacturing, assuming a discount rate of 12%. Should the company buy the new welding system?
2. **CONCEPTUAL CONNECTION** Assuming a required rate of return of 8%, calculate the NPV for Kaylin Day's investment. Should she invest? What if the estimated return was $45,000 per year? Would this affect the decision? What does this tell you about your analysis?
3. What was the required investment for Goates Company's project?

OBJECTIVE ❶ ❹

### Exercise 14-29    Internal Rate of Return

Each of the following scenarios is independent. Assume that all cash flows are after-tax cash flows.

a. Cuenca Company is considering the purchase of new equipment that will speed up the process for producing flash drives. The equipment will cost $7,200,000 and have a life of 5 years with no expected salvage value. The expected cash flows associated with the project follow:

| Year | Cash Revenues | Cash Expenses |
|------|--------------|---------------|
| 1 | $8,000,000 | $6,000,000 |
| 2 | 8,000,000 | 6,000,000 |
| 3 | 8,000,000 | 6,000,000 |
| 4 | 8,000,000 | 6,000,000 |
| 5 | 8,000,000 | 6,000,000 |

b. Kathy Shorts is evaluating an investment in an information system that will save $240,000 per year. She estimates that the system will last 10 years. The system will cost $1,248,000. Her company's cost of capital is 10%.

c. Elmo Enterprises just announced that a new plant would be built in Helper, Utah. Elmo told its stockholders that the plant has an expected life of 15 years and an expected IRR equal to 25%. The cost of building the plant is expected to be $2,880,000.

### Required:

1. Calculate the IRR for Cuenca Company. The company's cost of capital is 16%. Should the new equipment be purchased?
2. Calculate Kathy Short's IRR. Should she acquire the new system?
3. What should be Elmo Enterprises' expected annual cash flow from the plant?

## Exercise 14-30   Net Present Value and Competing Projects

OBJECTIVE ❶❻

ILLUSTRATING
RELATIONSHIPS

Spiro Hospital is investigating the possibility of investing in new dialysis equipment. Two local manufacturers of this equipment are being considered as sources of the equipment. After-tax cash inflows for the two competing projects are as follows:

| Year | Puro Equipment | Briggs Equipment |
|------|----------------|------------------|
| 1 | $320,000 | $120,000 |
| 2 | 280,000 | 120,000 |
| 3 | 240,000 | 320,000 |
| 4 | 160,000 | 400,000 |
| 5 | 120,000 | 440,000 |

Both projects require an initial investment of $560,000. In both cases, assume that the equipment has a life of 5 years with no salvage value.

**Required:**

1. Assuming a discount rate of 12%, compute the net present value of each piece of equipment.
2. A third option has surfaced for equipment purchased from an out-of-state supplier. The cost is also $560,000, but this equipment will produce even cash flows over its 5-year life. What must the annual cash flow be for this equipment to be selected over the other two? Assume a 12% discount rate.

## Exercise 14-31   Payback, Accounting Rate of Return, Net Present Value, Internal Rate of Return

OBJECTIVE ❶❷❸❹

Booth Company wants to buy a numerically controlled (NC) machine to be used in producing specially machined parts for manufacturers of tractors. The outlay required is $960,000. The NC equipment will last 5 years with no expected salvage value. The expected after-tax cash flows associated with the project follow:

| Year | Cash Revenues | Cash Expenses |
|------|---------------|---------------|
| 1 | $1,275,000 | $900,000 |
| 2 | 1,275,000 | 900,000 |
| 3 | 1,275,000 | 900,000 |
| 4 | 1,275,000 | 900,000 |
| 5 | 1,275,000 | 900,000 |

**Required:**

1. Compute the payback period for the NC equipment.
2. Compute the NC equipment's ARR.
3. Compute the investment's NPV, assuming a required rate of return of 10%.
4. Compute the investment's IRR.

## Exercise 14-32   Payback, Accounting Rate of Return, Present Value, Net Present Value, Internal Rate of Return

OBJECTIVE ❶❷❸❹

All scenarios are independent of all other scenarios. Assume that all cash flows are after-tax cash flows.

a. Kambry Day is considering investing in one of the following two projects. Either project will require an investment of $20,000. The expected cash flows for the two projects follow. Assume that each project is depreciable.

| Year | Project A | Project B |
|------|-----------|-----------|
| 1 | $ 6,000 | $ 6,000 |
| 2 | 8,000 | 8,000 |
| 3 | 10,000 | 10,000 |
| 4 | 10,000 | 3,000 |
| 5 | 10,000 | 3,000 |

*(Continued)*

b.  Wilma Golding is retiring and has the option to take her retirement as a lump sum of $450,000 or to receive $30,000 per year for 20 years. Wilma's required rate of return is 6%.

c.  David Booth is interested in investing in some tools and equipment so that he can do independent drywalling. The cost of the tools and equipment is $30,000. He estimates that the return from owning his own equipment will be $9,000 per year. The tools and equipment will last 6 years.

d.  Patsy Folson is evaluating what appears to be an attractive opportunity. She is currently the owner of a small manufacturing company and has the opportunity to acquire another small company's equipment that would provide production of a part currently purchased externally. She estimates that the savings from internal production will be $75,000 per year. She estimates that the equipment will last 10 years. The owner is asking $400,000 for the equipment. Her company's cost of capital is 8%.

**Required:**

1.  **CONCEPTUAL CONNECTION** What is the payback period for each of Kambry Day's projects? If rapid payback is important, which project should be chosen? Which would you choose?

2.  **CONCEPTUAL CONNECTION** Which of Kambry's projects should be chosen based on the ARR? Explain why the ARR performs better than the payback period in this setting.

3.  Assuming that Wilma Golding will live for another 20 years, should she take the lump sum or the annuity?

4.  Assuming a required rate of return of 8% for David Booth, calculate the NPV of the investment. Should David invest?

5.  Calculate the IRR for Patsy Folson's project. Should Patsy acquire the equipment?

 **OBJECTIVE 3**

## Exercise 14-33   Net Present Value, Basic Concepts

Wise Company is considering an investment that requires an outlay of $600,000 and promises an after-tax cash inflow 1 year from now of $693,000. The company's cost of capital is 10%.

**Required:**

1.  Break the $693,000 future cash inflow into three components: (a) the return of the original investment, (b) the cost of capital, and (c) the profit earned on the investment. Now compute the present value of the profit earned on the investment.

2.  **CONCEPTUAL CONNECTION** Compute the NPV of the investment. Compare this with the present value of the profit computed in Requirement 1. What does this tell you about the meaning of NPV?

 **OBJECTIVE 1 3 4**

 **ILLUSTRATING RELATIONSHIPS**

## Exercise 14-34   Solving for Unknowns

Each of the following scenarios are independent. Assume that all cash flows are after-tax cash flows.

a.  Thomas Company is investing $120,000 in a project that will yield a uniform series of cash inflows over the next 4 years.

b.  Video Repair has decided to invest in some new electronic equipment. The equipment will have a 3-year life and will produce a uniform series of cash savings. The NPV of the equipment is $1,750, using a discount rate of 8%. The IRR is 12%.

c.  A new lathe costing $60,096 will produce savings of $12,000 per year.

d.  The NPV of a project is $3,927. The project has a life of 4 years and produces the following cash flows:

| Year 1 | $10,000 | Year 3 | $15,000 |
| Year 2 | $12,000 | Year 4 | ? |

The cost of the project is two times the cash flow produced in Year 4. The discount rate is 10%.

**Required:**

1. If the internal rate of return is 14% for Thomas Company, how much cash inflow per year can be expected?
2. Determine the investment and the amount of cash savings realized each year for Video Repair.
3. For Scenario c, how many years must the lathe last if an IRR of 18% is realized?
4. For Scenario d, find the cost of the project and the cash flow for Year 4.

### Exercise 14-35   Net Present Value versus Internal Rate of Return

OBJECTIVE 6

Skiba Company is thinking about two different modifications to its current manufacturing process. The after-tax cash flows associated with the two investments follow:

| Year | Project I | Project II |
|------|-----------|------------|
| 0 | $(100,000) | $(100,000) |
| 1 | — | 63,857 |
| 2 | 134,560 | 63,857 |

Skiba's cost of capital is 10%.

**Required:**

1. Compute the NPV and the IRR for each investment.
2. **CONCEPTUAL CONNECTION** Explain why the project with the larger NPV is the correct choice for Skiba.

# PROBLEMS

Round all present value calculations to the nearest dollar.

### Problem 14-36   Basic Net Present Value Analysis

OBJECTIVE 1 3

Jonathan Butler, process engineer, knows that the acceptance of a new process design will depend on its economic feasibility. The new process is designed to improve environmental performance. On the negative side, the process design requires new equipment and an infusion of working capital. The equipment will cost $1,200,000, and its cash operating expenses will total $270,000 per year. The equipment will last for 7 years but will need a major overhaul costing $120,000 at the end of the fifth year. At the end of 7 years, the equipment will be sold for $96,000. An increase in working capital totaling $120,000 will also be needed at the beginning. This will be recovered at the end of the 7 years.

On the positive side, Jonathan estimates that the new process will save $400,000 per year in environmental costs (fines and cleanup costs avoided). The cost of capital is 12%.

**Required:**

1. Prepare a schedule of cash flows for the proposed project. (*Note:* Assume that there are no income taxes.)
2. Compute the NPV of the project. Should the new process design be accepted?

### Problem 14-37   Net Present Value Analysis

OBJECTIVE 1 3

Emery Communications Company is considering the production and marketing of a communications system that will increase the efficiency of messaging for small businesses or branch offices of large companies. Each unit hooked into the system is assigned a mailbox number, which can be matched to a telephone extension number, providing access to messages 24 hours a day. Up to 20 units can be hooked into the system, allowing the delivery of the same message to as many as 20 people. Personal codes can be used to make messages confidential. Furthermore, messages can be reviewed, recorded, cancelled, replied to, or deleted all during the same message playback. Indicators wired to the telephone blink whenever new messages are present.

*(Continued)*

To produce this product, a $1.75 million investment in new equipment is required. The equipment will last 10 years but will need major maintenance costing $150,000 at the end of its sixth year. The salvage value of the equipment at the end of 10 years is estimated to be $100,000. If this new system is produced, working capital must also be increased by $90,000. This capital will be restored at the end of the product's 10-year life cycle. Revenues from the sale of the product are estimated at $1.65 million per year. Cash operating expenses are estimated at $1.32 million per year.

**Required:**

1. Prepare a schedule of cash flows for the proposed project. (*Note:* Assume that there are no income taxes.)
2. Assuming that Emery's cost of capital is 12%, compute the project's NPV. Should the product be produced?

 **OBJECTIVE ❶ ❹**

### Problem 14-38    Basic Internal Rate of Return Analysis

Julianna Cardenas, owner of Baker Company, was approached by a local dealer of air-conditioning units. The dealer proposed replacing Baker's old cooling system with a modern, more efficient system. The cost of the new system was quoted at $339,000, but it would save $60,000 per year in energy costs. The estimated life of the new system is 10 years, with no salvage value expected. Excited over the possibility of saving $60,000 per year and having a more reliable unit, Julianna requested an analysis of the project's economic viability. All capital projects are required to earn at least the firm's cost of capital, which is 8%. There are no income taxes.

**Required:**

1. Calculate the project's IRR. Should the company acquire the new cooling system?
2. Suppose that energy savings are less than claimed. Calculate the minimum annual cash savings that must be realized for the project to earn a rate equal to the firm's cost of capital.
3. Suppose that the life of the new system is overestimated by 2 years. Repeat Requirements 1 and 2 under this assumption.
4. **CONCEPTUAL CONNECTION** Explain the implications of the answers from Requirements 1, 2, and 3.

 **OBJECTIVE ❶ ❸**

### Problem 14-39    Net Present Value, Uncertainty

Ondi Airlines is interested in acquiring a new aircraft to service a new route. The route will be from Tulsa to Denver. The aircraft will fly one round-trip daily except for scheduled maintenance days. There are 15 maintenance days scheduled each year. The seating capacity of the aircraft is 150. Flights are expected to be fully booked. The average revenue per passenger per flight (one-way) is $235. Annual operating costs of the aircraft follow:

| | |
|---|---|
| Fuel | $1,750,000 |
| Flight personnel | 750,000 |
| Food and beverages | 100,000 |
| Maintenance | 550,000 |
| Other | 100,000 |
| Total | $3,250,000 |

The aircraft will cost $120,000,000 and has an expected life of 20 years. The company requires a 12% return. Assume there are no income taxes.

**Required:**

1. Calculate the NPV for the aircraft. Should the company buy it?
2. In discussing the proposal, the marketing manager for the airline believes that the assumption of 100% booking is unrealistic. He believes that the booking rate will be somewhere between 70 and 90%, with the most likely rate being 80%. Recalculate the NPV by using an 80% seating capacity. Should the aircraft be purchased?

3. Calculate the average seating rate that would be needed so that NPV will equal zero.
4. **CONCEPTUAL CONNECTION** Suppose that the price per passenger could be increased by 10% without any effect on demand. What is the average seating rate now needed to achieve a NPV equal to zero? What would you now recommend?

## Problem 14-40    Review of Basic Capital Budgeting Procedures

OBJECTIVE ❶❷❸❹

Dr. Whitley Avard, a plastic surgeon, had just returned from a conference in which she learned of a new surgical procedure for removing wrinkles around eyes, reducing the time to perform the normal procedure by 50%. Given her patient-load pressures, Dr. Avard is excited to try out the new technique. By decreasing the time spent on eye treatments or procedures, she can increase her total revenues by performing more services within a work period. In order to implement the new procedure, special equipment costing $74,000 is needed. The equipment has an expected life of 4 years, with a salvage value of $6,000. Dr. Avard estimates that her cash revenues will increase by the following amounts:

| Year | Revenue Increases |
|------|-------------------|
| 1 | $19,800 |
| 2 | 27,000 |
| 3 | 32,400 |
| 4 | 32,400 |

She also expects additional cash expenses amounting to $3,000 per year. The cost of capital is 12%. Assume that there are no income taxes.

### Required:

1. Compute the payback period for the new equipment.
2. Compute the ARR.
3. **CONCEPTUAL CONNECTION** Compute the NPV and IRR for the project. Use 14% as your first guess for IRR. Should Dr. Avard purchase the new equipment? Should she be concerned about payback or the ARR in making this decision?
4. **CONCEPTUAL CONNECTION** Before finalizing her decision, Dr. Avard decided to call two plastic surgeons who have been using the new procedure for the past six months. The conversations revealed a somewhat less glowing report than she received at the conference. The new procedure reduced the time required by about 25% rather than the advertised 50%. Dr. Avard estimated that the net operating cash flows of the procedure would be cut by one-third because of the extra time and cost involved (salvage value would be unaffected). Using this information, recompute the NPV of the project. What would you now recommend?

## Problem 14-41    Net Present Value and Competing Alternatives

OBJECTIVE ❶ ❻

**Stillwater Designs** has been rebuilding Model 100, Model 120, and Model 150 **Kicker** subwoofers that were returned for warranty action. Customers returning the subwoofers receive a new replacement. The warranty returns are then rebuilt and resold (as seconds). Tent sales are often used to sell the rebuilt speakers. As part of the rebuilding process, the speakers are demagnetized so that metal pieces and shavings can be removed. A demagnetizing (demag) machine is used to achieve this objective. A product design change has made the most recent Model 150 speakers too tall for the demag machine. They no longer fit in the demag machine.

   **Stillwater Designs** has two alternatives that it is currently considering. First, a new demag machine can be bought that has a different design, eliminating the fit problem. The cost of this machine is $600,000, and it will last 5 years. Second, Stillwater can keep the current machine and sell the 150 speakers for scrap, using the old demag machine for the Model 100 and 120 speakers only. A rebuilt speaker sells for $295 and costs $274.65 to rebuild (for materials, labor, and overhead cash outlays). The $274.65 outlay includes the annual operating cash effects of the new demag machine. If not rebuilt, the Model 150 speakers can be sold for $4 each as scrap. There are 10,000 Model 150 warranty returns per year. Assume that the required rate of return is 10%.

*(Continued)*

**Required:**

1.  Determine which alternative is the best for Stillwater Designs by using NPV analysis.
2.  **CONCEPTUAL CONNECTION** Determine which alternative is best for Stillwater Designs by using an IRR analysis. Explain why NPV analysis is a better approach.

 OBJECTIVE **3 6**    Problem 14-42   **Basic Net Present Value Analysis, Competing Projects**

Kildare Medical Center, a for-profit hospital, has three investment opportunities: (1) adding a wing for in-patient treatment of substance abuse, (2) adding a pathology laboratory, and (3) expanding the outpatient surgery wing. The initial investments and the net present value for the three alternatives are as follows:

|  | Substance Abuse | Laboratory | Outpatient Surgery |
|---|---|---|---|
| Investment | $1,500,000 | $500,000 | $1,000,000 |
| NPV | 150,000 | 140,000 | 135,000 |

Although the hospital would like to invest in all three alternatives, only $1.5 million is available.

**Required:**

1.  Rank the projects on the basis of NPV, and allocate the funds in order of this ranking. What project or projects were selected? What is the total NPV realized by the medical center using this approach?
2.  **CONCEPTUAL CONNECTION** Assume that the size of the lot on which the hospital is located makes the substance abuse wing and the outpatient surgery wing mutually exclusive. With unlimited capital, which of those two projects would be chosen? With limited capital and the three projects being considered, which projects would be chosen?
3.  **CONCEPTUAL CONNECTION** Form a group with two to four other students, and discuss qualitative considerations that should be considered in capital budgeting evaluations. Identify three such considerations.

 OBJECTIVE **1 2 3 4 6**    Problem 14-43   **Payback, Net Present Value, Internal Rate of Return, Intangible Benefits, Inflation Adjustment**

Foster Company wants to buy a numerically controlled (NC) machine to be used in producing specially machined parts for manufacturers of trenching machines (to replace an existing manual system). The outlay required is $3,500,000. The NC equipment will last 5 years with no expected salvage value. The expected incremental after-tax cash flows (cash flows of the NC equipment minus cash flows of the old equipment) associated with the project follow:

| Year | Cash Benefits | Cash Expenses |
|---|---|---|
| 1 | $3,900,000 | $3,000,000 |
| 2 | 3,900,000 | 3,000,000 |
| 3 | 3,900,000 | 3,000,000 |
| 4 | 3,900,000 | 3,000,000 |
| 5 | 3,900,000 | 3,000,000 |

Foster has a cost of capital equal to 10%. The above cash flows are expressed without any consideration of inflation.

**Required:**

1.  Compute the payback period.
2.  Calculate the NPV and IRR of the proposed project.
3.  **CONCEPTUAL CONNECTION** Inflation is expected to be 5% per year for the next 5 years. The discount rate of 10% is composed of two elements: the real rate and the inflationary element. Since the discount rate has an inflationary component, the projected cash flows should also be adjusted to account for inflation. Make this adjustment, and recalculate the NPV. Comment on the importance of adjusting cash flows for inflationary effects.

## Problem 14-44    Cost of Capital, Net Present Value

OBJECTIVE ③

Leakam Company's product engineering department has developed a new product that has a 3-year life cycle. Production of the product requires development of a new process that requires a current $100,000 capital outlay. The $100,000 will be raised by issuing $60,000 of bonds and by selling new stock for $40,000. The $60,000 in bonds will have net (after-tax) interest payments of $3,000 at the end of each of the 3 years, with the principal being repaid at the end of Year 3. The stock issue carries with it an expectation of a 17.5% return, expressed in the form of dividends at the end of each year ($7,000 in dividends is expected for each of the next 3 years). The sources of capital for this investment represent the same proportion and costs that the company typically has. Finally, the project will produce after-tax cash inflows of $50,000 per year for the next 3 years.

### Required:

1. Compute the cost of capital for the project. (*Hint*: The cost of capital is a weighted average of the two sources of capital where the weights are the proportion of capital from each source.)
2. **CONCEPTUAL CONNECTION** Compute the NPV for the project. Explain why it is not necessary to subtract the interest payments and the dividend payments and appreciation from the inflow of $50,000 in carrying out this computation.

## Problem 14-45    Capital Investment, Advanced Manufacturing Environment

OBJECTIVE ① ⑥

"I know that it's the thing to do," insisted Pamela Kincaid, vice president of finance for Colgate Manufacturing. "If we are going to be competitive, we need to build this completely automated plant."

"I'm not so sure," replied Bill Thomas, CEO of Colgate. "The savings from labor reductions and increased productivity are only $4 million per year. The price tag for this factory—and it's a small one—is $45 million. That gives a payback period of more than 11 years. That's a long time to put the company's money at risk."

"Yeah, but you're overlooking the savings that we'll get from the increase in quality," interjected John Simpson, production manager. "With this system, we can decrease our waste and our rework time significantly. Those savings are worth another million dollars per year."

"Another million will only cut the payback to about 9 years," retorted Bill. "Ron, you're the marketing manager—do you have any insights?"

"Well, there are other factors to consider, such as service quality and market share. I think that increasing our product quality and improving our delivery service will make us a lot more competitive. I know for a fact that two of our competitors have decided against automation. That'll give us a shot at their customers, provided our product is of higher quality and we can deliver it faster. I estimate that it'll increase our net cash benefits by another $2.4 million."

"Wow! Now that's impressive," Bill exclaimed, nearly convinced. "The payback is now getting down to a reasonable level."

"I agree," said Pamela, "but we do need to be sure that it's a sound investment. I know that estimates for construction of the facility have gone as high as $48 million. I also know that the expected residual value, after the 20 years of service we expect to get, is $5 million. I think I had better see if this project can cover our 14% cost of capital."

"Now wait a minute, Pamela," Bill demanded. "You know that I usually insist on a 20% rate of return, especially for a project of this magnitude."

### Required:

1. Compute the NPV of the project by using the original savings and investment figures. Calculate by using discount rates of 14% and 20%. Include salvage value in the computation.
2. Compute the NPV of the project using the additional benefits noted by the production and marketing managers. Also, use the original cost estimate of $45 million. Again, calculate for both possible discount rates.
3. Compute the NPV of the project using all estimates of cash flows, including the possible initial outlay of $48 million. Calculate by using discount rates of 14% and 20%.
4. **CONCEPTUAL CONNECTION** If you were making the decision, what would you do? Explain.

OBJECTIVE     **Problem 14-46    Postaudit, Sensitivity Analysis**

Newmarge Products Inc. is evaluating a new design for one of its manufacturing processes. The new design will eliminate the production of a toxic solid residue. The initial cost of the system is estimated at $860,000 and includes computerized equipment, software, and installation. There is no expected salvage value. The new system has a useful life of 8 years and is projected to produce cash operating savings of $225,000 per year over the old system (reducing labor costs and costs of processing and disposing of toxic waste). The cost of capital is 16%.

**Required:**

1.  Compute the NPV of the new system.
2.  One year after implementation, the internal audit staff noted the following about the new system: (1) the cost of acquiring the system was $60,000 more than expected due to higher installation costs, and (2) the annual cost savings were $20,000 less than expected because more labor cost was needed than anticipated. Using the changes in expected costs and benefits, compute the NPV as if this information had been available 1 year ago. Did the company make the right decision?
3.  **CONCEPTUAL CONNECTION** Upon reporting the results mentioned in the postaudit, the marketing manager responded in a memo to the internal auditing department indicating that revenues had increased by $60,000 per year because of increased purchases by environmentally sensitive customers. Describe the effect that this has on the analysis in Requirement 2.
4.  **CONCEPTUAL CONNECTION** Why is a postaudit beneficial to a firm?

OBJECTIVE     **Problem 14-47    Discount Rates, Automated Manufacturing, Competing Investments**

Patterson Company is considering two competing investments. The first is for a standard piece of production equipment. The second is for computer-aided manufacturing (CAM) equipment. The investment and after-tax operating cash flows follow:

| Year | Standard Equipment | CAM Equipment |
|------|--------------------|---------------|
| 0 | $(500,000) | $(2,000,000) |
| 1 | 300,000 | 100,000 |
| 2 | 200,000 | 200,000 |
| 3 | 100,000 | 300,000 |
| 4 | 100,000 | 400,000 |
| 5 | 100,000 | 400,000 |
| 6 | 100,000 | 400,000 |
| 7 | 100,000 | 500,000 |
| 8 | 100,000 | 1,000,000 |
| 9 | 100,000 | 1,000,000 |
| 10 | 100,000 | 1,000,000 |

Patterson uses a discount rate of 18% for all of its investments. Patterson's cost of capital is 10%.

**Required:**

1.  Calculate the NPV for each investment by using a discount rate of 18%.
2.  Calculate the NPV for each investment by using a discount rate of 10%.
3.  **CONCEPTUAL CONNECTION** Which rate should Patterson use to compute the NPV? Explain.

OBJECTIVE     **Problem 14-48    Quality, Market Share, Automated Manufacturing Environment**

Fabre Company, Patterson Company's competitor, is considering the same investments as Patterson. Refer to the data in **Problem 14-47** above. Assume that Fabre's cost of capital is 14%.

**Required:**

1.  Calculate the NPV of each alternative by using the 14% rate.

2. **CONCEPTUAL CONNECTION** Now assume that if the standard equipment is purchased, the competitive position of the firm will deteriorate because of lower quality (relative to competitors who did automate). Marketing estimates that the loss in market share will decrease the projected net cash inflows by 50% for Years 3 through 10. Recalculate the NPV of the standard equipment given this outcome. What is the decision now? Discuss the importance of assessing the effect of intangible benefits.

# CASES

### Case 14-49   Capital Investment and Ethical Behavior

OBJECTIVE ❸

Manny Carson, certified management accountant and controller of Wakeman Enterprises, has been given permission to acquire a new computer and software for the company's accounting system. The capital investment analysis showed an NPV of $100,000. However, the initial estimates of acquisition and installation costs were made on the basis of tentative costs without any formal bids. Manny now has two formal bids, one that would allow the firm to meet or beat the original projected NPV and one that would reduce the projected NPV by $50,000. The second bid involves a system that would increase both the initial cost and the operating cost.

Normally, Manny would take the first bid without hesitation. However, Todd Downing, the owner of the firm presenting the second bid, is a close friend. Manny called Todd and explained the situation, offering Todd an opportunity to alter his bid and win the job. Todd thanked Manny and then made a counteroffer.

**Todd:** Listen, Manny, this job at the original price is the key to a successful year for me. The revenues will help me gain approval for the loan I need for renovation and expansion. If I don't get that loan, I see hard times ahead. The financial stats for loan approval are so marginal that reducing the bid price may blow my chances.

**Manny:** Losing the bid altogether would be even worse, don't you think?

**Todd:** True. However, if you award me the job, I'll be able to add personnel. I know that your son is looking for a job, and I can offer him a good salary and a promising future. Additionally, I'll be able to take you and your wife on that vacation to Hawaii that we've been talking about.

**Manny:** Well, you have a point. My son is having an awful time finding a job, and he has a wife and three kids to support. My wife is tired of having them live with us. She and I could use a vacation. I doubt that the other bidder would make any fuss if we turned it down. Its offices are out of state, after all.

**Todd:** Out of state? All the more reason to turn it down. Given the state's economy, it seems almost criminal to take business outside. Those are the kind of business decisions that cause problems for people like your son.

**Required:**

Evaluate the ethical behavior of Manny. Should Manny have called Todd in the first place? What if Todd had agreed to meet the lower bid price—would there have been any problems? Identify the parts of the Statement of Ethical Professional Practice (Chapter 1) that Manny may be violating, if any.

### Case 14-50   Payback, Net Present Value, Internal Rate of Return, Effects of Differences in Sales on Project Viability

OBJECTIVE ❷ ❸ ❹

Shaftel Ready Mix is a processor and supplier of concrete, aggregate, and rock products. The company operates in the intermountain western United States. Currently, Shaftel has 14 cement-processing plants and a labor force of more than 375 employees. With the exception of cement

*(Continued)*

powder, all materials (e.g., aggregates and sand) are produced internally by the company. The demand for concrete and aggregates has been growing steadily nationally. In the West, the growth rate has been above the national average. Because of this growth, Shaftel has more than tripled its gross revenues over the past 10 years.

Of the intermountain states, Arizona has been experiencing the most growth. Processing plants have been added over the past several years, and the company is considering the addition of yet another plant to be located in Scottsdale. A major advantage of another plant in Arizona is the ability to operate year round, a feature not found in states such as Utah and Wyoming.

In setting up the new plant, land would have to be purchased and a small building constructed. Equipment and furniture would not need to be purchased; these items would be transferred from a plant that opened in Wyoming during the oil boom period and closed a few years after the end of that boom. However, the equipment needs some repair and modifications before it can be used. The equipment has a book value of $200,000, and the furniture has a book value of $30,000. Neither has any outside market value. Other costs, such as the installation of a silo, well, electrical hookups, and so on, will be incurred. No salvage value is expected. The summary of the initial investment costs by category is as follows:

| | |
|---|---:|
| Land | $ 20,000 |
| Building | 135,000 |
| Equipment: | |
|    Book value | 200,000 |
|    Modifications | 20,000 |
| Furniture (book value) | 30,000 |
| Silo | 20,000 |
| Well | 80,000 |
| Electrical hookups | 27,000 |
| General setup | 50,000 |
|    Total | $582,000 |

Estimates concerning the operation of the Scottsdale plant follow:

| | |
|---|---:|
| Life of plant and equipment | 10 years |
| Expected annual sales (in cubic yards of cement) | 35,000 |
| Selling price (per cubic yard of cement) | $   45.00 |
| Variable costs (per cubic yard of cement): | |
|    Cement | $   12.94 |
|    Sand/gravel | 6.42 |
|    Fly ash | 1.13 |
|    Admixture | 1.53 |
|    Driver labor | 3.24 |
|    Mechanics | 1.43 |
|    Plant operations (batching and cleanup) | 1.39 |
|    Loader operator | 0.50 |
|    Truck parts | 1.75 |
|    Fuel | 1.48 |
|    Other | 3.27 |
|    Total variable costs | $   35.08 |
| Fixed costs (annual): | |
|    Salaries | $ 135,000 |
|    Insurance | 75,000 |
|    Telephone | 5,000 |
|    Depreciation | 58,200* |
|    Utilities | 25,000 |
|    Total fixed costs | $ 298,200 |

\* Straight-line depreciation is calculated by using all initial investment costs over a 10-year period assuming no salvage value.

After reviewing these data, Karl Flemming, vice president of operations, argued against the proposed plant. Karl was concerned because the plant would earn significantly less than the normal 8.3% return on sales. All other plants in the company were earning between 7.5 and 8.5% on sales. Karl also noted that it would take more than 5 years to recover the total initial outlay of $582,000. In the past, the company had always insisted that payback be no more than 4 years. The company's cost of capital is 10%. Assume that there are no income taxes.

**Required:**

1. Prepare a variable-costing income statement for the proposed plant. Compute the ratio of net income to sales. Is Karl correct that the return on sales is significantly lower than the company average?
2. Compute the payback period for the proposed plant. Is Karl right that the payback period is greater than 4 years? Explain. Suppose you were told that the equipment being transferred from Wyoming could be sold for its book value. Would this affect your answer?
3. Compute the NPV and the IRR for the proposed plant. Would your answer be affected if you were told that the furniture and equipment could be sold for their book values? If so, repeat the analysis with this effect considered.
4. Compute the cubic yards of cement that must be sold for the new plant to break even. Using this break-even volume, compute the NPV and the IRR. Would the investment be acceptable? If so, explain why an investment that promises to do nothing more than break even can be viewed as acceptable.
5. Compute the volume of cement that must be sold for the IRR to equal the firm's cost of capital. Using this volume, compute the firm's expected annual income. Explain this result.

## Relevant Costing, Cost-Based Pricing, Cost Behavior, and Net Present Value Analysis for NoFat

| Chapters | Objectives | Cornerstones |
|----------|-----------|--------------|
| 3 | 3-1 | 7-2 |
| 7 | 7-1 | 13-2 |
| 13 | 13-2 | 13-8 |
| 14 | 13-4 | 14-3 |
| | 14-1 | 14-5 |
| | 14-3 | |
| | 14-6 | |

*The purpose of this integrated exercise is to demonstrate how a special sales-relevant decision analysis relies on knowledge of cost behavior (including variable, fixed, and batch costs) and how the adoption of a long-term time horizon can affect the final decision.*

## Special Sales Offer Relevant Analysis

NoFat manufactures one product, olestra, and sells it to large potato chip manufacturers as the key ingredient in nonfat snack foods, including Ruffles, Lays, Doritos, and Tostitos brand products.[1] For each of the past 3 years, sales of olestra have been far less than the expected annual volume of 125,000 pounds. Therefore, the company has ended each year with significant unused capacity. Due to a short shelf life, NoFat must sell every pound of olestra that it produces each year. As a result, NoFat's controller, Allyson Ashley, has decided to seek out potential special sales offers from other companies. One company, Patterson Union (PU)—a toxic waste cleanup company—offered to buy 10,000 pounds of olestra from NoFat during December for a price of $2.20 per pound. PU discovered through its research that olestra has proven to be very effective in cleaning up toxic waste locations designated as Superfund Sites by the U.S. Environmental Protection Agency.[2] Allyson was excited, noting that "This is another way to use our expensive olestra plant!"

The annual costs incurred by NoFat to produce and sell 100,000 pounds of olestra are as follows:

| | |
|---|---|
| Variable costs per pound: | |
| Direct materials | $1.00 |
| Variable manufacturing overhead | 0.75 |
| Sales commissions | 0.50 |
| Direct manufacturing labor | 0.25 |
| Total fixed costs: | |
| Advertising | $3,000 |
| Customer hotline service | 4,000 |
| Machine set-ups | 40,000 |
| Plant machinery lease | 12,000 |

[1] Over 7 billion servings of Olean (the Procter & Gamble brand name for olestra) have been consumed. See further information at the Procter & Gamble website: www.olean.com/default.asp?p=products&id=fll.

[2] This exercise is based on facts reported in the business press [e.g., Nanci Hellmich and Bruce Horovitz, "Fat Substitute Olestra Eyed as Hazardous Waste Cleaner: Potato Chips Sales Fall Short," *USA TODAY* (May 31, 2001): 1A].

# EXPERIENCE MANAGERIAL DECISIONS
## with Google

You probably are familiar with the famous business phrase "Cash Is King." In fact, cash is so important that it has its own financial statement—the statement of cash flows. Cash flows, particularly their source and timing, are especially important for high-growth companies.

**Google** is one of the fastest growing companies in U.S. history. Many companies are pleased with double-digit growth (e.g., at least 10%). But from 2006 through 2009, Google's revenue grew at a triple-digit annualized rate. In addition, its stock price has skyrocketed from its initial public offering price of $85 in 2004 to over $600 per share by the end of 2009, making the two founders multibillionaires.[1] How has Google grown at such an amazing pace, and what are some of the impacts of this growth on the company?

Google's statement of cash flows contained in its annual report helps answer this question.[2] The statement shows that Google's cash balance increased during 2009 from a beginning balance of $8,656,670,000 to an ending balance of $10,197,590,000. The statement of cash flows breaks this total cash flow amount into three categories: operating, investing, and financing. Google's impressive growth is reflected partly in its cash flows from operating activities. Driven by soaring sales, Google's net cash *provided* by *operating* activities almost quadrupled from 2005 through 2009, increasing from $2,459,400,000 to $9,316,200,000. Also, the statement shows that heavy investments in marketable and nonmarketable securities explain the company's relatively large net cash outflows, as represented by the net amount of cash *used* for *investing* activities of $8,019,210,000. Finally, the statement of cash flows indicates that the company issued stock in 2009 that added $90,270,000 of cash from financing activities. Other financing activities provided $143,140,000. Therefore, these three important categories of cash inflows and outflows—operating, investing, and financing—go a long way in helping to explain Google's business activities and their impact on the king of all measures—cash!

> *"Google is one of the fastest growing companies in U.S. history. Many companies are pleased with double-digit growth, but from 2006 through 2009, Google's revenue grew at a triple-digit annualized rate."*

[1] http://moneycentral.msn.com/investor/charts/chartdl.aspx?Symbol=US%3aGOOG provides historical stock prices for Google accessed July 5, 2010.
[2] http://moneycentral.msn.com/companyreport?Symbol=US%3agoog provides the statement of cash flows for the years 2005 to 2009 accessed July 5, 2010.

# OVERVIEW OF THE STATEMENT OF CASH FLOWS

The cash information provided by **Google** illustrates that management needs to understand the sources and uses of cash within its own company to assess its financing capabilities. Google has tremendous cash resources which enables the company to easily invest in new product developments and expand its revenue-generating capability. For example, Google recently announced a cooperative venture with **DISH Network, LL** to develop an integrated multichannel and web TV platform.[3] In general, management should raise a number of questions relating to cash management. For example, can the company make necessary purchases or investments using cash generated from operations? Will the company need to borrow all or some of the cash it needs for various purposes? If borrowing is necessary, can the debt be serviced? Can some or all of the cash be raised by issuing additional capital stock?

Answers to these questions and others like them are not available in a company's income statement or balance sheet. A third financial statement—the statement of cash flows—does provide this information. All firms that are registered with the U.S. Securities and Exchange Commission (SEC) must issue a statement of cash flows.

## Cash Defined

*Cash* is defined as both currency and cash equivalents. **Cash equivalents** are highly liquid investments such as Treasury bills, money market funds, and commercial paper. Many firms, as part of their cash management programs, invest their excess cash in these short-term securities. Because of their high liquidity, these short-term investments are treated as cash for the statement of cash flows. For example, suppose that a company has $100,000 of cash and $200,000 of marketable securities on its beginning balance sheet. The total cash at the beginning of the year would be measured as $300,000.

## Sources and Uses of Cash

The **statement of cash flows** provides information regarding the sources and uses of a firm's cash (as illustrated in Exhibit 15.1). Activities that increase cash are sources of

---

( EXHIBIT 15.1 )

**Sources and Uses of Cash**

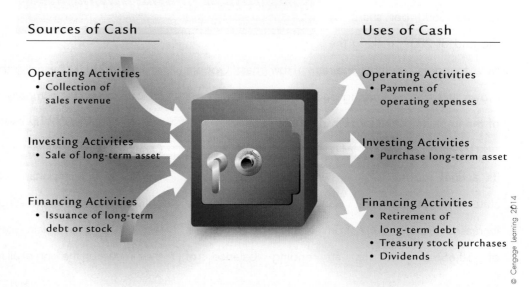

Sources of Cash

**Operating Activities**
- Collection of sales revenue

**Investing Activities**
- Sale of long-term asset

**Financing Activities**
- Issuance of long-term debt or stock

Uses of Cash

**Operating Activities**
- Payment of operating expenses

**Investing Activities**
- Purchase long-term asset

**Financing Activities**
- Retirement of long-term debt
- Treasury stock purchases
- Dividends

© Cengage Learning 2014

---

[3] http://moneycentral.msn.com/news/ticker/sigdev.aspx?Symbol=US%3aGOOG accessed, July 5, 2010.

cash and are referred to as **cash inflows**. Activities that decrease cash are uses of cash and referred to as **cash outflows**.

The statement provides additional information by classifying cash flows into three categories: cash flows from operating activities, cash flows from investing activities, and cash flows from financing activities.

- **Operating activities** are the ongoing, day-to-day, revenue-generating activities of an organization. Typically, operating cash flows involve increases or decreases in either current assets or current liabilities. Cash inflows from operating activities come from the collection of sales revenues. Cash outflows are caused by payment for operating costs. The difference between the two produces the net cash inflow (outflow) from operations.
- **Investing activities** are those activities that involve the acquisition or sale of long-term assets. Long-term assets may be productive assets (e.g., acquiring new equipment) or long-term activities (e.g., acquiring stock in another company).
- **Financing activities** are those activities that raise (provide) cash from (to) creditors and owners. Although interest payments could be seen as financing outflows, the statement includes these payments in the operating section.

This classification, referred to as the **activity format**, is the format that should be followed in preparing the statement of cash flows.

Cornerstone 15.1 shows how activities can be classified into the three categories and identified as sources or uses of cash.

## concept Q&A

Explain why disclosing the sources and uses of cash are so important for potential users of a statement of cash flows.

**Answer:**

Knowing the sources of cash—especially from operating activities—provides a user with a good idea of a company's financial strength and its long-term viability. The decision to invest in a company is much safer if a potential investor—be it a bank or buyer—knows how much cash is being produced, where it is coming from, and the requirements for using cash. A firm's value is inextricably tied to its cash flows.

## Classifying Activities and Identifying Them as Sources or Uses of Cash

CORNERSTONE

15.1

**Why:**

Operating activities, investing activities, and financing activities provide cash (cash inflows) and uses cash (cash outflows). Operating activities are day-to-day revenue generating activities. Investing activities involve the sale and acquisition of long-term assets. Financing activities are associated with cash flows involving creditors and investors.

**Information:**

During the last 2 years of operation, Wiggum Company engaged in the following activities:

1. issuing long-term debt
2. paying cash dividends
3. reporting unprofitable operations
4. issuing capital stock
5. reducing long-term debt
6. retiring capital stock
7. selling long-term assets (e.g., plant, equipment, and securities)
8. reporting profitable operations
9. purchasing long-term assets

**Required:**

Classify each of these activities as belonging to the operating, investing, or financing categories and identify them as sources or uses of cash.

**Solution:**

1. financing, source of cash
2. financing, use of cash
3. operating, use of cash
4. financing, source of cash
5. financing, use of cash
6. financing, use of cash
7. investing, source of cash
8. operating, source of cash
9. investing, use of cash

## Noncash Exchanges

Occasionally, investing and financing activities take place without affecting cash. These are referred to as **noncash investing and financing activities**. A direct exchange of noncurrent balance sheet items may occur. For example, land may be exchanged for common stock. These noncash transactions must also be disclosed in a supplementary schedule attached to the statement. The requirement to report noncash financing and investing activity is essentially an "all-financial-resources approach." Since the major purpose of the statement is to provide cash flow information, the noncash nature of these transactions should be identified and highlighted in the supplementary schedule.

## Methods for Calculating Operating Cash Flows

The two approaches for calculating operating cash flows are the *indirect method* and the *direct method.* The two methods differ only on how the cash flows from *operating activities* are calculated:

- The **indirect method** computes operating cash flows by *adjusting net income* for items that do not affect cash flows.
- The **direct method** computes operating cash flows by *adjusting each line on the income statement* to reflect cash flows.

For example, revenue on an accrual basis is adjusted to reflect only cash revenue. If the direct method is used, companies must also provide a supplementary schedule that shows how net income is reconciled with operating cash flows. This requirement means that direct method users must also provide the information associated with the indirect method. On the other hand, if the indirect method is used, there is no need to provide a line-by-line adjustment as found in the direct method. Not surprisingly, the indirect method is by far the most widely used.

**ETHICAL DECISIONS**    The need to report a strong cash position for obtaining loans and equity capital may invite potential abuse. For example, at the end of a fiscal year, early deliveries of goods sold on credit (to reduce inventories) coupled with deliberate one-time special arrangements for secretive cash side payments by a third party to cover the increase in accounts receivables would show a stronger cash position than a company really has. Of course, such behaviors are deceptive and unethical. Ethical professional practices require fair, objective, and accurate reporting. ●

OBJECTIVE ❷

Prepare a statement of cash flows using the indirect method.

# PREPARATION OF THE STATEMENT: INDIRECT METHOD

Five basic steps are followed in preparing a statement of cash flows:

**Step 1.** *Compute the change in cash for the period.* This figure is the difference between the ending and beginning cash balances shown on the balance sheets. It must equal the net cash inflow or outflow shown on the statement of cash flows.

**Step 2.** *Compute the cash flows from operating activities.* Use the period's beginning and ending balance sheets and information about other events and transactions to adjust the period's income statement to an operating cash flow basis.

**Step 3.** *Identify the cash flows from investing activities.* Use the period's beginning and ending balance sheets and information about other events and transactions to identify the cash flows associated with the sale and purchase of long-term assets.

**Step 4.** *Identify the cash flows from financing activities.* Use the period's beginning and ending balance sheets to identify the cash flows associated with long-term debt and capital stock.

**Step 5.** *Prepare the statement of cash flows based on the previous four steps.*

Exhibit 15.2 provides comparative balance sheets for the Lemmons Company. These comparative balance sheets provide essential information for preparing a statement of cash flows.

( EXHIBIT 15.2 )

**Balance Sheets: Lemmons Company**

| Lemmons Company<br>Comparative Balance Sheets<br>At December 31, 2013 and 2014 | | | | |
|---|---|---|---|---|
| | | | Net Changes | |
| | **2013** | **2014** | **Debit** | **Credit** |
| **Assets** | | | | |
| Cash | $ 70,000 | $ 175,000 | $105,000 | |
| Accounts receivable | 140,000 | 112,500 | | $ 27,500 |
| Inventories | 50,000 | 60,000 | 10,000 | |
| Plant and equipment | 400,000 | 410,000 | 10,000 | |
| Accumulated depreciation | (200,000) | (210,000) | | 10,000 |
| Land | 200,000 | 287,500 | 87,500 | |
| Total assets | $ 660,000 | $ 835,000 | | |
| **Liabilities and stockholders' equity** | | | | |
| Accounts payable | $ 120,000 | $ 95,000 | 25,000 | |
| Mortgage payable | | 100,000 | | 100,000 |
| Common stock | 75,000 | 75,000 | | |
| Paid-in capital in excess of par | 100,000 | 100,000 | | |
| Retained earnings | 365,000 | 465,000 | | 100,000 |
| Total liabilities and stockholders' equity | $ 660,000 | $ 835,000 | $237,500 | $237,500 |

© Cengage Learning 2014

## Step 1: Compute the Change in Cash

Cornerstone 15.2 shows how to compute the change in cash.

## Computing the Change in Cash

CORNERSTONE

15.2

**Why:**

The change in cash for a period is the difference between the ending and beginning cash balances of cash and cash equivalents on the balance sheet.

**Information:**

Exhibit 15.2 showed the following information on cash and cash equivalents for Lemmons Company:

| | | | Net Changes | |
|---|---|---|---|---|
| **Assets** | **2014** | **2013** | **Debit** | **Credit** |
| Cash | $175,000 | $70,000 | $105,000 | — |

**Required:**

Calculate the change in cash.

**Solution:**

$$\text{Change in Cash} = \text{Ending Cash Balance} - \text{Beginning Cash Balance}$$
$$= \$175,000 - \$70,000 = \$105,000$$

© Pixelfabrik/Alamy

In Cornerstone 15.2 (p. 679), notice that the change in cash flow is simply the change in cash, which for Lemmons is an increase of $105,000 from 2013 to 2014. This number serves as a control figure for the statement of cash flows. The sum of the operating, investing, and financing cash flows must equal $105,000.

## Step 2: Compute Operating Cash Flows

Income statements are prepared on an accrual basis. Thus, revenues and expenses that involve no cash inflows and outflows might be recognized. Also, cash inflows and outflows that are not recognized on the income statement might occur. The accrual income statement can be converted to an operating cash flow basis by making four adjustments to net income:

a. Add to net income any increases in current liabilities and decreases in noncash current assets.

b. Deduct from net income any decreases in current liabilities and increases in noncash current assets.

c. Add to or deduct from net income the remaining net income items that do not affect cash flows (e.g., add back noncash expenses).

d. Eliminate any income items that belong in either the investing or financing section.

Cornerstone 15.3 lists these four types of adjustments and illustrates how to calculate the operating cash flows that use them.

CORNERSTONE

## 15.3

## Calculating Operating Cash Flows Using the Indirect Method

**Why:**

Income statements are prepared on an accrual basis. Thus, net income is converted to operating cash flow by making adjustments for revenues and expenses that do not involve cash inflows and outflows.

**Information:**

Exhibit 15.2 (p. 679) showed the following information on current assets and liabilities for Lemmons Company:

|  |  |  | Net Changes | |
|---|---|---|---|---|
|  | **2013** | **2014** | **Debit** | **Credit** |
| **Current assets** |  |  |  |  |
| Accounts receivable | $140,000 | $112,500 |  | $27,500 |
| Inventories | 50,000 | 60,000 | $10,000 |  |
| **Current liabilities** |  |  |  |  |
| Accounts payable | 120,000 | 95,000 | 25,000 |  |

The income statement for Lemmons Company follows:

**Lemmons Company**
**Income Statement**
**For the Year Ended December 31, 2014**

| | |
|---|---|
| Revenues | $ 480,000 |
| Gain on sale of equipment | 20,000 |
| Less: Cost of goods sold | (260,000) |
| Less: Depreciation expense | (50,000) |
| Less: Interest expense | (10,000) |
| Net income | $ 180,000 |

*(Continued)*

**Required:**

Compute operating cash flows using the indirect method.

**Solution:**

| | |
|---|---|
| Net income | $180,000 |
| Add (deduct) adjusting items: | |
|    Decrease in accounts receivable | 27,500   (Type A adjustment) |
|    Decrease in accounts payable | (25,000) (Type B adjustment) |
|    Increase in inventories | (10,000) (Type B adjustment) |
|    Depreciation expense | 50,000   (Type C adjustment) |
|    Gain on sale of equipment | (20,000) (Type D adjustment) |
|      Net cash from operating activities | $202,500 |

Five adjusting items are used to compute operating cash flows for Lemmons Company. These five entries exhibit each of the four types of adjustments.

**Decrease in Accounts Receivable (Example of Type A Adjustment)** From Cornerstone 15.3, operating income is increased by a $27,500 decrease in accounts receivable. A decrease in accounts receivable represents a decrease in a noncash current asset. It indicates that cash collections from customers were greater than the revenues reported on the income statement by the amount of the decrease. Thus, to compute the operating cash flow, the decrease must be added to net income. To understand fully why this amount is added back to net income, consider the cash collection activity of Lemmons.

At the beginning of the year, Lemmons reported accounts receivable of $140,000 (Exhibit 15.2). This beginning balance represents revenues recognized during 2013 but not collected. During 2014, additional operating revenues of $480,000 were earned and recognized on the income statement. Lemmons, therefore, had a total cash collection potential of $620,000 ($140,000 + $480,000). Since the ending balance of accounts receivable was $112,500, the company collected cash totaling $507,500 ($620,000 − $112,500). The cash collected from operations was $27,500 greater than the amount recognized on the income statement ($507,500 vs. $480,000), an amount exactly equal to the decrease in accounts receivable. Thus, the change in accounts receivable can be used to adjust revenues from an accrual to a cash basis.

**Decrease in Accounts Payable and Increase in Inventories (Examples of Type B Adjustment)** Cornerstone 15.3 shows that the second adjusting item in the operating section reflects a decrease in accounts payable of $25,000 and the third an increase in inventories of $10,000. Taken together, these two items adjust the cost of goods sold to a cash basis. A decrease in accounts payable means that cash payments to creditors were larger than the purchases made during the period; the difference is the amount that accounts payable decreased. The total cash payment made to creditors, therefore, is equal to the purchases plus the decrease in accounts payable. Since inventories increased, purchases are larger than the cost of goods sold by the amount that inventories increased. Thus, by deducting both the decrease in accounts payable and the increase in inventories, the cost of goods sold figure is increased to reflect the cash outflow for goods during the period.

Using information from Exhibit 15.2, the following statement of costs of goods sold can be prepared for Lemmons. (In this statement, goods available for sale and purchases are obtained by working backwards from cost of goods sold.)

| | |
|---|---:|
| Beginning inventory | $ 50,000 |
| Purchases | 270,000 |
| Goods available for sale | $320,000 |
| Less: Ending inventory | (60,000) |
| Cost of goods sold | $260,000 |

Adding purchases to the beginning balance in accounts payable (from Exhibit 15.2, p. 679) yields the total potential payments to creditors: $390,000 ($270,000 + $120,000). Subtracting the ending balance of accounts payable (Exhibit 15.2) from the total potential payments gives the total cash payments for the year: $295,000 ($390,000 − $95,000). By deducting the decrease in accounts payable ($25,000) and the increase in inventories ($10,000), an additional $35,000 is deducted, bringing the cost of goods sold figure from $260,000 to $295,000. This amount equals the total cash payment for goods during 2014.

**Depreciation Expense (Example of Type C Adjustment)** While depreciation expense is a legitimate deduction from revenues to arrive at net income, it does not require any cash outlay. As a noncash expense, it should be added back to net income as part of the adjustment needed to produce operating cash flow.

**Gain on the Sale of Equipment (Example of Type D Adjustment)** The sale of long-term assets is a non-operating activity and should be classified in the section that reveals the firm's investing activities. Furthermore, the gain on the sale of the equipment does not reveal the total cash received. It gives only the cash received in excess of the equipment's book value. The correct procedure is to deduct the gain and report the full cash inflow from the sale in the investing section of the statement of cash flows.

## Step 3: Compute Investing Cash Flows

Investing activities include the purchase and sale of long-term assets (plant and equipment, land, and long-term securities). Cornerstone 15.4 shows how to compute investing cash flows for Lemmons. The company had three investing transactions in 2014, which are summarized in the investing section.

CORNERSTONE

15.4

## Computing Investing Cash Flows

**Why:**

Investing activities include the purchase and sale of long-term assets (plant, equipment, land, and long-term securities).

**Information:**

Equipment with a book value of $50,000 was sold for $70,000 (original purchase cost of $90,000). New equipment was purchased. Exhibit 15.2 showed the following information on investing transactions for Lemmons Company:

| | | | Net Changes | |
|---|---|---|---|---|
| **Long-Term Assets** | **2013** | **2014** | **Debit** | **Credit** |
| Plant and equipment | $ 400,000 | $ 410,000 | $10,000 | |
| Accumulated depreciation | (200,000) | (210,000) | | $10,000 |
| Land | 200,000 | 287,500 | 87,500 | |

*(Continued)*

**Required:**

Calculate the investing cash flows.

**Solution:**

| | |
|---|---:|
| Sale of equipment | $ 70,000[a] |
| Purchase of equipment | (100,000)[b] |
| Purchase of land | (87,500)[c] |
| Net cash from investing activities | $(117,500) |

[a] The sale of long-term assets is an investing activity. Thus, the receipt of the $70,000 should be reported in the investing section.

[b] There is no explicit information concerning the purchase price of equipment. The purchase price is inferred from the comparative balance sheet information as well as the information about the equipment originally costing $90,000 that was sold and removed from the books. The purchase price of the new equipment can be computed by the following procedure:

| | |
|---|---:|
| Beginning plant and equipment | $400,000 |
| Purchase of equipment | ? |
| Less: Sale of equipment | (90,000) |
| Ending balance, plant, and equipment | $410,000 |

The "plug figure" for the equipment purchase must be $100,000. (_Note:_ $40,000 of accumulated depreciation was deducted from the books, removing the accumulated depreciation associated with the equipment that was sold, and $50,000 was added to reflect the depreciation expense for 2014, giving a net increase of $10,000.)

[c] The comparative balance sheets reveal that land was purchased for $87,500. This transaction also should appear in the investing section.

## Step 4: Compute Financing Cash Flows

Issuance of long-term debt or capital stock can produce cash inflows. Retirement of debt or stock and payment of dividends produce cash outflows. Cornerstone 15.5 shows how to compute the financing cash flows for Lemmons.

## Computing Financing Cash Flows

**Why:**

Issuance of long-term debt or capital stock produces cash inflows. Retirement of long-term debt or stock and payment of dividends produce cash outflows.

**Information:**

Net income of $180,000 was earned in 2014. Exhibit 15.2 showed the following information on financing transactions for Lemmons Company:

| | | | Net Changes | |
|---|---:|---:|---:|---:|
| | 2013 | 2014 | Debit | Credit |
| Mortgage payable | | $100,000 | | $100,000 |
| Common stock | $ 75,000 | 75,000 | | |
| Paid-in capital in excess of par | 100,000 | 100,000 | | |
| Retained earnings | 365,000 | 465,000 | | 100,000 |

**Required:**

Compute the financing cash flows for 2014.

_(Continued)_

## CORNERSTONE
## 15.5

*(Continued)*

**Solution:**

| | |
|---|---:|
| Issuance of mortgage | $100,000[a] |
| Payment of dividends | (80,000)[b] |
| Net cash from financing activities | $ 20,000 |

[a] The comparative balance sheets show that the only change in long-term debt and capital stock accounts is the apparent issue of a mortgage during 2014. The proceeds from this mortgage should be shown as a source of cash in the financing section.

[b]

| | |
|---|---:|
| Retained earnings, end of 2013 | $365,000 |
| Net income (2014) | 180,000 |
| Total | $545,000 |
| Less retained earnings, end of 2014 | 465,000 |
| Dividends paid in 2014 | $ 80,000 |

Since dividends represent a return on the funds provided by stockholders, this amount should be shown in the financing section.

## Step 5: Prepare the Statement of Cash Flows

The outcomes of Steps 2 through 4 correspond to the individual sections needed for the statement of cash flows. Cornerstone 15.6 shows how to prepare this statement.

## CORNERSTONE
## 15.6

## Preparing the Statement of Cash Flows

**Why:**

The statement of cash flows summarizes the flows for operating, investing, and financing activities.

**Information:**

Refer to the information for Lemmons Company in Cornerstones 15.2 (p. 679) through 15.5.

**Required:**

Prepare a statement of cash flows for Lemmons.

**Solution:**

**Lemmons Company**
**Statement of Cash Flows**
**For the Year Ended December 31, 2014**

| | | |
|---|---:|---:|
| Cash flows from operating activities: | | |
| Net income | $ 180,000 | |
| Add (deduct) adjusting items: | | |
| Decrease in accounts receivable | 27,500 | |
| Decrease in accounts payable | (25,000) | |
| Increase in inventories | (10,000) | |
| Depreciation expense | 50,000 | |
| Gain on sale of equipment | (20,000) | |
| Net cash from operating activities | | $ 202,500 |

*(Continued)*

CORNERSTONE

**15.6**

*(Continued)*

| Cash flows from investing activities: | | |
|---|---|---|
| Sale of equipment | $ 70,000 | |
| Purchase of equipment | (100,000) | |
| Purchase of land | (87,500) | |
| Net cash from investing activities | | (117,500) |
| Cash flows from financing activities: | | |
| Issuance of mortgage | $ 100,000 | |
| Payment of dividends | (80,000) | |
| Net cash from financing activities | | 20,000 |
| Net increase in cash | | $ 105,000 |

Notice that the change in cash flow computed in Step 1 from the comparative balance sheets corresponds to the net increase in cash identified in the statement of cash flows. The computation produced by Step 1 serves as a control on the accuracy of Steps 2 through 4.

# YOU DECIDE    The Importance of Cash Flow Analysis for Acquisition Decisions

You are the Vice President of Finance for Karabekian Company. Terry Kitchen, the CEO, calls a meeting with you and Kilgore Trout, the Vice President of Operations. Kitchen is very interested in acquiring Flemington, a small, private company that manufactures a component used in the construction of Karabekian's major product. Kitchen expresses his view that the small company appears to be a good buy and will contribute to the long-run objective of vertical integration. He is curious, though, why the owner now appears eager to sell when the last time he was approached, he was strongly opposed to any deal. He wonders whether the company might now be having cash-flow problems.

Trout doubts that this could be the case and points out that the income statements for the past several years show stable profits. Moreover, the most recent balance sheet shows a small but positive cash balance and the working capital appears to be fairly stable. Kitchen then turns you and asks you the following:

**Do you agree with this analysis? Does this financial evidence mean there is no cash-flow problem? If not, then what do we need to know?**

The answer to the first question is definitely no. The positive cash balance on the balance sheet doesn't say much about cash

flows—nothing about the sources and uses of cash during the reporting period is known. Furthermore, Trout needs to be very cautious about interpreting stable profits and working capital. Many companies have reported stable profits and working capital for several periods and then have gone bankrupt in spite of these signals. In answer to the second question, before Kitchen commits formally to any acquisition, he needs to evaluate Flemington's current cash flows and assess its future cash flow potential. If the firm is in a current cash crisis, acquiring it will cost a great deal more than the purchase price. Also, if the firm is in a cash crisis, Kitchen still may be able to work out a deal but on much more favorable terms. You should advise Kitchen to get a statement of cash flows for the last 5 years. This statement should show cash flows from operations as well as cash flows from the firm's financing and investing activities.

**When trying to determine information about cash flows, the statement of cash flows is the most valuable source of information because it shows the cash flows from operating, financing, and investing activities.**

# THE DIRECT METHOD: AN ALTERNATIVE APPROACH

OBJECTIVE ❸

Calculate operating cash flows using the direct method.

The section of operating cash flows in Cornerstone 15.3 (p. 680) computes cash flows by adjusting net income for items that do not affect cash flows. This approach is known as the indirect method. Some individuals prefer to show operating cash flows as the difference between cash receipts and cash payments. To do so, each item on the accrual income statement is adjusted to reflect cash flows. Either approach to computing and presenting operating cash flows may be used; which to use is a matter of preference. However, if a company chooses the direct method, it must also present the indirect method in a separate schedule.

## Here's the Real Kicker

The statement of cash flows is a report required of all SEC-registered firms. **Stillwater Designs**, however, is not a public company and therefore is not subject to the requirement to produce a statement of cash flows. The management of Stillwater Designs does not see any value in producing this statement, and therefore the accounting department does not produce it. A daily cash position report is provided to management. Furthermore, it is a very easy matter to identify the source of the cash flows—either they come from operating, investing, or financing activities. Thus, if this information is ever explicitly needed, it can be provided.

Interestingly, Stillwater Designs' creditors have not demanded this statement as information needed for granting loans. Income statements and balance sheets have provided the needed information. Stillwater Designs' chief accountant, Jeanne Snyder, noted that bank officers tend to be much more interested in assets that can act as collateral such as accounts receivable and inventory.

The same adjustments and the same reasoning are used to produce the operating cash flows for both the direct and indirect methods. However, the presentation of the information is different. In the direct method, each line on the income statement is adjusted to produce a cash flow income statement. Cornerstone 15.7 shows how to compute operating cash flows using this approach for Lemmons.

**CORNERSTONE**

**15.7**

## Calculating Operating Cash Flows Using the Direct Method

**Why:**

The direct method calculates operating cash flows by adjusting each line of the income statement for revenues and expenses that do not involve cash inflows or outflows.

**Information:**

Exhibit 15.2 (p. 679) showed the following information on current assets and liabilities for Lemmons Company:

|  | 2013 | 2014 | Net Changes Debit | Net Changes Credit |
|---|---|---|---|---|
| **Current assets** |  |  |  |  |
| Accounts receivable | $140,000 | $112,500 |  | $27,500 |
| Inventories | 50,000 | 60,000 | $10,000 |  |
| **Current liabilities** |  |  |  |  |
| Accounts payable | 120,000 | 95,000 | 25,000 |  |

*(Continued)*

The income statement for Lemmons follows:

**Lemmons Company**
**Income Statement**
**For the Year Ended December 31, 2014**

| | |
|---|---:|
| Revenues | $ 480,000 |
| Gain on sale of equipment | 20,000 |
| Less: Cost of goods sold | (260,000) |
| Less: Depreciation expense | (50,000) |
| Less: Interest expense | (10,000) |
| Net income | $ 180,000 |

**Required:**

Calculate operating cash flows using the direct method.

**Solution:**

| | Income Statement | Adjustments | Cash Flows |
|---|---:|---:|---:|
| Revenues | $ 480,000 | $ 27,500[a] | $ 507,500 |
| Gain on sale of equipment | 20,000 | (20,000) | |
| Less: Cost of goods sold | (260,000) | (25,000)[b] | |
| | | (10,000)[c] | (295,000) |
| Less: Depreciation expense | (50,000) | 50,000 | |
| Less: Interest expense | (10,000) | | (10,000) |
| Net income | $ 180,000 | | |
| Net cash from operating activities | | | $ 202,500 |

[a] Decrease in accounts receivable.
[b] Decrease in accounts payable.
[c] Increase in inventories.

# WORKSHEET APPROACH TO THE STATEMENT OF CASH FLOWS

OBJECTIVE

Prepare a statement of cash flows using a worksheet approach.

As transactions increase in number and complexity, a worksheet becomes a useful and almost necessary aid in preparing the statement of cash flows. The approach minimizes confusion and allows careful consideration of all the details underlying an analysis of cash flows. One advantage of a worksheet is the fact that it uses a spreadsheet format, allowing the preparer to use a computer and spreadsheet software like Excel. Furthermore, a worksheet offers the user an efficient, logical means to organize the data needed to prepare a statement of cash flows. Although the worksheet itself is not the statement of cash flows, the statement can be easily extracted from the worksheet. To illustrate, refer to the comparative balance sheets of Portermart Company presented in Exhibit 15.3 (p. 688).

Cornerstone 15.8 shows how to prepare a worksheet for Portermart's statement of cash flows. Notice that the worksheet is divided into two major sections: one corresponding to the balance sheet classifications and one corresponding to the statement of cash flows classifications. Four columns are needed: two for the beginning and ending balances of the balance sheet and two to analyze the transactions that produced the changes in cash flows.

## concept Q&A

What are the advantages of a worksheet approach for preparing the statement of cash flows?

**Answer:**

A worksheet reduces confusion, provides a ready way to track the details of a cash flow analysis, and allows the use of spreadsheet programs.

( EXHIBIT 15.3 )

**Balance Sheets: Portermart Company**

| Portermart Company<br>Comparative Balance Sheets<br>At December 31, 2013 and 2014 | | | | |
| --- | --- | --- | --- | --- |
| | | | **Net Changes** | |
| | **2013** | **2014** | **Debit** | **Credit** |
| **Assets** | | | | |
| Cash | $ 90,000 | $183,000 | $ 93,000 | |
| Accounts receivable | 55,000 | 60,000 | 5,000 | |
| Inventory | 80,000 | 55,000 | | $ 25,000 |
| Plant and equipment | 130,000 | 100,000 | | 30,000 |
| Accumulated depreciation | (65,000) | (60,000) | 5,000 | |
| Land | 25,000 | 65,000 | 40,000 | |
| Total assets | $315,000 | $403,000 | | |
| **Liabilities and stockholders' equity** | | | | |
| Accounts payable | $ 40,000 | $ 60,000 | | 20,000 |
| Wages payable | 5,000 | 3,000 | 2,000 | |
| Bonds payable | 30,000 | 20,000 | 10,000 | |
| Preferred stock (no par) | 5,000 | 15,000 | | 10,000 |
| Common stock | 50,000 | 60,000 | | 10,000 |
| Paid-in capital in excess of par | 50,000 | 80,000 | | 30,000 |
| Retained earnings | 135,000 | 165,000 | | 30,000 |
| Total liabilities and stockholders' equity | $315,000 | $403,000 | $155,000 | $155,000 |

© Cengage Learning 2014

The columns for the analysis of transactions are the focus of the worksheet approach. Generally, a debit or credit in a balance sheet column produces a corresponding credit or debit in a cash flow column. Once all changes are accounted for, the statement of cash flows can be prepared (by using the lower half of the worksheet).

CORNERSTONE

**15.8**

## Preparing a Statement of Cash Flows Using a Worksheet Approach

**Why:**

As transactions increase in number and complexity, a worksheet is an efficient and logical way to organize the data needed to prepare a statement of cash flows.

**Information:**

Refer to the comparative balance sheets for Portermart Company in Exhibit 15.3. Other (2014) transactions include the following:

a.  Cash dividends of $10,000 were paid.
b.  Equipment was sold for $8,000. It had an original cost of $30,000 and a book value of $15,000. The loss is included in operating expenses.
c.  Land with a fair market value of $40,000 was acquired by issuing common stock with a par value of $10,000.
d.  One thousand shares of preferred stock (no par) were sold for $10 per share.

*(Continued)*

© Pixelfabrik/Alamy

The income statement for Portermart for 2014 follows:

| | | |
|---|---:|---|
| Sales | $ 400,000 | |
| Less: Cost of goods sold | (250,000) | |
| Gross margin | $ 150,000 | |
| Less: Operating expenses | (110,000) | |
| Net income | $  40,000 | |

**Required:**

Prepare a worksheet for Portermart Company.

**Solution:**

**Worksheet: Portermart Company**

| | 2013 | Transactions Debit | Transactions Credit | 2014 |
|---|---|---|---|---|
| **Assets** | | | | |
| Cash | $ 90,000 | (1) $93,000 | | $183,000 |
| Accounts receivable | 55,000 | (2)   5,000 | | 60,000 |
| Inventory | 80,000 | | (3) $25,000 | 55,000 |
| Plant and equipment | 130,000 | | (4)   30,000 | 100,000 |
| Accumulated depreciation | (65,000) | (4)   15,000 | (5)   10,000 | (60,000) |
| Land | 25,000 | (6)   40,000 | | 65,000 |
| Total assets | $315,000 | | | $403,000 |
| | | | | |
| **Liabilities and stockholders' equity:** | | | | |
| Accounts payable | $ 40,000 | | (7)   20,000 | 60,000 |
| Wages payable | 5,000 | (8)   2,000 | | 3,000 |
| Bonds payable | 30,000 | (9)   10,000 | | 20,000 |
| Preferred stock (no par) | 5,000 | | (10)   10,000 | 15,000 |
| Common stock | 50,000 | | (11)   10,000 | 60,000 |
| Paid-in capital in excess of par | 50,000 | | (11)   30,000 | 80,000 |
| Retained earnings | 135,000 | (13)   10,000 | (12)   40,000 | 165,000 |
| Total liabilities and stockholders' equity | $315,000 | | | $403,000 |
| Cash flows from operating activities: | | | | |
| Net income | | (12)   40,000 | | |
| Depreciation expense | | (5)   10,000 | | |
| Loss on sale of equipment | | (4)   7,000 | | |
| Decrease in inventory | | (3)   25,000 | | |
| Increase in accounts payable | | (7)   20,000 | | |
| Increase in accounts receivable | | | (2)   5,000 | |
| Decrease in wages payable | | | (8)   2,000 | |
| Cash flows from investing activities: | | | | |
| Sale of equipment | | (4)   8,000 | | |
| Cash flows from financing activities: | | | | |
| Reduction in bonds payable | | | (9)   10,000 | |
| Payment of dividends | | | (13)   10,000 | |
| Issuance of preferred stock | | (10)   10,000 | | |
| Net increase in cash | | | (1)   93,000 | |
| Noncash investing and financing activities: | | | | |
| Land acquired with common stock | | (11)   40,000 | (6)   40,000 | |

## Analysis of Transactions

The summary transactions on the worksheet will be explained by examining the items on the worksheet in order of their appearance (essentially equivalent to the numerical order of the entries). The entries are developed by considering each balance sheet item and the associated supplementary information.

**Change in Cash**  Entry (1) identifies the total change in cash during 2014.

| (1) | Cash | 93,000 | |
| | Net increase in cash | | 93,000 |

The actual cash balance increased from the beginning to the end of the year by $93,000.

**Change in Accounts Receivable**  Entry (2) reflects the increase in accounts receivable.

| (2) | Accounts receivable | 5,000 | |
| | Operating cash | | 5,000 |

Increasing accounts receivable means that revenues were recognized on the income statement but not collected. Thus, net income must be adjusted to show that cash inflows from revenues were less by this amount.

**Decrease in Inventory**  Entry (3) reflects the effect of a decrease in inventory on operating cash flow.

| (3) | Operating cash | 25,000 | |
| | Inventory | | 25,000 |

Operating cash should be increased since a decrease in inventory would be included in the cost of goods sold but would not represent a cash outflow.

**Sale of Equipment**  The sale of equipment affects two balance sheet accounts and two cash flow accounts. The effect is captured in Entry (4).

| (4) | Operating cash | 7,000 | |
| | Cash from investing activities | 8,000 | |
| | Accumulated depreciation | 15,000 | |
| | Plant and equipment | | 30,000 |

Operating cash shows an increase because the loss on the sale is a noncash expense and should be added back to net income to arrive at the correct cash provided by operating activities. The equipment is sold for $8,000. This sale produces a cash inflow that is recognized as a cash flow from investing activities. The other two entries reflect the fact that the original cost of the equipment and the accumulated depreciation have been removed from the company's books.

**Depreciation Expense**  Entry (5) shows an increase in operating cash flow because depreciation expense, a noncash expense, is added back to net income.

| (5) | Operating cash | 10,000 | |
| | Accumulated depreciation | | 10,000 |

Although the amount of depreciation expense is not explicitly given, it can be easily computed. The net decrease in the accumulated depreciation account is $5,000 (Exhibit 15.3, p. 688). The sale of the equipment decreased accumulated depreciation by $15,000 (accumulated depreciation removed is equal to original cost minus book value, or $30,000 – $15,000). Thus, the amount of depreciation expense recognized for the period must be $10,000. Depreciation expense increases accumulated depreciation—an increase of $10,000 and a decrease of $15,000 produce a net decrease of $5,000.

**Land for Common Stock**  Three balance sheet accounts are affected in the noncash transaction that acquires land in exchange for common stock. To balance transactions columns, two separate entries [(6) and (11)] are needed.

| | | | |
|---|---|---|---|
| (6) | Land | 40,000 | |
| | Noncash investing activities | | 40,000 |
| (11) | Noncash investing activities | 40,000 | |
| | Common stock | | 10,000 |
| | Paid-in capital in excess of par | | 30,000 |

**Accounts Payable**  Entry (7) provides the adjusting entry for an increase in accounts payable.

| | | | |
|---|---|---|---|
| (7) | Operating cash | 20,000 | |
| | Accounts payable | | 20,000 |

An increase in accounts payable means that some of the purchases were not acquired through the use of cash. Accordingly, the amount of the increase needs to be added back to net income.

**Wages Payable**  Wages payable decreased by $2,000 during 2014. This decrease means that the company had a cash outflow $2,000 larger than the wage expense recognized on the income statement. Entry (8) reflects this $2,000 decrease.

| | | | |
|---|---|---|---|
| (8) | Wages payable | 2,000 | |
| | Operating cash | | 2,000 |

**Bonds Payable**  Bonds payable decreased by $10,000, indicating a cash outflow belonging to the financing section. Entry (9) recognizes the reduction of debt and the associated cash outflow.

| | | | |
|---|---|---|---|
| (9) | Bonds payable | 10,000 | |
| | Cash flow from financing activities | | 10,000 |

**Preferred Stock**  Entry (10) reflects the cash inflow that resulted from the issuance of preferred stock.

| | | | |
|---|---|---|---|
| (10) | Cash flow from financing activities | 10,000 | |
| | Preferred Stock | | 10,000 |

**Net Income**  Net income is assigned to the operating cash flow section by Entry (12).

| | | | |
|---|---|---|---|
| (12) | Operating cash | 40,000 | |
| | Retained earnings | | 40,000 |

**Payment of Dividends**  The payment of dividends is given in Entry (13).

| | | | |
|---|---|---|---|
| (13) | Retained earnings | 10,000 | |
| | Cash flow from financing activities | | 10,000 |

( EXHIBIT 15.4 )

**Worksheet-Derived Statement of Cash Flows for Portermart Company**

| | | |
|---|---:|---:|
| **Cash flows from operating activities:** | | |
| Net income | $40,000 | |
| Add (deduct) adjusting items: | | |
| Depreciation expense | 10,000 | |
| Loss on sale of equipment | 7,000 | |
| Decrease in inventory | 25,000 | |
| Increase in accounts payable | 20,000 | |
| Increase in accounts receivable | (5,000) | |
| Decrease in wages payable | (2,000) | |
| Net cash from operating activities | | $ 95,000 |
| **Cash flows from investing activities:** | | |
| Sale of equipment | | $  8,000 |
| **Cash flows from financing activities:** | | |
| Reduction in bonds payable | $(10,000) | |
| Payment of dividends | (10,000) | |
| Issuance of preferred stock | 10,000 | |
| Net cash from financing activities | | $(10,000) |
| Net increase in cash | | $ 93,000 |
| Noncash investing and financing activities: | | |
| Acquisition of land issuing common stock | | $ 40,000 |

## The Final Step

Once the worksheet is completed, the final step in preparing the statement of cash flows is relatively straightforward. The lower half of the worksheet contains all of the sections needed. The debit column provides the cash inflows, and the credit column provides the cash outflows. The noncash section is an exception; either column may be used to provide the information. The only additional effort needed is to compute subtotals for each section. The statement of cash flows for Portermart is shown in Exhibit 15.4.

# SUMMARY OF LEARNING OBJECTIVES

**LO 1.**   Explain the basic elements of a statement of cash flows.

- Knowing a company's cash flows enables managers, investors, creditors, and others to assess the economic strength and viability of a company by evaluating its current cash flows and by assessing future cash flow potential.
- The Financial Accounting Standards Board (FASB), recognizing the need for cash flow information, recommend that all firms prepare a statement of cash flows.
- The activity format for a statement of cash flows has three sections: cash flows from operating activities, cash flows from investing activities, and cash flows from financing activities. Noncash financing and investing activities also are reported.
- The change in cash for a period is the difference between the beginning and ending balances of the cash account. The change in cash equivalents also is included in the change in cash.
- Operating activities are the main revenue-generating activities engaged in by the organization.
- Operating cash flows are computed by adjusting the period's net income for noncash expenses, accrual effects, and non-operating revenues or expenses.

- Investing activities involve the acquisition and sale of long-term assets.
- Financing activities involve raising outside capital through the issuance of debt and capital stock. Financing activities also involve the retirement of debt and capital stock.

**LO 2.**    Prepare a statement of cash flows using the indirect method.

- Compute the change in cash.
- Compute operating cash flows by adjusting net income for items that do not affect cash flows.
- Identify investing cash flows.
- Identify financing cash flows.
- Assemble the data into a statement of cash flows.
- Preparation of the statement relies on the beginning and ending balance sheets and information regarding other activities and events that may not be fully apparent from the balance sheets themselves.

**LO 3.**    Calculate operating cash flows using the direct method.

- Compute the change in cash.
- Compute operating cash flows by adjusting each line on the income statement to reflect cash flows.
- Identify investing cash flows.
- Identify financing cash flows.
- Assemble the data into a statement of cash flows.
- Preparation of the statement relies on the beginning and ending balance sheets and information regarding other activities and events that may not be fully apparent from the balance sheets themselves.

**LO 4.**    Prepare a statement of cash flows using a worksheet approach.

- Worksheets can be used to organize the preparation of the statement of cash flows.
- Worksheets offer increased efficiency in form and the added convenience of spreadsheet software packages.

CORNERSTONES

# KEY TERMS

Activity format, 677
Cash equivalents, 676
Cash inflows, 677
Cash outflows, 677
Direct method, 678
Financing activities, 677

Indirect method, 678
Investing activities, 677
Noncash investing and financing activities, 678
Operating activities, 677
Statement of cash flows, 676

# REVIEW PROBLEMS

## I. Statement of Cash Flows: Indirect Method

The following balance sheets are taken from the records of Golding Inc.:

|  | 2013 | 2014 |
|---|---|---|
| **Assets** | | |
| Cash | $130,000 | $150,000 |
| Accounts receivable | 25,000 | 20,000 |
| Plant and equipment | 50,000 | 60,000 |
| Accumulated depreciation | (20,000) | (25,000) |
| Land | 10,000 | 10,000 |
| Total assets | $195,000 | $215,000 |
| **Liabilities and equity** | | |
| Accounts payable | $ 10,000 | $  5,000 |
| Bonds payable | 8,000 | 18,000 |
| Common stock | 120,000 | 120,000 |
| Retained earnings | 57,000 | 72,000 |
| Total liabilities and equity | $195,000 | $215,000 |

Additional information is as follows: (a) Equipment costing $10,000 was purchased at year-end. No equipment was sold; (b) Net income for the year was $25,000; $10,000 in dividends were paid.

**Required:**

1. Prepare a statement of cash flows using the indirect method.

**Solution:**

1. Cash flow change: $150,000 – $130,000 = $20,000

2. Operating cash flows:

| | |
|---|---|
| Net income | $25,000 |
| Add (deduct): | |
| Decrease in accounts receivable | 5,000 |
| Depreciation expense | 5,000 |
| Decrease in accounts payable | (5,000) |
| Net cash from operating activities | $30,000 |

3. Cash from investing activities for purchase of equipment is $(10,000).

4. Cash from financing activities:

| | |
|---|---|
| Payment of dividends | $(10,000) |
| Issuance of bonds | 10,000 |
| Net cash from financing activities | $    0 |

5.

**Golding Inc.**
**Statement of Cash Flows**
**For the Year Ended December 31, 2014**

| | | |
|---|---:|---:|
| **Cash flows from operating activities:** | | |
| Net income | $ 25,000 | |
| Add (deduct) adjusting items: | | |
| Decrease in accounts receivable | 5,000 | |
| Depreciation expense | 5,000 | |
| Decrease in accounts payable | (5,000) | |
| Net cash from operating activities | | $ 30,000 |
| **Cash flows from investing activities:** | | |
| Purchase of equipment | | $(10,000) |
| **Cash flows from financing activities:** | | |
| Payment of dividends | $(10,000) | |
| Issuance of bonds | 10,000 | |
| Net cash from financing activities | | 0 |
| Net increase in cash | | $ 20,000 |

## II. Statement of Cash Flows: Direct Method

The following balance sheets are taken from the records of Golding:

| | 2013 | 2014 |
|---|---:|---:|
| **Assets** | | |
| Cash | $130,000 | $150,000 |
| Accounts receivable | 25,000 | 20,000 |
| Plant and equipment | 50,000 | 60,000 |
| Accumulated depreciation | (20,000) | (25,000) |
| Land | 10,000 | 10,000 |
| Total assets | $195,000 | $215,000 |
| **Liabilities and equity** | | |
| Accounts payable | $ 10,000 | $ 5,000 |
| Bonds payable | 8,000 | 18,000 |
| Common stock | 120,000 | 120,000 |
| Retained earnings | 57,000 | 72,000 |
| Total liabilities and equity | $195,000 | $215,000 |

Additional information is as follows: (a) Equipment costing $10,000 was purchased at year-end. No equipment was sold; (b) Net income for the year was calculated as follows:

| | |
|---|---:|
| Revenues | $ 500,000 |
| Cost of goods sold | (375,000) |
| Depreciation expense | (5,000) |
| Other expenses | (95,000) |
| Net income | $ 25,000 |

Dividends paid were $10,000.

## Required:

1. Prepare a statement of operating cash flows using the direct method.

## Solution:

1. Cash flows from operating activities:

| | Income Statement | Adjustments | Cash Flows |
|---|---:|---:|---:|
| Revenues | $ 500,000 | $ 5,000[a] | $ 505,000 |
| Cost of goods sold | (375,000) | (5,000)[b] | (380,000) |
| Depreciation expense | (5,000) | 5,000[c] | |
| Other expenses | (95,000) | | (95,000) |
| Net cash from operating activities | | | $ 30,000 |

[a] Decrease in accounts receivable.
[b] Decrease in accounts payable.
[c] Add back depreciation (noncash expense).

# DISCUSSION QUESTIONS

1. What are cash equivalents? How are cash equivalents treated in preparing a statement of cash flows?

2. The activity format calls for three categories on the statement of cash flows. Define each category.

3. Of the three categories on the statement of cash flows, which do you think provides the most useful information? Explain.

4. Explain the all-financial-resources approach to reporting financing and investing activities.

5. Why is it better to report the noncash investing and financing activities in a supplemental schedule rather than to include these activities on the body of the statement of cash flows?

6. What are the five steps for preparing the statement of cash flows? What is the purpose of each step?

7. Explain how a company can report a positive net income and yet still have a negative net operating cash flow.

8. Explain how a company can report a loss and still have a positive net operating cash flow.

9. In computing the period's net operating cash flows, why are increases in current liabilities and decreases in current assets added back to net income?

10. In computing the period's net operating cash flows, why are decreases in liabilities and increases in current assets deducted from net income?

11. In computing the period's net operating cash flows, why are noncash expenses added back to net income?

12. Explain the reasoning for including the payment of dividends in the financing section of the statement of cash flows.

13. What are the advantages in using worksheets when preparing a statement of cash flows?

14. Explain how the statement of cash flows can be prepared using the worksheet approach.

# MULTIPLE-CHOICE QUESTIONS

**15-1** Cash inflows from operating activities come from

   a. payment for raw materials.
   b. gains on the sale of operating equipment.
   c. collection of sales revenues.
   d. issuing capital stock.
   e. issuing bonds.

**15-2** Cash outflows from operating activities come from

   a. collection of sales revenues.
   b. payment for operating costs.
   c. acquisition of operating equipment.
   d. retirement of bonds.
   e. none of these.

**15-3** Raising cash by issuing capital stock is an example of

   a. a financing activity.
   b. an investing activity.
   c. an operating activity.
   d. a noncash transaction.
   e. none of these.

**15-4** Sources of cash include

   a. profitable operations.
   b. the issuance of long-term debt.
   c. the sale of long-term assets.
   d. the issuance of capital stock.
   e. all of these.

**15-5** Uses of cash include

    a.   cash dividends.

    b.   the sale of old equipment.

    c.   the purchase of long-term assets.

    d.   only a and b.

    e.   only a and c.

**15-6** The difference between the beginning and ending cash balances shown on the balance sheet

    a.   is added to net income to obtain total cash inflows.

    b.   serves as a control figure for the statement of cash flows.

    c.   is deducted from net income to obtain net cash inflows.

    d.   is the source of all investing and financing activities.

    e.   is both c and d.

**15-7** Which of the following adjustments helps to convert accrual income to operating cash flows?

    a.   Deduct from net income all noncash expenses.

    b.   Add to net income a decrease in inventories.

    c.   Add to net income a decrease in accounts payable.

    d.   Deduct from net income an increase in accounts payable.

    e.   None of the above.

**15-8** Which of the following adjustments to net income is needed to obtain cash flows?

    a.   Eliminate gains on sale of equipment.

    b.   Deduct from net income all noncash expenses (e.g., depreciation and amortization).

    c.   Deduct from net income any increases in current liabilities.

    d.   Add to net income any increases in inventories.

    e.   All of the above.

**15-9** An increase in accounts receivable is deducted from net income to obtain operating cash flows because

    a.   cash collections increased due to increasing sales.

    b.   cash collections from customers were less than the revenues reported.

    c.   cash collections decreased due to declining sales.

    d.   cash collections from customers were greater than the revenues reported.

    e.   None of the above.

**15-10** An increase in inventories is deducted from net income to arrive at operating cash flow because

    a.   cash payments to customers were larger than the purchases made during the period.

    b.   purchases are larger than the cost of goods sold by the amount that inventories increased.

    c.   cash payments to customers were less than the purchases made during the period.

    d.   purchases are less than the cost of goods sold by the amount that inventories increased.

    e.   All of the above.

**15-11** The gain on sale of equipment is deducted from net income to arrive at operating cash flows because

    a.   the sale of long-term assets is an operating activity.

    b.   the gain reveals the total cash received.

    c.   all of the cash received from the sale is reported in the operating section.

    d.   All of the above.

    e.   None of the above.

**15-12** Which of the following is an investing activity?

    a.   Issuance of a mortgage
    b.   Increase in accounts receivable
    c.   Purchase of land

    d.   Increase in inventories
    e.   All of these.

**15-13** Which of the following is a financing activity?

    a.   Increase in inventories
    b.   Purchase of land
    c.   Increase in accounts receivable

    d.   Issuance of a mortgage
    e.   All of these.

**15-14** Which method calculates operating cash flows by adjusting the income statement on a line-by-line basis?

    a.   Direct method
    b.   Indirect method
    c.   Working paper approach

    d.   Income method
    e.   None of these.

**15-15** A worksheet approach to preparing the statement of cash flows

    a.   is a useful aid.
    b.   uses a spreadsheet format.
    c.   offers an efficient and logical way of organizing the data.

    d.   allows an easy extraction of the needed data.
    e.   All of these.

**15-16** In a completed worksheet,

    a.   the debit column contains the cash inflows.
    b.   the debit column contains the cash outflows.
    c.   the credit column contains the cash inflows.
    d.   the credit column contains only operating cash flows.
    e.   None of the above.

# CORNERSTONE EXERCISES

OBJECTIVE ❶
CORNERSTONE 15.1

**Cornerstone Exercise 15-17    Activity Classification**

During the last 2 years of operations, Barnes Company had the following transactions:

a.  Purchased a new plant for $5,000,000.
b.  Issued bonds with a 6-year maturity date for $2,000,000.
c.  Reported profits of $7,000,000 for the most recent year.
d.  Sold equipment for $500,000.

e.  Paid cash dividends of $2,000,000.
f.  Sold a 30% interest in a company.
g.  Retired a long-term note payable.
h.  Reported a loss for the year ($500,000).
i.  Issued common stock for $1,000,000.

**Required:**

Classify each of these transactions as an operating activity, an investing activity, or a financing activity and indicate whether the activity is a source of cash or a use of cash.

OBJECTIVE ❷
CORNERSTONE 15.2

**Cornerstone Exercise 15-18    Change in Cash**

Blaylock Company provided the following information:

**Blaylock Company**
**Comparative Balance Sheets**
**At December 31, 2013 and 2014**

|  | 2014 | 2013 |
|---|---|---|
| Cash | $1,130,000 | $700,000 |

**Required:**

1. Calculate the change in cash.
2. Explain the role of the change in cash flow in the statement of cash flows.

### Cornerstone Exercise 15-19   Operating Cash Flows: Indirect Method

OBJECTIVE **2**
CORNERSTONE 15.3

Blaylock Company provided the following partial comparative balance sheets and the income statement for 2014.

**Blaylock Company**
**Comparative Balance Sheets**
**At December 31, 2013 and 2014**

|  | 2013 | 2014 |
|---|---|---|
| **Current assets:** | | |
| Accounts receivable | $750,000 | $582,500 |
| Inventories | 300,000 | 320,000 |
| **Current liabilities:** | | |
| Wages payable | 700,000 | 515,000 |

**Blaylock Company**
**Income Statement**
**For the Year Ended December 31, 2014**

| Revenues | $ 3,000,000 |
|---|---|
| Gain on sale of equipment | 100,000 |
| Less: Cost of goods sold | (1,920,000) |
| Less: Depreciation expense | (270,000) |
| Less: Interest expense | (10,000) |
| Net income | $   900,000 |

**Required:**

Compute operating cash flows using the indirect method.

### Cornerstone Exercise 15-20   Cash Flows from Investing Activities

OBJECTIVE **2**
CORNERSTONE 15.4

During the year, Blaylock Company sold equipment with a book value of $280,000 for $380,000 (original purchase cost of $480,000). New equipment was purchased.

Blaylock provided the following comparative balance sheets:

**Blaylock Company**
**Comparative Balance Sheets**
**At December 31, 2013 and 2014**

|  | 2013 | 2014 |
|---|---|---|
| **Long-Term Assets:** | | |
| Plant and equipment | $ 2,200,000 | $ 2,150,000 |
| Accumulated depreciation | (1,200,000) | (1,270,000) |
| Land | (1,000,000) | (1,437,500) |

**Required:**

Calculate the investing cash flows for the current year.

### Cornerstone Exercise 15-21   Cash Flows from Financing Activities

OBJECTIVE **2**
CORNERSTONE 15.5

Blaylock Company earned net income of $900,000 in 2014. Blaylock provided the following information:

*(Continued)*

**Blaylock Company**
**Comparative Balance Sheets**
**At December 31, 2013 and 2014**

|  | 2013 | 2014 |
|---|---|---|
| Bonds payable | — | 385,000 |
| Mortgage payable | 100,000 | — |
| Common stock | 375,000 | 375,000 |
| Pain-in capital in excess of par | 280,000 | 280,000 |
| Retained earnings | 1,825,000 | 2,325,000 |

**Required:**

Compute the financing cash flows for the current year.

OBJECTIVE **2**
CORNERSTONE 15.6

**Cornerstone Exercise 15-22   Statement of Cash Flows**

Refer to the information provided in **Cornerstone Exercises 15-19, 15-20,** and **15-21.**

**Required:**

1. Prepare a statement of cash flows for Blaylock for 2014.
2. What is the relationship between the statement of cash flows and the change in cash calculated in **Cornerstone Exercise 15-18**?

OBJECTIVE **3**
CORNERSTONE 15.7

**Cornerstone Exercise 15-23   Operating Cash Flows: Direct Method**

Roberts Company has provided the following partial comparative balance sheets and the income statement for 2014.

**Roberts Company**
**Comparative Balance Sheets**
**At December 31, 2013 and 2014**

|  | 2013 | 2014 |
|---|---|---|
| **Current assets:** |  |  |
| Accounts receivable | $350,000 | $281,500 |
| Inventories | 125,000 | 150,000 |
| **Current liabilities:** |  |  |
| Accounts payable | 300,000 | 237,500 |

**Roberts Company**
**Income Statement**
**For the Year Ended December 31, 2014**

| Revenues | $1,200,000 |
|---|---|
| Gain on sale of equipment | 50,000 |
| Less: Cost of goods sold | (650,000) |
| Less: Depreciation expense | (125,000) |
| Less: Interest expense | (25,000) |
| Net income | $ 450,000 |

**Required:**

Compute operating cash flows using the direct method.

OBJECTIVE **4**
CORNERSTONE 15.8

**Cornerstone Exercise 15-24   Worksheet Approach**

During 2014, Young Company had the following transactions:

a. Cash dividends of $10,000 were paid.
b. Equipment was sold for $4,800. It had an original cost of $18,000 and a book value of $9,000. The loss is included in operating expenses.

c.  Land with a fair market value of $25,000 was acquired by issuing common stock with a par value of $6,000.

d.  One thousand shares of preferred stock (no par) were sold for $7 per share.

Young provided the following income statement (for 2012) and comparative balance sheets:

| | |
|---|---:|
| Sales | $ 246,000 |
| Less: Cost of goods sold | (150,000) |
| Gross margin | $  96,000 |
| Less: Operating expenses | (66,000) |
| Net income | $  30,000 |

**Young Company**
**Comparative Balance Sheets**
**At December 31, 2013 and 2014**

| | 2013 | 2014 |
|---|---:|---:|
| **Assets** | | |
| Cash | $ 54,000 | $111,000 |
| Accounts receivable | 33,000 | 36,800 |
| Inventory | 48,000 | 33,000 |
| Plant and equipment | 78,000 | 60,000 |
| Accumulated depreciation | (39,000) | (36,000) |
| Land | 15,000 | 40,000 |
| Total assets | $189,000 | $244,800 |
| **Liabilities and stockholders' equity** | | |
| Accounts payable | $ 24,000 | $ 36,000 |
| Wages payable | 3,000 | 1,800 |
| Bonds payable | 18,000 | 11,000 |
| Preferred stock (no par) | 3,000 | 10,000 |
| Common stock | 30,000 | 36,000 |
| Paid-in capital in excess of par | 30,000 | 49,000 |
| Retained earnings | 81,000 | 101,000 |
| Total liabilities and stockholders' equity | $189,000 | $244,800 |

**Required:**

Prepare a worksheet for Young Company.

# EXERCISES

### Exercise 15-25   Activity Classification

Stillwater Designs is a private company and outsources production of its Kicker speaker lines. Suppose that Stillwater Designs provided you the following transactions.

OBJECTIVE **1**

a.  Sold a warehouse for $750,000.
b.  Reported a profit of $100,000.
c.  Retired long-term bonds.
d.  Paid cash dividends of $350,000.
e.  Obtained a mortgage for a new building from a local bank.

f.  Purchased a new robotic system.
g.  Issued a long-term note payable.
h.  Purchased a 40% interest in a company.
i.  Reported a loss for the year.
j.  Negotiated a long-term loan.

**Required:**

Classify each of these transactions as an operating activity, an investing activity, or a financing activity. Also, indicate whether the activity is a source of cash or a use of cash.

OBJECTIVE ❷      **Exercise 15-26    Adjustments to Net Income**

Consider the following independent events:

a.   Loss on sale of an asset
b.   Decrease in accounts receivable
c.   Increase in prepaid insurance
d.   Depreciation expense
e.   Decrease in accounts payable

f.   Uncollectible accounts expense
g.   Increase in wages payable
h.   Decrease in inventory
i.   Amortization of an intangible asset

**Required:**

Indicate whether each event will be added to or deducted from net income in order to compute cash flow from operations.

OBJECTIVE ❷      **Exercise 15-27    Adjustment for Prepaid Rent**

Jarem Company showed $189,000 in prepaid rent on December 31, 2013. On December 31, 2014, the balance in the prepaid rent account was $226,800. Rent expense for 2014 was $472,500.

**Required:**

1.   What amount of cash was paid for rent in 2014?
2.   **CONCEPTUAL CONNECTION** What adjustment in prepaid expenses is needed if the indirect method is used to prepare Jarem's statement of cash flows?

OBJECTIVE ❷      **Exercise 15-28    Operating Cash Flows**

During the year, Hepworth Company earned a net income of $61,725. Beginning and ending balances for the year for selected accounts are as follows:

|  | Account | |
|---|---|---|
|  | **Beginning** | **Ending** |
| Cash | $108,000 | $126,600 |
| Accounts receivable | 67,500 | 99,750 |
| Inventory | 36,000 | 52,500 |
| Prepaid expenses | 27,000 | 30,000 |
| Accumulated depreciation | 81,000 | 91,500 |
| Accounts payable | 45,000 | 55,125 |
| Wages payable | 27,000 | 15,000 |

There were no financing or investing activities for the year. The above balances reflect all of the adjustments needed to adjust net income to operating cash flows.

**Required:**

1.   Prepare a schedule of operating cash flows using the indirect method.
2.   Suppose that all the data in used Requirement 1 except that the ending accounts payable and cash balances are not known. Assume also that you know that the operating cash flow for the year was $20,475. What is the ending balance of accounts payable?
3.   **CONCEPTUAL CONNECTION** Hepworth has an opportunity to buy some equipment that will significantly increase productivity. The equipment costs $25,000. Assuming exactly the same data used for Requirement 1, can Hepworth buy the equipment using this year's operating cash flows? If not, what would you suggest be done?

OBJECTIVE ❷      **Exercise 15-29    Cash Flow from Investing Activities**

During 2013, Shorts Company had the following transactions:

a.   Purchased $200,000 of 10-year bonds issued by Makenzie Inc.
b.   Acquired land valued at $70,000 in exchange for machinery.

c.  Sold equipment with original cost of $540,000 for $330,000; accumulated depreciation taken on the equipment to the point of sale was $180,000.

d.  Purchased new machinery for $120,000.

e.  Purchased common stock in Lemmons Company for $55,000.

**Required:**

1.  Prepare the net cash from investing activities section of the statement of cash flows.

2.  **CONCEPTUAL CONNECTION** Usually, the net cash from investing activities is negative. How can Shorts cover this negative cash flow? What other information would you like to have to make this decision?

### Exercise 15-30    Cash Flow from Financing Activities

OBJECTIVE 2

Tidwell Company experienced the following during 2013:

a.  Sold preferred stock for $480,000.

b.  Declared dividends of $150,000 payable on March 1, 2014.

c.  Borrowed $575,000 from bank on a 2-year note.

d.  Purchased $80,000 of its own common stock to hold as treasury stock.

e.  Repaid 5-year bonds issued in 2008 for $400,000 due in December.

**Required:**

Prepare the net cash from financing activities section of the statement of cash flows.

---

*Use the following information for Exercises 15-31 and 15-32:*

Oliver Company provided the following information for the years 2013 and 2014:

**Oliver Company**
**Income Statement**
**For the Year Ended December 31, 2014**

| | |
|---|---:|
| Sales | $ 75,000 |
| Cost of goods sold | (20,000) |
| Depreciation expense | (2,000) |
| Other expenses | (13,000) |
| Net income | $ 40,000 |

**Oliver Company**
**Comparative Balance Sheets**
**At December 31, 2013 and 2014**

| | 2013 | 2014 |
|---|---:|---:|
| **Assets** | | |
| Cash | $ 24,600 | $ 64,600 |
| Accounts receivable | 5,400 | 9,200 |
| Inventory | 8,000 | 6,000 |
| Property, plant, and equipment | 160,000 | 175,000 |
| Accumulated depreciation | (18,000) | (20,000) |
| Land | 20,400 | 47,000 |
| Total assets | $200,400 | $281,800 |
| | | |
| **Liabilities and equity** | | |
| Accounts payable | $ 8,600 | $ 10,000 |
| Mortgage payable | — | 40,000 |
| Stockholders' equity | 191,800 | 231,800 |
| Total liabilities and equity | $200,400 | $281,800 |

### Exercise 15-31    Operating Cash Flows

Refer to the information for Oliver Company on the previous page.

**Required:**

1. Calculate the change in cash flows that serves as the control figure for the statement of cash flows.
2. Prepare a schedule that provides operating cash flows for the year 2014 using the indirect method.
3. Assume that you have all the information provided for Requirement 1 except that you only know the beginning balance of accounts receivable for 2014. Given this information and assuming that the operating cash flows for 2014 are $41,000, calculate the ending balance for accounts receivable.

### Exercise 15-32    Operating Cash Flows

Refer to the information for Oliver Company on the previous page.

**Required:**

Prepare a schedule that provides operating cash flows for the year 2014 using the direct method.

### Exercise 15-33    Classification of Transactions

Consider the following independent activities.

| | |
|---|---|
| a. Payment of a cash dividend | i. Decrease in accounts payable |
| b. Amortization of intangible asset | j. Increase in accounts receivable |
| c. Gain on disposal of equipment | k. Proceeds from the sale of land |
| d. Exchange of common stock for land | l. Increase in prepaid expenses |
| e. Increase in accrued wages | m. Retirement of a bond |
| f. Retirement of preferred stock | n. Purchase of a 60% interest in another company |
| g. Purchase of a new plant | |
| h. Depreciation expense | |

**Required:**

Classify the following transaction as operating activities, investing activities, financing activities, or financing/investing not affecting cash. If an activity is an operating activity, indicate whether it will be added to or deducted from net income to compute cash from operations.

---

*Use the following information for Exercises 15-34 and 15-35:*
The income statement for Piura Merchandising Corporation is as follows:

**Piura Merchandising Corporation**
**Income Statement**
**At December 31, 2013**

| | | |
|---|---:|---:|
| Sales | | $ 1,500,000 |
| Less: Cost of goods sold | | |
| Beginning inventory | $ 400,000 | |
| Purchases | 800,000 | |
| Ending inventory | (200,000) | |
| | | (1,000,000) |
| Less: Depreciation expense | | (100,000) |
| Less: Amortization of patent | | (20,000) |
| Less: Wages expense | | (80,000) |
| Less: Insurance expense | | (40,000) |
| Income before taxes | | $ 260,000 |
| Less: Income taxes (all current) | | (104,000) |
| Net income | | $ 156,000 |

Other information is as follows:

a.  Accounts payable decreased by $20,000 during the year.
b.  Accounts receivable increased by $20,000.
c.  All wages were paid at the beginning of the year; at the end of the year, wages payable had a balance of $12,000.
d.  Prepaid insurance increased by $24,000 during the year.

### Exercise 15-34   Operating Cash Flows

OBJECTIVE **2**

Refer to the information for Piura Merchandising Corporation above.

**Required:**

Prepare a schedule that provides the operating cash flows for the year using the indirect method.

### Exercise 15-35   Operating Cash Flows, Direct Method

OBJECTIVE **3**

Refer to the information for Piura Merchandising Corporation above.

**Required:**

Prepare a schedule of operating cash flows using the direct method.

# PROBLEMS

*Use the following information for Problems 15-36 and 15-37:*
Solpoder Corporation has the following comparative financial statements:

**Solpoder Corporation**
**Comparative Balance Sheets**
**At December 31, 2013 and 2014**

|  | 2013 | 2014 |
|---|---|---|
| **Assets** | | |
| Cash | $ 49,500 | $ 81,000 |
| Accounts receivable, net | 135,000 | 108,000 |
| Inventory | 27,000 | 54,000 |
| Plant and equipment | 180,000 | 180,000 |
| Accumulated depreciation | (36,000) | (45,000) |
| Total assets | $355,500 | $378,000 |
| **Liabilities and equity** | | |
| Accounts payable | $ 57,600 | $ 18,000 |
| Common stock | 190,800 | 207,000 |
| Retained earnings | 107,100 | 153,000 |
| Total liabilities and equity | $355,500 | $378,000 |

**Solpoder Corporation**
**Income Statement**
**For the Year Ended December 31, 2014**

| | |
|---|---|
| Sales | $ 297,000 |
| Less: Cost of goods sold | (175,500) |
| Gross margin | $ 121,500 |
| Less: Operating expenses | (58,500) |
| Net income | $ 63,000 |

Dividends of $17,100 were paid. No equipment was purchased or retired during the current year.

OBJECTIVE **2**    **Problem 15-36    Statement of Cash Flows, Indirect Method**

Refer to the information for Solpoder Corporation on the previous page.

**Required:**

Prepare a statement of cash flows using the indirect method.

OBJECTIVE **3**    **Problem 15-37    Statement of Cash Flows, Direct Method**

Refer to the information for Solpoder Corporation on the previous page.

**Required:**

Prepare a statement of cash flows using the direct method.

---

*Use the following information for Problems 15-38 and 15-39:*
The following financial statements were provided by Roberts Company:

**Roberts Company**
**Balance Sheets**
**At September 30, 2013 and 2014**

|  | 2013 | 2014 |
|---|---|---|
| **Assets** | | |
| Cash | $ 23,000 | $ 7,000 |
| Accounts receivable | 7,600 | 9,600 |
| Inventory | 20,800 | 18,000 |
| Plant and equipment | 40,000 | 60,000 |
| Accumulated depreciation | (10,000) | (16,000) |
| Total assets | $ 81,400 | $ 78,600 |

|  | 2013 | 2014 |
|---|---|---|
| **Liabilities and equity** | | |
| Accounts payable | $ 4,800 | $ 3,200 |
| Wages payable | 1,200 | 800 |
| Common stock | 50,000 | 50,000 |
| Retained earnings | 25,400 | 24,600 |
| Total liabilities and equity | $81,400 | $78,600 |

**Roberts Company**
**Income Statement**
**For the Year Ended September 30, 2014**

| | | |
|---|---|---|
| Sales | | $ 40,000 |
| Less: Cost of goods sold | | |
| Beginning inventory | $ 20,800 | |
| Purchases | 26,000 | |
| Ending inventory | (18,000) | (28,800) |
| Less: Wages expense | | (4,000) |
| Less: Advertising | | (2,000) |
| Less: Depreciation expense | | (6,000) |
| Net Income (Loss) | | $    (800) |

At the end of 2014, Roberts purchased some additional equipment for $20,000.

## Problem 15-38   Statement of Cash Flows, Indirect Method

OBJECTIVE ❸

Refer to the information for Roberts Company on the previous page.

**Required:**

Prepare a statement of cash flows using the indirect method.

## Problem 15-39   Statement of Cash Flows, Direct Method

OBJECTIVE ❸

Refer to the information for Roberts Company on the previous page.

**Required:**

Calculate operating cash flows using the direct method.

---

*Use the following information for Problems 15-40 and 15-41:*
Booth Manufacturing has provided the following financial statements.

**Booth Manufacturing**
**Comparative Balance Sheets**
**At December 31, 2013 and 2014**

|  | 2013 | 2014 |
|---|---|---|
| **Assets** | | |
| Cash | $   112,500 | $   350,000 |
| Accounts receivable | 350,000 | 281,250 |
| Inventories | 125,000 | 150,000 |
| Plant and equipment | 1,000,000 | 1,025,000 |
| Accumulated depreciation | (500,000) | (525,000) |
| Land | 500,000 | 718,750 |
| Total assets | $1,587,500 | $2,000,000 |
| **Liabilities and equity** | | |
| Accounts payable | $   300,000 | $   237,500 |
| Mortgage payable | — | 250,000 |
| Common stock | 75,000 | 75,000 |
| Paid-in capital in excess of par | 300,000 | 300,000 |
| Retained earnings | 912,500 | 1,137,500 |
| Total liabilities and equity | $1,587,500 | $2,000,000 |

**Booth Manufacturing**
**Income Statement**
**For the Year Ended December 31, 2014**

| | |
|---|---|
| Revenues | $1,200,000 |
| Gain on sale of equipment | 50,000 |
| Less: Cost of goods sold | (640,000) |
| Less: Depreciation expense | (125,000) |
| Less: Interest expense | (35,000) |
| Net income | $   450,000 |

Other information includes: (a) Equipment with a book value of $125,000 was sold for $175,000 (original cost was $225,000); and (b) Dividends of $225,000 were declared and paid.

---

*(Continued)*

OBJECTIVE  ❶ ❷

### Problem 15-40    Statement of Cash Flows, Indirect Method

Refer to the information for Booth Manufacturing on the previous page.

**Required:**

1. Calculate the cash flows from operations using the indirect method.
2. Prepare a statement of cash flows.
3. **CONCEPTUAL CONNECTION** Search the Internet to find a statement of cash flows. Which method was used—the indirect method or the direct method? How does the net income reported compare with the operating cash flows? To the change in cash flows?

OBJECTIVE  ❶ ❸

### Problem 15-41    Statement of Cash Flows: Direct Method

Refer to the information for Booth Manufacturing on the previous page.

**Required:**

Calculate operating cash flows using the direct method.

---

*Use the following information for Problems 15-42 and 15-43:*

The following balance sheets and income statement were taken from the records of Rosie-Lee Company:

**Rosie-Lee Company**
**Comparative Balance Sheets**
**At June 30, 2013 and 2014**

|  | 2013 | 2014 |
|---|---|---|
| **Assets** | | |
| Cash | $270,000 | $333,000 |
| Accounts receivable | 126,000 | 144,000 |
| Investments | — | 54,000 |
| Plant and equipment | 180,000 | 189,000 |
| Accumulated depreciation | (54,000) | (57,600) |
| Land | 36,000 | 54,000 |
| Total assets | $558,000 | $716,400 |
| **Liabilities and equity** | | |
| Accounts payable | $ 72,000 | $ 90,000 |
| Mortgage payable | 108,000 | — |
| Bonds payable | — | 90,000 |
| Preferred stock | 36,000 | — |
| Common stock | 180,000 | 288,000 |
| Retained earnings | 162,000 | 248,400 |
| Total liabilities and equity | $558,000 | $716,400 |

**Rosie-Lee Company**
**Income Statement**
**For the Year Ended June 30, 2014**

| | |
|---|---|
| Sales | $ 920,000 |
| Less: Cost of goods sold | (620,000) |
| Gross margin | $ 300,000 |
| Less: Operating expenses | (177,600) |
| Net income | $ 122,400 |

---

OBJECTIVE ❷ ❸

### Problem 15-42    Direct and Indirect Methods

Refer to the information for Rosie-Lee Company above. Additional transactions were as follows:

a. Sold equipment costing $21,600 with accumulated depreciation of $16,200 for $3,600.
b. Issued bonds for $90,000 on December 31.

c.  Paid cash dividends of $36,000.
d.  Retired mortgage of $108,000 on December 31.

**Required:**

1.  Prepare a schedule of operating cash flows using (a) the indirect method and (b) the direct method.
2.  Prepare a statement of cash flows using the indirect method.

**Problem 15-43    Statement of Cash Flows, Worksheet**                          OBJECTIVE **4**

Refer to the information for Rosie-Lee Company on the previous page. Additional transactions were as follows:

a.  Sold equipment costing $21,600 with accumulated depreciation of $16,200 for $3,600.
b.  Issued bonds for $90,000 on December 31.
c.  Paid cash dividends of $36,000.
d.  Retired a mortgage at a price of $108,000 on December 31.

**Required:**

Prepare a statement of cash flows using a worksheet similar to the one shown in **Cornerstone 15.8** (p. 688). Use the indirect method to prepare the statement.

---

*Use the following information for Problems 15-44 and 15-45:*
Balance sheets for Brierwold Corporation follow:

|  | Beginning Balances | Ending Balances |
|---|---|---|
| **Assets** | | |
| Cash | $ 100,000 | $ 150,000 |
| Accounts receivable | 200,000 | 180,000 |
| Inventory | 400,000 | 410,000 |
| Plant and equipment | 700,000 | 690,000 |
| Accumulated depreciation | (200,000) | (245,000) |
| Land | 100,000 | 150,000 |
| Total assets | $1,300,000 | $1,335,000 |
| **Liabilities and equity** | | |
| Accounts payable | $ 300,000 | $ 250,000 |
| Mortgage payable | — | 110,000 |
| Preferred stock | 100,000 | — |
| Common stock | 240,000 | 280,000 |
| Paid-in capital in excess of par | 360,000 | 420,000 |
| Retained earnings | 300,000 | 275,000 |
| Total liabilities and equity | $1,300,000 | $1,335,000 |

Additional transactions were as follows:

a.  Purchased equipment costing $50,000.
b.  Sold equipment costing $60,000 with a book value of $25,000 for $40,000.
c.  Retired preferred stock at a cost of $110,000 (the premium is debited to retained earnings).
d.  Issued 10,000 shares of common stock (par value, $4) for $10 per share.
e.  Reported a loss of $15,000 for the year.
f.  Purchased land for $50,000.

OBJECTIVE ❶ ❷     **Problem 15-44   Statement of Cash Flows: Indirect Method**

Refer to the information for Brierwold Corporation above.

**Required:**

Prepare a statement of cash flows using the indirect method.

OBJECTIVE ❸ ❹     **Problem 15-45   Statement of Cash Flows, Worksheet**

Refer to the information for Brierwold Corporation on the previous page.

**Required:**

Prepare a statement of cash flows using the worksheet approach. Use the indirect method to prepare the statement.

OBJECTIVE ❶ ❷     **Problem 15-46   Schedule of Operating Cash Flows: Indirect Method**

The income statement for the Mendelin Corporation is as follows:

| | | |
|---|---:|---:|
| Revenues | | $ 380,000 |
| Less: Cost of goods sold: | | |
| Beginning inventory | $ 50,000 | |
| Purchases | 200,000 | |
| Ending inventory | (34,000) | (216,000) |
| Less: Patent amortization | | (20,000) |
| Advertising | | (12,000) |
| Depreciation expense | | (60,000) |
| Wages expense | | (30,000) |
| Insurance expense | | (10,500) |
| Bad debt expense | | (6,400) |
| Interest expense | | (7,600) |
| Net income | | $ 17,500 |

Additional information is as follows:

a.   Interest expense includes $1,800 of discount amortization.
b.   The prepaid insurance expense account decreased by $2,000 during the year.
c.   Wages payable decreased by $3,000 during the year.
d.   Accounts payable increased by $7,500 (this account is for purchase of merchandise only).
e.   Accounts receivable increased by $10,000 (net of allowance for doubtful accounts).
f.   Inventory decreased by $16,000.

**Required:**

Prepare a schedule of operating cash flows using the indirect method.

OBJECTIVE ❶ ❷     **Problem 15-47   Statement of Cash Flows, Indirect Method**

The following balance sheets are taken from the records of Golding Company (numbers are expressed in thousands):

| | 2013 | 2014 |
|---|---:|---:|
| **Assets** | | |
| Cash | $130,000 | $150,000 |
| Accounts receivable | 25,000 | 20,000 |
| Plant and equipment | 50,000 | 60,000 |
| Accumulated depreciation | (20,000) | (25,000) |
| Land | 10,000 | 10,000 |
| Total assets | $195,000 | $215,000 |
| **Liabilities and equity** | | |
| Accounts payable | $ 10,000 | $ 5,000 |
| Bonds payable | 8,000 | 18,000 |
| Common stock | 120,000 | 120,000 |
| Retained earnings | 57,000 | 72,000 |
| Total liabilities and equity | $195,000 | $215,000 |

Additional information is as follows: (a) Equipment costing $10,000,000 was purchased at year-end. No equipment was sold; and (b) Net income for the year was $25,000,000; $10,000,000 in dividends were paid.

**Required:**

1. Prepare a statement of cash flows using the indirect method.
2. **CONCEPTUAL CONNECTION** Assess Golding's ability to use cash to acquire Lemmons Company. Consider the information in Exhibit 15.2 (p. 679) and Cornerstone 15.6 (p. 684) as part of your analysis.

---

*Use the following information for Problems 15-48 and 15-49:*
The following balance sheets were taken from the records of Blalock Company:

**At the Years Ended December 31**

| | 2013 | 2014 |
|---|---|---|
| **Assets** | | |
| Cash | $150,000 | $185,000 |
| Accounts receivable | 70,000 | 80,000 |
| Investments | — | 30,000 |
| Plant and equipment | 100,000 | 105,000 |
| Accumulated depreciation | (30,000) | (32,000) |
| Land | 20,000 | 30,000 |
| Total assets | $310,000 | $398,000 |
| **Liabilities and equity** | | |
| Accounts payable | $ 40,000 | $ 50,000 |
| Bonds payable | 60,000 | — |
| Mortgage payable | — | 50,000 |
| Preferred stock | 20,000 | — |
| Common stock | 100,000 | 160,000 |
| Retained earnings | 90,000 | 138,000 |
| Total liabilities and equity | $310,000 | $398,000 |

Additional transactions were as follows:

a. Sold equipment costing $12,000 with accumulated depreciation of $9,000 for $2,000.
b. Retired bonds at a price of $60,000 on December 31.
c. Earned net income for the year of $68,000; paid cash dividends of $20,000.

---

**Problem 15-48    Statement of Cash Flows**

OBJECTIVE 4

Refer to the information for Blalock Company above.

**Required:**

Prepare a statement of cash flows using the indirect method.

**Problem 15-49    Statement of Cash Flows, Worksheet**

OBJECTIVE 4

Refer to the information for Blalock Company above.

**Required:**

Prepare a statement of cash flows using the worksheet approach. Use the indirect method to prepare the statement.

# CASES

OBJECTIVE ❷❸❹ **Case 15-50    Direct and Indirect Methods**

The comparative balance sheets and income statement of Piura Manufacturing follow.

**Piura Manufacturing**
**Comparative Balance Sheets**
**For the Years Ended June 30, 2013 and 2014**

|  | 2013 | 2014 |
|---|---|---|
| **Assets** | | |
| Cash | $ 72,000 | $146,400 |
| Accounts receivable | 44,000 | 48,000 |
| Inventory | 64,000 | 44,000 |
| Plant and equipment | 104,000 | 112,000 |
| Accumulated depreciation | (52,000) | (48,000) |
| Land | 20,000 | 20,000 |
| Total assets | $252,000 | $322,400 |
| **Liabilities and equity** | | |
| Accounts payable | $ 32,000 | $ 48,000 |
| Wages payable | 4,000 | 2,400 |
| Bonds payable | 24,000 | 16,000 |
| Preferred stock (no par) | 4,000 | 12,000 |
| Common stock | 30,000 | 36,000 |
| Paid-in capital in excess of par | 50,000 | 76,000 |
| Retained earnings | 108,000 | 132,000 |
| Total liabilities and equity | $252,000 | $322,400 |

**Piura Manufacturing**
**Income Statement**
**For the Year Ended June 30, 2014**

| | |
|---|---|
| Sales | $ 320,000 |
| Less: Cost of goods sold | (200,000) |
| Gross margin | $ 120,000 |
| Less: Operating expenses | (88,000) |
| Net income | $  32,000 |

Additional transactions for 2014 were as follows:

a. Cash dividends of $8,000 were paid.
b. Equipment was acquired by issuing common stock with a par value of $6,000. The fair market value of the equipment is $32,000.
c. Equipment with a book value of $12,000 was sold for $6,000. The original cost of the equipment was $24,000. The loss is included in operating expenses.
d. Two thousand shares of preferred stock were sold for $4 per share.

**Required:**

1. Prepare a schedule of operating cash flows using (a) the indirect method and (b) the direct method.
2. Prepare a statement of cash flows using the indirect method.
3. Prepare a statement of cash flows using a worksheet similar to the one shown in Cornerstone 15.8 (p. 688).
4. Form a group with two to four other students, and discuss the merits of the direct and indirect methods. Which do you think investors might prefer? Should the FASB require all companies to use the direct method?

OBJECTIVE ❶❷❸ **Case 15-51    Management of Statement of Cash Flows, Ethical Issues**

Fred Jackson, president and owner of Bailey Company, is concerned about the company's ability to obtain a loan from a major bank. The loan is a key factor in the firm's plan to expand its operations. Demand for the firm's product is high—too high for the current production capacity to handle. Fred is convinced that a new plant is needed. Building the new plant, however, will require an infusion of new capital. Fred calls a meeting with Karla Jones, financial vice president.

**Fred:** Karla, what is the status of our loan application? Do you think that the bank will approve?

**Karla:** Perhaps, but at this point, there is a real risk. The loan officer has requested a complete set of financials for this year and the past 2 years. He has indicated that he is particularly interested in the statement of cash flows. As you know, our income statement looks great for all 3 years, but the statement of cash flows will show a significant increase in receivables, especially for this year. It will also show a significant increase in inventory, and I'm sure that he'll want to know why inventory is increasing if demand is so great that we need another plant. Both of these effects show decreasing cash flows from operating activities.

**Fred:** Well, it is certainly true that cash flows have been decreasing. One major problem is the lack of operating cash. This loan will solve that problem. Bill Lawson has agreed to build the plant for the amount of the loan but will actually charge me for only 95% of the stated cost. We get 5% of the loan for operating cash. Bill is willing to pay 5% to get the contract.

**Karla:** The loan may help with operating cash flows, but we can't get the loan without showing some evidence of cash strength. We need to do something about the increases in inventory and receivables that we expect for this year.

**Fred:** The increased inventory is easy to explain. We had to work overtime and use subcontractors to take care of one of our biggest customers. That inventory will be gone by the first of next year.

**Karla:** The problem isn't explaining the inventory. The problem is that the increase in inventory decreases our operating cash flows and this shows up on the statement of cash flows. This effect, coupled with the increase in receivables, depicts us as being cash poor. It'll definitely hurt our chances.

**Fred:** I see. Well, this can be solved. The inventory is for a customer that I know well. She'll do me a favor. I'll simply get her to take delivery of the inventory early, before the end of our fiscal year. She can pay me next year as originally planned.

**Karla:** Fred, all that will do is shift the increase from inventory to receivables. It'll still report the same cash position.

**Fred:** No problem. We'll report the delivery as a cash sale, and I'll have Bill Lawson advance me the cash as a temporary loan. He'll do that to get the contract to build our new plant. In fact, we can do the same with some of our other receivables. We'll report them as collected, and I'll get Bill to cover. If he understands that this is what it takes to get the loan, he'll cooperate. He stands to make a lot of money on the deal.

**Karla:** Fred, this is getting complicated. The bank will have us audited each year if this loan is approved. If an audit were to reveal some of this manipulation, we could be in big trouble, particularly if the company has any trouble in repaying the loan.

**Fred:** The company won't have any trouble. Sales are strong, and the problem of collecting receivables can be solved, especially given the extra time that the 5% of the loan proceeds will provide.

### Required:

1.  Form a group with two to four other students. Discuss the propriety of the arrangement that Fred has with Bill Lawson concerning the disbursement of the proceeds from the loan.
2.  In your group, discuss the propriety of the actions that Fred is proposing to improve the firm's statement of cash flows. Suppose that there is very little risk that the loan will not be repaid. Does this information affect your assessment?
3.  Assume that Karla is subject to the Institute of Management Accountant's (IMA) code of ethics. Look up this code, and identify the standards of ethical conduct that will be violated, if any, by Karla should she agree to cooperate with Fred's scheme.
4.  Using the IMA code of ethics, if you were in Karla's position, what would you do (suppose that Fred insists on implementing his plan)? Now, answer the question assuming that Fred is willing to consider alternative ways to solve the company's problems.

# 16

# Financial Statement Analysis

© Pixelfabrik/Alamy

After studying Chapter 16, you should be able to:

1. Analyze financial statements using two forms of common-size analysis: horizontal analysis and vertical analysis.

2. Explain why historical standards and industrial averages are important for ratio analysis.

3. Calculate and use liquidity ratios to assess the ability of a company to meet its current obligations.

4. Calculate and use leverage ratios to assess the ability of a company to meet its long- and short-term obligations.

5. Calculate and use profitability ratios to assess the extent to which a company's resources are being used efficiently.

© Hank Abernathy/Alamy

# EXPERIENCE MANAGERIAL DECISIONS
## with Apple

In response to a recent survey, 73% of college students ranked the iPod as the most "in" thing on campus—higher than anything else, including Facebook.com and specialty beverages.[1] In addition, Apple offers numerous other successful products, such as the iPad and iPhone. Not surprisingly, **Apple** has surpassed the 315 million units sold milestone for its iOS devices (includes the iPhone, iPad, and iPod family of products), making it one of the most successful companies in history. How has Apple achieved such amazing market penetration and does it have the capability to continue this impressive trend? Several common and easily computed financial statement ratios can begin to provide an answer to this question.

> *"**Apple** has surpassed the 315 million units sold milestone for its iOS devices."*

First, the current ratio of 1.61—a common liquidity ratio—indicates that as of the end of the year in which its App Store nearly reached the 25 billion download milestone, Apple had $1.61 of current assets for every $1 of current liabilities. Given that it has more current assets than current liabilities, it appears as though Apple is in a position to remain liquid and meet its short-term obligations.

Apple's inventory turnover, another liquidity ratio, shows that the company turned over its inventory 70.5 times during that year, which also means that on average its inventory sat on the shelf for only 5.2 days before being sold. Turning inventory into cash so quickly is very beneficial to the company because it can reinvest the cash back into the business, such as for research and development of the next generation iPad, iPhone or iPod.

Apple's debt ratio is 0.34, indicating that over 65% of its assets are financed using equity. Interestingly, over 70% of Apple's liabilities are current in nature. For example, trying to calculate the times-interest-earned ratio, another leverage ratio, for Apple would be impossible because Apple had no long-term debt in the year in which it surpassed the 315 million iOS units sold milestone and, therefore, no interest payments on long-term debt (a key part of the times-interest-earned ratio). Rather than taking on long-term debt, and the interest associated with such debt, Apple chose that year to raise the capital necessary to supplement its cash from operating activities by issuing $831 million worth of stock to investors.

Finally, the company's return on sales of 0.24, a profitability ratio, indicates that $0.24 of every $1.00 in sales revenue was left over as profit after accounting for all expenses.

In summary, several common financial statement ratios suggest that Apple was able to perform so effectively that year, in part, because of its impressive ability to turn inventory into cash quickly, avoid costly long-term debt, and raise significant capital through stock issuances to investors. Therefore, the next time you download a song, television episode, or movie from the iTunes Store, you can appreciate Apple's performance on these key financial statement ratios and be thankful for its part in revolutionizing the entertainment industry.

---

[1] Information compiled from Apple's 2011 Annual Report.

Financial statement analysis provides useful information for many users and purposes.

- **Creditors**: By using ratio analysis, common-size analysis, and other techniques, loan managers can assess the creditworthiness of potential customers. The formal analysis of financial statements can also provide a means to exercise control over outstanding loans.
- **Investors**: Investors need to analyze financial statements to assess the attractiveness of a company as a potential investment.
- **Managers**: Managers need to analyze their own financial statements to assess profitability, liquidity, debt position, and progress toward organizational objectives.

The analysis of financial statements is designed to reveal relationships among items on the financial statements and trends of individual items over time. By knowing these relationships and trends, users are in a better position to exercise sound judgment regarding the current or future performance of a company. The two major techniques for financial analysis are common-size analysis and ratio analysis.

## Here's The Real Kicker

Every month, **Kicker** holds a company-wide meeting of all employees. In addition to the introduction of new employees and general announcements, Kicker's owner shares financial information. Then, graphs showing the trend in sales and profits are posted on the bulletin board in the break room. Employees can check trends in financial information at their leisure. This information is important to Kicker employees because all of them are part of a comprehensive profit-sharing plan. Robust monthly sales and income will result in a bonus check to every employee that month. Yearly profits lead to another bonus check at year-end. Finally, Kicker also contributes to employees' 401(K) accounts. Since all of this is dependent on net income, each employee has a vested interest in keeping costs down and sales up.

**OBJECTIVE ❶**

Analyze financial statements using two forms of common-size analysis: horizontal analysis and vertical analysis.

## COMMON-SIZE ANALYSIS

A simple first step in financial statement analysis is comparing two financial statements. For example, the income statement for this year could be compared with the income statement for last year. To make the analysis more meaningful, percentages can be used. **Common-size analysis** expresses line items or accounts in the financial statements as percentages. The two major forms of common-size analysis are horizontal analysis and vertical analysis. Exhibit 16.1 illustrates vertical and horizontal analysis.

**( EXHIBIT 16.1 )**

**Common-Size Analysis**

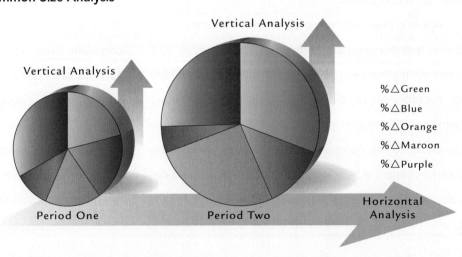

# Horizontal Analysis

Also called *trend analysis*, **horizontal analysis** expresses a line item as a percentage of some prior-period amount. This approach allows the trend over time to be assessed. In horizontal analysis, line items are expressed as a percentage of a base period amount. The base period can be the immediately preceding period, or it can be a period further in the past. Cornerstone 16.1 shows how to prepare common-size income statements by using the first year as the base period.

CORNERSTONE

16.1

## Preparing Common-Size Income Statements Using Base Period Horizontal Analysis

**Why:**

By comparing a given financial statement line item, such as sales or various expenses, as a percentage of some prior-period amount, managers can better identify trends in performance.

**Information:**

Simpson Company provided the following income statements for its first 3 years of operation:

|  | Year 1 | Year 2 | Year 3 |
|---|---|---|---|
| Net sales | $100,000 | $120,000 | $132,000 |
| Less: Cost of goods sold | (60,000) | (75,000) | (81,000) |
| Gross margin | $ 40,000 | $ 45,000 | $ 51,000 |
| Less: |  |  |  |
| Operating expenses | (20,000) | (24,000) | (29,000) |
| Income taxes | (8,000) | (9,000) | (10,000) |
| Net income | $ 12,000 | $ 12,000 | $ 12,000 |

**Required:**

Prepare common-size income statements by using Year 1 as the base period.

**Solution:**

Year 1 is the base year. Therefore, every dollar amount in Year 1 is 100% of itself.

$$\text{Percent for a Line Item} = \left( \frac{\text{Dollar Amount of Line Item}}{\text{Dollar Amount of Base Year Line Item}} \right) \times 100$$

Percent Year 1 Net Sales = ($100,000/$100,000) × 100 = 100%

Percent Year 2 Net Sales = ($120,000/$100,000) × 100 = 120%

Percent Year 3 Net Sales = ($132,000/$100,000) × 100 = 132%

|  | Year 1 | | Year 2 | | Year 3 | |
|---|---|---|---|---|---|---|
|  | **Dollars** | **Percent** | **Dollars** | **Percent** | **Dollars** | **Percent** |
| Net sales | $100,000 | 100% | $120,000 | 120.0% | $132,000 | 132.0% |
| Less: Cost of goods sold | (60,000) | 100 | (75,000) | 125.0 | (81,000) | 135.0 |
| Gross margin | $ 40,000 | 100 | $ 45,000 | 112.5 | $ 51,000 | 127.5 |
| Less: |  |  |  |  |  |  |
| Operating expenses | (20,000) | 100 | (24,000) | 120.0 | (29,000) | 145.0 |
| Income taxes | (8,000) | 100 | (9,000) | 112.5 | (10,000) | 125.0 |
| Net income | $ 12,000 | 100 | $ 12,000 | 100.0 | $ 12,000 | 100.0 |

Since the base year in Cornerstone 16.1 is Year 1, all line amounts in subsequent years are compared with the amount in the base year. For example, Year 3 sales are expressed as a percentage of Year 1 sales. By comparing each subsequent amount with the base period, trends can be seen. The data reveal that sales have increased by 32% over the 3 years. With such a large increase in sales, many would expect net income to experience a significant increase also. The percentage analysis, however, shows that net income has shown no change from the base period. Net income has stayed flat because expenses and taxes have also increased: cost of goods sold has increased by 35%, operating expenses by 45%, and taxes by 25%. As a result of the percentage analysis, the manager of the company might decide to focus more attention on controlling costs.

## Vertical Analysis

While horizontal analysis involves relationships among items over time, vertical analysis is concerned with relationships among items within a particular time period. **Vertical analysis** expresses the line item as a percentage of some other line item for the same period. With this approach, within-period relationships can be assessed. Line items on income statements often are expressed as percentages of net sales. Items on the balance sheet often are expressed as a percentage of total assets. Cornerstone 16.2 shows how to perform vertical analysis with the same example used in Cornerstone 16.1 (p. 717).

CORNERSTONE

# 16.2

## Preparing Income Statements Using Net Sales as the Base: Vertical Analysis

**Why:**

By comparing a given financial statement line item as a percentage of some other line item (such as sales or total assets) for the same time period, managers can better understand the relative size and importance of each item.

**Information:**

Simpson Company provided the following income statements for its first 3 years of operation:

|  | Year 1 | Year 2 | Year 3 |
|---|---|---|---|
| Net sales | $100,000 | $120,000 | $132,000 |
| Less: Cost of goods sold | (60,000) | (75,000) | (81,000) |
| Gross margin | $ 40,000 | $ 45,000 | $ 51,000 |
| Less: |  |  |  |
| Operating expenses | (20,000) | (24,000) | (29,000) |
| Income taxes | (8,000) | (9,000) | (10,000) |
| Net income | $ 12,000 | $ 12,000 | $ 12,000 |

**Required:**

Prepare common-size income statements by using net sales as the base.

**Solution:**

Since the analysis is based on net sales, net sales in each year equals 100% of itself. Then, every line item on the income statement is expressed as a percent of that year's net sales.

*(Continued)*

$$\text{Percent for a Line Item} = \left(\frac{\text{Dollar Amount of Line Item}}{\text{Dollar Amount of That Year's Sales}}\right) \times 100$$

Percent Year 1 Net Sales = ($100,000/$100,000) × 100 = 100%

Percent Year 2 Net Sales = ($120,000/$120,000) × 100 = 100%

Percent Year 3 Net Sales = ($132,000/$132,000) × 100 = 100%

**CORNERSTONE**

**16.2**

*(Continued)*

|  | Year 1 | | Year 2 | | Year 3 | |
|---|---|---|---|---|---|---|
|  | **Dollars** | **Percent*** | **Dollars** | **Percent*** | **Dollars** | **Percent*** |
| Net sales | $100,000 | 100% | $120,000 | 100.0% | $132,000 | 100.0% |
| Less: Cost of goods sold | (60,000) | 60 | (75,000) | 62.5 | (81,000) | 61.4 |
| Gross margin | $ 40,000 | 40 | $ 45,000 | 37.5 | $ 51,000 | 38.6 |
| Less: | | | | | | |
| Operating expenses | (20,000) | 20 | (24,000) | 20.0 | (29,000) | 22.0 |
| Income taxes | (8,000) | 8 | (9,000) | 7.5 | (10,000) | 7.6 |
| Net income | $ 12,000 | 12 | $ 12,000 | 10.0 | $ 12,000 | 9.1 |

\* Percentages are rounded to one decimal place.

In Cornerstone 16.2, sales are used as the base for computing percentages. Although the main purpose of vertical analysis is to highlight relationships among components of a company's financial statements, changes in these relationships over time can also be informative. For example, Cornerstone 16.1 (p. 717) reveals large increases in cost of goods sold and operating expenses over time. Over the 3-year period, cost of goods sold has increased by 35% ($21,000/$60,000), and operating expenses have increased by 45% ($9,000/$20,000). Cornerstone 16.2 compares these expenses with sales. This comparison reveals that much of the increase may be tied to increased sales. That is, Year 1 operating expenses represented 20% of sales, whereas in Year 3, they represented 22% of sales.

## Percentages and Size Effects

The use of common-size analysis makes comparisons more meaningful because percentages eliminate the effects of size. For example, Heisman Company earns $100,000 and Casciani Company earns $1 million, which company is more profitable? The answer depends to a large extent on the assets employed to earn the profits. If Heisman used an investment of $1 million to earn the $100,000, then the return expressed as a percentage of dollars is 10% ($100,000/$1,000,000). If Casciani used an investment of $20 million to earn its $1 million, the percentage return is only 5% ($1,000,000/$20,000,000). By using percentages, it is easy to see that the first firm is relatively more profitable than the second.

**concept Q&A**

Hornsby Company's net income is $1,000 one year and $1,500 the following year. Grabowski Company's net income is $10,000 one year and $12,000 the following year. What is the percentage increase from one year to the next for each company? Which company is doing better?

**Answer:**

Hornsby's net income has increased by 50%, while Grabowski's net income has increased by 20%. It is hard to say which is doing a better job. Because percentages abstract from size, users must exercise caution in their interpretation, particularly when the numbers involved are small. If the base is small, small changes in line items can produce large percentage changes. The percentage increase in net income is larger for Hornsby than for Grabowski. However, Hornsby increased its total earnings by only $500, while Grabowski increased its earnings by $2,000.

## RATIO ANALYSIS

Ratio analysis is the second major technique for financial statement analysis. Ratios are fractions or percentages computed by dividing one account or line-item amount by another. For example, operating income divided by sales produces a ratio that measures the profit margin on sales.

OBJECTIVE  **2**

Explain why historical standards and industrial averages are important for ratio analysis.

## Standards for Comparison

Ratios by themselves tell little about the financial well-being of a company. For meaningful analysis, the ratios should be compared with a standard. Only through comparison can someone using a financial statement assess the financial health of a company. Two standards commonly used are the past history of the company and industrial averages. Exhibit 16.2 illustrates the way a company might view both types of ratio comparison.

( EXHIBIT 16.2 )

**Ratio Analysis**

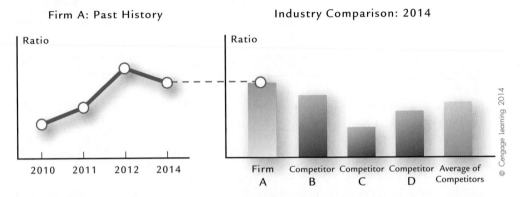

**Past History**   One way to detect progress or problems is to compare the value of a ratio over time. Doing so allows trends to be assessed. For example, ratios measuring liquidity may be dropping over time, signaling a deteriorating financial condition. The company's management can use this information to take corrective action. Investors and creditors, on the other hand, may use this information to decide whether or not to invest money in the company.

**Industrial Averages**   Additional insight can be gained by comparing a company's ratios with the same ratios for companies in the same business. To facilitate the comparison, a number of annual publications provide industrial figures. For example, Dun and Bradstreet report the median, upper quartile, and lower quartile for 14 commonly used ratios for more than 900 lines of business. The titles and publishers of some of the more common sources of industrial ratios are as follows:

- *Key Business Ratios*, **Dun and Bradstreet**
- *Standard & Poor's Industry Survey*, **Standard & Poor's**
- *Annual Statement Studies*, **Robert Morris Associates**
- *The Almanac of Business and Industrial Financial Ratios*, **Prentice-Hall**
- *Dow Jones-Irwin Business and Investment Almanac*, **Dow Jones-Irwin**

A number of online sources are also useful for obtaining competitive information on a company's ratios. Some of these are:

- **www.bizstats.com**
- **www.fidelity.com**
- **http://moneycentral.msn.com/investor/invsub/results/compare.asp?**
- **http://biz.yahoo.com/r/**

Even though the industrial figures provide a useful reference point, they should be used with care. Companies within the same industry may use different accounting methods, which diminishes the validity of the average. Other problems such as small sample sizes for the industrial report, different labor markets, the impact of extreme values, and terms of sale can produce variations among companies within the same industry. The industrial statistics should not be taken as absolute norms but rather as general guidelines for purposes of making comparisons.

## Classification of Ratios

Ratios generally are classified into one of three categories: liquidity, borrowing capacity or leverage, and profitability.

- **Liquidity ratios** measure the ability of a company to meet its current obligations.
- **Leverage ratios** measure the ability of a company to meet its long- and short-term obligations. These ratios provide a measure of the degree of protection provided to a company's creditors.
- **Profitability ratios** measure the earning ability of a company. These ratios allow investors, creditors, and managers to evaluate the extent to which invested funds are being used efficiently.

Some of the more common and popular ratios for each category will be defined and illustrated. Exhibits 16.3 and 16.4 (p. 722) provide an income statement, a statement of retained earnings, and comparative balance sheets for Payne Company, a manufacturer of glassware. These financial statements provide the basis for subsequent analyses.

( EXHIBIT 16.3 )

**Income Statement and Statement of Retained Earnings for Payne Company for Year 2**

**Payne Company**
**Income Statement**
**For the Year Ended December 31, Year 2**
**(dollars in thousands)**

|  | Amount | Percent |
|---|---|---|
| Net sales | $ 50,000 | 100.0% |
| Less: Cost of goods sold | (35,000) | 70.0 |
| Gross margin | $ 15,000 | 30.0 |
| Less: Operating expenses | (10,000) | 20.0 |
| Operating income | $ 5,000 | 10.0 |
| Less: Interest expense | (400) | 0.8 |
| Income before taxes | $ 4,600 | 9.2 |
| Less: Income taxes (50%)* | (2,300) | 4.6 |
| Net income | $ 2,300 | 4.6 |

*Includes both state and federal taxes.

**Payne Company**
**Statement of Retained Earnings**
**For the Year Ended December 31, Year 2**

| | |
|---|---|
| Balance, beginning of period | $ 5,324 |
| Net income | 2,300 |
| Total | $ 7,624 |
| Less: Preferred dividends | (224) |
| Dividends to common stockholders | (1,000) |
| Balance, end of period | $ 6,400 |

( EXHIBIT 16.4 )

**Comparative Balance Sheets for Payne Company for Years 1 and 2**

| Payne Company<br>Comparative Balance Sheets<br>For the Years Ended December 31, Year 1 and Year 2<br>(dollars in thousands) | | |
| --- | --- | --- |
| **Assets** | | |
| | **Year 2** | **Year 1** |
| Current assets: | | |
| Cash | $ 1,600 | $ 2,500 |
| Marketable securities | 1,600 | 2,000 |
| Accounts receivable (net) | 8,000 | 10,000 |
| Inventories | 10,000 | 3,000 |
| Other | 800 | 1,500 |
| Total current assets | $22,000 | $19,000 |
| Property and equipment: | | |
| Land | $ 4,000 | $ 6,000 |
| Building and equipment (net) | 6,000 | 5,000 |
| Total long-term assets | $10,000 | $11,000 |
| Total assets | $32,000 | $30,000 |
| **Liabilities and Stockholders' Equity** | | |
| Current liabilities: | | |
| Notes payable, short term | $ 3,200 | $ 3,000 |
| Accounts payable | 6,400 | 5,800 |
| Current maturity of long-term debt | 400 | 400 |
| Accrued payables | 2,000 | 1,876 |
| Total current liabilities | $12,000 | $11,076 |
| Long-term liabilities: | | |
| Bonds payable, 10% | 4,000 | 4,000 |
| Total liabilities | $16,000 | $15,076 |
| Stockholders' equity: | | |
| Preferred stock, $25 par, 7% | $ 3,200 | $ 3,200 |
| Common stock, $2 par | 1,600 | 1,600 |
| Additional paid-in capital* | 4,800 | 4,800 |
| Retained earnings | 6,400 | 5,324 |
| Total equity | $16,000 | $14,924 |
| Total liabilities and stockholders' equity | $32,000 | $30,000 |

*For common stock only.

© Cengage Learning 2014

OBJECTIVE ❸

Calculate and use liquidity ratios to assess the ability of a company to meet its current obligations.

# LIQUIDITY RATIOS

Liquidity ratios are used to assess the short-term debt-paying ability of a company. If a company does not have the short-term financial strength to meet its current obligations, it is likely to have difficulty meeting its long-term obligations. Accordingly, evaluation of the short-term financial strength of a company is a good starting point in financial analysis. Although there are numerous liquidity ratios, only the most common ones will be discussed in this section. These liquidity ratios are:

- current ratio
- quick or acid-test ratio
- accounts receivable turnover ratio
- inventory turnover ratio

# Current Ratio

The **current ratio** is a measure of the ability of a company to pay its short-term liabilities out of short-term assets. The current ratio is computed as follows:

$$\text{Current Ratio} = \frac{\text{Current Assets}}{\text{Current Liabilities}}$$

Since current liabilities must be paid within an operating cycle (usually within a year) and current assets can be converted to cash within an operating cycle, the current ratio provides a direct measure of the ability of a company to meet its short-term obligations. Payne Company's current ratio for Year 2 is computed as follows, using data from Exhibit 16.4:

$$\text{Current Ratio} = \frac{\$22,000,000}{\$12,000,000}$$
$$= 1.83$$

But what does a current ratio of 1.83 mean? Does the ratio of 1.83 signal good or poor debt-paying ability? Additional information is needed to interpret it. Many creditors use the rule of thumb that a 2.0 ratio is needed to provide good debt-paying ability. Based on this assessment, Payne does not have sufficient liquidity.

However, this rule has many exceptions. For example, the industrial norm might be less than 2.0. Suppose that the upper quartile, median, and lower quartile values of the current ratio for the glassware industry are 2.2, 1.7, and 1.3, respectively. Payne's current ratio of 1.83 is above the median ratio for its industry, suggesting that Payne does not have liquidity problems. More than half of the firms in its industry have lower current ratios. Information on the ratio's trend is also helpful. It is possible, for example, that Payne's current ratio for Year 2 is representative of what usually happens. By comparing this year's ratio with ratios for prior years, some judgment about whether or not it is representative can be made. For example, if the ratio in prior years has been reasonably stable with values in the 1.7 to 1.9 range, this year's ratio is representative. If the ratio has been declining for the past several years, the company's financial position could be deteriorating.

A declining current ratio is not necessarily bad, particularly if it is falling from a high value. A high current ratio may signal excessive investment in current resources. Some of these current resources may be more productively employed by reducing long-term debt, paying dividends, or investing in long-term assets. Thus, a declining current ratio may signal a move toward more efficient utilization of resources. But a declining current ratio coupled with a current ratio lower than that of other firms in the industry supports the judgment that a company is having liquidity problems.

# Quick or Acid–Test Ratio

For many companies, inventory represents 50% or more of total current assets. For example, Payne Company's inventory represents 45% of its total current assets. The liquidity of inventory often is less than that of accounts receivable, marketable securities, and cash. Inventory may be slow moving, nearly obsolete, or even pledged in part to creditors. Because including inventory may produce a misleading measure of liquidity, it is often excluded in computing liquidity ratios. For similar reasons, other current assets, such as miscellaneous assets, also are excluded.

The **quick** or **acid-test ratio** is a measure of liquidity that compares only the most liquid assets with current liabilities. Excluded from the quick ratio are nonliquid current assets such as inventories. The numerator of the quick ratio includes only the most liquid assets (cash, marketable securities, and accounts receivable).

---

## concept Q&A

This year, Bellows Company has the same level of current assets and current liabilities as last year. However, last year current assets were 50% cash and accounts receivable, while this year current assets are 75% inventories. How will the change in the current asset mix affect this year's current ratio? Quick ratio?

**Answer:**

The current ratio will be unaffected (i.e., this year's current ratio will equal last year's current ratio). The quick ratio will be lower this year than last year because cash and accounts receivable are lower than last year. *Hint:* Sometimes it helps to put numbers into this type of question. For example, you can choose to let last year's (as well as this year's) current assets equal $2,000 and to let last year's (as well as this year's) current liabilities equal $1,000. Then, the current ratio last year will be $2,000/$1,000 or 2. This year's current ratio is the same. The quick ratio for last year will be 1 ($1,000/$1,000), while this year's quick ratio will be 0.5 ($500/$1,000).

$$\text{Quick Ratio} = \frac{(\text{Cash} + \text{Marketable Securities} + \text{Accounts Receivable})}{\text{Current Liabilities}}$$

For Payne Company, the quick ratio is calculated as follows (using data from Exhibit 16.4, p. 722 for Year 2):

$$\text{Quick Ratio} = \frac{(\$1,600,000 + \$1,600,000 + \$8,000,000)}{\$12,000,000}$$

$$= \frac{\$11,200,000}{\$12,000,000}$$

$$= 0.93$$

Payne's quick ratio reveals that it does not have the capability to meet its current obligations with its most liquid assets; a ratio of 1.0 is the usual standard. Payne's quick ratio is not far below the standard level, and perhaps some attention should be paid to raise it somewhat.

Cornerstone 16.3 shows how to calculate the current ratio and the quick ratio.

**CORNERSTONE**

**16.3**

## Calculating the Current Ratio and the Quick (or Acid-Test) Ratio

**Why:**

The current ratio measures a company's liquidity by showing how many dollars of current assets it possesses relative to current liabilities. The quick ratio provides an even more direct assessment of liquidity by including in the numerator only the three assets that already are cash or typically are converted to cash most quickly.

**Information:**

Bordner Company has current assets equal to $120,000. Of these, $15,000 is cash, $30,000 is accounts receivable, and the remainder is inventories. Current liabilities total $50,000.

**Required:**

1. Calculate the current ratio.

2. Calculate the quick ratio (acid-test ratio).

**Solution:**

1. Current Ratio = Current Assets/Current Liabilities

   = $120,000/$50,000

   = 2.40

2. Quick Ratio = (Cash + Marketable Securities + Accounts Receivable)/Current Liabilities

   = ($15,000 + $0 + $30,000)/$50,000

   = 0.90

*Note:* Answer is rounded to two decimal places.

# Accounts Receivable Turnover Ratio

The extent of Payne's liquidity problem can be further investigated by examining the liquidity of its receivables, or how long it takes the company to turn its receivables into cash. A low liquidity of receivables signals more difficulty since the quick ratio would be overstated. The liquidity of receivables is measured by the **accounts receivable turnover ratio**, computed as follows:

$$\text{Accounts Receivable Turnover Ratio} = \frac{\text{Net Sales}}{\text{Average Accounts Receivable}}$$

Average accounts receivable is defined as follows:

$$\text{Average Accounts Receivable} = \frac{(\text{Beginning Receivables} + \text{Ending Receivables})}{2}$$

The average accounts receivable is based on the beginning and ending balances of accounts receivable because this matches the account to the period that corresponds to the income statement measure.

Payne Company's accounts receivable turnover is computed as follows (using data from Exhibits 16.3, p. 721 and 16.4, p. 722):

$$\text{Accounts Receivable Turnover} = \frac{\$50,000,000^*}{\$9,000,000}.$$
$$= 5.56 \text{ times per year}$$

*Average Receivables = ($10,000,000 + $8,000,000)/2

The accounts receivable turnover ratio can be taken further to determine the number of days the average balance of accounts receivable is outstanding before being converted into cash, which is calculated as follows:

$$\text{Turnover in Days} = \frac{365}{\text{Receivables Turnover Ratio}}$$

Payne Company's accounts receivable turnover in days is computed as follows (using data from Exhibits 16.3, p. 721, and 16.4, p. 722):

$$\text{Accounts Receivable Turnover in Days} = 365/5.56 = 65.6 \text{ days}$$

Payne's receivables are held for almost 66 days before being converted to cash.

Whether this is good or bad depends to some extent on what other companies in the industry are experiencing. The low turnover ratio suggests a need for Payne's managers to modify credit and collection policies to speed up the conversion of receivables to cash. This need is particularly acute if a historical analysis shows a persistent problem or a trend downward. Note that net sales were used to compute the turnover ratio. Technically, credit sales should be used. However, external financial reports do not usually break net sales into credit and cash components. Consequently, if a turnover ratio is to be computed by external users, net sales must be used. For many firms, most sales are credit sales, and the computation is a good approximation. If sales are mostly for cash, liquidity is not an issue. In that case, the ratio provides a measure of the company's operating cycle. Cornerstone 16.4 shows how to calculate the average accounts receivable, the accounts receivable turnover ratio, and the accounts receivable turnover in days.

**CORNERSTONE**

**16.4**

## Calculating the Average Accounts Receivable, the Accounts Receivable Turnover Ratio, and the Accounts Receivable Turnover in Days

**Why:**

These three ratios assess the speed at which a company converts its accounts receivable into cash.

**Information:**

Last year, Shuster Company had net sales of $750,000 and cost of goods sold of $400,000. Shuster had the following balances:

| | January 1 | December 31 |
|---|---|---|
| Accounts receivable | $ 98,500 | $101,500 |
| Inventories | 463,000 | 497,000 |

**Required:**

1. Calculate the average accounts receivable.

2. Calculate the accounts receivable turnover ratio.

3. Calculate the accounts receivable turnover in days.

**Solution:**

1. Average Accounts Receivables = (Beginning Receivables + Ending Receivables)/2

   = ($98,500 + $101,500)/2 = $100,000

2. Accounts Receivable Turnover Ratio = Net Sales/Average Accounts Receivable

   = $750,000/$100,000 = 7.5 times

3. Accounts Receivable Turnover in Days = Days in a Year/Accounts Receivable

   Turnover Ratio

   = 365/7.5 = 48.7 days

*Note:* Answer is rounded to one decimal place.

# YOUDECIDE Using Ratio Analysis to Improve Cash Management Decisions

You are a finance manager at **Macy's**, an international retailing company. One of your primary duties is management of the company's cash position.

**Which financial ratios would you most likely use in managing Macy's cash position? In addition to these ratios, what other factors would you consider?**

While numerous ratios are important in managing a company's cash position, the ones you might consider first would be the liquidity ratios because they address a company's ability to meet current obligations as they come due. For example, Macy's current ratio is a critical indicator of the extent to which the company has enough current assets to settle its current liabilities. Typically, having a current ratio greater than 1.0 is an important benchmark because it indicates that current assets exceed current liabilities. Looking at the quick ratio would add incremental insights into Macy's cash position because it focuses on the company's most liquid current assets—cash, marketable securities, and receivables. Examining the current and quick ratios in tandem, along with any other pertinent information such as the timing of cash inflows and outflows, paints a more complete picture of the company. For instance, a retailer might experience a seasonal preholiday decrease in its quick ratio as it builds inventory while accounts payable simultaneously increases faster than sales. These ratios would change again as the holiday season progresses and inventory is sold (increasing accounts receivable and eventually cash) and current liabilities are paid using cash generated from holiday sales.

Additional factors to consider include the company's customer credit granting policies, which affects credit sales and accounts receivable. Loosening credit policies usually increases credit sales and accounts receivable. However, if bad debts (i.e., customer payment defaults) increase as a result of selling on credit to customers with poor credit ratings, then such information should supplement the current and quick ratio analyses to best predict the company's future cash position.

**Effective cash management is particularly important during severe economic downturns; some companies even go so far as to prepare daily liquidity reports.**

## Inventory Turnover Ratio

Inventory turnover is also an important liquidity measure. The **inventory turnover ratio** is computed as follows:

$$\text{Inventory Turnover Ratio} = \frac{\text{Cost of Goods Sold}}{\text{Average Inventory}}$$

Average inventory is found as follows:

$$\text{Average Inventory} = \frac{(\text{Beginning Inventory} + \text{Ending Inventory})}{2}$$

This ratio tells an analyst how many times the average inventory turns over, or is sold, during the year. The number of days inventory is held before being sold can be computed as follows:

$$\text{Turnover in Days} = \frac{365}{\text{Inventory Turnover Ratio}}$$

The inventory turnover ratio for Payne Company is computed as follows, using data from Exhibits 16.3 (p. 721) and 16.4 (p. 722):

$$\text{Inventory Turnover} = \frac{\$35,000,000}{\$6,500,000^*}$$

$$= 5.38 \text{ times per year, or every } 67.8 \text{ days} \left(\frac{365}{5.38}\right)$$

*Average Inventory = (3,000,000 + $10,000,000)/2

Suppose that the glassware industry revealed the upper quartile, median, and lower quartile turnover figures in days to be 34, 57, and 79, respectively. Payne's turnover ratio is midway between the median and the lower quartile. The evidence seems to indicate that the turnover ratio is lower than it should be. A low turnover ratio may signal the presence of too much inventory or sluggish sales. More attention to inventory policies and marketing activities may be in order. Cornerstone 16.5 shows how to calculate the average inventory, the inventory turnover ratio, and the inventory turnover in days.

Let's return briefly to **Apple**, which was the focus of the chapter's opening vignette. Apple is a master at successfully launching new products. For example, it sold 1 million first generation iPhones during the first 74 days after launch. Was this successful launch performance a one-time aberration or was it indicative of a trend that would continue with future product launches? The next several big launches provided clear insights on this question as Apple subsequently launched its initial iPad and hit 1 million units sold in only 28 days, which continued with a total of

## Calculating the Average Inventory, the Inventory Turnover Ratio, and the Inventory Turnover in Days

**16.5**

**Why:**

These three ratios assess the speed at which a company converts its inventory into cash.

**Information:**

Last year, Shuster Company had net sales of $750,000 and cost of goods sold of $400,000. Shuster had the following balances:

|                     | January 1 | December 31 |
|---------------------|-----------|-------------|
| Accounts receivable | $98,500   | $101,500    |
| Inventories         | 83,000    | 87,000      |

**Required:**

1. Calculate the average inventory.

2. Calculate the inventory turnover ratio.

3. Calculate the inventory turnover in days.

**Solution:**

1. Average Inventory = (Beginning Inventory + Ending Inventory)/2

$$= (\$83,000 + \$87,000)/2$$

$$= \$85,000$$

2. Inventory Turnover Ratio = Cost of Goods Sold/Average Inventory

$$= \$400,000/\$85,000$$

$$= 4.7 \text{ times}$$

3. Inventory Turnover in Days = Days in a Year/Inventory Turnover Ratio

$$= 365/4.7$$

$$= 77.7 \text{ days}$$

*Note:* Answer is rounded to one decimal place.

3 million iPad unit sales during its first 80 days. Even more impressive was Apple's sales of 1.7 million iPhone 4 units during its first *three days* on the market! Following Apple's inventory turnover surrounding such astounding product launches provides insights regarding its ability to successfully sell its products after the initial "wow" factor subsides at some point after launch.

Apple's inventory turnover for the fiscal year prior to its launch of the iPad and iPhone 4 was 53.28 times, which means that, on average, its inventory remained on the shelf prior to being sold for only 6.85 days—less than one week. Apple's inventory turnover has increased even further since its launch of the iPad 2 and the iPhone 4S.

These results are impressive given that the majority of Apple's inventory consists of at least moderately expensive merchandise that customers likely retain for relatively long periods. In other words, to maintain such large inventory turnover results, Apple has succeeded in attracting customers to purchase multiple Apple products, sometimes of the same type (e.g., multiple laptops, iPods, iPads, or iPhones for the entire family).

# LEVERAGE RATIOS

OBJECTIVE 4

Calculate and use leverage ratios to assess the ability of a company to meet its long- and short-term obligations.

When a company incurs debt, it has the obligation to repay the principal and the interest. Holding debt increases the riskiness of a company. Unlike other sources of capital (e.g., retained earnings or proceeds from the sale of capital stock), debt carries with it the threat of default foreclosure and bankruptcy if income does not meet projections. Both potential investors and creditors need to evaluate a company's debt position. A potential creditor may find that the amount of debt and debt-servicing requirements of a company make it too risky to grant further credit. Similarly, the company may be too risky for some potential investors. Leverage ratios can help an individual to evaluate a company's debt-carrying ability.

## Times-Interest-Earned Ratio

The first leverage ratio uses the income statement to assess a company's ability to service its debt. This ratio, called the **times-interest-earned ratio**, is computed as follows:

$$\text{Times-Interest-Earned Ratio} = \frac{(\text{Income Before Taxes} + \text{Interest Expense})}{\text{Interest Expense}}$$

Income before taxes must be recurring income; thus, unusual or infrequent items appearing on the income statement should be excluded in order to compute the ratio. Recurring income is used because it is the income that is available each year to cover interest payments.

The times-interest-earned ratio for Payne Company is computed as follows, using data from Exhibit 16.3 (p. 721):

$$\text{Times-Interest-Earned Ratio} = \frac{(\$4,600,000 + \$400,000)}{\$400,000}$$
$$= \$5,000,000/\$400,000$$
$$= 12.5 \text{ times}$$

Since the assumed upper quartile for the glassware industry is 10.0, Payne's times-interest-earned ratio is among the highest in its industry. Payne does not have a significant interest expense burden.

Cornerstone 16.6 shows how to calculate the times-interest-earned ratio.

## Calculating the Times-Interest-Earned Ratio

**Why:**

Times-interest-earned is a profitability ratio that compares a company's earnings to its interest expense to assess how well the company can service its debt.

**Information:**

Calvin Company provided the following income statement for last year:

CORNERSTONE

16.6

*(Continued)*

**CORNERSTONE**

**16.6**

*(Continued)*

| | |
|---|---:|
| Sales | $900,000 |
| Cost of goods sold | 350,000 |
| Gross margin | $550,000 |
| Operating expenses | 270,000 |
| Operating income | $280,000 |
| Interest expense | 15,000 |
| Income before taxes | $265,000 |
| Income taxes | 80,000 |
| Net income | $185,000 |

**Required:**

Calculate the times-interest-earned ratio.

**Solution:**

$$\text{Times-Interest-Earned Ratio} = \frac{(\text{Income Before Taxes} + \text{Interest Expense})}{\text{Interest Expense}}$$

$$= (\$265,000 + \$15,000)/\$15,000$$

$$= 18.7 \text{ times}$$

*Note:* Answer is rounded to one decimal place.

## Debt Ratio

Investors and creditors are the two major sources of capital. As the percentage of assets financed by creditors increases, the riskiness of the company increases. The **debt ratio** measures this percentage and is computed as follows:

$$\text{Debt Ratio} = \frac{\text{Total Liabilities}}{\text{Total Assets}}$$

Since total liabilities are compared with total assets, the ratio measures the degree of protection afforded creditors in case of insolvency. Creditors often impose restrictions on the percentage of liabilities allowed. If this percentage is exceeded, the company is in default, and foreclosure can take place.

The debt ratio for Payne Company is calculated as follows, using data from Exhibit 16.4 (p. 722):

$$\text{Debt Ratio} = \frac{\$16,000,000}{\$32,000,000}$$

$$= 0.50$$

Payne's debt ratio indicates that 50% of its assets are financed by creditors.

Is this percentage good or bad? How much risk will the stockholders allow? Will creditors be willing to provide more capital? For guidance, we again turn to industrial figures. The upper quartile, median, and lower quartile figures are 0.47, 0.55, and 0.69, respectively. With respect to industrial performance, Payne's debt ratio is not out of line. In fact, Payne is close to the upper quartile figure of 0.47. This position might indicate that Payne still has the capability to use additional credit.

Another ratio useful in assessing the leverage used by a company is the debt-to-equity ratio. This ratio compares the amount of debt that is financed by stockholders and is calculated as follows:

---

### concept Q&A

Quickly estimate your total debts and your total assets. Calculate your own debt ratio. Do you expect it to change over the next 5 years? Why or why not?

**Answer:**

Answers will vary. As a student, your debt ratio is likely high because you're incurring student loan costs and living expenses, probably without full-time employment. However, this will likely change in the future when you graduate and are more likely to begin paying off debt instead of continuing to accrue it.

$$\text{Debt-to-Equity Ratio} = \frac{\text{Total Liabilities}}{\text{Total Stockholders' Equity}}$$

For Payne Company, the debt-to-equity ratio is calculated as follows, using data from Exhibit 16.4:

$$\text{Debt-to-Equity Ratio} = \$16,000,000/\$16,000,000$$

$$= 1.00$$

Creditors would like this ratio to be relatively low, indicating that stockholders have financed most of the assets of the firm. Stockholders, on the other hand, may wish this ratio to be higher because that indicates that the company is more highly leveraged and stockholders can reap the return of the creditors' financing.

Cornerstone 16.7 shows how to calculate the debt ratio and the debt-to-equity ratio.

## Calculating the Debt Ratio and the Debt-to-Equity Ratio

CORNERSTONE

**16.7**

**Why:**

These two ratios provide insights into the capital structure (i.e., debt or equity) used by a company to finance its assets.

**Information:**

Jemell Company's balance sheet shows total liabilities of $450,000, total stockholders' equity of $300,000, and total assets of $750,000.

**Required:**

1. Calculate the debt ratio for Jemell.

2. Calculate the debt-to-equity ratio for Jemell.

**Solution:**

1. $\text{Debt Ratio} = \dfrac{\text{Total Liabilities}}{\text{Total Assets}}$

   $= \$450,000/\$750,000$

   $= 0.60$, or 60%

2. $\text{Debt-to-Equity Ratio} = \dfrac{\text{Total Liabilities}}{\text{Total Stockholders' Equity}}$

   $= \$450,000/\$300,000$

   $= 1.50$

# PROFITABILITY RATIOS

Investors earn a return through the receipt of dividends and appreciation of the market value of their stock. Both dividends and market price of shares are related to the profits generated by companies. Since they are the source of debt-servicing payments, profits also are of concern to creditors. Managers also have a vested interest in profits. Bonuses, promotions, and salary increases often are tied to reported profits. Profitability ratios, therefore, are given particular attention by both internal and external users of financial statements.

OBJECTIVE ❺

Calculate and use profitability ratios to assess the extent to which a company's resources are being used efficiently.

## Return on Sales

Return on sales is the profit margin on sales. It represents the percentage of each sales dollar that is left over as net income after all expenses have been subtracted. **Return on sales** is one measure of the efficiency of a firm and is computed as follows:

$$\text{Return on Sales} = \frac{\text{Net Income}}{\text{Sales}}$$

Cornerstone 16.8 shows how to calculate the return on sales for Payne Company for Year 2.

CORNERSTONE

16.8

### Calculating the Return on Sales

**Why:**
Return on sales computes the cents from each sales dollar that remain after subtracting all expenses.

**Information:**
Refer to the information for Payne Company in Exhibit 16.3 (p. 721).

**Required:**
Calculate the return on sales.

**Solution:**
Return on Sales = $2,300,000/$50,000,000

= 0.046, or 4.6%

*Note:* Answer is rounded to three decimal places.

## Return on Total Assets

Return on assets measures how efficiently assets are used by calculating the return on total assets used to generate profits. **Return on total assets** is computed as follows:

$$\text{Return on Total Assets} = \frac{\text{Net Income} + [\text{Interest Expense}(1 - \text{Tax Rate})]}{\text{Average Total Assets}}$$

Average total assets is found as follows:

$$\text{Average Total Assets} = \frac{(\text{Beginning Total Assets} + \text{Ending Total Assets})}{2}$$

By adding back the after-tax cost of interest, this measure reflects only how the assets were employed. It does not consider the manner in which they were financed (interest expense is a cost of obtaining the assets, not a cost of *using* them).

Cornerstone 16.9 computes the return on assets for Payne Company for Year 2.

## Calculating the Average Total Assets and the Return on Assets

CORNERSTONE

16.9

**Why:**

Return on assets is a popular ratio that assesses the efficiency with which assets generate earnings.

**Information:**

Refer to the information for Payne Company in Exhibits 16.3 (p. 721) and 16.4 (p. 722).

**Required:**

1. Calculate the average total assets.

2. Calculate the return on total assets.

**Solution:**

1. Average Total Assets = ($30,000,000 + $32,000,000)/2

   = $31,000,000

2. Return on Total Assets = $2,300,000 + [$400,000(1 − 0.50)]/$31,000,000

   = ($2,300,000 + $200,000)/$31,000,000

   = $2,500,000/$31,000,000

   = 0.0806, or 8.06%

*Note:* The $400,000 of interest expense in the return on total assets numerator is given in Exhibit 16.3. Alternately, it can be calculated as follows:

   $4,000,000 of Bonds Payable (as shown in Exhibit 16. 4) × 10% = $400,000.

*Note:* Answer is rounded to four decimal places.

## Return on Common Stockholders' Equity

Return on total assets is measured without regard to the source of invested funds. For common stockholders, however, the return that they receive on their investment is of paramount importance. Of special interest to common stockholders is how they are being treated relative to other suppliers of capital funds. The **return on stockholders' equity** provides a measure that can be used to compare against other return measures (e.g., preferred dividend rates and bond rates) and is computed as follows:

$$\text{Return on Stockholders' Equity} = \frac{(\text{Net Income} - \text{Preferred Dividends})}{\text{Average Common Stockholders' Equity}}$$

For Payne Company, the beginning and ending common stockholders' equity require further calculations because the company has preferred stock. The preferred stock must be backed out of the total equity to get the common stockholders' equity. For Payne, the beginning and ending common stockholders' equity is calculated as follows:

$$\text{Beginning Common Stockholders' Equity} = \$14,924,000 - \$3,200,000$$
$$= \$11,724,000$$

$$\text{Ending Common Stockholders' Equity} = \$16,000,000 - \$3,200,000$$
$$= \$12,800,000$$

$$\text{Average Common Stockholders' Equity} = \frac{(\$12,800,000 + \$11,724,000)}{2}$$
$$= \$12,262,000$$

Cornerstone 16.10 calculates the return on stockholders' equity for Payne Company.

## Calculating the Average Common Stockholders' Equity and the Return on Stockholders' Equity

**Why:**

Return on stockholders' equity is a popular ratio among investors that calculates the earnings generated per dollar of stockholders' equity.

**Information:**

Refer to the information for Payne Company in Exhibits 16.3 (p. 721) and 16.4 (p. 722).

**Required:**

1. Calculate the average common stockholders' equity.

2. Calculate the return on stockholders' equity.

**Solution:**

1. Average Common Stockholders' Equity = ($11,724,000 + $12,800,000)/2

   = $12,262,000

   *Note:* Common stockholders' equity for each year is calculated by summing common stock, additional paid-in capital, and retained earnings (all three of which are shown in Exhibit 16.4). Therefore, common stockholders' equity for Year 1 = $1,600,000 + $4,800,000 + $5,324,000 = $11,724,000.

2. Return on Stockholders' Equity = ($2,300,000 − $224,000)/$12,262,000

   = $2,076,000/$12,262,000

   = 0.1693, or 16.93%

   *Note:* Preferred dividends = $3,200,000 of preferred stock × 7% preferred dividend rate = $224,000 (as shown in Exhibits 16.3 and 16.4).

   *Note:* Answer is rounded to four decimal places.

As we can see in Cornerstone 16.10, compared with the bond return of 10% and the preferred dividend rate of 7%, common stockholders are faring quite well. Furthermore, since the industrial average is about 14%, the rate of return provided common stockholders is above average.

# Earnings per Share

Investors also pay considerable attention to a company's profitability on a per-share basis. **Earnings per share** is computed as follows:

$$\text{Earnings per Share} = \frac{(\text{Net Income} - \text{Preferred Dividends})}{\text{Average Common Shares}}$$

Average common shares outstanding is computed by taking a weighted average of the common shares for the period under study. For example, assume that a company has 8,000 common shares at the beginning of the year. At the end of the first quarter, 4,000 additional shares are issued. No other transactions take place during the period. The weighted average is computed as follows:

|  | Outstanding Shares | Weight | Weighted Shares |
|---|---|---|---|
| First quarter | 8,000 | 3/12 | 2,000 |
| Last three quarters | 12,000 | 9/12 | 9,000 |
| Average common shares outstanding |  |  | 11,000 |

Cornerstone 16.11 shows how to compute earnings per share for Payne Company.

## Computing Earnings per Share

CORNERSTONE

16.11

**Why:**

Earnings per share is the ratio most frequently cited by the majority of investors because it calculates the earnings generated per share of common stock.

**Information:**

Refer to the information for Payne Company in Exhibits 16.3 (p. 721) and 16.4 (p. 722).

**Required:**

1. Compute the dollar amount of preferred dividends.

2. Compute the number of common shares.

3. Compute earnings per share for Payne Company.

**Solution:**

1. Preferred Dividends = $3,200,000 × 0.07 = $224,000

   (Recall that the preferred shares pay a dividend of 7% as shown in Exhibit 16.4.)

2. Number of Common Shares = $1,600,000/$2 = 800,000 shares

3. Earnings per Share = ($2,300,000 − $224,000)/800,000

   = $2,076,000/800,000

   = $2.60

*Note:* Answer is rounded to two decimal places.

Since the median value for the industry is about $3.47 per share, Payne's earnings per share is somewhat low and may signal a need for management to focus on increasing earnings.

## Price-Earnings Ratio

The **price-earnings ratio** is calculated as follows:

$$\text{Price-Earnings Ratio} = \frac{\text{Market Price per Share}}{\text{Earnings per Share}}$$

Price-earnings ratios are viewed by many investors as important indicators of stock values. If investors believe that a company has good growth prospects, then the price-earnings ratio should be high. If investors believe that the current price-earnings ratio is low based on their view of future growth opportunities, the market price of the stock may be bid up. However, the price-earnings ratio should be interpreted with caution as it is comprised of stock price—a highly volatile measure that is influenced by numerous factors, including investor psychology—and earnings—a number that can be manipulated to meet certain targets involving analyst expectations, managerial bonuses, and other organizational goals.

Cornerstone 16.12 shows how to compute the price-earnings ratio for Payne Company.

**CORNERSTONE**

**16.12**

## Computing the Price-Earnings Ratio

**Why:**

Price-earnings ratio varies widely across companies and compares the market price per share of stock to the earnings generated per share of common stock.

**Information:**

Assume that the price per common share for Payne Company is $15.

**Required:**

Compute the price-earnings ratio.

**Solution:**

Price-Earnings Ratio = $15.00/$2.60
= 5.7692, or 5.77

*Note:* Refer to Cornerstone 16.11 for an explanation of how to calculate the $2.60 earnings per share.

*Note:* Answer is rounded to two decimal places.

As Cornerstone 16.12 shows, Payne's stock is selling for 5.8 times its current earnings per share. This ratio compares with an industrial median value of 6.3. Thus, Payne's price-earnings ratio is lower than more than half of the firms in the industry.

## Dividend Yield and Payout Ratios

The profitability measure called **dividend yield** is computed as follows:

$$\text{Dividend Yield} = \frac{\text{Dividends per Common Share}}{\text{Market Price per Common Share}}$$

By adding the dividend yield to the percentage change in stock price, a reasonable approximation of the total return accruing to an investor can be obtained.

The **dividend payout ratio** is computed as follows:

$$\text{Dividend Payout Ratio} = \frac{\text{Common Dividends}}{(\text{Net Income} - \text{Preferred Dividends})}$$

The payout ratio tells an investor the proportion of earnings that a company pays in dividends. Investors who prefer regular cash payments instead of returns through price appreciation will want to invest in companies with a high payout ratio; investors who prefer gains through appreciation will generally prefer a lower payout ratio.

Cornerstone 16.13 computes the dividend yield and dividend payout ratio for Payne Company.

## Computing the Dividend Yield and the Dividend Payout Ratio

CORNERSTONE

16.13

**Why:**

The dividend yield and dividend payout ratios compare the amount of dividends a company declares relative to other popular measures of its profitability, such as the market price per share of common stock or earnings.

**Information:**

Assume that the market price per common share is $15. Refer to the information for Payne Company in Exhibits 16.3 (p. 721) and 16.4 (p. 722).

**Required:**

1. Compute the dividends per share.

2. Compute the dividend yield.

3. Compute the dividend payout ratio.

**Solution:**

1. Dividends per Share = $1,000,000/800,000 = $1.25

2. Dividend Yield = $1.25/$15.00

    = 0.0833, or 8.33%

3. Dividend Payout Ratio = $1,000,000/($2,300,000 − $224,000)

    = $1,000,000/$2,076,000

    = 0.4817

*Note:* Answer is rounded to four decimal places.

The Summary of Important Equations section at the end of the chapter (p. 739) provides an overview of the ratios discussed in this chapter.

## Impact of the Just-in-Time Manufacturing Environment

In the just-in-time (JIT) manufacturing environment, reducing inventories and increasing quality are critical activities. Both activities are essential for many companies to retain their competitive ability. Accordingly, users of financial statements should have a special interest in ratios that measure a company's progress in achieving the goals of zero inventories and total quality. As a company reduces its inventory, the inventory turnover ratio should increase dramatically. Traditionally, high inventory turnovers have had a negative connotation. It was argued that a high inventory turnover ratio might signal such problems as stockouts and disgruntled customers. In the JIT manufacturing environment, however, a high turnover ratio is viewed positively. High turnover is interpreted as a signal of success—of achieving the goal of zero inventories with all of the efficiency associated with that state (see Chapter 14).

As inventory levels drop, the current ratio also is affected. Without significant inventories, the current ratio will drop. In fact, it will approach the value of the quick ratio. Since many lenders require a 2.0 current ratio to grant and control a loan, some reevaluation of the use of this ratio is needed for customers with a JIT system. It may be necessary to rely more on the quick ratio or other alternative ratios (such as cash flow divided by current maturities of long-term debt).

A ratio that says something about quality also is desirable for JIT firms. The usual approach is to express quality costs as a percentage of sales. External users, however, may not have access to quality costs as a separate category. Warranty costs, returns and allowances, unfavorable materials quantity variances, and other quality costs that are readily identifiable from the financial statement can be added. This sum can then be divided by sales to give the external users some idea of the company's capability in this important area. Tracking this ratio over time will reveal the progress that the company is making. As quality improves, quality costs as a percentage of sales should decline.

## The Importance of Profitability Ratios to External Users of the Financial Statements

Of course, for ratio analysis to be useful, it is critically important that the underlying financial information be accurate. The purpose of financial statements prepared for outside users is to fairly represent the underlying economic position of the firm. Many external users, such as investors in the stock market, banks, and public agencies, rely on the financial statements to provide necessary information. A look back at the past 5 to 10 years shows many instances in which corporate heads, knowing the importance of various ratios, took unethical steps to make the information fit the desired ratio results rather than letting the ratios come from fairly generated information.

**ETHICAL DECISIONS**  **Enron** provides an excellent example of top management's obsession with ratio "doctoring." The focus of Enron top management was the company's stock price. In order to convince the stock market that Enron was a strong company, worthy of supporting the price set by the market, Enron officials took steps to report increasing income, even when income was decreasing. Of course, when the facts about Enron's actual earnings came out, the stock price tumbled, and the company resorted to bankruptcy. The demise of this company, one of the largest companies in the United States, had serious consequences for Enron investors and employees, as well as their families.[2] ●

---

[2] For an excellent, and readable, description of the environment and events leading up to Enron's fall, see Bethany McLean and Peter Elkind, *The Smartest Guys in the Room: The Amazing Rise and Scandalous Fall of Enron.* (Penguin Books, New York: 2003/2004).

# SUMMARY OF LEARNING OBJECTIVES

**LO 1.**    Analyze financial statements using two forms of common-size analysis: horizontal analysis and vertical analysis.

- Common-size analysis expresses accounts or line items in financial statements as percentages.
- Horizontal analysis compares line items from one period with another period, to assess trends.
- Vertical analysis compares one line item with another line item from the same time period, to assess relationships among financial statement items.

**LO 2.**    Explain why historical standards and industrial averages are important for ratio analysis.

- Ratios can be compared with a standard.
- The most common standards are historical values and industrial values.

**LO 3.**    Calculate and use liquidity ratios to assess the ability of a company to meet its current obligations.

- Liquidity ratios are used to assess the short-term debt-paying ability of a company.
- These ratios include the current ratio, the quick or acid-test ratio, the accounts receivable turnover ratio, and the inventory turnover ratio.

**LO 4.**    Calculate and use leverage ratios to assess the ability of a company to meet its long- and short-term obligations.

- Leverage ratios measure the ability of a company to meet long-term debt obligations.
- These ratios include the times-interest-earned ratio and the debt ratio.

**LO 5.**    Calculate and use profitability ratios to assess the extent to which a company's resources are being used efficiently.

- Profitability ratios relate the firm's earnings to the resources used to create those earnings.
- Profitability ratios include return on sales, return on total assets, earnings per share, the price-earnings ratio, dividend yield, and the dividend payout ratio.

# SUMMARY OF IMPORTANT EQUATIONS

**Liquidity ratios:**

1. $\text{Current Ratio} = \dfrac{\text{Current Assets}}{\text{Current Liabilities}}$

2. $\text{Quick Ratio} = \dfrac{(\text{Cash} + \text{Marketable Securities} + \text{Accounts Receivable})}{\text{Current Liabilities}}$

3. $\text{Accounts Receivable Turnover Ratio} = \dfrac{\text{Net Sales}}{\text{Average Accounts Receivable}}$

4. $\text{Average Accounts Receivable} = \dfrac{(\text{Beginning Receivables} + \text{Ending Receivables})}{2}$

5. $\text{Turnover in Days} = \dfrac{365}{\text{Receivables Turnover Ratio}}$

6. $\text{Inventory Turnover Ratio} = \dfrac{\text{Cost of Goods Sold}}{\text{Average Inventory}}$

7. $\text{Average Inventory} = \dfrac{(\text{Beginning Inventory} + \text{Ending Inventory})}{2}$

8. $\text{Turnover in Days} = \dfrac{365}{\text{Inventory Turnover Ratio}}$

**Leverage ratios:**

9. Times-Interest-Earned Ratio $= \dfrac{\text{(Income Before Taxes + Interest Expense)}}{\text{Interest Expense}}$

10. Debt Ratio $= \dfrac{\text{Total Liabilities}}{\text{Total Assets}}$

11. Debt-to-Equity Ratio $= \dfrac{\text{Total Liabilities}}{\text{Total Stockholders' Equity}}$

**Profitability ratios:**

12. Return on Sales $= \dfrac{\text{Net Income}}{\text{Sales}}$

13. Return on Total Assets $= \dfrac{\text{Net Income + [Interest Expense}(1 - \text{Tax Rate})]}{\text{Average Total Assets}}$

14. Average Total Assets $= \dfrac{\text{(Beginning Total Assets + Ending Total Assets)}}{2}$

15. Return on Stockholders' Equity $= \dfrac{\text{(Net Income - Preferred Dividends)}}{\text{Average Common Stockholders' Equity}}$

16. Earnings per Share $= \dfrac{\text{(Net Income - Preferred Dividends)}}{\text{Average Common Shares}}$

17. Price-Earnings Ratio $= \dfrac{\text{Market Price per Share}}{\text{Earnings per Share}}$

18. Dividend Yield $= \dfrac{\text{Dividends per Common Share}}{\text{Market Price per Common Share}}$

19. Dividend Payout Ratio $= \dfrac{\text{Common Dividends}}{\text{(Net Income - Preferred Dividends)}}$

**CORNERSTONES**

© Pixelfabrik / Alamy

# KEY TERMS

# REVIEW PROBLEMS

## I. Financial Statement Analysis

Shera Company just completed its second year of operations. The comparative income statements for these years are as follows:

|  | 2012 | 2013 |
|---|---|---|
| Sales revenue | $500,000 | $800,000 |
| Less cost of goods sold | 300,000 | 464,000 |
| Gross margin | $200,000 | $336,000 |
| Operating expenses | 80,000 | 164,000 |
| Interest expenses | 20,000 | 20,000 |
| Income before taxes | $100,000 | $152,000 |
| Income taxes | 34,000 | 51,680 |
| Net income | $ 66,000 | $100,320 |

Selected information from the balance sheet for 2013 is also given.

| | |
|---|---|
| Current assets | $100,000 |
| Long-term assets | 400,000 |
| Total assets | $500,000 |
| Current liabilities | $ 80,000 |
| Long-term liabilities | 220,000 |
| Total liabilities | $300,000 |
| Common stock | $100,000 |
| Retained earnings | 100,000 |
| Total equity | $200,000 |

Shera had 100,000 shares of stock outstanding. At the end of 2013, a share had a market value of $1.80. The shares outstanding have not changed since the original issue. Dividends of $30,000 were paid in 2013. Total assets have not changed during 2013.

**Required:**

1. Using 2012 as a base period, express all line items of the income statements as a percentage of the corresponding base period item.
2. Express each line item of the two income statements as a percentage of sales.
3. Comment on the trends revealed by the computations in Requirements 1 and 2.
4. Compute the following ratios for 2013: (a) current ratio, (b) debt ratio, (c) return on total assets, (d) times-interest-earned, (e) earnings per share, and (f) dividend yield.

**Solution:**

1. Horizontal analysis:

| | 2012 | Percent | 2013 | Percent |
|---|---|---|---|---|
| Sales revenue | $500,000 | 100.0% | $800,000 | 160.0% |
| Less cost of goods sold | 300,000 | 100.0 | 464,000 | 154.7 |
| Gross margin | $200,000 | 100.0 | $336,000 | 168.0 |
| Operating expenses | 80,000 | 100.0 | 164,000 | 205.0 |
| Interest expense | 20,000 | 100.0 | 20,000 | 100.0 |
| Income before taxes | $100,000 | 100.0 | $152,000 | 152.0 |
| Income taxes | 34,000 | 100.0 | 51,680 | 152.0 |
| Net income | $ 66,000 | 100.0 | $100,320 | 152.0 |

2. Vertical analysis:

| | 2012 | Percent | 2013 | Percent |
|---|---|---|---|---|
| Sales revenue | $500,000 | 100.0% | $800,000 | 100.0% |
| Less cost of goods sold | 300,000 | 60.0 | 464,000 | 58.0 |
| Gross margin | $200,000 | 40.0 | $336,000 | 42.0 |
| Operating expenses | 80,000 | 16.0 | 164,000 | 20.5 |
| Interest expense | 20,000 | 4.0 | 20,000 | 2.5 |
| Income before taxes | $100,000 | 20.0 | $152,000 | 19.0 |
| Income taxes | 34,000 | 6.8 | 51,680 | 6.5 |
| Net income | $ 66,000 | 13.2 | $100,320 | 12.5 |

3. The trends reflected by both the horizontal and vertical analyses are basically favorable. Sales have increased and, with the notable exception of operating expenses, expenses have not increased as rapidly as sales and have declined as a percentage of sales. Operating expenses, however, have more than doubled from 2012 to 2013 and have also increased as a percentage of sales.

4.  a. Current Ratio = $100,000/$80,000 = 1.25
    b. Debt Ratio = $300,000/$500,000 = 0.60, or 60%
    c. Return on Total Assets = {$100,320 + [$20,000(0.66)]}/$500,000 = 0.227, or 22.7%
    d. Times-Interest-Earned Ratio = $172,000/$20,000 = 8.6
    e. Earnings per Share = $100,320/100,000 = $1.00 per share
    f. Dividend Yield = $0.30/$1.80 = 0.167, or 16.7%

# DISCUSSION QUESTIONS

1. Name the two major types of financial statement analysis discussed in this chapter.

2. What is horizontal analysis? Vertical analysis? Should both horizontal and vertical analyses be done? Why?

3. Explain how creditors, investors, and managers can use common-size analysis as an aid in decision making.

4. What are liquidity ratios? Leverage ratios? Profitability ratios?

5. Identify two types of standards used in ratio analysis. Explain why it is desirable to use both types.

6. What information does the quick ratio supply that the current ratio does not?

7. Suppose that the accounts receivable turnover ratio of a company is low when compared with other firms within its industry. How would this information be useful to the managers of a company?

8. A high inventory turnover ratio provides evidence that a company is having problems with stockouts and disgruntled customers. Do you agree? Explain.

9. A loan agreement between a bank and a customer specified that the debt ratio could not exceed 60%. Explain the purpose of this restrictive agreement.

10. A manager decided to acquire some expensive equipment through the use of an operating lease even though a capital budgeting analysis showed that it was more profitable to buy than to lease. However, the purchase alternative would have required the issuance of some bonds. Offer some reasons that would explain the manager's choice.

11. Explain why an investor would be interested in a company's debt ratio.

12. Assume that you have been given the responsibility to invest some funds in the stock market to provide an annuity to an individual who has just retired. Explain how you might use the dividend yield and the dividend payout ratio to help you with this investment decision.

13. Explain how an investor might use the price-earnings ratio to value the stock of a company.

14. Why would investors and creditors be interested in knowing the dilutive effects of convertible securities on earnings per share?

15. Explain the significance of the inventory turnover ratio in a JIT manufacturing environment.

16. In a JIT manufacturing environment, the current ratio and the quick ratio are virtually the same. Do you agree? Why?

# MULTIPLE-CHOICE QUESTIONS

16-1 In examining Luke Company's current period income statement, you notice that Research and Development expenses are 62% of sales revenue. Luke has most likely provided

   a. a horizontal analysis.
   b. a vertical analysis using sales as the base.
   c. a horizontal analysis using sales as the base.
   d. a vertical analysis using net income as the base.
   e. none of the above.

16-2 An advantage of common-size analysis is that

   a. the size of dollar amounts impact the analysis.
   b. larger companies will have higher common-size percentages.
   c. it focuses only on vertical analysis.
   d. the effects of size are eliminated.
   e. it focuses only on horizontal analysis.

16-3 Fractions or percentages computed by dividing one account or line-item amount by another are called

   a. returns.
   b. industry averages.
   c. common-size statements.
   d. dividend yields.
   e. ratios.

16-4 The measures of the ability of a company to meet its current obligations are called

   a. ratios.
   b. liquidity ratios.
   c. leverage ratios.
   d. profitability ratios.
   e. percentage changes.

**16-5** Pedee Company's inventory turnover in days is 80 days. Which of the following actions could help to improve that ratio?

    a. Increase sales price.
    b. Increase manufacturing costs.
    c. Reduce cost of goods sold.
    d. Reduce average inventory.
    e. All of these.

**16-6** Etchey Company shows that 46% of its assets are financed by creditors. Which of the following shows this result?

    a. Current ratio
    b. Times-interest-earned ratio
    c. Debt ratio
    d. Inventory turnover in days
    e. Return on sales

**16-7** Profitability ratios are used by which of the following groups?

    a. Company managers
    b. Creditors
    c. Lenders
    d. Investors
    e. All of these.

**16-8** Fred and Torrie Jones are a retired couple looking for income. They are currently rebalancing their portfolio of stocks to include more with high dividends. Fred and Torrie will be most interested in which of the following?

    a. Current ratio
    b. Dividend payout ratio
    c. Return on assets
    d. Price-earnings ratio
    e. Dividend yield

**16-9** A small pizza restaurant, founded and owned by the Martinelli sisters, would be expected to have which of the following?

    a. Low inventory turnover and high gross margin
    b. Low accounts receivable turnover and low gross margin
    c. High price-earnings ratio
    d. High inventory turnover and low gross margin
    e. All of these.

**16-10** The after-tax cost of interest expense is used in calculating which of the following?

    a. Times-interest-earned
    b. Return on assets
    c. Debt ratio
    d. Inventory turnover ratio
    e. All of these.

# CORNERSTONE EXERCISES

*Use the following information for Cornerstone Exercises 16-11 and 16-12:*
Scherer Company provided the following income statements for its first 3 years of operation:

|  | Year 1 | Year 2 | Year 3 |
|---|---|---|---|
| Net sales | $1,000,000 | $1,100,000 | $1,300,000 |
| Less: Cost of goods sold | (300,000) | (310,000) | (364,000) |
| Gross margin | $ 700,000 | $ 790,000 | $ 936,000 |
| Less: Operating expenses | (421,000) | (484,000) | (591,500) |
| Income taxes | (111,600) | (122,400) | (137,800) |
| Net income | $ 167,400 | $ 183,600 | $ 206,700 |

## Cornerstone Exercise 16-11 Preparing Common-Size Income Statements by Using Base Period Horizontal Analysis

OBJECTIVE 1
CORNERSTONE 16.1

Refer to the information for Scherer Company on the previous page.

**Required:**

Prepare common-size income statements by using Year 1 as the base period. (*Note:* Round answers to the nearest whole percentage.)

## Cornerstone Exercise 16-12 Preparing Income Statements by Using Net Sales as the Base: Vertical Analysis

OBJECTIVE 1
CORNERSTONE 16.2

Refer to the information for Scherer Company on the previous page.

**Required:**

Prepare common-size income statements by using net sales as the base. (*Note:* Round answers to the nearest whole percentage.)

## Cornerstone Exercise 16-13 Calculating the Current Ratio and the Quick (or Acid-Test) Ratio

OBJECTIVE 3
CORNERSTONE 16.3

Chen Company has current assets equal to $5,000,000. Of these, $1,000,000 is cash, $2,250,000 is accounts receivable, $500,000 is inventory, and the remainder is marketable securities. Current liabilities total $4,000,000.

**Required:**

*Note:* Round answers to two decimal places.
1. Calculate the current ratio.
2. Calculate the quick ratio (acid-test ratio).

---

*Use the following information for Cornerstone Exercises 16-14 and 16-15:*
Last year, Nikkola Company had net sales of $2,299,500,000 and cost of goods sold of $1,755,000,000. Nikkola had the following balances:

|  | January 1 | December 31 |
|---|---|---|
| Accounts receivable | $142,650,000 | $172,350,000 |
| Inventories | 54,374,200 | 62,625,800 |

---

## Cornerstone Exercise 16-14 Calculate the Average Accounts Receivable, the Accounts Receivable Turnover Ratio, and the Accounts Receivable Turnover in Days

OBJECTIVE 3
CORNERSTONE 16.4

Refer to the information for Nikkola Company above.

**Required:**

*Note:* Round answers to one decimal place.
1. Calculate the average accounts receivable.
2. Calculate the accounts receivable turnover ratio.
3. Calculate the accounts receivable turnover in days.

## Cornerstone Exercise 16-15 Calculating the Average Inventory, the Inventory Turnover Ratio, and the Inventory Turnover in Days

OBJECTIVE 3
CORNERSTONE 16.5

Refer to the information for Nikkola Company above.

**Required:**

*Note:* Round answers to one decimal place.
1. Calculate the average inventory.
2. Calculate the inventory turnover ratio.

*(Continued)*

3. Calculate the inventory turnover in days.
4. **CONCEPTUAL CONNECTION** Based on these ratios, does Nikkola appear to be performing well or poorly?

**Cornerstone Exercise 16-16    Calculating the Times-Interest-Earned Ratio**

Paxton Company provided the following income statement for last year:

| | |
|---|---|
| Sales | $ 87,021,000 |
| Cost of goods sold | (62,138,249) |
| Gross margin | $ 24,882,751 |
| Operating expenses | (19,371,601) |
| Operating income | $ 5,511,150 |
| Interest expense | (875,400) |
| Income before taxes | $ 4,635,750 |
| Income taxes | (1,854,300) |
| Net income | $ 2,781,450 |

**Required:**

Calculate the times-interest-earned ratio. (*Note:* Round the answer to one decimal place.)

**Cornerstone Exercise 16-17    Calculating the Debt Ratio and the Debt-to-Equity Ratio**

Ernst Company's balance sheet shows total liabilities of $32,500,000, total stockholders' equity of $8,125,000, and total assets of $40,625,000.

**Required:**

*Note:* Round answers to two decimal places.
1. Calculate the debt ratio.
2. Calculate the debt-to-equity ratio.

---

*Use the following information for Cornerstone Exercises 16-18 through 16-23:*
The income statement, statement of retained earnings, and balance sheet for Somerville Company are as follows:

**Somerville Company**
**Income Statement**
**For the Year Ended December 31, 2014**

| | Amount | Percent |
|---|---|---|
| Net sales | $ 8,281,989 | 100.0% |
| Less: Cost of goods sold | (5,383,293) | 65.0 |
| Gross margin | $ 2,898,696 | 35.0 |
| Less: Operating expenses | (1,323,368) | 16.0 |
| Operating income | $ 1,575,328 | 19.0 |
| Less: Interest expense | (50,000) | 0.6 |
| Income before taxes | $ 1,525,328 | 18.4 |
| Less: Income taxes (40%)* | (610,131) | 7.4 |
| Net income | $ 915,197 | 11.0 |

\* Includes both state and federal taxes.

**Somerville Company**
**Statement of Retained Earnings**
**For the Year Ended December 31, 2014**

| | |
|---|---|
| Balance, beginning of period | $1,979,155 |
| Net income | 915,197 |
| Total | $2,894,352 |
| Less: Preferred dividends | (80,000) |
| Dividends to common stockholders | (201,887) |
| Balance, end of period | $2,612,465 |

### Somerville Company
### Comparative Balance Sheets
### At December 31, 2013 and 2014

|  | 2013 | 2014 |
|---|---|---|
| **Assets** | | |
| Current assets: | | |
| Cash | $2,875,000 | $2,580,000 |
| Marketable securities | 800,000 | 700,000 |
| Accounts receivable (net) | 939,776 | 690,000 |
| Inventories | 490,000 | 260,000 |
| Other | 93,000 | 74,261 |
| Total current assets | $5,197,776 | $4,304,261 |
| Property and equipment: | | |
| Land | $1,575,000 | $1,067,315 |
| Building and equipment (net) | 1,348,800 | 1,150,000 |
| Total long-term assets | $2,923,800 | $2,217,315 |
| Total assets | $8,121,576 | $6,521,576 |
| **Liabilities and Stockholders' Equity** | | |
| Current liabilities: | | |
| Notes payable, short term | $1,170,127 | $ 543,641 |
| Accounts payable | 298,484 | 101,500 |
| Current maturity of long-term debt | 3,000 | 2,000 |
| Accrued payables | 200,000 | 57,780 |
| Total current liabilities | $1,671,611 | $ 704,921 |
| Long-term liabilities: | | |
| Bonds payable, 10% | 500,000 | 500,000 |
| Total liabilities | $2,171,611 | $1,204,921 |
| Stockholders' equity: | | |
| Preferred stock, $25 par, 8% | $1,000,000 | $1,000,000 |
| Common stock, $1.50 par | 337,500 | 337,500 |
| Additional paid-in capital* | 2,000,000 | 2,000,000 |
| Retained earnings | 2,612,465 | 1,979,155 |
| Total stockholders' equity | $5,949,965 | $5,316,655 |
| Total liabilities and stockholders' equity | $8,121,576 | $6,521,576 |

\* For common stock only.

## Cornerstone Exercise 16-18   Calculating the Return on Sales

OBJECTIVE ⑤
CORNERSTONE 16.8

Refer to the information for Somerville Company above.

**Required:**

Calculate the return on sales. (*Note:* Round the answer to three decimal places.)

## Cornerstone Exercise 16-19   Calculating the Average Total Assets and the Return on Assets

OBJECTIVE ⑤
CORNERSTONE 16.9

Refer to the information for Somerville Company above. Assume a tax rate of 40%.

**Required:**

*Note:* Round answers to four decimal places.
1.   Calculate the average total assets.
2.   Calculate the return on assets.

## Cornerstone Exercise 16-20   Calculating the Average Common Stockholders' Equity and the Return on Stockholders' Equity

OBJECTIVE ⑤
CORNERSTONE 16.10

Refer to the information for Somerville Company above.                    *(Continued)*

**Required:**

*Note:* Round answers to four decimal places.
1. Calculate the average common stockholders' equity.
2. Calculate the return on stockholders' equity.

OBJECTIVE **5**
CORNERSTONE 16.11

### Cornerstone Exercise 16-21   Computing Earnings per Share

Refer to the information for Somerville Company on the previous page.

**Required:**

*Note:* Round answers to two decimal places.
1. Compute the dollar amount of preferred dividends.
2. Compute the number of common shares.
3. Compute earnings per share.

OBJECTIVE **5**
CORNERSTONE 16.12

### Cornerstone Exercise 16-22   Computing the Price-Earnings Ratio

Refer to the information for Somerville Company on the previous page. Also, assume that the price per common share for Somerville is $8.10.

**Required:**

Compute the price-earnings ratio. (*Note:* Round the answer to two decimal places.)

OBJECTIVE **5**
CORNERSTONE 16.13

### Cornerstone Exercise 16-23   Computing the Dividend Yield and the Dividend Payout Ratio

Refer to the information for Somerville Company on the previous page. Also, assume that the market price per common share is $8.10.

**Required:**

*Note:* Round answers to four decimal places.
1. Compute the dividends per share.
2. Compute the dividend yield.
3. Compute the dividend payout ratio.

## EXERCISES

*Use the following information for Exercises 16-24 and 16-25:*
Sundahl Company's income statements for the past 2 years are as follows:

**Sundahl Company**
**Income Statements**
**For the Years 1 and 2**

|  | Year 1 | Year 2 |
|---|---|---|
| Sales | $ 2,000,000 | $ 1,800,000 |
| Less: Cost of goods sold | (1,400,000) | (1,200,000) |
| Gross margin | $ 600,000 | $ 600,000 |
| Less operating expenses: |  |  |
| Selling expenses | $ (300,000) | $ (300,000) |
| Administrative expenses | (100,000) | (110,000) |
| Operating income | $ 200,000 | $ 190,000 |
| Less: Interest expense | (50,000) | (40,000) |
| Income before taxes | $ 150,000 | $ 150,000 |

OBJECTIVE **1**

### Exercise 16-24   Horizontal Analysis

Refer to the information for Sundahl Company above.

**Required:**

Prepare a common-size income statement for Year 2 by expressing each line item for Year 2 as a percentage of that same line item from Year 1. (*Note:* Round percentages to the nearest tenth of a percent.)

### Exercise 16-25   Vertical Analysis

OBJECTIVE ❶

Refer to the information for Sundahl Company on the previous page.

**Required:**

1.  Prepare a common-size income statement for Year 1 by expressing each line item as a percentage of sales revenue. (*Note:* Round percentages to the nearest tenth of a percent.)
2.  Prepare a common-size income statement for Year 2 by expressing each line item as a percentage of sales revenue. (*Note:* Round percentages to the nearest tenth of a percent.)

---

*Use the following information for Exercises 16-26 and 16-27:*
Cuneo Company's income statements for the last 3 years are as follows:

**Cuneo Company**
**Income Statements**
**For the Years 1, 2, and 3**

|                             | Year 1       | Year 2       | Year 3        |
| --------------------------- | ------------ | ------------ | ------------- |
| Sales                       | $1,000,000   | $1,200,000   | $ 1,700,000   |
| Less: Cost of goods sold    | (700,000)    | (700,000)    | (1,000,000)   |
| Gross margin                | $ 300,000    | $ 500,000    | $   700,000   |
| Less operating expenses:    |              |              |               |
| Selling expenses            | (150,000)    | (220,000)    | (250,000)     |
| Administrative expenses     | (50,000)     | (60,000)     | (120,000)     |
| Operating income            | $ 100,000    | $ 220,000    | $   330,000   |
| Less: Interest expense      | (25,000)     | (25,000)     | (25,000)      |
| Income before taxes         | $   75,000   | $  195,000   | $   305,000   |

---

### Exercise 16-26   Horizontal Analysis

OBJECTIVE ❶

Refer to the information for Cuneo Company above.

**Required:**

1.  Prepare a common-size income statement for Year 2 by expressing each line item for Year 2 as a percentage of that same line item from Year 1. (*Note:* Round percentages to the nearest tenth of a percent.)
2.  Prepare a common-size income statement for Year 3 by expressing each line item for Year 3 as a percentage of that same line item from Year 1. (*Note:* Round percentages to the nearest tenth of a percent.)

### Exercise 16-27   Vertical Analysis

OBJECTIVE ❶

Refer to the information for Cuneo Company above.

**Required:**

1.  Prepare a common-size income statement for Year 1 by expressing each line item as a percentage of sales revenue. (*Note:* Round percentages to the nearest tenth of a percent.)
2.  Prepare a common-size income statement for Year 2 by expressing each line item as a percentage of sales revenue. (*Note:* Round percentages to the nearest tenth of a percent.)
3.  Prepare a common-size income statement for Year 3 by expressing each line item as a percentage of sales revenue. (*Note:* Round percentages to the nearest tenth of a percent.)

OBJECTIVE ③

### Exercise 16-28   Current Ratio and Quick (Acid-Test) Ratio

Jordan Company provided the following information:

| | |
|---|---:|
| Current assets: | |
| Cash | $12,450,000 |
| Accounts receivable | 8,740,000 |
| Inventories | 8,150,000 |
| Total current assets | $29,340,000 |
| Current liabilities | $16,300,000 |

**Required:**

*Note:* Round answers to one decimal place.
1. Compute the current ratio.
2. Compute the quick (acid-test) ratio.

OBJECTIVE ③

### Exercise 16-29   Current Ratio and Quick (Acid-Test) Ratio

Upton Company has current assets equal to $3,600,000. Of these, $1,100,000 is cash, $1,300,000 is accounts receivable, and the remainder is inventories. Current liabilities total $3,000,000.

**Required:**

*Note:* Round answers to two decimal places.
1. Compute the current ratio.
2. Compute the quick (acid-test) ratio.

OBJECTIVE ③

### Exercise 16-30   Average Accounts Receivable, Accounts Receivable Turnover Ratio, Accounts Receivable Turnover in Days

Knowlton Company had net sales of $3,906,000. Knowlton had the following balances:

| | January 1 | December 31 |
|---|---|---|
| Accounts receivable | $419,000 | $398,100 |
| Inventories | 128,000 | 132,070 |

**Required:**

*Note:* Round answers to one decimal place.
1. Calculate the average accounts receivable.
2. Calculate the accounts receivable turnover ratio.
3. Calculate the accounts receivable turnover in days.

OBJECTIVE ③

### Exercise 16-31   Average Accounts Receivable, Accounts Receivable Turnover Ratio, Accounts Receivable Turnover in Days

Whalen Company had net sales of $6,500,300. Whalen had the following balances:

| | January 1 | December 31 |
|---|---|---|
| Accounts receivable | $1,100,400 | $965,800 |
| Inventories | 450,000 | 525,000 |

**Required:**

*Note:* Round answers to two decimal places.
1. Calculate the average accounts receivable.
2. Calculate the accounts receivable turnover ratio.
3. Calculate the accounts receivable turnover in days.

OBJECTIVE ③

### Exercise 16-32   Average Inventory, Inventory Turnover Ratio, Inventory Turnover in Days

Belt Company had net sales of $2,225,500,000 and cost of goods sold of $1,557,850,000. Belt had the following balances:

| | January 1 | December 31 |
|---|---|---|
| Inventories | $335,000,000 | $350,000,000 |

**Required:**

*Note:* Round answers to two decimal places.
1. Calculate the average inventory.
2. Calculate the inventory turnover ratio.
3. Calculate the inventory turnover in days.

### Exercise 16-33 Average Inventory, Inventory Turnover Ratio, Inventory Turnover in Days

OBJECTIVE 3

Delater Company had sales of $3,948,340 and a gross margin of $1,859,260. Delater had beginning inventory of $53,420 and ending inventory of $62,640.

**Required:**

*Note:* Round answers to one decimal place.
1. Calculate the average inventory.
2. Calculate the inventory turnover ratio.
3. Calculate the inventory turnover in days.

### Exercise 16-34 Profitability Ratios

OBJECTIVE 5

Bryce Company manufactures pet supplies. However, Bryce's electronic accounting system recently crashed and, unfortunately, only a partial recovery of the company's year-end accounting records (which included several profitability ratios) was possible. As a result, Bryce's controller, a bright young CMA named Jeanette, must compute various lost financial account balances using the recovered information listed below:

ILLUSTRATING
RELATIONSHIPS

- Long-term liabilities: $1,500,000
- Ending inventory is the same as beginning inventory.
- Gross margin: $3,000,000
- Net sales: $8,000,000
- Accounts receivable turnover: 50
- Ending accounts receivable is the same as beginning accounts receivable.
- Total liabilities: $2,000,000
- Current ratio: 2.5
- Cash: $600,000
- Quick ratio: 2.0
- Inventory turnover in days: 3.65

**Required:**

1. Calculate current liabilities.
2. Calculate current assets.
3. Calculate average accounts receivable.
4. Calculate marketable securities.
5. Calculate average inventory.

### Exercise 16-35 Times-Interest-Earned

OBJECTIVE 4

Tsao Company provided the following income statement for last year:

| | |
|---|---|
| Sales | $16,250,000 |
| Cost of goods sold | 6,500,000 |
| Gross margin | $ 9,750,000 |
| Operating expenses | 3,750,000 |
| Operating income | $ 6,000,000 |
| Interest expense | 500,000 |
| Income before taxes | $ 5,500,000 |
| Income taxes | 1,650,000 |
| Net income | $ 3,850,000 |

**Required:**

Calculate the times-interest-earned ratio.

OBJECTIVE **4**     **Exercise 16-36   Debt Ratio, Debt-to-Equity Ratio**

Busch Company's balance sheet shows total liabilities of $510,900, total equity of $126,000, and total assets of $636,900.

**Required:**

*Note:* Round answers to two decimal places.
1.   Calculate the debt ratio.
2.   Calculate the debt-to-equity ratio.
3.   **CONCEPTUAL CONNECTION** Based on the ratios calculated in Requirements 1 and 2, comment on the riskiness of Busch's financing decisions.

---

*Use the following information for Exercises 16-37 through 16-39:*
Juroe Company provided the following income statement for last year:

| | |
|---|---:|
| Sales | $11,300,000 |
| Cost of goods sold | 3,000,000 |
| Gross margin | $ 8,300,000 |
| Operating expenses | 3,800,000 |
| Operating income | $ 4,500,000 |
| Interest expense | 1,000,000 |
| Income before taxes | $ 3,500,000 |
| Income taxes | 1,400,000 |
| Net income | $ 2,100,000 |

Juroe's balance sheet as of December 31 last year showed total liabilities of $10,250,000, total equity of $6,150,000, and total assets of $16,400,000.

---

OBJECTIVE **4**     **Exercise 16-37   Times-Interest-Earned Ratio, Debt Ratio, Debt-to-Equity Ratio**

Refer to the information for Juroe Company above.

**Required:**

*Note:* Round answers to two decimal places.
1.   Calculate the times-interest-earned ratio.
2.   Calculate the debt ratio.
3.   Calculate the debt-to-equity ratio.

OBJECTIVE **5**     **Exercise 16-38   Return on Sales**

Refer to the information for Juroe Company above.

**Required:**

1.   Calculate the return on sales. (*Note*: Round the percent to two decimal places.)
2.   **CONCEPTUAL CONNECTION** Briefly explain the meaning of the return on sales ratio, and comment on whether Juroe's return on sales ratio appears appropriate.

OBJECTIVE **5**     **Exercise 16-39   Average Total Assets, Return on Assets**

Refer to the information for Juroe Company above. Also, assume that Juroe's total assets at the beginning of last year equaled $17,350,000 and that the tax rate applicable to Juroe is 40%.

**Required:**

*Note:* Round answers to two decimal places.
1.   Calculate the average total assets.
2.   Calculate the return on assets.

Use the following information for Exercises 16-40 and 16-42:

Rebert Inc. showed the following balances for last year:

|  | January 1 | December 31 |
|---|---|---|
| Stockholders' equity: | | |
| Preferred stock, $100 par, 8% | $ 4,000,000 | $ 4,000,000 |
| Common stock, $3 par | 3,000,000 | 3,000,000 |
| Additional paid-in capital* | 4,800,000 | 4,800,000 |
| Retained earnings | 4,000,000 | 4,250,000 |
| Total stockholders' equity | $15,800,000 | $16,050,000 |

\* For common stock only.

Rebert's net income for last year was $3,182,000.

### Exercise 16-40   Average Common Stockholders' Equity, Return on Stockholders' Equity   OBJECTIVE 5

Refer to the information for Rebert Inc. above.

**Required:**

1. Calculate the average common stockholders' equity.
2. Calculate the return on stockholders' equity.

### Exercise 16-41   Earnings per Share, Price-Earnings Ratio   OBJECTIVE 5

Refer to the information for Rebert Inc. above. Also, assume that the market price per share for Rebert is $51.50.

**Required:**

1. Compute the dollar amount of preferred dividends.
2. Compute the number of common shares.
3. Compute earnings per share. (*Note:* Round to two decimals.)
4. Compute the price-earnings ratio. (*Note:* Round to the nearest whole number.)

### Exercise 16-42   Dividend Yield Ratio, Dividend Payout Ratio   OBJECTIVE 5

Refer to the information for Rebert Inc. above. Also, assume that the dividends paid to common stockholders for last year were $2,600,000 and that the market price per share of common stock is $51.50.

**Required:**

1. Compute the dividends per share.
2. Compute the dividend yield. (*Note*: Round to two decimal places.)
3. Compute the dividend payout ratio. (*Note:* Round to two decimal places.)

# PROBLEMS

### Problem 16-43   Liquidity Analysis   OBJECTIVE 3

The following selected information is taken from the financial statements of Arnn Company for its most recent year of operations:

| | |
|---|---|
| Beginning balances: | |
| Inventory | $200,000 |
| Accounts receivable | 300,000 |
| Ending balances: | |
| Inventory | $250,000 |
| Accounts receivable | 400,000 |

*(Continued)*

| | |
|---|---|
| Cash | $100,000 |
| Marketable securities (short-term) | 200,000 |
| Prepaid expenses | 50,000 |
| Accounts payable | 175,000 |
| Taxes payable | 85,000 |
| Wages payable | 90,000 |
| Short-term loans payable | 50,000 |

During the year, Arnn had net sales of $2.45 million. The cost of goods sold was $1.3 million.

**Required:**

*Note*: Round all answers to two decimal places.
1. Compute the current ratio.
2. Compute the quick or acid-test ratio.
3. Compute the accounts receivable turnover ratio.
4. Compute the accounts receivable turnover in days.
5. Compute the inventory turnover ratio.
6. Compute the inventory turnover in days.

OBJECTIVE  **Problem 16-44   Leverage Ratios**

Grammatico Company has just completed its third year of operations. The income statement is as follows:

| | |
|---|---|
| Sales | $ 2,460,000 |
| Less: Cost of goods sold | (1,410,000) |
| Gross profit margin | $ 1,050,000 |
| Less: Selling and administrative expenses | (710,000) |
| Operating income | $   340,000 |
| Less: Interest expense | (140,000) |
| Income before taxes | $   200,000 |
| Less: Income taxes | (68,000) |
| Net income | $   132,000 |

Selected information from the balance sheet is as follows:

| | |
|---|---|
| Current liabilities | $1,000,000 |
| Long-term liabilities | 1,500,000 |
| Total liabilities | $2,500,000 |
| Common stock | $4,000,000 |
| Retained earnings | 750,000 |
| Total equity | $4,750,000 |

**Required:**

*Note:* Round answers to two decimal places.
1. Compute the times-interest-earned ratio.
2. Compute the debt ratio.
3. **CONCEPTUAL CONNECTION** Assume that the lower quartile, median, and upper quartile values for debt and times-interest-earned ratios in Grammatico's industry are as follows:

| | |
|---|---|
| Times-interest-earned: | 2.4, 5.4, 16.1 |
| Debt: | 0.3, 0.8, 2.4 |

How does Grammatico compare with the industrial norms? Does it have too much debt?

## Problem 16-45   Profitability Ratios

OBJECTIVE ② ⑤

The following information has been gathered for Malette Manufacturing:

| | | | |
|---|---|---|---|
| Net income | $5,000,000 | Common dividends | $1,200,000 |
| Interest expense | 400,000 | Average common shares outstanding | 800,000 shares |
| Average total assets | 60,000,000 | Average common stockholders' equity | $20,000,000 |
| Preferred dividends | 400,000 | Market price per common share | $40 |

Assume that the firm has no common stock equivalents. The tax rate is 34%.

### Required:

1. Compute the return on assets.
2. Compute the return on common stockholders' equity.
3. Compute the earnings per share.
4. Compute the price-earnings ratio.
5. Compute the dividend yield.
6. Compute the dividend payout ratio.

---

Use the following information for Problems 16-46 through 16-50:

Mike Sanders is considering the purchase of Kepler Company, a firm specializing in the manufacture of office supplies. To be able to assess the financial capabilities of the company, Mike has been given the company's financial statements for the 2 most recent years.

**Kepler Company**
**Comparative Balance Sheets**

| | This Year | Last Year |
|---|---|---|
| **Assets** | | |
| Current assets: | | |
| Cash | $      50,000 | $100,000 |
| Accounts receivable, net | 300,000 | 150,000 |
| Inventory | 600,000 | 400,000 |
| Prepaid expenses | 25,000 | 30,000 |
| Total current assets | $  975,000 | $680,000 |
| Property and equipment, net | 125,000 | 150,000 |
| Total assets | $1,100,000 | $830,000 |
| **Liabilities and Stockholders' Equity** | | |
| Current liabilities: | | |
| Accounts payable | $  400,000 | $290,000 |
| Short-term notes payable | 200,000 | 60,000 |
| Total current liabilities | $  600,000 | $350,000 |
| Long-term bonds payable, 12% | 100,000 | 150,000 |
| Total liabilities | $  700,000 | $500,000 |
| Stockholders' equity: | | |
| Common stock (100,000 shares) | 200,000 | 200,000 |
| Retained earnings | 200,000 | 130,000 |
| Total liabilities and stockholders' equity | $1,100,000 | $830,000 |

**Kepler Ctompany**
**Comparative Income Statements**

| | This Year | Last Year |
|---|---|---|
| Sales | $ 950,000 | $ 900,000 |
| Less: Cost of goods sold | (500,000) | (490,000) |
| Gross margin | $ 450,000 | $ 410,000 |
| Less: Selling and administrative expenses | (275,000) | (260,000) |
| Operating income | $ 175,000 | $ 150,000 |

*(Continued)*

| | This Year | Last Year |
|---|---|---|
| Less: Interest expense | (12,000) | (18,000) |
| Income before taxes | $ 163,000 | $ 132,000 |
| Less: Income taxes | (65,200) | (52,800) |
| Net income | $  97,800 | $  79,200 |
| Less: Dividends | (27,800) | (19,200) |
| Net income, retained | $  70,000 | $  60,000 |

OBJECTIVE **1**

### Problem 16-46    Horizontal Analysis

Refer to the information for Kepler Company above.

**Required:**

*Note*: Round all percentages to one decimal place.
1.  Compute the percentage change for each item in the balance sheet and income statement.
2.  **CONCEPTUAL CONNECTION** Comment on any significant trends.

OBJECTIVE **1**

### Problem 16-47    Vertical Analysis

Refer to the information for Kepler Company above.

**Required:**

*Note*: Round all percentages to one decimal place.
1.  Express each item in the asset section of the balance sheet as a percentage of total assets for each year.
2.  Express each item in the liabilities and equity section as a percentage of total liabilities and equity for each year.
3.  Express each item in the income statement as a percentage of sales for each year.

OBJECTIVE **2** **3**

### Problem 16-48    Liquidity Ratios

Refer to the information for Kepler Company above.

**Required:**

*Note*: Round all answers to two decimal places.
1.  Compute the following ratios for each year: (a) current ratio, (b) quick ratio, (c) receivables turnover (in days), and (d) inventory turnover (in days).
2.  **CONCEPTUAL CONNECTION** Has the liquidity of Kepler improved over the past year? Explain why industrial liquidity performance would be useful information in assessing Kepler's liquidity performance.

OBJECTIVE **2** **4**

### Problem 16-49    Leverage Ratios

Refer to the information for Kepler Company above.

**Required:**

*Note*: Round all answers to two decimal places.
1.  Compute the following for each year: (a) the times-interest-earned ratio and (b) the debt ratio
2.  **CONCEPTUAL CONNECTION** Does Kepler have too much debt? What other information would help in answering this question?

OBJECTIVE **2** **5**

### Problem 16-50    Profitability Ratios

Refer to the information for Kepler Company above. Also, assume that for last year and for the current year, the market price per share of common stock is $2.98. In addition, for last year, assets and equity were the same at the beginning and end of the year.

**Required:**

*Note*: Round all answers to two decimal places.
1. Compute the following for each year: (a) return on assets, (b) return on stockholders' equity, (c) earnings per share, (d) price-earnings ratio, (e) dividend yield, and (f) dividend payout.
2. **CONCEPTUAL CONNECTION** Based on the analysis in Requirement 1, would you invest in the common stock of Kepler?

## Problem 16-51 Profitability Analysis

OBJECTIVE 5

Albion Inc. provided the following information for its most recent year of operation. The tax rate is 40%.

| | | | |
|---|---|---|---|
| Sales | $100,000 | Preferred dividends | $300 |
| Cost of goods sold | 45,000 | Common dividends (paid December 31) | $8,000 |
| Net income | 10,500 | Common shares outstanding—January 1 | 30,000 shares |
| Interest expense | 350 | Common shares outstanding—December 31 | 40,000 shares |
| Assets—beginning balance | 120,000 | Average common stockholders' equity | $55,000 |
| Assets—ending balance | 126,000 | Market price per common share | $12 |

**Required:**

1. Compute the following: (a) return on sales, (b) return on assets, (c) return on stockholders' equity, (d) earnings per share, (e) price-earnings ratio, (f) dividend yield, and (g) dividend payout ratio.
2. **CONCEPTUAL CONNECTION** If you were considering purchasing stock in Albion, which of the above ratios would be of most interest to you? Explain.

## Problem 16-52 Analysis of Accounts Receivable and Credit Policy

OBJECTIVE 3

Based on customer feedback, Ted Pendleton, manager of Gray Company, which produces photo supplies, decided to grant more liberal credit terms. Ted chose to allow customers to have 60 days before full payment of the account was required. From 2010 through 2012, Gray's credit policy for sales on account was 2/10, n/30. In 2013, the policy of 2/10, n/60 became effective. By the end of 2014, Gray was beginning to experience cash flow problems. Although sales were strong, collections were sluggish, and the company was having a difficult time meeting its short-term obligations. Ted noted that the cash flow problems materialized after the credit policy was changed and wondered if there was a connection. To help assess the situation, he gathered the following data pertaining to the collection of accounts receivable (balances are end-of-year balances; the 2010 balance was the same as that in 2009):

| | 2010 | 2011 | 2012 | 2013 | 2014 |
|---|---|---|---|---|---|
| Accounts receivable | $100,000 | $120,000 | $100,000 | $150,000 | $190,000 |
| Net credit sales | 500,000 | 600,000 | 510,000 | 510,000 | 520,000 |

**Required:**

*Note*: Round answers to two decimal places.
1. Compute the number of times that receivables turned over per year for each of the 5 years. Also express the turnover in days instead of times per year.
2. **CONCEPTUAL CONNECTION** Based on your computation in Requirement 1, evaluate the effect of the new credit policy. Include in this assessment the impact on the company's cash inflows.
3. **CONCEPTUAL CONNECTION** Assume that the industry has an average receivables turnover of six times per year. If this knowledge had been available in 2012, along with knowledge of the company's receivable turnover rate, do you think that Ted Pendleton would have liberalized his company's credit policy?

OBJECTIVE ⑤     **Problem 16-53   Profitability Analysis for an Investment Decision**

Suppose that you are considering investing in one of two companies, each in the same industry. The most recent income statements for each company and other relevant information are as follows:

**Income Statements (in thousands)**

|  | McGregor Company | Fasnacht Company |
|---|---|---|
| Sales | $ 50,000 | $ 40,000 |
| Less: Cost of goods sold | (30,000) | (26,000) |
| Gross margin | $ 20,000 | $ 14,000 |
| Less: Selling and administrative expenses | (15,000) | (7,000) |
| Operating income | $ 5,000 | $ 7,000 |
| Less: Interest expense | (1,000) | (3,000) |
| Income before taxes | $ 4,000 | $ 4,000 |
| Less: Income taxes | (1,360) | (1,360) |
| Net income | $ 2,640 | $ 2,640 |
| Retained earnings | 8,000 | 6,000 |
|  | $ 10,640 | $ 8,640 |
| Less: Dividends | (840) | (1,040) |
| Ending retained earnings | $ 9,800 | $ 7,600 |
|  |  |  |
| Average total assets | $20,000,000 | $22,000,000 |
| Average common equity | $10,000,000 | $13,000,000 |
| Average common shares | 1,000,000 shares | 1,200,000 shares |
| Average preferred shares* | 300,000 shares | 100,000 shares |
| Market price per common share | $5.00 | $9.80 |

\* For both McGregor and Fasnacht, the preferred dividend is $1 per share.

**Required:**

*Note:* Round answers to two decimal places.

1. Compute the following for each company: (a) earnings per share, (b) dividend yield, (c) dividend payout ratio, (d) price-earnings ratio, (e) return on assets, and (f) return on stockholders' equity.
2. **CONCEPTUAL CONNECTION** In which of the two companies would you invest? Explain.

# CASES

OBJECTIVE      **Case 16-54   Manipulation of Ratios and Ethical Behavior**

Pete Donaldson, president and owner of Donaldson Mining Supplies, was concerned about the firm's liquidity. He had an easy time selling supplies to the local coal mines but had a difficult time collecting the receivables. He had even tried offering discounts for prompt payment. The outcome wasn't as expected. The coal mines still took as long to pay as before but took the discount as well. Although he had complained about the practice, he was told that other suppliers would provide the supplies for the same terms. Collections were so slow that he was unable to pay his own payables on time and was receiving considerable pressure from his own creditors.

The solution was a line of credit that could be used to smooth his payment patterns. Getting the line of credit was another matter, however. One bank had turned him down, indicating that he already had too much debt and that his short-term liquidity ratios were marginal. Pete had begun the business with $5,000 of his own capital and a $30,000 loan from his father-in-law. He was making interest payments of $3,000 per year to his father-in-law with a promise to pay the principal back in 5 years (3 years from now).

While mulling over his problem, Pete suddenly saw the solution. By changing accountants, he could tell the next accountant that the $30,000 had been donated to the business and therefore would be reclassified into the equity section. This would dramatically improve the debt ratio. He would simply not disclose the $3,000 annual payment—or he could call it a dividend. Additionally, he would not tell the next accountant about the $6,000 of safety gear that was now obsolete. That gear could be added back, and the current ratio would also improve. With an improved financial statement, the next bank would be more likely to grant the needed line of credit.

**Required:**

1.  Evaluate Pete Donaldson's ethical behavior.
2.  Suppose that you have been hired as the chief finance officer for Donaldson Mining Supplies. You have been told that the $30,000 has been donated to the company. During the second week of your employment, the father-in-law drops in unexpectedly and introduces himself. He then asks you how the company is doing and wants to know if his $30,000 loan is still likely to be repaid in 3 years. Suppose also that same day you overhear an employee mention that the safety equipment is no longer usable because regulations now require a newer and different model.
    a.   Assume that you have yet to prepare the financial statements for the loan application. What should you do?
    b.   Suppose that the financial statements have been prepared and submitted to the bank. In fact, that morning, you had received a call from the bank, indicating that a decision was imminent and that the line of credit would likely be approved. What should you do under these circumstances?
3.  Suppose that Pete invites you in as a consultant. He describes his problem to you. Can you think of a better solution?

### Case 16-55    Interpreting the Meaning of Ratios from the Financial Statements

OBJECTIVE ❷❸❹❺

Using the Internet, locate the most recent financial statements for two companies from the same industry. Find (or calculate) the ratios listed below, and compare the two companies. (If you cannot calculate a particular ratio, explain why.) Which company do you think is performing better? Why?
Ratios:

a.   Current ratio
b.   Quick ratio
c.   Accounts receivable turnover
     ratio
d.   Inventory turnover ratio
e.   Turnover in days
f.   Times-interest-earned ratio
g.   Debt ratio
h.   Debt-to-equity ratio

i.   Return on sales
j.   Return on assets
k.   Return on stockholders' equity
l.   Earnings per share
m.   Price-earnings ratio
n.   Dividend yield
o.   Dividend payout ratio

# GLOSSARY

## A

**absorption costing** a product-costing method that assigns all manufacturing costs to units of product: direct materials, direct labor, variable overhead, and fixed overhead.

**accounting rate of return** the rate of return obtained by dividing the average accounting net income by the original investment (or by average investment).

**accounts receivable turnover ratio** a ratio that measures the liquidity of receivables. It is computed by dividing net sales by average accounts receivable.

**accumulating costs** the way that costs are measured and recorded.

**activity** action taken or work performed by equipment or people for other people.

**activity analysis** the process of identifying, describing, and evaluating the activities an organization performs.

**activity attributes** nonfinancial and financial information items that describe individual activities.

**activity-based budgeting system (ABB)** a budget system that focuses on estimating the costs of activities rather than the costs of departments and plants and the use of multiple drivers, both unit-based and nonunit-based.

**activity-based costing (ABC) system** a cost assignment approach that first uses direct and driver tracing to assign costs to activities and then uses drivers to assign costs to cost objects.

**activity-based management** a systemwide, integrated approach that focuses management's attention on activities with the objective of improving customer value and the profit achieved by providing this value. It includes driver analysis, activity analysis, and performance evaluation, and draws on activity-based costing as a major source of information.

**activity dictionary** a list of activities described by specific attributes such as name, definition, classification as primary or secondary, and activity driver.

**activity drivers** factors that measure the consumption of activities by products and other cost objects.

**activity elimination** the process of eliminating nonvalue-added activities.

**activity flexible budgeting** predicting what activity costs will be as activity usage changes.

**activity format** a format for the statement of cash flows that reports cash flows for three categories: (1) cash flows from operating activities, (2) cash flows from investing activities, and (3) cash flows from financing activities.

**activity inputs** the resources consumed by an activity in producing its output (they are the factors that enable the activity to be performed).

**activity output** the result or product of an activity.

**activity output measure** the number of times an activity is performed. It is the quantifiable measure of the output.

**activity reduction** decreasing the time and resources required by an activity.

**activity selection** the process of choosing among sets of activities caused by competing strategies.

**activity sharing** increasing the efficiency of necessary activities by using economies of scale.

**actual cost system** an approach that assigns actual costs of direct materials, direct labor, and overhead to products.

**adjusted cost of goods sold** the cost of goods sold after all adjustments for overhead variances are made.

**administrative costs** all costs associated with research, development, and general administration of the organization that cannot reasonably be assigned to either selling or production.

**allocation** when an indirect cost is assigned to a cost object using a reasonable and convenient method.

**annuity** a series of future cash flows.

**applied overhead** overhead assigned to production using predetermined rates.

**appraisal costs** cost incurred to determine whether products and services are conforming to requirements.

**assigning costs** the way that a cost is linked to some cost object.

## B

**balanced scorecard** a strategic management system that defines a strategic-based responsibility accounting system. The Balanced Scorecard translates an organization's mission and strategy into operational objectives and performance measures for four different perspectives: the financial perspective, the customer perspective, the internal business process perspective, and the learning and growth (infrastructure) perspective.

**beginning work-in-process (BWIP)** consists of work done on partially completed units that represents prior-period work with the costs assigned to them being prior-period costs. Uses two approaches for dealing with the prior-period output and costs found in BWIP: the weighted average method and the FIFO method.

**break-even point** the point where total sales revenue equals total cost; at this point, neither profit nor loss is earned.

**budget committee** a committee responsible for setting budgetary policies and goals, reviewing and approving the budget, and resolving any differences that may arise in the budgetary process.

**budget director** the individual responsible for coordination and directing the overall budgeting process.

**budgetary slack** the process of padding the budget by overestimating costs and underestimating revenues.

**budgets** plans of action expressed in financial terms.

## C

**capital budgeting** the process of making capital investment decisions.

**capital investment decisions** the process of planning, setting goals and priorities, arranging financing, and identifying criteria for making long-term investments.

**carrying costs** the costs of holding inventory.

**cash budget** a detailed plan that outlines all sources and uses of cash.

**cash equivalents** highly liquid investments such as treasury bills, money market funds, and commercial paper.

**cash inflows** activities that increase cash and are sources of cash.

**cash outflows** activities that decrease cash and are uses of cash.

**causal factors** activities or variables that invoke service costs. Generally, it is desirable to use causal factors as the basis for allocating service costs.

**certified internal auditor (CIA)** the CIA has passed a comprehensive examination designed to ensure technical competence and has two years' experience.

**certified management accountant (CMA)** a certified management accountant has passed a rigorous qualifying examination, met an experience requirement, and participates in continuing education.

**certified public accountant (CPA)** a certified accountant who is permitted (by law) to serve as an external auditor. CPAs must pass a national examination and be licensed by the state in which they practice.

**coefficient of determination ($R^2$)** the percentage of total variability in a dependent variable that is explained by an independent variable. It assumes a value between 0 and 1.

**committed fixed cost** a fixed cost that cannot be easily changed.

**common costs** the costs of resources used in the output of two or more services or products.

**common fixed expenses** fixed expenses that cannot be directly traced to individual segments and that are unaffected by the elimination of any one segment.

**common-size analysis** a type of analysis that expresses line items or accounts in the financial statements as percentages.

**compounding of interest** paying interest on interest.

**constraints** mathematical expressions that express resource limitations.

**consumption ratio** the proportion of an overhead activity consumed by a product.

**continuous budget** a moving 12-month budget with a future month added as the current month expires.

**continuous improvement** searching for ways to increase the overall efficiency and productivity of activities by reducing waste, increasing quality, and reducing costs.

**contribution margin** sales revenue minus total variable cost or price minus unit variable cost.

**contribution margin income statement** the income statement format that is based on the separation of costs into fixed and variable components.

**contribution margin ratio** contribution margin divided by sales revenue. It is the proportion of each sales dollar available to cover fixed costs and provide for profit.

**control** the process of setting standards, receiving feedback on actual performance, and taking corrective action whenever actual performance deviates significantly from planned performance.

**control activities** activities performed by an organization to prevent or detect poor quality (because poor quality may exist).

**control costs** costs incurred from performing control activities.

**control limits** the maximum allowable deviation from a standard.

**controllable costs** costs that managers have the power to influence.

**controller** the chief accounting officer in an organization.

**controlling** the managerial activity of monitoring a plan's implementation and taking corrective action as needed.

**conversion cost** the sum of direct labor cost and overhead cost.

**core objectives and measures** those objectives and measures common to most organizations.

**cost** the amount of cash or cash equivalent sacrificed for goods and/or services that are expected to bring a current or future benefit to the organization.

**cost behavior** the way in which a cost changes when the level of output changes.

**cost center** a division of a company that is evaluated on the basis of cost.

**cost object** any item such as products, customers, departments, projects, and so on, for which costs are measured and assigned.

**cost of capital** the cost of investment funds, usually viewed as a weighted average of the costs of funds from all sources.

**cost of goods manufactured** the total product cost of goods completed during the current period.

**cost of goods sold** the total product cost of goods sold during the period.

**cost of goods sold budget** the estimated costs for the units sold.

**cost reconciliation** the final section of the production report that compares the costs to account for with the costs accounted for to ensure that they are equal.

**cost structure** A company's mix of fixed costs relative to variable costs.

**cost-volume-profit graph** a graph that depicts the relationships among costs, volume, and profits. It consists of a total revenue line and a total cost line.

**costs of quality** costs incurred because poor quality may exist or because poor quality does exist.

**creditors** loan managers who assess the creditworthinesss of potential customers through ratio analysis, common-size analysis, and other techniques.

**current ratio** a measure of the ability of a company to pay its short-term liabilities out of short-term assets.

**customer perspective** a balanced scorecard viewpoint that defines the customer and market segments in which the business will compete.

**customer value** realization less sacrifice, where realization is what the customer receives and sacrifice is what is given up.

**cycle time** the length of time required to produce one unit of a product.

# D

**debt ratio** the ratio that measures the percentage of a company's risk as the percentage of its assets financed by creditors increases. It is computed by dividing a company's total liabilities by its total assets.

**decentralization** the granting of decision-making freedom to lower operating levels.

**decision making** the process of choosing among competing alternatives.

**decision model** a specific set of procedures that, when followed, produces a decision.

**degree of operating leverage (DOL)** a measure of the sensitivity of profit changes to changes in sales volume. It measures the percentage change in profits resulting from a percentage change in sales.

**departmental overhead rate** estimated overhead for a single department divided by the estimated activity level for that same department.

**dependent variable** a variable whose value depends on the value of another variable.

**differential cost** the difference in total cost between the alternatives in a decision.

**direct costs** costs that can be easily and accurately traced to a cost object.

**direct fixed expenses** fixed costs that are directly traceable to a given segment and, consequently, disappear if the segment is eliminated.

**direct labor** the labor that can be directly traced to the goods or services being produced.

**direct labor budget** a budget showing the total direct labor hours needed and the associated cost for the number of units in the production budget.

**direct materials** materials that are a part of the final product and can be directly traced to the goods or services being produced.

**direct materials purchases budget** a budget that outlines the expected usage of materials production and purchases of the direct materials required.

**direct method** a method that allocates service costs directly to producing departments. This method ignores any interactions that may exist among support departments.

**discount factor** the factor used to convert a future cash flow to its present value.

**discount rate** the rate of return used to compute the present value of future cash flows.

**discounted cash flows** future cash flows expressed in present-value terms.

**discounting** the act of finding the present value of future cash flows.

**discounting models** capital investment models that explicitly consider the time value of money in identifying criteria for accepting and rejecting proposed projects.

**discretionary fixed costs** fixed costs that can be changed relatively easily at management discretion.

**dividend payout ratio** a ratio that is computed by dividing the total common dividends by the earnings available to common stockholders.

**dividend yield** a profitability measure that is computed by dividing the dividends received per unit of common share by the market price per common share.

**double-loop feedback** information about both the effectiveness of strategy implementation and the validity of assumptions underlying the strategy.

**driver** a factor that causes or leads to a change in a cost or an activity; a driver is an output measure.

**driver analysis** the effort expended to identify those factors that are the root causes of activity costs.

**dysfunctional behavior** individual behavior that conflicts with the goals of the organization.

# E

**earnings per share** earnings per share is computed by dividing net income less preferred dividends by the average number of shares of common stock outstanding during the period.

**economic order quantity (EOQ)** the amount that should be ordered (or produced) to minimize the total ordering (or setup) and carrying costs.

**economic value added (EVA)** a performance measure that is calculated by taking the after-tax operating profit minus the total annual cost of capital.

**ending finished goods inventory budget** a budget that describes planned ending inventory of finished goods in units and dollars.

**ending work-in-process (EWIP)** inventory that is not complete and attaching a unit cost to it requires defining the output of the period. A unit completed and transferred out during the period is not identical (or equivalent) to one in EWIP inventory, and the cost attached to the two units should not be the same.

**environmental costs** costs that are incurred because poor environmental quality exists or may exist.

**environmental detection costs** costs incurred to detect poor environmental performance.

**environmental external failure costs** costs incurred after contaminants are introduced into the environment.

**environmental internal failure costs** costs incurred after contaminants are produced but before they are introduced into the environment.

**environmental prevention costs** costs incurred to prevent damage to the environment.

**equivalent units of output** complete units that could have been produced given the total amount of manufacturing effort expended during the period.

**ethical behavior** choosing actions that are right, proper, and just.

**expenses** costs that are used up (expired) in the production of revenue.

**external failure costs** costs incurred because products fail to conform to requirements after being sold to outside parties.

## F

**failure activities** activities performed by an organization or its customers in response to poor quality (poor quality does exist).

**failure costs** the costs incurred by an organization because failure activities are performed.

**favorable (F) variances** variances produced whenever the actual amounts are less than the budgeted or standard allowances.

**FIFO costing method** a process-costing method that separates units in beginning inventory from those produced during the current period. Unit costs include only current-period costs and production.

**financial accounting** a type of accounting that is primarily concerned with producing information for external users.

**financial perspective** a balanced scorecard viewpoint that describes the financial consequences of actions taken in the other three perspectives.

**financing activities** those activities that raise (provide) cash from (to) creditors and owners.

**fixed costs** costs that, in total, are constant within the relevant range as the level of output increases or decreases.

**flexible budget** a budget that can specify costs for a range of activity.

**flexible budget variance** the sum of price variances and efficiency variances in a performance report comparing actual costs to expected costs predicted by a flexible budget.

**future value** the value that will accumulate by the end of an investment's life if the investment earns a specified compounded return.

## G

**goal congruence** the alignment of a manager's personal goals with those of the organization.

**gross margin** the difference between sales revenue and cost of goods sold.

## H

**high-low method** a method for separating mixed costs into fixed and variable components by using just the high and low data points. [*Note*: The high (low) data point corresponds to the high (low) output level.]

**horizontal analysis** also called trend analysis, this type of analysis expresses a line item as a percentage of some prior-period amount.

**hurdle rate** the rate that indicates the minimum ROI necessary to accept an investment.

## I

**incentives** the positive or negative measures taken by an organization to induce a manager to exert effort toward achieving the organization's goals.

**independent projects** projects that, if accepted or rejected, will not affect the cash flows of another project.

**independent variable** a variable whose value does not depend on the value of another variable.

**indifference point** the quantity at which two systems produce the same operating income.

**indirect costs** costs that cannot be easily and accurately traced to a cost object.

**indirect method** a method that computes operating cash flows by adjusting net income for items that do not affect cash flows.

**innovation process** a process that anticipates the emerging and potential needs of customers and creates new products and services to satisfy those needs.

**intercept** the fixed cost, representing the point where the cost formula intercepts the vertical axis.

**internal business process perspective** a balanced scorecard viewpoint that describes the internal processes needed to provide value for customers and owners.

**internal failure costs** costs incurred because products and services fail to conform to requirements where lack of conformity is discovered prior to external sale.

**internal rate of return** the rate of return that equates the present value of a project's cash inflows with the present value of its cash outflows (i.e., it sets the NPV equal to zero). Also, the rate of return being earned on funds that remain internally invested in a project.

**inventory turnover ratio** a ratio that is computed by dividing the cost of goods sold by the average inventory.

**investing activities** those activities that involve the acquisition or sale of long-term assets.

**investment center** a division of a company that is evaluated on the basis of return on investment.

**investors** those who analyze financial statements to assess the attractiveness of a company as a potential investment.

## J

**job** one distinct unit or set of units for which the costs of production must be assigned.

**job-order cost sheet** a subsidiary account to the work-in-process account on which the total costs of materials, labor, and overhead for a single job are accumulated.

**job-order costing system**   a costing system in which costs are collected and assigned to units of production for each individual job.

**joint products**   products that are inseparable prior to a split-off point. All manufacturing costs up to the split-off point are joint costs.

**just-in-time (JIT)**   a demand-pull system whose objective is to eliminate waste by producing a product only when it is needed and only in the quantities demanded by customers.

## K

**keep-or-drop decisions**   relevant costing analyses that focus on keeping or dropping a segment of a business.

## L

**labor efficiency variance (*LEV*)**   the difference between the actual direct labor hours used and the standard direct labor hours allowed multiplied by the standard hourly wage rate.

**labor rate variance (*LRV*)**   the difference between the actual hourly rate paid and the standard hourly rate multiplied by the actual hours worked.

**lead time**   the time required to receive the economic order quantity once an order is placed or a setup is started.

**lean accounting**   an accounting practice that organizes costs according to the value chain by focusing primarily on the elimination of waste. The objective is to provide information to managers that support this effort and to provide financial statements that better reflect overall performance, using financial and nonfinancial information.

**learning and growth (infrastructure) perspective**   a balanced scorecard viewpoint that defines the capabilities that an organization needs to create long-term growth and improvement.

**leverage ratios**   ratios that measure the ability of a company to meet its long- and short-term obligations. These ratios provide a measure of the degree of protection provided to a company's creditors.

**line positions**   positions that have direct responsibility for the basic objectives of an organization.

**liquidity ratios**   ratios that measure the ability of a company to meet its current obligations.

## M

**make-or-buy decisions**   relevant costing analyses that focus on whether a component should be made internally or purchased externally.

**managerial accounting**   the provision of accounting information for a company's internal users.

**managers**   those who analyze their own financial statements to assess profitability, liquidity, debt position, and progress toward organizational objectives.

**manufacturing cycle efficiency (MCE)**   measured as value-added time divided by total time. The result tells the company what percentage of total time spent is devoted to actual production.

**manufacturing organization**   an organization that produces tangible products.

**manufacturing overhead**   all product costs other than direct materials and direct labor. In a manufacturing firm, manufacturing overhead also is known as *factory burden* or *indirect* manufacturing costs. Costs are included as manufacturing overhead if they cannot be traced to the cost object of interest (e.g., unit of product).

**margin**   the ratio of net operating income to sales.

**margin of safety**   the units sold, or expected to be sold, or sales revenue earned, or expected to be earned, above the break-even volume.

**markup**   the percentage applied to a base cost; it includes desired profit and any costs not included in the base cost.

**master budget**   the collection of all area and activity budgets representing a firm's comprehensive plan of action.

**materials price variance (*MPV*)**   the difference between the actual price paid per unit of materials and the standard price allowed per unit multiplied by the actual quantity of materials purchased.

**materials requisition form**   a source document that records the type, quantity, and unit price of the direct materials issued to each job.

**materials usage variance (*MUV*)**   the difference between the direct materials actually used and the direct materials allowed for the actual output multiplied by the standard price.

**method of least squares (regression)**   a statistical method to find the best-fitting line through a set of data points. It is used to break out the fixed and variable components of a mixed cost.

**mixed costs**   costs that have both a fixed and a variable component.

**monetary incentives**   the use of economic rewards to motivate managers.

**mutually exclusive projects**   projects that, if accepted, preclude the acceptance of competing projects.

**myopic behavior**   behavior that occurs when a manager takes actions that improve budgetary performance in the short run but bring long-run harm to the firm.

## N

**net present value**   the difference between the present value of a project's cash inflows and the present value of its cash outflows.

**noncash investing and financing activities**   investing and financing activities that take place without affecting cash.

**nondiscounting models**   capital investment models that identify criteria for accepting or rejecting projects without considering the time value of money.

**nonmonetary incentives**   the use of psychological and social rewards to motivate managers.

**nonunit-level activity drivers**   factors that measure the consumption of nonunit-level activities by products and other cost objects.

**nonvalue-added activities**   all activities other than those that are absolutely essential to remain in business.

**nonvalue-added costs**   costs that are caused either by nonvalue-added activities or by the inefficient performance of value-added activities.

**normal cost of goods sold** the cost of goods sold before adjustment for any overhead variance.

**normal cost system** an approach that assigns the actual costs of direct materials and direct labor to products but uses a predetermined rate to assign overhead costs.

## O

**operating activities** the ongoing, day-to-day, revenue-generating activities of an organization.

**operating assets** assets used to generate operating income, consisting usually of cash, inventories, receivables, and property, plant, and equipment. Average operating assets are found by adding together beginning operating assets and ending operating assets, and dividing the result by 2.

**operating budgets** budgets associated with the income-producing activities of an organization.

**operating income** revenues minus operating expenses from the firm's normal operations. Operating income is before-tax income.

**operating leverage** the use of fixed costs to extract higher percentage changes in profits as sales activity changes. Leverage is achieved by increasing fixed costs while lowering variable costs.

**operations process** a process that produces and delivers existing products and services to customers.

**opportunity cost** the benefit given up or sacrificed when one alternative is chosen over another.

**ordering costs** the costs of placing and receiving an order.

**overapplied overhead** the amount by which applied overhead exceeds actual overhead.

**overhead budget** a budget that reveals the planned expenditures for all indirect manufacturing items.

**overhead variance** the difference between actual overhead and applied overhead.

## P

**parallel processing** a processing pattern in which two or more sequential processes are required to produce a finished good.

**participative budgeting** an approach to budgeting that allows managers who will be held accountable for budgetary performance to participate in the budget's development.

**payback period** the time required for a project to return its investment.

**performance report** a report that compares the actual data with planned data.

**period costs** costs that are expensed in the period in which they are incurred; they are not inventoried.

**physical flow schedule** a schedule that reconciles units to account for with units accounted for. The physical units are not adjusted for percent of completion.

**planning** a management activity that involves the detailed formulation of action to achieve a particular end.

**plantwide overhead rate** a single overhead rate calculated using all estimated overhead for a factory divided by the estimated activity level across the entire factory.

**postaudit** a follow-up analysis of an investment decision, comparing actual benefits and costs with expected benefits and costs.

**postpurchase costs** the costs of using, maintaining, and disposing of the product.

**postsales service process** a process that provides critical and responsive service to customers after the product or service has been delivered.

**predetermined overhead rate** an overhead rate computed using estimated data.

**present value** the current value of a future cash flow. It represents the amount that must be invested now if the future cash flow is to be received assuming compounding at a given rate of interest.

**prevention costs** cost incurred to prevent defects in products or services being produced.

**price** the revenue per unit.

**price-earnings ratio** the price-earnings ratio is found by dividing the market price per share by the earnings per share.

**price standards** the price that should be paid per unit of input.

**price (rate) variance** the difference between standard price and actual price multiplied by the actual quantity of inputs used.

**prime cost** the sum of direct materials cost and direct labor cost.

**process-costing system** a costing system that accumulates production costs by process or by department for a given period of time.

**process-value analysis** an approach that focuses on processes and activities and emphasizes systemwide performance instead of individual performance.

**process value chain** the innovation, operations, and postsales service processes.

**producing departments** units within an organization responsible for producing the products or services that are sold to customers.

**product (manufacturing) costs** costs associated with the manufacture of goods or the provision of services. Product costs include direct materials, direct labor, and overhead.

**product diversity** the situation present when products consume overhead in different proportions.

**production budget** a budget that shows how many units must be produced to meet sales needs and satisfy ending inventory requirements.

**production report** a document that summarizes the manufacturing activity that takes place in a process department for a given period of time.

**products** goods produced by converting raw materials through the use of labor and indirect manufacturing resources, such as the manufacturing plant, land, and machinery.

**profit center** a division of a company that is evaluated on the basis of operating income or profit.

**profit-volume graph** a graphical portrayal of the relationship between profits and sales activity in units.

**profitability ratios** ratios that measure the earning ability of a company. These ratios allow investors, creditors, and managers to evaluate the extent to which invested funds are being used efficiently.

**pseudoparticipation** a budgetary system in which top management solicits inputs from lower-level managers and then ignores those inputs. Thus, in reality, budgets are dictated from above.

**publicly traded companies** companies that issue stock traded on U.S. stock exchanges to which the Sarbanes-Oxley Act applies.

# Q

**quick or acid-test ratio** a measure of liquidity that compares only the most liquid assets to current liabilities.

# R

**realized external failure costs** environmental costs caused by environmental degradation and paid for by the responsible organization.

**reciprocal method** a method that simultaneously allocates service costs to all user departments. It gives full consideration to interactions among support departments.

**relevant costs** future costs that change across alternatives.

**relevant range** the range of output over which an assumed cost relationship is valid for the normal operations of a firm.

**reorder point** the point in time when a new order should be placed (or setup started).

**required rate of return** the minimum rate of return that a project must earn in order to be acceptable. Usually corresponds to the cost of capital.

**residual income** the difference between operating income and the minimum dollar return required on a company's operating assets.

**resource drivers** factors that measure the consumption of resources by activities.

**responsibility center** a segment of the business whose manager is accountable for specified sets of activities.

**return on investment (ROI)** the ratio of operating income to average operating assets.

**return on sales** a measure of the efficiency of a firm that is computed by dividing net income by sales.

**return on stockholders' equity** a measure that can be used to compare against other return measures (e.g., preferred dividend rates and bond rates). It is computed by dividing net income less preferred dividends by the average common stockholders' equity.

**return on total assets** the result of dividing net income plus the after-tax cost of interest by the average total assets.

**revenue center** a segment of the business that is evaluated on the basis of sales.

# S

**safety stock** extra inventory carried to serve as insurance against changes in demand. Safety stock is computed by multiplying the lead time by the difference between the maximum rate of usage and the average rate of usage.

**sales budget** a budget that describes expected sales in units and dollars for the coming period.

**sales mix** the relative combination of products (or services) being sold by an organization.

**Sarbanes-Oxley Act (SOX)** passed in 2002 in response to revelations of misconduct and fraud by several well-known firms, this legislation established stronger governmental control and regulation of public companies in the United States, from enhanced oversight (PCAOB), to increased auditor independence and tightened regulation of corporate governance.

**scattergraph method** a method to fit a line to a set of data using two points that are selected by judgment. It is used to break out the fixed and variable components of a mixed cost.

**segment** a subunit of a company of sufficient importance to warrant the production of performance reports.

**segment margin** the contribution a segment makes to cover common fixed costs and provide for profit after direct fixed costs and variable costs are deducted from the segment's sales revenue.

**sell-or-process-further decision** relevant costing analysis that focuses on whether a product should be processed beyond the split-off point.

**selling and administrative expenses budget** a budget that outlines planned expenditures for nonmanufacturing activities.

**selling costs** those costs necessary to market, distribute, and service a product or service.

**semi-variable** a type of cost behavior where the true total cost function is increasing at a decreasing rate.

**sensitivity analysis** the "what-if" process of altering certain key variables to assess the effect on the original outcome.

**sequential (or step) method** a method that allocates service costs to user departments in a sequential manner. It gives partial consideration to interactions among support departments.

**sequential processing** a processing pattern in which units pass from one process to another in a set order.

**service organization** an organization that produces intangible products.

**services** tasks or activities performed for a customer or an activity performed by a customer using an organization's products or facilities.

**single-loop feedback** information about the effectiveness of strategy implementation.

**slope** the variable cost per unit of activity usage.

**societal costs** (see unrealized external failure costs.)

**special-order decisions** relevant costing analyses that focus on whether a specially priced order should be accepted or rejected.

**split-off point** the point at which products become distinguishable after passing through a common process.

**staff positions** positions that are supportive in nature and have only indirect responsibility for an organization's basic objectives.

**standard cost per unit** the per-unit cost that should be achieved given materials, labor, and overhead standards.

**standard cost sheet** a listing of the standard costs and standard quantities of direct materials, direct labor, and overhead that should apply to a single product.

**standard hours allowed (*SH*)** the direct labor hours that should have been used to produce the actual output (Unit labor standard × Actual output).

**standard quantity of materials allowed (*SQ*)** the quantity of materials that should have been used to produce the actual output (Unit materials standard × Actual output).

**statement of cash flows** a statement that provides information regarding the sources and uses of a firm's cash.

**static budget** a budget for a particular level of activity.

**step cost** a cost that displays a constant level of cost for a range of output and then jumps to a higher level of cost at some point, where it remains for a similar range of output.

**stockout costs** the costs of insufficient inventory.

**strategic plan** the long-term plan for future activities and operations, usually involving at least five years.

**strategy** the process of choosing a business's market and customer segments, identifying its critical internal business processes, and selecting the individual and organizational capabilities needed to meet internal, customer, and financial objectives.

**sunk costs** costs for which the outlay has already been made and that cannot be affected by a future decision.

**support departments** units within an organization that provide essential support services for producing departments.

## T

**target cost** the difference between the sales price needed to achieve a projected market share and the desired per-unit profit.

**target costing** a method of determining the cost of a product or service based on the price (target price) that customers are willing to pay.

**testable strategy** a set of linked objectives aimed at an overall goal that can be restated into a sequence of cause-and-effect hypotheses.

**time ticket** a source document by which direct labor costs are assigned to individual jobs.

**times-interest-earned ratio** a leverage ratio that uses the income statement to assess a company's ability to service its debt. It is computed by dividing net income before taxes and interest by interest expense.

**total budget variance** the difference between the actual cost of an input and its planned cost.

**total quality management** a management philosophy in which manufacturers strive to create an environment that will enable workers to manufacture perfect (zero-defect) products.

**transfer price** the price charged for goods transferred from one division to another.

**transferred-in costs** costs transferred from a prior process to a subsequent process.

**treasurer** the individual responsible for the finance function; raises capital and manages cash and investments.

**turnover** the ratio of sales to average operating assets.

## U

**underapplied overhead** the amount by which actual overhead exceeds applied overhead.

**unfavorable (*U*) variances** variances produced whenever the actual input amounts are greater than the budgeted or standard allowances.

**unit-level activities** activities that are performed each time a unit is produced.

**unit-level activity drivers** factors that measure the consumption of unit-level activities by products and other cost objects.

**unrealized external failure costs** environmental costs caused by an organization but paid for by society.

**usage (efficiency) variance** the difference between standard quantities and actual quantities multiplied by standard price.

## V

**value-added activities** activities that are necessary for a business to achieve corporate objectives and remain in business.

**value-added costs** costs caused by value-added activities.

**value chain** the set of activities required to design, develop, produce, market, and deliver products and services to customers.

**variable budgets** (see flexible budget.)

**variable cost ratio** variable costs divided by sales revenues. It is the proportion of each sales dollar needed to cover variable costs.

**variable costing** a product-costing method that assigns only variable manufacturing costs to production: direct materials, direct labor, and variable overhead. Fixed overhead is treated as a period cost.

**variable costs** costs that, in total, vary in direct proportion to changes in output within the relevant range.

**variable overhead efficiency variance** the difference between the actual direct labor hours used and the standard hours allowed multiplied by the standard variable overhead rate.

**variable overhead spending variance** the difference between the actual variable overhead and the budgeted variable overhead based on actual hours used to produce the actual output.

**velocity** the number of units that can be produced in a given period of time (e.g., output per hour).

**vertical analysis** a type of analysis that expresses the line item as a percentage of some other line item for the same period.

## W

**weighted average costing method** a process-costing method that combines beginning inventory costs with current-period costs to compute unit costs. Costs and output from the current period and the previous period are averaged to compute unit costs.

**work distribution matrix** identifies the amount of labor consumed by each activity and is derived from the interview process (or a written survey).

**work in process (WIP)** the cost of the partially completed goods that are still being worked on at the end of a time period.

# CHECK FIGURES

Check Figures are given for selected problems.

## Chapter 2

**2-43** 1. Total direct materials = $7,810
2. Net income = $6,120
**2-44** 1. Total owed by Natalie = $30
2. Total cost for Mary = $17.50
**2-45** 2. Cost of goods manufactured = $224,950
3. Cost of goods sold = $226,050
**2-46** 1. Total product cost = $9,200,000
2. Operating income = $2,000,000
3. Gross margin = $2,860,000
**2-47** 1. Cost of goods manufactured = $24,725
2. Cost of goods sold = $27,160
**2-49** 1. Cost of goods manufactured = $910,000
**2-50** 3. Operating income = $332,100
**2-52** 2. Magazine total prime costs = $4,500
4. Operating income = $2,010
**2-53** 2. Tent sale loss = ($1,300)

## Chapter 3

**3-43** 2. Fixed receiving cost = $6,600
3. Receiving cost for the year = $295,200
**3-44** 2. Receiving cost = $25,180
**3-45** 2. Supplies variable rate = $6.50
4. Charge per hour = $75.69
**3-46** 2. Plan 2 unused minutes = 75
3. Plan 2 minutes used = 90
**3-47** 3. Variable rate = $4.50
**3-49** 1. 10 months' data intercept = 3,212
**3-50** 2. Variable power cost = $1.13 (rounded)
**3-51** 2. Fixed rate = $1,349

## Chapter 4

**4-40** 1. Break-even units = 63,400
2. Units for target profit = 103,400
4. Margin of safety in units = 21,600
**4-41** 2. Break-even units = 47,699
**4-42** 1. Break-even sales revenue = $11,538,731 (rounded) or $11,539,500
3. Profits underestimated = $642,900
5. Operating leverage = 5.32
**4-43** 2. Break-even basic sleds = 39,680
3. Increase in total contribution margin = $320,000

**4-44** 1. Margin of safety in units = 13,200
2. Operating income = $11,220
3. Units for target profit = 98,400
**4-45** 2. Revenue = $234,375
4. Break-even sales revenue = $250,000
**4-46** 1. Break-even sales revenue = $450,000
2. Desk lamps = 8,998
3. Operating leverage = 4.0
**4-47** 2. Operating income = $34,000
3. Trim kits = 32,444
**4-48** 1. Break-even units = 21,429
3. Operating income = $119,900
**4-49** 1. Contribution margin ratio = 0.22
3. Margin of safety = $330,000
4. Contribution margin from increased sales = $2,640
**4-50** 1. Price = $70
**4-51** 1. Contribution margin ratio = 0.25
2. Breakeven in units = 32,000
4. Margin of safety = $16,800
5. New operating income = $18,200
**4-52** 1. Macduff degree of operating leverage = 9
2. Duncan break-even point = $250,000
3. Macduff increase in profits = 270%
**4-53** 1. May current year contribution margin ratio = 0.5489
2. May prior year break-even sales = $24,590
3. May current year margin of safety = $6,522
**4-54** 1. Grade I sales = 224 cabinets
2. Grade II breakeven in units = 392
3. Additional contribution margin = $73,602
4. Increase in operating income = $25,365
**4-55** 1. First process breakeven = 5,000 cases
2. Units for equal profit = 25,000 cases

## Chapter 5

**5-46** 2. Total cost Job 741 = $148,230
4. Cost of goods sold = $234,882
**5-47** 1. Total = $10,575
**5-48** 2. Total cost of Carter job = $2,179
4. Gross margin = $3,309
**5-49** 1. Overhead rate = $6
2. Department B overhead rate = $4.125
**5-50** 2. Finishing overhead rate = $75 per machine hour
2. Total manufacturing cost Job 2 = $24,139
**5-51** 1. Total Ed's Job = $234
**5-52** 2. Ending Work in Process = $16,526
**5-53** 2. Total Job 519 = $3,448
**5-54** 1. Overhead rate = 175%
3. Cost of goods manufactured = $245,000

Chapter 6

6-46  1. Equivalent units of output = 402,000
      2. Units transferred out = 396,000
      3. Units transferred out = 49,500
6-47  1. Total units to account for = 180,000
      2. Equivalent units, conversion = 156,000
      3. Total cost per equivalent unit = $320
      4. Cost of EWIP = $7,440,000
6-48  1. Total cost per equivalent unit = $320
6-49  1. Total units to account for = 160,000
      2. Equivalent units of output = 144,000
      3. Unit cost = $5.20
6-50     Cost per equivalent unit = $5.20
6-51  1. Units to account for = 50,000
      2. Total Equivalent units = 46,250
      3. Unit cost = $0.60
      4. Cost of EWIP = $750
      5. Spoilage cost = $1,500
6-52     Cost per equivalent unit = $12.00
6-53     Cost per equivalent unit = $10.1994
6-54  1. Total equivalent units = 500,000
      2. Unit cost = $23.225
      3. Goods transferred out = $11,148,000
      5. Unit paraffin cost = $6.746
6-55  1. Unit cost = $5.74
6-56  1. Total cost of units transferred out = $160,940
6-57  1. Total cost of goods transferred out = $17,349
      2. Total cost of goods transferred out = $23,400
6-58  1. Cost of units started and completed = $15,573
      2. Cost of units started and completed = $23,174

Chapter 7

7-53  1. Unit cost = $0.60
      2. Duffel bags unit cost = $2.40 per unit
      3. Total per unit of Backpacks = $0.80 per unit
7-54  1. Model B overhead cost per unit = $6.75
      2. Model B overhead per unit = $7.49
      3. Model B overhead cost per unit = $8.38
7-55  1. Total cost = $120,000
      2. Basic unit cost = $87.50
7-56  1. Cost per patient day = $277
      2. Cost per patient day (complications) = $658
7-57  1. Average monthly fee = $6.78
      2. Cost per account (low) = $87.37
      3. Profit (high-balance) = $112.50

5-55  2. Applied overhead = $3,024
      5. Adjusted cost of goods sold = $634,340
5-56  2. Total Job 703 = $41,220
      4. Ending balance Work in Process = $40,900
5-57  1. Direct Total (laboratory) = $664,500
      2. Sequential (laboratory) = $663,825
5-58  1. Drilling rate = $15.30 per machine hour (direct);
         $16.23 (sequential)
5-59  2. May overhead assigned = $200
      3. Total cost = $475

7-58  2. Category I per-unit ordering cost = $0.08
      3. Total reduction = $4,950,000
7-59  1. Watson unit cost = $1,096.60
7-60  2. Potential reduction per unit = $7.10
      4. Total potential unit reduction = $8.35
      5. Greatest benefit = $12 price
7-61  1. Total nonvalue cost = $1,204,800
      2. Materials nonvalue-added cost = $164,000 U
7-62  1. Theoretical cycle time = 8 minutes
      2. Actual cycle time = 9.6 minutes
      3. Reduction = $16.67 per telescope

Chapter 8

8-35  2. Gross margin = $353,439
      4. Operating income = $77,439
      5. Absorption-costing income = $67,261
8-36  2. Ending inventory = $10,125
      3. Segment margin beauty shops = $38,500
8-37  1. Blender segment margin = $206,000
      3. Blender segment margin = $241,000
8-38  1. Unit cost = $4.23
      3. Contribution margin per unit = $3.92
      4. Operating income = $49,708
8-39  1. Musical product margin = ($1,850)
      2. Operating income (loss) = ($500)
      3. Operating income = $400
8-40  3. Total cost of current inventory policy = $4,680
      5. Carrying cost at EOQ = $900
      7. Cost of ordering 3,000 units = $4,860
8-41  1. Total cost = $1,750
      3. Reorder point = 200
      4. Total cost = $1,458

Chapter 9

9-46     Total cash, September = $203,462
9-47  1. i. Budgeted income before taxes = $4,971,260
         j. Cash budget ending balance (March) = $2,686,004
9-48  1. Total assets = $562,750
      2. Cash budget ending cash balance (Sept.) = $12,005
      3. Total assets = $565,605
9-50     Ending cash balance = $24,722
9-51  10. Income before taxes = $16,129,000
9-52  1. December materials to be purchased = 5,150 yards
9-53  1. September total cash = $79,446

Chapter 10

10-40  1. MUV = $10,500 F
       2. LRV = $0
       3. LEV = $13,200 F
10-41  2. LEV, Cutting = $300 U
10-42  1. Standard cost per unit = $126.88
       2. LEV = $2,457.60 U
       3. Average time = 0.768 per unit

**10-43** 1. Standard cost (normal) = $305 per patient day
       2. MUV (cesarean) = $30,000 F
       3. LEV (normal) = $3,200 U
       4. LEV = $11,200 U
**10-44** 1. UCL (labor) = $770,000
       2. Total liquid variance = $117,000 U
       3. LEV = $26,250 F
**10-45** 1. June UCL (labor) = $372,600 (efficiency standard)
       2. May LEV = $30,000 U (10%)
**10-46** 1. MPV = $2,213 U
       2. LEV = $1,000 F
       3. LRV = $0
**10-47** 1. MUV = $17,100 U
       2. LEV = $56,250 U
**10-48** 1. MUV = $100,000 U
       2. LEV = $24,000 U
       3. Net effect = $46,000 U

## Chapter 11

**11-43** 1. Direct labor hours = 40,000 hours
       2. Total variable costs = $120,000
**11-44** 1. Direct labor hours for 20% lower = 32,000
       2. Total overhead costs for 10% higher = $271,750
**11-45** 2. Total cost variance = $1,850 U
**11-46** 1. Total direct labor hours = 30,000
       2. Total overhead costs = $271,700
**11-47** 1. Variable = $685; Fixed = $13,000,000
       2. Optimistic income = $5,750,000
**11-48** 1. Total = $68,655
       2. Supplies, variable = $2.30
**11-49** 1. Total overhead costs (Formula 280) = $2,836.47
**11-50** 1. Total cost = $22,127
**11-51** 1. Total budgeted variance = $100,000 U
       2. Total budgeted variance = $6,000 F
**11-52** 1. Total budgeted variance = $2,500 F
       2. Unit cost = $15.29
       3. Total (20,000 moves) = $165,000
**11-53** 2. Total conversion cost variance = $184,360 F
**11-54** 1. SFOR = $3.60; SVOR = $2.40
       2. Total FOH variance = $15,600 U
       3. Volume variance = $25,200 U
       4. VOH efficiency variance = $1,680 F
**11-55** 1. VOH efficiency = $20,000 U
       2. FOH spending = $20,000 F
**11-56** 1. Standard variable overhead rate = $1.85
       3. Volume variance = $10,720 U
       4. Efficiency variance = $22,015 U
**11-57** 3. VOH spending variance = $7,996 U
       4. 0.26667 hour per unit
**11-58** 1. Total variance = $40,000 U
       2. Volume variance = $15,000 U;
          Efficiency variance = $15,000 U

## Chapter 12

**12-34** 1. ROI of radio project = 0.16
       2. Residual income of division with radio = $450,000

**12-35** 1. ROI Year 3 = 6.30%
       3. Turnover = 0.75
       4. Turnover = 0.83
**12-36** 1. Turbocharger ROI = 15%
       4. Residual income with neither = $289,000
**12-37** 2. ROI = 10.34% (rounded)
       4. Margin = 0.0913
       5. EVA with investment = $122,500
**12-38** 2. Minimum price = $53
**12-39** 1. Model SC67 contribution margin = $760,000
       5. Contribution margin = $320,000
**12-40** 2. Markup percentage = 42.5%
**12-43** 1. Theoretical cycle time = 30 minutes
       2. MCE = 60%
       3. Actual velocity = 1.2

## Chapter 13

**13-39** 1. Total net benefit = $100,000
**13-40** 1. Cost to make = $367,000
       4. Cost to make = $598,000
**13-41** 2. Additional income per pound = $21.025
**13-42** 1. Operating income = $6,100
       2. Operating income = $16,558
       3. Total segment margin = $29,620
**13-43** 1. Increase Pat's profit = $18,400
       2. Increase Steve's profit = $15,200
**13-44** 2. Markup = $2,646
**13-45** 1. Standard contribution margin per machine hour = $20
**13-46** 1. Loss per box = ($0.05)
**13-47** 1. Operating profit = $40,000
**13-48** 1. $300,000
**13-49** 1. Differential amount to process further = $4,900
**13-50** 1. Monthly cost for Community Bank = $5,773

## Chapter 14

**14-36** 2. NPV = $(697,095)
**14-37** 2. NPV = $9,751
**14-38** 1. IRR = 12%
       2. Cash flow = $50,521
       3. Minimum CF = $58,991
**14-39** 1. NPV = $40,032,752
       2. NPV = $3,171,066
       3. Seating rate = 79%
       4. Seating rate = 71%
**14-40** 1. Payback = 3.13 years
       2. ARR = 10.68%
       3. IRR = 14% (approximately)
       4. NPV = $(21,025)
**14-41** 1. NPV (scrap alternative) = $151,632
**14-43** 1. Payback period = 3.89 years
       2. NPV = $(88,298)
       3. NPV = $422,302
**14-44** 1. Cost of capital = 0.10
       2. NPV = $24,344
**14-45** 1. NPV (20% rate) = $(25,391,280)
       2. NPV (14%) = $4,374,962
       3. NPV (14%) = $1,374,962

**14-46** 1. NPV = $117,308
2. NPV = $(29,564)
3. NPV = $231,051
**14-47** 1. NPV (standard) = $190,719
2. NPV (CAM) = $761,686
**14-48** 1. NPV (CAM) = $198,560
2. NPV (Standard) = $95,524

## Chapter 15

**15-36**  Net cash from operating activities = $32,400
**15-38**  Net cash from operating activities = $4,000
**15-40** 1. Net cash from operating activities = $506,250
2. Net cash from investing activities = $(293,750)
**15-42** 1. Net cash from operating activities = $144,000
**15-44** 1. Net cash from operating activities = $10,000;
net cash from investing activities = $(60,000)
**15-46**  Net cash from operating activities = $111,800
**15-47** 1. Net cash from operating activities = $30,000,000;
net cash flow from investing activities = $(10,000,000)
**15-48**  Net cash from operating activities = $80,000;
net cash from investing activities = $(55,000)

## Chapter 16

**16-43** 1. Current ratio = 2.5
3. Average receivables = $350,000
5. Average inventory = $225,000
**16-44** 2. Total assets = $7,250,000
**16-45** 1. Return on assets = 0.088
3. Earnings per share = $5.75
5. Dividend yield = 0.0375
**16-46** 1. Percent change total assets = 32.5%
**16-47** 1. This year percent total current assets = 88.6%
2. Last year percent total liabilities = 60.2%
3. This year percent net income = 10.3%
**16-48** 1. b. Last year quick ratio = 0.71
d. Last year turnover in days = 296.75
**16-49** 1. b. Last year debt ratio = 0.60
**16-50** 1. a. Last year return on assets = 0.11
f. Last year dividend payout = 0.24
**16-51** 1. b. Return on assets = 8.7%
**16-52** 1. 2010 accounts receivables turnover = 5
2013 accounts receivables turnover = 4.08
**16-53** 1. a. McGregor EPS = $2.34
b. Fasnacht dividends per common share = $0.78
e. McGregor return on assets = 0.17

# INDEX

# Cornerstones

## Cornerstones for Chapter 1

N/A

## Cornerstones for Chapter 2

## Cornerstones for Chapter 3

## Cornerstones for Chapter 4

## Cornerstones for Chapter 5

## Cornerstones for Chapter 6

## Cornerstones for Chapter 7

## Cornerstones for Chapter 8

## Cornerstones for Chapter 9